SECOND EDITION

FAMILY LAW FOR NON-LAWYERS

By Kerry Weil Tripp

cognella® | ACADEMIC PUBLISHING

Bassim Hamadeh, CEO and Publisher
Kassie Graves, Director of Acquisitions and Sales
Jamie Giganti, Senior Managing Editor
Jess Estrella, Senior Graphic Designer
Carrie Montoya, Acquisitions Editor
Kaela Martin, Project Editor
Natalie Lakosil, Licensing Manager
Laureen Gleason, Production Editor
Joyce Lue, Interior Designer

Printed in the United States of America

ISBN: 978-1-5165-1539-4 (pbk) / 978-1-5165-1540-0 (br)

CONTENTS

PREFACE

At its core, family law covers matters of the family. While traditionally, each state makes its own family law, each deals with the same basic concepts but viewed from its own moral lens. Beyond that commonality, there is often overlap in the substantive laws created. Yet, more and more, with the involvement of the Supreme Court of the United States in family law cases, family law is becoming federal law, too.

Similar to most law schools, this book does not focus on the family law of a particular jurisdiction or state. The goal of this book is to provide an overview of the topics included in the law and some of the similarities and differences found throughout the country. Unlike law school textbooks, this book's audience is the non-lawyer—all of us from families who are interested in the impact of the law on the family. While this book is not intended to provide legal advice or legal training, hopefully it will be an enlightening and entertaining exposure to the traditional breadth of family law issues challenged by the cutting edge issues.

Kerry Tripp, J.D.
KTripp@umd.edu
University of Maryland, College Park
College Park, MD
2017

INTRODUCTION

Everyone has a family. As a result, unlike most areas of the law, we all have personal experience in this topic of law. As you prepare to read this book, most of you can guess what it should cover: Family or "domestic relations" law answers questions such as who can marry and the process of divorce. Many readers will pick up *Family Law for Non-Lawyers* believing it consists of a "how-to manual" on areas many people already have some familiarity with (e.g., marriage and divorce). It is not. Family law is most interesting when each step of the family is examined. From families' formation through birth or adoption, to dissolution in divorce or termination of parental rights, this book raises questions such as: what is a family from the law's perspective, and more importantly: why is this the perception? One's own examination of each stage of family through the legal prism involves personal perspectives and biases that exist from having been members and participants.

For example, we all have a mother. But looking at the issue of the parent/child relationship, a question arises: Are there "bad mothers?" Many are uncomfortable labeling a person as "bad." But from society's standpoint, is that not what the law does when it terminates parental relationships? Yet, many read the U.S. Constitution as preventing government interference in the privacy of family affairs. So, how do the Constitution's guarantees interface with legal action? From an individual perspective, would you think of someone as a bad parent? Like you, the government has reservations about questioning another person's parenting. Would having personal involvement with the issue (e.g., your daughter's teacher) likely cause more involvement or discourage it? What about having a family relationship (sister or spouse)? Would that make a difference? What about children who think they have a "bad mother"; does the law listen to them?

While most children complain about their parents—(as the mother of a teen, I know)—should the children be able to sue their mother for being a "bad parent?" If so, what should they ask the court to do about it—what is the remedy? If a person buys a bad car and the seller is sued in court, the buyer may get a different car that is as good as or even better than the original. What should be the legal remedy for children who sue their mother for being a bad parent? Should they get a new one? What kinds of complaints would the child need about their parent in order to win such a lawsuit? Would it require abuse—either sexual or physical? Is neglect sufficient? Does this include the mother in New York City who goes next door to visit while the child is sleeping and can be heard on the portable nursery monitor? Does it matter if she goes for cocktails? How about if she goes down the block to a restaurant, but is still within range of the baby monitor?

Most may not think of a mom in touch via monitor as their idea of a "bad mother" case, but is it? More likely, our mental image of a bad mother case involves failing to provide food, shelter, or education. But in 2009, siblings "Steven Miner, 23, and Kathryn Miner, 20, filed a lawsuit seeking $50,000 for emotional distress stemming from the damage of supposed bad mothering."[1] Their mother, Kimberly Garrity from Illinois, "was married and then divorced in 1995."[2] In their lawsuit, the siblings "alleged th[at] Garrity was a lousy mom because she failed to send money for birthdays, called her daughter home early from homecoming, and threatened to call police on Kimberly's 7 year old son, if he didn't buckle up in the car." "Steven also accused his mother of once smacking him on the head, saying that he still suffers from headaches. One of the exhibits in the case included a birthday card that Steven called 'inappropriate' because it failed to include cash or a check."[3] The card did include the inscription, "Son I got you this birthday card because it's just like you. Different from all the rest!" On the inside, Garrity wrote, "Have a great day! Love & Hugs, Mom xoxoxo."[4]

What should a court do with a case like this? The case was filed in the Cook County Circuit Court,[5] where it was dismissed. The siblings then took it up on appeal. Two years after filing their lawsuit, "an Illinois appellate court also dismissed it."[6] "In its ruling, the appellate court found that none of Garrity's behavior could be ruled 'extreme or outrageous.' Such alleged actions are unpleasant and perhaps insensitive, and some would arguably fall outside the realm of 'good mothering,' but they are not so shocking as to form a basis for a claim for intentional infliction of 'emotional distress,'" the court ruled.[7]

---

1 http://abcnews.go.com/US/adult-children-sue-mom-bad-parent/story?id=14407409#.UXKri0rYySo, "Illinois Mom Kimberly Garrity Wins 'Bad Mom' Case Over Her Kids" by Candice Smith, ABC News, August 30, 2011.
2 Ibid.
3 Ibid.
4 According to court documents cited by the *Chicago Tribune*, "The alleged offenses include failing to take her daughter to a car show, telling her then-7-year-old son to buckle his seat belt or she would contact police, 'haggling' over the amount to spend on party dresses and calling her daughter at midnight to ask that she return home from celebrating homecoming. http://articles.chicagotribune.com/2011-08-28/news/chi-bad-mothering-lawsuit-dismissed-20110828_1_mothering-emotional-distress-lawsuit, "Bad mothering lawsuit dismissed" by Steve Schmadeke, *Chicago Tribune*, August 28, 2011.
5 http://abcnews.go.com/US/adult-children-sue-mom-bad-parent/story?id=14407409#.UXKri0rYySo, "Illinois Mom Kimberly Garrity Wins 'Bad Mom' Case Over Her Kids" by Candice Smith, ABC News, August 30, 2011.
6 Ibid
7 Ibid.

Does it make any difference if after the divorce the children were "[r]aised in a $1.5 million home by their father?"[8] How about if "[t]he children's lawyer was Garrity's ex-husband and the children's father?"[9] In spite of the suit, the *Chicago Tribune* reports that Garrity, in court filings, said that she still loves her children.[10]

A quarter century ago, when I began to practice law in the 1980s, I had to dictate my thoughts to a secretary (yes, that's what we called them in the dark ages) who was twice my age and exponentially more legally experienced and probably more knowledgeable than I was. I was uncomfortable with this undeserved subservient relationship and glad that my class of young lawyers was the first to train on computers, learning to do legal research on the burgeoning cites of Westlaw and LexusNexus and to compose our briefs in word processing. The downside of this new technology was that individual secretaries were placed into "pools" to provide filing and phone service for groups of lawyers and a well-paying, respected job for women vanished. In the 1980s, my job provided me with a work cellphone; it was the size of a shoebox. Given this trip down memory lane, one can surmise that I am not the person to lecture on technology.

Yet, the first revision of this book was driven in part by the impact technology has on our lives and, by extension, on issues of family law. For most, there is no "private" life; we make our lives public voluntarily. Through selfies, Snapchat, tweets, Twitter, Facebook, GPS, and the ubiquitous cell phone, we share our lives and even our literal location with friends, family, and who knows who. No occasion is too small to deserve an up-to-the minute review. A deluge of emails can be sent with the touch of a finger without review, introspection, or personal interaction. Endless hours are spent "surfing the web" which, if we even bother to think about it at all, we believe to be anonymous. In reality, the data from these hours are actually being tracked, stored, and sold by businesses, the government or even a former partner with cheap tracking software. Whatever the benefits of all this free "information," one negative impact is that online actions are commonly used in family law matters. This book's revision would be remiss in not including a new final chapter on the impact of technology on family law issues. The issues that arise from this impact could fill a book in itself. Given, however, that I am a self-professed technology dinosaur, the chapter continues to highlight the impacts we are seeing today on some of the subjects of previous chapters.

As the earlier version of this book, the revised first edition, was going to press, the U.S. Supreme Court ruled that marriage was a constitutional right and recognized marriage equality. Immediately we knew there would be another revision. With the election of Donald J. Trump as President during this second revision and his Executive Orders reversing policy on abortion, LGTBQ and other issues concerning families and the upcoming appointment of a new Supreme Court Justice, the probability of a third revision looms again. For now, as those changing issues arise we raise them in the "As we go to press" sections to allow the reader to speculate how they will resolve. Stay tuned!

—KWT

---

8   Ibid.
9   Ibid.
10 Ibid.

THE BOOK'S GOALS AND A LEGAL PRIMER

A judge is sworn "to determine, not according to his own private judgment, but according to the known laws and customs of the land; not delegated to pronounce a new law, but to maintain and expound the old one."
—William Blackstone, Commentaries 69.[1]

[T]he province and duty of the judicial department [is] to say what the law is—not what it should be.
—Chief Justice John Marshall in *Marbury v. Madison*, 5 U.S. (1 Cranch) 137, 177, 2 L.Ed. 60 (1803).

THREE GOALS: ISSUE SPOTTING, LAWS, EFFECTS OF CHANGE

While this book is not intended to provide legal advice or give legal training, keep three major goals in sight when reading. First, learn to **issue spot**. Lawyers do this to identify the conflict that the court will resolve. In addition to spotting the issues or conflicts in this book, try to find them in everyday events. Second, learn the rules, or the **black-letter law** of family law. In law school, lawyers are trained to find the law in appellate cases. In this book, in addition to providing an overview of topics included in family law, the text will highlight some of the similarities and differences found in the laws throughout the country and in a "uniform" federal system. Also, while a few legal cases are included, they are designed to show a court's analysis or reasoning used in making a decision on the laws. Third, while reading these cases, remember that the law is not made in a vacuum; societal shifts impact and cause changes in the

---

1 From *Christopher v. Christopher*,—So.3d—, 2012 WL 6634435 (ALCiv.App. 2012) http://caselaw.findlaw.com/al-court-of-civil-appeals/1619072.html, from the concurring opinion of Judge Bryan.

law—especially in the area of family law. Think of what was happening in society that caused the law to change or the courts to change the law.

Beyond looking at the cases for what they say about society as a whole, it is easy to forget that each case involves real people with tangible interests in the case's outcome. As a result, many of the book's chapters provide a spotlight on the parties or lawyers in some landmark cases. Finally, in the "as we go to press" sections, the new Trump administration promises to change some major family law issues. As this book is being revised in the spring of 2017, most of the impact will not be known until after this book is published this summer. Therefore future editions (like this one did for this current second edition) will provide the answers. In the meantime, play "judge for the day" and use the discussions to decide how the issues will ultimately be resolved.

How a Case Gets to Court

Before digging into family law, it is useful to have a sufficient understanding of both the court system and laws. When someone does something that causes another person to be unhappy (often losing money) or causes an injury to another person—like when a bus hits a pedestrian—someone may want the court to resolve the issue. While the two people (or businesses, or a combination) may try to resolve the matter informally amongst themselves, if they cannot or choose not to, they may go to court. In that case, the person bringing (or filing) the lawsuit is called the **plaintiff**. The person having the lawsuit brought against them is called the **defendant**. Trials can involve either **civil matters,** where one person claims a wrong caused by another, or **criminal matters,** where the plaintiff is the government, e.g., *the State of Maryland v. the Defendant*. Most of the cases discussed in this text are civil matters except for abuse cases.

In order to get to court and have the lawsuit heard, the plaintiff will file a legal document called the **complaint**. In the complaint, the plaintiff alleges the facts of the problem and requests legal remedies from the court. In response, the defendant needs to respond to the allegations made in the complaint by filing a legal paper called an **answer** (or he may file a **motion**, e.g., to dismiss the case, etc.), in which he responds with his version of the story/ facts and may request his own legal remedies or solutions. The **parties** (collectively, the defendant and plaintiff) then have the court hear their versions of the facts.

The State Court System

Recall that the United States is unique among many countries because it has two court systems—a federal and a state system. Why have two different sets of courts? The United States Constitution established this system when trying to more efficiently manage[2] the union of individual states and to clarify functions of the central/national government. Under the Constitution, certain powers were given to the federal courts while some were reserved for state courts. This means that each

---

2   After the United States was established it was run under the Articles of Confederation which, notably, negotiated the peace treaty to end the Revolutionary War.

court system, federal and state, is responsible for hearing certain kinds of cases. Yet, neither is independent of each other, and systems often interact. **Federalism** is the sharing of powers between the two systems.[3]

Generally, state court systems are set up in a "hierarchy of courts," where the lowest courts are the trial courts. These "lower" courts may include a small claims court (for controversies involving smaller dollar claims, e.g., less than $5,000) or traffic court. At the higher level many states have trial courts for each district of the state that hear cases involving claims for larger dollar amounts (e.g., over $5,000).[4] The trial court is charged with hearing and weighing evidence presented by the parties and their lawyers. As the "trier of fact" the court will make a determination as to which facts are true. Once the facts are established, the trial court will apply appropriate laws and legal precedents to decide who "wins" the case.

Often someone is unhappy with the decision or thinks the case was decided in error. That person may file an appeal and becomes the **appellant**. The person to whom the appeal is filed against is the **appellee**. At the state court level, an appellant may have the automatic right to appeal to the next appellate court level, which requires the court to hear the appeal. When beginning to read legal cases, remember that the plaintiff at the trial court level may not be the appellant at the appellate court level. Generally, the plaintiff was unhappy with the situation and filed the lawsuit, but the appellant is unhappy with the court's decision and files the appeal. Each level of appeal means the appellant is the one who continues to be unhappy.

It is the appellate court's responsibility to review the trial court's decision and determine if there was an error. So what does an appellate court do? It reviews the application of the law and the legal precedent by the lower court. If the lower court involved a jury trial, the appellate court decides if the jury's decision was proper, based on the application of the appropriate law to the jury's determined facts. Remember: an appellate court does not retry the case; no new trial is conducted. Appellate courts accept the facts as determined by the trial court. So the job of the appellate court is not to decide who should win or lose the case, but to review it to make sure the decision was fair according to the law. The courts of appeal review cases and facts to see if there is an appealable issue. They decide if they want to hear the appeal in their court.

The cycle of an unhappy party continuing to challenge a court's ruling as error can continue on in the state appeals courts (only finally stopping at the Supreme Court of the United States). But often, beyond the initial appeal from the trial court to the appellate court level, appeals are not a matter of right. This means a legal request must be made (application to the court) and the court has to choose to take the case for review on appeal.

---

3 Wiktionary defines federalism as a "system of national government in which power is divided between a central authority and a number of regions with delimited self-governing authority."
4 Maryland, for example, has a small claims cap that requires all claims for money damages to total less than $5,000. Because the amount of the claim is so limited, often people do not hire lawyers, but represent themselves in court. http://www.courts.state.md.us/district/forms/civil/dccv001br.html

The Federal Court System

A similar hierarchy exists in the federal court system. After the trial in the district court, an appeal can be filed to the next level of court, the appellate court level. This is the United States court of appeal, or **circuit court** (in the U.S., several states combine to form about 14 circuits, including Washington, D.C.—there is not one per state); these are known as the intermediate appellate courts in the federal system. There is no automatic right to have an appeal to the circuit courts from the trial court. Therefore, a request must be made to the court to hear the appeal. If it is accepted, the appeal is usually heard by a group of three judges (except *en banc* decisions, when all of the justices hear a case). It is these appellate court decisions that are binding **precedent**. This means that the appellate court's decisions can be used to determine how other courts decide similar cases. Like state courts, if either the appellant or appellee thinks there was an error with the circuit court's decision, an attempt can be made to move to the next and final level of appeal: the Supreme Court of the United States.[5] The Supreme Court is, therefore, the highest court in the land. In order to have the Supreme Court hear a case, there must be a federal issue, and a **writ of certiorari** must be filed and accepted by a majority of the justices. The Supreme Court does not hear all requests for review. In fact, it hears the least number of cases of all the appeals courts. Each year the Supreme Court receives approximately 10,000 petitions for a writ of certiorari and it "grants and hears oral argument [in] about 75–80 cases."[6]

How Laws Are Made

Much like the court system, the American legislative system is a dual system, one for the state/local and one for the national/federal system. It, too, has a hierarchy. Working from the top down, the United States federal Constitution is the highest law in the land. The Constitution controls all other laws made in the United States (see Chapter 4 for more discussion). A state cannot pass a law that does not give constitutional protections. When looking at the Supreme Court cases included in this book, the issue is often to determine whether a regulation (or law) denies a right guaranteed by the U.S. Constitution. If it does, the court will strike/invalidate it.

The Congress and Senate, working in the District of Columbia, our nation's capital, make and pass laws dealing with federal issues that govern all of the states. Therefore, federal law is "uniform law," because it applies uniformly to all the states. The Constitution specifies which laws the United States Congress has the right to make. These include laws on matters like federal taxation, immigration, and bankruptcy. In the second system, each state makes its own laws because elected officials for each region should be more attuned to the morality and the needs and wants of their local communities. At the top of the hierarchy are state laws called **statutes**. These statutes (which are signed by the governor of the state) are then assembled into volumes that look like a set of encyclopedias and are referred to as the state's **code**. Because each state passes its

---

5   See, generally, Judgepedia at http://judgepedia.org/index.php/Main_Page
6   http://www.supremecourt.gov/faq.aspx#faqgi9

own laws, states may treat a subject matter differently from other states. In addition, local cities and communities also have authority to pass laws. One area of local law that impacts family law is zoning regulation (see, e.g., Chapter 2 on defining family through zoning laws). Zoning may include classifying what type of house is permitted in an area of the city or whether commercial properties are allowed. Moreover, community covenants may be as specific as to detail how far a shed or outbuilding can be built from one neighbor's property to another or if fences are allowed in the front yard. When reviewing state laws, remember that each law, regardless of level, must provide the citizens with the rights provided under the United States Constitution, or the law is unconstitutional and therefore invalid. Often, when reading the Supreme Court cases included in this book, this is the issue: Is the state's law unconstitutional?

Case Law versus Legislative Law

If a governing body (e.g., the president by executive order or the Congress) passes laws, is this the only way that laws are made in the United States? No. The United States, like a minority of countries, is a common law country.[7] The United States inherited its common law system from England. What differentiates the common law system is its use of precedent. Precedent refers to the body of past cases that are used to decide a current case. Under the doctrine of **stare decisis** (roughly translated from Latin as "to adhere to that which has already been decided"), previous court decisions/cases involving similar facts and questions of law will be used to decide similar cases today. A positive aspect of using precedent is that it gives an attempt at certainty under the law; once a principle of law has been put into place, it can be applied when similar facts occur in the future to give a similar decision. "Some legal theorists… argue precedent is important because it provides four things: predictability, reliability, efficiency, and equality."[8] "Critics argue that a legal system based on precedent is grounded in the past and slow to change," and those who seek to challenge the basis of the legal system are "seen as heretics by those who accept the legal system."[9]

A problem with using precedent is that courts are bound to use a prior court decision in making a current decision, even if the judge may want to decide this particular case differently. So, with all this emphasis on certainty under the law, can courts ever reject past decisions? Referring back to the book's introduction, the law does not operate in a vacuum. So when considerations of public policy require it, courts may reverse/overrule old cases to make laws that fit today's society. Think of some examples. In *Loving v. Virginia* (discussed in Chapter 5 on the Constitution), the Supreme Court of the United States overruled decades of prior decisions, which had prevented whites from marrying nonwhites.

---

7   "The civil family of law is actually the most common and is used in countries such as France, Italy, and Scotland." *Women and Justice*, 2nd ed., by Sheryl J. Grana, 2009, p. 32.

8   Ibid.

9   Ibid.

Jurisdiction: Where Should the Case Be Heard?

Now that it is clear how the court system works and how laws are made and applied, the next question is **jurisdiction,** the legal term that means to determine which court has the authority to hear a case. **Jurisdiction** asks the question of where family law cases should be heard. Are family law cases filed in federal courts or state courts? *Anastasi v. Anastasi,* 544 F. Supp. 866, 447 A.D., 173 (D.N.J. 1982) looks at this issue. In this case, a man and a woman were cohabitating (not married, just living together) in the state of New Jersey. After they broke up, the woman sued the man for money she felt he owed her because of an alleged claim "to provide plaintiff with all of her financial support and needs for the rest of her life" (Anastasi, p. 866). Jurisdiction asks the question: In which court should she file her case—federal or state?

If the woman had been married to the man, the state's divorce laws would probably apply. Because divorce laws are made in each state, the plaintiff would have filed in her state's court. In this case, however, the couple never married. When the woman filed her case, she chose state court and filed in New Jersey. The defendant responded by filing a motion requesting the case be moved to federal court (because the defendant did not live in the state of New Jersey). The federal court originally agreed that it had jurisdiction because this was not officially a domestic relations matter, but more "akin to a contract" or a promise to pay. The federal court's decision in *Anastasi* was based on another case (precedent); however, that case was overruled by the New Jersey Supreme Court. As a result, the *Anastasi* federal court changed its decision based on the conclusion "that in the present posture of New Jersey law this kind of case is within the domestic relations exception to jurisdiction and must be remanded" (sent back to the state court to decide). The *Anastasi* federal court wrote, "Not only does *Crowe v. DeGioia* announce a significant state interest in the consensual live-in relationship, it requires that in order to protect this interest a trial court must make the same kinds of inquiries that have traditionally brought into play the domestic relations exception to federal jurisdiction." Because the trial court will have to make the kinds of investigations that are usually involved in a family law case, the local state court is the best one to do it. Based on this "significant state interest," the federal court exercised the "domestic relations exception," which defers federal courts from hearing cases involving family matters. Thus, the rule is that cases involving domestic relations/family issues are better left to the state courts to decide.

Briefing a Case

Lawyers write briefs, which are summaries of their arguments for submission to the court. Students also write briefs, but to learn the skill of reading legal cases and to serve as a study guides for law exams. Legal opinions can be lengthy, so a brief summarizes a case. The discussion above of *Anastasia v. Anastasia* amounts to a brief.

Begin a student brief with the name of the case and the case cite. There are many ways and styles to brief a case. Keeping in mind that student briefs are for the student's use, any style can be adapted for the best fit. One method is called IRAC, which is the method used by the author of this book. The "I" in IRAC stands for the issue. After identifying the main **issue** the court is trying to decide, format it into a query beginning with the word "whether." For example, the issue in *Anastasi* was whether the federal court was the right court to hear a case involving the end of a cohabitational relationship. The "R" stands for the court's **ruling**, which should answer the question raised by the issue. In the *Anastasi* case, the court ruled that the federal court was not the correct court to hear the case. The "A" stands for **analysis**, the court's reasoning in deciding a case. Included in the analysis section is a summary of the relevant facts and, if needed, a procedural history of the case. For example, in the *Anastasi* case, the facts section would include that the couple cohabitated and were not married, and that it is the woman's appeal from the federal court's decision to hear the case. Caution: this is a summary, so it should only be a few sentences. The analysis section might include what influenced the court in making its decision, such as public policy, or even bias. In the *Anastasi* case, the court's decision was influenced by the New Jersey legislature's change in its views towards cohabitation and its findings that such relationships required many similar inquiries to divorce cases. Finally, the "C" is for the **conclusion/holding**. This should clarify the **black letter law** (court-made rules of law) that the courts base future decisions on. The black letter law in *Anastasi* is that the federal courts will defer to the state courts in cases involving family matters.

Remember, only appellate court rulings are precedent that can be used by other courts to decide other cases. However, in agreement with Mark Twain that the "truth is stranger than fiction" many of the cases included in this book were chosen for their, shall we say, arresting fact patterns or issues they decide. Unlike a law school textbook, which contains mostly Supreme Court and appellate court cases (cited for their precedent value), some cases in this book may not have precedent value and will not be used by the courts to decide other cases. Notwithstanding, *enjoy!*

WHAT IS A FAMILY?

A family is a unit composed not only of children but of men, women, an occasional animal, and the common cold.
—Ogden Nash[1]

Family isn't about whose blood you have. It's about who you care about.
—Trey Parker and Matt Stone, *South Park,*
"Ike's Wee Wee," 1998[2]

What is the family? Is it true, as Mary Catherine Bateson said, "The family is changing not disappearing? We have to broaden our understanding of it, look for the new metaphors."[3] As society has changed, defining family has become harder, but should it?

THE FORM FAMILY

What is a family? When asked to define family, many will include language to the effect that a "family is a group of people connected by blood or marriage or adoption." Society and the law have recognized this "traditional" family model for centuries. It is a **form** family because it is a family that is "formed" by its connections through blood (biologically), marriage, or adoption.

The form family is often described as a "single housekeeping unit." So what happens if the parents move out and go on strike? In Florida, in December 2004, "Cat Barnard [45], a stay-at-home mom, and her 56-year-old husband, a government social services worker, decided their children needed to learn about empathy and responsibility" so they went on strike. After trying

---

1   https://www.brainyquote.com/quotes/quotes/o/ogdennash159111.html
2   http://www.quotationspage.com/quote/32317.html
3   www.brainyquote.com/quotes/quotes/m/marycather390111.html

many ways to get their two children, 12 and 17, to do their chores, the parents moved out of the house and into a tent on the driveway. Mrs. Barnard even held up "handwritten signs that read 'Parents on Strike' and 'Seeking Cooperation and Respect!'" when the children walked by. "The Barnard [parents] slept on air mattresses in the tent during their strike and … barbecued while their children fended for themselves with frozen TV dinners inside the house. The parents only [went] inside to shower and use the bathroom."[4] Is this a form family? Why or why not?

THE FUNCTIONAL FAMILY

Many definitions of family might expand to include non-biological relatives or non-legally related people who have a "household tie" to each other or work together as one group. This expanded definition of family can become unwieldy. Distinguishing the difference between a "group of people," like students in a classroom, who are working to define family, but are not family by anyone's definition, in comparison to legally recognizing a group of people as a family is dependent on function. Being defined as a **functional** family requires that the members are together based on commitment to each other while they operate and behave like form families.

This is the dilemma that courts are faced with in trying to decide which groups deserve recognition as a family, and the legal benefits and protections that society awards them. Traditionally, the form family was the only recognized family by society, and thus the only group entitled to legal benefits. As society has changed, so has the appearance of families. Courts and legislatures have also started to expand their definitions of family.

The case of *City of Ladue v. Horn*, 720 S.W.2d 745 (1986), involved an Illinois couple and their children who bought a seven-bedroom, four-bath house in an area covered by a city ordinance, but were evicted because they were not a "family." The Ladue city ordinance specifically defined family under Zoning Ordinance 1175 as: "One or more persons related by blood, marriage, or adoption occupying a dwelling unit as an individual housekeeping organization."[5]

Why would a city have such an ordinance? Society uses laws to punish behaviors it does not want and reward behaviors it wants to encourage. Cities are given broad power in creating ordinances to regulate their local area, as long as they can show that they promote the health, safety,

---

4   "A well-intentioned neighbor reported the Barnards to sheriff's deputies, who checked up on the family three times Tuesday. They were satisfied that the children were safe. One of the children's teachers also stopped by the house, thinking she had been abandoned, after the teenager said that her parents had moved out of the house." Compare that to, "Passers-by from this bedroom community between Orlando and Daytona Beach have shouted out words of encouragement. One woman driving past the Barnard's house rolled down her car window Wednesday and shouted "'Good for you! You should put the kids outside!'" http://www.nbcnews.com/id/6677175/42465883#.UXL2zErYySo, Fed-up parents go on strike over kids' laziness," AP, ABCNEWS.com, December 9, 2004. The parents eventually called off the strike, having felt they made their point (especially with media support). No word on the impact on the children.
5   Other than family members related by blood, marriage or adoption, the city of Ladue allowed only one exception to the zoning ordinance, and that was for hired help, "'[a]ccommodations for domestic persons employed and living on the premises and home occupations.'" *City of Ladue v. Horn*, p. 745.

morals, and general welfare of the city and its residents. When challenged by the court to defend the ordinance, the city of Ladue broadly alleged that it met those requirements. The city argued that requiring single-family residences to be inhabited by traditional form families promotes community stability, and therefore protects property values of houses in the community. This created a higher tax base benefiting the city.

In the *Ladue* case, Joan Horn and E. Terrence Jones had a blended family. Joan and Terrence had children from prior relationships, but none together. While the older children were away at school, one of the children continued to live at home. The couple shared a common bedroom, joint bank accounts, health care expenses, and meals. They also entertained as a couple and disciplined one another's kids. Despite this outward appearance of "functioning" as a family and not having caused any problems in their community, the city of Ladue still asked the couple to vacate their home (after living there several years) because they were not within the definition of family as required under the city ordinance.

When the defendants refused to leave, the city sued to evict them from their home. The defendants argued that the term "family" had many different meanings and that their household was the functional and factual equivalent of a natural family. The couple reminded the court that they used their home for the identical purposes as families with biological and marital relationships in the neighborhood. They also made constitutional arguments about their rights to free association and privacy, in addition to prohibitions against discrimination. In the final ruling, the city's zoning ordinance was validated, and, approving the lower court's decision that the defendants did not meet the city's definition of family, the court required the occupants to leave their home. The court reinforced the power of a municipality to limit household residents to those related by blood, adoption, or marriage. It seems the court viewed the group as having no legal bond. Therefore, although they functioned like a family, they did not show requisite commitment to a "permanent relationship and perceived reciprocal obligations" necessary to demonstrate that a true family existed. Constitutional rights arguments did not apply because those are only applicable to families and the court found that this was not a family.[6]

Was the case decided correctly?[7] Would the same result occur today?[8] A 2006 case in the city of Black Jack, Missouri, a St. Louis suburb, had a similar fact pattern involving a cohabitating

6 http://usatoday30.usatoday.com/news/nation/2006-05-15-unmarried-family_x.htm, Parents, kids not necessarily "family" everywhere, by Martha T. Moore, *USA TODAY*, May 15, 2006.

7 Joan Kelly Horn said, "'It was, 'Get married or move out,'" says Horn, who later served in Congress in 1991 and 1992. "We were both pretty appalled." The couple married in 1987—on their own timetable, Horn says. They divorced in 1999. http://usatoday30.usatoday.com/news/nation/2006-05-15-unmarried-family_x.htm Parents, kids not necessarily "family" everywhere, by Martha T. Moore, *USA Today*, May 15, 2006.

8 April 25, 2006: In Manassas, Virginia, the city "could not change the rules on how much living space each resident requires; those are set by the state. But the city can regulate how buildings are used." So, in December 2005, the city "tightened" its code definition to limit "immediate relatives of the homeowner." While blood relatives like parents and children were acceptable, blood relatives like aunts, uncles, nieces, nephews, and cousins were not. "2.2.6.06: The way we live: A family or a crowd? Americans admire extended families—except when immigrants share a house in the suburbs," By Christopher Caldwell, *New York Times*, February 2, 2006, p. 9. Prince George's County Maryland enacted

couple. Olivia Shelltrack and Fondray Loving built a five-bedroom house in a new community. In 2005, the city prevented them from moving in by denying their occupancy permit. The city of Black Jack's ordinance defined family as those related by blood, marriage, and adoption or no more than three people, living together as a single nonprofit housekeeping unit. In this case, the unmarried couple had three children, two biological children and a third child from a prior relationship. Based on this, the clerk requested identification for all adults living in the house and birth certificates for all the children before issuing the occupancy permit.[9] The couple then appealed to the city's Board of Adjustments for an exemption, which was also rejected. Although at an open hearing the Zoning Board approved language amendments to the ordinance to define family as including two unrelated people with biological children, the City Council voted not to accept that proposed language.[10] It was then that the American Civil Liberties Union (ACLU) filed suit on behalf of the couple seeking an injunction, among other things, to bar the city from keeping the couple out of their home. Plaintiff Shelltrack said, "This ordinance is outdated. We are a family." "There's a mom, there's a dad, there's three children. We are a family." "Whether Shelltrack, a stay-at-home mom, and Loving, 33, who works for a payroll-administration company, are married 'should not be anybody's business, if I pay my taxes, if I'm able to buy the house,' she said."[11] Is she right?[12] At that time, Missouri law did not prohibit discrimination in housing based on marital status.[13] In February 2007, the city of Black Jack settled with Shelltrack and Loving, agreeing to pay them $28,000.[14] "In announcing the settlement, the city agreed to pay Shelltrack and Loving $5,500 each, plus $1,000 for each of their three children. (Their attorneys received

---

the Mini Dorm Ordinance in an effort to: "prevent or control the detrimental effects upon neighboring properties, such as illegal parking and saturation of available parking by residents of mini-dormitories, litter, and noise" that regulated rental properties within single to triple family houses to require certain square footage per person etc. if they rent to unrelated students at the nearby University of Maryland. Such regulation was upheld for allegations of equal protection and discrimination under the broad local zoning powers. *Kirsch v. Prince George's County*, 92 Md. App. 719 (1992).

9 "Move or get married," Anderson Cooper, CNN.com. In a similar denial, the city's mayor, Norman McCourt, was quoted as saying, "While it would be naive to say that we don't recognize that children are born out of wedlock frequently these days, we certainly don't believe that is the type of environment within which children should be brought into this world," http://www.cnn.com/CNN/Programs/anderson.cooper.360/blog/2006/04/move-or-get-married.html

10 http://www.aclu-em.org/downloads/BlackJackPetition.pdf, ACLU's Petition in the Circuit Court for the county of St. Louis, State of Missouri, asking for, among other things, an injunction against the city, in *Shelltrack and Loving v. the City of Black Jack et al.* (which included the zoning board and/or city council members who rejected a proposed amendment to the ordinance). This case reinforces the broad discretion and powers municipalities have in making ordinances as long as they are justified as promoting the responsibilities of good government.

11 Ibid.

12 http://usatoday30.usatoday.com/news/nation/2006-05-15-unmarried-family_x.htm, Parents, kids not necessarily "family" everywhere, by Martha T. Moore, *USA Today*, May 15, 2006.

13 http://usatoday30.usatoday.com/news/nation/2006-05-15-unmarried-family_x.htm, Parents, kids not necessarily "family" everywhere, by Martha T. Moore, *USA Today*, May 15, 2006. "Missouri housing laws, like those of at least 18 other states, do not prohibit discrimination based on marital status."

14 http://www.stltoday.com/suburban-journals/city-settles-lawsuit-with-black-jack-couple/article_9356fc40-d4a5-5e45-87cb-0c82933bb9af.html, "City settles lawsuit with Black Jack couple," Brian Flinchpaugh, STL.com, February 28, 2007.

$14,000).[15] After trying and failing, the city council unanimously adopted a new ordinance in September, redefining what constitutes a family. City officials said this resolved the situation. "The council also amended its housing code in August to include the same definition contained in the city's zoning code."[16]

While the case was going on, a neighbor, Larry Hensley, said, "Shelltrack and Loving should conform or move." He says that's what "he did 20 years ago when he moved from neighboring Florissant, which barred him from keeping bees in his backyard." Is keeping bees the same as getting married?[17]

The topic of marriage has come up between Shelltrack and Loving. About three years before the ACLU petition, "he proposed, and she said yes. But the couple has set no date for the wedding. Instead, they saved for a bigger house."[18] "We're happy with the way our lives are," Shelltrack says. "We don't feel that a piece of paper is going to change it. It's not going to make us better parents. It's not going to make us better neighbors."[19]

The decisions of the cities of Ladue and Black Jack to evict unmarried couples from their homes in single-family zoned communities might have been explained by the fact that neither city prohibited discrimination based on marital status. What would be the effect on a state that did not allow for this bias? Would an east coast state, aware of the history of discrimination, and therefore proactive in its attempts to remedy it, rule the same? A similar case in Prince George's County, Maryland, involved a Maryland Court of Special Appeals decision regarding an unmarried woman's attempt to purchase a unit in a cooperative housing development in 1981.

PRINCE GEORGE'S COUNTY V. GREENBELT HOMES, INC.
49 MD. APP. 314, 431 A.
AD 745 (M.D.APP 1981)

County appealed from decision of the Circuit Court, Prince George's County, James Magruder Rea, J., which granted cooperative housing development's motion for summary judgment in county's action to enforce order of the county human relations commission that development not discriminate

---

15   Ibid.
16   Ibid.
17   http://usatoday30.usatoday.com/news/nation/2006-05-15-unmarried-family_x.htm, Parents, kids not necessarily "family" everywhere, Martha T. Moore, *USA Today*, May 15, 2006.
18   Ibid.
19   Ibid.

against nonmarried couples. The Court of Special Appeals, Lowe, J., held that commission could not enforce order, under city ordinance outlawing housing discrimination based on marital status, restraining cooperative housing development from interpreting term "family" contained in mutual ownership contract to prohibit those couples not having legal marital status from living in the development since common-law marriages were not recognized in state as a legal status.

Judgment affirmed.
**746 LOWE, Judge.

Reluctant to plunge into the sea of matrimony, John Hemphill and Lynn Bradley were nonetheless eager to settle upon its shores. They had jointly contracted to purchase the right of "perpetual use and enjoyment" of a dwelling unit in a cooperative housing development known as Greenbelt Homes, Inc., situated in Prince George's County. Because the contract was "subject to an acceptance of the purchaser by Greenbelt Homes, Inc. as members," each applied for membership indicating on his application that they resided together and by the joint contract to purchase, inferentially intended to continue to do so in the dwelling unit described.

To their chagrin, they were denied membership "because (they) were not married." According to their precipitous complaint to the Human Relations Commission of Prince George's County, the spokesman for Greenbelt Homes, Inc., "said that in the past the Board (of Directors) has made exceptions to its policy of not selling to unmarried persons but never for an unmarried couple. He stated that not being married was the only reason for our rejection, that everything else was alright."

Anxious to fulfill its destiny as destroyer of discrimination, the Commission made ready to do battle, apparently to *316 provide surcease for the sensitivities of those whom they clept "Complainants."

The Complainants had not alleged that they had been deprived individually of membership, which under the by-laws stipulated that "Only one person per dwelling unit may be a member of the Corporation...."

They were concerned solely with the "policy" of not selling to unmarried couples which stemmed from the provision in the by-laws that excepted from the individual membership restriction, "that a husband and wife or other persons specifically authorized in any case by the Board of Directors may hold a membership jointly."

The Commission perceived discrimination from a different perspective. It noted that Greenbelt's Mutual Ownership Contract contained a covenant that "The member shall occupy the dwelling unit covered by this contract as a private dwelling from the date of occupancy... for himself and his immediate family...."

Focusing on the word "family" (while ignoring its immediately preceding restrictive adjective), the Commission rejected the "generally accepted" interpretation of "family" applied by Greenbelt Homes, and took "notice" that Webster's Seventh New Collegiate Dictionary (1967 edition) listed a series of definitions for "family" broad enough to cover not only "(a) group of persons of common ancestry," but also "a group of individuals living under one roof...," a "group of things related by common characteristics," "fellowship" and more pointedly, "A basic unit in society having as its nucleus two or more adults living together, and cooperating in the care and rearing of their own or adopted children."

*317 The Commission also took "notice" that as 10.0 of the Prince George's County Zoning Ordinance defines a family for housing occupancy purposes as, "An individual, or two or more persons related by blood or marriage, or a group of not more than five persons (excluding servants) not related by blood or marriage, living together as a single housekeeping group in a dwelling unit...."

The Commission further concluded that "Greenbelt Homes, Inc.'s claim (The Board of Directors acting as Greenbelt Homes, Inc.) that their verbally expressed, only, interpretation of 'family' being 'commonly accepted' is not valid."

It then held that Greenbelt's covenant, so interpreted, contravened a local ordinance against discrimination which proscribed "acting, or failing to act, or unduly delaying any action regarding any person because of ... marital status ... in such a way that such person is adversely affected in the area(s) of housing...." Prince George's County Code, s 2-186(3).

**747 Caught up in the cause which by now seemingly surpassed its "complainants" (who we empirically note have since married and become ensconced elsewhere), the Commission ordered (among other things):

"That Greenbelt Homes, Inc. revise their (sic) Membership Agreement and their (sic) Mutual Ownership Contract to eliminate any provisions which are contrary to federal, state and/or local laws and/or ordinances."

Our purpose in belaboring how the Commission arrived at its result is to emphasize by its omission that the Commission did not find that a covenant restricting membership to one's immediate "family" as that term is *318 "COMMONLY ACCEPTED" WOULD HAVE BEEN discriminating because of marital status. It found only that the definition applied by Greenbelt to its covenant was invalid and implicitly should be defined as broadly as any of Webster's alternatives, and at least as broadly as the Zoning Ordinance of which the Commission took "notice."

Pursuant to s 2-197 of its Code, Prince George's County filed suit for declaratory judgment and mandatory injunction in the Circuit Court for Prince George's County in equity to enforce the order of the Commission. Greenbelt Homes, Inc. answered and sought declaratory judgment as to the meaning of the terms "marital status" as used in the code and "family" as used in the Greenbelt covenants ...

The case was submitted on motions for summary judgment by both parties; that of the County was denied and that of Greenbelt granted. In its opinion, which we shall accept as the requested declaration, (Reddick v. State, 213 Md. 18, 31, 130 A.2d 762 (1957)), the judge did not define "family" as requested. In defining "marital status," however, he held that "People who are not married to one another do not have a marital status and for that reason it is clear that the legislative body did not intend for such to apply. If the County Council of Prince George's County wants that intent, the ordinance should be amended to prohibit marital status 'or lack thereof.'"

The issue raised on appeal by Prince George's County is "whether the appellee's practice of refusing to approve or enter into perpetual use agreements with unmarried heterosexual couples constitutes *319 marital status discrimination within the meaning of s 2-186(3), Prince George's County Code?"

But the issue is not nearly so conceptually broad. When we reflect upon the Human Relations Commission Order, it is that foundation with which we find primary fault. If we addressed the question asked in isolation, a simple affirmance would support the result of the Court's judgment but leave in limbo a highly questionable declaration which is the crux of this appeal. Significantly, Maryland's statute with regard to "Discrimination in Housing" also makes it an unlawful practice to discriminate in regard to housing "because of ... marital status" (Md.Ann.Code Art. 49B, s 20). A declaration regarding that term in context takes on added interpretative importance. It is noteworthy that the term "marital status" appears 100 times in the Annotated Code of Maryland scattered in some 31 different, although often related, sections. Since Judge Ross' proclamation that "People who are not married to one another do not have a marital status ..." is somewhat misleading, we will attempt to clarify the meaning of that term as used in the context of the housing discrimination law before addressing the Commission's erroneous definition of "family" in its even more restrictive context in the covenant. See Md. Rule 1085.

—Marital Status—

Under the facts presented, we point out that neither complainant (each of whom **748 was "single," "unmarried") was denied membership individually because of his or her individual marital status. While each separately had a marital status, collectively they did not. Only marriage as prescribed by law can change the marital status of an individual to a new legal entity of husband and wife. The law of Maryland does not recognize common law marriages (*Henderson v. Henderson*, 199 Md. 449, 454, 87 A.2d 403 (1952), or other unions of two or more persons such as concubinage, *320 syneisaktism, relationships of homosexuals or lesbians as legally bestowing upon two people a legally cognizable marital status. Such relationships are simple illegitimate unions unrecognized, or in some instances condemned, by the law. That public policy message rings out from the procedural prerequisites for legitimating "marriages," Md.Ann. Code Art. 62, and the statutory condemnation of other relationships, see, e.g., Md.Ann. Code Art. 27, s 18 (Bigamy) and ss 390 et seq. The obvious intent of our legislature is to encourage the proverbial concept that more belongs to a marriage than four bare legs in a bed.[FN1] Even contemporary discrimination laws are not intended to promulgate promiscuity by favoring relationships unrecognized by statute or case law as having legal status.

FN1. Wilson, The Oxford Dictionary of English Proverbs 513 (3d Ed. 1970)

Neither Mr. Hemphill nor Ms. Bradley was denied membership in Greenbelt Homes, Inc. because he or she was single. They were denied joint membership because neither Greenbelt nor the law of Maryland recognized their union as cloaking them with a "marital status." Greenbelt simply refused to acknowledge that the naked emperor was wearing clothes. The complainants who were not then married may not compel treatment as an entity (e.g., as tenants by the entireties, see *Lopez v. Lopez*, 250 Md. 491, 510, 243 A.2d 588 (1968); and cf.

McManus, et al. v. Summers, 290 Md. 408, 430 A.2d 80 (1981)), any more than a married couple may be treated as single for preferential tax treatment, see e.g., *Helvering v. Janney*, 311 U.S. 189, 61 S.Ct. 241, 85 L.Ed. 118 (1940). We are what we are, and it is in that capacity which we must be judged even when we seek the judgment.

—Family—

The crux of the Commission's order, however, was its finding that Greenbelt's "commonly accepted" definition of the term "family" is invalid. The Commission held that the term "family" as used in the contractual covenant included as a matter of law at the very least the two *321 complainants, but interpretatively as many as "five persons ... not related by blood or marriage, living together as a single housekeeping group in a dwelling unit," which it gleaned from the local zoning ordinance.

The Court of Appeals has noted that the statutory use and definition of the word "family" may be (and often is) limited to the purposes of a specific act. *Hicks v. Hatem*, 265 Md. 260, 264 n. 1, 289 A.2d 325 (1972). In that case the Court of Appeals was interpreting the use of the term "family" in the household exclusion provision of insurance contract, just as we are here concerned with an exclusionary provision in a contract. There the Court agreed with Greenbelt's observation of the "commonly accepted" interpretation of terms: "It would thus appear that in common parlance and usage the word 'family' more frequently connotes the existence of a marital or blood relationship, or a legal status approximating such relationship." Id. at 264, 289 A.2d 325 (Emphasis added).

Noting that common law marriages are not recognized in Maryland as a "legal status," the Court held that an unmarried woman living without consanguinal ties within an insured's household did not "in this State" possess a legal status, which was the equivalent of being a "family" member. It would seem to follow that the Greenbelt covenant meant what Greenbelt intended it to mean, rather than what the Commission wanted it to mean. From at least as early as 1833, we are told that in construing covenants they must be viewed in context and in accordance with the intention of the covenantors. **749 See, *Watchman v. Crook*, 5 G & J 239 (1833) ...

It is apparent that the Commission's declaration of invalidity of Greenbelt's definitional application of the term "family" was an error of law affecting its decision. Md.Ann. Code Art. 41, s 255(f)(4); or, if found as a fact, it was unsupported by competent material, and substantial evidence in view of the entire record as submitted. Md.Ann. Code Art. 41, s 255(f)(5). It follows that without regard to the judge's rather broad definitional reasoning regarding the meaning of "marital status," he did not err in refusing to enforce the defective order of the Commission at the insistence of the County.

Finally, we cannot conclude without noting that the Court of Appeals has given recognition sub silentio to the Greenbelt Homes, Inc. policy complained of by the original parties in this case as "never (authorizing joint membership) for an unmarried couple." Although not written in either the light or the shadow of the recent influx of discrimination laws, the Court of Appeals was by no means offended by this same appellee's termination of membership of a single woman who "persistently and grossly" violated her contract by (among other things) living with "an adult man" to whom she was related neither by blood nor marriage. The Court affirmed the termination of her interest for such "objectionable conduct." Green v. Greenbelt Homes, Inc., 232 Md. 496, 194 A.2d 273 (1963).

Judgment Affirmed. Costs to be Paid By Appellant Prince George's County.

Was the court right to decide the case this way? What do you think of the court's statement that, "[t]he obvious intent of our legislature is to encourage the proverbial concept that more belongs to a marriage than four bare legs in a bed? (p. 747)" How about the court's disparaging remarks on same-sex relationships as viewed 25 years ago?

In the case of *Braschi v. Stahl Assoc. Co.*, 74 NY2d 201, (1989), the court applied a definition of family similar to *Ladue* and *Greenbelt Homes*, but this was a New York ordinance in the context of a pending eviction from a rent-controlled apartment which involved a same-sex couple. Would the court decide differently because same-sex couples could not marry in New York at that time; whereas, the heterosexual couples in the Horn and Loving cases had the choice?

BRASCHI V. STAHL ASSOCS. CO.
74 N.Y.2D 201, (1989)

Summary

Appeal, by permission of the Appellate Division of the Supreme Court in the First Judicial Department, from an order of that court, entered August 4, 1988, which (1) reversed, on the law, an order of the Supreme Court (Harold Baer, Jr., J.), entered in New York County, granting a motion by plaintiff for a preliminary injunction and enjoining defendant from evicting plaintiff from the apartment at which he currently resides, and (2) denied plaintiff's motion. The following question was certified by the Appellate Division: "Was the order of this Court, which reversed the order of the Supreme Court, properly made?"

Braschi v. Stahl Assocs. Co., 143 AD2d 44, reversed.
Opinion of the court
Titone, J.

In this dispute over occupancy rights to a rent-controlled *206 apartment, the central question to be resolved on this request for preliminary injunctive relief (see, CPLR 6301) is whether appellant has demonstrated a likelihood of success on the merits (see, *Grant Co. v. Srogi, 52 NY2d 496, 517*) by show-ing that, as a matter of law, he is entitled to seek protection from eviction under New York City Rent and Eviction Regulations 9 NYCRR 2204.6 (d) (formerly New York City Rent and Eviction Regulations § 56 [d]). That regulation provides that upon the death of a rent-control tenant, the landlord may not dispossess "either the surviving spouse of the deceased tenant or some other member of the deceased tenant's family who has been living with the tenant" (emphasis supplied). Resolution of this question requires this court to determine the meaning of the term "family" as it is used in this context.

I.

Appellant, Miguel Braschi, was living with Leslie Blanchard in a rent-controlled apartment located at 405 East 54th Street from the summer of 1975 until Blanchard's death in September of 1986. In November of 1986, respondent, Stahl Associates Company, the owner of the apartment building, served a notice to cure on appellant contending that he was a mere licensee with no right to occupy the apartment since only Blanchard was the tenant of record. In December of 1986 respondent served appellant with a notice to terminate informing appellant that he had one month to vacate the apart-ment and that, if the apartment was not vacated, respondent would commence summary proceedings to evict him.

Appellant then initiated an action seeking a permanent injunction and a declaration of entitle-ment to occupy the apartment. By order to show cause appellant then moved for a preliminary injunction, pendente lite, enjoining respondent from evicting him until a court could determine whether he was a member of Blanchard's family within the meaning of 9 NYCRR 2204.6 (d). After examining the nature of the relationship between the two men, Supreme Court concluded that appellant was a "family member" within the meaning of the regulation and, accordingly, that a preliminary injunction should be issued. The court based this decision on its finding that the long-term interdependent nature of the 10-year relationship between appellant and Blanchard "fulfills any definitional criteria of the term 'family.'"

(1) The Appellate Division reversed, concluding that *207 section 2204.6 (d) provides noneviction protection only to "family members within traditional, legally recognized familial relationships" (143 AD2d 44, 45). Since appellant's and Blanchard's relationship was not one given formal recognition by the law, the court held that appellant could not seek the protection of the noneviction ordinance. After denying the motion for preliminary injunctive relief, the Appellate Division granted leave to appeal to this court, certifying the following question of law: "Was the order of this Court, which reversed the order of the Supreme Court, properly made?" We now reverse *[discussion of court's reason for taking the case and statutory interpretation omitted by the author]*...

III ...

The present dispute arises because the term "family" is not defined in the rent-control code and the legislative history is devoid of any specific reference to the noneviction provision. All that is known is the legislative purpose underlying the enactment of the rent-control laws as a whole.

Rent control was enacted to address a "serious public emergency" created by "an acute shortage in dwellings," which resulted in "speculative, unwarranted and abnormal increases in rents" (L 1946ch 274, codified, as amended, at McKinney's Uncons Laws of NY § 8581 et seq). These measures were designed to regulate and control the housing market so as to "prevent exactions of unjust, unreasonable and oppressive rents and rental agreements and to forestall profiteering, speculation and other disruptive practices tending to produce threats to the public health * * * [and] to prevent uncertainty, hardship and dislocation" (id.). Although initially designed as an emergency measure to alleviate the housing shortage attributable to the end of World War II, "a serious public emergency continues to exist in the housing of a considerable number of persons" (id.) ... Consequently, the Legislature has found it necessary to continually reenact the rent control *209 laws, thereby providing continued protection to tenants.

To accomplish its goals, the Legislature recognized that not only would rents have to be controlled, but that evictions would have to be regulated and controlled as well (id.)....

... [R]espondent argues that the term "family member" as used in 9 NYCRR 2204.6 (d) should be construed, consistent with this State's intestacy laws, to mean relationships of blood, consanguinity and adoption in order to effectuate the over-all goal of orderly succession to real property. Under this interpretation, only those entitled to inherit under the laws of intestacy would be afforded noneviction protection (see, EPTL 4-1.1). Further, as did the Appellate Division, respondent relies on our decision in Matter of Robert Paul P. (63 NY2d 233), arguing that since the relationship between appellant and Blanchard has not been accorded legal status by the Legislature, it is not entitled to the protections of section 2204.6 (d), which, according to the Appellate Division, applies only to "family members within traditional, legally recognized familial relationships" ...

Respondent's reliance on Matter of *Robert Paul P.* (supra) is also misplaced, since that case, which held that one adult cannot adopt another where none of the incidents of a filial relationship is evidenced or even remotely intended, was based solely on the purposes of the adoption laws (see, Domestic Relations Law § 110) and has no bearing on the proper interpretation of a provision in the rent-control laws ...

Contrary to all of these arguments, we conclude that the term family, as used in 9 NYCRR 2204.6 (d), should not be rigidly restricted to those people who have formalized their relationship by obtaining, for instance, a marriage certificate or an adoption order. The intended protection against sudden eviction should not rest on fictitious legal distinctions or genetic history, but instead should find its foundation in the reality of family life. In the context of eviction, a more realistic, and certainly equally valid, view of a family includes two adult lifetime partners whose relationship is long term and characterized by an emotional and financial commitment and interdependence. This view comports both with our society's traditional concept of "family" and with the expectations of individuals who live in such nuclear units (see also, *829 Seventh Ave. Co. v. Reider, 67* NY2d 930, 931–932 [interpreting 9 NYCRR 2204.6 (d)'s additional "living with" requirement to mean living with the named tenant "in a family unit, which in turn connotes an arrangement, whatever its duration, bearing some indicia of permanence or continuity" (emphasis supplied)]). In fact, Webster's Dictionary defines "family" first as "a group of people united by certain convictions or common affiliation" (*Webster's Ninth New Collegiate Dictionary* 448 [1984]; see, Ballantine's Law Dictionary 456 [3d ed. 1969] ["family" defined as "(p)rimarily, the collective body of persons who live in one house and under one head or management"]; *Black's Law Dictionary* 543 [Special Deluxe 5th ed. 1979]). Hence, it is reasonable to conclude that, in using the term "family," the Legislature intended to extend protection to those who reside in households having all of the normal familial characteristics. Appellant Braschi should therefore be afforded the opportunity to prove that he and Blanchard had such a household. *212

This definition of "family" is consistent with both of the competing purposes of the rent-control laws: the protection of individuals from sudden dislocation and the gradual transition to a free market system. Family members, whether or not related by blood, or law who have always treated the apartment as their family home will be protected against the hardship of eviction following the death of the named tenant, thereby furthering the Legislature's goals of preventing dislocation and preserving family units which might otherwise be broken apart upon eviction. This approach will foster the transition from rent control to rent stabilization by drawing a distinction between those individuals who are, in fact, genuine family members, and those who are mere roommates (see, Real Property Law § 235-f; *Yorkshire Towers Co. v. Harpster, 134 Misc 2d 384*) or newly discovered relatives hoping to inherit the rent-controlled apartment after the existing tenant'sdeath.[FN4]

FN3 We note, however, that the definition of family that we adopt here for purposes of the noneviction protection of the rent-control laws is completely unrelated to the concept of "functional family," as that term has developed under this court's decisions in the context of zoning ordinances (see, *Baer v. Town of Brookhaven*, 73 NY2d 942; *McMinn v. Town of Oyster Bay*, 66 NY2d 544; *Group House v. Board of Zoning & Appeals*, 45 NY2d 266). Those decisions focus on a locality's power to use its zoning powers in such a way as to impinge upon an individual's ability to live under the same roof with another individual. They have absolutely no bearing on the scope of noneviction protection provided by section 2204.6 (d) …

The determination as to whether an individual is entitled to noneviction protection should be based upon an objective examination of the relationship of the parties. In making this assessment, the lower courts of this State have looked to a number of factors, including the exclusivity and longevity of the relationship, the level of emotional and financial commitment, the manner in which the parties have conducted their everyday lives and held themselves out to society, and the *213 reliance placed upon one another for daily family services (see, e.g., *Athineos v. Thayer*, NYLJ, Mar. 25, 1987, at 14, col 4 [Civ Ct, Kings County], affd NYLJ, Feb. 9, 1988, at 15, col 4 [App Term, 2d Dept] *[orphan never formally adopted but lived in family home for 34 years]*; *2–4 Realty Assocs. v Pittman*, 137 Misc 2d 898, 902 *[two men living in a "father-son" relationship for 25 years]*; *Zimmerman v. Burton*, 107 Misc 2d 401, 404 *[unmarried heterosexual life partner]*; *Rutar Co. v. Yoshito*, No. 53042/79 [Civ Ct, NY County] *[unmarried heterosexual life partner]*; *Gelman v. Castaneda*, NYLJ, Oct. 22, 1986, at 13, col 1 [Civ Ct, NY County] *[male life partners]*). These factors are most helpful, although it should be emphasized that the presence or absence of one or more of them is not dispositive since it is the totality of the relationship as evidenced by the dedication, caring and self-sacrifice of the parties which should, in the final analysis, control. Appellant's situation provides an example of how the rule should be applied.

Appellant and Blanchard lived together as permanent life partners for more than 10 years. They regarded one another, and were regarded by friends and family, as spouses. The two men's families were aware of the nature of the relationship, and they regularly visited each other's families and attended family functions together, as a couple. Even today, appellant continues to maintain a relationship with Blanchard's niece, who considers him an uncle.

In addition to their interwoven social lives, appellant clearly considered the apartment his home. He lists the apartment as his address on his driver's license and passport, and receives all his mail at the apartment address. Moreover, appellant's tenancy was known to the building's superintendent and doormen, who viewed the two men as a couple.

Financially, the two men shared all obligations including a household budget. The two were authorized signatories of three safe-deposit boxes, they maintained joint checking and savings accounts, and joint credit cards. In fact, rent was often paid with a check from their joint checking account. Additionally, Blanchard executed a power of attorney in appellant's favor so that appellant could make necessary decisions—financial, medical and personal—for him during his illness. Finally, appellant was the named beneficiary of Blanchard's life insurance policy, as well as the primary legatee and coexecutor of Blanchard's estate. Hence, a court examining these facts could reasonably conclude that these men were much more than mere roommates. *214

In as much as this case is before us on a certified question, we conclude only that appellant has demonstrated a likelihood of success on the merits, in that he is not excluded, as a matter of law, from seeking noneviction protection. Since all remaining issues are beyond this court's scope of review, we remit this case to the Appellate Division so that it may exercise its discretionary powers in accordance with this decision.

Accordingly, the order of the Appellate Division should be reversed and the case remitted to that court for a consideration of undetermined questions. The certified question should be answered in the negative.

While appellate courts still continue to give deference to local zoning ordinances that promote "the health, safety, morals and general welfare" of the community, the concern in using these traditional "family" definitions is that they are really justifications of discrimination or bias. For example, "senior" communities or retirement villages can keep out families who they think are too young.[20] Is that fair? What are some other examples where a community may be legally segregated?

CHAPTER SOURCE

Wadlington, W., and O'Brien, R. C. (2007). *Domestic Relations Cases and Materials*, 6th ed. Foundation Press.

---

20 The Way We Live Now, "Childproof. Why is a segregated community O.K. when kids are the ones-excluded? Christopher Caldwell, *New York Times Magazine*, August 13, 2006.

PRIVATE ORDERING—COHABITATION

Try to live your life so that you wouldn't be afraid
to sell the family parrot to the town gossip.
—Will Rogers[1]

Private ordering refers to people structuring their relationships and their desires to meet their own needs outside of what the law provides. Couples who choose to cohabitate,[2] deciding to live together outside of marriage, are private ordering. They are voluntarily rejecting society's traditionally recognized relationship of marriage. Instead, cohabitating couples are creating a lifestyle and relationship that fits their own needs. In doing so, they are rejecting the legal, social, and financial benefits that society has bestowed on married couples to encourage the institution. Or are they? A problem arises when cohabitating couples ask society (through the courts) to recognize their relationship, even though it does not fit within the rules prescribed by society regarding legally recognized relationships. Is that like refusing to buy insurance, but then demanding protection after a disaster? Or should the courts recognize such relationships as an efficient way to change society, when the law has been too slow?

Traditionally, society disapproved of couples living together outside of marriage. To dissuade such behavior, states passed laws including prohibitions against sodomy, fornication, and birth control (see Chapter 13). While most states have abolished their criminal laws against cohabitation, the stigma against it often remains. In the *Watts v. Watts* case, the court wrote, "[w]hen the legislature abolished criminal sanctions for cohabitation in 1983, it nevertheless added a section to the criminal code stating that while the state does not regulate private sexual activity

---

1 The Quotations Page, http://www.quotationspage.com/quote/22209.html
2 Wiktionary defines cohabitation as: "1. An emotional and physical intimate relationship which includes a common living place and which exists without legal or religious sanction; 2. The act of living together … 4. (biology) The act of two species living together in the same habitat. http://en.wiktionary.org/wiki/cohabitation"

of consenting adults, the state does not condone or encourage sexual conduct outside of the institution of marriage."[3]

In 2005, cohabitation was illegal in seven states: Florida, Michigan, Mississippi, North Carolina, North Dakota, Virginia, and West Virginia—which covered almost 1 million people.[4] Now, only two states criminalize a couple's choice to live together: Mississippi and Michigan.[5] States that still make cohabitation illegal generally ignore couples violating the law and selectively fail to criminally prosecute them. In the 1990s, the effects of Virginia law were felt by a 73-year-old day care provider and her boyfriend of 16 years. "Darlene K. Davis ... of Norfolk, [Virginia] ... nearly lost her daycare license after a state inspector learned she and her boyfriend ... lived together. According to Davis the inspector told her, 'You live in sin.'" Only after the ACLU filed suit against the state was the matter resolved, after nine months.[6] Virginia's 136-year-old law against "lewd and lascivious cohabitation" §18.2-345 of Virginia Code specified that "If any persons, not married to each other, lewdly and lasciviously associate and cohabit together ... each of them shall be guilty of a Class 3 misdemeanor"—punishable by a fine up to $500. When Virginia abolished that law[7] in 2013, census data showed that about 140,000 Virginians were cohabitating. Clearly, the law was not enforced. The law also prohibited anyone, married or not, from engaging in 'open and gross lewdness,' meaning sex acts in public. That aspect of the law still stands.[8] In 1979 Florida suspended a company's liquor license after finding that six company employees were "in cohabitating relationships." By 2016 Florida repealed its 1868 law making it "a second degree misdemeanor-punishable by up to 60 days in jail and a $500 fine."[9]

CALIFORNIA'S *MARVIN* CASES

California's three *Marvin v. Marvin* cases beginning in the 1970s were seminal cases regarding court recognition of privately ordered relationships involving heterosexual cohabitation. The case went from the trial court's dismissal based on the stigma of a meretricious relationship all the way

---

3   *Watts v. Watts* (1987), 137 Wis.2d 506, 405 N.W.2d 303, 56 USLW 2011, FN 10.
4   "Cohabitating Americans in 7 states run afoul of the law," Sharon Jayson, *USA Today*, July 17, 2005. http://usatoday30.usatoday.com/life/lifestyle/2005-07-17-state-law_x.htm
5   http://www.essence.com/2016/04/08/whoa-its-still-illegal-unmarried-couples-live-together-two-states
6   Ibid.
7   http://www.wjla.com/articles/2013/02/va-house-panel-backs-repeal-of-cohabitation-law-85332.html# ixzz2RsGeNaQw, "Va. House panel backs repeal of cohabitation law," ABCNEWS7, Mike Conneen, AP for News 7, on February 16, 2013.
8   "Bill would legalize cohabitation in Virginia," Laura Vozzella, The *Washington Post*, January 27, 2013. http://www. washingtonpost.com/local/va-politics/bill-would-legalize-cohabitation-in-virginia/2013/01/27/ba65ef94-68d2-11e2-95b3-272d604a10a3_story.html. Contrast that to Spain where six Swiss tourists were fined $135 each when they were caught having an orgy in a moving van. "'Having sex in the back of a van is not illegal,'" said a police spokesman. "Not wearing a seat belt is." *The Week*, August 22, 2014, P. 4.
9   www.tampbay.com/blogs/the-buzz-florida=politics/after148-years=cohabitation=legal-again--in-florida/2272119/anti-cohabitation

up to the California Supreme Court and then back down to the trial court on remand. Because of the combination of the Hollywood celebrity involved and the questions it raised on the fabric of the institution of marriage, it was probably one of the most watched family law cases of the time.

In the first *Marvin v. Marvin*, (I) 557 P2.d 106 (CA 1976), the California Supreme Court was asked to determine whether the courts would award compensation to a woman whose cohabitational relationship ended. The couple comprised of the Hollywood actor, Lee Marvin, and Michelle Triola Marvin. "She met Lee Marvin in 1964 when she had a part in the movie 'Ship of Fools,' which came out the next year. They began dating, and within a few months Marvin left his wife and began staying at Michelle's Hollywood apartment. In January 1965 they moved into a house he found for them in Malibu."[10] "In May 1970 she legally added 'Marvin' to her name, but the next month the actor had her evicted from the Malibu house."[11] "In November 1971, he cut off a monthly allowance he had been paying to Michelle."[12] In February 1972, Triola Marvin took Lee Marvin to court. "[S]he testified that Lee Marvin, who won an Academy Award for best actor in 'Cat Ballou' (1965) during their relationship, had asked her to give up her career and said he would take care of her."[13] Having "calculated that her former boyfriend had earned $3.6 million during the six years of their cohabitation … [S]he sued for half of that sum, $1.8 million."[14]

The couple lived together for seven years, but never intended to marry. What was she entitled to when they broke up? When the lower trial court was asked to decide the matter, they agreed with defendant Lee Marvin that the case should be dismissed. He argued—as had been successfully done for centuries—that even if such an agreement existed, which he denied, it was immoral because it was based on sex—a meretricious relationship. The trial court, without hearing the case, agreed that cohabitation agreements are founded on the parties' sexual relationship, and, therefore unenforceable. Michelle Triola Marvin continued to appeal until the case reached the California Supreme Court.

At the California Supreme Court in *Marvin* I, the court was asked again to look at the issue of whether California would recognize nonmarital agreements for support and property division. Rejecting years of precedent that found agreements between two unmarried people living together as immoral, the court said that such relationships were more than just about sex. The court felt that such relationships were similar to other relationships, and therefore the contract may be enforceable if it had not been based specifically on illicit sexual services. In this landmark case, the court recognizes equitable rights and remedies in a live-in relationship, as long as the

---

10   http://www.latimes.com/news/obituaries/la-me-michelle-triola-marvin31-2009oct31,0,2805574.story (Obituary, *Los Angeles Times*, October 31, 2009)
11   Ibid.
12   Ibid.
13   Ibid.
14   Ibid. At the trials, "[b]oth Marvins took the stand, providing numerous moments of high drama. He said he never loved her; she said he proposed marriage twice. He said she threatened suicide; she said he made her pregnant three times and paid for one abortion. (One pregnancy ended in miscarriage, and two were terminated.) Marvin … said the second abortion left her unable to bear children."

reason for the contract was not based just on sexual consideration. Perhaps this case was one of the first to recognize private ordering.

In *Marvin v. Marvin* (II), 122 CA App 3d 871 (1981), having determined that these cases may require a legal remedy, the case was remanded back to the lower court to determine whether compensation was due based on the facts and the alleged oral agreement in this particular case. Making clear that it was not deciding this case using the laws of divorce, and not finding an express or implied contract, the *Marvin* II court awarded about $104,000 to Michelle Triola Marvin. The court said that Michelle could use it for economic rehabilitation—a term that is recognized in divorce cases when a stay-at-home mom needs to refresh her job skills to become self-sufficient after the divorce. The newspapers nicknamed Michelle's award "palimony."

Lee Marvin then filed an appeal of the $104,000 award to Michelle in *Marvin v. Marvin* (III) 176 CA Rptr. 555 (CA Ct. App. 1981). The appellate court reversed the *Marvin* II court and took away the award of $104,000. While the court acknowledged that the *Marvin* I court ruled that compensation may be due from the breakup of a cohabitation relationship, the *Marvin* III court said that did not apply in this particular situation because Michelle had benefited both socially and economically from her seven-year relationship with a celebrity. Therefore, she had not suffered any damages at the time of the breakup, and they revoked Lee Marvin's obligation to pay Michelle Triola Marvin the $104,000.[15] While both sides claimed victory, Michelle Marvin perhaps won the best sound bite: "If a man wants to leave his toothbrush at my house, he better bloody well marry me."[16] When discussing the *Marvin* cases and the issue of "palimony," Ruth Bader Ginsburg, later appointed to the U.S. Supreme Court, said in 1979 when she was a Columbia University law professor: "It illustrates the further breakdown of the legal line between married and unmarried union."[17]

Whatever happened to Michelle and Lee? In October of 1970, the same year he broke up with Michelle, Lee "married his childhood sweetheart, Pamela Feeley."[18] Michelle Triola subsequently had a 30-year relationship with talented comedian and actor (think Disney's *Mary Poppins*), Dick Van Dyke, until her death in October 2009. Interestingly, in his book *My Lucky Life In and Out of Show Business*, Van Dyke refers to that court award and withdrawal of the $104,000 payment as the death knell to his own long-term marriage. When Van Dyke met Michelle, he was still married and later began a relationship with her. According to the book, beginning on page 222, when Michelle was "extremely upset after years of fighting a fight" in the *Marvin* lawsuits, Van Dyke gave her the money. When his wife found out, she started the process for divorce.[19]

---

15 *My Lucky Life In and Out of Show Business: A Memoir*, by Dick Van Dyke, 2011 by Point Productions, Inc. (beginning on page 222).

16 Michele Triola Marvin died in October 2009. http://www.latimes.com/news/obituaries/la-me-michelle-triola-marvin31-2009oct31,0,2805574.story (Obituary, *Los Angeles Times*, October 31, 2009).

17 Ibid.

18 Ibid.

19 *My Lucky Life In and Out of Show Business: A Memoir*, by Dick Van Dyke, 2011 by Point Productions, Inc. (beginning on page 222).

Thus, in the *Marvin* I case, the California courts ignored centuries of public policy in ruling that unmarried cohabitants should be allowed to make contract claims against their partners as long as the claim existed independently of their sexual relationship and was supported by separate consideration. With this legal recognition of cohabitation relationships and the possible remedies, including divorce-like alimony payments of "palimony," is the status of marriage weakened? The *Marvin* court was careful to point out in the case that it recognized the important role marriage played in society, but said that recognizing nonmarital relationships would not deprecate the status. It also made clear that it was recognizing the legal rights created, not based on marriage and divorce laws, but based on contract. Is it a good idea to uphold these private arrangements?

In 1979, the Illinois Supreme Court looked at the same issue in the case of *Hewitt v. Hewitt*, 394. N.E.2d 1204 (IL 1979). In the *Hewitt* case, the couple met while students at Grinnell College. When the woman became pregnant, they moved in together and remained together for the next 15 years, raising three children together. Although they never applied for a marriage license, they acted as a married couple. During their time together, the man earned an advanced degree and set up his practice, using money from the woman's parents to do so. The woman, in addition to raising the children, did bookkeeping and occasional work in the man's practice. After 15 years, the woman decided she wanted to leave the relationship and originally filed a motion for divorce (mistakenly believing they had been married during this time). When her husband filed a motion to dismiss her claim because they had not been married, the court agreed, but allowed her to amend her complaint to ask for half of the accumulated property they had obtained during the time they lived together.

In arguing that she should be awarded some of the property obtained during their relationship, the woman said it would be unfair for her to receive nothing and for him to receive everything. She also argued that they were a functional family (indeed, she thought they were a form family) for 15 years. Therefore, their outwardly conventional appearance was not an affront to public policy. On appeal, the Illinois Supreme Court did not agree with her and rejected her claim for any property rights. The state was very clear that to do otherwise would only encourage avoidance of marriage and create an attractive alternative. Because society and the state had an interest in encouraging people to marry, the court rejected her claim. The court's decision was further based on the fact that the Illinois state legislature had recently rejected no-fault divorce and made clear its support of the traditional family. Indeed, the *Hewitt* court said that it would not enforce a contract between the cohabitating couples even if it had been written, because the state did not want to encourage private ordering behavior.

Thus, the *Hewitt* court continued to rule that contracts between cohabitating couples are against public policy. In contrast to the *Hewitt* case, the case of *Watts v. Watts*, 405 N.W.2d 303 (WI 1987) found that "[n]onmarital cohabitation does not render every agreement between cohabiting parties illegal and does not automatically preclude one party from seeking judicial relief" when possibly allowing the enforcement of an express or implied, in fact, contract or the possibility of recovery based upon unjust enrichment (the moral principle that one who has received benefit has a duty to make restitution, where retaining benefit would be unjust).

WATTS V. WATTS 137 WIS.2D 506, 405N.W.2D 303, 56 USLW2011 (1987)

Unmarried cohabitant brought action for accounting and share of accumulated property under family law statutes, theory of marriage by estoppel, theory of express or implied in fact contract, theory of constructive trust based upon unjust enrichment, and partition theory. The Circuit Court, Dane County, William D. Byrne, J., dismissed complaint for failure to state claim. Cohabitant appealed. The Court of Appeals certified case. The Supreme Court, Shirley S. Abrahamson, J., held that: (1) unmarried cohabitants were not "family" within meaning of statute that authorizes division of property in action affecting family; (2) doctrine of marriage by estoppel was inapplicable; and (3) cohabitant stated claims for breach of express or implied in fact contract, unjust enrichment, and partition.

Reversed and remanded.

Public policy did not preclude unmarried cohabitant from asserting contract claim against other party so long as claim existed independently of sexual relationship and was supported by separate consideration. W.S.A. 765.001, 944.01.

Unmarried cohabitant stated claim for accounting of property acquired during relationship and partition, where she alleged that cohabitants were engaged in joint venture or partnership, they purchased real and personal property as husband and wife, they intended to share all property acquired during relationship, and cohabitant contributed to acquisition of property. W.S.A. 820.01 et seq., 842.01 et seq., 842.02(1).

Shirley s. Abrahamson, Justice.

This is an appeal from a judgment of the circuit court for Dane County, William D. Byrne, Judge, dismissing Sue Ann Watts' amended complaint, pursuant to *510 sec. 802.06(2)(f), Stats. 1985–86, for failure to state a claim upon which relief may be granted … For the reasons set forth, we hold that the complaint states a claim upon which relief may be granted. Accordingly, we reverse the judgment of the circuit court and remand the cause to the circuit court for further proceedings consistent with this opinion.

The case involves a dispute between Sue Ann Evans Watts, the plaintiff, and James Watts, the defendant, over their respective interests in property accumulated during their nonmarital cohabitation relationship, which spanned 12 years and produced two children. The case presents an issue of first impression and comes to this court at the pleading stage of the case, before trial and before the facts have been determined.

The plaintiff asked the circuit court to order an accounting of the defendant's personal and business assets accumulated between June 1969 through December 1981 (the duration of the parties' cohabitation) and to determine plaintiff's share of this property. The circuit court's dismissal of plaintiff's amended complaint is the subject of this appeal. The plaintiff rests her claim for an accounting and a share in the accumulated property on the following legal theories: (1) she is entitled to an equitable division of property under sec. 767.255, Stats. 1985–86; (2) the defendant is estopped to assert as a defense to plaintiff's claim under sec. 767.255, that the parties are not married; (3) the plaintiff is entitled to damages for defendant's breach of an express contract or an implied-in-fact contract between the parties. …FN1

FN1. The complaint also includes five tort claims based on allegations regarding the defendant's conduct after the termination of their relationship. The parties stipulated to the dismissal of the tort claims and they are not the subject of the appeals.

The circuit court dismissed the amended complaint, concluding that sec. 767.255, Stats. 1985–86, authorizing a court to divide property, does not apply to the division of property between unmarried persons. Without analyzing the four other legal theories upon which the plaintiff rests her claim, the circuit court simply concluded that the legislature, not the court, should provide relief to parties who have accumulated property in nonmarital cohabitation relationships. The circuit court gave no further explanation for its decision.

We agree with the circuit court that the legislature did not intend sec. 767.255 to apply to an unmarried couple. We disagree with the circuit court's implicit conclusion that courts cannot or should not, without express authorization from the legislature,**306 divide property between persons who have engaged in nonmarital cohabitation. Courts traditionally have settled contract and property disputes between unmarried persons, some of whom have cohabited. Nonmarital cohabitation does not render every agreement between the cohabiting parties illegal and does not automatically preclude one of the parties from seeking judicial relief, such as statutory or common law partition, damages for breach of express or *512 implied contract, constructive trust and quantum meruit where the party alleges, and later proves, facts supporting the legal theory. The issue for the court in each case is whether the complaining party has set forth any legally cognizable claim …

We test the sufficiency of the plaintiff's amended complaint by first setting forth the facts asserted in the complaint and then analyzing each of the five legal theories upon which the plaintiff rests her claim for relief.

I.

The plaintiff commenced this action in 1982. The plaintiff's amended complaint alleges the following *513 facts, which for purposes of this appeal must be accepted as true. The plaintiff and the defendant met in 1967, when she was 19 years old, was living with her parents and was working full time as a nurse's aide in preparation for a nursing career. Shortly after the parties met, the defendant persuaded the plaintiff to move into an apartment paid for by him and to quit her job. According to the amended complaint, the defendant "indicated" to the plaintiff that he would provide for her.

Early in 1969, the parties began living together in a "marriage-like" relationship, holding themselves out to the public as husband and wife. The plaintiff assumed the defendant's surname as her own. Subsequently, she gave birth to two children who were also given the defendant's surname. The parties filed joint income tax returns and maintained joint bank accounts asserting that they were husband and wife. The defendant insured the plaintiff as his wife on his medical insurance policy. He also took out a life insurance policy on her as his wife, naming himself as the beneficiary. The parties purchased real and personal property as husband and wife. The plaintiff executed documents and obligated herself on promissory notes to lending institutions as the defendant's wife.

During their relationship, the plaintiff contributed childcare and homemaking services, including cleaning, cooking, laundering, shopping, running errands, and maintaining the grounds surrounding the parties' home. Additionally, the plaintiff contributed personal property to the relationship which she owned at the beginning of the relationship or acquired through gifts or purchases during the relationship. She served as hostess for the defendant for social and *514 business-related events. The amended complaint further asserts that periodically, between 1969 and 1975, the plaintiff cooked and cleaned for the defendant and his employees while his business, a landscaping service, was building and landscaping a golf course.

From 1973 to 1976, the plaintiff worked 20–25 hours per week at the defendant's office, performing duties as a receptionist, **307 typist, and assistant bookkeeper. From 1976 to 1981, the plaintiff worked 40–60 hours per week at a business she started with the defendant's sister-in-law, then continued and managed the business herself after the dissolution of that partnership. The plaintiff further alleges that in 1981 the defendant made their relationship so intolerable that she was forced to move from their home and their relationship was irretrievably broken. Subsequently, the defendant barred the plaintiff from returning to her business.

The plaintiff alleges that during the parties' relationship, and because of her domestic and business contributions, the business and personal wealth of the couple increased. Furthermore, the plaintiff alleges that she never received any compensation for these contributions to the relationship and that the defendant indicated to the plaintiff both orally and through his conduct that he considered her to be his wife and that she would share equally in the increased wealth.

The plaintiff asserts that since the breakdown of the relationship the defendant has refused to share equally with her the wealth accumulated through their joint efforts or to compensate her in any way for her contributions to the relationship.

II.

The plaintiff's first legal theory to support her claim against the property accumulated during the *515 cohabitation is that the plaintiff, defendant, and their children constitute a "family," thus entitling the plaintiff to bring an action for property division …

The plaintiff asserts that the legislature intended secs. 767.02(1)(h) and 767.255, which usually govern division of property between married persons in divorce or legal separation proceedings, to govern a property division action between unmarried cohabitants who constitute a family. …

In a supplemental submission, and at oral argument, the plaintiff analogized its interpretation of sec. 767.255 to this court's adoption of a broad definition of "family" in the context of zoning and land use. See, e.g. *Crowley v. Knapp*, 94 Wis.2d 421, 437, 288 N.W.2d 815 (1980), in which this court stated that a "family" in that context "may mean a group of people who live, sleep, cook, and eat upon the premises as a single housekeeping unit." In Crowley, the court adopted a definition of "family" serving that public policy favoring the free and unrestricted use of property.

By contrast, the plaintiff here has failed to convince us that extending the definition of "family" in this case to include unmarried cohabitants will further in any way the expressed public policy of ch. 767 to promote marriage and the family.

FN5. The "Family Code" is comprised of ch. 765, Marriage; ch. 766, Marital Property; ch. 767, Actions Affecting the Family; and ch. 768, Actions Abolished.

The plaintiff relies on *Warden v. Warden*, 36 Wash.App. 693, 676 P.2d 1037 (1984), to support her claim for relief under secs. 767.02(1)(h) and 767.255. In *Warden*, the Washington court of appeals held that the statute providing guidelines for property division upon dissolution of marriage, legal separation, etc., could also be applied to divide property acquired by unmarried cohabitants in what was "tantamount to a marital family except for a legal marriage."**308 Warden, 36 Wash.App. at 698, 676 P.2d at 1039. *Warden* is remarkably similar on its facts to the instant case. The parties in Warden had lived together for 11 years, had two children, held themselves out as husband and wife, acquired property together, and filed joint tax returns. On those facts, the Washington court of appeals held that the trial court correctly treated the parties as a "family" within the meaning of the Washington marriage dissolution statute. In addition, the trial court had considered such statutory factors as the length and purpose of the parties' relationship, their two children, and the contributions and future *517 prospects of each in determining their respective shares of the property.

Although the Warden case provides support for the plaintiff's argument, most courts which have addressed the issue of whether marriage dissolution statutes provide relief to unmarried cohabitants, have either rejected or avoided application of a marriage dissolution statute to unmarried cohabitants. See, e.g., *Marvin v. Marvin*, 18 Cal.3d 660, 681, 134 Cal.Rptr. 815, 557 P.2d 106 (1976); …

While we agree with the plaintiff that some provisions in ch. 767 govern a mother, father, and their children, regardless of marriage, FN7 upon our analysis of sec. 767.255 and the Family Code, we *518 conclude that the legislature did not intend sec. 767.255 to extend to unmarried cohabitants.

FN10. When the legislature abolished criminal sanctions for cohabitation in 1983, it nevertheless added a section to the criminal code stating that while the state does not regulate private sexual activity of consenting adults, the state does not condone or encourage sexual conduct outside the institution of marriage. The legislature adopted the language of sec. 765.001 that "[m]arriage is the foundation of family and society. Its stability is basic to morality and civilization, and of vital interest to society and this state." Sec. 944.01, Stats. 1985–86.

On the basis of our analysis of sec. 767.255 and the Family Code which revealed no clear evidence that the legislature intended sec. 767.255 to apply to *520 unmarried persons, we decline the invitation to extend the application of sec. 767.255 to unmarried cohabitants. We therefore hold that the plaintiff has not stated a claim for property division under sec. 767.255 … [*Argument III on marriage by estoppels is omitted by the author.*]

IV.

The plaintiff's third legal theory on which her claim rests is that she and the defendant had a contract to share equally the property accumulated during their relationship. The essence of the complaint is that the parties had a contract, either an express or implied in fact contract, which the defendant breached.

Wisconsin courts have long recognized the importance of freedom of contract and have endeavored to protect the right to contract. A contract will not be enforced, however, if it violates public policy. A declaration that the contract is against public policy should be made only after a careful balancing, in the light of all the circumstances, of the interest in enforcing a particular promise against the policy **310 against enforcement. Courts should be reluctant to frustrate a party's reasonable expectations without a corresponding benefit to be gained in deterring "misconduct" or avoiding inappropriate use of the judicial system …

The defendant appears to attack the plaintiff's contract theory on three grounds. First, the defendant apparently asserts that the court's recognition of plaintiff's contract claim for a share of the parties' property contravenes the Wisconsin Family Code. Second, the defendant asserts that the legislature, not the courts, should determine the property and contract rights of unmarried cohabiting parties. Third, the defendant intimates that the parties' relationship was immoral and illegal and that any recognition of a contract between the parties or plaintiff's claim for a share of the property accumulated during the cohabitation contravenes public policy.

The defendant rests his argument that judicial recognition of a contract between unmarried cohabitants for property division violates the Wisconsin Family Code on *Hewitt v. Hewitt*, 77 Ill.2d 49,

31 Ill.Dec. 827, 394 N.E.2d 1204, 3 A.L.R. 4th 1 (1979). In *Hewitt* the Illinois Supreme Court concluded that judicial recognition of mutual property rights between unmarried cohabitants would violate the policy of the Illinois Marriage and Dissolution Act because enhancing the attractiveness of a private arrangement contravenes the Act's policy of strengthening and preserving the integrity of marriage. The Illinois court concluded that allowing such a contract claim would weaken the sanctity of marriage, put in doubt the rights of inheritance, and open the door to false pretenses of marriage. *Hewitt*, 77 Ill.2d at 65, 31 Ill.Dec. at 834, 394 N.E.2d at 1211.

We agree with Professor Prince and other commentators that the Hewitt court made an unsupportable inferential leap when it found that cohabitation *523 agreements run contrary to statutory policy and that the Hewitt court's approach is patently inconsistent with the principle that public policy limits are to be narrowly and exactly applied. FN14

FN14. Prince, Public Policy Limitations in Cohabitation Agreements: Unruly Horse or Circus Pony, 70 Minn.L.Rev. 163, 189–205 (1985).

Furthermore, the Illinois statutes upon which the Illinois Supreme Court rested its decision are distinguishable from the Wisconsin statutes. The Illinois Supreme Court relied on the fact that Illinois still retained "fault" divorce and that cohabitation was unlawful. By contrast, Wisconsin abolished "fault" in divorce in 1977 and abolished criminal sanctions for nonmarital cohabitation in 1983. FN15

FN15. Both Illinois and Wisconsin have abolished common law marriages. In our view this abolition does not invalidate a private cohabitation contract. Cohabitation agreements differ in effect from common law marriage. There is a significant difference between the consequences of achieving common law marriage status and of having an enforceable cohabitation agreement.

In *Latham v. Latham*, 274 Or. 421, 426-27, 547 P.2d 144, 147 (1976), the Oregon supreme court found that the Legislature's decriminalization of cohabitation represented strong evidence that enforcing agreements made by parties during cohabitation relationships would not be contrary to Oregon public policy.

The defendant has failed to persuade this court that enforcing an express or implied in fact contract between these parties would in fact violate the Wisconsin Family Code. The Family Code, chs. 765–68, Stats. 1985–86, is intended to promote the institution of marriage and the family. We find no indication, however, that the Wisconsin legislature intended the Family Code to restrict in any way a court's resolution *524 of property or contract disputes between unmarried cohabitants.

The defendant also urges that if the court is not willing to say that the Family Code proscribes contracts between unmarried **311 cohabiting parties, then the court should refuse to resolve the contract and property rights of unmarried cohabitants without legislative guidance. The defendant asserts that this court should conclude, as the Hewitt court did, that the task of determining the rights of cohabiting parties is too complex and difficult for the court and should be left to the legislature. We are not persuaded by the defendant's argument. Courts have traditionally developed principles of contract and property law through the case-by-case method of the common law. While ultimately the legislature may resolve the problems raised by unmarried cohabiting parties, we are not persuaded that the court should refrain from resolving such disputes until the legislature gives us direction. *Our survey of the cases in other jurisdictions reveals that Hewitt is not widely followed. [FN 16 omitted by the author and emphasis added.]*

We turn to the defendant's third point, namely, that any contract between the parties regarding property division contravenes public policy because the contract is based on immoral or illegal sexual activity. The defendant does not appear to make this *525 argument directly. It is not well developed in the brief, and at oral argument defendant's attorney indicated that he did not find this argument persuasive in light of the current community mores, the substantial number of unmarried people who cohabit, and the legislature's abolition of criminal sanctions for cohabitation. Although the parties in the instant case cohabited at a time when cohabitation was illegal, the defendant's counsel at oral argument thought that the present law should govern this aspect of the case. Because illegal sexual activity has posed a problem for courts in contract actions, we discuss this issue even though the defendant did not emphasize it.

Courts have generally refused to enforce contracts for which the sole consideration is sexual relations, sometimes referred to as "meretricious" relationships. See In Matter of Estate of Steffes, 95 Wis.2d 490, 514, 290 N.W.2d 697 (1980), citing Restatement of Contracts Section 589 (1932). Courts distinguish, however, between contracts that are explicitly and inseparably founded on sexual services and those that are not. This court, and numerous other courts, FN17 have concluded that "a bargain between two people is not illegal merely because there is an illicit relationship between the two so long as the bargain is independent of the illicit relationship and the illicit relationship does not constitute any part of the consideration bargained for and is not a condition of the bargain." *Steffes*, supra, 95 Wis.2d at 514, 290 N.W.2d 697. *[FN 17 and citations omitted by the author.]*

*526 While not condoning the illicit sexual relationship of the parties, many courts have recognized that the result of a court's refusal to enforce contract and property rights between unmarried cohabitants is that one party keeps all or most of the assets accumulated during the relationship, while the other party, no more or less "guilty," is deprived of property which he or she has helped to accumulate. See e.g., *Glasgo v. Glasgo*, 410 N.E.2d 1325, 1330 (Ind.App.1980); *Latham v. Latham*, 274 Or. 421, 426, 547 P.2d 144 (1976); **Marvin v. Marvin**, supra, 18 Cal.3d at 682, 134 Cal.Rptr. at 830, 557 P.2d at 121; *West v. Knowles*, 50 Wash.2d 311, 315-16, 311 P.2d 689 (1957). *[Emphasis added by the author.]*

The *Hewitt* decision, which leaves one party to the relationship enriched at the expense of the other party who had contributed to the acquisition of the property, **312 has often been criticized by courts and commentators as being unduly harsh. FN18 Moreover, courts recognize that their refusal to enforce what are in other contexts clearly lawful promises will not undo the parties' relationship and may not discourage others from entering into such relationships. *Tyranski v. Piggins*, 44 Mich. App. 570, 577, 205 N.W.2d 595 (1973). A harsh, per se rule that the contract and property rights of unmarried cohabiting parties will not be recognized might actually encourage a partner with greater income potential to avoid marriage in order to retain all accumulated assets, leaving the other party with nothing. See *527 *Marvin v. Marvin*, supra, 18 Cal.3d at 683, 134 Cal.Rptr. at 831, 557 P.2d at 122. *[Emphasis added by the author; Footnote 18 and citations omitted by the author.]*

One Wisconsin case which requires discussion in this context is *Smith v. Smith*, 255 Wis. 96, 38 N.W.2d 12, 14 A.L.R.2d 914 (1949). In *Smith*, one of the parties to a common law marriage discovered that such marriages were not legal, demanded that the defendant marry her, was refused, and sought equitable property division. The court denied her claim. Although we find the harsh result in *Smith* troubling, we need not overrule it because *Smith* is distinguishable from the instant case.

The plaintiff in Smith was seeking equitable property division under the marriage dissolution statutes. Like the court in *Smith*, we have decided that those statutes are unavailable to an unmarried person. The plaintiff in this case, however, rests her claim on theories of recovery other than those of the plaintiff in *Smith*. The *Smith* court ruled that the plaintiff had based her claim for property division solely on the fact of the couple's illegal common law marriage. Smith, supra, 255 Wis. at 100, 38 N.W.2d 12. In other words, the plaintiff in that case had not alleged facts necessary to find that the couple had agreed to share their property, independent from their sexual relationship. Id.

In *Smith*, the problem was inadequate pleading by the plaintiff. In this case, the plaintiff has alleged many facts independent from the parties' physical relationship which, if proven, would establish an express contract or an implied in fact contract that the parties agreed to share the property accumulated during the relationship.

*528 The plaintiff has alleged that she quit her job and abandoned her career training upon the defendant's promise to take care of her. A change in one party's circumstances in performance of the agreement may imply an agreement between the parties. *Steffes*, supra, 95 Wis.2d at 504, 290 N.W.2d 697; *Tyranski*, supra, 44 Mich.App. at 574, 205 N.W.2d at 597.

In addition, the plaintiff alleges that she performed housekeeping, childbearing, childrearing, and other services related to the maintenance of the parties' home, in addition to various services for the defendant's business and her own business, for which she received no compensation. Courts have recognized that money, property, or services (including housekeeping or childrearing) may constitute adequate consideration independent of the parties' sexual relationship to support an agreement to share or transfer property. ... *[Cites omitted by the author.]*

FN19. Until recently, the prevailing view was that services performed in the context of a "family or marriage relationship" were presumed gratuitous. However, that presumption was rebuttable. See *Steffes*, 95 Wis.2d at 501, 290 N.W.2d at 703-704. In *Steffes*, we held the presumption to be irrelevant where the plaintiff can show either an express or implied agreement to pay for those services, even where the plaintiff has rendered them "with a sense of affection, devotion and duty." Id. 95 Wis.2d at 503, 290 N.W.2d at 703–704. For a discussion of the evolution of thought regarding the economic value of homemaking services by cohabitants, see Bruch, Property Rights of De Facto Spouses Including Thoughts on the Value of Homemakers' Services, 10 Fam.L.Q. 101, 110-14 (Summer 1976).

**313 *529 According to the plaintiff's complaint, the parties cohabited for more than twelve years, held joint bank accounts, made joint purchases, filed joint income tax returns, and were listed as husband and wife on other legal documents. Courts have held that such a relationship and "joint acts of a financial nature can give rise to an inference that the parties intended to share equally." *Beal v. Beal*, 282 Or. 115, 122, 577 P.2d 507, 510 (1978). The joint ownership of property and the filing of joint income tax returns strongly implies that the parties intended their relationship to be in the nature of a joint enterprise, financially as well as personally. See *Beal*, 282 Or. at 122, 577 P.2d at 510; *Warden v. Warden*, supra, 36 Wash.App. at 696–97, 676 P.2d at 1038.

Having reviewed the complaint and surveyed the law in this and other jurisdictions, we hold that the Family Code does not preclude an unmarried cohabitant from asserting contract and property claims against the other party to the cohabitation. We further conclude that public policy does not necessarily preclude an unmarried cohabitant from asserting a contract claim against the other party to the cohabitation so long as the claim exists independently of the sexual relationship and is supported by separate consideration. Accordingly, we conclude that the plaintiff in this case has pleaded the facts necessary to state a claim for damages resulting from the defendant's breach of an express or an implied in fact contract to share with the plaintiff the property accumulated through the efforts of both parties during their relationship. Once again, we do not judge the merits of the plaintiff's claim; we merely hold that she be given her day in court to prove her claim.

*530 V.

The plaintiff's fourth theory of recovery involves unjust enrichment. Essentially, she alleges that the defendant accepted and retained the benefit of services she provided knowing that she expected to share equally in the wealth accumulated during their relationship. She argues that it is unfair for the defendant to retain all the assets they accumulated under these circumstances and that a constructive trust should be imposed on the property as a result of the defendant's unjust enrichment. In his brief, the defendant does not attack specifically either the legal theory or the factual allegations made by the plaintiff.

Unlike claims for breach of an express or implied in fact contract, a claim of unjust enrichment does not arise out of an agreement entered into by the parties. Rather, an action for recovery based upon unjust enrichment is grounded on the moral principle that one who has received a benefit has a duty to make restitution where retaining such a benefit would be unjust. *Puttkammer v. Minth*, 83 Wis.2d 686, 689, 266 N.W.2d 361, 363 (1978).

Because no express or implied in fact agreement exists between the parties, recovery based upon unjust enrichment is sometimes referred to as "quasi contract," or contract "implied in law" rather than "implied in fact." Quasi contracts are obligations created by law to prevent injustice. *Shulse v. City of Mayville*, 223 Wis. 624, 632, 271 N.W. 643 (1937). [*Footnote 20 omitted by the author.*]

In Wisconsin, an action for unjust enrichment, or quasi contract, is based upon proof of three elements: (1) a benefit conferred on the defendant by the plaintiff, (2) appreciation or knowledge by the defendant of the benefit, and (3) acceptance or retention of the benefit by the defendant under circumstances making it inequitable for the defendant to retain the benefit. *Puttkammer*, supra, 83 Wis.2d at 689, 266 N.W.2d 361; Wis.J.I. Civil No. 3028 (1981).

The plaintiff has cited no cases directly supporting actions in unjust enrichment by unmarried cohabitants, and the defendant provides no authority against it. This **314 court has previously extended such relief to a party to a cohabitation in Estate of Fox, 178 Wis. 369, 190 N.W. 90, 31 A.L.R. 420 (1922). In Fox, the plaintiff was a woman who had believed in good faith that she was married to the decedent, when in fact she was not. The court found that the decedent "husband" had "by fraudulent representations induced the plaintiff to enter into the illicit relationship." Fox, supra, 178 Wis. at 372, 190 N.W. 90. Under those circumstances, the court reasoned that it was "just and logical" to infer "from the nature of the transaction" that "the supposed husband [can be] held to have assumed to pay [for services rendered by his 'spouse'] because in point of law and equity it is just that he should pay." Id.

In Fox, the court expressly refused to consider whether the same result would necessarily follow in other circumstances. Thus, Fox does not supply explicit support for the plaintiff's position here where she does not claim that she thought the parties were actually married.

The *Steffes* case, however, does provide additional support for the plaintiff's position. Although Steffes involved a claim for recovery in contract by an *532 unmarried cohabitant for the value of services she performed for the decedent, the same equitable principles that governed that case would appear to apply in a case where the plaintiff is seeking recovery based upon unjust enrichment. In *Steffes*, the court cited with approval a statement by the trial judge that "[t]he question I have in mind is why should the estate be enriched when that man was just as much a part of the illicit relationship as she was and not let her have her fair dues. I don't understand that law that would interpret unjust enrichment that way and deprive one and let the other benefit and do it on the basis that there was an illicit relationship but not equally held against the both. ..." *Steffes*, supra, 95 Wis.2d at 508, 290 N.W.2d 697.

As part of his general argument, the defendant claims that the court should leave the parties to an illicit relationship such as the one in this case essentially as they are found, providing no relief at all to either party. For support, the defendant relies heavily on *Hewitt v. Hewitt*, supra, and the dissent in *Steffes*, to argue that courts should provide no relief whatsoever to unmarried cohabitants until the legislature provides specifically for it. See *Steffes*, supra, 95 Wis.2d at 521–22, 290 N.W.2d 697 (Coffey, J., dissenting).

As we have discussed previously, allowing no relief at all to one party in a so-called "illicit" relationship effectively provides total relief to the other, by leaving that party owner of all the assets acquired through the efforts of both. Yet it cannot seriously be argued that the party retaining all the assets is less "guilty" than the other. Such a result is contrary to the principles of equity. Many courts have held, and we now so hold, that unmarried cohabitants may raise claims based upon unjust enrichment *533 following the termination of their relationships where one of the parties attempts to retain an unreasonable amount of the property acquired through the efforts of both. *[The cites of Footnote 21 are omitted by the author.]*

In this case, the plaintiff alleges that she contributed both property and services to the parties' relationship. She claims that because of these contributions the parties' assets increased, but that she was never compensated for her contributions. She further alleges that the defendant, knowing that the plaintiff expected to share in the property accumulated, "accepted the services rendered to him by the plaintiff" and that it would be unfair under the circumstances to allow him to retain everything while she receives nothing. We conclude that the facts alleged are sufficient to state a claim for recovery based upon unjust enrichment … *[Arguments on constructive trust and partition omitted by the author.]*

Second, as we have previously said, the defendant relying on Hewitt groups all of the plaintiff's claims together, including the partition claim, labels them "marriage-like claims," and argues that the court should not grant relief relating to the parties' accumulated property in cases of nonmarital cohabitation. We have already discussed the defendant's position and concluded that we are not persuaded by it.

In this case, the plaintiff has alleged that she and the defendant were engaged in a joint venture or partnership, that they purchased real and personal property as husband and wife, and that they intended to share all the property acquired during their relationship. In our opinion, these allegations, together with other facts alleged in the plaintiff's complaint (e.g., the plaintiff's contributions to the acquisition of their property) and reasonable inferences therefrom, are sufficient under Wisconsin's liberal notice pleading rule to state a claim for an accounting of the property acquired during the parties' relationship and partition. We do not, of course, presume to judge the merits of the plaintiff's claim. Proof of her allegations must be made to the circuit court. We merely hold that the plaintiff has alleged sufficient facts in her complaint to state a claim for relief statutory or common law partition.

*538 In summary, we hold that the plaintiff's complaint has stated a claim upon which relief may be granted. We conclude that her claim may not rest on sec. 767.255, Stats. 1985–86, or the doctrine of "marriage by estoppel," but that it may rest on contract, unjust enrichment or partition. Accordingly, we reverse the judgment of the circuit court, and remand the cause to the circuit court for further proceedings consistent with this opinion.

The judgment of the circuit court is reversed and the cause remanded.

In *Watts*, the court uses its equity (or fairness) powers to allow recovery for the woman after the breakup of her cohabitation. The *Watts* court upholds a claim of unjust enrichment, because the woman allegedly contributed both property and services to the relationship that increased their joint assets and she was not compensated. Moreover, the court felt the man accepted those services knowing that his partner expected to share in accumulated property. Two different results, from two Midwestern states, about ten years apart—why? Which court used the *Marvin* theory to decide its case? Should it have? The majority of states today would probably make rulings more similar to the *Watts* decision than the *Hewitt* outcome. That being said, the majority of courts, like the *Watts* court, would use their equity powers to find a way to allocate a share of the assets after a long cohabitation relationship ends. Why did the case of *Steelman v. Hirsch*, 473 F. 3d 124, (2007) not follow this precedent?

In *Steelman v. Hirsch*, 473 F.3d 124 (2004), "romantic partners, who exchanged vows, lived together, and worked side-by-side in a dog-grooming business known as 'Hair of the Dog' in Asheville, North Carolina... anticipated spending their lives together, but when the romantic relationship ended, the professional relationship collapsed as well." One of the two partners sued the other in Federal Court for an ownership interest in the company and compensation for work performed. The Federal Court dismissed the case based on the federal employment claims because she was not an employee. Interestingly, the federal judge in a southern state that opposed marriage equality encouraged the plaintiff to file under state law based on possible claims for "breach of contract... quantum meruit or unjust enrichment". "State law has provided mechanisms for dealing with the dissolution of domestic and business relationships for centuries". Sounds like language from the *Marvin* cases. Now that Marriage Equality is the law of the land, what would be the impact on Steelman's claims?

From the *Marvin* cases forward, the courts made clear that in awarding compensation for the breakup of cohabiting couples, the courts were not doing so under the rights recognized by marriage. Yet, in the forty years since those cases were decided, marriage rates in the U.S. continue to decline and cohabitation rates climb. If society is recognizing relationship commitment beyond the requirements of marriage, is it time to extend other benefits of marriage? For example, consortium refers to the "love, companionship, society, sexual relations, support, services, and solace"[20] that traditionally derived from a marriage. Thus, if a wife is injured in a car accident, the husband could sue the negligent driver for the loss of companionship while his spouse healed. Should consortium be extended to cohabiting couples in committed relationship? In *Lozoya v. Sanchez* in 2003, the New Mexico Supreme Court extended consortium rights to a cohabitating couple who had lived together for 30 years and married after the accident. While this was the only state to do so, some states recognize the claim for other unmarried people such as grandparents and siblings. Yet, if we extend it beyond marriage where do we stop? What about others who claim an impact from another's injury? "'One would also envision that the injured person has cousins, co-workers, drinking buddies and softball team members who may lose his society, companionship and guidance. For that matter, the dead or injured person may have been having an affair with his married neighbor, who also may suffer a loss of consortium."

---

20 *Denil v. Integrity Mutual Insurance Co.* (Wis.App.1986) 135 Wis2d373. Traditionally this claim was only allowed by the husband at a time when women were viewed as the husband's property. See chapter 10.

AS WE GO TO PRESS

In New York, Theodora Lee Corsell, 67, sued James Greenwald, 88, for $2 million claiming he failed to pay her for professional services. "Here's what makes it interesting. The woman is the man's former mistress."[21] Greenwald had approached her about seven years prior in her professional capacity as a "retired fund raiser and non-profit worker" and asked her to handle some personal and charitable matters for him.[22] Corsell agreed, believing she would be compensated.[23] Her duties varied from distributing unused New York Giants tickets to promoting his unpublished memoir.[24] Their relationship developed into an affair[25] and Corsell was never paid. Corsell claims that she "'had an expectation of being compensated based on… Greenwald's affirmative representations' to her."[26] Greenwald promised her, "'I owe you everything and I will compensate you,'"[27] and that the "reasonable value" of her "services" were $2 million.[28] She claims she's due the money because her "professional services … were separate and apart from … the parties' romantic relationship."[29]

In 2016, Greenwald moved to dismiss the case but the judge[30] denied the motion after hearing that Corsell not only "fed the defendant, cleaned the defendant and took care of him after he had a 'cerebral hemorrhage' but also managed his business affairs including saving him $500,000 in a legal dispute."[31] Greenwald later counter-sued Corsell, claiming she made unauthorized payments and to recover $63,000 which he claims is the amount of the rent on the apartment he had rented

---

21   https://www.aol.com/article/2015/06/08/mistress-sues-ex-lover-for-unpaid-services/21192810/

22   Quoting Corsell's lawyer, Donald Kravet at the hearing on the motion to dismiss. http://nypost.com/2016/10/03/man-countersues-ex-mistress-after-wife-refused-him-a-divorce/

23   Ibid.

24   Corsell alleges that she helped Greenwald defend against a $3 million threat by another "of Greenwald's mistresses" who threatened to tell Greenwald's wife, according to court papers. http://www.nydailynews.com/new-york/mistress-media-exec-files-1m-lawsuit-ex-lover-article-1.2247966 Also, "Corsell said she worked with Greenwald and Clair to compile information on (Greenwald's wife's) purchases, telephone use and activities but the divorce never happened because Greenwald's wife resisted, telling her husband: 'I will see them bury you six feet under before I grant you a divorce. I'm the last Mrs. Greenwald,' according to court papers.'" http://nypost.com/2015/06/06/mistress-sues-her-ex-lover-for-not-leaving-his-wife/ In addition, "Corsell claims she saved Greenwald thousands of dollars by resolving a coop board dispute over his leaking Park Avenue penthouse and by getting lower legal fees for him in 2007 when an insurance carrier refused to pay out for fire damages in a Trump Plaza apartment that Greenwald had rented for her." http://www.nydailynews.com/new-york/mistress-media-exec-files-1m-lawsuit-ex-lover-article-1.2247966. http://courts.state.ny.us/Reporter/3dseries/2010/2010_52394.htm

25   Greenwald rented her an apartment but continued to live with his wife in their residence. http://nypost.com/2015/06/06/mistress-sues-her-ex-lover-for-not-leaving-his-wife/

26   http://www.nydailynews.com/new-york/mistress-media-exec-files-1m-lawsuit-ex-lover-article-1.2247966

27   As alleged in her law suit. https://www.aol.com/article/2015/06/08/mistress-sues-ex-lover-for-unpaid-services/21192810/

28   http://www.nydailynews.com/new-york/mistress-media-exec-files-1m-lawsuit-ex-lover-article-1.2247966

29   Ibid.

30   Manhattan Supreme Court Judge Eileen Rakower. http://nypost.com/2016/10/03/man-countersues-ex-mistress-after-wife-refused-him-a-divorce/

31   Ibid.

for Corsell when she refused to leave it after they split up in 2014. Plaintiff denies the claims.[32] Which parts of the cases are similar to others in the chapter and what is the difference? How might a New York judge decide?

CHAPTER SOURCE

Wadlington, W., and O'Brien, R. C. (2007). *Domestic Relations Cases and Materials*, 6th ed. Foundation Press.

---

32   Ibid.

LOVE NOTES: FAMILY LAW CONTRACTS

The most difficult aspect of the prenuptial agreement is informing your future wife (or husband): I love you very much, but just in case things don't work out, this is what you will get in the divorce. There are basically three types of women and reactions. One is the good woman who very much loves her future husband, solely for himself, but refuses to sign the agreement on principle. I fully understand this, but the man should take a pass anyway and find someone else. The other is the calculating woman who refuses to sign the prenuptial agreement because she is expecting to take advantage of the poor, unsuspecting sucker she's got in her grasp. There is also the woman who will openly and quickly sign a prenuptial agreement in order to make a quick hit and take the money given to her.

—Donald Trump[1]

Okay, okay, I know this is about as popular as a root canal and doing your taxes combined, but I need you to hear me out on this. When you are preparing to get married I hope your life is full of absolute hopefulness and joy, and fun. My argument for why you and your soon-to-be spouse need a pre-nup agreement has absolutely nothing to [do with] the genuine warm fuzzies you are feeling now. I am merely asking you to protect yourself from the what-ifs of life. Think, I am a kill-joy? Well if I am, I am batting about .500: With the divorce rate near 50 percent that means that one out of every two marriages could probably end a whole lot more gracefully if there was a pre-nup. Or to put it another way; if there was a 50 percent chance you might get hurt in an accident, wouldn't you buy insurance?

—Suze Orman[2]

---

1   *"The Art of the Comeback (from the chapter, the Art of the Prenup),"* https://www.washingtonpost.com/news/book-party/wp/2015/08/05/donald-trump-on-women-sex-marriage-and-feminism/?utm_term=.5b4f70b01122.   In 1991, Trump's first wife, Ivana received "$10 million, the 45-room Greenwich, Connecticut mansion, a Manhattan apartment at Trump Plaza on Third Avenue, $300,000 annually in child support, $350,000 a year in alimony, and use of the Trumps' Florida mansion, Mar-a-Lago, for one month a year." http://articles.baltimoresun.com/1991-03-25/features/1991084035_1_ivana-trump-donald-and-ivana-divorce-settlement

2   http://apps.suzeorman.com/igsbase/igstemplate.cfm?SRC=DB&SRCN=&GnavID=21&SnavID=39&TnavID=52. "Young, Fabulous and Broke," by Suze Orman.

RELATIONSHIP AGREEMENTS

Sheldon Cooper to Amy Farrah Fowler, "I present to you the Relationship Agreement." Amy, "It's so romantic." Sheldon, "Mutual indemnification always is."[3] In Sheldon Cooper's 31-page relationship agreement he specifically sets out the rights and responsibilities of "the boyfriend" and "the girlfriend" including, under section 5, regarding holding hands, "which is only allowed (a) when either party is in danger of falling off of a cliff, (b) when either party is deserving of a hearty handshake after winning a Nobel Prize, or (c) for moral support during a flu shot."[4] While it gets a good laugh on the show, is it really far from the truth? Do relationships need detailed contracts to work? Before Priscilla Chan moved to California to be near her boyfriend Mark Zuckerberg of Facebook, "the couple forged a relationship agreement where she 'insisted on at least one date night and 100 minutes together a week, not in his apartment or at the Facebook office.'"[5]

Family law establishes the rights and responsibilities of many family relationships, but what about those who want to engage in private ordering by making the terms of their relationship outside of what the law provides (see Chapter 3)? During various stages of a relationship, couples can create written agreements to clarify their rights and responsibilities or modify the ones the law provides for them, but should the courts enforce them? This chapter covers some of the various types of written agreements that may be used by a family to clarify their relationships; these agreements allow treatment that is different from what the law would provide. In addition to relationship agreements, this chapter includes discussions of cohabitation agreements; prenuptial or premarital agreements; postnuptial or postmarital agreements; and separation/settlement agreements in anticipation of divorce.[6]

1. COHABITATION AGREEMENTS

If the Marvins, Michelle Triola and Lee, had a written agreement supporting her claim that he would support her for life, would the court enforce it? Should it? Should couples who cohabitate, choosing to live together outside of marriage, have their agreements about those relationships enforced? Because these couples have decided to privately order their relationships, choosing

---

3   *The Big Bang Theory*, CBS. "The Flaming Spittoon Acquisition" episode referring to the 31 page agreement of the rights and responsibilities of the boyfriend and girlfriend. The Big Bang Theory Wiki http://bigbangtheory.wikia.com/wiki/The_Relationship_Agreement

4   The Big Bang Theory Wiki http://bigbangtheory.wikia.com/wiki/The_Relationship_Agreement

5   "Just call it a pre-nup", Jan Hoffman, *The New York Times*, May 27, 2012, P. 9.

6   Even a marriage involves signing a marriage contract. Other types of family law contracts occur as families evolve, such as more specialized "love notes" developed especially for gay and lesbian couples, (e.g., between a birth mother and known sperm donor and/or between the child's two mother over parenting rights and duties) or in adoptions. Those are beyond the scope of this book.

to reject society's encouragement of marriage, should society now recognize that relationship in order to legally enforce their rights? On the other hand, if the agreements the cohabitating couples make are contracts, society usually enforces contracts.

A cohabitation agreement is different than Sheldon Cooper's relationship agreement because it is for people who plan to live together.[7] As more couples cohabitate rather than marry, it may be smart to create a cohabitation agreement, especially as the law has not caught up with this societal reality (see chapter 3). Because cohabitation agreements are generally not used to shelter assets, like a prenuptial agreement, they can focus on the couple's requests about behaviors during their relationship. What if the agreement is for one partner's care and companionship in exchange for the other's agreement to pay support? Should that be enforced? The initial prohibition against cohabitation agreements was that they were immoral, and that living together outside of marriage was all about sex. As Lee Marvin responded in the *Marvin* I case, agreements based on cohabitation were viewed as paying for sex and against public policy. Recall that in *Marvin* I, the California Supreme Court disagreed, finding that cohabitation relationships involved many similar elements of a marriage relationship, including—but not only—sex. (See discussion of the *Marvin* cases, Chapter 3.) If additional services are mentioned as consideration for payments, and those services are "inextricably connected to his providing sexual services," then the whole agreement is void. *Jones v. Daly*, 122 CA App. 3d 500 (1981) where the agreement provided, in part, that one partner "would render his services as a <u>lover</u>, companion, homemaker, ..." (emphasis added) and "plaintiff allowed himself to be known to the general public as the lover and cohabitation mate of defendant."

If, however, the contract is based on "non-meretricious consideration,"[8] it may be, sometimes begrudgingly, enforceable. "The state is not thusly condoning the lifestyles of homosexuals or unmarried live-ins; it is merely recognizing their constitutional private property and contract rights." *Posik v. Layton*, 695 So.2d 759, 761 (FL Dist. Ct. App. 1997). Today's courts may find such cohabitation agreements enforceable if, like any other contract, they are: informed, voluntary, and not based on fraud, misrepresentation, or duress.

What kinds of things might be included in a cohabitation agreement? While they can include who walks the dog and the number of hours required away from the office, such contracts can generally include anything not against public policy. They often contain terms regarding the obligation to provide financial support for one partner, especially if there is income disparity. Although a contract, it is questionable if a court would enforce some of the requirements under Sheldon's Relationship Agreement or even a cohabitation agreement if the behavior requests

---

7   Indeed many episodes later when Sheldon said Amy could not move in with him, she called the relationship agreement a "ridiculous contract". "The Spoiler Alert Segmentation" (S06E15) The Big Bang Theory Wiki http://bigbangtheory.wikia.com/wiki/The_Relationship_Agreement. While it is assumed that Zuckerberg and his wife Chan signed a prenuptial agreement, the timing of their nuptials may have been their best planning; they married the day of the Facebook IPO which will help establish the value of their assets before the wedding especially in a community property state like California (see discussion of division of assets in a divorce, chapter 12).

8   "Meretricious" is from the Latin *meretrix*, meaning harlot or prostitute.

were too extreme. To answer the question, if the Marvin's had a written cohabitation agreement promising her support for life while she lived with him as his girlfriend, would it be enforceable? Probably not, because Mr. Marvin was married to someone else at the time he moved in with Michelle, therefore such a contract would probably be against public policy.[9]

2. PRENUPTIAL OR PREMARITAL AGREEMENTS

Celebrities have them, why don't you? Only about four percent of people admit to having a **prenuptial** or in some states antenuptial agreement, yet 15 percent of divorced people wish they had one.[10] Originally, prenuptial agreements, known as "prenups" or premarital agreements, were a way for the rich and famous to keep their money from their spouses during divorce. Now, the document can also be used to work out a fair agreement before the animosity of divorce. In addition, older couples who want to save assets for children from prior relations, may also utilize prenups. A majority of states now recognize their validity. With about 40 percent of marriages ending in divorce, should more couples have one?

Prenups are contracts made in contemplation of marriage to determine what will happen after the marriage occurs, usually focusing on how assets will be distributed at death or divorce.[11] Prenups are different from typical contracts for three reasons. First, they are made by a couple anticipating marriage—not the typical "arm's-length" business transaction. Second, because marriage is encouraged by society, the courts are more inclined to look at the question of fairness than the usual *caveat emptor* (let the buyer beware) commercial contract. Third, because these contracts depend on the occurrence of a future event (divorce), the passage of time may make them unfair. Most states have adopted the Uniform Premarital Agreement Act (UPAA), which recognizes private ordering under a premarital agreement and the effect on couples, should they divorce.

Earlier courts in the 1960s and 1970s were reluctant to enforce prenups because they felt it encouraged or induced divorce (if, however, the agreements were conditioned on death, that would be acceptable). (See generally, *Posner v. Posner* (FL S.CT 1970) 233 So.2d 381, below). With the recognition of private ordering, most courts will enforce them if, like regular commercial contracts, they are in writing, signed by both parties, voluntary (not made under duress or coercion), do not involve fraud or misrepresentation, provide full disclosure of assets, and are fair and reasonable (not unconscionable) at the time they are signed or enforced. Due to the increase in private ordering many courts are declining to evaluate fairness as long as full disclosure of assets and liabilities has been made. What does full disclosure of assets require?

---

9   http://www.latimes.com/news/obituaries/la-me-michelle-triola-marvin31-2009oct31,0,2805574.story,   (Obituary, *Los Angeles Times*, October 31, 2009.)
10   Uniform Premarital Agreement Act. (UPAA), 1983.
11   Ibid.

Generally, knowledge of assets and debt, but if parties lived with each other before, some of that knowledge may be imputed.

In *Blige v. Blige*, a Georgia court looked at the validity of the prenuptial agreement, requested by the husband the day before the wedding. What did the court decide?

BLIGE V. BLIGE[10]
656 S.E.2D 822 (2008)

SUPREME COURT OF GEORGIA

SEARS, Chief Justice.

Meagan Taylor Blige filed a complaint for divorce against Willie Taylor Blige in 2005. The trial court set aside the parties' antenuptial agreement based on Mr. Blige's failure to make a fair and complete disclosure of his assets, income, and liabilities, and the jury returned a verdict awarding Ms. Blige $160,000 representing her equitable interest in the marital home. Mr. Bilge filed an application for discretionary review, which this Court granted pursuant to its pilot project in family law cases. We have determined that the trial court did not err in setting aside the antenuptial agreement for non-disclosure and that the jury did not err in awarding Ms. Blige $160,000 as her equitable interest in the marital property. Accordingly, we affirm.

1. The Bliges had a child together in 1994 and married in 2000. They did not live together before the marriage. The day before the wedding, Mr. Blige took his bride-to-be to an office building to meet with an attorney he had hired for her. The attorney handed her a fully drafted antenuptial agreement, read through it with her, and asked her to sign it, which she did. Mr. Blige signed the antenuptial agreement later, and the parties were married the following day as scheduled.

The antenuptial agreement provided that Mr. Blige would retain as his sole and separate property 19.5 acres of land in Bryan County that he had previously purchased "together with any house or structure which may be situated upon said property." There was no house or structure situated on the property when the parties married, but Mr. Blige had hidden away $150,000 in cash that he planned to use to build a home there after the wedding. Ms. Blige knew Mr. Blige worked as a delivery truck driver and approximately what he made. However, Mr. Blige never told Ms. Blige about the $150,000 in cash, and she had no knowledge of the money from any other source.

On July 26, 2005, Ms. Blige filed a complaint for divorce in the Bryan County Superior Court. In his answer and counterclaim, Mr. Bilge sought enforcement of the antenuptial agreement. Ms. Bilge moved to have it set aside for failure to comply with the legal requirements for antenuptial agreements, and the trial court conducted a pretrial evidentiary hearing on the issue. After hearing from both Mr. Blige and Ms. Blige, the trial court found as fact that Mr. Blige failed to make a fair and clear disclosure of his income, assets, and liabilities to Ms. Blige before the execution of the antenuptial agreement. On November 7, 2006, the trial court entered an order setting aside the antenuptial agreement, and a jury trial on property division ensued.

The evidence before the jury showed that Mr. Blige put the $150,000 in cash he had concealed from Ms. Blige toward the construction *824 of an enormous home on the Bryan County property. The cost to complete the construction of the home was approximately $280,000, and by the time of trial, it was worth approximately $375,000 to $400,000. At the conclusion of the evidence, the jury returned a verdict awarding Mr. Blige the Bryan County property and house minus $160,000 to be paid to Ms. Blige representing her equitable interest in the marital property. The jury assigned each party the debts held in his or her own name and held that Mr. Blige would be responsible for the mortgage on the house. On February 15, 2007, the trial court entered a final judgment and decree of divorce incorporating the jury's equitable division of the marital property. Mr. Blige appealed.

2. Until 1982, antenuptial agreements were unenforceable in Georgia divorce proceedings as being contrary to public policy. Then, in Scherer v. Scherer, this Court concluded that Georgia courts were no longer justified in applying a rule of per se invalidity to antenuptial agreements entered into in contemplation of divorce. At the same time, we recognized the importance of marriage as a social institution and the vital public policy interests that can be undermined by antenuptial agreements. Accordingly, we held that antenuptial agreements would henceforth be enforceable in Georgia divorce proceedings, but only if certain prerequisites are met.

Taking the law of other jurisdictions as our guide, we devised a three-part test for-determining whether a particular antenuptial agreement is enforceable under Georgia law. We held that the party seeking enforcement bears the burden of proof to demonstrate that: (1) the antenuptial agreement was not the result of fraud, duress, mistake, misrepresentation, or nondisclosure of material facts; (2) the agreement is not unconscionable; and (3) taking into account all relevant facts and circumstances, including changes beyond the parties' contemplation when the agreement was executed, enforcement of the antenuptial agreement would be neither unfair nor unreasonable. The Scherer test, as refined and clarified by our later case law, continues to govern the enforceability of antenuptial agreements.

The three-part test we adopted in Scherer is consistent with the standards governing the enforcement of antenuptial agreements that prevail throughout most of the nation today. As one commentator has explained:

> Generally accepted guidelines for analyzing antenuptial agreements determine whether they are enforceable. The contract must meet the usual requirements of offer, acceptance, and consideration, and there is often an implied, sometimes express, requirement of fundamental fairness. The agreement cannot violate a statute or clear public policy. If the circumstances have changed beyond the parties' contemplation at the time they entered into the agreement, it may not be enforceable. Usually both parties must *825 fully disclose their assets at the time of the agreement....

We evaluate a trial court's determination regarding the enforceability of an antenuptial agreement under the familiar abuse of discretion standard of review.

On appeal, Mr. Blige contends the trial court erred in setting aside the antenuptial agreement under the first prong of the Scherer test, i.e., the agreement must not be the result of fraud, duress, mistake, misrepresentation, or nondisclosure of material facts. To satisfy the first prong of the Scherer test, the party seeking enforcement must show both that there was "a full and fair disclosure of the assets of the parties prior to the execution of the [antenuptial] agreement," and that the party opposing enforcement entered into the antenuptial agreement "[freely], voluntarily, and with full understanding of its terms after being offered the opportunity to consult with independent counsel." Thus, Georgia law, like that of virtually every other State in the Union, imposes an affirmative duty of disclosure on both parties to an antenuptial agreement. In essence, the law writes into every antenuptial agreement a provision requiring both parties to disclose all material facts. Absent "full and fair disclosure" of the parties' financial condition prior to execution, enforcement of the antenuptial agreement would violate Georgia public policy.

The trial court specifically found that Mr. Blige did not make a "fair and clear disclosure of his income, assets and liabilities before the parties signed [the] antenuptial agreement" as required by the first prong of the Scherer test. The evidence presented at the pretrial hearing showed that at the time of the parties' marriage, Mr. Blige made his living as a vending and delivery person for Savannah Coca-Cola. His base pay was $10 an hour. A year before the nuptials, Mr. Blige purchased 19.5 acres of land in rural Bryan County for $85,000. He owned no other property. Ms. Blige did not live with Mr. Blige before the marriage, and it was undisputed that he never told her prior to the execution of the antenuptial agreement that he had $150,000 in cash in his possession. To the contrary, there are indications in the record that Mr. Blige actively hid his true financial status from Ms. Blige before the marriage and for some time thereafter. Thus, the evidence in the record amply supports the trial court's finding that Mr. Blige failed to disclose a fact material to the antenuptial agreement i.e., the $150,000 in cash he had hidden away and therefore did not make a full and fair disclosure of his financial status before the signing of the antenuptial agreement as required by the first prong of the Scherer test.

Mr. Blige claims that in spite of his nondisclosure of the $150,000 in cash, the trial court was required to enforce the antenuptial *826 agreement under our recent decision in Mallen v. Mallen. However, Mallen is easily distinguishable on the facts, at least with respect to the disclosure requirement. First, in Mallen, the trial court, after hearing all the evidence, exercised its discretion to uphold the antenuptial agreement, while here, the trial court exercised its discretion to do the opposite. Second, in Mallen, the parties attached financial disclosure statements to the antenuptial agreement itself that accurately reflected their assets and liabilities and that clearly revealed the tremendous disparity between the net worths of the prospective spouses (approximately $10,000 versus at least $8.5 million); there was no exchange of financial disclosure statements between the Bliges. Third, the Mallens had lived together for four years before the execution of the antenuptial agreement, and we specifically held that Ms. Mallen "was aware from the standard of living they enjoyed that he [i.e., Mr. Mallen] received significant income from his business and other sources." By contrast, Ms. Blige never moved in with Mr. Blige, even after the marriage, and there was nothing in Mr. Blige's lifestyle to indicate that he might have enormous sums of cash stashed away somewhere.

Mr. Blige argues that Mallen requires trial courts to enforce an antenuptial agreement, even where the spouse seeking enforcement did not make a full and fair disclosure, if the spouse resisting enforcement failed to "exercise reasonable diligence in ascertaining the assets" of the other before the execution of the antenuptial agreement. Thus, according to Mr. Blige, Mallen recognized a generalized "duty to ... inquir[e]" into the financial status of one's prospective spouse, and absent such inquiry, a challenge to the enforceability of the antenuptial agreement is barred.

Mr. Blige's reading of Mallen turns Scherer's disclosure requirement on its head. Mallen did not purport to overrule the portion of the first prong of the Scherer test that asks whether the antenuptial agreement was "obtained through ... nondisclosure of material facts." In Mallen itself, both, the majority and dissenting opinions directly quoted this portion of the decision in Scherer. In decisions rendered both before and after Mallen, we have repeatedly recognized that Scherer imposes an affirmative duty of full and fair disclosure of all material facts on parties entering into an antenuptial agreement. As noted above, this is the prevailing rule throughout the United States.

To support his claim that Mallen created a "duty of inquiry," Mr. Blige relies on a single passage from Mallen quoting a New Jersey trial court's description in dicta of what California law regarding the enforceability of antenuptial agreements "appear[ed]" to be in *827 1986. It is worth noting that the DeLorean case has never once been relied on or even cited by any California appellate court in construing California law regarding the enforcement of antenuptial agreements. Moreover, while California, like Georgia, does not consider individuals planning to wed to be in a "fiduciary" or "confidential" relationship, California law nevertheless imposes an affirmative duty of disclosure as part of its test for determining the enforceability of antenuptial agreements.

While the DeLorean court's interpretation of California law was off the mark, we agree with that court's statement which it recognized to be the law of New Jersey that the "better rule" is that the "burden is not on either party to inquire, but on each to inform, for it is only by requiring full disclosure of the amount, character, and value of the parties' respective assets that courts can ensure intelligent waiver of the statutory [and other] rights involved," and that "[w]hen a spouse has a duty to fully and completely disclose his financial wealth[,] we would eviscerate and render meaningless that duty if we imposed upon the other spouse a duty to investigate." In short, the "duty of inquiry", envisioned by Mr. Blige is incompatible with the duty of full and fair disclosure recognized by Scherer and its progeny.

Finally, in Mallen, we did not rest our decision upholding the trial court's enforcement of the antenuptial agreement on Ms. Mallen's failure to inquire into Mr. Mallen's financial status prior to the execution of the antenuptial agreement. Instead, we concluded that the omission of Mr. Mallen's income from the financial statement he attached to the antenuptial agreement was not material given the unique circumstances of that case. We emphasized the fact that Ms. Mallen had lived with Mr. Mallen for four years before she signed the, antenuptial agreement, that the financial disclosure statement Mr. Mallen attached to the antenuptial agreement revealed him to be a wealthy man with significant income-producing assets, and that Ms. Mallen was well aware from the standard of living they enjoyed prior to the marriage that Mr. Mallen received substantial income from the business bearing his name and other sources.

The evidence supports the trial court's finding that Mr. Blige failed to make a full and fair disclosure of his assets, income, and liabilities to Ms. Blige prior to the execution of the antenuptial agreement, and nothing in Mallen or Ms. Blige's actions or inactions prior the execution of the antenuptial agreement excuses Mr. Blige's nondisclosure. Accordingly, the trial court properly held that Mr. Blige failed to establish the first prong of the Scherer test, and it did not abuse its discretion in setting aside the antenuptial agreement.

3. Mr. Blige also contends the evidence presented at trial does not support the jury's verdict awarding Ms. Blige $160,000 for her equitable interest in the marital property. We have independently reviewed the record on appeal, and it supports the jury's verdict. This argument is meritless.

Judgment affirmed.
All the Justices concur. (NOTES OMITTED BY AUTHOR)

Do you think the Georgia court was influenced by the fact that the state was reluctant to recognize these agreements for fear that they encouraged divorce?

If the parties have a reasonable time to review and sign the prenup before the wedding—say, 30 days—most courts would enforce it. Courts have been asked to determine if asking for a signature on a prenup on the eve of the wedding amounts to duress. The alternative is delaying the wedding for time to think it over. While earlier courts may have objected, most courts do not void wedding-eve prenups, especially if there was time to review it beforehand. What if the parties are marrying to legitimize a child? This probably would not affect the court's decision. What if the woman is presented with the prenup shortly before her "fiancée visa" is about to expire? In the case of *Azarova v. Schmidt*, 2007-Ohio 653 (OH Ct. App 2007), a 22-year-old Ukrainian "mail-order" bride traveled to the United States on a three-month visa that would allow her to stay only if she married within 90 days of entry. One week before her visa expired, the woman married a 38-year-old man, but five days before the wedding (about two weeks before the visa expired), she signed an eight-page prenup[12] prepared by her fiancé's lawyer. The fiancé, who had been married before, told her she could get a lawyer to review the agreement. She did not (later claiming she had no money to pay a lawyer). The woman claimed she had to read the agreement by using an English-to-Russian dictionary, and that she cried when meeting with the fiancé's lawyer. In invalidating the agreement, the appellate court affirmed the lower court's finding that she signed it under duress, considering the impact of time and her lack of language skills; the decision allowed for equitable distribution of the marital assets.

As raised in the *Azarova* case, should an attorney approve a prenup? It's a very good idea, but probably not required. Some states require the opportunity to visit counsel, but do not insist on it. Could the same attorney approve it for both spouses? Because of the possible conflict of interest, this is probably not a good idea.

In the case of *In re Marriage of Bonds*, 99 Cal. Rptr. 2d 252 (CA 2000), baseball player Barry Bonds married at the beginning of his career and insisted on a prenup agreement before he married. The prenup said that each spouse's earnings and property would remain separate. When they divorced, Bonds was making $8 million per year. His wife challenged the prenup as unfair because she did not have a lawyer, but the California court rejected her argument. (Under California law, the court will find invalid a waiver of spousal support if the spouse was not represented by independent counsel.) Contrast that to New York Giants star Michael Strahan, who had to pay his wife $15.3 million, more than half of his net worth. Under the terms of their prenup, he gave her "50 percent of their joint marital assets and 20% of his yearly income from each year they were married."[13] In addition, the court ordered Strahan to pay "hundreds of thousands of dollars in child support." According to his ex-wife, Strahan's lawyers wrote the agreement.

What kinds of terms included in a prenup are enforceable? Courts are often willing to enforce limits or total denial of financial support from one spouse to the other. But, what happens if one partner makes a lot of money and they live very well during the relationship? Would an agreement refusing to pay any support still be enforceable? If that clause creates an injustice, like

---

12 Schmidt attached to the agreement an exhibit that listed his assets and their approximate values. Included on this list were two houses, an IRA account, a checking account, a TSP Retirement account, and stocks. The agreement stated that Azarova did not have any assets to disclose.

13 www.ESPN.com, "Strahan ordered to abide by prenup, pay $15.3 M," January 13, 2007.

leaving the partner destitute or substantially below the standard of living they maintained during the relationship, courts may void it as against public policy.

Most people think of prenups as a way to protect either spouse's property. They can include not only how property will be disposed of in a divorce or death, but also who is responsible for the property during the life of the marriage (e.g., paying taxes on it or selling it). Spouses might include specifics like who does the dishes or what the penalty is for adulterous behavior. "Prenups can even outline what is expected of a spouse's behavior."[14] "Some prenups address issues such as adultery, frequency of intimacy, limitations of weight gain, the scheduling of housekeeping and provisions for pets."[15] Many states do not allow such demands if they become too extreme, such as requirements on weight or clothing choices. In one prenup, the husband agreed to pay his wife $25,000 for each year she did not do cocaine, including the terms for drug testing.[16] Courts generally will not enforce agreements specifying custody of children or which religion to raise future children. State laws also control child support, so prenups are most likely not valid on this issue.

What about gender issues? Should courts be careful to empower a demure spouse against the dominating partner? What if a 23-year-old unemployed nurse marries a 39-year-old doctor and the prenup limits her to support of $200 a week, with a maximum amount of $25,000? Should the court acknowledge some sort of inherent power imbalance voiding such an agreement? In *Simeone v. Simeone*, 581 A. 2d 162, 525 PA 392 (1990), the court rejected "[p]aternalistic presumptions and protections that arose to shelter women from the inferiorities and incapacities which they were perceived as having in earlier times" enforcing a similar contract.

In a March 2013 case, "Elizabeth Petrakis of New York's Long Island recently won a major and rare divorce battle after a New York Appellate Court tore up the prenuptial agreement she signed with her husband that hung only on a verbal promise." In 1998, six weeks before her wedding, Mrs. Petrakis, 39, was presented with what her lawyer called a "heavy handed" prenup that would give her $25,000 for every year she was married, but nothing more. "I put my foot down and said I wasn't signing it," Mrs. Petrakis said. ... "But four days before tying the knot, she agreed to sign the prenup after her fiancé, 41-year-old Peter Petrakis, promised he would get rid of the prenup once the two began to have children." Petrakis, a commercial property developer, is worth an estimated $20 million. "[O]n February 20, Elizabeth Petrakis got the news she had

---

14 http://usatoday30.usatoday.com/money/perfi/basics/2010-03-08-prenups08_CV_N.htm, "Prenuptial agreements: Unromantic, but important," Laura Petrecca, for *USA Today*, March 11, 2010. Citing to a February 2010 Harris Interactive poll for *USA Today* on the opinion of adults in the United States regarding prenuptial agreements. Among other things, the poll found that 4 percent of married people have a prenup and that 15 percent of divorced Americans regretted not having a prenup.

15 Ibid.

16 *USA Today*, http://usatoday30.usatoday.com/money/perfi/basics/2010-03-08-prenups08_CV_N.htm, "Prenuptial agreements: Unromantic, but important," Laura Petrecca, *USA Today*, March 11, 2010, quoting Robert Nachshin, co-author of the prenup guide "*I Do, You Do ... But Just Sign Here*": 'I had a client who was willing to pay his wife a special amount each year provided she didn't do cocaine.' 'The agreement was to pay her $25,000 a year. He had the right to drug test her, and if she was clean, she was able to get $25,000.'" "The wife stayed off the drugs, and over the last 10 years she received $250,000."

been waiting for: the court ruled that Peter Petrakis had fraudulently induced Elizabeth to sign the prenup."[17]

3. POSTNUPTIAL OR POSTMARITAL AGREEMENTS

Postnuptial or **post-marital** agreements are made by the parties during a valid marriage. Generally, they are designed to privately order the terms of marriage, which the law already covers. While courts were reluctant to allow married couples to bypass legal provisions for marriage, with the advent of recognition of other forms of private ordering, that has become less of a concern. Now, postnuptial agreements are recognized as an inducement for one spouse to remain in the marriage.

Post-marital agreements may be made for any reason (in *Posner v. Posner*, below, the wife asked for one to distribute her property to her daughters from a prior marriage), including a modification of potential alimony obligations, should the spouses ever divorce. Often, such agreements are made to induce one spouse, with a valid reason for leaving an ailing marriage, to remain in the marriage. When one spouse threatens to leave (and has a reason to do so), generally, the party who wants to remain in the marriage offers a valuable asset to finalize the agreement. Postnuptial agreements are generally enforced like a regular commercial contract. The consideration (or value exchanged) for the agreement may be one spouse's consent to remain in a marriage rather than proceed with a divorce—giving it another try. These agreements should be enforceable. Courts generally do not consider post-marital agreements as duress against the other party. While it is true that a postnuptial agreement is the result of one spouse threatening to leave the other, the courts recognize the contract as the inducement for that spouse to remain and make good faith efforts to stay in the marriage.

POSNER V. POSNER,
233 SO. 2D 381
(FL.SCT 1970)

The Florida Supreme Court gives a thorough general history of the court's evolution in recognition of postmarital agreements in *Posner v. Posner*, and reminds that while a valid postmarital agreement may be treated like a regular contract, an award under it may be increased or decreased because of the passage of time and any change in conditions.

---

17 http://abcnews.go.com/blogs/headlines/2013/03/long-island-woman-wins-groundbreaking-prenup-battle/ "Long Island Woman Wins 'Groundbreaking' Prenup Battle," Joanna Suarez for ABCNews.com, March 11, 2013.

W ife brought suit for alimony, support of children and decree that an antenuptial agreement was void, and husband counterclaimed for divorce. The Circuit Court, Dade County, Ralph O. Cullen, J., granted divorce to husband and awarded alimony and child support to wife pursuant to antenuptial contract, and wife appealed. The Third District Court of Appeal, 206 So.2d 416, held that alimony provision of antenuptial contract was not binding on chancellor awarding alimony, and rehearing was granted on petition for certiorari. The Supreme Court, Roberts, J., held that antenuptial agreement respecting alimony in event of divorce or separation of parties, if made under proper conditions, was a valid and binding agreement, but subject to be increased or decreased under changed conditions.

ROBERTS, Justice.

This cause is before the court on rehearing granted on petition for certiorari to review the decision of the Third District Court of Appeal in *Posner v. Posner*, Fla.App.1968, 206 So.2d 416. Both parties had appealed to the appellate court for reversal of the decree of the Chancellor entered in a divorce suit—the wife having appealed from those portions of the decree awarding a divorce to the husband and the sum of $600 per month as alimony to the wife pursuant to the terms of an antenuptial agreement between the parties, and the husband having attacked, by cross-appeal, the award of $600 per month support money for each of the two minor children of the parties.

The three appellate judges who considered the appeals agreed upon the affirmance of the decree of divorce to the husband and the award for child support of $1,200 per month. However, each took a different position respecting the antenuptial agreement concerning alimony. Their respective views were (1) that the parties may validly agree upon alimony in an antenuptial agreement but that the trial court is not bound by their agreement; (2) that such an agreement is void as against public policy; and (3) that an antenuptial agreement respecting alimony is entitled to the same consideration and should be just as binding as an antenuptial agreement settling the property rights of the wife in her husband's estate upon his death. They have certified to this court, as one of great public interest, the question of the validity and binding effect of an antenuptial agreement respecting alimony in the event of the divorce or separation of the parties. We have concluded that jurisdiction should be accepted, as authorized by Section 4(2), Article V, Florida Constitution, F.S.A.

At the outset we must recognize that there is a vast difference between a contract made in the market place and one relating to the institution of marriage.

It has long been the rule in a majority of the courts of this country and in this State that contracts intended to facilitate or promote the procurement of a divorce will be declared illegal as contrary to public policy. See *Gallemore v. Gallemore*, 1927, 94 Fla. 516, 114 So. 371; *Allen v. Allen*, 1933, 111 Fla. 733, 150 So. 237. The reason for the rule lies in the nature of the marriage contract and the interest of the State therein.

At common law, the so-called 'matrimonial causes', including divorce, were cognizable only in the Ecclesiastical Courts. Because of the Church's view of the sanctity of the nuptial tie, a marriage valid in its inception would not be dissolved by an absolute divorce A vinculo matrimonii, even for adultery—although such divorces could be granted by an Act of Parliament. Therefore, the divorce was only from bed and board, with an appropriate allowance for sustenance of the wife out of the husband's estate. See *Ponder v. Graham*, 1851, 4 Fla. 23; Chitty's Blackstone, Vol. I, Ch. XV, 432, 441. We have, of course, changed by statute the common-law rule respecting the indissolubility of a marriage valid in its inception; but the concept of marriage as a social institution that is the foundation of the family and of society remains unchanged. See 38 Am.Jur., Marriage, Sec. 8, p. 185. *383 Since marriage is of vital interest to society and the state, it has frequently been said that in every divorce suit the state is a third party whose interests take precedence over the private interests of the spouses. See *Underwood v. Underwood*, 1868, 12 Fla. 434; *Light v. Meginniss*, 1945, 156 Fla. 61, 22 So.2d 455; *Pickston v. Dougherty*, Fla.App.1959, 109 So.2d 577; *Wall v. Wall*, Fla.App.1961, 134 So.2d 288.

The state's interest in the preservation of the marriage is the basis for the rule that a divorce cannot be awarded by consent of the parties, see *Underwood v. Underwood*, supra, 12 Fla. 434, as well as the doctrine of corroboration applicable in divorce suits, see *Pickston v. Dougherty*, Fla.App.1959, 109 So.2d 577. In the *Underwood* case this court said that it 'would be aiming a deadly blow at public morals to decree a dissolution of the marriage contract merely because the parties requested it;' and in the *Pickston* case it was noted that the 'prime object of the corroboration doctrine is to prevent collusion and to forestall any attempt which might otherwise be made to destroy the marital relationship falsely.'

And it is this same public policy that is the basis for the rule that an antenuptial agreement by which a prospective wife waives or limits her right to alimony or to the property of her husband in the event of a divorce or separation, regardless of who is at fault, has been in some states held to be invalid. See the cases collected in the annotation in 57 A.L.R.2d 942 et seq.; 27 Am.Jur., Husband and Wife, Sec. 275, p. 881, and Sec. 326, p. 923; *Werlein v. Werlein*, 1965, 27 Wis.2d 237, 133 N.W.2d 820; *Crouch v. Crouch*, 1964, 53 Tenn.App. 594, 385 S.W.2d 288; *Motley v. Motley*, 1961, 255 N.C. 190, 120 S.E.2d 422. The reason that such an agreement is said to 'facilitate or promote the procurement of a divorce' was stated in *Crouch v. Crouch*, supra, as follows:—

> *Such contract could induce a mercenary husband to inflict on his wife any wrong he might desire with the knowledge his pecuniary liability would be limited. In other words, a husband could through abuse and ill treatment of his wife force her to bring an action for divorce and thereby buy a divorce for a small fee less than he would otherwise have to pay.*

Antenuptial or so-called 'marriage settlement' contracts by which the parties agree upon and fix the property rights which either spouse will have in the estate of the other upon his or her death have, however, long been recognized as being conducive to marital tranquility and thus in harmony with public policy. See *Del Vecchio v. Del Vecchio*, Fla.1962, 143 So.2d 17, in which we prescribed the rules by which the validity of such antenuptial or postnuptial property settlement agreements should be tested. Such an agreement has been upheld after the death of the spouse even though it contained also a provision settling their property rights in the event of divorce or separation—the court concluding that it could not be said this provision 'facilitated or tended to induce a separation or divorce.' See In re *Muxlow's Estate*, 1962, 367 Mich. 133, 116 N.W.2d 43.

In this view of an antenuptial agreement that settles the right of the parties in the event of divorce as well as upon death, it is not inconceivable that a dissatisfied wife—secure in the knowledge that the provisions for alimony contained in the antenuptial agreement could not be enforced against her, but that she would be bound by the provisions limiting or waiving her property rights in the estate of her husband—might provoke her husband into divorcing her in order to collect a large alimony check every month, or a lump-sum award (since, in this State, a wife is entitled to alimony, if needed, even though the divorce is awarded to the husband) rather than take her chances on being remembered generously in her husband's will. In this situation, a valid antenuptial agreement limiting property rights upon death would have the same meretricious effect, insofar as the public policy in *384 question is concerned, as would an antenuptial divorce provision in the circumstances hypothesized in *Crouch v. Crouch*, supra, 385 S.W.2d 288.

There can be no doubt that the institution of marriage is the foundation of the familial and social structure of our Nation and, as such, continues to be of vital interest to the State; but we cannot blind ourselves to the fact that the concept of the 'sanctity' of a marriage—as being practically indissoluble, once entered into—held by our ancestors only a few generations ago, has been greatly eroded in the last several decades. This court can take judicial notice of the fact that the ratio of marriages to divorces has reached a disturbing rate in many states; and that a new concept of divorce—in which there is no 'guilty' party—is being advocated by many groups and has been adopted by the State of California in a recent revision of its divorce laws providing for dissolution of a marriage upon pleading and proof of 'irreconcilable differences' between the parties, without assessing the fault for the failure of the marriage against either party.

With divorce such a commonplace fact of life, it is fair to assume that many prospective marriage partners whose property and familial situation is such as to generate a valid antenuptial agreement settling their property rights upon the death of either, might want to consider and discuss also—and agree upon, if possible—the disposition of their property and the alimony rights of the wife in the event their marriage, despite their best efforts, should fail. In *Allen v. Allen*, supra, 150 So. at page 238, this court said that the agreements relating to divorce that are held to be illegal as contrary to public policy are those 'withdrawing opposition to the divorce or not to contest it or to conceal the true cause thereof by alleging another' and that they 'have no reference to bona fide agreements relating to alimony or the adjustment of property rights between husband and wife, though in contemplation of divorce, if they are not directly conducive to the procurement of it.'

We know of no community or society in which the public policy that condemned a husband and wife to a lifetime of misery as an alternative to the opprobrium of divorce still exists. And a tendency to recognize this change in public policy and to give effect to the antenuptial agreements of the parties relating to divorce is clearly discernible. Thus, in *Hudson v. Hudson*, Okl.1960, 350 P.2d 596, the court simply applied to an antenuptial contract respecting alimony the rule applicable to antenuptial contracts settling property rights upon the death of a spouse and thus tacitly, if not expressly, discarded the contrary-to-public-policy rule.

Sanders v. Sanders, 1955, 40 Tenn.App. 20, 288 S.W.2d 473, involved an antenuptial contract providing that the parties would poll their separate properties and make future acquisitions in their joint names, and that the party filing a suit for divorce would forfeit his or her interest in the properties. The court construed the provision for forfeiture as applicable only in the event that a divorce suit was not filed in good faith and held that, as so construed, the contract was not promotive of divorce and was valid.

In *LeFevers v. LeFevers,* 1966, 240 Ark. 992, 403 S.W.2d 65, the validity of an antenuptial agreement providing that, in the event of divorce, the wife should be restored to her own property rights and have one-half of the net gain made by the joint efforts of the parties during marriage, was not questioned—the contest being only as to the proper interpretation of the contract.

In re *Muxlow's Estate,* 1962, 367 Mich. 133, 116 N.W.2d 43, was a contest between the heirs of the deceased spouses, in which the heirs of the deceased husband relied upon an antenuptial agreement limiting the husband's financial obligations to the wife in the event of divorce and the share of his estate to which she would be entitled *385 at his death. The agreement was upheld, the court stating that it could not be held that any effective provision in the agreement 'provided for, facilitated, or tended to induce a separation or divorce * * *.'

Strandberg v. Strandberg, 1967, 33 Wis.2d 204, 147 N.W.2d 349, was a divorce case in which an antenuptial agreement providing for the division of property in the event of divorce or separation was held to be void; however, it was held, also, that it could be admitted into evidence 'and considered for a limited purpose as one of the circumstances in determining the equities of the division.'

The trend of recent cases involving postnuptial agreements is well summarized by the court in *Schulz v. Fox,* 1959, 136 Mont. 152, 345 P.2d 1045, 1050, as follows:—

> *The conclusion to be drawn from these cases is that any agreement the purpose of which is to facilitate the granting of a divorce without proper grounds existing, is void, but that where proper grounds do exist, an agreement with respect to a property settlement, when not brought about by duress or coercion, cannot be said to perpetrate a fraud upon the court and will not be held void. *** All of the well reasoned cases we have read look to the collusive intent, that is, as to whether the divorce was on proper grounds and as to whether the Court's interest in the continuity of the marriage status or support of spouse and children has been protected.*

We have given careful consideration to the question of whether the change in public policy towards divorce requires a change in the rule respecting antenuptial agreements settling alimony and property rights of the parties upon divorce and have concluded that such agreements should no longer be held to be void Ab initio as 'contrary to public policy.' If such an agreement is valid when tested by the stringent rules prescribed in *Del Vecchio v. Del Vecchio,* supra, 143 So.2d 17, for ante- and post-nuptial agreements settling the property rights of the spouses in the estate of the other upon death, and if, in addition, it is made to appear that the divorce was prosecuted in good faith, on proper grounds, so that, under the rules applicable to postnuptial alimony and property settlement agreements referred to above, it could not be said to facilitate or promote the procurement of a divorce, then it should be held valid as to conditions existing at the time the agreement was made.

> *The question of the future binding effect of such antenuptial agreements when presented to the Chancellor for approval and incorporation in the final decree, and the question of the modification thereof upon a showing of a change in circumstances after the entry of the decree of divorce, should be decided under applicable statutory law and judicial decisions relating to postnuptial contracts settling the alimony and/or property rights of the parties.*

Section 61.14, Florida Statutes, F.S.A. (Ch. 16780, 1935) among other things, provides:—

> *(1) When a husband and wife have entered or hereafter enter into an agreement for payments for, or instead of, support, maintenance or alimony, whether in connection with an action for divorce or separate maintenance or with any voluntary property settlement or when a husband is required by court order to make any payments to his wife, and the circumstances of the parties or the financial ability of the husband has changed since the execution of such agreement or the rendition of the order, either party may apply to the circuit court of the circuit in which the parties, or either of them, resided at the date of the execution of the agreement or reside at the date of the application or in which the agreement was executed or in which the order was rendered, for a judgment decreasing or increasing the amount of support, maintenance or alimony, *386 and the court has jurisdiction to make orders as equity requires with due regard to the changed circumstances and the financial ability of the husband, decreasing or increasing or confirming the amount of separate support, maintenance or alimony provided for in the agreement or order. ...*

In summary, we hold that the antenuptial agreement, if entered into under the conditions outlined in *Del Vecchio v. Del Vecchio*, supra, 143 So.2d 17, was a valid and binding agreement between the parties at the time and under the conditions it was made, but subject to be increased or decreased under changed conditions as provided in s 61.14, Florida Statutes, F.S.A.

Accordingly, the decision under review is quashed with instructions to the District Court of Appeal, Third District, to vacate that portion of the final decree of the trial court relating to alimony and support money and remand same for further proceedings in the trial court not inconsistent with this opinion.

It is so ordered.

While it is true that courts will enforce a postmarital agreement for a troubled marriage where one spouse agrees to stay and try again, courts may not agree to enforce such an agreement if the marriage is intact. In the case of *Bratton v. Bratton*, 136 S.W.3d 595 (TN 2004), at the time of their marriage on June 26, 1982, "Dr. had completed his first year of medical school, and Ms. Bratton was employed as a research technician." "On June 27, 1983, Dr. Bratton handwrote and signed the following letter: I, Michael W. Bratton, being of sound mind and being married to Cynthia L. Bratton hereby promise never to be the cause of a divorce between us. In the event that I do not fulfill my promise, I will give Cindy 50% of my present belongings and 50% of my net future earnings." That handwritten agreement was followed by a formal property settlement agreement on August 26, 1983, which stated if, "in the event the husband was "guilty of statutory grounds for divorce under the statutes of the state the parties are domiciled and the [w]ife institutes divorce proceedings," then the husband would give the wife one half of everything. Although both parties differed as to the reason for the agreements, "Dr. Bratton testified that it was Ms. Bratton who contacted an attorney to have the agreement drafted and brought it home for him to sign. At first he refused, but then he relented when she threatened to leave him if he did not sign it. Both parties testified that at the time the agreement was signed, they were not having any marital difficulties." The Court of Appeals ruling invalidated the agreement as void and against public policy when treating the agreement under contract terms since the marriage was intact. The court found that it lacked consideration by Ms. Bratton giving her no reason to leave it at that time.

What happens if one spouse offers to stay in exchange for the promise of an asset at divorce, but shortly thereafter divorces anyway, because she never really intended to stay? Because the agreement was not made in good faith, it would probably not be enforced.

Today's courts continue to enforce post-marital agreements, provided "each spouse had meaningful choice; some factors to be considered are whether each party was represented by independent counsel, whether each party had adequate time to review agreement, whether parties understood terms of agreement and their effect, and whether parties understood their financial rights in absence of agreement," as the Wisconsin Supreme Court ruled in *Button v. Button* in 1986.

BUTTON V. BUTTON
131 WI2D 84, 388 N.W.2D 546
(S.CT WIS 1986)

Parties sought divorce. The Circuit Court, Walworth County, Robert D. Read, J., divided property upon divorce in accordance with terms of postnuptial property agreement and wife appealed. After taking jurisdiction of the appeal upon certification by the Court of Appeals, 126 Wis.2d 521, 378 N.W.2d

294, the Supreme Court, Shirley S. Abrahamson, J., held that: (1) property agreement is inequitable, and thus not binding, if parties have not reasonably disclosed their financial status, if agreement was not entered into voluntarily and freely, or if substantive provisions of agreement were not fair to each spouse, and (2) fairness of substantive provisions of agreement is determined at time of agreement and, if circumstances significantly change, also at time of divorce.

Reversed and remanded.
SHIRLEY S. ABRAHAMSON, Justice.

This is an appeal from a judgment of the circuit court for Walworth county, Circuit Judge Robert D. Read, dividing property upon divorce in accordance with the terms of a written property agreement which the circuit court found binding under sec. 767.255(11), ... Sec. 767.255 provides for division of property upon divorce. The statute requires the court to presume that certain property shall be divided equally between the parties but authorizes the court to alter this distribution after considering certain factors, including any written agreement between the parties. The statute provides that a written agreement for property distribution shall be binding upon the court and the court shall presume any agreement to be equitable as to both parties. No written agreement shall be binding, however, where the terms of the agreement are inequitable as to either party, Sec. 767.255 provides, inter alia, as follows:

"Upon every judgment of annulment, divorce or legal separation ... the court shall divide the property of the parties and divest and transfer the title of any such property accordingly ... Any property shown to have been acquired by either party prior to or during the course of the marriage as a gift, bequest, devise or inheritance ... shall remain the property of such party. ... The court shall presume that all other property is to be divided equally between the parties, but may alter this distribution without regard to marital misconduct after considering:

"(11) Any written agreement made by the parties before or during the marriage concerning any arrangement for property distribution; such agreements shall be binding upon the court except that no such agreement shall be binding where the terms of the agreement are inequitable as to either *88 party. The court shall presume any such agreement to be equitable as to both parties."

The circuit court concluded that the provisions in the parties' 1974 postnuptial written agreement dividing the property in the event of a divorce were binding under sec. 767.255 (11), Stats. 1983–84, but that the provisions waiving support and alimony were "not enforceable as being against public policy and contrary to the laws of the State of Wisconsin." Florence S. Button appeals only from that part of the judgment directing a division of property pursuant to the 1974 written agreement; neither party appeals from that part of the judgment awarding limited maintenance.

As a result of dividing the property at the dissolution of this 14-year marriage according to the 1974 agreement, the circuit court awarded Mrs. Button assets valued at $7,882.10 and awarded Mr. Button assets valued at $255,103.99. The circuit court's entire finding relating to the division of property in the event of divorce is as follows:

> "The Court notes that Mrs. Button was 54 years of age when she signed the June 19, 1974 agreement, some five **548 years after the initial agreement and the marriage of the parties. The court also notes that she had already given her daughter $12,000 from funds brought to the marriage by her from funds she received at the time of the death of her first husband. She clearly wanted to be able to dispose of her own property as she saw fit and it is reasonable to assume she understood that Mr. Button would be able to do the same thing as a result of this agreement. In light of the entire record, the Court is convinced that Mrs. Button was well aware of the consequences of the June 19, 1974 agreement *89 and it is enforceable as written with regard to the distribution of the property."

The court of appeals certified the following issue: "When is equitableness of an antenuptial or postnuptial agreement [under sec. 767.255 (11)] to be determined—as of the time of execution of the agreement or as of the time of divorce?" Although the circuit court found the agreement equitable, it did not state whether it examined the agreement as of the date of execution or as of the divorce.

The parties present a second issue, namely, what constitutes an equitable agreement? The circuit court apparently considered four factors: Mrs. Button's age, Mrs. Button's transfer to her child of property which she brought into the marriage, Mrs. Button's desire to retain the power to dispose of her separate property, and Mrs. Button's awareness of the consequences of the postnuptial agreement.

This court is addressing both of these issues for the first time. We conclude that an agreement is inequitable under sec. 767.255 (11) if it fails to satisfy any one of the following requirements: each spouse has made fair and reasonable disclosure to the other of his or her financial status; each spouse has entered into the agreement voluntarily and freely; and the substantive provisions of the agreement dividing the property upon divorce are fair to each spouse. The first two requirements must be assessed as of the time of the execution of the agreement. As we shall explain, the third requirement is also assessed as of the time of the execution of the agreement and, if circumstances significantly changed since the agreement, then also at the divorce.

*90 Because the circuit court did not consider and apply the three requirements discussed herein, we reverse that part of the judgment ordering property division on the basis of the written agreement and remand the cause to the circuit court to consider whether the terms of the written agreement are inequitable and not binding under sec. 767.255 (11) under the test set forth herein.

The relevant facts are as follows. The parties married on September 12, 1969, having known each other for approximately five years prior to their marriage. Both parties had been married previously; Mrs. Button had one adult child from her prior marriage and Mr. Button had three adult children. When they were married, Mrs. Button was 50 years old, and Mr. Button 61 years old. Mrs. Button began the divorce action in 1983.

Prior to the marriage, Mrs. Button had acquired some personal property and other assets with a total worth of no more than $3,000 and a life insurance policy on the life of her former husband in the amount of $12,000. Mr. Button had an upholstery business, a stock portfolio, personal property and real estate upon which a duplex residence and the business were located. He had inherited a substantial part of this property and, under sec. 767.255, inherited property is considered separate property not generally subject to division upon divorce.

The parties entered into a written prenuptial agreement on August 15, 1969. While this prenuptial agreement is not the agreement in issue here, the facts relating to the execution of the 1969 agreement are stated because they may bear on the determination of whether the 1974 agreement is inequitable.

*91 Mrs. Button testified that there was no discussion of Mr. Button's finances prior to their marriage, although she was aware **549 that he owned a duplex house, an upholstery business, a car, and a snowmobile. Mrs. Button also testified that Mr. Button's attorney told her that "if [you] wanted to take it to another attorney [you] could, but if [you] did that then you would say that you didn't trust Charles and Charlie said that's right and [the attorney] said the same thing." Mrs. Button also stated that she did not read the agreement before signing it. Mr. Button's attorney testified that he believed that both parties understood the agreement, although he has no record of any financial disclosures being made between the parties. Mr. Button testified that he did not make any financial disclosures to Mrs. Button. Neither Mrs. Button nor Mr. Button's attorney had any recollection of Mrs. Button's being advised of the rights she was surrendering by signing the agreement.

Mrs. Button testified that soon after their marriage, Mr. Button instructed her to stop working outside the home because her contribution to the marriage would be greater if she devoted all her time to being a homemaker. Mrs. Button had been employed as a produce worker at a supermarket. Mr. Button denied that he made this demand. Mrs. Button did cease to work outside the home within 6 months after the marriage. She testified that she worked hard in the house. After the marriage, Mr. Button continued working outside the home as an upholsterer.

In 1970 Mrs. Button received $12,000 from the life insurance policy on the death of her first husband. These funds were held in her own name until 1974, when she placed the funds in a joint account with her *92 daughter. In 1982, apparently after the parties separated, Mrs. Button transferred $12,000 to her daughter. Mrs. Button's daughter testified that she used these funds for Mrs. Button.

In June 1974, after Mr. Button sold his upholstery business to his son for $85,000, the parties signed a postnuptial agreement, which expressly rescinded and terminated the 1969 prenuptial agreement. Mr. Button's assets had appreciated in value during the marriage to approximately $110,000. Mrs. Button's assets were essentially the same as before marriage, except that sometime during the marriage Mr. Button gave her a joint interest in shares of stock having a value of $3,000. During the marriage Mr. Button paid for the household expenses and vacation trips from his income and property.

The 1974 agreement—which is the agreement to be tested under sec. 767.255 (11)—was drafted by Mr. Button's attorney. Mrs. Button did not have independent counsel. She testified that the agreement was never explained to her and that no financial disclosures were made. Mrs. Button also testified, however, that she was generally aware of Mr. Button's property, that they filed joint tax returns and that she had access to copies of the returns. She also testified that she was unfamiliar with tax returns, having never prepared one herself. Furthermore, Mr. Button acknowledged that the full extent of his financial holdings could not be discerned from his tax returns.

The 1974 postnuptial agreement provided that in the event of a divorce all property owned by either party prior to marriage would remain the separate property of that party and that all property acquired after the marriage would be deemed the separate property*93 of the party acquiring the property. In the event of divorce, Mrs. Button was to accept as full property settlement her own articles of personal property, her own separate property and one-half of all properties acquired jointly by the parties.

At the time of divorce Mrs. Button was in ill health, confined to a skilled care nursing home receiving public assistance. In addition to receiving $255,103 in property, Mr. Button was working parttime after the divorce.

We now turn to the question of what is an inequitable agreement for purposes of sec. 767.255 (11). The statute does not define inequitable. We must interpret inequitableness**550 in light of the language and purpose of sec. 767.255 (11). FN2

FN2. Commentators have disagreed regarding the extent to which and the manner in which courts should review marital agreements. See, e.g., Clark, Antenuptial Contracts, 50 U.Colo.L.Rev. 141 (1979); Klarman, Marital Agreements in Contemplation of Divorce, 10 U.Mich.J.L. Reform 397 (1977); Oldham & Caudill, A Reconnaissance of Public Policy Restrictions upon Enforcement of Contracts between Cohabitants, 18 Fam.L.Q. 93 (1984); Oldham, Premarital Contracts Are Now Enforceable, Unless ... , 21 Houston L.Rev. 757 (1984); Sharp, Fairness Standards and Separation Agreements: A Word of Caution on Contractual Freedom, 132 U.Pa.L.Rev. 1399 (1984); Comment, Antenuptial Contract to Circumvent Equitable Distribution in New Jersey under the Revised Divorce Act, 12 Rutgers L.J. 283 (1981).

Sec. 767.255 (11) permits marital partners to reach their own agreements about financial arrangements. Sec. 767.255 (11) states that the court is to presume the agreement dividing property is equitable. We read this provision, which puts the burden of production of evidence and the burden of persuasion on *94 the spouse challenging the agreement, as demonstrating the legislature's interest in giving effect to the parties' agreement to the extent possible.

The legislature has recognized that prenuptial and postnuptial agreements dividing property serve a useful function. They allow parties to structure their financial affairs to suit their needs and values and to achieve certainty. This certainty may encourage marriage and may be conducive to marital tranquility by protecting the financial expectations of the parties. The right to enter into an agreement regulating financial affairs in a marriage is important to a large number of citizens.

Sec. 767.255 (11), however, sets forth a competing public policy. While sec. 767.255 (11) embodies the public policy of freedom of contract, it also empowers a divorce court to override the parties' agreement if the agreement is inequitable. This latter policy reflects the unique role of the marriage contract in society. Marriage is not simply a contract between two parties. Marriage is a legal status in which the state has a special interest. Certain rights and obligations dictated by the state flow from marriage, and the legislature requires a divorce court to scrutinize an agreement between the spouses carefully. The parties are free to contract, but they contract in the shadow of the court's obligation to review the agreement on divorce to protect the spouses' financial interests on divorce.

After studying the language and purpose of sec. 767.255 (11), we conclude that an agreement is inequitable under 767.255(11) if it is unfair either in its procurement or in its substantive provisions.

*95 Fairness in procurement depends on two factors: whether each spouse makes fair and reasonable disclosure to the other spouse of his or her financial status, and whether each spouse enters into the agreement voluntarily and freely. Obviously these two factors are determined as of the date of the execution of the contract. If the parties fail to satisfy either of these factors, the agreement is inequitable under sec. 767.255(11).

An agreement is inequitable if either spouse has not made fair and reasonable disclosure to the other of his or her assets, liabilities and debts. A party might not have entered into the agreement had she or he known the facts. Where it can be shown that a spouse had independent knowledge of the opposing spouse's financial status, this independent knowledge serves as a substitute for disclosure. This case does not raise the question of whether a spouse may waive disclosure and we do not decide that issue.

The public interest requires that a financial agreement between spouses or prospective spouses be executed under conditions of candor and fairness. Married persons and persons about to marry stand in a confidential relationship and must deal fairly with each other. Fair and reasonable disclosure of financial status is a significant aspect of the duty of fair dealing.

An agreement is also inequitable if it is not entered into voluntarily and freely. In determining whether the agreement was **551 entered into voluntarily and freely, the relevant inquiry is whether each spouse had a meaningful choice. Some factors a circuit court should consider are whether each party was represented by independent counsel, whether each party *96 had adequate time to review the agreement, whether the parties understood the terms of the agreement and their effect, and whether the parties understood their financial rights in the absence of an agreement. If the agreement was not entered into voluntarily and freely, the agreement is inequitable under sec. 767.255 (11).

The first two requirements are issues of "procedural fairness." The third requirement is an issue of "substantive fairness." Substantive fairness is an amorphous concept. We can set forth general principles, but the courts must determine substantive fairness on a case by case basis. In determining substantive fairness a court must be mindful of the two principal legislative concerns reflected in sec. 767.255 (11)—the protection of the parties' freedom to contract and the protection of the parties' financial interests at divorce. Sec. 767.255 (11) allows parties freedom to contract but does not allow them to ignore the state's interest in protecting the financial interests of the parties at divorce.

An agreement need not approximate a division a circuit court might make under sec. 767.255 to meet the requirement of substantive fairness. If the parties are permitted to do only that which a circuit court would do under sec. 767.255, the parties would not have a meaningful right to contract or to divide their property as they wish. A party should be able to enter into an agreement, for example, which preserves property acquired before marriage for persons other than the spouse. To meet the requirement of substantive fairness an agreement need not divide the property in conformity with how a divorce court would divide the property, but it should in some manner appropriate to the circumstances of the parties take into account that *97 each spouse contributes to the prosperity of the marriage by his or her efforts.

In framing the agreement the parties should consider the circumstances existing at the execution of the agreement and those reasonably foreseeable. The parties should consider that the duration of the marriage is unknown and that they wish the agreement to govern their financial arrangements whether the marriage lasts a short time or for many years. The parties should consider such factors as the objectives of the parties in executing an agreement, the economic circumstances of the parties, the property brought to the marriage by each party, each spouse's family relationships and obligations to persons other than to the spouse, the earning capacity of each person, the anticipated contribution by one party to the education, training or increased earning power of the other, the future needs of the respective spouses, the age and physical and emotional health of the parties, and the expected contribution of each party to the marriage, giving appropriate economic value to each party's contribution in homemaking and child care services.

In assessing the fairness of the substantive terms of the agreement, a circuit court considers these factors and evaluates the terms of the agreement from the perspective of the parties at the execution of the agreement. We conclude that the court should look at the substantive fairness of the agreement as of the time it was made if the court is to give effect to the parties' freedom to contract. At execution the parties know their property and other relevant circumstances and are able to make reasonable predictions about the future;*98 they should then be able to draft a fair agreement considering these factors. [Footnote 3 omitted.]

By contrast, others have read sec. 767.255 (11) to mean that the assessment of the validity of the agreement is to be made as of the date the agreement was executed. Thus in Hengel v. Hengel, 122 Wis.2d 737, 745, 365 N.W.2d 16 (Ct.App.1985), the parties interpreted the statute to require the validity of the agreement to be determined as of the time of execution. The court of appeals conducted its analysis of the agreement in that case as of the time of execution without exploring or ruling on the correctness of the parties' position …

**552 Clearly an agreement fair at execution is not unfair at divorce just because the application of the agreement at divorce results in a property division which is not equal between the parties or which a court might not order under sec. 767.255. If, however, there are significantly changed circumstances after the execution of an agreement and the agreement as applied at divorce no longer comports with the reasonable expectations*99 of the parties, an agreement which is fair at execution may be unfair to the parties at divorce.

Using this approach to assess substantive fairness, a circuit court would look at the fairness of the substantive terms of the agreement as of the execution of the agreement and, if there have been significantly changed circumstances after the execution of the agreement, at divorce. This approach protects the parties' freedom to contract and the parties' financial interests at divorce.

To summarize, an agreement is inequitable under sec. 767.255 (11) if it fails to satisfy any one of the three requirements: each spouse has made fair and reasonable disclosure to the other about his or her financial status; each spouse enters into the agreement voluntarily and freely; the substantive terms of the agreement dividing the property upon divorce are fair to each spouse.

The circuit court's determination of inequitableness under sec. 767.255 (11), as does the circuit court's determination of a property division under 767.255, requires the circuit court to exercise its discretion. A discretionary determination must be made on the basis of the facts and the applicable law. A discretionary determination must be the product of a rational mental process by which the facts of record and the law relied upon are stated and considered together for the purpose of achieving a reasoned and reasonable determination. The decision will be upheld by an appellate court if the circuit court considered the relevant law and facts and set forth a process of logical reasoning.

*100 Because the circuit court has not considered this agreement in this case under the three-part test we have set forth, we remand the cause to the circuit court to exercise its discretion under the test set forth herein.

Accordingly, we reverse the judgment dividing the property on the basis of the agreement and remand the cause for further proceedings not inconsistent with this decision. In reaching its decision the circuit court should consider the entire record in this matter and may reopen the proceedings for further testimony or briefing if it so elects.

The judgment is reversed and the cause is remanded to the circuit court.

---

4. SEPARATION AND SETTLEMENT AGREEMENTS

Separation agreements are made by spouses after they legally separate in anticipation of divorce. Also known as settlement agreements, the married couple creates them after they decide to divorce or dissolve their marriage, as a way to divide up their assets. Like the other types of agreements already discussed, the courts originally voided such agreements because they felt they would encourage divorce. This was especially true when courts made divorces hard to obtain. With the advent of "no-fault" divorce and with society's increasing acceptance of private ordering, the courts encourage divorcing parties to reach an agreement outside of the court's involvement. A problem may arise if the agreement is breached because the only remedy is enforcement under contract law. Even when the parties have worked out an agreement, the court still has the power to modify it especially in areas involving children.

What was the effect of property settlement agreements on same-sex couples, before Marriage Equality, if their state did not recognized their marriage that was valid in another state? In *Gonzalez v. Green*, 831 NY.S.2d 856 (2006), "plaintiff and defendant had been same sex domestic partners since in or about 2001 when the defendant, a person of considerable assets and income, invited the plaintiff to move in with him. The plaintiff was a student with little or no income at the time. During the course of their relationship the defendant gave the plaintiff expensive gifts, including two automobiles and a ski house in the plaintiff's name. In 2005 the couple, whose primary residence was in Westchester, New York, decided to take advantage of recent Massachusetts legislation that permits people of the same sex to marry. They arranged for and took part in a marriage ceremony to each other in Massachusetts on February 14, 2005." At that time, Massachusetts had a law that stated marriages for non-residents were not valid if their home state did not recognize same-sex marriages. (New York did not.) As a result, the defendant argued that the marriage was principally symbolic in nature.

When their relationship dissolved in September of 2005, the defendant's attorney drafted a "separation agreement" which was signed by both. The agreement "recites in relevant part that 'the parties desire to confirm their separation and make arrangements in connection therewith, including the settlement of their property rights, and other rights and obligations growing out of the marriage relation'" and the parties agreed, among other things, to "a one-time payment by defendant to plaintiff of the sum of $780,000.00, described as 'the only support, maintenance, or other form of payment by either party hereto to the other.'" When the agreement was challenged, the New York Supreme Court did not find the marriage valid but did hold that the separation agreement was enforceable as a contract at the end of a relationship.

The case of *Glickman v. Collins*, 13 CA3d 852, 120 Cal.Rptr. 76, 533 P.2d 204 (1975) has an interesting twist to the typical separation agreement. In this case, Gerald and Claire were married. Gerald had an affair with Hilda and wanted a divorce from Claire. In their separation agreement, the couple worked out the terms of Gerald's spousal support payments (alimony) to Claire. Claire put in a twist by only agreeing to the divorce if Hilda agreed to guarantee Claire's support payments, should Gerald fail to make them. All agreed. The couple signed the property settlement agreement. Hilda signed a guarantee of the support payments. After the divorce, Hilda and Gerald married, but later divorced. When Gerald stopped making his support payments to Claire, she sued him. The court awarded her about $9,000, which Gerald was not able to pay. Claire then sued Hilda under her guarantee and the court found Hilda liable for the amount of Gerald's debt. Hilda then appealed the case arguing that she should not have to pay because the property settlement agreement should be void against public policy because it encouraged divorce. The appellate courts affirmed the lower court's decision to hold Hilda responsible for Gerald's support payments to Claire. In so doing they rejected Hilda's argument that the separation agreement induced their divorce finding that the marriage was already broken. "If the marriage had so deteriorated that legitimate grounds for divorce existed and if there was little hope of reconciliation, the dissolution of such marriage is not contrary to public policy." So, the latter ex-wife had to pay the former ex-wife's alimony.

It is curious. On one hand, people have moved away from the law's prescriptions for marriage to define their own expectations in relationships. Yet, on the other, people are quick to look to the law to tell them how to deal with the relationships that they created. Is this the product of helicopter parents that did too much?

Are there any other relationships where society may want to create a contract? How about the "hook up"—sex without a relationship? "The more casual sex becomes, the more we demand that our institutions and government police the line between what's consensual and what isn't."[18] The issues of consent in a sexual relationship are hot topics of debate on college campuses today. Some argue that poor communication should not turn sex into a crime.[19] Meanwhile legal scholars try to create model laws.

At the same time, some industrious attorneys have suggested "pre-sexual agreements." Under this newest of "love note," people (usually celebrities) may have a potential sexual partner stipulate via a pre-printed form that she (he):

- Is at least 18
- Is not under the influence of mind-altering drugs
- Does not have a sexually transmitted disease
- Freely consents to the sexual acts and/or
- Will not bring criminal charges against the person asking for the agreement.

I assume the idea is that you would purchase a form contract as an app for your cellphone and download it each time. This has led some to quip that, "[a]thletes are going to carry consent forms just like they carry condoms."[20] Are these contracts effective? Especially, as pointed out prior, when a sexual partner can withdraw consent at any time. Obviously, these agreements are so new that they have not been tested in court. Should the courts enforce them?

ADDITIONAL SOURCES

http://family.findlaw.com/marriage/top-10-reasons-a-premarital-agreement-may-be-invalid.html, Lisa C. Johnson, Esq., July 2010, legal zoom.

Weisberg, D. Kelly. *Emanuel Law Outlines*, Family Law. (2011).

---

18 "Regulating Sex, as mores become more free, we increasingly want the state to decide what is allowed." Judith Shhulevitz, *The New York Times Sunday Review*, page 1. June 28, 2105,

19 Ibid., p. 6. Nancy Gertner, senior lecturer at Harvard Law School and a retired judge is quoted, "If there's no social consensus about what the lines are" then affirmative consent "has no business being in the criminal law."

20 http://www.si.com/vault/2003/12/29/357624/forms-of-endearment-want-to-have-sex-with-an-athlete-just-sign-here

THE CONSTITUTION AND FAMILY LAW

5

Our constitution protects aliens, drunks and U.S. Senators.[1]
—Will Rogers

Aspx#faqgi9![2]

spx#faqgi9!—Surely, swearing at an overflowing toilet must be a constitutional right. Yet, in Pennsylvania, a woman who allegedly shouted obscenities at her toilet as it overflowed from the second floor, was cited for disorderly conduct by the police. In Scranton, Pennsylvania, Dawn Herb, "a single mother of four, expressed her frustration with the toilet, [when] her neighbor, a Scranton police officer, overheard [her] through an open window. After ordering Ms. Herb to 'shut the f—k up,' the off-duty cop called police who cited her for using obscene language under Pennsylvania's disorderly conduct statute" for which "she could receive up to 90 days jail time and a $300 fine."[3] Is it illegal to swear in the house? The answer is in the United States Constitution.

THE CONSTITUTION

As the Constitution states in Article 6, it is the "supreme law of the land." This means that all laws in the United States must agree with the Constitution. It is a set of organizing principles that grant and limit the powers of our government, listing the people's rights and liberties. Because

---

1   http://www.quotationspage.com/search.php3?Search=Constitution&startsearch=Search&Author=&C=mgm&C=motivate&C=classic&C=coles&C=poorc&C=lindsly, The Quotations Page.

2   Although aspx#faqgi9! was put in to illustrate a censored cussing, it is actually the end of the Web page to the Supreme Court of the United States, http://www.supremecourt.gov/faq.aspx#faqgi9

3   http://www.aclupa.org/our-work/legal/legaldocket/commonwealth-v-herb/, containing the Court's order in *Commonwealth v. Herb*, case No. NT0000758-07, heard December 10, 2007, in front of Judge Terrence V. Gallagher.

of its importance to our nation, it deserves to have some historical background. Who wrote the Constitution? Most guess Thomas Jefferson, but it was James Madison. The Constitution was written in Philadelphia in the summer of 1787. Curiously, in a country that values transparency in its democracy, the Constitution was created in secret. The delegates did not tell anybody what they were doing. They pulled down the shades in the hot Philadelphia summer to keep the creation of the document under wraps. They ended up with a document that consists of three parts: the Preamble (introduction), seven Articles, and eventually 27 Amendments. Most are familiar with the Preamble, which reads: "We the people of the United States, in order to form a more perfect union, establish justice, insure domestic tranquility, provide for the common defense, promote the general welfare, and secure the blessings of liberty to ourselves and our posterity, do ordain and establish this Constitution for the United States of America."

Next, the Constitution contains seven Articles, with subsections. The first Article deals with the legislative branch, or Congress. The second concerns the executive branch, or the president. The third is the judicial branch, which includes federal judges and federal/national courts. The fourth Article deals with how states relate to one another and to the federal government. The fifth Article states how to amend or change the Constitution. The sixth Article, as noted above, clarifies that the Constitution is the supreme law of the land. The seventh Article discusses the ratification or approval process for the Constitution.

There are five major concepts to the Constitution. The first is the separation of powers. The delegates feared giving too much power to any single person or group and decided to create three branches of government. They are: the executive (the president), the legislative (Congress), and the judicial (the courts). Also fearing the danger of power concentrated in one of those branches, the delegates created a system of checks and balances. This limits the power of each branch so that no single branch can overpower the other. The checks and balances also foster interdependency, where one branch may need another branch's approval in order to do its job. Additionally, the Constitution enumerates, or lists, the powers of the federal government. Finally, the Constitution deals with the issue of federalism, the division of powers between the federal and state governments.

THE AMENDMENTS

As the forefathers anticipated, the Constitution was not perfect when it was written. There are 27 Amendments today. (The 21st, involves a repeal of the 18th, which made it illegal for Americans to drink alcohol.) Looking at some of the Amendments reveals what the drafters and the country wanted from this supreme law of the land.

A. The First Amendment

The First Amendment, probably the most well known, actually includes four rights: the freedom of religion, speech, press, and assembly. Freedom of religion has two parts. Most people remember the first part—that in the United States people are free to worship as they please.[4] The second part of that Amendment, called the Establishment Clause (but probably more accurately the anti-establishment clause) clarifies that the government cannot establish or have an official religion.[5] Remember, many of the pilgrims came to America because of religious persecution. England, at that time, had one main religion: the official Church of England. Membership in this church impacted everything from employment to jail. The second freedom contained in the First Amendment is the freedom of assembly. This allows Americans to freely gather peacefully. The third, freedom of the press, guarantees the government will not censor newspapers or media. Finally, free speech allows the right to speak openly (with some limits—you cannot yell "fire" in a crowded theater, thus putting people at risk) without fear of government reprisal.[6]

B. The Second Amendment

The Second Amendment might also be familiar since it involves the issue of gun ownership. Remember, the Preamble of the Constitution states that part of the document's responsibilities is to provide for the common defense[7]. The Second Amendment raises the issue of whether the right

---

4 For example, the Supreme Court has held that public schools cannot require children to salute the U.S. flag if such an action conflicts with their religious beliefs.

5 Yet, in May, 2014, the Supreme Court ruled "non-believers and those of other religions had no reason to be unduly disturbed if a government meeting opened with a Christian prayer. Without more overt actions, there was no reason to see such invocations as government endorsement of a particular religion. Offended adults could simply leave that portion of the meeting or quietly let the time pass without being seen as endorsing the religious message delivered, wrote Justice Anthony Kenney." "After ruling on prayer at meetings, could crosses be justices' next religious issue to bear?", Robert Barnes, *The Washington Post,* May 12, 2014, A11.

6 The boundaries of using free speech were tested by the Westboro Baptist Church with its anti-gay picketing at military funerals (and even the funeral of Fred Rogers, of PBS' Mr. Roger's Neighborhood because he had "neglected to warn young viewers that sodomy is a sin"). Although the behaviors "inflamed the nation", and "even managed to offend the conscience of the Ku Klux Klan, which staged protests to counter Westboro's demonstrations" the protests were protected free speech according to the Supreme Court. Later, laws allowing the creation of buffer areas near the sites of funerals were upheld. "Obituary of Fred Phelps Sr.", Adam Bernstein, *The Washington Post,* March 20, 2014. Obscenity falls under this amendment and still causes questions as to its protected status as free speech. On February 4, 2015, Virginia legislatures voted on a bill to keep "obscene materials" away from prison inmates. "Morrissey votes against ban on smut in prison", Jenna Portnoy, *The Washington Post,* February 5, 2015, p.B2

7 "Sure, there are cases where guns are successfully used for self-defense, but a study in the journal *Injury Prevention* found that the purchase of a handgun was associated with 2.4 times the risk of being murdered and 6.8 times the risk of suicide". "We have 300 million guns circulating in America." "Just since 1968, it has been calculated, more Americans have died from gunfire than have died in all the wars in our country's history." Since the 1990s the Japanese government teaches its "citizens traveling to the United State the word 'freeze'" after a 16-year old Japanese exchange student in Louisiana who had been invited to a Halloween party but went to the wrong door was killed when the homeowner came out with a gun, shouted "freeze" (which the student did not understand) and shot the student in the chest. "Stranger Danger and Guns", Nicholas Kristof, *The New York Times*, September 28, 2014, P. 11.

to bear arms (guns)[8] concerns an individual homeowner's gun rights or those of a militia intended to defend the community. The specific language reads, "A well regulated militia being necessary to the security of a free state, the right of the people to keep and bear arms, shall not be infringed." You decide.

C. The Third Amendment

The Third Amendment limits the obligation to quarter (keep) soldiers in private homes. The Amendment prevents Americans from being forced to keep government soldiers in their private homes without the homeowner's consent. To understand the Third Amendment, look back to Colonial times in America. Before our independence, England sent soldiers to maintain order in the colonies. When they arrived, the English government ordered American colonists to house and feed English soldiers. This practice continued until the end of the Revolution.

D. The Fourth Amendment

Familiar from televised police dramas; the Fourth Amendment is the "search and seizure" amendment. It limits the government's right to search Americans, including their houses, and has been extended to cars and other private places. The government must first demonstrate reasonable cause by obtaining a court-ordered warrant. The Fourth Amendment reads: "The right of the people to be secure in their homes, houses, papers, and effects, against unreasonable searches and seizures, shall not be violated, and no warrants shall issue, but upon probable cause, supported by oath or affirmation, and particularly describing the place to be searched and the persons or things to be seized."

E. The Fifth Amendment

The Fifth Amendment addresses capital (murder) cases, but includes the well-known right against self-incrimination. No one can be forced to testify against him or herself in a criminal case brought

---

8   In 2013, Florida granted a new trial to a woman sentenced to 20 years in prison after she fired a warning shot during an argument with her abusive husband. "New Trial granted in 'warning' shot case", *The Washington Post,* September 27, 2013, p.A3. Indeed, the right to gun ownership has led to other interesting twists. Former Virginia Attorney General Ken Cuccinelli went to work as a lawyer in private practice in the "Virginia Self Defense Law"—a firm focused on defending Second Amendment rights. For less than $10 per month, the law firm will "defend clients facing firearms charges stemming from an act of self-defense and those who have been 'harassed by law enforcement for lawfully carrying their weapon.'" Their slogan is "Defending those who defend themselves" and their web site reads, "Don't be a victim! Don't let these realities become your family's fiscal nightmare!" There are limits to being defended after shooting someone under the pre-paid legal plan. "If they pick up a weapons charge while dealing drugs or engaging in some other sort of illegal activity", all bets are off. The firm has an out through, what Cuccinelli calls the 'sex, drugs, rock-n-roll clause.'" "Defense law firm defending gun right", Laura Vozzella, *The Washington Post,* February 27, 2014. http://www.washingtonpost.com/local/virginia-politics/cuccinelli-3-others-start-virginia-self-defense-law-firm-defending-gun-rights/2014/02/27/fdce2b8e-9fbd-11e3-b8d8-94577ff66b28_story.html

by the government. It also prevents double jeopardy, which is trying a person more than once for the same crime. Another often recognized right in this Amendment is that no person shall be "deprived of life, liberty, or property without due process of the law."

F. The Ninth and Tenth Amendments[9]

The Ninth Amendment reads, "The enumeration in the Constitution of certain rights shall not be construed to deny or disparage others retained by the people." The Tenth Amendment reads, "The powers not delegated to the United States by the Constitution, nor prohibited by it to the states, are reserved to the states respectively, or to the people." Thus, the people reserve the right to and are entitled to the rights not listed in the Constitution as applicable to the government.

G. The 14th Amendment

The 14th Amendment has two parts—due process and equal protection clauses. First, the amendment begins by broadly defining who is considered an American citizen. Next, under the due process clause, it states, "nor shall any state deprive any person of life, liberty, or property, without due process of law; nor deny to any person within its jurisdiction the equal protection of the laws" without insuring fair legal procedures are followed. Due process has two meanings: Substantive due process requires the government to give due process before taking away a constitutional right (thus protecting those rights). The second, procedural due process refers to legal procedures or rules that establish that which must be impartially and fairly applied to all, rich or poor. Thus, Americans have the right to be treated fairly under a body of law that will be applied fairly, not arbitrarily, to different groups of people.

Looking at these Amendments as a whole, it seems clear that the Framers' intent in drafting the Constitution and the Amendments was to limit the government's interference in people's lives and to reserve the majority of rights for the people. This makes sense, given the historical context of when the Constitution was written. America had just fought a war to free itself from England. The last thing the colonists wanted was to put themselves, again, in a subservient position to one ruler. When translating a document created in the 1700s to modern society, try to understand the context of the Founders' period. Clearly, they could not anticipate the modern advancements of today's society. Therefore it's a challenge to apply the Constitution to issues raised by modern advances. How does the Constitution apply to family law? Family law is decided in state courts and has been slow in changing. This is partly because society is comfortable with the old rules that reflected the morality of the community, but also because relying on legislature to change family law means risking the next election. As a result, for over 200 years, from the formation of the country, family laws (viz., marriage law) have changed very little until, arguably, two decisions by the United States Supreme Court in the 1960s.

---

9 The Sixth, Seventh, and Eighth amendments deal with important rights like the right to trial or bail, but are not typically a part of family law cases.

RIGHT TO PRIVACY

Griswold v. Connecticut 381 U.S. 479 (1965)

The case of *Griswold v. Connecticut* involved the medical director/doctor along with the executive director of the Planned Parenthood League of Connecticut who gave information and medical advice to married couples regarding methods of birth control (no pills or medical products were provided). They were found guilty of aiding and abetting the couples' illegal use of birth control and were fined $100 each. In Connecticut (and in most states at the time), there was a prohibition against utilizing anything that might prevent conception. Anyone who violated this law would be criminally punished, including the doctors and pharmacists who helped other people obtain birth control. If most states had rules preventing the use of birth control, could these laws be unconstitutional?

GRISWOLD V. CONNECTICUT
381 U.S. 479 (1965)

Supreme Court of the United States (1965)
381 U.S. 479, 85 S.Ct. 1678, 14 L.Ed.2d 510

Defendants were convicted of violating the Connecticut birth control law. The Circuit Court in the Sixth Circuit, Connecticut, rendered judgments, and the defendants appealed. The Appellate Division of the Circuit Court affirmed, and defendants appealed. The Connecticut Supreme Court of Errors, 151 Conn. 544, 200 A.2d 479, affirmed, and the defendants appealed. The Supreme Court, Mr. Justice Douglas, held that the Connecticut law forbidding use of contraceptives unconstitutionally intrudes upon the right of marital privacy.

Reversed.

*480 Mr. Justice DOUGLAS delivered the opinion of the Court.

Appellant Griswold is Executive Director of the Planned Parenthood League of Connecticut. Appellant Buxton is a licensed physician and a professor at the Yale Medical School who served as Medical Director for the League at its Center in New Haven—a center open and operating from November 1 to November 10, 1961, when appellants were arrested.

They gave information, instruction, and medical advice to married persons as to the means of preventing conception. They examined the wife and prescribed the best contraceptive device or material for her use. Fees were usually charged, although some couples were serviced free.

The statutes whose constitutionality is involved in this appeal are ss 53–32 and 54–196 of the General Statutes of Connecticut (1958 rev.). The former provides:

> *Any person who uses any drug, medicinal article or instrument for the purpose of preventing conception shall be fined not less than fifty dollars or imprisoned not less than sixty days nor more than one year or be both fined and imprisoned.*

Section 54-196 provides:

> *Any person who assists, abets, counsels, causes, hires or commands another to commit any offense may be prosecuted and punished as if he were the principal offender.*

The appellants were found guilty as accessories and fined $100 each, against the claim that the accessory statute as so applied violated the Fourteenth Amendment. The Appellate Division of the Circuit Court affirmed. The Supreme Court of Errors affirmed that judgment. 151 Conn. 544, 200 A.2d 479. We noted probable jurisdiction. 379 U.S. 926, 85 S.Ct. 328, 13 L.Ed.2d 339.

We think that appellants have standing to raise the constitutional rights of the married people with whom they had a professional relationship...

Coming to the merits, we are met with a wide range of questions that implicate the Due Process Clause of the Fourteenth Amendment... We do not sit as a super-legislature to determine the wisdom, need, and propriety of laws that touch economic problems, business affairs, or social conditions. This law, however, operates directly on an intimate relation of husband and wife and their physician's role in one aspect of that relation.

The association of people is not mentioned in the Constitution nor in the Bill of Rights. The right to educate a child in a school of the parents' choice—whether public or private or parochial—is also not mentioned. Nor is the right to study any particular subject or any foreign language. Yet the First Amendment has been construed to include certain of those rights.

By *Pierce v. Society of Sisters*, supra, the right to educate one's children as one chooses is made applicable to the States by the force of the First and Fourteenth Amendments. By *Meyer v. State of Nebraska*, supra, the same dignity is given the right to study the German language in a private school. In other words, the State may not, consistently with the spirit of the First Amendment, contract the spectrum of available knowledge. The right of freedom of speech and press includes not only the right to utter or to print, but the right to distribute, the right to receive, the right to read [Cites omitted by the author.]... And so we reaffirm the principle of the Pierce and the Meyer cases.

In *NAACP v. State of Alabama*, 357 U.S. 449, 462, 78 S.Ct. 1163, 1172, we protected the 'freedom to associate and privacy in one's associations,' noting that freedom of association was a peripheral First Amendment right. Disclosure of membership lists of a constitutionally valid association, we held, was invalid 'as entailing the likelihood of a substantial restraint upon the exercise by petitioner's members of their right to freedom of association.' Ibid. In other words, the First Amendment has a penumbra where privacy is protected from governmental intrusion. In like context, we have protected forms of 'association' that are not political in the customary sense but pertain to the social, legal, and economic benefit of the members. *NAACP v. Button*, 371 U.S. 415, 430–431, 83 S.Ct. 328, 336–337. In *Schware v. Board of Bar Examiners*, 353 U.S. 232, 77 S.Ct. 752, 1 L.Ed.2d 796, we held it not permissible to bar a lawyer from practice, because he had once been a member of the Communist Party. The man's 'association with that Party' was not shown to be 'anything more than a political faith in a political party' (id., at 244, 77 S.Ct. at 759) and was not action of a kind proving bad moral character. Id., at 245–246, 77 S.Ct. at 759–760.

Those cases involved more than the 'right of assembly'—a right that extends to all irrespective of their race or ideology. *De Jonge v. State of Oregon*, 299 U.S. 353, 57 S.Ct. 255, 81 L.Ed. 278. The right of 'association,' like the right of belief (*West Virginia State Board of Education v. Barnette*, 319 U.S. 624, 63 S.Ct. 1178), is more than the right to attend a meeting; it includes the right to express one's attitudes or philosophies by membership in a group or by affiliation with it or by other lawful means. Association in that context is a form of expression of opinion; and while it is not expressly included in the First Amendment its existence is necessary in making the express guarantees fully meaningful.

The foregoing cases suggest that specific guarantees in the Bill of Rights have penumbras, formed by emanations from those guarantees that help give them life and substance. See *Poe v. Ullman*, 367 U.S. 497, 516–522, 81 S.Ct. 1752, 6 L.Ed.2d 989 (dissenting opinion). Various guarantees create zones of privacy. The right of association contained in the penumbra of the First Amendment is one, as we have seen. The Third Amendment in its prohibition against the quartering of soldiers 'in any house' in time of peace without the consent of the owner is another facet of that privacy. The Fourth Amendment explicitly affirms the 'right of the people to be secure in their persons, houses, papers, and effects, against unreasonable searches and seizures.' The Fifth Amendment in its Self-Incrimination Clause enables the citizen to create a zone of privacy which government may not force him to surrender to his detriment. The Ninth Amendment provides: 'The enumeration in the Constitution, of certain rights, shall not be construed to deny or disparage others retained by the people.'

The Fourth and Fifth Amendments were described in *Boyd v. United States*, 116 U.S. 616, 630, 6 S.Ct. 524, 532, 29 L.Ed. 746, as protection against all governmental invasions 'of the sanctity of a man's home and the privacies of life.' FN* **1682 We recently referred*485 in *Mapp v. Ohio*, 367 U.S. 643, 656, 81 S.Ct. 1684, 1692, 6 L.Ed.2d 1081, to the Fourth Amendment as creating a 'right to privacy, no less important than any other right carefully and particularly reserved to the people.' See Beaney, The Constitutional Right to Privacy, 1962 Sup.Ct.Rev. 212; Griswold, The Right to be Let Alone, 55 Nw.U.L.Rev. 216 (1960).

FN* The Court said in full about this right of privacy: 'The principles laid down in this opinion (by Lord Camden in *Entick v. Carrington*, 19 How.St.Tr. 1029) affect the very essence of constitutional liberty and security. They reach further than the concrete form of the case then before the court, with its adventitious circumstances; they apply to all invasions on the part of the government and its employees of the sanctity of a man's home and the privacies of life. It is not the breaking of his doors, and the rummaging of his drawers, that constitutes the essence of the offense; but it is the invasion of his indefeasible right of personal security, personal liberty and private property, where that right has never been forfeited by his conviction of some public offense,—it is the invasion of this sacred right which underlies and constitutes the essence of Lord Camden's judgment. Breaking into a house and opening boxes and drawers are circumstances of aggravation; but any forcible and compulsory extortion of a man's own testimony, or of his private papers to be used as evidence to convict him of crime, or to forfeit his goods, is within the condemnation of that judgment. In this regard the fourth and fifth amendments run almost into each other.' 116 U.S., at 630, 6 S.Ct., at 532…

The present case, then, concerns a relationship lying within the zone of privacy created by several fundamental constitutional guarantees. And it concerns a law which, in forbidding the use of contraceptives rather than regulating their manufacture or sale, seeks to achieve its goals by means [*of*] having a maximum destructive impact upon that relationship. Such a law cannot stand in light of the familiar principle, so often applied by this Court, that a 'governmental purpose to control or prevent activities constitutionally subject to state regulation may not be achieved by means which sweep unnecessarily broadly and thereby invade the area of protected freedoms.' *NAACP v. Alabama*, 377 U.S. 288, 307, 84 S.Ct. 1302, 1314, 12 L.Ed.2d 325. Would we allow the police to search the sacred precincts of marital bedrooms for telltale signs of the use of contraceptives? The *486 very idea is repulsive to the notions of privacy surrounding the marriage relationship.

We deal with a right of privacy older than the Bill of Rights—older than our political parties, older than our school system. Marriage is a coming together for better or for worse, hopefully enduring, and intimate to the degree of being sacred. It is an association that promotes a way of life, not causes; a harmony in living, not political faiths; a bilateral loyalty, not commercial or social projects. Yet it is an association for as noble a purpose as any involved in our prior decisions. *[Author's emphasis added.]*

Reversed.

381 U.S. 479, 85 S.Ct. 1678, 14 L.Ed.2d 510

In the *Griswold* case, the court looked at various amendments and concluded that taken as a whole, they amount to a "right to privacy" based on the Constitution. The Supreme Court recognized the intention of including these amendments was to protect citizens from government intrusion into their lives. In so finding, the 1960s Supreme Court argued that there is no place more personal than in the private sexual lives of married people. In the *Griswold* case, the state focused on the abettors: the doctor who helped the married couple obtain birth control and provided medical advice, penalizing them with a fine. What would be the effect of the law on people who actually used birth control? As the court writes:

> Would we allow the police to search the sacred precincts of marital bedrooms for telltale signs of the use of contraceptives? The very idea is repulsive to the notions of privacy surrounding the marriage relationship.
>
> We deal with a right of privacy older than the Bill of Rights—older than our political parties, older than our school system. Marriage is a coming together for better or for worse, hopefully enduring, and intimate to the degree of being sacred. It is an association that promotes a way of life, not causes; a harmony in living, not political faiths; a bilateral loyalty, not commercial or social projects. Yet it is an association for as noble a purpose as any involved in our prior decisions.
>
> *Griswold v. Connecticut*

Eisenstadt v. Baird 405 U.S. 438 (1972)

Less than ten years later, the Supreme Court decided the right to privacy should extend to unmarried people too. Should there be a difference between married and unmarried people under the law when dealing with birth control? Should the government deny birth control to punish sex outside of the marriage relationship? In the 1972 case of *Eisenstadt v. Baird*,[10] the Supreme Court looked at a Massachusetts "law that makes it a felony for anyone to give away a drug, medicine, instrument, or article for the prevention of conception except in the case of (1) a registered physician administering or prescribing it for a married person or (2) an active registered pharmacist furnishing it to a married person presenting a registered physician's prescription." So, married couples could use birth control (pursuant to *Griswold*), but unmarried people could not.

As part of a lecture on overpopulation to a group of Boston University college students, William Baird, neither a doctor nor a pharmacist, discussed birth control alternatives. After the lecture, he gave an unmarried woman a pack of vaginal foam (a contraceptive). He was arrested and convicted. "The Massachusetts Supreme Judicial Court unanimously set aside the conviction for exhibiting contraceptives on the ground that it violated Baird's First Amendment rights, but by a four-to-three vote sustained the conviction for giving away the foam. *Commonwealth v. Baird*, 355 Mass. 746, 247 N. E. 2d 574 (1969)." The *Eisenstadt* case worked its way up to the Supreme Court of the United States on appeal. In reviewing the Massachusetts law under the 14th Amendment Equal Protection Clause, the Supreme Court wrote in *Eisenstadt v. Baird*, 405 U.S. 438, (1972):

---

10 http://laws.lp.findlaw.com/getcase/us/405/438.html

EISENSTADT V. BAIRD
405 U.S. 438 (1972)

The question for our determination in this case is whether there is some ground of difference that rationally explains the different treatment accorded married and unmarried persons under Massachusetts General Laws Ann., c. 272, 21 and 21A. 7 For the reasons that follow, we conclude that no such ground exists.

First. Section 21 stems from Mass. Stat. 1879, c. 159, 1, which prohibited, without exception, distribution of articles intended to be used as contraceptives. In *Commonwealth v. Allison*, 227 Mass. 57, 62, 116 N. E. 265, [405 U.S. 438, 448] 266 (1917), the Massachusetts Supreme Judicial Court explained that the law's "plain purpose is to protect purity, to preserve chastity, to encourage continence and self restraint, to defend the sanctity of the home, and thus to engender in the State and nation a virile and virtuous race of men and women." Although the State clearly abandoned that purpose with the enactment of 21A, at least insofar as the illicit sexual activities of married persons are concerned, see n. 3, supra, the court reiterated in *Sturgis v. Attorney General,* supra, that the object of the legislation is to discourage premarital sexual intercourse. Conceding that the State could, consistently with the Equal Protection Clause, regard the problems of extramarital and premarital sexual relations as "[e]vils... of different dimensions and proportions, requiring different remedies," *Williamson v. Lee Optical Co.*, 348 U.S. 483, 489 (1955), we cannot agree that the deterrence of premarital sex may reasonably be regarded as the purpose of the Massachusetts law.

It would be plainly unreasonable to assume that Massachusetts has prescribed pregnancy and the birth of an unwanted child as punishment for fornication, which is a misdemeanor under Massachusetts General Laws Ann., c. 272, 18. Aside from the scheme of values that assumption would attribute to the State, it is abundantly clear that the effect of the ban on distribution of contraceptives to unmarried persons has at best a marginal relation to the proffered objective. What Mr. Justice Goldberg said in *Griswold v. Connecticut*, supra, at 498 (concurring opinion), concerning the effect of Connecticut's prohibition on the use of contraceptives in discouraging extramarital sexual relations, is equally applicable here. "The rationality of this justification is dubious, particularly in light of the admitted widespread availability to all persons in the State of Connecticut, unmarried as well as married, of birth-control devices for the [405 U.S. 438, 449] prevention of disease, as distinguished from the prevention of conception." See also id., at 505–507 (WHITE, J., concurring in judgment). Like Connecticut's laws, 21 and 21A do not at all regulate the distribution of contraceptives when they are to be used to prevent, not pregnancy, but the spread of disease. *Commonwealth v. Corbett*, 307

Mass. 7, 29 N. E. 2d 151 (1940), cited with approval in *Commonwealth v. Baird*, 355 Mass., at 754, 247 N. E. 2d, at 579. Nor, in making contraceptives available to married persons without regard to their intended use, does Massachusetts attempt to deter married persons from engaging in illicit sexual relations with unmarried persons. Even on the assumption that the fear of pregnancy operates as a deterrent to fornication, the Massachusetts statute is thus so riddled with exceptions that deterrence of premarital sex cannot reasonably be regarded as its aim.

Moreover, 21 and 21A on their face have a dubious relation to the State's criminal prohibition on fornication. As the Court of Appeals explained, "Fornication is a misdemeanor [in Massachusetts], entailing a thirty dollar fine, or three months in jail. Massachusetts General Laws Ann. c. 272 18. Violation of the present statute is a felony, punishable by five years in prison. We find it hard to believe that the legislature adopted a statute carrying a five-year penalty for its possible, obviously by no means fully effective, deterrence of the commission of a ninety-day misdemeanor." 429 F.2d, at 1401. Even conceding the legislature a full measure of discretion in fashioning means to prevent fornication, and recognizing that the State may seek to deter prohibited conduct by punishing more severely those who facilitate than those who actually engage in its commission, we, like the Court of Appeals, cannot believe that in this instance Massachusetts has chosen to expose the aider and abettor who simply gives away a contraceptive to [405 U.S. 438, 450] 20 times the 90-day sentence of the offender himself. The very terms of the State's criminal statutes, coupled with the de minimis effect of 21 and 21A in deterring fornication, thus compel the conclusion that such deterrence cannot reasonably be taken as the purpose of the ban on distribution of contraceptives to unmarried persons.

Second. Section 21A was added to the Massachusetts General Laws by Stat. 1966, c. 265, 1. The Supreme Judicial Court in *Commonwealth v. Baird*, supra, held that the purpose of the amendment was to serve the health needs of the community by regulating the distribution of potentially harmful articles. It is plain that Massachusetts had no such purpose in mind before the enactment of 21A. As the Court of Appeals remarked, "Consistent with the fact that the statute was contained in a chapter dealing with 'Crimes Against Chastity, Morality, Decency and Good Order,' it was cast only in terms of morals. A physician was forbidden to prescribe contraceptives even when needed for the protection of health. *Commonwealth v. Gardner*, 1938, 300 Mass. 372, 15 N. E. 2d 222." 429 F.2d, at 1401. Nor did the Court of Appeals "believe that the legislature [in enacting 21A] suddenly reversed its field and developed an interest in health. Rather, it merely made what it thought to be the precise accommodation necessary to escape the Griswold ruling." Ibid.

Again, we must agree with the Court of Appeals. If health were the rationale of 21A, the statute would be both discriminatory and overbroad. Dissenting in *Commonwealth v. Baird*, 355 Mass., at 758, 247 N. E. 2d, at 581, Justices Whittemore and Cutter stated that they saw "in 21 and 21A, read together, no public health purpose. If there is need to have a physician prescribe (and a pharmacist dispense) contraceptives, that need is as great for unmarried persons as for married persons." [405 U.S. 438,

451] The Court of Appeals added: "If the prohibition [on distribution to unmarried persons]... is to be taken to mean that the same physician who can prescribe for married patients does not have sufficient skill to protect the health of patients who lack a marriage certificate, or who may be currently divorced, it is illogical to the point of irrationality." 429 F.2d, at 1401. 8 Furthermore, we must join the Court of Appeals in noting that not all contraceptives are potentially dangerous. 9 As a result, if the Massachusetts statute were a health measure, it would not only invidiously discriminate against the unmarried, but also be overbroad with respect to the married, a fact that the Supreme Judicial Court itself seems to have conceded in *Sturgis v. Attorney General*, 358 Mass., at—, 260 N. E. 2d, at 690, where it noted that "it may well be that certain contraceptive medication and devices constitute no hazard to health, in which event it could be argued that the statute swept too broadly in its prohibition." "In this posture," as the Court of [405 U.S. 438, 452] Appeals concluded, "it is impossible to think of the statute as intended as a health measure for the unmarried, and it is almost as difficult to think of it as so intended even as to the married." 429 F.2d, at 1401.

But if further proof that the Massachusetts statute is not a health measure is necessary, the argument of Justice Spiegel, who also dissented in *Commonwealth v. Baird*, 355 Mass., at 759, 247 N. E. 2d, at 582, is conclusive: "It is at best a strained conception to say that the Legislature intended to prevent the distribution of articles 'which may have undesirable, if not dangerous, physical consequences.' If that was the Legislature's goal, 21 is not required" in view of the federal and state laws already regulating the distribution of harmful drugs. See Federal Food, Drug, and Cosmetic Act, 503, 52 Stat. 1051, as amended, 21 U.S.C. 353; Mass. Gen. Laws Ann., c. 94, 187A, as amended. We conclude, accordingly, that, despite the statute's superficial earmarks as a health measure, health, on the face of the statute, may no more reasonably be regarded as its purpose than the deterrence of premarital sexual relations.

Third. If the Massachusetts statute cannot be upheld as a deterrent to fornication or as a health measure may it, nevertheless, be sustained simply as a prohibition on contraception? The Court of Appeals analysis "led inevitably to the conclusion that, so far as morals are concerned, it is contraceptives per se that are considered immoral—to the extent that Griswold will permit such a declaration." 429 F.2d, at 1401–1402. The Court of Appeals went on to hold, id., at 1402:

To say that contraceptives are immoral as such, and are to be forbidden to unmarried persons who will nevertheless persist in having intercourse, means that such persons must risk for themselves an unwanted pregnancy, for the child, illegitimacy, and [405 U.S. 438, 453] for society, a possible obligation of support. Such a view of morality is not only the very mirror image of sensible legislation; we consider that it conflicts with fundamental human rights. In the absence of demonstrated harm, we hold it is beyond the competency of the state.

We need not and do not, however, decide that important question in this case because, whatever the rights of the individual to access to contraceptives may be, the rights must be the same for the unmarried and the married alike.

If under Griswold the distribution of contraceptives to married persons cannot be prohibited, a ban on distribution to unmarried persons would be equally impermissible. It is true that in Griswold the right of privacy in question inhered in the marital relationship. Yet the marital couple is not an independent entity with a mind and heart of its own, but an association of two individuals each with a separate intellectual and emotional makeup. If the right of privacy means anything, it is the right of the individual, married or single, to be free from unwarranted governmental intrusion into matters so fundamentally affecting a person as the decision whether to bear or beget a child. See Stanley v. Georgia, 394 U.S. 557 (1969). 10 See also Skinner v. Oklahoma, [405 U.S. 438, 454] 316 U.S. 535 (1942); Jacobson v. Massachusetts, 197 U.S. 11, 29 (1905). [Author's emphasis added.]

On the other hand, if Griswold is no bar to a prohibition on the distribution of contraceptives, the State could not, consistently with the Equal Protection Clause, outlaw distribution to unmarried but not to married persons. In each case the evil, as perceived by the State, would be identical, and the under inclusion would be invidious.

Mr. Justice Jackson, concurring in Railway Express Agency v. New York, 336 U.S. 106, 112–113 (1949), made the point:

> The framers of the Constitution knew, and we should not forget today, that there is no more effective practical guaranty against arbitrary and unreasonable government than to require that the principles of law which officials would impose upon a minority must be imposed generally. Conversely, nothing opens the door to arbitrary action so effectively as to allow those officials to pick and choose only a few to whom they will apply legislation and thus to escape the political retribution that might be visited upon them if larger numbers were affected. Courts can take no better measure to assure that laws will be just than to require that laws be equal in operation.

Although Mr. Justice Jackson's comments had reference to administrative regulations, the principle he affirmed has equal application to the legislation here. We hold that by providing dissimilar treatment for married and unmarried persons who are similarly situated, Massachusetts [405 U.S. 438, 455] General Laws Ann., c. 272, 21 and 21A, violate the Equal Protection Clause. The judgment of the Court of Appeals is Affirmed.

In *Eisenstadt v. Baird*, the Supreme Court found the Massachusetts law unconstitutional and extended the married couple's right of privacy to single people under the 14th Amendment's

Equal Protection Clause. The Court found it unreasonable to treat two similarly situated groups, unmarried people and married people, differently when a state is deciding who should legally be allowed to use birth control. Thus, the Supreme Court discounts the argument that the state was reasonably trying to discourage unmarried sex, because, "[t]he deterrence of fornication, a 90-day misdemeanor under Massachusetts law, cannot reasonably be regarded as the purpose of the statute, since the statute is riddled with exceptions making contraceptives freely available for use in premarital sexual relations and its scope and penalty structure are inconsistent with that purpose" (*Eisenstadt*, p. 439).

Harking back to *Griswold*, the Supreme Court writes,

> If under Griswold the distribution of contraceptives to married people cannot be prohibited, a ban on distribution to unmarried people would be equally impermissible. It's true that in Griswold the right of privacy question is inherent to the marital relationship. Yet, the marital couple is not an independent entity with a mind and heart of its own but an association of two individuals each with a separate intellectual emotional relationship.

The Supreme Court clarifies that a married couple is not a separate entity but two individuals and so, the right to privacy must extend "to the individual married or single."

Before leaving *Eisenstadt*,[11] remember the court's statement: "If the right of privacy means anything, it is the right of the individual, married or single, to be free from unwarranted governmental intrusion into matters so fundamentally affecting a person as the decision whether to bear or beget a child." When will that language come up again in the context of family law?

FUNDAMENTAL RIGHT TO MARRY

Loving v. Virginia 388 U.S.1 (1967)

The Supreme Court brought change to the traditional law of marriage in the 1967 case of *Loving v. Virginia*. In this case, childhood sweethearts, Richard Loving, a white man, and Mildred Jeter, a black woman, wanted to get married. She was pregnant.[12] But the state law in Virginia (and many states) did not allow him to marry outside of the white race. Traditionally, under family law, the

---

11 March 22, 2017, marks the 45th anniversary of single people legally using birth control.

12 "Obituaries, Quiet Va. Wife Ended Interracial Marriage Ban," Patricia Sullivan, May 6, 2008, *Washington Post*. "The case legalized (white's) interracial marriages in Virginia and 15 other states." In a 2016 interview with one of the Loving's attorneys, Philip Hirschkop said, "It was a difficult time to be a black woman married to a white man. It would have been much harder as a black man and a white woman. They might have been hanged for that.'" "A long time love for civil rights," DeNeen L. Brown, *The Washington Post*, December 11, 2016, C1.

government encouraged marriage and created many inducements for its citizens to get married. These anti-miscegenation laws prohibiting the alleged interbreeding of what were presumed to be two distinct human races—whites and nonwhites—had been around for decades.[13]

> The couple traveled 90 miles to cross the border into the District of Columbia—where interracial marriages were legal. After they married, they returned to Virginia. There, the police arrested them for violating the state law. By their own widely reported accounts, Mrs. Loving and her husband, Richard, were in bed in their modest house in Central Point in the early morning of July 11, 1958, five weeks after their wedding, when the county sheriff and two deputies, acting on an anonymous tip, burst into their bedroom and shined flashlights in their eyes. A threatening voice demanded, "Who is this woman you're sleeping with?"

> Mrs. Loving answered, "I'm his wife."

> Mr. Loving pointed to the couple's marriage certificate that hung on the bedroom wall. The sheriff responded, "That's no good here."[14]

> After Mr. Loving spent a night in jail and his wife several more, the couple pleaded guilty to violating the Virginia law, the Racial Integrity Act. Under a plea bargain, their one-year prison sentences were suspended on the condition that they leave Virginia and not return together… for 25 years.[15]

Judge Leon M. Bazile, in language Chief Justice Warren would recall, said that if God had meant for whites and blacks to mix, he would have not placed them on different continents. Judge Bazile reminded the defendants that "As long as you live you will be known as a felon."

They paid court fees of $36.29 each, moved to Washington and had three children. They returned home occasionally, never together. Times were tough financially and the Lovings missed family, friends, and their easy country lifestyle in the rolling Virginia hills.

By 1963 Mrs. Loving could not stand the ostracism any longer. Inspired by the civil rights movement and its march on Washington, she wrote Attorney General Robert F. Kennedy and

---

13 Interestingly, Virginia's law did allow whites to marry people with a one-sixteenth or less of American Indian blood, in deference to Pocahontas (who under Virginia legend saved Captain John Smith when the Virginia Company was the first to colonize English America and who later married John Rolfe—possibly the first recorded interracial marriage). (See Wadlington, W., and O'Brien, R. C. (2007). *Domestic Relations Cases and Materials*, 6th ed. Foundation Press., pg. 155, FN 4)

14 http://www.nytimes.com/2008/05/06/us/06loving.html?_r=0, Obituary of "Mildred Loving, Who Battled Ban on Mixed-Race Marriage, Dies at 68," Douglas Martin, *New York Times*, May 6, 2008.

15 Ibid.

asked for help. He wrote her back, referring her to the American Civil Liberties Union (ACLU). The ACLU took the case. Its lawyers, Bernard S. Cohen and Philip J. Hirschkop, faced an immediate problem: the Lovings had pleaded guilty and had no right to appeal. They asked Judge Bazile to set aside his original verdict. When he refused, they appealed. The Virginia Supreme Court of Appeals upheld the lower court's decision and the case went to the United States Supreme Court.

Mr. Cohen recounted telling Mr. Loving about various legal theories applying to the case. Mr. Loving replied, "Mr. Cohen, tell the court I love my wife, and it is just unfair that I can't live with her in Virginia."[16]

On appeal to the Supreme Court of the United States the Virginia law was struck down as unconstitutional (along with over 24 other states' laws[17] that also prevented whites from marrying outside their race). Although the Supreme Court acknowledged that the states had the right to set marriage policy, the Court reasoned that a law that only prevented whites from marrying outside of their race had no other purpose than to promote white supremacy.

In addition to striking down Virginia's law, the Court went further to find a fundamental right to marry; a right that the state cannot unreasonably interfere with. The Supreme Court found that the defendants had the right and freedom to marry which is one of the "vital personal rights essential to the orderly pursuit of happiness by free men." In what other area of family law might the fundamental right to marry be an issue?

Zablocki v. Redhail 434 U.S. 374 (1978)

The last case included in this family constitutional law review is *Zablocki v. Redhail*, because it serves as a good reminder that the Constitution applies to all, not just the rich. In *Zablocki*, the Supreme Court again looked at the issue of the right to marry. Under a Wisconsin law, the state would not give a marriage license if the applicant had unpaid court-ordered child support. The law allowed a judge to give permission to marry, but only if all child support payments were current and the child was not receiving public benefits (e.g., welfare). Plaintiff Redhail had one child from a prior nonmarital relationship for whom he owed child support. When Redhail applied for a license to marry a different woman, the state's licensing clerk denied his request. Redhail sued, challenging the constitutionality of the law. What constitutional arguments could he raise?

Redhail acknowledged that he had not paid child support payments and that the child was on public assistance. He argued that the law was unfair, because even if he paid all of his child support debts, the child would still probably be on welfare because Redhail was poor. Under due process and equal protection arguments under the 14th Amendment, Redhail argued that the right to marry should not be impacted by failure to pay child support. It was a right freely given

---

16 Ibid.
17 Curiously, Alabama was the last state to officially repeal its interracial marriage ban, but not until 1999. "State Rep. Phil Crigler said that, although he personally opposes interracial marriages, he will vote for the bill. He said the bill was just racial grandstanding, since the law prohibiting such marriages is not enforced." " Alabama considers lifting interracial marriage ban ", CNN, http://www.cnn.com/US/9903/12/interracial.marriage/

to people who did not have child support payments or kept up with those payments. The Supreme Court, relying on *Loving v. Virginia*, agreed that the fundamental right to marry was guaranteed to all under the Constitution and therefore should not be denied to groups because they lacked money. Thus, for richer or for poorer, the Constitution prevents the states from preventing marriage based on financial issues.

CONCLUSION

How should Dawn Herb's case be decided? She is the woman in Pennsylvania who was cited for swearing at her overflowing toilet. She was inside her own home and alleged that she was not drunk or acting in an outrageous way. The toilet was overflowing and leaking sewage into her kitchen while she was yelling. Although there is no mention of toilets or cussing in the Constitution, there is a right to free speech under the First Amendment. Thus, the constitutional query in Herb's case is: does the right to free speech extend to shouting obscenities at your overflowing toilet in your home even if your neighbors overhear? In ruling on Herb's petition filed by the American Civil Liberties Union (ACLU) on December 13, 2007, Judge Gallagher found Dawn Herb not guilty of violating a state law against using obscenity, ruling that although her language "may be considered by some to be offensive, vulgar and imprudent... such representations are protected speech pursuant to the First Amendment." "In October 2008, Herb and the City of Scranton reached a settlement in which Herb received $19,000 in damages and attorneys' fees."[18]

In 2014, Ocean City, Maryland posted signs on its boardwalk before the beach that read, "No profanity please". What is the effect of such signs?

---

18   http://www.aclupa.org/legal/legaldocket/womancitedforswearingattoi.htm, containing the Court's order in *Commonwealth v. Herb*, Case No. NT0000758-07, heard December 10, 2007, before Judge Terrence V. Gallagher. What about swearing on your parking ticket when you send it in for payment? When a Connecticut student was ticketed for speeding in upstate New York, he "sent back a payment form with a scribbled five-word expression of vulgarity, and crossed out the town's name. Instead of Liberty, the man wrote 'Tyranny.'" The court required the man to drive back to the town, where he was "summarily lectured by a judge, arrested and held for several hours on charges of aggravated harassment." When he sued the town and its police officers, "a federal judge, Cathy Seibel, in White Plains, ruled that his First Amendment rights had been violated, and allowed his lawsuit to proceed." https://www.nytimes.com/2015/09/16/nyregion/us-judge-upholds-right-to-scrawl-nasty-note-on-speeding-ticket-payment.html?_r=0 The Village of Liberty subsequently settled the suit for $75,000, The plaintiff will receive "$30,000 in damages while his attorneys, with the New York Civil Liberties Union, will get $45,000". http://www.recordonline.com/news/20160225/75k-settlement-approved-in-suit-over-rights-of-driver-who-wrote-obscenities-on-speeding-ticket.

Was a Florida judge using the same grounds when he ruled that a school district broke union rules when it fired a high school teacher for routinely cursing at her students" (including "repeatedly using the F-word in class and calling her students 'lazy n—s'"). The judge ruled that firing the teacher was "improper because large classes put her in an 'untenable situation' making it difficult to 'maintain her composure and professionalism.'" "Only in American", *The Week*, August 22, 2014.

6 MARRIAGE EQUALITY— SAME-SEX MARRIAGE

But you want us to step in and render a decision based on an assessment of the effects of this institution, which is newer than cell phones or the Internet? I mean we—we are not—we do not have the ability to see the future.
—Supreme Court Justice Samuel Alito[1]

You're saying, no, state said two kinds of marriage; the full marriage, and then this sort of skim-milk marriage.
—Supreme Court Justice Ruth Bader Ginsburg[2]

While it could have stopped its decision by merely striking down the state's racism, the Supreme Court of the United States in *Loving v. Virginia* went on to find a fundamental right to marry. Inherent in the Constitution is the right to pick a marriage partner without governmental interference. Yet, same-sex couples have struggled to win this fundamental right for their relationships. Even with the initial increasing recognition by some states, the struggle at the federal level was difficult. As was the case in the first and revised first editions of this book, an unprecedented change in attitude toward recognition of same-sex marriage continues to sweep the country both to embrace it and thwart it. When the Supreme Court made the decision to recognize marriage equality, it was supported by a majority of the public,[3] up from 27% when the first national poll was taken in 1996.[4] Moreover, at the time of the decision, over 37 states plus the District of Columbia allowed same-sex marriage,[5] which meant that a

---

1 Hearing on March 26, 2013, in the case of *Hollingsworth v. Perry*.
2 Ibid.
3 "Gay-marriage moves riles conservatives", Karen Tumulty, *The Washington Post*, October 7, 2013, p A5.
4 "A 40-year courtship", Andrea Ford, *Time*, April 8, 2013, p. 23.
5 Compare this to only four states legalizing it when the first edition of this book was published only four years ago in 2013.

substantial majority of people lived in a state that recognized marriage equality,[6] covering about 70 million people.[7]

As the first wave of states legalized same-sex marriage in 2013, Democratic legislators started to openly come on board. Even "as most Republican leaders in Congress and elsewhere stayed relatively silent" it "underscores the extent to which support for gay marriage has expanded in the decade since President George W. Bush supported a constitutional amendment to ban such unions."[8] This revolution heated up following the Supreme Court's decisions in 2013 that dealt with marriage equality in California and under the Defense of Marriage Act (DOMA). The Court did reverse DOMA, in part, and required the federal government to recognize same-sex marriages where the states allowed them, but left in place DOMA's permission for states to choose whether to recognize or not such marriages from other states. Presented with a split in the federal appeals courts, with the majority rejecting state prohibitions against marriage equality and only one federal appellate decision refusing to do so, the Supreme Court in 2015 recognized marriage equality as a civil right in the case of *Obergefell v. Hodges*.

HISTORY OF RECOGNITION OF SAME-SEX MARRIAGE

In previous editions, this chapter explored the issue of "what is marriage?" by looking at what had so far fallen short of marriage in many states. Because this has been one of family law's major issues throughout our lifetime, we will continue to trace it from its inception to the final recognition as a constitutional right. In the legal hierarchy, with marriage at the top, same-sex couples arguably owe their success in obtaining legally recognized rights of marriage because of private ordering (see Chapter 3).[9] The difference is that in private ordering, couples demanded society's recognition of their committed relationships outside of marriage through the courts. In the same-sex marriage movement, business, not the courts, was the catalyst and gay couples desperately wanted the court's approval of their relationships but the court refused to give it.

---

6   As of February 2015, HRC estimates that over 70% of the U.S. population lives in a state where same-sex marriage is legal. http://www.hrc.org/resources/entry/percent-of-population-living-in-states-with-marriage-equality

7   Human Rights Campaign estimates that as many as 70 million people will be living in states with same-sex marriage. Ibid.

8   "Gay-marriage moves riles conservatives", Karen Tumulty, *The Washington Post*, October 7, 2013, p A5.

9   In 2012, 52 percent of all employers offered domestic partner health benefits, with the percentage varying widely by region and industry, according to a nationally representative sample of about 3,000 employers surveyed by benefit consultant Mercer. The *Village Voice* newspaper in New York is credited with being the first private employer to offer workers domestic partner benefits in 1982. http://www.pbs.org/newshour/rundown/2012/05/many-businesses-offer-health-benefits-to-same-sex-couples-ahead-of-laws.html, "Many Businesses Offer Health Benefits to Same-Sex Couples Ahead of Laws," Julie Appleby, PBS News.

A. Domestic Partnerships[10]

The lowest tier of the "what is marriage?" hierarchy, Domestic Partnerships, originated as a recruiting tool for businesses. Eager to attract the best and brightest from their competitors, some businesses thought it was a good business decision to offer the benefits that their married heterosexual couples received to committed couples who did not want to marry or could not (including homosexuals). After self-identifying, the couples would register with the company's human resources office as a domestic partnership and receive *some* of the economic benefits (like health insurance for the nonemployee or sick leave for the employee to take care of the partner). When the domestic partnership relationship ended, much like in a traditional divorce, the domestic partner/employee filled out another form with the company's human resources office to terminate the designation and the benefits stopped.

Domestic partnerships provided two things. First, they bestowed third-party recognition on the couple's committed status. Second, they expanded the rights that are associated with a committed relationship (marriage), but in a very limited sense. Domestic partnerships were common in the competitive atmosphere of the Silicon Valley, California, where start-up computer companies were competing for the most innovative talent. Today, a majority of Fortune 500 businesses offer similar benefits.

This business practice inspired many local governments to pass laws recognizing same-sex relationships. Vermont was the first state to offer coverage to state workers in 1995.[11] As of 2010, at least 22 states (plus D.C.) had "a law, policy, court decision or union contract that provide state employees with domestic partner benefits."[12] Yet, society was only partly giving recognition, because the rights, while expanding, were still very limited to certain economic benefits.[13] Even so, the federal government taxed these benefits (which it does not do for heterosexual married couples).

---

10 Although not recognized by any state law, was California's possibility of "palimony" awards for same-sex cohabitating couples the first rung on the ladder to marriage? As discussed in Chapter 3, the *Marvin v. Marvin* cases coined the term "palimony" to mean alimony-like compensation for couples who cohabitate outside of marriage and then break up. In a 1982 suit, dubbed "Gaylimony," Scott Thorson sued pianist Wladziu Valentino ("Liberace"), requesting compensation of $113 million from their five-year relationship. The court dismissed the portion of the case on the alleged agreement because it was based on a sexual nature and against public policy. http://transcripts.cnn.com/TRANSCRIPTS/0208/12/lkl.00.html, "Transcript of Larry King interviewing Scott Thorson," August 12, 2002. The case settled out of court, reportedly for $95,000, two cars, and two pet dogs. As part of that relationship, Thorson claimed that Liberace promised to adopt and care for him.

11 Ibid., in 1995, Vermont became the first to offer coverage to state workers. Thus, some states began to give recognition to the status, not a marriage, of the couples.

12 National Conference of State Legislatures, December 2014. http://www.ncsl.org/research/health/state-employee-health-benefits-ncsl.aspx#Partner Most of this is moot, as the courts continue to require states to recognize same-sex marriage. Yet, it could be impacted again, depending on the current Trump administration.

13 Since Maryland starting marrying same-sex couples in 2013, the state is eliminating benefits to domestic partners effective the end of 2013. Is that fair?

What happens if a local government recognizes same-sex relationships but the state does not? In *Tyma v. Montgomery County*, 801 A.2d. 148 (MD Ct of App 2001), the court allowed the small town of Takoma Park, Maryland (a home-rule municipality) to adopt an ordinance extending similar benefits to the domestic partners of its employees as it did to its married employees—even though the state, which regulated marriage, did not allow it at the time.[14] In what other cases in this book did the court defer to a local government's ordinance powers? (See Chapter 2.)

B. Reciprocal Beneficiaries: The First Court to Require Same-Sex Marriage

In *Baehr v. Miike* (formerly *Baehr v. Lewin*), 74 Haw 530 (1992), Hawaii's highest court was the first ever to rule that excluding same-sex couples from marriage was discrimination based on improper sexual classifications. In so doing, the court became the first to demand a compelling state interest before a state could deny same-sex couples a license to marry. The court acknowledged that the definition of marriage could change and that "customs change with an evolving social order," so the Hawaiian high court remanded the case back to the trial court to determine whether the state could justify this discrimination in denying marriage licenses. The state argued that its definition of marriage precluded discrimination, but the court said it was "circular and unpersuasive." In 1996, the Circuit Court of Hawaii rejected the state's argument and agreed that denying marriage licenses to same-sex couples was unjustifiable; as a result, it required the state to award marriage licenses to same-sex couples. When the state appealed that decision, it was on its way back to the highest court for review.[15] Before that court could act, the state legislature took a step that would become often repeated; it redefined marriage to exclude same-sex couples. Mindful of the political pressure of having Hawaii be the first state (court ordered) to require same-sex marriage, the state legislature proposed amending the state's constitution to define marriage as between a man and a woman. The constitutional amendment was approved by the voters; the next year, the state's highest court ruled that the constitutional amendment prevented it from allowing same-sex couples to marry. The Hawaii legislature, however, mindful of the court's original ruling that same-sex couples were entitled to the benefits of marriage, passed a second law creating a new classification for committed same-sex couples' relationships, Reciprocal Beneficiaries. This classification afforded couples even more economic benefits, but not marriage. (Interestingly, the designation was not limited to same-sex couples and might include a son and his widowed mother). Benefits included health plans, preferential real estate holding status, inheritance, and funeral and death benefits.

---

14   The ordinance was limited to Takoma Park's personnel policies, so it was not making "marriage" laws, which would be the purview of the state. Takoma Park is in the forefront again with its recent passage of a law allowing 16-year olds to vote. Takoma Park grants 16-year-olds right to vote. Lindsay A. Powers, *The Washington Post*, May 24, 2013   http://www.washingtonpost.com/local/takoma-park-grants-16-year-olds-right-to-vote/2013/05/14/b27c52c4-bccd-11e2-89c9-3be8095fe767_story.html

15   http://www.lambdalegal.org/in-court/cases/baehr-v-miike

C. Civil Unions

In *Baker v. State*, 744 A.2d 864 (Vt. 1999), the Vermont Supreme Court ruled that denying same-sex couples marriage licenses or the opportunity to enter into a similar legally recognized relationship violated Vermont's constitution (under its Common Benefits clause, which is somewhat like the federal Equal Protection clause of the 14th Amendment). Finding no basis for "the continued exclusion of same-sex couples from the benefits incident to a civil marriage license under Vermont law,"[16] the court instructed the Vermont legislature to deal with the ruling. Like Hawaii, the Vermont legislature passed "An Act Relating to Civil Unions" in 2000 to define a civil marriage as between a man and a woman and then created a "civil union," which would be identical to marriage in every aspect but the name. Thus, same-sex couples had obtained all the legal benefits of marriage,[17] but not the legal name recognition. Is this enough? Is the glass half empty, because this is the modern "separate but equal," establishing second-class citizenship? Or is the glass half full, because with the award of equal benefits, same-sex couples reach the top of the marriage hierarchy?

Since that time, hundreds of same-sex couples traveled to Vermont for civil unions, most from other states. In 2005, other states like New Jersey, New Hampshire, and Connecticut followed suit and passed civil union laws, often as a precursor to recognition of civil marriage. Colorado, the last to join in April 2013, changed its laws to allow civil unions, but at that time it was just not enough.

STATE LEGISLATION

Maryland was the first state to rewrite its constitution to define marriage as between and man and a woman in 1973.[18] Many states followed it or like Hawaii, did so to avoid a state court decision finding denial of same-sex marriages discriminatory. At least 30 state legislatures passed -laws defining marriage as between a man and woman, including North Carolina in 2012.

These laws prevent same-sex couples from asking the court if their constitutional rights were violated when denied marriage licenses. Voters regularly supported such legislation when given the opportunity on a ballot. It took until the elections of 2012 for the tide to start to turn, when Maryland and Maine voters approved their state legislatures' new laws making same-sex marriage legal.

---

16   http://writ.news.findlaw.com/grossman/20090413.html, "The Vermont Legislature, Inventor of the 'Civil Union,' Grants Full Marriage Rights to Same-Sex Couples: Why It Decided Civil Unions Were Not Sufficient to Ensure Equality," Joanna L. Grossman, April 13, 2009.

17   But was that true? The court in *Baker* counted over a thousand times in Vermont law where marital status was relevant to the allocation of rights and obligations.

18   "A 40-year courtship", Andrea Ford, *Time*, April 8, 2013, p. 23.

CITY ACTION

On February 13, 2004, in San Francisco, Gavin Newsom, the newly elected mayor, received international attention when he challenged the state of California's law prohibiting same-sex marriages by directing the city's employees to issue marriage licenses to same-sex couples. When a San Francisco Superior Court judge refused to stop the marriages, more than 4,000 same-sex couples were married while Governor Arnold Schwarzenegger worked to stop it. That took two months.[19] On August 12, 2004, the California Supreme Court voided all of the licenses, ruling 5 to 2 that Newsom had exceeded his authority and was legally wrong to act. It did not decide the underlying issue on the constitutionality of denying the marriage licenses.[20] Was the mayor doing the right thing by taking the law into his own hands?

THE CASES

At the time the legislatures were dealing with the issues of same-sex relationships and marriage, they often acted in response to court decisions. Probably the first legal challenge for same-sex marriage was by Minnesota law student Jack Baker, who sued after he was denied the right to marry Michael McConnell in 1970. He lost.[21] In 1974, in the case of *Singer v. Hara*, 522 P.2d 1187 (Wash. Ct. App. 1974) (review denied 84 Wash. 2d 1008), two adult males applied for a marriage license in their state of Washington. When the state refused to give them a license, they challenged that denial under the state's equal rights amendment. The appellate court agreed with the lower court's ruling that because the definition of marriage is between a man and a woman, their request was denied, not on the basis of discrimination, but because they did not fit within the definition. The court stressed the concept of nature and the purpose of marriage, which is procreation and raising children. In denying the claim, couples who were unable to procreate naturally were outside of the definition of marriage and therefore did not qualify. According to the court, what the couples proposed was not marriage. The court reasoned that the couples were not being denied the right to marry on the basis of sex, but on physical characteristics.

---

19   In March 2004, the California Supreme Court, in the case of *Lockyer v. City and County of San Francisco*, 17 Cal. Rptr.3d 225 (2004) 95 P.3d 459, 33 Cal.4th 1055, barred the city of San Francisco from issuing any more marriage licenses to same-sex couples. Afterward, the city sued the state's attorney general (who had said, he did not "personally support policies that give lesser legal rights and responsibilities to committed same-sex couples")

20   In 2005, a New York court ruled that the mayor of New Paltz New York, Jason West, also defied the state's law in marrying same-sex couples and was charged with 19 misdemeanors for violating the state's marriage laws with possible sentences of a fine and up to one year in jail. Though never tried, an injunction was issued against him permanently preventing him from presiding over same-sex marriages. Adding to the confusion on this issue, those marriages were never invalidated and could still be valid today.http://www.nytimes.com/2011/06/20/nyregion/gay-couples-recall-a-pivotal-day-in-new-paltz.html?_r=0, "Awaiting a Big Day, and Recalling One in New Paltz," Shaila Dewan, *New York Times*, June 19, 2011.

21   "A 40-Year Courtship," Andrea Ford, *Time*, April 18, 2013, p. 20.

The Supreme Court of the United States' first involvement in this issue was in a case involving sexual acts between consenting adults. In the case of *Bowers v. Hardwick*, 478 U.S. 186 (1986), when a policeman saw two men engaging in consensual homosexual sodomy, he arrested them for violating a Georgia criminal statute prohibiting sodomy. Although the state's prosecutor decided not to prosecute, the defendant, Michael Hardwick sued in federal court to have the statute declared invalid and unconstitutional. The court dismissed his case. The 11th Circuit Court of Appeals, however, reversed that ruling and found the Georgia statute unconstitutional, ruling that the statute violated Hardwick's "fundamental rights because his homosexual activity was a private and intimate association." Georgia's Attorney General, Michael J. Bowers, appealed to the U.S. Supreme Court, where a divided court (5 to 4) reversed that 11 Circuit decision and did not find a right to privacy. In his concurring opinion, Chief Justice Warren Burger wrote, "In constitutional terms there is no such thing as a fundamental right to commit homosexual sodomy." (197) The dissents in the *Bowers* case wrote that just because history has held sodomy to be immoral, there is no reason to continue to agree with it[22] and reminded the Court that the strategy did not work when dealing with issues including abortion, biracial marriages, and segregation.

In the case of *Lawrence v. Texas,* 539 U.S. 558 (2003), the United States Supreme Court looked at a case similar to *Bowers*, involving a Houston police officer who entered a private residence after a false claim of a weapons disturbance. Once inside petitioner Lawrence's apartment, the policeman saw two adult males engaging in private, consensual sex and arrested them. They were convicted of deviant sexual intercourse, which violated the Texas statute forbidding two persons of the same sex to engage in specified intimate sexual conduct and were fined $200, plus court costs of $141. They appealed.

When the Texas Court of Appeals affirmed the lower court's conviction, it referenced the *Bowers* precedent. In overruling the *Bowers* case, the Supreme Court of the United States ruled that the Texas statute that criminalized certain sexual acts by same-sex people was a violation of the Due Process Clause. In so doing, Justice Anthony Kennedy, writing for the 6–3 majority[23], wrote, "To say that the issue in *Bowers* was simply the right to engage in certain sexual conduct demeans the claim the individual put forward, just as it would demean a married couple were it to be said marriage is simply about the right to have sexual intercourse." "When sexuality finds overt expression in intimate conduct with another person, the conduct can be but one element in a personal bond that is more enduring. The liberty protected by the Constitution allows homosexual persons the right to make this choice." By using the constitutionally protected right

---

22   Referring to a quote from Justice Holmes, "[i]t is revolting to have no better reason for a rule of law than that so it was laid down in the time of Henry IV".

23   Justice Scalia, Chief Justice Rehnquist, and Justice Thomas dissented. Justice Scalia did not want to depart from the *Bowers* precedent, and argued that the states should be able to make their own moral judgment about homosexual conduct and criminalize it if they chose.

of privacy and intimacy, many people believe the *Lawrence* decision cleared the path for state recognition of same-sex marriages.[24]

STATE RECOGNITION OF SAME-SEX MARRIAGE

Massachusetts was the first state to legalize same-sex marriage.[25] In the case of *Goodridge v. Department of Public Health*, 440 Mass. 309, 798 N.E. 2d 941 (2003), when several same-sex couples were denied marriage licenses, they sued the state claiming they were denied equal protection under the law. The couples pointed out the many benefits associated with marriage that they were denied, such as property rights and tax benefits. The state replied that it had a legitimate governmental interest in upholding the institution of marriage, focusing again on procreation. The state reasoned that since same-sex couples could not naturally further that goal, the state had an interest in disallowing their marital rights. The Massachusetts Supreme Court, however, overruled that decision, saying that the state's reasoning did not amount to sufficient justification to allow discrimination, especially with assisted reproductive methods available today.

---

24 In June 2005, Baltimore City Circuit Court Judge Brooke Murdock ruled that Maryland's 1973 statute, which defined marriage as between a man and a woman, violated the state's constitution. The case was filed in August 2005 by the ACLU, on behalf of several same-sex couples who had been denied marriage licenses. Plaintiffs Lisa Polyak and Gitanjali Deane had been together for 25 years. Polyak said at the time of the birth of their second child, "that their status as an unmarried couple was driven home" when the doctor made her leave the birthing room of their child. While Judge Murdock said that tradition was important, it could not justify discrimination. Murdock's opinion was immediately stayed (preventing issuance of any same-sex marriage licenses in Maryland) until a higher court reviewed her decision. The state attorney general immediately appealed the decision to an intermediate court, but the highest court agreed to hear the matter first. The Maryland Court of Appeals, in the case of *Conaway v. Deane and Polyak*, 932 A2d 571 (2007), ruled against the right to same-sex marriage, clarifying that marriage has always been between a man and a woman only.

25 In 1975 a clerk in Boulder Colorado "checked the law and didn't see anything that said they (a gay couple) couldn't" so she issued a marriage license to the couple who married in a gay friendly church the next day. The marriage was even mentioned on the Johnny Carson's *Tonight Show*. Then, they applied to U.S. immigration to allow the Austrian spouse to get a visa and received this chilling response, "You have failed to establish that a bona fide marital relationship can exist between two faggots." The couple sued but because the federal government did not allow same-sex marriages and it had jurisdiction over the immigration issue, the couple lost. When they tried again, requesting a "hardship exemption" to avoid deportation (his home country was hostile to gays), the 9th Circuit Court of Appeals did not find a showing of extreme hardship. Interestingly, Supreme Court Justice Anthony Kennedy, later the author of *Lawrence v. Texas* and *Windsor*, was one of the judges on that appeals panel at the time and wrote the opinion including, "Deportation rarely occurs without personal distress and emotional hurt." After a letter to President Obama by the living partner in the marriage, the director of U.S. Citizenship and Immigration Services wrote him a letter that said, "This agency should never treat any individual with the disrespect shown toward you...You have my sincerest apology for the years of hurt caused by the deeply offensive and hateful language used..."On a lighter side, before the lawyers made her stop issuing marriage licenses to gay couples, a man came in and said, 'If a man can marry a man and a woman can marry a woman, why can't a tired old cowboy marry his best friend?'" He had his horse Dolly with him. The clerk asked how old the horse was and the man said 8. Then the clerk quipped, "I am sorry. Dolly's underaged." "A same-sex marriage, 'exile' and a final twist", Robert Barnes, *The Washington Post*, April 19, 2015, P. 1.

Does allowing same-sex marriage lessen the status of marriage? Some argue that marriage formed through natural laws have been ratified by every culture through generations and therefore should resist change. Others argue that marriage is a social contract and should be defined by society. Is nothing short of marriage enough? What was the effect of some states allowing same-sex couples to make it to the top of the ladder and grab the brass ring of full marriage? When gay couples objected to Vermont's awarding them civil unions—even though they were equivalent to marriage, because it was just not enough—will being "married" make a difference?[26]

SAME-SEX MARRIAGE IN CANADA
The Impact of Legal Marriage on the First Cohort of Gay and Lesbian Canadians to Wed
By Heather MacIntosh, Elke D. Reissing, and Heather Andruff

INTRODUCTION

In the last three decades, most Western countries have seen important steps in the advancement of equal rights and protection for all citizens. With respect to gay and lesbian individuals, the Trudeau government's removal of homosexuality from Canada's criminal code in 1969 was an early and significant change. However, it was not until 1996 that it became illegal to discriminate against persons on the basis of their sexual orientation. Following a court decision in 1999, both the federal and provincial governments introduced bills amending laws related to family law, adoption, pension benefits, and income tax to give couples in same-sex relationships the same rights and obligations as heterosexual couples in common-law relationships. Equality for Gays and Lesbians Everywhere (Egale) argued that this change was still not sufficient and that legal recognition of same-sex relationships was necessary to achieve equality.

On June 10, 2003, a ruling of the Court of Appeal for Ontario deemed the definition of marriage (a union of a man and a woman) unconstitutional and redefined marriage to include the "voluntary

---

26 Since *Goodridge*, 37 states and the District of Columbia now allow same-sex marriages. As society moves toward acceptance of same-sex marriage, should we stop calling it that? When same-sex couples were given the rights and benefits of marriage in Vermont, it was called a civil union; that was not enough. If same-sex couples are allowed to marry, they are married, just like heterosexuals. In order to end the discrimination, isn't it time to just call it marriage?

union for life of two persons to the exclusion of all others." City halls across Ontario were quickly flooded with same-sex couples seeking marriage licenses reflecting a fear that the ruling would be appealed and the opportunity to be legally married lost. British Columbia followed suit on July 8, 2003, and Quebec on March 19, 2004. The federal government's passage of the Civil Marriage Act on July 20, 2005, extended the right to marry to same-sex partners across Canada. This legislation created the first cohort of same-sex couples in North America to become legally married. It also provided a unique opportunity to examine the effects of the legalization of same-sex marriage in Canada.

The present quantitative and qualitative study explored these effects in a sample of 26 lesbian and gay married couples. Themes of interest in the study are reflected in the background literature reviewed below.

The Impact of Marriage on Same-Sex Couples

Practical Benefits

The practical benefits of legal marriage for same-sex couples include those related to family law, pension and health benefits, income tax, inheritance and power of attorney, and immigration law. These rights are afforded immediately to married couples without the waiting period required of common-law couples. Same-sex married couples are bound by the same responsibilities as heterosexual married couples including decision-making in medical or legal emergencies, spousal support, child support, and division of property upon dissolution of marriage. A recent survey of 558 individuals in same-sex marriages in Massachusetts conducted by the Massachusetts Department of Public Health (Ramos, Goldberg, & Badgett, 2009) found that 85% of participants listed legal recognition as one of their top three reasons for getting married. In a phenomenological study of 22 married or soon to be married same-sex couples from Canada and around the world, Alderson (2004) highlighted the importance of practical and legal benefits to the couples interviewed. The legal benefits that these couples identified as having had a particularly significant impact in their relational lives were the opportunities to create families through adoption, to automatically have the right to care for a partner in the case of illness or injury, and to act on other legal matters.

Social Support

Zicklin (1995) hypothesized that public and legal marriage for same-sex couples living in the United States would increase social support for these couples because of the higher social recognition afforded to legally married couples. As Zicklin anticipated, this has now been shown to be the case in several studies (e.g., Ramos et al., 2009; Balsam, Beauchaine, Rothblum, & Solomon, 2008; Lannutti, 2008). Given that many gay and lesbian couples lack family support (e.g., Kurdek, 2005; 2006), legal marriage might challenge families and public opinion to be more accepting. Family members who opposed a couple's cohabiting outside of marriage might be less negative toward gay or lesbian couples who were legally married and more inclined to provide support (Ramos et al., 2009). Social support from family and friends has been shown to influence commitment to the relationship in gay and lesbian couples in that partners with higher levels of social support also demonstrate higher levels of commitment (Kurdek, 2008a).

Prior to the legalization of same-sex marriage in Canada, a national poll found that 49% of Canadians supported the legalization of same-sex marriage and 46% opposed. Among those aged from 18 to 40, that support was 60% (The Strategic Counsel, 2002). A more recent Angus Reid poll conducted in September 2009 showed that 61% of Canadians supported the legalization of same-sex marriage and an additional 23% were supportive of same-sex unions (Angus Reid Strategies, 2009). Only 11% felt that same-sex couples should not have any legal recognition.

In some cases, marriage can also have a negative effect on social support for same-sex couples. For example, Lannutti's (2008) qualitative interviews with 26 female couples in Massachusetts in which one partner was bisexual found that some of the bi-women felt that family members (particularly parents) were very unsupportive of their decision to marry. It appeared in some cases that family members may have tolerated the same-sex relationship prior to marriage in the hope that the bisexual partner would once again have relationships with men. Embarrassment at having a lesbian or bisexual daughter was also given as a reason for lack of parental support.

Relationship Satisfaction

Kurdek (2003) has extensively examined the correlates of relationship satisfaction in gay and lesbian couples in the United States. The comparison groups have been both homosexual and heterosexual couples. The findings have consistently indicated that similar factors are correlated with relationship satisfaction in heterosexual, gay and lesbian relationships (e.g., Kurdek, 2005; 2006). These factors include arguing about issues related to power and intimacy, attachment styles and behaviors, commitment, and relationship history. Gottman et al. (2003) have also assessed the correlates of relationship satisfaction and dissolution in gay and lesbian couples and found that similar factors predicted satisfaction in heterosexual and gay/lesbian couples.

In their comparative study of cohabiting, married, and remarried heterosexual couples in the U.S., Skinner, Barh, Crane, and Call (2002) found that the cohabiting couples reported lower relationship happiness and fairness. Moore, McCabe, and Brink (2001) similarly reported that married heterosexual couples in Australia had higher levels of intimacy and relationship satisfaction than cohabiting couples. With respect to relationship quality in unmarried same-sex couples, Balsam et al. (2008) compared 203 same-sex couples in civil unions, 84 same-sex couples who were not in civil unions and 55 heterosexual married couples in Vermont. Whether they were in civil unions or not, the sample-sex couples reported more positive relationship quality and less conflict than the heterosexual married participants. However, same-sex couples not in civil unions were more likely to have ended their relationships on three-year follow-up than those who were in civil unions. Wienke and Hill's (2009) comparative study of 282 partnered gay and lesbian couples and 6,734 legally married heterosexual couples in the U.S. asked about general life happiness rather than relationship happiness or satisfaction in particular. They found that the partnered gay men and lesbian women reported less general happiness with their lives than did the married heterosexual participants.

In another approach to Studying relationship quality of partners in different types of cohabiting relationships, Kurdek (2008b) followed 95 lesbian couples, 92 gay male couples, 226 heterosexual couples without children, and 312 heterosexual couples with children. Participants in these cohabiting relationships were contacted every year for 10 years to determine patterns of relationship quality based on the Dyadic Adjustment Scale. Lesbian couples showed the overall highest level of relationship quality and gay male couples showed significantly higher levels of relationship quality compared to heterosexual couples with children. In addition, relationship quality for both gay male and lesbian couples remained constant over the course of the study whereas heterosexual couples showed an accelerated decline in relationship quality at the beginning of cohabitation followed by a second period of accelerated decline if the couple was living with children.

Alderson's (2004) phenomenological exploration provided the first insights into relationship functioning in a predominantly Canadian sample of legally married same-sex couples. Participants in this study noted an increase in commitment and connection, a finding replicated by Ramos et al. (2009) who found that 72% of their sample felt more committed to their partners following marriage and by Lannutti (2008) whose participants expressed greater feelings of love and a closer emotional bond to their partner following legal marriage. With regard to the feeling among some same-sex couples that their relationships seem more egalitarian than they observe in heterosexual couples, Solomon, Rothblum, and Balsam's (2005) study of the division of finances and household tasks among 336 members of same-sex civil unions, 238 members of same-sex couples not in civil unions, and 413 married heterosexual couples in Vermont is of interest. These authors found that lesbian and gay male couples, both those in civil unions and those not, were more egalitarian with respect to money and housework, than heterosexual married couples. Kurdek (2005; 2006) noted similar findings with respect to division of household labor and has also suggested that satisfaction with the division of household labor increases both relationship satisfaction and relationship stability (Kurdek, 2007).

Coming Out

Disclosure of sexual orientation and relationship status has been consistently associated with measures of positive menial health and relationship satisfaction in gay and lesbian persons, and with decreases in internalized homophobia (e.g., Jordan, 2000; Rosario, Hunter, Maguen, Gwadz, & Smith, 2001; Saphira & Glover, 2001). Cabaj and Purcel (1998) hypothesized that legalized marriage would increase disclosure and have a positive impact on relationship satisfaction and internalized homophobia. While this has shown to be the case for some, other individuals have described feelings of anguish when their loved ones respond with anger (e.g., Alderson, 2004; Lannutti, 2008). Same-sex couples who appreciate the formal recognition of a legal marriage may be less hesitant to disclose their same-sex relationship. This was noted in one study where more than 80% of participants indicated that being in a same-sex marriage had caused them to be more likely to come out to coworkers and healthcare providers (Ramos et al., 2009). Further, it has been shown that lesbian women in civil unions demonstrate significantly higher levels of "being out" than lesbian women not in civil unions (Solomon, Rothblum, & Balsam, 2004). Finally, level of "being out" has been shown to be a positive predictor of relationship quality in men such that those men who were more likely to be out demonstrated greater relationship quality at follow-up (Balsam et al., 2008).

Rationale for the Current Study

The literature reviewed above indicates that many gay and lesbian couples who have married experience not only the practical benefits related to the laws affecting married couples and the social benefits of acknowledgement and societal acceptance but also the relational benefits of increased relationship satisfaction (e.g., Alderson, 2004). In these respects, legal marriage appears to bring to same-sex couples many of the positive benefits experienced by heterosexual couples when they marry. Since this is a new area of research, the particular ways in which legal marriage has impacted on same-sex couples who were previously in long-term relationships warrants further investigation. The current study thus used both qualitative and quantitative methodology to assess the impact of marriage on members of the first cohort of legally-married, Canadian same-sex couples.

METHODS

Participants

Participants were recruited through gay, lesbian, bisexual and transgendered (GLBT) newspapers (e.g., Capital XTra), GLBT advocacy groups and web sites (e.g., Egale) and pro-same-sex marriage web sites (e.g., Canadians for Equal Marriage). Recruitment began in Ontario in response to the initial legislative change and expanded to British Columbia (B.C.) in response to requests from couples who had seen the call for participants on various web sites and who wanted to participate in the study.

Procedures

Couples who initiated contact through e-mail were e-mailed a package containing information about the study and what participants would be asked to do. Those who contacted us through telephone were provided with this information verbally. Inclusion criteria included (a) being legally married, (b) having lived together for a minimum of one year, and (c) no physical violence in the relationship. Couples who met these criteria and were participating from outside the Ottawa area were e-mailed a questionnaire package, information letter, and consent form. Questionnaires were returned by e-mail through a secured server or mail, and consent forms were sent back by mail to ensure that a signed original was in the file. The first author carried out telephone interviews with both members of the couple on the phone at the same time. Couples in the Ottawa area who were interviewed in person were given the information and consent forms and completed the questionnaires at the time of the interview. This study was approved by the Research Ethics Board of the University of Ottawa.

Measures

In addition to requesting demographic information, the questionnaire included the two research instruments described below.

Relationship Satisfaction

Relationship satisfaction was measured using the Dyadic Adjustment Scale (DAS, Spanier, 1976). This is a widely used self-report index of global couple adjustment with well-established psychometric properties. Johnson and O'Conner (2001) used the DAS in a study examining parenting in same-sex couples and found that the norms for their study were consistent with published test norms for married heterosexual couples. The DAS may also have utility for comparing same-sex and hetero-sexual couples because it is somewhat gender neutral in that it primarily uses the terms "partner" and "couple" throughout.

Attachment Security

Security and comfort with closeness in relationships was measured using the Experiences in Close Relationships-Revised (ECR-R, Brennan, Clark, & Shaver, 1998). The ECR-R is a 36-item measure of adult attachment in romantic relationships with well-established psychometric properties. The measure can be used to measure attachment along two attachment dimensions: avoidance and anxiety. Reliability of the items in both dimensions is high with alphas of .94 for the avoidance dimension and .91 for the anxiety dimension.

Semi-Structured Interview

The semi-structured, open-ended interview was designed to assess the impact of legal marriage on the couple. Three questions were asked in all of the interviews. These questions were used to stimulate discussion and couples were given time to expand upon their responses prior to being asked a successive question. The questions were: "What were your reasons for getting married?", "How did this change your relationship?", and "What impact did legal marriage have on your family?" Other questions were not structured and were emergent based on the content of the discussions. Interviews lasted between half an hour and an hour and both members of the couple were present in the room or on the phone. Couples were allowed to answer the questions with as much or as little detail as they were comfortable and to take the interview off to different topics that were not included in the interviewer's list of questions. All interviews were carried out by the first author.

Thematic Analysis

Thematic analysis is particularly suited to the relatively new study of same-sex marriage because it is an emergent rather than hypothesis driven methodology. It is appropriate for research topics where no established theories exist, and/or the theories are not specific enough or relevant to the area one is investigating, and/or the research questions are difficult to study with traditional research design and methods (e.g., Fereday & Muir-Cochrane, 2006). Thematic analysis is a qualitative methodology that can be utilized to organize qualitative data into patterns with the goal of eventually developing theories or models to account for phenomena or to' explain change (e.g., Taylor & Bogdan, 1984). In the present study, all interviews were transcribed by the principal investigator and the initial screening for general categories and sub-themes was undertaken throughout this process. Two additional independent raters were then asked to read the transcripts and identify categories and themes. All three raters then met, discussed the findings, and agreed on three general global themes, one of which was further broken down into three sub-themes.

RESULTS

Participant Characteristics

Fifty-two individuals completed the quantitative measures, 20 lesbian and 6 gay couples. Due to time zone differences, work schedules and parenting responsibilities, only 15 couples were available to participate in the interview and be included in the qualitative analyses.

The mean age of all couples was 48.8 years (range = 23–72 years). The average number of years together was 10.8 years (range = 1–35 years). Five couples had children with one to three children per couple. Twenty-two of the participants reported having had a previous heterosexual relationship. A majority of participants had a post-secondary education (33.4% post graduate, 26.7% undergraduate degree, 11.7% community college diploma) with 6.7%: A majority of participants had a post-secondary education (33.4% post graduate, 26.7% undergraduate degree, 11.7% community college diploma) with 6.7% having a high school diploma and 3.3% having less than a high school diploma. Most had incomes over $75,000 per year with 63.3% above $75,000, 30% at $25–75,000 and 3.3% less than $25,000.

Relationship Satisfaction

Results of the Dyadic Adjustment Scale measurement indicated that the 26 same-sex couples had a mean relationship satisfaction score of 126.71 with a standard deviation of 8.94. The population mean on this scale for married heterosexual couples is 114 (Spanier, 1976). Cronbach's alpha for these responses was .926. Thus, the same-sex marriage group in the present study had significantly higher levels of relationship satisfaction than did the sample of married, heterosexual couples reported on by Spanier, $t\,(26) = 7.25, < .001$.

Attachment Security

The population mean chosen for comparison on the Experiences in Close Relationships-Revised measure was the Married Population Norm as this is the most rigorous norm for this measure. Other available norms were for clinical populations experiencing psychological and relational distress. Results of the ECR-R suggest that these married heterosexual couples were reporting levels of Attachment Anxiety with an average of 1.79 out of a possible 3.00 $t\,(26) = -13.59, p < .001$ and Attachment Avoidance with an average of 1.60 out of a possible 3.00 $t\,(26) = -13.832, p < .001$ (Brennan, Clark, & Shaver, 1998). Cronbach's alpha for these responses was .611. The same-sex marriage group reported significantly less attachment-related anxiety and avoidance than married norms, $t(26\ anx) = -13.59, p < .001$ and $t(26\ avoid) = -13.832, p < .001$ respectively. In addition, all of the couples in the present study fell within the "secure" range of attachment compared to 70% for the normative heterosexual married couples.

Qualitative Interview Findings

In total, 15 couple interviews were carried out either by telephone or in person. Analysis of differences in interview length, general responsiveness of participants, and content did not reveal any qualitative differences based on method of interview. The three global themes that emerged from every interview were characterized as Social elements, Relational elements, and Political elements. Each theme is described below with representative quotes reflecting representative ideas and thoughts from participants that led to the thematic characterizations.

Social Elements

All of the participants described social elements related to the impact of being legally married on them personally and/or on their relationships. The three sub-themes that fell under the Social category were: (I) the Language of Marriage, (2) Being Out, and (3) Rights and Responsibilities.

Sub-theme 1: The Language of Marriage

Ninety-two percent of participants discussed the impact of the language of marriage as an element of their experience of becoming legally married. Almost all indicated that words such as spouse, marriage, wife, husband, and daughter-in-law, were understood by everyone and that through this language they felt understood and known by their friends and families in a different way that created a new and deeper acceptance of their partnerships. For most, this language had a very positive influence.

> *The language of marriage helped us feel more a part of this world. Everyone knows what it means. It helps others start to realize that a relationship is a relationship and we are dealing with the same issues that everyone else deals with. It helped me realize, the word marriage, what was important to me; getting married, having a wedding. The language was really intentional; showing others that that's what we mean. (Tessa, 37)*

Only two couples discussed the negative impact of language. In both cases, their families had previously been only minimally tolerant of their relationship and marriage broke the limits of tolerance and caused a breach in their relationships with these family members.

A majority of female participants described their experiences with the word "wife." They discussed how this has been a patriarchal word throughout history and illustrated their struggle with deciding whether to use this word or not. A number of women joked that they would like to have a wife but would not like to be one. A lot of humor and thought was put into these decisions and the majority of participants had chosen to continue using the word spouse or partner. A smaller number of participants chose to reclaim the word wife in a more positive frame or to make up their own word.

> *... for me it's like reclaiming the word queer or dyke, taking something that's been used as a negative and defining itself (Grace, 56)*

Participants indicated that there was no more mystery about their relationships as everyone knows that a marriage is about a lifelong emotional and sexual relationship that is primary and equal to the relationships that heterosexual couples have with their partners.

> *The word has taken us from being legal partners to being wives with the status that the word conveys, it puts this relationship into a context that everyone, homophobic or not can understand. (Chris, 50)*

Sub-theme 2: Being Out

Three quarters of participants commented on the fact that legalized marriage had an impact on their level of being out. In particular they felt more comfortable and entitled to be out but also a sense of responsibility about the need to be out. They talked about an increased personal level of social awareness and felt that this had come about as a result of their being more out and in particular, as a result of their public declaration of marriage.

> *It's a problem cause if you're going to have a gay wedding you need to tell people you're gay! It's not that people didn't know, it's that I wasn't silent anymore. (Sue, 36)*

Participants discussed the impact that legal marriage had on their own levels of internalized homophobia and the external homophobia of others. In fact, a number of participants observed that they had not even been aware that they had any internalized homophobia until it came time to announce their marriage. They talked about coming out again in a new way with a newfound sense of pride and a decreased level of internalized homophobia.

> *We would have thought that we were really even on the scale of internalized homophobia. I've been out for 25 years and we're out to friends, family, at work in community but this resurfaced issues and dynamics with the decision to wed publicly. I moved from a place of being grateful to feeling entitled… from "Am I really allowed to tell people to come to my wedding" to celebrating, revelling in, and claiming the legitimacy. I used to simply feel grateful for being accepted but now I feel entitled and legitimate. It was another layer of coming out. (Pat, 48)*

Seventy-two percent of participants discussed how the language of marriage and the increased "outness" of being married had the combined impact of creating normalization for their relationships and for same-sex couples in general and that these things led to social change. They felt that being out, proud and having affirmed their relationships publicly through marriage showed the world more about their relationships. Further, they noted that simply living their married lives publicly and openly demonstrated that their relationships were no different than those of their heterosexual peers.

Marriage opens the door for people to know that we're not really any different from any other couple who decides to make a commitment to each other... and that we get up, go to work, pay our bills, buy gas for our cars, help our kids, and just live ordinary, everyday lives... I would invite anyone to come into our home to see just how very ordinary we really are! (Helen, 50)

In effect, these participants felt that living their lives and loving publicly has led to greater levels of acceptance and support from their communities.

People have said that having experienced our wedding, they are more willing to challenge other people when the subject comes up which is very affirming. (Will, 40)

Sub-theme 3: Rights and Responsibilities

Three quarters of the participants indicated that the rights and responsibilities of marriage were important to them and that this had an impact on them since getting married. They felt that they and their relationships were full participants in society in the sense that the ability to file taxes together as spouses and to have the immediate practical benefits of marriage, such as receiving immediate spousal health insurance benefits, had given them a newfound sense of empowerment and inclusion in a system that they had been restricted from in the past. These couples embraced the opportunity to be responsible for their partner in all of the legal and social ways that come with marriage and articulated a deep sense of belongingness and feelings of entitlement that had historically been denied to them and their relationships.

Relational Elements

All of the participants described experiencing an impact on their relationship through the act of legally marrying their partner. In particular this impact was felt in the areas of family and safety or security. While all couples talked about the impact that legal marriage had on their sense of commitment, the majority reported that it had not changed their level of commitment.

The legal ceremony did not change our level of commitment at all... our first commitment ceremony three years ago had a tremendous impact... the unlegal deepened our commitment and the courts simply caught up to us. (Bryn, 37)

Ninety-two percent of participants discussed the impact that legal marriage had on their sense of family and almost all of them described feeling more open to or ready for the idea of having children.

They also felt more entitled to apply to adopt and many were, in fact, either in the process of beginning adoption applications or assisted fertilization and some were already pregnant. Among the couples contemplating having children, a number had previously decided not to have children and indicated that being legally married had changed something for them that allowed them for the first time to imagine that they could become parents.

> *Adoption and parentage was a big part of getting married. We felt it would legitimize us as co-parents and make the child feel more secure. (Leslie, 42)*

Most participants talked about family from the perspective of creating family and bringing family together. Some talked with animation and emotion about their experiences of being welcomed into the family of their partner and a number recounted how previously anxious or unaccepting parents had introduced their child's partner to others as their daughter-in-law or son-in-law. Most described this kind of experience as one of the impacts of legal marriage that was tremendously enriching. For example, a woman whose partner's rural father had been very uncomfortable and even negative when his daughter came out to the family describes how over time he had changed his attitude and openly embraced the marriage of his daughter and included her as a full member of the family.

> *It's the reason that everyone gets married, to feel a part of each other's family… we really are… we stopped to get a coffee and I thought he'd want to stay in the truck so I offered to go in and get it but he said he wanted to go in to show off his new daughter-in-law.*
> *I call her father "Dad" now and he gets a kick out of it… he calls us his girls. (Abbie, 38)*

In contrast, two couples experienced further distancing from already strained family relationships because their families saw in legal marriage the kind of public profession of love from which they had to withdraw. The couples told these stories with sadness but also with a sense of having made a decision to move forward in deepening their relationship with a full understanding of the potential consequences.

Eighty-six percent of participants also discussed the impact that legal marriage had on their level of safety and security in the relationship with most describing this as a newfound sense of peaceful-ness and feeling relaxed and at ease in the relationship in ways that they had not before. Among the many who talked about an increased feeling of closeness, a majority indicated that they had been overwhelmed and tremendously surprised that it was even possible to feel closer to the partner they had been with for many years. This is an interesting observation in relation to the couples that did not necessarily feel any greater level of commitment; possibly something did increase in terms of emotional closeness and security. Some couples expressed both awe and anger at the amazement of actually being able to feel closer to someone that they had loved for so long and then at realizing that they had been denied this feeling throughout their relationship.

> *The minute we got married all of the conversation about security and houses and money stopped... the bottom line was that when you get married you are taking on a responsibility for that person and if something happens to her it is my problem... I finally felt safer, more secure and knew that she was not going to walk out the door. (Sue, 36)*

> *I had no idea that I could feel any closer to him than I already did after 35 years together. It is unbelievable and I can't believe that we have been denied this experience all of these years. (Len, 68)*

Political Elements

All of the couples talked about the political climate around same-sex marriage and the impact that this element of the issue has had on them. All couples described the importance of being granted legal rights of marriage and full equality in society. In terms of legal rights, all of the participants described their feeling of finally being protected by society. They described a profound sense of safety and security in knowing that they would be able to have the right to make decisions for an ill partner, care for children together and have the benefits related to inheritance and insurance. Almost all talked about the importance of being married for access to parental rights and their desire to be given equal rights under the law in cases of adoption and automatic parental rights to a child born into the marriage. As mentioned above, many of the participants were in the process of starting families at the time of the interviews and these issues were foremost on their minds.

> *We did insemination a couple of days ago. We were going to do this anyway but I wanted to be legally married before the baby was born. From a legal perspective I want to be legally protected and secure. (Donna, 39)*

Most participants also talked about their feeling that legal marriage had the impact of legitimizing their relationships. They reported feeling like they finally existed and were accepted by society and not just by their immediate social circle.

> *I think that changing the law has set a moral standard by which people's attitudes are changing; it does legitimize it... like corporal punishment. In Sweden they changed the laws and it changed from 90% of people believing that it was okay to hit their kids to only 10% in less than twenty years... it is insisting that cultural change be instigated by government. (Sandra, 43)*

It really changed the status that I am allowed to claim in the world. *(Dale, 39)*

In discussing the political issues related to same-sex marriage, 92% of participants indicated that offering same-sex couples civil unions instead of marriage was not acceptable to them and certainly not equal. These couples expressed deep concern about the possibility of a political watering down of the judgment that denying marriage to same-sex couples is unconstitutional.

> *If civil unions were what was there for everyone then fine but if same-sex couples can only have civil unions where heterosexual couples can have marriage, it isn't fair. It is the same as having to sit at the back of the bus. (Lynn, 39)*

DISCUSSION

Participants in the present study were among the first same-sex couples to get legally married in Canada. Our findings indicate that they experienced primarily positive consequences subsequent to marriage and it is therefore not surprising that this sample showed significantly higher levels of relationship satisfaction and attachment security compared to heterosexual married population norms. While others have reported comparatively high levels of relationship satisfaction and happiness in cohabiting same-sex couples (e.g., Balsam et al., 2008; Kurdek, 2008b), another explanation for this finding may be that couples in this sample have been in committed relationships for extended periods of time and have undoubtedly weathered the inevitable struggles of long-term relationships in a social environment that may not have always been supportive. High scores on attachment and relationship satisfaction may therefore reflect the fact that these are highly successful couples who simply renewed their commitment by getting married legally.

Our qualitative analyses documented the overall positive experience of marriage for these couples as reflected in the three overarching thematic elements that emerged from their observations: (a) Social elements, (b) Relational elements, and (c) Political elements.

Socially, participants indicated that the language of marriage had an important impact in helping the people in their lives to better understand and validate their relationship. Marriage also increased their level of being out, decreased their own internalized homophobia, and apparently decreased externalized homophobia in the people around them. In many cases, participants were not even aware that they had residual internalized homophobia after having been out for many years. They welcomed taking on the rights and responsibilities of legal marriage and felt that this allowed them to finally be full participants in society.

Relationally, most participants indicated that legal marriage had not deepened their level of commitment to their partners but it did have the effect of helping them feel more fully a part of each other's families. Participants noted that legal marriage had deepened their feelings of closeness to their partners and peacefulness in their relationships and were struck by this unexpected outcome.

They said they could not have imagined feeling any closer to their partners after many years of committed deep relationship.

Politically, participants found in the legal right to marry the feeling of being protected by society in terms of inheritance, power of attorney, parenting rights, and other areas where marriage protects partners. In this sense, marriage had a profound impact on their sense of security and entitlement. They were clear that a civil union was not the same as or equal to a legal marriage that provided couples with a measure of equality and legitimization.

In areas where comparisons are possible, the foregoing observations are generally comparable to those in the few other studies of the impact of legal marriage on same sex couples (Alderson, 2004; Lannutti, 2008; Ramos, et al., 2009). One difference is that Alderson (2004) and Ramos et al. (2009) found that their participants felt more committed to their partners whereas that feeling was less apparent in the present study although our couples did comment on an increased sense of closeness to their partner and a greater feeling of peace and relaxation about their relationship status.

Perceived Implications of Same Sex Marriage

Although our participants decided to marry for personal reasons, as did the couples studied by Alderson (2004) and Ramos et al. (2009), they also recognized that the positive effects on their relationships also had the potential to impact on society through increased exposure and normalization. People who had witnessed their marriages and who continued to support them had become more willing to speak out against homophobia and to support governmental initiatives that legalized and now protect same-sex relationships. However, participants also expressed concern that same-sex marriage could have a negative impact on queer culture in that the inclusion of gay and lesbian couples in the traditions of heterosexual society might cause divisions within the GLBTQ community. Would advocates for same-sex marriage and those who reject marriage as sublimation into the dominant patriarchal society become split off from each other? Another concern was that some members of the GLBTQ community who might not be prepared for marriage would decide too quickly, without having contemplated the consequences, and marry simply because they have the opportunity.

Limitations and Summary Observations

Our comparison of relationship satisfaction and attachment-related anxiety, avoidance and security in heterosexual married couples and same-sex married couples may have been limited by the age of the measure (Spanier, 1976) and by the fact that the scale used was designed for heterosexual respondents. Researchers should now consider psychometric validation of measures on couple function and satisfaction for gay and lesbian married couples. Another limitation was that our participants were highly self-selected couples who were committed and secure enough to make the decision about getting married once the opportunity was available to them. Future investigations may benefit from a comparison group of heterosexual married couples and a sample of same-sex couples chosen to be demographically representative of married couples in general.

While it is important to understand the impact of legalized marriage on this first cohort, over time it will also be necessary to examine the impact of access to marriage on the next generation of LGBT youth. For example, it will be interesting to follow the relational lives of youth who are coming of age in this period of change and increased rights. Future research might also study matched heterosexual and gay and lesbian couples who met their partners after the legalization of same-sex marriage to determine the impact of marriage on couples who had always had marriage as a legal option.

Overall, our assessment of the impact of legal marriage on Canadian same-sex couples demonstrated positive impact across the personal, interpersonal, and political realities of the couples. The fact that participants reported feeling legitimized, understood, supported and protected by both society and their communities suggests a compelling impact that extends beyond the individuals to encompass the larger society

REFERENCES

Alderson, K. (2004). A phenomenological investigation of same-sex marriage. *The Canadian Journal of Human Sexuality, 13,* 107–122.

Angus Reid Strategies. (2009). *Canada more open to same-sex marriage than U.S., UK.* Retrieved from http://www.angus-reid.com/polls/view/canada_more_open_to_same_sex_marriage_than_us_uk/

Balsam, K.F., Beauchaine, T. P., Rothblum, E. D., & Solomon, S.E. (2008). Three-year follow-up of same-sex couples who had civil unions in Vermont, same-sex couples not in civil unions, and heterosexual married couples. *Developmental Psychology, 44,* 102–116. doi:10.1037/0012-1649.44.1.102

Brennan, K.A., Clark, C.L., & Shaver, P.R. (1998). Self-report measurement of adult attachment: An integrative overview. In J.A. Simpson & W.S. Rholes (Eds.), *Attachment theory and close relationships* (46–76). New York, NY: Guilford Press.

Cabaj, R., & Pureel, D. (1998). *On the road to same-sex marriage; A supportive guide to psychological, political and legal issues.* San Francisco, CA: Jossey-Bass.

Fereday, J., & Muir-Cocbrane, E. (2006). Demonstrating rigor using thematic analysis: A hybrid approach of inductive and deductive coding and theme development. *International Journal of Qualitative Methods, 5,* 1–11.

Gottman, J.M., Levenson, R. W., Gross, J., Frederickson, B., McCoy, K., Rosenthal, L., Ruef, A., & Yoshimoto, D. (2003). Correlates of gay and lesbian couples' relationship satisfaction and relationship dissolution. *Journal of Homosexuality, 45,* 23–43. doi:10,1300/J082v45n01_02

Johnson, S.M., & O'Connor, E. (2001). *For lesbian parents: Your guide to helping your family grow up happy, healthy, and proud.* New York, NY: Guilford Press.

Jordan, K.M. (2000). Substance abuse among gay, lesbian, bisexual, transgender, and questioning adolescents. *School Psychology Review, 29,* 201–207.

Kurdek, L. (2003). Differences between gay and lesbian cohabiting couples. *Journal of Social and Personal Relationships, 20,* 411–436. doi:10.1177/02654075030204001

Kurdek, L.A. (2004). Are gay and lesbian cohabitating couples *really* different from heterosexual married couples? *Journal of Marriage and Family, 66,* 880–900. doi:10.1111/j.0022-2445.2004.00060.x

Kurdek, L.A. (2005). What do we know about gay and lesbian couples? *Current Directions in Psychological Science, 14,* 251–254. doi:10.1111/j.0963-7214.2005.00375.x

Kurdek, L.A. (2006). Differences between partners from heterosexual, gay, and lesbian cohabiting couples. *Journal of Marriage and Family, 68,* 509–528. doi:10.1111/j.1741-3737.2006.00268.x

Kurdek, L.A. (2007). The allocation of household labor by partners in gay and lesbian couples. *Journal of Family Issues, 28,* 132–148. doi:10.1177/0192513X06292019

Kurdek, L.A. (2008a). A general model of relationship commitment: Evidence from same-sex partners. *Personal Relationships, 15,* 391–405. doi:10.1111/j.1475-68U.2008.00205.x

Kurdek, L.A. (2008b). Change in relationship quality for partners from lesbian, gay male, and heterosexual couples. *Journal of Family Psychology, 22,* 701–711. doi:10.1037/0893-3200.22.5.701

Lannutti, P.J. (2008). "This is not a lesbian wedding": Examining same-sex marriage and bisexual-lesbian couples. *Journal of Bisexuality, 7,* 237–260. doi:10.1080/15299710802171316

Moore, K.A., McCabe, M., & Brink, R. (2001). Are married couples happier in their relationships than cohabiting couples? Intimacy and relationship factors. *Sexual and Relationship Therapy, 16,* 35–46. doi:10.1080/14681990020021548

Ramos, C., Goldberg, N.G, Badgett, M.V.L. (2009). *The effects of marriage equality in Massachusetts: A survey of the experiences and impact of marriage on same-sex couples.* Los Angeles, CA: The Williams Institute, UCLA.

Rosario, M., Hunter, J., Maguen, S., Gwadz, M., & Smith, R. (2001). The coming-out process and its adaptational and health-related associations among gay, lesbian, and bisexual youths: Stipulation and exploration of a model. *American Journal of Community Psychology, 29,* 113–160.

Saphira, M., & Glover, M. (2001). The effects of coming out on relationships and health. *Journal of Lesbian Studies, 5,* 183–194.

Skinner, K.B., Bahr, S.J., Crane, R.D., & Call, V.R. (2002). Cohabitation, marriage, and remarriage: A comparison of relationship quality over time. *Journal of Family Issues, 23,* 74–90. doi:10.1177/0192513X02023001004

Solomon, S.E., Rothblum, E.D., & Balsam, K.F. (2004). Pioneers in partnerships: Lesbian and gay male couples in civil unions compared with those not in civil unions, and married heterosexual siblings. *Journal of Family Psychology, 18,* 275–286. doi:10.1037/0893-3200.18.2.275

Solomon, S.E., Rothblum, E.D., & Balsam, K.F. (2005). Money, housework, sex, and conflict: Same-sex couples in civil unions, those not in civil unions, and heterosexual married siblings. *Sex Roles, 52,* 561–575. doi:10.1007/s11199-005-3725-7

Spanier, G. B. (1976). Measuring dyadic adjustment: New scales for assessing the quality of marriage and similar dyads. *Journal of Marriage and the Family, 38,* 15–28.

Taylor, S.J., & Bogdan, R. (1984) *Introduction to qualitative research methods: The search for meanings.* New York, NY: John Wiley & Sons.

The Strategic Counsel. (2002). *Canadian attitudes on the family: Focus on the family Canadian national survey.* Toronto, ON: Author.

Wienke, C., & Hill, G.J. (2009). Does the "marriage benefit" extend to partners in gay and lesbian relationships? Evidence from a random sample of sexual active adults. *Journal of Family Issues, 30,* 259–289. doi:10.1177/0192513X08324382

Zicklin, G. (1995). Deconstructing legal rationality: The care of lesbian and gay family relationships *Marriage and Family Review, 21,* 55–76.

FEDERAL LAW

In 1996, the United States Congress passed the Defense of Marriage Act (DOMA), declaring in its legislative history that it "was motivated by the Hawaiian lawsuit"[27] and the concern that if Hawaii or any state allows same-sex marriage, other states would be forced to recognize it. In 2013, Supreme Court justice Elena Kagan, quoting the legislative record from DOMA, said, "Well, is what happened in 1996—and I'm going to quote from the House report here—is that 'Congress decided to reflect to honor a collective moral judgment and to express moral disapproval of homosexuality.'"[28] President Bill Clinton signed DOMA into law. Under DOMA: 1) the federal law defined marriage as between two people of the opposite sex (and therefore would not recognize a state's valid same-sex marriage); and 2) stated that no state could be required to recognize a same-sex marriage from another state, even if the latter state allowed same-sex marriage. (This is contrary to the Full Faith and Credit Act,[29] which says, generally, that states should respect the "public acts, records, and judicial proceedings of every other state". As a result, a marriage that is valid in one state has typically been valid in all others, preventing the need to re-marry every time one leaves the state to enter another state.) The Government Accounting Office said there were over 1,000 federal laws affected by marital status.[30]

Fearing that DOMA was not enough, congressional conservatives—and then President George W. Bush—proposed federal Constitution amendments several times to bar same-sex marriage. In 2004, the Senate voted on such a measure several times but failed to obtain the two-thirds majority vote necessary to amend the United States Constitution.[31] Prior to re-election, President

---

27 http://www.lambdalegal.org/in-court/cases/baehr-v-miike
28 Justice Elena Kagan on March 27, 2013, in the case of *United States v. Windsor.*
29 Article IV, Section 1 of the United States Constitution
30 Under DOMA same-sex partners of federal workers were not eligible for coverage under the Federal Employees Health Benefits Program (FEHB) because the Defense of Marriage Act, according to the FEHB website.
31 Remember, the Constitution has only been amended 27 times in over 200 years; it is a difficult thing to accomplish.

Bush held a rare press conference touting the need to revise the constitutional ban against same-sex marriages, but never followed up on it.[32] On June 7, 2006, the Senate defeated a similar constitutional amendment.[33] What would it mean if the United States Constitution expressly prohibited same-sex marriages? Is marriage for the states or the federal government to decide?

SOME COMPLICATED EFFECTS OF THE MIXED MARRIAGE LAWS

DOMA raised lots of complications. For example, if someone is in a same-sex relationship, from a state that allows same-sex marriage, how should she file her federal taxes—married filing jointly (which is true under her state law, but not the federal law) or single (which is true under the federal law, but not her state law)? Suppose she is legally married in one state, and then the couple moves to another that does not recognize their marriage. In January 23, 2005, when asked by the District of Columbia's tax office, the D.C. attorney advised same-sex couples (legally married in other states) that it was okay to file a joint tax return in the District.[34] After that opinion, concerns about the Districts willingness to recognize out-of-state, same-sex marriages as valid, created doubts. By May 5, 2005, the city added to the confusion and changed its opinion and warned that it was not okay to file a joint tax form. Some Republicans in Congress had warned the District that such action would cause a backlash in Congress. At that time, D.C. law specifically forbade recognition of same-sex marriage, so the only taxpayers who could file jointly in the District were those who had been married in a way that was recognized under federal law—defined as a union between one man and one woman.

What about divorce? If you were married in a state that allowed marriage equality, but wanted to get divorced in another state that did not recognize you as married, what happened? In 2015, the Texas Supreme Court upheld an Austin "same-sex" divorce even though Texas did not recognize their 2004 Massachusetts marriage. The Texas Attorney General moved to block the divorce because "it would implicitly recognize marriage equality, which the Texas voters rejected in 2005."[35] Was the Texas court influenced by the timing of the case, which was decided just as the U.S. Supreme Court was deciding on the constitutionality of marriage equality?

---

32   At that time, Vice President Richard Cheney felt the issue should be left to the states, like all marriage issues. Since then, one of his daughters has married her same-sex spouse and adopted a child. More recently, in March 2013, Senator Rob Portman of Ohio, one of DOMA's biggest proponents, rejected it in support of his gay son. Views evolve on both sides of the political spectrum. While an activist, President Obama endorsed same-sex marriage in the 1990s. Eight years later, he rejected it. In 2015, his "administration told the Supreme Court that the Constitution does not allow states to prohibit gay couples from marring." "Obama's words on same-sex marriage are a major shift from him", Juliet Eilperin and Robert Barnes, *The Washington Post*, March 7, 2015, P.A6/

33   In October 2014, Senator Ted Cruz a Republican from Texas, "vowed to introduce a constitutional amendment allowing states to ban gay marriage." "Gay-marriage move riles conservatives", Karen Tumulty, *The Washington Post*, October 7, 2013, p A5.

34   At that time, Washington, D.C., did not allow same-sex marriage; it now does.

35   www.txcourts.gov/media/1001370/110114.pdf

On the flip side, as more states embraced marriage equality, some lawsuits were filed against service providers who, based on religious reasons, refused to provide services for gay weddings. For example: in Vermont in 2005, the Wildflower Inn refused to accommodate a lesbian wedding; in 2006, a New Mexico photo studio declined to photograph a commitment ceremony; and bakers in Colorado and Oregon refused to make wedding cakes for gay couples. Each was charged with complaints under their states' anti-discrimination laws. When recognizing same-sex marriages, some states included exemptions for religious leaders and organizations opposed to same-sex marriage from having to perform such weddings. Such exemptions do not apply here, however, because these are private businesses, not religious ones. While the owners of the businesses may have religious objections to gay unions, their businesses must still comply with state laws against discrimination based on sexual orientation. In the Colorado case (where same-sex marriage was not legal at the time) a baker refused to make a wedding cake for a same-sex ceremony (for a couple legally married in Massachusetts, but who wanted to have a celebration ceremony in their home-state of Colorado) and the couple complained. The baker argued that it violated his first amendment rights and the couple argued it violated state anti-discrimination laws. An administrative law judge ruled against the baker, Jack Phillips, and the commission upheld that decision.[36] The baker said he did not discriminate. "'I clearly told them that I would make them birthday cakes, shower cakes, cookies and brownies,'" he said. "I just don't do cakes for same sex weddings."[37] Phillips said he would just stop making wedding cakes as a result.[38] This was also the case in Washington when the owner of Arlene's Flowers[39] refused to provide the flowers for the wedding of a gay couple, who were long-time customers who had spent thousands of dollars at her shop. The owner refused, citing "her relationship with Jesus Christ."[40] In 2013, Washington State sued the florist in Benton County Superior Court, alleging that the refusal to service customers was a violation of the state's anti-discrimination law.[41] In February 2015, the Oregon Bureau of Labor

36 "Baker appeals order to provide gay wedding cakes", *A.P.*, July 17, 2014 http://www.denverpost.com/news/ci_26166540/baker-appeals-order-provide-gay-wedding-cakes

37 "Masterpiece Cakes shop owner Jack Phillips appeals order to provide same-sex wedding cakes", July 17, 2014 http://www.thedenverchannel.com/news/local-news/masterpiece-cakeshop-owner-jack-phillips-appeals-order-to-provide-same-sex-wedding-cakes

38 Citing one of the commissioner's comments, that "to me it is one of the most despicable pieces of rhetoric that people can use — to use their religion to hurt others", the baker appealed to the Colorado Court of appeals, but that court also ordered him to stop discriminating. "Cake maker who refused to bake for gay wedding labeled a 'Nazi' by Colo. civil rights officials", Valerie Richardson, *The Washington Times*, January 12, 2015 http://www.washingtontimes.com/news/2015/jan/12/colorado-cake-case-pits-religion-against-tolerance/?page=all See also," The U.S. at a glance...", *The Week*, August 28, 2015, P5. "In its 66-page ruling, [the appellate panel] said Phillips was prohibited 'from picking and choosing customers based on their sexual orientation."

39 Who curiously is named Baronelle Stutzman. Ibid.

40 Ibid. Although she was fined $1,000 for the violation, a GoFundMe site crowd funded over $90,000 for her." "Amid Indiana controversy, donations soar for Washington florist who refused gay wedding", Paige Cornwell, *The Seattle Times*, April 4, 2015

41 In April 2015, A GoFundMe site "netted the florist more than $80,000 from an online crowd funding page dedicated to "'protect her and her livelihood.'". A similar crowd funding site raised a reported $800,000 for an Indiana pizza store that had never been sued for failing to provide services for a gay wedding, it just reported that it would not in response to Indiana's proposed Religious Freedom Restoration Act (RFRA). "Washington Florist who

found a baker guilty of discrimination when she said that, "the couple's union was an 'abomination unto the lord'" and refused to sell any cakes for gay weddings.[42] The baker has since closed the store and bakes from home, but was fined $135,000 for her discrimination. [43,44] In 2015, in Montgomery County Maryland, a company declined to provide a DJ for a gay man's birthday party because they were "a Christian organization and it would go against our faith."[45] It seems these cases make clear that while the owners of businesses may be religious, their businesses are not; so the owners must comply with the state's anti-discrimination law. What will be the effect on these cases with the U.S. Supreme Court's decision in *Burwell v. Hobby* Lobby, decided in June 2014? In *Burwell*, the Supreme Court ruled that requiring "family-owned corporations to pay for insurance coverage for contraception under the Affordable Care Act violated a federal law protecting religious freedom."[46] "The contraceptive coverage requirement was challenged by two corporations whose owners say they try to run their businesses on Christian principles: Hobby Lobby, a chain of craft stores, and Conestoga Wood Specialties, which makes wood cabinets. The requirement has also been challenged in 50 other cases…Justice Alito (writing for the majority) said the requirement that the two companies provide contraception coverage imposed a substantial burden on their religious liberty."[47] Justice Alito claimed that this opinion should be narrowly applied to "closely held corporations, each controlled by a family member."[48] This seems to pierce the corporate shell, making it merely a vehicle for tax advantage with no ideology disadvantage.

---

refused gay wedding", Paige Cornwell, *The Seattle Times*, April 4, 2015. http://www.seattletimes.com/seattle-news/amid-indiana-controversy-donations-soar-for-washington-florist-who-refused-gay-wedding/

42 "Bakery risks large fine for anti-gay discrimination", Sara Roth, *U.S.A. Today*, February 3, 2015.http://www.usatoday.com/story/news/2015/02/02/bakery-same-sex-oregon-fined-wedding-cake/22771685/

43 After the story broke about the bakery citing religious objections to making a cake for a gay couple's wedding, five reporters from local newspapers called the bakery to request cakes for fictional occasions. The bakery agreed to make cakes for researchers cloning human stem cells (actually two similar cakes—or "two little clone cakes"); a pagan solstice party for a "coven" (with a pentagram decoration); a divorce party; and a baby shower for a woman with two children outside of marriage. "The cake wars", Martin Cizmar, *The Willmette Weekly*, May 29,2013. http://www.wweek.com/portland/article-20698-the-cake-wars.html But in April 2015, the tide turned again, when A GoFundMe site compensated her for more than her losses. "Washington Florist who refused gay wedding", Paige Cornwell, *The Seattle Times*, April 4, 2015 http://www.seattletimes.com/seattle-news/amid-indiana-controversy-donations-soar-for-washington-florist-who-refused-gay-wedding/; See also, "Talking Points", *The Week*, July 17, 2015, P 16.

44 In 2016, a graduate student in Missouri State University's counseling program sued the school "claiming he was wrongfully dismissed from the program because of his religious beliefs…his unwillingness to counsel same-sex couples." The University settled the case by refunding him the $25,000 in lost tuition. http://www.news-leader.com/story/news/local/2017/01/09/msu-settles-lawsuit-student-who-wouldnt-counsel-gay-couples/96340566/

45 The company's written policy states, "'we will not be involved in any event involving homosexual celebration or activity. We follow biblical morality.'" The company also says it will "not play vulgar music or tolerate provocative dancing or be involved with strippers" "'fortune tellers, psychics, or magicians.'" https://www.washingtonpost.com/news/acts-of-faith/wp/2015/06/12/a-maryland-dj-has-refused-to-work-a-birthday-party-for-a-gay-man-we-ought-to-obey-god-rather-than-men/?utm_term=.4ac2829fe88e

46 "Supreme Court Rejects Contraceptives Mandate for Some Corporations", Adam Liptak, *The New York Times*, June 20, 3014. http://www.nytimes.com/2014/07/01/us/hobby-lobby-case-supreme-court-contraception.html?_r=0

47 Ibid.

48 Ibid.

If it was, as Justice Ginsberg's dissent countered, "a decision of startling breadth,"[49] will that mean that family owned small businesses too will be able to claim religious freedoms in refusing to make cakes, provide flowers, or take photos at same-sex marriages?[50]

Almost if as on cue, as this book was being updated for the revised first edition in April 2015, Indiana and then Arkansas tried to pass Religious Freedom Restoration Acts (RFRA) which were based on a federal law "to restore the compelling interest test" to situations where religion is substantially burdened even by a neutral, generally applicable law." Indiana's law was signed by then Governor, and now Vice President Mike Pence. [51] Because of "the Supreme Court's interpretation of the federal RFRA in last year's *Hobby Lobby* case...where the court for the first time made clear that closely held corporations, as well as individuals, can assert religious rights" and the tensions created with the "rapid legalization of same-sex marriage and the publicity" given to the types of cases listed above,[52] these state's proposed laws that allowed corporations to assert religious rights and object to providing service (neither required the government to be a party to the discrimination suit either). "Under the Arkansas bill, religious rights can be invoked to obtain an injunction or damages against an individual (not the government) who insists that I comply with a regulation that violates my beliefs."[53] As of February 2017, more than a dozen states have proposed "religious freedom" bills. For example, in February, Alabama, proposed the "'Child Placing Agency Inclusion Act,' which would give faith-based adoption and foster agencies the right to use their religion to guide their child placement decisions."[54] President Trump has suggested, "that the nation's religious liberties have eroded considerably." Yet, in February 2017, he "declined to sign an executive order that would have given businesses and individuals of faith broad leeway to opt out of laws that conflict with their religion."[55]

In the previous edition of this book, I finished by asking what would be the effect of the Hobby Lobby case on the 1983 *Bob Jones University* case, where two Christian Universities "claimed

---

49   Ibid.

50   Citing to page 94 of the opinion, Justice Ginsberg asked, "Would the exemption the Court holds RFRA demands for employers with religiously grounded objections to the use of certain contraceptives extend to employers with religiously grounded objections to blood transfusions (Jehovah's Witnesses); antidepressants (Scientologists); medications derived from pigs, including anesthesia, intravenous fluids, and pills coated with gelatin (certain Muslims, Jews, and Hindus); and vaccinations (Christian Scientists, among others)?", Ibid.

51   In one light-hearted moment, marijuana smokers challenged Indiana's law by forming the First Church of Cannabis and announcing that they will smoke at services. "Controversy of the Week", *The Week*, June 19, 2015, P. 4.

52   The Federal Government passed a RFRA in 1993 which applied to both the federal and state governments, but the Supreme Court later limited that to the federal government only so each state must pass its own. Today, 19 states have such laws. "10 things you need to know to really understand RFRA in Indiana and Arkansas, Howard M. Friedman, *The Washington Post*, April 1, 2015., http://www.washingtonpost.com/news/acts-of-faith/wp/2015/04/01/10-things-you-need-to-know-to-really-understand-rfra-in-indiana-and-arkansas/

53   Ibid.

54   "Raft of states drafting religious opt-out bills that critics call discriminatory", *Washington Post*, February 9, 2017, P A16. Oklahoma and South Dakota have introduced similar bills and North Dakota, Virginia and Michigan, already have such laws in place. Ibid.

55   Ibid.

that their racially discriminatory policies were based on their religious beliefs" and therefore the government could not require them to admit people of color to their schools. The Supreme Court denied the argument but the Regan administration defended the case up to the Supreme Court. Chuck Cooper was Regan's lawyer that argued this case in support of discrimination. As I write this edition, President Trump is appointing Mr. Cooper to a senior position at the Justice Department

INTERNATIONAL RECOGNITION

Internationally, twenty-one other countries recognized marriage equality before the United States, including Argentina, Belgium, Brazil, Canada, Denmark, Estonia, Finland, France, Iceland, Ireland, Luxembourg, Netherlands, New Zealand, Norway, Portugal, Slovenia, South Africa, Spain, Sweden, and Uruguay.[56] Even conservative Chile, which did not legalize divorce until 2004, recognized civil unions in the country and gay marriages from outside of it, in April, two months before the U.S.[57]

MARCH 2013 U.S. SUPREME COURT HEARINGS

In back-to-back hearings, the Supreme Court of the United States reviewed the issue of same-sex marriage in spring 2013. Two different challenges—one to a state law overridden by voter referendum and the second to the Federal DOMA law—gave the Court the opportunity to decide if same-sex marriage is a civil right.

1. CHALLENGE TO STATE LAW—"PROP 8"—*HOLLINGSWORTH V. PERRY*

The first case, *Hollingsworth v. Perry*, involved a challenge to California's Proposition 8, a voter referendum that voted to overturn a California Supreme Court ruling that declared the right to marry for same-sex couples. Under Proposition 8, marriage was defined as between a man and woman and it passed by a narrow margin of 52 percent of the vote.

KNOW THE PLAINTIFFS

Jeff Zarrillo and Paul Katami of Burbank, California, were one of the same-sex couples who challenged the state's law against same-sex marriage.[58] At the time of the case, the couple lived together with their French bulldogs and had been together for 12 years (they wanted children,

---

56   https://www.washingtonpost.com/graphics/world/gay-rights/
57   "The World at a Glance", *The Week*, April 24, 2015.
58   Kris Perry and Sandy Stier from the San Francisco area are also named in the suit; they are raising four sons, p. 17, *Washington Post*, March 10, 2013. "Pair's Prop 8 Challenge heads to Supreme Court,", p. 1,

but only after they were married).[59] "Zarrillo is a 'Jersey boy' raised in the township of Brick and a graduate of Montclair State University. He was a movie theater manager, having worked at movie theaters since his college days. Katami, from San Francisco, has a master's of fine arts from UCLA and was fitness trainer. At the time of the case, the couple 'would [have] like[d] to get married. Proposition 8 [said] they may not.'"[60] "'They are a real couple... They live in a house in the suburbs, with kids going by on skateboards and playing catch in the front yard, and they've got their two dogs and they go to work. It's so remarkably normal in a way.'"[61] "[H]ow could somebody be afraid of people like me and Jeff?" Katami asked.[62]

MEET THE LAWYERS

Perhaps gaining even more attention than the plaintiffs (and various defendants) were the attorneys, Ted Olson and David Boies. The two first made national attention when they represented opposing sides in *Bush v. Gore*, effectively deciding the presidential election. Ted Olson had been President George W. Bush's[63] solicitor general when he argued the government's cases at the U.S. Supreme Court. In a twist, Olsen was working with a group that wanted the Supreme Court's ruling to extend beyond the legality of Prop 8 to establish the constitutionality of the fundamental right to marriage as applied to all same-sex couples in all states. In cases like these, with the potential to challenge landmark issues, the lawyers carefully choose the lead plaintiffs. "We talked to quite a few couples," said Theodore Boutros, a partner of Olson's in Los Angeles. He said the discussions were extensive. "We wanted them to know that we expected this to be a major case for marriage equality... and that we were trying to change the public dialogue and that they would really be in the public eye."[64]

THE CASE

California's history on same-sex marriage is a somewhat tortured one. Like many states in 2000, California's voters passed Proposition 22, which restricted marriages to between a man and a woman. As discussed above, Mayor Gavin Newsom probably jump-started the political review of the issue in 2004 when he unilaterally allowed the city of San Francisco to issue marriage licenses in violation of the state's prohibition. Later, when the California legislature

---

59   *Washington Post*, March 10, 2013. "Pair's Prop 8 Challenge heads to Supreme Court."
60   Ibid.
61   *Washington Post*, March 10, 2013, "Pair's Prop 8 Challenge heads to Supreme Court," quoting Adam Umhoefer, executive director of the American Foundation for Equal rights. The group organized to challenge Prop. 8, p. 17.
62   *Washington Post*, March 10, 2013. "Pair's Prop 8 Challenge heads to Supreme Court."
63   Bush had proposed the federal constitutional amendment to bar same-sex marriage.
64   "[L]egitimate justifications for traditional marriage are long-established, even if sometimes forgotten or deemed old-fashioned." *Washington Post*, March 10, 2013. "Pair's Prop 8 Challenge heads to Supreme Court."

passed bills[65] that allowed same-sex marriage status in the state, they were vetoed by Governor Arnold Schwarzenegger in 2005 and 2007.[66] In the second veto, the governor threw down the gauntlet to the state's supreme court to change the law under Proposition 22.[67]

In May 2008, in *In re Marriage Cases*, the California Supreme Court held that the state's current law limiting marriage to opposite-sex applicants violated the California constitution. On June 16, 2008, California began granting marriage licenses to same-sex couples who were now able to marry in the state. Opponents of same-sex marriage then worked to get the issue on California's ballot referendum as Proposition 8 (Prop 8)[68] to allow the state's voters to decide if they wanted to have same-sex marriage or not. In November 2008, the same year California overwhelmingly voted for the first black president, Barack Obama,[69] it also passed Proposition 8, which restricted marriage to a man and a woman. As of that date, California stopped issuing marriage licenses to same-sex couples. Many lawsuits were filed against Prop 8. In *Strauss v. Horton* (2009), California's highest appellate court deemed Proposition 8 valid. What would become of those same-sex marriages that had been performed while it was legal, and then not? In *Strauss*, the court held that the marriages, which occurred before Prop 8 passed, were valid. Thus, some same-sex couples were legally married by a state that did not allow same-sex marriage.

"Respondents, same-sex couples who wish to marry, filed suit in federal court, challenging Proposition 8 under the Due Process and Equal Protection Clauses of the Fourteenth Amendment, and naming as defendants California's Governor and other state and local officials responsible for enforcing California's marriage laws,"[70] Governor Schwarzenegger's attorney general, Jerry Brown, said Prop 8 was unconstitutional and refused to defend it. "[S]o the District Court allowed petitioners—the initiative's official proponents—to intervene to defend it. After a bench trial, the court declared Proposition 8 unconstitutional and enjoined the [state through its] public officials named as defendants from enforcing the law."[71] When Brown succeeded Schwarzenegger as governor,[72] he

---

65 "The 2007 vetoed measure, AB43, was the third try by Assemblyman Mark Leno… to create a gender-neutral marriage bill. The act would have amended state law to define marriage as a civil contract between two persons… Leno said the governor missed a "lifetime opportunity to show extraordinary leadership and be a real-life action hero." http://www.sfgate.com/bayarea/article/Schwarzenegger-vetoes-same-sex-marriage-bill-again-2497886.php, "Schwarzenegger vetoes same-sex marriage bill again," Jill Tucker, *Chronicle*.

66 Ibid.

67 Governor Schwarzenegger also challenged the voters to do so under a ballot. Ibid.

68 It is relatively easy to get a proposition on the ballot in California; it just needs the support of as few as 5% of the voters. In 2015, however, the California courts relieved the then Attorney General, now U.S. Senator, Kamala Harris, of the obligation to process a ballot initiative that "advocated killing anyone who engages in sex with a person of the same gender" in the so-called Sodomite Suppression Act, submitted by a California lawyer. "Judge allows rejection of anti-gay ballot measure", *Washington Post*, June 25, 2015, p. A3.

69 Obama has evolved his position while serving two terms as president, from supporting civil unions to being the first sitting president to affirmatively support same-sex marriage.

70 *Hollingsworth v Perry* 570 U.S.—(2013)

71 Ibid.

72 Edmund Gerald "Jerry" Brown, Jr.'s political career is legend, having been elected as California's 34th governor from 1975 to 1983, then elected attorney general from 2007 to 2011, and then reelected as the current, and 39th governor.

upheld his campaign promises and again refused to defend the case of *Perry v. Brown*[73]. The proponents of Prop 8, however, wanted to defend its invalidation and asked "the California Supreme Court whether official proponents of a ballot initiative have authority to assert the State's interest in defending the constitutionality of the initiative when public officials refuse to do so?"[74] When the California Supreme Court held that they did have standing, the Ninth Circuit Court of Appeals concluded that petitioners had standing under federal law to defend Proposition 8's constitutionality. After all that work, however, it did not go well, because the Court of Appeals affirmed the District Court's order[75] in which Judge Vaughn R. Walker in August 2010 struck down "Proposition 8." Thus, California again began issuing marriage licenses to same-sex couples when it was, again, legal in the state.

The Ninth Circuit's three-judge appellate panel ruled that Prop 8 was unconstitutional because ballots that allow the people to vote to amend the state's constitution (affecting constitutional rights) were unconstitutional (agreeing with the 9th Circuit, but in a more limited opinion). With the state unwilling to appeal that decision, supporters of Prop 8 filed a writ of certiorari with the U.S. Supreme Court, which was accepted and the case was heard on March 26, 2013. On June 26, 2013, when the U.S Supreme Court decided the case in *Hollingsworth v. Perry* 570 U.S. ___(2013), it followed precedent and ruled that the state of California had standing (the right to bring the case) and when it failed to do so, the sponsors of the Prop 8 ballot did not have the right to appeal an adverse ruling on it. There was no pronouncement by the Supreme Court on the legality of marriage equality.

2. THE DOMA CASE—*U.S. V. WINDSOR*

The second 2013 case the U.S. Supreme Court used to examine the issue of marriage equality involved a challenge to the 1996 DOMA[69] in *U.S. v. Windsor*. Edith Windsor, a former college math major who became one of the first, and few, female IBM computer programmers, and Thea Spyer, a psychologist, lived together as a couple for over 40 years[70] in New York (which did not allow same-sex marriages at the time) and were married in Ontario, Canada, in 2007 (which legalized same-sex marriages in 2005). When Spyer died in 2009, she left her large estate to Windsor who was required to pay $363,053 in inheritance taxes to the Internal Revenue Service. Had they been a heterosexual couple, Windsor would not have had to pay a dime as spouses inherit from each other tax-free. As Windsor quipped, "'If Thea was Theo, I would not have had to pay' those taxes."[76] In her case, her attorneys argued that she too should not have to pay the tax, as she was a "surviving spouse." Under section 3 of DOMA, however, the federal government limited the term "spouse" to marriages between a man and woman.[77] The I.R.S. rejected her argument and ordered payment of the estate taxes, which she paid.

---

73   The case was initially named *Perry v. Schwarzenegger*, who was California's governor at the time of the filing.
74   *Hollingsworth v Perry* 570 U.S.—(2013)
75   Ibid.
76   Ibid.
77   DOMA barred federal recognition of same-sex married couples and therefore denied them benefits (including tax benefits) even though at the time of *Windsor*, there were nine states where same-sex marriage was legal.

On November 9, 2010, Windsor filed a lawsuit against the federal government in the U.S. District Court for the Southern District of New York, and sought a refund because DOMA singled out legally married same-sex couples for "differential treatment compared to other similarly situated couples without justification."[5] Much like the Prop 8 cases, U.S. Attorney General Eric Holder believed DOMA was unconstitutional and refused to defend DOMA's section 3 on behalf of the Obama administration. Also, as in Prop 8, another group (BLAG[78]), stepped up to defend the law. On June 6, 2012, Judge Barbara S. Jones ruled that Section 3 of DOMA was unconstitutional under the due process guarantees of the Fifth Amendment and ordered the federal government to refund Windsor's inheritance tax payment. The U.S. Second Circuit Court of Appeals affirmed that decision on appeal[79]

BLAG then filed a writ of certiorari to the U.S. Supreme Court, which looked at the issue of whether Section 3 of DOMA violated the Fifth Amendment's guarantee of equal protection for same-sex partners? In their arguments, Windsor's attorneys reminded the court that marriage was an issue left to the state and that Windsor and Spyer's marriage was valid in New York (which recognized other jurisdiction's valid same-sex marriages even though it did not allow same-sex marriage in the state). Windsor's attorneys argued that for the federal government under DOMA to refuse to recognize a state recognized marriage it amounted to "second-class citizenship, or at least second-class marriages, that the Equal Protection Clause of the Constitution forbids."[80] Among the arguments for the defenders of DOMA was one raised in *Hollingsworth*, that "'the core purpose and defining characteristic of the institution of marriage always has been the creation of a social structure to deal with the inherently procreative nature of the male-female relationship.' This inherent difference between same-sex and opposite-sex couples is just one of the rational justifications for their unequal treatment under federal law."[81] On June 26, 2013, in a 5–4 decision, the Supreme Court struck down Section 3 of DOMA as unconstitutional, "as a deprivation of the liberty of the person protected by the Fifth Amendment." Again, Justice Anthony Kennedy writing for the majority, wrote that to treat state approved marriages differently between heterosexuals and same-sex couples, "demean[ed] the couple, whose moral and sexual choices the Constitution protects."[82]

---

78   The U.S. House of Representative's Republican leadership hired former President George W. Bush's Solicitor General Paul Clement to defend DOMA through the Bipartisan Legal Advisory Group (BLAG). This caused the Court to decide whether Congress had standing to defend DOMA (where in *the Hollingsworth case*, the court decided the case based on a lack of standing) to bring the case before reviewing the DOMA arguments. Unlike *Hollingsworth*, however, the Obama administration agreed with Congress that it did have standing, so the Supreme Court had to appoint a private lawyer to argue that Congress does not.

79   The U.S. Second Circuit Court of Appeals unanimously affirmed the decision on October 18, 2012.

80   "DOMA Challenge Tests Federal Definition of Marriage", Nina Totenberg, *NPR*, March 26, 2013. http://www.npr.org/2013/03/27/175295410/doma-challenge-tests-federal-definition-of-marriage

81   Ibid.

82   Before the case was decided some, including this author, speculated that the liberal justices who thought that Justice Kennedy, the swing vote on many issues and the author of *Lawrence v. Texas*, would rule similarly in this case. After the arguments, he seemed to indicate that he had always felt that the case should not have been granted. He also said, "A democracy should not be dependent for its major decisions on what nine unelected people for a narrow legal background have to say." "High Court Could Take Cautious Path on Gay Marriage." Robert Barnes, *Washington Post*, March 25, 2013, p. A3. Others speculated that it "seem that the conservative members of the court, making a

3. A CONSTITUTIONAL RIGHT, *OBERGEFELL V. HODGES*

After the 2013 *Windsor* case, several cases were filed in the federal circuit appellate courts challenging state bans on gay marriage. The first three federal appellate courts to review those cases interpreted *Windsor* as indicating that such bans were unconstitutional and marriage bans were voided from Virginia to Utah allowing gay couples to legally marry in 37 states, plus D.C.[83,84] By the fall of 2014, over 30 states had petitioned the Supreme Court to decide whether there was a constitutional right for same-sex couples to marry. But on March 5, 2015, the justices declined to take up those cases. This caused some to speculate that the conservative justices were worried that the battle to stop such marriages was lost. Certainly with thousands of couples getting married under these court rulings, it would make it difficult to void these marriages should the Supreme Court decide to rule against them. Others wondered if the court just wanted to take "incremental steps" in allowing the law to work through the states.[85] A month later, on November 6, 2014, the U.S. Court of Appeals for the 6th Circuit in Cincinnati, ruling 2 to 1,[86] upheld bans against gay marriage when it allowed the states of Kentucky, Michigan, Ohio, and Tennessee[87] to limit marriage to heterosexuals. Presented with a "split" in the decisions, the Supreme Court decided to review the issue by consolidating six cases from four states. On April 28, 2015, the U.S. Supreme Court heard two and one-half hours [88] of arguments in *Obergefell v. Hodges* which concentrated

---

calculation that their chances of winning would not improve with time, were behind the decision to take up the volatile subject?" So, given that it takes four votes to decide to take a case and five votes to decide it at the Supreme Court, "The 'aha' moment came after Justice Anthony M. Kennedy suggested that the court should dismiss the case. Justice Antonin Scalia tipped his hand. 'It's too late for that now, isn't it?' he said, a note of glee in his voice. 'We have crossed that river,' he said." "Justice Scalia, almost certainly joined by Justices Clarence Thomas and Samuel A. Alito Jr., apparently made a twofold calculation: that their odds of winning would not improve as same-sex marriage grows more popular and more commonplace, and that Justice Kennedy, who is likely to write the decision in the case concerning the 1996 law, would lock himself into rhetoric and logic that would compel him to vote for a constitutional right to same-sex marriage in a later case" leaving Chief Justice John G. Roberts Jr. as the deciding vote. http://www.nytimes. com/2013/03/30/us/supreme-courts-glimpse-at-thinking-on-same-sex-marriage.html?pagewanted=all&_r=0, Supreme Court Memo "Who Wanted to Take the Case on Gay Marriage? Ask Scalia," Adam Liptakfor, *New York Times*.

83   "More high-profile cases on high court's schedule", Robert Barnes, *Washington Post*, March 6, 2015, p. A3.

84   If the 5th Circuit rules soon that number could increase to 50 states from Florida to Alaska.

85   *"Move may reflect the court's preference for small steps"*, Robert Barnes, *The* Washington Post, October 7, 2014, p. A1.

86   Rejecting the other court's reliance on the *U.S. v. Windsor* case, it emphasized the "principle of democratic actions", encouraging change through the political process "in which the people, gay and straight alike, become the heroes of their own stories by meeting each other not as adversaries in a court system but as fellow citizens seeking to resolve a new social issue in a fair-minded way." In the dissenting opinions, Senior Judge Margaret Craig Daughtrey wrote that the majority opinion "would make an engrossing TED Talk, or possibly, and introductory lecture in Political Philosophy" but that it ignored the judge's obligation to protect the constitutional rights of minorities." "Panel Upholds bans on gay marriage, Robert Barnes, *The Washington Post*, November 7, 2014, A1.

87   While the other states involved the rights of same-sex couples to marry, the Ohio appeal focused on the undisturbed issue in the DOMA case, their refusal to recognize out-of-state same-sex marriages that are valid in the states that preformed them. "Same-sex marriage-Advocates decry inconsistent laws", *The Washington Post*, November 15, 2014, A3.

88   Indicating the importance of the decision, the Court made the unusual move and made the recorded legal arguments available to the public that same day.

on two issues: 1) whether states may limit marriage to the traditional definition of a man and a woman and 2) whether states must recognize valid same-sex marriages performed in other states.

The latter issue is based on two Ohio cases in which the state would not list a partner on a death certificate as a spouse, even though the couple was legally married in another state. In *Obergefell*, James Obergefell and John Arthur lived together for 22 years until John died of ALS disease. They decided to marry after the Supreme Court struck down DOMA in *Windsor* but because of John's deteriorating health, it took Herculean efforts (a medically equipped plane) to fly to Maryland to marry (because their home state of Ohio had not legalized gay marriage).

When John's health would not allow him to leave the plane, they were married on the airport tarmac. On return, Ohio indicated that it would not list Jim on John's death certificate as his surviving spouse. Because Ohio did not allow same-sex marriages and under DOMA's remaining provision, Ohio was not required to recognize another state's valid same-sex marriage. At Obergefell's request, on July 22, 2013, the federal court in Ohio granted a restraining order preventing Ohio from denying his status on John's death certificate and at John's death in October, his death certificate listed James as his surviving spouse.[89] Ohio appealed that ruling and it is one of the cases that raised the issue of whether a state is allowed to not recognize a valid same-sex marriage from another state (when generally states recognize valid marriages from other states) along with whether states can continue to refuse to issue marriage licenses to same-sex couples, thus barring their marriages.

In a 5 to 4 ruling the Supreme Court concluded that the dignity of marriage and the Constitution's 14th's Amendment's Due Process clause required that same-sex couples be allowed to marry in all states in *Obergefell v. Hodges*. 576 US _ (2015). Writing for the majority, Justice Kennedy said:

> In forming a marital union, two people become something greater than once they were. As some of the petitioners in these cases demonstrate, marriage embodies a love that may endure even past death. It would misunderstand these men and women to say they disrespected the idea of marriage. Their plea is that they do respect it, respect it so deeply that they seek to find its fulfillment for themselves. Their hope is not to be condemned to live in loneliness, excluded from one of civilization's oldest institutions. They ask for equal dignity in the eyes of the law. The Constitution grants them that right. The judgment of the Court of Appeals for the Sixth Circuit is reversed. It is so ordered.

An estimated 123,000 same-sex marriages have occurred since Justice Kennedy wrote those words for a total estimated one-half million same-sex marriages involving one million Americans[90].

---

89 "*Obergefell, et al. v. Hodges* - Freedom to Marry in Ohio," ACLU, March 17, 2015 https://www.aclu.org/lgbt-rights/obergefell-et-al-v-hodges-freedom-marry-ohio.

90 Based on a Gallup survey http://www.cbsnews.com/news/same-sex-marriages-us-supreme-court-ruling-estimate/

AS WE GO TO PRESS

In the same June 2015 week that the White House was bathed in a rainbow of colors for the Supreme Court's recognition of marriage equality, our nation watched South Carolina remove its Confederate flag, a symbol of slavery, and the Supreme Court voted to keep the Affordable Care Act. Yet, only three months before, then Governor of Indiana, now Vice President, Mike Pence signed Indiana's broad "religious freedom law" that allows businesses to turn away gay and lesbian customers[91] and in June, a California lawyer obtained enough voter's signatures to propose a ballot initiative that "advocated killing anyone who engages in sex with a person of the same gender."[92] The Obergefell decision does not protect LGBTQ Americans from job discrimination, allow them to adopt their children, or even find a bathroom. So where will we go from here?

CHAPTER SOURCE

Wadlington, W., and O'Brian, R.C. *Domestic Relations Cases and Materials*, 6th ed. (2007). Foundation Press.

---

91   http://www.cnn.com/2015/03/25/politics/mike-pence-religious-freedom-bill-gay-rights/
92   "Judge allows rejection of anti-gay ballot measure", *Washington Post*, June 25, 2015, p. A3.

7

COURTSHIP

He is the cheese to my macaroni[1]
—Juno MacGuff in *Juno*

A gift given by a man to a woman on condition that she embark on the sea of matrimony with him is not different from a gift based on the condition that the donee sail on any other sea. If, after receiving the provisional gift, the donee refuses to leave the harbor—if the anchor of contractual performance sticks in the sands of irresolution and procrastination—the gift must be restored to the donor.
—Justice Musmanno in *Pavlicic v. Vogtsberger*, 136 A.2d 127, 130 (Pa. 1957).

A multi-millionaire like Kim Kardashian is not hurting for money, so why did she refuse to give back her reported $2-million "rectangular diamond weighing approximately 16.21 carats, flanked on either side by trapeze-cut diamonds each weighing 1.80 carats, set in platinum"[2] engagement ring when she filed to divorce her first husband, Kris Humphries? Was it determined by a pre-nuptial agreement? Or is there a state law to determine the issue of who gets the diamond engagement ring when couples break it off?[3]

---

1 Juno MacGuff (played by Ellen Page), the movie "Juno" 2007 directed by Jason Reitman and written by Diablo Cody 2007. "Time" called it the "Juno Effect" when in 2008 17 high school students in Massachusetts became pregnant. "Pregnancy Boom at Gloucester High", Kathleen Kingsbury, *Time*, June 18, 2008. content.time.com/time/magazine/article/0,9171,1816486,00.html

2 According to a Christie's Auction House website. "Kim Kardashian's Engagement Ring from Kris Humphries Sells at Auction", Jessica Derschowitz, *CBS News*, October 15, 2013. http://www.cbsnews.com/news/kim-kardashians-engagement-ring-from-kris-humphries-sells-at-auction/

3 http://www.huffingtonpost.com/2012/11/30/kim-kardashian-kris-humph_n_2219637.html#slide=1771030, Kim "Kardashian, Kris Humphries: Engagement Ring Causing Drama in Divorce," November 30, 2012.

BREACH OF THE PROMISE TO MARRY

It is an age-old ritual to court, to romance, to woo. The mating ritual is universal to all animals, including humans.[4] So, when two people get engaged, should a person be able to sue when the partner breaks off the wedding?

In the ancient case of *Wrightman v. Coates*, 15 MA 1, 8 Am. Dec. 77 (1818), the Massachusetts Supreme Court looked at this issue and agreed that the woman could sue her fiancé, especially "when one of the parties wantonly and capriciously refuses to execute the contract" of marriage.[5] Beyond the breaking of the engagement, the facts are irrelevant. The court writes in the flowery language of old that there is "no more suitable grounds of application to the tribunals of justice for compensation, than that of a violated promise to enter into a contract, on the faithful performance of which the interest of all civilized country so essentially depends."[6] "A deserted female, whose prospects in life may be materially affected by the treachery of the man to whom she has plighted her vows, will always receive from a jury the attention which her situation requires."[7]

Surely, in 1818, it was not in the public's interest for engaged couples to call off a wedding, especially because marriage at that time was, in effect, a woman's job. Early-19th-century author Jane Austen reminds us that without the opportunity for real employment, a woman hoped to marry, and especially to "marry up." While private ordering is not part of the social fabric, the court is still willing to jump in and clear up an arrangement made by consenting adults. These ancient cases involve stereotypes of damsels in distress and villainous fiancés, but what would the results be today?

If courts treat a promise to marry like any other contract, then these promises are similar to commercial contracts. It is the court's responsibility to enforce contracts and when it does so in a commercial context, damages often include specific performance—e.g., forcing the person to buy the car. Surely, the courts would not intend such a remedy for breaching the promise to marry—they would not force someone to marry when they have decided not to marry.

In *Miller v. Ratner*, 114 MD. App. 18, 688 A.2d 976 (1997), the Maryland Court of Special Appeals looked at this issue for the first time in over 50 years. The court traced Maryland's history on breaches of promises to marry that existed at common law, but were abolished by the state in 1945. As a result, the appellate court affirmed the circuit court's granting of summary judgment to the defendant to dismiss the case.

---

4 In 2015, Mandy Len Catron's essay "To Fall in Love With Anyone, Do This" appearing in *Modern Love* "told how to find love" by replicating a 20-year old-experiment by psychologist Arthur Aron where two strangers "asked each other 36 increasingly personal questions followed by a four-minute staring session to see if doing so would lead to intimacy and love. Afterward over 8 million people worldwide." "The 36 Questions: An Answer to their Prayers?" Daniel Jones, *The New York Times Modern Love*", February 15, 2015, P.6. Worldwide tried the test.

5 *Domestic Relations*, 6th ed. Wadlington and O'Brien, p. 180.

6 Ibid.

7 Ibid.

For purposes of the motion, the court presumed the plaintiff/appellant's facts as true, including some "allegations of atrocious conduct." "Ms. Miller, and appellee, William Ratner, began to live together, apparently at his request. Appellant, at his request, substantially altered her lifestyle. After living with appellee for approximately three years, appellant became seriously ill with breast cancer. He initially supported her, but later rejected her and ordered her to leave his house. She refused." "She alleges that, while she was ill from undergoing radiation treatments, Warren repeatedly woke her up in the middle of the night admonishing her to leave. She alleges that Warren's brother Dennis, also an appellee, telephoned her during the same period, calling her a "bitch, whore, and a one-breasted woman." He told her that his brother "deserves a whole woman, not a one breasted woman." Eventually, she moved out and sued.

The appellate court looked at many issues from the case, including the question of whether the contract she and Ratner entered into was a contract to marry. The court began by looking at the plaintiff's complaint, which asserted: "There was a mutual understanding that the defendant and plaintiff were making a permanent commitment that *would* be followed by marriage." "The plaintiff relied upon the defendant's *promises* and moved into what the defendant referred to as 'our home'... *In anticipation of their marriage*, the defendant told [her] that he had 'plenty of money' and that he would take care of her.'" (Court's emphasis retained.) A later scheduling conference statement filed by plaintiff alleged, in part, that she and appellee Warren Ratner "were engaged to be married."

In declining to allow the plaintiff's case for breach of promise to marry, the court writes,

> Although I have sympathy for Ms. Miller [appellant], I fail to see how the Court would uphold this contract as enforceable when we do have a statutory scheme that is outlined in detail for married partners upon the dissolution of marriage, *why this plaintiff would be able to come into court as an unmarried person and enforce this contract when it was never considered by the legislature to be valid.*[8]

As part of its opinion, the court traces Maryland's history of the breach of promise to marry claim.

---

8   The court then looked at the plaintiff's claim for intentional infliction of emotional distress by the appellee's alleged outrageous behavior and denied that, too. The court wrote, "As far as the intentional infliction of mental distress, I have reviewed the cases. I have looked at all the labor dispute ones, and I would agree with [appellee's attorney] that every relationship that breaks up has emotional distress, but I do not believe that our Court of Appeals at this time is willing to, under these facts, uphold a cause of action for intentional infliction of mental distress".

Affirmed...

*978 CATHELL, Judge.

In 1945, the Legislature abolished the cause of action for breach of promise to marry. In the fifty-one years since, there has been no Maryland reported case in which the abolishment of that cause of action has been at issue. This, then, shall be the first.

In the Circuit Court for Montgomery County, Judge Martha G. Kavanaugh granted Warren Ratner's and Dennis Ratner's,[FN1] appellees, motions for summary judgment against Lonnie Miller, appellant. In the posture of this case, we must presume the accuracy of all factual allegations made by appellant, the party against whom the motion was granted. Accordingly, we shall recount some of the factual matters presented to the trial judge as if true, with the realization that their truthfulness has not been litigated. Our discussion may, therefore, include some of appellant's allegations of atrocious conduct on the part of appellees. While, as we have said, for the purpose of this appeal, we shall presume them to be true, we will be relying on just that presumption, not proven facts.

Ms. Miller and appellee, Warren Ratner, began to live together, apparently at his request. Appellant, at his request, substantially altered her lifestyle. After living with appellee for approximately three years, appellant became seriously ill with breast cancer. He initially supported her, but later rejected her and ordered her to leave his house. She refused. *22 She alleges that Warren, and his brother Dennis, then conspired to inflict emotional distress upon her in order to cause her to vacate Warren Ratner's house (and his life).

She alleges that, while she was ill from undergoing radiation treatments, Warren repeatedly woke her up in the middle of the night admonishing her to leave. She alleges that Warren's brother Dennis, also an appellee, telephoned her during the same period, calling her "bitch," "whore," and a "one-breasted woman." He told her that his brother "deserves a whole woman, not a one breasted woman." He told Ms. Miller on at least one occasion, "fuck you." She further alleges that Warren repeatedly told her she was a financial burden and that she was going to die. She proffered that Warren threatened her with bodily harm if she did not leave his house and told her that if she did not voluntarily vacate his house, he would have her put out by the "Woodridge boys."

Eventually, she moved out. Thereafter, she obtained a job with Universal Debit Credit. She alleges, even then, that appellees "continued to torment her" by causing her not to get the business of The Hair Cuttery, an entity owned by appellees or by a corporation evidently controlled by them. She also alleges that Warren filed a false claim in the bankruptcy proceedings she ultimately was forced to file.

Appellant presents twelve questions:

1. Was the contract Plaintiff and Defendant Warren Ratner entered into a contract to marry?
2. Was illicit sexual intercourse consideration for the contract the Plaintiff and Defendant Warren Ratner entered into?
3. Was Defendant Warren Ratner acting adversely to Creative Hairdressers, Inc. or within the scope of his authority when he interfered with the Plaintiff's prospective advantage?
4. Was Defendant Warren Ratner's conduct toward the Plaintiff intentional or reckless?
5. Was Defendant Warren Ratner's conduct toward the Plaintiff extreme and outrageous?
6. *23 Was there a causal connection between Defendant Warren Ratner's wrongful conduct and the Plaintiff's emotional distress?
7. Did the Plaintiff suffer severe emotional distress due to Defendant Warren Ratner's conduct?
8. Did Defendant Warren Ratner conspire with Defendant Dennis Ratner to commit an unlawful act?
9. **979 Was Defendant Dennis Ratner's conduct toward the Plaintiff intentional or reckless?
10. Was Defendant Dennis Ratner's conduct toward the Plaintiff extreme and outrageous?
11. Was there a causal connection between Defendant Dennis Ratner's wrongful conduct and the Plaintiff's emotional distress?
12. Did the Plaintiff suffer severe emotional distress due to Defendant Dennis Ratner's conduct?

We shall respond only to those questions necessary to our resolution of the main issues.

We begin by examining appellant's Complaint and amended complaints. The original complaint provided in paragraph four that Warren Ratner asked her to move in with him. In paragraphs five and six, appellant asserted that:

5.... *There was a mutual understanding that the defendant and the plaintiff were making a permanent commitment that would be followed by marriage.*

6. *The plaintiff relied upon the defendant's promises and moved into what the defendant referred to as "our home...." In anticipation of their marriage, the defendant told [her] that he had "plenty of money" and that he would take care of her.* [Emphasis added.]

In Count I of the original complaint, Breach of Contract, the foregoing provisions were incorporated "as if they were fully repeated and set forth again" therein. They were also, likewise, incorporated in Count II, Tortious Interference with Prospective Advantage, and Count III, Intentional Infliction of Emotional Distress. Thereafter, appellant filed a Scheduling *24 Conference Statement, in which she alleged, in part, that she and appellee Warren Ratner "were engaged to be married."

Subsequently, an Amended Complaint was filed. In that amended complaint appellant reiterated:

> 5. . . . *There was a mutual understanding that the defendant and the plaintiff were making a permanent commitment that would be followed by marriage.*
>
> 6. *The plaintiff relied upon the defendant's promises and moved. . . . In anticipation of their marriage, the defendant told the plaintiff. . . that he would take care of her.* [Emphasis added.]

Again, appellant incorporated those statements into each of her counts, stating, as she did in the original complaint, that the allegations were incorporated "as if they were fully repeated and set forth again herein."

Thereafter, appellant filed a Second Amended Complaint. That complaint added an Intentional Infliction of Emotional Distress count, in which appellant incorporated, "as if fully set forth herein, the entire Amended Complaint," thereby adding the above statements about marriage promises to that new count. (Emphasis added.) Subsequently, appellant filed a Third Amended Complaint that added a civil conspiracy count. In it, she again incorporated "as if fully set forth herein, the entire amended complaint and Second Amended Complaint," thereby incorporating into the civil conspiracy count the marriage promises we have above quoted. (Emphasis added.)

Warren Ratner filed a Motion for Summary Judgment as to Counts I, II, III, and IV of the Third Amended Complaint. Count I was the Breach of Contract count against Warren, Count II was the Tortious Interference with Prospective Advantage count against Warren, and Count III was the Intentional Infliction of Emotional Distress count against Warren. Count IV alleged a civil conspiracy by both Warren and Dennis Ratner to "inflict" severe emotional distress on Ms. Miller.

In Warren Ratner's motion, his counsel argued that appellant's "claims" were, in substance, claims for breach of promise*25 to marry and that these were barred under the law of Maryland; that her breach of contract claim was not actionable "because it [was] based on consideration for illicit sexual intercourse;" and that appellant was precluded from maintaining a claim for intentional infliction of emotional distress because she had not suffered a severely disabling injury from appellees' conduct. Warren Ratner also disclaimed **980 liability for tortious interference with prospective advantage as a matter of law.

Dennis Ratner also filed a Motion for Summary Judgment on his behalf as to the counts against him. He incorporated Warren's position and arguments and further expounded upon them as deemed necessary.

Ultimately, the trial judge granted both motions for summary judgments. She opined:

Although I have sympathy for Ms. Miller [appellant], I fail to see how the Court would uphold this contract as enforceable when we do have a statutory scheme that is outlined in detail for married partners upon the dissolution of marriage, why this plaintiff would be able to come into court as an unmarried person and enforce this contract when it was never considered by the legislature to be valid.

As far as the intentional infliction of mental distress, I have reviewed the cases. I have looked at all the labor dispute ones, and I would agree with Mr. Brault [counsel for Warren Ratner] that every relationship that breaks up has emotional distress, but I do not believe that our Court of Appeals at this time is willing to, under these facts, uphold a cause of action for intentional infliction of mental distress.

I think allowing this lawsuit to go forward would open the floodgates, and I am not willing at this point to make this public policy.

So, for that reason, I am going to grant summary judgment motions on all counts. *[Emphasis added.]*

While the trial court's comment can be construed to be a comment on the "palimony" issue, its comments, especially the comment as to an unmarried person enforcing a contract *26 "never considered by the legislature to be valid" can be equally construed to be applicable to the law enacted by the Legislature in 1945 that then declared such contracts "absolutely void."

We shall affirm the trial court's grant of summary judgment in favor of appellees…

We note again that if appellant's representations are accurate and true, the actions and words of appellees were at the least reprehensible. Appellant's representations, however, may not be accurate. Because of the posture of the case, our function is to determine whether the trial court erred in granting summary judgment even if it, and we, assume appellant's representations as to appellees' conduct are true. In other words, if such vile conduct did occur, is it actionable. Can appellees be sued for it?

We shall break down our consideration of the case to (1) appellees' assertions that this is really a case for breach of promise to marry, especially as to those counts that traditionally would constitute that type of cause of action or inferentially could, and (2) if necessary, to appellees' assertion that whatever counts are not directly resolvable by the application of the Maryland bar against suits for a breach of promise to marry are otherwise unmaintainable under the circumstances here present. We look first to the statute that prohibits *28 actions for a breach of promise to marry and the Legislature's purpose in enacting it.

The common-law causes of action for breach of promise to marry and for alienation of affections were first abolished in this State in 1945 by the enactment of Chapter 1010, House Bill 341. The prohibitions as to both causes of action have been codified together throughout all of the subsequent statutory history. The original act included an express statement of public policy that was included in the first several reenactments, but not specifically included, although acknowledged, in later codifications. We include that original declaration of policy here in order to emphasize the importance that the General Assembly attached to the abolition of these causes of action.

PROHIBITED ACTIONS

1. (Declaration of Public Policy of State.) The remedies heretofore provided by law for the enforcement of actions based upon alleged alienation of affections and alleged breach of promise to marry, having been subjected to grave abuses, causing extreme annoyance, embarrassment, humiliation and pecuniary damage to many persons wholly innocent and free of any wrongdoing, who were merely the victims of circumstances and such remedies having been exercised by unscrupulous persons for their unjust enrichment, and such remedies having furnished vehicles for the commission or attempted commission of crime and in many cases having resulted in the perpetration of frauds, it is hereby declared as the public policy of the State that the best interests of the people of the State will be served by the abolition of such remedies.[FN2]

FN2. During the same general period, several states also abolished both causes of action. They include Florida, New York, Pennsylvania, Alabama, California (perhaps), Indiana, Massachusetts, Michigan, New Hampshire, New Jersey, North Carolina, Colorado (perhaps), Maine, Nevada, Wyoming. (Some of the states have special provisions, sometimes case created, permitting suits to recover engagement rings and other property transferred to the other party.) Consistent with the statement of policy by the Maryland Legislature are comments by other state courts as to those states' public policy. The Supreme Court of Florida stated:

> [T]he legislature… [may] regulate… any right growing out of [the marriage] relation…. Perhaps the strongest argument in support of the act [the Florida statute prohibiting breach of promise suits] is that perverted sexual relations are often found lurking in these cases, and when it comes to measuring perverted chastity in terms of "heart balm", society has not yet set up a standard as it has with peanuts and popcorn and other tangibles….

> … [W]hen they [breach of promise actions] became an instrument of extortion and blackmail, the legislature… may… abolish them.

Rotwein v. Gersten, 160 Fla. 736, 36 So.2d 419, 421 (1948). The Court of Appeals of New York opined: "… [W]e view the marriage engagement as a period of probation, so to speak and if that probation results in… incompatibility of tastes and temperament… and incurable repugnance of one to the other… duty requires that the match be broken off…."

Thoughtful people… have long realized that the scandals growing out of actions to recover damages for breach of promise to marry constituted a reflection upon the courts and a menace to the marriage institution, and thereby a danger to the state….

Because experience has demonstrated that the maintenance of [such] actions… have resulted in injury to the marriage institution and thereby interfered with the general welfare, the Legislature, in order to correct the evil… had authority to abolish the cause of action….

The Legislature... has determined... that marriages should not be entered into because of the threat or danger of an action to recover money damages and the embarrassment and humiliation growing out of such an action.

Fearon v. Treanor, 272 N.Y. 268, 5 N.E.2d 815, 816–17 (1936).

In a number of states, the right of action for breach of promise to marry has been abolished by statute (commonly referred to as "heart balm" statutes).... It has been said that a state legislature has plenary power... to determine as a matter of public policy that marriages should not be entered into because of the danger or threat of an action for breach of promise. The purpose of such statutes is to avert the perpetuation of fraud by adventurers or adventureress [sic] who were prone to use the threat of a breach of promise of marriage action to compel over apprehensive and naive defendants to make lucrative settlements in order to avoid the embarrassing and lurid notoriety which accompanied litigation of this character.

12 Am.Jur. 2d Breach of Promise § 18 (1964) (footnotes omitted).

**982 *29 1945 Md. Laws, Chap. 1010; Md.Code (1951), Art. 75C, § 1; Md.Code (1957), Art. 75C, § 1.

*30 We suspect that we would be hard pressed to find a stronger expression of a legislative entity's attitude of repugnance towards a cause of action in statutory language. Moreover, the legislature attempted to make sure that the causes of actions therein abolished could not thereafter be incidentally recreated or resurrected by subsequent act. It provided what we perceive to be an attempt to foreclose waiver and estoppel issues by limiting, perhaps us, and perhaps even itself, from undoing the effects of the legislation when it included a provision we do not recall seeing with any great frequency in other legislative acts. Chapter 1010 provided:

> 4. *(Legal Effect of Certain Acts Hereafter Occurring.) No act hereafter done within this State shall operate to give rise, either within or without this State, to any of the rights of action abolished by this Article.*

The Act declared, in very broad language (perhaps even broad enough had it survived to this date to foreclose efforts to create "palimony" actions [FN3]), that certain contracts were void as against public policy:

> FN3. *The term "palimony" somehow arose out of* Marvin v. Marvin, 18 Cal.3d 660, 134 Cal.Rptr. 815, 557 P.2d 106 (1976), *although the term was never used in that case.*

All contracts and instruments of every kind, name, nature or description, which may hereafter be executed within this State in payment, satisfaction, settlement or compromise of any claim or cause of action abolished or barred by this Article, whether such claim or cause of action arose within or without this State, are hereby declared to be contrary to the public policy of this State and absolutely void. It shall be unlawful to cause, induce or procure any person to execute such a contract or instrument; or cause, induce or procure any person to give, pay, transfer or deliver any money or thing of value in payment, satisfaction, settlement or compromise of any such claim or cause of action;[FN4] or to *31 receive, take or accept any such money or thing of value as such payment, satisfaction, settlement or compromise. It shall be unlawful to commence or **983 cause to be commenced, either as party or attorney, or as agent or otherwise in behalf of either, in any court of this State, any proceeding or action seeking to enforce or recover upon any such contract or instrument, knowing it to be such, whether the same shall have been executed within or without this State; provided, however, that this action shall not apply to the payment, satisfaction, settlement or compromise of any causes of action which are not abolished or barred by this Article, or any contracts or instruments heretofore executed or to the bona fide holder in due course of any negotiable instrument which may be hereafter executed...

It then went even further by providing criminal penalties for violations of the Act:

> *7. (Penalties.) Any person who shall violate any of the provisions of this Article shall be guilty of a misdemeanor which shall be punishable by a fine of not less than One Thousand Dollars ($1,000) nor more than Five Thousand Dollars ($5,000), or by imprisonment for a term of not less than one (1) year not more than five (5) years, or by both such fine and imprisonment, in the discretion of the Court...*

We have included this rather extensive review of the predecessor statutes for two primary purposes: (1) to emphasize what we view as the extraordinarily strong statement of public policy that is evidenced by (i) the statement first found in the original enactment and repeated and/or reaffirmed since then, (ii) the initial effort by the General Assembly to forbid any future modifications (apparently by the judiciary) of its prohibitions, and

(iii) the creation of a criminal offense with severe criminal sanctions for those attempting to ignore the proscription, including attorneys—criminal sanctions that remained intact until recently; and (2) to emphasize that the prohibitions against both breach of promise to marry and alienation of affections actions were originally enacted together under the same strong public policy statement and criminal penalty sanctions, and have remained together, if not as twins as close siblings, throughout all of the rest of the history of the statute.

Accordingly, in our resolution of these issues, we shall remain cognizant of the strong statement of public policy and, until relatively recent times, the criminal character of attempts to circumvent the law. We shall also consider closely those cases involving alienation of affections, as we perceive them to be so closely related as to have strong precedential value in respect to breach of promise to marry cases.

*34 As we previously noted, in the fifty-one years since the statute prohibiting cases for breach of promise to marry was enacted, there has, apparently, been no reported Maryland case construing it.[FN7] As we shall indicate later, our finite review of foreign jurisdictions indicates that there has not been developed a substantial body of law elsewhere relating specifically to the application of statutory proscriptions to breach of promise to marry cases, although there are several cases we will address. Most of the limited foreign consideration, like Maryland's case-law treatment of this type of proscription, has been generally limited to cases involving the statutory prohibitions of alienation of affections actions and, to some extent, actions for criminal conversation. We shall rely for some guidance on the treatment of those causes of action given their close association with breach of promise to marry actions. We initially note that our late Chief Judge Gilbert briefly noted, as dicta, in the fraud case of *Collection & Investigation Bureau of Maryland, Inc. v. Linsley*, 37 Md.App. 66, 68, 375 A.2d 47 (1977), the historical origins of the bar to breach of promise actions. Speaking to the original enactment of the Statute of Frauds by the English Parliament during the reign of King Charles II, 1660–1688, Chief Judge Gilbert stated:

> FN7. *Counsel for the parties informed us that they had found none. We, too, have found none.*

Other provisions of § IV of the Statute [of Frauds] have been lifted from that act and are now codified in various articles of the Maryland Code annotated, or as in the case of suits for breach of promise barred as a cause of action, unless the plaintiff is pregnant. [Citing then section 5-301(a) of the Courts & Judicial Proceedings Article; footnote omitted.]

It appears that the bar has been a part of English jurisprudence since the 1600's. If so, Maryland's prohibition was somewhat belated.

The earliest mention in Maryland cases we have found of the statutory prohibition of breach of promise to marry and *35 alienation of affections suits occurred in the deceit case of *Babb v. Bolyard*, 194 Md. 603, 607–08, 72 A.2d 13 (1950), in which the Court of Appeals noted:

> *The common law of torts, like the Statute of Frauds, reflects the public policy that the cause of justice should not be thwarted by a pursuit of abstract justice which does more harm than good. The same public policy is embodied and expressed in Chapter 1010 of the Acts of 1945, which abolishes rights of action for breach of promise to marry and for alienation **985 of affections. By mention of this act we do not intimate that any provision of the act is or is not constitutional.* [Citation omitted.]

Another of the few early mentions of the statutory proscription at issue here was in the defamation and criminal conversation case of *Di Blasio v. Kolodner*, 233 Md. 512, 197 A.2d 245 (1964). In an earlier suit, Kolodner's client, Rezek, (Kolodner was an attorney) brought suit against Di Blasio alleging that Di Blasio had "debauched and carnally knew" the client's wife and had impregnated her. There were several counts in the original suit, all encompassed by the criminal conversation allegations. Di Blasio, in the original suit, moved for judgment on the ground that the criminal conversation action was really an alienation of affections action and that such actions had been abolished. Rezek asserted that it was a criminal conversation action, which had not been abolished. Subsequently, while the criminal conversation suit was pending, Di Blasio sued Rezek and Kolodner for libel based on their allegations against him in the original action.

The Court, in the second action, found it necessary to discuss the statute abolishing actions for alienation of affections and breach of promise to marry. The Court first discussed parts of the Legislature's public policy statement that we have heretofore recounted. It then noted that alienation of affections and criminal conversation are separate, though closely related, torts. Following the lead of the Supreme Court of Pennsylvania, and citing that court's cases, the Di Blasio Court held that the tort of criminal conversation had not been abolished. The Court, in doing so, and in *36 comparing the public policy statements of the Pennsylvania and Maryland statutes, noted that "our public policy is declared only as to the causes of action mentioned [breach of promise and alienation of affection]." The Court (albeit probably as dicta in that it was describing a statute it was holding did not apply to its case) then opined:

> We find no reason for holding that the General Assembly did not mean exactly what it said—no more and no less—with regard to the kinds of causes of action which it undertook to abolish. It will be observed that even as to one of such causes of action which it did undertake to abolish generally—breach of promise to marry—it carefully made an exception "in cases wherein pregnancy exists." Our Art. 75 C says nothing whatever about causes of action for criminal conversation, and we think that they are not abolished by it....

The Court of Appeals later abolished the tort of criminal conversation in Kline v. Ansell, 287 Md. 585, 414 A.2d 929 (1980). It noted the statutory prohibitions of Chapter 1010 of the Acts of 1945:

> An examination of the judicial and legislative history of this cause of action in Maryland shows that in 1945 the Legislature enacted chapter 1010, Laws of Maryland 1945, which abolished, among other things, the cause of action for alienation of affections. That action, which arose when a person induced a married woman to leave her husband or otherwise interfered with the marital relationship, even though no act of adultery was committed, was recognized long ago as separate and distinct from the action for criminal conversation. See Annarina v. Boland, 136 Md. 365, 374 [111 A. 84] (1920); Callis v. Merrieweather, 98 Md. 361, 363, 365 [57 A. 201] (1904). In 1964, this Court held that the Legislature, assumably aware of our decisions, Supervisor of Assessments v. Southgate Harbor, 279 Md. 586, 591–92 [369 A.2d 1053] (1977); Herbert v. Gray, 38 Md. 529, 532 (1873), did not abolish the separate and distinct action for *38 criminal conversation when it abolished the action for alienation of affections. Di[ ]Blasio v. Kolodner, 233 Md. 512, 520 [197 A.2d 245] (1964). In 1976, this Court recognized that the husband's action for criminal conversation was related to the State's special interest in the domestic relations of its citizens and remained viable. Geelhoed [v. Jensen],

277 Md. [220,] 233 [352 A.2d 818 (1976)]. As recently as 1977, the Legislature, again assumably aware of our decisions, rejected House Bill 170 which expressly provided that the action for criminal conversation be abolished. Journal of Proceedings of the Senate of Maryland, Regular Session 1977, pp. 3034, 3514; Journal of Proceedings of the House of Delegates of Maryland, Regular Session 1977, pp. 162, 2397, 290 (citations omitted).

The Kline Court, after noting the passage in 1977 of Article 46 of the Maryland Declaration of Rights, Maryland's "Equal Rights Amendment," commented that the action of criminal conversation could only be brought by and against men and therefore any "previous implicit approval by this Court... is eradicated." 287 Md. at 593, 414 A.2d 929. The Court then abolished the action.

In Kline, the Court there additionally opined as to the reasons for abolishing the action of criminal conversation. These reasons are similar to those given by several authorities for abolishing actions for breach of promise to marry and alienation of affections:

The action for criminal conversation is notorious for affording a fertile field for blackmail and extortion because it involves an accusation of sexual misbehavior. Criminal conversation actions may frequently be brought, not for the purpose of preserving the marital relationship, but rather for purely mercenary or vindictive motives. An award of damages does not constitute an effective deterrent to the act of adultery, and it does not effectively help to preserve or restore a marital relationship in which adultery has already occurred. Indeed, a contested trial may destroy a *39 chance to restore a meaningful relationship. In addition, this action, which eliminates all defenses except the husband's consent and which imposes liability without any regard to the quality of the marital relationship, is incompatible with today's sense of fairness. Most important, today's sense of the increasing personal and sexual freedom of women is incompatible with the rationale underlying this action. For all of these reasons, this **987 harsh cause of action has been considered to be unreasonable and anachronistic. (cites omitted)...

The more recent case of Figueiredo-Torres v. Nickel, 321 Md. 642, 584 A.2d 69 (1991), was one of the few cases in which the Court permitted an action similar to alienation of affections to be maintained, but only because of a professional relationship upon which the cause could be separately and independently grounded. It involved an action brought for professional negligence against a psychologist who had treated a husband and wife. The husband and wife alleged that Nickel, the psychologist, committed malpractice by advising the husband to be distant from and not to have sexual relations with his wife, while at the same time, Nickel was having sexual relationships with the woman. Nickel argued that the act he had committed was either criminal conversation or alienation of affections, or both and that these causes of action had been abolished in Maryland.[FN8] Nickel argued that the complaint against him was a mere "refitting of the abolished actions into other forms." Refusing to find the action to be prohibited, the Court of Appeals focused on the professional relationship of the parties that was independent *40 of Nickel's personal relationship with the wife. The Court noted:

> *FN8. Ms. Miller argues that cases involving alienation of affections have left the door open to other causes of action that, even if fundamentally arising out of the personal relationship encompassed by the anticipation of marriage, are, nevertheless, viable for other reasons. To some extent, we agree. The professional malpractice case, as we shall see, can be such a case. But the few cases have been carefully limited by factors not present in the case sub judice. We discuss this issue further, infra.*

We do not agree with Nickel's contention that the affair was his private concern wholly separate from his professional practice. The trier of fact may find it was professional malpractice for a psychologist engaged in marriage counseling to maintain a sexual relationship with his patient's spouse. See *Mazza v. Huffaker*, 61 N.C.App. 170, 300 S.E.2d 833, 838, petition for discretionary review denied, 309 N.C. 192, 305 S.E.2d 734 (1983). We doubt that the standard of care exercised by a reasonable psychologist permits the practitioner to treat a patient in the confines of the office and then undermine that treatment outside the therapy session.... At trial, Torres [the husband] should be given the opportunity to establish likewise that a psychologist's duty to his patient does not stop at the office door. See also *Rowe v. Bennett*, 514 A.2d 802, 804 (Me.1986)....

On the surface, the allegations of improper sexual conduct set forth in Torres' complaint may constitute criminal conversation; [FN9]however, if in addition, the sexual activity violated the professional standard of care which Nickel owed to Torres, it is sufficient to support a cause of action for professional negligence. [*Emphasis added.*]

> *FN9. The Court had abolished criminal conversion actions prior to this time.*
> Figueiredo-Torres, 321 Md. at 650-51, 584 A.2d 69.

We have examined closely and extensively the record forwarded to us for any indication that Ms. Miller's cause of action is based on anything other than her previous personal relationship with Warren Ratner that was, according to the averments of her complaints—made by her applicable to all counts—and her subsequent deposition testimony, based on their "permanent commitment that would be followed by marriage" and "promises... [i]n anticipation of their marriage." At one point, a document proffered by her contained her assertion that she and Warren were engaged to be *41 married. We have found no indication of any other fundamental relationship between the parties or other basis for the actions filed.

What appellant attempts to do in this case is similar to what the plaintiff attempted to do in *Gasper v. Lighthouse*, Inc., 73 Md.App. 367, 533 A.2d 1358 (1987), cert. denied, 311 Md. 718, 537 A.2d 272 (1988). That case involved an action by a husband against a marriage counselor, who the husband asserted had caused a divorce by having sexual relations with the husband's wife. The husband sued the counselor and the counselor's **988 employer, Lighthouse, Inc., for breach of their contractual obligation to "help the plaintiff and his wife solve the marital difficulties"; malicious breach of contract; breach of fiduciary duty; two counts of negligence; intentional infliction of emotional distress; malicious interference with the marriage contract of the husband and his wife; and loss of consortium. We noted that the question there before us was whether "a husband can do indirectly what he cannot do directly"—i.e., bring a suit that was, although not in those terms, for alienation of affections and criminal conversation. Id. at 370, 533 A.2d 1358. After noting that the abolition of actions for criminal conversation and alienation of affections did not preclude traditional contract and tort actions, we stated:

> *What is precluded, however, is the refitting of the abolished actions into other forms. One cannot sue to recover for injuries arising from "defilement of the marriage bed" or from an interference with the marriage by simply casting the defendant's conduct as a breach of contract, or negligence, or some other intentional tort. It is that kind of sham that the case law prevents. See, in general, Nicholson v. Han, 12 Mich.App. 35, 162 N.W.2d 313 (1968); Destefano v. Grabrian, 729 P.2d 1018 (Colo.Ct.App.1986); Goldberg v. Musim, 162 Colo. 461, 427 P.2d 698 (1967); Lund v. Caple, 100 Wash.2d 739, 675 P.2d 226 (1984); Arnac v. Wright, 163 Ga.App. 33, 292 S.E.2d 440 (1982); Harrington v. Pages, 440 So.2d 521 (Fla.Dist.Ct.App.1983).*

*42 Gasper, 73 Md.App. at 372, 533 A.2d 1358. After disposing of several of the counts, we looked at the real basis for the professional malpractice counts:

> *Counts IV and V sound in professional malpractice. Such an action may well lie against a marriage counselor who fails to exercise reasonable care in the performance of his or her calling. See Restatement (Second) of Torts § 299A. But, as with the breach of contract action, we have to examine not merely the form of the action but its real basis. It is clear from the incorporation of the underlying allegations and the absence of any other articulated negligence that the sole basis of these actions was Derby's cuckolding activity. It is therefore precluded. Destefano v. Grabrian, supra, 729 P.2d 1018. Likewise Count VI. Lund v. Caple, supra, 675 P.2d 226, and cf. Harrington v. Pages, supra, 440 So.2d 521.*

Gasper, 73 Md.App. at 373–74, 533 A.2d 1358 (emphasis added); see also *Homer v. Long*, 90 Md.App. 1, 17, 599 A.2d 1193 (affirming trial court's dismissal of negligent misrepresentation and fraud claims brought by nonpatient husband against psychiatrist who was treating husband's wife and having sexual relations with her "because... the real injury for which recovery is sought is either the adultery or the breakup of the marriage"), cert. denied, 326 Md. 177, 604 A.2d 444 (1992).

Likewise, in the case sub judice, each and every count contained in appellant's complaints incorporated that her action was, at least in part, based upon "a permanent commitment... followed by marriage" and "promises" and that Warren Ratner "[i]n anticipation of their marriage... would take care of her." For us to reverse the grants of summary judgment in favor of appellees would require this Court to ignore the underlying bases, proffered by Ms. Miller herself, for all of her claims....

In a case in which the plaintiff was attempting to extend loss of consortium claims to persons who were engaged, we rejected the claim and commented on the prohibition at issue in the case sub judice. Judge Bloom, writing for the Court, noted in *Gillespie-Linton v. Miles*, 58 Md.App. 484, 496, 473 A.2d 947 (1984):

> *We also note that the General Assembly has abrogated the right to sue for breach of a promise to marry. Md. Cts. & Jud. Proc.Code Ann. § 5-301. "It would be anomalous to permit a[n engaged] person to recover for the loss of consortium yet deny that same person recovery for the loss of those same marital benefits upon the failure to carry out the promise of marriage."* Hendrix [*v. General Motors Corp., 146 Cal.App.3d 296]* 193 Cal.Rptr. [922,] 924 [(1983)] (citations omitted). *Furthermore, any decision to extend to unmarried persons legal rights previously held only by married persons would necessitate identifying and weighing competing notions of public policy, social mores, and moral values. Such a decision is best left to the General Assembly. "Only the Legislature responsible to the electorate should have the power to make such a radical change in the fabric of society." Id., 193 Cal.Rptr. at 925* (citation omitted).

In the present case, the purpose of the statute was extensively presented as a part of it, and thus its purpose—to abolish actions for breach of promise to marry and alienation *45 of affections—is not even open to argument. Nor do we have to decipher whether the Legislature intended it to be remedial and liberally construed—it told us so. Were we to be in any way still uncertain, the General Assembly resolved that uncertainty by the unusual (in our view) inclusion in the original statute of a provision preventing anyone from changing it and providing for serious criminal penalties for anyone attempting to circumvent it, penalties that remained as part of the statute until less than eleven years ago. Appellant here would have us restrict that which was clearly intended to be applied broadly. In view of the statute and the cases we have cited, we are bound to apply the statute liberally to ensure that it is not being circumvented by artful **990 pleading and artful framing of other causes of action.

Foreign jurisdictions are generally in accord with the views we have expressed herein and in our prior cases. Several have held that other causes of action were really alienation of affections claims. There are, however, a few cases that directly address breach of promise issues.

Judge Mary F. Spicer, in a poem opinion, stated in *Irvin v. Smith*, 71 Ohio Misc.2d 18, 654 N.E.2d 189 (Ohio Ct.C.P.1993), that the plaintiff, Doris Irwin, had been promised marriage by the defendant, Jimmie Smith, but that The Court determines upon proper review That Doris' complaint is an amatory action; That the same is barred by R.C. 2305.29, And thus denies Doris satisfaction...

Among the other cases we have found directly dealing with breach of promise to marry is *Zaragoza v. Capriola,* 201 N.J.Super. 55, 492 A.2d 698 (Ch. Div.1985). There, the plaintiff, noting that the "defendant continually stated he wished to marry her and provide a family for her daughter and their son," sued defendant and sought pendente lite support for herself and the payment of all expenses of the home in which she was living. The court found for the defendant, holding "that any claim predicated upon defendant's alleged failure to live up to his promises of marriage must necessarily fail." Id. at 702.

*46 In *Waddell v. Briggs,* 381 A.2d 1132 (Me.1978), parents filed suit on behalf of their minor daughter for breach of promise to marry and infliction of mental suffering. The court noted Maine's statute prohibiting the bringing of breach of promise to marry actions for direct or indirect damages and held that a party "cannot circumvent the statute by suing in tort for fraud or other tortious conduct, instead of bringing an action based on breach of [promise to marry] contract." Id. at 1136–37 (footnote omitted).

We have found two cases with unusual factual circumstances in which other tortious actions have been permitted even though promises of marriage existed between the parties. In *Lampus v. Lampus,* 541 Pa. 67, 660 A.2d 1308 (1995), the man, knowing that his prior divorce had been declared invalid, nevertheless, entered into another marriage. Upon his death, the woman discovered that her marriage had been bigamous and asserted claims for breach of promise to marry, and for deceit, negligent misrepresentation, concealment, and negligence. The court upheld the lower court's dismissal of the breach of promise to marry claim but allowed the woman to maintain the remaining counts. The court held that the Heart Balm Act was not intended to preclude an action to recover damages because of a failure to inform a purported spouse of a bigamous marriage, and its specific language cannot be interpreted to abolish causes of action therefor.... The tort claims do not arise from the decedent's failure to marry her, but from the decedent's negligent or intentional conduct in failing to apprise her of the invalidity of the foreign divorce decree.... A claim of tortious conduct which is not based upon an individual's failure to keep a promise to marry is actionable. Only the first count was based upon the fracture of the marriage contract; the remaining counts [were] based upon the decedent's conduct after he had fulfilled his promise to marry.

Id. at 1311.

A similar case was *Jackson v. Brown,* 904 P.2d 685 (Utah 1995). There, the man was also already married when he *47 promised to marry the woman. He did not tell her of his married status. Nevertheless, he participated with her in planning the wedding and obtaining a marriage license, but on the morning of the wedding told her he would not marry her—he still did not tell her he was already married. She sued him for breach of promise to marry and for intentional infliction of emotional distress. In Utah, there was no statute prohibiting breach of promise suits. The court then, in essence, abolished the cause of action but preserved what could be termed a right to maintain palimony actions—"losses... may be recoverable under a theory of reasonable reliance or breach of contract." Id. at 687. The court permitted the maintenance of an action **991 for intentional infliction of emotional distress because the man knew he was already married, and thus could not marry the woman when he proposed to her, obtained the marriage license, and planned the wedding. These actions, the Utah court held, might be sufficiently "'...outrageous and intolerable in that they offend... generally accepted standards of decency and morality.'" Id. at 688.

In the case sub judice, there was neither evidence, nor averments, that there was any legal impediment to a marriage between Lonnie Miller and Warren Ratner. Nor was there any allegation that when the initial promises in respect to marriage were made, they were not sincere. The case at bar is a pure "change of mind" case. It is exactly that type of case that heart balm statutes are intended to prohibit. Once Warren Ratner conveyed his change of mind to appellant and asked her to leave his house, his subsequent conduct has to be viewed as conduct designed to assert his legal rights to cause her to remove herself from the house.

In both Lampus and Jackson, the defendants had deceitfully concealed their marital status when they induced the woman to marry, i.e., move in to live with them in anticipation of marriage. Although we do not so hold, such actions may well constitute a deceit that might, even in this State, support a tortious action because a person would fraudulently be caused to change his or her position in reliance on an intentional misrepresentation of the promisor's then present status. It *48 would not be an action for failure to keep a promise, but an action grounded in deceit and fraud. The first instance, failing to keep a promise to marry, is a breach of promise to marry; the second, making a misrepresentation of one's marital status in order to cause one to change her position may, in some circumstances, constitute the tort of deceit. In any event, the factual situations in Lampus and Jackson are manifestly inapposite to those facts extant in the case at bar. As to foreign cases that have held that certain claims were in reality prohibited alienation of affections or criminal conversation actions, see *Goldberg v. Musim*, 162 Colo. 461, 427 P.2d 698 (1967) (loss of consortium); *Destefano v. Grabrian*, 729 P.2d 1018 (Colo.Ct.App.1986), modified, 763 P.2d 275 (Colo.1988) (negligence, intentional infliction of emotional distress); *Harrington v. Pages*, 440 So.2d 521 (Fla.Dist.Ct.App.1983) (emotional distress); *Arnac v. Wright*, 163 Ga.App. 33, 292 S.E.2d 440 (1982) (intentional interference with marriage contract); Nicholson v. Han, 12 Mich.App. 35, 162 N.W.2d 313 (1968) (negligence, fraud, battery); *Lund v. Caple*, 100 Wash.2d 739, 675 P.2d 226 (1984) (loss of consortium).

[In her argument before the Court, Ms. Miller attempts to assert that, in spite of the averments and testimony as to promises and anticipation of marriage, the promises of support are independent grounds for maintaining a breach of contract action. We initially note again that nonmarital partners can certainly be subject to suit for promises made independent of promises to marry so long as the actions are not shams intended to circumvent the actions prohibited by statute. Actions to establish constructive or resulting trusts, in replevin, for conversion, to enforce purchase agreements are a few that come to mind. FN10 Additionally, there is what has come to *49 be termed as a "palimony" action, which may also incorporate some of those specific actions we have just noted. Although we do not here decide, such an action, under appropriate circumstances, may be maintainable in this State.

FN10. In *Gikas v. Nicholis*, 96 N.H. 177, 71 A.2d 785 (1950) that court permitted an action to recover an engagement ring. The court noted that in prohibiting breach of promise suits, the Legislature had not intended "to permit the unjust enrichment" of a party. The court limited its holding to engagement rings. That view, that actions can be maintained to recover engagement gifts, also finds support in several older cases: *Norman v. Burks*, 93 Cal.App.2d 687, 209 P.2d 815 (1949); *De Cicco v. Barker*, 339 Mass. 457, 159 N.E.2d 534 (1959); *Beberman v. Segal*, 6 N.J.Super. 472, 69 A.2d 587 (Law Div.1949).

We shall briefly discuss the distinction between actions involving unmarried companions that do not violate the prohibition by discussing two cases involving palimony-type actions beginning with the most famous, although not the first, California palimony case—**992 *Marvin v. Marvin*, 18 Cal.3d 660, 134 Cal.Rptr. 815, 557 P.2d 106 (1976).[FN11] The accepted facts in Marvin did not include allegations of promises to marry or promises in anticipation of marriage. In fact, one of Lee Marvin's arguments on appeal was that because Michelle was claiming that Lee had promised to support her and to pool property, the action was so similar to a breach of promise to marry that it should be prohibited even if no promise to marry had been made. At the time the parties agreed to live together, the defendant, Lee Marvin, was already married to somebody else. Under the posture of that case, certain facts were accepted. They included that the parties entered into an oral contract that provided that while they lived together, "they would combine their efforts and earnings and would share equally" in any property acquired during that period. Id. at 819, 557 P.2d at 110. The contract also provided that they would hold themselves out to the public as husband and wife and that the plaintiff, Michelle, would be Lee's "companion, homemaker, housekeeper and cook." Id. The plaintiff agreed to give up her career, and Lee was to provide for her "financial support and needs for the rest of her life." Id. There was no allegation of any promise to marry or of any *50 anticipation of marriage when the parties entered into the agreement.

FN11. *Trutalli v. Meraviglia*, 215 Cal. 698, 12 P.2d 430 (1932), and *Vallera v. Vallera*, 21 Cal.2d 681, 134 P.2d 761 (1943), mentioned in Marvin, supra, appear to be the initial California palimony cases. Additionally, there are numerous pre-Marvin California cases permitting nonmarital partners to enforce contracts for the distribution of property.

Kozlowski v. Kozlowski, 80 N.J. 378, 403 A.2d 902 (1979), was a palimony action in which the New Jersey court approved breach of contract actions between adults who contract to live together so long as the contract is in no way based upon a promise to marry. The man in that case, when asking the woman to live with him,[FN12] "made it clear that he did not intend to marry her." Id. at 905. "She moved back into the house… knowing that he refused to take steps toward marriage." Id. The court, in upholding the trial court's decision, noted that "society's mores have changed… an agreement between adult parties living together is enforceable to the extent it is not based… on a promise to marry." Id. at 908.

FN12. They had previously lived together, broken up, and he then asked her to move back in. The case involved only the second arrangement.

In respect to such actions, we perceive an inherent difficulty in maintaining a palimony action in this State when a plaintiff concedes that the relationship was based on promises and commitments to marry or in anticipation of marriage, even though the cases discussed in *Attorney Grievance Comm'n v. Ficker*, 319 Md. 305, 316–23, 572 A.2d 501 (1990), and *Unitas v. Temple*, 314 Md. 689, 701 n. 6, 552 A.2d 1285 (1989), do not foreclose the possibility of such actions. In light of Maryland's statutory prohibition, however, a complaint, in order to survive a motion for summary judgment, will have to be carefully framed, based upon proper and supportable allegations, and devoid of factual circumstances implicating the applicability of section 3–102 of the Family Law Article.

[The palimony cases that we have examined have one thing in common. They exist in a factual précis that is completely free of any taint of a breach of promise to marry. So long as persons initiate and maintain their relationships based upon promises of marriage, and its anticipation, rights arising out of those promises or agreements cannot escape the *51 bar by being recast as agreements between nonmarital partners. That is not to say that if the agreement to marry is terminated and the relationship either continues or recommences, as in Kozlowski, under a new agreement, in which no promises to marry are made and which does not anticipate a marriage, that a contractual action might not be sustainable. Moreover, while we do not so decide, it is not difficult to surmise that breach of contract actions between nonmarital partners completely free of promises in anticipation of marriage, might also be viable. In either case, it might be necessary, under the facts of a given case, to address the issue of meretricious sexual services. In some states, that issue has become de minimis, but it is unclear which direction **993 Maryland will take on this issue. As we indicate elsewhere, we need not concern ourselves in this case with whether the promises here made also contemplated meretricious conduct.

We shall accept what we perceive to be the dictates of the statute (considering its history), the mandate of Maryland's alienation of affections cases, persuaded by the weight of the law elsewhere, and liberally construe this remedial statute to insure that no proscribed actions are maintained in Maryland, whether attired in the full raiment of the prohibited action or disguised as another type of action. We have earlier remarked that in each and every count of Ms. Miller's complaint, she specifically averred that she moved into Warren Ratner's house and began her relationship with him because the two of them were "making a permanent commitment that would be followed by marriage" and that she "relied upon the defendant's promises... [i]n anticipation of their marriage." Moreover, she stated elsewhere that they were engaged to be married. We perceive that these statements, considering the strong public policy of this State, would be sufficient, under the circumstances here present, to constitute a claim for breach of promise to marry and that would be barred.FN13 There are additional undisputed facts that support our position *52 and make it even more clear that the real cause of action here presented is statutorily barred.

Appellant, while being questioned by Warren Ratner's counsel, stated in deposition:

[MR. BRAULT:]... *I want to make sure I understand, is it your contention that there was a suggestion to the point that you felt that there was an agreement that Mr. Warren Ratner would marry you?*

[APPELLANT:] *We did have an agreement.*

[MR. BRAULT:] *That agreement was to marry?*

[APPELLANT:] *Yes.*

[MR. BRAULT:]... *[Y]ou, in addition, had an agreement that he would support you financially into the future?*

[APPELLANT:] *Yes....*

[MR. BRAULT:]... *[W]as that regardless of marriage?*

[APPELLANT:] *Regardless.*

[MR. BRAULT:] *And to what extent did you understand that he was to support you?*

[APPELLANT:] *Well, he had a prenuptial drawn up.*[FN14]

FN14. *A prenuptial agreement is an agreement entered into in anticipation of marriage.*

BY MR. BRAULT:

Q. You moved in because you felt you had a commitment for your future support and to marry you in the future?

A. Yes.

Q. Did you discuss a date for the marriage or place for the marriage?

A. Warren had discussed with me and many friends that he wanted to surprise me and we would get married on the 19th of some month, and he said it was going to be a surprise.

*53 Q. So when you moved in you had no specific date on which the marriage was to occur?

A. No, we were just working towards learning about each other and planning for a future.

In *Lewis v. State*, 71 Md.App. 402, 406, 526 A.2d 66 (1987), Judge Alpert, for this Court, quoted Lord Brougham, from Wellman, The Art of Cross Examination 21:

> *The issue of a cause rarely depends upon a speech and is but seldom even affected by it. But there is never a cause contested, the result of which is not mainly dependent upon the skill with which the advocate conducts his cross-examination.* [Footnote omitted.]

Mr. Brault's cross-examination[FN15] did what effective cross-examinations are designed to do. It elicited truth. Although Ms. Miller **994 now argues that the issues here present are not based on a breach of promise to marry, she previously asserted otherwise. All her complaints, in every count, assert, at least in important part, that her grievances arise out of promises of and in anticipation of marriage—a marriage that, because of Warren Ratner's change of heart (or mind), did not occur. She also testified in deposition that the arrangement between her and Warren was an arrangement in contemplation of marriage based upon a promise to marry.

FN15. Mr. Brault apparently took the deposition of appellant. Accordingly, he cross-examined her as an adverse party.

Upon our review of Ms. Miller's averments when the motions for summary judgment were granted, the alleged atrocious actions of Warren and Dennis did not occur until Warren Ratner had terminated the relationship and ordered Ms. Miller to leave his house, and she refused to leave. Thus, not only was their relationship based upon their promises in anticipation of marriage, the unilateral termination was a rejection (a breach) of those promises and a nullification of the anticipation of the parties. It could not be more clear.

The emotional distress appellant alleges she suffered resulted from the breaching of Warren Ratner's promise to *54 marry her and his attempts at terminating their relationship and evicting her from the house. The mental distress counts are therefore fatally tainted with the ramification of the prohibited breach of promise action. They, likewise, under the circumstances here present, cannot be maintained...

FN16. This statute is over fifty years old. The world of female/male relationships and gender issues in all areas of our society may have changed more in the last thirty years than in America's prior history. The state of marriage as an essential element of our society may or may not be considered as fundamentally important now as in prior times. Where it will finally settle, if it does, remains generally unclear. Living arrangements of many kinds continue to evolve. While controversial efforts are being made elsewhere to reclassify marriage, lesser changes may be more appropriately functional. Moreover, there may be a need to consider the feasibility of providing methods for people who are not marriage partners to be able to present certain of their conflicts to the courts.

These statutory prohibitions we construe today apply to the marriage relationship, i.e., a man and a woman who have promised to marry or are married. Thus, other parties in other arrangements, including parties who cannot legally marry, may effectively be able to avoid the prohibitions, which in turn would conceivably confer rights to them that those who can legally marry do not have. If two parties cannot legally marry, and they know it, a breach of promise between them might not logically be a present breach of promise to marry. It is not our function (thankfully) to consider those issues best addressed by the people's direct representatives, the Legislature.

We shall, therefore, at this point, affirm the trial court's granting of judgment in favor of appellee as to all counts of the various complaints, except as to the tortious interference *55 with prospective advantage count, which we shall address separately. We further explain.

All of the counts alleging breach of contract and intentional infliction of emotional distress were based upon Warren Ratner's attempt to terminate the relationship that we have found was based in major part on a promise to marry and in anticipation of marriage. Dennis Ratner's conduct, by itself, although, if true, is reprehensible, does not independently satisfy the elements of the torts.

To the extent it is based on his attempt to help his brother terminate the relationship, it may come under the broad ambit of the prohibition. We note that appellant's count for civil conspiracy related to the infliction of severe emotional distress count and that appellant stated therein that the actions taken that caused her such distress were done by Dennis Ratner and Warren Ratner **995 "together, [so that] they could cause the Plaintiff to leave the home that she had been living in with Defendant Warren Ratner for almost three (3) years." Appellant alleged no possessory or ownership-based right to occupy the property; she relied solely on her relationship with Warren Ratner. However vile and repugnant the Ratner's [sic] actions were, if true, Warren Ratner nevertheless had the legal right to ask her to leave and to cause her to leave. That his brother helped him to do what he had a right to do does not create any separate action against Dennis Ratner for intentional infliction of emotional distress.

Even if we did not hold that appellant's claims for intentional infliction of severe emotional distress are fatally tainted with the breach of promise aspect of her case, we would nevertheless sustain the trial court's judgment on those counts...

FN17. Ms. Miller's physical health problems—cancer—did not result from the Ratner's [sic] conduct. It predated the actions here complained of and appears to have been at least one of the factors causing that alleged conduct.

In resolving the issue, the Court of Appeals first noted the tort's elements:

**996 To establish a cause of action for intentional infliction of emotional distress, four essential elements are necessary:

1. "The conduct must be intentional or reckless;
2. The conduct must be extreme and outrageous;
3. There must be a causal connection between the wrongful conduct and the emotional distress;
4. The emotional distress must be severe."

Id. at 734, 602 A.2d 1191 (quoting *Harris v. Jones*, 281 Md. 560, 566, 380 A.2d 611 (1977)). It then continued:

> *All four elements must be shown. We have acknowledged that "'[i]n developing the tort of intentional infliction of emotional distress, whatever the relationship between the parties, recovery will be meted out sparingly, its balm reserved for those wounds that are truly severe and incapable of healing themselves.'" Figueiredo-Torres v. Nickel, 321 Md. 642, 653 [584 A.2d 69] (1991) (quoting Hamilton [v. Ford Motor Credit Co., 66 Md.App. [46,] 61, 502 A.2d 1057 (1986)]).*

For conduct to meet the test of "outrageousness," it must be "so extreme in degree, as to go beyond all possible bounds of decency, and to be regarded as atrocious, and *58 utterly intolerable in a civilized community." *Harris*, 281 Md. at 567 [380 A.2d 611] (quoting Restatement (Second) of Torts § 46 comment d (1965)). Whether the conduct complained of meets this test is, in the first instance, for the court to determine; in addressing that question, the court must consider not only the conduct itself but also the "personality of the individual to whom the misconduct is directed." *Harris*, 281 Md. at 568 [380 A.2d 611]. This high standard of culpability exists to screen out claims amounting to "mere insults, indignities, threats, annoyances, petty oppressions, or other trivialities" that simply must be endured as part of life. Id. at 567 [380 A.2d 611] (quoting Restatement (Second) of Torts § 46, comment d (1965))....

We have upheld claims for intentional infliction of emotional distress only three times and only in cases which involved truly egregious acts. See *Figueiredo-Torres v. Nickel*, 321 Md. 642 [584 A.2d 69] (1991) (psychologist had sexual relations with the plaintiff's wife during the time when he was treating the couple as their marriage counselor); *B. N. v. K. K.*, 312 Md. 135 [538 A.2d 1175] (1988) (physician did not tell nurse with whom he had sexual intercourse that he had herpes); *Young v. Hartford Accident & Indemnity*, 303 Md. 182 [492 A.2d 1270] (1985) (worker's compensation insurer's "sole purpose" in insisting that claimant submit to psychiatric examination was to harass her and force her to abandon her claim or to commit suicide)....

Batson, 325 Md. at 734-35, 602 A.2d 1191 (emphasis added; some citations omitted).

The three cases cited by the Court in Batson—involving (1) a psychiatrist's sexual relations with a wife at the same time he was providing marriage counseling to the couple; (2) a doctor's failure to disclose to a nurse with whom he was having sexual relations that he had an incurable sexually transmitted disease; and (3) an insurer's "sole purpose" in requiring a claimant to undergo a psychiatric examination was to harass her and force her either to abandon her claim or to *59 commit suicide—are all, as we perceive them, more repugnant than what occurred here.

The verbal language directed to Ms. Miller, and the conduct was solely verbal, although it included threats, was for the purpose of pressuring appellant to leave Warren's house, where, regardless of the morality of his position, she had no legal right to remain. Considering that the appellees had the legal right to require appellant to leave, we do not perceive their verbal actions alone to be, as nauseating as they are if true, of such egregiousness so as to satisfy the elements of the tort. Accordingly, had we not sustained the trial court's judgment on this issue for the reasons we earlier stated, we would affirm it for this reason.[FN18]

FN18. The allegations as to Warren Ratner filing a claim in her bankruptcy matter does not, in and of itself, under the cases we have described, constitute a sufficient basis for the maintenance of a claim for intentional infliction of emotional distress, although it might constitute grounds for other types of relief not presented in the case at bar.

**997 Because we have based our decision on the statutory prohibition against breach of promise actions and appellant's failure to meet the essential elements of the tort of intentional infliction of emotional distress, we shall not address appellees' alternate argument that the alleged contract was based upon an "illicit sexual" relationship. We are, therefore, spared the necessity of entering that jungle to determine what, in 1997, remains illicit or is meretricious.[FN19]

FN19. *The Random House Dictionary of the English Language* 897 (unabr. ed. 1983) defines "meretricious" as "alluring by a show of flashy or vulgar attractions;... based on pretense, deception, or insincerity pertaining to or characteristic of a prostitute."...

*62 Resolution

We shall affirm. The primary basis for our affirmance is the statute itself, its stated purpose, its remedial nature, and the history of its original passage and subsequent reenactments. We note, however, that we, as judicial officers, do not approve of the actions, if true, allegedly committed by appellees. We have no way of knowing whether the allegations are accurate. We also recognize the great harm that can be done to a person falsely accused of such actions.[FN22] For purpose of this review, we were required to presume that Ms. Miller's assertions were true. Moreover, we are reminded that

FN22. The difficulty in determining the truthfulness of such statements was one of the reasons that the cause of action was abolished fifty years ago. [j]udicial power is never exercised for the purpose of giving effect to the will of the Judge; always for the purpose of giving effect to the will of the Legislature; or, in other words, to the will of the law.

Osborn v. Bank of United States, 22 U.S. [9 Wheat.] 738, 866, 6 L.Ed. 204 (1824).

We affirm.

Judgment Affirmed; All Costs to Be Paid by Appellant

Miller v. Ratner makes clear that Maryland does not allow claims for breach of the promise to marry, which keeps with the modern concept that marriage is not a social elevation for women. Only a few states still recognize this claim.

GIFTS IN CONTEMPLATION OF MARRIAGE

Another issue that comes up surrounding courtship is the question of gifts in contemplation of marriage. Usually the gift associated with the human courtship ritual is an engagement ring, which is traditionally given by a man to a woman. What does the law dictate should happen to the ring when an engaged couple calls off a wedding? If the break up is mutual, the couple can often work it out. If one party is jilted by the other, will the courts intervene to allow the return of the ring? Traditionally, based on the common law approach, the courts looked at fault to determine ownership of the engagement ring. Whoever was at fault by breaking off the engagement would lose the ring. Is a fault-based system fair? Suppose the ring had sentimental value to the fiancé's family? Suppose the person who broke the engagement was justified?

Moreover, if states have abolished claims for breach of promise to marry, do those states still want to decide who gets the wedding ring? In *Brown v. Thomas*, 127 Wis. 2d 318 (WI Ct. App. 1985), the appellate court looked at this issue and overruled the lower court's dismissal of a man's complaint for the return of an engagement ring after the courtship ended. In citing the legislative history of the state's decision to abolish claims for breach of promise to marry, the court writes, "The action for breach of promise encourages marriages that should not take place and its abolishment is in keeping with the philosophy that legislation should be designed to promote stability in marriage. As a remedy which permits monetary recovery [sic] the action sanctions conduct that borders on extortion." The court found that breach of promise to marry claims often involved allegations of emotional damages, which the court felt a claim for return of the ring was not. As to the claim of the ring, the appellate court wrote, "[a]lthough it appears that this suit is one of first impression in Wisconsin, there is sufficient precedent in our case law, as well as the decided weight of authority in other jurisdictions, to recognize the inherent validity of his claim." The Wisconsin court relied on the conditional gift theory and wrote, "The inherent symbolism of this gift forecloses the need to establish an express condition that marriage will ensure. Rather, the condition may be implied in fact or imposed by law in order to prevent unjust enrichment." If the condition (marriage) is not fulfilled, the court reasoned the gift/ring should be returned to make the ring giver whole. The court pointedly ignored any allegations of fault regarding the breakup, saying it was irrelevant to its decision. Is that a good ruling?

Compare that ruling, based on the modern legal concept that the ring was a conditional gift, received on the condition that the marriage would occur, to *Clippard v. Pfefferkorn*, 168 S.W. 3d 616 (MO Ct. App. 2005), where as recently as 2005, a court relied on the determination of fault to decide who would keep an engagement ring. The facts in this case were a little more complicated because the $13,500 ring was given a few days before Christmas, so the nature of the gift had to be determined. The couple had been dating for four or five months when the plaintiff proposed marriage to the defendant and gave her the ring. Once the court was assured that it was an engagement ring, it used a fault-based standard to determine if it should be returned. Finding that the plaintiff terminated the relationship about six weeks after giving the ring to the defendant, "because [she] was not the 'right' person and [due] to the influence of his brother, sisters, and parents," the defendant was allowed to keep the ring.

Senator Sam Rayburn famously said, "There is no education in the second kick of a mule."[9] Does the number of times a couple gets engaged and exchanges the same ring make a difference? Should there be some theory of "combat pay" for repeated break ups? The Pennsylvania case of *Lindh v. Surman* looks at such facts involving a $17,400 engagement ring, under such circumstances.

---

9   http://www.azquotes.com/quote/1223220

In August 1993, Rodger Lindh (Rodger) proposed marriage to Janis Surman (Janis). Rodger presented her with a diamond engagement ring that he had purchased for $17,400. Janis accepted the marriage proposal and the ring. Two months later, Rodger broke the engagement and asked Janis to return the ring. She did so. Rodger and Janis later reconciled, with Rodger again proposing marriage and again presenting Janis with the engagement ring. Janis again accepted the proposal and the ring. In March 1994, Rodger again broke the engagement and asked Janis to return the ring. This time, she refused. Rodger sued her, seeking recovery of the ring or a judgment for its value. The trial court held in Rodger's favor and awarded him damages in the amount of the ring's value. When Janis appealed, the Pennsylvania Superior Court affirmed the award of damages and held that when an engagement is broken, the engagement ring must be returned, even if the donor broke the engagement. Janis appealed to the Supreme Court of Pennsylvania.

Newman, Justice [W]e are asked to decide whether a donee of an engagement ring must return the ring or its equivalent value when the donor breaks the engagement. We begin our analysis with the only principle on which [the] parties agree: that Pennsylvania law treats the giving of an engagement ring as a conditional gift. In *Pavlicic v. Vogtsberger* (Sup. Ct. Pa. 1957), the plaintiff supplied his ostensible fiancée with numerous gifts, including money for the purchase of engagement and wedding rings, with the understanding that they were given on the condition that she marry him. When the defendant left him for another man, the plaintiff sued her for recovery of these gifts. Justice Musmanno explained the conditional gift principle: A gift given by a man to a woman on condition that she embark on the sea of matrimony with him is no different from a gift based on the condition that the donee sail on any other sea. If, after receiving the provisional gift, the donee refuses to leave the harbor—if the anchor of contractual performance sticks in the sands of irresolution and procrastination—the gift must be restored to the donor.

[T]he parties disagree, however, [over] whether fault [on the part of the donor] is relevant to determining return of the ring.

[Janis] contends that Pennsylvania law... has never recognized a right of recovery in a donor who severs the engagement. [She maintains that] if the condition of the gift is performance of the marriage ceremony, [a rule allowing a recovery of the ring] would reward a donor who prevents the occurrence of the condition, which the donee was ready, willing, and eagerly waiting to perform. Janis's argument that... the donor [should not be allowed] to recover the ring where the donor terminates the engagement has some basis in [decisions from

Pennsylvania's lower courts and in treatises]. This Court, however, has not decided the question of whether the donor is entitled to return of the ring where the donor admittedly ended the engagement.

[T]he issue we must resolve is whether we will follow the fault-based theory argued by Janis, or the no-fault rule advocated by Rodger. Under a fault-based analysis, return of the rings depends on an assessment of who broke the engagement, which necessarily entails a determination of why that person broke the engagement. A no-fault approach, however, involves no investigation into the motives or reasons for the cessation of the engagement and requires the return of the engagement ring simply upon the nonoccur[r]ence of the marriage.

The rule concerning the return of a ring founded on fault principles has superficial appeal because, in the most outrageous instances of unfair behavior, it appeals to our sense of equity. Where one [of the formerly engaged persons] has truly "wronged" the other, justice appears to dictate that the wronged individual should be allowed to keep [the ring] or have [it] returned, depending on whether [the wronged] person was the donor... or the donee. However, the process of determining who is "wrong" and who is 'right," when most modern relationships are complex circumstances, makes the fault-based approach less desirable. A thorough fault-based inquiry would not... end with the question of who terminated the engagement, but would also examine that person's reasons. In some instances the person who terminated the engagement may have been entirely justified in his or her actions. This kind of inquiry would invite the parties to stage the most bitter and unpleasant accusations against those whom they nearly made their spouse. A ring-return rule based on fault principles will inevitably invite acrimony and encourage parties to portray their ex-fiancées in the worst possible light. Furthermore, it is unlikely that trial courts would be presented with situations where fault was clear and easily ascertained. The approach that has been described as the modern trend is to apply a no-fault rule to engagement ring cases. Courts that have applied [this rule] have borrowed from the policies of their respective legislatures that have moved away from the notion of fault in their divorce statutes. [A]ll fifty states [have] adopted some form of no-fault divorce. We agree with those jurisdictions that have looked toward the development of no-fault divorce law for a principle to decide engagement ring cases. [In addition, the] inherent weaknesses in any fault-based system lead us to adopt a no-fault approach to resolution of engagement ring disputes.

Decision of Superior Court in Favor of Rodger Lindh Affirmed.

Cappy, Justice, dissenting The majority urges adoption of [the no-fault rule] to relieve trial courts from having the onerous task of sifting through the debris of the broken engagement in order to ascertain who is truly at fault. Are broken engagements truly more disturbing than cases where we ask judges and juries to discern possible abuses in nursing homes, day care centers, dependency proceedings involving abused children, and criminal cases involving horrific, irrational injuries to innocent victims? The subject matter our able trial courts address on a daily basis is certainly of equal sordidness as any fact pattern they may need to address in a simple case of who broke the engagement and why.

I can envision a scenario whereby the prospective bride and her family have expended thousands of dollars in preparation for the culminating event of matrimony and she is, through no fault of her own, left standing at the altar holding the caterer's bill. To add insult to injury, the majority would also strip her of her engagement ring. Why the majority feels compelled to modernize this relatively simple and ancient legal concept is beyond the understanding of this poor man. [A]s I see no valid reason to forego the [fault-based rule] for determining possession of the engagement ring under the simple concept of conditional gift law, I cannot endorse the modern trend advocated by the majority.[10]

In the age of no-fault divorce, should courts determine fault of an engagement breakup? Some states laws clarify non-intervention. Yet, should the value of the ring make a difference? Sport celebrities have dealt with expensive gifts in contemplation of marriage claims. "Former Buffalo Sabres player Matthew Barnaby reached an out-of-court settlement... of a lawsuit against his ex-fiancée and reclaimed an engagement ring worth $50,000.... Dallas Cowboys receiver Roy Williams sued his ex-fiancée over a $77,000 engagement ring but got the ring back without going to court." With such jaw-dropping amounts involved, does the ring take on the status of other similar priced objects like cars or houses?

On May 3, 2013, Buffalo Bills football star Mario Williams filed a lawsuit in Houston against his former fiancée, seeking the return of a 10-carat diamond engagement ring reportedly worth $785,000. "For some perspective, the median home price in Buffalo is $94,000—more than eight times less than the price of the ring."[11] Williams, 28, had signed a six-year, $100 million contract with $50 million in guaranteed money with the Bills, which made him the highest-paid defensive player in National Football League history and, by far, the highest-paid in Bills' history. In the lawsuit, Williams alleged that his former fiancée ended the engagement and that she had agreed that "if the wedding was ever called off, she would return the ring that Williams bought for her." Williams also accused her of being a spendthrift and then the case turned ugly when she released some of his text messages. In January 2014, they settled the case keeping the terms confidential and issuing mutual apologies.[12]

In December 2014, ex-Redskins wide receiver Laveranues Coles sued for the return of a "reportedly 5.6-carat diamond appraised at $240,000. Coles proposed in February, allegedly found out in March that his betrothed was interested in another and the whole thing got called off in June."[13] Coles made a request for the ring back and then sued in Virginia. His former fiancée (who did not respond to his request for the ring back before the suit), asked the court to dismiss the case arguing that Virginia's

---

10   http://highered.mcgraw-hill.com/sites/dl/free/0073377643/336398/ch23_Lindh_vs_Surman.html
11   He alleged that "he gave his fiancée an American Express credit card to pay for living expenses. He contended that she ran up $108,000 in charges on the card in 2012." "Mario Williams Sues to get Back $785,000 Engagement Ring", Ryan Wilson, *CBSSports.com*, May 6, 2013. http://www.cbssports.com/nfl/eye-on-football/22207169/mario-williams-sues-to-get-back-785000-engagement-ring
12   "Mario Williams, former fiancée agree to settlement on $785K ring", Josh Katowitz, *CBSSports*, January 3, 2014. http://www.cbssports.com/nfl/eye-on-football/24396478/mario-williams-former-fiancee-agree-to-settlement-on-785k-ring
13   "Ex-Redskins player Coles sues to get back ring", Tom Jackman. *The Washington Post*, December 13, 2014, P. B3. Coles' lawyer argued that, "breach of promise to marry is a specific common law action. There are economic damages...and [involves] keeping rings for their enrichment" when distinguishing it from heart balm laws that were "designed to allow people to leave the altar without facing liability for economic damages".

"heart balm" statute which says that no civil action shall lie or be maintained…"for alienation of affection, breach of promise to marry, or criminal conversion" controlled. But "Virginia courts have not always applied that statute to contested engagement rings, with some ruling that the ring is a conditional gift and the breach of promise to marry violates the condition of the agreement." Virginia's Supreme Court has never ruled on the issue, so perhaps this case will make precedent?[14]

Back to our celebrity case involving Kardashian's engagement ring from Humphries—what should be the result? California has a specific law on the issue of courtship. California Civil Code, Section 1590 states that if either money or property is given in anticipation of marriage, and the recipient calls off the marriage, the ring should be returned to the giver. In the Kardashian/Humphries case, however, they were married (for at least 72 days) so this rule does not apply. In this case, after the divorce, the diamond ring, valued at about $2 million was returned to Humphreys and he subsequently auctioned it at Christie's for $749,000. According to the auction website, a portion of the proceeds would go to charity.[15]

More men are receiving and wearing engagement rings. Is this a positive trend? If only men give engagement rings to women, how will the tradition continue in same-sex relationships? What if a couple exchanges other kinds of property at engagement (e.g., a goat)? Should the same rules apply? In one case, a man got a vasectomy at the request of his fiancée during their engagement. Could he request reimbursement when she broke off the wedding?

HESS V. JOHNSTON[14]
NO. 20060497-CA.
(UTAH 2007)

OPINION

Hess appeals the trial court Plaintiff Layne D. Hess appeals the trial court's order dismissing his complaint, with prejudice, for failure to state a claim upon which relief can be granted, see Utah R. Civ. P. 12(b)(6). Defendant Jody Johnston cross-appeals, arguing that the trial court committed error

---

14 Ibid.

15 The final sale price far exceeded the auction catalogue's expected price of between $300,000 and $500,000 (less than the $ 2 million reported cost). "Kim Kardashian's Engagement Ring from Kris Humphries Sells at Auction", Jessica Derschowitz, *CBS News*, October 15, 2013, http://www.cbsnews.com/news/kim-kardashians-engagement-ring-from-kris-humphries-sells-at-auction/

when it denied her motion for sanctions under rule 11 of the Utah Rules of Civil Procedure, see Utah R. Civ. P. 11. We affirm.

BACKGROUND 1

2 Hess and Johnston started dating in mid-April 2004 and within three months, they decided to marry. Johnston found an engagement ring she liked, and Hess commissioned a jeweler to craft one like it. The couple planned to marry sometime in November 2004, but mutually decided that they would take their time in planning the wedding to ensure their finances were in order.

3 About this time, Johnston told Hess that, during their engagement, she wanted to go on some trips and wanted Hess to have a vasectomy. Hess complied with these requests. Hess began by paying for the couple to take a seven-day cruise to Alaska at the end of July. In August, Hess underwent the vasectomy procedure requested by Johnston. And in September, after Johnston expressed an interest in traveling to France to introduce Hess to friends she had met while living there years earlier, Hess paid for the couple to travel to France for three weeks. Before leaving on the trip, Hess paid the balance on the custom engagement ring so that he could present Johnston with it while in France. After returning from France, Hess and Johnston twice rescheduled the wedding, first, from November 2004 to May 5, 2005, and then to July 9, 2005. In October 2004, Johnston also asked Hess to help purchase a vehicle for her son. Hess contributed $2400 toward the automobile.

4 In late April 2005, without any forewarning or explanation, Johnston returned the engagement ring to Hess and informed him that she would not be his wife. Hess attempted, numerous times, to obtain an explanation from Johnston, but she refused to offer any excuse for breaking off the engagement.

5 In November 2005, Hess brought suit against Johnston seeking restitution under four different legal theories: (1) conditional gift, (2) unjust enrichment, (3) promissory estoppel or reasonable reliance, and (4) breach of contract. Central to all the claims is the argument that but for Johnston's promise to marry him, Hess would not have paid for the engagement ring, the Alaskan cruise, the trip to France, or the vehicle for Johnston's son. Hess sought restitution in the form of reimbursement for Johnston's portion of the travel expenses, the medical costs of the vasectomy and a reversal procedure, the money given toward the vehicle, and the difference between the purchase price of the engagement ring and its eventual sale price. In response, Johnston sought sanctions under rule 11 of the Utah Rules of Civil Procedure and moved to dismiss the complaint, with prejudice, for failure to state a claim upon which relief can be granted. The trial court denied the motion for sanctions but dismissed the complaint on the ground that Utah has abolished the common law cause of action for breach of a promise to marry. Both parties appeal...

ANALYSIS

9 Johnston argues that Jackson v. Brown, 904 P.2d 685 (Utah 1995), clearly abolished the cause of action for breach of a promise to marry, including claims of the type asserted by Hess. Therefore, she reasons that sanctions were proper because, given the settled state of the law, Hess would not have brought his claims had he first made the reasonable inquiry required by rule 11.[2] We disagree. First, we begin by noting that "the reasonable inquiry analysis does not hinge solely on whether the law is clear. [Instead, t]he focus should be on what the attorney actually did in researching the law." Barnard, 846 P.2d at 1236–37. Second, and perhaps more importantly, we disagree with Johnston's contention that Jackson clearly bars Hess's claims. Instead, we read Jackson as expressly acknowledging the possibility that some economic claims arising out of a failed engagement may still be viable.

10 In Jackson, the Utah Supreme Court examined the common law cause of action for breach of a promise to marry. See 904 P.2d at 686–87. In abolishing that claim from Utah's common law, the court first examined the history of the cause of action, noting that it "arose over four hundred years ago," when marriage was viewed primarily as an economic transaction. Id. at 686. Because of the economic nature of matrimony, the cause of action for breach of promise provided an economic remedy to persons who had relied to their detriment on a recanted promise of marriage. See id. The court noted, however, that over time "American marriage customs ha[ve] so changed as to be totally unlike those prevailing when breach of promise first became actionable." Id. The court reasoned that because modern concepts of marriage focus primarily on emotion—not economics—the breach of promise cause of action had lost its historical moorings such that "an action developed to remedy the economic losses resulting from the withdrawal of a marriage promise [was being] used in this day and age to redress the emotional losses that follow[ed]." Id. at 687 (emphasis added). The supreme court found this use of a breach of promise claim antithetical to modern policy considerations and held that the cause of action was no longer "the proper vehicle" to recover for emotional damages where the "losses complained of are pride, love, and esteem." Id. Rather, the court held that recovery for emotional damages was properly pursued only through a claim for intentional infliction of emotional distress and only if the strict elements of such a claim could be established. See id. at 687–88.

11 Despite abolishing the cause of action for breach of a promise to marry, the Jackson court specifically left open the question of whether economic damages arising from a broken engagement could ever be recovered under alternate legal theories. All the justices agreed that, despite abolishing the cause of action for breach of a promise to marry, "no injury to a plaintiff, upon proper showing, goes unremedied." Id. at

687. A majority of the court, however, postponed deciding which legal theories would support recovery of economic damages stemming from a broken engagement.   See id. at 688 (Stewart, J., concurring, joined by Zimmerman, C. J. & Russon, J.) (stating that the issue of what theories would support a recovery of economic damages "should be addressed only when it is properly presented to [the c]ourt and properly argued by the parties"). Alternatively, Justice Durham, joined by Justice

Howe, anticipated the question and suggested that "any economic losses suffered because of [plaintiff's] reasonable reliance upon [defendant's] promise to marry may be recoverable under a theory of reasonable reliance or breach of contract." Id. at 687 (Durham, J., concurring, joined by Howe, J.).

12 Because Jackson did not clearly foreclose claims for purely economic damages, we cannot say that Hess's reading of the law, alone, supports the conclusion that he did not make a reasonable inquiry into the claims, defenses, and other legal contentions contained in the complaint. Rule 11 does not "require the attorney to reach the correct legal position from the research. It is enough that the attorney's reading of the law is a reasonable one." Barnard, 846 P.2d at 1236. Therefore, we affirm the trial court's denial of Johnston's motion for rule 11 sanctions...

A. CONDITIONAL GIFT

14 Assuming, without deciding, that Utah would allow recovery of engagement gifts under a theory of conditional gift, Hess's claims fail as a matter of law because he has not alleged facts that could establish that the travel, vasectomy,3 or money for the vehicle were conditioned on the marriage taking place.4 Instead, Hess urges this court to adopt the position that any gift given during the engagement period carries an implied condition of marriage. We decline to do so. If we were to imply a condition on all gifts given during the engagement period, every gift would be recoverable regardless of the size, cost, significance, or nature of the gift, and without regard to the surrounding circumstances under which the gift was given.

Surely, the donor will give some gifts during the engagement period that are intended as absolute gifts. However, with an implied condition, the donor would have to expressly indicate that he does not expect the gift back in order to make an absolute gift * turn[ing] traditional gift law on its head.

Cooper v. Smith, 155 Ohio App.3d 218, 2003-Ohio-6083, 800 N.E.2d 372, at ¶26.

15 Because we do not accept Hess's contention that all gifts given during the engagement period carry an implied condition of marriage, and because "one asserting the delivery [of a gift] was made on some condition has the burden of establishing such condition" as an element of recovery under a conditional gift theory, Fierro v. Hoel, 465 N.W.2d 669, 671 (Iowa Ct.App.1990), we examine Hess's complaint for allegations that could support his contention that the gifts were conditional.

16 Hess's complaint states that, in retrospect, Hess would not have made the expenditures but for Johnston's promise to marry him. But this assertion, relying on hindsight, even if true, is not sufficient to establish that the gifts were conditioned on the marriage taking place. "Whether a gift is conditional or absolute is a question of the donor's intent, to be determined from any express declaration

by the donor at the time of the making of the gift or from the circumstances." 38 Am.Jur.2d Gifts § 72 (1999) (emphasis added).

17 Here, Hess's complaint fails to include any facts that could demonstrate, either expressly, by the circumstances, or by the nature of the gifts that his intent was to condition the gifts on the marriage taking place. Cf. Mace v. Tingey, 106 Utah 420, 149 P.2d 832, 834 (1944) (evaluating "the intention of the donor, the situation and relationship of the parties, the kind and character of the property, and the things said, written or done" in determining whether an irrevocable gift was given (emphasis omitted)). First, Hess does not allege that he expressly conditioned the gifts when he gave them. Second, the alleged circumstances existing at the time the gifts were made do not imply that the gifts were conditional. See, e.g., Maiorana v. Rojas, 787 N.Y.S.2d 678, 3 Misc.3d 1107, No. 94988KCV2003, 2004 WL 1258073, 2004 N.Y. Misc. LEXIS 669 (N.Y. Civ.Ct. June 3, 2004) (concluding that ring was not conditional gift when circumstances showed it was given on donee's birthday). But see, e.g., Fanning v. Iversen, 535 N.W.2d 770, 772 (S.D.1995) (holding that circumstances surrounding gift of money implied a condition of marriage where check memo indicated money was for wedding expenses). When evaluating the circumstances surrounding the gift, some jurisdictions will examine the purpose of the gift and inquire whether that purpose can be achieved only by the marriage taking place. See, e.g., Wagener v. Papie, 242 Ill.App.3d 354, 182 Ill.Dec. 417, 609 N.E.2d 951, 953–54 (1993) (examining circumstances surrounding gift/sale of family home to future son-in-law and finding that purpose of gift—to use home as marital home—would be frustrated when the marriage did not ensue); Cooper, 155 Ohio App.3d 218, 800 N.E.2d 372, at 25–27, 32 (finding gift of improvements to the donee's home were not conditional where donor "merely presumed" but did not articulate the intention that they would live in the improved home after they wed); Restatement of Restitution § 58 cmt. c & illus. 5 (1937) (noting that the gift of a car to a putative future son-in-law for the purpose of a honeymoon road trip may be recoverable because the purpose may only be achieved if the marriage ensues). Here, the facts alleged cannot support the conclusion that the purposes of the gifts were frustrated when the wedding did not take place. The complaint states that the purpose of the Alaskan cruise was to travel for pleasure before the wedding. The same purpose applied to the Paris trip, which also had the added purpose of allowing Johnston an opportunity to introduce Hess to her friends. The vasectomy was for the purpose of mutuality in birth control.5 And, the gift of money to Johnston's son was for the purpose of allowing him to purchase a vehicle. All of these purposes were achieved despite the fact that the parties did not marry. Thus, Hess's complaint fails to state any facts that suggest the circumstances surrounding these gifts implied they were conditioned on the marriage.

18 Finally, the nature of the gifts does not give rise to an inference that they were inherently conditional. Some jurisdictions have recognized that gifts, like engagement rings, carry with them an implied condition of marriage due to the inherent symbolism of the gift. See, e.g., Fierro, 465 N.W.2d

at 671 ("The inherent symbolism of [an engagement ring] forecloses the need to establish an express condition that marriage will ensue."); Heiman v. Parrish, 262 Kan. 926, 942 P.2d 631, 634 (1997) ("[E] ngagement rings should be considered, by their very nature, conditional gifts given in contemplation of marriage."); see also Restatement of Restitution § 58 cmt. c (noting that a donor may be entitled to restitution "if the gift is an engagement ring, a family heirloom or some other thing intimately connected with the marriage"). Here, the nature of the gifts—trips, a vasectomy, and cash given to a third party—carry no inherent inference that they were conditioned on the marriage.

19 Thus, even if Utah recognized recovery under a theory of conditional gift, which we do not decide today, Hess's claim for recovery would be barred because none of the alleged facts support the conclusion that at the time he made the gifts, he did not intend for them to take effect until the marriage ensued. Instead, the facts alleged in the complaint can only be read to support the conclusion that Hess intended an unconditional gift. We do recognize that the alleged facts suggest that the reason Hess gave the unconditional gifts was because he and Johnston were engaged. However, the reason for a gift should not be confused with a donor's intent that the gift be revocable. "'Many gifts are made for reasons that sour with the passage of time.' Unfortunately, gift law does not allow a donor to recover/revoke an inter vivos gift simply because his or her reasons for giving it have 'soured.'" Cooper v. Smith, 155 Ohio App.3d 218, 2003-Ohio-6083, 800 N.E.2d 372, at ¶ 25 (quoting Albanese v. Indelicato, 25 N.J. Misc. 144, 51 A.2d 110 (1947)); see also Restatement of Restitution § 58 (1937) ("A person who has conferred a benefit upon another, manifesting that he does not expect compensation therefor, is not entitled to restitution merely because his expectation that an existing relation will continue or that a future relation will come into existence is not realized, unless the conferring of the benefit is conditioned thereon."). We therefore affirm the trial court's dismissal of Hess's cause of action for recovery under a theory of conditional gift...

C. PROMISSORY ESTOPPEL

22 Like unjust enrichment, promissory estoppel is an equitable remedy and should be employed where injustice can be avoided only by enforcement of the promise. To state a claim for promissory estoppel, Hess must allege four elements:

> (1) [t]he plaintiff acted with prudence and in reasonable reliance on a promise made by the defendant; (2) the defendant knew that the plaintiff had relied on the promise which the defendant should reasonably expect to induce action or forbearance on the part of the plaintiff or a third person; (3) the defendant was aware of all material facts; and (4) the plaintiff relied on the promise and the reliance resulted in a loss to the plaintiff.

Youngblood v. Auto-Owners Ins. Co., 2007 UT 28, 16, 158 P.3d 1088 (quotations omitted). Here, Hess has failed to allege facts that would support the first element, that he acted with prudence and reasonable reliance on Johnston's promise to marry.

23 A promise to marry is unique in that it is not generally considered enforceable, but instead is made for the purpose of "allow[ing] a couple time to test the permanency of their feelings." Fierro v. Hoel, 465 N.W.2d 669, 672 (Iowa Ct.App.1990). Thus, the fact that the engagement period is, in essence, a test period makes reliance on the promise of marriage inherently problematic because "[w]hen either party lacks assurance, for whatever reason, the engagement should be broken." Id.; see also Jackson v. Brown, 904 P.2d 685, 687 (Utah 1995) ("It is certainly the policy of the state to uphold marriage vows. However, we see no benefit in discouraging or penalizing persons who realize, before making these vows, that for whatever reason, they are unprepared to take such an important step.").8 This is especially true when, as here, the couple had not even set an actual date for their nuptials.9 Cf. Gilbert v. Barkes, 987 S.W.2d 772, 777 (Ky.1999) (holding that recovery was unavailable because where no wedding date is set, the plaintiff could not "affirmatively demonstrate the parties' final and serious intent to enter into marriage"). Without foreclosing the possibility that, in some instances, the acts undertaken in reliance on a promise of marriage can be so intertwined with the promise itself that reliance may be reasonable,10 in this instance, Hess's complaint fails to allege facts that can support the conclusion that he was acting prudently and reasonably on Johnston's promise of marriage. All that can be inferred from the facts alleged in the complaint is that Hess made several irrevocable gifts during the engagement period. Thus, this is not a situation where "injustice can be avoided" only by awarding restitution damages, Skanchy v. Calcados Ortope SA, 952 P.2d 1071, 1077 (Utah 1998), and Hess's promissory estoppel claim fails as a matter of law.

D. BREACH OF CONTRACT

24 Similarly, even assuming without deciding that Jackson v. Brown, 904 P.2d 685 (Utah 1995), does not preclude a claim for breach of contract based on reciprocal promises to marry, Hess's claim fails because his allegations cannot support a conclusion that the damages were causally related to the breach.

25 Hess does not allege that Johnston made any promise to repay him if the marriage did not ensue; she never promised to pay for half of the travel, or to bear the cost of the vehicle herself. The only promise Johnston made was to marry Hess. Thus, in order to recover general damages, Hess would be required to show that the damages or injuries he sustained "flow[ed] naturally from the breach" of that promise. Machan v. UNUM Life Ins. Co. of Am., 2005 UT 37, ¶ 15, 116 P.3d 342

(quotations omitted). Or, to recover consequential damages, Hess must demonstrate that the damages he sustained were "reasonably within the contemplation of, or reasonably foreseeable, by the parties at the time the contract was made." Id. (quotations omitted). Under the circumstances of this case, none of the allegations show how restitution for gifts of travel, a vasectomy, and money to a third party flow naturally from a breach of a promise to marry or were reasonably contemplated by the parties at the time they decided to wed. As previously discussed, none of these gifts or the circumstances under which they were given suggest that they were in any way conditioned on the promise to marry being fulfilled. Additionally, neither the travel, the vasectomy, nor the gift of money to Johnston's son were preparatory acts required to be performed under the contract to marry. To hold otherwise would give rise to a claim for breach of contract—albeit for economic damages instead of emotional damages—"any time a person, for whatever reason, cancels or indefinitely postpones wedding plans." Jackson, 904 P.2d at 687. This result is clearly "contrary to the public policy of this state" because "such an action [would] be readily amenable to abuse [and] would discourage individuals with legitimate doubts or concerns about a planned wedding from cancelling the event." Id. Therefore, Hess's claims for restitution under a breach of contract theory were properly dismissed as a matter of law.

CONCLUSION

26 Rule 11 sanctions are inappropriate where, as here, counsel's interpretation of existing law is reasonable and there is no other evidence demonstrating counsel's failure to make a 'reasonable inquiry required by rule 11. Therefore, the trial court's denial of Johnston's motion for sanctions was proper. It was also proper for the trial court to dismiss Hess's complaint because the facts alleged could not support recovery of restitution under any of the grounds pleaded.

27 Affirmed.

FOOTNOTES...

3. Under the facts of this case, it is not necessary to address whether a vasectomy, undertaken by one person in a relationship, can ever be a "gift" to the other person in the relationship.

4. We note the possible exception of the engagement ring. See, e.g., Fierro v. Hoel, 465 N.W.2d 669, 671 (Iowa Ct.App.1990) ("An engagement ring given in contemplation of marriage is an impliedly conditional gift."); Heiman v. Parrish, 262 Kan. 926, 942 P.2d 631, 634 (1997) ("Once it is established the ring is an engagement ring, it is a conditional gift."). However, because Johnston returned the ring, Hess received back exactly that which he gave. Consequently, he has already received restitution,

and this court need not address whether the gift of an engagement ring carries with it an implied condition of marriage requiring its return when the wedding does not ensue.

5. Johnston had already undergone a tubal ligation, but remained concerned about the possibility of pregnancy.

6. Hess has not alleged that Johnston fraudulently promised to marry him...

8. After all, [w]hat fact justifies the breaking of an engagement? The absence of a sense of humor? Differing musical tastes? Differing political views? The painfully learned fact that marriages are made on earth, not in heaven. They must be approached with intelligent care and should not happen without a decent assurance of success. When either party lacks that assurance, for whatever reason, the engagement should be broken. No justification is needed. Either party may act. Fault, impossible to fix, does not count. *Fierro v. Hoel*, 465 N.W.2d 669, 672 (Iowa Ct.App.1990).

9. Hess does allege that in late 2004 the couple eventually set an actual wedding date for May 5, 2005. However, at the time the trips were taken, the vasectomy was performed, and the money was given to Johnston's son, the couple had not yet set an actual date for a wedding but were, instead, tentatively planning to marry sometime in November 2004.

10. As noted in Jackson v. Brown, 904 P.2d 685 (Utah 1995), it may be reasonable, under certain circumstances, to rely on another's promise of marriage when undertaking "normal expenses attendant to a wedding." Id. at 687. However, we do not reach that question because Hess is not seeking recovery of expenses directly related to a wedding.

McHUGH, Judge:

28 WE CONCUR: JAMES Z. DAVIS and GREGORY K. ORME, Judges.

Did the court make the right decision?

CHAPTER SOURCES

Wadlington, W., and O'Brien, R.C. (2007). *Domestic Relations*, 6th ed., p. 180. Foundation Press.
Weisberg, D. Kelly. (2011). *Emanuel Legal Lines*, Family Law.

WAYS TO STRENGTHEN MARRIAGE—REDEFINING MARRIAGE

Anything that makes marriage more treasured, we're for. It should be harder to get in and harder to get out so that it's elevated and treasured.
—Kelly J. Shackelford, Free Market Foundation president.[1]

Make marriage harder if you want to. Outlaw those Vegas chapels with neon wedding bells, require marriage applications modeled after tax forms, but leave divorce alone.[2]
—Ann Patchett

"While the divorce rate is down from its peak of almost one in two marriages in the early 1980s,"[3] today, about 40 percent of marriages end in divorce. Is there a way to avoid such a high rate of matrimonial failure? Perhaps society could redefine marriage or its expected length to make it more successful. Various modifications of marriage and divorce laws have been proposed with varying degrees. What would work?

COVENANT MARRIAGES

Lately, there has been some organized support by groups advocating for **covenant marriages**. These groups argue that because some states redefined marriage while legalizing same-sex unions, states should allow a new definition of marriage: the covenant marriage. The purpose of the covenant marriage is to make divorce more difficult by requiring fault, but with limited reasons

---

1   http://www.nytimes.com/2007/04/15/us/15marriage.html?pagewanted=print&_r=0, "Texas Legislators Push Marital Counseling," New York Times.com, April 15, 2007.
2   "Ann Patchett, "This is the story of a happy marriage", Harper Collins, 2013, p. 68.
3   "In the Season of Marriage, a Question. Why Bother?" Opinion, Andre J. Cerlin, *New York Times*, April 28, 2013, p. 7.

for divorce.[4] Louisiana was the first state to recognize covenant marriages, which allow two people of the opposite sex to contract that they will only dissolve their marital union through agreed-upon, limited grounds for divorce. Kansas, Alabama, Texas, and Arizona have adopted or attempted to pass covenant marriage laws, too. What kinds of things would parties covenant/agree to in order to obtain a divorce? The grounds are similar to fault-based divorce (see Chapter 11), but focus on adultery. Are covenant marriages just a revival of the fault-based system for divorce? Perhaps the irony of covenant marriage is that it's touted as a "reform movement," but really just advocates private ordering that is guaranteed state recognition. By this type of private ordering, proponents get the best of both worlds: a way to satisfy their needs beyond the state's ideals for the marriage relationship, while ensuring the state's approval. Finally, is it troubling that the term "covenant" is a central tenet for certain Christian religions, raising a concern about the separation of church and state?[5]

When adopting "covenant" marriages, states allow couples to, in effect, contract the terms of their marriage (beyond what the state allows). Should contract-like penalties apply? If one spouse commits adultery within a covenant marriage, would it be better to allow an automatic divorce? Should the adulterer pay a penalty or perform community service? Indeed, some proponents of covenant law want to include the right to designate penalties for violation. One such proponent believes an adulterer would lose all rights to marital assets and custody of the children. Would there be an impact on child support and custody arrangements, which are now regulated by the state, if couples control the terms of their marriage and divorce?

Under Arizona's covenant law,[6] passed in 1998, couples who volunteer for covenant marriage must get a special covenant marriage license. At the marriage license office, the couple signs an affidavit and a Declaration of Intent to Enter into a Covenant Marriage, which affirms they have met the statutory requirements. The cost for covenant marriage licenses is the same as traditional marriage licenses. Arizona has a provision to allow married couples to convert their traditional marriage to a covenant marriage, without the need to remarry, by signing a marriage license affidavit, a Declaration of Intent to Enter into a Covenant Marriage, and paying a $26.50 fee. Although a few states allow covenant marriage, it is not clear if these marriages have had an effect on the divorce rate.[7]

---

4 http://www.nytimes.com/2007/04/15/us/15marriage.html?pagewanted=print&_r=0, "Texas Legislators Push Marital Counseling," NewYorkTimes.com April 15, 2007.

5 For example, according to its webpage, Focus on the Family's central tenet is that the "covenant is the heart of the marriage mystery," and covenant is also the "fundamental tool that God has designed to construct and order His relationship with man." Would these same groups, who have successfully suggested the language to the states that allow covenant marriage, be such strong advocates if it was just called a contract marriage? http://www.focusonthefamily.com/marriage/gods_design_for_marriage/marriage_gods_idea/covenant_the_heart_of_the_marriage_mystery.aspx. Similarly, is there an issue concerning the state's requiring marriage counseling from a minister before obtaining a covenant marriage license?

6 (A.R.S. 25-901-906) http://www.usmarriagelaws.com/search/united_states/arizona/covenant_marriage.shtml

7 http://www.nytimes.com/2007/04/15/us/15marriage.html?pagewanted=print&_r=0, "Texas Legislators Push Marital Counseling," NewYorkTimes.com, April 15, 2007.

When author Ann Patchett interviewed author Elizabeth Gilbert (*Eat, Pray, Love*) about topics on marriage, Gilbert referred to covenant marriage as "super vows" and said, "[t]he idea was to offer couples an option: they could essentially choose between 'marriage lite,' with an easy, no-fault divorce option, or 'marriage for life,' the full handcuffs. Curiously enough, medieval Germans had the same package of options. Back then, as now, the vast majority of couples—given the choice—select the lighter bond. Even in the heat of love, it's as though we all understand that the future is a mystery, and it's best to keep your options open, just in case, God forbid, it doesn't last."[8]

TERM MARRIAGES

In **term marriages**, spouses agree to a specific length or term for their marriage commitment (often opting out of the traditional "death do us part"). Once the period—say, three years—expires, if the couple is happy, they stay married and can renew for an additional time period. If not, the couple splits by default. Should marriage be like a cell phone plan?

In 2011, the Mexico City Assembly proposed a reform in the civil marriage code that would allow marriage licenses that are valid for a specific term to automatically expire, unless the couple decided to renew. The intention was "to avoid the torturous process of divorce."[9] This was an attempt by Mexico's politicians to deal with the country's high rate of divorce—about 50 percent. Because most of Mexico's divorces occur in the first two years of a marriage, the couple would have to agree to at least a two-year term under the proposal. The idea of term marriage is that it supposedly takes stress away from the couple in ending their marriage. Additionally, it would relieve stress from the court system, which handled a large number of divorce cases. Term marriages in Mexico would lower divorce rates because they do not require divorce proceedings. Is this just smoke and mirrors? "The [Catholic] church criticized the proposed change." "This reform is absurd. It contradicts the nature of marriage," said Hugo Valdemar, spokesman for the Mexico City Archdiocese (which has "the world's second largest Catholic population after Brazil.") "It's another one of these electoral theatrics the assembly tends to do that are irresponsible and immoral."[10]

ENJOYMENT MARRIAGES

A mut'ah, or an **enjoyment marriage**, is a temporary union cleaved by Shiite Muslims that is sanctioned under Islamic law. Following the U.S. invasion of Iraq, this thousand-year-old Shiite

---

8   "Eat, Pray, Love, Then Commit", Ann Patchett, *The Wall Street Journal.* January 2, 2010.

9   http://www.guardian.co.uk/world/2011/sep/30/mexico-city-fixed-term-marriages, "Mexico City considers fixed-term marriage licenses," *Guardian*, September 30, 2011.

10   Ibid.

practice was revived there and in other parts of the region as a way, it was claimed, to provide for war widows. In an enjoyment marriage, a man and woman negotiate the terms of their arrangement. Often, the man is married, but to a pregnant woman who cannot have sex with him. Therefore he would contract with an unmarried woman or widow who "wanted" companionship. As a temporary wife she would receive a small amount of money up front and additional monthly payments for expenses about twice a week or as agreed upon over the term of the enjoyment marriage (often the next eight months). Under this arrangement, the man could summon the woman to a rented house to "enjoy" their marriage. Different than a term marriage, under the mut'ah, the man agrees to pay the woman. It also allows men, not women, to have multiple "marriages." According to Shiite religious law, this arrangement can last for a few minutes or several years. A man can have an unlimited number of mut'ahs while retaining his permanent wife at the same time. There is no written contract or official ceremony. Is this religious freedom, or economic exploitation?[11]

GERIATRIC MARRIAGE

In a **geriatric marriage**, time is of the essence. Some states have proposed a modification of marriage that allows older people to enter into the marital union faster and with fewer legal incidences. Considering a senior's limited number of years, the proposals shorten the period to get married and to get out of marriages. Geriatric marriages may include provisions for adult children from prior relationships, which allow them to inherit and bypass typical inter-spousal transfers upon death and under a will.

RAISE THE MARRIAGE AGE

No U.S. state has made a move to raise the age for marriage as a way to lower the divorce rate. (In all but one state a person can marry without parental consent at age 18. In Nebraska the age is 19.) Should this be considered? As each generation's crude death rate continues to rise in most developed countries, is it plausible that someone married at 18 will live happily with another for 60 years until they die?

When discussing marriage, which was the subject of her book, author Elizabeth Gilbert said, "Marriage is a strange combination of dream and reality, and we spend our lives as couples trying to negotiate that divide. I will say this, because I think it is the single most important piece of information in the whole story: Marriage is not a game for the young... Don't get married when you're 20 years old, for reasons I am certain I do not need to explain. Maturity brings—among other things—the ability to sustain and survive enormous contradictions and disappointments.

---

11 "Temporary 'Enjoyment Marriages' In Vogue Again with Some Iraqis," Nancy Trejos, *Washington Post*, January 20, 2007 (front page, 19).

Marriage is—among other things—a study in contradiction and disappointment, and inside that reality there is space for us to truly learn how to love. But it is wise to check at least a few of our most idealistic youthful dreams at the door before entering."[12] What age would signify the maturity needed? Is age the best standard for a successful long marriage?

PREMARITAL COUNSELING REQUIREMENTS

In 2007, in addition to a covenant marriage proposal, a Texas legislator proposed a law to encourage all couples (not just those volunteering for covenant marriage) to undergo premarital education. Under the proposal, Texas would waive the $30 marriage license fee and the 72-hour waiting period (between obtaining the marriage license and getting married)[13] for couples who took an eight-hour premarital instruction course called "Twogether in Texas."[14] Alternatively, the Texas proposal said it might increase the marriage license fee to $100 for those who do not take the course. Is this a marriage tax that discourages marriage? Would that cause an equal protection problem?

Under Arizona's covenant law,[15] couples must obtain a notarized statement from the clergy or marriage counselor who provided their premarital counseling, affirming the couple was informed of the nature and purpose of a covenant marriage and the limited terms for ending the marriage (which differ from traditional civil marriage). Under Georgia law, a qualifying premarital education program consists of at least six hours of instruction on marital issues including: conflict management, communication skills, financial responsibilities, child and parenting responsibilities, and extended family roles. Couples must complete the program together within 12 months of their marriage. Counselors, including marriage and family therapists and social workers, are all recognized by the state to perform the premarital education programs.[16] In Minnesota, couples who have 12 hours of premarital education will get the cost of the marriage license reduced from $115 to $40. Minnesota permits religious officials to conduct the programs; a licensed or ordained minister or designee authorized to solemnize marriage (under MS 517.18) or licensed to practice marriage and family therapy (under MS 148.33). What becomes of the certificates filed at the marriage-licensing bureau with the application for the marriage license? In Minnesota, the law requires the local registrar to keep statements of completion (which are submitted for the marriage license) for seven years.[17]

---

12 "Eat, Pray, Love, Then Commit", Ann Patchett, *The Wall Street Journal*. January 2, 2010.
13 http://www.nytimes.com/2007/04/15/us/15marriage.html?pagewanted=print&_r=0, "Texas Legislators Push Marital Counselling," NewYorkTimes.com, April 15, 2007.
14 http://twogetherintexas.com/UI/HomePage.aspx
15 (A.R.S. 25-901-906) http://www.usmarriagelaws.com/search/united_states/arizona/covenant_marriage.shtml
16 Georgia Code Chapter 10A of Title 43.
17 MS 517.08 subd1.

Could a state require premarital counseling? How about if counseling is an option, but has financial inducements, as Texas and Minnesota propose? Is this too much governmental intervention in the family or with the fundamental right to marry? Another proposal was to encourage couples who are filing for divorce to attend a ten-hour crisis marriage counseling course. This instruction includes conflict management and forgiveness skills. Is it better to have counseling before marriage or before divorce?

FINANCIAL COUNSELING

Effective January 1999 in Pinellas County, Florida couples must consider the consequences of divorce before they can marry. Prospective brides and grooms are now required to read a small booklet, which describes how a court would divide assets and child support payments. The couple must attend a four-hour course to improve communication, financial, and parenting skills before marriage. In exchange, licenses are available for less than $93.50. With proof of counseling, the court clerks are allowed, by law, to waive the three-day waiting period in the event of a hardship case.[18]

EXTEND THE SEPARATION PERIOD

Another Texas proposal was to extend the waiting period for a no-fault divorce to six months, an increase from the current two-month period. What effect would this have on the divorce rate? Could it impact court determinations of custody and child support? Is it in the children's best interest?[19] Texas does allow a reduction of the newly extended waiting period to three months, if the divorcing couple participates in ten hours of marital counseling.

DIVORCE SCHOOL

As of November 2014, Oklahoma requires couples who divorce on grounds of incompatibility to go through an education program before being allowed to divorce if their children are younger than 18. This program is "aimed at educating parents about the effects of divorce on children and advising them about reconciliation."[20] According to one of the bill's sponsors, "If you are going

---

18 http://www.usmarriagelaws.com/search/united_states/florida/marriage_licenses/pinellas_county_saint_petersburg.shtml

19 http://www.nytimes.com/2007/04/15/us/15marriage.html?pagewanted=print&_r=0, "Texas Legislators Push Marital Counselling," *NewYorkTimes.com*, April 15, 2007.

20 "Oklahoma to require divorce school for couples with children", Heide Brandes, *Reuters*, June 5, 2014.Contrast this to Oklahoma's "marriage classes", its legislative initiative to prevent poverty (caused by single parenthood) through the "marriage cure" or promoting marriage's benefits to single women. https://www.google.com/search?q=%E2%80

through the whole divorce process and have kids, if we can do anything to keep people together, we should. Marriage is a lifelong contract with the state and with your children." [21] The program costs between $15 and $60, but allows couples to opt out for compelling circumstances."

In all these attempts to strengthen or even restore marriage, "[e]verything tried—from marriage-education programs to changes in the way marriage is treated in tax and benefit programs—has had little or no effect."[22] It is probable that the high divorce rate is more fundamental than a few days or weeks of counseling or other built-in marriage delays can resolve. What is the answer? Could it be that in an era where couples marry for love, the answer is divorce when they fall out of love?

%9CThe+Marriage+Cure.+Is+wedlock+really+a+way+out+of+poverty%3F%E2%80%9D++Katherine+Boo&ie=utf-8&oe=utf-8

21   Ibid. Citing bill sponsor Senator Rob Standridge (R).
22   "Beyond Marriage", Isabel V. Sawhill, *The New York Times*, September 13, 2014, Sunday Review, p1

9

MARRIAGE

The fact is, marriage is this magic thing. I mean forget all the financial stuff—marriage...
symbolizes commitment and love like nothing else in the world.
And it's known all over the world. I mean, wherever you go, if you're married,
that means something to people, and it meant a difference in feeling the next day.
—Edie Windsor, Plaintiff in *U.S. v. Windsor*[1]

I married the first man I ever kissed. When I tell my children that,
they just about throw up.
—Barbara Bush[2]

MARRIAGE DEFINED

"Love and marriage, love and marriage, go together like a horse and carriage," Frank Sinatra famously sang.[3] While that simile defined marriage for a whole generation of 1950s Americans, it is not true according to the law. For hundreds of years, courts have said love appears to be irrelevant to marriage.[4] The institution of marriage has existed since the beginning of history in every culture. The courts often remark that marriage exists as a

---

1 In *the U.S. v. Windsor*, the U.S. Supreme Court struck down section 3 of DOMA allowing the federal government to recognize valid same-sex marriages from the states. "Meet The 83-Year-Old Taking On The U.S. Over Same-Sex Marriage", Nina Totonger, *NPR*. March 21, 2013http://www.npr.org/2013/03/21/174944430/meet-the-83-year-old-taking-on-the-u-s-over-same-sex-marriage.

2 www.brainyquote.com/quotes/quotes/b/barbarabus161533.html

3 "Love and Marriage," written by Sammy Cahn and Jimmy van Heusen.

4 This is the theory proposed by some groups opposed to same-sex marriage. They argue that if marriage is about love, what is to stop people from marrying their brothers, whom they love? Under this argument, which the court accepted for centuries, marriage is really about procreation, which same-sex couples cannot do without assistance.

unique commitment between two people. Historically, marriages were arranged as "commercial" transactions with the transfer of money in the form of dowries, which promoted the joining of families, not just spouses. In *Hyde v. Hyde* in 1866[5], which involved a potentially polygamous union, Judge Penzance famously said, "I conceive that marriage, as understood in Christendom, may for this purpose be defined as the voluntary union for life of one man and one woman, to the exclusion of all others." How is this working out?

How should marriage be defined? In 1972, Maryland was the first state to restrict its definition of marriage to a man and a woman. Now that same-sex marriage is legal in Maryland and all other states (see Chapter 6), this definition has been revised. The Uniform Marriage and Divorce Act, Section 20, also defined marriage as "a personal relationship between a man and a woman arising out of a civil contract to which the consent of the parties is essential." If, the old classification of the parties as a man and a woman was wrong, at least the number of parties—two—is accurate, right?

The late and much beloved Princess of Wales, Diana, said, "There were three people in the marriage, so it was quite crowded."[6] Is three too many in a marriage? In a classic case, *Maynard v. Hill*, 125 U.S. 190 (1888), the court defined marriage as a relationship between three parties: the two spouses and the state. Marriage was defined as unique because it is both a contract between two people and a status recognized between those two people and the state (government). While recognizing the state's rights to regulate marriage, the U.S. Supreme Court wrote that marriage "…is something more than a mere contract. The consent of the parties is… essential to its existence but when the contract to marry is executed by the marriage, a relation between the parties is created which they cannot change…. The relation once formed, the law steps in and holds the parties to various obligations and liabilities…."

When *Maynard* held that the state is a party to the marriage, it said that the state becomes so only after the marriage occurs. But the state does involve itself into marriages in the sense that it prevents those that it believes should not occur, as discussed infra. Can it ever be that the state would involve itself in requiring a couple to marry? In the 30's and 40's courts sometimes gave a petty criminal the option to go to jail or join the army. It is unclear if that was to straighten him out or just to get him out of the court's jurisdiction. What about a judge who orders a man to marry or go to jail in 2015? In Texas after a man pled guilty to a misdemeanor assault charge (he punched his girlfriend's ex-boyfriend), the judge gave him a choice of going to jail for two years or marrying his 20-year-old girlfriend as part of his probation (he also was required to write a Bible verse 25 times "'If a man digs a pit, he will fall into it' Proverbs 26:27")[7]. Is this constitutional?

---

5   http://webdb.lse.ac.uk/gender/Casefinaldetail.asp?id=1&pageno=9

6   http://www.nytimes.com/2005/02/11/world/europe/charles-calls-end-to-the-affair-hell-happily-wed-his-camilla.html?_r=0

7   When the judge insisted that he ask his girlfriend to marry she was flustered and embarrassed in the courtroom. Later when she told her father what happened in court Kenneth Jaynes said, "'I was really upset. Judge Rogers stepped into my family and tried to tell them what to do without any regard for me or anything. This isn't his decision.' "Man gets a choice: Marry her or go to jail", Tony Marco, CNN, August 8, 2015. www.cnn.com/2015/08/07/us/texas/-judge-marriage-sentence/

Some courts remark that marriages exist as a unique commitment of two people. As discussed in Chapter 7, the couple forms the marriage contract during courtship. With a proposal ("will you marry me?"), an offer of marriage is made. The reply ("Yes!"), is the acceptance. The consideration (value exchanged) can be a ring or simply a promise to marry. How is a marriage contract different from a typical commercial contract, say, to buy a car? It is different because it creates a status—the forming of a new relationship makes it harder to break. Also, once this relationship is formed, the government holds the couple to various obligations and liabilities. How much do you know about the contract of marriage? This chapter should give you some knowledge.

IS MARRIAGE DEAD?

More than 40 percent of new mothers are unmarried.[8] When they do marry, it is often the result of the birth of a child during cohabitation.[9] But even such weddings, previously called "shot gun weddings," are on the decline; instead, impending birth only causes the couple to begin cohabitation in "shot gun cohabitations."[10] About 50 percent of couples who "drift into parenthood unintentionally… and are cohabitating at the time of their child's birth" will split up by the time their child is 5 years old.[11] Certainly the change in cultural norms is reflected in these statistics. "Single men and women in the late 19th centuries rarely lived together without marrying, and very few had children. The social norms against cohabitation and childbearing outside of marriage were strong. During the past few generations, these norms have weakened. It is now commonplace for unmarried young adults to cohabit and broadly acceptable for them to have children."[12] So has cohabitation turned mainstream or "can marriage be restored as the standard way to raise children?"[13] Should it?

On one side of the argument to support marriage are "conservatives who see marriage as sacred and the key to a society based on traditional values".[14] Economist Isabel V. Sawhill was also an influential voice on the side of marriage when supporting her view with data "which shows that marriage promotion programs haven't worked and that children born to married parents tend to fare far better in life than do children in other family arrangements."[15] On the other side of the

---

8   "Beyond Marriage", Isabel V. Sawhill, *The New York Times*, September 14, 2015, Sunday Review, p.2.
9   Ibid.
10   "More couples who become parents are living together but not marrying, data show", Hope Yen, *The Washington Post*, January 7, 2014. About 18.1 percent of all single women who became pregnant opted to move in with their boyfriends before the child was born, according to 2006-2010 data from the government's National Survey of Family Growth, the latest available. That is compared with 5.3 percent who chose a post-conception marriage. As recently as the early 1990s, 25 percent of such couples got married.
11   Ibid.
12   "The real reason richer people marry", Andrew J. Cherlin, *The New York Times*, December 7, 2014, Sunday Review p3. "
13   "Beyond Marriage", Isabel V. Sawhill, *The New York Times*, September 14, 2015, Sunday Review, p.2.
14   "An objection to the status quo", Brigid Schulte, *The Washington Post*, January 4, 2015, C1.
15   Ibid.

argument against marriage as the status quo are, among others, economists "who dismissed the institution as an oppressive vestige of patriarchy"[16] and those who argue "that we should accept the new reality and support single parents by providing more child care, health care, food and cash assistance."[17] So why has Sawhill now joined the other side? "The genie is out of the bottle. What we need instead is a new ethic of responsible parenthood. If we combine an updated social norm with greater reliance on the most effective forms of birth control, we can transform drifters into planners and improve children's life prospects. Unless we come to grips with what is happening to marriage and parenting, progress will be limited."

One's income seems to make a difference in marriage matters. "Among 20 to 49-year old men in 2013, 56 percent of professional, managerial and technical workers were married, compared with 31 percent of service workers" per the census.[18] "College—educated men and women can pool two incomes and provide a solid financial foundation for a marriage. In contrast...there are declines in marriage among high school graduates who are stuck in the middle of the labor market, where they can no longer find the kind of steady, decently paying employment that supported their grandparents' marriages."[19] "The latest results seem to indicate that marriage, as a context for childbearing and childrearing is increasingly reserved for America's middle- and upper-class populations."[20] Sawhill notes that for centuries, the human need for closer relationships was fulfilled by marriage, which guaranteed the survival of women, who, for the most part, were prohibited from making a living. For men, marriage was a cornerstone, signifying entry to adult life. But as women have gained economic independence, marriage does neither of those things anymore."[21] Yet, many, including Sawhill, suggest that education and job opportunities would help, but cultural changes are also driving the statistics.

Is it true, as Sawhill now advocates, that it's time that society stops trying to revive marriage and instead tries to figure out what will replace it?[22] As she says, is "[m]arriage disappearing?"[23] According to Sawhill, "the institution will evolve, and must evolve with the times"[24] especially for the sake of

16 Ibid.

17 "Beyond Marriage", Isabel V. Sawhill, *The New York Times*, September 14, 2015, Sunday Review, p.2.

18 The real reason richer people marry", Andrew J. Cherlin, *The New York Times*, December 7, 2014, Sunday Review p3. The author argues that the marriage gap may be based, at least in part, on the wage gap between the two groups. He also cites cultural changes as impacting the decision to marry.

19 Ibid.

20 "More couples who become parents are living together but not marrying, data show", Hope Yen, *The Washington Post, January 7, 2014,* quoting Daniel Lichter, a Cornell sociologist and past president of the Population Association of America.

21 "An objection to the status quo", Brigid Schulte, *The Washington Post*, January 4, 2015, C1-5. Unfortunately, "marrying up" in social status may not be the answer either. Research done by Jessi Streib found that "marrying outside your economic class can fuel fights about everything from home décor to free time." Sometimes, however, "class" allowed couples to draw strength from their differences. "They were drawn to their middle-class partners because they offered the promise of a stable future." "For richer or poorer," Jessi Streib, *The Washington Post*, March 29, 2015, P. B3.

22 Ibid. p.5

23 Ibid, p5.

24 Ibid.

children.[25] Sawhill thinks maybe Scandinavian-style long-term cohabiting may be next.[26] Given that cohabitation and children born outside of marriage is a cultural norm, why is cohabitation status not on birth certificates? One step would be to include this option so that policy debates over the government safety net for poor households are less skewed and such families can receive the support they need.[27] In what other ways can society support these relationships?[28]

PREGLIMONY
BY SHARI MOTRO

Unmarried lovers who conceive are strangers in the eyes of the law. If the woman terminates the pregnancy, the man owes her nothing. If she takes the pregnancy to term, the man's obligation to support her is limited. The law reflects this lovers-as-strangers presumption by making a man's obligation towards a woman with whom he conceives derivative of his paternity-related obligations; his duty is towards his child, not towards the woman in her own right. Thus, a pregnant woman's lost wages and other personal costs are her private problem, and if there is no child at the end of the pregnancy, there is no one—from a legal perspective—that the man must support.

The law also endorses this lovers-as-strangers default in the way in which it treats men who do support their pregnant lovers. It does this through the tax code. Current tax law likely regards payments between unmarried lovers as gifts or as child support. This characterization not only misses

---

25   One-third of American children are living in a single-parent family where child poverty rates are four times as high as in two-parent families." Ibid.

26   Ibid.

27   Ibid.

28   Sawhill also proffers the idea that if "instead of 'drifting' into mistimed and unwanted pregnancies outside of marriage, people had to consciously; 'plan' to have children by using long-acting reversible contraceptives" or "if in place of traditional marriage there was at least a new 'ethic of responsible parenthood,'" which "means not having a child before you and your partner really want one and have thought about how you will care for that child" people could use contraceptives that are 40 times more effective than condoms and 20 times more effective than the pills. These would allow people to opt out and plan when they will have a child. That means not having a child before both partners really want one and have thought about how you will care for that child. But these contractions for women cost as much as $1000. Sawhill also advocates more child care options and a higher minimum wage. The old social norm was, "Don't have a child outside of marriage." The new norm needs to be, "Don't have a child until you and your partner are ready to be parents." "Beyond Marriage", Isabel V. Sawhill, *The New York Times*, September 14, 2015, Sunday Review, p.2.

the mark descriptively, it also misses an opportunity to reward and encourage a behavior that is critically important in an age when sex and procreation outside of marriage are common.

This Article argues that the law should develop a new framework for addressing the unique relationship between unmarried lovers who conceive and that tax reform offers a practical and relatively modest first step for doing so. To this end, it proposes that Congress create a pregnancy-support deduction to benefit taxpayers who already support pregnant women, thereby extending to them the same deduction we now give taxpayers who pay alimony.

INTRODUCTION

We have alimony. We have palimony. Why don't we have *preg*limony? Under current law, a man has no legal obligation towards a woman with whom he conceives until paternity is established. This almost always happens after and only *if* a pregnancy is taken to full term. If the pregnancy ends in abortion, the woman is entirely on her own. If she gives birth, the man may be required to reimburse her for a portion of prenatal and birthing medical expenses, but other pregnancy-related costs—like her lost wages—are seen as her personal problem. In many cases, women never invoke even these limited retroactive entitlements for fear of alienating men already reluctant to meet their child support obligations.

Why is this a problem? First, unless both parties understood their encounter as a no-strings-attached proposition, the current rule is unfair. It puts a disproportionate share of the costs of both parties' actions on the woman alone. Second, it gives men who assume their partner will terminate an unwanted pregnancy no economic incentive to be vigilant about birth control. Of course, conscientious men have plenty of other reasons to prevent an unwanted pregnancy, but the fact that abortion is free for men leaves some unconcerned about pregnancy prevention, contributing to the perception that birth control is a woman's responsibility.[1] Finally, the current paradigm disregards the relational implications of conception. Some pregnancies result from what is clearly a no- strings-attached encounter, but often the sex[2] that produces a pregnancy takes place in the context of a relationship in which certain baseline responsibilities are assumed. Data on men's involvement in pregnancy and

---

1   See Jennifer A. Reich & Claire D. Brindis, *Conceiving Risk and Responsibility: A Qualitative Examination of Men's Experiences of Unintended Pregnancy and Abortion,* 5 INT'L J. MEN'S HEALTH 133, 140 (2006) (noting that in a study of men whose sexual partners had undergone an abortion, the majority stated that "pregnancy prevention is the primary responsibility of women").

2   Since the focus of this Article is on pregnancy, "sex" or "sexual relations" generally refers to penile-vaginal penetration. There are, of course, many other types of sex. Susan Appleton has argued that the legal and cultural focus on heterosexual intercourse to the exclusion of other types of physical intimacy reflects a deep-seated disregard for women's pleasure. *See* Susan Frelich Appleton, *Toward a "Culturally Cliterate" Family Law?*, 23 BERKELEY J. GENDER L. & JUST. 267, 285-86 (2008).

abortion is scant,[3] but it does suggest that many abortions and most births take place in the context of relationships that involve some expectation of care and support.[4]

Current scholarship on the legal relationship between unmarried lovers who conceive is virtually nonexistent,[5] judicial commentary on the scope of unwed fathers' pregnancy-related obligations is sparse, and many state courts have been silent on the issue.[6] Uncertainty abounds, leaving unmarried lovers who conceive to muddle through on their own. In the past, when marriage was the primary site for procreation, the problem was relatively modest. Today, with over one-third of births[7] and two-thirds of abortions[8] occurring outside of marriage, the status quo is untenable.

In a prior work—*The Price of Pleasure*[9]—I argued that the lovers-as-strangers paradigm that now governs out-of-wedlock pregnancy should be replaced with a relational default. This default would require unmarried lovers who conceive to share both the direct and indirect financial burdens of the pregnancy regardless of its outcome. It would not apply to pregnancies resulting from non-consensual sex (including sex involving fraud or deceit) for which we have (albeit imperfect) criminal and tort frameworks, and couples who don't want to be governed by the relational paradigm would be free to opt out of it. No-strings-attached sex isn't inherently wrong; it's just the wrong legal default.

---

3   See *infra* note 34.

4   See *infra* note 35.

5   A number of scholars have begun to critique the law's hands-off approach to sexual fraud. But these scholars do not focus on pregnancy in particular and they are unconcerned with consensual sex that involves no fraud or deceit. See Martha Chamallas, *Consent, Equality, and the Legal Control of Sexual Conduct*, 61 S. CAL. L. REV. 777, 830-35 (1988) (arguing that criminal law is not "at a point where deception is generally regarded as an impermissible inducement to sex"); Jane E. Larson, *"Women Understand So Little, They Call My Good Nature 'Deceit'": A Feminist Rethinking of Seduction*, 93 COLUM. L. REV. 374, 381 (1993) (arguing that the existing adjudicatory system is capable of "identify[ing] the absence of authentic consent required under [a] theory of sexual fraud"); Michelle Oberman, *Sex, Lies, and the Duty to Disclose*, 47 ARIZ. L. REV. 871, 889 (2005) ("The post-seduction norm of nondisclosure [that enables sexual fraud] represents a degree of complacency with regard to bald-faced lying that is almost unparalleled in the common law governing tort and contract."); Lea VanderVelde, *The Legal Ways of Seduction*, 48 STAN. L. REV. 817, 892-93 (1996) (exploring the history of seduction under the law and treatment of sexual fraud under the Field Codes).

The work of Linda Hirshman and Jane Larson does address the imbalance at the heart of the default code governing consensual heterosexual sex, but Hirshman and Larson do not focus on conception. *See* LINDA R. HIRSHMAN & JANE E. LARSON, HARD BARGAINS: THE POLITICS OF SEX 281 (1998).

6   Sheri Motro, "Preglimony," Stanford Law Review, vol. 63, no. 3, pp. 647-697. Copyright © 2011 by Stanford University. Reprinted with permission. Provided by ProQuest LLC. All rights reserved.

7   FED. INTERAGENCY FORUM ON CHILD & FAMILY STATISTICS, AMERICA'S CHILDREN IN BRIEF 4 (2008); *see also* Jeffrey A. Parness & Zachary Townsend, *For Those Not John Edwards: More and Better Paternity Acknowledgments at Birth*, 40 U. BALT. L. REV. 51, 86 (2010) ("In 2007, the number of children in the United States born out of wedlock exceeded 1.7 million, more than nineteen times the estimated number of children born out of wedlock in 1940.").

8   *An Overview of Abortion in the United States*, GUTTMACHER INST., http://www.guttmacher.org/media/presskits/2005/06/28/abortionoverview.html (last visited Oct. 26, 2010).

9   Shari Motro, *The Price of Pleasure*, 104 NW. U. L. REV. 917 (2010).

I continue to maintain that comprehensive reform along these lines represents an important long-term ideal, but I also recognize that imposing a mandatory pregnancy-support obligation on unmarried men presents both administrative and philosophical challenges that require further study. In this Article, therefore, I develop a simpler, more immediately practical framework through which we may begin to recognize the unique relationship between unmarried lovers who conceive: tax reform.

The law is silent on the proper tax treatment of pregnancy-related payments, but current principles suggest that they may be either gifts or child support for tax purposes. Neither of these characterizations matches the realities of the relationship between lovers who conceive, and neither triggers tax consequences because gifts and child support are nondeductible to the payor and excludible by the recipient. As a result, the current rule misses an opportunity to reward and encourage men who are already inclined to support their pregnant lovers. In addition, it implicitly endorses a view of lovers as legal strangers.

This Article proposes that Congress create a pregnancy-support deduction—a provision that would extend to taxpayers who support pregnant women the same benefits we now give taxpayers who pay alimony. Part I lays out the problem—when unmarried sexual partners conceive they often view the pregnancy as a shared responsibility, but the law treats them as strangers. As a result, the current legal approach to reproduction is unjust, it is expressly harmful, and it sets up the wrong incentives. Part II explores possibilities for reform—bolstering marriage as the gateway to sex, increasing public support for pregnant women, and giving women a legally enforceable entitlement to support from the men with whom they conceive. Ultimately, I conclude that these possibilities are unworkable, utopian, or unlikely to materialize in the near term. Part III therefore turns to the pregnancy-support deduction—a relatively simple amendment to the Internal Revenue Code with immediate effects. The deduction would incentivize greater pregnancy-related support and treat unmarried lovers more equitably by implicitly recognizing that they are neither spouses nor complete strangers, but rather something in between.

I. THE LOVERS-AS-STRANGERS PARADIGM

A. The Current Law of Conception

Our legal tradition has not been kind to unmarried love. Under the common law, men had no legal obligations towards the women with whom they conceived out of wedlock.[10] Today, the same rule holds in cases in which the woman terminates an unintended pregnancy—the man owes her nothing. When the woman takes the pregnancy to term, most states require unwed fathers to participate in the "reasonable expenses" of pregnancy,[11] which are generally limited to expenses that directly benefit

---

10 *See* People *ex rel.* Lawton v. Snell, 111 N.E. 50, 51 (N.Y. 1916); *In re* Cirillo's Estate, 114 N.Y.S.2d 799, 801 (Sur. Ct. 1952); Jelen v. Price, 458 N.E.2d 1267, 1270 (Ohio Ct. App. 1983).

11 *See, e.g.*, CAL. FAM. CODE § 7637 (West 2010) (an unwed father may be directed "to pay the reasonable expenses of the mother's pregnancy and confinement"); R.I. GEN. LAWS § 15-8-1 (2010) ("The father of a child which is or

the subsequently born child. This is because most states frame pregnancy-related obligations as an element of a man's child support obligations[12] or as part of a parentage order,[13] not as a duty to-wards the woman in her own right. The rationale behind this approach stems from the now widely accepted imperative that children of unmarried parents should not be relegated to the legal no-man's-land of "illegitimacy."[14] All fifty states now require both parents to support their offspring regardless of marital status.[15] Since a child's prebirth health cannot be disentangled from the health of the expectant mother, child support begins in utero.[16] Accordingly, most cases dealing with the scope of these pregnancy-related obligations focus on prenatal and birthing medical expenses,[17] as does the Uniform Parentage Act, which provides that:

---

may be born out of lawful wedlock is liable to the same extent as the father of a child born in lawful wedlock... for the reasonable expense of the mother's pregnancy and confinement... ."); VA. CODE ANN. § 20-49.8(A) (2010) ("A judgment or order establishing parentage... may direct either party to pay the reasonable and necessary unpaid expenses of the mother's pregnancy and delivery or equitably apportion the unpaid expenses between the parties."); State ex rel. Reitenour, 807 A.2d 1259, 1262 (N.H. 2002) (relying on N.H. REV. STAT. ANN. § 168-A:1 (2002) in holding that "[o]nce paternity has been established, the father of a child born out of wedlock is liable for the 'reasonable expense of the mother's pregnancy and confinement'").

12   See, e.g., 750 ILL. COMP. STAT. ANN. 45/14 (West 2010); MASS. GEN. LAWS ANN. ch. 209C, § 9 (West 2010); MISS. CODE ANN. § 93-9-7 (2010).

13   See, e.g., CAL. FAM. CODE § 7637; COLO. REV. STAT. § 19-4-116(3)(a) (2010); VA. CODE ANN. § 20-49.8(A).

14   See AM. LAW INST., PRINCIPLES OF THE LAW OF FAMILY DISSOLUTION § 3.01, at 464 (2002) ("[I]t is now generally accepted that children of informal and formal relationships must be treated equally with respect to the amount and duration of child support.").

15   See Jeffery W. Santema, Annotation, Liability of Father for Retroactive Child Support on Judicial Determination of Paternity, 87 A.L.R. 5th 361, 379-80 (2001) ("The parents of a child born out of wedlock have an obligation to support the child.... It is the fact of paternity or maternity, not that of marriage, that obligates the parents to nourish and rear the child. Hence, the support rights of children born out of wedlock are the same as those of children born in wedlock.").

16   See Coxwell v. Matthews, 435 S.E.2d 33, 34 (Ga. 1993) ("[T]he duty to protect and maintain a child includes the duty to ensure that the child receives adequate medical care prior to and during birth.").

17   See, e.g., id. at 34 (holding that a claim for $15,459 in pregnancy- and birth-related medical expenses may be made in an action to determine the paternity of a child and affirming the trial court's order that the father reimburse the mother for the entire amount); Sisneroz v. Polanco, 975 P.2d 392, 398-99 (N.M. Ct. App. 1999) (holding that the mother of a child born out of wedlock had standing to seek reimbursement for pregnancy and birthing expenses while recognizing the trial court's discretion to grant or deny pregnancy and birthing costs); State ex rel. Dep't of Health & Human Res. v. Carpenter, 564 S.E.2d 173, 176 (W. Va. 2002) (requiring a biological father to reimburse the Department of Health and Human Resources for $4,879 in birth and medical expenses paid on behalf of the mother); Kathy L.B. v. Patrick J.B., 371 S.E.2d 583, 587 (W. Va. 1988) (requiring a child's biological father to reimburse the mother for birth expenses); see also, e.g., MASS. GEN. LAWS ANN. ch. 209C, § 9(a) ("An order may be entered requiring a parent chargeable with support to reimburse the mother... for medical expenses attributable to the child or associated with childbirth or resulting from the pregnancy."); N.D. CENT. CODE § 14-20-48 (2010) (adopting language from section 621(d) of Uniform Parentage Act); OKLA. STAT. tit. 10, § 7700-621 (2010) (adopting same section 621(d) language); TEX. FAM. CODE ANN. § 160.621 (West 2010) (also adopting section 621(d) language); id. § 160.636(g) ("On a finding of parentage, the court may... on a proper showing, order a party to pay an equitable portion of all of the prenatal and postnatal health care expenses of the mother and the child."); UTAH CODE ANN. § 78B-15-613 (LexisNexis 2010) (adopting language from section 621(d) of Uniform Parentage Act); WASH. REV.

Copies of bills for genetic testing and for prenatal and postnatal health care for the mother and child which are furnished to the adverse party [to a paternity proceeding] not less than 10 days before the date of a hearing are admissible to establish:... that the charges were reasonable, necessary, and customary.[18] *Case law generally disregards other costs like lost wages,*[19] *childbirth classes,*[20] *and maternity clothes.*[21]

B. The Problem with the Status Quo

This legal status quo is troubling for three main reasons. First, it is unfair. When a woman who isn't prepared to be a mother discovers she's pregnant, the weeks and months that follow can be extremely difficult. If she chooses to terminate the pregnancy, the physical and emotional risks of the procedure

---

CODE ANN. § 26.26.570 (West 2010) (adopting same section 621(d) language); WYO. STAT. ANN. § 14-2-813 (2010) (adopting same section 621(d) language).

18   UNIF. PARENTAGE ACT § 621(d) (amended 2002), 9B U.L.A. 346 (2001 & Supp. 2008).

19   Many jurisdictions have been silent on the issue, but Minnesota, Montana, and Ohio have construed the Uniform Parentage Act not to include lost wages as part of the reasonable expenses associated with the birth. *See* Bunge v. Zachman, 578 N.W.2d 387, 389 (Minn. Ct. App. 1998); *In re* Paternity of W.L., 855 P.2d 521, 523-24 (Mont. 1993); Jelen v. Price, 458 N.E.2d 1267, 1270 (Ohio Ct. App. 1983). *But see* Horner v. Dible, No. S-93-44, 1994 WL 319071, at *3 (Ohio Ct. App. June 30, 1994) (affirming the trial court's award of lost wages under new statutory language). Lost wages are also not included in reasonable expenses of pregnancy in Arkansas. *See* Taylor v. Finck, 211 S.W.3d 532, 537 (Ark. 2005).

20   *See, e.g., In re* Baby Girl D., 517 A.2d 925, 929 (Pa. 1986) (construing the "reasonable lying-in expenses" language to mean that Lamaze classes, prenatal care, and sonograms are not chargeable to the adopting parents to reimburse for expenses on behalf of the natural mother). The court in *Taylor* relied on this holding to deny reimbursement to a birth mother for such expenses from the birth father. 211 S.W.3d at 537.

21   *See, e.g., Taylor,* 211 S.W.3d at 537 ("Lying-in expenses normally would not include items such as maternity clothes, lost wages, or counseling."). A minority of states extend a man's pregnancy-related obligations beyond the narrow scope guided by the best interests of the child to encompass duties to the woman in her own right. Most notably, Delaware's domestic relations statute dedicates an independent code section to the "[d]uty to support woman with child conceived out of wedlock." DEL. CODE ANN. tit. 13, § 504 (2010). This provision empowers judges to allocate the costs of pregnancy and birth as they see fit. Despite this broad statutory language, however, there is little indication that Delaware courts have awarded pregnant women anything in excess of the amount typically available in other states under the child support rubric: reimbursement for medical expenses directly related to pregnancy and childbirth. *See* DCSE/J. O'C. v. D.U., No. CN07-03863, 2009 WL 1205835, at *2 (Del. Fam. Ct. Mar. 18, 2009) (discussing only out-of-pocket delivery expenses in connection with a man's pregnancy-related obligation).

alone are significant.[22] When an abortion causes an infection, the long-term effects may be serious, even fatal.[23] For many women, an abortion is also logistically and financially hard to obtain.[24]

As for a pregnancy taken to term, the consequences go far beyond the monetary charges of visits to the obstetrician/gynecologist and the delivery room. Pregnancy may of course be an inspiring and joyful experience, but even smooth pregnancies come with routine difficulties that are more extensive than is generally recognized—including prolonged bouts of nausea and vomiting, back pain, and fatigue.[25] Pregnancy also limits a woman's freedom of movement and it transforms her public identity. Reva Siegel captures some of the effects of pregnancy on a woman's personhood:

> *A woman may find that pregnancy comes to embody her social identity to others, who may treat her with love and respect or, alternatively, abuse her as a burden, scorn her as unwed, or judge her as unfit for employment.... Pregnancy, and the period of lactation that follows it, are not merely burdensome, disruptive, or even consuming forms of work. They amplify the gendered judgments and constraints to which women are already subject, exposing them to material and dignitary injuries having nothing*

---

22 These include abdominal cramping, irregular bleeding, nausea, vomiting, and diarrhea. *See* ELIZABETH RING-CASSIDY & IAN GENTLES, WOMEN'S HEALTH AFTER ABORTION 2-3 (2002); *Abortion—Before, During, and After an Abortion: When to Call a Doctor*, WEBMD, http://women.webmd.com/tc/abortion-before-during-and-after-an-abortion-when -to-call-a-doctor (last updated Sept. 29, 2008); *Possible Physical Side Affects* [sic], AM. PREGNANCY ASS'N, http://www.americanpregnancy.org/unplannedpregnancy/possibleside effects.html (last updated Sept. 2007). On the psychological effects of abortion and debates surrounding the extent and relevance of these effects, see Reva B. Siegel, Lecture, *The Right's Reasons: Constitutional Conflict and the Spread of Woman-Protective Antiabortion Argument*, 57 DUKE L.J. 1641 (2008); Jeannie Suk, *The Trajectory of Trauma: Bodies and Minds of Abortion Discourse*, 110 COLUM. L. REV. 1193 (2010); and *Emotional Reactions After an Abortion*, WEBMD, http://www.webmd.com/hw-popup/emotional-reactions-after-an-abortion (last updated Sept. 29, 2008).

23 *See* F. GARY CUNNINGHAM ET AL., WILLIAMS OBSTETRICS 247 (22d ed. 2005) ("Although serious complications of abortion most often occur with criminal abortion, even spontaneous abortion and legal elective abortion continue to be associated with severe and even fatal infections. Severe hemorrhage, sepsis, bacterial shock, and acute renal failure have all developed in association with abortion but at a much lower frequency. Uterine infection is the usual outcome, but parametritis, peritonitis, endocarditis, and septicemia may all occur." (citations omitted)); RING-CASSIDY & GENTLES, *supra* note 21, at 2; Joel Brind et al., *Induced Abortion as an Independent Risk Factor for Breast Cancer*, 50 J. EPIDEMIOLOGY & COMMUNITY HEALTH 481 (1996); David A. Grimes, *Sequelae of Abortion*, *in* MODERN METHODS OF INDUCING ABORTION 95, 101-02 (David T. Baird et al. eds., 1995).

24 Most U.S. counties do not have abortion providers. This means that women must travel, sometimes for hours, to the nearest clinic. Once they arrive, an abortion typically costs several hundred dollars, and public funding for abortions is limited. As a result of their difficulties reaching a clinic and raising the money for the procedure, pregnant women who are both poor and young are more likely to undergo later-term—and therefore riskier—abortions. *See The New Health Care Reform Legislation: Pros and Cons for Reproductive Health*, GUTTMACHER INST. (Mar. 29, 2010), http://www.guttmacher.org/media/inthenews/2010/03/29/index.html.

25 I discuss these effects in further detail in *The Price of Pleasure. See* Motro, *supra* note 8, at 923-24.

to do with the physiology of reproduction, and entangling them in relationships that profoundly define their identity and life prospects.[26]

After childbirth, a woman may require weeks, sometimes months to recover, especially if she is among the one-third of mothers who now give birth through a cesarean—which is major abdominal surgery.[27] Possible complications and long-term risks of pregnancy and childbirth include chronic vaginal and bowel infections, incontinence, and diabetes. All of these effects compounded together tend to interfere with a woman's ability to provide for herself, if only temporarily, and the scope of workplace protections for pregnant women is limited. As Joanna Grossman explains,

> *[t]he plight of pregnant workers today rests... primarily... in the failure of current law to account for the physical, medical, and social realities of pregnancy. Pregnancy discrimination law provides absolute protection for women only if they retain full work capacity during the period of pregnancy and childbirth. A pregnant woman who seeks to continue working through pregnancy, but experiences a temporary diminishment or alteration of capacity due to the physical effects of pregnancy, will encounter limited protection in the law.*[28]

---

26 Reva Siegel, Reasoning from the Body: *A Historical Perspective on Abortion Regulation and Questions of Equal Protection*, 44 STAN. L. REV. 261, 374-75 (1992) (footnotes omitted); *see also* ANNIE MURPHY PAUL, ORIGINS: HOW THE NINE MONTHS BEFORE BIRTH SHAPE THE REST OF OUR LIVES 167 (2010) ("We're used to thinking of adolescence as a time when our bodies are changing, when our emotions are unruly—well, pregnancy is very similar.... It's a very disorderly time, when a lot of things are in flux. But that fluidity also opens up new opportunities for positive change.... You have to let yourself fall apart, and then put the pieces back together in a different way." (quoting therapist Catherine Monk)).

27 *See Cesarean Section—Topic Overview*, WEBMD, http://www.webmd.com/baby/tc/cesarean-section-topic-overview (last updated Feb. 24, 2010) ("[I]t may take 4 weeks or longer to fully recover [after a C-section]."). On recovery of the perineal area in particular, see Frederick R. Jelovsek, *Vaginal Conditions After Delivery*, WOMEN'S HEALTH RESOURCE, http://www.wdxcyber.com/npreg14.htm (last visited June 6, 2010) ("One study that looked at how long, on the average, it took women to recover various functions after normal vaginal delivery found that the median time (time for 50% of subjects) 'for perineal comfort in general (including walking and sitting) was 1 month (range, 0-6 months); 20% of women took more than 2 months to achieve general perineal comfort. For comfort during sexual inter- course, the median time was 3 months (range, 1 to more than 12 months); 20% of women took longer than 6 months to achieve comfort during sexual intercourse.'" (emphasis omitted)).

28 Joanna L. Grossman, *Pregnancy, Work, and the Promise of Equal Citizenship*, 98 GEO. L.J. 567, 570 (2010); *see also id.* at 578 ("An important, yet under-examined, aspect of pregnant women in the modern workplace is the potential for conflict between the physical effects of pregnancy and paid work.... Historically, women 'with child' were presumed incapable of work, particularly in the later stages of pregnancy.... Today, the opposite presumption is often applied—uncomplicated pregnancy has no meaningful physical effects that bear on a woman's ability to work. The presumption of incapacity and the presumption of uninterrupted capacity are, however, both flawed.").

Annie Murphy Paul illustrates the disconnect between pregnant women's reality and their roles in society through what she calls the myth of the Pregnant Superwoman:

> *This imaginary superhero never needs to sit down and take the weight off her feet, or catch her breath at the top of the stairs. She runs a marathon in her third trimester and works twelve-hour days until her water breaks. She's just like a nonpregnant mortal, in fact, only better, and she has become the unattainable standard against which women measure themselves during pregnancy.*
>
> *... [The myth of the Pregnant Superwoman] is perpetuated in part by pregnant women themselves: she reassures us with her cheerful invulnerability, her bulletproof resistance to all the changes—physical and emotional and logistical—that come along with having a child. Her fearless independence allows us to evade the fact that pregnancy and childrearing do make us more dependent on others, in the heat of a disaster and in the heart of everyday life. In short, the Pregnant Superwoman embodies the insistence that pregnancy doesn't change anything, a fable that may hold as much appeal for pregnant women as it does for spouses and employers. She tells us that, for nine months more, we can hold off the tidal wave of change we know is coming—but at the cost of slighting the needs that have already arisen, and ignoring the changes that are already here.[29]*

These realities combined with our heavy reliance on the nuclear family as a form of "social insurance"[30] mean that when the man is not forthcoming and the pregnancy is complicated (both physically and in its impact on a woman's work life), the law leaves a single pregnant woman to shoulder most of the burdens alone. When a man goes beyond his legal call of duty and regards the pregnancy as a shared responsibility, the law casts his contributions as optional gifts, gratuitous acts of kindness, which leads some women to refuse the help they deserve out of pride.[31] As we shall see, tax law reinforces this message. For sexual partners who do not already share their income but who

---

29   PAUL, *supra* note 25, at 59, 73-74; *see also* Sylvia A. Law, Rethinking Sex and the *Constitution*, 132 U. PA. L. REV. 955, 955-56 (1984) ("The power to create people is awe-some. Men are profoundly disadvantaged by the reality that only women can produce a human being and experience the growth of a child in pregnancy. Pregnancy and childbirth are also burdensome to health, mobility, independence, and sometimes to life itself, and women are profoundly disadvantaged in that they alone bear these burdens.").

30   *See* Anne Alstott, *Private Tragedies? Family Law as Social Insurance*, HARV. L. & POL'Y REV. 3 (2010).

31   I have not found in-depth studies of support patterns among unmarried lovers, but the 1960 novel *The L-Shaped Room* provides one beautifully subtle rendering of the complex and layered emotions involved. *See* LYNNE REID BANKS, THE L-SHAPED ROOM 240 (1960) ("'What's your trouble, my lad?'" the heroine asks the stirring in her womb after meeting Terry, the man with whom she conceived, for the first time since their affair. "'Should I have taken the money he wanted to give us? Why not? you ask. A good question.' Well, why not? He hadn't offered it out of a sense of duty. Or had he? I didn't much care. What mattered was that I hadn't wanted it.... 'It would have given him some claim on you,' I said to the bump under my hand, 'and such claims can't be bought with money.' But I knew that wasn't the only reason. I looked at the stove, snarling like the part of me that had wanted Terry to see all this—the five long flights, the darkness, the smell, the landing taps; I had wanted to punish him. But that feeling had gone—so quickly. I drew back my lips and snapped my teeth happily at the stove. I felt pleased with myself. It would have been so easy to

nevertheless view pregnancy as a shared responsibility, the law also gives virtually no guidance as to a reasonable or equitable baseline for pregnancy-related support. Partners must essentially make up their own rules as they go, which can put tremendous pressure on men and women alike.

The second problem with the status quo is that it sets up the wrong incentives. Studies show that adolescent men who expect to pay child support should their partner become pregnant have fewer partners, less frequent intercourse, and are more likely to use contraceptives.[32] But in some relationships, men assume—sometimes reasonably—that a woman will terminate an unwanted pregnancy. How does the fact that abortion frees men not only of child support but also of any responsibility towards the woman figure into what happens in the bedroom?

Decisions about sex, contraception, and abortion take place in the shadow of the law's allocation of their attendant risks. It is only logical that one way to reduce unintended pregnancies might be to raise the stakes for men, to make sure *all* pregnancies have concrete consequences for both parties involved.

Thus, increasing support for pregnant women regardless of the pregnancy's outcome is likely, over time, to change abortion from being used as a form of birth control that lets men off the hook into a last resort that both parties are invested in preventing. It may also reduce abortions obtained under the pressure of short-term economic considerations.[33]

To be sure, responsible men don't need external incentives to do the right thing; they do their best to prevent pregnancy, and when their efforts fail they don't leave their partner in the lurch, even when their legal duties are minimal or nil. But for some men, the bottom line matters.

Third and finally, by viewing nonmarital pregnancies through the prism of paternity rather than as giving rise to an obligation toward the woman herself, the current rule not only underestimates the real costs of pregnancy, it also ignores the relational implications of conception. True, not all conceptions happen in the context of an ongoing relationship, and casual lovers who mutually intend and expect a no-strings-attached encounter (i.e., those who expect to have no responsibilities vis-à-vis each other should pregnancy occur) should be permitted to set their own rules. But using the lovers-as-strangers paradigm as the baseline governing all nonmarital conceptions flies in the face

---

hate Terry, to take advantage of his vulnerable position; it would have been so easy to take the money, and to justify taking it. I wasn't pleased because I'd resisted the temptation to take it. I was pleased because I hadn't wanted it.").

32 *See* Chien-Chung Huang & Wen-Jui Han, *Child Support Enforcement and Sexual Activity of Male Adolescents*, 69 J. MARRIAGE & FAM. 763 (2007); Chien-Chung Huang & Wen-Jui Han, *Perceptions of Child Support and Sexual Activity of Adolescent Males*, 27 J. ADOLESCENCE 731 (2004).

33 A recent study suggests that child support enforcement decreases the incidence of abortion. *See* Jocelyn Elise Crowley, Radha Jagannathan & Galo Falchettore, The Effect of Child Support Enforcement on Abortion in the United States 22-23 (unpublished manuscript) (on file with author). For data on the higher incidence of abortion among poor women, see HEATHER D. BOONSTRA ET AL., GUTTMACHER INST., ABORTION IN WOMEN'S LIVES 20 (2006), *available at* http://www.guttmacher.org/pubs/2006/05/04/AiWL.pdf ("The abortion rate among women living below the federal poverty level… is more than four times that of women living above 300% of the poverty level… ."); and Annie Murphy Paul, *Is the Recession Causing More Abortions?*, SLATE (May 15, 2009), http://www.doublex.com/section/health-science/recession-causing-more-abortions.

of most people's reality. For one, most conceptions result not from birth control failures during a single encounter but from repeated acts of unprotected intercourse.[34] Also, though further research is needed,[35] studies suggest that most unmarried fathers are involved to some extent during the birth of their child, and boyfriends commonly pay for or contribute to the cost of an abortion.[36] Unless the sex was mutually understood as implying no ongoing responsibilities should conception occur, when the man abandons his pregnant lover we generally think he has done something wrong, that he has violated a basic moral code.

Why then is a lovers-as-strangers paradigm our legal default?

One way to make sense of the current rule is as an example of what Robin West sees as the hyperindividualistic starting point—the "separation thesis"—that underlies modern American jurisprudence.[37] We imagine ourselves as disconnected self-sufficient beings; we believe that we are essentially and fundamentally free-floating independent selves. Accordingly, we think that the greatest danger we face is that other individuals will interfere with or violate our otherwise blissfully isolated independence. This "separation thesis" drives us to fortify ourselves with laws that preserve values like autonomy and privacy, while ignoring other values that are equally essential to human

---

34 *See* JENNIFER J. FROST, JACQUELINE E. DARROCH & LISA REMEZ, GUTTMACHER INST., IMPROVING CONTRACEPTIVE USE IN THE UNITED STATES 1 (2008), *available at* http://www.guttmacher.org/pubs/2008/05/09/ ImprovingContraceptiveUse.pdf ("Slightly more than half of unintended pregnancies occur among women who were not using any method of contraception in the month they conceived, and more than four in 10 occur among women who used their method inconsistently or incorrectly. Only one in 20 are attributable to method failure."); EILEEN L. MCDONAGH, BREAKING THE ABORTION DEADLOCK: FROM CHOICE TO CONSENT 51-53 (1996).

35 *See* ARTHUR B. SHOSTAK & GARY MCLOUTH, MEN AND ABORTION: LESSONS, LOSSES, AND LOVE 5 (1984) (finding that eight-five percent of sociological research on abortion "dealt with women, or the fetus, or the state, etc.—anything except the men involved"); Reich & Brindis, *supra* note 1, at 134 ("Some research has been conducted regarding the perceptions of men's roles in contraception, reproduction, or pregnancy in general, but far less research has been conducted in the area of men's experiences with abortion." (citations omitted)).

36 35. One study of unmarried parents in Oakland, California, revealed that most unmarried parents were romantically involved when their child was born and that about half were living together. SARAH MCLANAHAN ET AL., PUB. POLICY INST. OF CAL., FRAGILE FAMILIES ONE YEAR LATER: OAKLAND, CALIFORNIA 7 (2002), *available at* http://www.ppic.org/content/pubs/op/op_1002smop.pdf. Approximately eighty percent of the mothers in the survey "reported that the father had contributed financial support or helped in other ways (such as providing transportation) during the pregnancy." *Id.* at 10; *see also* MAUREEN R. WALLER, MY BABY'S FATHER: UNMARRIED PARENTS AND PATERNAL RESPONSIBILITY 2-3 (2002) ("Approximately 33 percent of all births in the United States now occur to unmarried parents... [and] about half of these parents are living together at the time of their child's birth."). Another survey of men in abortion clinic waiting rooms revealed that most paid for all or some of the procedure. *See* SHOSTAK & MCLOUTH, *supra* note 34, at 36. Note, however, that data on how many men accompany their partner to the clinic are contradictory. *Compare* Reich & Brindis, *supra* note 1, at 135 ("One recent study found that only 22-25% of women came or left the abortion procedure with the man by whom they became pregnant." (citing Britta Beenhakker et al., *Are Partners Available for Post-Abortion Contraceptive Counseling? A Pilot Study in a Baltimore City Clinic*, 69 CONTRACEPTION 419 (2004))), *with* SHOSTAK & MCLOUTH, *supra* note 34, at 17 n.1 (finding that men accompanied their partners to abortion clinics approximately half of the time).

37 *See* Robin West, *Jurisprudence and Gender*, 55 U. CHI. L. REV. 1, 2 (1988).

flourishing like intimacy and mutual responsibility.[38] Human beings are social animals, we are all inescapably interdependent, we are mutually bound, and we need one another. Thus, West argues that building and cultivating a "connection thesis" to counterbalance the prevailing separation bias is critical to creating a more humane jurisprudence.

Applying this framework to our problem, pregnancy and the sexual act that precedes it are the ultimate embodiment of human beings' capacity for connectedness. A system that treats a woman and the man with whom she conceives as legal strangers is profoundly out of touch with the emotional, spiritual, and moral dimensions of human experience. In some cases, this legal lacuna legitimates the view that an unintended pregnancy is a woman's problem. In others, the law's failure to provide a script, a framework for couples to deal with a difficult situation that clearly implicates both parties, may contribute to the pressure to marry when alternative forms would yield better long-term consequences.[39] Finally, by remaining silent on this issue, the law misses an opportunity to sanction and encourage, indeed to *normalize*, pregnancy support within unmarried couples.[40]

In sum, the lovers-as-strangers paradigm belongs in the past. It is out of step with broadly accepted mores regarding men's responsibility toward a lover undergoing an abortion, and its minimalist approach to pregnancies taken to term is unfair, unwise, and untrue to human experience.

---

38   West casts this opposition in gendered terms. In her view, the separation bias is inherently male, while connection is inherently female. Women, unlike men, "are not essentially, necessarily, inevitably... separate from other human beings.... [W]oman [sic] are 'essentially connected'...." *Id.* at 2-3. West locates women's essential connectedness in their "critical material experiences," including pregnancy and breastfeeding. *Id.* at 3; *see also* Robin L. West, *The Difference in Women's Hedonic Lives: A Phenomenological Critique of Feminist Legal Theory*, 15 WIS. WOMEN'S L.J. 149, 210 (2000).
I do not know whether separation is essentially masculine or connection is essentially feminine, but I do believe that the ultimate conclusion West draws from these categories is crucial to the knot we are trying to unravel. Her most compelling insight is that connectedness expresses an important, undervalued truth that is critical to the happiness of both men and women. Though she emphasizes the differences between the sexes, West also thinks that both men and women are animated by both connection and separation. It is the tension between the two, she says, that is essential to our nature. *See* West, *supra* note 36, at 15-19.
39   *See infra* notes 50-54 and accompanying text.
40   Supporting and encouraging pregnancy support should be especially popular among those dedicated to responsible fatherhood initiatives. *See* Senator Barack Obama, Remarks at the Apostolic Church of God (June 15, 2008) (transcript available at http://my.barackobama.com/page/community/post/stateupdates/gG5nFK) ("We need fathers to realize that responsibility does not end at conception."); *White House Launches Father- hood Initiative*, NPR (Aug. 11, 2009), http://www.npr.org/templates/story/story.php?storyId=111770004 ("Obama's faith-based office will go around the country holding town hall meetings to discuss the importance of fatherhood and speak with community organizations about what policies best work to build strong families.").

II. POSSIBLE SOLUTIONS

In this Part, I turn from the problem to possible solutions. Ultimately, I conclude that the main existing framework for addressing the special relationship between a man and a woman who conceive—marriage—is not a panacea. Nor are utopian proposals to do away with civil marriage and shift the burden of supporting reproduction from the private realm of the family to the state. A third possibility is to create a new legal status specifically designed to address the unique situation of unmarried lovers who conceive. This option is promising, but requires further development before it may be implemented.

A. Marriage

The legal vacuum in which unmarried lovers who conceive find themselves might be seen as a symptom of another, broader crisis: the crisis afflicting the institution of marriage. The very purpose of marriage, some believe, is to regulate the unique relational consequences of heterosexual reproduction.[41] The most visible recent manifestation of this view has arisen in the context of the debates surrounding gay marriage. "[A]n orderly society requires some mechanism for coping with the fact that sexual intercourse commonly results in pregnancy and childbirth," wrote dissenting Massachusetts Supreme Judicial Court Justice Robert Cordy in *Goodridge v. Department of Public Health*,[42] and "[t]he institution of marriage is that mechanism."[43] According to this frequently quoted argument,[44] marriage should be limited to heterosexuals because the raison d'être of marriage—regulating accidental procreation—is a nonissue for gay and lesbian lovers.

Applying this theory of marriage to the problem, the most appropriate response might be to bolster the tried-and-true institution we already have for addressing the issue rather than reinventing the wheel. From this perspective, marriage is women's insurance policy against being left in the lurch. Marriage guarantees a minimal level of mutual support, at least de jure.[45] A pregnant woman married

---

41 For a discussion and critique of the channeling function of marriage, see Appleton, *supra* note 2, at 276-85.

42 798 N.E.2d 941, 995 (Mass. 2003) (Cordy, J., dissenting); *see also id.* at 969 (majority opinion) (holding that a bar against same-sex marriage violated the state's constitution).

43 *Id.* at 995 (Cordy, J., dissenting).

44 See Kerry Abrams & Peter Brooks, Marriage as a *Message: Same-Sex Couples and the Rhetoric of Accidental Procreation*, 21 YALE J.L. & HUMAN. 1, 3-4 (2009) (surveying and critiquing the widespread influence of Justice Cordy's decision).

45 Note however that economically dependent spouses generally have few mechanisms for enforcing their entitlements during marriage. Spouses' economic rights generally vest at divorce. For a discussion of spouses' limited economic rights during an ongoing marriage, see Alicia Brokars Kelly, *Money Matters in Marriage: Unmasking Interdependence in Ongoing Spousal Economic Relations*, 47 U. LOUISVILLE L. REV. 113 (2008–2009). *See also* Katharine Silbaugh, *Turning Labor into Love: Housework and the Law*, 91 NW. U. L. REV. 1, 34 (1996) (explaining that spouses' duty of mutual support is "not directly enforceable between the parties when married" but "may be enforceable during a marriage only by third party creditors who may sue one spouse for certain very narrow categories of debts undertaken by the other"). Even at divorce, while property distribution determinations may take childcare contributions into account, they do not look at pregnancy and the "labor" of child-birth for purposes of determining spouses' contributions to the marriage.

to the man with whom she conceives is thus marginally safer than a pregnant woman who is unwed. Women who want their relationship to be governed by a set of rules that depart from the no-strings-attached default are free to make their commitment official and legally binding. Indeed, some people believe that society deliberately provides additional incentives for them to do so—including sizable tax benefits[46]—and that partners who choose not to commit deserve to face the consequences of their actions alone. From this perspective, changing the default governing unmarried lovers to include minimal relational duties might further erode the fragile institution by removing one of the remaining imperatives to get married.

The historical accuracy of the theory of marriage as primarily aimed at regulating accidental reproduction is subject to debate.[47] Its current relevance, however, is clearly dubious. The overwhelming majority of Americans today have sex outside of marriage.[48] Even the abstinence movement within

---

46 Contrary to popular belief, Congress did not create the "marriage bonus" in order to promote marriage. Nevertheless, politicians and activists have grown to defend it as though Congress did. See Shari Motro, A New "I Do": Towards a Marriage-Neutral Income Tax, 91 IOWA L. REV. 1509, 1529 (2006) [hereinafter Motro, A New "I Do"]. For discussion of tax and other marriage-based benefits, see Appleton, supra note 2, at 273 ("By licensing marriage and attaching to it material and status-based benefits, the state singles out the favored, 'legitimate' site for sexual activity, and clearly communicates its preference for monogamy...." (footnote omitted)); Tara Siegel Bernard & Ron Lieber, The Costs of Being a Gay Couple Run Higher, N.Y. TIMES, Oct. 3, 2009, at A1; and Shari Motro, Op-Ed., The State of the Unions; Single and Paying for It, N.Y. TIMES, Jan. 25, 2004, § 4, at 15.

47 In fact, as Kerry Abrams and Peter Brooks argue, rather than guaranteeing all pregnant women a minimal level of support, marriage limited men's responsibility to just one of their companions. "In the English legal tradition," they write, "[m]arriage... functioned not as a check on the wildness of male heterosexuality but as a way for men to maintain sexual freedom without adverse financial consequences... " Abrams & Brooks, supra note 43, at 9. Marriage obviously provided no protections to mistresses, prostitutes, or slaves. See Larson, supra note 5, at 389-90 ("[Victorian] conventions of female sexual modesty protected 'respectable' women only at the expense of prostitutes, enslaved women, and domestic servants, against whom male sexual interest was redirected."); see also STEPHANIE COONTZ, MARRIAGE, A HISTORY 35 (2005) ("The story that marriage was invented for the protection of women is still the most widespread myth about the origins of marriage."); id. at 31 ("Probably the single most important function of marriage through most of history... was its role in establishing cooperative relationships between families and communities."); id. at 34-49 (discussing the invention of marriage); NANCY F. COTT, PUBLIC VOWS: A HISTORY OF MARRIAGE AND THE NATION 16 (2000) ("As an intentional and harmonious juncture of individuals for mutual protection, economic advantage, and common interest, the marriage bond resembled the social contract that produced government."). For a summary of judicial critiques of the theory, see Courtney Megan Cahill, The Genuine Article: A Subversive Economic Perspective on the Law's Procreationist Vision of Marriage, 64 WASH. & LEE L. REV. 393, 410-12 (2007); and Law, supra note 28, at 957-58.

48 See Naomi Cahn & June Carbone, Red Families v. Blue Families 60 (George Washington Univ. Law Sch. Pub. Law & Legal Theory, Working Paper No. 343, 2007), available at http://papers.ssrn.com/sol3/papers.cfm?abstract_id=1008544 ("Social science research... suggests that well over 90% of all adults engage in sex before they marry... "). As Cahn and Carbone show, the main cultural divide in America today seems to be not between unmarried youth who abstain and those who are sexually active. Rather, the main division is in how people tend to handle an unplanned pregnancy. Conservatives tend toward the "shotgun wedding" while liberals are more likely to terminate the pregnancy. The unintended pregnancy rate is highest among young unmarried women. See Stanley K. Henshaw, Unintended Pregnancy in the United States, 30 FAM. PLAN. PERSP. 24, 27 (1998); Melinda Beck, The Birth-Control Riddle, WALL ST. J., Apr. 20, 2010, at D1 ("One out of every two American women aged 15 to 44 has at least one unplanned

conservative Christian communities has delayed the age of first intercourse only marginally.[49] Some studies show that teens who take chastity pledges are also less likely to use birth control, presumably because "the use of birth control implies that one thought about sex beforehand; one *planned* for it."[50] As the age of first intercourse falls and the age of first marriage rises, the real world relevance of marriage as gatekeeper becomes increasingly tenuous.

Not only does marriage fail to deter nonmarital sex, the solution it offers young people who marry *because* of an accidental pregnancy—the preferred fallback in conservative communities—may also be less than ideal. A "shotgun marriage" will guarantee the woman a baseline level of support,[51] but early marriages (particularly those "compelled by an improvident pregnancy") are more likely than other marriages to end in divorce.[52] Furthermore, the financial and emotional costs of dissolving a failed marriage may outweigh the temporary security it provides during pregnancy. Marriage provides a useful way to formalize intimate relations between lovers who would choose to marry regard- less of the risk of procreative accidents. By standardizing a basket of rights and responsibilities between adults who intend to unite for life, it absolves couples of the need to deliberate and negotiate over every aspect of their union. Its maximalist one-size-fits-all defaults designate spouses as each others' primary beneficiaries, caretakers, guardians, agents, and representatives in all aspects of life—financial, medical, spiritual. In this capacity, spouses replace parents and siblings as a person's most significant legal relation. Though pregnancy and co-parenting are life-altering undertakings, marriage binds people to a broader, more extensive commitment than is needed to protect lovers who conceive and their unplanned children. Thus when pregnancy is accidental, couples whose actual emotional relationship is not one of lifelong commitment may be better served by an intermediate

---

pregnancy in her lifetime. Among unmarried women in their 20s, seven out of 10 pregnancies are unplanned."); *see also* Rob Stein, *Rise in Teenage Pregnancy Rate Spurs New Debate on Arresting It*, WASH. POST, Jan. 26, 2010, at A4.

49   *See* LAUREN F. WINNER, REAL SEX: THE NAKED TRUTH ABOUT CHASTITY 17 (2005) ("In 2001, a study of 6,800 students showed that virgins who took the [True Love Waits abstinence] pledge were likely to abstain from sex for eighteen months longer than those who did not take the pledge. This... means simply that a lot of abstinence pledgers are having sex at nineteen instead of eighteen."); Heather D. Boonstra, *Advocates Call for a New Approach After the Era of "Abstinence-Only" Sex Education*, GUTTMACHER POL'Y REV., Winter 2009, at 6, 8.

50   WINNER, *supra* note 48, at 17. More broadly, rather than functioning as an insurance policy against unintended procreation, marriage is more commonly the form of choice for couples who *intend* to conceive. "Many people today marry," write Kerry Abrams and Peter Brooks, once they think they have found the person they want to procreate with, not because they have decided to have sex for the first time and want to insure themselves against "accidents," but because they have been (irresponsibly?) engaging in sex for quite some time and only now are ready to settle down and have a child. Abrams & Brooks, *supra* note 43, at 32.

51   The scope of this Article is limited to unmarried conception, but the treatment of pregnancy in marriage and divorce law, while better, is also lacking.

52   Cahn & Carbone, *supra* note 47, at 60; *see also id.* at 26 ("[D]ivorce risk... increases with younger age of marriage, lower economic status, and having a baby either prior to marriage or within the first seven months after marriage. Accordingly, family strategies that either emphasize marrying young, or marriage as the solution to an improvident pregnancy are likely to increase rates of divorce, all other things being equal." (footnote omitted)).

status that is calibrated to their situation.[53] The "shotgun" practice is at best an incomplete answer to the problem. Finally, even when parties are already married when they conceive, being married does not necessarily improve the woman's position because it may lock her into a harmful relationship,[54] with the only alternative—divorce—having potentially devastating economic consequences.[55]

In sum, Justice Cordy and those who follow his lead are correct that accidental procreation demands attention. We do need legal institutions that recognize and support its consequences. But marriage is not the ultimate answer. A more coherent and honest approach would acknowledge the crossroads at which we stand. Marriage as we know it does not and cannot set the code for all unplanned pregnancies. An alternative form is needed.[56]

B. Collective Responsibility Toward Pregnant Women

Another possibility is to follow Martha Fineman's lead and go to the opposite extreme: abolish marriage altogether and instead privilege only caretaker-dependent relationships.[57] Fineman starts from the premise that dependency is an inevitable aspect of our nature. "Far from being a 'pathological' condition... it is an inevitable part of the human condition. It is universal—a developmental and shared experience. All of us were dependent as children, and many of us will become dependent as

---

53 *See id.* at 59 ("[M]arriage at younger ages is a risky enterprise. It has historically required a high degree of community-reinforced socialization into marital roles—including stereotypical gender roles, male financial contributions and female dependence—to succeed. New research emphasizes that full emotional maturity does not occur until the mid-twenties, and the less than fully mature early twenties brain (especially if male) is primed for risk- taking and sexual experimentation. At the same time, the modern economy provides fewer opportunities for the men who are ready to start families in their early twenties to move into productive employment." (footnotes omitted); *see also* HIRSHMAN & LARSON, *supra* note 5, at 276 ("Rather than try to force sexual actors into marriage, we choose to modify the anarchic state of nature that characterizes nonmarital sexual bargaining."). *But see* Elizabeth S. Scott, *Marriage, Cohabitation and Collective Responsibility for Dependency*, 2004 U. CHI. LEGAL F. 225, 235 (noting that "even broken marriages provide financial and relationship benefits for dependent family members").

54 *See* JEANNIE SUK, AT HOME IN THE LAW 13-16 (2009) (discussing the marital home as a site of violence, the limitations of available legal remedies, and the difficulties women face in leaving abusive marriages).

55 *See* ANN CRITTENDEN, THE PRICE OF MOTHERHOOD 149-61 (2001); MARTHA ALBERTSON FINEMAN, THE NEUTERED MOTHER, THE SEXUAL FAMILY AND OTHER TWENTIETH CENTURY TRAGEDIES (1995); Appleton, *supra* note 2, at 296-97 (describing family law's failure to deliver on the presumed promises of marriage).

56 For a broader argument that family law should recognize and support friendships that do not resemble marriage or marriage-like relationships, see Laura A. Rosenbury, *Friends with Benefits?*, 106 MICH. L. REV. 189 (2007).

57 *See generally* FINEMAN, *supra* note 54. For related arguments, see Alstott, *supra* note 29, at 6 (showing "how family law operates—despite its traditional private-law label—as social insurance for affective life" and asking "whether public programs ought to address, more explicitly, the consequences of risks traditionally covered by family law—risks of divorce, nonmarriage, parenthood, and childhood"); and Appleton, *supra* note 2, at 274-76 (critiquing family law's sex-centricity).

we age, fall ill, or are disabled."[58] To be human is to be dependent; to be human is to be vulnerable.[59] It follows that all humans need to be cared for at some point in their lives. The people who do this caretaking—usually women[60]—in turn need to be supported themselves because "caretaking requires the sacrifice of autonomy and entails compromises that negatively affect economic and market possibilities."[61] As Robin West puts it:

> *Emotionally and morally women may benefit from the dependency of the fetus and the infant upon us. But materially we are more often burdened than enriched by that dependency. And because we are burdened, we differentially depend more heavily upon others, both for our own survival, and for the survival of the children who are part of us. Women, more than men, depend upon relationships with others, because the weakest of human beings—infants—depend upon us.*
>
> *Thus, motherhood leaves us vulnerable: a woman giving birth is unable to defend herself against aggression; a woman nursing an infant is physically exposed; a woman nurturing and feeding the young is less able to feed herself. Motherhood leaves us unequal....*[62]

The question then becomes, who bears the responsibility for these "inevitable dependents"[63] (the children, the ill, the elderly) and the "derivative dependenc[ies]"[64] of their caretakers? Currently, Fineman argues, we are myopically focused on sexual affiliations between men and women (i.e., marriage and its approximations) as the primary legally significant intimate connection and the framework through which we address dependency.[65] "Marriage has historically served as the 'natural' repository for dependencies," she writes. "The family is the institution to which children, the elderly, and the ill

---

58 Martha Albertson Fineman, *Why Marriage?*, 9 VA. J. SOC. POL'Y & L. 239, 269 (2001).

59 *See* Martha Albertson Fineman, Essay, *The Vulnerable Subject: Anchoring Equality in the Human Condition*, 20 YALE J.L. & FEMINISM 1, 8 (2008) ("I want to claim the term 'vulnerable' for its potential in describing a universal, inevitable, enduring aspect of the human condition that must be at the heart of our concept of social and state responsibility."); *id.* at 12 ("The vulnerable subject approach does what the one-dimensional liberal subject approach cannot: it embodies the fact that human reality encompasses a wide range of differing and interdependent abilities over the span of a lifetime. The vulnerability approach recognizes that individuals are anchored at each end of their lives by dependency and the absence of capacity.").

60 *See* FINEMAN, *supra* note 54, at 162-63 ("Women, wives, mothers, daughters, daughters-in-law, sisters are typically the socially and culturally assigned caretakers. As caretakers they are tied into intimate relationships with their dependents. The very process of assuming caretaking responsibilities creates dependency in the caretaker—she needs some social structure to provide the means to care for others.").

61 Fineman, *supra* note 57, at 270.

62 West, *supra* note 37, at 210.

63 Fineman, *supra* note 57, at 269.

64 Id. at 270.

65 See id. at 243.

are referred; it is the way that the state has effectively 'privatized' dependencies that otherwise might become the responsibility of the collective unit or state."[66]

Fineman argues that this is the wrong approach because romantic relationships do not, in fact, protect dependent caretakers. Though she notes that marriage on an individual level is so specific in practice that any attempt at a generalized definition of the institution is meaningless,[67] she emphasizes that historically, marriage has worked to disadvantage women.[68] A family law that privileges sexual affiliates also casts other intimate forms as deviant, eclipsing discussion about the pressing problems of dependency throughout society, not just amongst pairs.[69] Thus, it exacerbates dependencies by masking them.[70] Most importantly, relegating dependency to the nuclear family is wrong because "dependency is of concern well beyond the family. Dependency work is of benefit to the entire society."[71] This is true not only because primary caretakers' circumstances influence the children who will become the future citizens of our world but also because the conditions of pregnant women influence their fetuses[72]—potentially replicating and perpetuating economic inequalities.[73] Thus Fineman would abolish marriage as a legal category,[74] recognize "the parent-child relationship as the quintessential or core family connection [to be subsidized and supported], and focus on how policy can strengthen this tie."[75] In sum, Fineman's vision leaves behind the obsession with the marital tie and is built around the caretaker and dependent relationship. It is this relationship that should be subsidized and protected.

---

66   Id. at 268; *see also* FINEMAN, *supra* note 54, at 226 ("In our individualistic society, the state relies on the family—allocating to it the care and protection of society's weaker members and the production and education of its future citizens.").

67   *See* Fineman, *supra* note 57, at 241 ("Except in extreme situations, there are no legal enforcement mechanisms to ensure compliance with standards of conduct imposed generally across marriages. The result might be characterized as creating a vacuum of legally mandated meaning for marriage—a vacuum that is to be filled with various non-legal, sometimes conflicting, individual aspirations, expectations, fears, and longings." (footnote omitted)).

68   *See id.* at 247 ("[M]arriage has not been a neutral social, cultural, or legal institution. It has shaped the aspirations and experiences of women and men in ways that have historically disadvantaged women." (footnote omitted)).

69   *See id.* at 246 ("Marriage, as the preferred societal solution, has become the problem. The very existence of this institution eclipses discussion and debate about the problems of dependency and allows us to avoid confronting the difficulty of making the transformations necessary to address these problems.").

70   *See id.*

71   *Id.* at 268.

72   *See* PAUL, *supra* note 25, at 155 ("Increased rates of premature delivery and low birth weight among babies born to depressed pregnant women have been firmly established by research. Now scientists are exploring a startling but still speculative notion: that a pregnant woman's emotional state can influence the fetus's developing brain and nervous system, potentially shaping the way the offspring will experience and manage its own emotions—a kind of maternal impressions redux.").

73   *See id.* at 210 ("In recent years, [Douglas] Almond notes, early-life health measures of blacks have stagnated; black infants are two and a half times more likely to have low birth weight as white infants, and are more than twice as likely to die before age one. Given the potentially lasting effects of prenatal experience, Almond warns, it may be the case that 'a future of racial inequality is being programmed.'").

74   FINEMAN, *supra* note 54, at 228.

75   Fineman, *supra* note 57, at 245.

Recognizing both the inevitability of dependency and the society preserving work that caretakers do in meeting the demands of that dependency, [she] argue[s] for the restructuring of our workplaces to accommodate a "dually responsible" worker, and the reinvigoration of our state so that caretaking and market work... are compatible, accomplishable tasks. Only when this is accomplished will we have a society in which dependency is fairly and justly managed.[76]

As Fineman herself acknowledges, however, her project is utopian.[77] Public support for single pregnant women remains limited,[78] and support for unmarried women seeking an abortion, already scant, is on the decline.[79] This is not to say that efforts to increase collective responsibility for dependency are futile, and advances in this direction are being made. For example, provisions in the recently passed health reform law benefiting pregnant women and teens (read in isolation from the law's abortion-related provisions) are a positive development.[80] But in the current climate, even the most generous

---

76   Id. at 271 (footnotes omitted).

77   FINEMAN, *supra* note 54, at 232.

78   See Rachel Benson *Gold, Recession Taking Its Toll: Family Planning Safety Net Stretched Thin as Service Demand Increases*, GUTTMACHER POL'Y REV., Winter 2010, at 8, 11-12 (examining the recession's harsh impact on women of reproductive age and acknowledging that many women, even before the recession, were uninsured without sufficient public support for family planning). Indeed, even California, a state once touted for its "landmark healthcare programs," has proposed limiting the state's Medicaid program for pregnant women by reducing eligibility requirements from 200% to 133% of the poverty level. *See* Tom Eley, *U.S. States Slash Medicaid*, GLOBAL RES. (Feb. 22, 2010), http://www.globalresearch.ca/index.php?context=va&aid=17743; *see also* Shane Goldmacher & Evan Halper, *Schwarzenegger's Revised Budget Plan Is Expected to Eliminate Health Programs*, L.A. TIMES, May 13, 2010, at AA1.

79   Since 1976, Congress has passed various versions of legislation known as the Hyde Amendment, which prohibits the use of federal funding to pay for abortions except when a mother's life is in danger, or in the case of rape or incest. Act of Sept. 30, 1976, Pub. L. No. 94-439, § 209, 90 Stat. 1418, 1434. Although abortion remains legally permissible, the Hyde Amendment makes it difficult for women without independent resources to obtain one. *See* Heather Boonstra & Adam Sonfield, *Rights Without Access: Revisiting Public Funding of Abortion for Poor Women*, GUTTMACHER REP. ON PUB. POL'Y, Apr. 2000, at 8, 10 ("[R]estrictions on funding have considerable impact on women's reproductive decisions.... [P]regnancies that would have otherwise been aborted are instead carried to term.... [W]omen who are able to raise the money needed for an abortion do so at a great sacrifice to themselves and their families."); Lawrence B. Finer & Stanley K. Henshaw, *Disparities in Rates of Unintended Pregnancy in the United States, 1994 and 2001*, 38 PERSP. ON SEXUAL & REPROD. HEALTH 90, 95 (2006) (noting that even though indigent women are two times as likely not to have health insurance, "the only federal stream of dollars dedicated to family planning services for low-income women[] declined between 1994 and 2001"); GUTTMACHER INST., FACTS ON INDUCED ABORTION IN THE UNITED STATES 2 (2011), http://www.guttmacher.org/pubs/fb_induced_abortion.pdf ("About 20% of abortion patients report using Medicaid to pay for abortions (virtually all in states where abortion services are paid for with state dollars)."); NAT'L ABORTION FED'N, PUBLIC FUNDING FOR ABORTION: MEDICAID AND THE HYDE AMENDMENT 2 (2006), http://prochoice.org/pubs_research/ publications/downloads/about_abortion/public_funding.pdf ("Barriers to abortion access such as the lack of providers, state laws delaying women from receiving timely care, and funding restrictions like the Hyde Amendment fall disproportionately on low-income women who have limited resources with which to overcome these obstacles.").

80   *See The New Health Care Reform Legislation: Pros and Cons for Reproductive Health*, *supra* note 23 (stating that the "16 million more Americans to join Medicaid by 2019 [under the health care reform will]... receive the program's guarantee of family planning services without cost sharing, along with coverage for its comprehensive package of reproductive health services beyond family planning").

public program is unlikely to adequately support the pregnant unwed. Thus, in addition to working towards increasing public pregnancy-related benefits, something more is needed. Furthermore, as I explain in the next Subpart, *regardless* of such public support, women and the men with whom they conceive form a special relationship that demands its own legal category.

Marriage is changing, but it is not going away. In fact, its variations are multiplying, and the theme unifying its progeny—civil unions, domestic partnerships, and the infinite variety of marriages defined by individually crafted premarital agreements—continues to be the sexually affiliated dyad. Rather than focus on futile attempts to stem the tide, we should recognize it as reality. As long as marriage and marriage-like privileges exist for some citizens, extending them to a greater diversity of relationships is preferable to the status quo.[81]

C. Mandatory Preglimony and the Relational Default

Nonmarital intimate relationships used to inhabit a legal no-man's-land. Over the past few decades, however, courts and legislatures have begun to recognize unmarried partners who live together as forming a unique type of relationship under theories that parallel contractual and equity-based theories of marriage. Where a couple formalizes their domestic partnership and then one partner abandons the other, "palimony"[82] relief to the abandoned partner may be granted under contract principles.[83] Where a couple has made no explicit agreement formalizing their commitment, many jurisdictions nevertheless recognize that a partnership was formed and provide protections when the relationship breaks down under either an implied contract theory[84] or an equity-based status approach.[85]

A similar logic applies to sexual partners who conceive, whether or not they live together. From a contractual perspective, partners who conceive should be recognized under the rubric of a distinct

---

81   I also support retracting these privileges from economically independent spouses. *See infra* note 188.

82   The *Oxford English Dictionary* traces the term back to the late 1970s, linking it with the California Supreme Court landmark case *Marvin v. Marvin*, which recognized support rights arising from a cohabitation relationship. *See* 557 P.2d 106 (Cal. 1976); *Palimony Definition*, OED.COM, http://oed.com/view/Entry/136318 (last visited Jan. 6, 2010).

83   Most jurisdictions that recognize domestic partners as forming a legally significant relationship follow the contractual approach introduced in *Marvin v. Marvin*. Under this approach, divorce-type property distribution rules apply to separating domestic partners who have explicitly agreed to formalize their union in a marriage-like relationship.

84   *See* Scott, *supra* note 52, at 258; Shahar Lifshitz, Married Against *Their Will* 11-13 (Bar-Ilan Univ. Pub. Law & Legal Theory Working Paper Series, Paper No. 06-09, 2009), *available at* http://ssrn.com/abstract=1352043.

85   A minority of jurisdictions and the American Law Institute's *Principles of Family Dissolution* reject the contractual approach in favor of a status-based solution. Contract is seen as a poor vehicle for regulating intimate relations for two main reasons. First, as ALI chief reporter Ira Ellman put it, "people do not think of their intimate relationships in contract terms." Ira Mark Ellman, *"Contract Thinking" Was* Marvin's *Fatal Flaw*, 76 NOTRE DAME L. REV. 1365, 1373 (2001). Second, the contract rubric fails to address the equitable claims of abandoned partners where no implied agreement can be reasonably inferred. *Id.* at 1372 & n.39.

legal relationship because, in many sexual relationships, an agreement to assume mutual obligations of support and communication can be inferred. In these types of relationships, each sexual connection implies a promise, an engagement of sorts to maintain some semblance of a relationship, some minimal modicum of collective responsibility and care should the woman become pregnant.

But even where such an agreement cannot be inferred, sexual partners who conceive should be legally responsible to each other for normative reasons. When a man and a woman have non-reproductive sex, they knowingly engage in an act that has a reasonable possibility of radically interfering with the woman's life, and disproportionately so. If neither party expects an ongoing commitment, a lovers-as-strangers rule is appropriate. But where their expectations diverge, the current default exacerbates imbalances in power and risk. In these types of relationships, when an unwanted pregnancy occurs, fairness requires that the material cost should be distributed between the two parties.

Fineman is right that dependency is inevitable and that its burdens extend to caretakers. She may also be right that the world would be a better place if women could have sexual relationships with whomever they wished, and for however long, relying on kinship ties and community support when they became pregnant. But the "sexual family"[86] persists as the dominant form in our society because sex and procreation *are* related and because—whether we are biologically or culturally programmed to do so—fathers and mothers tend to have a special relationship with each other. I agree with Fineman that the "core family connection"—the primary connection that deserves legal recognition and support—should not be marriage or sexual affiliation.[87] But I do not think the mother/child or caretaker/dependent relationship is the only relationship that should matter. Rather, in addition to the vertical relationship between care-taker and dependent, the horizontal relationship between individuals who share responsibility for a dependent is also critical.[88] A pregnant woman and the man with whom she conceives inhabit a murky middle ground between complete strangers and co-parents. Regardless of whether life begins at conception or whether a fetus can be said to be a "dependent," a pregnant woman *is* providing for a potential dependent. This reality diminishes her ability to survive on her own and creates a special relationship between her and the man with whom she conceived.

A man's obligation towards his pregnant lover might be analogized to the support obligations of a breadwinner towards a dependent spouse. Naturally, a sexual relationship implies a much lower level of commitment than betrothal, but, I would like to suggest, it falls along the same spectrum. Sex implies a baseline level of responsibility—a promise. In some communities, conception is tantamount

---

86   Fineman uses this term "to emphasize that our societal and legal images and expectations of family are tenaciously organized around a sexual affiliation between a man and a woman." FINEMAN, *supra* note 54, at 143.
87   Fineman, *supra* note 57, at 245.
88   As I have argued elsewhere, I also believe that horizontal relationships between adults who do not share a dependent, but who share their resources, should be recognized under a separate rubric. *See* Motro, *A New "I Do," supra* note 45.

to an engagement to marry. In others, the man is expected to do much less, but few people think he has no responsibilities. Accordingly, the justifications behind continued postdissolution support in the marital context—alimony—parallel the justifications behind my proposed pregnancy-support obligation—preglimony.

One common justification for alimony is contract based. Marriage implies a promise to share economic resources for life. When that promise is broken, the dependent spouse is entitled to an ongoing share of the higher-earning spouse's income because he or she has relied on the marital unity promise and reasonably expected to be supported over time. An alternative justification awards alimony based on a rehabilitative theory—alimony's function is to tide dependent spouses over until they can "get back on their feet" and support themselves. A related theory links alimony to needs that result "from the unfair allocation of the financial losses arising from the marital failure."[89] A final rationale frames alimony in restitutionary terms: its function is to make whole a spouse who sacrificed career opportunities in order contribute to the marriage in nonmonetary ways.[90]

Each of these theories is relevant for the unmarried couple facing a pregnancy. Again, sex can be viewed as a promise of sorts; when the promise is broken and pregnancy support is not forthcoming, preglimony ensures that the breaching party pays his fair share. Preglimony will also ensure that a pregnant woman who is temporarily unable to provide for herself will be taken care of during a transitional period. Third, it ensures that the financial losses arising from the sexual relationship will be allocated fairly. And finally, if the assumption of risk is a type of "contribution" to a relationship, preglimony ensures that the man contributes too if the woman becomes pregnant. (In this sense, preglimony might be understood as a way to prevent unjust enrichment.)[91]

How might a mandatory preglimony regime work in practice? I explore this question in further detail in *The Price of Pleasure*.[92] My main goal in that piece was to introduce the principle of a relational default to replace the current lovers-as-strangers paradigm governing nonmarital conception. Specifically, I argued that the material costs of pregnancy, childbirth, miscarriage, and abortion should be shared by both the woman and the man with whom she conceives. That article also laid out a range of possibilities for how the amount of a man's preglimony obligation might be set. One possibility is that it be based on the costs associated with each particular pregnancy broadly defined, including not only medical costs but also indirect costs like lost wages, maternity clothes, and childbirth classes. Alternatively, the preglimony obligation might be based on a more objective standard, like the length of the pregnancy and/or the parties' financial situation. The relational default would not apply to pregnancies conceived through rape or fraud and partners who do not want to be governed by the

89   AM. LAW INST., *supra* note 13, § 5.02 cmt. a, at 789.
90   For further discussion of justifications for alimony, see DOUGLAS E. ABRAMS ET AL., CONTEMPORARY FAMILY LAW 548-52 (2006); and KATHARINE K. BAKER & KATHARINE B. SILBAUGH, FAMILY LAW 135-46 (2009).
91   I credit Susan Appleton for this insight.
92   *See* Motro, *supra* note 8.

relational standard would be free to opt out of it. These exceptions not- withstanding, preglimony would apply to most nonmarital pregnancies. Again, no-strings-attached sex isn't inherently wrong; it's just the wrong legal default.

The most frequent objection I hear to the full-blown preglimony proposal is the fear that it will shift the decision-making power over abortion to men. Specifically, since pregnancy support (and child support) will likely be lower if the woman terminates the pregnancy, the concern is that pregli- mony will increase abortions. In my opinion, this objection collapses a critical distinction. Yes, once men have to pay they will be brought into the conversation and have an opportunity to share their feelings and preferences. In this sense, they will have *a* say, but that does not mean they will have *the final* say over abortion. Opening the door to greater male participation in women's reproductive deci- sions is dangerous only if we assume that the imbalance of power so heavily tilts towards the man that he will always, by definition, steamroll over the woman's preferences. But preliminary data on the influence of child support enforcement on the incidence of abortion suggests that the opposite may be true—abortions drop as child support enforcement rises.[93] To be sure, the concern that once men participate in bearing the costs of pregnancy they may pressure women to have (or not to have) an abortion is relevant in some cases. It is *possible* that these cases justify a lovers-as-strangers default, but over the long haul, the current rule may do more harm than good. "Protecting" women by as- signing to them most of the material burdens of pregnancy and abortion perpetuates the perception that pregnancy is a woman's problem and shuts men out of a process that implicates them in profound ways. Pregnancy that results from consensual sex where the partners have not agreed on a no-strings-attached arrangement concerns both parties to the act. Ideally, the law should treat it accordingly.

Nevertheless, the mandatory preglimony proposal requires further study before it can be imple- mented. Among the most pressing challenges is devising valuation, administration, and enforcement mechanisms that are not prohibitively expensive. Another challenge parallels a challenge common in the child support context: The goal of the child support system is to ensure that all parents support their children. But child support obligations that exceed a parent's realistic ability to pay sometimes work to alienate parents from children and to snowball the already indigent into more dire financial turmoil.[94] Preglimony that is not carefully calibrated to each situation might have similar effects. Finally, there is a danger that calls for mandatory preglimony will result in a backlash. Specifically,

---

93   The number of abortions *falls* as the expectation that men will have to pay child support rises because women are "encouraged by the potential economic security that the father may provide." Crowley, Jagannathan & Falchettore, *supra* note 32, at 22. A similar dynamic may lead pregnant women who are considering an abortion because they are worried about loss of income due to their pregnancy to take the pregnancy to term once they know additional preglimony support will be coming.

94   For a discussion of the negative effects of the current child support paradigm on never-married poor fathers, see Solangel Maldonado, *Deadbeat or Deadbroke: Redefining Child Support for Poor Fathers*, 39 U.C. DAVIS L. REV. 991 (2006).

some fringe men's rights groups already challenge mandatory child support rules by arguing that men should have a right to a so-called "financial abortion."[95] These activists believe that a man should be able to "buy" his way out of child support obligations by paying his pregnant partner a sum equal to the cost of an abortion. Although no legal authority takes their claims seriously,[96] mandatory preglimony may increase support for these attitudes.

While we are studying these issues, however, there is something simpler and less controversial we can do more quickly. As a first step towards recognizing and integrating the relational paradigm, we can support and reward men who already participate in the costs of pregnancy through the tax code. Unlike a mandatory pregnancy-support regime paralleling the cumbersome alimony and child support systems, tax reform offers a much leaner alternative. By creating an incentive for support rather than imposing sanctions for failure to support, it sidesteps thorny enforcement issues and encourages cooperation rather than conflict. Incentivizing rather than requiring support also responds to some men's fear that they will be duped into impregnating a woman. Though mandatory preglimony as I envision it would not apply where the woman engaged in foul play (e.g., lying about birth control) evidentiary challenges make this exception difficult to enforce. Tax reform based on voluntary preglimony avoids this problem.

To be clear, the remainder of this Article proposes to use tax law for the narrow purpose of bolstering public support for the *relational* aspects of pregnancy. Again, in an ideal world, greater public support for pregnant women regardless of their relational status would be forthcoming. Thus, I would support a tax credit available to all pregnant women in need—including those estranged from the man with whom they conceived as well as those whose partner is also poor.[97] But at this time, public

---

95 *See* Kim Shayo Buchanan, Lawrence v. Geduldig: *Regulating Women's Sexuality*, 56 EMORY L.J. 1235, 1245 (2007); John Tierney, Op-Ed., *Men's Abortion Rights*, N.Y. TIMES, Jan. 10, 2006, at A25; Sherry F. Colb, *Should Men Have the Right to a "Financial Abortion"? A Biological Father Cries Sex Discrimination When Forced to Pay Child Support for an Unwanted Baby*, FINDLAW (Mar. 21, 2006), http://writ.news.findlaw.com/colb/20060321.html; Stephanie Fairyington, *The Parent Trap: Paternal Rights and Abortion*, ELLE.COM (May 17, 2010), http://www.elle.com/Life-Love/Society-Career-Power/The-Parent-Trap-Paternal-Rights-and-Abortion. For *New York Times* readers' comments on the issue, *see* Readers' Comments to *A Father's Reproductive Rights: What Happens When a Man Makes His Intentions Clear Before a Child Is Conceived or Born?*, N.Y. TIMES MOTHERLODE BLOG, http://community.nytimes.com/comments/parenting. blogs.nytimes.com/2010/05/17/a-fathers-reproductive-rights/ (last visited Aug. 15, 2010). Many commenters assert that a man should have no right to prevent a women from having an abortion and should be required to pay child support for a child he does not want, while some argue a man's opposition to a woman's decision to take a pregnancy to term should exempt him from having to pay child support.

96 Anne M. Payne, Annotation, *Parent's Child Support Liability as Affected by Other Parent's Fraudulent Misrepresentation Regarding Sterility or Use of Birth Control, or Refusal to Abort Pregnancy*, 2 A.L.R. 5th 337, 348 (1992) ("To date, the courts have refused to deem a woman's decision to bear a child despite the objections of the child's father, even where he has offered to pay for an abortion, to create an unconstitutional infringement on the father's federal or state equal protection or due process rights." (citation omitted)).

97 Some "65 percent of unmarried fathers have incomes below $20,000, with about 19 percent reporting incomes below $5,000." WALLER, *supra* note 35, at 49.

support for indigent pregnant women remains limited.[98] So long as community assistance to these women remains at its current level, tax law can help incentivize and normalize greater financial support by men who do have the means to participate meaningfully in the fallout of pregnancy. The solution I offer gets at only a subset of the relevant cases: situations in which the pregnant woman earns significantly less than the man with whom she conceived. Thus it provides no help to poor couples, equal-earner couples, women whose income exceeds that of their partners, and most young couples. Instead, it begins with relatively low-hanging fruit—high-income men already predisposed to contribute to their pregnant lovers' welfare—pursuing a viable, symbolically potent first step towards breaking the silence on this issue.

III. THE PREGNANCY-SUPPORT DEDUCTION

When unmarried lovers conceive and the man helps support the woman through pregnancy, miscarriage, or abortion, how is this support treated for tax purposes? How should it be?[99] Current tax law is silent on preglimony payments, but it most likely treats them as neither deductible to the payor nor includible by the recipient. By contrast, married and divorced taxpayers who support each other and whose incomes diverge can shift high-bracket income to a lower bracket, producing a tax benefit. As I argue below, preglimony is more like an intraspousal transfer or alimony than a transfer between strangers, friends, or siblings. It should be treated accordingly.

A. The Current Income Tax Treatment of Pregnancy-Related Transfers

1. A primer on the taxation of personal transfers

Before we turn to the ideal treatment of preglimony, let's take a brief tour of the basic principles undergirding our income tax system so we may consider the full range of possibilities. The current income tax system measures income by "accessions to wealth."[100] In general, this means that receipts are taxable and expenditures are not deductible unless they represent the costs of producing

---

98   See *supra* Part II.B.
99   I limit the scope of this Article to the income tax consequences of pregnancy- related transfers and disregard any gift tax implication because in most cases the transfers either fall below the yearly gift tax exclusion amount ($13,000 for 2010) or include payments for medical care which, if paid directly to the provider, are exempted from gift taxes.
100   Comm'r v. Glenshaw Glass Co., 348 U.S. 426, 431 (1955). The normative base for the *Glenshaw* formulation and for the current tax system is the Haig-Simons definition of income as the sum of consumption and savings. *See* HENRY C. SIMONS, PERSONAL INCOME TAXATION: THE DEFINITION OF INCOME AS A PROBLEM OF FISCAL POLICY 50 (1938).

income.[101] Tax law does, however, deviate from this principle. Some receipts may be excluded from income despite the fact that they raise the taxpayer's wealth, and some expenditures may be deducted despite the fact that they are clearly personal in nature. Thus, when one taxpayer transfers property to another, four consequences may result. Assuming the taxpayers are not married and that one is not a dependent of the other,[102] the transfer may:

(a) be neither includible by the recipient nor deductible to the payor (as when an individual gives a gift to another individual[103]);

(b) result in taxable income to the recipient and a deduction to the payor (this is what happens when an employer compensates an employee working in her business[104]);

(c) result in taxable income to the recipient without a corresponding deduction allowance to the payor (as when an individual compensates a housekeeper, gardener, or other purveyor of personal services[105]); or

(d) produce no taxable income to the recipient and be deductible to the payor (as when an individual makes a charitable contribution[106]).

The significance of each possibility may be demonstrated as follows. Assume a payor whose taxable income is $100,000 transfers $20,000 to a recipient whose taxable income is $60,000. Assume also, for simplicity, a rate schedule with only two brackets. Taxable income that does not exceed $80,000 is taxed at a ten percent rate, taxable income above $80,000 is taxed at a thirty-five percent rate.

---

101   *See* 26 U.S.C. § 262(a) (2006).
102   If the woman qualifies as the man's dependent, the tax system provides several benefits. Section 213(a) gives the payor a deduction for certain medical expenses paid on behalf of a dependent, § 151 provides a personal exemption for dependents, and § 21 provides a credit for the costs of household and dependent care services if the dependent is incapable of caring for herself. (The credit is available if the services procured are necessary for the supporting taxpayer's gainful employment. Thus, an employed man whose pregnant domestic partner is confined to bed rest can receive a credit for hiring a nurse on her behalf.) For a more detailed list of tax benefits available to taxpayers providing for a dependent, see Theodore P. Seto, *The Unintended Tax Advantages of Gay Marriage*, 65 WASH. & LEE L. REV. 1529, 1543 n.35 (2008). *See also* 26 U.S.C. § 223 (allowing a deduction for amounts paid into a health savings account on behalf of a dependent).
103   *See* 26 U.S.C. § 102.
104   *See id.* §§ 61(a)(1), 162.
105   *See id.* §§ 61(a)(1), 262.
106   *See id.* § 170.

FIGURE 1[107]

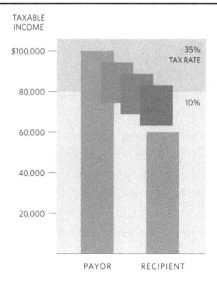

The four possible treatments are:

FIGURE 2

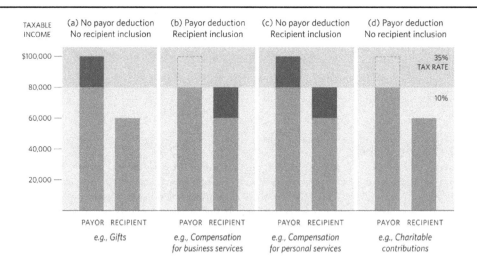

---

107 Graphic design by Jonathan Corum.

Thus, a transfer may be taxed once (alternatives (a) and (b)), twice (alternative (c)), or not at all (alternative (d)). From the taxpayers' collective perspective, (c) is the worst outcome and (d) is the best. If, as in alternatives (a) and (b), the transfer is taxable income to only one of the two taxpayers, the overall tax liability associated with it will be lower if the liability falls on the taxpayer whose marginal rate is the lower of the two. It follows that if, as in the illustration, the recipient is in a lower bracket than the payor, the transfer will be subject to a lower tax rate if it is includible by the recipient and deductible by the payor than if it is excludible by the recipient and nondeductible to the payor. That is, all else being equal, (b) is better for the taxpayers as a "team" than (a).

It is in order to prevent this "income-shifting" advantage that Congress does not extend the deduction/inclusion rule in scenario (b) to most personal transfers. Rather, income is generally taxable to the individual who earns it[108] or who owns the property that generates it[109] *even if* she assigns that income to another individual.[110] As Justice Holmes famously put it, fruits may not be "attributed to a different tree from that on which they grew."[111]

Congress has carved out one major exception to this assignment of income prohibition: marriage. Regardless of whether spouses in fact share their incomes, they are effectively treated as if each spouse earned half of their combined income, at least at lower income levels. It accomplishes this result through a rate structure for married taxpayers filing jointly that uses brackets approximately twice as wide as those applied to individuals.[112] Another way of describing the effective result is that tax law assumes that the high earner transferred to the low earner enough income so as to make the spouses equal, and blesses the assumed transfer with the deduction/inclusion alternative of scenario (b). For couples whose incomes diverge significantly, this produces a marriage bonus (i.e., it makes them better off than an unmarried couple whose transfers are treated as nondeductible/excludible gifts as in (a)).[113] Extending the benefit beyond marriage, tax law also permits a divorced spouse paying alimony (usually the higher earner) to deduct the payment provided the recipient (the low earner) includes it;[114] thus, the taxes on the payment are based on the recipient's lower marginal rate. Child

---

108   *See* Comm'r v. Culbertson, 337 U.S. 733, 739-40 (1949); Helvering v. Eubank, 311 U.S. 122, 124-25 (1940); Lucas v. Earl, 281 U.S. 111, 114-15 (1930).
109   *See* Helvering v. Horst, 311 U.S. 112, 117-20 (1940); Blair v. Comm'r, 300 U.S. 5, 12-14 (1937).
110   *See generally* 3 BORIS I. BITTKER & LAWRENCE LOKKEN, FEDERAL TAXATION OF INCOME, ESTATES AND GIFTS ¶ 75.2 (2d ed. 1991).
111   *Earl*, 281 U.S. at 115. For a critique of the fruit-and-the-tree metaphor, see Patricia A. Cain, *The Story of Earl: How Echoes (and Metaphors) from the Past Continue to Shape the Assignment of Income Doctrine*, *in* TAX STORIES: AN IN-DEPTH LOOK AT TEN LEADING FEDERAL INCOME TAX CASES 275, 276-79 (Paul L. Caron ed., 2003).
112   For a more detailed discussion of the way in which the rate structure produces a marriage bonus for unequal earners and a marriage penalty for equal earners, see EDWARD J. MCCAFFERY, TAXING WOMEN 12-19 (1997); and Motro, *A New "I Do," supra* note 45, at 1560-68.
113   The joint return reduces their overall tax liability because with a progressive rate structure, the tax on two people earning $50,000 is less than the tax on one person earning $100,000.
114   *See* 26 U.S.C. §§ 71, 215 (2006). The deduction/inclusion of alimony is the default treatment, but taxpayers may elect to designate payments as nondeductible to the payor and excludible by the recipient. *Id.* § 71(a), (b)(1)(B).

support payments, by contrast, are seen as inherently personal, and as such they are nondeductible to the payor and excludible to the receiving custodial parent.[115]

FIGURE 3

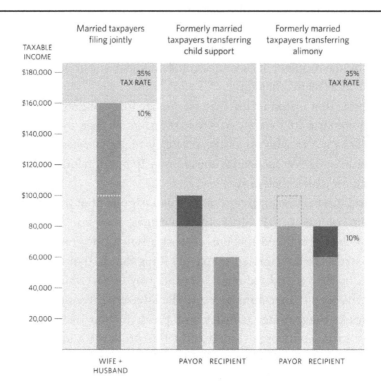

2. *The current taxation of preglimony*

No authority has addressed the proper income tax treatment of pregnancy-related transfers.[116] Current law regarding these types of payments is therefore a matter of conjecture. If asked to rule on the issue,

---

115 Bittker and Lokken explain that the underlying theory for this rule is that "child support payments do not reflect a diversion [of] income from one spouse to the other because they are not for the payee's benefit." 3 BITTKER & LOKKEN, *supra* note 109, ¶ 77.1.7; *see also* Knight v. Comm'r, 64 T.C.M. (CCH) 1519, 1523 (1992) (explaining that the child support a man pays to the mother of his child "goes toward the support of their children, not for her benefit or enjoyment as is the case of alimony" and that "personal, living, and family expenses (including the cost of supporting one's child) are not deductible by any taxpayer" (citing 26 U.S.C. § 262 (1988))). *But see infra* note 156 and accompanying text.

116 The IRS has also been silent regarding the broader issue of other support payments between unmarried couples either during the partnership or after dissolution. *See* Patricia A. Cain, *Taxing Families Fairly*, 48 SANTA CLARA L. REV. 805, 829 (2008).

the Internal Revenue Service might characterize them as either child support or as gifts, depending on the jurisdiction and on the particular circumstances of the pregnancy. In either case, the payments would be nondeductible to the payor and excludible by the recipient. In short, both alternatives are essentially disregarded for tax purposes.

a. Child support characterization

In jurisdictions that frame a man's pregnancy-related obligations as an element of child support, payments made pursuant to this obligation might be treated accordingly for tax purposes (i.e., he would not be permitted to deduct the payments and the woman would not be required to include them).[117] This is because federal income tax consequences generally track state law's characterization of a given event.[118] Child support characterization is also consistent with the Tax Court's holding that pregnancy-related medical payments made by adoptive parents on the birth mother's behalf may be treated as payments on behalf of their unborn "dependent" if the payments can be disentangled from payments necessary for the care of the mother.[119]

This Article addresses only income tax issues. Gift tax issues arise only with respect to payments that exceed $13,000, the annual gift tax exclusion amount for 2010. 26 U.S.C. § 2503(b)(1) (2006); Rev. Proc. 2009-50, 2009-45 I.R.B. 617. For many unmarried lovers who conceive, this means the only relevant question concerns income tax treatment.

117   See 26 U.S.C. § 71(c); Knight, 64 T.C.M. (CCH) at 1523 ("[C]hild support payments are neither deductible by the payor nor taxable to the recipient…. [N]o parent may deduct the cost of supporting his or her child; no distinction is made between parents who are married or unmarried, parents who are married to each other or to others, or parents having or not having custody of the child."). In the surrogate motherhood context, some attorneys advise surrogates not to include payments they receive from the intended fathers under the theory that these payments are child support. On the other hand, some scholars argue these payments are compensation. See Bridget J. Crawford, Taxation, Pregnancy, and Privacy, 16 WM. & MARY J. WOMEN & L. 327, 343-45 (2010); Bridget J. Crawford, Taxing Surrogacy, in CHALLENGING GENDER INEQUALITY IN FISCAL POLICY MAKING: COMPARATIVE RESEARCH ON TAXATION (Åsa Gunnarsonn et al. eds., forthcoming May 2011) (manuscript at 2), available at http://papers.ssrn.com/sol3/papers.cfm?abstract_id=1422180.117. See United States v. Mitchell, 403 U.S. 190, 194-96 (1971); Poe v. Seaborn, 282 U.S. 101, 110 (1930); see also Cain, supra note 115, at 838-39.

118   See United States v. Mitchell, 403 U.S. 190, 194-96 (1971); Poe v. Seaborn, 282 U.S. 101, 110 (1930); see also Cain, supra note 115, at 838-39.

119   See Kilpatrick v. Comm'r, 68 T.C. 469, 472-73 (1977). Kilpatrick deals with whether adoptive parents were allowed to deduct the expenses incurred for medical services rendered to their son's natural mother under 26 U.S.C. § 213, which provides a deduction for certain medical care expenses incurred on behalf of a taxpayer's dependent. The court acknowledged that "medical care rendered to an expectant mother may, under certain circumstances, constitute medical care rendered to her child." 68 T.C. at 472 (emphasis added). "Prior to the child's birth," the court explains, "the health of the mother is so intimately connected with the health of the child that to say a service rendered to one could never be a service rendered to the other belies believability." Id. at 472-73. However, the court placed the burden on the adoptive parents seeking to take the deduction to prove that "the expenses in question were directly or proximately related to the 'diagnosis, cure, mitigation, treatment, or prevention of disease' in the unborn child." Id. at 473 (quoting Havey v. Comm'r, 12 T.C. 409, 412 (1949)). In the absence of such proof, it held the entire amount to be a nondeductible personal expense. Id.; see also Hornish v. Comm'r, 37 T.C.M. (CCH) 919 (1978) (denying deduction to adoptive parents for failure to prove what portion, if any, of delivery fees constituted medical care for the child).

However, the characterization of pregnancy-related payments as child support might be challenged as inconsistent with another aspect of the tax system: the treatment of the gestational period for purposes of determining personal exemptions. If pregnancy-related transfers are indeed child support, the pregnant woman should be eligible to take a dependency deduction in her capacity as the custodial parent.[120] The Court of Federal Claims, however, has clearly held that a taxpayer is not entitled to a dependency exemption for a tax year in which an "unborn child" is still in utero.[121]

b. Gift characterization

Even if pregnancy-related payments classified as child support for state law purposes are not deemed to be child support for federal tax purposes,[122] they might still be neither includible by the recipient nor deductible to the payor under the theory that they constitute gifts. The same holds for pregnancy-related payments made pursuant to state laws that do not frame the obligation as an element of child support but rather as an obligation towards the woman herself.[123] Gift treatment might also apply to payments that exceed those required by any jurisdiction's law (including support for a woman undergoing and recovering from an abortion). This is true despite the fact that the circumstances in which these payments are made may, but often do not, match the law's official test for tax-free gifts, which hinges on the payor's intent.

Under the test coined in *Commissioner v. Duberstein*, to qualify as a gift for income tax purposes the payment must arise out of "detached and disinterested generosity."[124] It must be made "out of affection, respect, admiration, charity or like impulses."[125] Pregnancy-related payments rarely fit this bill. When they come from the man who is "responsible" because he feels it is his duty they are inherently *not* detached and disinterested. The case clearly states that a payment that arises from either a legal

---

120   *See* 26 U.S.C. § 152(c).

121   Cassman v. United States, 31 Fed. Cl. 121, 123-24 (1994). In a brief filed in *Magdalin v. Commissioner*, 96 T.C.M. (CCH) 491 (2008), *aff'd*, No. 09-1153, 2009 WL 5557509 (1st Cir. Dec. 17, 2009), *Cassman* was cited for the proposition that "an unborn child is not a dependent." *See* Katherine Pratt, *Deducting the Costs of Fertility Treatment: Implications of* Magdalin v. Commissioner *for Opposite-Sex Couples, Gay and Lesbian Same-Sex Couples, and Single Women and Men*, 2009 WIS. L. REV. 1283, 1315.

122   For examples of situations in which federal income tax treatment does not track state law, see *Boyter v. Commissioner*, 668 F.2d 1382, 1388 (4th Cir. 1981) (holding that a divorce that is valid under state law may nevertheless be deemed invalid for federal income tax purposes under the sham transaction doctrine); Deborah A. Geier, *Simplifying and Rationalizing the Federal Income Tax Law Applicable to Transfers in Divorce*, 55 TAX LAW. 363, 363 n.3 (2002) ("[P]ayments subject to the inclusion/deduction scheme [of alimony for federal tax purposes] may not actually constitute 'alimony' under state law, so long as the payment satisfies the federal tax definition of 'alimony' in section 71(b)."); and Deborah H. Schenk, *Simplification for Individual Taxpayers: Problems and Proposals*, 45 TAX L. REV. 121, 135 (1989) ("[T]he Code provides a special federal definition of an abandoned spouse so that a taxpayer who is married for state law purposes may be single for federal purposes.").

123   *See supra* note 20.

124   363 U.S. 278, 285 (1960) (quoting Comm'r v. LoBue, 351 U.S. 243, 246 (1956)).

125   *Id.* (quoting Robertson v. United States, 343 U.S. 711, 714 (1952)).

or a moral obligation cannot qualify for gift treatment.[126] The *Duberstein* test also precludes from gift treatment payments proceeding from the "'incentive of anticipated benefit' of an economic nature."[127] In some instances, payments towards an abortion are very much self-interested. Surely there are some men who support their pregnant lovers purely out of love and generosity, but in many instances an element of duty is present as well. Thus, the gift treatment of many of these payments does not fit well with the doctrine.

Pregnancy-related transfers between lovers might nevertheless be treated as gifts because other payments between sexual partners have been classified as gifts by several courts in the past.[128] Another reason why these payments might be nondeductible to the payor and excludible by the recipient is that the alternative leads to a counterintuitive result. In theory, every accession is income unless it is explicitly exempted[129] and all personal expenditures are nondeductible unless specifically covered by a deduction allowance. Thus, if pregnancy- related payments are not gifts, there is a possibility that the payments would be included in the recipient's income and nondeductible to the payor as in illustration (c) above. They would be taxed the same way we tax a person paying for a housekeeper or any other provider of services that are personal in nature—both the payor and the recipient would bear a liability.[130] In practice however, many transfers that do not fall neatly into the official definition of gifts and which are made in nonbusiness contexts are routinely disregarded by taxpayers and by the Internal Revenue Service alike.[131] As Boris Bittker and Lawrence Lokken put it in the context of their discussion of intrafamily transfers that would not qualify as gifts under the law's technical definition, such transfers "can be properly viewed as excludable by a higher authority than the language of § 102(a)—a supposition, so obvious that it does not require explicit mention in the [Internal Revenue] Code, that Congress never intended to tax them."[132]

In sum, current principles suggest that pregnancy-related payments are either child support or gifts for tax purposes. As such, they have no tax consequences to either the payor or the recipient.

---

126 *Id.* ("[I]f the payment proceeds primarily from 'the constraining force of any moral or legal duty'... it is not a gift." (quoting Bogardus v. Comm'r, 302 U.S. 34, 41 (1937))).

127 *Id.* (quoting *Bogardus*, 302 U.S. at 41).

128 *See* 1 BITTKER & LOKKEN, *supra* note 109, ¶ 10.2.7 (surveying case law classifying "[t]ransfers of cash and property by a taxpayer to a companion or sexual partner... as tax-free gifts or taxable compensation, depending on whether the recipient appears to be a beneficiary of generosity or a purveyor of services").

129 Section 61 of the Internal Revenue Code clearly provides that "[e]xcept as otherwise provided... gross income means all income from whatever source derived." 26 U.S.C. § 61(a) (2006); *see also supra* note 99.

130 Indeed, some theorists believe this is the correct treatment of all gifts, but their approach has not held sway. *See, e.g.*, SIMONS, *supra* note 99, at 56-58, 125-28.

131 *But see* Wendy Gerzog Shaller, *On Public Policy Grounds, a Limited Tax Credit for Child Support and Alimony*, 11 AM. J. TAX POL'Y 321, 329 (1994) ("Taxing the payment to both the payor and the payee is exactly what happens when... personal liabilities [other than alimony] are paid. When money changes hands between taxpayers and there is no gift involved, ordinarily the money is taxed to each successive taxpayer who has been enriched.").

132 1 BITTKER & LOKKEN, *supra* note 109, ¶ 10.2.

While neutral on its face, this result has harmful consequences. First, as an expressive matter, treating pregnancy-related payments as child support disregards the effects of pregnancy on the woman. Both child support and gift characterizations also disregard the reality that these payments tend to stem, at least in part, from the man's sense of his moral obligation to the woman herself. Second, from a utilitarian perspective, the current treatment misses a relatively simple opportunity to reward and encourage men who are inclined to help support their pregnant partners.

Finally, while the gift/child support theory is reasonable, it is not certain. For reasons discussed above, if the IRS eventually reviews the tax status of pregnancy-related payments, it could take the position that they are neither gifts nor child support. In that case, they might be properly taxed twice (i.e., they may not be deductible to the payor and they may be taxable income to the recipient).[133] The result would put couples who conceive in a worse position than all other taxpayers exchanging gifts. It would effectively treat the woman as the man's employee—like a housekeeper, she would be receiving gross income in exchange for performing a personal nondeductible service for him—an improbable but nevertheless disturbing outcome.[134]

B. The Pregnancy-Support Deduction

How then *should* preglimony be taxed? First, it should be clear that not taxing the transfers at all (i.e., providing a deduction/exclusion option similar to that applicable to charitable contributions (scenario (d))) is not a relevant option. It may seem appealing at first glance, but this approach would create a new type of marriage penalty because a high-earning man and a low-earning pregnant woman who share income would pay more if they marry than they would if, as unmarried, he can deduct and she can exclude the transfers.[135] Again, taxing the transfer twice as in scenario (c) is an unlikely result considering current practices.[136] It would also be punitive and administratively cumbersome as it would require detached and disinterested gifts to pregnant women to be disentangled

---

133   For arguments in favor of treating alimony as nondeductible to the payor and includible by the recipient, see Geier, *supra* note 121, at 368 ("[I]f we view the matter from the recipient's side alone, and if alimony is considered within the *Glenshaw Glass* notion of 'in- come' as an undeniable accession to wealth, *etc.*, then it would be includable by the recipient. At the same time, the payor earning wages from which the alimony was paid would have to include the wages in gross income, since compensation for services rendered is specifically listed as 'income' in section 61(a)(1). Moreover, the payor would arguably be denied a deduction for the payment under a strict definition of 'income' in the familiar Schanz-Haig-Simons sense, under which only outlays incurred to produce includable income are properly deductible (with personal consumption outlays being nondeductible, and thus taxed)."); and *id.* at 430.

134   For a discussion of why alimony is not taxed twice (i.e., to both payor and recipient), see *id.* at 368-71.

135   To remedy this result a new credit or deduction for pregnant spouses might be introduced, but for simplicity I will bracket this alternative and assume the current tax treatment of spouses as a given.

A deduction/exclusion would also be inconsistent with the current charitable contributions framework, which permits a deduction only for gifts to eligible charitable entities, not to individuals. 26 U.S.C. § 170(a), (c) (2006).

136   *See supra* notes 128-31 and accompanying text.

from duty-inspired preglimony. The remaining choice, therefore, is to move from the status quo (no deduction/no inclusion) to an income-shifting option (deduction/inclusion), which would produce a benefit in cases in which the payor's income is higher than the recipient's.

FIGURE 4

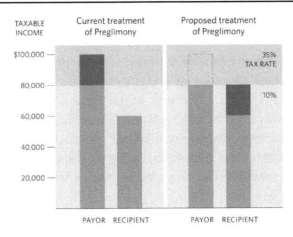

As we have seen, current tax law does not apply the general prohibition against income shifting to married taxpayers and to former spouses paying alimony. It allows married taxpayers to shift income by means of a special rate schedule applicable only to spouses filing jointly.[137] It allows former spouses agreeing on an alimony arrangement to elect to treat the payments as deductible to the payor and includible by the recipient.[138]

Though the justifications for both of these special rules are problematic, as long as they remain in force, similar treatment should extend to unmarried lovers who conceive. The next Subpart surveys the main critiques of marriage- and divorce-based income-shifting benefits, and introduces a novel theory for why they remain deeply entrenched despite voluminous criticism they have received. This theory suggests preglimony should be treated comparably. Then, I turn to utilitarian justifications for a deduction/inclusion approach to preglimony.

---

137   *See supra* notes 111-12 and accompanying text.
138   26 U.S.C. §§ 62(a)(10), 71(a)-(b), 215(a). To qualify for this treatment the payments must be in cash and they must be made pursuant to a divorce or separation instrument. *Id.* § 71(a)-(b).

1. *Theoretical justification*

Marriage-based joint filing has been the subject of much criticism,[139] which I will not review here, except to reiterate[140] that the most compelling rationale for retaining it—an assumption that marriage serves as a proxy for economic unity—is faulty. In most states, spouses have no obligation to share income during marriage, and many marriages are clearly (sometimes *contractually*) not fifty-fifty propositions. There is no defensible reason to assume that spouses whose union is governed by a premarital agreement separating their economic identities actually share to the point of equalizing their incomes, and there is no reason to then exempt these imaginary transfers from the assignment of income doctrine.

The deduction/inclusion option available to former spouses paying alimony also rests on a shaky foundation. The original rationale for the rule was to mitigate the effects of marginal rates as high as ninety-one percent in the early 1940s.[141] The force of this rationale diminished as the rate structure became less steeply progressive, but scholars point to other theories for the system's endurance[142] including mitigating the financial hardship of divorce,[143] promoting equity between "wealthy" and "less wealthy" divorcing couples,[144] and incentivizing higher alimony payments.[145] The leading theory is that the rule essentially extends to former spouses the income-splitting benefits to which they

---

139 *See* MCCAFFERY, *supra* note 111, at 11-85; Pamela Gann, *Abandoning Marital Status as a Factor in Allocating Income Tax Burdens*, 59 TEX. L. REV. 1 (1980); Marjorie E. Kornhauser, *Love, Money, and the IRS: Family, Income-Sharing, and the Joint Income Tax Return*, 45 HASTINGS L.J. 63 (1993); Edward J. McCaffery, *Taxation and the Family: A Fresh Look at Behavioral Gender Biases in the Code*, 40 UCLA L. REV. 983 (1993); Lawrence Zelenak, *Doing Something About Marriage Penalties: A Guide for the Perplexed*, 54 TAX L. REV. 1, 3 (2000); Lawrence Zelenak, *Marriage and the Income Tax*, 67 S. CAL. L. REV. 339 (1994) [hereinafter Zelenak, *Marriage and Tax*].
140 *See* Motro, *A New "I Do," supra* note 45.
141 *See* Geier, *supra* note 121, at 371-72; Gerzog Shaller, *supra* note 130, at 322.
142 *See* Gerzog Shaller, *supra* note 130, at 322-23 (noting that since the original enactment of the alimony provision "its repeal, which could be seen as a natural concomitant with the enactment of lower rates, has not been seriously contemplated" (footnote omitted)).
143 *See* Geier, *supra* note 121, at 396 ("Since divorce frequently strains liquidity to the breaking point anyway, in the view of the Task Force, such a harsh result, *i.e.*, divorce *per se* pushing incomes into higher brackets, should be avoided, if possible." (quoting AM. BAR ASS'N'S DOMESTIC RELATIONS TAX SIMPLIFICATION TASK FORCE, THE "INCOME-SHIFTING" PRINCIPLE IN PROPOSALS FOR SIMPLIFICATION OF DOMESTIC RELATIONS TAX LAW 5 (1983))); *id.* at 435 ("Divorce is usually accompanied by financial hardship (and it triples the chances of bankruptcy). Therefore, Congress should avoid adopting what would amount to a mandatory divorce tax 'penalty' in many cases."). Geier makes the related argument that taxing the payments twice would also affirmatively discourage divorce. *See id.* at 370.
144 *See id.* at 435 ("[A] mandatory exclusion/nondeduction rule would also introduce a disparity between less wealthy couples, where support payments must come from future wages of the payor, and wealthy couples, who could still engage in significant income- shifting by transferring income-producing assets to the payee to fund support.").
145 *See id.*; Michael Waggoner, *IRC § 71 May Impoverish Children, Endanger Ex-Wives, and Disrupt Federalism*, 46 FAM. CT. REV. 574 (2008).

were entitled during marriage because divorce does not end their economic[146] or legal[147] relationship. Since marriage-based joint filing approximates income splitting, former spouses should be entitled to continue to shift the tax burden associated with income they share post-divorce to the party who actually benefits from the income (i.e., the recipient).

None of these theories is compelling. If the goal is to mitigate the financial hardship of divorce, the deduction/inclusion of alimony is a particularly inefficient mechanism for providing relief. The benefit it produces rises as income differentials between spouses rise, which also correlates with higher overall income; lower-income couples are more likely to be equal earners and thus unable to benefit from the deduction/inclusion at all. A better way to mitigate hardships would be to provide a phased out credit for taxpayers whose household income drops as a result of divorce.

The rule does promote equity between taxpayers who own income- producing assets and those whose main income-generating asset is their career. This is because without the deduction/inclusion of alimony, property owners could transfer assets to their former spouses, effectively shifting these assets' income streams to the recipient's lower tax bracket, whereas professionals would have to pay taxes on their wage income first (at their own presumably higher rates) before transferring them to the lower-bracket alimony recipient.[148] But this disparity exists between every transfer of cash as compared with income-generating property. It's not clear why having been married should justify equalizing the earned/unearned income differential when it is largely ignored throughout the rest of the tax system.

Incentivizing higher alimony payments is a laudable goal, but the extent to which the deduction/inclusion accomplishes this goal is unclear. Also, as I will discuss in further detail shortly, the same

---

146   *See* Cain, *supra* note 115, at 828 ("The underlying principle [for the alimony rule] is that the now-divided family will only be taxed once on the income that is used to support its prior members. This principle is consistent with the notion that the spousal unit is a single economic unit for federal tax purposes."); Geier, *supra* note 121, at 369-70 ("[T]he... appropriate way to think about the payment [of alimony is to]... view both taxpayers *together*. In an intact marriage, by analogy, amounts earned by one spouse and paid to another are ignored for tax purposes (*i.e.*, they are neither includable by the recipient nor deductible by the payor)... Therefore, the amounts are taxed only once between the two. We could reason that the amounts should continue to be taxed only once, even though the family is no longer intact, because of the clear and direct relationship of the payments to the former legal relationship of the parties (or the continuing legal relationship, in the case of a paternity payment to support a child after a divorce or otherwise outside of marriage)." (footnote omitted)); Gerzog Shaller, *supra* note 130, at 324 n.15; Laurie L. Malman, *Unfinished Reform: The Tax Consequences of Divorce*, 61 N.Y.U. L. REV. 363, 392 (1986) ("To the extent that family law continues the former spouses' economic unit through alimony payments, the tax laws should also treat the former spouses as a continuing, single tax unit after divorce."); Schenk, *supra* note 121, at 164 ("Although the marital relationship ends, the economic relationship does not and thus, the taxation of the earnings should not change.").
147   *See* Geier, *supra* note 121, at 370.
148   *See id.* at 396 ("[E]liminating income-shifting would discriminate between well-to-do couples with income-producing property, who would effectively be able to continue to engage in income-shifting by transferring such property in satisfaction of support obligations, and less wealthy couples.").

argument—indeed a more compelling argument—can be made with respect to child support payments and preglimony.

Finally, the main theoretical rationale for the deduction/inclusion of alimony—that the tax treatment of alimony should extend the effective income shifting accomplished through the joint return during marriage—is incoherent. The first problem is that it assumes marriage-based joint filing is justified. But even if we assume that a large enough number of spouses share income to a significant extent[149] *and* if we take this assumption as sufficient justification for joint filing,[150] the argument does not track when applied to alimony because alimony (though actually paid) rarely results in a fifty-fifty income split. We support and reward marriage not on the theory that spouses share *some* of their income (as unmarried taxpayers do quite frequently), but rather because we assume they share *everything*.[151] Marriage deserves special treatment, the argument goes, because when two people join their fates, society is better off. Marriage is worth supporting because it binds individuals into an economic partnership of equals.[152] Divorce does not end spouses' economic relationship, but it does change it quite explicitly *away* from the fifty-fifty presumption and toward an unequal model. If alimony replicated a community-property-style marriage,[153] the deduction/inclusion rule might make

---

149   *But see* Kornhauser, *supra* note 138, at 80 ("The theoretical justification for the joint return—the belief that married couples share resources—is largely unsupported by empirical evidence."); *id.* at 91 ("[N]either assertions of pooling nor nominal arrangement of assets in a pooling manner accurately reflect the reality of financial arrangements. Behind the facade of sharing is a deep-seated, though often subtle, control of the income by the earner spouse.").

150   *See* Boris I. Bittker, *Federal Income Taxation and the Family*, 27 STAN. L. REV. 1389, 1420-22 (1975); Zelenak, *Marriage and Tax*, *supra* note 138, at 353 ("If one accepts the premise that the crucial question in determining the appropriate taxable unit is 'Does this person pool his income with another person for the purpose of shared consumption (and savings)?' then requiring joint returns for married couples and separate returns for unmarried persons is an easy-to-administer rule that gets it right most of the time.").

151   *See* Motro, *A New "I Do," supra* note 45, at 1541-42 & nn.108-09 (critiquing Henry Smith's proposal for partial income splitting in marriage based on individually determined ratios, Henry E. Smith, *Intermediate Filing in Household Taxation*, 72 S. CAL. L. REV. 145, 183 (1998)).

152   On the equality principle in marriage, see Carolyn J. Frantz & Hanoch Dagan, *Properties of Marriage*, 104 COLUM. L. REV. 75, 91 (2004) ("People may engage in many joint enterprises where equality is not necessary. Joint owners in a business, for instance, may divide the ownership interest 70-30 without raising any alarm. But it would be perverse to conceive of a marriage of this sort, where one spouse has a recognized controlling interest in the property that partially constitutes the marriage, and, correspondingly, in marital decisions... Disparity in the control of marital property moves beyond simple inequality—which an individual may rightly choose as a means to other ends—to subordination, which systematically denies the importance of whatever ends that individual chooses. As subordination in marriage is a threat to a spouse's basic personhood, the marital community must be bounded by a commitment to equality.").

153   For persuasive arguments that it should, see Jana B. Singer, *Divorce Reform and Gender Justice*, 67 N.C. L. REV. 1103, 1117 (1989) (proposing that divorcing couples be required to share income for a set period of time after the divorce); and Joan Williams, *Is Coverture Dead? Beyond a New Theory of Alimony*, 82 GEO. L.J. 2227, 2260-61 (1994) (arguing for postdivorce income equalization for the duration of children's dependence plus one additional year for every two years of marriage beginning at the date of divorce).

sense. Since it rarely does, extending the income shifting of marriage to alimony is indefensible.[154] Lots of taxpayers share some of their income on a regular basis. It is unclear why having been married should change the tax treatment of similarly personal transfers.

Several scholars who have written about the current iteration of the rule also believe that the taxation of postdivorce transfers is flawed in its disparate treatment of alimony and child support.[155] For one, the two types of payments are practically impossible to distinguish.[156] More importantly, the same extension-of-marriage argument for the deduction/inclusion of alimony holds with respect to child support.[157]

In sum, the justifications for both marriage- and alimony-based benefits are weak, and yet these benefits are so firmly entrenched they are taken for granted as permanent aspects of the income tax system.

Perhaps, however, there is another—subterranean, rarely articulated—reason behind the current tax treatment of both alimony and marriage that helps explain these benefits' longevity. Perhaps the real reason we think married and divorced taxpayers deserve a special benefit is that we use marriage as a proxy not for economic unity, but for procreation. Perhaps marriage is a proxy for the special type of dependency and identity transformation that tends to accompany the co-parenting relationship.[158]

---

154 Thus, the alimony rule is difficult to defend for reasons that are slightly different from the problem at the heart of marriage-based income splitting. Whereas marriage-based income splitting relies on the questionable presumption that most spouses share income equally, the alimony rule extends a benefit specifically limited to taxpayers who (presumably) share equally to taxpayers who explicitly share *un*equally.

155 *See* Geier, *supra* note 121, at 432 ("[T]he parties should be given full power to decide who, between them, should be taxed on all cash transfers incident to divorce."); *id.* at 411-30; Gerzog Shaller, *supra* note 130, at 321 ("[T]here are public policy reasons to eliminate the distinctions between them and to allow a limited credit for both types of payments."); Malman, *supra* note 145, at 379-80; Schenk, *supra* note 121, at 162 (proposing that child support and alimony should not be differentiated for federal tax purposes to eliminate complexities resulting from the difficulty distinguishing the two); Waggoner, *supra* note 144; Laura Bigler, Note, *A Change Is Needed: The Taxation of Alimony and Child Support*, 48 CLEV. ST. L. REV. 361, 361-62 (2000).

156 This argument appears in almost every critique of the current system.

157 The theoretical justification for the nondeductibility/exclusion of child support is that supporting one's child is inherently personal; the costs of raising a child are not deductible during marriage, nor should they be after divorce. The problem with this line of reasoning is that it ignores the fundamental difference between the nondeductibility of child raising costs *by a married couple* and the nondeductibility of child support *by an exspouse*. The former ensures that the underlying income is taxed to the couple rather than escaping taxation altogether; the latter determines that it is taxed to the payor rather than to the recipient. The alternative to nondeductibility of child support is deductibility *coupled with* inclusion to the recipient, which would be entirely consistent with the treatment of the costs of raising a child during marriage because joint filing during marriage accomplishes (approximately) the same thing as a deduction/inclusion postdivorce. Viewing the couple together, the deduction of child support wouldn't really be a deduction at all, but rather an income-shifting mechanism. For a similar argument, see Geier, *supra* note 121, at 369-70, 431.

158 I do not mean to suggest that policymakers have deliberately or consciously used marriage as a proxy for procreation. The existence of children is, of course, quite easy to determine directly. But marriage may serve as a convenient and comfortable way for us to privilege "responsible procreation" without confronting the prevalence of nonmarital children. On the stigma associated with "irresponsible reproduction," see Linda C. McClain, *"Irresponsible" Reproduction*, 47 HASTINGS L.J. 339 (1996). Marriage also expresses a view that all spouses, even elderly couples

Thus, we give married one-earner couples a benefit as compared with unmarried couples with the same income distribution because we imagine the married couple to be composed of a husband supporting the mother of his children. Even if he doesn't literally split his income with her, they are a unit in a sense that goes deeper than mere economics. He need not "assign" his income to her to legitimate the income-splitting tax result. To turn Holmes's metaphor on its head, taxing father and mother as one (i.e., as if each earned half of their combined income) does not effectively attribute the fruits "to a different tree from that on which they grew" because procreation turns two trees into one. In a sense what I'm suggesting is that we subconsciously retain some vestige of coverture, or some religious sensibility that husband and wife are "one flesh." This unity is most apparent during the gestational period—when the combination of both parents' genetic material is physically inside the expectant wife-mother—but it extends to childbirth, and to the nursing period, and is also true as children grow.

If the marriage dissolves and the man continues to support his former wife, again, we may treat these transfers in a special way because we imagine the former wife as a mother—the woman who carried, gave birth to, and who is caring for the man's children. This is not to say that alimony is really child support in disguise. Rather, quite apart from supporting one's child—paying for education, health care, housing—supporting a woman who is also the mother of one's child is in some sense supporting one's self. Transfers to her simply do not fit into any of the categories applicable to taxpayers who are not parents of the same child. They are not compensation paid to an employee, they are not gifts arising out of detached generosity in the absence of any legal or moral obligation, and they are not charity. In a sense, they are not "transfers" at all.

To be clear, I am not taking a position here on whether procreation does in fact justify the income-shifting benefits of marriage and alimony. I am simply suggesting that if this procreation hypothesis has merit (i.e., if the true reason we support marriage is because we use it as a proxy for the co-parenting relationship) the same treatment should extend to all transfers between unmarried co-parents generally and, most relevantly for our purposes, to lovers who conceive regardless of whether a child is ultimately born.[159]

---

who have never had children, are potentially procreative, which those who see procreation as essential to the human experience may find comforting.

As we saw in Part II.A, courts denying same-sex couples' right to marry have often relied on the argument that the main purpose of marriage is to regulate accidental procreation. Another, related argument used in this context focuses not on *accidental* procreation specifically, but on the essential feature of marriage being procreation more generally. *See* Adams v. Howerton, 486 F. Supp. 1119, 1124 (C.D. Cal. 1980) ("[T]he main justification in this age for societal recognition and protection of the institution of marriage is procreation, perpetuation of the race."); Baker v. Nelson, 191 N.W.2d 185, 186 (Minn. 1971) ("The institution of marriage as a union of man and woman, uniquely involving the procreation and rearing of children within a family, is as old as the book of Genesis."); Singer v. Hara, 522 P.2d 1187, 1195 (Wash. Ct. App. 1974) ("[M]arriage exists as a protected legal institution primarily because of societal values associated with the propagation of the human race.").

159 It also suggests that income-shifting benefits should not be automatically available to childless spouses and former spouses, but this issue is outside the scope of this Article. As I have argued elsewhere, I believe that joint filing

Conception is a marriage of sorts. It is the union of two individuals' bodies to create a third potential life. While this potential life is in gestation, and whether or not it is in fact born, a man who supports the woman carrying it is different from a man supporting a stranger, a friend, or a sister. He is supporting a person—the woman—who is bearing his own flesh, including if the woman ultimately terminates the pregnancy. During the weeks or months of the pregnancy, man and woman are existentially bound.

2. Utilitarian Justifications

Even if my procreation hypothesis is wrong (i.e., if marriage-based tax benefits are not our collective subconscious's way of supporting "responsible procreation") extending alimony treatment to preglimony makes sense for utilitarian reasons. First, the policy will encourage support for pregnant women.[160] By setting a minimal baseline for acceptable support, the rule will also have positive expressive effects, shaming those who leave their pregnant lovers to fend for themselves.[161] Imagine Internal Revenue Service Form 1040 (and TurboTax's corresponding prompts) modified to include preglimony as well as alimony. The appearance of the term alone (to be defined in the form's instructions as per the model statute below[162]) will link pregnancy with financial obligation in the minds of taxpayers from the time they begin filing their taxes.

Champions of marriage may, at first glance, worry that the pregnancy-support deduction might undermine marriage by offering a "marriage-lite" alternative, subsidizing out-of-wedlock childbearing. But the limited timeframe for deductibility means that in reality the revenue costs of the subsidy will be quite small. Furthermore, by "hooking" steady couples to the benefits of income splitting, the

---

should be limited to taxpayers who are legally committed to sharing income equally regardless of marital status. *See* Motro, *A New "I Do,"* *supra* note 45. Taken together, this project and my former work recommend that childless couples be permitted to file jointly only if they are legally committed to sharing income and that co-parents be permitted to shift income through a deduction/inclusion mechanism so long as they are transferring more than a minimal threshold amount.

160   *Cf.* Bigler, *supra* note 154, at 379 (arguing for extending the deduction/inclusion treatment of alimony to child support payments in order to "encourage 'deadbeat dads' to pay their support obligations").

161   Some commentators may object that the tax code is the wrong vehicle for achieving this symbolic goal because it is the wrong vehicle for social engineering more broadly. This is not the place to revisit debates on the proper role of tax law in setting social norms. It is worth noting, however, that Congress routinely and deliberately uses the tax system to shape economic and social behavior. *See* Maureen B. Cavanaugh, *On the Road to Incoherence: Congress, Economics, and Taxes*, 49 UCLA L. REV. 685, 687 (2002) ("[G]overnments generally (and Congress in particular), have frequently used both tax incentives and disincentives in an effort to address important social problems."); Stanley S. Surrey, *Tax Incentives as a Device for Implementing Government Policy: A Comparison with Direct Government Expenditures*, 83 HARV. L. REV. 705, 705 (1970). Given that tax expenditures have grown from $45 billion in 1968 to $1 trillion for fiscal years 2001 to 2005, Stanley Surrey's comments are as true today as they were when he first advocated a strong presumption against their use. For a discussion of the influence of tax law on gender relations in particular, see MCCAFFERY, *supra* note 111.

162   *See infra* pp. 696-97.

deduction might create an additional incentive to marry. It may, in other words, function as a step towards marriage—instead of marriage lite, marriage with training wheels.[163]

On the flip side, this supposed benefit may, at first glance, figure as a negative aspect of the proposal in light of the ways in which marriage-based tax benefits exacerbate power imbalances along gendered lines. (For example, the current income tax system penalizes two-earner married couples whereas it privileges couples composed of one exclusive breadwinner. This creates an incentive for the low, so-called "secondary" earner—usually the wife—to forgo paid work, eventually becoming entirely dependent on her husband.)[164] Rather than chipping away at this problem, preglimony arguably extends it. Admittedly, this will be true in some cases. In others, however, preglimony benefits may help ill-suited partners forestall and ultimately avoid an unhappy marriage. More broadly, preglimony's promise is that it can expose the inherent contradictions at the heart of a marriage-centered view of friendship, family, and community. Whereas marriage is an arbitrary eligibility criterion for special tax treatment, pregnancy presents a crystal clear *limited* moment during which a gendered view of men and women's different economic capabilities, needs, and deserts is appropriate.[165] Marriage is not special; pregnancy and nursing an infant are.[166] By isolating the obvious, undeniable temporary dependency that comes along with procreation, preglimony can begin to strip away the *imagined* dependency that often follows women throughout their lives.[167]

Finally, over time the combination of these effects may create a more robust pregnancy-support norm that will influence sexual behavior. That is, if the government's preferential treatment of significant pregnancy support helps make it socially mandatory, the fear of such responsibility may incentivize men who do not want to become fathers to be more vigilant about birth control.[168]

---

163 *Cf.* WILLIAM N. ESKRIDGE, JR. & DARREN R. SPEDALE, GAY MARRIAGE: FOR BETTER OR FOR WORSE? (2006) (using Scandinavian countries' experience with gay marriage to suggest that alternatives to traditional heterosexual marriage may bolster rather than undermine the institution).

164 *See* MCCAFFERY, *supra* note 111, at 19-23 (discussing the tax system's secondary- earner bias); Nancy C. Staudt, *Taxing Housework*, 84 GEO. L.J. 1571, 1574 (1996) (examining "the possibility of valuing and taxing nonmarket labor in the same manner as market labor"); *see also* Silbaugh, *supra* note 44, at 44–55 (1996) (surveying a variety of ways in which the tax system contributes to the law's failure to value unpaid work).

165 Discussions with Laura Rosenbury and Adam Rosenzweig helped me in identifying and thinking about this issue.

166 For a related argument, see CRITTENDEN, *supra* note 54, at 268 (proposing that the birth or adoption of a child should turn spouses into full economic partners).

167 *See supra* Part II.B.

168 After conception occurs, it is unclear whether and how the deduction/inclusion of preglimony may influence the incidence of abortion. It would apply whether or not the pregnancy is taken to term, but if the existence of the tax benefit and its expressive effects causes men to support a pregnancy taken to term more robustly than they currently do such that the woman receives more in after-tax dollars, this may decrease abortions undertaken because of financial pressures. *Cf.* Crowley, Jagannathan & Falchettore, *supra* note 32, at 22–23 (finding that increased child support correlates with fewer abortions).

C. How It Would Work

The administrative mechanism for the pregnancy-support deduction would mirror that used in the alimony context, except that whereas alimony payments must be made pursuant to divorce or separation, preglimony payments would have to be made to a pregnant woman.[169] Like in the alimony context, the deduction/inclusion treatment would be elective.[170] Proof of the pregnancy or abortion from a health care provider would be required. This administrative burden on the taxpayers would create an incentive for pregnant women to seek medical care, a net positive.[171] (Thus, the pregnancy discovered through a home pregnancy-test kit that ends in spontaneous miscarriage would only be eligible for preglimony tax treatment if medical proof of the pregnancy were available.)

Whereas alimony tax treatment requires that parties not live together,[172] parties would be permitted to deduct/include preglimony regardless of whether they live together. In this respect, preglimony is qualitatively different from both alimony and palimony, which are triggered by the dissolution of a relationship. Preglimony is triggered by pregnancy. It *may* coincide with the end of a relationship, but it may take place in the context of an intact relationship and it may solidify a relationship.[173] In a sense,

---

169   See notes 181-84 and accompanying text for a discussion of whether the payor must be the man with whom the woman conceived.

170   Unlike in the alimony context, however, the default would be that preglimony payments are nondeductible to the payor and excludible by the recipient, because the deduction/inclusion alternative requires formal and deliberate cooperation, which will not always be possible. Additionally, women should be able to keep their pregnancy private if they wish to do so. For an argument that the default rule for alimony should also be nondeductible/excludible, see Waggoner, *supra* note 144, at 579.

171   For a discussion of the risks to both woman and newborn child when a pregnant woman receives no prenatal care, see MATERNAL & CHILD HEALTH BUREAU, U.S. DEP'T. OF HEALTH & HUMAN SERVS., A HEALTHY START: BEGIN BEFORE BABY'S BORN, *available at* ftp://ftp.hrsa.gov/mchb/prenatal.pdf ("Babies born to mothers who received no prenatal care are *three* times more likely to be born at low birth weight, and *five* times more likely to die, than those whose mothers received prenatal care."); and John L. Kiely & Michael D. Kogan, *Prenatal Care, in* FROM DATA TO ACTION: CDC'S PUBLIC HEALTH SURVEILLANCE FOR WOMEN, INFANTS, AND CHILDREN 105, 105 (1994), *available at* http://www.cdc.gov/reproductivehealth/ProductsPubs/DatatoAction/pdf/rhow8.pdf ("Inadequate use of prenatal care has been associated with increased risks of low-birth-weight births, premature births, neonatal mortality, infant mortality, and maternal mortality." (citation omitted)). *But see* Cassman v. United States, 31 Fed. Cl. 121, 129 (1994) (Taxpayers are not entitled to a deduction based on conception because, among other reasons, allowing a deduction would "create confusion because of the uncertainty regarding the date when a particular conception occurs.... A live birth [by contrast]... results in the issuance of a birth certificate, which is a universally accepted and administratively efficient document of identification.... If the court held... that the dependent exemption was available as of the date of conception, then the exemption would be available for pregnancies that never resulted in live births and the issuance of a birth certificate, including those pregnancies ending in miscarriages, induced abortions, and stillbirths. In the absence of any clear evidence of congressional intent to do otherwise, the court must spare taxpayers and the I.R.S. the administrative burden of establishing that such pregnancies occurred or did not occur.").

172   *See* 26 U.S.C. § 71(b)(1)(C) (2006).

173   Susan Appleton and Cheryl Block alerted me to the significance of these distinctions.

preglimony might be seen as a term marriage of sorts—a time-bound commitment of mutual respect and of material support from the man to the woman.[174]

To take advantage of the deduction/inclusion rule, the payor and the pregnant recipient will need to cooperate. Both will need to retain documentary proof of the pregnancy and of the amount of the transfers, though an itemized record linking each transfer to particular costs would not be required.[175] The taxpayers will also need to coordinate so their respective deductions and inclusions are consistent. To be recognized as alimony for tax purposes, payments must be made under a divorce or separation instrument (i.e., under a decree or written agreement).[176] Similarly, preglimony tax treatment would require parties to agree in writing that payments represent pregnancy-related support and that they wish to designate them as deductible to the payor and includible to the recipient.[177] While this imposes another administrative burden, again, it also creates a beneficial incentive; it encourages partners to communicate and reach agreement about their circumstances.

One concern is that taxing women on the preglimony they receive could leave them with less support than they would have gotten under the current no deduction/no inclusion rule. This would happen in cases in which the deductibility of preglimony does not incentivize a significantly higher payment. A simple deduction/inclusion rule would also reward even the most ungenerous contributions, sending the wrong message. To avoid this result, the deduction should be limited to payors whose pregnancy support exceeds a certain threshold set so as to produce a reasonable after-tax award for the woman. One possibility is to extend deduction/inclusion treatment to any transfer to a pregnant woman that exceeds a standard dollar amount fixed for all pregnancies. Alternatively, the minimal threshold might vary depending on the length of the pregnancy. It might also depend on the payor and the recipient's economic circumstances. Finally, at the maximalist end of the spectrum, the rule could require that the man transfer enough of his yearly income to the woman so as to equalize their earnings. That is, only if lovers are prepared to share fifty-fifty, as if they were married in a community property state, should they be entitled to the income-shifting benefit.[178]

---

174   I am not suggesting a similarity to the term "marriage" in Islamic law, which contemplates more robust obligations. *See generally* SHAHLA HAERI, LAW OF DESIRE: TEMPORARY MARRIAGE IN SHI'I IRAN (1989).

175   For one, requiring itemization would be administratively burdensome. More importantly, the physical, professional, and emotional effects of pregnancy are so diverse that parsing apart pregnancy-related expenses from other expenses would be nearly impossible. Finally, even if it were possible to draw such a distinction, since many of the burdens of pregnancy cannot be ameliorated, payments used toward non-pregnancy-related ends—whether indulgences or investments for the future—should be given the same support and encouragement as payments used for strictly pregnancy-related ends.

176   26 U.S.C. § 71(b)(2).

177   In order to reduce fraud or collusion, in addition to proof of the pregnancy, the payor and recipient might also be required to include with their return a cosigned statement recording their agreement and understanding of the tax consequences to each. I credit Wendy Gerzog for this suggestion.

178   The advantage of this requirement is that it would encourage significant support. The disadvantage is that it would provide no incentive for those who are prepared to share significantly but not to the point of fifty-fifty division. It would also subject unmarried partners to a higher sharing standard than we apply to spouses, an incongruous result.

The modest revenue effects of the existing alimony rule[179] suggest that the costs of even the most expensive version of the new rule would likely be small. Nevertheless, should the potential revenue impact of an unlimited deduction rule prove to be a concern, a maximum cap on amounts eligible for deduction/inclusion treatment might be set.[180] Another reason for considering a cap is the possibility that if an unequal-earner unmarried couple splits income entirely (i.e., if the payor shares enough to put both parties on equal footing) it would be in a better after-tax position than a married couple.[181]

Finally, lawmakers will need to determine whether proof linking the preglimony payor with the recipient's pregnancy would be required. Requiring such proof would ensure that the benefit is narrowly tailored to apply only to unmarried heterosexual lovers who conceive (as opposed to same-sex couples and other types of relationships that involve economic support). This would make the proposal more politically promising than its alternative. In an ideal world, however, a more expansive alternative is preferable. One reason is administrative. Though in utero genetic testing is available, it is risky and expensive.[182] Thus, if proof linking the payor with the pregnancy were required, a couple wishing to avoid the risky test might have to forgo its preglimony benefits initially and amend their returns once testing becomes safe (i.e., once the pregnancy ends in birth, abortion, or miscarriage).[183]

Finally, it would create a marriage penalty because the rate schedule for married taxpayers filing jointly approximates but does not replicate "pure" income splitting.

179   See Malman, *supra* note 145, at 398-99 ("Statistics indicate… that the revenues at stake in the alimony deduction are not large. For example, only 0.6% of all returns filed claimed a deduction for alimony payments. In contrast, 48.3% of all returns filed took ad- vantage of the joint return tables. Moreover, the potential for a significant revenue impact is more hypothetical than real. Although divorced women are generally in lower tax brackets than their male counterparts, studies indicate that cash awards to former spouses are relatively few in number and small in size, and often remain uncollected. Even where substantial annual payments are made, the resulting increase in the recipient's income narrows the difference between the former spouses' marginal tax rates and thus lessens the revenue impact." (footnotes omitted)); *see also* Waggoner, *supra* note 144, at 579-80 (concluding that the revenue loss following a reform extending the deduction/inclusion treatment of alimony to child support and lump sum payments is difficult to calculate but, regardless of the cost, in light of the dangers of the current rule to the custodial spouse and the children, "it may be an appropriate area for some federal revenue loss").

180   I credit Wendy Gerzog for this insight, though she would rather the cap apply only to the deduction, not the inclusion amount.

181   This is because joint filing *approximates* but does not quite replicate pure income splitting. *See* Gerzog Shaller, *supra* note 130, at 328 (discussing the "divorce bonus"). To prevent the resulting "marriage penalty," the income-shifting benefit derived from the pregnancy-support deduction might be capped at the benefit that would have accrued to the couple were they married.

182   See *Paternity Testing*, AM. PREGNANCY ASS'N, http://www.americanpregnancy.org/prenataltesting/paternity-testing.html (last updated Nov. 2007) ("Prenatal DNA testing done in conjunction with other prenatal testing involves some risk associated with how the testing is conducted, whether amniocentesis or CVS. These tests are often discour-aged for the sole reason of seeking paternity because of the increased miscarriage risks."). The cost of paternity testing generally "range[s] from $400.00 to $2,000.00. Prenatal testing is often more costly than testing done after a baby is born because of the additional doctor and hospital-related fees." *Id.*

183   If, for example, the couple conceives in November of year 1 and miscarries in May of year 2, the support payments made in November and December of year 1 would not be taken into account in each partner's year 1 tax returns filed in April. Then, after the miscarriage, a test linking the man to the ill-fated pregnancy would enable them

The test also creates additional costs. This level of administrative hassle and added cost would make the program prohibitively complex and burdensome to many taxpayers.

Another reason for not requiring that the payor prove a genetic connection to the pregnancy is equitable. Recent (albeit controversial) family law trends diminish the focus on blood ties for purposes of determining paternity in favor of more functional approaches.[184] We recognize that to be a parent, one need not have a biological relationship with a child; likewise, to be a supportive partner to a pregnant woman, one need not be the person with whom she conceived. Thus, ideally, a pregnant woman and her lesbian partner should be eligible for the deduction, as should a woman and a man other than the one with whom she conceived.[185] But again, the more expansive the eligibility criteria the less likely the proposal is to be politically viable. Not requiring that the payor be the man with whom the woman conceived also broadens the targets of the reform beyond the main issue addressed in this Article—the relational consequences of pregnancy. In any case, if no genetic link is required, to be consistent with broader tax policy considerations aimed at preventing intrafamily income shifting,[186] an exception would need to be made limiting the deduction/inclusion treatment to unrelated parties.[187]

The proposal would only benefit couples in which the payor's income is higher than the pregnant woman's and the value it bestows will increase as the rate differential between the two increases. Thus, the pregnancy-support deduction will not significantly help low-income taxpayers whose incomes are more likely to be comparable and whose rate differentials, if any, tend to be smaller. But as we have seen, calls for more robust public assistance for the unmarried poor have gone largely

---

to amend their year 1 returns to take advantage of the benefit—an administrative hassle that would effectively make the program impractical for most couples.

184   *See* Lehr v. Robertson, 463 U.S. 248, 266-67 (1983) (holding that a biological father's legal rights with respect to his child are contingent on whether he established a relationship with the child); *see also* Michael H. v. Gerald D., 491 U.S. 110, 113 (1989) (plurality opinion) (denying a biological father's paternity rights when the mother was married to another man when she gave birth because "a child born to a married woman living with her husband is presumed to be a child of the marriage").

185   Indeed, one possibility is to allow multiple people to shift income to a single pregnant woman, which would represent a step in the direction of recognizing broader collective responsibilities rather than focusing on the nuclear family as the main form of social insurance. *See supra* Part II.B. The multiple-party version of the proposal would also accommodate polyamorous forms. *See* Elizabeth F. Emens, *Monogamy's Law: Compulsory Monogamy and Polyamorous Existence*, 29 N.Y.U. REV. L. & SOC. CHANGE 277, 284-85 (2004) (suggesting that the law should give greater attention and consideration to polyamorous alternatives to marriage and monogamy). It is not, however, likely to attract broad support.

186   *See generally* 3 BITTKER & LOKKEN, *supra* note 109, ¶ 75.2.

187   Thus payments from parents to their daughter would not be eligible for deduction/inclusion treatment. Payments formally characterized as transfers from parents to their son's girlfriend would also be ineligible as they would be viewed as gifts from parents to son followed by preglimony payments from the son to his girlfriend. The gifts to the son would be nondeductible and excludible (as all gifts are). The payments from the son would be eligible for preglimony tax treatment but the benefit would most likely be lost (because if the son needs his parents to pay, his marginal rate is likely to be low, in which case no income- shifting benefit would be available).

unheeded in favor of a model privatizing care for dependents.[188] The fact is that the world in which we live leaves many pregnant women to fend for themselves. Unless and until society steps in more robustly, incentivizing men to shoulder more of the burden is preferable to the status quo, and though it will only affect the well-off, its symbolic effects are likely to spread more broadly.

In light of the fact that pregnancy's effects often extend over more than one year, the benefit might apply during the year of conception plus the subsequent year or two—either as a standard matter or depending on whether the pregnancy was taken to term and whether the birth mother retained custody of the child. This may seem fair, but it would require distinguishing extended preglimony from nondeductible child support, which, as we saw in the divorce context, is practically impossible. In this sense, the preglimony debate may revive arguments for making child support deductible as well, which would be a positive development. More broadly, the long-term effects of pregnancy and child- bearing raise an even thornier question: If the reason we support marriage through the tax code is as a proxy for procreation, why not create a *motherhood* or primary-caregiver support deduction as well as a pregnancy-support deduction?[189] Again, like the issues discussed in Part II.B above, the answer to this question turns on how we as a society wish to treat unmarried parents more broadly, a subject that has been studied by other scholars. Regardless of these broader issues, however, recognizing and rewarding preglimony in isolation would be valuable in itself. The relational aspects of nonmarital pregnancies, which marriage enthusiasts and critics alike agree present opportunities for reform, have been largely ignored. I hope this project helps bring them out of the shadows and into the public debate.

The provision I envision might be worded as follows:

Pregnancy-Related Payments

(a) *General Rule.*—Pregnancy-related payments, designated as such by both the payor and the transferee, shall be includible in the gross income of the recipient and deductible by the payor.

(b) *Pregnancy-Related Payments Defined.*—For purposes of this section, the term "pregnancy-related payments" means any payment in cash if—

(1) such payment is received by a pregnant person[190] (as defined in subsection (c)) within the later of [one year] of the start of the pregnancy or [one year] of the birth a child, and

---

188   *See supra* Part II.B.

189   Elsewhere I have argued that joint filing should be limited to taxpayers who are legally obligated to share their income, regardless of marital status. *See* Motro, *A New "I Do," supra* note 45. I continue to support this reform. In addition, I agree with critics who have argued that child support paid subsequent to a divorce should receive the same tax treatment as alimony. *See supra* note 154. I would also support extending this treatment to unmarried co-parents.

190   The provision should be gender neutral to avoid uncertainties that might arise with respect to intersexual, transgendered, and other individuals whose sexual identity is ambiguous or subject to dispute. For a discussion of

(2) the payment exceeds [dollar amount, percentage of payor's adjusted gross income, or other minimal threshold].

(c) *Pregnant Person Defined.*—For purposes of this section the term "pregnant person" means a person deemed to be pregnant by a physician in a licensed hospital (or in a medical care facility which is related to, or the equivalent of, a licensed hospital).

CONCLUSION

Unmarried partners who conceive respond to pregnancy in a range of different ways. Some get married. Others face pregnancy and its repercussions—whether it ends in abortion, miscarriage, or childbirth—together without marrying. A third group views conception as the woman's private affair.

The law effectively treats all sexual partners who are not married as falling into the third category; it treats all lovers as strangers. When pregnancy ends in abortion, it requires nothing of the man. When pregnancy progresses to term, the law requires male participation only in the bare essentials of bringing a child into the world. Its requirements fall short of the type of support that would be provided by a man who views the pregnancy itself—in addition to the potential child it creates—as a joint responsibility.

This Article begins to bring the law up to date with this now commonplace sensibility. Pregnancy results from a connection between two people; its burdens should be borne by both parties to the act. Translating this moral intuition into a comprehensive legal regime is complicated and controversial; it will take some time. But there is something we can begin to do now: the law can and should respect lovers who already regard conception as a joint responsibility by treating the economics of the pregnancy accordingly. The pregnancy-support deduction offers a first step in this direction.

Preglimony is a new word; it is not a new practice. It's time the law noticed.

STATE REGULATION OF MARRIAGE

A final decision on the ability of marriage to remain the standard of society is beyond the scope of this book, but if *Loving v. Virginia* finds a fundamental right to marry (see Chapter 5), how does the state regulate marriage? The dual nature of the legal civil marriage contract allows the state to regulate it. While each state regulates marriage as appropriate for its community, there are certain capacities and some prohibitions that remain common to most including issues surrounding age, kinship, mental capacity, fraud, and polygamy.

---

intersexuality and sex discrimination, see Julie A. Greenberg, *Intersex and Intrasex Debates: Building Alliances to Challenge Sex Discrimination*, 12 CARDOZO J.L. & GENDER 99 (2005).

ACHIEVING MARITAL STATUS

License

All states' first involvement in the status of marriage is to require a couple to obtain a marriage license. Generally, little information is required to obtain a marriage license—often, a driver's license and/or proof of identification (some states may also require proof of divorce if previously married).[29] While some states do not charge a fee for marriage licenses, many states charge anywhere from $18 in Indiana up to $115 in Minnesota. As a tourist magnet for beach weddings, Delaware charges $100 for out-of-state couples—double the $50 in-state fee. Michigan also requires nonresidents to pay $10 more than residents.[30]

Most states do not require either party to be a resident of the state. Many states have a waiting period to give the couple a short time to think over their decision to marry after the license has been obtained. It can vary from one day in Illinois, three days in Maryland, or five days in Minnesota. Some states, like Nevada and New Mexico, do not have a waiting period. Alabama does not have a waiting period, but does require a 60-day period between divorce and remarriage. In the case of *Krug v. Krug*, 292 AL 498, 296 So.2d 715 (1974), a woman violated the terms of her divorce which required that she not marry within 60 days of the divorce order. Unfortunately, her new husband left to serve in the Vietnam War shortly after their marriage and died. His parents challenged the validity of the marriage when the wife made an inheritance claim. The court resolved the case by finding that the couple was married under common law and allowed her to inherit. (See discussion of common law marriage below.) Dallas, Texas has a waiting period of three days, but allows a waiver for those in the military. Generally, it is a good idea not to wait too long before obtaining a marriage license, because marriage licenses often expire within a few months if not used, although Manhattan, New York extends the expiration period for active military personnel. A license is generally valid only in the county in which it was issued and cannot be used in another state.

Most states no longer require a blood test, though Montana still requires a rubella blood test. In 2007, the law allowed couples to opt out by signing an informed consent. Mississippi requires both parties get a blood test to screen for syphilis within 30 days of the wedding. Many states, including Massachusetts, stopped requiring medical exams in 2005. Such requirements raised privacy challenges, so many states eliminated them.

---

29   In some states, family information is required. In Indiana, the clerk requests family information for the State Library for genealogical purposes, including both parties' full names, last known address, and birthplace of each parent. In Louisiana and Mississippi, the application requires the highest grade completed in school for bride and groom. North Carolina makes optional the listing of race.

30   Minnesota's $115 licensing fee is reduced to $45 after the couple completes a premarital education program (see Chapter 8).

Solemnization

After the license, the ceremony is the next step in the marriage process. All marriages must be solemnized. Generally, the only central requirement of the ceremony is each party's acknowledgement that each accept the other as a spouse. Many states still require at least one witness, some require two (Nebraska); others, like Virginia, do not require any. Wyoming requires a witness who knows the couple just to obtain a marriage license. There is no minimum age for a witness. However, in selecting a witness, a good choice is someone who would be competent to testify in a court proceeding as to what he or she witnessed should it ever be necessary.

The question of who can officiate a marriage can be complicated—especially if courts have to determine who qualifies as a "minister." It is curious, in a country with rules against the separation of church and state, that the government relies on religious institutions to perform wedding ceremonies, especially as marriage is a fundamental institution in society. In many European countries, like Portugal, it is often typical for parties to be married by a justice of the peace who represents the country's government followed by a religious ceremony and reception. The former is the official marriage. Of course, states generally recognize various civil officers who can solemnize a marriage like the mayor, a judge, or a court clerk.

States often define who can be a minister, but it can vary by county within the state. The traditional definition includes officials of a religious order, but also allows a deputy clerk or judge to officiate. Often, the state will keep a registrar of authorized officiates who have registered to perform marriages within the state. Virginia requires religious officiates to be authorized by a circuit court and show evidence of regular communion with the religious society of which he or she is a reputed member. Virginia even specifies what to do if the couple belongs to a religious society which does not ordain ministers.[31] Maine allows lawyers from the state to officiate. California recognizes shamans or medicine men from Native American tribes to perform marriages. Some counties allow ship captains to perform them, but California does not, while it does allow captains of the Salvation Army.[32]

New Hampshire makes it clear that even authorized officiates cannot conduct their own marriage ceremonies. Colorado is one of a small number of states that allows self-solemnization, or performing your own marriage (C.R.S. §14-2-109(1)). To do this, a couple need only indicate such on the marriage certificate form, on the third line, indicating "themselves."[33]

Some jurisdictions allow the mayor to marry people, but only in the town where he or she serves. New York's mayor, Michael Bloomberg, has only served as an officiant on three occasions. He was the official for his predecessor, Rudolph W. Giuliani's, third wedding. Mayor Bloomberg also officiated his daughter's wedding. His jurisdiction is limited to Manhattan, so the couple was married there and had another ceremony in upstate New York the next day for invited guests.

---

31   Section 20–26, Code of Virginia, Domestic Relations.
32   California Department of Public Health. http://www.cdph.ca.gov/certlic/birthdeathmar/Pages/FAQforMarriageLicenseCeremonyInfo.aspx
33   http://www.usmarriagelaws.com/search/united_states/colorado/marriage_licenses/denver_county.shtml

Although he swore off the role, the mayor officiated the first same-sex marriage in New York's City Hall after working to change the state's laws banning them.[34]

New York does not permit Internet-ordained ministers to solemnize marriage licenses. In the case of *Ranieri v. Ranieri*, 146 A2d 34, 539 N.Y.S.2d 382 (1989),[35] the New York court invalidated a marriage performed by a minister for the Universal Life Church. The court stated, "it could never be that the legislature intended to qualify for licensing to marry someone whose title and status could be so casually and cavalierly acquired". In the case, the plaintiff married the defendant, 57, and left him after 84 days to file for divorce based on cruel and inhuman behavior. Because the court invalidated the marriage based on the unauthorized officiant, the court also voided their ante-nuptial agreement, in which they each waived their rights and claims acquired by reason of the marriage. The consideration for this agreement was the impending marriage. The defendant also agreed to give the Plaintiff $90,000 within 90 days of the marriage. All were invalid. Later, the New York City Clerk's office decided to register ULC ministers and allow them to perform marriages in the City. With court precedent to the contrary, these marriages may be at risk.[36]

In some states, like Massachusetts (by special permission) and Vermont (by paying $100), non-ministers can be ordained for the purpose of officiating a wedding ceremony. Delaware does not require ministers to be licensed, but they must register with the state. In California, anyone can become "ordained" in a matter of minutes on a website—or even from the back of a matchbook. Known as the "deputy for a day" program, if the California county allows it, the person does not have to be a California resident or even register with the state.[37] Nontraditional officiants are increasingly common in a more modern society. It is a way to personalize the wedding in a less religious culture. Often, people look for someone with a close connection to them. When Sunshine McCoury and Greg Stein married in 2002, they asked their friend, Chris Brewster, a former chief lifeguard in San Diego, to officiate. Mr. Stein said, "We were getting married at the beach, so having a lifeguard to do it seemed right."[38]

34   "Political Turns Personal: Mayor Will Officiate at Gay Advisers' Wedding," Michael Barbaro, July 7, 2011, http://www.nytimes.com/2011/07/08/nyregion/bloomberg-to-preside-at-gay-aides-wedding.html?_r=0

35   http://www.ulcseminary.org/forum/uploads/RanierivRanieri.pdf

36   Fran Drescher of the TV show "The Nanny", is a ULC minister and specializes in preforming same-sex marriages in New York. "Still Dictating Orders, This Time at the Altar", Linda Marx, *The New York Times Wedding*, March 11, 2012, p. 19.

37   California does not have such a registration and therefore takes no responsibility for verification of credentials, leaving it to the parties. See, generally, California Family Code, Section 400-402. Is that a good idea?

38   Some unofficial officiants are more flexible regarding their fees. A minister ordained online can charge from $375–$800, but some may do it for "a bottle of tequila." "Finding Just the Right Match for the Do You's," Elaine Zimmerman, *New York Times* Celebrations, May 1, 2005, p. 21.

Renewal of Vows

Some previously married couples want to renew their vows. Do they need a new marriage license? Probably not, since they are already married. Most states do not issue a new marriage license to couples who want to renew their vows. New Jersey does issue a new marriage license and waives the usual waiting period upon proof of the prior marriage. Texas specifically orders the court clerk to give a new marriage license to couples who are renewing their vows. More intriguingly, Texas law requires the court clerk to issue a marriage license to couples who are secretly married and now wish to "marry" more publicly.

LEGAL WAYS TO MARRY IN NONTRADITIONAL WAYS

1. Proxy Marriage

A **proxy marriage** is a way for two people to have a valid ceremony, even if one of them is not present in the same jurisdiction; even if they are not in the same state or country. "Yet, solemnization of marriage, or the celebration of the marriage ceremony or rites comprehends a personal appearance together by the contracting parties before one authorized by law to celebrate marriage ceremonies, and that the marriage ceremonies or rites be entered into and performed by the parties to such marriage together with the minister or other person authorized to perform such in the presence of each other and one or more witnesses, in order that the fact of the marriage contract may have due publication for the sake of notoriety and the certainty of its being made."[39] *Torres v. Torres* 144 NJ Super 540, 366 A.2d 713 (1976).

Proxy marriages are more common in the "global community" of Europe than in the United States.[40] While most jurisdictions require both parties of a wedding to be physically present at the time of the ceremony, some jurisdictions will allow a proxy marriage in which one of the parties is not present, but is represented by a stand-in or proxy on their behalf. While some states, such

---

[39] http://www.leagle.com/xmlResult.aspx?xmldoc=1976684144NJSuper540_1620.xml&docbase=CSLWAR1-1950-1985

[40] In a "proxy marriage" that is highly contested, a man formerly engaged to actress Gina Lollobrigida and 34 years her younger (when they met in 1984, he was 23 and she was 57. She was famously quoted as saying "that is the perfect age between a man and a woman".) "went ahead with their wedding using a stand-in for Gina. According to Lollobrigida, this was entirely unbeknownst to her…[He] claims that she had willingly signed all necessary paperwork and agreed to marry him by proxy in order to avoid media spectacle, and that they were happily married. Lollobrigida says that he was able to arrange the proxy marriage using a power of attorney she had once granted him to take care of a different legal matter." In January 2013, she filed several lawsuits objecting to the "wedding". His case "seemed to be bolstered when an attorney who had represented Lollobrigida for several years, Giulia Citani, stepped forward to claim that prior to the ceremony she had traveled with Lollobrigida to Barcelona, where the prospective bride signed papers to authorize the ceremony." "I can tell you she is legally married'". "'You have to remember that Gina is 85 so she sometimes has trouble remembering things.'" Since then, her son has requested a court appointed administrator to manage her business decisions. "Twilight of the Goddess" James Reginato, *Vanity Fair*, February 2015, pg. 126, 134-5.

as Colorado, allow proxy marriage,[41] Missouri and Texas do not. Generally, proxy marriages, known as "picture marriages," were disfavored because they were often abused in illegal immigration by allowing people to marry foreign partners. Proxy marriages are often revived during periods of war. In 2004, Governor Arnold Schwarzenegger of California revived his state's proxy marriage law during the Iraqi war to allow soldiers in the Middle East to marry their sweethearts back home. In Texas if one spouse is incarcerated, and therefore unable to be present for the wedding ceremony, he can file a prison proxy form.

In *Torres v. Torres aka Rodriguez*, 366 A. 2d 382 (1989),[42] the New Jersey court heard a case of first impression of the validity of a proxy marriage. The Plaintiff was a Cuban national at the time of the marriage and knew the defendant in Cuba for some time before escaping to the United States on May 8, 1967. The Defendant, also a Cuban national, remained domiciled in Cuba, where proxy marriages were allowed. The Plaintiff took up residence in New Jersey. In the case, the Plaintiff swore that he sent his proxy to Cuba on October 28, 1967 and a ceremony of marriage took place with a designated stand-in representing the plaintiff. The authenticity of the proxy was not challenged, and so the court found that the proxy marriage met the state's solemnization requirements via the proxy legal requirements in Cuba. The court also said that solemnization requirements could be met by a showing of commitment. The court found that such a commitment existed in this case because the husband went to "great lengths" to get married. The wife came to the United States and lived with the man for seven years, had a child with him, and shared his surname. In the eyes of the public, these people constituted a family unit.

2. Common-Law Marriage or Informal Marriage

Everyone has heard the story of somebody's aunt who lived with her boyfriend for X number of years in X-state, and therefore it was considered "common-law marriage." But, what does this mean? There seems to be some misperception about the applicability of this right. Common-law marriage, unlike traditional marriage, requires no ceremony or license. If your state permits it, and the parties are otherwise qualified to marry, a common-law marriage may be imposed.

Common-law, or informal marriage, comes from the common-law doctrine, or rule, which acknowledged that there are two ways to marry: the traditional way (license and ceremony) or under the common law. In *Meister v. Moore*, 96 U.S. 76 (1877), the Supreme Court gave a good explanation of the historical basis for the common-law right to marry in the United States. Common-law marriage was a way for the state to impose a married status upon couples even when they had failed to do so. To say it another way, common-law marriage is a way to achieve

---

41 http://www.usmarriagelaws.com/search/united_states/colorado/marriage_licenses/pitkin_county.shtml.   Aspen, Colorado, allows proxy marriage (if either the groom or bride cannot appear due to illness, is out of the state of Colorado, or incarcerated).

42 http://www.leagle.com/xmlResult.aspx?xmldoc=1976684144NJSuper540_1620.xml&docbase=CSLWAR1-1950-1985.

marital status, not a distinct type of marriage. Common-law married couples are still married couples—they just got there in a different way.

Even more confusingly, the requirements for common-law marriage vary among the states that still allow it. Most require that the couple be eligible to marry (more on that below), agree or intend to get married (but never do the traditional way), hold themselves out as married, and often require that the marriage be consummated. Texas provides two ways to be informally married. First, the couple must sign a Declaration and Registration of Informal Marriage and declare that they are married because they intended to be; then they live and hold themselves out to others as husband and wife. Under the second option, no signature on a document is required. The couple must only agree that they are married, live together, and hold themselves out to others as a married couple. How many people will use Texas's first option? It seems unlikely that Texans who reject traditional marriage, and choose to privately order their relationship, will file papers with the government to marry under the common law.

The common law in Aspen, Colorado states that if you claim "We are married," then it is true. The specifics of the law provides:[43] "A common law marriage is established when the parties mutually consent to be husband and wife. Common law marriage does not require any license, ceremony or documentation to be legal. Parties to a common law marriage are entitled to all rights, privileges and responsibilities of a legal and binding marriage. If the parties need documentation of a marriage, it is recommended that they file a signed, notarized affidavit, attesting to the marriage, with the county clerk and recorder in the county where they reside. This affidavit will be filed as a document, not as a marriage record. Only legal divorce or death of one of the parties may terminate common law marriage." (Emphasis added.)

Indeed, the simplest things could be evidence of marriage in Aspen, such as "Maintenance of a joint checking and/or savings account; joint ownership of property; Mutual financial support; Filing of joint income tax returns; Registration as husband and wife on applications, leases, contracts, registers, etc.; Use of the man's surname by the woman" provide evidence that a heterosexual couple who live together intended to get married—even though they never took any of the steps (see below) necessary to traditionally do so.[44, 45]

Today, when obtaining a marriage license is as easy as taking the bus to town, does it really make sense for the state to presume couples who are cohabitating for a certain period of time

---

43   http://www.usmarriagelaws.com/search/united_states/colorado/marriage_licenses/pitkin_county.shtml

44   http://www.usmarriagelaws.com/search/united_states/colorado/marriage_licenses/pitkin_county.shtml.

45   It is curious that while Aspen County seems to say that anyone could just say they were married, and they were—they really meant anyone but same-sex couples. Could it be constitutional to have such a loose requirement for marriage, but still be rigid in excluding same-sex couples? Is this fair? As the rest of the country started to confront the issue of allowing same-sex marriage, Colorado passed a law allowing same-sex couples the right to a civil union in the spring of 2013. Although some argued this "eras[ed] a generation of anguish for supporters of gay rights in what once was dubbed "'the hate state'" is it too little too late? http://www.denverpost.com/breakingnews/ci_22841921/colorado-civil-unions-hickenlooper-takes-up-pen-sign#ixzz2Si8kpt9l "Colorado civil unions bill signed by Gov. John Hickenlooper at History Colorado Center," Lynn Bartels, denverpost.com, March 21, 2013.

really intend to marry and then impose the status of marriage on them? States that rejected common-law marriages, or never allowed them in the first place, probably did so because they do not want to be in the business of picking and choosing who is married. If the state deems a couple common-law married under its existing common-law rules, is there common-law divorce? No, as Aspen County points out. Remember, common-law marriage is not a distinct type of marriage—it is marriage—just achieved in a nontraditional way. Therefore, although a couple may have become common-law married, getting out of it may be complicated because they will still need to get a divorce (or die).

Most states have rejected the common-law right to marriage. As a result, only about a dozen states allow common-law marriage today. The states that still recognize common-law marriage are: Alabama, Colorado, Iowa, Kansas, Montana, Rhode Island, South Carolina, Utah, Texas, and the District of Columbia. Georgia, Idaho, Ohio, and Pennsylvania abolished the law about two decades ago, but any common-law marriages occurring during this time may still be effective. Maryland, and many other states, never allowed them. The majority of states have specifically rejected common-law marriage by statute. Yet, most states will recognize a valid common-law marriage from another state. States choosing who is married is complicated enough, but when a person is already married, then lives with someone else, then holds themselves as married to one another—is this considered a common-law marriage? Are they committing bigamy, which is against public policy (see below)? In *Boswell v. Boswell*, 497 So.2d 479 (1986), a woman moves in with a man while she is already married to another man she never divorced. During the time she lived with the new man, her husband died. The Alabama Supreme Court in 1986 was willing to recognize the woman and the man's cohabitation relationship as a common-law marriage so that she could inherit from her "common law husband" at his death. In so doing, the court avoided the polygamy concerns by making the common-law marriage effective the day her husband died. Do the court's gyrations in *Boswell* support the argument for abolishing common-law marriage? Or is it the creepy age of marital consent issue raised in Colorado's *Marriage of J. M. H.* case below, that should be the death knell?

3. Putative Marriage

Under the doctrine of **putative marriage**, the court may impose a marriage on a couple whose own marriage was flawed, unbeknownst to them. The law has always had a special deference for "good faith" efforts. A putative marriage is a statutory device designed to prevent the hardship that occurs when parties to a marriage are ignorant of some impediment that invalidates their marriage. States may impose a putative marriage when one spouse, usually a widow, would harshly be denied economic rights from a long-term relationship that she did not know was invalid. By imposing a putative marriage, she will be deemed married and allowed to collect the pension or whatever financial benefit that she would have earned if she had been legally married as she thought she was. When there is a flaw in the marriage process, the courts try to achieve equity and fairness. Of course, once the flaw is known, the parties should marry to remedy the problem. Which do you think the courts should impose: a marriage by common law (when the couple made no effort to marry), or by putative, (when they couple tried to marry, but messed it up)?

4. Confidential Marriage

Generally, marriage licenses and registrations are public records and available for public review. A few states allow **confidential marriage,** which means there is no public record of the marriage. Confidential marriage allows the parties to go through the formalities of marriage (see below), but all the personal information of the marriage (the records of the marriage, including all the personal information on the license, and the issuance of the license itself) remains confidential. This information is only made public by court order or notarized request of either party. At one time, this type of marriage was popular with Hollywood stars as a way to keep their bachelor status for publicity purposes, while actually maintaining a traditional family life. While both California and Texas allow confidential marriage, Texas allows parties to have their marriage back-dated, while California generally recognizes the marriage from the day the confidential marriage license is properly filed. Why does California prevent minors from having a confidential marriage?

WHO CAN MARRY?

Void, Voidable, and Annulment

Who can marry? From a legal perspective, a better question may be who is not allowed to marry? While under *Loving v. Virginia* (see Chapter 5), there is a fundamental right to marry, state laws provide limitations. What happens if a couple violates one of the restrictions on marriage? The marriage may be void, or voidable. A **void marriage,** *void ab initio,* or from the beginning, means that one of the conditions required for marriage was missing. The marriage cannot be ratified. Void marriages are, therefore, invalid without a court order. Void marriages often offend a major public policy.

A **voidable marriage** also fails to meet a condition of marriage, but it is deemed valid unless it is set aside by a timely request to the court. What does timely mean? The parties to a voidable marriage can ratify it. Often, consummation after having knowledge of the violation is sufficient to demonstrate ratification under the law. Generally, voidable marriages offend a lesser public policy. Once parties are made aware of the defect in their marriage, they need to deal with it.

Rudolph (Rudy) W. Giuliani, former mayor of New York, had his first wedding annulled after 14 years because he married his second cousin.[46]

An **annulment** is when the court formally voids a marriage. If a marriage is voidable and one party chooses to void, it is necessary to go to court and obtain the court's order of an annulment. Once an annulment is entered, it is like erasing a whiteboard—the marriage is wiped clean from the public record as if it never existed.

What kinds of conditions would make a marriage void or voidable? What might a spouse find out that would be sufficient to void the marriage? Often issues of age, kinship, fraud, and mental or physical capacity might be included, as well as having another spouse. What else?

Conditions of Marriage

While each state sets out the conditions or prohibitions necessary for a marriage by statute, this book will include the restrictions most common to each state. Generally, in placing conditions that restrict marriage, the states are trying to ensure that someone has the capacity to enter into marriage and is fit enough to safely procreate and raise children, which has been the traditional legal rationale for marriage. Do these conditions satisfy this purpose?

1. Age

Every state sets a specific minimum age requirement necessary in order for two people involved to be married. Under common law, a marriage under the age of seven is void. Marriages from ages seven to 14 were valid. New Hampshire does not allow nonresidents under 18 to marry; it also prohibits marriage of female residents below the age of 13 or males below the age of 14 from marrying. Originally, states tied the marriage age to the ability to procreate and bear children. So under common law, there were two different ages: A woman could be married at 12 while a man had to wait until he was 14 (when he could provide for his family). Of course, in the old days, when marriage was more of a financial investment or coming together of powerful families, a betrothal could take place years earlier when the marriage was arranged while the actual marriage waited until the parties were of childbearing age.

Today, most states recognize 18 years as the age of maturity to marry. Mississippi requires parental consent for anyone under 21. Is maturity matched by age? Is serving in the military a better determinant? In Alaska, people under the age of 18 need parental consent to marry, but if the person is actively serving in the military, the parental consent requirement is waived. What if it were based on passing a driver's test or SAT scores? Now that people live so much longer than they did 100 years ago, should the age be raised higher than 18?

Many states had two different age requirements for each sex that allowed marriage with parental consent. For example, with a parent's consent, a boy who was at least 16 years old could

---

46   http://www.washingtonpost.com/wp-dyn/content/article/2006/03/07/AR2006030701768.html, "On 'Feeling Thermometer,' Giuliani Is the Hottest," Michael Powell and Zachary A. Goldfarb, *Washington Post*, March 8, 2006. See also, http://nymag.com/news/features/28517/index5.html

marry, but a girl only had to be at least 14 years old (or 15 and 17). Should states be allowed to set different age minimums for different genders? If so, why? In the case of *Moe v. Dinkins*, 533 F. Supp. 623 (S.D.N.Y 1981), a New York statute required males between ages 16 and 18 and females between 14 and 18 obtain permission from both parents to marry, if both parents were living. Women between the ages of 14 and 16 could obtain judicial approval if they could not get both of their parents' permission. In *Moe*, the girl was 15 and wanted to marry to a boy who was 18. They had a one-year-old, non-marital child together and were living with the baby as an independent family unit. When the girl became pregnant again with their second out-of-marriage child, she wanted to marry the boy. This required her to obtain permission from her mother (a widow) in order to marry the father of her children. The mother refused to allow it (allegedly because she did not want to give up the welfare payments she collected as a result of the dependent girl). The young couple sued, saying that the requirement of parental permission violated their liberty interest guaranteed by the due process clause of the 14th Amendment. The New York court agreed with the state's law and rejected the plaintiffs' claim. Because she was still a minor, the court stressed the importance of the parental role in child rearing—even when her mother did not appear to act in her best interest. Of course, the court would argue that the girl was not being denied the fundamental right to marry; it was only delayed until she turned 18 and was permitted to marry on her own. While 18 is thought of as the minimum age to marry, as the *Moe* case demonstrates, most states allow younger people to marry with their parents' permission. Some states will even allow a young person to marry without her parent's approval if she obtains a judge's approval. Missouri allows a person under age 15 to marry with a county judge's approval. The statute states that the judge should grant approval only upon a showing of "good cause" and that unusual conditions make the marriage "advisable." Given this, it sounds like child brides should be rare. Yet, between 2000 and 2010, in 38 states, more than 167,000 children "some as young as 12" were married "mostly to men 18 or older."[47] When 70% of child marriages end in divorce, why are they allowed? New Jersey proposed a law to prevent marriage below 18 years of age. A similar bill in Maryland did not pass.[48]

Common-law marriage (see above) may further complicate the issue of minimum age to marriage. In *In re the Marriage of J. M. H., and Willis Rouse v. Concerning Weld County Department of Human Services*, Case No 04CA0740 CO Ct App (2006), the appellant, Rouse, was not able to make an appearance at the trial and had to appear by telephone from the county jail because he was "incarcerated and awaiting trial on a charge of sexual assault on a child, and was serving a sentence for escape and parole violation." According to Rouse, he and minor J. M. H. began living together in April 2002 (when she was 14). In April 2003, when J. M. H. was 15 years old, they

---

47 "Why do we still let 12-year-olds get married", Fraidy Reiss, *Washington Post Outlook*, 2/13/17, B1. The children cannot run away from these forced marriages because the police will return them back to their parents and hostels will call their parents. Child protective services "caseworkers point out that preventing legal marriage is not in their mandate." Ibid., B5

48 Ibid.

applied for a marriage license in Adams County. Rouse also asserts, although J. M. H. was subject to a dependency and neglect proceeding brought by the Weld County Department of Human Services, that she was emancipated. J. M. H.'s mother offered her signed and notarized consent to the marriage, and accompanied Rouse and J. M. H. to the county clerk's office to obtain a marriage license. The deputy clerk approved the application and forwarded it to the county clerk for registration. The county clerk also approved the application and mailed it back to Rouse and J. M. H., stating they were fully registered as a legally married couple as of April 28, 2003.

In February 2004, the department filed a petition to declare the marriage invalid, asserting that J. M. H. was 15, the application was not approved by a parent, and the various criminal matters in which Rouse was involved. "Rouse responded by asserting that he and J. M. H. were legally married at common law and, in the alternative, that they had a valid ceremonial marriage because they had obtained a marriage license in Adams County." The trial court "held that a person under the age of sixteen must obtain judicial approval for a valid common law or ceremonial marriage." The case was then appealed. The Colorado Court of Appeals agreed with Rouse's contention "that the trial court erred in holding that a person under the age of sixteen must seek judicial approval to be married, even if that marriage is at common law."[49] In invalidating the trial court's ruling, the court did not set a specific minimum age for common-law marriage.

While the *J. M. H.* case brushed aside the underlying issue of the sexual relationship, when Matthew Koso, 22, married his pregnant girlfriend Crystal, 14, the state of Nebraska did not. "The Nebraska attorney general accuses Mr. Koso of being a pedophile; they say it is true love." Because Nebraska would not allow the marriage of a 14-year-old, the Kosos crossed the border into Kansas, which allows such marriages with parental consent, and they married. When they returned to live in Nebraska, the state charged Matthew Koso with statutory rape. What should the courts do in situations where older men impregnate younger girls and marry them? Once they are married, should the state give its usual deference to an intact family?[50]

2. Kinship

Should you be allowed to marry your brother or your mother? How about your uncle or cousin? Why does society prohibit marriage to immediate family members? When people are related through blood, marriage, or adoption, our society prohibits them from marrying each other. Perhaps, given the ecclesiastical history of marriage law, the prohibition is biblically related. Leviticus 18:6–18 prohibits brothers and sisters from marrying. Is the prohibition on incest more than an enforcement of some religions' prohibitions? While science has raised concerns about genetic mutations from inbreed populations, in a population as diluted as the United States with so few family marriages,

---

49 http://www.courts.state.co.us/Courts/Court_of_Appeals/opinion/2006/2006q2/04CA0740.pdf

50 http://www.nytimes.com/2005/08/30/national/30baby.html?pagewanted=all&_r=0, "Rape Charge Follows Marriage to a 14-Year-Old," Jodi Wilgoren, *New York Times*, August 30, 2005.

does it really have statistical validity? Whatever the reason, marrying a too-close relative is void. Such marriages can be challenged by the members. But should they? The Cousins United to Defeat Discriminating Laws through Education (C.U.D.D.L.E) advocates that marriage should be legal between cousins. C.U.D.D.L.E. cites new scientific research which disproves the genetic concerns and argues that cousin marriages have a lower rate of health risk than smoking and drinking which are not illegal. Maryland and many states allow first cousins to marry. If close cousin marital relationships are allowed in some states, would parent/child marital relationships be allowed too if the parent did not raise the biological child? In New Mexico, a mother and her 19-year old son were facing jail time for their admitted sexual relationship that began 18 years after she placed her newborn son up for adoption at birth. They reunited through an internet search and the mother picked him up at his adoptive house.[51]

Kinship marriage can be challenged by anyone, including the police if a crime has been committed. Many states have limited their restrictions based on affinity or relationship through marriage, but generally, consanguinity, or relationships based on blood relations has been retained.[52] As the definition of family expands, what are the effects of this prohibition on the nuclear family? In the case of *Israel v. Allen*, 195 CO 264 (1978), after a man and woman were married, he adopted her 13-year-old daughter, Tammi, and lived in Denver, Colorado. At that time, he had a son, Martin, who was 18 years old and living in Washington. When Martin and Tammi later decided to marry, Colorado would not give them a marriage license because they had a common father, which made them brother and sister. The Colorado statute specifically included such relationships by adoption. The Colorado Supreme Court agreed to strike the part of the law that included the language including the adoptions. Should there be a difference if the child was adopted at an advanced stage or an infant?

3. Physical Capacity

Traditionally, it is expected that spouses will have sexual relations and be able to raise the children produced. As a result, at the turn of the last century, states prohibited marriage for people who had certain medical conditions that were thought to be inheritable, such as epilepsy, or transmittable, like venereal disease. Most states have abolished such restrictions, so now, the cases involving physical capacity to marry mostly focus on a spouse's impotence. A spouse is expected to be able to copulate and produce children. Impotence may make a marriage voidable although the spouses have to be careful not to ratify it once the condition is known.

The question of an annulment may arise if a person is not aware of the other spouse's physical defect or condition, and it goes to the essentials of the marriage. This area of physical capacity to

---

51   http://www.foxnews.com/world/2016/08/08/new-mexico-mother-and-son-face-jail-time-for-incestuous-relationship.html

52   In Georgia, marriage licenses are denied to uncles and nieces, but cousins are permitted to marry. Nevada allows "cousins of half-blood." Virginia precludes kin marriages by blood or adoption. Indiana and Utah have an exception to prohibiting cousins to marry if they are first cousins who are both at least 65 years of age, or in Utah, if over the age of 55 and they can prove sterility. In Rhode Island, a woman, by the way, may marry her uncle, providing she is Jewish.

create children has also been raised in cases involving a transsexual spouse. In the Kansas case of *In the Matter of the Estate of Marshall G. Gardiner,* 273 KS 191, 42 P.3d 120 (2003), the Kansas Supreme Court rejected a more expansive definition of female when determining if a marriage to a transsexual spouse was valid.[53]

The *Gardiner* court found that the words "sex," "marriage," "male," and "female" in everyday understanding do not encompass transsexuals. The court found that the common, ordinary meaning of "persons of the opposite sex" contemplates what is commonly understood to be a biological man and a biological woman, and that a post-operative male-to-female transsexual did not fit the common definition of female. In so doing, the Kansas Supreme Court cited to the state legislature's declaration that the public policy of this state is to recognize only traditional marriage between two parties who are of the opposite sex. They found that a marriage between a post-operative male-to-female transsexual and a man is void as against public policy. As a result, the court rejected a transsexual woman's right to inherit from her husband's estate.[54]

The *Gardiner* court relied on the strict chromosome test that was used in the *Corbett* case, from English case law. In the case of *M. T. v. J. T.,* 355 A.2d 204 (NJ Super. Ct. App. Div. 1976), the New Jersey court, while looking at a similar issue, ignored the traditional English case law in the *Corbett case*[55] that said sex is biologically determined based on chromosomes at birth. That decision has been challenged by members of the medical community. In *M. T.,* the New Jersey court adopted a congruence of anatomy and psyche, finding that it was necessary to determine whether the person's anatomy was incongruent with his psyche and therefore functioning as a gender-neutral person that may include results of surgical intervention. As a result, the *M. T.* court recognized her as female and allowed the divorce to go forward. That finding has been challenged in several states.

While the *M. T.* case has been challenged by other courts such as the Kansas courts, should it be? The United Kingdom had originally used the strict chromosome test to make such determinations, but the U.K. passed the Gender Recognition Act of 2004[56] to expand the factors involved in making such decisions based on human rights laws. Many U.S. courts seem to rely on the outdated U.K. law, should they become more current?

---

53 The Court of Appeals reversed and remanded for the district court's determination whether J'Noel was male or female at the time the marriage license was issued. See In re *Estate of Gardiner,* 29 Kan.App. 2d 92, 22 P.3d 1086 (2001). The court of appeals directed the district court to consider a number of factors in addition to chromosomes.
54 http://www.stanford.edu/~mrosenfe/In_Re_Gardiner_Kansas_2002.pdf
55 In *Corbett v. Corbett* (UK), April Ashley was a post-operative male-to-female transsexual who had undergone sex reassignment surgery before marrying male Corbett. When they split up, the husband wanted the marriage voided because the definition of marriage under English law marriage was that of a union between a man and a woman. Thus, he claimed that the Corbetts were both males, thus making their relationship not a marriage. The English judge looked at biological tests involving chromosomes, glands, and the genitalia in ruling for the husband.
56 http://www.gires.org.uk/GRA.php, which allows transgendered people to obtain a certificate for recognition of a gender, including obtaining a new birth certificate with the appropriate gender designation.

4. Mental Capacity

"In the past, stigmas against people with intellectual impairments led to forced sterilization and laws prohibiting them from marriage. In some states those laws remain though they are rarely enforced."[57]

Many states prevent marriage with a person who is "mentally incompetent," as the term is used in Kentucky. For those states that look at the issue of mental capacity, they are trying to ensure that both parties understand the nature of the marriage proceedings, the meaning of marriage, and their responsibilities underneath it. In Indiana, if a person has been judged to be of an unsound mind, proof of removal of that adjudication is acceptable to allow the marriage to go forward. In some states, such marriages may be ratified during a lucid period. Most states, including Indiana, will not issue a marriage license to anyone under the influence of drugs or alcohol. These laws attempt to determine if the spouses have sufficient capacity to consent to marriage. Obviously, if a person is so impaired by alcohol or drugs, that capacity is lacking, such marriages can be annulled. There is an urban legend that after getting married at the courthouse a wife asked her husband to go to the local bar to celebrate. When she walked into the bar, she yelled to the bartender, "See, I married him. Now where is my $10?" Surely a marriage should be voided if it is made in jest to win a bet or play a game.

5. Fraud

If a marriage is a civil contract, then the parties must consent to it. If either party consents by reason of fraud, the marriage is voidable. What kind of fraud would be necessary to void a marriage? Often, the fraud, the misrepresentation of a material fact, must "go to the essence of the marriage"—procreation. Courts have voided marriages in which the wife was pregnant at the time of marriage without notifying her spouse of the pregnancy. What about a marriage in which the wife told the husband that the child was his, but later it is determined that it was not? Is this a marriage that should be annulled for fraud?

---

57   "What Love Is", Ellen McCarthy, *Washington Post Magazine*, February 10, 2013, pp. 8, 13, is an uplifting article on this issue.

JOSEPH M. ELLIS, Judge.

William Jerry Blair (Husband) appeals from a judgment entered in the Circuit Court of Platte County denying his petition for annulment of his marriage to Nancy Blair[1] (Wife). For the following reasons, we affirm.

In July 1976, Husband and Wife had sexual intercourse on one occasion after having worked together for a couple of years. At that time, Wife was married to Jim Farra and was also involved in a long-standing sexual relationship with Sam Kelly.

Subsequently, Wife gave birth to a son, Devin, on April 26, 1977. Husband visited Wife in the hospital shortly after Devin's birth, but did not discuss the paternity of the child with her and had no further contact with Wife until 1979.

In January 1979, Wife contacted Husband, told him that he was Devin's father, and asked whether he had any history of disease in his family that might affect Devin later in life. Husband met with Wife and Devin, and he resumed a sexual relationship with Wife a few days later. In March 1979, Wife separated from Mr. Farra and filed a petition for dissolution of that marriage. Subsequently, Wife became pregnant with Husband's child, and on March 13, 1980, Wife gave birth to their daughter, Oralin.

Wife's marriage to Mr. Farra was dissolved in December 1980. Several days after her divorce from Mr. Farra became final, Husband and Wife were married on December 22, 1980. Husband later adopted both Devin and Oralin.

On November 20, 2001, Wife filed a petition for dissolution of her marriage to Husband. Husband filed his answer and cross-petition on December 26, 2001.

On April 11, 2002, Husband filed an amended answer and cross-petition requesting that the marriage be annulled. In support of his annulment claim, Husband averred that Wife had fraudulently represented to him before their marriage that he was Devin's father and had thereby induced him to marry her. Subsequent testing proved that Husband was indeed not Devin's father and that he was the son of Sam Kelly.

The trial court heard the matter on November 25, 2002. On January 8, 2003, the trial court entered its judgment denying Husband's petition for an annulment and dissolving the marriage between Husband and Wife. Husband filed a motion for new trial on February 5, 2003. On May 5, 2003, the trial court denied Husband's motion for new trial and entered its Amended Judgment and Decree of Dissolution of Marriage.

In its amended judgment, like the initial judgment, the trial court denied Husband's request for an annulment. In support of its denial of an annulment, the court found: (1) that Wife had believed that Devin was Husband's son during their courtship and at the time of marriage;(2) that Husband would have married Wife even if he had known the representation to be false and that the representation was not material to his decision to marry her; (3) that Husband did not detrimentally rely upon Wife's statement; (4) that Wife did not intend for her representation about Devin's paternity to be relied upon by Husband; (5) that even if the marriage had been the result of a misrepresentation related to Devin's paternity, Husband failed to prove any damages, actual or punitive, resulting from the alleged misrepresentation; (6) that Husband had "unclean hands" sufficient to deny equitable relief because Husband had fraudulently represented to Wife that he loved her prior to marriage; and (7) Husband was precluded from equitable relief because of the doctrine of laches based upon the fact that Husband failed to take any action toward the paternity of Devin, even though at times he questioned Devin's paternity. Husband brings five points on appeal challenging the trial court's denial of his petition for annulment…

"The annulment of a marriage voids the marriage ab initio." *Eyerman v. Thias*, 760 S.W.2d 187, 189 (Mo.App. E.D.1988). "In the eyes of the law it is as if the marriage never existed." Id. "[A]nnulment of marriage is the exception and not the rule, and must be granted only upon extraordinary facts." *Woy v. Woy*, 737 S.W.2d 769, 774 (Mo.App. W.D.1987). "[T]he burden of proving the invalidity of a marriage rests upon him who asserts such invalidity, and a marriage will not be declared invalid except upon clear, cogent and convincing proof."[3] In re *Marriage of Burnside*, 777 S.W.2d 660, 664 (Mo.App. S.D.1989).

As grounds for granting an annulment, Husband asserted that Wife perpetrated a fraud upon him regarding Devin's paternity. In order to establish fraud, Husband was required to plead and prove the following elements: (1) a representation by Wife; (2) its falsity; (3) its materiality; (4) Wife's knowledge of its falsity or ignorance of its truth; (5) Wife's intent that the representation be acted upon by Husband; (6) Husband's ignorance of the falsity of the representation; (7) Husband's reliance on the truth of the representation; (8) Husband's right to rely on the representation; and (9) that Husband sustained consequent and proximate injury. *Charley v. Fant*, 892 S.W.2d 811, 812 (Mo.App. W.D.1995). Moreover, "'[p]ublic policy demands that integrity of the marriage contract be preserved so far as possible, and fraud necessary to avoid a marriage must be such as is deemed vital to the marriage relationship.'" *Woy*, 737 S.W.2d at 772.

In its judgment, the trial court found that Wife's representations as to Devin's paternity were not material to Husband's decision to marry her and that Husband would have married her even if he had known that those representations were false. In one of his points on appeal, Husband contends that these findings are not supported by sufficient evidence and are against the weight of the evidence.

Husband notes that he testified at trial that he would not have married Wife if he had known that he was not Devin's father and contends that the trial court was required to accept that testimony as true. In making this assertion, Husband disregards our standard of review, which requires this court to view the evidence and all reasonable inferences drawn therefrom in the light most favorable to the judgment and to disregard all evidence and inferences to the contrary. *Stuckmeyer*, 117 S.W.3d at 690. "We defer to the trial court where there is conflicting evidence, and will affirm the judgment even if there is evidence which would support a different conclusion." *McAllister v. McAllister*, 101 S.W.3d 287, 290 (Mo.App. E.D.2003).

Because the trial court is in a better position to assess such factors as sincerity, character, and other intangibles that are not apparent in a trial transcript, we must defer to the trial court's determinations related to the credibility of the witnesses. Id. at 290–91. "'The trial judge has absolute discretion as to the credibility of witnesses and the weight of their testimony is a matter for the trial court, and its findings on witness credibility are never reviewable by the appellate court.'" Id. at 291 (quoting *Milligan v. Helmstetter*, 15 S.W.3d 15, 24 (Mo.App. W.D.2000)). "The trial court is free to accept or reject all, part, or none of the testimony of a witness. And, it may disbelieve testimony even when it is uncontradicted." Id. (internal citations omitted).

Accordingly, the trial court was not required to accept Husband's own self-serving testimony that he would not have married Wife but for her representations related to Devin's paternity. Indeed, the overall gist of Husband's testimony appears to have been that he would never have seen Wife again after their one-night-stand if it had not been for her calling and telling him that he had a child and that the marriage was, therefore, the result of that representation. Such testimony does not establish that Husband relied upon the representations regarding Devin's paternity in deciding whether to marry Wife, only that it played a part in his decision to begin a relationship with her.

Sufficient evidence in the record supports the trial court's determination that Husband would have married Wife regardless of the representation as to Devin's paternity. Wife testified that Husband was crazy about her and that she was certain that he would have left his girlfriend and had a relationship with her regardless of Devin's paternity. Husband admitted on cross-examination that, during the two-year courtship the couple had between Wife's initial phone call and their marriage, he fell in love with Wife. In addition, nine months before their marriage, Oralin, who is undisputedly Husband's child, was born. The trial court could reasonably have inferred that Oralin's paternity would have been sufficient to cause Husband to marry Wife.[4] Furthermore, testimony from both Husband and Wife reflects that Husband had questions about Devin's paternity prior to marriage, that he married her anyway, and that he subsequently adopted both children.

Based upon the foregoing testimony, the trial court could more than reasonably have found that Husband would have married Wife regardless of Wife's representations related to Devin's paternity. Such a finding is supported by sufficient evidence and is not against the weight of the evidence. Point denied.

Having determined that this ground for the trial court's denial of Husband's request for an annulment is not erroneous, we need not address Husband's remaining points related to the trial court's other grounds for its decision.[5] See Eckhoff, 71 S.W.3d at 622 (noting that this court must affirm the trial court's judgment if "cognizable under any theory").

The judgment is affirmed.

FootNote1. In the trial court's decree dissolving Husband and Wife's marriage, the court granted Wife's request that her name be changed from Nancy Blair back to Nancy Asheton.

In *Blair*, the court looked at the issue of whether the woman fraudulently induced a marriage by telling the man her child was his. What happens when the couple marries based on a promise to have a child or not during the marriage? Will the court annul a marriage when one party refuses to have children? In the New Jersey case of *VJS v. MJB*, 249 NJ Super. 318. 592 A.2d 328 (1991), Judge Krafte wrote, "It is axiomatic that, given proper proof, a party will be entitled to an annulment when the spouse refuses to have children." In the *VJS* case, the court was asked to decide if "the converse is also true, i.e., given proper proof, a party will be entitled to an annulment when the spouse insists on having children, contrary to the express agreement of the parties prior to marriage that they would not have children." The court wrote, "Defendant refused to engage in sexual intercourse utilizing any form of contraception. Defendant misrepresented his agreement not to have children and intended that plaintiff rely on same, which in fact she did when she exchanged vows with defendant. This is a suit for annulment of a marriage on the ground that defendant committed a fraud as to an essential of the marriage contract whereby he possessed a preconceived, uncommunicated determination at the time of the marriage to have children in the face of an express agreement with plaintiff not to have children." In determining that this amounted to fraud, which goes to the "essentials of the marriage," the court voided the marriage.[58]

6. Force or Duress

Of course, a marriage based on force or duress is against public policy and could be annulled. Generally, this arises in federal government immigration cases. The outdated term "shotgun wedding" would also be voidable.

---

58 http://www.leagle.com/xmlResult.aspx?page=2&xmldoc=1991567249NJSuper318_1536.xml&docbase=CSLWAR2-1986-2006&SizeDisp=7

7. Monogamy

The law requires monogamy—marriage is a "one-per-customer rule." Thus, if a person is already married and marries another person, the second marriage is void. Bigamy is when a person is married to two people at the same time. Such behavior is criminal in all 50 states (although this law is frequently not enforced). The case of *State (of North Carolina) v. Lynch* 272 S.E.2d 349 (1980) raises the issue of a legally recognized officiant when looking at the issue of bigamy.

STATE V. LYNCH
NO. 31.
272 S.E.2D 349 (1980)

STATE of North Carolina v. James Roberts LYNCH.

Supreme Court of North Carolina.

December 2, 1980.

Rufus L. Edmisten, Atty. Gen. by Norma S. Harrell, Associate Atty. Gen., Raleigh, for the State.

Eubanks, Walden & Mackintosh by Bruce A. Mackintosh, Winston-Salem, for defendant appellant.

HUSKINS, Justice:

The question we address upon this appeal is whether the evidence of the crime of bigamy is sufficient to withstand defendant's motion for nonsuit. We hold the evidence insufficient to go to the jury, and defendant's motion for nonsuit should have been granted....

Bigamy is a statutory crime in all fifty states. See Slovenko, *The De Facto Decriminalization of Bigamy,* 17 J. of Fam.L. 297, 307-08 (1979) (Appendix contains list of bigamy statutes). Bigamy was not an offense at common law. It was an offense against society punishable under ecclesiastical law. *State v. Burns* 90 N.C. 707 (1884); 4 W. Blackstone, Commentaries * 163; but see, *State v. Williams,* 220 N.C. 445, 17 S.E.2d 769 (1941), *rev'd on other grounds, Williams v. North Carolina,* 317 U.S. 287, 87 L.Ed. 279, 63 S.Ct. 208 (1942). It was made a statutory offense in the reign of James I. 2 James I, c.11 (1604). This English statute was the prototype for the first North Carolina bigamy statute of 1790. 1790 N.C.Sess. Laws c.11.

[272 S.E.2d 353]

Our bigamy statute is presently codified at G.S. 14-183 and reads as follows:

If any person, being married, shall marry any other person during the life of the former husband or wife, every such offender, and every person counseling, aiding or abetting such offender, shall be guilty of a felony, and shall be imprisoned in the State's prison or county jail for any term not less than four months nor more than ten years. Any such offense may be dealt with, tried, determined and punished in the county where the offender shall be apprehended, or be in custody, as if the offense had been actually committed in that county. If any person, being married, shall contract a marriage with any other person outside of this State, which marriage would be punishable as bigamous if contracted within this State, and shall thereafter cohabit with such person in this State, he shall be guilty of a felony and shall be punished as in cases of bigamy. Nothing contained in this section shall extend to any person marrying a second time, whose husband or wife shall have been continually absent from such person for the space of seven years then last past, and shall not have been known by such person to have been living within that time; nor to any person who at the time of such second marriage shall have been lawfully divorced from the bond of the first marriage; nor to any person whose former marriage shall have been declared void by the sentence of any court of competent jurisdiction.

A person commits bigamy when being lawfully married he purports to marry another person.

The issue raised in this nonsuit question is whether defendant contracted a marriage to Mary Alice Bovender while lawfully married to Sandra Lynch. This case turns upon whether the marriage to Sandra Lynch was a valid marriage under the laws of this State.

The existence of a valid prior marriage must be proved beyond a reasonable doubt by the State. The question of its validity must be determined by the law of the state in which the ceremony was performed. If the prior marriage was void, the second marriage was not bigamous. 2 Wharton's Criminal Law § 236 (14 ed. 1979).

Marriage is an institution controlled by the individual states. *Jones v. Bradley,* 590 F.2d 294, 296 (9th Cir. 1979); *see also Boddie v. Connecticut,* 401 U.S. 371, 91 S.Ct. 780, 28 L.Ed.2d 113 (1971). "There are three parties to a marriage contract-the husband, the wife and the State." *Ritchie v. White,* 225 N.C. 450, 453, 35 S.E.2d 414, 415 (1945).

Marriage, or the relation of husband and wife, is in law complete when parties, able to contract and willing to contract, actually have contracted to be man and wife in the forms and with the solemnities required by law. It is marriage-it is this contract, which gives to each right or power over the body of the other, and renders a consequent cohabitation lawful. And it is the abuse of this formal and solemn contract, by entering into it a second time when a former husband or wife is yet living, which the law forbids because of its outrage upon public decency, its violation of the public economy, as well as its tendency to cheat one into a surrender of the person under the appearance of right. A man takes a wife lawfully when the contract is lawfully made. He takes a wife unlawfully when the contract is unlawfully made; and this unlawful contract the law punishes.

State v. Patterson, 24 N.C. 346, 355-56 (1842). To constitute a valid marriage in this State, the requirements of G.S. 51-1 must be met. That statute provides:

[272 S.E.2d 354]

The consent of a male and female person who may lawfully marry, presently to take each other as husband and wife, freely, seriously and plainly expressed by each in the presence of the other, and in the presence of an ordained minister of any religious denomination, minister authorized by his church, or of a magistrate, and the consequent declaration by such minister or officer that such persons are husband and wife, shall be a valid and sufficient marriage: Provided, that the rite of marriage among the Society of Friends, according to a form and custom peculiar to themselves, shall not be interfered with by the provisions of this Chapter: Provided further, that marriages solemnized and witnessed by a local spiritual assembly of the Baha'is, according to the usage of their religious community, shall be valid; provided further, marriages solemnized before March 9, 1909, by ministers of the gospel licensed, but not ordained, are validated from their consummation.

A common law marriage or marriage by consent is not recognized in this *State. State v. Alford*, 298 N.C. 465, 259 S.E.2d 242 (1979); *State v. Samuel*, 19 N.C. 177 (1836). Consent is just one of the essential elements of a marriage. The marriage must be acknowledged in the manner and before some person prescribed in G.S. 51-1. *State v. Wilson*, 121 N.C. 650, 28 S.E. 416 (1897). In order to have a valid marriage in this State, the parties must express their solemn intent to marry in the presence of (1) "an ordained minister of any religious denomination," or (2) a "minister authorized by his church" or (3) a "magistrate."

In this case, the State is required to establish beyond a reasonable doubt that Chester A. Wilson was an ordained minister of a religious denomination or a minister authorized by his church. Though the marriage license is competent evidence tending to prove a marriage, *State v. Melton*, 120 N.C. 591, 26 S.E. 933 (1897), the absence or presence of a marriage license is of minimal consequence in establishing a valid marriage to support a bigamy prosecution. *State v. Robbins*, 28 N.C. 23 (1845); see also G.S. 51-6 to -21. The subjective intent of defendant to indeed marry the person alleged to be his first wife is also of minimal consequence. Bigamy is an offense even though unwittingly committed. *State v. Goulden*, 134 N.C. 743, 47 S.E. 450 (1904). The admission of defendant that he was previously married is competent evidence tending to establish the marriage. State v. Goulden, supra; *State v. Melton*, supra; *State v. Wylde*, 110 N.C. 500, 15 S.E. 5 (1892). The marriage defendant admitted he entered into or intended and the marriage which is at least licensed by the State or which is apparent by reputation in the community must, however, comply with G.S. 51-1. We conclude the State has failed to meet this burden and the motion for nonsuit consequently should have been allowed.

It is not within the power of the State to declare what is or is not a religious body or who is or is not a religious leader within the body. *State v. Bray*, 35 N.C. 289 (1852). In Bray, a bigamy case which brought into question the validity of the first marriage, Chief Justice Ruffin addressed the wording of the North Carolina marriage statute:

The statute, without assuming to pronounce dogmatically who were true ministers of the gospel, meant to give a catholic rule, by admitting everyone to be so, to this purpose, who, in the view of his own church, hath the cure of souls by the ministry of the Word, and any of the sacraments of God, according to its ecclesiastical polity, implying spiritual authority to receive or deny any desiring to be partakers thereof, and to administer admonition or discipline, as he may deem the same to be the soul's health of the person and the promotion of godliness among the people. When to such a ministry is annexed, according to the canons, or statutes of the particular church, the faculty of performing the office of solemnizing matrimony, the qualification of the minister is sufficient, within the statute.

35 N.C. at 295-96. Whether defendant is married in the eyes of God, of himself or of any ecclesiastical body is not our concern. Our concern is whether the marriage is one the State recognizes. "[A] marriage pretendedly celebrated before a person not authorized would be a nullity." *State v. Wilson,* 121 N.C. 650, 656-57, 28 S.E. 416, 418 (1897). A ceremony solemnized by a Roman Catholic layman in the mail order business who bought for $10.00 a mail order certificate giving him "credentials of minister"

[272 S.E.2d 355]

in the Universal Life Church, Inc.-whatever that is-is not a ceremony of marriage to be recognized for purposes of a bigamy prosecution in the State of North Carolina. The evidence does not establish— rather, it negates the fact-that Chester A. Wilson was authorized under the laws of this State to perform a marriage ceremony.

The State has failed to prove a prior marriage within the meaning of G.S. 51-1. The second marriage was therefore not bigamous. Defendant's motion for nonsuit should have been granted. The decision of the Court of Appeals is

REVERSED.

BROCK, J., took no part in the consideration or decision of this case

---

Many states have Enoch Arden statutes, named after the Lord Tennyson character in his 1864 narrative poem. In this story, a man is presumed dead at sea after his ship was wrecked, but he returns home after ten years to the quiet village where he had lived with his wife and family. Despite all his struggles to return, he leaves quietly when he sees that she is happily married and later dies of a broken heart.[59] Some states will not prosecute a spouse for remarrying after a period of time if their original spouse has been missing and presumed dead (even if he reappears later). State statutes may allow such a presumption after an absence of five to seven years. But under these laws, the second marriage is made valid and the original marriage is voided without

---

59 The poem was supposedly based on a real story, but many liken it to the myth of Odysseus. Odysseus had a long absence during the Trojan War due to being lost at sea when one of the gods gave him a bag of wind, but this story has a happier ending as his wife loyally awaited his return.

divorce after the time period. This is in direct contrast with bigamy or polygamy cases in which the second marriage is void.

Polygamy is the practice of intentionally marrying many wives at the same time. The 1878 Supreme Court case of *Reynolds v. United States*, 98 U.S. 145 (1878), upheld a federal statute that criminalized the behavior of polygamy in Utah. In this case, Reynolds argued against such laws based on his First Amendment freedom of religion challenge. Reynolds was a member of the Mormon religion which, at that time, encouraged multiple marriages.[60] After Utah became a territory, it agreed to outlaw such behavior. While Reynolds argued that he was still entitled to his religious objection allowing his behavior, the court disagreed with him. The Supreme Court indicated that while he was entitled to believe whatever he wanted, by putting that belief into an illegal action, he would be prosecuted. While usually deferential to the states on the issue of marriage, polygamy and same-sex marriage are two areas for which the federal government has set marriage prohibitions (see Chapter 6). Now that marriage equality is the law, should polygamy be? In the *Obergefell* case legalizing gay marriage, Chief Justice John Roberts wrote in his dissent, "Although the majority randomly inserts the adjective 'two' in various places, it offers no reason at all why the two-person element of the core definition of marriage may be preserved while the man-woman element may not. Indeed, from the standpoint of history and tradition, a leap from opposite-sex marriage to same-sex marriage is much greater than one from a two-person union to plural unions, which have deep roots in some cultures around the world." [61] Do you agree? In 2010, this country shined a spotlight on polygamist marriages, especially in the cases against the Fundamentalist Church of Jesus Christ of Latter-Day Saints. This breakaway sect was formerly run by Warren Jeffs, who was at one time on the FBI's most wanted posters and is now serving a life sentence in Texas for child sex abuse and bigamy.[62] (See Chapter 17.) In a further

---

60 "It's Official: Mormon Founder Had Up to 40 Wives", Laurie Goodstein, *The New York Times*, November 11, 2014. "Mormon leaders have acknowledged for the first time that the church's founder and prophet, Joseph Smith, portrayed in church materials as a loyal partner to his loving spouse Emma, took as many as 40 wives, some already married and one only 14 years old." Many Mormons knew "that Smith's successor, Brigham Young practiced polygamy...but they did not know the full truth about Smith." "For his wife, Emma, polygamy was 'an excruciating ordeal.'" http://www.nytimes.com/2014/11/11/us/its-official-mormon-founder-had-up-to-40-wives.html?_r=0

61 *Obergefell v. Hodges,* (U.S. 2015) 576 U.S. ___, see chapter 6.

62 http://www.nytimes.com/2011/11/09/us/fredrick-jessop-sentenced-for-polygamist-marriages. html?ref=warrensjeffs&_r=0, "Texas: 10-Year Sentence for Polygamist Marriages," AP, November 8, 2011. In *U.S. v. Lyle Jeffs,* et. al, in Utah, the federal government sued members of the polygamous group for a multi-million dollar food stamp fraud and money laundering. The group raised a religious defense under the Mormon "'law of consecration'". "Seth Jeffs (Warren's brother) testified....they believe everything on earth belongs to God, which is why members must donate everything they own to a community storehouse" where the leaders decide how to distribute it. The leader's diverted food stamp money to personal items including a tractor and luxury vehicle. The judge "decided the case doesn't violate the[ir] religious freedoms". "Judge rules against polygamous sect in food-stamp fraud case", Lindsay Whitehurst, http://www.Philly.com/new, updated November 15, 2016. Another of Warren's brothers was also a defendant in the case, but he slipped off his house-arrest bracelet with olive oil and was on the lam until his capture in 2017. A 2016 email from the food storehouse manager to one of the defendant church officials that was submitted into evidence in the case read, "'The inventory looks pretty bleak. We did not get much today. Many orders went out with no eggs and no fruit. Number of orders to be filled: 116. Number of people to be served: 1,563. Produce in stock: 0.'"

effort to keep up the pressure, the U.S. Justice Department filed a civil rights lawsuit against two polygamous towns along the Utah-Arizona border, claiming discrimination against people who are not members of the Fundamentalist Church of Jesus Christ of Latter-Day Saints. "The lawsuit comes after the Legislatures in Utah and Arizona failed to pass bills aimed at abolishing the Colorado City Police Department, which serves both towns. The Arizona bill was being pushed by the state's attorney general, Tom Horne, who said Colorado City police officers who are members of the church flout the law. According to the lawsuit officers allow sect members to destroy crops and vandalize property of nonmembers. Federal officials also say the officers keep underage brides from running away and accuse the cities of refusing to provide electricity and water to nonmembers."[63]

Prior to this, in 2005, the Utah Supreme Court was asked whether to remove a judge who was openly married to three women. Judge Walter Steed "was found to be a polygamist by the state's Judicial Conduct Commission." The judge's attorneys argued that while "drug abuse might be grounds for removal, what the judge does in the privacy of his own home should not."[64] Should the polygamist judge be allowed to pass judgment on the legality of other people's behavior from the bench?

Should polygamy still be prohibited? In January, 2013, the "Sister Wives" lawsuit, brought by the polygamous family on TV's TLC involving Kody Brown and his four "wives" was filed in Utah federal court. The Brown family alleged that despite the *Reynolds* precedent, they had a first amendment right to freedom of religion to enter into their polygamist marriage and they challenged the Utah law after the state filed a criminal charge against them. Indeed, their attorney argued that after *Lawrence*, the government should stay out of a family's private relationships.[65] When U.S. District Court Judge Clark Waddoups made his ruling in December 2013 striking down part of Utah's polygamy law, many lamented that this decision, along with recognition of same-sex marriage, was the end of marriage. But a closer reading of this opinion shows that Judge Waddoups merely said that Brown and the women could continue to cohabitate together. Brown had only married his first wife in a state recognized marriage; the other three were religious marriages, which had no legal effect even though they lived as a family. The Utah law not only outlawed "true polygamy, which is the practice of claiming

---

Another email read, "Some of the orders went out looking pretty sad. For a while we only had celery, peppers, and potatoes. At 3 p.m. we received one bin of oranges. At 5 p.m. the oranges were gone." *Harper's* magazine, "Hungry Souls", December 2016, p. 18.

63 http://www.nytimes.com/2012/06/22/us/utah-polygamous-towns-are-sued.html, "Utah: Polygamous Towns Are Sued," AP for *New York Times*, June 22, 2012.

64 http://www.nbcnews.com/id/9904689/ns/us_news-crime_and_courts/t/utah-high-court-hears-case-polygamous-judge/#.UYaFSkrYySo, "Utah high court hears case of polygamous judge," AP, nbcnews.com, November 2, 2005.

65 http://www.examiner.com/article/sister-wives-polygamy-lawsuit-addressed-federal-court, "Sister Wives Polygamy lawsuit addressed in federal court," by Scott Paulson, *Examiner*, January 18, 2013. See also, "One Big, Happy Polygamous Family," Jonathan Turley (attorney for the Big Love family), op. ed., *New York Times*, July 20,2011, http://www.nytimes.com/2011/07/21/opinion/21turley.html arguing under *Lawrence v. Texas*, the government should stay out of a family's private relationships.

more than one legal spouse at a time. It also prohibited cohabitation by unmarried people with multiple sexual partners."[66] Thus, the court upheld Utah's anti-polygamy laws but recognized that such law could not limit a family's right to cohabitate together. Even so, the state of Utah has filed an appeal of that case.[67]

INTERNATIONAL POLYGAMY

Many cultures and people around the world practice polygamy. What is the effect should they want to immigrate to the United States? In the case of *Fuad Farfan Ali Al Sharabi and Fathiya Abdo Alhaj Maamoon v. Heinauer*, Not Reported in F.Supp.2d, 2011 WL 3955027 (N.D.CA. 2011), the court had to determine the effects of a polygamous marriage recognized in its native country of Yemen, when the husband wanted to immigrate to the United States with his second wife. In this case, the man married his first wife, then later a second, before he came to the United States and requested asylum status. After, he maintained that he wanted to bring his wife over under a Refugee/Asylee Relative Petition. The problem was that the wife he wanted to bring to the U.S. was his second wife. He argued that because he had legally divorced his first wife, he should be able to bring over the second. All parties agreed that his polygamous marriage was valid in Yemen. All also agreed that his divorce of his first wife was also valid in Yemen. The problem was that the divorce occurred after he married his second wife and after he arrived in the United States. As a result, the U.S. District court found that his second marriage was void under U.S. anti-polygamy laws and denied his request. In so doing, the court cited the proposition that even if the marriage is valid where celebrated, it is void as against public policy in the United States because it is a polygamous marriage; therefore, it cannot be recognized as a valid marriage for immigration purposes. (AR 39) The *Al Sharabi* court also wrote, "U.S. law does not allow polygamy. If you were married before, you and your spouse must both show that you ended (terminated) all previous marriages before your current marriage. In cases of legal marriage to two or more spouses at the same time, or marriages overlapping for a period of time, you can file only for your first spouse."[68]

Before leaving the subject of prohibitions on marriage, what would be so unforgivable in a marriage as to not only need to dissolve it (divorce), but obliterate it (annulment)? While a review of any online dating website may lead one to conclude that the mating ritual is fraught with puffery, what could be so despicable that its failure to mention would cause all to agree to void the marriage upon its discovery? What if a spouse finds out that her husband was a Nazi?

---

66   The appeal if accepted will be held in the 10th Circuit U.S. Court of Appeals in Denver "Utah's anti-polygamy law: When a Man loves 4 Women", Editorial, *Los Angeles Times,* December 19, 2013.
67   Utah appeals ruling on anti-polygamy laws in 'Sister Wives" case", Brady McCombs, *The Salt Lake Tribune,* October 16, 2014. http://www.sltrib.com/news/polygamy/1689789-155/utah-ruling-law-families-family-multiple
68   Ibid

A ction by wife for annulment of marriage. From an order of the Appellate Division of the Supreme Court in the First Judicial Department, Charles D. Breitel, J. P., 22 A.D.2d 468, 256 N.Y.S.2d 615, entered February 18, 1965, which (1) reversed, on the law, an order of the Supreme Court at Special Term, Gerald P. Culkin, J., entered in New York County, denying a motion to dismiss the second cause of action contained in the amended complaint, and (2) granted the motion, the plaintiff appealed. The Court of Appeals, Van Voorhis, J., held that a wife's amended complaint alleging husband's alleged concealment from wife prior to marriage that during World War II he had been [an] officer in German army and member of Nazi party, that he was fanatically anti-Semitic and believed in extermination of Jewish people and that he would require her to give up her Jewish friends, and that husband during courtship maintained an apparent absence of fanatic anti-Semitism stated cause of action for annulment of marriage.

Order of Appellate Division reversed and that of Special Term reinstated.
Desmond, C. J., and Burke and Scileppi, JJ., dissented.
**818 VAN VOORHIS, Judge.

This is an annulment suit. The question is one of pleading. The appeal presents solely whether the second cause of action in the wife's amended complaint is sufficient in law. Special Term denied the defendant husband's motion to dismiss for insufficiency, stating: 'Whether the issue herein refers to matters vital to the marriage relationship must be determined at the trial.' The Appellate Division reversed, holding that the fraud alleged in the second cause of action was not vital to the marriage relationship. An earlier complaint had been dismissed at Special Term, with leave to plead over, in an opinion by Loreto, J., the reasoning of which would sustain the sufficiency of this cause of action in the amended complaint which is now before us.

*193 The material portions of this cause of action allege that the parties were married at New York City on June 28, 1963 (this annulment action was begun April 22, 1964) and that at and before the marriage the defendant husband falsely and fraudulently concealed from the plaintiff that he had been an officer in the German Army and a member of the Nazi party during World War II, and 'was fanatically anti-Semitic; that he believed in, advocated, approved and even applauded Hitler's 'Final Solution' of the Jewish question, namely the extermination of the Jewish people; and that he would require plaintiff to 'weed out' all of her Jewish friends and to cease socializing with them.' The next paragraph alleges that plaintiff married defendant believing him to be without ***366 fanatic anti-Semitism and without the belief that the Jewish people should be exterminated, 'all of which he had at the date thereof, and during the marriage and all of which he expressed after and during the marriage so as to make the marital relationship unworkable.' The next paragraph further alleges: 'That plaintiff relied on defendant's apparent normal character, high moral beliefs and absence of fanatic anti-Semitism and would not have married him had she known prior to the aforementioned marriage that the defendant had been a member of the Nazi Party, was fanatically anti-Semitic, believed that all Jews should be exterminated, and that he would require plaintiff to cease socializing with all her Jewish friends, and had the defendant not been guilty of said fraudulent concealment... ' [5] Bearing these principles in mind, we hold that this portion of the amended complaint states a cause of action. In *Shonfeld v. Shonfeld* (260 N.Y. 477, 184 N.E. 60) an annulment was granted under section 1139 of the Civil Practice Act (now Domestic Relations Law, Consol.Laws, c. 14, s 140, subd. (e)), husband against wife, where the former had stated that he was in no position to marry because he was not able to make a living, in response to which the defendant had stated fraudulently that, if it was merely a matter of sufficient money to establish **819 him in a business of his own, she had enough, if such an opportunity presented itself. The opportunity did arise, but she refused to advance the money before marriage, and the trial court had found as facts that the representations thus made were false, were believed and relied upon, and induced the plaintiff's consent to the marriage, and that if they had not ***367 been made he would not have consented. The case reached this court in the posture that a decree of annulment had been refused upon the ground that these representations did not go 'to the essence of the marriage contract.'

The decree was granted in this court upon the ground that, if the true facts had been known to the husband, he would not have entered into the marriage. 'The obligation of a husband to support a wife is no less lightly to be entered into than the other obligations of the marital relation. The ability to support is correspondingly important. *** The business which defendant's mythical money was to establish was plaintiff's only prospect of supporting her. The misrepresentation was not a mere exaggeration or misstatement of her means or prospects, which might or might not be an incentive to marriage. It was a definite statement of an existing fact without which, as defendant clearly understood, no marriage was presently practicable' *(supra, p. 482, 184 N.E. p. 62)*.

The development of the law of annulment was reviewed, the court pointing out (pp. 476–480, 184 N.E. p. 61) that the fraud need no longer 'necessarily concern what is commonly called the essentials of the marriage relation the rights and duties connected with cohabitation and consortium attached by law to the marital *195 status. *(di Lorenzo v. di Lorenzo, supra (174 N.Y. 467, 67 N.E. 63); Beard v. Beard, 238 N.Y. 599, 144 N.E. 908; Domschke v. Domschke, 138 App.Div. 454, 122 N.Y.S. 892).* Any fraud is adequate which is 'material, to that degree that, had it not been practiced, the party deceived would not have consented to the marriage' *(di Lorenzo v. di Lorenzo, supra, p. 471 of*

174 N.Y., 67 N.E. 63, 64), and is 'of such a nature as to deceive an ordinarily prudent person.' *(Id., page 474 of 174 N.Y., 67 N.E. 63, 65.)' (See Woronzoff-Daschkoff v. Woronzoff-Daschkoff, 303 N.Y. 506, 511, 104 N.E.2d 877, 880).* Although it is not enough to show merely that one partner married for money and was disappointed *(Woronzoff-Daschkoff v. Woronzoff-Daschkoff, supra, 303 N.Y. p. 512, 104 N.E.2d p. 880),* and the decisions upon the subject of annulment of marriage have not always been uniform, there have been circumstances where misrepresentation of love and affection, with intention to make a home, were held sufficient *(Schinker v. Schinker, 271 App.Div. 688, 68 N.Y.S.2d 470),* likewise in case of fraudulent misrepresentations concerning the legitimacy of children of the wife by a supposedly prior marriage *(Domschke v. Domschke, 138 App.Div. 454, 122 N.Y.S. 892),* or concerning prior marital status *(Smith v. Smith, 273 App.Div. 987, 77 N.Y.S.2d 902).* Concealment of prior marital status was held to be sufficient in Costello v. Costello *(155 Misc. 28, 279 N.Y.S. 303),* concealment of affliction with tuberculosis in Yelin v. Yelin *(142 Misc. 533, 255 N.Y.S. 708)* and *Sobol v. Sobol (88 Misc. 277, 150 N.Y.S. 248);* failure to ***368 reveal treatment of a mental disorder (schizophrenia, catatonic type) was held to be enough in *Schaeffer v. Schaeffer (20 Misc.2d 662, 192 N.Y.S.2d 275);* material misrepresentation of age in Tacchi v. Tacchi *(47 Misc.2d 996, 195 N.Y.S.2d 892);* fraudulent promise to become a United States citizen in Siecht v. Siecht, Sup. *(41 N.Y.S.2d 393),* where after years of married life the husband learned that his wife was a member of the Deutsche Bund and that her failure to become a citizen had been deliberate because of disloyalty to the United States. In *Laage v. Laage (176 Misc. 190, 26 N.Y.S.2d 874),* an annulment was granted to a wife by reason of the husband's false representation that he was a naturalized American citizen, after she had stated to him that she would not marry a German-born alien. In **820 *Brillis v. Brillis (207 Misc. 104, 137 N.Y.S.2d 32, affd. 3 A.D.2d 662, 158 N.Y.S.2d 780),* a marriage was annulled where the evidence established that the defendant did not intend, at the time when he induced plaintiff's consent to the marriage, to establish a home for his wife and to support her, and that his purpose in entering into the marriage, unknown to plaintiff, was to facilitate his re-entry *196 into the United States from Greece as a non-quota immigrant. In *Harris v. Harris (201 App.Div. 880, 193 N.Y.S. 936),* an annulment was granted on account of the concealment by the husband of previous criminal activities. A recent annulment suit in this court was *Sophian v. Von Linde (22 A.D.2d 34, 253 N.Y.S.2d 496, affd. 16 N.Y.2d 785, 262 N.Y.S.2d 505, 209 N.E.2d 823 (July 9, 1965)).* Although a third cause of action was sustained that the defendant misrepresented his intentions to have normal sexual relations with his wife, the first cause of action was also sustained (see opinion at *Appellate Division, p. 35, 253 N.Y.S.2d p. 497)* based on misrepresentation by the defendant of his age, origin and ancestry. We affirmed, notwithstanding the dissent of two Justices at the Appellate Division based on *Lapides v. Lapides (254 N.Y. 73, 80, 171 N.E. 911)* and other decisions holding or purporting to hold that misrepresentations of the nature alleged in the Sophian first cause of action were not vital to the marriage relationship.

[6] Marriage is a civil contract (Domestic Relations Law, s 10) and, as stated in *Shonfeld v. Shonfeld* (*supra, 260 N.Y. p. 479, 184 N.E. p. 61):* 'The essentials of marriage as a civil contract are, therefore, (a) consent by (b) parties having statutory capacity to give it. Any lack in those essentials makes the marriage void (*Domestic Relations Law*, ss 5 and 6) or voidable (Id. s 7). If either party consents by reason of fraud there is no reality of consent. Hence the marriage is voidable (Id. s 7, subd. 4) and an action may be maintained to annul it.'

Under these principles, if the facts stated in the second cause of action of this amended complaint are true (as we are bound to assume for the purposes of this appeal), the trier of the fact might well conclude that ***369 there was no reality to the consent of plaintiff to this marriage. Allowing the pleading the broad construction to which it is entitled under the law, defendant had not merely been a member of the Nazi party and an officer in the German Army during World War II, which in themselves would be insufficient to sustain an annulment, but also, as an individual, he was fanatically anti-Semitic and supported the extermination of the Jewish people. In spite of the fact that he believed in, advocated and approved such genocide, he nevertheless, during courtship, according to the complaint, maintained an 'apparent *** absence of fanatic anti-Semitism' from which it would appear that, if true, he put on a false front *197 to obtain plaintiff's hand in that he dissembled his genocidal beliefs by seemingly associating agreeably with Jews.

Plaintiff alleges that she relied on this, and would not have married him had she known his true nature, in these respects, which he manifested 'after and during the marriage so as to make the marital relationship unworkable.'

These allegations go beyond merely requiring 'a wife, in order to preserve marital harmony, to give up friendships which she had made in the past', or asking the courts to 'lay down a viable line of separation between political and philosophical views too extreme to be concealed during the courting relationship from those not so extreme which may be concealed intentionally or inadvertently without impairing the agreement to marry' as said by the Appellate Division majority (22 *A.D.2d, p. 471, 256 N.Y.S.2d p. 618*). A fanatical conviction, to be effectuated where possible through the mobilization of superior force, that a race or group of people living in the same community should be put to death as at Auschwitz, Belsen, Dachau or Buchenwald, evinces a diseased mind and makeup which parallels the ground for annulment stated **821 in subdivision (c) of section 140 of the Domestic Relations Law, where a party to the marriage is an idiot or lunatic.

The continuation of defendant's addiction to this anti-social and fanatical objective after and during marriage, which had been concealed and inferentially misrepresented during courtship, would so plainly make the marital relationship unworkable in this jurisdiction, where the marriage was contracted, that it would depart from the realities to conclude that it was not essential to this married relationship, or that, to defendant's knowledge, plaintiff would have consented to the marriage without its concealment. At least the trier of the fact could so find if evidence is adduced to sustain the allegations of the second cause of action in this pleading. As was said in the dissenting opinion at the Appellate Division, quoting from Justice Loreto at Special Term, "These are more than distasteful beliefs; they are absolutely repugnant and insufferable ***. A fraud with respect to such beliefs, inducing marriage, is one ***370 affecting a vital aspect of the marital relationship. At least, it may be so determined upon a trial. It might well be found to be 'material to that degree that, had it not been practiced, the party deceived would not have consented to the marriage' and *198 is of such a nature as to deceive an 'ordinarily prudent person' *(di Lorenzo v. di Lorenzo, 174 N.Y. 467, 471, 473 (67 N.E. 63, 64, 65, 63 L.R.A. 92); Shonfeld v. Shonfeld, 260 N.Y. 477 (184 N.E. 60))*."

We are not called upon at this stage of the litigation to determine whether plaintiff will succeed in establishing these allegations at the trial. She should not be denied her day in court, however, on the basis that it could not be found at the trial that the facts alleged, if established by evidence, would go to the essence of her consent to marry him.

The order appealed from should be reversed and that of Special Term reinstated, without costs.

DESMOND, C. J., and BURKE and SCILEPPI, JJ., dissent and vote to affirm upon the majority opinion at the Appellate Division.

Order reversed, etc.

Is the discovery that her husband concealed his former life during World War II as an officer in the German army and a member of the Nazi party, and that he was fanatically anti-Semitic and he believed in the extermination of the Jewish people and he required her to give up her Jewish friends (while failing to mention any of this during the courtship), enough to have the marriage annulled?[69]

Twenty-six year-old Afton Elaine Burton, who goes by the name Star, wanted to marry eighty-year old Charles Manson, notorious mass-murder who is serving life in prison for seven murders, including the murder of Sharon Tate. They applied for a marriage license and the prison assigned a wedding coordinator to handle the paperwork for a marriage which 10 non-inmate guests may attend, plus an outside officiant. Manson is not "entitled to family visits, a euphemism for conjugal visits."[70] California Department of Corrections spokeswoman Terry Thornton said

---

69 There was a dissenting opinion. Interestingly, in their biography of Salinger in 2016, authors Shane Salerno and David Shields Salerno allege that Salinger had his first marriage annulled because his wife "was allegedly a Gestapo informant" Some challenge the evidence of the claim. http://www.thedailybeast.com/articles/2013/09/02/15-revelations-from-new-j-d-salinger-biography.html

70 "Charles Manson plans prison wedding", Linda Deutsch *AP.*, http://news.yahoo.com/ap-exclusive-charles-manson-gets-marriage-license-215524033.html The couple did not marry and their marriage license expired in 2015. Rumor was that the fiancée wanted to display Manson's body Lenin-like in a glass tomb after his death. http://nypost.com/2015/02/08/charles-mansons-fiancee-wanted-to-marry-him-for-his-corpse-source/

"In most cases… the Department of Corrections approves of such weddings as 'a tool of family reunification and social development.' But Manson is a unique case… including three violations for possession of a weapon, threatening staff and refusal to provide a urine sample."[71] Can the state prohibit this marriage?

---

71 Ibid.

10

HOW DOES MARRIAGE AFFECT WOMEN?

When Mr. Bumble tries to pass the guilt of the stolen locket and ring off on his wife, Mr. Brownlow informs him that in the eyes of the law Bumble was the more guilty of the two because the law assumes that his wife operated under his direction.[1]

"If the law supposes that," said Mr. Bumble, squeezing his hat emphatically in both hands, "the law is a ass—a idiot. If that's the eye of the law, the law is a bachelor; and the worst I wish the law is, that his eye may be opened by experience—by experience."
—Charles Dickens, *Oliver Twist*, Ch. 51, 1838.

1 + 1 = 1

In the song "Bargain," when *The Who* famously wrote, "In life one and one don't make two," they were probably thinking of man's suffering at the loss of his woman, but they might as well have been summarizing the law's view on marriage for women. Under common law, when a woman married a man they became one; the one being the husband. Under the common law doctrine of coverture, meaning to cover (as to be distinguished from an uncovered single woman), the wife merged into the husband's being;[2] as a result, the woman became the husband's property or chattel. Chattel, from the word cattle, can mean movable property (personal property, not real estate).[3] In Europe and the Middle East, the groom paid the bride's parents for his bride (a negotiated amount of money or property) and so she was his possession, no different

---

1 http://charlesdickenspage.com/twist.html
2 http://wiki.answers.com/Q/What_is_the_historical_meaning_of_chattel_and_chattel_law
3 E.g., in the Old Testament of the Bible, the Ten Commandments listed in Exodus 20:17, the tenth Commandment forbids coveting any of the man's "property," including his wife.

from cattle.[4] Thus, under common law, the act of marriage amounted to a legal disability for women when their legal identity disappeared and merged into their husband's.[5]

Under common law, an unmarried woman had most of the rights of a man, excluding the right to vote. As *The Who* wrote, she suddenly became legally disabled with unrecognized legal status when she married. Under this **fiction of oneness**, or marital unity, an unmarried woman's legal identity merged with her husband's identity at the time they married. This equation of "1+1=1" yielded one legally recognized person and that one was the husband. It prevented wives from keeping their names, any earnings acquired in employment, owning or managing their own property, choosing their place of residence, contracting, working outside of the home, bringing a lawsuit, or getting an education.

Beyond church doctrine, perhaps this disenfranchisement was the result of traditional commerce and business. With the advent of industrialization at the turn of the last century, men went into the workforce and women stayed home to raise children. But as women increasingly joined the workforce, the law was slow to modernize in recognition of this change in status. Courts today still struggle to recognize the modern relationship between husband and wife. In contemporary society, as in centuries past, the perception of women influences their treatment by the justice system. Sheryl J. Grana wrote in *Women and Justice*, 2010, "[a]s law and justice do not operate in a vacuum; the people, conditions and ideas of an era influence the rights, roles and responsibilities of women."

WOMEN'S LAST NAMES/MAIDEN NAMES

A. Name Change at Marriage

Probably nowhere else is the evidence of marital unity's continuation into today's society more symbolic than the tradition of a woman adopting her husband's last name at marriage. By giving up her maiden name or surname[6]—and therefore her own identity—she is known only as his wife.

In the case of *Stuart v. Board of Supervisors*, 266 MD 440 (1972) in Howard County, Maryland, a man and woman married in a ceremonial marriage after signing a prenuptial agreement which included, among other things, their agreement that the wife would retain her birth name. When the woman attempted to register to vote with the county board of elections, she was denied the right to do so unless she used her husband's last name. The local board of elections' supervisors told her that Maryland law required her to use her husband's name now that she was married. They also informed her that refusal would cause her voter registration to be canceled. When the woman sued against this

---

4   History is replete with financial marriages, including arranged royal marriages.

5   Even the expression "man and wife," and not "husband and wife," is part of many traditional religious wedding ceremonies.

6   Even the historic term for the woman's birth name, the maiden name—further emphasizes the difference in status between the married woman and the unmarried one at common law. England recently passed a law outlawing the use of the word "maiden" on legal forms requiring information on names.

disenfranchisement, she argued that Maryland law did not require it, and that it was her decision as reflected in a modern society. The appellate court agreed with her and said as long as the woman was not using her name fraudulently to avoid creditors, she was entitled to vote in the state using her birth name. This case illustrates that the fiction of oneness continued under modern law as late as the mid-1970s. Even the registrar of voters confused common law custom with the legal requirements, thus reflecting the legal merging of the woman into the husband via his name, while she loses the identity of her own name. While a majority of women continue to take their husband's surname at marriage, a woman may choose to retain her name.[7] In addition, many women hyphenate their names so that their birth name merges with their husband's. Some couples use the marriage occasion to create a new name out of whole cloth that symbolizes their new life together.[8] For instance, former Los Angeles Mayor Antonio Villaraigosa (born Antonio Villar) and his now ex-wife, Corina Raigosa, combined their names when they were married in 1987. What should happen when they divorced? With the increasing availability of same-sex marriages, where will this tradition lead?

B. Name Changes during Marriage

Anyone can change their name by common law (adopting a new name and using it consistently, but not to defraud creditors) or pursuant to statute which is more reliable and efficient. Even after taking her husband's last name at marriage, a woman can still return to her maiden name during the marriage.

C. Name Changes at Divorce

Can a husband require his ex-wife to not use his surname after divorce? Should she require his permission to do so? Historically, some cases refused to allow a wife to return to her maiden name without her husband's consent. Many couples now use milestones as the reason for a name change, including divorce.

D. Husband's Name Change

It still remains more difficult for a husband to take his wife's last name. "Before Michael Buday married his fiancée, Diana Bijon, he decided to honor her family by bucking tradition and taking her last name." "Under California state law, he needed to pay more than $300, go to court, file a petition, and publicly advertise his name change for four weeks in a local newspaper. If he had simply gone with tradition, it would have cost only $50 to $80."[9] California is one of 44 states with unequal name change laws for people getting married. Only six states: Georgia, Hawaii, Iowa, Massachusetts, New York, and North Dakota, explicitly allow a man to change his name through marriage with the same ease as a woman. "California has the perfect marriage

---

7   In many states, when a couple applies for a marriage license the state may include a reminder of the statutory requirements for a name change.

8   "Mr. and Mrs. Bothofus," Roxanne Hawn, *New York Times*, March 4, 2005.

9   http://abcnews.go.com/US/LegalCenter/story?id=2778930&page=1#.UYakd0rYySo, "Man Fights to Take Wife's Name in Marriage," Michelle Rittner, ABC News, January 8, 2007.

application for the 17th century," said Mark Rosenbaum, legal director of the ACLU of Southern California. "The laws reflect a mind-set that the wife is to be subordinate to the husband."[10]

SUPPORT AND NECESSITIES

Under common law, a woman gave her husband everything she had. In exchange for a wife giving her husband all of her property, wages, and legal identity at marriage, the husband agreed to support her for life. Support was generally restricted to the necessities of life, such as food, shelter, clothing, transportation, housing and furniture, and medical treatment. Under the common law rule, if a husband failed to provide his wife with the proper necessities, a third party (e.g., storeowner) who gave the wife those necessities could sue the husband for their value. In addition to paying her marital debts, the husband would also be responsible for any of her premarital debts. Under equal protection, the obligation to support is usually attributed to both spouses. Today, necessities may include a lawyer or even a cell phone.

Would a modern court hold a husband liable for his wife's purchase of furniture for the house under the common law doctrine created in the 1800s? In *Sharpe Furniture Inc. v. Buckstaff* 299 M.W. 2d 219 (Wis. 1980), the court looked at this question when the wife bought a new sofa for the marital home, but failed to make the payments.

SHARPE FURNITURE, INC., A WISCONSIN CORPORATION, PLAINTIFF-RESPONDENT
V.
JOHN D. BUCKSTAFF, JR., AND KAREN BUCKSTAFF, HIS WIFE, DEFENDANTS-APPELLANTS-PETITIONERS.
99 WIS.2D 114 (1980)
299 N.W.2D 219

BEILFUSS, C. J.

This is a review of a decision of the court of appeals which affirmed the judgment of the circuit court for Winnebago county. The judgment was entered against the defendants John D. Buckstaff, Jr., and his wife, Karen Buckstaff, requiring payment of sums due on the purchase of goods from the plaintiff, Sharpe Furniture, Inc., a Wisconsin corporation engaged in the business of retail furniture sales.

---

10   Ibid.

This controversy centers around the purchase of a sofa from Sharpe Furniture, Inc. (Sharpe). The purchase was made by Karen Buckstaff on August 15, 1973. On that date, Mrs. Buckstaff signed in her own name a special order for a "Henredon 6800 Sofa." Under the *116 terms of the order she was to pay $621.50 within 60 days after the item was received from the factory. Interest at a rate of 1.5 percent per month was charged on the unpaid balance after that 60-day period. No representations were made to Sharpe at the time of the purchase that Mrs. Buckstaff was acting on behalf of her husband in purchasing the furniture. Indeed, John Buckstaff had previously written to the local credit bureau service to advise that office that he would not be responsible for any credit extended to his wife.

The Henredon sofa was received from the factory and delivered to the residence of the defendants on February 8, 1974. This piece of furniture has been a part of the Buckstaff home ever since its delivery. Despite this fact, neither John Buckstaff nor his wife have tendered payment for the sofa.

On November 20, 1975, Sharpe commenced this action against both Buckstaffs. The parties agreed to allow the trial court to decide the dispute on the basis of the undisputed facts as they appeared in the trial memorandum submitted by counsel. In addition to the facts already stated above, the informal stipulation of the parties reveals that John Buckstaff, Jr., is the president of Buckstaff Company of Oshkosh, Wisconsin. Mrs. Buckstaff is a housewife. Mr. Buckstaff earns a substantial income and the Buckstaff family is one of social and economic prominence in the Oshkosh area. It was further set forth that Mr. Buckstaff has always provided his wife with the necessaries of life and has never failed or refused to provide his wife with items which could be considered necessaries.

On the basis of these facts, the trial court found that Karen Buckstaff was liable on her contract and that John Buckstaff was also liable for the amount due on the sofa under the common law doctrine of necessaries. Judgment was entered accordingly. The court of appeals *117 affirmed. John Buckstaff now seeks review of the decision of the court of appeals. Karen Buckstaff has not sought appellate relief from the entry of the judgment against her.

There are two issues which we must consider in reviewing the decision of the court of appeals:

1. Whether, under the common law doctrine of necessaries and in the absence of any contractual obligation on his part, a husband may be held liable for sums due as payment for necessary items purchased on credit by his wife.
2. Whether, in an action for recovery of the value of necessaries supplied on credit to a wife, it is essential for the plaintiff-creditor to prove either that the husband has failed, refused or neglected to provide the items which have been supplied by the plaintiff-creditor or that the items supplied were reasonably needed by the wife or the family.

Before proceeding to a discussion of the merits of this case, we examine the substance of the doctrine of necessaries.

The Wisconsin Supreme Court restated the common law rule of necessaries early on in the history of the jurisprudence of this state. In 1871, in the case of *Warner and Ryan v. Heiden*, 28 Wis. 517, 519 (1871), the court wrote:

"The husband is under legal obligations to support his wife, and nothing but wrongful conduct on her part can free him from such obligation. If he fails to provide her with suitable and proper necessaries, any third person who does provide her therewith, may maintain an action against him for the same. 1 Bishop on Mar. and Div., sec. 553. The same learned author, in the next section (sec. 554), thus defines what are necessaries which the husband is bound to furnish to his wife: `And, in general, we may say, that necessaries are such articles of food, or apparel, or medicine, or such medical attendance and *118 nursing, or such provided means of locomotion, or provided habitation and furniture, *or such provision for her protection in society,* and the like, as the husband, considering his ability and standing, ought to furnish to his wife for her sustenance, and the preservation of her health and comfort.'"[1]

This doctrine traditionally required the creditor to show that he supplied to the wife an item that was, in fact, a necessary and that the defendant had previously failed or refused to provide his wife with this item. *See, e.g., Eder v. Grifka,* 149 Wis. 606, 610, 136 N.W. 154 (1912). *See also* Brown, *The Duty of the Husband to Support the Wife,* 18 Va. L. Rev. 823, 824-35 (1932). When such a showing was made, the creditor was entitled to recovery as against the husband despite the fact that the husband had not contractually bound himself by his own act or by the act of an agent. The doctrine of necessaries is not imposed by the law of agency.[2] This duty is placed upon a husband by virtue of the legal relationship of marriage.[3] It arises as an obligation placed on him as a matter of public policy.

The appellant challenges the continued vitality of this common law rule. Mr. Buckstaff charges that the necessaries doctrine conflicts with contemporary trends toward equality of the sexes and a sex neutral society.

He further argues that the doctrine is an outdated and inefficient means of compelling support. It is argued that various social welfare agencies and governmental institutions have replaced the doctrine of necessaries as a mechanism for the maintenance of the members of a household.

It is true that the necessaries rule has been justified in the past on the basis of a social view of the married *119 woman as a person without legal capacity.[4] However, the nature of the woman's obligations under the necessary rule in relation to the obligation of her husband is not at issue here. That question has been treated in our decision in *Estate of Stromsted,* 99 Wis.2d 136, 299 N.W. 2d 226 (1980), wherein we concluded the husband was primarily liable for necessities and the wife secondarily liable. The question presented in this case involves a consideration of the nature of the husband's obligation. We must decide whether such a liability imposed upon the husband furthers a proper purpose in contemporary society.

We are of the opinion that the doctrine of necessaries serves a legitimate and proper purpose in our system of common law. The heart of this common law rule is a concern for the support and the sustenance of the family and the individual members thereof. The sustenance of the family unit is accorded a high order of importance in the scheme of Wisconsin law. It has been codified as a part of our statutes, *see e.g.*, sec. 767.08, Stats., and it has been recognized as a part of our case law. *See Zachman v. Zachman*, 9 Wis.2d 335, 338, 101 N.W.2d 55 (1960). The necessaries rule encourages the extension of credit to those who in an individual capacity may not have the ability to make these basic purchases. In this manner it facilitates the support of the family unit and its function is in harmony with the purposes behind the support laws of this state. The rule retains a viable role in modern society.

We view the nature of the husband's liability as a contractual duty implied in law, *i.e.*, a quasi-contractual obligation.... the elements of such action were listed as:

"`... (1) a benefit conferred upon the defendant by the plaintiff, (2) appreciation by the defendant of the fact of such benefit, and (3) acceptance and retention by the defendant of the benefit, under circumstances such that it would be inequitable to retain the benefit without payment of the value thereof.'"

We conclude that when an item or service is obtained for the benefit of the family which is necessary and no payment for that item or service has been made, the elements of an action for an implied-in-law contract exist and the husband is primarily liable.

In light of the proper function of the necessaries rule in relation to the support of the family, in the absence of an express contract to the contrary, we hold that a husband incurs the primary obligation, implied as a matter of law, to assume liability for the necessaries which have been procured for the sustenance of his family.

Mr. Buckstaff's second argument is that, as a matter of law, he is not liable for the necessaries purchased by his wife because Sharpe did not plead or prove that he as a husband failed, refused or neglected to provide a sofa for his wife. It is also argued that liability cannot be found in the face of the parties' stipulation which states that Mr. Buckstaff has always provided his wife with the necessaries of life and has never failed or refused to provide her with items which would constitute necessaries.

There are three leading cases in Wisconsin concerning the nature of a creditor's action under the law of necessaries. *121 The most recent of these cases was decided in 1924.

The law of necessaries was first recognized in the case of *Warner and Ryan v. Heiden*, 28 Wis. 517 (1871).[5] In that case the court ruled that a husband could be held liable for attorney's fees incurred by his wife in the course of defending against a criminal charge. *Id.* at 521. Such legal fees were viewed as necessaries for which the husband was responsible.

In the case of *Eder v. Grifka*, 149 Wis. 606, 136 N.W. 154 (1912), it was held that, besides demonstrating that necessaries were furnished by the creditor to the defendant's spouse, a plaintiff-creditor must also plead and prove that the defendant willfully refused to provide the necessaries for his wife. The court wrote:

"A husband is not *ipso facto* liable for all necessaries that may be furnished his wife. It is only under circumstances and conditions showing a necessity that they be furnished her by others, such as his misconduct compelling her to leave him and their home, *his willful refusal to provide for her*, or his deserting her, that the husband is liable for them." *Id.* at 610. (Emphasis added.)

In the absence of these special circumstances, the rule of *Eder* allowed no recovery for the creditor. The merchant sold to the wife at his own risk.

The merchant's burden of proof was modified by the decision in *Simpson Garment Co. v. Schultz,* 182 Wis. 506, 196 N.W. 783 (1924). The *Simpson Garment Company* decision involved a defendant whose wife purchased a coat, a dress and a slip for her daughter. The daughter was about to graduate from high school and lacked the proper attire for the commencement exercises. The wife pledged the defendant's credit in order to purchase the *122 items and when her husband refused to pay, a lawsuit was commenced. The defendant was found liable for the cost of the garments. In discussing the plaintiff's *prima facie* burden, the court said:

"When a merchant sues a husband for necessaries sold to his wife or some member of his family, it is incumbent upon him to show, among other things, (1) that the articles purchased were such as are suitable for the wife or member of the family in view of the family's social position in the community in which they live and in view of the defendant's financial ability to pay for them; and (2) that the articles sold were reasonably needed by the wife or member of the family to whom they were sold at the time of the sale." *Id.* at 509–10.

The *Simpson Garment Company* rule required only that the creditor show that the item was "reasonably needed" by the wife or family, and not that the husband willfully refused to provide his wife with the necessary item as suggested by *Eder v. Grifka, supra.*

In applying the rule of the *Simpson Garment Company* decision to the case at bar, the creditor Sharpe must prevail over Mr. Buckstaff's two-pronged attack on the judgment. The latter's arguments are directed at the second element of the necessaries doctrine, *i.e.,* reasonable need of the family. Buckstaff's first argument, that the court's judgment of liability is invalid in the absence of a finding of refusal or neglect by a husband, must be rejected. Under *Simpson Garment Company,* the refusal or neglect of the husband is not an element essential to recovery by the creditor. Mr. Buckstaff's second contention is that the sofa should not be considered a necessary in view of the stipulation that he as a husband provided his wife with all necessaries. Whether or not, as a general matter, a man provides his wife with necessaries is irrelevant to a determination of whether a particular item is reasonably needed under the *Simpson Garment Company* rule. 182 Wis. at 510. This stipulation, which *123 is phrased in terms of the conclusion which it seeks to establish, is not probative of whether the sofa in issue was reasonably needed.

We have reviewed the stipulation of the parties in this matter and we are satisfied that ample evidence supported the trial court's conclusion that the Henredon sofa was a legally necessary item. The Buckstaffs are a prominent family and their socio-economic standing justifies a finding that the sofa at issue here was a suitable and proper item for their household. With reference to the element of reasonable need, we note that the sofa has been in use in the Buckstaff home since its delivery. Such continued use gives rise to an inference of reasonable need. This inference is not rebutted by the stipulation stating that Mr. Buckstaff provided his wife with "all necessaries."

Several spousal agency theories have been advanced as a ground for liability by both the respondent and by the Wisconsin Merchants Federation as *amicus curiae.* Having found that Mr. Buckstaff is liable on the independent ground provided by the necessaries rule, we need not reach these questions.

By the Court. — The decision of the court of appeals is affirmed.

SHIRLEY S. ABRAHAMSON, J. (*concurring*).

I join the court in retaining the doctrine of necessaries and imposing liability on Mr. Buckstaff for the cost of the sofa. I do not agree, however, with that portion of the opinion in which the court adopts a rule placing primary liability on the husband to the creditor for necessaries supplied to the family.

*124 This case presents neither a novel fact situation nor a novel question of law. I believe that resolution of this case requires the court to do no more than apply the common law doctrine of necessaries to the facts. Mrs. Buckstaff is a full-time homemaker; her contribution to the support of the family is her domestic labor. Apparently she has no earnings or property in her own name. Mr. Buckstaff is employed outside the home. He has income and property in his own name. Mrs. Buckstaff ordered the sofa for the family home, but she did not personally promise to pay for the sofa. On these facts the law in Wisconsin imposes the duty to support on the husband. The common law doctrine of necessaries which arises from and is ancillary to the duty to support allows a merchant to collect the cost of the necessary goods from the husband after extending credit to the wife. As the *125 majority points out, the elements of the common law doctrine of necessaries have been proved in this case. Imposing liability for the sofa on Mr. Buckstaff comports not only with the common law doctrine of necessaries but also with the Wisconsin law of support which follows the contemporary trend toward equality of the sexes.

I recognize, as does the majority, that if the common law doctrine of necessaries is to survive as a rule of law it must be modified in accordance with the developing laws recognizing equal rights and responsibilities of both marital partners and the changes in the economic and social conditions of society. The common law doctrine of necessaries was premised on the legal disability of the married woman and on the husband's duty to support. Today, the married woman is free to contract, sec. 766.15, Stats., *Baum v. Bahn Frei Mut. B. & L. Assoc.*, 237 Wis. 117, 295 N.W. 14 (1941), and the duty of support rests not on the husband alone but on both the husband and wife. Sec. 767.08, Stats. While these changes in the law will require an alteration of the doctrine of necessaries, I would leave that alteration to a case in which the application of the common law doctrine conflicts with the married women statutes and the support statutes. This is not the case.

I believe the court has erred in adopting a flat, general rule which places primary liability on the husband to the creditor who supplies necessaries to the family. In my opinion, the rule suffers from two infirmities: First, the rule is not in harmony with the legislatively established public policy of this state which is to impose the obligation to support on both the husband and wife on the basis of their respective economic resources and not on one spouse or the other on the basis of gender. *See* secs. 767.08(1), 767.25, 767.26, Stats.; sec. 52.055, Stats., amended by sec. 8, ch. 352, Laws of 1979. Second, *126 the rule discriminates against men and thus contravenes the state and federal constitutional guarantees of equal protection of law. These constitutional provisions apply to the decisions of the courts, just as they do to the acts of the state legislature. *Shelley v. Kraemer,* 334 U.S. 1, 17 (1948); *New York Times Co. v. Sullivan,* 376 U.S. 254, 265 (1964).

I am persuaded that the majority rule which effects an unequal distribution of economic benefits and burdens on the basis of gender cannot pass muster under the federal and Wisconsin constitutions. (citations omitted) The New Jersey Supreme Court similarly concluded that a rule imposing liability for necessaries solely on *127 the husband was unconstitutional under the federal and state constitutions, reasoning as follows:

"Under the [common law] rule, even a husband who is economically dependent on his wife would be liable for the necessary expenses of both spouses, while the wife would not be liable for either. In perpetuating additional benefits for a wife when the benefits may not be needed, the rule runs afoul of the equal protection clause. *Orr, supra,* 440 U.S. at 282-283, 99 S. Ct. at 1113, 59 L. Ed2d at 321.

"We recognize that in many instances the present rule correctly operates to favor a needy wife. Even wives who have entered the work force generally earn substantially less than their husbands.... However, that is an insufficient reason to retain a gender based classification that denigrates the efforts of women who contribute to the finances of their families and denies equal protection to husbands. *Weinberger v. Weisenfeld, supra,* 420 U.S. at 645, 95 S. Ct. at 1232, 43 L. Ed.2d at 523.

"Although the New Jersey Constitution does not contain an equal protection clause, the same result follows as under the United States Constitution. The relevant section of the New Jersey Constitution provides 'All persons are by nature free and independent, and have certain natural and unalienable rights, among which are those of enjoying and defending life and liberty, of acquiring, possessing, and protecting property, and of pursuing and obtaining safety and happiness.' Art. 1, sec. 1, par. 1. In interpreting that section, this Court stated that it provides comparable or superior protection against unequal protection of the law. *Peper v. Princeton University Board of Trustees,* 77 N.J. 55, 79 (1978) (discrimination on the basis of gender in private employment may deny equal protection of the laws under Art. 1, sec. 1, par. 1 of the New Jersey Constitution). For reasons previously set forth, we conclude that the rule concerning necessaries with its inherent discrimination against husbands constitutes a denial of equal protection of the laws under the New Jersey Constitution." *Jersey Shore Medical Center-Fitkin Hospital v. Estate of Sidney Baum,* 84 N.J. 137, 417 A.2d 1003, 1008-1009 (1980).

*128 I believe the reasoning of the New Jersey Supreme Court is applicable to the rule adopted by the majority.

For the reasons I have set forth, I concur in the disposition of the case but not in the rule adopted by the court imposing primary liability for necessaries on the husband.[4]

Was the husband right when he argued "that the necessaries doctrine conflicts with contemporary trends toward equality of the sexes and a sex neutral society" and is based on outdated "social view of women"?

PROPERTY OWNERSHIP

One of the most severe legal disabilities for married women at common law was the requirement that she give her husband her interest (ownership or rents) in real property. Even if she owned real estate before she married, it became her husband's at marriage. Mississippi passed one of the first acts to protect the rights and property of married women on February 15, 1839.[11]

The same was true for personal property. The 1848 New York Married Women's Property Act provided a model to other states with its comprehensive expansion of the rights of married women to keep their personal property and real estate at marriage, along with gifts of property received during marriage.

AN ACT for the effectual protection of the property of married women, Passed April 7, 1848.

The People of the State of New York, represented in Senate and Assembly do enact as follows:

Sec. 1. The real and personal property of any female who may hereafter marry, and which she shall own at the time of marriage, and the rents issues and profits thereof shall not be subject to the disposal of her husband, nor be liable for his debts, and shall continue her sole and separate property, as if she were a single female.

Sec. 2 The real and personal property, and the rents issues and profits thereof of any female now married shall not be subject to the disposal of her husband; but shall be her sole and separate property as if she were a single female except so far as the same may be liable for the debts of her husband heretofore contracted.

Sec. 3. It shall be lawful for any married female to receive, by gift, grant devise or bequest, from any person other than her husband and hold to her sole and separate use, as if she were a single female, real and personal property, and the rents, issues and profits thereof, and the same shall not be subject to the disposal of her husband, nor be liable for his debts.

---

11   The Gilder Lehrman Institute of American History, http://www.gilderlehrman.org/history-by-era/first-age-reform/timeline-terms/first-married-women%E2%80%99s-property-act

Sec. 4. All contracts made between persons in contemplation of marriage shall remain in full force after such marriage takes place.[12]

Although the property rights acts helped to remove the strong bite of marital disability in commerce, its vestiges lingered under the law for many years.

HOME, SWEET HOME

The fiction of oneness not only prevented a woman's right to own real property, it denied her the right to pick the place to call home. At common law, a woman's lack of legal capacity meant that she could not pick or change her domicile. Domicile is a legal term dealing with jurisdiction based on a person's relationship to the state. The place of domicile impacts many family law cases including custody, divorce, and adoption. As one, at common law, the husband's domicile was the wife's domicile. Not until the 1970s, when dealing with cases of wives living separately from their husbands, did the courts begin to acknowledge a wife's legal capacity to establish her own domicile separate from that of her husband.

CAREERS/EMPLOYMENT

There was a common law rule that a husband was entitled to his wife's earnings. Only when the Married Women's Property Acts were passed did the wages and earnings of a married woman acquired in any employment "which she carries on separately from her husband," become her sole and separate property again.

Under marital unity, the husband decided for his wife if she could get an education. It was not until 1869 that a woman was allowed to practice law (before, the courts thought women were not designed for its confrontational nature).[13] Because many professions were not available to women, this reinforced the commercial concept of men working outside the home and women staying at home to raise children (thus continuing their financial dependence). Arguably, anti-nepotism policies that prevented one spouse from employing the other, or any relative, negatively impacted a married woman's employment possibilities. As the husband was usually the first employed, the wife could not be hired. In the twenty-first century, women make up a large percentage of the workforce, but still receive less pay than men in every country in the world. In the U.S., to put it in perspective, "pay equity day," April 14 is how far past December 31 of the prior year that women must work to earn as much as a man did in the previous calendar year. This should hardly be a

---

12   Library of Congress. http://memory.loc.gov/ammem/awhhtml/awlaw3/property_law.html, citing to 1848 *New York Laws* 307, Ch. 200.
13   Contrast this to Saudi Arabia where women were granted the right to obtain licenses to practice law in 2011.

surprise, when in 2014, the Montana legislature demeans women when making a dress code for its members that instructed female lawmakers to "be sensitive to skirt lengths and necklines."[14]

WOMEN AND CRIME

Most horrifyingly, the fiction of oneness gave license to a husband's criminal acts against his wife. If a woman is legally subsumed to her husband at marriage, can a husband commit a crime against himself? The courts wrestled with this issue for many years while finding marital exceptions to criminal law. In the field of domestic violence, courts have decided issues ranging from spousal testimony at trial to rape and theft. While the law has changed on this issue, change has come shockingly slowly.

A. Married Women's Testimony

The fiction of oneness is clearly illustrated by the court's disallowance of testimony between a husband and wife. Much like the privilege between lawyer/client or doctor/patient, the law carved an exception to witness testimony, or an "evidentiary privilege," that prevented wives from testifying against their husbands in criminal cases. In the lawyer/client privilege, the lawyer is prevented from giving testimony against his client at trial. This is designed to encourage clients to tell their attorney everything during their representation without fear it could be used against them later. Similarly, the husband/wife privilege is designed to encourage free communication and confidence during the marriage without fear that it will later be used against one of them. The purpose was to induce marital harmony. As a result, state and federal law bar a wife from testifying against her husband during a criminal proceeding.

When viewed through the lens of marital unity, the Fifth Amendment of the Constitution comes into play. There is a right against self-incrimination (a right not to testify against oneself). If, under common law, a wife merges and becomes one with her husband, the court reasoned that a husband could not be forced to testify against himself; by extension, his wife could not be required to testify against him either. The courts were also concerned about the credibility of a wife's testimony. What woman would rat out her husband? The court was concerned that only a vengeful wife would do so, and the testimony would then be tainted.

---

14 "Montana Legislature Dress Code Angers Women", Jack Healy, *The New York Times*, National December 14, 2014, P. 31. Disparity for women in the workforce was also raised in 2014 in the case of Peggy Young who sued the United Parcel Service claiming that "her pregnancy cost her her job". Although she lost in two Maryland courts, the Supreme Court heard argument in December 2014. "When AWorker Becomes Pregnant", Brigid Schulte, *The Washington Post*, Monday December 1, 2104, P. B1 In another case in San Francisco, a jury did not agree when a junior partner sued her venture capital firm for gender discrimination, putting the spot light on how women are treated in Silicon Valley. "Jury rejects 'boys' club bias claims", Todd C. Frankel & Andrea Peterson, *The Washington Post*, March 28, 2015, P. A13.

From a modern perspective, it seems a curious rationale to protect criminal behavior. While states still maintain an exclusionary privilege between husbands and wives, the federal court has started to pull away, but only in limited circumstances. In the case of *Trammel v. United States*, 445 U.S. 40 (1980), the Supreme Court reviewed the marital exception to testimony in a modern context and found that a wife could decide whether to serve as a witness in a criminal case against her husband and give testimony on the criminal actions that she witnessed in the presence of others, even if her husband objected. To decide otherwise would hark back to the fiction of oneness in which the husband spoke for both himself and his wife under the law. Is society poorly served when a woman witnesses a crime but is not allowed to testify against her husband who was involved in criminal activity?

In 2005, the marital evidentiary privilege was raised by a partner in a same-sex relationship. Stephen Signorelli, 60, pleaded "not guilty" to a grand larceny charge. He asked a court to bar the testimony of former superintendent Frank Tassone if his case went to trial. Tassone was his partner. Signorelli "said the court should treat them like spouses." Stephen Signorelli, a Long Island school superintendent, was charged with embezzling $11.2 million from the school district. His partner, Tassone, pleaded guilty to stealing at least $1 million; as part of that plea, he was willing to provide evidence against Signorelli. In arguing that the marital privilege laws should apply in their situation, Signorelli said they had been "loving partners for 33 years"; had a "solemn religious ceremony at sea to memorialize their relationship and love for each other" (referring to a commitment ceremony they had in the Caribbean); that they were "beneficiaries of each other's wills"; they could be seen in each other's family photographs; and shared every single Thanksgiving, Christmas, and other holiday together. The two were registered as domestic partners in New York City. At that time, same-sex marriage was not legal in the state.[15]

What should the court decide? Remember, this case was in Nassau County (state court), but if it was tried in federal court, even if same-sex marriage were legal, what would DOMA's impact be on the case? Which other case in this book is similar to this one?

With more people living in relationships outside of marriage, should this rule extend to domestic partners? In a domestic partner violence case involving extraordinary testimony, the court was able to convict on rape and abduction charges based on the courtroom testimony of a woman who had died more than a year earlier. While the couple was once engaged, they broke it off before the night "he threw her on her bed, beat and choked her, ripped her clothes off and then raped her... and then about an hour later he sexually assaulted her again." The next day when she tried to leave for work, he abducted her in his car but she was eventually set free and he was arrested. After the preliminary hearing in which the woman testified to the events, "the woman committed suicide... distraught about what happened to her." Although the defendant did not get a chance to cross-examine on the testimony, it was eventually allowed as evidence at the trial when a friend of the victim read her preliminary hearing testimony in court.[16]

---

15   "Gay Partner Seeks Spousal Privilege in New York Case," *Los Angeles Times*, November 25, 2005.
16   "Man gets 67 years for rape, abduction", Justin Jouvenal, *The Washington Post*, January 31, 2015, B2.

B. Violence Against Women

Not surprisingly, if a married woman was viewed as her husband's property (like an ox), violence occurred often and went unpunished. In the 1970s, the federal government focused on the issue of wife abuse and passed the Violence Against Women Act. That act has been updated and broadened several times since. Yet, violence against women (and men) in domestic relations continues to be a major social issue.[17]

HISTORY

Common law recognized a man's right to discipline his wife as needed. In *State v. Rhodes*, 1868, a husband was found innocent because, the judge said, "The defendant had a right to whip his wife with a switch no larger than his thumb," and in another case, in 1874, *State v. Oliver*, the judge cited the "old doctrine, that a husband had a right to whip his wife, provided he used a switch no longer than his thumb," but continued that this was "not law in North Carolina. Indeed, the Courts have advanced from that barbarism."

Domestic violence is abuse, or threats of abuse, when the person who was being abused and the abuser are, or have been, in an intimate relationship. It is also when the abused person and the abuser are closely related by blood, or by marriage. California's domestic violence laws define abuse as physically hurting or trying to hurt someone (whether intentionally or recklessly); sexual assault; making someone reasonably afraid that they or someone else will be seriously hurt (threats or promises to harm); or behavior such as harassing, stalking, hitting; disturbing the peace, or destroying personal property. Physical abuse includes hitting, kicking, shoving, pushing, pulling hair, throwing things, scaring, following, or preventing persons from freely coming and going. It can also include physical abuse of family pets.[18]

In 2014, the issue of domestic partner violence came to the forefront in professional sports.[19] The Baltimore Ravens cut running back Ray Rice after a hotel "surveillance video surfaced showing Rice knocking his then-fiancée unconscious" in an elevator and the National Football League was criticized for not doing more until it suspended him "indefinitely"[20] and promised

---

17   "Most of the women in lockup—about 75 percent—have been severely, physically abused, according to the Correctional Association of New York. "Domestic violence puts some women on the path to incarceration", Petula Dvorack, *The Washington Post*, September 16, 2014, P. B1.

18   http://www.courts.ca.gov/selfhelp-domesticviolence.htm

19   Not all the violence is on the field. After losing a bet on the winner of a Monday Night Football game in 2013, a husband tasered his wife using the stun gun "twice on her butt and once on her thigh and that there were burn marks." "Man uses stun gun after bet on Packers game", WiscNews November 5, 2013 http://www.wiscnews.com/news/local/article_0c1853b0-84e4-5f07-92df-d415eaaff170.html. Afterward, the wife called the police and the man was arrested; the court later ordered him to pay a $250 fine for use of an electric weapon, "Bears fan who tasered wife fined", ESPN Chicago .com http://espn.go.com/blog/chicago/bears/post/_/id/4689985/bears-fan-who-tasered-wife-fined

20   "Rice is cut after video emerges", Mark Maske, *The Washington Post*, September 9, 2014. P.1. Shortly after the assault, they were married. In the three years since his suspension from the League, Rice has not even received a

to focus on the issue. Carolina Panthers defensive end Greg Hardy was convicted on charges of assaulting a female and communicating threats and appealed. Although Hardy was allowed to play in the first game of the season after the Rice video came out, he was suspended indefinitely by the team until his case was resolved.[21] Eleven other players have been arrested since 2005, but were allowed to continue to play. Since then, the NFL created its "so-called improved domestic violence policy [that] calls for a six-game suspension without pay for a first-time offender, and for a more severe penalty if 'the act was committed against a pregnant woman or in the presence of a child'".[22] Yet, Giants kicker Josh Brown was signed after the League was aware of his "2015 arrest for assaulting his wife (police and the court record documented that he assaulted her nearly two dozen times, including at least once…when she was pregnant)."[23] After the League investigated for 10 months, Brown was suspended for one game. Indeed, the League's investigators "blamed the victim. Brown's wife failed to cooperate." Should such investigations "put… the onus on an abused woman to make the case against her abuser—to the abuser's employer, no less"?[24] Worse yet, "[t]he Giants knew about Brown's past, even before they re-signed him before the season."[25] "'He's admitted to us that he's abused his wife in the past."[26] Then, further details of the case were made public, including Brown's journals where he "admitting abusing his wife and viewing her as a slave."… "'I have controlled her by making her feel less human than me, Brown wrote…I have disregarded my stepsons' feelings, and they have witnessed me abusing their mother.'"[27] Brown was eventually banned from the NFL, but "is eligible to receive the remaining $720,480 of his 2016 contract through termination pay."[28] Others have protested the League's inaction, including players' mothers[29] and Melissa Mark-Viverito, New York City Council's Speaker who "spearheaded a public service campaign, #NotAFan"[30] where top athletes and coaches spoke out against domestic violence. Interestingly, neither the Giants nor the Jets agreed to participate.[31]

"workout invitation…despite being a former Pro Bowl" player. He is now an advocate for domestic violence victims and has pledged to donate any money he makes in the NFL to domestic violence causes. http://www.cbssports.com/nfl/news/josh-brown-eligible-for-termination-pay-still-faces-nfl-ban-after-release/

21   Eleven other players were arrested since 2005, but they were allowed to continue to play. "NFL Arrests Database", *USA Today,* http://www.usatoday.com/sports/nfl/arrests/

22   http://www.cbssports.com/nfl/news/josh-brown-eligible-for-termination-pay-still-faces-nfl-ban-after-release/

23   https://www.nytimes.com/2016/10/22/sports/football/nfl-domestic-violence-josh-brown-new-york-giants.html?_r=0

24   Ibid.

25   Ibid.

26   Ibid., Quoting Giant's co-owner John K. Mara.

27   Ibid, quoting Brown's diaries.

28   http://www.cbssports.com/nfl/news/josh-brown-eligible-for-termination-pay-still-faces-nfl-ban-after-release/

29   https://www.nytimes.com/2016/10/22/sports/football/nfl-domestic-violence-josh-brown-new-york-giants.html?_r=0

30   Ibid.

31   Ibid.

But partner violence is not limited to football. The New York Yankees hired pitcher Aroldis Chapman, "even though he was being investigated for domestic violence."[32] NASCAR suspended driver Kurt Busch indefinitely "after a judge said the former champion almost surely choked and beat an ex-girlfriend" and that there was "a 'substantial likelihood' of more domestic violence from him in the future."[33] But domestic partner violence is an issue for both men and women in professional sports. For example, in April 2015-"two engaged WNBA stars—Phoenix Mercury star Brittney Griner and the Tulsa Shock's Glory Johnson—were arrested after a domestic dispute."[34] The WNBA suspended each player for the first seven games of the season.[35] "Yet, when Congress wrote a letter urging professional sports leagues to clarify their domestic violence policies after the Ray Rice incident last year, the WNBA was not on the list of recipients." Domestic violence effects everyone, heterosexuals, gays, children, and the police that have to respond.

Since the 1970s, the federal government acknowledged domestic violence as a major social problem and began to deal with its impact on families. The federal government encouraged states to create their own domestic violence protection and education programs. Since this time, all states have created programs to combat it. In 1994, Congress passed the Violence Against Women Act (VAWA).[36] This act created criminal sanctions for interstate domestic violence. It also provided federal funds to help prosecute domestic abuse crimes and sexual assaults while also assisting victims of those crimes.[37] The VAWA also expanded the authority of tribal courts to

---

32 Ibid.

33 "Auto Racing, Kurt Busch is suspended indefinitely by NASCAR" *The Washington Post Sports*, February 21, 2015, p. D2

34 "Brittney Griner, Gloria Johnson and the WNBA's domestic violence problem", Justin Wm. Moyer, April, *The Washington Post,* 2015. http://www.washingtonpost.com/news/morning-mix/wp/2015/04/24/brittney-griner-glory-johnson-and-the-wnbas-domestic-violence-problem/. Three weeks later, Griner married Johnson. The next month, Griner filed for an annulment because, "[i]n the week prior to the wedding, I attempted to postpone the wedding several times until I completed counseling, but I still went through with it. I now realize that was a mistake." The day before, Johnson-Griner had announced that she was pregnant. Johnson's agent, A.J. Fisher, said his client was blindsided by the announcement. Johnson was "extremely hurt and blindsided" by Griner's decision. "'She loves Brittney and made a huge sacrifice to carry a child, put her career on hold, invest in their relationship and their future'", Fisher said. https://www.washingtonpost.com/news/early-lead/wp/2015/06/06/brittney-griner-files-to-annul-marriage-to-newly-pregnant-glory-johnson/?utm_term=.394a40722fe5

35 https://www.washingtonpost.com/news/early-lead/wp/2015/06/06/brittney-griner-files-to-annul-marriage-to-newly-pregnant-glory-johnson/?utm_term=.394a40722fe5

36 When the act expired in 2011, there was a year of bipartisan fighting until Congress reauthorized the VAWA and President Obama signed it into law in February of 2013. This version of the act extended protections to gays, lesbians, and transgender individuals. It also helps victims of domestic violence who are undocumented immigrants. The act provides for a "U visa," which gives victims temporary legal status if they help police investigate the crime. It strengthens penalties for sex trafficking.

37 Outrageously, violence may occur on the other side of the bench. In 2014, the judge of a Montgomery Alabama U.S. District Court called the police because her husband, the federal judge, was "'beating on me'" and she had "cuts on her mouth and forehead. The judge was arrested and jailed on misdemeanor battery charges. After 24 weekly counseling sessions, the charges were dismissed. But the 11 Circuit U.S. Court of Appeals began an investigation." Federal judges are judges for life, meaning that they must be impeached to be removed. Does this meet the standard?

prosecute non-Indian offenders.[38] The act also works to prevent sexual assaults on college campuses by providing funding for programs at rape crisis centers near college campuses. In 2014, this issue became head-line news,[39] in part because of the Obama administration's focus on the reportedly high incidents of sexual assaults and other sexual misconduct on college campuses.[40] The Education Department's office for Civil Rights began investigations into "dozens of colleges and universities," from Harvard and its Law School to American University, alleging they failed to provide their students with a safe learning environment. This caused institutions of higher education to revise their sexual misconduct policies, including changing the burden of proof in determining whether a violation occurred as a "preponderance of evidence" (or more likely than not) from the old standard that required a higher level of evidence. Many questioned why colleges would hear rape allegations under a student "honor code" and suggested that these types of violent crimes (like other felonies or murder) are best dealt with in the criminal courts with Constitutional safeguards and a goal of removing predators from society. In 2015, Virginia's legislature debated a mandate that would require all campus sexual assaults to be reported to law enforcement. States have also passed "Scarlet Letter" laws. Virginia and New York require a student found responsible for sexual assault by a campus tribunal to have his/her college transcript permanently notated, even if the student withdraws from the college while the investigation is

---

38   Native American women are two and a half times more likely to be raped than those in the general population. Editorial, *Los Angeles Times*, March 1, 2013. Voting for women, and against violence—Congress finally reauthorizes the Violence Against Women Act, broadening its protections, http://www.latimes.com/news/opinion/editorials/la-ed-violence-against-women-act-20130301,0,4863376.story The VAWA also expanded the authority of tribal courts to prosecute non-Indian offenders. Previously, cases of rape by non-Indians toward Native Americans were prosecuted in federal court. Already overworked, the closest U.S. Attorney's office may be hundreds of miles from the reservation; it was time consuming and expensive for federal prosecutors to travel to the crime site and conduct witness interviews. As a result, valuable evidence or testimony might not be collected or the cases would lag. Opposition to the reauthorization of the act included a belief that states should continue to handle such matters.

39   Rightfully so, with cases like one in 2013 involving a dorm-room gang rape and charges against some Vanderbilt University football players whose defense was, "their judgment was warped by a campus culture where drunken sex was commonplace". "Vanderbilt gang-rape defense puts blame on campus culture", Sheila Burke and Travis Loller, *The Washington Post*, January 25, 2015, p. A4. Of the four football players charged in 2013, two, went to trial twice; a mistrial was declared after a guilty verdict because of concerns of "juror's honesty" in January 2015, but both were later convicted. http://www.tennessean.com/story/news/2016/09/13/state-appeals-sentence-vanderbilt-rape-case/90317248/ One of those convicted, Cory Batey, is currently serving a 15-year prison sentence, but state prosecutors requested that that sentence be revisited on a motion in 2016. 15 years was the minimum sentence and the State wanted the maximum of 25. The remaining two players were attempting to reach a plea agreement. Ibid. Compare this to Brigham Young University in Utah, where a woman was charged with an honor code violation when reporting her rape. The day she reported being raped from an on-line date to the school's Title IX director, she also received an honor code violation allegation for its strict rules against pre-marital sex. The honor code" priz[es] chastity, honesty and virtue. It requires modest dress on campus, discourages consensual sex outside marriage and, among other things, prohibits drinking, drug use, same-sex intimacy and indecency, as well as sexual misconduct."

40   The Obama Administration cites statistics that one in five women who attend college will be sexually assaulted before graduation, but that number and the study that supports it, have been challenged. "Confusion About College Sexual Assault", *The New York Times*, Editorial Page, February 8, 2015, p.A10.

underway.[41] Shockingly, in the 2015 reports, "Ninety-one percent of college campuses disclosed zero reported incidences of rape in 2014."[42] Even victim's rights groups have challenged the statistically low expulsion rates for these crimes and questioned the conflict presented when a college has to balance resolution against its reputation.[43] Should rape be treated like cheating in college?

C. Protective Orders: Restraining Orders/Peace Orders

Perhaps the most frequently used tools against domestic violence are **protective orders**. Also known as restraining orders, or peace orders, they are used to help victims/survivors of domestic violence keep their attackers away from them and to prevent future attacks. Generally, the parties must be in a close personal relationship such as being married, registered domestic partners, divorced, separated in anticipation of divorce, dating or have dated, living together or have lived together (but more than roommates), parents (together) of a child, closely related by blood or legally (such as a parent, child, brother, sister, grandmother, grandfather, or in-law).[44] Rude behavior and threats are generally not sufficient reasons to order a protective order. Often, emotional abuse or damage to property does not satisfy the grounds for a restraining order unless there is also fear of physical injury.

A protective order is a court order that tells an abuser to stay away from a victim. Generally, court systems award protective orders (POs) in a two-step process. First, a victim/survivor applies to a designated court on an expedited basis and testifies that the abuser has already abused her and/or there is substantial likelihood of violence occurring in the future or "ongoing" violence. If the court finds grounds to issue a restraining order, it will be a temporary restraining order (TRO). Often, the defendant becomes aware of the PO request after the judge signs the TRO and he receives a copy (often by hand delivery by the sheriff's office). TROs are usually granted on an *ex parte* (without notice, giving an opportunity for the abuser to respond). Constitutional issues have been raised about the denial of a full hearing on the charge. Courts generally find that while this is a concern, it is acceptable to override the Constitution's due process requirements of the 14th Amendment because those protections will be provided in the second stage of the final protective order hearing

---

41   https://www.washingtonpost.com/news/grade-point/wp/2015/07/20/a-scarlet-letter-for-students-implicated-in-sex-assaults-d-c-bill-sparks-debate/?utm_term=.8ce584e883ab

42   http://www.aauw.org/article/clery-act-data-analysis/. "With about 11,000 campuses disclosing annual crime data, an overwhelming majority of schools certified that in 2014 they did not receive a single report of a rape."

43   A "Journal of Psychology, Public Policy and Law" study found that when the Education Department audits a college, the reports of sexual assault rise by 44%, but falls back to the lower rate after the period of scrutiny. This is not true of other crimes like robbery and burglary. This study was conducted from 2001 to 2012 for 4-year collages with at least 10,000 students. Ibid.

44   If the accused does not fit into the category of close personal relationship, other types of restraining orders may be available, (e.g., workplace or neighbor).

After a TPO is issued and the defendant receives a copy of the order, the defendant can request a hearing. The hearing must be conducted within a short period of time (two to 21 days). This allows an opportunity for a full hearing (lawyers, witnesses, etc.) and proof must be made (with pictures and so forth) by the victim/survivor of prior abuse and/or the danger of future abuse. Thus, although there are constitutional concerns about granting TROs without allowing the defendant due process, justice is delayed not denied. This is especially true in balancing the potential risk of tragedy occurring if the initial request is not acted upon quickly. At the second hearing, the court will determine if the TRO will stay in effect (be made permanent) or if any changes to its terms are necessary. If no hearing is requested, the restraining order may become permanent. Permanent generally means that it is good for one year and can be subsequently presented for yearly renewals.

What can a protective order prevent? Traditionally, POs remove the defendant from the home or authorize a police officer to "stand by" for 25 minutes while the victim removes personal articles to leave the home. Many include geographic restrictions on the defendant (e.g., to stay 500 feet from the victim's home or office). In today's society, with more reliance on technology, domestic violence protective orders may include restrictions on placement of GPS systems (which amounts to stalking), as well as video surveillance of the spouse's bedroom (which amounts to harassment). Similarly, restrictions on e-mail messages and texting may be necessary. Protective orders may extend to the victim's children which can temporarily impact custody (including preventing pickup at day care or school).[45] Some states (e.g., Oregon) prevent the defendant from having a gun. Are there any limits on what the restraining order can restrict?

In the case of *St. v. Williams v. Marsh* ,626 S.W. 2d 223 (MO 1982), the restraining order included geographic restrictions against the accused husband, a former Golden Gloves boxer. It also made determinations regarding custody and visitation and imposed financial support obligations. In allowing the restraining order as constitutional, the court indicated that the due process concerns are dealt with swiftly when the full hearing is conducted on the final order.

If the respondent/defendant violates the terms of the restraining order, the victim should call the police, tell them of the order's existence, and an officer will arrest the defendant if there is "probable cause" (a good reason to believe) that a violation has occurred. The respondent can then be charged with contempt of court for failing to obey a court order and, if found guilty, can be fined, placed on probation, or put in jail for up to six months. Other penalties could include a warning, probation, a suspended sentence, or a sentence of less than the maximum. Restraining orders often set the amount of bail before the hearing if the defendant is arrested for violating it. Sometimes, an abuser may be released from jail if it appears likely that they will reappear for the court hearing on the contempt charge. A condition of the release may be that the abuser agrees not to go near the victim (precisely what the court's order had already decreed). For these reasons, some argue that a restraining order is a paper tiger: it does not guarantee the victim's safety.

---

45 If custody issues are involved, the hearing for the permanent injunction will be held quickly, within five to 12 days.

In contrast to *Warren*, where the temporary restraining order was intended to keep the parties apart, in *Williams v. State of Alaska*, 151 P.3d 460 (Alaska App 2006), the husband, who was under a TRO for domestic violence against his wife, wanted to move back to the marital home while on pre-trial release and his wife also wanted him back. When the court refused to allow it, the appeals court did allow it saying that the marital status created a right to live with his wife in the marital home. The court said that judges often have to predict whether a person would be a danger in the future and, since this case involved only one instance of violence, (the husband strangled the wife, but eventually let go) the court allowed him to return.

Most people would feel that restraining orders, even with the questions regarding temporary constitutional deprivations, are necessary to prevent tragic circumstances and possible irreparable harm. But what happens when a court goes too far? In December 2005, a Santa Fe, New Mexico court issued a temporary restraining order against CBS late-night television host, David Letterman. The temporary restraining order was granted to Colleen Nestler, even though she had never met Letterman, who lived in New York. In requesting the order, Ms. Nestler's application included statements that Letterman forced her to go bankrupt causing mental cruelty and sleep deprivation since 1994. She also alleged that Letterman used code words and gestures to convey his desires for her and that he began sending her thoughts of love from his television show. She claimed he asked her to be his wife during a televised teaser for a show by saying, "Marry me, Oprah!" She alleged that Oprah was the first of many code names that he had for her and that the vocabulary increased and changed with time.[46]

If some view protective orders as paper tigers that really provide no protection against an abusive partner, what should domestic violence victims do? Should they just call the police? Maybe not or they could be evicted. Across the country many cities have enacted nuisance, crime-free or disorderly behavior ordinances that penalize tenants and landlords when residents repeatedly access police services, even when the tenants are victims.[47] An Arizona law prevents landlords from renting to tenants who call the police 4 times or more within 30 days or face civil or criminal consequences.[48] These ordinances impact women of color especially.[49] Do they violate the First Amendment's right to petition the government, which includes the right to call the police in an emergency?[50]

---

46 "Letterman lawyers contest fan's restraining order," Associated Press for *Washington Post*, December 22, 2005.
47 http://www.chicagotribune.com/suburbs/daily-southtown/opinion/ct-sta-kadner-tenants-st-0227-20150226-column.html
48 "How 911 can abuse women", Sandra S. Park, *USA Today*, October 15, 2015, 7A.
49 Ibid. St. Louis' nuisance law stopped mostly low income African-American women who were victims of domestic violence from calling the police.
50 Ibid.

D. Crimes against Persons

Can a man be criminally charged with raping his wife? To most, this seems like a rhetorical question. But it was not until the 1980s that courts were willing to criminally convict husbands for such a vicious crime. Under common law, a man was entitled to his wife's interest in society, companionship, and sexual relationship. Only after the women's liberation movement were the traditional rights and duties of marriage questioned. In the case of *Warren v. State of Georgia*, 336 S.E.2d 221 (GA 1985), when a husband raped his wife, his defense was that it was impossible for him to be guilty of raping her because they were married. When she had said, "I do," it negated her ability to say "no." Adopting the traditional marital unity, his time-tested argument was that when a woman married her husband, they became one in all domestic matters. If the two were as one, it would not be possible for him to rape her. Noting that the law had no written exceptions for spouses in the definition of rape, the *Warren* court rejected the husband's argument and convicted him.[51]

Yet, the wheels continue to turn slowly on this issue. The first conviction for marital sexual assault in Prince George's County, Maryland, did not occur until 2005. Valentine Selwyn Boston was sentenced to seven years in prison for second-degree attempted rape, second-degree assault, false imprisonment, and violating a protective order. According to the case, the wife had a restraining order against her husband, but he was permitted to stay in the same house as long as he was not violent. They slept in separate bedrooms, but when the wife came into her bedroom, the husband "jumped up from beside her bed, holding what she believed to be a knife." She kicked it out of his hand, but he then "attempted to rape her. [He] bit the inside of her knee and choked her." When he let up, he followed her as she went to the bathroom and "said he wanted sex;" "she submitted because she feared he would become more violent." Under this "consent" the county was unable to charge him with rape.[52] Still, some states require higher levels of violence or allow lesser penalties for marital rape. Also, some states still have marital exclusions for statutory rape (defined as sex with a minor, but not prosecuted if the couple is married. See age restrictions in marriage discussion in Chapter 9).

But what happens when a man has sex with his wife who is in a coma. Can she consent?

---

51 In another early case to decide this issue, *Commonwealth v. Chretien*, 417 NE2d 1203 (Mass 1981), the husband was convicted of raping his wife while they were separated for divorce, but before the final order of divorce was entered. In its ruling, the court noted that the language of the common law rape statute of 1800 "appears to include a reflection of the common law principle that a man cannot, as a matter of law, rape his wife. '[T]he husband cannot be guilty of a rape committed by himself upon his lawful wife, for by their mutual matrimonial consent an [*sic*] contract the wife hath given up herself in this kind unto her husband, which she cannot retract…. [I]n marriage she hath given up her body to her husband'…." citing to 1 Hale, Pleas of the Crown 628 (1800).
52 "7-Year Term for Marital Sex Assault" Ruben Castaneda, *The Washington Post*, June 12, 2005, P. C3.

Decided May 3, 1985.
Rehearing Denied May 30, 1985.

Attorney(s) appearing for the Case

Wade C. Hoyt III, for appellant.
F. Larry Salmon, District Attorney, Deborah D. Haygood, Stephen F. Lanier, Assistant District Attorneys, for appellee.

BANKE, Chief Judge.

The appellant appeals the denial of his motion for new trial following his conviction of rape.

The factual setting of this case is unusual to the point of being bizarre. The appellant and the victim had been living together for approximately a year and a half, when she suffered a brain injury as the result of a motor vehicle accident and lapsed into a coma from which she has apparently never recovered. The appellant admits that one night several weeks after the accident he had sexual relations with the victim as she lay comatose in her hospital bed. His "defense" to the charge of rape was that because he and the victim had enjoyed a loving sexual relationship prior to her injury, it is reasonable to assume she would have consented had she been capable of doing so. *Held*:

Rape is defined by OCGA § 16-6-1 (a) as "carnal knowledge of a female forcibly and against her will." The phrase "against her will" has been interpreted to mean "without her consent." See *Gore v. State,* 119 Ga. 418, 419 (46 SE 671) (1903); *Drake v. State,* 239 Ga. 232, 233 (236 S.E.2d 748) (1977). Also, it has been held that "[s]exual intercourse with a woman whose will is temporarily lost from intoxication, or unconsciousness arising from use of drugs or other cause, or sleep, is rape. (Cits.)" *Paul v. State,* 144 Ga.App. 106 (2) (240 S.E.2d 600) (1977).

Based on these principles, we are constrained to hold that the evidence in this case was sufficient to enable a rational trier of fact to find the appellant guilty of rape beyond a reasonable doubt. See generally *Jackson v. Virginia,* 443 U.S. 307 (99 S.C. 2781, 61 LE2d 560) (1979); *Crawford v. State,* 245 Ga. 89 (1) (263 S.E.2d 131) (1980). Penetration was established by the unequivocal testimony of two hospital employees to the effect that they had observed the appellant in the act of "sexual intercourse" with the victim. Assuming *arguendo* that a legal presumption of consent might arise from proof that the appellant and the victim were united in a common law marriage, the evidence as to the existence of such a relationship was conflicting, and the jury was authorized to conclude that no such marriage relationship existed. Finally, the evidence did not establish as a matter of law that the appellant acted without criminal intent. "As pointed out in *Towler v. State*, 24 Ga.App. 167 (4) (100 SE 42) [1919], the intent with which an act is done is peculiarly a question of fact for determination by the jury, and although a finding that the accused had the intent to commit the crime charged may be supported by evidence which is exceedingly weak and unsatisfactory the verdict will not be set aside on that ground. (Cits.)" *Mallette v. State*, 119 Ga.App. 24, 27 (165 S.E.2d 870) (1969). See also *Schwerdtfeger v. State*, 167 Ga.App. 19,

[174 Ga. App. 914]

20 (305 S.E.2d 834) (1983).

2. The trial court did not err in excluding as irrelevant the appellant's proffered testimony concerning the specifics of his prior sexual relationship with the victim, nor did the court err in refusing to give the appellant's requested charge on the defense of consent, there being no question that the victim was incapable of communicating such consent. See *Paul v. State*, 144 Ga.App. 106 (2), supra.

3. The trial court did not err in admitting two photographs of the victim taken as she lay on a hospital bed in a nursing home a few weeks after the incident, where the photographs were identified as depicting her in substantially the same condition she was in on the date in question. Although the photographs were not, strictly speaking, necessary to prove any material fact in the case, there was nothing about them that can reasonably be characterized as gruesome, inflammatory, or prejudicial. "Photographs which are relevant to any issue in the case are admissible even though they may have an effect upon the jury. (Cits.)" *Ramey v. State*, 250 Ga. 455, 456 (298 S.E.2d 503) (1983). See also *Brown v. State*, 250 Ga. 862, 866-867 (302 S.E.2d 347) (1983).

Judgment affirmed. McMurray, P. J., and Benham, J., concur.[53]

Does it make any difference that Georgia recognized common law marriage at the time? Or that Brown sat by her bed for forty-two days waiting for her to wake up and took pills so he could stay awake?[54] Do you agree with Browns' defense attorney's closing statement, "I told the jury that they could go back and do the right thing. That it didn't matter what the law said, they weren't accountable to anyone but themselves. By then, Dennis had been in jail half a year, and there wasn't much left to punish. I said, 'Dennis Brown has had about all the justice one person could stand.'"[55]

---

53   https://www.courtlistener.com/opinion/1211005/brown-v-state/
54   *Paper Trails*, Pete Dexter, 2007, HarperCollins, pg.221
55   Ibid. Quoting Brown's attorney, Wade Hoyt.

Compare this to a case that raised the issue in a tragic circumstance when a husband was charged with sexual abuse when he had sex with his demented spouse in her nursing home. In April 2015, a jury found the 78-year-old state legislator not guilty. Iowa prosecutors based the accusations on the fact that the wife's doctors had told her husband that her Alzheimer's prevented her from giving consent.[56] As the population ages, consent will continue to be an issue.

E. Battered Partner Defense

In addition to domestic violence as physical abuse, in some states like California, verbal, emotional, or psychological abuse suffices. Often, abusers use control and isolation in combination with other forms of abuse.[57] The battered partner defense is used as a defense to murder when a partner admits the action, but claims it was done in self-defense, because of a history of abuse and fear of imminent danger or serious bodily harm. In 2004, a judge in Maryland sentenced a woman to ten years in prison, but suspended all but 198 days of her sentence (the time she had already spent in jail) because he "was convinced by a diagnosis that she suffered from battered spouse syndrome." In the case, the woman shot her husband while he was asleep after she discovered videotapes showing him sexually abusing her daughter (whom they later found was pregnant with his child). In making his sentence, the judge called her husband, the murder victim, "a horrible human being."[58] Was justice served?

F. Property Crimes against a Spouse

Can a husband steal his wife's property? The act of stealing requires taking something you do not own (you cannot steal from yourself). So, under common law when a woman gave all of her property interests to her husband when they married, there was no recognized crime of a husband stealing from his wife. What about in current society? If your spouse sells household items to pay for a drug habit, will the court convict him of stealing? In the case of *Cladd v. State*, 398 So. 2d 442 (FL 1981), despite the age-old saying that "what's hers is mine," the court was able to convict a husband of theft when he broke into his wife's apartment and stole some of her items. The conviction was probably granted because they were estranged and living separately.

Someone who intentionally breaks all the things in your house could be charged with a crime such as vandalism. But if a spouse intentionally breaks the same property in the marital home, is that criminal? The California courts are looking at this issue in *People v. Wallace* 123 Cal. App.4th 144 (2004).

---

56 "Former Iowa Legislator Henry Raythons, 78, found not guilty of sexually abusing wife with Alzheimer's", Sarah Kaplan, *The Washington Post*, April 23, 2015, http://www.washingtonpost.com/news/morning-mix/wp/2015/04/23/former-iowa-legislator-henry-rayhons-78-found-not-guilty-of-sexually-abusing-wife-with-alzheimers/
57 http://www.courts.ca.gov/selfhelp-domesticviolence.htm
58 "He was never going to harm my daughter again," Eric Rich, *Washington Post*, November 12, 2004, pp. B1 and B4.

THE PEOPLE, Plaintiff and Respondent, v. ANTHONY LEROY WALLACE, Defendant and Appellant.
GOMES, J.

FACTUAL AND PROCEDURAL BACKGROUND

One summer evening in Fresno, Anthony LeRoy Wallace's wife of two months, Arlissa Pointer Wallace, caught him smoking crack cocaine, called him a crack head, and told him to leave the house she had bought six or seven years before the marriage and had refinanced shortly after the marriage. fn. 1 Although she had kept the house in her name, Wallace presumably had acquired a small community property interest through mortgage payments with community property funds.

Instead of leaving, however, Wallace began tearing up the house. Frightened, Pointer kept her distance from him as she opened the living room curtains in the hope a neighbor might see and call the police. He kept breaking things. Twice she dialed 911, but twice she hung up, fearing things would get much worse if he knew she had called. He left before the police arrived. She told a police officer that the only thing he had not broken in the house was his own stereo and that everything else in the house belonged to her. A couple of hours later, alerted by a neighbor to "incredible pounding, very, very loud noise" from the house, police officers found Wallace inside the house breaking things again. Only after he challenged three armed and uniformed officers to fight did they subdue him with a taser and arrest him.

At trial, an expert witness testified to over $ 9,000 of damage to the house and to over $ 6,000 of damage to the furniture and furnishings. A jury found Wallace guilty of felony vandalism and of two misdemeanors—being under the influence and resisting, delaying, or obstructing an officer ("resisting")—[123 Cal.App.4th 147] and found two assault with a deadly weapon priors true as both serious felony priors and prison term priors. (Pen. Code, 148, subd. (a)(1), 245, subd. (a)(1), 594, subd. (b)(1), 667.5, subd. (b), 1192.7, subd. (c); Health & Saf. Code, 11550, subd. (a).) fn. 2 The court sentenced him to a 25-to-life term for felony vandalism, a consecutive term of one year on each of his two prison term priors, and time served on each of his two misdemeanors. (?? 594, subd. (b)(1), 667, subds. (b)-(j), 667.5, subd. (b), 1170.12, subds. (a)-(d).)

INTRODUCTION

Wallace argues that as a matter of law he cannot be guilty of vandalizing either community property or his spouse's separate property inside the marital home. In the published portion of our opinion, we will reject his argument and embrace the emerging rule imposing criminal liability on a spouse for intentionally causing harm to property in which the other spouse has an interest, whether the property is individual or marital, whether the harm occurs outside or inside the marital home.

DISCUSSION

1. Scope of Vandalism Statute

The question before us is whether a spouse can be guilty of vandalizing community property and the other spouse's separate property inside the marital home. Wallace asks us to answer that question in the negative on the basis of "the common law rule that a person's home is his or her castle" and the language in the vandalism statute (? 594) that a vandal can deface, damage, or destroy only property that is "not his or her own." The Attorney General asks us to answer that question in the affirmative, arguing that vandalism is not a crime that threatens property rights only in a particular place, that the criminal law protects each owner's interest in community property against nonconsensual damage by the other, and that Pointer's separate property suffered most of the harm anyway. [123 Cal.App.4th 148]

[1] In *People v. Kahanic* (1987) 196 Cal. App. 3d 461 [241 Cal. Rptr. 722] (*Kahanic*), we held that the vandalism statute applies to community property on the rationale that the "essence of the crime is in the physical acts against the ownership interest of another, even though that ownership is less than exclusive." (*Id.* at p. 466.) Citing *Kahanic*, a proposed vandalism instruction from the Judicial Council's Task Force on Jury Instructions requires proof that the accused "did not own the property" or "owned the property with someone else." (See Task Force on Jury Instructions, Cal. Jud. Council, Criminal Jury Instructions (July 5, 2004 Draft) (Task Force) Inst. No. 1995, pp. 1–2.)

However, Wallace argues that with the vandalism in *Kahanic* occurring outside the marital home the case is inapposite to the issue here whether "the common law rule that a person's home is his or her castle" precludes criminal liability for vandalizing property in one's own home. He analogizes that issue to the question whether a person can burglarize his or her own home and notes the California Supreme Court relied on the common law rule to hold that the burglary statute applies only to "a person who has no right to be in the building." (*People v. Gauze* (1975) 15 Cal.3d 709, 714 [125 Cal. Rptr. 773, 542 P.2d 1365].) Emphasizing that "burglary and the lesser related offenses of trespass and vandalism *are* 'closely related' " (*People v. Farrow* (1993) 13 Cal.App.4th 1606, 1625-1626 [16 Cal. Rptr. 2d 844], citing *People v. Geiger* (1984) 35 Cal.3d 510 [199 Cal. Rptr. 45, 674 P.2d 1303], overruled by

People v. Birks (1998) 19 Cal.4th 108, 112-113, 136 [77 Cal. Rptr. 2d 848, 960 P.2d 1073]), he argues that as one can neither burgle nor trespass in one's own home, neither can one vandalize property in one's own home.

[2] Wallace's argument ignores three key differences between vandalism, on the one hand, and burglary and trespass, on the other. First, one can commit vandalism anywhere (see 594 fn. 3), but one can commit burglary and trespass only by entering into a specific place (see 459, fn. 4, 602). Second, one cannot commit vandalism without defacing, damaging, or destroying property (see 594), but one can commit burglary and trespass without harming any [123 Cal.App.4th 149] property at all (459, 602 fn. 5). Third, the harm that vandalism by a spouse necessarily inflicts to community property or to the other spouse's separate property ousts the other spouse of his or her ownership interest in a way that neither burglary nor trespass necessarily does. Together, those differences foil Wallace's endeavor to broaden to vandalism the rule that applies to burglary and trespass.

[3] Instead, on the question before us, we broaden our holding in *Kahanic* to embrace the emerging rule imposing criminal liability on a spouse for intentionally causing harm to property in which the other spouse has an interest, whether the property is individual or marital, whether the harm occurs outside or inside the marital home. (*Kahanic, supra,* 196 Cal. App. 3d at p. 466; see, e.g., *Jackson v. United States* (D.C. 2003) 819 A.2d 963, 964-967 (*Jackson*) [spouse [123 Cal.App.4th 150] criminally liable for harm to marital property at marital home under statute prohibiting harm to property "not his or her own"]; *State v. Superior Court* (Ct. App. 1997) 188 Ariz. 372 [936 P.2d 558, 559] [spouse criminally liable for harm to joint tenancy property of both spouses under statute prohibiting damage to "property of another person"]; *State v. Coria* (2002) 146 Wn. 2d 631 [48 P.3d 980, 981-985] (*Coria*) [spouse criminally liable for harm to community property at marital home under statute prohibiting damage to "property of another"]; *Hughes v. State* (Alaska Ct.App. 2002) 56 P.3d 1088, 1094-1095 [spouse criminally liable for harm to marital property at marital home under statute prohibiting damage to "property of another"]; *Ginn v. State* (2001) 251 Ga.App. 159 [553 S.E.2d 839, 840, 842] [spouse criminally liable for harm to marital property at marital home under statute prohibiting damage to "any property of another"]; *State v. Sevelin* (Ct.App. 1996) 204 Wis.2d 127 [554 N.W.2d 521, 522-523] [spouse criminally liable for harm to marital property at marital home under statute prohibiting damage to "any physical property of another"]; *State v. Zeien* (Iowa 1993) 505 N.W.2d 498, 498-499 [spouse criminally liable for harm to marital property at marital home under statute prohibiting damage to property "by one who has no right to so act"]; *People v. Schneider* (App.Ct. 1985) 139 Ill. App. 3d 222 [487 N.E.2d 379, 379-381, 93 Ill. Dec. 712] [spouse criminally liable for harm to marital property under statute prohibiting damage to "any property of another"]; but see *Horn v. State* (Ala.Crim.App. 2004)—So. 2d—[2004 Ala. Crim. App. LEXIS 88, 2004 WL 924682] [spouse not criminally liable for harm to marital property under statute prohibiting "damages to property"]; *State v. Powels* (Ct.App. 2003) 2003 NMCA 90, 134 N.M. 118 [73 P.3d 256, 257-259] [spouse not criminally liable for harm to marital property under statute prohibiting damage to "any real or personal property of another"]; *People v. Person* (N.Y.App.Div. 1997) 239 A.D.2d 612 [658 N.Y.S.2d 372, 373] (*Person*) [spouse not criminally liable for harm to marital property under statute prohibiting damage to

property of another person] *fn. 6*; see generally Lutz & Bonomolo, *My Husband Just Trashed Our Home; What Do You Mean That's Not a Crime?* (1997) 48 S.C. L.Rev. 641, 651 ["[W]hen a husband destroys property that he owns jointly with his wife, not only does he destroy his property, which he may have a right to destroy, but he simultaneously destroys his wife's undivided one hundred percent interest in the property, which he does not have a right to destroy."]; cf. Carpenter, *Of the Enemy Within, The Castle Doctrine, and Self-Defense* (2003) 86 Marq. L.Rev. 653, 693 ["The innocent cohabitant still has an identifiable interest in the protection that the sanctuary might offer and should not be denied its safe harbor because someone else may share in its possession. [Footnote.]"].) [4] Accordingly, we answer in the affirmative the question before us and [123 Cal.App.4th 151] hold that a spouse can be guilty of vandalizing community property and the other spouse's separate property inside the marital home.

[5] Finally, on the premise that the Family Code confers on each spouse "absolute power of disposition" of community personal property until service of a reciprocal temporary restraining order to the contrary (Fam. Code, ?? 1100, 2040, subd. (a)(2)), Wallace argues that as he and Pointer were not engaging in family law litigation, but rather were cohabiting as husband and wife, he cannot as a matter of law be guilty of vandalizing community personal property. Case law from other states applies the emerging rule to spouses cohabiting and presumably not engaging in family law litigation at the time of the vandalism (see, e.g., *State v. Superior Court, supra,* 936 P.2d at p. 559; *Coria, supra,* 48 P.3d at p. 981; *Ginn v. State, supra,* 553 S.E.2d at p. 840; *State v. Sevelin, supra,* 554 N.W.2d at p. 522) as well as to spouses no longer cohabiting and either estranged or contemplating, if not actually engaging, in family law litigation at the time of the vandalism (see, e.g., *Jackson, supra,* 819 A.2d at p. 964; *State v. Zeien, supra,* 505 N.W.2d at p. 498; *Hughes v. State, supra,* 56 P.3d at p. 1089; *People v. Schneider, supra,* 487 N.E.2d at pp. 379-380.) Wallace articulates, and we perceive, no sound reason in public policy or the law for the astounding notion that the criminal law should afford protection to some spouses but not to others. We decline to so limit our holding. *fn. 7*

2.-10. *fn.* * [Not certified for publication.] [123 Cal.App.4th 152]

DISPOSITION

The resisting conviction is ordered stricken from the judgment, which is modified to show 269 days of presentence custody credit, 134 days of presentence conduct credit, and 403 total days of presentence credit. The matter is remanded with directions to the court to issue and forward to the appropriate persons an abstract of judgment amended accordingly. Wallace has no right to be present at those proceedings. (See *People v. Price* (1991) 1 Cal.4th 324, 407-408 [3 Cal. Rptr. 2d 106, 821 P.2d 610].) Otherwise the judgment is affirmed.

Levy, Acting P. J., and Cornell, J., concurred.

(Some footnotes omitted by author) FN 3. Section 594, subdivision (a) provides: "Every person who maliciously commits any of the following acts with respect to any real or personal property not his or her own, in cases other than those specified by state law, is guilty of vandalism: [?] (1) Defaces with graffiti or other inscribed material. [?] (2) Damages. [?] (3) Destroys."

FN 4. Section 459 provides in part: "Every person who enters any house, room, apartment, tenement, shop, warehouse, store, mill, barn, stable, outhouse or other building, tent, vessel..., floating home..., railroad car, locked or sealed cargo container..., trailer coach..., any house car..., inhabited camper..., vehicle... when the doors are locked, aircraft..., or mine or any underground portion thereof, with intent to commit grand or petit larceny or any felony is guilty of burglary."

CONTRACTS WITH THIRD PARTIES

The common-law marital disability prevented women from entering into contracts. If the married woman only existed through her husband, only he had the legal right to enter into a contract. Thus, any contract a woman entered into was void and unenforceable under the law. This prevented a woman from buying something at the local store without her husband present to authorize it. Eventually, the system developed to allow the woman to buy "on her husband's account" which was authorized by him. Only after the passage of various state laws called the Married Women's Property Acts, did a wife have some authority to buy necessities from a merchant. Connecticut's law allowing a woman to make a will in 1809 was one of the first times a woman's right to contract was recognized.[59] When women got the right to contract after the 1890s, many of the marital disabilities began to disappear.

LAWSUITS WITH THIRD PARTIES

Under the common law fiction of oneness, a woman could not sue or be sued. If a wife committed a crime in her husband's presence, it was presumed to be at his direction and he was part of the lawsuit. (See Bumble's plight, above, when his wife steals something and he is held responsible for it in Dickens' *Oliver Twist*.) For personal property torts, the same pattern was required.

Likewise, when dealing with crimes or torts (personal violations) by a married woman at common law, she could not be sued because she gave up her legal identity to her husband when she married. He would be the one who would be legally fined. He also had all the money, so there was no reason to sue the wife. Similarly, a married woman could not bring a lawsuit against someone at common law unless she joined with her husband as the plaintiff. Only under the

---

59   Library of Congress, http://memory.loc.gov/ammem/awhhtml/awlaw3/property_law.htm

various Married Women's Property Acts did the wife gain the right to sue and be sued in her own name, without joining her husband. The courts were slow to change from this interpretation. It was in the mid-20th century that the last state eliminated this concept.

CONTRACTS WITH SPOUSES

While the law returned the right to contract and/or sue third parties to married women at the end of the 1800s, it still prevented them from contracting with their spouses, under "contractual incapacity." Yet, did preventing a wife from making an agreement that was enforceable by the courts just reinforce her disenfranchisement? Certainly, the doctrine of interspousal immunity, where spouses could not legally be held responsible to each other under the law, redefined marital unity. This doctrine was largely abolished by the states beginning in the 1940s. Today, courts enforce agreements between spouses, including postmarital contracts (see Chapter 4). Yet, this concept of interspousal immunity carried over into modern society longer than one may think.

In 1980, the New Jersey courts dealt with the issue of whether a wife's contract with her husband would be enforceable after her husband was murdered. In the case of *Romeo v. Romeo*, 418 A.2d 358 (NJ 1980), a woman purchased a tavern/restaurant in Newark, New Jersey after she married. He began to work full-time for her. One of his duties was to go to the bank to cash paychecks for their local factory worker customers. One day, the wife gave the husband checks and cash to take to the bank. That afternoon, he was found dead by a policeman in the passenger seat of her car with two gunshot wounds to his head and only a few dollars on him. The police concluded that he was ambushed after going to the bank and driven to an isolated area where he was robbed and shot.

Later, the wife filed for dependent benefits from Worker's Compensation because her husband died in the course of his employment. When the compensation judge analyzed the facts, he was concerned because the employment contract that served as the basis for the claim was between husband and wife. He looked at the issue of whether the doctrine of interspousal immunity would prevent enforcing a contract between a husband and wife. The court cited a 1949 New Jersey case denying an employment contract because it was between a husband and wife, as the employee and employer. According to that case, the statutory right of recovery did not apply when employer and employee were married. The court denied enforcement of the contract based on interspousal immunity. The compensation judge, however, noted that the doctrine of interspousal immunity had been abolished and allowed the wife's claim for benefits.

On appeal to New Jersey's appellate division, the court determined that the problem with an employment between a husband and wife is not the doctrine of interspousal immunity, but the simple question of contractual capacity. That court writes, "[A] contract of hire between spouses is utterly void and unenforceable at law". The court noted two reasons for this common-law rule: Contracts between husband and wife have been deemed objectionable, not only because they are inconsistent with the common-law doctrine of unity of person and interest, "but because they introduce the disturbing influence of bargain and sale into the marriage relation, and induce a separation rather than a unity of interests". The appellate court also looked to old cases which reasoned that "the act [has] **not so far severed the unity of person and interest of husband and wife in the law** as that their contracts *inter se* are enforceable at law" to conclude that any "contracts for hire" (employment contracts) between a husband and wife were utterly void in the 1970s, New Jersey. In 1980, the New Jersey Supreme Court reviewed the case on appeal and overruled the appellate court to allow the woman worker's compensation for the loss of her husband, who was also her employee.

TORTS AGAINST SPOUSES

Obviously, at common law, a woman could not sue her husband because she gave up her legal identity to her husband when she married. But, like a woman's right to contract with a spouse, it was not abolished under the Married Women's Property Acts. Indeed, these changes were very slow to evolve. Sometimes, courts will rely on old rules—even today.

In 2006, in California, when a woman's husband backed into the family car while driving a city truck, the city dismissed his claim for damages since he was at fault. His wife then sued the city. In response, City Attorney Steve Schwabauer said, "[t]here is no basis for Rhonda Gokey's claim, either, because she can't, in essence, sue her husband." "You can sue your spouse for divorce, but you can't sue your spouse for negligence," Schwabauer said. "They're a married couple under California law. They're one entity. It's damage to community property." When asked why she sued the city for more money than her husband, the woman said, "I'm not as nice as my husband is."[60]

The common law doctrine of "interspousal immunity" prevented tort suits between spouses, supposedly based upon concerns of encouraging inter-family fighting and the possibility of collusion and fraud between the spouses (usually against their insurance company). Torts are non-criminal suits ranging from negligence to assault. In the case of *McCullough v. Godwin*, from the Texas Court of Appeals, No. 12-05-00422-CV, February 9, 2007, the courts applied the doctrine of parental immunity in denying an ex-wife's suit against her ex-husband for allowing their son to drown in a lake while he had him for visitation.[61] Most states have abolished interspousal immunity today and allow spouses to sue each other. Insurance companies, however, generally add a "family exclusion" in their coverage to prevent spouses from suing each other like the *Gokey* case.

---

60 http://www.lodinews.com/news/article_b4438667-e0d0-594a-9a17-284bcc46fe87.html, "City rejects claim by own employee, so wife files another," Ross Farrow, lodinews.com, March 14, 2006.
61 http://caselaw.findlaw.com/tx-court-of-appeals/1013312.html

G. Your Cheatin' Spouse

What happens if the third party the spouse wants to sue is a mistress and the injury incurred is the alleged collapse of the marriage? Should the spurned spouse be able to sue, and how should compensation be determined? Historically, under common law, damages could be awarded to a husband on the loss of his wife due to the actions of another because his wife was considered chattel.[62] Known as "heart balm" actions, these claims were first aid for a broken heart. Courts recognized claims against another for interfering in a marriage under two forms: alienation of affection and criminal conversion.[63]

1. CRIMINAL CONVERSION

The existence of criminal conversion claims reinforces a husband's common law right to his wife as property. Proof of sexual intercourse is required for such a claim. Thus, if a man had sexual relations with someone's wife her husband could be paid for the loss of her virtue—that was harm enough! While courts justified this concept under the theory that a man may have to raise and financially support another man's children under such circumstances, most states have abolished it.

In the case of *Misenheimer v. Burris*, 183 NC App 408, (2007), the North Carolina Supreme Court upheld the determination of the lower court which found the defendant liable to the plaintiff for criminal conversion of the plaintiff's wife even though the affair occurred after the wife separated for divorce. In making its decision, the North Carolina Supreme Court also affirmed that the three-year time period to bring such an action (the statute of limitations) only began to run when the husband became aware that the affair occurred, not when the affair began. The court also affirmed the limited waiver of the clergy evidentiary privilege, which was used to try to determine the date the husband became aware of the wife's affair.

---

62   In certain Middle Eastern societies, women (and women in some Orthodox Jewish cultures) are still considered chattel, having no legal existence outside their husbands, fathers, sons, and brothers. A husband owns his wife and any children of the marriage. In some areas, that chattel status is modified to only include sexual and reproductive rights that are owned by husbands. http://wiki.answers.com/Q/What_is_the_historical_meaning_of_chattel_and_chattel_law
63   These suits should not be confused with loss of consortium claims which result from the "inability of one's spouse to have normal marital relations... (an euphemism for sexual intercourse). Such loss arises as a claim for damages when a spouse has been injured and cannot participate in sexual relations for a period of time or permanently due to the injury, or suffers from mental distress, due to a defendant's wrongdoing, which interferes with usual sexual activity." Thus, the uninjured spouse... joins in the injured mate's lawsuit against the person who injured the spouse. http://legal-dictionary.thefreedictionary.com/loss+of+consortium

2. ALIENATION OF AFFECTION

Alienation of affection claims were brought against a third party who lured a spouse away or caused loss of affection for the spouse. Elements of the claim required: 1) Wrongful conduct by the defendant with the plaintiff's spouse; 2) Loss of affection by the spouse for the plaintiff; 3) A causal relationship between the defendant's conduct and the loss of consortium; 4) Damages (humiliation, loss of affection, mental distress).

In North Carolina, 60-year-old Cynthia Shackelford sued her husband's mistress under an alienation of affection claim. Alienation of affection allows a spouse to sue the third party who had an affair with their spouse. Shakelford claimed that their affair caused her spouse to fall out of love with her. In March 2010, the jury awarded Shackelford $5 million in compensatory damages and $4 million in punitive damages. After Shackelford became suspicious of her husband's late nights at work, suspicious credit card charges, and cell phone bills, she hired a private investigator. "She set her sights on him. She knew he was married," said Shackelford.

North Carolina had about 200 alienation of affection claims filed in 2005. Only a handful of states still allow such lawsuits. Why have the majority of states eliminated them? Perhaps it is the tenuous connection between the affair and the breakup of the marriage. The plaintiff's husband, Mr. Shackelford, 62, wrote that he had "numerous affairs going back to the first two years" of his marriage and that the couple had "significant problems in their marriage for years, including three rounds of marital counseling that failed." As for the states that still allow it, alienation of affection will probably be around for another 100 years. Recently, North Carolina's legislature debated abolishing it, but declined to do so for fear of looking like they supported adultery.[64]

Forget the mistress, can one spouse sue the other for transmission of a venereal disease during the marriage? In *Endres v. Endres* (2004–281), 180 VT 640; 912 A.2d 975 (2006), the Vermont Supreme Court overruled the lower courts' rulings dismissing a wife's claim against her husband for infecting her with the human papillomavirus (HPV) after he had an extramarital affair. Although the court did not rule on the merits of the case, it agreed to allow her to present evidence of her claims against her husband for negligence, battery, and intentional infliction of emotional distress.[65]

---

64   http://abcnews.go.com/Business/wife-wins-million-husbands-alleged-mistress/story?id=10151957#. UYcu7ErYySp, "Wife Wins $9 Million from Husband's Alleged Mistress," Alice Gomstyn, *ABC News*, March 22, 2010.
65   These cases should be distinguished from those in which a person with HIV or AIDS knowingly has unprotected sex with unaware partners. In Montgomery County, Maryland, a man was sentenced to 18 months in jail for two counts of reckless endangerment for such behavior (charges of knowingly transferring HIV were dropped in a plea deal). On two occasions, the 28-year-old man met a woman in a bar and did not tell her that he had HIV before having unprotected sex with her. In one case, before they had sex he asked the women if she was on birth control and she asked him if he had any STDs; he said no. Maryland law makes it a crime to knowingly transfer or try to transfer HIV, but not other STDs such as herpes, gonorrhea, or syphilis (but the deliberate or reckless transmission of these diseases can result in charges of assault or aggravated assault.) "Judge orders jail in HIV cases, Dan Morse, *The Washington Post*, March 31, 2015, P. B1. In 2014 a minister in Alabama was forced to resign when he "confessed to having sex with church members and neglecting to tell them he had AIDS. As part of his confession, "He confessed to "having sex with

In conclusion, while vestiges of the common law fiction of oneness still linger in the legal system, the courts and the law are slowly chipping away at it. The federal courts did so in the husband and wife privilege, although shockingly late. Not until the 1980s did criminal courts begin to do so on issues of physical crimes, like rape, committed by husbands against their wives. Without all states pursuing these cases more aggressively, there is still much work to do. Similarly, in the area of personal property theft by a husband of a wife's property, the courts still do not intervene unless the couple is already living separately. While many argue that equal protection has eliminated legal burdens for women, surprisingly, in this new millennium, the law still has far to go to abolish the effects of marriage on women.

MEDICAL DECISION MAKING

Generally, under the law, an adult makes his or her own decision about health care treatments. When that person becomes incapacitated (either mentally or physically) and is no longer able to make those decisions, another adult must step in. Many states have natural death acts that allow a person to make decisions about medical treatment during a terminal illness in advance of becoming incompetent. By writing a legal document, a person can direct medical treatment with specifics of care (e.g., palliative care only) or may designate a surrogate to make those decisions for the person.[66] If a person fails to do so, states have a hierarchy as to who should be authorized to make those decisions. Generally, if an adult is unmarried, his/her parents (if alive) are legally authorized or a sibling if the parents are dead. If the adult is married, the spouse would be the one (even if the parties were legally separated, but not divorced). There are few decisions more personal and painful than those of a medical nature, and rightfully, the law generally allows families to decide them in a private way. But what happens if the family does not agree? Should the courts intervene and make the decision for them? If so, which court should have jurisdiction: federal or state? Is this ever a matter for more intense government intervention?

The Florida case of Terri Schiavo looks at this difficult issue and provides some answers. After she collapsed on her bathroom floor and was unable to be revived by medical personnel, Schiavo remained on life support for eight years in what doctors had determined was a persistent vegetative state until her husband decided to remove her feeding tube, which would end her life. Without any documentation from her, such as a medical directive or living will, under Florida law, Michael Schiavo, her husband, was legally authorized to make a treatment decision. He later testified that in conversations with Terri during their marriage, she told him that she would not want to be kept alive artificially. Terri's parents did not want the feeding tube removed and fought

---

church members in the church building, but not in the sanctuary". "Minister barred from church in sex scandal", *The Washington Post Digest*, October 17, 2014, P. A2.

66   This is different than laws granting the right to die (also called assisted suicide) which exist in less than a handful of states, including Oregon. In 2015, 29-year old Brittany Maynard who suffered from terminal brain cancer shed light on the issue when she moved to Oregon to use its laws. She very publically announced her intention to die with dignity.

his efforts. After a judge ordered the tube removed, a legal struggle between the parents and the husband ensued. Throughout the fight, the parents made allegations of abuse, conflicts of interest, and even attempted to act on behalf of their daughter to obtain a divorce. In October 2003 a Florida judge, saying there was no hope of recovery, ordered the tube removed again.

Then Florida governor Jeb Bush signed "Terri's law," allowing the governor to have the tube reinserted. The Florida Supreme Court struck down that law, finding that Governor Bush exceeded his authority. After the Florida State Supreme Court refused to hear Governor Bush's appeal, the tube was again ordered removed. Two days later, the United States Congress and President George Bush became involved. Called by the media the "Easter Miracle," on March 2005, at about midnight, Congress passed a law requiring the federal courts to review the case *de novo* (without deference/regard to the Florida state court rulings or record). President George Bush signed it into law in the late-night hours. The 11th Circuit Court of Appeals (federal) invalidated the law and called the actions of Congress improper, and in a "manner demonstrably at odds with the Founding Fathers' blueprint for the governance of a free people" (the Constitution).[67]

The Schiavo case attracted a lot of celebrity interest. Consumer advocate Ralph Nader opined that "we don't allow dogs to be starved" and the Reverend Jesse Jackson came in a white stretch limousine to visit Ms. Schiavo in hospice. Even then senator Barack Obama voted in support of the law, which he later acknowledged was a mistake in a presidential debate with Hillary Rodham Clinton.

Contrast this case to a matter in Northern Virginia when a woman who died from a stroke while she was pregnant was kept alive after being pronounced clinically dead by a joint decision of her husband and her parents.[68] Although she was kept artificially alive to serve as surrogate for the unborn child, the child died shortly after its birth.[69]

The inability of committed same-sex couples to make medical decisions for each other is one of the arguments in favor of marriage equality as the case of *In re Guardanship of Atkins* case illustrates.[70] In this case, two men met at college and were in a "committed and loving relationship" for 25 years until one of the partners became incapacitated and eventually had a stroke. His parents objected to their relationship and his mother said, "no amount of evidence could convince her that Patrick and Brett were happy together or that they had a positive and beneficial relationship." When the other partner attempted to visit the hospital (or even telephone), the

---

67   http://www.sptimes.com/2005/03/31/Tampabay/From_ordinary_girl_to.shtml, Obituary of Terri Schiavo, "From ordinary girl to international icon," Kelly Benham, *St. Petersburg Times*, March 31, 2005.

68   http://usatoday30.usatoday.com/news/nation/2005-06-15-saving-baby-cover_x.htm, "Woman kept alive in hopes of saving baby," Richard Willing, *USA Today*, June 25, 2005.

69   Compare this to the Supreme Court of Rhode Island's decision in *In re Doe*, 533 A.2d 523 (R.I.1987), as to whether an incompetent person could exercise her right to decide whether or not to have an abortion. Relying on other jurisdictions' doctrine, which allows a judge to try to determine what the incompetent's decision would have been had she been competent, it upheld the trial court's determination that the incompetent young woman would have decided to terminate her pregnancy. Id. at 526–27.

70   868 N.E. 2d 878 (Ind. App 2007)

parents prevented it and moved for guardianship of their son, which was granted. The other partner requested visitation from the court in order to visit. While the lower court denied his request because it was opposed by his parents, who were legally the ones to make decisions, the appellate court recognized the value of their relationship and allowed the visitation. If they were allowed to marry in Indiana at that time, medical decisions (and financial ones) would have been made by his spouse.

CHAPTER SOURCES

Wadlington, W., and R. C. O'Brien. (2007). *Domestic Relations*, 6th ed. Foundation Press. Weisberg, D. Kelly. (2011). *Emanuel Law Outlines*, Family Law.

DIVORCE

The only thing more unthinkable than leaving was staying; the only thing more impossible than staying was leaving. I didn't want to destroy anything or anybody. I just wanted to slip quietly out the back door, without causing any fuss or consequences, and then not stop running until I reached Greenland.
—Elizabeth Gilbert, *Eat, Pray, Love*

When I meet a man I ask myself, "Is this the man I want my children to spend their weekends with?"
—Rita Rudner [1]

MATRIMONIAL BREAKDOWN

"Is divorce contagious?" A 2010 research study indicated that it might be in close social groups. "Think of getting divorced like a virus, because it spreads in more or less the same way."[2] "Being friends with someone who gets divorced makes someone 147 percent more likely to get divorced themselves. A person who has a sibling who gets divorced is 22 percent more likely to also split from his spouse."[3] This results from the change of the social group's perception of divorce as a stigma to the possibility of an appropriate option. Some argue that the law's change to a "no fault" system of divorce may encourage this perception.

After remaining static for decades, divorce laws in the United States have changed dramatically over the past 30 years. Going from a public policy that discouraged divorce under fault-based

---

1   www.brainyquote.com/quotes/quotes/r/ritarudner122726.htm
2   Quoting University of California, San Diego professor James Fowler on "Good Morning America," "Is Divorce Contagious? How you can Beat the Bug," Jay Shaylor, ABCNews, July 20, 2010 http://abcnews.go.com/GMA/HealthyLiving/divorce-contagious/story?id=11198347
3   Ibid.

grounds for divorce to the current "no-fault" system, current laws on dissolving a marriage may have revolutionized society's thoughts on marital commitment. Now, a small movement to resist that revolution is starting to take hold in some states.

After the Revolution, as our newly formed country began to deal with the reality of failing marriages, no laws were yet established. Rather than use this historic opportunity to create new laws on divorce, the colonial civil courts borrowed from European and English ecclesiastical courts' common law, which treated marriage as an indivisible bond before God. As a result, divorce was viewed as against public policy. Later, divorce was allowed by court order, but only upon proof of a spouse's marital fault. Thus, states began to recognize limited "fault"-based grounds for divorce. Even if both spouses wanted a divorce, they still had to prove to a judge's satisfaction that one of them committed the necessary marital fault to obtain the divorce.

Because each state chooses the marital misdeeds that trigger a divorce (which reflect the communities' morals), the list can be extensive. The law requires that "grounds" (reasons prescribed by law) for divorce must exist and be proven to the court, even if the husband and wife agree that a marriage should end. States began to adopt their own fault-based grounds for divorce, sometimes with lengthy specific listings, ranging from habitual alcoholism to impotence. In New York, for example, you can file for divorce if your spouse goes to jail for three or more years—but, if your spouse was released more than five years ago, you cannot. Some states, like Tennessee, still have a lengthy list of fault-based grounds (including indignities that make the spouse's life intolerable).[4] Illinois allows divorce for a spouse infected with a sexually transmitted disease.[5] Virginia and West Virginia specifically include "adultery or sodomy outside of marriage" as a ground for divorce.[6] West Virginia still includes the grounds of buggery and a "false accusation of adultery or homosexuality,"[7] and New Jersey describes the fault as "deviant sexual conduct."[8] Despite the state-by-state variety, as the states were creating their divorce standards, all states generally adopted three major fault-based grounds: 1) adultery; 2) cruelty; and 3) desertion/abandonment.

A. Adultery

Probably based on the Ten Commandments, given the ecclesiastical (church) based background of American divorce, it is not surprising that adultery was and continues to be on most states' lists as a marital misbehavior worthy of divorce. While many states retain it as separate grounds for divorce, it currently only accounts for a small number of the total divorces granted. This is somewhat ironic, given the high incidences of reports of adultery in marriages today. In some states, an adulterous affair during the divorce process can be grounds for a fault-based divorce.

---

4   Sections 36-4-101-3 of the Tennessee Code.
5   750 Illinois Complied Statutes—Chapter 5—Section 401.
6   Virginia Code—Title 20—Sections: 20–91.
7   West Virginia Code—Sections: 48-5-202 and 48-5-209.
8   New Jersey Statutes—Title 2 A—Chapters: 34–2.

Generally, the legal definition of **adultery** is when a married person has voluntary sexual intercourse with another person who is not his or her own spouse.[9] Defining adultery is generally easy; proof of adultery, however, can be much more difficult. In the old days, proving adultery may have been easy when it involved the wife becoming pregnant while the husband had no access to her (e.g., away in the military or on a sailing ship). Otherwise, the courts required a witness or proof of the opportunity to commit the act with another or "having the disposition" to do it; pictures of kissing or handholding in public may suffice. Still, corroboration of the testimony of a spouse is often necessary to prove adultery and friends or neighbors may be called as witnesses. Courts often had strict standards for a spouse to prove adultery as it could impact the amount of financial support provided after the divorce.

The use of adultery as a fault-based ground for divorce was much more common in 20th-century divorce litigation. Cases often involved photographs taken by a private detective of the husband exiting a hotel room (from a door with a number on it) on the arm of a woman in a negligee—thus creating the evidence of the disposition. In a system that required one innocent party in divorce, historians estimate that in many consensual divorce cases, whether through their attorneys or alone, the couples would agree on which fault to claim in order to end their marriage.

B. Cruelty

The second most common ground for fault-based divorce was **cruelty**. Unlike adultery, cruelty was complex to define. In South Dakota, extreme cruelty is defined as the infliction of grievous bodily injury or grievous mental suffering upon one party to the marriage.[10] A modern view of cruelty requires bodily harm or reasonable apprehension of it, which endangers life, limb, or health, and renders the couple living together as a unsafe or improper. Are words alone sufficient? Generally, it must be much more than "not getting along" or incompatibility. Some states may place limitations on the acts. For example, in New York, the acts must be within the past five years. Is a single act sufficient to meet the standard? Generally, the courts say "no." What if it involves an outrageous act of extreme brutality—such as attempted murder?

Sex can be a big factor in proving cruelty during fault-based divorce litigation because sex has such a significant role in marriage under the law. Courts vary, however, on whether acts of unreasonable demands for sexual intercourse,[11] refusing to have sex, or embarrassingly false accusations of sexual infidelity amount to cruelty. Despite its many definitions, many states rightfully continue to include cruelty as grounds for no-fault divorce.

---

9   E.g., Maryland Code Family Law Section 7-103.
10   South Dakota Laws—Volume 9A—Title 25, Chapters 4-2-18.
11   Under the Tennessee divorce statute, what do indignities that make the spouse's life intolerable include? See, Sections 36-4-101-3 of the Tennessee Code.

C. Desertion/Abandonment

Desertion or abandonment has also been a traditional ground for fault-based divorce that continues in many states. While many have heard of the father who says he is "going for a gallon of milk" and is never seen again, the legal definition of abandonment has several requirements. It requires both the act of leaving plus intention to abandon.

Abandonment:

1. voluntary separation by one spouse from the other;
2. with the intent not to resume marital cohabitation;
3. without consent of the other spouse;
4. without justification; and
5. for a specific period of time.

Generally, state laws on desertion require the spouse to be gone from one to five years. It must be uninterrupted and the other spouse must have wanted the missing spouse to return. Would a person leaving who has been abused by her spouse be considered abandonment? No; there is justification for the behavior.

Constructive Abandonment

Maryland and some other states have recognized **constructive desertion** as a ground for no-fault divorce. Under this doctrine, one spouse's conduct must be so intolerable toward the other that they feel forced to leave the marital home. Constructive abandonment differs from abandonment because the leaving spouse does so as a result of the remaining spouse's actions. Originally, this fault-based ground for divorce was created by the courts for when cruelty was not available or required proof of serious physical harm. Recently, Virginia changed its law stating constructive abandonment can occur without the spouse leaving the home. In Maryland, having an affair with a same-sex partner (not within the definition of adultery) could be constructive abandonment.

Because marital relations are such an important part of civil marriage under the law, the refusal to engage in marital sex (without justification) may constitute constructive desertion. In *Handshoe v. Handshoe*, 560 Sp. 2d 182 (Miss 1990), the spouses admitted to not having sex (together) for 12 years upon the wife's insistence. The couple disagreed as to why. The wife blamed the truck-driving husband who had long absences from the home. "Mrs. Handshoe then moved Mr. Handshoe out of the master bedroom, and later she gave all his clothes away to Goodwill." He claimed that he worked to keep the marriage together. When the husband sued for divorce, each made claims of constructive desertion. The court found for the husband and granted the divorce. Contrast this to *Davis v. Davis*, 889 NYS.2d 611 (NY App. Div. 2009), where the wife did not allege absence of conjugal relations, but the husband would not celebrate holidays with her (e.g., Valentine's Day, Thanksgiving, her birthday), refused to go to the "movies, shopping, restaurants, and church services, once left her at the emergency room, removed her belongings from the marital bedroom and otherwise ignored her." The court would not recognize her claim of "social abandonment." Should social abandonment in a marriage be enough for a divorce?

INSANITY

Insanity can be both a ground for[12] and a defense to divorce.[13] Typically, when states include it as a ground for divorce, they require it to be "incurable." Others specify that the spouse must be confined to an institution for the mentally ill or be certified insane by a certain number of doctors. Generally, the state statute sets a length of time the spouse must have been insane, with the average length of time between three to five years. Today, some states use insanity as the **only** grounds for fault-based divorce. Insanity is a double-edged sword, however, because some states preclude divorce if one of the spouses is insane.

DEFENSES TO FAULT GROUNDS FOR DIVORCE

In order to obtain a fault-based divorce, the spouse has to prove:
1. corroboration—(including pictures/witness accounts);
2. an innocent party (who committed no marital fault);
3. no defense by the respondent mitigating or equalizing the fault of the other party.

Under the basic fault approach, only an innocent party could obtain a divorce based on the fault of the other spouse. If the petitioner was also at fault, no divorce could be granted. The defenses allowed the spouse accused of the fault grounds to challenge the innocence of the other spouse. If successful, the court would deny the divorce request. Thus, defenses would be a strong weapon in thwarting a spouse's attempt at divorce. Why would a spouse choose to defend against a divorce knowing that, at least as far as the other spouse is concerned, the marriage is over? Perhaps it was for love or the courts' attribution of a spouse's fault/non-fault in awarding property and alimony.

---

12 In the 1960s, 29 states recognized insanity as a fault base for divorce, with the time frame varying by state (viz., generally, the prior three to five years.) *Washington and Lee Law Review*, Vol. 18 [1961], Iss. 2, Art. 18 FN 29, page 328 (http://scholarlycommons.law.wlu.edu/wlulr/vol18/iss2/18,).
13 What about a spouse who commits adultery while insane? Under the M'Naghten rule used in homicide cases, it would seem that the fault-based culpability required for adultery should be negated by the mental incompetency. For a lengthy discussion of this issue, see "Insanity as a Defense or Ground of Divorce," *Washington and Lee Law Review*, September 1, 1961; but an older court, concerned about the possibility that a husband might have to raise a child created from the relationship, denied it as a defense. The court based its ruling excluding insanity defenses from adultery charges on the moral seriousness of the adultery charge and the thought that an innocent husband might be forced to accept the offspring resulting from such immoral conduct. This rule was criticized by other jurisdictions and later ignored. *Manley v. Manley*, 47 Pa. D. & C.2d 164 (Del. Co. 1950).

The defenses a spouse could raise against an allegation of marital fault for a fault-based divorce include the four most common:

1. recrimination;
2. connivance;
3. collusion; and
4. condonation.

Reconciliation, similar to condonation, was a less common defense.

A. Recrimination

Recrimination is a defense in a fault-based divorce when the party requesting the divorce has committed an equally egregious offense. Thus, there is no innocent party; both parties are at fault. In most states, any recognized fault-based marital misconduct by the spouse filing for divorce can be used as a defense by the other spouse to preclude a divorce. While New Jersey recently abolished this defense, in some states, recrimination only applies in adultery allegations (in which both spouses committed adultery).

B. Condonation

Condonation is the conditional forgiveness by one spouse of the other spouse's marital offense that otherwise could be used as grounds for divorce. Generally, it requires the resumption or continuation of marital cohabitation to imply forgiveness on the part of the non-offending spouse. For example, a wife discovers her husband's adultery, but after candy, flowers, and much begging for forgiveness, she forgives (and sleeps with) him. This would bar her from alleging adultery in a later divorce action. If, however, the husband has an affair again, it serves as a new ground for divorce. Why do some states say that the act of sexual relations alone does not show condonation? It is just an effort to "save the marriage."

In the case of *Edwards v. Edwards*, 501 S.W.2d 283 (1973), after a husband returned home to find another man "leaving his home putting his clothes on; that, at this time, [his wife] stated that she loved [the other man] and he loved her, but promised that she would not see or talk to him again," the court considers the wife's defense of condonation to the adultery charge in the divorce case.

EDWARDS V. EDWARDS
501 S.W. 2ND 283 (1973)

TODD, Judge.

The defendant, Ruby Louise Hulsey Edwards, has appealed from a decree awarding 286*286 a divorce to her husband, the plaintiff, William Eugene Edwards, granting to said husband the care, custody and control of the three minor children of the parties, divesting out of the defendant and vesting in the plaintiff all of the joint property of the parties.

On October 11, 1972, plaintiff filed his petition for divorce, charging adultery and cruel and inhuman treatment.

On October 13, 1972, defendant filed an original petition for divorce charging cruel and inhuman treatment.

On October 28, 1972, defendant filed her answer to plaintiff's petition requesting that her original petition, supra, be considered a counter complaint.

No answer was ever filed to the original petition of defendant.

The final decree, entered on January 2, 1973, reflects that the cause was heard on December 28, 1972,—"… upon the original petition, the answer and cross-petition and answer thereto, the proof in open court, exhibits to the pleadings, argument of counsel, and the entire record in this cause, from all of which it appears to the satisfaction of the Court that the allegations contained in the original bill as to cruel and inhuman treatment have been sustained by the proof, that the allegations contained in the original bill as to adultery are not well taken and that the allegations in the cross-petition have not been sustained by the proof, and it further appearing that the original petitioner, William Eugene Edwards is, and the Defendant Ruby Edwards is not, the fit and proper person to have the care, custody and control of the minor children, Robin Renee Edwards, Phyllis Denise Edwards and Robert Allen Edwards."

Said decree granted an absolute divorce to William Eugene Edwards, together with custody of the three children with visitation rights to the mother on two Saturdays each month "at the home of her parents and provided she does not take the children to Pegram, Tennessee."

All interest of the wife in a 2.8 acre tract, household goods, auto, a truck, and a horse was divested out of her and vested in the plaintiff husband, subject to his assumption of mortgage indebtedness.

The first three assignments assert that there is no evidence to support the award of a divorce, or that the evidence preponderates against the award.

To a large degree, the evidence is uncontroverted.

The parties are a young couple with three young children, aged 3, 5, and 7. The parties resided in the community of Ridgetop, on a 2.8 acre tract given them by the father of plaintiff on which tract they had built a substantial home on which there is now a mortgage of $12,000.00. Plaintiff worked regularly at the Dupont plant in Old Hickory, and defendant worked at a garment factory in Greenbrier.

In the course of various activities related to horses, the parties became acquainted with a couple named Andy and Beth Greer, who resided at Pegram, Tennessee.

Plaintiff testified without direct contradiction that in July, 1971, he returned to his home and found Andy Greer leaving his home putting his clothes on; that, at this time, defendant stated that she loved Andy and he loved her, but promised that she would not see or talk to him again.

In August 1971, there was a severe altercation in the home, at which time defendant was slapped (according to plaintiff) or beaten (according to defendant), requiring the attention of a doctor. Plaintiff says the altercation resulted from defendant's request, "take me to Andy Greer." Defendant denies this, and insists that there was no cause for the beating except 287*287 that she had been at her parents' house and plaintiff had been taking pills which caused him to act strangely.

Subsequently, plaintiff asserts, and defendant denies that defendant admitted to regular and repeated telephone conversations with Andy Greer.

The immediate, precipitating causes of this suit occurred on October 4, 1972. Defendant testified that, a few days before October 4, Andy Greer telephoned her at her work and she agreed to meet him "to talk"; that, on October 4, 1972, she reported to work at 7:00 a.m., but shortly after 8:00 a.m. she complained of illness and was excused from work for the day; that she telephoned her sister and requested that she come and transport her to Rivergate Mall for shopping; that Andy Greer met them at Rivergate at about 9:00 a.m. and her sister agreed to return for her at 2:00 p.m.; that she (defendant) and Andy "drove around and talked" from 9:00 a.m. until 2:00 p.m. when they returned to Rivergate Mall where they found not only her sister, but also plaintiff and certain other members of the family; that, because of threatening words and gestures of plaintiff, she (defendant) and Andy Greer drove away; that they "drove around and talked" until about midnight when they went to the home of a mutual friend in Nashville where defendant was permitted to stay 2 1/2 weeks; and that she did not return to her home during said period because she was "scared."

The testimony of plaintiff and other participants in this episode of October 4, 1972, simply affirms, from their various points of view, the foregoing details given by defendant.

On said date, the three children were taken to the home of the parents of plaintiff where they have remained, except for visitation permitted by the Trial Court.

In the Trial Court, and in this Court, defendant has insisted **that the July, 1971, incident involving Andy Greer at the home of the parties should not be considered because of intervening cohabitation and the plea of condonation. Such plea is effective as to the charge of adultery**, but said incident forms an integral part of the background of subsequent events which are alleged to constitute cruel and inhuman treatment.

Defendant insists:

> "... it would appear that the only incriminating evidence presented by the appellee is his statement that his wife had stated to him that she was in love with a certain Andy Greer, and that on one occasion, with no provocation or reason whatsoever, she stated that she wanted to go down to Mr. Greer's home, all of which was totally and completely unbelievable, particularly in view of the many discrepancies in appellee's testimony. The only other incriminating evidence presented at the trial of this cause, was the appellee's testimony that he saw his wife in the truck of a certain Andy Greer at a shopping center in the middle of the afternoon in Davidson County, Tennessee, none of which could possibly constitute any legal grounds for divorce on the basis of cruel and inhuman treatment."

It is probably true that a wife's unexplained presence in a vehicle with another man on a single occasion would not be grounds for divorce. However, accepting as true all of the testimony of plaintiff, that man was the same man who had been seen leaving plaintiff's home putting on his clothes, whom defendant had promised never to see or talk to again, and with whom defendant admitted regular telephone conversations. Additionally, under plaintiff's version of the facts, the prolonged absence from home, following the October 4, 1972 incident, was not justified by any wrongful acts on his part and produced severe and sustained anxiety on the part of plaintiff and the children.

This is not among the strongest cases for divorce but, this Court cannot say that 288*288 the facts alleged and proven do not constitute grounds for divorce or that the evidence preponderates against the conclusions of fact reached by the Trial Judge.

It is true that defendant offered impressive evidence of abusive treatment of her by the plaintiff. Some, he admitted in part, but this he attempted to justify or excuse by the conduct of defendant which she denied.

What does the *Edwards* court's recognition of a cruelty based marital fault against the wife (even when the parties agree that the husband had hit her) say about Tennessee's view of adultery?

C. Collusion

Collusion is when there is an agreement between spouses, who both want the divorce (but have not committed fault-based behavior to get one), that one of the spouses will charge the other with a marital offense while the other will not defend against it. In an effort to end their marriage, both spouses intentionally agree to create the story of the fault behavior. Sometimes, the spouses would actually act out the behavior after agreement, in order to show the necessary grounds. Collusion amounts to a fraud on the court.

D. Connivance

Connivance is when one spouse, with a corrupt intent, consents to the other spouse's commission of a marital offense that is a ground for a fault-based divorce. Generally, it is used in adultery-based divorce actions. An example is when spouses are in an open marriage and one spouse gives the other permission to commit adultery. That behavior cannot be used as fault grounds in a divorce because the spouse was not "at fault." Connivance is different from collusion because, even though both spouses agree to the wrongdoing, the spouses did not agree that the goal was a divorce.

RECONCILIATION

Similar to condonation, **reconciliation** is a defense that involves forgiveness by the spouse who filed for divorce. It is loosely used to describe any forgiveness that leads to resumption of the marriage relationship. While it is often used interchangeably with condonation to refer to actions that occurred before the divorce was filed, reconciliation more often involves conduct that happened after the divorce was filed and before it became final. Many use it to mean the spouses "kissed and made up."

What is the result if a spouse successfully uses a defense to a requested divorce? It results in the court denying the divorce case and at least one spouse, who does not want to be married, being forced to remain in the marriage. This could lead to more power imbalances in fault-based divorces if the spouse wanting a divorce negotiates deferentially to the other spouse in order to get it.

Not only does a fault-based system determine who can obtain a divorce, but the courts often use it in making financial determinations in the case. In adultery cases, as discussed above, courts punished offending spouses by requiring more support payments and, in effect, made restitution to the offended spouses by providing greater financial support or property distribution. Does a fault-based system encourage courts to be punitive, and is that appropriate for noncriminal divorce actions? Should fault impact custody determinations or amounts of child support awarded?

"NO-FAULT" DIVORCE

As demonstrated in the *Edwards v. Edwards* case, a successful defense can prevent the award of a fault-based divorce request. In a case where both parties are equally at fault, should the court's solution be to deny the divorce? While this did reinforce the original public policy, to discourage divorce, does it keep with modern feelings on marriage being about love? If the love is lost, should this be enough to get a divorce? Also, is it the job of a judge to hear all of the marital dirty laundry? Should the government pass judgment on marital habits if there are no threats or violence? Is this healthy for spouses; for their children?

Unhappy spouses did not think so. It is believed that a large portion of fault-based divorces were "cooked up" by the spouses to ensure they would be granted legal marital dissolution. In effecting a fraud on the courts, the spouses would either fabricate grounds for divorce (e.g., agreeing that the husband would admit to an adultery) or agree not to raise a valid defense to such allegation. Or the spouses would work with their attorneys to determine which fault-based grounds would most easily give them the divorce they desired.

In an effort to avoid this harsh effect and get out of the divorce business of reviewing couples' behavior, California, in the 1950s, developed the doctrine of comparative rectitude. Under this theory, courts would still hear the allegations of marital misbehavior, but instead of requiring an innocent party they would weigh the alleged misbehavior and award the divorce to the "less guilty" spouse if both were at fault. This led some states to start ranking the severity of marital faults in a hierarchy where certain faults outweighed "lesser" ones.[14]

California's comparative rectitude doctrine, however, still required the courts to actively evaluate the most personal aspects of a marriage. In an effort to avoid this "daytime talk show–like" behavior, the state decided to totally revamp its divorce system. In 1969, California proposed what is commonly referred to as "no-fault" divorce.[15] It allowed divorces without requiring the parties to demonstrate marital fault. No-fault also eliminated the need for defenses to divorce.

This was an unusual step, by a state to make such a drastic revision of hundreds of years of American divorce law. As previously discussed, family law has been slow to modernize; usually society has changed long before the courts catch up. When California reviewed divorce, it totally revised it, including name changes. California proposed renaming divorce "marital dissolution." Next, it removed the element of marital fault. Using the terminology of "irreconcilable differences," it empowered the spouses to demonstrate their desire for a divorce that would be respected by the courts.

In essence, in "no-fault" divorce courts acknowledge that when spouses were recognized as legally mature to make the decision to wed, they should also be able to determine when the marriage is no longer functioning. Today, all states allow no-fault divorce (many still retain the fault-based option too.) States vary as to the term associated with it, be it California's "irretrievable breakdown," "irreconcilable differences," or incompatibility. Both parties can agree to this state of their marriage or just one party. Generally, if one spouse wants a divorce he will be able to obtain it—it just may take some time (see below). By making these allegations to the courts, in essence, it means that the marriage is not functioning and that the parties do not believe in the future, it will ever do so. In addition to empowering the participants, the no fault system eliminates the need for emotionally harmful and expensive litigation.

---

14   The spouses had to be careful because, if, before the divorce was finalized one spouse decided not to honor the "agreement," the spouse could raise collusion as a defense, thus stopping the divorce (and, one would think, the careers of the participating attorneys).

15   While considered revolutionary in American family law, the idea of no fault divorce had been used in France after its revolution overthrowing the monarchy. Liberte, based on ideas of equality for all, allowed a system of divorce based on request. Only when Napoleon created his French Empire did the system return to disallowing divorce. It took France until the 1970s to begin to implementing a divorce system again.

SEPARATION

Under the fault-based system, divorce was immediate; there was no waiting period in order to obtain a divorce other than how long it took the case to grind through the heavily burdened divorce court. Under "no-fault," however, most states require a "separation" period before the court will grant the divorce. Perhaps in an effort to "quantify" divorce requests, most states have a provision that allows spouses who separate for a state specified period of time to obtain a divorce based on that passage of time. Once the spouses give testimony that they have been separated for the required period, the divorce court can dissolve their marriage via court order. Some states may require that a legal (court filed/ordered) separation agreement be on file to start the period. Certainly, the spouse must have the intention to leave the marriage in order to begin the separation period and the other spouse should be aware of this.

The length of the separation periods vary and sometimes depend on circumstances. Some states have a shorter separation period if both spouses agree to divorce. In some states, the separation period is six months, if uncontested and no children, or a year if they have children. In California, the length of the marriage may also impact the separation period; so marriages of short duration (less than five years), without children, have a more summary dissolution. Many state statutes require less than 18 months of separation (e.g., Uniform Marriage and Divorce Act). Is that long enough for the spouses to determine if they are making the right decision and cannot live as a married couple any longer? In 2011, Maryland modified its separation period from two years in a contested divorce (when one spouse does not want the divorce), to one year. Is this a good idea?

What does living apart and/or separation mean? In some states, this means the spouses must have separate living accommodations. In others, it means they can live under "the same roof" if they do not have sex. In Kentucky and the District of Columbia, it is alright for the separating spouses to live under the same roof if the spouses do not share bed or food. Is the purpose of the law effectuated if the spouses live under the same roof, but have separate lives (separate bedrooms, no cooking or eating meals together)? As the economy went into recession, this option was increasingly considered.

Finally, as discussed before, because of the legal importance of sexual relations in marriage, what is the effect of the spouses' continued sexual relationship with each other during the separation period? Many states (including Maryland) affirm that sexual intercourse restarts the separation period. Does this discourage attempts at reconciliation? In Delaware, "temporarily sleeping in the same bedroom and resumption of sexual relations" does not toll the separation period as long as the spouses have not "occupied the same bedroom or had sexual relations with each other within the 30-day period immediately preceding the filing date."[16] Which is better?

---

16 Delaware Code—Title 13—Chapters: 1505.

EFFECTS OF MARITAL TORTS

Marital torts include spousal transmission of a venereal disease, sexual assault, false imprisonment, infliction of emotional distress, and wiretapping without knowledge or consent. If a spouse has such a claim, should they be allowed to raise it during divorce? What would be the effect? Would the compensation received, if the claim was successful, be in addition to a share of marital assets or affect that distribution? Would it be better to try the case outside of the divorce action or is that a waste of the court's resources? Finally, is a family court judge the correct judge to decide a tort case?

Given the outrageous nature of these actions, it is hard to understand how courts might dismiss them as part of the husband and wife relationship, but still the fiction of oneness (see Chapter 10) survives. In *Twyman v. Twyman* the Texas Supreme Court looked at some of these issues in a claim for infliction of emotional distress based on a husband's demands for bondage sex.

TWYMAN V. TWYMAN
855 S.W.2D 619, 61 USLW 2748
(TX SCT 1993)

Wife filed suit for divorce and for infliction of emotional distress. The 353rd District Court, Travis County, B. F. Coker, J., held for wife, and husband appealed. The Austin Court of Appeals, 790 S.W.2d 819, Gammage, J., affirmed, and further appeal was taken. The Supreme Court, Cornyn, J., held that: (1) although there is no cause of action for negligent infliction of emotional distress, tort of intentional infliction of emotional distress is recognized, and (2) such claim can be brought in divorce proceeding.
Reversed and remanded.

OPINION
CORNYN, Justice.

In this case we decide whether a claim for infliction of emotional distress can be brought in a divorce proceeding. Because the judgment of the court of appeals is based on negligent infliction of emotional distress, and cannot be affirmed on that or any other basis, we reverse the judgment of that court and remand this cause for a new trial in the interest of justice. Tex.R.App.P. 180. We deem a new trial appropriate because of our recent decision that no cause of action for negligent infliction of emotional distress exists in Texas. Today, however, we expressly adopt the tort of intentional infliction of emotional distress, and hold that such a claim can be brought in a divorce proceeding.

I.

Sheila and William Twyman married in 1969. Sheila filed for divorce in 1985. She later amended her divorce petition to add a general claim for emotional harm without specifying whether the claim was based on negligent or intentional infliction of emotional distress. In her amended petition, Sheila alleged that William "intentionally and cruelly" attempted to engage her in "deviate sexual acts." FN1 Following a bench trial, the court rendered judgment dissolving the marriage, dividing the marital estate, awarding conservatorship of the children to Sheila, ordering William to pay child support, and awarding Sheila $15,000 plus interest for her claim for emotional distress. William appealed that portion of the judgment based on emotional distress, contending that interspousal tort immunity precluded Sheila's recovery for negligent infliction of emotional distress. The court of appeals affirmed the judgment, holding that Sheila could recover for William's negligent*621 infliction of emotional distress. 790 S.W.2d 819.

FN1. At trial, Sheila testified that William pursued sadomasochistic bondage activities with her, even though he knew that she feared such activities because she had been raped at knife-point before their marriage. The trial court found that William "attempted to emotionally coerce [Sheila] in 'bondage' on an ongoing basis..." and "engaged in a continuing course of conduct of attempting to coerce her to join in his practices of 'bondage' by continually asserting that their marriage could be saved only by [Sheila] participating with him in his practices of 'bondage.'" *[Discussion on the tort of intentional infliction of emotional distress.]...*

II.

We now consider whether the cause of action for intentional infliction of emotional distress may be brought in a divorce proceeding. FN13 In Bounds v. Caudle, this court unanimously abolished the doctrine of interspousal immunity for intentional torts. 560 S.W.2d 925 (Tex.1977). Ten years later, we abrogated interspousal immunity "completely as to any cause of action," FN14 including negligence actions for personal injuries. *Price v. Price*, 732 S.W.2d 316, 319 (Tex.1987). Under the rules established in *Caudle and Price*, there appears to be no legal impediment to bringing a tort claim in a divorce action based on either negligence or an intentional act such as assault or battery....

FN14. CHIEF JUSTICE PHILLIPS' statement that "all conduct actionable between strangers is [not] automatically actionable between spouses" cannot be reconciled with this language. See 855 S.W.2d at 627 (Phillips, C.J., dissenting).

The more difficult issue is when the tort claim must be brought and how the tort award should be considered when making a "just and right" division of the marital estate. See Tex.Fam.Code§ 3.63(b). Of the states that have answered this question, several have held that the tort case and the divorce case must be litigated separately. See e.g. *Walther v. Walther*, 709 P.2d 387, 388 (Utah 1985); *Windauer v.*

O'Connor, 107 Ariz. 267, 485 P.2d 1157 (1971); *Simmons v. Simmons,* 773 P.2d 602, 605 (Colo.Ct.App.1988). Other states require joinder of the two actions. See, e.g. *Tevis v. Tevis,* 79 N.J. 422, 400 A.2d 1189, 1196 (1979); Weil v. Lammon, 503 So.2d 830, 832 (Ala.1987).

We believe that the best approach lies between these two extremes. As in other civil actions, joinder of the tort cause of action should be permitted, FN16 but subject to the principles of res judicata. FN17 See *625 *Barr v. The Resolution Trust Corp.,* 837 S.W.2d 627, 631 (Tex.1992) (reaffirming the transactional approach to res judicata analysis). See also Tex.R.Civ.P. 51; *Henriksen v. Cameron,* 622 A.2d 1135 (Me.1993). Of course, how such claims are ultimately tried is within the sound discretion of the trial court. See Tex.R.Civ.P. 174. But joinder of tort claims with the divorce, when feasible, is encouraged. Resolving both the tort and divorce actions in the same proceeding avoids two trials based at least in part on the same facts, and settles in one suit "all matters existing between the parties." FN18 Mogford, 616 S.W.2d at 940 (citing *Parkhill* Produce *Co. v. Pecos Valley S. Ry.,* 348 S.W.2d 208, 209 (Tex. Civ.App.—San Antonio 1961) writ ref'd n.r.e. per curiam, 163 Tex. 88, 352 S.W.2d 723 (1961)). (FN 16–18)

When a tort action is tried with the divorce, however, it is imperative that the court avoid awarding a double recovery. FN19 When dividing the marital estate, the court may take into account several factors, including the fault of the parties if pleaded. See *Murff v. Murff,* 615 S.W.2d 696, 699 (Tex.1981). The trial court may also consider "such factors as the spouses' capacities and abilities, benefits which the party not at fault would have derived from continuation of the marriage, business opportunities, education, relative physical conditions, relative financial condition and obligations, disparity of ages, size of separate estates, and the nature to the property." Id. See also *Young v. Young,* 609 S.W.2d 758, 761 (Tex.1980); *Bell v. Bell,* 513 S.W.2d 20, 22

(Tex.1974). However, a spouse should not be allowed to recover tort damages and a disproportionate division of the community estate based on the same conduct. Therefore, when a factfinder awards tort damages to a divorcing spouse, the court may not consider the same tortious acts when dividing the marital estate. Contrary to CHIEF JUSTICE PHILLIPS' contention, an award for tortious conduct does not replace an analysis of the remaining factors to be considered when the trial court divides the marital estate. 855 S.W.2d at 626 (Phillips, C.J., dissenting). The court may still award a disproportionate division of property for reasons other than the tortious conduct. To avoid the potential problem of double recovery, the factfinder should consider the damages awarded in the tort action when dividing the parties' property. If a jury is used to render an advisory division of the parties' estate, the judge should limit, by appropriate instruction, the jury's consideration of the alleged tortious acts and later consider the award of damages in determining a just and right division of the marital estate. FN20 *[Footnotes 19–21 omitted.]...*

After considering the pleadings, the evidence, and the arguments of the attorneys, the Court finds the facts and law support judgment for Petition [sic] in her tort for negligent infliction of emotional distress upon Petitioner.

Additionally, the trial court made a disproportionate property division based on William's cruel treatment and adultery. It appears that such an award may allow Sheila a double recovery based on the same conduct. A new trial conducted in accordance with the principles announced in this decision should rectify this problem.

GONZALEZ, Justice, concurring.

What happened to Sheila Twyman in this case involves grossly offensive conduct which warrants judicial relief and the length of time it took this Court to decide this case is regrettable. However, the actions of William Twyman in engaging in bondage activities with Sheila Twyman, under the rationale that such activities were necessary to the future of their marriage, were all intentional in nature. None of William Twyman's actions could be in any way described as negligent, or careless, or accidental...

PHILLIPS, Chief Justice, concurring and dissenting.

I join in the Court's recognition of the tort of intentional infliction of emotional distress. Unlike negligent infliction of emotional distress, which we rejected in *Boyles v. Kerr*, 855 S.W.2d 593 (Tex.1993), recovery for intentional infliction of emotional distress is permitted in almost every other state....

In recognizing this tort, however, I would not extend it to actions between spouses or former spouses for conduct occurring during their marriage. Although this Court has abolished interspousal immunity, *Price v. Price*, 732 S.W.2d 316 (Tex.1987); *Bounds v. Caudle*, 560 S.W.2d 925 (Tex.1977), it does not necessarily follow that all conduct actionable between strangers is automatically actionable between spouses. Several courts in other jurisdictions have expressly made such a reservation when abolishing interspousal immunity. For example, the Utah Supreme Court wrote in abolishing interspousal immunity:

The marriage relation is created by the consent of both of the parties; inherently within such relationship is the consent of both parties to physical contacts with the other, personal dealings and ways of living which would be unpermitted and in some cases unlawful as between other persons... *[Citations omitted.]* In accordance with these sentiments, I believe that a tort which is grounded solely on a duty not to inflict emotional distress should not be cognizable in the context of marriage.

Married couples share an intensely personal and intimate relationship. When discord arises, it is inevitable that the parties will suffer emotional distress, often severe. In the present case, for example, Ms. Twyman testified that she suffered "utter despair" and "fell apart" upon learning that her husband was seeing another woman. She further testified that "[t]he mental anguish was unbelievable to realize, hoping every time, when he went off to Houston, that he was just going to fly and not be with her." Yet Ms. Twyman seeks no recovery for this distress, and apparently cannot do so under Texas law. Cf. Tex.Fam.Code §§ 4.05; 4.06. In such circumstances, the fact finder is left to draw a virtually impossible distinction between recoverable and disallowed injuries.

Furthermore, recognition of this tort in the context of a divorce unnecessarily restricts the trial court's discretion in dividing the marital estate. Prior to today's opinion, the trial court could, but was not required to, consider fault in dividing the community property. See *Murff v. Murff*, 615 S.W.2d 696, 698 (Tex.1981). The court had broad discretion to weigh any fault along with other appropriate factors, such as relative financial condition, disparity of ages, and the needs of the children. *628 Id. at 698–699. Now, however, where fault takes the form of "outrageous" conduct intentionally or recklessly inflicted, it becomes a dominant factor that must be considered at the expense of the other factors. Unlike battery, fraud, or other torts resting on more objective conduct, a colorable allegation of intentional infliction of emotional distress could arguably be raised by one or both parties in most intimate relationships. FN1 As the court noted in *Chiles v. Chiles*, 779 S.W.2d 127, 131 (Tex.App.—Houston *[14th Dist.]* 1989, writ denied):

While we recognize the trial court may consider fault in the distribution of community property, we believe permitting such separate damages *[for intentional infliction of emotional distress]* in divorce actions would result in evils similar to those avoided by the legislature's abrogation of fault as a ground for divorce...

Perhaps because of these difficulties, the tort of intentional infliction of emotional distress has not been generally recognized in the marital context. Although most states, like Texas, have abolished interspousal immunity, it appears that, until today, only two state supreme courts have expressly held that intentional infliction of emotional distress may be applied to marital conduct. See *Henriksen*, supra; *Davis v. Bostick*, 282 Or. 667, 580 P.2d 544 (1978). Moreover, these two decisions do not appear to represent typical actions for the recovery of emotional distress damages. In *Henriksen*, the husband inflicted on his wife not only verbal abuse but also physical attacks, including multiple assaults and rapes. 622 A.2d at 1139. Similarly in *Bostick*, the husband broke his wife's nose, choked her, and threatened her with a loaded pistol. 580 P.2d at 545–46. To the extent that emotional distress results from a physical attack or threat of attack, it is already compensable under tort theories previously recognized in Texas. The court in Henriksen apparently recognized the risk of spurious claims in the divorce context, noting that "to protect defendants from the possibility of long and intrusive trials on meritless claims, motions for summary judgment should... be viewed sympathetically in interspousal cases." 622 A.2d at 1139. By contrast, it is far from clear that Texas' strict summary judgment standard will allow our trial courts to use this procedure in weeding out meritless or trivial claims.

I recognize that a few intermediate appellate courts have also applied the tort to spousal disputes...

Just as I join the Court's decision to recognize a tort now available in nearly every American jurisdiction, I depart from the Court's decision to extend that tort to a type of dispute where it is not generally applied in other states. I fail to understand how, lexigraphically or logically, it can be "medieval" or "archaic" to decline to adopt a position which has been expressly embraced by only two other state supreme courts. *629 855 S.W.2d at 643 (Spector, J., dissenting). I therefore would reverse the judgment of the court of appeals and render judgment that Sheila Twyman take nothing on her tort claim.

HECHT, Justice, concurring and dissenting.

The wrongful conduct for which the common law offers redress by an award of damages should be defined by standards sufficiently objective and particular to allow a reasonable assessment of the likelihood that certain behavior may be found to be culpable, and to adjudicate liability with some consistency in the various cases that arise. The tort of intentional or reckless infliction of emotional distress which the Court adopts for the first time today does not meet these standards. As proof, even the Court itself is unable to say whether the conduct complained of in this case either is, might be, or is not tortious. The fault lies in the principal element of the tort, the requirement that a defendant's conduct be outrageous. Outrageousness, like obscenity, is a very subjective, value-laden concept; what is outrageous to one may be entirely acceptable to another. To award damages on an I-know-it-when-I-see-it basis is neither principled nor practical… FN1. As Justice Potter Stewart observed concerning "hard core" pornography: "I shall not today attempt further to define the kinds of material I understand to be embraced within that shorthand description; and perhaps I could never succeed in intelligibly doing so. But I know it when I see it, and the motion picture involved in this case is not that." *Jacobellis v. Ohio*, 378 U.S. 184, 197, 84 S.Ct. 1676, 1683, 12 L.Ed.2d 793 (1964) (Stewart, J., concurring)…

In my view, intentional or reckless infliction of emotional distress is too broad a rubric to describe actionable conduct, as this case illustrates. Accordingly, I dissent from the Court's decision to remand this case for trial on such a cause of action. I concur only in the reversal of the court of appeals' judgment allowing recovery for negligent infliction of emotional distress…

The cases thus far decided have found liability only where the defendant's conduct has been extreme and outrageous. It has not been enough that the defendant has acted with an intent which is tortious or even criminal, or that he has intended to inflict emotional distress, or even that his conduct has been characterized by "malice," or a degree of aggravation which would entitle the plaintiff to punitive damages for another tort. Liability has been found only where the conduct has been so outrageous in character, and so extreme in degree, as to go beyond all possible bounds of decency, and to be regarded as atrocious, and utterly intolerable in a civilized community. Generally, the case is one in which the recitation of the facts to an average member of the community would arouse his resentment against the actor, and lead him to exclaim, "Outrageous!"

The liability clearly does not extend to mere insults, indignities, threats, annoyances, petty oppressions, or other trivialities. The rough edges of our society are still in need of a good deal of filing down, and in the meantime plaintiffs must necessarily be expected and required to be hardened to a certain amount of rough *631 language, and to occasional acts that are definitely inconsiderate and unkind. There is no occasion for the law to intervene in every case where some one's feelings are hurt. There must still be freedom to express an unflattering opinion, and some safety valve must be left through which irascible tempers may blow off relatively harmless steam.

This language describes a very narrow category of behavior which, to summarize, does not include insults, indignities, threats, annoyances, petty oppression, rough language, inconsiderate or unkind acts, or conduct which is only tortious, criminal, intended to inflict emotional distress, malicious, or worthy of punitive damages. Outrageous conduct is "extreme", "beyond all possible bounds of decency", "atrocious", and "utterly intolerable in a civilized community."

How much worse than criminal or malicious must conduct be to be beyond all possible bounds of decency, and not merely offensive, deplorable or even unbearable, but utterly intolerable in a civilized community? Only the most extremely egregious conduct would seem to qualify. Applying comment d, is it extreme and outrageous conduct—for one person to tell another, as a practical joke, that the other's spouse has been badly injured in an accident and is in the hospital with both legs broken?—for a man, knowing of another person's pathological fear of men in women's clothing, to dress as a woman to surprise and startle the other person?—for the president of a rubbish collectors association to summon a member to a meeting, accuse him of working in another member's exclusive territory, and threaten that if he does not pay over what he has earned he will be physically beaten and his business destroyed?—for a man to give a woman a bathing suit which dissolves in water, leaving her naked in front of strangers?—for a person to "hex" the farm of a superstitious landowner to force him to sell it? Many would agree that one or more of these situations involves truly outrageous conduct, but I doubt whether there would be much consensus among judges, let alone juries, that the conduct in every instance is "beyond all possible bounds of decency" and "utterly intolerable in a civilized community." Those who considered one such situation to fall into this narrow category might even object to equating it with others of these examples. In some instances, conduct is more or less reprehensible depending upon the setting in which it occurred and the personalities involved. If comment d were taken literally, truly outrageous conduct would be rare indeed, yet the illustrations in the comments to section 46, taken from actual cases, reflect a less exacting view of outrageousness: in all of these examples a court has determined the conduct to be outrageous, giving rise to liability. The Restatement's illustrations of outrageous conduct suggest that comment d, though rigid in word, is much more flexible in application.

The vice in such indeterminacy is not that the tort sweeps too broadly, resulting in liability more often than it should. A review of the cases in which intentional or reckless infliction of emotional distress is alleged indicates that while the claim is routinely asserted, it is seldom successful. See Annotation, Modern Status of Intentional Infliction of Mental Distress as Independent Tort; "Outrage", 38 A.L.R.4th 998 (1985). The vice in the nebulous standard of outrageousness is rather that it results in erratic decisions which appear to have no unifying principle. The cases reveal no clear patterns of application of the standard, nor should they be expected to. What is outrageous unavoidably depends upon the sensitivities of the person asked to decide and to some extent the community in which the conduct occurs. "The term 'outrageous' is neither value-free nor exacting." Daniel Givelber, The Right to Minimum Social Decency and the Limits of Evenhandedness: Intentional Infliction of Emotional

Distress by Outrageous Conduct, 82 Colum.L.Rev. 42, 51 (1982). Because outrageousness is a subjective, almost personal, notion, its application is as much a matter of who decides as of what happened.

Proving that conduct is or is not outrageous is virtually impossible. What evidence*632 is there which tends to prove that certain behavior was or was not outrageous? The issue is certainly not a factual one, like whether the traffic light was red or green, on which a witness can be called to testify. It is a matter of opinion, but it involves no "scientific, technical, or other specialized knowledge" as to which a witness could be qualified as an expert "by knowledge, skill, experience, training, or education". Tex.R.Civ.Evid. 702. The only possible evidence which could be offered on the issue would be the opinion of a lay witness, but it is difficult to conceive of an instance in which a lay opinion would be helpful to a determination of outrageousness and thus admissible. See Tex.R.Civ.Evid. 701. The rules would certainly not allow witness after witness to be called to testify one by one that, "Yes, in my opinion defendant's conduct was outrageous," or "No, in my opinion it was not." Quite simply, the principal element of the tort of intentional or reckless infliction of emotional distress is something on which testimony cannot be offered and which can neither be proved nor disproved...

Whether a judge or a jury decides the issue of outrageousness, neither has a standard for doing so. Without evidence or rules to guide a decision, both can resort only to their own views, and their own prejudices. Opinions about outrageous conduct may vary widely in various contexts. An employee may accuse his employer of behaving outrageously in terminating him, an insured may accuse his insurer of denying a claim outrageously, or a debtor may accuse a creditor of outrageous conduct in attempting to collect the debt. That class of persons to which each plaintiff or defendant belongs will almost certainly not share the same view of the alleged conduct as that class which includes the other party. To be sure, there will be a few instances when almost everyone is in accord, but in the vast majority of cases, creditors, for example, are less likely to be outraged by aggressive debt collection than debtors. What rule or standard can a judge or jury use to resolve such disputes? There is none. The composition of the jury, whether of bankers or borrowers, is likely to play heavily in the verdict delivered...

... Evidence is always available on the standard of care to which a reasonable person can be expected to adhere in a given situation; in many cases, such as professional malpractice, such evidence is required. The jury is obliged to confine its deliberations to that evidence and cannot create its own standard of care. Thus, jurors who regularly drive in excess of the speed limit cannot equate ordinary care with their own conduct. But evidence of what is outrageous in a given situation is never available. Jurors are not only permitted to judge a defendant's conduct by their own personal experiences; they are required to do so.

There are also moral overtones to outrageousness that are absent in ordinary care. Conduct which negligently causes an accident is not "beyond all possible bounds of decency" and "utterly intolerable in a civilized community." In a negligence action a jury must decide whether the defendant was careless; in an action for intentional or reckless infliction of emotional distress, the jury must decide whether the defendant was bad. A finding that conduct was outrageous is qualitatively different from a finding that it was negligent.

The Court's sole response to all these criticisms is this: we trust juries to decide. This truism simply does not address the problems raised by the standardless tort the Court recognizes. The issue is not whether juries are qualified to decide fact issues—certainly they are—but what standards they are to employ in doing so. In a society ruled by law and not by men, we do not allow judges or juries to base adjudications on personal predilections. This is not a matter of trust, but of power properly exercised. We trust juries to judge according *634 to the law; we trust no one to judge according to his own views...

*635 Texas law does not permit a divorce court to divest a spouse of separate property in dividing the marital estate. *Eggemeyer v. Eggemeyer,* 554 S.W.2d 137 (Tex.1977). Allowing a tort action between spouses in connection with the dissolution of the marriage circumvents this bar. Although the Court does not address this issue, the damages assessed against a spouse for intentional infliction of emotional distress should be paid out of that spouse's share of the community or his or her separate property. Damages could not be paid out of the balance of the community without punishing the aggrieved spouse. I assume the Court intends that both compensatory and punitive damages may be awarded for the tort, as for other intentional torts. Damages paid from one spouse's separate property awards the other spouse more than would otherwise be allowed in a divorce action. While it is already possible for one spouse to recover damages from the other's separate property for an intentional tort, such as battery, the adoption of intentional or reckless infliction of emotional distress greatly expands the circumstances in which such recovery may be had, further distorting the basic community property system.

Awarding one spouse tort damages against the other in the context of divorce also creates a problem of double recovery. The fault of a spouse contributing to the breakup of a marriage may be considered by the divorce court in dividing the marital estate. *Murff v. Murff,* 615 S.W.2d 696 (Tex.1981). But the aggrieved spouse should not be awarded both tort damages and a disproportionate share of the community for the same conduct of the other spouse. It is difficult to imagine how wrongful conduct which contributes to the breakup of the marriage can be segregated from that which is tortious to prevent double recovery. If the tort claim is tried to the court, the judge may attempt to separate the property division from the damages award. But if the tort claim is tried to a jury, who does not have authority to divide the property, it is impossible for either the judge or the jury to take into account the other's actions. The judge cannot instruct the jury that he has decided to make an uneven division of the property on account of fault without commenting on the weight of the evidence in the tort trial; nor can the judge determine from a jury verdict what conduct should not be considered in dividing the property. The judge may request an advisory verdict on the division of property and instruct the jury to consider tort damages separately, but even when this is feasible, the trial court must follow the advisory verdict or the effect of the instruction will be lost. In sum, allowance of a tort of intentional or reckless infliction of emotional distress in a divorce proceeding creates serious trial management problems which affect the substantive rights of the parties.

There can be little doubt that both spouses in a great many divorce cases will allege intentional or reckless infliction of emotional distress against each other. The Family Law Section of the State Bar of Texas, in an amicus brief, endorses this assessment. Whenever the tort is alleged, the parties will be entitled to a jury trial. At present, the right to a jury trial in divorce cases is very limited. The likely increase in the number of jury trials in such cases can only delay the resolution of divorce cases in many courts. The Court does not consider this potential impact of its ruling.

Allowing a tort action between spouses in divorce also presents the problem of whether attorney's fees may be charged on a contingent basis. Ordinarily, an attorney may not charge a contingent fee in a divorce proceeding, but may do so in a tort action. When the actions are combined, the alleged fault giving rise to the tort claim will also affect other issues in the divorce proceeding, including property division, custody, and support. Segregation of the time an attorney spends on these matters is virtually impossible. As a practical matter, contingent fees must either become the principal compensation for attorneys in divorce cases involving tort claims, or else they must be disallowed in such situations altogether.

The standard of outrageousness is certainly no easier to apply in the marital *636 context than in other contexts, as the facts of this case illustrate. Sheila Twyman's claim of intentional infliction of emotional distress is based upon the following testimony at trial, which was mostly undisputed. William, a Navy pilot, and Sheila, a college graduate with a degree in nursing, were married in 1969. In 1975, on two or three occasions at William's suggestion, the couple engaged in what they referred to as "light bondage"—tying each other to the bed with neckties during their sexual relations. Sheila testified that William did not force her to participate in these activities. After the last occasion Sheila told William she did not like this activity and did not want to participate in it further. She revealed to him that she associated the activities with the horrible experience of having been raped at knifepoint earlier in her life. William never again suggested that she engage in the activities, nor was the subject discussed again for ten years. In 1985 Sheila inadvertently discovered that William was consulting with a psychologist. When she asked him why, he told her that he was involved with another woman. William told Sheila that if she could only have done bondage, nothing else would have mattered. For the remainder of the year the couple sought counseling. At times during this period William made derogatory remarks to Sheila about her sexual ability, comparing her to his girlfriend. On their counselor's advice, William and Sheila discussed William's bondage fantasies, and Sheila again tried to participate in bondage activities with William. But she found the activity so painful and humiliating that she could not continue it. Their last encounter, which did not include bondage activities, was so rough that she was injured to the point of bleeding. At one point Sheila was distressed to discover that their ten-year-old son had found magazines William kept hidden, which portrayed sadomasochistic activities. Eleven months after she first learned of William's affair, Sheila separated from him and filed for divorce. Throughout that period, Sheila testified, she experienced utter despair, devastation, pain, humiliation and weight loss because of William's affair and her feelings that the marriage could have survived if only she had engaged in bondage activities.

To recover damages Sheila must prove that William's conduct was outrageous—that is, "extreme", "beyond all possible bounds of decency", "atrocious", and "utterly intolerable in a civilized community." Although outrageousness is, according to the plurality opinion and the Restatement, a question for the court in the first instance, this Court refuses to say whether William's conduct was or was not outrageous. If it was not, as a matter of law, then there is no need to remand this case for further proceedings. If William's conduct was outrageous, or if that issue must be decided by a jury, then it is unclear what components of the conflict between Sheila and William were actionable. There is no question from the record that Sheila claims to have suffered bitterly, but there appear to have been three causes: William's affair, his interest in bondage, and the breakup of the marriage. If the first or last causes constitute outrageous behavior, then there a tort claim may be urged successfully in most divorces. Allowing recovery based upon the first cause of Sheila's emotional distress is simply to revive the old action for alienation of affections abolished by the Legislature. Tex.Fam.Code § 4.06. I doubt whether the Court intends this result. If William's outrageous conduct was attempting to interest Sheila in sexual conduct which he considered enjoyable but she, in her words, "did not like", then again, this tort may be very broad indeed.

The sexual relationship is among the most intimate aspects of marriage. People's concepts of a beneficial sexual relationship vary widely, and spouses may expect that some accommodation of each other's feelings will be necessary for their mutual good. Any breach of such an intimate and essential part of marriage may be regarded as outrageous by the aggrieved spouse and will often be the cause of great distress. There are many other aspects of marriage which are likewise sensitive. How money is to be spent, how children are *637 to be raised, and how time is to be allocated are only a few of the many areas of conflict in a marriage. Not infrequently disagreements over these matters are deep and contribute to the breakup of the marriage. If all are actionable, then tort claims will be commonplace in divorce cases, and judges and juries with their own deeply felt beliefs about what is proper in a marital relationship will face the hard task of deciding whether one spouse or another behaved outrageously with no standards but their own to guide.

The inquiry which must be made to determine whether a spouse's conduct is outrageous entails too great an intrusion into the marital relationship. Although courts are already called upon to consider fault in divorce actions, allowance of tort claims requires a more pervasive inspection of spouses' private lives than should be permissible. In this case the parties were called to testify in detail and at length about the most private moments of their marriage. If the court's only concern were the degree to which a spouse's fault had contributed to the demise of the marriage, the inquiry into each spouse's conduct need not have been so detailed. To recover damages, however, Sheila was required to testify at length before a jury, and to rebut her claim, William was obliged to answer in equal detail. The prospect of such testimony in many divorces is too great an invasion of spouses' interests in privacy, and promises to make divorce more acrimonious and injurious than it already is…

IV

Finally, I must say a word in response to Justice Spector's dissenting opinion, the principal thesis of which is that the Court has denied recovery for negligent infliction of emotional distress in this case because of an institutional bias against women. "It is no coincidence", Justice Spector contends, that both this case and *Boyles v. Kerr*, 855 S.W.2d 593 (Tex.1993), involve claims for emotional distress by women against men. Post at 642. Actually, it is just that: a coincidence.

It is a further coincidence that another case we decide today, *Valenzuela v. Aquino*, 853 S.W.2d 512 (Tex.1993), in which we also deny recovery for negligent infliction of emotional distress, does not involve claims solely by women against men. That case involves a claim by Dr. Aquino and his family for damages caused by anti-abortion picketers demonstrating in front of his home. Our refusal to allow recovery for negligent infliction of emotional distress in Valenzuela contradicts Justice Spector's assertions of bias. Accordingly, Justice Spector does not attempt to argue that our decision in Valenzuela is motivated by prejudice in favor of abortion or against doctors, or by any other bias. There is no more basis for the assertion that the views against recognition of the tort in the present context are born of a latent antagonism to women.

Further, Justice Spector's assertions are somewhat antagonistic toward one another. She states: "In the judicial system dominated by men, emotional distress claims have historically been marginalized." Post at 642. She also claims, however: "From the beginning, tort recovery for infliction of emotional distress has developed primarily as a means of compensating women for injuries inflicted by men insensitive to the harm caused by their conduct." Post at 642. It is not entirely clear how the justice system can have developed a tort primarily to compensate claims by women at the same time that the system was dominated by men intent upon marginalizing women's claims. Justice Spector herself states that "[n]either the Fort Worth Court of Appeals, nor any of the other courts at the time *[in 1918]* were primarily concerned with protecting women's rights." Post at 643. If, as I will concede, the justice system has been historically dominated by men, and if, as I am willing to assume, those men were not always sympathetic to *639 women's claims, then development of theories for recovering damages for emotional distress cannot have been due primarily to a desire to compensate women. There must be other factors which better explain the development of the law.

There is evidence of such factors. It cannot be denied that differentiations have been drawn between the emotional distress suffered by men and that suffered by women. Some early cases and commentaries explicitly recognized the distinction between a female plaintiff and a male plaintiff suffering a similar injury, and commentators indicated that the gender of the plaintiff is one of the relevant factors in determining liability. See, e.g., *Fort Worth & Rio Grande Ry. Co. v. Bryant*, 210 S.W.

556 (Tex.Civ.App.—Fort Worth 1918) (in which a daughter recovered for exposure to coarse language in a train depot, but her father did not); FN3 Calvert Magruder, Mental and Emotional Disturbance in the Law of Torts, 49 Harv.L.Rev. 1033, 1046 (1936) (suggesting that the plaintiff's gender should play a part in the determination of defendant's liability). Prosser stated the idea clearly: "There is a difference between violent and vile profanity addressed to a lady, and the same language to a Butte miner and a United States marine." William L. Prosser, Intentional Infliction of Mental Suffering: A New Tort, 37 Mich.L.Rev. 874, 887 (1939) (footnote omitted). This language was modified to reflect the "eggshell plaintiff" concept in the comment c to section 48 of the Restatement, which states that "language addressed to a pregnant or sick woman may be actionable where the same words would not be if they were addressed to a United States Marine."

FN3. One may argue that this case reflects a patronizing view of women, or as Justice Spector does, that it is a case decided without particular regard for gender. Either way, the point is that recovery for emotional distress did not develop, in Justice Spector's words, "primarily" to compensate women, but for other reasons.

One may argue that these attempted differentiations of emotional distress reflect a patronizing view of women. FN4 Or one may also argue that the differentiations were drawn without particular regard for gender. But there is no evidence that ensuring recovery for uniquely female claims, because of any uniquely female characteristics, has been a primary factor in recognizing recovery for such injuries. The earliest cases to hold defendants liable for the infliction of mental suffering involved common carriers and innkeepers who were held to have breached an implied contract to be polite. W. Page Keeton, et al., Prosser and Keeton on the Law of Torts, § 12, at 57 (5th ed. 1984). Neither the cases nor the commentaries gives any indication that women more frequently pursued this cause of action. See, Annotation, Right to Recover for Mental Pain and Anguish Alone, Apart from other Damages, 23 A.L.R. 361 (1923), and cases cited therein. (In one of the cases awarding punitive damages to a male plaintiff, the facts showed that the conductor of a railroad had permitted the train to become overcrowded without informing the passengers that some would have to stand. The conductor intentionally humiliated a passenger who refused to give up his ticket before being provided an alternate seat by saying that a lady would be asked to give up her seat to him. *Cave v. Seaboard Air Line Ry.*, 94 S.C. 282, 77 S.E. 1017 (1913).)

FN4. Justice Spector construes my acknowledgment of the logical possibility of this argument as an endorsement. I do not make this argument, nor do I believe that the evidence for it is convincing. My point is that while this argument can be made with some support, there is no support for Justice Spector's argument that recovery for emotional distress has developed primarily to compensate women.

In the first successful cases against defendants other than common carriers, the defendants' actions were found to have caused physical injuries as a result of emotional distress in the absence of physical impact. See John E. Hallen, *Hill v. Kimball*—A Milepost in the Law, 12 Tex.L.Rev. 1, 7–8 (1933). The cases frequently involved female plaintiffs, and Prosser described the pattern that quickly emerged as follows:

*640 Nearly all of the plaintiffs have been women, usually in that delicate condition whose standardized consequences have typified mental suffering cases with the "customary miscarriage."

William L. Prosser, Intentional Infliction of Mental Suffering: A New Tort, 37 Mich.L.Rev. 874, 888 (1939); see also Hubert Winston Smith, Relation of Emotions to Injury and Disease: Legal Liability for Psychic Stimuli, 30 Va.L.Rev. 193, at Appendix B (1944) (listing a large number of cases involving miscarriage). No reason is suggested for the large number of cases involving miscarriages either by Prosser or other commentators that identify the pattern. Prosser, Intentional Infliction of Emotional Distress, at 888 & n. 81; Green, 'Fright Cases,' 27 Ill.L.Rev. 761, (1933). However, it is possible that the reason for the frequency of such cases was the requirement of a physical manifestation of injury to recover for emotional distress. Thus the fact that the majority of the cases involved women plaintiffs does not reveal anything except the fact that men do not miscarry.

Although miscarriage was the most common type of injury for which recovery was awarded in the early cases, other physical manifestations of emotional harm gave rise to recovery. See Hubert Winston Smith, Relation of Emotions to Injury and Disease: Legal Liability for Psychic Stimuli, 30 Va.L.Rev. 193, at Appendix B (1944) (categorizing over 300 cases by type of injury alleged). Contrary to the dissent's suggestion, however, the reasoning supporting recovery in these cases did not develop "[f]rom the beginning" to provide "a means of compensating women for injuries inflicted by men insensitive to the harm caused by their conduct." Post at 642. Rather, the cases permitted recovery for physical injury resulting from the negligent actions of the defendants, regardless of the fact that the injury resulted from emotional trauma. The duty imposed in these cases was a duty not to inflict foreseeable physical injury by whatever means; the early cases did not impose a duty not to inflict the emotional trauma itself. See *Boyles v. Kerr*, 855 S.W.2d 593, 599 & n. 4 (Tex.1993).

Even from this very abbreviated overview, to the extent that any pattern can be discerned in this history, it is not one of a struggle for recognition of women's rights, but of either a condescending and patronizing view of women, or a development of the law without particular regard for gender. Arguments for allowance of claims for emotional distress owe their support to far more factors than the relationships between men and women. FN5 The tort the Court recognizes today will have marked impact on marital relationships, but it will have far broader impact on the many other relationships it will affect. To assert, as Justice Spector does, that the principal effect of today's decision falls upon women, overlooks the broader reality which, as I have explained, is the basis for my concern.

FN5. I do not insist, with "astonishment" "masculine" or otherwise, contrary to Justice Spector's charge, that "with a few possible exceptions, women have played no distinct part in the development of tort recovery for emotional distress." Post at 643. It cannot be denied that some early cases of recovery for emotional distress involved claims by women. My point is that recovery was not allowed "primarily" to ensure compensation for women, but for other reasons. The tort the Court acknowledges today has significance in many contexts that do not involve women's issues. Justice Spector's attempts to limit this case to such issues fail.

***

> For all the foregoing reasons, I dissent from the opinion and judgment of the Court.
> Justice ENOCH joins in this concurring and dissenting opinion.
> SPECTOR, Justice, dissenting.

Over five years ago, a trial court issued a divorce decree that included an award to Sheila Twyman of $15,000 for the years of abuse she had suffered at the hands of her husband. At the time, the award was consistent with prevailing Texas law. Today, the plurality sets aside the trial court's award and sends Sheila Twyman back to start the process over in a new trial. Because justice for Sheila Twyman has been both delayed and denied, I dissent.

*641 I.

At trial, Sheila testified that her husband, William Twyman, introduced bondage activities into their relationship after their marriage. Sheila told William that she could not endure these activities because of the trauma of having been raped several years earlier. She also informed William that she had been cut with a knife during the rape, and had been placed in fear for her life. Although William understood that Sheila equated bondage with her prior experience of being raped, he told Sheila that if she would not satisfy his desires by engaging in bondage, there would be no future to their marriage.

As a result, Sheila experienced "utter despair" and "devastation," as well as physical problems—weight loss and, after one encounter, prolonged bleeding that necessitated gynecological treatment. The pain and humiliation of the bondage activity caused her to seek help from three professional counselors.

The trial court found that William "engaged in a continuing course of conduct of attempting to coerce [Sheila] to join in his practices of 'bondage' by continually asserting that [their] marriage could be saved only by [Sheila] participating with [William] in his practices of 'bondage.'" The trial court also determined that Sheila's suffering was certainly foreseeable from William's continuing course of conduct, "in light of his existing knowledge of her long-existing emotional state, which was caused by her having been forcibly raped prior to their marriage." Finally, the trial court found that Sheila's mental anguish was a direct proximate result of William's sexual practices.

Based on the pleadings, evidence, and arguments, the trial court concluded that the facts and the law supported Sheila's recovery of $15,000 for William's negligent infliction of emotional distress. The court of appeals, in an opinion by Justice Gammage, affirmed the trial court's judgment under prevailing tort law and noted that this court had expressly approved the recovery of damages on a negligence claim in a divorce action. 790 S.W.2d 819, 823 (citing *Price v. Price*, 732 S.W.2d 316 (Tex.1987)).

This court, however, has now rejected Texas law established to provide redress for injuries of the kind inflicted by William Twyman. While allowing some tort claims to be brought in a divorce action, the plurality forbids recovery for negligent infliction of emotional distress, and insists that Sheila Twyman proceed on a theory of intentional infliction of emotional distress.

II.

Today's decision is handed down contemporaneously with the overruling of the motion for rehearing in *Boyles v. Kerr*, 855 S.W.2d 593 (Tex.1993), in which this court reversed a judgment in favor of a woman who was surreptitiously videotaped during intercourse, then subjected to humiliation and ridicule when the tape was displayed to others. In Boyles, as in this case, a majority of this court has determined that severe, negligently-inflicted emotional distress does not warrant judicial relief—no matter how intolerable the injurious conduct. The reasoning originally articulated in Boyles, and now implied in this case, is that "[t]ort law cannot and should not attempt to provide redress for every instance of rude, insensitive, or distasteful behavior"; providing such relief, the Boyles majority explained, "would dignify most disputes far beyond their social importance." 36 Tex. S.Ct.J. 231, 233–234 (Dec. 2, 1992). FN1

FN1. On rehearing, the Boyles majority has reworded slightly its discussion but reiterated its reasoning and result. The majority's overriding concern there has remained the avoidance of relief for "merely rude or insensitive behavior." 855 S.W.2d 593, 602.

Neither of these cases involves "rude, insensitive, or distasteful behavior"; they involve grossly offensive conduct that was appropriately found to warrant judicial relief. The decision in Boyles overturns well-reasoned case law, and I strongly agree with the dissenting opinion in that case. For the same reasons, I strongly disagree with the plurality here; the rule embodied *642 in Boyles is no less objectionable when applied to the facts of this case. Sheila Twyman is entitled to recover the amount awarded by the trial court for the injuries inflicted by her husband.

III.

It is no coincidence that both this cause and Boyles involve serious emotional distress claims asserted by women against men. From the beginning, tort recovery for infliction of emotional distress has developed primarily as a means of compensating women for injuries inflicted by men insensitive to the harm caused by their conduct. In "[t]he leading case which broke through the shackles," FN2 a man amused himself by falsely informing a woman that her husband had been gravely injured, causing a serious and permanent shock to her nervous system. *Wilkinson v. Downton*, 2 Q.B.D. 57 (1897). Similarly, in the watershed Texas case, a man severely beat two others in the presence of a pregnant woman, who suffered a miscarriage as a result of her emotional distress. *Hill v. Kimball*, 76 Tex. 210, 13 S.W. 59 (1890). By World War II, the pattern was well-established: one survey of psychic injury claims found that the ratio of female to male plaintiffs was five to one. Hubert Winston Smith, Relation of Emotions to Injury and Disease: Legal Liability for Psychic Stimuli, 30 Va.L.Rev. 193 (1944).

FN2. William L. Prosser, Insult and Outrage, 44 Cal.L.Rev. 40, 42 (1956).

Even today, when emotional distress claims by both sexes have become more widely accepted, women's claims against men predominate. Of the thirty-four Texas cases cited by the plurality—all decided since 1987—women's claims outnumbered men's by a ratio of five to four; FN3 and only four of the thirty-four involved any female defendants. FN4 Of those cases involving relations between two individuals—with no corporations involved—five involved a woman's claim against a man; FN5 none involved a man's claim against a woman.

FN3. The plurality downplays this fact by miscategorizing two cases involving women's emotional distress claims: *Resolution Trust Corp. v. Cook,* 840 S.W.2d 42 (Tex.App.—Amarillo 1992, writ denied) (claim asserted only on behalf of wife) and *Godinet v. Thomas,* 824 S.W.2d 632 (Tex.App.—Houston [14th Dist.] 1991, writ denied) (survivorship claim brought on behalf of deceased woman)(FN 4–5 omitted)...

I do not argue that women alone have an interest in recovery for emotional distress. However, since the overwhelming majority of emotional distress claims have arisen from harmful conduct by men, rather than women, I do argue that men have had a disproportionate interest in downplaying such claims.

Like the struggle for women's rights, the movement toward recovery for emotional distress has been long and tortuous. See Peter A. Bell, The Bell Tolls: Toward Full Tort Recovery for Psychic Injury, 36 U.Fla.L.Rev. 333, 336–40 (1984). In the judicial system dominated by men, emotional distress claims have historically been marginalized:

> *The law of torts values physical security and property more highly than emotional security and human relationships. This apparently gender-neutral hierarchy of values has privileged men, as the traditional owners and managers of property, and has burdened women, to whom the emotional work of maintaining human relationships has commonly been assigned. The law has often failed to compensate women for recurring harms—serious though they may be in the lives *643 of women—for which there is no precise masculine analogue.*

Martha Chamallas and Linda K. Kerber, Women, Mothers, and the Law of Fright: A History, 88 Mich.L.Rev. 814 (1990). Even Prosser recognizes the role of gender in the historical treatment of claims like that involved in *Hill v. Kimball*:

It is not difficult to discover in the earlier opinions a distinctly masculine astonishment hat any woman should ever allow herself to be frightened or shocked into a miscarriage.

W. Page Keeton et al., Prosser and Keeton on the Law of Torts § 12, at 55–56 (5th ed. 1984).

Displaying a comparable "masculine astonishment," the dissenting opinion by Justice Hecht insists that, with a few possible exceptions, women have played no distinct part in the development of tort recovery for emotional distress. As a general matter, Justice Hecht questions how a legal system dominated by men could develop a tort to compensate women even while marginalizing women's claims. The answer is amply illustrated by the present case: to provide some appearance of relief for Sheila Twyman, the court recognizes the tort of intentional infliction of emotional distress; but in doing so, it restricts her to a theory which, as Justice Hecht observes, is "seldom successful." 855 S.W.2d at 631.

Justice Hecht acknowledges that in the early cases, recovery for emotional distress "frequently involved female plaintiffs." 855 S.W.2d at 631. However, rather than viewing this phenomenon as an indication of actual, serious injuries, Justice Hecht suggests that it may have been due to a patronizing attitude on the part of the courts.

There is little doubt that some of the case law in this area, as in any other, reflects a patronizing view of women. More often, though, the case law reflects the logical application of existing law to a wide range of claims. For example, in the only case cited by Justice Hecht to illustrate an arguably patronizing view of women, there was evidence that men employed by a railroad had humiliated a man's ten-year-old daughter by subjecting her to obscene language; but there was no evidence that the language had humiliated the father. *Fort Worth & Rio Grande Ry. Co. v. Bryant,* 210 S.W. 556 (Tex.Civ.App.—Fort Worth 1918, writ ref'd). There is nothing patronizing about holding a railroad company responsible for the harm caused by its employees' conduct.

I would group Bryant with the many other common carrier cases that were decided, in Justice Hecht's terms, "without particular regard for gender." 855 S.W.2d at 639. Neither the Fort Worth Court of Appeals, nor any of the other courts at the time were primarily concerned with protecting women's rights. But in Bryant, as in so many of the other cases, the evolution of the law regarding emotional distress claims did enable a female to recover for emotional harm inflicted by men. This fact does not reflect a charitable desire to help women; it reflects the fact that the serious emotional distress claims usually involved injuries inflicted by men upon women.

Given this history, the plurality's emphatic rejection of infliction of emotional distress claims based on negligence is especially troubling. Today, when the widespread mistreatment of women is being documented throughout the country—for instance, in the areas of sexual harassment FN6 and domestic violence FN7—a majority of this court takes a step backward and abolishes one way of righting this grievous wrong.

FN6. During the 1980s, complaints of sexual harassment nearly doubled. Susan Faludi, Backlash: The Undeclared War Against American Women, at xvi, 464 (1991) (citing statistics from U.S. Equal Employment Opportunity Commission, "National Database: Charge Receipt Listing," 1982–88; "Sexual Harassment," 1981–89). A 1988 survey found that 42 percent of federally-employed women said they had been sexually harassed, and a U.S. Navy survey the same year found that more than half the women in the navy were victims of sexual harassment. Id. at 525.

FN7. See American Medical Association Council on Scientific Affairs, "Violence Against Women: Relevance for Medical Practitioners," 267 J.Am.Med.Ass'n 3184, 3185 (1992).

*644 IV.

Rather than dismissing Sheila's claim outright, the plurality remands this cause to the trial court to allow Sheila to seek recovery under an alternative theory. I agree that Sheila is entitled to pursue a claim based upon intentional infliction of emotional distress, as set out in section 46 of the Restatement (2d) of Torts.

However, in restricting recovery for emotional distress to claims based upon intent, the plurality, joined by Justice Gonzalez's concurring opinion, demonstrates a basic misunderstanding of claims like those presented by Susan Kerr and Sheila Twyman. While recognizing that recovery should be allowed for conduct intended to inflict injury, the plurality fails to acknowledge the severe emotional distress often caused unintentionally.

This court has previously made clear that the distinguishing feature of an intentional tort is "the specific intent to inflict injury." *Reed Tool Co. v. Copelin*, 689 S.W.2d 404, 406 (Tex.1985) (citing Restatement (2d) of Torts § 8A (1965)); see also Rodriguez v. Naylor Indus., 763 S.W.2d 411, 412 (Tex.1988). This definition of an "intentional" injury is echoed in the portion of the Restatement governing intentional infliction of emotional distress:

> *The rule stated in this Section applies where the actor desires to inflict severe emotional distress, and also where he knows that such distress is certain, or substantially certain, to result from his conduct.*
>
> *Restatement (2d) of Torts § 46 cmt. i (1965).*

Unfortunately, in many cases, severe emotional distress is caused by an actor who does not actually desire to inflict severe emotional distress, and who is even oblivious to the fact that such distress is certain, or substantially certain, to result from his conduct. It may well be the case, for example, that William Twyman never actually intended to inflict emotional distress upon Sheila, and never expected the injury that his conduct caused. Rather, he may have insisted on bondage activities solely for the purpose of satisfying his own desires. Similarly, Dan Boyles may have videotaped his activities with Susan Kerr not for the purpose of injuring her, but rather for the purpose of amusing himself and his friends.

I do not argue, as the plurality asserts, that "the emotional harm William caused was foreseeable but not substantially certain to occur." 855 S.W.2d at 624. I do argue, though, that Sheila's recovery for William's conduct should not depend upon proof of William's sensitivity. To apply a standard based on intent is to excuse William's conduct so long as he believed his actions were harmless.

Brutish behavior that causes severe injury, even though unintentionally, should not be trivialized. Foreclosing recovery for such behavior may prevent litigation of frivolous claims; but it also denies redress in exactly those instances where it is most needed.

V.

While the plurality would allow some possibility of recovery for injuries like Sheila Twyman's, the dissenting opinions by Chief Justice Phillips and Justice Hecht would allow none at all. Adopting the medieval view of marital relations, Chief Justice Phillips argues that spouses should be shielded from liability for even the most outrageous acts against one another. This view echoes William Twyman's assertion at trial that, by consenting
to marriage, Sheila Twyman assumed the risk of physical injury and emotional harm. Fortunately, in Texas, this archaic view has been soundly rejected; interspousal immunity has been abolished "completely as to any cause of action." *Price v. Price*, 732 S.W.2d 316, 320 (Tex.1987). Insulating spouses from liability, we have noted, "would amount to a repudiation of the constitutional guarantee of equal protection of the laws." Id. Thus, recovery for intentional infliction of emotional distress should be available to spouses and non-spouses alike, as other states have recognized. FN8

FN8. The state supreme court that reexamined this issue most recently noted, "Courts around the country have recognized that public policy considerations should not bar actions for intentional infliction of emotional distress between spouses or former spouses based on conduct occurring during the marriage." *Henriksen v. Cameron*, 622 A.2d 1135, 1140 (Me.1993) (citations omitted)…

VI.

The claim asserted by Sheila Twyman was based on a simple premise: her husband should be held accountable for the foreseeable consequences of his conduct. The courts below, in applying the law, understood the nature and extent of such conduct; the plurality does not. Tragically, the lack of understanding shown today will only lead to more delay and more injustice.

Justice DOGGETT joins in this dissenting opinion.

ANNULMENTS DISTINGUISHED

Annulments are different from divorces. In a divorce, the marriage is recognized and then dissolved by court order. In contrast, an annulment (see Chapter 9) is a legal order invalidating the marriage because an underlying flaw means the marriage never existed. Like fault-based divorce, annulments are granted in limited circumstances, but their purpose is to void, not to dissolve a marriage. Before the advent of no-fault divorce, annulments were a popular way to dissolve a marriage when both parties wanted out, but did not have fault-based reasons to do so.

AFFECTS OF DIVORCE ON RELIGION

Divorce can impact religion in many ways. For example, a 2013 study found that children of religious couples are much more likely to leave the religion if their parents get divorced. [17] In addition, civil court ordered divorces affect many religions. In the Indian Hindu religion, "divorce is stigmatized as 'a shameful admission of failure'" where families are "shunned, locked(ed) out of social and religious events" and even making it difficult for children of divorced parents to get married in the future.[18] For women, this divorce taboo has severe financial impacts when the woman is viewed as a "pariah or harbinger of bad luck. She may be left with no place to go and no means of supporting herself and her children."[19] Court-ordered divorces affect the Catholic religion too, where marriages are presumed valid and lifelong. Unless a spouse dies, the church requires a divorced Catholic to get an annulment or church court/tribunal declared declaration of nullity before remarrying in the Catholic church. If the tribunal determines "something essential was missing from the couple's relationship from the moment of consent" or time of the marriage, the church can declare that a "valid marriage was never actually brought about on the wedding day."[20] In October 2015, Catholic Bishops from around the world began a discussion regarding the church's treatment of civil divorce and although no changes were announced, they agreed to meet again to determine whether to make changes to the church's views, "including the place of divorced worshipers in the church."[21] An estimated 28% of Catholics adults divorce,

---

17   Based on a Baylor University study published in the *Journal for the Scientific Study of Religion* showing that adults who lived with just one parent during their formative years are more than twice as likely to disaffiliate than those who grew up with continuously married parents. The study found that the children are twice as likely to become estranged from their church as adults compared to people whose parents didn't get divorced. "Study" Religious Parents Divorce May Cause Children to Leave Church", Jason Koebler, *U.S. News and World Report*, March 5, 2013 http://www.usnews.com/news/articles/2013/03/05/study-religious-parents-divorce-may-cause-children-to-leave-the-church

18   "Some communities need more divorce, not less", Sharadha Bain, *The Washington Post*, March 15, 2015, PB3.

19   Ibid.

20   "For Your Marriage an initiative of the United States Conference of Catholic Bishops" http://www.foryourmarriage.org/catholic-marriage/church-teachings/annulments/

21   "As Vatican Revisits Divorce, Faithful Long for Acceptance", Michael Paulson, *The New York Times*, January 25, 2015. P. 1.

but only 15% of those go through the church's annulment process.[22] The Philippines, based on the Catholic Church's dominate influence, is the last major country that does not allow divorce. There, residents must either obtain a religious annulment from the Catholic Church or an expensive civil annulment (see chapter 9) based on limited grounds including mental incapacity at the time of marriage. This led one man to joke, "You know, it's only about 10,000 or 15,000 pesos to hire a hit man to kill your spouse—much less than an annulment".[23] Some members of the New York Orthodox Jewish religion, however, were not joking. Orthodox Jewish women cannot get divorced unless their husbands consent through a document called a "get." Some women allege, "get abuse" when their "husbands demand a larger share of the couple's communal property before granting the divorce."[24] In 2013, New Jersey charged 11 members of "a violent ring that included two rabbis" who would threaten and torture (including the use of hand cuffs, surgical blades, screwdrivers, and cattle prods) Jewish husbands in order to extort a "get" for their ex-wives. Two brothers from the gang testified to undercover FBI agents that "[b]asically what we are going to be doing is kidnapping a guy for a couple of hours and beating him up and torturing him and then getting him to give the get." The service cost up to $60,000. [25] Six of the members, including one of the rabbis pleaded guilty. In April 2015, a New Jersey jury found the second Orthodox rabbi, nicknamed the "Prodfather" and two other men "guilty of conspiring to kidnap Jewish husbands and violently forc[ing] them to grant their wives religious divorces." When talking to undercover FBI agents, the Rabbi said, "We prefer not to leave a mark." At the trial, the defenses' attorney argued they were "champions of women's rights."[26]

WHERE TO FILE FOR DIVORCE?

Unlike marriage, divorce requires a court order; therefore, it is important to file a request for divorce in the proper state that has jurisdiction (authority) over the spouses. This is especially important because the spouses want the court's order to be recognized in other states. This is the concept of **full force and credit** under the law as provided by the Constitution. While law school classes and textbooks are full of the intricacies of establishing proper jurisdiction, to avoid getting unnecessarily technical, at least one of the parties must have sufficient nexus or connection to the state. States require that a spouse be a resident of the state which means the spouse lives in

---

22   Ibid.
23   "Left in limbo when the honeymoon's over" Tom Hundley and Ana P. Santo, *The Washington Post*, October 12, 2014, P.A12.
24   "Brothers Avrohom and Moshe Goldstein Plead Guilty in 'Get' Extort Scheme", Reuters, *The Jewish Daily Forward*, March 11, 2014. http://forward.com/articles/194289/brothers-avrohom-and-moshe-goldstein-plead-guilty/
25   Ibid, quoting one of the brothers.
26   The Rabbi also talked about what the men should do if the husband was so scared he suffered a heart attack. "'Take a right turn and let him die" he told an undercover agent." One member of the alleged gang, the son of one of the Rabbis, was found not guilty. "N.J. jury finds Orthodox rabbi guilty of kidnap-divorce plot. Reuven Blau, *New York Daily News,* April 21, 2015.

that state and has done so for a specified period of time.[27] The spouse must be **domiciled** in that state with intentions to remain there. Evidence of such intent may include registering to vote, paying local taxes, or obtaining a driver's license. This was more of an issue when divorces were based on fault grounds as some spouses would choose to forum shop, going to states with short residence requirements like Florida or Nevada. In the case of *Gutierrez v. Gutierrez*, Docket No. Kno-06-574, (Maine Supreme Court 2007),[28] the Maine Supreme Court found that a summer home was an insufficient jurisdiction for filing a divorce petition, because the residence was only occupied short periods of time (a few months).

DIVORCE ABROAD

The topic of which foreign divorces are recognized in the United States is beyond the breadth of this textbook. **Comity** looks at the issue of whether a foreign order is recognized and honored in the United States. With globalization, many very rich couples live and have assets in many countries, so where should they file their divorce case? The answer can have a major impact on how the assets are divided. Currently, "London has become the world capital of divorce—a global magnet for those who possess both astronomical sums of money and a burning contempt for their spouses."[29] Because England's courts generally split marital assets 50/50 and provide for lifetime alimony, non-working or lower earning spouses are strategically filing divorce cases there.[30] Former Miss Malaysia and her "wealthy fashion tycoon" husband have spent "millions of dollars in legal fees [trying] to decide where they'll ultimately divide the hundreds of millions left in the bank: Malaysia or England." She is a "67-year-old mother of five" who argues that her "primary residence is the family's sylvan estate outside London, where she keeps 700 pairs from her 1,000-strong shoe collection." In 2014, an English court agreed with her that she had sufficient contact with England and agreed to take the case. "But just weeks later, a Malaysian court sided with her husband—a major shareholder in the retailer Laura Ashley—and ruled the case should actually be heard there." "It's an undignified race to the courthouse door."[31]

---

27 Residency and some other requirements differ for members of the military to accommodate deployments and frequent transfers.

28 http://caselaw.findlaw.com/me-supreme-judicial-court/1466387.html

29 "The appeal of disunion under the Union Jack", Griff Witte & Karla Adam, *The Washington Post*, December 26,2014, P.1.

30 This favorable jurisdiction is not available through-out Britain. Scotland (and other European countries) has a separate legal system that limits alimony to only a few years. Ibid.

31 Citing Timothy Scott. Ibid. "Multimillion-dollar divorce settlement have brought reluctant members of the British comedy troupe Monty Python out of retirement and back on the road for tours and reunions. One member, Terry Jones, recently told the press that despite big proceeds from the shows, he may have to sell his north London mansion to keep up with the payments to his ex-wife."

States may reject a foreign divorce for many reasons including insufficient residency requirements.[32] For example, the Dominican Republic has no residency (or even waiting periods) for foreigners to obtain a divorce, provided both spouses request it (only one has to show up at the court hearing). Many states may not recognize these quickie divorces. Obviously, other countries would not be able to offer quick divorces if there was not a demand. Given that demand, should divorce be made easier? In Guam, for example, if both spouses sign a form consenting to jurisdiction while filing the divorce petition, they can obtain a divorce in about a month. Guam does have a 90-day residency requirement, but if both spouses request the divorce and consent to jurisdiction, the court will presume it is satisfied—and only the spouses could raise the jurisdiction issue. Attending the hearing is not required. Expedited requests of a few days may be available for an extra fee. As Guam is a U.S. territory (with U.S. jurisdiction) the order is valid in the U.S. If there are property issues, these can be resolved in the United States at a later hearing after the Order of Divorce is issued from Guam.[33] Is allowing mail-order divorce a good idea?

THE STATUS OF DIVORCE REQUIREMENTS— GOING AWAY FROM NO-FAULT

So what has been the effect of the no-fault revolution? All states have some form of no fault/marital breakdown as a ground for divorce. Some states keep both no-fault and fault-based grounds. Does this dual system create confusion? No-fault was supposed to eliminate attribution of fault in the distribution of assets at divorce. One advantage of a fault-based system is that without a separation period it may allow for a quicker divorce. No-fault makes it easier for spouses to cooperate and work out the terms of their divorce privately. This also takes the burden off of courts. Thus, the problems of the old no-fault system have been remedied. Under it, if both or even one spouse wants a divorce, they will eventually get it. Has this led to the rise of the national divorce rate to just under half of all marriages? Have we made divorce too easy? Remember, society makes getting married easy in order to encourage it. Is this, in effect, saying that society encourages divorce? Is there something wrong with that if it brings happiness?[34]

There have been recent efforts to revisit divorce as a result of these questions. Some new state requirements are designed to encourage reconciliation or at least confirm that the parties want a divorce. For example, courts have upheld mandatory mediation sessions for spouses in

---

32 England has a one-year residency requirement." Ibid.

33 http://www.legalzoom.com/marriage-divorce-family-law/divorce/divorcing-overseas-hot-spots, "Divorcing Overseas: Hot Spots for Quickie Divorces," by Leanne Phillips, September 2008.

34 Perhaps someone better remind this man that divorce is easy to obtain. In Kansas City, Kansas, a 70-year old man robbed a bank and then "took the money and took a seat in the bank lobby". When questioned by the arriving police, the robber told them that he told his wife, "he'd rather be in jail than home". http://www. duluthnewstribune.com/news/crime/4110121-alleged-bank-robber-70-chooses-prison-over-living-wife. Ironically, he was sentenced to home confinement. https://www.usnews.com/news/best-states/kansas/articles/2017-06-13/kansas-husband-who-robbed-bank-to-avoid-wife-given-probation.

contested divorce cases. In some states, like Oregon, short-term couples' counseling is available to families with minor children, assisting in disputes in their relationship, separation, divorce adjustment, or co-parenting. The mandate of many states for court-ordered divorce education seminars for spouses and minor children have been upheld. Finally, some states are attempting to modify divorce by allowing covenant marriages (see Chapter 9). This allows couples to agree or covenant that they will not divorce unless certain limited marital fault behaviors occur. Is this a return to the fault-based divorce system?

CHAPTER SOURCES

Legal Zoom New York: Making it easier to say "I don't?" by Alice Graves. http://www.legalzoom.com/marriage-divorce-family-law/divorce/new-york-making-it-easier

Wadlington, W., and O'Brien, R. C. (2007). *Domestic Relations*, 6th ed. Foundation Press.

12 DIVIDING THE ASSETS AFTER DIVORCE

I think a lot of times divorce can be like circumcision with a weed whacker.
—Robin Williams[1]

I'm a marvelous housekeeper. Every time I leave a man I keep his house.
—Zsa Zsa Gabor[2]

Have you ever seen a personal check for almost a billion dollars? On January 5, 2015, Harold Hamm, an oilman, wrote his ex-wife a personal check for $975,790,317.77; this was his offer to pay the full cash value of the court ordered billion-dollar divorce judgment, which ended their 26-year marriage (there was no prenuptial agreement). Better yet, his ex-wife, Sue Ann Arnall[3] (she went back to her maiden name after the divorce) rejected it. Her lawyers were concerned that her appeal of the divorce court ruling would be rejected if she accepted the check. During their two and a half year divorce trial, Ms. Arnall's attorney's argued that she was entitled to at least $5 billion of the $11 billion her husband had made in his oil company during their marriage. While the appeal continues, Ms. Arnall may also request alimony from the court. Astonishingly, the $995.5 million[4] in cash plus additional assets is not the largest divorce award ever made.[5]

---

1   As said to Ellen DeGeneres: http://www.hammersbaltazar.com/blog/hey-arnold-want-to-avoid-circumcision-with-a-weed-wacker-ask-robin-williams-about-collaborative-law/#.UhIv7H9ELTo, Hammer's & Baltazar

2   https://www.brainyquote.com/quotes/quotes/z/zsazsagabo125051.html

3   She went back to her birth or "maiden" name after the divorce. "Harold Hamm offers $975 mlm divorce check; ex-wife rejects it", *Cnbc.com*, January 6, 2015.

4   The court ordered the amount be paid with "roughly $320 million" by the end of 2014, and monthly installments of "$7 million or more" thereafter. It is alleged that Mr. Hamm borrowed the money to write the check. "Harold Hamm's $975 Million Uncashed Divorce Check? How About Deducting It?", Robert W. Wood, *Forbes.com* January 8, 2015. http://www.forbes.com/sites/robertwood/2015/01/08/harold-hamms-975-million-uncashed-divorce-check-how-about-deducting-it/

5   For total divorce ordered payments, perhaps media mogul Rupert Murdoch paid the highest amount. His second divorce cost $1.7 billion, which included both pre- and postnuptial agreements; the specifics were sealed by the New

While the old fault-based system of divorce was an attorney full-employment act, the advent of no-fault divorce has moved this to litigation on dividing up the assets.[6] Now, parties may spend disproportionately on attorneys' fees, paying more than the value of the assets retained. Of course, all is fair in love and war—so much of the suspicion and distrust may be more symbolic than realistic. Private ordering, such as a prenuptial agreement, may preclude all of this. Since prenups are still uncommonly used, the spouses may often work out (privately order) the terms of property distribution (and parenting) in an agreement that the divorce court can approve as part of the final divorce decree (see Chapter 4). While the couple may have been dewy-eyed in the early years of marriage, this sentiment is probably gone by the time of divorce. Often communication has deteriorated by this point, but couples may rely on a mediator to help them reach an agreement that creates a "win/win" for both.

DISTRIBUTING PROPERTY IN A DIVORCE

How should property be divided at divorce? Many suggest a modern marriage is a partnership and the assets should be split on a 50/50 basis. Others say that factors such as each spouse's station in life, age, and health should be factored in. What about the length of the marriage? What about punishing the spouse who cheated or committed some other marital fault? A 50/50 split is the rule in community property states. Factoring in other considerations to arrive at a decision on a case-by-case basis is the rule in equitable distribution states. Those who want to extract a financial penalty should be comforted that, while fault-based divorces are declining, courts sometimes still extract "justice."

DIVIDING ASSETS IN DIVORCE

Betty and Bob 1

Meet Betty and Bob, a hypothetical divorcing couple:

Betty and Bob have been married for 12 years; have two sons, and cited "irreconcilable differences" in their mutual decision to divorce. Complicating the dissolution of their marriage is a restaurant that they both run; she is the manager and he is the award-winning chef. They started the restaurant—their dream—after they married, when they both left their jobs as accountants. The restaurant is a big success and is very popular, but the industry is fickle, about 50 percent of all restaurants fail. Although they will no longer be married, their work relationship will continue (as well as co-parenting their two sons). The tensions surrounding the separation are affecting

---

York court, but included the division of hundreds of millions of dollars in real estate. "Rupert Murdoch, Pie-Catching Wife Finalize Divorce", Alan Farnham, *Good Morning America*, November 20, 2014. http://abcnews.go.com/Business/rupert-murdoch-wife-reach-divorce-settlement/story?id=20952190

6   This chapter ignores the issues of child support and parenting, which will be covered in later chapters.

their work. They would like to get the divorce resolved and have already worked out the issues of custody and child support. Now, they need to divide their property and financial obligations, as well as the distribution of labor in the restaurant.

Bob and Betty have been more like roommates or coworkers than a married couple lately and this is what motivated the divorce. Also, Bob was working late at night to close the restaurant after the dinner service. He had also been busy taking care of his sick mother, who just passed away. He feels badly that he has not been at home to see the boys as much as he would like. Bob seems to have some emotional connections to particular items. For example, he thinks fondly of the times he and the boys sailed in the family sailboat and he hopes to take some time away from the restaurant to sail more often. He has moved out of the family home and needs some furniture. In addition to the division of the restaurant, Bob would like to receive:

Italian marble table: $4,000
Half of the $100,000 cash savings
Gold watch from before marriage: $800
Diamond ring that Betty wears, which belonged to his mother: $8,000
Viking Refrigerator: $5,000
Car: $15,000
Sailboat: $50,000
Most of the furniture: $15,000

Betty resented Bob's time away from the house. Now that he is not around due to their separation, she is happier. She enjoys having the house with the boys and would like to stay there. She also has fond memories of the times she spent woodworking with the boys in the basement and would like the workshop items. She would also like to receive:

Italian marble table: $4,000
All of the $100,000 cash savings
All of the jewelry: $10,000
All of the photographs
Antique mirror: $1,000
Car $15,000
Table saw and shop equipment: $8,000
RV from before marriage: $70,000
Waterproof TV: $4,000.

How will they divide up their stuff to finalize the divorce? First, they must determine what their assets are.

WHAT IS AN ASSET?

While the definition of an asset as something of value seems obvious at first blush, sometimes the answer can be surprising.

KULP V. KULP
920 A.2D 867, 2007 PA SUPER 70 (PA 2007)

Background: During divorce action, husband sought interim counsel fees, costs and expenses and special and/or injunctive relief concerning the disposition of the ashes of parties' deceased child. The Court of Common Pleas, Schuylkill County, Civil Division, No. S-2327-2004, Smith, J., directed that child's cremated remains be divided into two separate urns and each party be allowed to place his or her urn at a site of his or her choice, and husband appealed.

Holdings: The Superior Court, No. 269 MDA 2006, Musmanno, J., held that:

1. trial court's order was an appealable collateral order, and
2. trial court abused its discretion in using its equitable powers to override the desires of one of the next of kin as to the division of child's remains and in ordering that child's remains be divided between husband and wife.

Vacated and remanded

Trial court's order directing that cremated remains of parties' deceased child be divided into two separate urns and each party be allowed to place his or her urn at a site of his or her choice was an appealable collateral order in parties' divorce action; the order relating to disposition of child's remains was separable from and collateral to the main cause of action, which involved divorce and the equitable distribution of marital property, the right involved was too important to be denied review, and the question presented was such that, if review was postponed until final judgment in the case, the right might be irreparably lost. Rules App.Proc., Rule 313(b), 42 Pa.C.S.A.

Appellate courts review an order disposing of a petition for special relief under an abuse of discretion standard of review.

The law does not prohibit a trial court from ordering the division of cremated remains where a dispute over the remains arises.

OPINION BY MUSMANNO, J.:

1 David D. Kulp, Jr. ("Husband") appeals from the Order, which directed that the cremated remains of the deceased son of Husband and Georgene Kulp ("Wife") be divided into two separate urns, and allowed each party to place their urn at a site of his/her choice. FN1 We vacate the Order and remand for further proceedings. [Footnote omitted.]

2 The trial court set forth the pertinent facts of this case as follows:

[Husband] has appealed our January 13, 2006 Order equally dividing the cremation*869 ashes of [the parties'] only son ["Son"] into two separate urns with each party having the discretion to place their urn at a site of their choice... The parties are involved in a divorce action filed by [Wife]... on December 1, 2004. During the litigation[,] on August 15, 2005, [Husband] had sought interim counsel fees, costs and expenses and special and/or injunctive relief concerning the disposition of the ashes of [Son]. On October 21, 2005, the Court conducted a hearing on the issues raised by [Husband].

At the conclusion of the hearing[,] we entered [an] order dated October 21, 2005 in which we, among other things, directed [Son's] ashes to remain in the marital residence pending this Court's final order and directing the parties to submit memorand[a] of law on the disposition of the ashes.... After review of the parties' memorand[a], by way of December 8, 2005 Order, we directed the parties to appear for a conference in our courtroom on January 11, 2006 and to present each party's position with regard to the following alternatives:

1. That the ashes be buried in a memorial park or cemetery of mutual choice within Schuylkill County with a portion remaining in a keepsake for each party;
2. That the ashes be placed in an above-ground urn niche in a memorial park or cemetery of mutual choice within Schuylkill County;
3. That the ashes contained in the present urn be divided and placed in two separate urns with each party placing their individual urn at a site of their choosing.

We conducted the conference on January 11, 2006 and then entered the Order at issue. A timely appeal was taken by [Husband] contemporaneously with [Husband] filing a Request for Reconsideration. We denied the reconsideration request.

Trial Court Opinion, 4/6/06, at 1–2. Husband raises the following issues on appeal:

4. Did the trial court abuse its discretion by considering the ashes of the parties' deceased child to be property of the parties and divisible contrary to 20 Pa.C.S.A. § 305(c)?
5. Did the trial court abuse its discretion by ignoring and foregoing a factual analysis regarding reinterment per Pettigrew v. Pettigrew, 207 Pa. 313, 56 A. 878 (1904) and other supporting authorities?... [Procedural issues omitted.]

We also conclude that the right involved is too important to be denied review, and that the question presented is such that, if review is postponed until final judgment in the case, the right may be irreparably lost. The right sought by Husband is the right to keep Son's remains intact and not divided. Husband also seeks to have Son's remains moved to a burial site. Due to the nature of the remains, and the hostility between the parties as demonstrated by the record, the relief which Husband seeks may be irreparably lost if review is postponed until final judgment in the case. Thus, we conclude that all three prongs of the collateral order doctrine are present in this case. Therefore, we will review the trial court's Order.

6. Husband contends that the trial court abused its discretion by considering the remains of Son to be the parties' property and thus divisible, and by ignoring and foregoing a factual analysis regarding reinterment. We review an order disposing of a petition for special relief under an abuse of discretion standard of review. See *Johnson v. Johnson*, 908 A.2d 290, 295 (Pa. Super.2006). In addition, we note that, in matrimonial cases, the Divorce Code provides that the court shall have full equity power and jurisdiction and may issue injunctions or other orders which are necessary to protect the interests of the parties or to effectuate the purposes of this part and may grant such other relief or remedy as equity and justice require against either party or against any third person over whom the court has jurisdiction and who is involved in or concerned with the disposition of the cause.

23 Pa.C.S.A. 3323(f).

7. Husband relies on section 305(c) of the Probate, Estates, and Fiduciaries ("PEF") Code to assert that there is no property right in a decedent's remains. Husband also relies on *Pettigrew v. Pettigrew*, 207 Pa. 313, 56 A. 878 (1904) and *Novelli v. Carroll*, 278 Pa.Super. 141, 420 A.2d 469 (1980), in support of his argument. In addition, Husband asserts that the testimony before the trial court establishes that the parties had agreed to eventually bury Son's remains in a cemetery, specifically, Higher-Ups Cemetery.

8. Control of a decedent's remains is governed by section 305 of the PEF Code, which provides in pertinent part as follows:

§ 305. Right to dispose of a decedent's remains

(a) General rule.—The determination of the final disposition of a decedent's remains shall be as set forth in this section unless otherwise specifically provided by waiver and agreement of the person entitled to make such determination under this section, subject to the provisions of a valid will executed by the decedent and section 8611(a) (relating to persons who may execute anatomical gift).

Disposition of the remains of a deceased spouse.—Absent an allegation of enduring estrangement, incompetence, contrary intent or waiver and agreement which is proven by clear and convincing evidence, a surviving spouse shall have the sole authority in all matters pertaining to the disposition of the remains of the decedent.

*871 (c) Disposition of the remains of others.—If there is not a surviving spouse, absent an allegation of enduring estrangement, incompetence, contrary intent or waiver and agreement which is proven by clear and convincing evidence, the next of kin shall have sole authority in all matters pertaining to the disposition of the remains of the decedent.

20 Pa.C.S.A. § 305. Thus, according to the PEF Code, where a deceased person does not have a surviving spouse, the next of kin have the sole authority in matters concerning disposition of a decedent's remains "absent an allegation of enduring estrangement, incompetence, contrary intent or waiver and agreement." Id. § 305(c). FN2

FN2. "Next of kin" are defined as "[t]he spouse and relatives by blood of the deceased in order that they be authorized to succeed to the deceased's estate under Chapter 21 (relating to intestate succession) as long as the person is an adult or an emancipated minor." Id. § 305(e). Under the intestate statutes, if a decedent has no surviving spouse, then his estate goes to his issue, and if no issue, to his parents. 20 Pa.C.S.A. § 2103.

9. The Pettigrew case, upon which Husband relies, is a central case in Pennsylvania law concerning burial rights. In Pettigrew, the Court held that the paramount right to control the body of a deceased person for interment is in the surviving spouse, and if there is no spouse, in the next of kin. Id. at 315, 56 A. 878. The Court summarized its holding as follows:

The result of a full examination of the subject [of disposition of human remains] is that there is no universal rule applicable alike to all cases, but each must be considered in equity on its own merits, having due regard to the interests of the public, the wishes of the decedent, and the rights and feelings of those entitled to be heard by reason of relationship or association. Subject to this general result, it may be laid down: First. That the paramount right [of control of the body for interment] is in the surviving husband or widow, and, if the parties were living in the normal relations of marriage, it will require a very strong case to justify a court in interfering with the wish of the survivor. Secondly. If there is no surviving husband or wife, the right is in the next of kin in the order of their relation to the decedent, as children of proper age, parents, brothers and sisters, or more distant kin, modified, it may be, by circumstances of special intimacy or association with the decedent. Thirdly[.] How far the desires of the decedent should prevail against those of a surviving husband or wife is an open question, but as against remoter connections, such wishes especially if strongly and recently expressed, should usually prevail. Fourthly. With regard to a reinterment in a different place, the same rules should apply, but with a presumption against removal growing stronger with the remoteness of connection with the decedent, and reserving always the right of the court to require reasonable cause to be shown for it.

Id. Thus, Pettigrew requires, in determining the disposition of a decedent's remains, that each case be considered on its own merits, the wishes of the decedent and the interests of the public be considered, the rights and feelings of the surviving spouse or next of kin are paramount, and a party seeking reinterment must demonstrate reasonable cause for such reinterment.

10. In Novelli v. Carroll, 278 Pa.Super. 141, 420 A.2d 469, this Court expanded the factors that must be considered by a court in deciding a request for reinterment. FN3 *872 The Court set forth the following factors: (1) the degree of relationship that the party seeking reinterment bears to the decedent and the strength of that relationship; (2) the degree of relationship that the party seeking to prevent reinterment bears to the decedent; (3) the desire of the decedent, including the "general presumption that the decedent would not wish his remains to be disturbed," or a specific statement of desire by the decedent; (4) "the conduct of the party seeking reinterment, especially as it may relate to the circumstances of the original interment;" (5) the conduct of the person seeking to prevent reinterment; (6) "the length of time that has elapsed since the original interment;" FN4 and (7) the strength of the reasons offered in favor of and in opposition to reinterment. Id. at 472–74.

FN3. A question arises as to whether the instant case involves an original interment or a reinterment. Son's cremated remains have not been "interred" in the earth, but rather have been placed in the marital home since the cremation. On the other hand, Husband is seeking to relocate Son's remains from their original location. On this basis, we find it helpful to take guidance from case law regarding reinterment.

FN4. "Generally, the sooner the person seeking reinterment acts after the original interment, the better the chance of obtaining reinterment." Id. at 474.

11. The language of section 305 of the PEF Code supports Husband's position that the right to dispose of a decedent's remains is not a property right, but rather an "authority" to dispose of the remains. The Pettigrew case also supports this position. However, the question of whether the Court has the power to order division of the remains is not answered by the conclusion that the remains are not property. Here, the parties who have the authority to dispose of Son's remains are Son's next of kin, his parents. The next of kin disagree as to the appropriate disposition of the remains. Therefore, Husband sought the assistance of the court. As Wife has pointed out, a court hearing a case under the Divorce Code has "full equity power and jurisdiction" to issue injunctions or other necessary orders and to grant such relief "as equity and justice require." 23 Pa.C.S.A. § 3323(f).

12. Although there are no appellate cases involving division of cremated remains in this jurisdiction, we note that at least two other jurisdictions have permitted the division of such remains. In *Estate of K. A.*, 807 N.E.2d 748 (Ind.App.2004), the appellate court approved a trial court's order directing that the cremated remains of the deceased child of the parties be divided

equally between the parties. The appellate court reasoned that (1) division of the remains was consistent with the deceased child's own wishes that her remains be scattered in three different states; (2) the Indiana Code governing final disposition of remains does not distinguish between custodial and non-custodial parents; thus, the custodial parent, did not have a superior right to determine the disposition of the remains; and (3) testimony was offered that "the practice of dividing the remains of a decedent among the survivors is common and acceptable in the funeral service industry." Id. at 751; see also *Stewart v. Schwartz Brothers-Jeffer Memorial Chapel*, Inc., 159 Misc.2d 884, 606 N.Y.S.2d 965 (1993) (expressing approval, in a dispute over whether the decedent desired cremation, of the parties' agreement to allow cremation of the decedent's body and to split the cremated remains).

13. In our view, the law does not prohibit a trial court from ordering the division of cremated remains where a dispute over the remains arises. Nevertheless, the issue is an extremely sensitive *873 one. While the division of cremated remains may be common in the funeral industry and may be acceptable in many instances to the next of kin, in other cases, as in the case of Husband herein, the next of kin may believe that the division of cremated remains is offensive. The question thus presented is whether the trial court in the instant case abused its discretion in ordering the division of Son's remains.

14. As recognized by the Court in Pettigrew, the rights and feelings of the next of kin are paramount, where there is no surviving spouse, in determining the disposition of a decedent's remains. Pettigrew, 56 A. at 880. In the instant case, the parties stand on equal footing as Son's next of kin. See 20 Pa.C.S.A. § 305(c); see also Estate of K. A., 807 N.E.2d at 751 (holding that, under Indiana law, one of two divorced parents does not have a superior right to determine the disposition of their child's remains). Given the extremely sensitive nature of this issue, and Husband's opposition to division of the remains, we conclude that the trial court abused its discretion in using its equitable powers to override the desires of one of the next of kin as to the division of Son's remains.

15. As to the issue of the placement of Son's remains, the factors set forth in Pettigrew and expanded in Novelli govern. The trial court did not specifically discuss these factors in its decision.

16. Because of our conclusion that the trial court abused its discretion in ordering that son's remains be divided, we vacate the trial court's Order, and remand for re-consideration of the issue of placement of Son's cremated remains. On remand, the trial court shall consider and apply the factors set forth in Pettigrew and Novelli to the facts of this case.

17. Order vacated; case remanded for further proceedings in accordance with this Opinion; Superior Court jurisdiction relinquished.

How does the *Kulp* court determine their deceased son's ashes should be treated in the divorce? Do they have a special nature that deserves special treatment?[7]

Sometimes, the issue is not only what the asset is, but whether it must have "value." Generally, when thinking of dividing the assets at divorce, things like the house, car, bank accounts, clothing, and personal items come to mind. But in today's society, when financial issues may be a major cause for divorce, many couples do not have substantial assets to divide. If a couple must divide up marital assets, should they also have to split the debt (or obligations) of their married life? Courts are increasingly including the responsibility of debt along with the benefits of assets when calculating property resolutions in divorce.[8] When the real estate market was soaring, divorcing couples often sold their homes for a profit and used the extra money (equity) to finance their post-divorce lives. Often, the battle during the divorce would be over who would keep the house (seen as an astute financial investment). After the 2008 economic recession, when many houses were worth less than the couple had paid, divorcing couples fought over who would have to *keep* the house in the divorce.

Courts have included anything from the goodwill of a business (e.g., client lists and business relationships) to a stock option that may be exercised in the future as an asset. What if a married spouse is in a car accident and wins a lawsuit for the injury after the divorce? (Generally, personal injury awards are personal to the one who was injured.) What if one spouse had earned a graduate degree while the other spouse continued to work to support the household—does this have value that should be divided at the divorce? Any student reading this book would hope that earning a degree has more than an intrinsic value when it comes time to pay student loans. Most courts, however, are reluctant to classify an advanced degree as a marital asset because of uncertainties of its value. In New York, however, the courts may recognize this value. In *O'Brien v. O'Brien*, 489 N.E.2d 712 (N.Y. 1985), a woman teacher marries a man who, "[a]t the time of marriage… was a college dropout, and except for a brief period of employment, attended school throughout the vast majority of his married life." As part of the husband's education to become a medical doctor, the wife gave up her job and moved to Mexico so that the husband could attend medical school while the wife worked, sometimes two or three jobs, to support them. Three years later, they returned to New York for the husband to do his residency. Two months after he earned his medical license, he filed for divorce. Based on expert projections at trial offered by the wife, the court determined that the medical degree was marital property and awarded the woman about $188,000. The court acknowledged that this was a "unique case" influenced by the fact that there were no other marital assets to split up and the wife had made a substantial financial contribution to allow the husband to obtain his medical degree. "When a spouse finances another's education, and thus high earning capacity, it is unfair to deny her a share of this asset which would not exist

---

7   Compare this case to the opposite spectrum of the cycle of life, the cases dealing with the division of frozen sperm or pre-embryos in divorces like *Hecht v. Kane* and *Davis v. Davis* (see Chapter 15).

8   *Hardy v. Hardy*, 311 S.C. 433 429 S.E. 2d 811 (1993), imposing some of the husband's credit card debt on the wife at divorce.

but for her efforts."[9] Is a graduate degree property? Can it be held in the hand or inherited? Is this approach supported by the concern that an advanced degree is really only the product of intelligence, skill, and hard work? Most courts do not agree with the *O'Brien* decision and do not allow the division of a degree as property at a divorce.

WHEN ARE MARITAL ASSETS CREATED?

Asset classification is also complicated by the issue of the time when it was acquired. Most think of marital assets as assets obtained by the couple during their marriage. But the time lines can be blurred. One would think that the date of the wedding would mark the clear beginning of the period, but what if the couple lived together for a long time before marriage? Would the bakery they started before their marriage be included in the marital assets? What if only one of them started the bakery pre-marriage, but the other spouse eventually worked there full time, then the couple married? Or what if the bakery belonged to the wife before the marriage, but the husband started to work there after the marriage? This issue may become more common as same-sex couples, who are now allowed to marry, convert their status to marriage from long-term domestic partnerships. Often, these raise complicated questions and require third party experts, like accountants, to trace the funds involved over the duration of the relationship.

On the other end, courts also need to determine whether the date of the marriage demarcation should be modified; when should the marital period end? Sometimes, couples separate years in advance of the final divorce decree; if the spouses have not agreed, the courts will need to clarify this cut-off date as well. Should it be the date the couple separated? The day the husband moved out? What happens if he moves in or out again later? This determination can be costly if a spouse buys a winning lottery ticket during this period.

VALUATING THE ASSETS

Once the issue of classifying assets and time periods is resolved, the court will need to determine the value. This is time consuming and expensive. First, the spouse must produce detailed inventories so both can agree on the quantities involved. Often, a third party expert is needed to appraise the value of the assets, which adds another layer of expenses (they usually charge a percentage of the value assessed). How do quarreling spouses agree on which appraiser to use? Sometimes each spouse does his/her own appraisal, further raising the costs and delay.

---

9   From the N.Y Supreme Court's lower review in *O'Brien v. O'Brien,* **114 Misc. 2d 233—NY: Supreme Court 1982.**

Betty and Bob 2

With this new knowledge on classifying assets, how should Betty and Bob's assets be classified?

IDENTIFY SEPARATE PROPERTY

First, identify any "separate property". Separate property is property that a spouse owned before the marriage. It may also include property obtained during the marriage as a gift or inheritance.[10] For Betty, that would include the RV worth $70,000. For Bob, it includes his gold watch worth $4,000. Although the diamond ring is from his mother, since she just passed away and the ring was used as the engagement ring for Betty, how should it be treated? It will probably be classified as a gift to Betty, which she could keep after the divorce.

What about Bob's Cordon Bleu award that he earned after they married—is that an asset? Under the majority rule, professional degrees are generally not considered assets (but Betty may ask for reimbursement if she sacrificed to maintain the home while he was in culinary school to earn it).

What about the credit card debt? Betty has a store card that she had before they married and which carries about $3,000 balance each month. They also have a joint Visa card that they use for the household and the restaurant. Under the *Hardy* case, most courts today would consider dividing debt along with assets.

This leaves the "pot" of pure marital assets of:

The house and furniture
The restaurant and business
Jewelry
$100,000 cash
A car worth $15,000
The sailboat, worth $50,000
The workshop

IDENTIFY THE MARITAL PROPERTY?

Generally, courts will presume that all property created during the couple's married life is marital property, unless the spouses separate that property during the life of the marriage (e.g., keeping a separate bank account or a safety deposit box).

---

10   Separate property is generally that which each spouse had before a marriage, plus any property obtained during the marriage acquired by gift or inheritance, exchanged for separate property or subject to a valid agreement of the parties. For purposes of this book, the system is simplified. For example, separate property can be commingled (mixed in) with the other assets and lose its "separate" status during the marriage.

DIVISION OF PROPERTY

Common Law

Historically, under the common law, the "title" theory was used to determine ownership of property. So the spouse, who bought it, owns it. If the property (real estate) has a title or deed that is in the name of both the husband and wife, they would both have a half-interest in it. Thus, in the early part of the last century, when men worked and women stayed home to raise the children, the husband would have purchased the assets in his own name and could retain them at divorce. No wonder divorce was seen as a bad deal for women.

Due to the obvious inequity that a title system placed on stay-at-home mothers, there was a transition to allowing more flexibility by the judge in determining property distribution at divorce. To overcome this penalty on women and as guidance to the courts, states established legal guidelines for the courts to use in dividing marital assets at divorce. Many clarified that the contribution of the stay-at-home mother had value, but the law "giveth with one hand and taketh away with the other." Under fault-based divorce, the court would often factor in a spouse's marital fault in distributing the assets—especially if the fault was adultery. In a fault-based system of divorce, court cases involved lengthy determinations of the issue of fault, because of its effect on the property distribution issues.

Even under today's no-fault system, some courts may still look at fault in making a property distribution. The question of spousal support in the case of *Congdon v. Congdon,* 40 VA. App. 255, 578 S.E.2d 833 (2003), was decided on Code § 20-107.1(B), which provides that "no permanent maintenance and support shall be awarded from a spouse if there exists in such spouse's favor a ground of divorce under the provisions of subdivision (1) of § 20-91, which includes adultery subject to the exception that such a denial "would constitute a manifest injustice, based upon the respective degrees of fault during the marriage and the relative economic circumstances of the parties." Although the wife admits that she committed adultery, negative allegations were also made against her husband, John.

> # CONGDON V. CONGDON
> ## 40 VA. APP. 255,
> ## 578 S.E.2D 833 (2003)

The evidence also portrayed John as a profane and verbally abusive man. John frequented "strip joints and topless bars" and told Lynn about, among other things, the "oil wrestlers" that performed at these places. He would indiscriminately engage in these conversations in the presence of his children and Lynn's family, at times even "boasting or bragging about those places." "It was not an infrequent topic of conversation." John went to these places, he explained to one witness, "because they have the best p—." John "frequently talked crudely about sexual type things." He carried on with this practice "[p]retty much the same the whole 20 years."

John also directed his profanity toward his children. In one instance, John's son Michael had accidentally kicked his father's head while both were lying on a bed watching television. Though realizing it was simply an accident, John "started yelling. God damn you, Michael. Why in the f— did you kick me in the face. Why did you f—ing have to kick me in the face?" In response, Michael ran out of the house. On another occasion, John was having a "food fight" with his twelve-year-old daughter when John accidentally got hit in the eye. He "started screaming. God damn you. God damn, you hit me in the eye." His daughter "just sat there and started crying," not at all understanding her father's outburst. Other times John would come home from work angry and declare, in ear-shot of his children, that "one of the girls at the office" was a "bitch or a c—." His use of vulgarity, in the presence of his family and others, "was quite frequent."

Several witnesses who knew John and Lynn over the years testified that they had never once seen John show any affection or any kindness toward Lynn. Over the course of the marriage, John chronically complained (both to Lynn and others) about Lynn's weight, appearance, housekeeping, and spending habits. John referred to Lynn as "Witch." He was a "heavy drinker," sometimes starting as early as "10:00 in the morning." Because John maintained strict control over the financial accounts, Lynn was not "privy to the family finances at any time during the marriage." John particularly disliked Lynn's family and threatened on one occasion to move her out of town if she did not "stop speaking with her parents."

Despite these problems, John and Lynn enjoyed considerable financial security. John has a college degree, a stable and long-term career in a family trucking business, an annual salary exceeding $250,000, and additional income from corporate dividends and family related gifts. John's interests in stocks, real estate, and tangible assets exceeded $6 million. In contrast, Lynn has not held a full time job since the early years of her marriage, choosing instead to stay at home to raise their three children. She has no college degree, giving her a future earning capacity far below her husband's. At the time of trial, Lynn was earning $10.00 an hour as a receptionist. (pg. 832)

The trial court also heard evidence that John's stock in his family business increased in value over the course of the marriage. Conceding that John acquired the shares as a gift from his family and thus should be considered separate property, Lynn argued that under Code § 20-107.3(A)(3)(a) the appreciation portion of the stock's present value should be treated as marital property. In reply, John presented extensive testimony on the internal management of the business and the role of six other key employees in the company's success.

After the close of the evidence, the trial court issued a comprehensive letter opinion detailing each aspect of the court's rulings on divorce grounds, equitable distribution, and spousal support. On the first issue on appeal, the adultery bar against spousal support, the court invoked the "manifest injustice" exception in Code § 20-107.1(B). After considering the additional factors in Code § 20-107.1(E), the court awarded support of $2,300 per month to Lynn to continue until her death or remarriage. On the second issue on appeal, the classification (marital or separate property) of the stock appreciation, the court found that 90% of the increase in value should be deemed separate property given the extensive efforts of other key employees and the extent of "passive growth" in the stock value…

On the "respective degrees of fault" issue, the evidence before the trial judge pits Lynn's admitted adultery against John's twenty-year showing of base and profane behavior, not only with his wife, but with his children and his extended family. We believe a reasonable jurist could put John's "fault" in a league apart from the type of mere incivility or petulance of manners ordinarily alleged, and often proved, in nearly every contested divorce case. We thus dismiss as exaggerated John's argument that sustaining the trial court's finding on these facts would effectively write the "respective degrees of fault" factor out of Code § 20-107.1(B). Nor do we believe, as John contends, that the trial court's finding essentially declares that John's behavior "amounted to a justification for adultery." The law does not excuse, condone, or justify Lynn's infidelity. But neither does the law turn a blind eye to John's behavior, which multiple witnesses described as both unrestrained and longstanding.

On the second factor, the "relative economic circumstances of the parties," Code § 20-107.1(B), the trial court found "extreme disparities in their relative economic situations, both in terms of earning capacity, current incomes and other economic assets and resources." Ample evidence supports this finding. John has a secure job with a family company paying over $250,000 a year plus corporate dividends and family related gifts. John's interests in stocks, real estate, and tangible assets exceeds $6 million. On the other hand, Lynn has no separate assets of any significance and holds down a $10.00-an-hour job as a receptionist.

For these reasons, the trial court was not plainly wrong in finding, by clear and convincing evidence, that denying spousal support under Code § 20-107.1(B) would constitute a "manifest injustice" based upon the respective degrees of fault attributable to John and Lynn as well as their disparate financial circumstances. Because credible evidence supports that conclusion, we affirm the trial court on this issue.

Should the *Congdon* appellate court take the factual findings of the husband's behavior into consideration when determining an award of spousal support? About half of the states take fault into consideration when allocating assets as necessary to promote accountability for bad conduct.[11]

COMMUNITY PROPERTY VERSUS EQUITABLE DISTRIBUTION APPROACHES

While each state has its own system, for simplicity's sake, this book focuses on the two general systems of community property and common law/equitable distribution.

COMMUNITY PROPERTY

The **community property** states recognize a married couple's efforts as a joint and equal effort—like a partnership—and so the property is each of theirs, not just the property of one. The eight states that use the community property system include Arizona, California, Idaho, Louisiana, New Mexico, Nevada, Texas, Washington, and Wisconsin. Under this system, each spouse keeps his or her separate property at divorce. The couple then splits the remaining community property equally. Fault is irrelevant and ignored.

EQUITABLE DISTRIBUTION

The remaining and substantial majority of states are some form of **equitable distribution** states. The goal of this system is to allow the judge to determine a fair distribution of the assets based on each case. Although each state has a statute that details the factors a court may look at when making its determination, the judge still has substantial latitude to determine fairness. Remember, equitable does not mean equal or 50/50, it means fair under the circumstances.

Many states have adopted the Uniform Marital and Divorce Act (UMDA) from 1970 and amended it. The UMDA focuses on four factors for the court to weigh when making an asset distribution: "1. The contribution of each spouse to that property (including homemaking services); 2. The value of the property set apart to each spouse; 3. The duration of the marriage; and 4. The economic circumstances of each spouse at the time of dissolution, including the desirability of awarding the family home to the primary custodian of the children." Also, another difference is that in community property states, separate property is off limits for division, while in many equitable distribution states, the courts may have to reach back and use some or all of the property to ensure a fair division. Today, lending guidelines require most banks to include both spouses on

---

11 *Domestic Relations*, 6th ed. Wadlington and O'Brien, Foundation Press 2007.

loans, and most property is jointly owned in a marriage, so this is not as much of an issue. Now, marital property is seen as all property from the marriage, no matter how held.[12]

The advent of no-fault divorce has encouraged couples to work together to resolve the issues surrounding their divorce and avoid the expense of the court deciding those issues. Reflected in these modern systems for dividing assets is the elimination of fault-based penalties and often the long-term obligation of one spouse to continue to financially support the other spouse after the marriage is over. Some states are still slow to reject financial punishment for marital fault.[13] A Virginia law precludes awarding spousal support when a spouse commits adultery (unless it would result in an injustice.)

Modern Approach

Today, many courts are accepting the "partnership model," which recognizes the modern marriage as a partnership. Both parties contribute in their own way, and there is at least an implied agreement that such contributions are accepted by both as equal.[14] As a result, long-term alimony, or spousal support (see below) awards are not generally made under the theory that each partner has a unique skill that was used during the marriage and available for the future when the marriage dissolves. Is this a fair exchange?

---

12   For purposes of this book, this is a simplified presentation of the law. There are certainly many exceptions to the "equal division" rule; if, for example:

One spouse misappropriates the community property, whether before or during a pending divorce.

One spouse has incurred educational debts. This is the same as separately incurred debt. On divorce, the spouse takes his or her GSL loans with him or her.

One spouse incurred tort liability NOT based on activity for the benefit of the marital community.

A personal injury award is community property during the marriage, but on divorce is awarded to the injured spouse.

"Negative community" refers to a situation where the community liabilities and debts exceed the available assets to pay the liabilities and debts. Here, the relative ability of spouses to pay the debt is considered. The interest here is to protect creditors. http://family.findlaw.com/marriage/what-s-mine-is-mine-what-s-yours-is-mine-who-owns-what-in.html

13   *Domestic Relations*, 6th ed., Wadlington and O'Brien, Foundation Press 2007. About 14 state statutes authorize the court to divide all the property of one spouse at divorce without regard to when, how, or by whom the property was acquired.

14   English courts generally allow the 50/50 split indicating value for both the non-working parent raising the children and the working spouse. In a March 2015 case, the English courts extended that idea beyond the assets at the time of the divorce to allow the "ex-wife of a man who later made millions" to at least attempt to claim some of that value. The "new-age" travelers met at Stonehenge where a group was protesting against nuclear weapons, had a baby, got married and 10-years later divorced. A few years later, the man built a windmill "out of scrap to power the old ambulance in which he still lived". Thirty years later, he had built up his electricity company to be worth 90 million British pounds. The woman who had raised their child now claims that she is entitled to some of that and the English Supreme Court agreed to at least allow her to make a claim in court for it. Should she succeed, the case will send a strong message of recognition of the value of a parent staying home to raise the children. "Finally divorced women who bring up the children have some legal value", Anne Perkins, *The Guardian*, March 2015. http://www.theguardian.com/commentisfree/2015/mar/11/divorced-women-children-legal-value-supreme-court

Spousal Support/Alimony

In an effort to protect women from the effects of divorce, especially under the title system when men worked outside of the home and women raised the children, a system for awarding alimony was created. Working women have reduced the need to provide traditional alimony/spousal support at divorce.

Reflecting the fiction of oneness and the husband's obligation to provide for and support his wife for life, alimony (from the Latin for sustenance) was awarded to the wife who sacrificed her career to stay at home (often to raise the children) while the husband worked outside of the home. Courts were sympathetic to the idea of providing for the wife after marriage since she had limited ways to do so for herself. Generally, the rule was that if one spouse needed it and the other could provide it, alimony was awarded. Two kinds of alimony were traditionally recognized in divorce. The first, *pendent lite* (meaning pending the litigation), was temporary alimony, which provided financial support during the period from when the parties separated until the final court hearing on the divorce. While some states may have statutory guidelines for calculating spousal support *pendent lite*, many spouses work out their own terms. (Often, the terms of the temporary support serves as the basis for the final order of support). The second type of alimony, permanent alimony, is the court-ordered amount awarded at the time the divorce is granted. Under fault-based divorce, alimony awards may be increased or decreased based on the fault of the parties involved (especially adultery). Today, courts are guided by many factors, including fairness.

Now, courts generally do not award long-term support obligations in divorce cases, which thwart the intent of divorce to allow a "clean break." Moreover, the norm of women working has reduced the need to provide traditional alimony at divorce. Now known as maintenance or spousal support, either spouse may have to pay support to the other.[15]

Generally, the possibility of spousal support depends on the facts of the case. As a rule of thumb, the courts used to award it according to need and the ability to pay. There are additional factors, such as children (although child support was created to deal with this factor), unequal income/employment, length of the marriage, and the spouse's age or health (serious mental or physical problems may be the exception to a short-term award). Now, support is generally for rehabilitation or reimbursement alimony. In rehabilitation awards, the court may grant a larger monthly amount for a limited period (a year or two) to allow the spouse to get back on her feet and find a way to earn support. Reimbursement support may occur when a spouse has sacrificed for the other's benefit so that the support helps to pay back this cost. This is common in cases in which one spouse worked while the other earned an advanced educational degree. While in the *O'Brien v. O'Brien* case discussed above, the court held that the graduate degree was an asset of the marriage, states typically reject this theory and reimburse instead.[16]

15 *Orr v. Orr* (1979). The Supreme Court invalidated a state law requiring husbands, but not wives, to pay alimony.
16 In Texas, spousal support is awarded in only extremely limited circumstances. The Uniform Marriage and Divorce Act rejects permanent spousal support in most situations.

EFFECTS OF REMARRIAGE/DEATH

Many state laws traditionally required alimony/support awards to continue until death or remarriage of the wife (to fulfill the husband's common law duty of support). Although states were probably paternal in making these requirements, does the later requirement unfairly penalize the wife? Does it allow her husband (who is free to marry without financial penalty) to control his ex-wife beyond the divorce? Is this an extension of the fiction of oneness?

What happens if the wife remarries, but then that marriage is annulled? Courts split on whether husband number one will have to resume paying alimony to his ex-wife. What happens if the wife cohabitates with someone else? Does this trigger the penalty? California's law has a rebuttable presumption that cohabitation reduces the wife's financial need. But if divorce is granted during that moment when the marriage is over, it has been determined that the wife needs support and the husband can pay it, what difference should future events make? Certainly, divorce agreements should clarify these issues.

One curious case illustrates the effects of these rules. Before they left, Beth Rice had t-shirts printed that said "Vegas Wedding Weekend, June 10–13, 2004." "Beth Rice and Stanley Blacker of Florida stood in front of 50 guests in a Las Vegas wedding chapel [and] went through a traditional Jewish ceremony where they exchanged rings and then left for a vacation together in Europe. They returned to a shared home with her children who call him 'stepfather.'" When her ex-husband sued to end his $5,000 per month alimony payments because Beth had remarried, she said that she did not. She admitted that she intended to get married, but when her husband refused to modify the child support she received, she "decided not to officially get married and 'told guests that despite what [the] program said, the event [was] no longer a wedding but [a] commitment ceremony.'" She never obtained a marriage license, so are they married?

At the hearing on the husband's suit to end alimony, Beth said, "He's not my husband." "We are living together. We are cohabitating. We saw no reason we could not cohabitate." The Florida court agreed and held that they were not married, so her ex-husband had to continue to pay alimony from their divorce five years before. The court noted that without the license, the couple had none of the benefits of marriage; they could not file a joint tax return, or collect social security benefits. In ruling, the court wrote that while it thought that a *de facto* marriage had occurred, this is not sufficient under Florida law "to terminate the alimony" and left the issue for the Florida legislature. While the court wrote, "If it walks like a duck and quacks like a duck, it is most certainly a duck," and while they "are a family now"... "[t]his was a ceremony. This was not a wedding."[17] Perhaps the court felt, "what happens in Vegas stays in Vegas."

Compare this case to the *Stroud v. Stroud* case from Virginia. Why did the two courts decide so differently?

---

17   http://www.sptimes.com/2005/01/27/Tampabay/I_take_thee__unless_i.shtml, "I take thee... unless it messes up my alimony," by Brady Dennis for *Tampa Bay Times*, January 27, 2005.

Background: Ex-husband brought action to terminate spousal support. The Circuit Court, Fairfax County, M. Langhorne Keith, J., found that ex-husband had not established cohabitation by the preponderance of the evidence. Ex-husband appealed, and ex-wife cross-appealed.

Holdings: The Court of Appeals, James W. Haley, Jr., J., held that:

1. word "person" as used in the spousal support termination provision of parties' property settlement agreement included individuals of both sexes, and
2. evidence was sufficient to show that ex-wife's relationship with her girlfriend constituted cohabitation in a situation analogous to marriage for purposes of terminating ex-husband's spousal support obligation.

Affirmed in part, reversed in part, and remanded.
JAMES W. HALEY, JR., Judge.

*365 I.

The primary issues here for resolution are (1) whether the evidence compels the conclusion that the terms of a property settlement agreement ("PSA") terminating spousal support upon "cohabitation with any person... in a situation analogous to marriage" have been met, and (2) if so, whether such a clause involving a relationship among persons of the same sex is operative as a matter of law in Virginia.

Joseph Anthony Stroud ("husband") maintains that the trial court: (1) erred in finding that husband had not established cohabitation by the preponderance of the evidence, and (2) erred in finding as a matter of law in Virginia that individuals of the same sex cannot cohabitate in a situation analogous to marriage. We agree and reverse on these issues.

Debra Lyn Stroud ("wife") has assigned as error the trial court decision (1) to permit the introduction of evidence concerning the parties' negotiations before execution of the PSA, and (2) to deny her request for attorney's fees. We affirm on these issues.

*366 II.

The parties were divorced by decree entered April 7, 1999. That decree ratified, affirmed, and incorporated a PSA dated March 22, 1999. The PSA required husband to pay wife $4,000 per month spousal support. The PSA continued: "[T]he aforesaid payments shall end upon the death of either party, the remarriage of Wife and/or her cohabitation with any person to whom she is not related by blood or marriage in a situation analogous to marriage for a period of thirty (30) or more continuous days…." Husband alleges the "person" here involved, who triggered the spousal support termination clause, was a female we identify as "Robyn."

In opening statements, wife's attorney noted that the issues in controversy included her "cohabitation with any person" and Virginia law concerning same-sex relationships. At trial, husband offered a pre-execution draft of the PSA, and testimony concerning the same. The trial court admitted both, concluding the PSA was ambiguous and such evidence, concerning "negotiations for a settlement," was admissible to discern the parties' intent in the use of the word "person" in the PSA. Wife has assigned this ruling as cross-error, maintaining the admission of the evidence violated the parol evidence rule. We disagree.

In this case, a foundational issue was whether the parties intended, by the use of the word "person" in the context of the PSA, only individuals of different sexes, or individuals of both sexes. We hold the word "person" can be understood in either way by an objectively reasonable standard and, accordingly, that word is ambiguous as it is used in the PSA.

Subsequent to the trial court's ruling on admissibility, husband testified that drafts of a proposed PSA "had already bounced back and forth several times [before] we finalized it on March 16th… and it was signed on March 22nd." Introduced into evidence was a draft PSA in which the support termination clause read "cohabitation with a male in a situation analogous to marriage…." (. Husband testified, "I remember scratching that out and putting in 'person,' and submitting that to my attorney, who submitted it to [wife's attorney's] office."

Likewise, relevant to interpreting the word "person" in the PSA is evidence offered by wife. On direct examination by her counsel, wife testified as follows:

Q. You testified a moment ago that you don't live with [Robyn] in a relationship analogous to a marriage. Are there reasons for that?

A. Yeah. The most important reason is the fact that I signed an agreement with [husband] in 1999 that said that I would not cohabit with anyone in a situation analogous to marriage for 30 consecutive days, and I was very aware of that and I kept track…

III.

FACTS

The evidence considered by the trial court with respect to cohabitation was essentially undisputed. That evidence included wife's written response to husband's request for admissions, a transcript of wife's deposition, a Christmas letter written by Robyn, and a **147 stipulation of facts entered into by the parties concerning the observations of private detectives. Relevant to this opinion are also the facts that wife owned a home, and Robyn owned a home on a different street.

Responding to husband's request, wife admitted the following: (1) Robyn stayed overnight in her house "an average of 5 nights per week for a period in excess of one year"; (2) Robyn "sleeps in the same bed" with her; (3) Robyn keeps clothes in wife's bedroom closet and toiletries in wife's bedroom's bathroom; (4) she engages "in consensual sexual acts" with Robyn; (5) she and Robyn have exchanged rings; (6) she and Robyn have been on vacation trips together to Europe and places in this country, and "share accommodations" on those trips; (7) Robyn washes dishes and laundry at wife's home, possesses a key to and drives wife's car, and attends church with wife; (8) she loaned Robyn $8,000 or $9,000 without written evidence of the debt or a repayment schedule; (9) Robyn is listed as the emergency contact on applicable forms for wife, and for wife's three daughters; and (10) Robyn tells these children she loves them and purchases gifts for them.

Relevant to the above admissions is a Christmas letter, dated December 29, 2004, that Robyn sent to friends and family members. In that letter Robyn relates in detail present*370 activities and future plans concerning the three children. She writes,

[T]he rewards of watching three teenagers grow and mature are endless.

On a personal note, [wife] and I are doing well. Each day presents a new parenting challenge but together we can and have both the joy and the frustrations of raising three girls.... [Wife] is still working in the office... and comes home every day with a new story.... When she is not working, she is busily putting food on the table, doing laundry, and making sure the pantry is stocked. We could not live without her.

I am the most spoiled of us all! Many of you always said that I was born with a silver spoon in my mouth.... I like to think that I know a good thing when I find it!

At trial Robyn, on many occasions after being reminded of her answers in discovery depositions, testified as an adverse witness that: (1) "[w]hen you've been in a relationship with someone as long as [wife] and I have, I think [that being a co-parent to wife's three children is] a side part to it... "; (2) she considered the three children as if they were her three children because "they're the closest I'm ever going to have to having children"; (3) she acknowledged there was "an understanding of fidelity" between her and wife and viewed herself and wife "as a couple"; (4) she acknowledged that wife is "certainly someone I'm in a relationship with" and that there had been an exclusive or faithful sexual relationship between the two for "[t]hree years or so maybe"; (5) she "routinely" wears the diamond ring she received from wife; and (6) she keeps "an accordion file" of her personal records at wife's house.

Robyn further admitted that, with respect to the residential property she owned, she rents the same to a woman with children for $900 per month, that her tenant paid all the utilities, that her tenant had complete use of the entire house, except for Robyn's bedroom and bathroom, for herself and "[h]er children and other guests." Robyn did not dispute any *371 of the answers wife had submitted in response to husband's request for admissions.

Both wife and Robyn explained why they did not present themselves as a couple to the public:

> Robyn: "what I share with Debb[y] is… against the law in Virginia… [and] I am in a profession where I'm not protected by the law because of that."

******

Wife: "I'm a Fairfax County public school employee and they don't exactly welcome me with open arms if I'm having a relationship of some kind with a woman."

The uncontradicted evidence, offered by both wife and Robyn, is that neither has an ownership interest in, or mortgage obligation on, the real property of the other, that they do not share bank accounts or investment **148 portfolios, and that neither is a beneficiary of retirement benefits, established trusts, life insurance, or the will of the other.

At trial the parties entered into a stipulation as to the observations of private detectives retained by husband. That stipulation, taken from the transcript, is summarized as follows: Private detectives "placed [wife's] house under surveillance for a period of… 34 days… [from] January 18, 2005 through February 20, 2005… [and Robyn] stayed overnight at [wife's] residence… [during that time period] with the exception of… four days." Further, Robyn "did not spend any appreciable time at her own house. There is the possibility that she may have gone there to pick up mail or something, but she didn't return to her house during that period of time… [and if she did so] it would be immaterial to the issue at hand…."

Robyn testified, with respect to the four-day interval, that she left from wife's home and was driven to the airport for a "business" trip, that she toured the University of Georgia, that wife picked her up at the airport, and that she returned directly to wife's home.

*372 At the conclusion of this undisputed evidence and argument, the trial court stated:

And so I keep finding myself in equipoise… it's cohabitation, analogous to a marriage, and the other, "'s not cohabitation, analogous to a marriage, and it seems to me that's the classic definition of a failure to prove something by the preponderance of the evidence…

V. SUFFICIENCY OF THE EVIDENCE AS TO COHABITATION

Citing References In Schweider, the Supreme Court of Virginia stated:

> We have said that the term "cohabit" means "to live together in the same house as married persons live together, or in the manner of husband and wife." Johnson v. Commonwealth, 152 Va. 965, 970, 146 S.E. 289, 291 (1929). While *373 engaging in sexual relations is a factor in determining cohabitation,

"'matrimonial cohabitation' consists of more than sexual relations. It also imports the continuing condition of living together and carrying out the mutual responsibilities of the marital relationship." Petachenko v. Petachenko, 232 Va. 296, 299, 350 S.E.2d 600, 602 (1986).

243 Va. at 248, 415 S.E.2d at 137.

In *Pellegrin v. Pellegrin*, 31 Va.App. 753, 763-66, 525 S.E.2d 611, 616–17 (2000), this Court enunciated four non-exclusive factors demonstrative of the "mutual responsibilities of the marital relationship."

(1) "Common residence." Id. at 764, 525 S.E.2d at 616. The trial court in the instant case concluded that wife and Robyn "maintain separate residences." Yet the undisputed facts show that, at a minimum, Robyn has spent five nights a week for over a year in wife's home, keeps clothes, toiletries, and personal files in wife's home, washes her clothes and dishes in wife's home, and possesses a key to the same. Wife's home is **149 where Robyn eats her meals. The stipulation in this case was that Robyn spent 34 consecutive days, with the exception of the four-day business trip, in wife's home, and, to the extent Robyn even went to her own property, those visits were "immaterial to the issue at hand." Even concerning the four-day interval, Robyn left from and returned to wife's house. FN2 With respect to Robyn's property, the entire house, with the exception of a bedroom and adjoining bathroom, are rented to a woman who has full use of the same for herself, her children, and her guests. Finally, in the Christmas letter, Robyn writes that wife "comes home every day with a new story.… " Since wife does not stay at Robyn's, Robyn's reference to "home" can only mean wife's residence, the location where wife returns and relates a new story every day. We conclude husband has established by the *374 preponderance of the evidence that Robyn and wife share a common residence.

FN2. As the trial court commented: "But if you're living with someone and you left on a business trip and you come back and you don't go to your apartment or house, you go right back to living with the other person, aren't you still cohabiting?"

(2) "Intimate or romantic involvement." Id. For five nights a week for at least a year, Robyn has slept in wife's bed in wife's home and engaged in "consensual sexual acts." Robyn testified that there had been an "exclusive or faithful sexual relationship" for "three years" and that they have exchanged diamond rings. We conclude that husband has established by the preponderance of the evidence that Robyn and wife are involved in an intimate or romantic relationship.

(3) "The provision of financial support." Id. at 765, 525 S.E.2d at 617. It is true in this case that wife and Robyn do not presently share bank accounts, investment portfolios, or the obligation on their respective home mortgages. Nonetheless, Robyn is, as we have concluded above, presently sharing a common residence with wife and one to which she contributes no financial support. To this extent, then, wife is providing financial support to Robyn. Moreover, that common residence permits Robyn to rent her property for $900 per month, with the tenant paying all utilities, and thus providing over $10,000 annual rent income to Robyn. We further note that wife lent Robyn $8,000 or $9,000 without

written evidence of the indebtedness or a repayment schedule, thus providing financial support in the past. Finally, the fact that neither wife nor Robyn has provided for financial support in futuro, by way of retirement, insurance or estate benefits, is of no moment. We are concerned with present, not future, financial arrangements. As Robyn wrote in the Christmas letter, wife is busy "putting food on the table," and Robyn is "the most spoiled" and one who "know[s] a good thing when [she] find[s] it." We conclude that husband has established by the preponderance of the evidence that wife is providing and has provided financial support for Robyn. FN3

FN3. We further note that the provision of financial support is not a condition precedent to the existence of an arrangement of cohabitation analogous to a marriage. Rather, "[f]inancial support is but one of a number of factors" which may support such an analogy. See Frey v. Frey, 14 Va.App. 270, 272, 416 S.E.2d 40, 41 (1992).

(4) "Duration and continuity of the relationship and other indicia of permanency." Id. By Robyn's testimony, she *375 and wife have been in a "long" relationship for "three years or so." She characterizes the relationship as "exclusive or faithful." In the Christmas letter Robyn recites, "Each day presents a new parenting challenge but together we can and have endured both the joy and the frustrations of raising three girls." In that letter, Robyn details the present activities of the children, plans for their futures, and expresses her joy "in watching [these] teenagers grow and mature...." Robyn testified she considered herself a "co-parent" to these children, ones who are "the closest I'm ever going to have to having children." It is clear Robyn considers herself a surrogate parent to wife's children, and the evidence does not disclose any action on wife's part to diminish such a status. Wife has designated Robyn as the emergency contact for these children, as well as for herself. Robyn and wife routinely wear the diamond **150 rings each gave the other. Wife's answers to requests for admissions did not challenge any of this factual evidence.

At trial, in response to her counsel's questions, wife only denied that she had ever entered into a "contract... verbal or in writing [as to either] the longevity... or the permanency of [her] relationship" and that they had any "ceremony" marking that relationship. Despite the absence of a contract or ceremony, it is clear that Robyn and wife view their relationship as a durable, continuing, and permanent one, and one that includes the joint raising of wife's children. From these undisputed facts we conclude that husband has established by the preponderance of the evidence the requisite relationship between wife and Robyn.

In concluding husband had failed to prove the existence of a situation analogous to marriage, the trial court noted that wife and Robyn did not present themselves to the public as a couple. In so doing, that court may have relied upon dicta in *376 Pellegrin, where it was noted that some foreign jurisdictions considered such display a factor "of a more circumstantial nature" in determining the existence of a relationship analogous to marriage. Pellegrin, 31 Va.App. at 766, 525 S.E.2d at 617. That being said, the testimony of both wife and Robyn makes clear why they did not present themselves to the public in general as a couple. To do so, they noted, could result in an adverse or terminal effect upon their jobs. Thus, we find the trial court's reliance on this factor in its decision unpersuasive.

Finally, we compare the evidence in the instant cause with that set forth in Penrod v. Penrod, 29 Va.App. 96, 510 S.E.2d 244 (1999), where a spousal support termination clause defined remarriage as cohabiting and living with a member of the opposite sex in a sexual relationship for a period in excess of sixty days. There we affirmed the trial's finding that the termination provisions had been met.

Wife admitted staying at Hardman's house three or four times a week over a period of years, sleeping in the same room and sometimes in the same bed. Wife also admitted that she kept numerous items of personality, including clothing, at Hardman's home. Hardman and wife vacationed together, usually at Hardman's expense. Hardman gave wife gifts, including a diamond ring. While wife testified that the relationship with Hardman was not sexual, other evidence... indicated that Hardman and wife were involved in a long-term intimate and monogamous relationship. Wife admitted in her deposition that she consciously caused breaks in the time she stayed at Hardman's home because of the "sixty consecutive days" requirement in the parties' agreement. FN4

FN4. Exactly as did wife in this cause. See Part II of this opinion, noting wife's testimony that she would "keep track" of the days to avoid the 30-day portion of the PSA.

Id. at 101, 510 S.E.2d at 246.

A court's findings "must be based upon evidence concerning the overall nature of the relationship, not merely a *377 piecemeal consideration of individual factors...." Id. It is our view that the evidence supporting the trial court's decision in Penrod is substantially less compelling than the uncontradicted evidence here. Although the trial court's conclusion is to the contrary, we think the undisputed evidence establishes, as a matter of law, that wife's relationship with Robyn constituted cohabitation in a situation analogous to marriage. See, e.g., *Schweider*, 243 Va. at 250, 415 S.E.2d at 138. Accordingly, the conclusion of the trial court that husband failed to prove that relationship by the preponderance of the evidence is reversed.

VI.

FOR PURPOSES OF CONTRACT INTERPRETATION, MAY INDIVIDUALS OF THE SAME SEX COHABIT IN A SITUATION ANALOGOUS TO MARRIAGE UNDER VIRGINIA LAW?

The trial court was persuaded that "in Virginia, where marriage between persons of the same sex is barred—'cohabit' has to mean between people of the opposite sex... as a matter of law, in Virginia, people of the same sex cannot cohabit, and that's how the PSA was written."

**151 In reaching this conclusion the trial court specifically relied upon a 1994 opinion of the Attorney General. 1994 Op. Atty. Gen. Va. 60. There the General opined that Code § 18.2-57.2(A), which criminalizes assault and battery in a situation where the defendant and victim cohabit, is not applicable to same sex cohabitation.

Initially we note that an Opinion of the Attorney General, while entitled to due consideration, is not binding upon a court. *Beck v. Shelton*, 267 Va. 482, 492, 593 S.E.2d 195, 200 (2004). See also *Virginia Beach v. Virginia Rest.* Ass'n, Inc., 231 Va. 130, 135, 341 S.E.2d 198, 201 (1986). That being said, in this case we are concerned with a contract between a man and a woman, husband and wife, not a statute defining or to be interpreted as defining "cohabitation," which is the subject of the Opinion on which the trial court relied.

*378 Such a distinction was emphasized by this Court in *O'Hara v. O'Hara*, 45 Va.App. 788, 613 S.E.2d 859 (2005). There, the issue was the correct standard of proof of cohabitation—preponderance of the evidence or clear and convincing evidence—applicable to a property settlement agreement. We held:

> *Accordingly, Code § 20-109(A), and its clear and convincing burden of proof, does not apply to this case involving the enforcement of a negotiated agreement between husband and wife. Rather, because this case involves an action to enforce a contract between the parties, husband's burden was to prove by a preponderance of the evidence that wife habitually cohabited with another person in a relationship analogous to a marriage for one year or more, not to prove cohabitation by clear and convincing evidence.*
>
> *Id. at 796, 613 S.E.2d at 863.*

The language of the PSA also contains the phrase "analogous to marriage." A relationship "analogous to marriage" does not mean a "marriage." Rather, "analogous" is defined as "similar in some way." Webster's Dictionary 17 (Michael Agnes ed., Wiley Publishing, Inc. 2002). See also The American Heritage Dictionary of the English Language 65 (3d ed. 1992). This Court defined "similar" in Frederick Fire & Rescue v. Dodson, 20 Va.App. 440, 446, 457 S.E.2d 783, 786 (1995) (quoting Black's Law Dictionary 1383 (6th ed. 1990)):

> *The word similar "is generally interpreted to mean that one thing has a resemblance in many respects, nearly corresponds, is somewhat like, or has a general likeness to some other thing but is not identical in form and substance."*

Our analysis of the phrase "analogous to marriage" in the PSA is based upon the factual relationship of wife and Robyn, and explicitly does not purport to grant, or comment upon, any legal status of that relationship.

Succinctly stated, that relationship, as established by the facts, is similar "but not identical in form and substance" to a marriage.

*379 For a congruent reason, wife's reliance on brief on the provisions of Code § 20-45.2 and Code § 20-45.3 is misplaced. The former prohibits same sex marriages in Virginia. The latter prohibits same sex civil unions, partnership contracts, or other arrangements purporting to grant the privileges and obligations of marriage. As stated above, our holding in this case explicitly does not grant any legal status to the relationship between wife and Robyn.

Accordingly, neither the trial court nor this Court is required to review the relationship between wife and Robyn with respect to matters of public policy as set forth in those statutes. Indeed, wife specifically testified that she and Robyn had never entered into a "contract" with respect to their relationship, nor participated in any "ceremony" concerning the same. In short, Code §§ 20-45.2 and 20-45.3 are irrelevant to the issue here raised. Thus, we do not address their application.

In accordance with the foregoing, we hold the trial court erred in concluding that, for the purposes of interpreting the contract between husband and wife, same sex individuals may not cohabit in Virginia as a matter of law. The cause is remanded to the trial court for entry of a decree conforming to this opinion.

**152 VII.
Affirmed in part, reversed in part, and remanded.

THE SEPARATION AGREEMENT AND DIVORCE DECREE

As the *Rice* case illustrates, careful detail must be given when drafting a separation agreement, especially when dealing with the issue of support (see Chapter 4). It is often necessary to "refer to and merge in" the language of the separation agreement with the final divorce decree in order to be effective. Problems arise when a court with jurisdiction over the two parties does not make a support maintenance award in the divorce case. The court will not make an initial reward once the case is over. A better strategy is to make a small award and reserve the issue for subsequent review or modification when necessary.

In probably one of the more bizarre challenges to payment of maintenance after a divorce, a husband requested that the court terminate his financial responsibility to his ex-wife after he alleged that she hired a hit man to try to kill him. "Before the December 1997 dissolution of their marriage, Joseph and Ida Richardson executed a separation agreement, which they agreed would be incorporated into the dissolution decree. The separation agreement provided that husband would pay wife $2,425 per month in maintenance until either wife remarried or either party died." The agreement stated, in part, that its terms "shall not be subject to modification or change, regardless of the relative circumstance of the parties." The trial court incorporated this agreement into its dissolution judgment and decree and specifically stated that maintenance was not modifiable. In 2004, the husband filed a motion to modify the judgment. In Count II of his motion, he sought to terminate his maintenance obligation, alleging his ex-wife had sought out someone to burglarize his home and attempted to hire someone to murder him. He alleged his ex-wife therefore breached their separation agreement and waived her claim to maintenance. The trial court dismissed Count II, finding that the husband failed to state a claim on which relief might be granted; the appellate court confirmed this ruling.

Betty and Bob 3

With a general knowledge of the two systems of divorce, how might Betty and Bob divide their assets to finalize their divorce?

In Community Property States

If Bob and Betty reside in a community property state (there are only a few of them), it might be easier to divide the property because the rules are clearer; each spouse should take one half of the assets:

A. Remove Separate Property to Each Owner

First, the separate property is taken back by each of the couple, so that Betty removes the RV and Bob takes his gold watch.

B. The Debt

Before they decide to divide up the assets from the available cash, they may want to pay off all of the debt (to stop any accruing interest), because it is a small amount. A strong argument could be made that Betty has to pay her own debt on the credit card she had before the marriage. As to the larger Visa card debt, which was marital, they should probably split it 50/50.

C. Divide the Marital Property 50/50

Under a community property system, Bob and Betty should divide the remaining property so that each takes one-half.

The house: If they each have a one-half interest in the house, they could sell it and split the equity (profit). Say the house is worth $400,000, and they have a mortgage (debt) of $200,000 on it. When they sell it for $400,000, they will need to pay the bank for the loan of $200,000, which leaves them with $200,000 in equity. This will be divided in half, so that they each receive $100,000 from the sale of the house. Another option is for Betty to live in the house (and pay the mortgage, taxes, and all of the maintenance) until the boys leave for college; then they can sell the house and split the proceeds.

The furniture: Used furniture generally has little value. As the couple will be setting up two different houses, they should work out an agreement to divide it in half. Perhaps they can agree to each take the items they want first. So, the chef husband might take the Viking refrigerator worth $5,000 and the wife could take the table worth $4,000. Or, if they both still want the table, they will need to work something out or sell it and divide the profit in half. After that, they will continue to negotiate the division of the remaining furniture and household items.

Because the husband needs furniture for his new place, he might take more, plus the TV, and give his wife the jewelry worth $10,000.

Jewelry: See above.

$100,000 cash: The cash could easily be divided in half.

Car: Worth $15,000, the car will need to be sold or one spouse could buy the other's half (from part of the cash, see above).

Workshop: Perhaps the husband could offer the woodshop to his wife in exchange for buying out her half of the car.

The sailboat: Worth $50,000, the sailboat will have to be sold or the husband, if he wants to keep it, could offer to buy the wife's half interest in it (he will be responsible for its upkeep and docking fees, etc.).

The Restaurant: While the couple may negotiate the above division of property on a rough 50/50 basis, they will probably need professional help in dividing their business. They should hire an appraiser to assess the value of the business. Because neither is likely to trust the other's appraiser, they should agree to find a neutral appraiser. They may want to select one from a neutral court-approved list for example. Because businesses often have a strong following of clients, things like client lists and goodwill have value and should be considered in the distribution of assets. The couple must negotiate their salaries with each other now that the profits will no longer go toward a marital household. If they can successfully agree to a 50/50 split in the business, the court will probably approve their proposed property settlement agreement.

In Equitable Distribution States

If they are in an equitable distribution state, which is more likely as there are more of them, they will need to divide their property fairly. Remember that equitable does not mean equal (50/50)—it means fair.

A. First, Remove Separate Property to Each Owner

Under equitable distribution, which is different from a community property system, the courts may take back some separate property from one spouse or both if it is needed to ensure a fair settlement of the property. Other courts would allow the spouses to take their separate property as long as it was not commingled (mixed in and used with the family assets or increased in value because of family contributions). So, for our analysis, each in effect removes and holds on to his or her separate property in case the court needs it again. Betty takes the RV (and makes payments on it), while Bob takes and holds the gold watch.

B. Second, Pay the Debt

Before they decide to divide the assets, they may want to use some of the cash to pay off their debt (to stop any accruing interest), because it is a small amount. Once the couple decides their ratio (see below), they can then decide where the debt belongs on each side of the ledger.

C. Third, Divide the Marital Property Fairly:

The Restaurant: Under this distribution, it would probably be best to decide the issues surrounding the restaurant/business first as it raises questions about income. Unlike a community property state, under an equitable distribution state, the spouses' contributions to the business and marriage are not presumed to be equal in value. So, in this scenario, each party's contribution to the business will be evaluated and quantified. Again, the couple should find an appraiser who is knowledgeable in the restaurant industry to make an inventory and assign a value to the restaurant as a going concern. Bob's skills as a chef probably raise the value of the restaurant when considering factors like goodwill and customer lists. It is likely that he would take at least a 60/40 split, even 70/30, of the profits (after expenses). Once this ratio is valued, it may impact other issues like rehabilitation alimony (see below), if Betty wants to go back to school for an MBA to earn more than her 40 or 30 percent share of the family business by working elsewhere.

The House: As discussed above, the parties may agree that Betty and the boys can live in the house until the boys leave for college; then, they can sell it and split the proceeds. Since there is not much money available now, the parties may need to sell the house to generate some. If the house is worth $400,000 and they have a $200,000 mortgage on it (which shows the loan amount), when they sell it, they should get $200,000 in equity (the sale price, less any debt).[18]

The Furniture: Again, used furniture generally has little value. As the couple will be setting up two different houses, they should work out an agreement to divide it fairly between themselves. Should they be selling the house, the furniture and household items may be less necessary.

The Jewelry (see above): They need to find an equitable division—not necessarily a 50/50 split, —but 50/50 could end up being the fair amount.

$100,000 Cash: The liquid money could be divided in the ratio they decide for the restaurant, or the wife could forego the cash to buy the husband's interest in the house, which would allow her to stay there regardless of the boy's domicile.

The car worth $15,000: It will either have to be sold, or one of them could buy the other's share (from part of the cash, see above).

Workshop: It is unlikely that the husband will fight for this, unless the negotiations become nasty, then anything goes!

Sailboat: Worth $50,000, this will be sold and split under an agreed formula, or the husband could offer to buy the wife's interest in it (after which he will be responsible for its upkeep, docking fees, etc.).

Separate property: If the couple is unable to reach an amicable settlement of their asset division and they go to court, some courts in equitable distribution states may reach back and use their separate property (e.g. by forcing the sale of the RV) to make a fair division of the assets.

---

18   Like all of this financial discussion, this is simplified to make the basic concepts easily understood. In real life, expenses like real estate agent fees, taxes, etc., would lower the equity the couple receives from the sale of the house.

ONE FINAL NOTE

Remember that the parties can privately order their asset distribution under either system, but if they do, they will need to write an agreement and present it to the judge to review for fairness (see Chapter 4 on contracts). If the parties cannot work it out themselves (with the assistance of the restaurant appraiser/consultant), they might need a family mediator to help them find a "win/win" arrangement. Lastly, if no agreement is reached, they may choose to "roll the dice" and let the court decide. But at court, there are no guarantees for either spouse as the equitable distribution system leaves a lot of flexibility to the judge to ensure fairness. Also, the last alternative will be expensive, because they will need to hire lawyers and experts.

MISCELLANEOUS ISSUES IN DIVORCE

Legal Fees

While not a part of asset distribution, attorneys' fees do impact the cost of divorce. This is doubled because each spouse should have his/her own attorney. What happens if one spouse does not work and makes little or no money (or disproportionately less than the other)? Should this spouse be penalized and have to go without an attorney? Generally, in this type of situation, the spouse can request the court to order the spouse with the greater income to pay all or part of the attorney's fees. What happens if no one works (or at least reports no taxable income)? The court can still order the spouse with the greater assets to pay the other's legal fees.

Economic Fault

Different from the fault-based behavior that serves as a reason for divorce, a spouse who engages in economic fault, or misappropriation of marital assets, can be punished at the time the court distributes the assets. Economic fault occurs when one spouse disposes of marital assets for less than fair market value during the divorce. Proof of this allows the divorce court to reimburse the other spouse for the value attributed to the misconduct. Similarly, dissipation of assets occurs when one spouse wastes marital assets solely for his own benefit while the marriage is dissolving. For example, if one spouse spends extravagantly, or has hidden or fraudulently conveyed assets, this may be discovered during the divorce when the spouses provide financial disclosure of their assets as the basis for the distribution.

Fifty-year-old Steven K. Zinnel was ordered to pay a fine of $500,000 and forfeit assets worth more than $2.8 million when he declared bankruptcy and hid his assets to avoid paying child support and alimony following a contentious divorce in California. "Zinnel had concealed millions of dollars in assets by putting them in other people's names. Even after that, he laundered money through shell corporations in order to disguise income that otherwise would have increased his child support obligation.[19] He was also sentenced to 17 years in prison. [20] Ironically, his crimes were only discovered after he requested that the FBI investigate his ex-wife". During the Bureau's investigation, his crimes were discovered.[21]

Name Change

While not legally required, a woman often changes her last name to her husband's when they marry. When the spouses divorce and the woman wants to return to her maiden name, the courts may grant the right to such a name change in the final divorce decree. What happens if the spouse no longer wants the other to use the marital last name, should he be able to force her to change it back?

Pets

Often pets are an integral part of a family; when divorce occurs, the spouses may fight over who gets to keep the pet. Should this issue be included in the child custody section of this book? Traditionally, the law views a pet as personal property[22]; therefore, ownership is determined under the state's property law (the pet goes to the spouse who owns it). Bucking this tradition, "Alaska became the first state to enact pet-custody legislation, which allows a court to consider the animal's well-being. The measure, which defines animals as a 'vertebrate living creature not a human being' was signed into law last year and took effect in January" 2017.[23] Unsettlingly, in proposed Wisconsin legislation, the judge would be able to award the pet to either spouse or

---

19   "Gold River Man who Hid Assets in Divorce, Bankruptcy gets 17-year Sentence" Denny Walsh, *The Sacramento Bee*, March 4, 2014, http://www.sacbee.com/news/local/article2592433.html#storylink=cpy

20   Ibid. His lawyer helped him launder the money from his corporations during the divorce and bankruptcy and then back to him afterward through her company, "Done Deal Inc., her attorney-client trust account and her personal bank account". She received a 10 year and one month sentence in prison and was fined $200,000 following her conviction at trial on two counts of money laundering. "Attorney sentenced to prison for helping Gold River businessman conceal assets", Cathy Locke, *The Sacramento Bee*, March 20, 2014, http://www.sacbee.com/news/local/crime/article2594413.html#storylink=cpy

21   Ibid. The California 3rd District Court of Appeal "had an equally negative impression of Zinnel when the divorce case came before it. In a 2008 ruling, the justices commented on Zinnel's 'unstated but apparent view that if he can conceal his finances long enough he will not have to support his children.'" After his conviction, Zinnel called his son (whom he attempted to defraud to avoid child support) "from jail and, in a recorded conversation, told the boy that 'Daddy got railroaded' and 'this all started because of your mom.'"

22   In a unanimous decision, the Georgia Supreme Court took a step towards valuing pet bonds beyond mere property value. When a dog died due to the kennel's alleged negligence, the court ruled that the owners were not limited to fair market value of the pet (the cost to replace it) but could also be compensated for medical expenses incurred in trying to save it. The court made clear that under Georgia law, "the owners can't seek damages based on the sentimental value of the animal to its owner. He said the unique human-animal bond, while cherished, is beyond legal measure." http://bigstory.ap.org/article/ac07bdaabdec4572870428abbfb717a4/georgia-high-court-rules-against-kennel-negligence-case

23   https://www.nytimes.com/2017/03/23/us/divorce-pet-custody-dog-cat.html?_r=0

choose to send it to the pound. Whichever spouse arrived at the shelter first could get the pet, but if they wait too long, the pet could be adopted by someone else—or worse.[24]

In a 2010 case in Maryland, a judge ordered a divorcing couple to split custody of their dog, "a recognition, experts say, that pets stand apart from other property."[25] "In the case, both Craig and Gayle Myers wanted Lucky, a suspected Lhasa Apso-Shih Tzu mix that Craig Myers found living under a construction trailer in 2008 and brought to the couple's Dunkirk home." After the Meyers separated a year later, they each wanted to keep the dog. The judge "heard testimony… which included details like who takes the dog to the vet and who has more time to take care of the dog".[26] Lucky was not in the divorce court for the hearing.

In San Diego a divorcing couple fought over their dog Gigi. After they were awarded joint custody, the couple disputed the arrangement in court for "two years (for a) cost (of) about $150,000 in legal fees. It involved a court-ordered 'bonding study' conducted by an animal behaviorist and a videotape, 'A Day in the Life of Gigi,' showing the dog spending time with (the wife), who was ultimately awarded sole custody in 2000."[27] In 2014 lawyers reported a "27 percent increase in pet-custody cases over the five previous years, with 20 percent of respondents citing an increase in cases where judges had deemed pets an asset in a divorce"[28].

---

24   Wisconsin bill outlines rules for pet custody, by P. J. Huffstutter, *Los Angeles Times* http://seattletimes.com/html/nationworld/2003789763_pets15.html Sharing Fido: Does your state have pet custody laws? Tim Clarke, September 2008, legal zoom.

25   "Split custody of dog recognizes changing role of family pet", Andrea F. Siegel *The Baltimore Sun*, July 18, 2010, http://articles.baltimoresun.com/2010-07-18/news/bs-md-pet-custody-law-20100718_1_animal-law-pets-animal-legal-defense-fund "Some jurisdictions have decided that the pet owners' emotional attachment should be weighed when making animal custody decisions. In a publicized New Jersey ruling last year, an appellate court overturned a judge's decision to grant one member of a formerly engaged couple ownership of a pug, with an order to pay the pooch's purchase price of $1,500 to the other. In rehearing the case, the judge awarded them shared custody, with Dexter shuttling between the two homes every five weeks, according to news accounts."

26   Ibid., Quoting Mark W. Carmean, Craig Myers' lawyer. Joyce Tischler of the California-based Animal Legal Defense Fund said, "We ask the court to consider that animals are not toasters. The toaster does not care which house it goes to, but animals do. Who takes the dog to the veterinarian, who walks, feeds the dog — the animal might prefer to be with that person,… We ask the judge to consider the animal's interests. I'm not saying that's an easy thing to do. Broken homes are difficult for everybody." One the other hand, "[s]ome family lawyers fear that looking at a pet's best interest in every contested pet 'custody' case would be problematic. Dorothy R. Fait, a Rockville family law practitioner who had a divorce case with a similar dispute a decade ago (the couple agreed to shared dog time) said the question is 'the law of unintended consequences.' "'What happens if somebody doesn't obey the order and return the dog at the end of six months? Are you going to put somebody in jail if they don't turn over the dog?… When you really think about it, do you really want to take it to next level?'"

27   https://www.nytimes.com/2017/03/23/us/divorce-pet-custody-dog-cat.html?_r=0

28   Ibid., Citing a survey in 2014 by the American Academy of Matrimonial Lawyers.

ATTORNEY REPRESENTATION

With the advent of no-fault divorce, when the parties no longer need to prove marital-based misconduct to obtain a divorce but can do so by mutual agreement, should a court still be necessary to obtain a divorce? What about just sending the papers and avoiding any court appearances? It would save the court time and the parties' money on attorneys' fees. The more contested the divorce, the more expensive it becomes for the parties involved. (This is all the more reason to work out the terms of the divorce amicably through mediation and/or a settlement/property agreement.) Remember, a divorce cannot be awarded by consent of the parties. *Posnor v. Posnor,* (S.Ct Fla 1970) 233 So.2d 381.

Should two spouses who are amicably obtaining a divorce use the same attorney in a dual representation to save money? Probably not. Many states consider such dual representation unethical. What conflicts of interest would this involve? What about if the couple had used the lawyer before in another matter (e.g., buying a business)? The concern would be that confidential information could have been shared if the matter was related closely enough to the divorce.[29]

Given all this, does it make sense for people to represent themselves (without a lawyer) in a divorce case? Increasingly the courts are being confronted with *pro se* litigants (unrepresented) in divorce cases with estimates of 80 to 90 percent of cases involving at least one unrepresented party.[30] "Popular opinion holds that the reason for the increase in *pro se* appearances is the high cost of attorneys and litigation."

But that may be misguided. In one survey, people chose to represent themselves because their cases were simple with only one "clear cut issue," not because they could not afford an attorney. It is estimated that only about one-third of *pro se* litigants cannot afford a lawyer.[31] Other surveys show that people in prior divorce cases had bad outcomes with an attorney and chose not to use one in the next divorce case. Certainly lack of financial resources, especially in divorce cases, is a factor. A 2013 study of judges said they saw "a significant uptick in the number of people representing themselves since the 2008 economic recession." "In that same survey, 62 percent of judges said the outcomes for people without counsel were worse."[32]

---

29 Much like cases of a spouse having sex with a psychologist or minister who was counseling the couple, unfortunately, there are some cases where an attorney has sex with his client. Only relatively recently have the states started to regulate this behavior, and even so, it is with mixed results. Some have a *pro se* prohibition against any sexual relationship with a client. In New York, that ban is only limited to family lawyers. *Emanuel Law Lines*, *Family Law*, D. Kelly Weisberg, 2011. What other regulations should there be?

30 "The *Pro Se* Phenomenon", Drew A. Swank, Esq., *BYU Journal of Public Law*, Vol 19. 373 (2005). http://digitalcommons.law.byu.edu/jpl/vol19/iss2/4/ "Even more spectacular than the number of *pro se* litigants is the growth rate of *pro se* litigation." In 1971 only 1% of divorce litigants in California were *pro se*. By 2005 the rate had increased to 75%.

31 Ibid. See list of reasons people go *pro se*.

32 Washington state intends to address this issue with a new class of legal professionals called "limited license legal technicians". The "nurse practitioners of the legal world", these supercharged paralegals will take a year of classes at a community college and a licensing exam which will allow them to do legal research for their clients and prepare court documents. "California, Oregon, Colorado and New Mexico say they may follow Washington's lead." "Who says you need a law degree to practice law?", Robert Ambrogi, *The Washington Post*, March 15, 1015, B5.

In one of perhaps the most expensive (and well published, perhaps for its controversial exchanges) divorces in history, the wife, Heather Mills, represented herself against her soon-to-be-ex-husband, former Beatle Paul McCartney. When it was over, the court granted the divorce and awarded Ms. Mills, McCartney's wife of less than four years, almost $50 million—or about $34,000 per day of marriage (not including the $70,000 per year McCartney pays for child support). Ms. Mills did not use a lawyer and represented herself. After the verdict, Ms. Mills said, "These people [referring to the barristers and judges] are in a club"… "It's like they want to stay together and they don't want to see a litigant in person doing well."[33] How did she do? Would that opinion change if she claimed he was worth $1.6 billion?

This is the "text of statement released by the [British] Family Court on the financial settlement for Heather Mills in her divorce from Paul McCartney":

This is a summary of the judgment handed down today (17 March 2008). It is not a summary of every issue in the judgment. This summary forms no part of the judgment. The court ruled that the judgment should be published but upon Ms. Mills' application granted a stay of such publication pending her appeal to the Court of Appeal.

The fundamental issue was what financial provision should be made for Ms. Mills. She sought an award of almost 125 million pounds ($250 million). Sir Paul proposed that the wife should exit the marriage with assets of 15.8 million pounds ($31.6 million) inclusive of any lump sum award.

The judge decided that the husband should pay the wife a lump sum of 16.5 million pounds ($33 million) which together with her assets of 7.8 million pounds ($15.6 million) (which include her current properties) means that she exits her marriage with total assets of 24.3 million pounds ($48.6 million) inclusive of a deemed figure of 500,000 pounds ($1 million) referable to her overspending in the period of separation.

The judge found that the total value of all the husband's assets, including his business assets, was about 400 million pounds ($800 million). There was no evidence at all before him that he was worth 800 million pounds ($1.6 billion).

The judge found that although the parties met in 1999 and formed a relationship, the parties did not cohabit from March 2000 but did so from the date of the marriage (11 June 2002). The parties separated in April 2006. The length of the marriage was just under four years.

The judge refused to permit either party to raise as an issue the alleged conduct of the other on the broad ground that it was irrelevant.

The judge, in undertaking the exercise prescribed by section 25 of the Matrimonial Causes Act, 1973, decided that the needs of the wife were a factor of magnetic importance.

---

33 http://www.cnn.com/2008/SHOWBIZ/03/17/mccartney.mills/, "McCartney's ex-wife awarded almost $50 million," CNN.com, March 17, 2008.

The lump sum of 16.5 million pounds ($33 million) is made up of a sum of 14 million pounds ($28 million) as the capitalized figure for the wife's income needs, which the judge assessed at 600,000 pounds ($1.2 million) per annum, and a sum of 2.5 million pounds ($5 million) for the wife to buy a property in London.

Financial provision for Beatrice consists of a periodical payments order of 35,000 pounds ($70,000) per annum, the husband agreeing to pay for her nanny and her school fees.

The court made an order in the following terms:

> Save for the release of the judgment and Order dated 17 March 2008 the Wife and the Husband and any persons acting on their behalves are strictly prohibited from publishing, disclosing, or in any way revealing without the consent of the other, the evidence, correspondence, transcripts, judgments or Orders in the proceedings concerning (a) the child of the family, (b) the main suit, (c) the cross-applications for ancillary relief, and (d) any marital confidences. If consent is not forthcoming then the party seeking publication shall be entitled to seek the permission of a Family Division Judge to do so.[34]

So, how *did* Heather Mills do as her own attorney?

CHAPTER SOURCES

http://family.findlaw.com/marriage/what-s-mine-is-mine-what-s-yours-is-mine-who-owns-what-in.html, "Who Owns What in Marital Property?"

Wadlington, W., and O'Brien, R. C. (2007). *Domestic Relations*, 6th ed. Foundation Press.

Weisberg, D. Kelly. (2011). *Emanuel*

---

[34] http://www.cnn.com/2008/SHOWBIZ/Music/03/17/mccartney.ruling/index.html, "Text of Family Court statement on Mills-McCartney settlement," CNN.com, March 17, 2008.

BIRTH CONTROL

Familiarity breeds contempt—and children.
—Mark Twain[1]

Humans are the only animals that have children on purpose with the exception of guppies,
who like to eat theirs.
—P. J. O'Rourke[2]

INVOLUNTARY OR VOLUNTARY DECISIONS

Today, most people take the availability and use of birth control for granted. For this generation, it is unthinkable that the government would interfere in such a personal decision as whether or not to utilize it. Most assume it is a right. Similarly, until the late 1800s, birth control was generally not a legal issue until moral crusaders classified it as obscene and persuaded governments to criminalize it. At the turn of the next century, the issue of birth control focused on involuntary decision-making—when the government could force a person not to reproduce by sterilization. The eugenics (from Greek, eugenēs, meaning wellborn)[3] movement that swept the country was a way to promote the more fit members of the human race and decrease those considered carriers of "defective" genetic traits. In the latter half of the 20th century, beginning in the 1970s, challenges were raised against the government's prohibition on voluntary use of birth control. Society continues to wrestle with birth control issues, including the question of

---

1   *www.twainquotes.com/Familiarity.html*
2   www.brainyquote.com/quotes/quotes/p/pjorour163103.html
3   *The Genius Factory*, David Plotz, Random House, 2005, has a good general discussion of the eugenics movement.

what age birth control should be available without a doctor's prescription, even while science encourages its availability for public health.

BUCK V. BELL, 274 U.S. 200 (1927)

Know the Plaintiff

Carrie Buck was 17-years old and living with a foster family when she became pregnant (Carrie claimed it was by the Dobbs' son, a point not raised at her trial). Since the age of three, Carrie had grown up with the foster family of J. T. and Alice Dobbs after Virginia institutionalized her mother, Emma Buck, who had prostituted herself to support her three children after her husband died. (At the trial, the court mistakenly received evidence that Carrie was illegitimate.) On April 1, 1920, Emma Buck was brought before the local justice of the peace, Charles D. Shackleford, in Charlottesville, Virginia, for evaluation. Based on some *pro forma* questioning, she "was committed to Virginia Colony for the Epileptics and Feebleminded" in Lynchburg, Virginia.

Carrie's school records show five years of normal progress until the Dobbs family withdrew her so she could provide domestic services for their house. When Carrie was 17, her foster parents had her committed to the same institution in which her mother resided shortly after Carrie gave birth to her non-marital child.[4] The Dobbs and the medical professionals claimed Carrie was "feebleminded to lowest grade moron class."[5] The state wanted to use Carrie Buck as a test case for a new eugenics law that allowed Virginia to sterilize unfit members of society to prevent the spread of their defective genes. Like her mother, Carrie was brought before Justice of the Peace Shackleford on a commitment hearing to determine whether she would join her mother at the Colony.[6]

Know the Defendant

When the Virginia Colony for the Epileptics and Feebleminded, located in Lynchburg, Virginia, opened its doors in 1910, it was the largest asylum in the United States. It was originally intended to be a home for epileptics, the mentally disabled, and the severely disabled. In 1912, Virginia Colony superintendent Albert Priddy lobbied the Virginia General Assembly for funds to expand the Colony to provide residential space for those deemed "feebleminded."

Such a determination was subjective at best but, as asserted by Priddy, it was considered a hereditary quality, which merited segregation from the rest of society in order to prevent proliferation. The authorizing legislation specifically directed the admission of "women of child-bearing

---

4   http://www.hsl.virginia.edu/historical/eugenics/3-buckvbell.cfm,

5   Transcripts from the Circuit Court of Amherst County hearing on the petition to sterilize Carrie Buck. http://digitalarchive.gsu.edu/cgi/viewcontent.cgi?article=1030&context=col_facpub

6   The Dobbs institutionalized Carrie when her daughter Vivian was born and then raised Vivian in their own home just as they had Carrie.

age, from twelve to forty-five years of age as the first patients." "As the population of the Colony grew, Priddy began to focus on a way to prevent patient reproduction that was more cost effective than long-term segregation from the general population. In 1914, he contributed to a report to the General Assembly entitled *Mental Defectives in Virginia*, proposing large-scale institutional sterilization for Virginia's feebleminded."[7] Albert Priddy died before appeals were heard in the *Buck v. Bell* case. Dr. J. H. Bell became superintendent of the Virginia Colony and his name replaced Priddy's as party to the suit in the appeals process.[8]

Procedural History

Virginia's Eugenical Sterilization Act of 1924 provided in part:[9]

> *An Act of Virginia, approved March 20, 1924, recites that the health of the patient and the welfare of society may be promoted in certain cases by the sterilization of mental defectives, under careful safeguard, &c.; that the sterilization may be effected in males by vasectomy and in females by salpingectomy, without serious pain or substantial danger to life; that the Commonwealth is supporting in various institutions many defective persons who, if now discharged, would become [p. 206] a menace, but, if incapable of procreating, might be discharged with safety and become self-supporting with benefit to themselves and to society, and that experience has shown that heredity plays an important part in the transmission of insanity, imbecility, &c.[10]*

The right of the state to perform sterilization procedures was first challenged and heard in the Circuit Court of Amherst County. Three men who had known each other for years, Albert Priddy, the superintendent of the Virginia Colony, Aubrey E. Strode, who drafted Virginia's sterilization law, and Irving P. Whitehead, decided to use Carrie Buck as a test case for the new eugenics law with the theory that the procedure would be easy to implement after she was sterilized. In response, Buck answered that the law did not provide due process, amounting to cruel and unusual punishment, which violated equal protection.[11] As might be expected from the cozy relationship between the men involved, Whitehead did not put much effort into his representation of Carrie Buck at the trial. While Aubrey E. Strode presented more than a dozen witnesses including four

---

7   http://www.hsl.virginia.edu/historical/eugenics/3-buckvbell.cfm
8   Ibid.
9   *Buck v. Bell*, 274 U.S. 200 (1927).
10   Interestingly, in 1924, Virginia passed another eugenics law at the same time; the first being the Racial Integrity Act, which defined a white person as having no trace of black blood and made it illegal for whites and non-Caucasians to marry. That law was later the basis of the case of *Loving v. Virginia*. Virginia House Joint Resolution No. 607, 2001 (see Chapter 5).
11   Transcripts from the Circuit Court of Amherst County hearing on the petition to sterilize Carrie Buck, 1–50. http://digitalarchive.gsu.edu/cgi/viewcontent.cgi?article=1030&context=col_facpub

'expert' witnesses in the field of eugenics to prove Carrie's 'feeblemindedness,"[12] Whitehead did not call any witnesses and did very little to challenge the speculative and hearsay testimony of witness[es] or to challenge the "science" of eugenics presented by the medical doctor experts.

Strode called Anne Harris, a District Nurse from Charlottesville, who testified that Emma Buck "was living in the worst neighborhoods, and that she was not able to, or would not, work and support her children, and that they were on the streets more or less." Strode asked, "What about the character of her offspring [Carrie]?" Harris replied, "Well, I don't know anything very definite about the children, expect they don't seem to be able to do any more than their mother."[13] Various teachers were called to give testimony about Carrie's relatives (some with ambiguous testimony such as "I don't know very much about Mr. Dudley. He strikes me as being right peculiar and that's all I do know about him)."[14]

Harry H. Laughlin, an expert in eugenics from Long Island's Carnegie Institute of Washington, was not present at the trial but his responses to written questions about the "science of eugenics" were submitted into evidence. Although he never met any members of the Buck family, he confidently reasserted Priddy's statements that the family belonged to "the shiftless, ignorant, and worthless class of anti-social whites of the South." He focused on Emma Buck's syphilis as evidence of her moral degeneracy and stated falsely that Carrie was an illegitimate baby.[15]

Another witness was a Red Cross social worker that the Dobbs family had arranged during Carrie's pregnancy, Mrs. Wilhelm, who was asked, "[F]rom your experience as a social worker, if Carrie were discharged from the Colony still capable of child-bearing, is she likely to become the parent of deficient offspring?" Wilhelm replied, "I should judge so. I think a girl of her mentality is more or less at the mercy of other people.... Her mother had three illegitimate children, and I should say that Carrie would be very likely to have illegitimate children" (even though she had never met her mother and Carrie was not illegitimate). Strode concluded, "So that the only way that she could likely be kept from increasing her own kind would be by either segregation or something that would stop her power to propagate."[16] When Wilhelm was asked about Carrie's daughter, Vivian, Wilhelm said, "It seems difficult to judge probabilities of a child as young as that [eight months], but it seems to me not quite a normal baby... There is a look that is not quite normal, but just what it is I can't tell."[17]

Dr. Priddy testified last against Carrie Buck and summarized the state's true intent with the eugenics law, that she "would cease to be a charge on society if sterilized. It would remove one potential source of the incalculable number of descendants who would be feebleminded. She would contribute to the raising of the general mental average and a standard."[18] The treatment

---

12   Ibid. 1-101.
13   Ibid. 1–50.
14   Ibid. 51–100.
15   Ibid. 1–50.
16   Ibid. 51–100.
17   Ibid.
18   Ibid.

was to help rid the state of future "misfits" not because it was medically requested by or needed by Carrie Buck.

In a historical photograph taken the day before the trial, "Mrs. Alice Dobbs, the foster mother of Carrie Buck's daughter, Vivian, holds Vivian while flashing a coin past the baby's face in a test to assess her intelligence. The infant, perhaps distracted by the camera, didn't follow the coin with her eyes and thus was declared an imbecile."[19]

Based on the testimony (erroneous and otherwise) presented at Carrie Buck's trial, the Amherst County Circuit Court ruled that it was in the best interest of the state ["the health of the patient and the welfare of society may be promoted"] for Carrie Buck to be sterilized under the state's new law.

In November of 1925, the Virginia Supreme Court of Appeals affirmed the ruling of the Amherst County Circuit Court that allowed the state to sterilize Carrie Buck. A petition for certiorari was filed requesting an appeal to the Supreme Court of the United States[20] in the 1927 case of *Buck v. Bell*. What will the Supreme Court rule on the government's right to sterilize a woman under the eugenics movement?

BUCK V. BELL, 274
U.S. 200 (1927)

Mr. JUSTICE HOLMES delivered the opinion of the Court.

This is a writ of error to review a judgment of the Supreme Court of Appeals of the State of Virginia, affirming a judgment of the Circuit Court of Amherst County, by which the defendant in error, the superintendent of the State Colony for Epileptics and Feeble Minded, was ordered to perform the operation of salpingectomy upon Carrie Buck, the plaintiff in error, for the purpose of making her sterile. 143 Va. 310. The case comes here upon the contention that the statute authorizing the judgment is void under the Fourteenth Amendment as denying to the plaintiff in error due process of law and the equal protection of the laws.

Carrie Buck is a feeble minded white woman who was committed to the State Colony above mentioned in due form. She is the daughter of a feeble minded mother in the same institution, and the mother of an illegitimate feeble minded child. She was eighteen years old at the time of the trial of

---

19   A. H. Estabrook was the person who initiated this test of the infant's intelligence and took the picture. See http://www.hsl.virginia.edu/historical/eugenics/3-buckvbell.cfm

20   http://www.hsl.virginia.edu/historical/eugenics/3-buckvbell.cfm,

her case in the Circuit Court, in the latter part of 1924. An Act of Virginia, approved March 20, 1924, recites that the health of the patient and the welfare of society may be promoted in certain cases by the sterilization of mental defectives, under careful safeguard, &c.; that the sterilization may be effected in males by vasectomy and in females by salpingectomy, without serious pain or substantial danger to life; that the Commonwealth is supporting in various institutions many defective persons who if now discharged would become 206*206 a menace but if incapable of procreating might be discharged with safety and become self-supporting with benefit to themselves and to society; and that experience has shown that heredity plays an important part in the transmission of insanity, imbecility, &c. The statute then enacts that whenever the superintendent of certain institutions including the above named State Colony shall be of opinion that it is for the best interests of the patients and of society that an inmate under his care should be sexually sterilized, he may have the operation performed upon any patient afflicted with hereditary forms of insanity, imbecility, &c., on complying with the very careful provisions by which the act protects the patients from possible abuse.

The superintendent first presents a petition to the special board of directors of his hospital or colony, stating the facts and the grounds for his opinion, verified by affidavit. Notice of the petition and of the time and place of the hearing in the institution is to be served upon the inmate, and also upon his guardian, and if there is no guardian the superintendent is to apply to the Circuit Court of the County to appoint one. If the inmate is a minor notice also is to be given to his parents if any with a copy of the petition. The board is to see to it that the inmate may attend the hearings if desired by him or his guardian. The evidence is all to be reduced to writing, and after the board has made its order for or against the operation, the superintendent, or the inmate, or his guardian, may appeal to the Circuit Court of the County. The Circuit Court may consider the record of the board and the evidence before it and such other admissible evidence as may be offered, and may affirm, revise, or reverse the order of the board and enter such order as it deems just. Finally any party may apply to the Supreme Court of Appeals, which, if it grants the appeal, is to hear the case upon the record of the trial 207*207 in the Circuit Court and may enter such order as it thinks the Circuit Court should have entered. There can be no doubt that so far as procedure is concerned the rights of the patient are most carefully considered, and as every step in this case was taken in scrupulous compliance with the statute and after months of observation, there is no doubt that in that respect the plaintiff in error has had due process of law.

The attack is not upon the procedure but upon the substantive law (author's emphasis added). It seems to be contended that in no circumstances could such an order be justified. It certainly is contended that the order cannot be justified upon the existing grounds. The judgment finds the facts that have been recited and that Carrie Buck "is the probable potential parent of socially inadequate offspring, likewise afflicted, that she may be sexually sterilized without detriment to her general health and that her welfare and that of society will be promoted by her sterilization," and thereupon makes the order. In view of the general declarations of the legislature and the specific findings of the Court, obviously we cannot say as matter of law that the grounds do not exist, and if they exist they justify the result.

We have seen more than once that the public welfare may call upon the best citizens for their lives. It would be strange if it could not call upon those who already sap the strength of the State for these lesser sacrifices, often not felt to be such by those concerned, in order to prevent our being swamped with incompetence. It is better for all the world, if instead of waiting to execute degenerate offspring for crime, or to let them starve for their imbecility, society can prevent those who are manifestly unfit from continuing their kind. The principle that sustains compulsory vaccination is broad enough to cover cutting the Fallopian tubes. Jacobson v. Massachusetts, 197 U.S. 11. Three generations of imbeciles are enough. *[Author's emphasis added.]*

208*208 But, it is said, however it might be if this reasoning were applied generally, it fails when it is confined to the small number who are in the institutions named and is not applied to the multitudes outside. It is the usual last resort of constitutional arguments to point out shortcomings of this sort. But the answer is that the law does all that is needed when it does all that it can, indicates a policy, applies it to all within the lines, and seeks to bring within the lines all similarly situated so far and so fast as its means allow. Of course so far as the operations enable those who otherwise must be kept confined to be returned to the world, and thus open the asylum to others, the equality aimed at will be more nearly reached.

Judgment affirmed.
MR. JUSTICE BUTLER dissents.

"THE ATTACK IS NOT ON THE PROCEDURE BUT UPON THE SUBSTANTIVE LAW."[21]

With only one judge dissenting, the U.S. Supreme Court affirmed the Virginia court's ruling to allow the state to involuntarily sterilize a woman. The constitutional issue presented to the Court was whether the 14th Amendment prevented the government from sterilizing a person who had committed no crime as a denial of due process and equal protection. With the affirmation of the constitutionality of the Virginia law, on October 19, 1927, Dr. Bell sterilized Carrie Buck— she was the first person to be sterilized under Virginia's new law. Soon after her sterilization, Carrie Buck was paroled from the Virginia institution. Carrie Buck married two times afterwards but could never have children. Her subsequent letters and actions confirmed that she was of, at least, average intelligence.

By the 1930s, most states had eugenic sterilization laws and more than 35,000 people were sterilized by the government which targeted all sorts of alleged "misfits."[22] It took Virginia until 1974 to repeal the sterilization statute. In 2001, Virginia apologized for its behavior during the

---

21   *Buck v. Bell*, 274 U.S. 200 (1927).
22   After *Buck v. Bell*, Virginia sterilized 7325 people, 62% of whom were women. https://www.uvm.edu/~lkaelber/eugenics/VA/VA.html

eugenics movement and referred to the "now-discredited pseudo-science of eugenics," in House Joint Resolution No. 607, "Expressing the General Assembly's regret for Virginia's experience with eugenics."[23] In 2015, Virginia agreed to reparations for victims of its eugenics law promising $25,000 for each victim or her estate.[24] "When someone is denied the ability to have a family, that's a tragedy, but when it's denied to them by their government, that is a scandal and a wrong that needs to be made right." More than 7,000 Virginians were sterilized by the state under the law. Only 11 were alive at the time of the reparations.[25]

Certainly this is a "repugnant part of our…history."[26] During the Nuremberg war trials, Nazi lawyers cited *Buck v. Bell* as acceptable precedent for the sterilization of two million people in its *Rassenhygiene* (race hygiene) program.[27] Should involuntary sterilization ever be permissible?

Is our eugenics ideology really gone when in 2014 an Arizona Republican official said "women on Medicaid should be sterilized?"[28] Or when that same year, in the case of child endangerment, hit and run driving, and driving on a suspended license, a Virginia judge sentenced a man to either 20 months in prison or five years of probation and a vasectomy.[29] The judge acknowledged that the vasectomy provision was "primarily due to the fact he had seven or eight children, all by different women, and we felt it might be in the commonwealth's interest for that to be part of the plea agreement."[30]

VOLUNTARY DECISIONS

While the first half of the 20th century involved decisions on government sterilization to prevent reproduction, the latter half dealt with the government's efforts to prevent voluntary decisions

---

23   Virginia House Joint Resolution No. 607, 2001.

24   Quoting Delegate Benjamin L. Cline. Virginia was the second state (behind North Carolina) to compensate such individuals of the 30 or so states that involuntarily sterilized. "Lawmakers agree to pay those sterilized by state", Jenna Portnoy, *The Washington Post*, February 28, 2015.

25   After his cousin hit him in the head with a rock triggering epileptic-like seizures, E. Lewis Reynolds was classified at age 13 as a "defective person" and sterilized. He went on to serve in the military for 30 years and marry but never have children or grandchildren. At 83 years of age, he was waiting to receive his restitution. https://www.washingtonpost.com/local/va-politics/va-eugenics-victims-would-receive-compensation-for-sterilization-under-proposed-bill/2013/01/30/eebad4de-6b0d-11e2-95b3-272d604a10a3_story.html?utm_term=.afcb65559aad

26   Ibid, quoting Virginia State Delegate Patrick A. Hope.

27   http://digitalarchive.gsu.edu/col_facpub/45/, Georgia University Digital Archives.

28   ""You put me in charge of Medicaid, the first thing I'd do is get (female recipients) Norplant, birth-control implants, or tubal ligations.…Then, we'll test recipients for drugs and alcohol, and if you want to (reproduce) or use drugs or alcohol, then get a job." Quoting Russell Pearce, a former Republican state senator who resigned in response to those comments as the Arizona GOP's vice chair. "Arizona Republican Resigns after Arguing that Women on Medicaid Should Be Sterilized", Adam Edelman, "*Daily News*", September 15, 2014. http://www.nydailynews.com/news/politics/arizona-republican-resigns-arguing-women-medicaid-sterilized-article-1.1940389

29   As part of the deal, he had to agree not allowed to undergo a reversal of the procedure until the five years of his probation was over.

30   "VA man agrees to get Vasectomy as Part of Plea Deal", *Fox News* June 24, 2014. http://insider.foxnews.com/2014/06/24/va-man-required-get-vasectomy-part-plea-deal

by individuals to prevent reproduction. In 1873, Anthony Comstock, "a vice crusader and ex-dry good salesman"[31] rallied Congress to pass federal laws banning the mailing of obscene materials and their circulation. Obscene materials were defined to include contraceptives and abortifacients. Caught up in the frenzy, many states passed their own laws outlawing birth control. Thus, doctors were prevented from prescribing birth control to their patients and, in extreme cases, the use of such devices was illegal. Courts upheld these "Comstock laws" under the exercise of the police powers until a Connecticut law was found unconstitutional in 1965.[32]

The government continued to interfere with the citizens' rights to use birth control up until the 1960s. Only in the case of *Griswald v. Connecticut*, 381 U.S. 479 (1965), did the U.S. Supreme Court strike down the states' strict bans on the use or distribution of birth control to citizens, even by their doctors and pharmacists. Finding a right to privacy in the penumbras of the Amendments to the Constitution, the Supreme Court went on to decide that marital status is irrelevant to the right to obtain and use birth control in *Eisenstadt v. Baird*, 405 U.S.438 (1972). (See Chapter 5 for more detailed analysis of the Supreme Court decisions.)[33]

Minors

The Supreme Court found a right to privacy in the decision of adults as to whether or not to use birth control, but what about minors? Does this constitutional right of privacy extend to them in using birth control? Yes; minors have rights to obtain information and use birth control. While states may argue that restricting minors' rights to birth control may deter sexual promiscuity, in *Carey v. Population Services. Int'l*, 431 U.S. 68 (1977), the Court rejected that argument, but in deference to the parental role in decision making for children the, Court restricted the right as applied to children.

Funding

Even though the 1960s ruling in *Griswald* indicates that the government should not be involved in the private decision-making on contraception use, politics continue to impact the topic. Politics allowed a religious exemption for companies not to provide contraception coverage under the

---

31 *Emanuel Law Outlines, Family Law*, by D. Kelly Weisberg, 2011, p. 226.

32 Ibid.

33 Contrast these cases determining a fundamental right to privacy from government intrusion in personal decisions about having children to modern issues on birth control. In 2013, New York legislatures debated whether prisoners, including rapist and sex offenders, should get Viagra at taxpayer expense and years later the debate continues. http://www.nbcnews.com/id/7946129/ns/us_news/t/sex-offenders-get-medicaid-paid-viagra/#.UX2UZ0rYySo, "Sex offenders get Medicaid-paid Viagra" NBCNews.com, May 22, 2005. "[S]cores of convicted rapists and other high-risk sex offenders in New York have been getting Viagra paid by Medicaid for the last five years." How about a clinic that advertised a free pizza for obtaining a vasectomy during college basketball's "March Madness Tournament". www.cbsnews.com/2102-504763_162-57398849.html?tag=con "Mass. clinic offers free pizza for vasectomy during March Madness," CBS News staff, March 16, 2012.

Affordable Health Care Act. It was "an element [in President] Obama's health care overhaul law that required most employers to cover birth control, free of charge for female workers as a preventive service. That controversy led to lawsuits that threatened to embroil Obama's health care law."[34] The Obama administration eventually worked to find a compromise on the rule for religious groups.[35] In 2014, Michigan lawmakers created a new law that requires women to purchase a separate insurance policy for abortion coverage, even in the case of rape or incest. It was derided as "rape insurance" because "it essentially forces victims of sexual assault to pay-out-of-pock for an abortion procedure unless they thought ahead and purchased a separate insurance rider."[36]

How much has the nation changed on the issue of contraception? What has changed since the shameful period of our nation's history of eugenics for which *Buck v. Bell* was the poster child? At the turn of the last century we dealt with our poor and vulnerable by "negative eugenics," hoping to eliminate them from the race. In perhaps one of its darkest hours, science twisted genetics into a pseudoscience to accomplish its political and societal goals. While states have abolished their sterilization laws, has society learned anything about the dangers of using twisted science or ignoring science altogether?

In 2013, federal judge Edward Korman in the U.S. District Court of New York required the federal government to make Plan B, a form of emergency contraception, the so-called "morning-after" drug[37] available to females of any age without prescription.[38] A previous 2011 decision by Health and Human Services Secretary Kathleen Sebelius had barred over-the-counter sales of Plan B to girls younger than 17 and required that they must also have a prescription. Under

---

34 http://www.huffingtonpost.com/2013/04/06/obama-morning-after-pill_n_3028949.html, "Obama Faces Choice on Morning-After Pill Restrictions," by Josh Lederman and Lauran Neergaard, *Huffington Post,* April 6, 2013. In April 2013, Virginia delegate Bob Marshall proposed to allow private insurance providers, who participated in the new federal health care plans, to deny coverage to women for an abortion. Which constitutional arguments could you make for and against such bills? Do they violate equal protection because only women can become pregnant? What about states' equal rights laws that prevent discrimination against women? Or do these bills satisfy equal protection because both men and women can use contraceptives? At the federal level, Senator Roy Blunt attached an amendment relating to contraception to a U.S. Senate transportation bill in February 2013. http://www.huffingtonpost.com/2013/04/04/virginia-abortion-bill_n_3014934.html, "Virginia Abortion Bill Blocks Coverage in Health Care Exchange," Jim Nolan, *HuffPost DC,* April 4, 2013. http://www.huffingtonpost.com/2012/11/26/bob-marshall-virginia-abortion_n_2192979.html, Bob Marshall: "Virginia GOP Pressures Me '7 Days a Week' to Drop Anti-Abortion Agenda," Laura Bassett.

35 In the *Hobby Lobby* case in 2014, the U.S. Supreme Court extended this exemption to corporations with "sincere religious views." (See chapter 5).

36 This would also require parents to purchase the plans for their minor daughters. "Senators continue fight against Michagna's new 'rape insurance' law", *CBSDetroit,* June 16, 2014. http://detroit.cbslocal.com/2014/06/16/senators-continue-fight-against-michigan-rape-insurance-law/

37 The Web definition for Plan B is "a large dose of estrogen taken orally within 24 to 72 hours after intercourse; prevents implantation of a fertilized ovum and so acts as a contraceptive; commonly used after rape or incest." wordnetweb.princeton.edu/perl/webwn (retrieved April 7, 2013).

38 http://www.huffingtonpost.com/2012/11/26/bob-marshall-virginia-abortion_n_2192979.html, Bob Marshall: "Virginia GOP Pressures Me '7 Days a Week' to Drop Anti-Abortion Agenda," Laura Bassett.

the new ruling,[39] Plan B would be on the shelf and available to all women at any age without a prescription.[40]

What ties the Plan B case to *Bell* and many other contraception rulings is the continued manipulation of science for politics and policy. The scientists at the Food and Drug Administration, responsible for approving the safety of drugs, recommended approving the use of the drug as "safe and effective in adolescent females" and said that it could be used properly by young women without consulting a doctor."[41] Indeed, the judge noted that Plan B would be among the safest over-the-counter drugs. Was the Obama administration relying on some pseudoscience (about girl's maturity in decision making perhaps) in ignoring the scientists' findings? Or is it enough for Obama to say, "[a]s the father of two daughters, I think it is important for us to make sure that we apply some common sense to various rules when it comes to over-the-counter medicine," when he endorsed Sebelius's decision? In the Judge's lengthy "ruling [he]accused the Obama administration in no uncertain terms of letting the president's pending re-election cloud its judgment when it set the age limits in 2011."[42] "The motivation for the secretary's action was obviously political," Judge Korman wrote in reference to Health and Human Services Secretary Kathleen Sebelius, who made the 2011 decision. "'[s]Science has finally prevailed over politics, to the benefit of millions of women across the United States.'"[43]

Yet, on May 1, 2013 the Obama administration refused to follow the court's order. Instead, the administration approved over-the-counter sales of the pill for girls age 15 years and above.[44] In response, the *Washington Post* wrote, "the administration's move represents a historic liberalization of contraception rules—perhaps the most significant since the morning-after was approved 14 years ago."[45] Just before the May 2013 appeals deadline, the Obama administration filed an appeal of Judge Korman's order. By June, the Justice Department dropped its appeal.[46] Should our

---

39   The court's order requires the FDA to lift the "age restrictions within 30 days." The Obama administration waivered as to whether it would appeal the ruling.

40   "Plan B ruling reanimates a political tug of war," Sarah Kliff and Brady Dennis, *Washington Post*, April 6, 2013, p 1.

41   "Plan B ruling reanimates a political tug of war," Sarah Kliff and Brady Dennis, *Washington Post*, April 6, 2013, pp. 1 and A2.

42   http://www.huffingtonpost.com/2013/04/06/obama-morning-after-pill_n_3028949.html, "Obama Faces Choice on Morning-After Pill Restrictions," by Josh Lederman and Lauran Neergaard, *Huffington Post*, April 6, 2013.

43   www.cbsnews.com/2102-504763_162-57398849.html?tag=con, "Mass. clinic offers free pizza for vasectomy during March Madness," CBS News staff, March 16, 2012, quoting Nancy Northup, President of the Center for Reproductive Rights, which initiated the lawsuit in 2005, p. A2.

44   "As the father of two daughters, I think it is important for us to make sure that we apply some common sense to various rules when it comes to over-the-counter medicine," Obama said in 2011 when he endorsed Sebelius's decision. http://www.huffingtonpost.com/2013/04/06/obama-morning-after-pill_n_3028949.html, "Obama Faces Choice on Morning-After Pill Restrictions," Josh Lederman and Lauran Neergaard, Huffington Post, April 6, 2013.

45   "FDA move on Plan B falls short of court order," Sarah Kliff and Zachary A. Goldfarb, for the Washington Post, May 1, 2013, p 1.

46   "Obama Administration drops fight to keep age restrictions on Plan B sales", Brady Dennis & Sarah Kliff, *The Washington Post*, June 10, 2013 http://www.washingtonpost.com/national/health-science/obama-administration-drops-fight-to-keep-age-restrictions-on-plan-b-sales/2013/06/10/a296406e-d22a-11e2-a73e-826d299ff459_story.html

government policy be driven by science in the twenty-first century? Is it right that Plan B should be sold next to toothpaste if scientists think it is safe? Or out of a campus vending machine, as it is sold at Shippensburg College in Pennsylvania? Finally, if we as a country have moved on from our eugenics past and recognized our prejudices toward the poor and vulnerable, should we have learned to provide Plan B and other forms of voluntary contraception for free to ensure that finances do not limit access?

AS WE GO TO PRESS

The Supreme Court decided not to hear the case of *Zubik v. Burwell*, 578 U.S. ___ (2016) but instead, uniquely sent the case back to the parties to allow them to attempt to resolve it outside of the court. The parties were the Obama administration representing the Affordable Care Act (ACA aka Obama Care) and the plaintiffs, many religious organizations, colleges and schools, including the Little Sisters of the Poor, a group of Catholic nuns who run homes for the elderly. Under the ACA, insurance companies were required to provide women with preventative care, including contraceptives without requiring a copayment. The Little Sisters raised religious objections to covering their employees' birth control as against the Catholic Church's religious convictions. Yet, the ACA included a "religious exemption". To claim it, the religious organization could file paperwork and it would not pay for the cost of the employees' contraception coverage (that would be done by a cost sharing mechanism with the government and the insurance company).[47] But the Sisters argued that the government was placing a "substantial burden" on them by requiring them to file the paperwork. By doing so, the Sisters argued it made them complicate in providing birth control. The government disagreed, saying a secular third-party provided the coverage so, the government argued, religious freedom claims were moot. Instead, the government and women's rights groups argued the religious organizations were attempting to infringe on woman's rights by limiting their access to birth control.

Perhaps part of the reason the Supreme Court did not rule in this case was that the Supreme Court was short one justice after Justice Scalia's unexpected death in 2016 and the Republican

---

47   The difference here and the *Hobby Lobby* case is the ACA offered the religious exemption to "religious organizations" like the Sisters. Under *Hobby Lobby*, with Justice Scalia on the Supreme Court, this exemption was extended to "closely held" corporations that were not religious organizations, but whose owners had strong religious beliefs. Contrast this with Hobby Lobby's July 2017 settlement agreement to forfeit thousands of artifacts that seemed to have been stolen from Iraq and pay a $3 million fine to resolve a civil action the Justice Department brought against the company. The DOJ alleged that Hobby Lobby treasures were intentionally falsely labeled as "samples" and smuggled from other countries as part of an elaborate scheme to defraud and obtain the items. This was done after the company's expert warned it in 2009 "'that the acquisition of cultural property likely from Iraq, including cuneiform tablets and cylinder seals, carries a risk that such objects may have been looted from archaeological sites in Iraq,' the DOJ said. http://www.cnn.com/2017/07/05/us/hobby-lobby-ancient-artifacts-trnd/index.html. See also https://www.theatlantic.com/politics/archive/2017/07/hobby-lobby-smuggled-thousands-of-ancient-artifacts-out-of-iraq/532743/.   Ironically, Hobby Lobby purchased the stolen artifacts for its Bible Museum.

Party's refusal to vote on President Obama's nominee for a replacement. As we go to press, President Trump has promised to nominate a pro-life judge to the Supreme Court, which would break the possible 4-4 tie of the now 8 Justices. (A tie ruling would affirm the lower court rulings giving different states different rules on the issue of federal health care). Also, as I write, the Republican Congress has just proposed the American Health Care Act to repeal and replace Obama Care.[48] As groups are forming up to support and oppose the AHCA, what will happen to the health insurance protections for coverage of woman's contraception?

---

48 At this time, the AHCA does not change the coverage for woman's preventative health care, which includes contraception coverage, but it does impact woman's health care in other ways by defunding Planned Parenthood, one of the country's largest providers of preventative health care to woman (and men) and cutting back on Medicaid and private insurance for abortions.

ABORTION

We are totally opposed to abortion under any circumstances. We are also opposed to abortifacient drugs and chemicals like the Pill and the IUD, and we are also opposed to all forms of birth control with the exception of natural family planning.
—Judie Brown, president, American Life Lobby[1]

If men could get pregnant, abortion would be a sacrament.
—Florynce Kennedy[2]

ROE V. WADE, 410 U.S. 113 (1973)
KNOW THE PLAINTIFF

"'Norma McCorvey, "Roe" in *Roe v. Wade,* is dead at 69'" read the headlines in the U.S. on February 18, 2017.[3] The press eulogized her as "a complicated protagonist in a legal case that became a touchstone in the culture wars, celebrated by champions as an affirmation of women's freedom and denounced by opponents as the nationwide legalization of murder of the unborn.[4] How did it end that way?

In the summer of 1970, an unmarried 22-year-old woman, Norma McCorvey, a carnival worker living in Texas, was pregnant after a brief affair. This was her third pregnancy. Distraught

1   http://www.quotationspage.com/search.php3?homesearch=Abortion&startsearch=Search, The Quotations Page, www.quotationspage.com
2   womenshistory.about.com/od/... /Florynce-Kennedy-quotes.htm
3   http://www.usatoday.com/story/news/nation/2017/02/18/norma-mccorvey-roe-roe-v-wade-dead-abortion/98093844/
4   https://www.washingtonpost.com/national/norma-mccorvey-jane-roe-of-roe-v-wade-decision-legalizing-abortion-dies-at-69/2017/02/18/24b83108-396e-11e6-8f7c-d4c723a2becb_story.html?utm_term=.d638581e2988

at the prospect of bearing a third child, McCorvey decided that she wanted an abortion in a medical setting by a licensed doctor. However, abortion was illegal in Texas, as in most states, except to save the life of the mother.

Ms. McCorvey was "born Norma Lea Nelson in Simmesport, Louisiana, on September 22, 1947, four ounces shy of seven pounds."[5] She wrote that her mother wanted "to terminate the pregnancy. Told she was too far along, my mother was left with no other choice but to have me."[6] Nicknamed "Pixie," McCorvey was "short and slight."[7] "Her mother... was physically abusive. Her brother... was mentally ill. Her father... a TV repairman was soon gone, rarely to return."[8] McCorvey went to "Catholic boarding school" and "then after minor brushes with the law, briefly to reform school."[9] Her mother summed up McCorvey's youth: "She drank and she took dope and she slept with women."[10]

McCorvey was married and pregnant by 16, but her husband was violent and she divorced him before her daughter was born.[11] That daughter, Melissa, was born in May 1965. After being arrested for abandoning her child[12], McCorvey granted custody of Melissa to her mother.[13]

"In 1967, at age 19, she became pregnant for the second time. At birth the baby was given up to an adoptive couple whose identity has been kept private."[14] "In September 1969, the month she turned 22, McCorvey became pregnant for the third time. She told her doctor... that she did not want to bring this pregnancy to term."[15,16] "And she could not afford to travel

---

5 "The Accidental Activist," Joshua Prager, *Vanity Fair*, February 2013, p. 110.

6 Citing to McCorvey's memoir, *I Am Roe*, in "The Accidental Activist," Joshua Prager, *Vanity Fair*, February 2013, p. 110.

7 "The Accidental Activist," Joshua Prager, *Vanity Fair*, February 2013, p. 111.

8 Ibid. As McCorvey tells it, "[H]er early life had been a Dickensian nightmare. By her own account, she was the unwanted child of a broken home, a ninth-grade dropout who was raped repeatedly by a relative, and a homeless runaway and thief consigned to reform school." https://www.nytimes.com/2017/02/18/obituaries/norma-mccorvey-dead-roe-v-wade.html?_r=0

9 Ibid.

10 Ibid. She was "[b]isexual but primarily lesbian. https://www.nytimes.com/2017/02/18/obituaries/norma-mccorvey-dead-roe-v-wade.html?_r=0

11 Ibid.

12 https://www.nytimes.com/2017/02/18/obituaries/norma-mccorvey-dead-roe-v-wade.html?_r=0

13 "McCorvey alleges in *I Am Roe* that her mother "kidnapped Melissa, tricking Norma into signing adoption papers on the pretense that the papers had to do with insurance." While McCorvey said the adoption occurred because she was a lesbian, her mother said it was caused by McCorvey's drinking and drug use. McCorvey admits to all of it. "The Accidental Activist," Joshua Prager, *Vanity Fair*, February 2013, p. 113.

14 Ibid.

15 Ibid., p. 112.

16 There seems to be some confusion as to whether McCorvey told her doctor that the pregnancy was the product of rape. "Another woman in the waiting room, upon hearing Norma's story, told her that she ought to tell the doctor that she had been raped, for the news might well make the difference." "Still Standing: The Resilience of *Roe v. Wade*", by Jeffrey Toobin, *New Yorker*, November 28, 2005, p. 72, citing to *Liberty and Sexuality* by David J. Garrow, 1994. "Thus misinformed, the doctor referred McCorvey to a local lawyer considering a challenge to the Texas abortion law" (*New Yorker*, p. 72). "[McCorvey] told the press that she had become pregnant after being raped," but in her book, *I Am Roe*, she said "the actual father was a consensual partner." (*VF*, p. 114) McCorvey also "made headlines in 1987 when she told the columnist Carl T. Rowan that she had lied when she told reporters in 1970 that her pregnancy had

to any of the six states where abortion was legal."[17,18] Her doctor referred her to an adoption lawyer.[19]

That lawyer referred McCorvey to two female lawyers, Linda Coffee and Sarah Weddington, who had an interest in challenging Texas' abortion statute.[20] Lawyers choose their plaintiffs carefully when they intend to challenge landmark laws. "It had to be a pregnant woman waiting to get an abortion. She couldn't have the funds to travel to California or New York for a legal abortion. And we had to have someone who could take the publicity. We weren't able to guarantee her anonymity."[21]

"Five months pregnant at the time, McCorvey seemed a perfect plaintiff."[22] As plaintiff, she was given the pseudonym Jane Roe and the Dallas County district attorney Henry Wade was named the defendant; the case was filed in federal court in Dallas, Texas, because of the constitutional question of privacy raised. The case was later modified to a class action in order to include all similarly situated pregnant women who were denied legal abortion procedures under Texas law.

As Roe was several months pregnant when the case was filed and legal cases and appeals are lengthy, she never received the medical procedure of an abortion. She became "ironically, a symbol of the right to a procedure that she herself never underwent."[23] Texas prevented Jane Roe's request for medical assistance because the Texas Criminal Abortion law of 1857 prohibited it:

> If any person shall administer to any woman any drug or medicine, or shall use towards her any violence or means whatever externally or internally, and thereby procure an abortion, he shall be confined in the penitentiary not less than two nor more than five years.

---

been the result of a gang rape". https://www.nytimes.com/2017/02/18/obituaries/norma-mccorvey-dead-roe-v-wade.html?_r=0 In any event, her lawyers "never mentioned an alleged rape in court, and it formed no part of their legal argument… But pro-life activists now asserted that the *Roe* ruling hinged on a falsehood." "The Accidental Activist," Joshua Prager, *Vanity Fair*, February 2013, p. 114.

17 Those states were Alaska, California, Hawaii, New York, Oregon, and Washington.

18 Ibid., p. 112.

19 "Months before meeting… McCorvey, [that lawyer] filed a suit taking aim at an anti-sodomy law in Texas. The case, *Alvin L. Buchanan v. Charles Batchelor*, concerned a male client convicted of having consensual oral sex with another man." Although successful in challenging Texas's sodomy law, the case was overturned by the U.S. Supreme Court in 1971. Ibid., p. 110–113.

20 Ibid., p. 113. Both were advocates for women's issues. "Weddington, for her part, had firsthand experience with abortion laws in Texas, having felt compelled to go to Mexico for an abortion during law school."

21 Ibid., p. 110, quoting Coffee talking to a reporter in 1983.

22 Ibid. Four months later, she gave birth to a daughter and surrendered her for adoption. https://www.nytimes.com/2017/02/18/obituaries/norma-mccorvey-dead-roe-v-wade.html?_r=0. The girl was about two and half years old by the time the Supreme Court decided the case. http://www.economist.com/news/obituary/21717339-jane-roe-roe-v-wade-was-69-obituary-norma-mccorvey-jane-roe-roe-v-wade

23 Ibid., p. 110,111 and 115. After many years as serving as the symbol for women's right to choose, "in August 119, McCorvey was baptized and became a member or a Christian pro-life congregation." "'The poster child has jumped off the poster.'" said the head of Texans United for Life. During the November 2012 elections, "McCorvey received $1,000 to appear in a Florida television ad paid for by Randall Terry, the founder of Operation Rescue, who ran (unsuccessfully) as an independent for election to the U.S. House of Representative from Florida. "'Do not vote for Barack Obama', McCorvey said against a background of images of aborted fetuses." Ibid. p. 167.

The law criminalized all abortion procedures except to save the life of the woman. That meant that any medical provider (or nonmedical person) who provided the medical procedure could be punished with prison time. As a result, McCorvey's choices were limited and dangerous. First, she could travel out of state to another state that did not prohibit abortions. Roe, however, was a carney who worked the rides at a carnival[24] and said she did not have the money to do so, which eliminated this option. Second, she could take the risk of going to a non-medical environment to see someone who was not medically trained to perform the procedure; this was known as receiving a "back-alley abortion." In her declaration in support of her request for the procedure, McCorvey's affidavit stated:

> I believe the enforcement of the Texas Criminal Abortion Law against licensed physi-
> cians has forced me into the dilemma of electing whether to bear an unwanted child or
> risk my life submitting to an abortion at the hands of unqualified personnel outside of
> a clinical setting.[25]

Procedural History

In the lower court, the plaintiff alleged that the Texas law violated her constitutional right to privacy to make a decision without government interference in an area that was so intimate as to "whether to bear or beget a child,"[26] and that the law was unconstitutionally vague. As a result, McCorvey requested the court declare the law unconstitutional and grant an injunction restraining Texas from enforcing the void law. The Texas D.A. responded that the Constitution did not mention the word abortion (or even a privacy right), so no such right could exist. "The hearing began in May and ended on June 17 when a three-judge panel struck down the Texas abortion statutes."[27] After the U.S. District Court for Texas ruled in favor of Roe, the state, through Wade, immediately appealed to the U.S. Supreme Court, so the law remained in effect.[28]

Justice Harry Blackmun, writing for the Supreme Court's majority (voting seven to two), announced the decision of the U.S. Supreme court on January 22, 1973.[29] The opinion in *Roe* starts by acknowledging the controversial and difficult nature of the issue.

---

24 "Still Standing: The Resilience of *Roe v. Wade*," Jeffrey Toobin, *New Yorker*, November 28, 2005, p. 72, citing to *Liberty and Sexuality*, David J. Garrow, 1994.

25 Great Decisions of the U.S. Supreme Court, Edited by Maureen Harrison and Steve Gilbert, Barnes & Noble, 2003.

26 *Eisenstadt v. Baird*, 405 U.S. 438 (1972).

27 "The Accidental Activist," by Joshua Prager, *Vanity Fair*, February 2013, p. 113.

28 Ibid., p. 113. Oral arguments were held "in December 1971. And after Justices Lewis Powell and William Rehnquist replaced the retiring justices Hugo Black and John Harlan, oral arguments were heard again, the following October." Three months later the decision arrived.

29 An anniversary date that continues to inspire large protests on both sides of the issue in front of the Supreme Court—. See photographs in http://www.washingtonpost.com/local/march-for-life-arrives-in-washington/2013/01/25/1b7bcfc4-672a-11e2-9e1b-07db1d2ccd5b_gallery.html#photo=20, "March for Life Arrives in Washington," by Brendan Smialowski, *Washington Post*, January 25, 2013.

We forthwith acknowledge our awareness of the sensitive and emotional nature of the abortion controversy, of the vigorous opposing views, even among physicians, and of the deep and seemingly absolute convictions that the subject inspires. One's philosophy, one's experiences, one's exposure to the raw edges of human existence, one's religious training, one's attitudes toward life and family and their values, and the moral standards one establishes and seek to observe, are all likely to influence and to color one's thinking and conclusions about abortion.

[The Constitution] is made for people of fundamentally differing views, and the accident of our finding certain opinions natural and familiar or novel and even shocking ought not to conclude our judgment upon the question whether statutes embodying them conflict with the Constitution of the United States.[30]

The beginning of the *Roe* opinion traces the history of abortion in the United States. Under common law, abortion was legal until "quickening (the first recognizable movement of the fetus in utero appearing usually from the 16th to the 18th week of pregnancy)—[it] was not an indictable offense." With this as the historical background, Justice Blackmun then outlined the concepts of the majority's decision.

ROE V. WADE, 410 U.S. 113, (1973)

(Case Notes Included for Summary Purposes)

Action was brought for a declaratory and injunctive relief respecting Texas criminal abortion laws, which were claimed to be unconstitutional. A three-judge United States District Court for the Northern District of Texas, 314 F.Supp. 1217, entered judgment declaring laws unconstitutional and an appeal was taken. The Supreme Court, Mr. Justice Blackmun, held that the Texas criminal abortion statutes prohibiting abortions at any stage of pregnancy except to save the life of the mother are unconstitutional; that prior to approximately the end of the first trimester the abortion decision and its effectuation must be left to the medical judgment of the pregnant woman's attending physician, subsequent to approximately the end of the first trimester the state may regulate abortion procedure in ways reasonably related to maternal health, and at the stage subsequent to viability the state may regulate

---

30 *Roe v. Wade* 410 U.S. 113, 93 S.Ct. 705, 35 L.Ed.2d 147 (1973), 708

and even proscribe abortion except where necessary in appropriate medical judgment for preservation of life or health of mother.

Right of personal privacy or a guarantee of certain areas or zones of privacy does exist under Constitution, and only personal rights that can be deemed fundamental or implicit in the concept of ordered liberty are included in this guarantee of personal privacy; the right has some extension to activities relating to marriage. U.S.C.A.Const. Amends. 1, 4, 5, 9, 14, 14, § 1.

Constitutional right of privacy is broad enough to encompass [the] woman's decision whether or not to terminate her pregnancy, but the woman's right to terminate pregnancy is not absolute since state may properly assert important interests in safeguarding health, in maintaining medical standards and in protecting potential life, and at some point in pregnancy these respective interests become sufficiently compelling to sustain regulation of factors that govern the abortion decision. U.S.C.A.Const. Amends. 9, Word "person" as used in the Fourteenth Amendment does not include the unborn. U.S.C.A.Const. Amend. 14.

Prior to approximately the end of the first trimester of pregnancy, the attending physician in consultation with his patient is free to determine, without regulation by state, that in his medical judgment the patient's pregnancy should be terminated, and if that decision is reached such judgment may be effectuated by an abortion without interference by the state.

From and after approximately the end of the first trimester of pregnancy, a state may regulate abortion procedure to extent that the regulation reasonably relates to preservation and protection of maternal health.

If state is interested in protecting fetal life after viability, it may go so far as to proscribe abortion during that period except when necessary to preserve the life or the health of the mother.

State criminal abortion laws like Texas statutes making it a crime to procure or attempt an abortion except an abortion on medical advice for purpose of saving life of the mother regardless of stage of pregnancy violate due process clause of Fourteenth Amendment protecting right to privacy against state action. U.S.C.A.Const. Amend. 14; Vernon's Ann.Tex.P.C. arts. 1191–1194, 1196.

Conclusion that Texas criminal abortion statute proscribing all abortions except to save life of mother is unconstitutional meant that the abortion statutes as a unit must fall, and the exception could not be struck down separately for then the state would be left with statute proscribing all abortion procedures no matter how medically urgent the case. Vernon's Ann.Tex. P.C. arts. 1191–1194, 1196.

A pregnant single woman (Roe) brought a class action challenging the constitutionality of the Texas criminal abortion laws, which proscribe procuring or attempting an abortion except on medical advice for the purpose of saving the mother's life. A licensed physician (Hallford), who had two state abortion prosecutions pending against him, was permitted to intervene. A childless married couple (the Does), the wife not being pregnant, separately attacked the laws, basing alleged injury on the future possibilities of contraceptive failure, pregnancy, unpreparedness for parenthood, and impairment of the wife's health. A three-judge District Court, which consolidated the actions, held that Roe and Hallford, and members of their classes, had standing to sue and presented justiciable controversies. Ruling that declaratory, though not injunctive, relief was warranted, the court declared the abortion statutes void as vague and overbroadly infringing those plaintiffs' Ninth and Fourteenth Amendment rights. The court ruled the Does' complaint not justiciable. Appellants directly appealed to this Court on the injunctive rulings, and appellee cross-appealed from the District Court's grant of declaratory relief to Roe and Hallford. Held:

1. While 28 U.S.C. s 1253 authorizes no direct appeal to this Court from the grant or denial of declaratory relief alone, review is not foreclosed when the case is properly before the Court on appeal from specific denial of injunctive relief and the arguments as to both injunctive and declaratory relief are necessarily identical. Pp. 711–712.
2. Roe has standing to sue; the Does and Hallford do not. Pp. 712–715.
    (a) Contrary to appellee's contention, the natural termination of Roe's pregnancy did not moot her suit. Litigation involving pregnancy, which is 'capable of repetition, yet evading review,' is an exception to the usual federal rule that an actual controversy *114 must exist at review stages and not simply when the action is initiated. Pp. 712–713.
    (b) The District Court correctly refused injunctive, but erred in granting declaratory, relief to Hallford, who alleged no federally protected right not assertable as a defense against the good-faith state prosecutions pending against him. Samuels v. Mackell, 401 U.S. 66, 91 S.Ct. 764, 27 L.Ed.2d 688. Pp. 713–714.

**708 (c) The Does' complaint, based as it is on contingencies, any one or more of which may not occur, is too speculative to present an actual case or controversy. Pp. 714–715.

3. State criminal abortion laws, like those involved here, that except from criminality only a life-saving procedure on the mother's behalf without regard to the stage of her pregnancy and other interests involved violate the Due Process Clause of the Fourteenth Amendment, which protects against state action the right to privacy, including a woman's qualified right to terminate her pregnancy. Though the State cannot override that right, it has legitimate interests in protecting both the pregnant woman's health and the potentiality of human life, each of which interests grows and reaches a 'compelling' point at various stages of the woman's approach to term. Pp. 726–732.
    (a) For the stage prior to approximately the end of the first trimester, the abortion decision and its effectuation must be left to the medical judgment of the pregnant woman's attending physician. Pp. 731–732.
    (b) For the stage subsequent to approximately the end of the first trimester, the State, in promoting its interest in the health of the mother, may, if it chooses, regulate the abortion procedure in ways that are reasonably related to maternal health. Pp. 731–732.

(c) For the stage subsequent to viability the State, in promoting its interest in the potentiality of human life, may, if it chooses, regulate, and even proscribe, abortion except where necessary, in appropriate medical judgment, for the preservation of the life or health of the mother. Pp. 732–733.

4. The State may define the term 'physician' to mean only a physician currently licensed by the State, and may proscribe any abortion by a person who is not a physician as so defined. Pp. 732–733.

5. It is unnecessary to decide the injunctive relief issue since the Texas authorities will doubtless fully recognize the Court's ruling *115 that the Texas criminal abortion statutes are unconstitutional. P. 733.

314 F.Supp. 1217, affirmed in part and reversed in part.
*116 Mr. Justice BLACKMUN delivered the opinion of the Court.

This Texas federal appeal and its Georgia companion, *Doe v. Bolton,* 410 U.S. 179, 93 S.Ct. 739, 35 L.Ed.2d 201, present constitutional challenges to state criminal abortion legislation. The Texas statutes under attack here are typical of those that have been in effect in many States for approximately a century. The Georgia statutes, in contrast, have a modern cast and are a legislative product that, to an extent at least, obviously reflects the influences of recent attitudinal change, of advancing medical knowledge and techniques, and of new thinking about an old issue.

We forthwith acknowledge our awareness of the sensitive and emotional nature of the abortion controversy, of the vigorous opposing views, even among physicians, and of the deep and seemingly absolute convictions that the subject inspires. One's philosophy, one's experiences, one's exposure to the raw edges of human existence, one's religious training, one's attitudes toward life and family and their values, and the moral standards one establishes and seeks to observe, are all likely to influence and to color one's thinking and conclusions about abortion.

In addition, population growth, pollution, poverty, and racial overtones tend **709 to complicate and not to simplify the problem.

Our task, of course, is to resolve the issue by constitutional measurement, free of emotion and of predilection. We seek earnestly to do this, and, because we do, we *117 have inquired into, and in this opinion place some emphasis upon, medical and medical-legal history and what that history reveals about man's attitudes toward the abortion procedure over the centuries. We bear in mind, too, Mr. Justice Holmes' admonition in his now-vindicated dissent in Lochner v. New York, 198 U.S. 45, 76, 25 S.Ct. 539, 547, 49 L.Ed. 937 (1905):

'(The Constitution) is made for people of fundamentally differing views, and the accident of our finding certain opinions natural and familiar, or novel, and even shocking, ought not to conclude our judgment upon the question whether statutes embodying them conflict with the Constitution of the United States.'

I

The Texas statutes that concern us here are Arts. 1191–1194 and 1196 of the State's Penal Code, FN1 Vernon's Ann.P.C. These make it a crime to 'procure an abortion,' as therein *118 defined, or to attempt one, except with respect to 'an abortion procured or attempted by medical advice for the purpose of saving the life of the mother.' Similar statutes are in existence in a majority of the States. FN2

FN1. 'Article 1191. Abortion 'If any person shall designedly administer to a pregnant woman or knowingly procure to be administered with her consent any drug or medicine, or shall use towards her any violence or means whatever externally or internally applied, and thereby procure an abortion, he shall be confined in the penitentiary not less than two nor more than five years; if it be done without her consent, the punishment shall be doubled. By 'abortion' is meant that the life of the fetus or embryo shall be destroyed in the woman's womb or that a premature birth thereof be caused. 'Art. 1192. Furnishing the means 'Whoever furnishes the means for procuring an abortion knowing the purpose intended is guilty as an accomplice. 'Art. 1193. Attempt at abortion 'If the means used shall fail to produce an abortion, the offender is nevertheless guilty of an attempt to produce abortion, provided it be shown that such means were calculated to produce that result, and shall be fined not less than one hundred nor more than one thousand dollars. 'Art. 1194. Murder in producing abortion' If the death of the mother is occasioned by an abortion so produced or by an attempt to effect the same it is murder. 'Art. 1196. By medical advice 'Nothing in this chapter applies to an abortion procured or attempted by medical advice for the purpose of saving the life of the mother. 'The foregoing Articles, together with Art. 1195, compose Chapter 9 of Title 15 of the Penal Code. Article 1195, not attacked here, reads: 'Art. 1195. Destroying unborn child 'Whoever shall during parturition of the mother destroy the vitality or life in a child in a state of being born and before actual birth, which child would otherwise have been born alive, shall be confined in the penitentiary for life or for not less than five years.'... [Footnotes of the 26 states with anti-abortion laws similar to Texas are omitted.]

**710 *119 Texas first enacted a criminal abortion statute in 1854. Texas Laws 1854, c. 49, s 1, set forth in 3 H. Gammel, Laws of Texas 1502 (1898). This was soon modified into language that has remained substantially unchanged to the present time. See Texas Penal Code of 1857, c. 7, Arts. 531–536; G. Paschal, Laws of Texas, Arts. 2192—2197 (1866); Texas Rev.Stat., c. 8, Arts. 536–541 (1879); Texas Rev. Crim.Stat., Arts. 1071–1076 (1911). The final article in each of these compilations provided the same exception, as does the present Article 1196, for an abortion by 'medical advice for the purpose of saving the life of the mother.' [Footnote 3 omitted.]

*120 II

Jane Roe, FN4 a single woman who was residing in Dallas County, Texas, instituted this federal action in March 1970 against the District Attorney of the county. She sought a declaratory judgment that the

Texas criminal abortion statutes were unconstitutional on their face, and an injunction restraining the defendant from enforcing the statutes.

FN4. The name is a pseudonym.

Roe alleged that she was unmarried and pregnant; that she wished to terminate her pregnancy by an abortion 'performed by a competent, licensed physician, under safe, clinical conditions'; that she was unable to get a 'legal' abortion in Texas because her life did not appear to be threatened by the continuation of her pregnancy; and that she could not afford to travel to another jurisdiction in order to secure a legal abortion under safe conditions. She claimed that the Texas statutes were unconstitutionally vague and that they abridged her right of personal privacy, protected by the First, Fourth, Fifth, Ninth, and Fourteenth Amendments. By an amendment to her complaint Roe purported to sue 'on behalf of herself and all other women' similarly situated.

James Hubert Hallford, a licensed physician, sought and was granted leave to intervene in Roe's action. In his complaint he alleged that he had been arrested previously for violations of the Texas abortion statutes and *121 that two such prosecutions were pending against him. He described conditions of patients who came to him seeking abortions, and he claimed that for many cases he, as a physician, was unable to determine**711 whether they fell within or outside the exception recognized by Article 1196. He alleged that, as a consequence, the statutes were vague and uncertain, in violation of the Fourteenth Amendment, and that they violated his own and his patients' rights to privacy in the doctor-patient relationship and his own right to practice medicine, rights he claimed were guaranteed by the First, Fourth, Fifth, Ninth, and Fourteenth Amendments.

John and Mary Doe, FN5 a married couple, filed a companion complaint to that of Roe. They also named the District Attorney as defendant, claimed like constitutional deprivations, and sought declaratory and injunctive relief. The Does alleged that they were a childless couple; that Mrs. Doe was suffering from a 'neural-chemical' disorder; that her physician had 'advised her to avoid pregnancy until such time as her condition has materially improved' (although a pregnancy at the present time would not present 'a serious risk' to her life); that, pursuant to medical advice, she had discontinued use of birth control pills; and that if she should become pregnant, she would want to terminate the pregnancy by an abortion performed by a competent, licensed physician under safe, clinical conditions. By an amendment to their complaint, the Does purported to sue 'on behalf of themselves and all couples similarly situated.'

FN5. These names are pseudonyms.

The two actions were consolidated and heard together by a duly convened three-judge district court. The suits thus presented the situations of the pregnant single woman, the childless couple, with the wife not pregnant, *122 and the licensed practicing physician, all joining in the attack on the Texas criminal abortion statutes. Upon the filing of affidavits, motions were made for dismissal and for summary judgment. The court held that Roe and members of her class, and Dr. Hallford, had standing to sue and presented justiciable controversies, but that the Does had failed to allege facts sufficient to state a present controversy and did not have standing. It concluded that, with respect to the requests for a declaratory judgment, abstention was not warranted. On the merits, the District Court held that the 'fundamental right of single women and married persons to choose where to have children is protected by the Ninth Amendment, through the Fourteenth Amendment,' and that the Texas criminal abortion statutes were void on their face because they were both unconstitutionally vague and constituted an overbroad infringement of the plaintiffs' Ninth Amendment rights. The court then held that abstention was warranted with respect to the requests for an injunction. It therefore dismissed the Does' complaint, declared the abortion statutes void, and dismissed the application for injunctive relief. 314 F.Supp. 1217, 1225 (N.D.Tex.1970). *[Discussion on injunctive relief and standing omitted.]....*

IV

*124 [2] Headnote Citing References A. Jane Roe. Despite the use of the pseudonym, no suggestion is made that Roe is a fictitious person. For purposes of her case, we accept as true, and as established, her existence; her pregnant state, as of the inception of her suit in March 1970 and as late as May 21 of that year when she filed an alias affidavit with the District Court; and her inability to obtain a legal abortion in Texas...

But when, as here, pregnancy is a significant fact in the litigation, the normal 266-day human gestation period is so short that the pregnancy will come to term before the usual appellate process is complete. If that termination makes a case moot, pregnancy litigation seldom will survive much beyond the trial stage, and appellate review will be effectively denied. Our law should not be that rigid. Pregnancy often comes more than once to the same woman, and in the general population, if man is to survive, it will always be with us. Pregnancy provides a classic justification for a conclusion of nonmootness. It truly could be 'capable of repetition, yet evading review.' *Southern Pacific Terminal Co. v. ICC*, 219 U.S. 498, 515, 31 S.Ct. 279, 283, 55 L.Ed. 310 (1911). See Moore v. Ogilvie, 394 U.S. 814, 816, 89 S.Ct. 1493, 1494, 23 L.Ed.2d 1 (1969); *Carroll v. President and Commissioners of Princess Anne,* 393 U.S. 175, 178–179, 89 S.Ct. 347, 350, 351, 21 L.Ed.2d 325 (1968); *United States v. W. T. Grant Co.,* 345 U.S. 629, 632–633, 73 S.Ct. 894, 897–898, 97 L.Ed. 1303 (1953).

We, therefore, agree with the District Court that Jane Roe had standing to undertake this litigation, that she presented a justiciable controversy, and that the termination of her 1970 pregnancy has not rendered her case moot.

B. Dr. Hallford. The doctor's position is different. He entered Roe's litigation as a plaintiff-intervenor, alleging in his complaint that he:

> '(I)n the past has been arrested for violating the Texas Abortion Laws and at the present time stands charged by indictment with violating said laws in the *126 Criminal District Court of Dallas County,

Texas to-wit: (1) The State of Texas v. James H. Hallford, No. C-69-5307-IH, and (2) The State of Texas v. James H. Hallford, No. C-69-2524-H. In both cases the defendant is charged with abortion...'
[Discussion of doctor's application to intervene omitted and the dismissal of the other Doe plaintiffs.]

V

The principal thrust of appellant's attack on the Texas statutes is that they improperly invade a right, said to be possessed by the pregnant woman, to choose to terminate her pregnancy. Appellant would discover this right in the concept of personal 'liberty' embodied in the Fourteenth Amendment's Due Process Clause; or in personal marital, familial, and sexual privacy said to be protected by the Bill of Rights or its penumbras, see *Griswold v. Connecticut*, 381 U.S. 479, 85 S.Ct. 1678, 14 L.Ed.2d 510 (1965); *Eisenstadt v. Baird*, 405 U.S. 438 (1972); id., at 460, 92 S.Ct. 1029, at 1042, 31 L.Ed.2d 349 (White, J., concurring in result); or among those rights reserved to the people by the Ninth Amendment, *Griswold v. Connecticut*, 381 U.S., at 486, 85 S.Ct., at 1682 (Goldberg, J., concurring). Before addressing this claim, we feel it desirable briefly to survey, in several aspects, the history of abortion, for such insight as that history may afford us, and then to examine the state purposes and interests behind the criminal abortion laws.

VI

It perhaps is not generally appreciated that the restrictive criminal abortion laws in effect in a majority of States today are of relatively recent vintage. Those laws, generally proscribing abortion or its attempt at any time during pregnancy except when necessary to preserve the pregnant woman's life, are not of ancient or even of common-law origin. Instead, they derive from statutory changes effected, for the most part, in the latter half of the 19th century.

*130 1. Ancient attitudes. These are not capable of precise determination. We are told that at the time of the Persian Empire abortifacients were known and that criminal abortions were severely punished. FN8 We are also told, however, that abortion was practiced in Greek times as well as in the Roman Era, FN9 and that 'it was resorted to without scruple.' FN10 The Ephesian, Soranos, often described as the greatest of the ancient gynecologists, appears to have been generally opposed to Rome's prevailing free-abortion practices. He found it necessary to think first of the life of the mother, and he resorted to abortion when, upon this standard, he felt the procedure advisable. FN11 Greek and Roman law afforded little protection to the unborn. If abortion was prosecuted in some places, it seems to have been based on a concept of a violation of the father's right to his offspring. Ancient religion did not bar abortion. FN12

FN8. A Castiglioni, A. History of Medicine 84 (2d ed. 1947), E. Krumbhaar, translator and editor (hereinafter Castiglioni). *[Other footnotes and other citations omitted.]...*

2. The Hippocratic Oath. What then of the famous Oath that has stood so **716 long as the ethical guide of the medical profession and that bears the name of the great Greek (460(?)–377(?) B.C.), who has been described *131 as the Father of Medicine, the 'wisest and the greatest practitioner of his art,' and the 'most important and most complete medical personality of antiquity,' who dominated the medical schools of his time, and who typified the sum of the medical knowledge of the past? FN13 The Oath varies somewhat according to the particular translation, but in any translation the content is clear: 'I will give no deadly medicine to anyone if asked, nor suggest any such counsel; and in like manner I will not give to a woman a pessary to produce abortion,' FN14 or 'I will neither give a deadly drug to anybody if asked for it, nor will I make a suggestion to this effect. Similarly, I will not give to a woman an abortive remedy.' FN15

Although the Oath is not mentioned in any of the principal briefs in this case or in *Doe v. Bolton*, 410 U.S. 179, 93 S.Ct. 739, 35 L.Ed.2d 201, it represents the apex of the development of strict ethical concepts in medicine, and its influence endures to this day. Why did not the authority of Hippocrates dissuade abortion practice in his time and that of Rome? The late Dr. Edelstein provides us with a theory: FN16 The Oath was not uncontested even in Hippocrates' day; only the Pythagorean school of philosophers frowned upon the related act of suicide. Most Greek thinkers, on the other hand, commended abortion, at least prior to viability. See Plato, Republic, V, 461; Aristotle, Politics, VII, 1335b 25. For the Pythagoreans, however, it was a matter of dogma. For them the embryo was animate from the moment of conception, and abortion meant destruction of a living being. The abortion clause of the Oath, therefore, 'echoes Pythagorean doctrines,' *132 and '(i)n no other stratum of Greek opinion were such views held or proposed in the same spirit of uncompromising austerity.' FN17…

Dr. Edelstein then concludes that the Oath originated in a group representing only a small segment of Greek opinion and that it certainly was not accepted by all ancient physicians. He points out that medical writings down to Galen (A.D. 130–200) 'give evidence of the violation of almost every one of its injunctions.' FN18 But with the end of antiquity a decided change took place. Resistance against suicide and against abortion became common. The Oath came to be popular. The emerging teachings of Christianity were in agreement with the Pythagorean ethic. The Oath 'became the nucleus of all medical ethics' and 'was applauded as the embodiment of truth.' Thus, suggests Dr. Edelstein, it is 'a Pythagorean manifesto and not the expression of an absolute standard of medical conduct.' FN19…

This, it seems to us, is a satisfactory and acceptable explanation of the Hippocratic Oath's apparent rigidity. It enables us to understand, in historical context, a long-accepted and revered statement of medical ethics.

3. The common law. It is undisputed that at common law, abortion performed before 'quickening'— the first recognizable movement of the fetus in utero, appearing usually from the 16th to the 18th week of pregnancy FN20—was not an indictable offense. FN21 The absence*133 of a **717 common-law crime for pre-quickening abortion appears to have developed from a confluence of earlier philosophical, theological, and civil and canon law concepts of when life begins. These disciplines variously

approached the question in terms of the point at which the embryo or fetus became 'formed' or recognizably human, or in terms of when a 'person' came into being, that is, infused with a 'soul' or 'animated.' A loose consensus evolved in early English law that these events occurred at some point between conception and live birth. FN22 This was 'mediate animation.' Although *134 Christian theology and the canon law came to fix the point of animation at 40 days for a male and 80 days for a female, a view that persisted until the 19th century, there was otherwise little agreement about the precise time of formation or animation. There was agreement, however, that prior to this point the fetus was to be regarded as part of the mother, and its destruction, therefore, was not homicide. Due to continued uncertainty about the precise time when animation occurred, to the lack of any empirical basis for the 40–80-day view, and perhaps to Aquinas' definition of movement as one of the two first principles of life, Bracton focused upon quickening as the critical point. The significance of quickening was echoed by later common-law scholars and found its way into the received common law in this country.... [Footnotes omitted.]...

FN22. Early philosophers believed that the embryo or fetus did not become formed and begin to live until at least 40 days after conception for a male, and 80 to 90 days for a female. See, for example, Aristotle, Hist.Anim. 7.3.583b; Gen.Anim. 2.3.736, 2.5.741; Hippocrates, Lib. de Nat.Puer., No. 10. Aristotle's thinking derived from his three-stage theory of life: vegetable, animal, rational. The vegetable stage was reached at conception, the animal at 'animation,' and the rational soon after live birth. This theory, together with the 40/80 day view, came to be accepted by early Christian thinkers. The theological debate was reflected in the writings of St. Augustine, who made a distinction between embryo inanimatus, not yet endowed with a soul, and embryo animatus. He may have drawn upon Exodus 21:22. At one point, however, he expressed the view that human powers cannot determine the point during fetal development at which the critical change occurs. See Augustine, De Origine Animae 4.4 (Pub.Law 44.527). See also W. Reany, The Creation of the Human Soul, c. 2 and 83–86 (1932); Huser, The Crime of Abortion in Canon Law 15 (Catholic Univ. of America, Canon Law Studies No. 162, Washington, D.C., 1942). Galen, in three treatises related to embryology, accepted the thinking of Aristotle and his followers. Quay 426–427. Later, Augustine on abortion was incorporated by Gratian into the Decretum, published about 1140. Decretum Magistri Gratiani 2.32.2.7 to 2.32.2.10, in 1 Corpus Juris Canonici 1122, 1123 (A. Friedberg, 2d ed. 1879). This Decretal and the Decretals that followed were recognized as the definitive body of canon law until the new Code of 1917. For discussions of the canon-law treatment, see Means I, pp. 411–412; Noonan 20–26; Quay 426–430; see also J. Noonan, Contraception: A History of Its Treatment by the Catholic Theologians and Canonists 18–29 (1965).

Whether abortion of a quick fetus was a felony at common law, or even a lesser crime, is still disputed. Bracton, writing early in the 13th century, thought it homicide. FN23 But the later and predominant**718 view, following the great common-law scholars, has been that it was, at most, a lesser offense. In a frequently cited *135 passage, Coke took the position that abortion of a woman 'quick with childe' is 'a great misprision, and no murder.' FN24 Blackstone followed, saying that while abortion after quickening had once been considered manslaughter (though not murder), 'modern law' took a less severe view. FN25 A recent review of the common-law precedents argues, however, that those precedents contradict Coke and that even post-quickening abortion was never established as a common-law crime. FN26 This is of some importance because while most American courts ruled, in holding or dictum, that abortion of an unquickened fetus was not criminal under their received common law, FN27 others followed Coke in stating that abortion*136 of a quick fetus was a 'misprision,' a term they translated to mean 'misdemeanor.' FN28 That their reliance on Coke on this aspect of the law was uncritical and, apparently in all the reported cases, dictum (due probably to the paucity of common-law prosecutions for post-quickening abortion), makes it now appear doubtful that abortion was ever firmly established as a common-law crime even with respect to the destruction of a quick fetus.

4. The English statutory law. England's first criminal abortion statute, Lord Ellenborough's Act, 43 Geo. 3, c. 58, came in 1803. It made abortion of a quick fetus, s 1, a capital crime, but in s 2 it provided lesser penalties for the felony of abortion before quickening, and thus preserved the 'quickening' distinction. This contrast was continued in the general revision of 1828, 9 Geo. 4, c. 31, s 13. It disappeared, however, together with the death penalty, in 1837, 7 Will. 4 & 1 Vict., c. 85, s 6, and did not reappear in the Offenses Against the Person Act of 1861, 24 & 25 Vict., c. 100, s 59, that formed the core of English anti-abortion law until the liberalizing reforms of 1967. In 1929, the Infant Life (Preservation) Act, 19 & 20 Geo. 5, c. 34, came into being. Its emphasis was upon the destruction of 'the life of **719 a child capable of being born alive.' It made a willful act performed with the necessary intent a felony. It contained a proviso that one was not to be *137 found guilty of the offense 'unless it is proved that the act which caused the death of the child was not done in good faith for the purpose only of preserving the life of the mother.'

A seemingly notable development in the English law was the case of *Rex v. Bourne*, (1939) 1 K.B. 687. This case apparently answered in the affirmative the question whether an abortion necessary to preserve the life of the pregnant woman was excepted from the criminal penalties of the 1861 Act. In his instructions to the jury, Judge MacNaghten referred to the 1929 Act, and observed that that Act related to 'the case where a child is killed by a willful act at the time when it is being delivered in the ordinary course of nature.' Id., at 691. He concluded that the 1861 Act's use of the word 'unlawfully,' imported the same meaning expressed by the specific proviso in the 1929 Act, even though there was no mention of preserving the mother's life in the 1861 Act. He then construed the phrase 'preserving the life of the mother' broadly, that is, 'in a reasonable sense,' to include a serious and permanent threat to the mother's health, and instructed the jury to acquit Dr. Bourne if it found he had acted in a good-faith belief that the abortion was necessary for this purpose. Id., at 693–694. The jury did acquit.

Recently, Parliament enacted a new abortion law. This is the Abortion Act of 1967, 15 & 16 Eliz. 2, c. 87. The Act permits a licensed physician to perform an abortion where two other licensed physicians agree (a) 'that the continuance of the pregnancy would involve risk to the life of the pregnant woman, or of injury to the physical or mental health of the pregnant woman or any existing children of her family, greater than if the pregnancy were terminated,' or (b) 'that there is a substantial risk that if the child were born it would suffer from such physical or mental abnormalities as *138 to be seriously handicapped.' The Act also provides that, in making this determination, 'account may be taken of the pregnant woman's actual or reasonably foreseeable environment.' It also permits a physician, without the concurrence of others, to terminate a pregnancy where he is of the good-faith opinion that the abortion 'is immediately necessary to save the life or to prevent grave permanent injury to the physical or mental health of the pregnant woman.'

5. The American law. In this country, the law in effect in all but a few States until mid-19th century was the pre-existing English common law. Connecticut, the first State to enact abortion legislation, adopted in 1821 that part of Lord Ellenborough's Act that related to a woman 'quick with child.' FN29 The death penalty was not imposed. Abortion before quickening was made a crime in that State only in 1860. FN30 In 1828, New York enacted legislation FN31 that, in two respects, was to serve as a model for early anti-abortion statutes. First, while barring destruction of an unquickened fetus as well as a quick fetus, it made the former only a misdemeanor, but the latter second-degree manslaughter. Second, it incorporated a concept of therapeutic abortion by providing that an abortion was excused if it 'shall have been necessary to preserve the life of such mother, or shall have been advised by two physicians to be necessary for such purpose.' By 1840, when Texas had received the common law, FN32 only eight American States *139 had **720 statutes dealing with abortion. FN33 It was not until after the War Between the States that legislation began generally to replace the common law. Most of these initial statutes dealt severely with abortion after quickening but were lenient with it before quickening. Most punished attempts equally with completed abortions. While many statutes included the exception for an abortion thought by one or more physicians to be necessary to save the mother's life, that provision soon disappeared and the typical law required that the procedure actually be necessary for that purpose.... [Footnotes omitted.]

Gradually, in the middle and late 19th century the quickening distinction disappeared from the statutory law of most States and the degree of the offense and the penalties were increased. By the end of the 1950's a large majority of the jurisdictions banned abortion, however and whenever performed, unless done to save or preserve the life of the mother. FN34 The exceptions, Alabama and the District of Columbia, permitted abortion to preserve the mother's health. FN35 Three States permitted abortions that were not 'unlawfully' performed or that were not 'without lawful justification,' leaving interpretation of those standards to the courts. FN36 In *140 the past several years, however, a trend toward liberalization of abortion statutes has resulted in adoption, by about one-third of the States, of less stringent laws, most of them patterned after the ALI Model Penal Code, s 230.3,FN37 set forth as Appendix B to the opinion in *Doe v. Bolton,* 410 U.S. 205, 93 S.Ct. 754.

FN34. Criminal abortion statutes in effect in the States as of 1961, together with historical statutory development and important judicial interpretations of the state statutes, are cited and quoted in Quay 447–520. See Comment, A Survey of the Present Statutory and Case Law on Abortion: The Contradictions and the Problems, 1972 U.Ill.L.F. 177, 179, classifying the abortion statutes and listing 25 States as permitting abortion only if necessary to save or preserve the mother's life... [Footnotes omitted.]

It is thus apparent that at common law, at the time of the adoption of our Constitution, and throughout the major portion of the 19th century, abortion was viewed with less disfavor than under most American statutes currently in effect. Phrasing it another way, a woman enjoyed a substantially broader right to terminate a pregnancy than she does in most States today. At least with respect to the early stage of pregnancy, **721 and very possibly without such a limitation, the opportunity *141 to make this choice was present in this country well into the 19th century. Even later, the law continued for some time to treat less punitively an abortion procured in early pregnancy. (The AMA position is omitted for space reasons and because it changes from "deploring abortion " in 1857 and then "'[e]xcept for periodic condemnation of the criminal abortionist, no further formal AMA action took place until 1967" when the Committee on Human Reproduction urged the adoption of a policy opposing induced abortion, except when there is 'documented medical evidence' of a threat to the health or life of the mother, or that the child 'may be born with incapacitating physical deformity or mental deficiency,' or that a pregnancy 'resulting from legally established statutory or forcible rape or incest may constitute a threat to the mental or physical health of the *143 patient,' two other physicians 'chosen because of their recognized professional competency have examined the patient and have concurred in writing,' **722 and the procedure 'is performed in a hospital accredited by the Joint Commission on Accreditation of Hospitals".' Thereafter, there was a "'polarization of the medical profession on this controversial issue'; 'the remarkable shift in testimony' in six months, felt to be influenced 'by the rapid changes in state laws and by the judicial decisions which tend to make abortion more freely available;' and a feeling 'that this trend will continue.'" "On June 25, 1970, the House of Delegates adopted preambles [that] emphasized "'the best interests of the patient,'" "'sound clinical judgment,'" and "'informed patient consent,'" in contrast to "'mere acquiescence to the patient's demand '"and resolutions "that abortion is a medical procedure that should be performed by a licensed physician in an accredited hospital only after consultation with two other physicians and in conformity with state law, and that no party to the procedure should be required to violate personally held moral principles." FN38 [Citations and further footnotes omitted.]

VII

Three reasons have been advanced to explain historically the enactment of criminal abortion laws in the 19th century and to justify their continued existence.

*148 It has been argued occasionally that these laws were the product of a Victorian social concern to discourage illicit sexual conduct. Texas, however, does not advance this justification in the present case, and it appears that no court or commentator has taken the argument seriously. FN42 The appellants and amici contend, moreover, that this is not a proper state purpose at all and suggest that, if it were, the Texas statutes are overbroad in protecting it since the law fails to distinguish between married and unwed mothers.... [Footnote 42 and citations omitted.]

A second reason is concerned with abortion as a medical procedure. When most criminal abortion laws were first enacted, the procedure was a hazardous one for the woman. FN43 This was particularly true prior to the *149 development of antisepsis. Antiseptic techniques, of course, were based on discoveries by Lister, Pasteur, and others first announced in 1867, but were not generally accepted and employed until about the turn of the century. Abortion mortality was high. Even after 1900, and perhaps until as late as the development of antibiotics in the 1940's, standard modern techniques such as dilation and curettage were not nearly so safe as they are today. Thus, it has been argued that a State's real concern in enacting a criminal abortion law was to protect the pregnant woman, that is, to restrain her from submitting to a procedure that placed her life in serious jeopardy....

**725 Modern medical techniques have altered this situation. Appellants and various amici refer to medical data indicating that abortion in early pregnancy, that is, prior to the end of the first trimester, although not without its risk, is now relatively safe. Mortality rates for women undergoing early abortions, where the procedure is legal, appear to be as low as or lower than the rates for normal childbirth. FN44 Consequently, any interest of the State in protecting the woman from an inherently hazardous procedure, except when it would be equally dangerous for her to forgo it, has largely disappeared. Of course, important state interests in the areas of health and medical standards do remain. *150 The State has a legitimate interest in seeing to it that abortion, like any other medical procedure, is performed under circumstances that insure maximum safety for the patient. This interest obviously extends at least to the performing physician and his staff, to the facilities involved, to the availability of after-care, and to adequate provision for any complication or emergency that might arise. The prevalence of high mortality rates at illegal 'abortion mills' strengthens, rather than weakens, the State's interest in regulating the conditions under which abortions are performed. Moreover, the risk to the woman increases as her pregnancy continues. Thus, the State retains a definite interest in protecting the woman's own health and safety when an abortion is proposed at a late stage of pregnancy, [Footnote 44 and citations omitted.]...

The third reason is the State's interest—some phrase it in terms of duty—in protecting prenatal life. Some of the argument for this justification rests on the theory that a new human life is present from the moment of conception. FN45 The State's interest and general obligation to protect life then extends, it is argued, to prenatal life. Only when the life of the pregnant mother herself is at stake, balanced against the life she carries within her, should the interest of the embryo or fetus not prevail. Logically, of course, a legitimate state interest in this area need not stand or fall on acceptance of the belief that life begins at conception or at some other point prior to life birth. In assessing the State's interest, recognition may be given to the less rigid claim that as long as at least potential life is involved, the State may assert interests beyond the protection of the pregnant woman alone. *[Footnote 45 and citations omitted.]*...

*151 Parties challenging state abortion laws have sharply disputed in some courts the contention that a purpose of these laws, when enacted, was to protect prenatal life. FN46 Pointing to the absence of legislative history to support the contention, they claim that most state laws were designed solely to protect the woman. Because medical advances have lessened this concern, at least with respect to abortion in early pregnancy, they argue that with respect to such abortions the laws can no longer be justified by any state interest. There is some scholarly support for this view of original purpose. FN47 The few state courts **726 called upon to interpret their laws in the late 19th and early 20th centuries did focus on the State's interest in protecting the woman's health rather than in preserving the embryo and fetus. FN48 Proponents of this view point out that in many States, including Texas, FN49 by statute or judicial interpretation, the pregnant woman herself could not be prosecuted for self-abortion or for cooperating in an abortion performed upon her by another. FN50 They claim that adoption of the 'quickening' distinction through received common *152 law and state statutes tacitly recognizes the greater health hazards inherent in late abortion and impliedly repudiates the theory that life begins at conception. *[Footnotes 46–50 and citations omitted.]*...

It is with these interests, and the weight to be attached to them, that this case is concerned.

VIII

The Constitution does not explicitly mention any right of privacy. In a line of decisions, however, going back perhaps as far as *Union Pacific R. Co. v. Botsford,* 141 U.S. 250, 251, 11 S.Ct. 1000, 1001, 35 L.Ed. 734 (1891), the Court has recognized that a right of personal privacy, or a guarantee of certain areas or zones of privacy, does exist under the Constitution. In varying contexts, the Court or individual Justices have, indeed, found at least the roots of that right in the First Amendment, *Stanley v. Georgia,* 394 U.S. 557, 564, 89 S.Ct. 1243, 1247, 22 L.Ed.2d 542 (1969); in the Fourth and Fifth Amendments, *Terry v. Ohio,* 392 U.S. 1, 8-9, 88 S.Ct. 1868, 1872–1873, 20 L.Ed.2d 889 (1968), *Katz v. United States,* 389 U.S. 347, 350, 88 S.Ct. 507, 510, 19 L.Ed.2d 576 (1967); *Boyd v. United States,* 116 U.S. 616, 6 S.Ct. 524, 29 L.Ed. 746 (1886), see *Olmstead v. United States,* 277 U.S. 438, 478, 48 S.Ct. 564, 572, 72 L.Ed. 944 (1928) (Brandeis, J., dissenting); in the penumbras of the Bill of Rights, *Griswold v. Connecticut,* 381 U.S., at 484–485, 85 S.Ct., at 1681–1682; in the Ninth Amendment, id., at 486, 85 S.Ct. at 1682 (Goldberg, J., concurring); or in the concept of liberty guaranteed by the first section of the Fourteenth Amendment, see *Meyer v. Nebraska,* 262 U.S. 390, 399, 43 S.Ct. 625, 626, 67 L.Ed. 1042 (1923). These decisions make it clear that only personal rights that can be deemed 'fundamental' or 'implicit in the concept of ordered liberty,' *Palko v. Connecticut,* 302 U.S. 319, 325, 58 S.Ct. 149, 152, 82 L.Ed. 288 (1937), are included in this guarantee of personal privacy. They also make it clear that the right has some extension to activities relating to marriage, *Loving v. Virginia*, 388 U.S. 1, 12, 87 S.Ct. 1817, 1823, 18 L.Ed.2d 1010 (1967); procreation, *Skinner v. Oklahoma*, 316 U.S. 535, 541–542, 62 S.Ct. 1110, 1113–1114, 86 L.Ed. 1655 (1942); contraception, *Eisenstadt v. Baird*, 405 U.S., at 453–454, 92 S.Ct., at 1038–1039; *153 id., at 460, 463–465, 92 S.Ct. at 1042, 1043–1044 (White, J., concurring in result); family relationships, *Prince v. Massachusetts*, 321 U.S. 158, 166, 64 S.Ct. 438, 442, 88 L.Ed. 645 (1944); and child rearing and education, **727 *Pierce v. Society of Sisters*, 268 U.S. 510, 535, 45 S.Ct. 571, 573, 69 L.Ed. 1070 (1925), *Meyer v. Nebraska,* supra.

This right of privacy, whether it be founded in the Fourteenth Amendment's concept of personal liberty and restrictions upon state action, as we feel it is, or, as the District Court determined, in the Ninth Amendment's reservation of rights to the people, is broad enough to encompass a woman's decision whether or not to terminate her pregnancy. The detriment that the State would impose upon the pregnant woman by denying this choice altogether is apparent. Specific and direct harm medically diagnosable even in early pregnancy may be involved. Maternity, or additional offspring, may force upon the woman a distressful life and future. Psychological harm may be imminent. Mental and physical health may be taxed by child care. There is also the distress, for all concerned, associated with the unwanted child, and there is the problem of bringing a child into a family already unable, psychologically and otherwise, to care for it. In other cases, as in this one, the additional difficulties and continuing stigma of unwed motherhood may be involved. All these are factors the woman and her responsible physician necessarily will consider in consultation.

On the basis of elements such as these, appellant and some amici argue that the woman's right is absolute and that she is entitled to terminate her pregnancy at whatever time, in whatever way, and for whatever reason she alone chooses. With this we do not agree. Appellant's arguments that Texas either has no valid interest at all in regulating the abortion decision, or no interest strong enough to support any limitation upon the woman's sole determination, are unpersuasive. The *154 Court's decisions recognizing a right of privacy also acknowledge that some state regulation in areas protected by that right is appropriate. As noted above, a State may properly assert important interests in safeguarding health, in maintaining medical standards, and in protecting potential life. At some point in pregnancy, these respective interests become sufficiently compelling to sustain regulation of the factors that govern the abortion decision. The privacy right involved, therefore, cannot be said to be absolute. In fact, it is not clear to us that the claim asserted by some amici that one has an unlimited right to do with one's body as one pleases bears a close relationship to the right of privacy previously articulated in the Court's decisions. The Court has refused to recognize an unlimited right of this kind in the past. *Jacobson v. Massachusetts*, 197 U.S. 11, 25 S.Ct. 358, 49 L.Ed. 643 (1905) (vaccination); *Buck v. Bell,* 274 U.S. 200, 47 S.Ct. 584, 71 L.Ed. 1000 (1927) (sterilization).

We, therefore, conclude that the right of personal privacy includes the abortion decision, but that this right is not unqualified and must be considered against important state interests in regulation. [*Author's emphasis added.*]

We note that those federal and state courts that have recently considered abortion law challenges have reached the same conclusion. A majority, in addition to the District Court in the present case, have held state laws unconstitutional, at least in part, because of vagueness or because of overbreadth and abridgment of rights. *Abele v. Markle,* 342 F.Supp. 800 (D.C.Conn.1972), appeal docketed, No. 72-56; *Abele v. Markle,* 351 F.Supp. 224 (D.C.Conn.1972), appeal docketed, No. 72-730; *Doe v. Bolton,* 319 F.Supp. 1048 (N.D.Ga.1970), appeal decided today, 410 U.S. 179, 93 S.Ct. 739, 35 L.Ed.2d 201; *Doe v. Scott,* 321 F.Supp. 1385 (N.D.Ill.1971), appeal docketed, No. 70-105; *Poe v. Menghini,* 339 F.Supp. 986 (D.C.Kan.1972); *YWCA v. Kugler,* 342 F.Supp. 1048 (D.C.N.J.1972); *155 *Babbitz v. McCann,* 310 F.Supp. 293 (E.D.Wis.1970), appeal dismissed, 400 U.S. 1, 91 S.Ct. 12, 27 L.Ed.2d 1 (1970); *People v. Belous,* 71 Cal.2d 954, 80 Cal.Rptr. 354, 458 P.2d 194 (1969), cert. denied, 397 U.S. 915, 90 S.Ct. 920, 25 L.Ed.2d 96 (1970); *State v. Barquet,* 262 So.2d 431 (Fla.1972).

Others have sustained state statutes. **728 *Crossen v. Attorney General,* 344 F.Supp. 587 (E.D.Ky.1972), appeal docketed, No. 72-256; *Rosen v. Louisiana State Board of Medical Examiners,* 318 F.Supp. 1217 (E.D.La.1970), appeal docketed, No. 70-42; *Corkey v. Edwards,* 322 F.Supp. 1248 (W.D.N.C.1971), appeal docketed, No. 71-92; *Steinberg v. Brown,* 321 F.Supp. 741 (N.D.Ohio 1970); *Doe v. Rampton,* 366 F.Supp. 189 (Utah 1971), appeal docketed, No. 71-5666; *Cheaney v. State, Ind.,* 285 N.E.2d 265 (1972); *Spears v. State,* 257 So.2d 876 (Miss.1972); *State v. Munson,* S.D., 201 N.W.2d 123 (1972), appeal docketed, No. 72-631.

Although the results are divided, most of these courts have agreed that the right of privacy, however based, is broad enough to cover the abortion decision; that the right, nonetheless, is not absolute and is subject to some limitations; and that at some point the state interests as to protection of health, medical standards, and prenatal life, become dominant. We agree with this approach.

Where certain 'fundamental rights' are involved, the Court has held that regulation limiting these rights may be justified only by a 'compelling state interest,' *Kramer v. Union Free School District,* 395 U.S. 621, 627, 89 S.Ct. 1886, 1890, 23 L.Ed.2d 583 (1969); *Shapiro v. Thompson,* 394 U.S. 618, 634, 89 S.Ct. 1322, 1331, 22 L.Ed.2d 600 (1969); *Sherbert v. Verner,* 374 U.S. 398, 406, 83 S.Ct. 1790, 1795, 10 L.Ed.2d 965 (1963), and that legislative enactments must be narrowly drawn to express only the legitimate state interests at stake. *Griswold v. Connecticut,* 381 U.S., at 485, 85 S.Ct., at 1682; *Aptheker v. Secretary of State,* 378 U.S. 500, 508, 84 S.Ct. 1659, 1664, 12 L.Ed.2d 992 (1964); *Cantwell v. Connecticut,* 310 U.S. 296, 307–308, 60 S.Ct. 900, 904–905, 84 L.Ed. 1213 (1940); see *156 *Eisenstadt v. Baird,* 405 U.S., at 460, 463–464, 92 S.Ct., at 1042, 1043–1044 (White, J., concurring in result).

In the recent abortion cases, cited above, courts have recognized these principles. Those striking down state laws have generally scrutinized the State's interests in protecting health and potential life, and have concluded that neither interest justified broad limitations on the reasons for which a physician and his pregnant patient might decide that she should have an abortion in the early stages of pregnancy. Courts sustaining state laws have held that the State's determinations to protect health or prenatal life are dominant and constitutionally justifiable.

IX

The District Court held that the appellee failed to meet his burden of demonstrating that the Texas statute's infringement upon Roe's rights was necessary to support a compelling state interest, and that, although the appellee presented 'several compelling justifications for state presence in the area of abortions,' the statutes outstripped these justifications and swept 'far beyond any areas of compelling state interest.' 314 F.Supp., at 1222–1223. Appellant and appellee both contest that holding. Appellant, as has been indicated, claims an absolute right that bars any state imposition of criminal penalties in the area. Appellee argues that the State's determination to recognize and protect prenatal life from and after conception constitutes a compelling state interest. As noted above, we do not agree fully with either formulation.

A. The appellee and certain amici argue that the fetus is a 'person' within the language and meaning of the Fourteenth Amendment. In support of this, they outline at length and in detail the well-known facts of fetal development. If this suggestion of personhood is established, the appellant's case, of course, collapses, *157 for the fetus' right to life would then be guaranteed specifically by the Amendment. The appellant conceded as much on reargument. FN51 On the other hand, the appellee conceded on reargument FN52 that no case could be cited **729 that holds that a fetus is a person within the meaning of the Fourteenth Amendment. [Footnotes 51–52 and citations omitted.]...

The Constitution does not define 'person' in so many words. Section 1 of the Fourteenth Amendment contains three references to 'person.' The first, in defining 'citizens,' speaks of 'persons born or naturalized in the United States.' The word also appears both in the Due Process Clause and in the Equal Protection Clause. 'Person' is used in other places in the Constitution: in the listing of qualifications for Representatives and Senators, Art, I, s 2, cl. 2, and s 3, cl. 3; in the Apportionment Clause, Art. I, s 2, cl. 3; FN53 in the Migration and Importation provision, Art. I, s 9, cl. 1; in the Emolument Clause, Art, I, s 9, cl. 8; in the Electros provisions, Art. II, s 1, cl. 2, and the superseded cl. 3; in the provision outlining qualifications for the office of President, Art. II, s 1, cl. 5; in the Extradition provisions, Art. IV, s 2, cl. 2, and the superseded Fugitive Slave Clause 3; and in the Fifth, Twelfth, and Twenty-second Amendments, as well as in ss 2 and 3 of the Fourteenth Amendment. But in nearly all these instances, the use of the word is such that it has application only postnatally. None indicates, with any assurance, that it has any possible prenatal application. FN54

FN53. We are not aware that in the taking of any census under this clause, a fetus has ever been counted.

FN54. When Texas urges that a fetus is entitled to Fourteenth Amendment protection as a person, it faces a dilemma. Neither in Texas nor in any other State are all abortions prohibited. Despite broad proscription, an exception always exists. The exception contained in Art. 1196, for an abortion procured or attempted by medical advice for the purpose of saving the life of the mother, is typical. But if the fetus is a person who is not to be deprived of life without due process of law, and if the mother's condition is the sole determinant, does not the Texas exception appear to be out of line with the Amendment's command? There are other inconsistencies between Fourteenth Amendment status and the typical abortion statute. It has already been pointed out, n. 49, supra, that in Texas the woman is not a principal or an accomplice with respect to an abortion upon her. If the fetus is a person, why is the woman not a principal or an accomplice? Further, the penalty for criminal abortion specified by Art. 1195 is significantly less than the maximum penalty for murder prescribed by Art. 1257 of the Texas Penal Code. If the fetus is a person, may the penalties be different?

All this, together with our observation, supra, that throughout the major portion of the 19th century prevailing legal abortion practices were far freer than they are today, persuades us that the word 'person,' as used in the Fourteenth Amendment, does not include the unborn. FN55 This is in accord with the results reached in those few cases where the issue has been squarely presented. *McGarvey v. Magee-Women's Hospital,* 340 F.Supp. 751 (W.D.Pa.1972); *Byrn v. New York City Health & Hospitals Corp.,* 31 N.Y.2d 194, 335 N.Y.S.2d 390, 286 N.E.2d 887 (1972), appeal docketed, No. 72-434; *Abele v. Markle,* 351 F.Supp. 224 (D.C.Conn.1972), appeal docketed, No. 72-730. Cf. *Cheaney v. State, Ind.,* 285 N.E.2d, at 270; *Montana v. Rogers,* 278 F.2d 68, 72 (CA7 1960), aff'd sub nom. *Montana v. Kennedy,* 366 U.S. 308, 81 S.Ct. 1336, 6 L.Ed.2d 313 (1961); *Keeler v. Superior Court,* 2 Cal.3d 619, 87 Cal.Rptr. 481, 470 P.2d 617 (1970); *159 State v. Dickinson,* 28 Ohio St.2d 65, 275 N.E.2d 599 (1971). Indeed, our decision in *United States v. Vuitch,* 402 U.S. 62, 91 S.Ct. 1294, 28 L.Ed.2d 601 (1971), inferentially is to the same effect, for we there would not have indulged in statutory interpretation favorable to abortion in specified circumstances if the necessary consequence was the **730 termination of life entitled to Fourteenth Amendment protection.

FN55. Cf. the Wisconsin abortion statute, defining 'unborn child' to mean 'a human being from the time of conception until it is born alive,' Wis.Stat. s 940.04(6) (1969), and the new Connecticut statute, Pub. Act No. 1 (May 1972 Special Session), declaring it to be the public policy of the State and the legislative intent 'to protect and preserve human life from the moment of conception.'

This conclusion, however, does not of itself fully answer the contentions raised by Texas, and we pass on to other considerations.

B. The pregnant woman cannot be isolated in her privacy. She carries an embryo and, later, a fetus, if one accepts the medical definitions of the developing young in the human uterus. See Dorland's Illustrated Medical Dictionary 478–479, 547 (24th ed. 1965). The situation therefore is inherently different from marital intimacy, or bedroom possession of obscene material, or marriage, or procreation, or education, with which Eisenstadt and Griswold, Stanley, Loving, Skinner and Pierce and Meyer were respectively concerned. As we have intimated above, it is reasonable and appropriate for a State to decide that at some point in time another interest that of health of the mother or that of potential human life, becomes significantly involved. The woman's privacy is no longer sole and any right of privacy she possesses must be measured accordingly.

Texas urges that, apart from the Fourteenth Amendment, life begins at conception and is present throughout pregnancy, and that, therefore, the State has a compelling interest in protecting that life from and after conception. We need not resolve the difficult question of when life begins. When those trained in the respective disciplines of medicine, philosophy, and theology are unable to arrive at any consensus, the judiciary, at this point in the development of man's knowledge, is not in a position to speculate as to the answer.

*160 It should be sufficient to note briefly the wide divergence of thinking on this most sensitive and difficult question. There has always been strong support for the view that life does not begin until live birth. This was the belief of the Stoics. FN56 It appears to be the predominant, though not the unanimous, attitude of the Jewish faith. FN57 It may be taken to represent also the position of a large segment of the Protestant community, insofar as that can be ascertained; organized groups that have taken a formal position on the abortion issue have generally regarded abortion as a matter for the conscience of the individual and her family. FN58 As we have noted, the common law found greater significance in quickening. Physicians and their scientific colleagues have regarded that event with less interest and have tended to focus either upon conception, upon live birth, or upon the interim point at which the fetus becomes 'viable,' that is, potentially able to live outside the mother's womb, albeit with artificial aid. FN59 Viability is usually placed at about seven months (28 weeks) but may occur earlier, even at 24 weeks. FN60 The Aristotelian theory of 'mediate animation,' that held sway throughout the Middle Ages and the Renaissance in Europe, continued to be official Roman Catholic dogma until the 19th century, despite opposition to this 'ensoulment' theory from those in the Church who would recognize the existence of life from *161 the moment of conception. FN61 The latter is now, of course, the official belief of the Catholic Church. As one brief amicus discloses, this is a view strongly held by many non-Catholics as well, and by many physicians. Substantial **731 problems for precise definition of this view are posed, however, by new embryological data that purport to indicate that conception is a 'process' over time, rather than an event, and by new medical techniques such as menstrual extraction, the 'morning-after' pill, implantation of embryos, artificial insemination, and even artificial wombs. [Footnotes 51–66 and citations omitted.]…

In areas other than criminal abortion, the law has been reluctant to endorse any theory that life, as we recognize it, begins before life birth or to accord legal rights to the unborn except in narrowly defined situations and except when the rights are contingent upon life birth. For example, the traditional rule of tort law denied recovery for prenatal injuries even though the child was born alive. FN63 That rule has been changed in almost every jurisdiction. In most States, recovery is said to be permitted only if the fetus was viable, or at least quick, when the injuries were sustained, though few *162 courts have squarely so held. FN64 In a recent development, generally opposed by the commentators, some States permit the parents of a stillborn child to maintain an action for wrongful death because of prenatal injuries. FN65 Such an action, however, would appear to be one to vindicate the parents' interest and is thus consistent with the view that the fetus, at most, represents only the potentiality of life. Similarly, unborn children have been recognized as acquiring rights or interests by way of inheritance or other devolution of property, and have been represented by guardians ad litem. FN66 Perfection of the interests involved, again, has generally been contingent upon live birth. In short, the unborn have never been recognized in the law as persons in the whole sense.

X

In view of all this, we do not agree that, by adopting one theory of life, Texas may override the rights of the pregnant woman that are at stake. We repeat, however, that the State does have an important and legitimate interest in preserving and protecting the health of the pregnant woman, whether she be a resident of the State or a non-resident who seeks medical consultation and treatment there, and that it has still another important and legitimate interest in protecting the potentiality of human life. These interests are separate and distinct. Each grows in substantiality as the woman approaches *163 term and, at a point during pregnancy, each becomes 'compelling.'

With respect to the State's important and legitimate interest in the health of the mother, the 'compelling' point, in the light of present medical knowledge, is at approximately the end of the first trimester. This is so because of the now-established medical **732 fact, referred to above at 725, that until the end of the first trimester mortality in abortion may be less than mortality in normal childbirth. It follows that, from and after this point, a State may regulate the abortion procedure to the extent that the regulation reasonably relates to the preservation and protection of maternal health. Examples of permissible state regulation in this area are requirements as to the qualifications of the person who is to perform the abortion; as to the licensure of that person; as to the facility in which the procedure is to be performed, that is, whether it must be a hospital or may be a clinic or some other place of less-than-hospital status; as to the licensing of the facility; and the like.

This means, on the other hand, that, for the period of pregnancy prior to this 'compelling' point, the attending physician, in consultation with his patient, is free to determine, without regulation by the State, that, in his medical judgment, the patient's pregnancy should be terminated. If that decision is reached, the judgment may be effectuated by an abortion free of interference by the State.

With respect to the State's important and legitimate interest in potential life, the 'compelling' point is at viability. This is so because the fetus then presumably has the capability of meaningful life outside the mother's womb. State regulation protective of fetal life after viability thus has both logical and biological justifications. If the State is interested in protecting fetal life after viability, it may go so far as to proscribe abortion *164 during that period, except when it is necessary to preserve the life or health of the mother.

Measured against these standards, Art. 1196 of the Texas Penal Code, in restricting legal abortions to those 'procured or attempted by medical advice for the purpose of saving the life of the mother,' sweeps too broadly. The statute makes no distinction between abortions performed early in pregnancy and those performed later, and it limits to a single reason, 'saving' the mother's life, the legal justification for the procedure. The statute, therefore, cannot survive the constitutional attack made upon it here.

This conclusion makes it unnecessary for us to consider the additional challenge to the Texas statute asserted on grounds of vagueness. See *United States v. Vuitch*, 402 U.S., at 67–72, 91 S.Ct., at 1296–1299.

XI

To summarize and to repeat:

> A state criminal abortion statute of the current Texas type, that excepts from criminality only a life-saving procedure on behalf of the mother, without regard to pregnancy stage and without recognition of the other interests involved, is violative of the Due Process Clause of the Fourteenth Amendment.
>
> (a) For the stage prior to approximately the end of the first trimester, the abortion decision and its effectuation must be left to the medical judgment of the pregnant woman's attending physician.
>
> (b) For the stage subsequent to approximately the end of the first trimester, the State, in promoting its interest in the health of the mother, may, if it chooses, regulate the abortion procedure in ways that are reasonably related to maternal health.
>
> (c) For the stage subsequent to viability, the State in promoting its interest in the potentiality of human life *165 may, if it chooses, regulate, and even proscribe, abortion except where it is necessary, in appropriate medical judgment, for the preservation of the life or health of the mother. [*Author's emphases added.*]
>
> The State may define the term 'physician,' as it has been employed in the preceding paragraphs of this Part XI of this opinion, to mean only a physician currently licensed by the **733 State, and may proscribe any abortion by a person who is not a physician as so defined.

In *Doe v. Bolton*, 410 U.S. 179, 93 S.Ct. 739, 35 L.Ed.2d 201, procedural requirements contained in one of the modern abortion statutes are considered. That opinion and this one, of course, are to be read together. FN67

FN67. Neither in this opinion nor in *Doe v. Bolton*, 410 U.S. 179, 93 S.Ct. 739, 35 L.Ed.2d 201, do we discuss the father's rights, if any exist in the constitutional context, in the abortion decision. No paternal right has been asserted in either of the cases, and the Texas and the Georgia statutes on their face take no cognizance of the father. We are aware that some statutes recognize the father under certain circumstances. North Carolina, for example, N.C.Gen.Stat. s 14–45.1 (Supp.1971), requires written permission for the abortion from the husband when the woman is a married minor, that is, when she is less than 18 years of age, 41 N.C.A.G. 489 (1971); if the woman is an unmarried minor, written permission from the parents is required. We need not now decide whether provisions of this kind are constitutional.

This holding, we feel, is consistent with the relative weights of the respective interests involved, with the lessons and examples of medical and legal history, with the lenity of the common law, and with the demands of the profound problems of the present day. The decision leaves the State free to place increasing restrictions on abortion as the period of pregnancy lengthens, so long as those restrictions are tailored to the recognized state interests. The decision vindicates the right of the physician to administer medical treatment according to his professional judgment up to the points where important *166 state interests provide compelling justifications for intervention. Up to those points, the abortion decision in all its aspects is inherently, and primarily, a medical decision, and basic responsibility for it must rest with the physician. If an individual practitioner abuses the privilege of exercising proper medical judgment, the usual remedies, judicial and intra-professional, are available.

XII

Our conclusion that Art. 1196 is unconstitutional means, of course, that the Texas abortion statutes, as a unit, must fall. The exception of Art. 1196 cannot be struck down separately, for then the State would be left with a statute proscribing all abortion procedures no matter how medically urgent the case.

Although the District Court granted appellant Roe declaratory relief, it stopped short of issuing an injunction against enforcement of the Texas statutes. The Court has recognized that different considerations enter into a federal court's decision as to declaratory relief, on the one hand, and injunctive relief, on the other. *Zwickler v. Koota,* 389 U.S. 241, 252–255, 88 S.Ct. 391, 397–399, 19 L.Ed.2d 444 (1967); *Dombrowski v. Pfister,* 380 U.S. 479, 85 S.Ct. 1116, 14 L.Ed.2d 22 (1965). We are not dealing with a statute that, on its face, appears to abridge free expression, an area of particular concern under Dombrowski and refined in *Younger v. Harris,* 401 U.S., at 50, 91 S.Ct., at 753.

We find it unnecessary to decide whether the District Court erred in withholding injunctive relief, for we assume the Texas prosecutorial authorities will give full credence to this decision that the present criminal abortion statutes of that State are unconstitutional.

The judgment of the District Court as to intervenor Hallford is reversed, and Dr. Hallford's complaint in intervention is dismissed. In all other respects, the judgment *167 of the District Court is affirmed. Costs are allowed to the appellee.

It is so ordered.
Affirmed in part and reversed in part.
Mr. Justice STEWART, concurring.
Mr. Justice REHNQUIST, dissenting.

The Court's opinion brings to the decision of this troubling question both extensive historical fact and a wealth of legal scholarship. While the opinion thus commands my respect, I find myself nonetheless in fundamental disagreement with those parts of it that invalidate the Texas statute in question, and therefore dissent.

I

The Court's opinion decides that a State may impose virtually no restriction on the performance of abortions during the first trimester of pregnancy. Our previous decisions indicate that a necessary predicate for such an opinion is a plaintiff who was in her first trimester of pregnancy at some time during the pendency of her lawsuit. While a party may vindicate his own constitutional rights, he may not seek vindication for the rights of others. *Moose Lodge No. 107 v. Irvis,* 407 U.S. 163, 92 S.Ct. 1965, 32 L.Ed.2d 627 (1972); *Sierra Club v. Morton,* 405 U.S. 727, 92 S.Ct. 1361, 31 L.Ed.2d 636 (1972). The Court's statement of facts in this case makes clear, however, that the record in no way indicates the presence of such a plaintiff. We know only that plaintiff Roe at the time of filing her complaint was a pregnant woman; for aught that appears in this record, she may have been in her last trimester of pregnancy as of the date the complaint was filed.

Nothing in the Court's opinion indicates that Texas might not constitutionally apply its proscription of abortion as written to a woman in that stage of pregnancy. Nonetheless, the Court uses her complaint against the Texas statute as a fulcrum for deciding that States may *172 impose virtually no restrictions on medical abortions performed during the first trimester of pregnancy. In deciding such a hypothetical lawsuit, the Court departs from the longstanding admonition that it should never 'formulate a rule of constitutional law broader than is required by the precise facts to which it is to be applied.' *Liverpool, New York & Philadelphia S.S. Co. v. Commissioners of Emigration,* 113 U.S. 33, 39, 5 S.Ct. 352, 355, 28 L.Ed. 899 (1885). See also *Ashwander v. TVA,* 297 U.S. 288, 345, 56 S.Ct. 466, 482, 80 L.Ed. 688 (1936) (Brandeis, J., concurring).

II

Even if there were a plaintiff in this case capable of litigating the issue which the Court decides, I would reach a conclusion opposite to that reached by the Court. I have difficulty in concluding, as the Court does, that the right of 'privacy' is involved in this case. Texas, by the statute here challenged, bars the performance of a medical abortion by a licensed physician on a plaintiff such as Roe. A transaction resulting in an operation such as this is not 'private' in the ordinary usage of that word. Nor is the 'privacy' that the Court finds here even a distant relative of the freedom from searches and seizures protected by the Fourth Amendment to the Constitution, which the Court has referred to as embodying a right to privacy. *Katz v. United States,* 389 U.S. 347, 88 S.Ct. 507, 19 L.Ed.2d 576 (1967).

If the Court means by the term 'privacy' no more than that the claim of a person to be free from unwanted state regulation of consensual transactions may be a form of 'liberty' protected by the Fourteenth Amendment, there is no doubt that similar claims have been upheld in our earlier decisions on the basis of that liberty. I agree with the statement of Mr. Justice STEWART in his concurring opinion that the 'liberty,' against deprivation of which without due process the Fourteenth *173 Amendment protects, embraces more than the rights found in the Bill of Rights. But that **737 liberty is not guaranteed absolutely against deprivation, only against deprivation without due process of law. The test traditionally applied in the area of social and economic legislation is whether or not a law such as that challenged has a rational relation to a valid state objective. *Williamson v. Lee Optical Inc.,* 348 U.S. 483, 491, 75 S.Ct. 461, 466, 99 L.Ed. 563 (1955). The Due Process Clause of the Fourteenth Amendment undoubtedly does place a limit, albeit a broad one, on legislative power to enact laws such as this. If the Texas statute were to prohibit an abortion even where the mother's life is in jeopardy, I have little doubt that such a statute would lack a rational relation to a valid state objective under the test stated in Williamson, supra. But the Court's sweeping invalidation of any restrictions on abortion during the first trimester is impossible to justify under that standard, and the conscious weighing of competing factors that the Court's opinion apparently substitutes for the established test is far more appropriate to a legislative judgment than to a judicial one.

The Court eschews the history of the Fourteenth Amendment in its reliance on the 'compelling state interest' test. See *Weber v. Aetna Casualty & Surety Co.,* 406 U.S. 164, 179, 92 S.Ct. 1400, 1408, 31 L.Ed.2d 768 (1972) (dissenting opinion). But the Court adds a new wrinkle to this test by transposing it from the legal considerations associated with the Equal Protection Clause of the Fourteenth Amendment to this case arising under the Due Process Clause of the Fourteenth Amendment. Unless I misapprehend the consequences of this transplanting of the 'compelling state interest test,' the Court's opinion will accomplish the seemingly impossible feat of leaving this area of the law more confused than it found it.

*174 While the Court's opinion quotes from the dissent of Mr. Justice Holmes in *Lochner v. New York,* 198 U.S. 45, 74, 25 S.Ct. 539, 551, 49 L.Ed. 937 (1905), the result it reaches is more closely attuned to the majority opinion of Mr. Justice Peckham in that case. As in Lochner and similar cases applying substantive due process standards to economic and social welfare legislation, the adoption of the compelling state interest standard will inevitably require this Court to examine the legislative policies and pass on the wisdom of these policies in the very process of deciding whether a particular state interest put forward may or may not be 'compelling.' The decision here to break pregnancy into three distinct terms and to outline the permissible restrictions the State may impose in each one, for example, partakes more of judicial legislation than it does of a determination of the intent of the drafters of the Fourteenth Amendment.

The fact that a majority of the States reflecting, after all the majority sentiment in those States, have had restrictions on abortions for at least a century is a strong indication, it seems to me, that the asserted right to an abortion is not 'so rooted in the traditions and conscience of our people as to be ranked as fundamental,' *Snyder v. Massachusetts*, 291 U.S. 97, 105, 54 S.Ct. 330, 332, 78 L.Ed. 674 (1934). Even today, when society's views on abortion are changing, the very existence of the debate is evidence that the 'right' to an abortion is not so universally accepted as the appellant would have us believe.

To reach its result, the Court necessarily has had to find within the Scope of the Fourteenth Amendment a right that was apparently completely unknown to the drafters of the Amendment. As early as 1821, the first state law dealing directly with abortion was enacted by the Connecticut Legislature. Conn.Stat., Tit. 22, ss 14, 16. By the time of the adoption of the Fourteenth *175 Amendment in 1868, there were at least 36 laws enacted by state or territorial legislatures limiting **738 abortion. FN1 While many States have amended or updated *176 their laws, 21 of the laws on the books in 1868 remain in effect today. FN2 Indeed, the Texas statute **739 struck down today was, as the majority notes, first enacted in 1857 *177 and 'has remained substantially unchanged to the present time.' Ante, at 710. [Footnote 1 and citations omitted.]…

FN2. Abortion laws in effect in 1868 and still applicable as of August 1970:1. Arizona (1865).2. Connecticut (1860).3. Florida (1868).4. Idaho (1863).5. Indiana (1838).6. Iowa (1843).7. Maine (1840).8. Massachusetts (1845).9. Michigan (1846).10. Minnesota (1851).11. Missouri (1835).12. Montana (1864).13. Nevada (1861).14. New Hampshire (1848).15. New Jersey (1849).16. Ohio (1841).17. Pennsylvania (1860).18. Texas (1859).19. Vermont (1867).20. West Virginia (1848).21. Wisconsin (1858).

There apparently was no question concerning the validity of this provision or of any of the other state statutes when the Fourteenth Amendment was adopted. The only conclusion possible from this history is that the drafters did not intend to have the Fourteenth Amendment withdraw from the States the power to legislate with respect to this matter.

III

Even if one were to agree that the case that the Court decides were here, and that the enunciation of the substantive constitutional law in the Court's opinion were proper, the actual disposition of the case by the Court is still difficult to justify. The Texas statute is struck down in toto, even though the Court apparently concedes that at later periods of pregnancy Texas might impose these selfsame statutory limitations on abortion. My understanding of past practice is that a statute found *178 to be invalid as applied to a particular plaintiff, but not unconstitutional as a whole, is not simply 'struck down' but is, instead, declared unconstitutional as applied to the fact situation before the Court. *Yick Wo v. Hopkins*, 118 U.S. 356, 6 S.Ct. 1064, 30 L.Ed. 220 (1886); *Street v. New York*, 394 U.S. 576, 89 S.Ct. 1354, 22 L.Ed. 572 (1969).

For all of the foregoing reasons, I respectfully dissent.

Roe is probably the most famous family law case.[31] Supreme Court Justice Harry A. Blackmun, writing for the majority, said that a woman had the right to abortion "free of interference by the State" "but that this right is not unqualified and must be considered against important state interests in regulation." While *Roe* has never been overturned, after over 40 years, later cases have significantly limited its scope.[32]

In *Planned Parenthood of Southeastern Pennsylvania v. Casey*, the Court pulled back on the constitutional protections found in *Roe* and, in so doing, rejected its trimester test for a new test that looks at the reasonableness of the state's regulation of abortion prior to viability (viz., are the regulations designed to help the woman or just discourage her from getting the procedure?). After viability, states are permitted to regulate abortions, as long as the exception remains for the woman's life and health.[33] Under *Casey*'s new test, state regulations must not constitute an "undue burden" on the woman. This means that the regulation must be necessary for the health of the woman and not a roadblock created to deter her access to the procedure.

ABORTION LAW AFTER *ROE*

1. Undue Burden

After *Roe*, the Supreme Court in *Planned Parenthood of Southeastern Pennsylvania v. Casey*, 505 U.S. 833 (1992), limited state regulations that would cause an undue burden to a woman's right to choose. "An undue burden occurs when a state regulation has the purpose or effect of placing a substantial obstacle in the path of the woman." *Casey*, at 876.

---

31   "Through eight Presidential elections and the nominations of thirteen [U.S. Supreme Court] Justices (some of which failed, at least in part, because of the nominees' views on *Roe*) no other controversies involving the Constitution—about such issues as civil rights or the relationship between church and state—have generated as much discussion as the holding, in Roe, that women have a right under the Constitution to terminate their pregnancies." "Still Standing: The Resilience of Roe v. Wade," Jeffrey Toobin, *New Yorker*, November 28, 2005, p. 70.

32   Many feminists felt that the decision should have been left to the individual state legislatures, which were slowly changing the laws to legalize abortion. Supreme Court Justice Ruth Bader Ginsburg, then an attorney in New York, said these lawsuits had, "[h]alted a political process that was moving in a reform direction." Ibid., p 72. In hindsight, this may have avoided decades of controversy. On the other hand, "only a ruling by the Supreme Court could establish a nationwide right to choose abortion, and at that time it was clear that several Justices wanted to protect abortion." Ibid., p. 72—especially in keeping with recent cases finding a right to privacy in contraception use. (See Chapter 5.)

33   505 U.S. 833 (1992), the majority opinion written by Justice Sandra Day O'Connor.

2. Viability and the Trimester Requirements

In *City of Akron v. Akron Center for Reproductive Health*[34], Justice Sandra Day O'Connor[35] criticized *Roe*'s trimester requirements and emphasis on viability. She wrote, in her dissent, that the state's interest in both the maternal health and potential for life should exist throughout pregnancy. Later in *Webster v. Reproductive Health Services*, 492 U.S. 490 (1989), a plurality of the Court further restricted *Roe* by finding that abortion was not a fundamental right, but a liberty interest under the 14th Amendment's due process clause and officially abandoned *Roe*'s trimester and viability standards. Also in the case of *Planned Parenthood of Southeastern Pennsylvania v. Casey*, the Supreme Court rejected the trimester plan, simplifying that a woman has a right to an abortion without government interference before viability, but after the viability period, the government may restrict abortions (except therapeutic—for saving the life or health of the woman—while protecting the maternal health balanced with the potential for life).

The majority of states have laws that restrict abortions after a certain number of weeks, but each year that number gets lower. Now, some states are proposing "fetal pain" (supposedly when a fetus can experience pain) and "fetal heart beat" laws (supposedly when a heartbeat can be detected) that prevents the procedure as early as six weeks. The scientific validity of these claims is disputed.[36] Yet, Wisconsin passed a 20-week "fetal pain" bill in 2015, with no exceptions for rape and incest.[37] In 2013, when North Dakota banned another "fetal heartbeat" request the governor, Jack Dalrymple said, "Although the likelihood of this measure surviving a court challenge remains in question, this bill is nevertheless a legitimate attempt by a state legislature to discover the boundaries of *Roe v. Wade*."[38] In March 2013, Arkansas's legislature passed the "Human Heartbeat Protection Act" (over the governor's veto) that bans abortions after 12 weeks of pregnancy.[39] The law would penalize doctors who performed abortions on woman more than 12 weeks pregnant unless she was a rape or incest victim or her life or the fetus' life was in danger.[40]

Arkansas governor Mike Beebe said he vetoed the bill "because it violates the precedent set by the Supreme Court's 1973 *Roe v. Wade* decision, which protects women's constitutional right to have an abortion until the fetus is viable outside the womb (usually around 24 weeks). 'In short, because it would impose a ban on a woman's right to choose an elective, non-therapeutic abortion well before viability, Senate Bill 134 blatantly contradicts the United States Constitution, as interpreted by the Supreme Court.... When I was sworn in as governor I took an oath to preserve, protect, and defend both the Arkansas Constitution and the Constitution of the United States.

---

34   462 U.S. 416 (1983)

35   "TFWSCJ," as she refers to herself ("the first woman Supreme Court justice").

36   https://www.theatlantic.com/health/archive/2017/01/ultrasound-woman-pregnancy/514109/

37   "Wisconsin Ban on abortions after 20 weeks passes", *Washington Post*, July 10, 2015, p.A3.

38   http://www.foxnews.com/politics/2013/03/26/north-dakota-governor-approves-6-week-abortion-ban/

39   http://www.nytimes.com/2013/03/07/us/arkansas-adopts-restrictive-abortion-law.html?pagewanted=all&_r=0, "Arkansas adopts a ban on abortions after twelve weeks," Eric Eckholm.

40   http://www.huffingtonpost.com/2013/03/06/arkansas-12-week-abortion-ban_n_2821739.html Arkansas, "12-Week Abortion Ban Becomes Law," Laura Bassett.

I take that oath seriously.'"[41] In 2015, the 9th Circuit Court of Appeals struck down a 20-week abortion ban from Idaho as unconstitutional and the 8th Circuit also struck down Arkansas' 20-week "fetal heart beat ban". In its ruling the 8th Circuit ruled that "abortion restrictions must be based on a fetus' ability to live outside the womb, not the presence of a fetal heartbeat that can be detected weeks earlier."[42] In 2016, the Supreme Court declined to review earlier court decisions blocking North Dakota's 6-week ban and Arkansas' 12-week ban.[43]

In Ohio a "fetal heartbeat" bill resembling that in Arkansas was defeated in the legislature[44] in 2013, but reintroduced in 2016. Interestingly, the legislature proposed two bills; one for a ban at 20 weeks and the other for six weeks. Former Republican Presidential candidate and then Governor, John Kasich, vetoed the "heartbeat bill" but signed the 20 week bill, almost making the 20 week bill seem sensible.[45] In January 2017 Congressional Republicans introduced a federal heartbeat bill.

3. Mootness

What happened to the legal case when Norma McCorvey's pregnancy was over in *Roe v. Wade*? The beginning of the Supreme Court's opinion addresses the **mootness** issue (is the issue still ripe for review or has it become academic) raised by defendants because Roe was no longer pregnant at the time of the lower court ruling at the Federal District Court on May 22 or the following June 17, 1971, when the Court's opinion and judgment were filed. The court addressed this by acknowledging that "despite the use of the pseudonym, Roe is not a fictitious person" and also accepts as true that she was pregnant at the "inception of her suit in March 1970 and as late as May 21 of that year when she filed an alias affidavit with the District Court." The Supreme Court acknowledged that in "federal cases an actual controversy must exist at each stage of appellate... review" and not just on the date the action was filed. Due to the nature of this case it presented the necessary "case or controversy." "But when, as here, pregnancy is a significant fact in the litigation, the normal 266-day human gestation period is so short that the pregnancy will come to term before the usual appellate process is complete. If that termination makes a case moot, pregnancy litigation seldom will survive much beyond the trial state, and appellate review will be effectively denied. Our law should not be that rigid. Pregnancy often comes more than once to the same woman, and in the general population, if man is to survive, it will always be with us. Pregnancy provides a classic justification for a conclusion of lack of mootness. It truly could be capable of repetition, yet evading review."[46]

---

41   Ibid.
42   "Arkansas Court Strikes down abortion restriction", *Washington Post,* May 28, 2015, pA3
43   "Ohio bill would ban abortion at heartbeat", Sandhya Somashekhar, *Washington Post*, December 8, 2016, pA8.
44   http://www.nytimes.com/2013/03/07/us/arkansas-adopts-restrictive-abortion-law.html?pagewanted=all&_r=0
45   https://www.washingtonpost.com/news/post-nation/wp/2016/12/13/ohio-governor-vetoes-heartbeat-bill-but-signs-into-law-another-abortion-restriction/?utm_term=.74927735a3db
46   *Roe v. Wade*, 410 U.S. 113 (1973).

DISCUSSION AND FUTURE OF ROE

After making its medically driven trimester analysis in finding a woman's constitutional right to choose an abortion under the 14th Amendment in *Roe*, over the next 40 years, the Supreme Court and many state courts and legislatures have attempted to carve out limits. "Since 2011, state politicians have enacted more than 200 restrictions" on abortions—"more restrictions in the past three years than were enacted in the previous decade".[47] *Planned Parenthood v. Casey* limited state regulations that would cause an "undue burden" or when "a state regulation has the purpose or effect of placing a substantial obstacle in the path of the woman." *Casey*, at 876. Which of these is an "undue burden?"

1. The Father's Rights in Abortion

The law does not recognize legal rights of men who father children in abortion decisions. While there is hope that the decision would be made jointly by the couple, no prior written consent is required for a woman to exercise her right to choose. As the Court wrote, "the state cannot constitutionally delegate to a spouse that power which the state, itself, is prohibited from exercising during the first trimester" under *Roe* in *Planned Parenthood v. Danforth*, 428 U.S. 52 (1976).

The Supreme Court struck down the states' attempts to require spousal notification before obtaining an abortion. In 1988, Pennsylvania passed a law requiring married women who sought an abortion to indicate that they had notified their husband of their intentions to abort the fetus. This law exempted spousal notification requirements when the father was not the husband, when he could not be located, when the pregnancy resulted from reported spousal rape, or if the woman feared the notification could cause her bodily injury. Of all the laws challenged in this case, which included imposing a 24-hour waiting period, the informed consent requirement was the only one invalidated by the Supreme Court.[48] *Planned Parenthood of Southeastern Pennsylvania v. Casey*, 505 U.S. 833 (1992).[49] Yet, in February 2017, Oklahoma proposed a bill that requires woman to

---

47 "Abortion out of reach", Nancy Northup, *The Washington Post*, October 12, 2014, P. A21. Indeed, during the short time of one midterm election cycle, 31 states enacted new restrictions on abortion. "Harper's Index", *Harper's Magazine*, November 2014, P.9.

48 Justice Samuel Alito was one of the judges on the Pennsylvania Court of Appeals that approved the *Casey* restrictions on abortion, including the requirement of husband's consent for a wife's abortion. In his 1985 application for a promotion in President Reagan's Justice Department, now Supreme Court justice Alito wrote that he was "particularly proud" to have participated in writing a brief to the Supreme Court arguing that "the Constitution does not protect a right to an abortion." "Still Standing: The *Resilience of Roe v. Wade*," Jeffrey Toobin, *New Yorker*, November 28, 2005, p. 72, citing to *Liberty and Sexuality*, David J. Garrow, 1994.

49 In *Dubay v. Wells*, 506 F.3d 422 (6th Cir. 2007) a biological father challenged Michigan's paternity laws after he told a woman that he did not want to have the child she was pregnant with. The father, Dubay, claims at the beginning of their relationship he told the child's mother that he did not want to have children and she replied that she was infertile and using contraception. The relationship deteriorated and then the woman told Dubay she was pregnant. He claims that he consistently told her he did not want to have the child and they broke off their relationship before the child was born. Dubay claimed that the law violated the 14th amendment's equal protection and due process clauses

get the written consent of the fetus' father in order to obtain an abortion.[50] What issue does this raise from an earlier chapter?

2. Minors' Rights to Abortion

Under *Planned Parenthood v. Danforth*, 428 U.S. 52 (1976), states may not prevent a minor from terminating a pregnancy. Yet her rights are more limited than an adult's. Courts have upheld state laws requiring parental consent and/or notification; making this distinction based in part on the importance of parental decision making for minors (see Chapter 18). In so doing, the court requires that if parental consent is required, there must be a judicial bypass option. In *Bellotti v. Baird*, 443 U.S. 622 (1979), the Massachusetts legislature required a judge to make the decision because a minor, alone, is too immature to make the decision to have an abortion. Based on the legal emphasis on the parental role in decision making for children, states have been more successful in enforcing parental notification requirements—especially when a judicial bypass option is available.[51] Courts have reviewed cases when parents have prevented children from getting abortions, when parents have taken children across state lines to get an abortion (against the wishes of the minor child), and when non-parents have transported minors out of state for the procedure. In 2007, the U.S. House of Representatives passed H.R. 1063, the "Child Interstate Abortion Notification Act," making it a federal offense for anyone other than a child's parent to take the child out of state to obtain an abortion, but the Senate refused to pass it.

In 2013, a ten-weeks-pregnant, 16-year-old girl sued her parents in Texas to prevent them from forcing her to get an abortion. "When the pregnancy was confirmed, the teenager's father allegedly 'became extremely angry, was insistent that R. E. K. was not having the baby, and that the decision was not up to her, according to the lawsuit.'" "The teen claimed in the lawsuit that her parents had taken away her phone, pulled her out of school, forced her to get two jobs and took away her car in an effort to 'make her miserable so that she would give in to the coercion and have the abortion.'" A family court granted her an injunction against her parents that will last for the term of the pregnancy. In addition, the "girl will be able to use her car to go to school, work and medical appointments." Interestingly, the "parents will be liable for half of the hospital bill when she gives birth, unless she is married to the baby's 16-year-old father."[52]

Compare this to the parents of a pregnant 19-year-old in Portland, Maine who pleaded not guilty to kidnapping, assault, and terrorizing in what prosecutors said was an attempt to force her to have an

---

because, among other reasons, the woman was the only one who got to make the decision and therefore he should not have to pay child support under it. Because he did not have the ability to influence the woman's decision to terminate the pregnancy, he requested the court's assistance but the court, like most others, rejected these claims.

50   https://www.washingtonpost.com/news/post-nation/wp/2017/02/14/oklahoma-bill-would-require-father-of-fetus-to-approve-abortion/?utm_term=.151561b8cad7

51   *Planned Parenthood of Southeastern Pennsylvania v. Casey*, 505 U.S. 833 (1992)

52   http://abcnews.go.com/blogs/headlines/2013/02/texas-teen-wins-right-to-give-birth-over-parents-objections/, "Texas Teen Wins Right to Give Birth Over Parents' Objections," Alyssa Newcomb, *ABC News*, February 19, 2013.

abortion. "Nicholas and Lola Kampf were accused of tying up their daughter Katelyn, forcing her into their car, and heading toward New York for an abortion. They were arrested… at a shopping center in Salem, N.H., after Katelyn fled and called police on a cell phone."[53] "Katelyn Kampf described a harrowing experience that ensued on September 15, 2006 after her parents learned the [she] was pregnant with a mixed-race baby. Kampf is white. Reme Johnson, her boyfriend, is black." "She said her parents tied her up, and her mother spit in her face before putting her in the car. After she escaped in New Hampshire, police found a .22-caliber rifle, duct tape, and rope in the parents' car."[54] "At one point I did make it out the door, and I ran down the driveway," she said. "I didn't make it a hundred feet. My dad chased me and tackled me in the driveway…. I was screaming for help."[55] At the time of the arrest, the parents contended… that they "learned the day before their arrest that their daughter was pregnant. They packed their car for a trip to Florida but their plans changed because of the pregnancy."[56] "While the Kampfs could have faced up to 30 years in prison if convicted of kidnapping, they agreed to plead guilty to misdemeanor assault and disorderly conduct charges for which they did not serve jail time, but were ordered to undergo court-ordered counseling." Katelyn Kampf's son, D'Andre Johnson, was born in January 2007, but Kampf remains worried about the father, Reme Johnson, who was scheduled to be deported to his native South Africa, because of felony convictions for crimes including receiving stolen property.[57]

3. Waiting Periods

Since the Supreme Court's ruling that a 24-hour waiting period is not an undue burden[58] some state courts have extended the waiting period. "Waiting period" refers to the time that is required to lapse between when the woman meets with her health care provider to sign her consent for an abortion and when the procedure is allowed to be performed. Is it an undue burden on a woman to have to meet with her doctor and then return the next day (or even later) for the procedure? What if there is only one clinic in the state? Does repeated travel amount to an undue burden? What if travel back and forth is too far or transportation is unavailable? What about the financial burden of spending a night in a hotel? Are these unreasonable?

---

53 http://www.deseretnews.com/article/650201156/Parents-say-they-didnt-kidnap-daughter-to-force-her-to-abort. html?pg=all, "Parents say they didn't kidnap daughter to force her to abort," AP, *Deseret News*, October 24, 2006.
54 http://www.boston.com/news/local/articles/2007/10/11/plea_seen_in_case_against_parents/, "Plea seen in case against parents," David Sharp, AP, *Boston Globe*, October 11, 2007.
55 Ibid.
56 http://www.deseretnews.com/article/650201156/Parents-say-they-didnt-kidnap-daughter-to-force-her-to-abort. html?pg=all, "Parents say they didn't kidnap daughter to force her to abort," AP, *Deseret News*, October 24, 2006.
57 http://www.boston.com/news/local/articles/2007/10/11/plea_seen_in_case_against_parents/, "Plea seen in case against parents," David Sharp, AP, *Boston Globe*, October 11, 2007.
58 Thus overruling *City of Akron v. Akron Center for Reproductive Health*, 462 U.S. 416 (1983) which found a waiting period unconstitutional and serves no state interest by imposing an "arbitrary and inflexible" waiting period.

As of 2014, "one half of the states have waiting periods."[59] Most are 24 hours, but Utah requires 72 hours while providing exceptions for rape, incest, and other circumstances. Missouri's waiting period is also 72 hours, but it does not have an exception for rape or incest. South Dakota's three-day (72-hour) waiting period does not include weekends and holidays, which means it could be up to five or six days in practice. In this same state, there is no waiting period for a person to buy a gun.[60]

4. Hospital Requirements

Recent state legislation has been successful in requiring surgical or hospital-like settings to perform abortion procedures. In South Dakota, the state successfully reduced the number of abortion clinics to one, based on laws requiring expensive and strict standards for outpatient clinics that performed abortions. States like Texas[61], Ohio, North Carolina, and Virginia[62] passed similar laws. Virginia's abortion clinic regulations imposed strict building standards similar to those for constructing new hospitals. Specifications include expensive reconstruction which ranged from specific hallway widths to accommodate wheel chairs (which are not needed for the procedure), closet sizes, parking and HVAC requirements, and hands-free sinks and applied to both newly constructed clinics and those that had historically operated legally. The new regulations will force clinics "to spend large sums on renovation that abortion rights advocates say are medically unnecessary."[63] After at least one abortion clinic shut down but in 2015, the newly elected Democratic attorney general issued an opinion that made the rules apply to new construction only. Do these strict and often-unnecessary restrictions endanger women by making access to abortion more difficult?[64] Does this lead "to later term—and consequently

---

59 "Banishing abortion, one rule at a time", Ruth Marcus, *The Washington Times*, October 5, 2014, P.A19.
60 "Waiting period for abortions extended", *The Washington Post*, December 12 2014, P. A3. See also, "Waiting Periods in South Dakota: Guns v. Abortions" Kate Sheppard" http://www.motherjones.com/mojo/2013/03/waiting-periods-south-dakota-guns-v-abortions. "South Dakota has only one abortion provider, a Planned Parenthood clinic in Sioux Falls, and its doctors fly in from out of state. Women already travel from as far as six hours away to reach the clinic. While the clinic has said that it has been able to find a way to make the 72-hour waiting period work, it thinks this new law will make it next to impossible for many women to access an abortion." http://www.motherjones.com/mojo/2013/03/south-dakota-women-cant-think-weekends, "In South Dakota, Women Can't Think on Weekends," Kate Sheppard.
61 Texas' law was famously filibustered for 12 hours by state Senator Wendy Davis but was subsequently passed.
62 Virginia (under new governor Terri McCullough) began reviewing these laws in 2014 "Health Board to vote on overhaul of abortion clinic rules", Jenna Portnoy, *The Washington Post,* December 4, 2014. P.B4. New Health Board appointee, Mary Margaret Whipple, was quoted as saying "'I really feel that it is better to let the medical profession practice medicine than have the legislature practicing medicine.'"
63 http://www.nytimes.com/2013/04/13/us/virginia-abortion-clinic-rules-get-final-approval.html?_r=0,   "Virginia Abortion Clinic Rules Get Final Approval," Erik Eckholm, *New York Times*, April 12, 2013.
64 Women in Texas after the ban, had to "pay more money and wait longer." https://www.nytimes.com/2016/03/20/us/women-cite-longer-wait-and-higher-costs-for-abortions-in-texas.html

riskier—procedures?"[65] In Texas, 2013 regulations required abortion clinics to satisfy "building codes and hygiene standards as surgical facilities, and for abortion doctors to have admitting privileges at nearby hospitals."[66] As a result of Texas' restrictions, the number of abortion clinics in the state went from 40 to seven in two years. "In practice, these rulings mean that about one in six Texas women seeking an abortion will live more than 150 miles from the nearest clinic.[67] There will be no facilities in the huge swath of the state west and south of San Antonio."[68] "Some would face a round trip of 1,000 miles to get an abortion in their home state."[69] How far does one have to travel for the medical procedure of an abortion for it to be an undue burden?[70]

After two lower courts ruled in favor of Texas' strict regulations, in 2016, the U.S. Supreme Court ruled in *Whole Woman's Health v. Hellerstedt* 579 U.S. __(U.S. 2016) that the Texas laws were an excessive burden on women's rights to legal abortion. Justice Breyer wrote for the majority in finding that the Texas regulations were medically unnecessary and unconstitutional. This was the Supreme Court's most important decision on abortion in "25 years". "At least 25 states have at least one of the two regulations that were covered in... the ruling."[71] In a separate opinion, Justice Ginsburg wrote, "When a State severely limits access to safe and legal procedures, women in desperate circumstances may resort to unlicensed rouge practitioners, *faute de mieux*, at great risk to their health and safety."

5. Declarations That Life Begins at Conception

While *Roe* acknowledges the decision of when life begins is best not left to lawyers[72], recent state legislative efforts have attempted to require statements that life begins at conception. When

---

65   "Banishing abortion, one rule at a time", Ruth Marcus, *The Washington Times*, October 5, 2014, P.A19, citing to an American College of Obstetricians and Gynecologists open letter to the Texas legislature that read in part, "The fact is that abortion is one of the safest medical procedures, with minimal-less than 0.5 percent-risk of major complications that might need hospital care."

66   Controversy of the week", *The Week*, March 11, 2016, P.6.

67   https://www.theatlantic.com/health/archive/2015/11/texas-self-abort/416229/

68   Ibid.

69   Abortion out of reach", Nancy Northup, *The Washington Post*, October 12, 2014, P. A21. Indeed, during the short time of one midterm election cycle, 31 states enacted new restrictions on abortion. "Harper's Index", *Harper's Magazine*, November 2014, P.9.

70   In addition, poverty and lack of health care access "led nearly 2 percent of Texas women to try to induce their own abortions using medicine, teas, vitamins, and other measures" "Digest", *Washington Post*, November 18, 2015, A3

71   https://www.washingtonpost.com/politics/supreme-court-strikes-down-texas-abortion-clinic-restrictions/2016/06/27/ba55d526-3c70-11e6-a66f-aa6c1883b6b1_story.html?utm_term=.a855b7536073

72   The majority rejected the view, pressed by opponents of liberalized abortion, that a fetus becomes a "person" upon conception and is thus entitled to the due process and equal protection guarantees.
"The word 'person,' as used in the 14th Amendment, does not include the unborn," Justice Blackmun wrote, although states may acquire "at some point in time" of a pregnancy an interest in the "potential human life" that the fetus represents, to permit regulation. It is that interest, the court said, that permits states to prohibit abortion after the fetus has developed the capacity to survive. https://www.nytimes.com/2017/02/18/obituaries/norma-mccorvey-dead-roe-v-wade.html?_r=0

confronted with this requirement in a Missouri law which would force the doctor to read a statement proclaiming life begins at conception, the Supreme Court did not address this contradiction to *Roe*, but said it was just the state's "value judgment."

6. Late-Term Abortions and Time Limitations

In *Stenberg v. Carhart*, the Court held that a Nebraska ban on later-term abortions with no exception for the woman's health was unconstitutional. These abortions (called an intact dilation and evacuation, or D & E, by doctors and by anti-abortionists as "partial-birth abortions") were made illegal in 2003 and punishable by up to two years in prison or a fine for knowing violation, when Congress passed the Partial-Birth Abortion Ban Act (PBABA), Pub. L. No. 198-105, 117 Stat. 1201, 18 U.S.C. section 1531.[73] Subsequently, in *Gonzales v. Carhart*, 550 U.S. 124 (2007), the Court upheld the federal ban on late-semester abortions even when no exception was made for the health of the woman. Many objected to Justice Kennedy's suggestion that the late-term abortion ban protects women from remorse in hindsight. Justice Ginsburg criticized these paternalistic comments in her dissent when she wrote that taking away women's reproductive choice is not a means to protect women.

Since then, many states passed laws banning abortions after 20 weeks of pregnancy (from the prior 26 week ban). Texas' state Senator, Wendy Davis, earned national attention when she filibustered this bill a few weeks before the Texas legislature met in a special session to finally pass it.[74] In 2015, the Republican-controlled U.S. Congress debated the Pain-Capable Unborn Child Protection Act" which would ban abortions after 20 weeks. An exception would be allowed for raped woman only if they reported the crime to law enforcement. The bill was dropped when some Republican woman objected to its restrictive language.[75] The urgent vote on the bill, which required the suspension of normal committee, was set to coincide with the anniversary of the *Roe* decision.

7. Gender Preference/Sex-Selective Abortions

While more of a topic for an international family law book, some legislatures in this county have proposed bills to make it a criminal offense for doctors to knowingly perform a sex-selective abortion. Eight states currently ban the practice.[76] Critics argued that the bill was designed to intimidate doctors, violate doctor-patient confidentiality, and encourage physicians to racially profile women who are seeking abortions, since the practice of sex-selective abortions is common in South Asian countries that have a cultural preference for boys.[77]

---

73 *Emanuel Law Outlines, Family Law,* by D. Kelly Weisberg (2011) p. 244.

74 "Abortion Setting a 20-week limit" *The Week*, July 19, 2013, P. 14. Arguably support for this bill was the result of the Kermit Gosnell murder trial in which a "Philadelphia abortion doctor killed well-developed fetuses six or more months into pregnancy" citing to Kirsten Pwers in *TheDailyBeast.com*.

75 "GOP discord halts vote on abortion bill", Ed O'Keefe, *The Washington Post*, January 22, 2015, P. A3.

76 https://www.theatlantic.com/politics/archive/2016/05/sex-disability-race-selective-abortion-indiana/482856/

77 http://www.huffingtonpost.com/2013/01/04/virginia-abortion-contraception_n_2410445. html, "Virginia Abortion, Contraception Bills Proposed in New Legislative Session," Linda Bassett.

Also in 2013, as part of its three-part abortion law, North Dakota became the first state to ban abortions based "on genetic defects such as Down syndrome.[78] "The measures... are fueled in part by an attempt to close the state's sole abortion clinic, in Fargo."[79] On March 2016, then Governor of Indiana and now Vice President of the United States signed a bill into law that made it the second state to ban abortions "fetal genetic abnormalities such as Down syndrome." The law also prohibits abortions based on "race, sex or ancestry."

What is the impact of this law if women have a right under *Roe* not to give a reason (or to make one up) to access the legal medical procedure. The penalty would fall on the doctors who could be "sued for wrongful death or face discipline from the state medical licensing board."[80]

8. Limits on Doctors' Scripts

In *City of Akron v. Akron Center for Reproductive Health*, 462 U.S. 416 (1983) the Supreme Court struck down a statute that required doctors to notify patients of fetal development or physical and emotional complications allegedly resulting from an abortion procedure, but this was overruled in *Casey*, when the Supreme Court looked at the issue of informed consent requiring doctors to inform their patients about effects on their health in abortion procedures. Since then, the 8th Circuit Federal Court of Appeals upheld a 2005 South Dakota law that requires doctors to tell women seeking abortions that the procedure causes an increased risk of suicide, in a seven to four vote (in which all seven were appointed by former anti-abortion president George W. Bush). Planned Parenthood challenged the requirement on a free-speech violation and argued the information was not based on reliable research. A 2008 Johns Hopkins review of various studies on the link between abortion and suicide concluded that the highest quality studies showed few, if any, differences between the mental health of women who had abortions and women who had not.[81]

Similarly, an appellate court overruled a prior appellate decision and upheld a South Dakota law requiring doctors to tell an abortion seeker that a woman "has an existing relationship with that unborn human being and that the relationship enjoys protection under the United States Constitution and under the laws of South Dakota." The lower court judge found the wording misleading; she said a relationship, in the eyes of the law, can only exist between people. Thus, the ruling upheld the Supreme Court' earlier decision that the unborn are not legally considered people.[82]

---

78 http://www.politico.com/story/2013/03/north-dakota-6-week-abortion-ban-89324.html
79 "North Dakota passes Arkansas for the Strictest Abortion Bill," *Washington Post,* March 27, 2013, p. A3. When sued on this issue, North Dakota backed down and chose another way to ban abortions. http://www.chicagotribune.com/news/nationworld/midwest/ct-indiana-abortion-ban-genetic-abnormalities-20160324-story.html
80 Ibid.
81 http://www.huffingtonpost.com/2012/07/24/south-dakota-abortion-suidice-law-appeals-court_n_1699615.html, Laura Bassett, "South Dakota Law Linking Abortion, Suicide Upheld in Court."
82 http://www.huffingtonpost.com/2011/09/02/south-dakota-mother-fetus-relationship-law_n_947504.html, "SouthDakota Can Require Doctors to Tell Women Seeking Abortions That They Have 'Existing Relationship'

9. Funding

Anti-abortion supporters have worked since *Roe* to limit the right of choice by defunding it. Ever since 1977, when Representative Henry Hyde introduced a law in the U.S. Congress to prevent the use of federal funds (via the Medicaid program) by indigents to pay for the medical procedure of abortion, courts have accepted the limitation as not amounting to an undue burden. Thus, unlike other legal medical procedures, federal funding for abortion is eliminated, including for women who serve in the military and for female military dependents (requiring them to travel off base to access the legal procedure of abortion). Women serving in the Middle East have even had to travel to another country. Similarly, public hospitals and employees have been prohibited to perform or assist in elective abortions. (See *Webster v. Reproductive Health Services.*) So-called "gag rules" have also prevented the use of federal funds at federal clinics for abortion counseling or referrals. (President Bill Clinton later rescinded these rules.) After President George W. Bush prevented international family planning agencies from accepting federal funding for counseling, advocating, or offering abortions, President Barack Obama had rescinded this "global gag rule."[83] But shortly after the Woman's March the day after his inauguration, President Trump reinstated and expanded the ban. The ban "prohibits any involvement with abortion in order for an NGO (non-governmental organization) to receive funding from the U.S. for family planning. This means that an organization can't even use *its own money*—not only in providing abortions, but for a physician counseling his/her patient as to the best care for her, or referring a patient to another place for that necessary medical care. It means that patients won't have condoms to reduce HIV transmission. Trump extended it to [prevent]... *all global health funding*, not just family planning."[84] Domestically, the fight against abortion involves defunding Planned Parenthood and Medicaid. Planned Parenthood is one of the country's largest providers of preventive care to women and men. Medicaid is a government program to provide care for the poor. In 2013, Virginia State Senator Thomas A. Garrett introduced a bill to stop Medicaid payments for abortions for low-income women unless "the fetus would be born with a gross and totally incapacitating physical deformity or mental deficiency." Virginia law allows Medicaid coverage for abortion in cases of rape, incest, severe fetal abnormalities, or when the life of the mother is in danger.[85] In 2013, when Congress threatened to shut down the federal government over budget issues, funding of Planned Parenthood was one of the problems. In 2017 Republicans formed a House panel "to investigate the procurement of human fetal tissue for medical research that recommended

---

with Fetus, Court Rules," Kristi Eaton. The South Dakota law also required women seeking abortions undergo counseling at pregnancy help centers that discourage abortion. http://www.huffingtonpost.com/2011/06/30/south-dakota-abortion-law-injunction_n_888253.html, "South Dakota Abortion Law: Federal Judge Grants Planned Parenthood Preliminary Injunction," Dirk Lammers.

83 *Emanuel Law Outlines, Family Laws*, D. Kelly Weisberg (2011), p. 241.

84 https://www.forbes.com/sites/judystone/2017/01/25/trump-is-hell-bent-on-punishing-women-with-yuge-global-gag-rule/#4e655deb1c75

85 http://www.huffingtonpost.com/2013/01/04/virginia-abortion-contraception_n_2410445.html, "Virginia Abortion, Contraception Bills Proposed in New Legislative Session," Linda Bassett.

stripping federal funds from Planned Parenthood."[86] This was based on a debunked video created by anti-abortionist activists. The panel was formed in 2015 after Republicans again threatened to shut down the federal government. Also, the recently proposed American Heath Care Act requires Planned Parenthood be defunded or lose reimbursement for preventative services it provides. Yet, in 2017, a federal judge blocked Texas from removing Planned Parenthood from the state's Medicaid program over the videos. Similar rulings were made in Arkansas, Alabama, Mississippi and Kansas. As we go to press, Congress passed, "Republican legislation letting states deny federal family planning money to Planned Parenthood and other abortion providers." The vote was so close that a tie-breaking vote by Vice President Mike Pence had to vote to break the tie.[87]

10. Face Laws and Freedom to Access Clinics

Anti-abortion activists have prevented women from entering abortion clinics through intimidation, even murdering doctors who perform abortions, going so far as to murder a doctor while he attended church.[88] "[S]ince 1991, at least ten people—5 doctors, 2 receptionists, an escort and a security guard—have been murdered and 17 people wounded, including 8 doctors."[89] In response, Congress passed the Freedom of Access to Clinic Entrances Act (FACE), 18 U.S.C. section 248 (2006) which provides both criminal and civil penalties for the "use of force, threat of force, or physical obstruction" aimed at injuring, intimidating, or interfering with any patients or providers of reproductive health services.[90] These laws have withstood appellate court scrutiny on free speech and equal protection. In *Planned Parenthood of Columbia/Willamette, Inc. v. American Coalition of Life Activists*, 290 F2d 1058 (9th Cir. 2002), cert. denied, 539 U.S. 958 (2003), the appellate court used FACE to stop the publication of "wanted posters" with the pictures and addresses of abortion providers. The appellate court designated these as "true threats" made with the intent to intimidate the providers and referenced prior incidents, including the murder of some doctors targeted by the group.[91]

---

86   https://www.pressreader.com/usa/the-washington-post/20170105/281848643279873 The Hyde Amendment prevents Planned Parenthood from being reimbursed for abortion procedures, but defunding will eliminate all reimbursement for the preventative care it provides, including cancer screenings. The videos referred to Planned Parenthood being reimbursed for its costs when a woman donates medical tissue for research, which is a common procedure for fertility clinics too. "Why wage war on abortion but not IVF patients?" Margo Kaplan, op-ed, *Washington Post*, August 16, 2015, p B4.

87   http://www.foxnews.com/politics/2017/03/30/pence-breaks-senate-tie-on-planned-parenthood-funding-bill.html

88   In 1994 in Brookline, Massachusetts, a gunman opened fire at two abortion clinics, killing two receptionists and wounding at least five other people. In March of 1993, Dr. David Gunn was murdered outside an abortion clinic in Pensacola, Florida. In 1991, a women's health clinic receptionist was shot and paralyzed from the waist down. On May 31, 2009, Dr. George Tiller was murdered at his church in Wichita, Kansas. "Clinic Buffer Zones at Risk" NOW http://now.org/resource/clinic-buffer-zones-at-risk-in-massachusetts-case-before-supreme-court/

89   Ibid., citing to the Feminist Majority Foundation.

90   *Emanuel Law Outline, Family Laws*, D. Kelly Weisberg (2011), p. 241.

91   Ibid.

In 2014, the U.S. Supreme Court looked again at the free speech issues in FACE laws in *McCullen v. Coakley* 573 U.S. ____ (2014)[92] when a group of "sidewalk counselors" challenged Massachusetts's law that made it a crime to stand on a sidewalk within 35 feet of an abortion clinic. They objected that this prevented them from "offering information about alternatives to abortions and helping to pursue those options" and that "escorts" who help to get clients of the centers through the buffer zones further prevent their ability to counsel. This time the U.S. Supreme Court voided the legal restrictions because sidewalks are public ways and are traditionally open for free speech activity. While the Court acknowledged that the buffer served a "legitimate interest in maintaining public safety" it "imposed serious burdens on petitioner's speech" depriving them of their two primary methods of communication with arriving patients: close personal conversations and distribution of literature". The Court viewed them not as protestors (who were permitted to protest outside of the buffer, thus using the free speech) but "to engage in personal, caring, consensual conversations with women." Are patients really "consenting" to "counseling" as they try to exercise their legal right to abortion? Some argue that past actions of murder are more the behaviors of terrorist. Yet, *McCullen* did not overrule *Roe*.

11. *Roe:* Eliminated at the State Level?

In South Dakota voters rejected statewide ballot measures in 2006 and 2008 that would have banned most abortions in the state–a direct challenge to *Roe v. Wade*. Despite this, South Dakota passed a law in March 2013 to outlaw abortions in the state. The state's voters previously rejected abortion bans at the polls in 2006 and 2008 by a 12-point margin, both times. Despite the voters' objections, South Dakota's government continues to pass laws restricting abortion rights and make the state's taxpayers pay for the legal cases to defend the laws. "The state's 2012 budget proposal [included] a little over $1 million for the 'Extraordinary Litigation Fund,' and of that $750,000 [was] to cover the costs related to the Planned Parenthood case through June. If the state loses it will also have to pay Planned Parenthood's legal fees." A legal fund set up by the state for private donations only contained about $63,000.[93]

Yet, abortion rates have dropped by 12 percent since 2010 across the U.S. The decline has occurred in both 'red' states that have passed new abortion restrictions and 'blue' states with no new restrictions.[94]

---

92   http://www.google.com/url?sa=t&rct=j&q=&esrc=s&source=web&cd=2&ved=0CCYQFjAB&url=http%3A%2 F%2Fwww.supremecourt.gov%2Fopinions%2F13pdf%2F12-1168_6k47.pdf&ei=qZk1VZadN6fPsQTQ8IH4CA& usg=AFQjCNEAEJSlmkT5yqg7s3NdnpNoW7bTXA&sig2=fRVeQAWWnyaWER8CaD9NBA&bvm=bv.91071109 ,d.cWc

93   http://www.motherjones.com/mojo/2011/12/south-dakota-taxpayer-defend-abortion-laws,   "South   Dakota Spends Big Taxpayer Bucks to Defend Anti-Abortion Laws," Kate Sheppard.

94   *The Week*, June 19, 2015, p. 14.

12. Fetal Homicide Laws

Roe reserved a decision on the question as to when life begins and deferred to precedent; the unborn have never been found to be people. Anti-abortionists have argued that if a fetus had the same legal rights to government protection as a living pregnant woman, *Roe* would fail. So far, the group has been successful in getting the courts to recognize the "killing" of a fetus during the commission of a crime on the pregnant woman through passage of federal and state laws. For the first time, the federal government conferred legal rights to a fetus when Congress passed the Unborn Victims of Violence Act, 18 U.S.C. section 1841 (2004 and 2006).[95] Eventually, dubbed "Laci and Conner's Law" (named after Laci Peterson and Conner, her unborn son—Laci was pregnant and killed by her husband on Christmas Eve to conceal his affair) it became law (Public Law 108-212) in 2004. The act makes it a criminal offense to kill or injure an unborn child (in any stage of gestation) during the commission of a federal crime against the pregnant woman. For the first time, this law recognized two people as victims of a crime. Similarly, a majority of states have fetal homicide laws, making it a crime to harm a fetus and the pregnant woman (the requirements of the stage of pregnancy vary).[96]

What is the logical extreme of these laws? Under the Irish constitution, "the unborn have the same right to life as the mother. Abortion is illegal except in cases where the mother's life is at 'real and substantial risk' due to medical complications or the threat of suicide."[97] In 2014, an Irish woman in her twenties with two other children was "clinically brain-dead" after suffering a head injury in a fall in November. She was declared dead on December 9 and her family and partner requested that her life support be removed. The doctors, however, were afraid to discontinue treatment because the woman was 18 weeks pregnant. The doctors thought it would subject them to being charged under the law for failing to promote the life and health for the unborn, so they asked the court for guidance. Meanwhile, the woman, "a corpse" was kept alive.[98] The court accepted the medical testimony that the chance of the fetus surviving was minimal and wrote "to maintain and continue the present somatic support for the mother would deprive her of dignity

---

95   In 1999 then Congressman (now Senator) Lindsey Graham, (R-S.C.), introduced the Unborn Victims of Violence Act to "establish federal legal status for unborn children when their pregnant mothers are the victims of violent crime." The proposed law "would apply only to federal crimes against pregnant women, as well as crimes committed under the jurisdiction of the U.S. military, and Graham said the measure would have no impact on related state laws." It passed the House but failed in the Senate. http://cnsnews.com/news/article/author-unborn-victims-bill-optimistic-passage#sthash.foImKkix.dpuf, "Author on Unborn victim bill optimistic about its passage" Scott Hogenson, CBSNews.com, July 7, 2008

96   *Emanuel Law Outline, Family Law*, D. Kelly Weisberg, 2011, p. 248.

97   "Irish court; Pregnant, clinically dead patient can be taken off life support", Peter Taggart, *CNN*, December 26, 2014. http://www.cnn.com/2014/12/26/world/europe/ireland-life-support-ruling/

98   "Brain-dead pregnant woman's life support can be switched off, Irish court rules", Henry McDonald, *The Guardian*, December 25, 2014. http://www.theguardian.com/world/2014/dec/26/ireland-court-rules-brain-dead-pregnant-womans-life-support-switched-off. The 8th Amendment of the Irish constitution "acknowledges the right to life of the unborn and, with due regard to the equal right to life of the mother, guarantees in its laws to respect and, as far as practicable by its laws, to defend and vindicate that right."

in death". The court also wrote that there was no reason medial or ethical reason "for continuing with a process described as verging on the grotesque."[99]

13. Fetal Personhood Laws

In March 2013, U.S. Senator Rand Paul and 2016 Republican presidential candidate, introduced so-called "fetal personhood" federal legislation that would completely outlaw abortion in the United States. The "Life at Conception Act" would declare that human life begins at conception providing fertilized eggs with the same legal status as born persons.[100] States have recently offered new laws recognizing fetuses as people under the law. In March 2013, North Dakota passed a "fetal personhood" amendment, which granted legal personhood rights to embryos at the moment of fertilization[101] and Colorado "passed Amendment 67, which would have included unborn fetuses as 'children' in the state's criminal code.[102] If voters approved the measure (they did not) it would effectively outlaw abortion in the state, with no exceptions for rape, incest, or risk of life to the mother. The law also raises questions about the legality of several forms of birth control.[103] Virginia tried to pass a state fetal personhood law in 2012, but it was blocked before a vote. The sponsor of this bill, Delegate Bob Marshall, vowed to tie the bill to other legislation in an effort to get it passed.[104] Senator Paul has used this tactic, too—having tried to attach a

---

99   Irish court; Pregnant, clinically dead patient can be taken off life support", Peter Taggart, *CNN*, December 26, 2014. http://www.cnn.com/2014/12/26/world/europe/ireland-life-support-ruling/

100   http://www.rawstory.com/rs/2013/03/17/sen-rand-paul-introduces-fetal-personhood-bill-to-outlaw-abortion/, "Sen. Rand Paul introduces 'fetal personhood' bill to outlaw abortion," Eric W. Dolan. See also, http://www.care2.com/causes/civil-liberties-hero-rand-paul-proposes-fetal-personhood-again.html, "Civil Liberties 'Hero' Rand Paul Proposes Fetal Personhood. Again," Jessica Pieklo, who points out that Paul once said he opposed the Civil Rights Act, believes it is the 14th Amendment, the very vehicle that makes the Civil Rights Act a reality, that gives Congress the power to declare life begins at conception.

101   http://www.thedailybeast.com/articles/2013/03/24/north-dakota-s-fetal-personhood-amendment-why-i-voted-against-it.html, "North Dakota's Fetal Personhood Amendment: Why I Voted Against It," State representative Kathy Hawken. "So far this year, we have taken up six different bills to end safe and legal abortion in our state. Some are the broad, so-called 'personhood' amendments that could also interfere with personal, private medical decisions ranging from abortion to fertility treatment; others ban abortion at different stages in pregnancy. One would effectively ban abortion in the state with overregulation that local doctors have said is medically unnecessary. One abortion ban was even amended to include a ban on funding for programs like the one that provides sex education to at-risk teens in Fargo"—the very programs designed to prevent the need for abortions. See also, http://www.thedailybeast.com/cheats/2013/03/22/north-dakota-passes-personhood-amend.html

102   Voters in Colorado voted against it 63 to 37 percent in support and similarly North Dakota voted against it 64 to 36 percent in favor. "Fetal personhood laws defeated in Colorado and North Dakota", Zach Schonfeld, *Newsweek*, November 5, 2014. http://www.newsweek.com/fetal-personhood-laws-defeated-colorado-and-north-dakota-282545

103   The law also raises questions about the legality of several forms of birth control.

104   Virginia Delegate Bob Marshall "will use backdoor methods to advance his legislation. He said he is 'always looking for bills to amend' with abortion-related stipulations in order to force members to go on record in support or opposition. 'For example, I might amend a bill that deals with life insurance to say the child killed in utero should be recognized as a legal person," he said. "Just put that in there and stipulate it. I've seen massive shifts on lobbying and delegates pulling their bills because they know I'll amend them and that I know how to do it in a germane way."

fetal personhood amendment to a flood insurance bill.[105] The North Carolina legislature attached abortion restriction bills to a bill to prohibit the threat of sharia law.[106]

14. Elimination of the Doctor-Patient Protections-Ultrasounds

Did the Virginia legislature attempt to totally eliminate *Roe*'s emphasis on the doctor and the patient-client relationship? In March 2012, Virginia's legislature passed a bill (but later withdrew it after national attention) requiring women wanting an abortion to have an "invasive procedure: a transvaginal sonogram. A probe—with a lubricated condom covering it—is inserted into a woman's vagina. The probe is attached to a monitor to show images in real time."[107] A proposed amendment to allow women to either consent to have the procedure or her physician to opt out, failed. Thus, in Virginia women would have been "forcibly penetrated for no medical reason."[108] The law also required a woman's doctor to "certify whether she did or did not 'avail herself of the opportunity' to view the ultrasound or listen to the fetal heartbeat." The certification would have been included in the patient's medical record, even if she opposed it.[109]

"So the problem is not just that the woman and her physician (the core relationship protected in *Roe*)[110] no longer matter at all in deciding whether an abortion is proper. It is that the physician is being commandeered by the state to perform a medically unnecessary

Marshall said it doesn't bother him that his antiabortion amendments might kill or stall an important bill that would otherwise pass, because in his opinion, no matter could be more important than ending abortion. "You're talking about human beings being killed," he said. "What higher considerations do I put out there?" http://www.huffingtonpost.com/2012/11/26/bob-marshall-virginia-abortion_n_2192979.html, "Bob Marshall: Virginia GOP Pressures Me '7 Days a Week' to Drop Anti-Abortion Agenda," Laura Bassett.

105   Ibid.

106   Abortion Setting a 20-week limit" *The Week*, July 19, 2013, P. 14.

107   http://prospect.org/article/pre-abortion-sonograms-make-their-way-law, "Pre-abortion sonograms make their way into law," Abbey Rapoport.

108   "I am not the first person to note that under any other set of facts, that would constitute rape under the federal definition." http://www.slate.com/articles/double_x/doublex/2012/02/virginia_ultrasound_law_women_who_want_an_abortion_will_be_forcibly_penetrated_for_no_medical_reason.html, "Virginia's Proposed Ultrasound Law Is an Abomination: Under the new legislation, women who want an abortion will be forcibly penetrated for no medical reason. Where's the outrage?" Dahlia Lithwick. I guess they were all out of scarlet letters in Richmond [Virginia]," (http://www.slate.com/articles/double_x/doublex/2012/02/virginia_ultrasound_law_women_who_want_an_abortion_will_be_forcibly_penetrated_for_no_medical_reason.html,

109   In response to Virginia's vaginal probe bill, State Senator Janet D. Howell "decided to push back on the measure, which she said is adding to the cost and... opening [women] up for emotional blackmail... Howell offered an amendment that would require any man seeking a prescription for erectile dysfunction medication first submit to a rectal examination... Her amendment was defeated 22–18." http://dcist.com/2012/01/ultrasounds_before_abortions_only_i.php, "Ultrasounds Before Abortions? Only if Men Get Rectal Exams for Viagra, Virginia Lawmaker Says," Benjamin R. Freed.

110   Eleven states have laws requiring the doctors performing abortions in clinics have admitting-privileges at a local hospital. This too is requiring clinics to shut down. Mississippi would have shut its last remaining clinic if the court had not overridden this provision in its laws. "Admitting privileges laws give abortion foes potent tool", Sandhya Somashekhar, *The Washington Post*, August 2014, P. 1.

procedure upon a woman, despite clear ethical directives to the contrary. There is no evidence at all that the ultrasound is a medical necessity, and nobody attempted to defend it on those grounds."[111]

"Five states have enacted "'informed consent'" laws, which require doctors to show their patients ultrasound images, and in some cases to describe the images, before performing an abortion. Two of those laws have been struck down by state courts. Twenty other states require a doctor to at least *offer* to show a woman seeking an abortion ultrasound."[112] In Virginia's proposed bill victims of rape and incest could only avoid the forced ultrasound if they made a prior report to the police. But Texas did not even allow that exemption. In 2015, the Supreme Court upheld the 4th Circuit(federal) court of appeals' 2014 rejection of North Carolina's law's requiring woman to have an ultrasound before an abortion because it violated free speech by requiring doctors provide the image even if the woman averted her eyes or clearly chose not to listen. The court wrote that the first amendment prohibits regulations that compel speech.[113]

15. Doctor's Visiting Privileges

Many states had laws requiring that doctors performing abortions in clinics have admitting-privileges at a local hospital. This is opposed by the American Medical Association and the American College of Obstetricians and Gynecologists "because it has nothing to do with its ostensible purpose of improving patient safety."[114] This too is requiring clinics to shut down. Mississippi would have shut its last remaining clinic if the court had not overridden this provision in its laws.[115] In Alabama, a federal judge struck the state's admitting-privileges requirement, noting that the law would "create a significant risk that some women would pursue dangerous, illegal abortions."[116] *Whole Woman's Health v. Hellerstadt* ruled that such requirements were unreasonable burdens.

---

111 The author cites to the language of Justice Anthony Kennedy in *Gonzales v. Carhardt* that this just gives women "more information" in making their decision to have an abortion. http://www.slate.com/articles/double_x/doublex/2012/02/virginia_ultrasound_law_women_who_want_an_abortion_will_be_forcibly_penetrated_for_no_medical_reason.html, "Virginia's Proposed Ultrasound Law Is an Abomination" Under the new legislation, women who want an abortion will be forcibly penetrated for no medical reason. Where's the outrage?" Dahlia Lithwick.

112 https://www.theatlantic.com/health/archive/2017/01/ultrasound-woman-pregnancy/514109/ In Tennessee if the woman declines to look at the ultrasound the "technician has to explain, "the results, including a medical description of the dimensions of the embryo or fetus, presence of a heartbeat, arms, legs, external members and internal organs" and the woman must be provided with a copy to obtain an abortion. "Bill introduced to Tennessee State House, requires ultrasound before an abortion", Cameron Taylor, 6ABC.con, November 14, 2014 http://www.tennessean.com/story/news/politics/2014/11/14/bill-require-ultrasound-abortion/19026477/.

113 "Justices deny N.C. bid to restore abortion law", Robert Barnes, *Washington Post,* June 16, 2015, p A2.

114 "Abortion out of reach", Nancy Northup, *The Washington Post*, October 12, 2014, P. A21.

115 "Admitting privileges laws give abortion foes potent tool", Sandhya Somashekhar, *The Washington Post*, August 2014, P. 1.

116 "Abortion out of reach", Nancy Northup, *The Washington Post*, October 12, 2014, P. A21.

16. Justifiable Homicide?

South Dakota, Nebraska, and Iowa all proposed similarly worded bills to expand justifiable homicide statutes to include covering "killings" committed in the defense of an unborn child. Critics of the bills including law enforcement officials warned that these measures could invite violence against abortion providers and possibly provide legal cover to the perpetrators of such crimes. "The bills are so loosely worded, abortion-rights advocates say, that a pregnant woman could seek out an abortion and a boyfriend, husband—or, in some cases, just about anyone—could be justified in using deadly force to stop it."[117]

In a 1999 case in Michigan a woman, 17-weeks pregnant with quadruplets, killed her boyfriend after he punched her twice in the stomach.[118] Jaclyn Kurr, who eventually miscarried quadruplets while serving her jail term, was convicted of manslaughter based partly on the fact that she had a history of criminal offenses."[119] During the case, Kurr's lawyers cited Michigan's "defense of others law" and tried to argue that Kurr was defending "the fetus" which could not defend itself. The trial court barred that argument because medical testimony showed that the fetus was not viable at 17 weeks. (Under *Roe*, the judge concluded that in order for Kurr to present a "defense of others" theory, there had "to be a living human being existing independent" of Kurr.)[120] In 1999 a Michigan appeals court overturned Kerr's conviction on the grounds that the jury was not properly instructed on the "defense of others" theory.[121] Should a woman have the right to kill another in protection of the unborn at any stage of development?

17. Abortion Inducing Medicine?

In June 2014, the 9th Circuit (federal) court of appeals decided to block a 2012 Arizona law preventing women from taking the most common abortion-inducing drug after the seventh week of pregnancy. Mifepristone is prescribed with a second drug, misoprostol. Originally, in 2000 the FDA approved it in a larger dose and limited its use to the fifth week of pregnancy. Since that time plaintiffs argued, "doctors have found that mifepristone is effective in much smaller doses that are beneficial to women and can be used for an additional two weeks into the pregnancy." Despite that, Arizona's law required the 7-week standard not the new 9th-week standard. The 9th Circuit ruled in *Humble v. Planned Parenthood of Arizona*, (9th Cir. June 3, 2014) No. 14-15234[122]

---

117 http://www.motherjones.com/politics/2011/02/americans-united-life-justifiable-homicide-bills, "Revealed: The Group Behind the Bills That Could Legalize Killing Abortion Providers," Nick Baumann and Daniel Schulman, *Mother Jones*, February 28, 2011.

118 Ibid.

119 Ibid.

120 http://www.foxnews.com/story/2002/11/21/court-may-tackle-question-when-life-begins/#ixzz2WTpF4eLd, Court May Tackle Question of When Life Begins, "Court may tackle the question of when life begins" FoxNews.com, November 21, 2002

121 Ibid.

122 http://www.google.com/url?sa=t&rct=j&q=&esrc=s&source=web&cd=2&ved=0CCQQFjAB&url=http%3 A%2F%2Fcdn.ca9.uscourts.gov%2Fdatastore%2Fopinions%2F2014%2F06%2F03%2F14- The Supreme Court

that the burden imposed on the woman's right to abortion outweighs "the strength of the state's justification for the law."

In 2015, Georgia police arrested and charged a 23-year old woman with malice murder after the death of her five-and-a-half-month-old fetus which she delivered after taking an abortion pill she bought online. Kenlissa Jones took a Cytotec abortion pill known as Misoprostol. The child was delivered on Jones' way to the hospital but only lived for 30 minutes. She was then taken to jail and spent three days there before being released. The county's district attorney later dropped the charges "in a statement that Georgia law does not permit the prosecution of a woman for the termination of her own pregnancy."[123]

In Virginia, in 2017, a woman was charged with a rarely used law (from 1950) that "prohibits giving a pregnant woman a drug or taking any action 'with intent to destroy her unborn child'."[124] Virginia indicted a 43-year old woman and accused her of self-aborting in the third trimester and charged with the felony, after skeletal fetal remains were found in her backyard. The woman, who already has a grown child, "told investigators she gave birth to a baby boy in the house, but he died afterward, and she buried him in the backyard." How will the police investigate this? Will all miscarriages be investigated in Virginia?[125]

In contrast to many state's attempts at "death by a thousand lashes" for the right to abortion, a clinic in Montgomery County Maryland opened in 2015 and advertises that it "pushes to de-stigmatize the nation's most controversial medical procedure by talking about it openly and unapologetically." With a spa-like environment, the clinic "specializes in the abortion pill." "In Los Angeles County, groups sent women door-to-door to talk about their abortion experiences in the hope of changing minds." In an attempt to "put a human face on abortion," some "Democratic lawmakers have publicly acknowledged having undergone the procedure."[126]

While *Roe* passed its 40th anniversary in 2013, "The number of U.S. states that have fewer abortion providers today than in 1978 is 48."[127] This substantial attrition is attributed to, in part, state regulations making it harder for a woman to get an abortion. Could all those regulations be "reasonable?" Moreover, these conflicting movements have created a patchwork of abortion rights throughout the states. Have we moved back to before *Roe* where a woman's option may only be to leave her home state and go to another one in order to obtain the legal procedure of abortion? "Is

---

declined to review that decision in December 2014. 15624.pdf&ei=cTw1VaSAGMK_ggTm8IC4BA&usg=AFQjCNEV eQbUFVUiq6zBGsymi30QR6LRXg&sig2=Wgwg03b1S-TZYceqS2l2rQ&bvm=bv.91071109,d.eXY

123   https://www.washingtonpost.com/news/morning-mix/wp/2015/06/10/woman-charged-with-murder-didnt-have-any-money-to-get-an-abortion-the-legal-way-brother-says/?utm_term=.6be4eb32435a

124   http://thewashingtonpost.newspaperdirect.com/epaper/viewer.aspx

125   Ibid.

126   "Maryland clinic to offer abortion, without shame", Sandhya Somashekhar, *The Washington Post,* March 31 2015, P. 1.

127   "Harper's Index," *Harper's Magazine*, May 2013, p. 15.

it true that '[t]he Supreme Court will have to resolve this issue… if the protections of *Roe v. Wade* are to retain any meaning at all?'"[128]

AS WE GO TO PRESS

"Donald Trump's election, and the presumption that he'll appoint conservative Supreme Court justices, spurred Ohio Republicans to pass what would effectively be the nation's strictest time-based abortion law, a[n Ohio] legislator said" as it passed the "Fetal Heartbeat Law" in 2016. In February 2017, an Oklahoma representative called woman the "host" as he proposed a bill to require the father's consent to a woman's abortion.[129]

Then Governor, now Vice President Mike Pence signed the "dignity for the unborn" law for his state in 2016 added a requirement that "mandates that the only way to dispose of an aborted fetus is through burial or cremation."[130] While campaigning, Donald Trump said that women who have abortions should suffer "some form of punishment"[131] and promised that he would load the Supreme Court with "pro-life" justices to overturn *Roe v. Wade* so that it will go back to the states to make the decision on abortion rights. Already, Trump appointed an anti-*Roe* Supreme Court nominee, Neil Gorsuch. Clearly, the right to an abortion will be the family law issue most likely to be impacted after this book is written.[132] Yet, "the abortion rate in the United States fell to its lowest level since… historic *Roe v. Wade. Moreover,* abortion declined in almost every state, and "having fewer clinics didn't always translate into having fewer abortions."[133]

---

128 Quoting Nancy Northup, president of the Center for Reproductive Rights, "Ruling forces 13 Texas abortion clinics to close abruptly", Sandhya Somashekhar, *The Washington Post*, October 4, 2014, P. A3.

129 https://www.washingtonpost.com/news/post-nation/wp/2017/02/14/oklahoma-bill-would-require-father-of-fetus-to-approve-abortion/?utm_term=.4aeec9ec00de

130 agotribune.com/news/nationworld/midwest/ct-indiana-abortion-ban-genetic-abnormalities-20160324-story.html

131 https://www.nytimes.com/2016/03/31/us/politics/donald-trump-abortion.html

132 Will Freakonomics' argument that Roe's right to abortion helped to lower the crime rate be a part of the debate? *Freakonomics, A Rogue Economist Explores The Hidden Side of Everything*, Levitt and Dubner, 2005, P 139-140

133 http://www.npr.org/sections/thetwo-way/2017/01/17/509734620/u-s-abortion-rate-falls-to-lowest-level-since-roe-v-wade, quoting the studies' principal researcher, Rachel Jones.

15 ASSISTED REPRODUCTIVE TECHNOLOGIES

"Riding the underground tram from the Senate Office Building to the Senate dining room, Senator Robert Wilson (D-Vermont) turned to Senator Dianne Feinstein (D-California) and said, 'I think we ought to be more proactive on this genetic thing. For example, we should consider a law that would prevent young women from selling their eggs for profit.'

'Young girls are already doing that, Bob,' Feinstein said. 'They sell their eggs now.'

'Why, to pay for college?'

'Maybe a few. Mostly, they do it to buy a new car for their boyfriend, or plastic surgery for themselves.'

Senator Wilson looked puzzled. 'How long has that been going on?' he said.

'A couple of years now,' Feinstein said.

'Maybe in California…"

'Everywhere, Bob. A teenager in New Hampshire did it to make bail for her boyfriend.'

'And this doesn't trouble you?'

'I don't like it,' Feinstein said. 'I think it's ill-advised. I think medically the procedure has danger. I think these girls may be risking their reproductive futures. But what would be the basis for banning it? Their bodies, their eggs.' Feinstein shrugged. 'Anyway, the boat's sailed, Bob. Quite a while ago.'"[1]

—Next

"[O]ne long episode of 'Oprah': 'The surrogate took our baby.' 'Our baby has three mothers; which is the real one?' 'My ex-wife stole our IVF embryos and had a baby.'"[2]

—"The Stork Market: How making babies has become a $3 billion industry—and an unregulated mess"

---

1 *Next*, by Michael Crichton, Harper Collins, 2006, pp. 385–386.

2 "The Stork Market: How making babies has become a $3 billion industry—and an unregulated mess," David Plotz, reviewing the book, *The Baby Business How Money, Science, and Politics Drive the Commerce of Conception*, by Debora L. Spar, *Washington Post Book Review*, February 26, 2006.

SPERM DONATION AND ASSISTED REPRODUCTIVE TECHNOLOGY (ART)

With the turn of the new century, the focus of family law moved to facilitate reproduction, not prevent it, as it had in the last two centuries. Because science pushes the boundaries on this topic seemingly daily, it has become fodder for pop culture as well. From television celebrity, Oprah, to best-selling author/medical doctor, Michael Crichton, assisted reproduction has become this generation's "science fiction." There are now various new ways to create children outside of the body or even in another person's body. "Thanks to fertility treatment, babies are conceived these days in so many different ways that it can be hard to keep track. Regardless of how they came into being, when they're born, they're all children—except when the Supreme Court rules that they're not."[3]

The idea of creating a child outside of the natural way, or outside of the body, has existed for centuries. "[T]he first modern gestation and delivery of a child conceived through artificial insemination [was] recorded in 1790."[4] Yet, the law is always racing to catch up to the ever changing scientific field of assisted conception. With the advent of the ability to freeze sperm and the first successful human pregnancy using frozen human sperm in 1953,[5] the business of having babies has created a new and profitable industry[6] and brought with it a new set of legal and ethical issues. Yet, in the United States, the industry is generally unregulated.[7]

1. Sperm Donation: Artificial Insemination (AI)

Sperm donation, the oldest of these technologies, is when a man (generally in a clinical setting) gives, or "donates," his sperm to be used by an unknown woman to become pregnant. This is known as Artificial Insemination by Donor (AID). Originally, donor sperm was used by married couples whose infertility problems were due to the husband's sperm (e.g. low sperm count, possible genetic diseases, etc.), and donor sperm was needed. With today's advanced technologies, the husband's sperm may be assisted and used (called artificial insemination by husband or AIH) or mixed with a donor's sperm, known as combined or confused (called CID). Now the majority of donor sperm is used by unmarried women and same-sex couples. Sperm banks were created to collect and house donated sperm so that purchasers can browse catalogues to select their ideal

---

3 "Supreme Court Rules against Benefits for Posthumously Conceived Kids," Bonnie Rochman, *Time*, May 24, 2012 (referring to the *Astrue v. Capato* case discussed infra).

4 "Reproductive Rights and Technology," Rachel Krantz, p. 92. http://www.scribd.com/doc/17619885/reproductiverights9780816045464 0816045461

5 Ibid., p. 93.

6 "The Stork Market: How making babies has become a $3 billion industry—and an unregulated mess," David Plotz, reviewing the book, *The Baby Business: How Money, Science, and Politics Drive the Commerce of Conception*, by Debora L. Spar, in *Washington Post Book Review*, February 26, 2006.

7 *Reproductive Rights and Technology*, Rachel Krantz, p. 93.

sperm.[8] Many of the donor's characteristics, from education to height, will affect the cost of the sperm—generally from $50 to $150 per vial.

While courts originally found that a woman who was artificially inseminated with sperm other than her husband's amounted to an adulterous relationship, this is no longer true. Similarly, children conceived by donor sperm are generally legitimized by state statute, especially if the husband consents to the wife's procedure.

Donation

But is it really a donation? Men receive payment for the donation of their sperm in the United States. In Canada, where men truly donate sperm (without payment), there can be a shortage. Would American men donate sperm without compensation? If so, would that improve the quality of the donors? Is sperm donation different from organ donation? If not, why do we pay for sperm and make it illegal to give an organ for money? Should there be a difference?[9]

Natural or Biological Father—Not Legal Father

Fathers' Rights

In 2005, "Sperm bank officials estimate[d] the number of children born to donors at about 30,000 a year, but because the industry is largely unregulated, no one really knows."[10] So, if a sperm donor is the biological father of the child produced by the AI, does the child have a right to a parent-child relationship? Will the child get financial support? Alternatively, will the donor have rights to a relationship with the child? Generally, sperm donors are required to sign consent forms giving up their paternal interest in any children resulting from the sperm donation. Also, the form contractually prevents him from having any legal responsibility to the children produced, including the obligation to pay child support.

What happens when a child is produced for the family with a donor, not the husband's sperm—who is the father? Generally, the law finds that the husband is the father of the child (and therefore the child is legitimate). While the industry has pretty loose regulations, most states give more rights when AI is conducted by a licensed doctor. What happens if the state's law requires the husband to sign a consent form, in part to help clarify these issues when the wife goes for AI treatments, but he fails to do so? Should this make a difference as to whether he is considered the father of any children that result from the treatments? Worse yet, if the couple later divorces, would he (the non-biological, but intended father) have to pay child support like a biological

---

8   See *The Genius Sperm Bank*, by David Plotz, Random House, 2006 for a good general history of the sperm banking industry.

9   In Iran it is legal to sell body organs because there is a shortage. Should such an argument justify sperm sales? "Human Organs for sale, legally in…which country?" Stephen J. Dubner, April 29, 2008. Freakonomics.com/2008/04/29/human-organs-for-sale-legally-in-which-country/

10   "Hello, I'm Your Sister. Our Father Is Donor 150," *New York Times*, November 20, 2005, p. 1.

father would—when he is not? These were the facts in the case of *Laura G. v. Peter G.*, where the court upheld that the "presumption of legitimacy of a child born during marriage was applicable to require defendant husband to pay child support for a child conceived by artificial insemination during the marriage, notwithstanding the absence of his written consent to the insemination procedure as required."

LAURA G. V. PETER G. (2007)
15 MISC.3D 164, 830 N.Y.S.2D 496, 2007 NY SLIP OP. 27011

Background: In divorce proceedings, child's law guardian moved that father be required to pay child support.

Holdings: 1—husband's failure to provide written consent to his wife's artificial insemination was not ground for relieving husband of his child support obligation, and (2) husband was equitably estopped form denying his paternity.

Motion Granted

Eugene E. Peckham, J.

This case began with submission of findings and judgment for an uncontested divorce in March 2006. The grounds for divorce stated in the complaint were based upon a separation agreement filed in the Delaware County Clerk's Office on November 12, 2004.

Upon review, that agreement contained the following provisions:

*"WHEREAS, the wife is currently expecting, but each of the parties acknowledges that the unborn child is not the biological child of the husband, but was conceived through a mutually agreed upon course of artificial insemination; and **2*

"WHEREAS, with respect to the unborn child the parties intend and agree that Peter G. shall in no way be deemed a 'responsible relative' in connection with any claim of reimbursement for monies expended by any government agency on behalf of either the unborn child, including after birth expenses, or Laura G., and he shall in no way be financially responsible in any way for said child or to Laura G. on behalf of that child." (Emphasis added.)

The complaint stated: "There are three children to this marriage: Connor...; Breanna...; Alyssa...." Alyssa is the unborn child referred to in the separation agreement.

Upon review of the papers submitted for the uncontested divorce, the court determined a law guardian should be appointed to protect the best interests of Alyssa. The law guardian submitted a "Memorandum of Law and Law Guardian's Recommendation." In that memorandum she argued in the alternative either that the defendant father should be deemed to be Alyssa's father because there was substantial compliance with the provisions of Domestic Relations Law § 73 or that the defendant should be required to pay child support because of equitable estoppel or implied agreement to the artificial insemination.

Domestic Relations Law § 73 provides as follows:

"1. Any child born to a married woman by means of artificial insemination performed by persons duly authorized to practice medicine and with the consent in writing of the woman and her husband, *166 shall be deemed the legitimate, natural child of the husband and his wife for all purposes.

"2. The aforesaid written consent shall be executed and acknowledged by both the husband and wife and the physician who performs the technique shall certify that he ha[s] rendered the service."

3. Certain facts in this case are not disputed. Defendant is vice-president of a bank (record at 140) and plaintiff is self-employed as a day-care worker at home (record at 37). The parties were married on December 9, 1995. After the first two children were born, Connor and Breanna, defendant had a vasectomy. Subsequently the parties discussed having a third child. In February or March 2004, defendant consulted a doctor about the possibility of reversing the vasectomy. After that consultation he decided not to have it done due to the "medical consequences." The doctor also told him there were "other avenues" to have a child and that his wife should consult her doctor and he went home and told his wife about it. (Record at 130–131, 198–199.)

On or about April 1, 2004, plaintiff called her doctor's office and spoke to his nurse and was given phone numbers for sperm banks. (Record at 23.) Thereafter plaintiff contacted the sperm bank and received a document entitled "Frozen Donor Semen Specimen Agreement." Both plaintiff and defendant signed the agreement and returned it to the sperm bank on or about April 7, 2004. (Law guardian mem, exhibit 2.) Next the plaintiff received catalogs of potential donors listing their characteristics such as hair and eye color. She picked a donor with characteristics similar to her husband. (Record at 69–70, 195–196.) Defendant saw her reviewing the catalogs. (Record at 189–190.) On or about May 2 and 3, 2004, she was inseminated by Dr. Agneshwar and subsequently became pregnant. (Record at 16.) Alyssa was born January 13, 2005. Defendant knew she was going to the doctor to be inseminated and took care of the other **3 two children while she did so. (Record at 204–205.) There was no written consent executed in the manner contemplated by Domestic Relations Law § 73.

After plaintiff became pregnant the parties' marital difficulties increased to the point that the separation agreement was signed on November 10, 2004. After the separation agreement was signed defendant moved out of the marital residence. (Record at 108.)

As previously stated, the complaint alleged there were three children of the marriage, which was denied in the answer. Just *167 before the uncontested divorce papers were submitted in March 2006, the parties entered into a stipulation dated March 9, 2006, which reaffirmed the separation agreement and then calculated defendant's obligation for child support based upon two children.

In a letter decision dated October 24, 2006, the court held that the provisions of the separation agreement purporting to absolve defendant from liability for child support for Alyssa were void as against public policy citing *Werther v Werther* (9 Misc 3d 1114[A], 2005 NY Slip Op 51543[U] [2005]).

A hearing was ordered limited to the issues of child support and paternity for Alyssa. That hearing was held on November 1, 2006 and briefs were submitted thereafter.

Clearly the public policy of New York in custody and support proceedings is that the paramount concern is the best interests of the child. (Domestic Relations Law §§ 70, 240; Matter of *Shondel J. v Mark D.*, 7 N.Y.3d 320 [2006].) The court's determination of the best interests of the child prevails over any agreement of the parties. "No agreement of the parties can bind the court to a disposition other than that which a weighing of all the factors involved shows to be in the child's best interests." (*Eschbach v Eschbach*, 56 NY2d 167, 171 [1982].) Similarly in Werther the court held:

> "In the context of child support, the Court must act as parens patriae, and retains jurisdiction to act in the child's best interests. Without question, a provision in an agreement eliminating a party's child support obligation is void as against public policy…. Accordingly, that portion of the agreement waiving [the] child support obligation is set-aside." (9 Misc 3d 1114[A], 2005 NY Slip Op 51543[U], *7; Matter of Perera v Perera, 251 AD2d 885 [3d Dept 1998].)

Three issues are presented for decision: (1) Is strict compliance with the provisions of Domestic Relations Law § 73 required? (2) If strict compliance is not required, has consent of defendant been proved by clear and convincing evidence? (3) Is defendant responsible to pay child support for Alyssa?

Is Strict Compliance with Domestic Relations Law § 73 Required?

In *Anonymous v Anonymous* (NYLJ, Jan. 18, 1991, at 21, col 6 [Sup Ct, NY County]), it was held that strict compliance with the statute was required. An earlier Appellate Division decision was to the contrary. (*168 State of New York ex rel. H. v P.*, 90 AD2d 434 [1st Dept 1982].) In State ex rel. *H. v P.* the husband had been determined to be sterile and the wife underwent artificial insemination on 10 occasions, became pregnant and a daughter was born. There was no statement as required by Domestic Relations Law § 73. When marital difficulties arose, the wife claimed the child was conceived "during a dalliance with an unnamed individual on a business trip to California" (at 435). The Court, relying in part on the presumption of legitimacy of a child born during marriage, rejected exclusive reliance on Domestic Relations Law § 73 and held the wife was estopped from denying the husband's paternity.

Alan Scheinkman, in discussing the Anonymous case in his Practice Commentaries to Domestic Relations Law § 73 says:**4

"The Anonymous court's insistence that there be strict compliance with Domestic Relations Law § 73 appears unduly rigid. Where it is clear that the father gave an oral consent or gave a written consent that was defective in form, there seems little reason to illegitimate the child because of a technical defect… In those situations, it seems inappropriate to allow a husband to evade his commitments to his wife and the child through a technical defect." (Alan Scheinkman, Practice Commentaries, McKinney's Cons Laws of NY, Book 14, Domestic Relations Law § 73, at 311–312.)

Scheinkman also says:

"In its opinion, the Anonymous court noted that the physician who had performed the insemination testified he had performed many inseminations and had never informed any of his patients as to the requirements of Domestic Relations Law § 73. The court wrote that it was apparent that the Legislature had relied upon physicians to advise their patients of the protections that the law would provide." (Practice Commentaries, supra at 311.)

However, physicians are not providing such advice to their patients. This is confirmed by the testimony of Dr. Agneshwar, the physician who performed plaintiff's insemination, who clearly had no idea of the statutory provisions and testified he had no forms for the husband or wife to consent to insemination. (Record at 17–18.)

Subsequent to the enactment of Domestic Relations Law § 73 the Legislature adopted amendments to sections 418 and 532 of the Family Court Act regarding use of DNA tests in paternity *169 and support proceedings. A provision of both those sections is the following: "No such test shall be ordered, however, upon a written finding by the court that it is not in the best interests of the child on the basis of res judicata, equitable estoppel or the presumption of legitimacy of a child born to a married woman." (Family Ct Act § 418 [a]; § 532 [a]; L 1990, ch 818, § 12; L 1997, ch 398, § 80.)

Both parties agree Alyssa was conceived by artificial insemination and so the court finds there is no need for a DNA test. (Cf. State ex rel. *H. v P.*, supra.) The clear implication of the amendments to sections 418 and 532 of the Family Court Act is that the written consent requirement of Domestic Relations Law § 73 does not apply in paternity and support proceedings where there is a presumption of legitimacy or an equitable estoppel. Since Alyssa was conceived and born during the marriage of the parties, the presumption is that she is the legitimate child of both parties. (Family Ct Act § 417; State ex rel. *H. v P.*, supra.) As will be seen later, equitable estoppel also is applicable to this case.

Neither the statute itself nor the legislative memoranda in the Bill Jacket indicate any requirement that the procedures in Domestic Relations Law § 73 are the only way to establish the legitimacy of a child born by artificial insemination. The fact that strict compliance is not required is demonstrated by the fact that the statute does not have a provision for filing anywhere the written consent set forth in the statute, nor is there any penalty on anyone for failing to follow the statute. (Mem of Attorney General Louis J. Lefkowitz, Bill Jacket, L 1974, ch 303, at 3–4; Assembly Introducer Mem in Support, L 1974, ch 303, at 18.) If the Legislature had intended to make the procedures in Domestic Relations Law § 73 the only way to provide for the legitimacy or support of a child born by artificial insemination it **5 could easily have included such enforcement procedures in the statute, but there are none.

The only conclusion that can be drawn from the legislative history of Domestic Relations Law § 73 and the amendments to Family Court Act §§ 418 and 532 is that consent of the husband can still be proved in the same manner as it was before the statute was passed. At common law a husband was required to support a child conceived by artificial insemination with third-party donor sperm and born during marriage with his consent.

There was no requirement of a writing to prove consent. (Matter of Gordon, 131 Misc 2d 823 [Sur Ct, Bronx County 1986].)

*170 This court agrees with Scheinkman that it is inappropriate to illegitimatize a child for lack of strict compliance with the requirements of Domestic Relations Law § 73. Where, as will be seen here, the husband has consented to the insemination procedure, he should not be allowed to deny support to the child that results.

It is held that strict compliance with the procedure set forth in Domestic Relations Law § 73 is not required and consent by the husband of a married woman to artificial insemination may be proved by other clear and convincing evidence.

Is There Clear and Convincing Proof of Consent by Defendant?

Plaintiff testified several times, both on direct and cross-examination, that the defendant absolutely agreed both to artificial insemination and to having a third child. (Record at 50–51, 62, 64, 67–68.) This is confirmed to some extent by the testimony of Nurse Glenn. (Record at 22–23, 31.)

Plaintiff's actions were not totally consistent, as she admits that she signed the separation agreement and a later stipulation with its provision that her husband was not responsible for the child. She explained this in her testimony as follows:

"Q: Okay. There was no provision in the separation agreement for any custody, joint custody or any kind of visitation, is there?

"A: He didn't want to be her father, he said at that point, so I said you can't make someone be a father so I wasn't going to push it. I couldn't fight him on it. I couldn't afford to fight him on it. I wasn't going to push it. I just let it go." (Record at 75, 83–84.)

Whether or not she agreed to the provisions of the separation agreement relating to Alyssa is not relevant in any event, because, as pointed out above, the court's determination of the best interests of the child override any agreement of the parents. (*Eschbach v Eschbach, supra; Werther v Werther, supra.*)

The court finds the testimony of plaintiff to be credible. The testimony of defendant, on the other hand, is not credible as it was evasive and contradictory.

Defendant took the position in his testimony that he felt the marriage was dysfunctional and that they needed to go to counseling before having another child. (Record at 98–99, 133, 185–188.) Yet he never demanded that they do so before having another child. (Record at 188, 192.) He also testified that he told his wife he definitely did not want a third child. (Record at *171 99–100.) Yet many of his other statements and actions contradict these assertions made in his testimony. He may have been reluctant to have a child, but, as his testimony shows, he vacillated, but never flat out refused.**6

First, he consulted a physician regarding possible reversal of his vasectomy and, when the doctor told him that his wife should see her doctor about other avenues to having a child, he reported that to his wife. (Record at 199.) Second, after plaintiff saw her doctor and presented the "Frozen Donor Semen Specimen Agreement" he signed it. (Law guardian mem, exhibit 2; record at 135–136.) He claims he signed under duress (record at 104), but nevertheless admits that he read the agreement before signing it. (Record at 134.) Third, he also signed the portion of the agreement for payment by credit card and he paid the bills out of their joint checking account. (Law guardian mem, exhibit 2; record at 78–79.) Fourth, after the agreement was returned he knew his wife was reviewing catalogs with donor characteristics and that she picked a donor with characteristics similar to his. (Record at 70–71, 154, 195–196.) Fifth, he knew when she went to the doctor's appointment to have the insemination performed (record at 140, 200–202) and he did not tell her not to do it. (Record at 201, 207.) He took care of the other two children while she was at the doctor. (Record at 205.) Sixth, after the insemination was performed, despite his objections, he continued to live with his wife and to sleep with her. (Record at 140–142.) Seventh, he read and signed the separation agreement that included the provision stating that Alyssa "was conceived through a mutually agreed upon course of artificial insemination." (Record at 166.) He was asked at least four times about whether there was a mutual agreement to the insemination and each time he evaded a direct answer to the question. (Record at 106, 139, 166–167, 180–181.) Lastly, after plaintiff became pregnant while they were living together and before they separated, he admitted on cross-examination that he assumed he would take the role of father and never told plaintiff he would not support the unborn child. (Record at 74, 176, 180.)

Plaintiff's testimony is supported by the testimony of Nurse Glenn and by the documentary evidence, the donor semen agreement and the separation agreement, both of which defendant admitted he read and signed. (Record at 134, 140–142.) As the vice-president of a bank (record at 148) the court must assume he understood what he read in the separation agreement and the frozen donor semen agreement. The court finds that Alyssa *172 "was conceived through a mutually agreed upon course of artificial insemination." Defendant repeatedly evaded answering directly as to whether that statement was true and correct, which must be held against him. Defendant's actions, vacillating though they may have been, implied consent to the artificial insemination and his wife testified credibly that he actually did consent. Since Alyssa was conceived and born during the parties' marriage by an agreed upon insemination the court holds the evidence is clear and convincing that she is the legitimate child of both plaintiff and defendant. (State ex rel. *H. v P.*, supra; Family Ct Act § 417; Domestic Relations Law § 73.)

Is Defendant Responsible to Pay Child Support for Alyssa?

An additional reason for holding defendant responsible to support Alyssa is the doctrine of equitable estoppel. The elements of equitable estoppel are whether there has been representation, reliance and detriment. As just stated by the Court of Appeals:

"The purpose of equitable estoppel is to preclude a person from asserting a right after having led another to form the reasonable belief that the right would not be asserted, and loss or prejudice to the other would result if the right were asserted. The law imposes the doctrine as a matter of fairness. Its purpose is to prevent someone from enforcing rights that would work injustice on the person against whom enforcement is sought and who, while justifiably relying on the opposing party's actions, has been misled into a detrimental change of position." **7 (Matter of *Shondel J. v Mark* D., supra at 326.)

Plaintiff testified that defendant was a very indecisive person and was also indecisive about having another child, but that he agreed to it.

"Q: Is it fair to say defendant did not want to have another child?
"A: He was up in the air. I don't know for sure that he said no. He was very indecisive.
"Q: Fair to say that he didn't say yes?
"A: He did say yes. He absolutely said yes, we will have the third child, absolutely.
"Q: When did he say that?
"A: Amongst our discussion to keep our marriage together" (record at 62, 64, 67).

*173 The fact of defendant's indecisiveness and equivocation is confirmed by his own inconsistent actions and testimony in at least the eight items discussed above. Particularly, this is shown by his evasion of an answer to the question of whether the insemination was mutually agreed upon. (Record at 106, 139, 166–167, 180–181.)

Thus it is clear to this court that plaintiff's testimony that he represented to her that he agreed to having another child by insemination is correct. She relied upon this representation by proceeding with the insemination, pregnancy and birth. The detriment in a legal sense is the birth of the child and the costs of Alyssa's support. "[P]aternity by estoppel is now secured by statute in New York (see Family Ct Act § 418 [a]; § 532 [a])" (Matter of *Shondel J. v Mark D.*, supra at 326).

The Court of Appeals also said in *Shondel J.* (at 330) "the issue does not involve the equities between the two adults; the case turns exclusively on the best interests of the child." It goes without saying that the best interest of Alyssa is to have a mother and a father who both love and support her, or, if that is not possible, at least a father who is obligated to provide child support for her. Defendant is estopped from denying his paternity of Alyssa.

Even if the decision is incorrect that defendant must be treated as Alyssa's father, he is still obligated to pay child support due to equitable estoppel. For example in Matter of *Campbell v Campbell* (149 AD2d 866 [3d Dept 1989]) the parties had two children. Subsequently, the father discovered that he was "medically incapable of fathering children" and petitioned to modify his child support (at 867). The Court said he "seeks to bastardize the children for the sole purpose of promoting his own self-interest in avoiding further support payments" and held that the petition to modify support was properly dismissed (id.).

In another unique case a woman who held herself out as a man entered into a marriage with another woman and subsequently they had two children by artificial insemination. She affixed her name to an agreement as the husband stating the children were hers. When the couple split up the court held the woman/husband was estopped and therefore liable for child support based upon her representations. (Matter of *Karin T. v Michael T.,* 127 Misc 2d 14 [Fam Ct, Monroe **8 County 1985].) In similar fashion defendant is estopped from refusing to pay child support as between him and his wife because she relied on his *174 representations to her detriment. (Domestic Relations Law § 240; Family Ct Act § 413; Matter of *Shondel J. v Mark D.,* supra.)

But he is also estopped because of his actions in relation to Alyssa and in her best interests. As previously set forth after plaintiff became pregnant and before they separated, defendant admitted that he would assume the role of father and did not say absolutely he would not support the child. (Record at 73–74, 176, 180.)

Most important is the relationship which has developed between Alyssa and defendant since her birth. Both parties testified she calls him "Daddy Pete." (Record at 55, 165.) Plaintiff also testified credibly in answer to questions posed to her on cross-examination:

"Q: Okay. But you say that defendant spends time with Alyssa?
"A: All the time.
"Q: Could you tell me how much time?
"A: Every day.
"Q: How much time every day?
"A: Whenever he's at the house. He is at the house all the time.
"Q: He's at your house?
"A: He comes in the door, 'Where's my hug, Alyssa?' Don't you *[referring to defendant]* dare lie. Every day.

"Q: Okay.

"A: He comes in her bedroom at night and helps put her to bed." (Record at 77.)

The Court of Appeals held in *Shondel J. v Mark D.* (supra at 327), "Where a child justifiably relies on the representations of a man that he is her father with the result that she will be harmed by the man's denial of paternity, the man may be estopped from asserting that denial." From plaintiff's testimony it is clear a loving relationship has developed between Alyssa and defendant. Alyssa will be harmed by termination of that relationship. The Court of Appeals stated in Shondel J. that the Appellate Divisions have repeatedly held that where a parent-child relationship has developed the doctrine of equitable estoppel prevents the father from denying the relationship and from refusing to pay child support. (Matter of *Sarah S. v James T.*, 299 AD2d 785 [3d Dept 2002]; *175 Matter of *Jennifer W. v Steven X.*, 268 AD2d 800 [3d Dept 2000]; *Brian B. v Dionne B.*, 267 AD2d 188 [2d Dept 1999]; *Mancinelli v Mancinelli*, 203 AD2d 634 [3d Dept 1994]; **9 *Campbell v Campbell, supra.*) It is held that defendant is estopped in the best interests of Alyssa and must pay child support for her.

The bottom line is that defendant may have been reluctant to have another child, but he vacillated and never clearly and unequivocally said "no" to his wife. In her testimony she said he said "yes," and the court finds that testimony believable. Defendant has now made a commitment to his wife and child Alyssa. That commitment must be honored. Since he participated in bringing Alyssa into this world, however reluctantly, he should be held responsible as her father for child support.

Defendant stated his income is $63,000 per year (stipulation dated Mar. 8, 2006), which after subtracting Social Security and child support paid for another child of $60 every two weeks, leaves parental income of $56,620. Plaintiff's income is $20,000 per year (stipulation dated Mar. 8, 2006), which is $18,470 after Social Security. Total parental income after Social Security is $75,090. Defendant's share of the income is 75% and plaintiff's is 25%. Child support for three children at the Child Support Standards Act percentage of 29% is $21,776 of which defendant's portion is $16,332 or $314.07 per week. It is therefore ordered that defendant shall pay to plaintiff the sum of $314.07 every week for child support for Connor, Breanna and Alyssa.

CHILDREN'S RIGHTS

In the United States, the sperm bank industry has historically kept sperm donors' identities secret. As a result of anonymity, children born from sperm donor fathers may never know who their father is. Is this fair? The adoption industry has moved to make its records available to adoptive children after a certain age. Should the same apply for sperm donor children? In Canada, "Olivia Pratten wanted to know the identity of her sperm-donor father case," but was prevented from doing so because the clinic destroyed the records. In 2008, she filed a class action (on behalf of other similarly situated donor children) to prevent destruction of records and require all donors be identified. While the B.C. Supreme Court agreed with her, its Court of Appeal overruled that decision on appeal. In its ruling, the Appeals court wrote, "'There are many non-donor offspring who do not know their family history or the identity of their biological father because of decisions taken by others, or because of the circumstances of their conception,' the ruling said. However desirable it may be that persons have access to information about their biological origins, Ms. Pratten has not established that such access has been recognized as so 'fundamental' that it is entitled to independent constitutionally protected status under the Charter."[11]

The article, "Hello, I'm Your Sister. Our father Is Donor 150,"[12] refers to the Donor Sibling Registry, "a web site that is helping to open a new chapter in the oldest form of assisted reproductive technology."[13] The site allows potential donor half siblings to locate each other and allows donors to identify themselves as looking for potential children created from their sperm (this is a very small part of the site). The popularity of the site (for siblings who call themselves "diblings") "speaks to the sustained power of biological ties."[14] Children are curious, "even if all the information about the father that is known is his code number used by the bank for identification purposes and the fragments of personal information provided in his donor profile."[15] Also, "Donor-conceived siblings, who sometimes describe themselves as 'lopsided' or 'half-adopted' can provide clues to make each other feel more whole, even if only in the form of physical details."[16] Mothers also look for each other when they share donors. One mother even "sent a leftover vial of sperm to another mother who wanted to have a second child and found there was no 401 sperm left to buy."[17] As the half-donor siblings and their mothers find each other are they extending the definition of family?

The donor internet site also allowed at least one donor-child to locate his donor father, who did not waive his contractual anonymity. By sending a DNA sample to a commercial genetic database service, a 15-year-old boy was able to get a Y chromosome match to just two men (who both seemed to be related, with different spellings of similar names). Because his mother had received the donor's birth place and date from the sperm bank, the boy paid another online service, OmniTrace.com, to research a list of all people born on that date. He then cross referenced the two lists and found one man with that last name. The results of the son and donor father meeting were kept confidential.[18] Should the donor father be able to sue for breach of contract? If so, who? Is it the donor son, the donor mother, the sperm bank? Or should donors expect that

---

11   http://qparent.com/2012/12/03/canadian-provincial-court-of-appeal-reverses-2011-decision-on-sperm-donor-disclosure/, "Parent, Canadian Court Reverses 2011 Decision on Sperm Donor Disclosure," Jennifer Tribe, December 3, 2012.

12   "Hello, I'm Your Sister. Our Father is Donor 150," *New York Times*, November 20, 2005, p. 1.

13   Ibid., p.1.

14   Ibid., p. 20.

15   Ibid., pp. 1, 20.

16   Ibid., p. 20.

17   Ibid.

18   "Found on the Web, with DNA: A Boy's Father," Rob Stein, *Washington Post*, November 13, 2005, p. A9.

children created by their DNA might find them? What if the child has a medical condition and needs to know her father's genetics for treatment? Should courts allow donor children to know their donor father's identity?

Some sperm banks are creating a system where the identification of the father could be made available to the donor child when they reach 18 years of age. Does this seem fair? Is it fair that the sperm from such fathers costs more? Does this make certain sperm banks even more elitist?

Does it make a difference if the identity of a sperm donor is known to the woman? If it is a coworker? A friend? Generally, anonymous donors have no obligations as long as the sperm is administered to the woman by a medical doctor. Known donors, however, generally do not have the same protections.

Should donor-created children at least be allowed to know their donor's medical history? In March 2015, Utah became the first state to allow sperm-donor created children access to their donor-father's medical histories.[19] If other states in the U.S. continue to refuse this under the theory of anonymity, should the law require donors to have better medical testing? "Generally, donors are tested only for sexually transmitted diseases. There are no laws requiring testing for genetic disorders or requiring that donors—usually in their 20s at the time of donation—update medical information as they age and inherited diseases may surface."[20]

POSTHUMOUSLY CONCEIVED CHILDREN

What happens if a man dies and his sperm has been frozen? If he leaves a will, courts generally treat sperm like they do other property (think stamp collection) and distribute it under the terms of the will.[21] Is sperm the same as property or is it something else? Some courts have treated this as something different—pre-life—or even as persons for whom "custody" must be determined.

Sometimes, when a man is anticipating chemotherapy, other severe medical treatments, or heading off to war, he may deposit sperm so that it will not be impacted by the treatments or other exposure (or perhaps in anticipation that he may not return). If he survives no legal problems arise. What if he dies? Are children considered illegitimate if they are created after their father's death?

Perhaps the case of *Astrue v. Capato* **132 S.Ct. 2021** (2012), most clearly illustrates the burden ART places on today's courts that are "wrestl[ing] with how to interpret a law written in 1939 and apply it to modern technology never imagined back then." In March of 2012, the U.S.

---

19 In what may help determine a genetic marker for autism, three of six families who used the same donor had children that were autistic and one more of the children was showing signs but had not been diagnosed. "Autistic children linked to same sperm donor", Randi Kaye, *CNN*, April 2, 2008. http://www.cnn.com/2008/HEALTH/conditions/04/02/autism.sperm.donor.index.html?eref=rss_us

20 "Fertility answers raise new questions", Michael Ollove, *The Washington Post*, April 14, 2015, P E1.

21 *Hecht v. Kane*, 59 Cal. Rptr. 2d 222 (Ct. App. 1996), a man left his frozen sperm to his girlfriend after he committed suicide and his family objected.

Supreme Court heard arguments on a case where the husband, Robert Capato, was diagnosed with esophageal cancer, so he froze his sperm before the operation.[22] This was done because cancer treatments may damage sperm. The treatment was unsuccessful and he died. In making his sperm donation, Robert wrote a note, clarifying that "this is my child even if it's conceived later."[23] His wife Karen "carried out the couple's plan to conceive using Robert's sperm… [and] [i]n 2003, she gave birth to twins and filed for survivors' benefits for the children based on her late husband's Social Security taxes."[24] The Social Security Administration denied the claim, contending that because the twins could not inherit under Florida state law, where the couple lived, the children were ineligible for survivors' benefits. A federal appeals court in Philadelphia disagreed, saying the 1939 Social Security Act confers benefits on all biological offspring of a married couple. The Supreme Court agreed to review the decision.

According to the government's case, "since 1940, the Social Security Administration has determined a child's eligibility for survivors benefits based on whether that child can inherit under state law." The Capatos' attorneys argued that the twins were surely their "'children' as they were biologically related to the parents and since they were a married couple, the children born to them were theirs." At the hearings, "the Justices Antonin Scalia and Anthony Kennedy both raised an issue not before the court—whether a child conceived in vitro can be properly called a survivor since the child never lived with or was dependent on the deceased."[25] The Capatos argued that the statute was intended to apply to all legitimate children, even though it does not use the word biological, because that was what the majority of children were at that time, so that was what Congress intended. If that was true, Justice Ruth Bader Ginsburg inferred, "[b]ut at the time this statute was written, 'Wasn't it also understood that the marriage ends when a parent dies?'"[26] When it appeared that the Court would defer to the agency in its ruling, the Capatos' attorney said, "The problem is that we're dealing with new technologies that Congress… wasn't anticipating."[27,28] At the hearing, Justice Sonia Sotomayor also asked, "'What happens if the decedent is the mother?'"… "'Does marriage matter only if it's the father?'"[29]

22 http://www.npr.org/2012/03/19/148935151/justices-weigh-ivf-technology-against-1939-law, Nina Totenberg for NPR's All Things Considered, March 19, 2012.

23 Ibid., but under state law it did not have bearing.

24 Ibid.

25 http://www.npr.org/2012/03/19/148935151/justices-weigh-ivf-technology-against-1939-law, Nina Totenberg for NPR's All Things Considered, March 19, 2012.

26 Ibid.

27 Quoting Rothfeld, the Capatos' lawyer.

28 "The transcript of Monday morning's oral argument included, in alphabetical order, the words 'illegitimate,' 'insemination,' 'marital,' 'offspring,' 'reproduced,' 'reproduction,' 'reproductive,' 'sperm,' 'unmarried,' 'wedlock,' 'wife' and 'wives.' And that's not even getting into Justice Sonia Sotomayor's description of 'biological input' into the procreative process." http://articles.washingtonpost.com/2012-03-19/opinions/35448169_1_karen-capato-capato-twins-sperm-donor. "Supreme Court conceives of life after death," Dana Milbank, *Washington Post*, March 19, 2012.

29 Ibid.

Two months later, the court denied the Capatos' request, deferring to the SSA. The SSA looks to the state law on intestate inheritance (without a will). The SSA recognizes only those children who would be heirs, which the twins were not, because they were not born while their father was alive (they were conceived nine months after his death and presumably born a full year and a half after his death). "The case is now going back to the Court of Appeals to determine domicile—where the family is considered to have lived—at the time of Robert Capato's death. While Florida's law does not permit posthumously conceived children to inherit, other states have more flexible laws—leaving open the possibility that they could eventually wind up with the benefits that clearly would have been theirs had they been conceived before their father died."[30]

The *Capato* case is in keeping with past cases that seemed to say that it is fine to create posthumous children, but do not expect the government/tax payers to be financially responsible for them. Do you agree, or should all biological children be considered children under the broad modern definition of children?[31] If so, should there be a time limit on when the woman must use the sperm? Scientifically, the sperm could be kept frozen forever, as long as the storage charges are paid. Is there an ethical issue?

MISTAKES WERE MADE

In this fast growing industry, with unknown numbers of children being created, coupled with its general lack of regulation, mistakes occur. A sampling from 2014 alone shows the extremes:

In Ohio, a lesbian couple sued a Chicago-area fertility clinic for "wrongful birth", because it sent Black sperm instead of White sperm. Although they have a healthy 2-year-old baby girl, the couple sued because their daughter "is already facing racial prejudice in Uniontown, a community of 3,300 people—97 percent of whom are white."[32] The couple discovered the error when they "decided to reserve more sperm from that donor so Zinkon could one day have a child related to the one Cramblett was carrying." It was simple human error; the sperm bank employee has misread the handwritten order. "The clinic allegedly sent an apology letter and a refund for the wrong batch."[33]

---

30   http://www.npr.org/2012/03/19/148935151/justices-weigh-ivf-technology-against-1939-law, Nina Totenberg for NPR's All Things Considered, March 19, 2012.
31   Contrast *Capato* to *Gillett-Netting v. Barnhart*, 371 F.3d 593 (9th Cir. 2004), where the court held that posthumously conceived children are children under the Social Security Act.
32   "White women sues sperm bank after she mistakenly gets black donor's sperm", By Lindsey Bever, *The Washington Post*, October 2, 2014. http://www.washingtonpost.com/news/morning-mix/wp/2014/10/02/white-woman-sues-sperm-bank-after-she-mistakenly-gets-black-donors-sperm/
33   "'Jennifer was crying, confused and upset,' according to the court papers. 'All of the thought, care and planning that she and Amanda had undertaken to control their baby's parentage had been rendered meaningless. In an instant, Jennifer's excitement and anticipation of her pregnancy was replaced with anger, disappointment and fear.' [Her] attorney, Thomas Intili, told NBC News his client "did not encounter any African-American people until she entered college. Not all her friends and family members are racially sensitive." Ibid

"Was your child fathered by Thomas Lippert?", is a website a mother created when she discovered that her daughter was not fertilized by her husband's sperm during their fertility treatments and who wanted to encourage "others to have their children tested to... avoid half-siblings... potentially engaging in romantic relationships, as well as for family medical history." [34] After discovering the unmatched DNA when doing some genetic testing for genealogy purposes, they then determined that the daughter's biological father was Thomas Lippert who worked at the sperm bank the couple had used for fertility treatments. The clinic had previously closed, but it is believed that Lippert switched out his sperm for her husband's. Lippert is a felon, having served two years in prison for "kidnapping a college student, keeping her in a box and performing electrical experiments on her."

2. EGG DONATION

Donations

Egg donation programs have been around since the 1980s. Any college newspaper likely contains ads to buy eggs for $5000, even $10,000. In New York, AI centers advertise for egg donors at the movies. Donors generally must be between 21–34 years old.[35] Higher SAT scores, Ivy League schools, even race or height might substantially increase the basic fee. Is this modern eugenics? As discussed above, donating eggs, similar to sperm donation, could raise some psychological issues for any children produced from the eggs. Unlike the sperm industry, egg donation involves a complicated medical procedure. As a result, egg donors are often limited to six donations.[36] But "egg donation isn't an easy way to make a quick buck. It's a time consuming medical procedure, with risks. Donors will spend weeks taking fertility drugs. Medications can cause hot flashes, headaches and vision problems. Donors also have to have frequent blood tests and ultrasounds. And it takes several days to recover after the eggs are harvested."[37] During that time, donors are advised not to have sex as they may be highly susceptible to pregnancy.

---

34 "DNA tests show felon used own sperm at fertility clinic", Nathan Giannini, July 10, 2014, *Newsy*, July 10, 2014, http://www.newsy.com/videos/dna-test-shows-felon-used-own-sperm-at-fertility-clinic/ Sometimes called, "accidental incest," some are concerned about the industry's failure to limit the number of children a donor can produce children while could occur when unknowing diblings meet. "Fertility answers raise new questions," Michael Ollove, *The Washington Post*, April 14, 2015, P E1.

35 http://www.cbsnews.com/2100-500165_162-4517178.html, "More Women Selling their Eggs," CBSNews.com, February 11, 2009.

36 "[P]robably [there was] at least a 40 percent increase in the number of people who are donating eggs... absolutely... it's due to people looking for money in the poor economy." Quoting the Center for Egg Options' Nancy Block. Ibid.

37 "That's a lot of money," Block says. "It's great for school. It's great for the mortgage. It's great... great to help their families out. And you know, it's... it's something that they feel good about." http://www.cbsnews.com/2100-500165_162-4517178.html, "More Women Selling their Eggs," CBSNews.com, February 11, 2009.

Compensation

Like the sperm industry, the egg donation industry pays for the "donation." When the U.S. economy entered a recession in the last few years, the number of women donating eggs increased substantially. Is this any different from the people who sell plasma?[38,39] Even with psychological screening, how can the center determine what the woman's future attachment to any child produced might be? (Like sperm donors, egg donors must sign away any legal right to children produced.)

SEX SELECTION, OR MORE?

Via two methods, potential parents can determine the sex of their future children by removing a single cell from a three-day-old embryo. "Only embryos of the desired sex are implanted into the womb."[40] "[U]sing techniques developed to help couples who are infertile or at risk for having babies with genetic diseases, some clinics are offering the techniques to couples with no medical reasons."[41] Should parents have the right to choose—after all, they are paying for it? Or is this one step further toward designer babies where parents can pick many traits, such as eye and hair color.[42] While nothing is perfect, what happens if the wrong sex arrives? Can the parents return the child? Recently, deaf potential parents in Maryland IV clinics have been requesting "deaf" eggs. Is this different?

EGG FREEZING

In 2012, the American Society for Reproductive Medicine[43] removed its "experimental" recommendation for egg freezing[44] and although the group does not recommend it for "elective use",

---

38   Ibid.

39   Contrast this to England where egg donors got a "pay raise" in April 20, 2012, from £250 to £750 per cycle; so many egg donations were made that the historic waiting lists were eliminated (attributed also to the poor economy). "IVF waiting lists down as egg donors get 'pay' rise: Surge in hard-up women offering to sell their eggs for £750 due to recession,'" *Daily Mail* online, July 17, 2012, http://www.dailymail.co.uk/health/article-2174846/Surge-hard-women-offering-sell-eggs.html

40   "A Boy for You, a Girl, for Me: Technology Allows Choice," Rob Stein, *Washington Post*, December 14, 2004, p. 1.

41   Ibid.

42   Ibid., p. 15.

43   The ASRM develops standards for fertility clinics in the U.S.

44   The group won't recommend the treatment for elective use, however, until more research is conducted. The American College of Obstetricians and Gynecologists endorsed the move, emphasizing that women should not rely on the procedure "for the sole purpose of circumventing reproductive aging." "How fear fuels the business of egg freezing", Danielle Paquette. *The Washington Post*, March 6, 2015, http://www.washingtonpost.com/business/economy/how-fear-fuels-the-business-of-egg-freezing/2015/03/06/87fd068c-c294-11e4-9271-610273846239_story.html

the request for the procedure has doubled since then.[45] Elective egg freezing for non-medical reasons[46] is now becoming a heavily marketed industry, especially for working women who are delaying childbearing (or even relationships) for their career.[47] A typical round of egg-freezing costs about $10,000, with an additional $500 or more in fees each year for storage. Two rounds are usually necessary to harvest about 20 eggs, which is ideal. Capitalizing on this, a company created in 2013, EggBanxx is the first service (they serve as a middleman between the provider and the client) to offer financing to women interested in egg freezing. For selected guests, they hold parties to raise the idea that include speeches by experts in the field. After attending one such session, a 38-year-old woman at an "egg freezing party" in Beverly Hills looked like she would use the $30,000 she had "tucked away over decades" for a down payment on her house for the procedure. Some question the ethics of this. Once you pay your fees, there is no guarantee of a baby. Indeed, the older the egg banker, the lower the likelihood of success.[48]

In employment, "[e]gg freezing has even been described as a key to 'leveling the playing field' between men and women: Without the crushing pressure of a ticking biological clock, women have more freedom in making life choices." Author Emma Rosenblum wrote "Not since the birth control pill has a medical technology had such potential to change family and career planning." Or, is this "a ploy to entice women to sell their souls to their employer, sacrificing childbearing years for the promise of promotion?"[49] Does this sound like a great job perk? In October 2014, Apple and Facebook began to offer a new employee benefit: female employees could freeze their eggs and the companies would pay up to $20,000 towards the expense of the (non-medical) procedure.[50] But does this send a message that being a mom is incompatible with being a valued employee?

---

45   "Perk up Facebook and Apple now pay for women to freeze eggs", Danielle Friedman, ABCNews, October 14, 2014. http://www.nbcnews.com/news/us-news/perk-facebook-apple-now-pay-women-freeze-eggs-n225011.

46   For non-medical use, as to be distinguished for freezing prior to medical treatments for cancer etc.

47   China bans single women from freezing their eggs; only married couples are allowed and only under limited circumstances. China claims the policy is to prevent trafficking of the eggs. In 2013, a popular Chinese actress admitted traveling to the U.S. to freeze some of her eggs, "as a backup plan". "The world at a glance…" *The Week*, August 14, 2015, p. 9.

48   Some medical experts argue that it will take 10 years to determine the success rates of the procedure including the impacts on the child's health. Shady Grove Fertility in Rockville, Maryland, the largest fertility clinic in the country, has on average up to 3,750 frozen eggs freezing on any given day and has a "success rate defined as a 20-week gestation period or a birth, for elective procedures" at about 40 percent but it is significantly lower for women closer to 40. "How fear fuels the business of egg freezing," Danielle Paquette. *The Washington Post*, March 6, 2015, http://www.washingtonpost.com/business/economy/how-fear-fuels-the-business-of-egg-

49   "Perk up Facebook and Apple now pay for women to freeze eggs", Danielle Friedman, ABCNews, October 14, 2014. http://www.nbcnews.com/news/us-news/perk-facebook-apple-now-pay-women-freeze-eggs-n225011.

50   Ibid.

3. IN VITRO FERTILIZATION

In vitro fertilization is when the ovum (egg) is fertilized outside of the woman's body. The complicated medical procedure involves a doctor removing the ova and placing it in a medium where it can be fertilized.[51] This embryo is then implanted into another woman's uterus (or back into the egg donor). Before it is implanted, should this embryo be considered property? If so, how should it be divided if the intending couple divorces? Some courts have treated embryos as something different than sperm—pre-life, or even persons for whom "custody" must be determined. The case of *Davis v. Davis*, was one of the first cases involving the disposition of the cryogenically preserved product of in vitro fertilization (IVF), commonly referred to as "frozen embryos," created by a husband and wife who were divorcing.[52] The appellee, Junior Lewis Davis, wanted the frozen embryos destroyed. His soon-to-be-ex-wife, Mary Sue, wanted control of the embryos "with the intent to have them transferred to her own uterus, in a post-divorce effort to become pregnant."[53] Eventually, she remarried, but wanted to use the embryos to donate to another infertile couple to honor all of her years of fertility treatments. The lower court, "[b]ased on its determination that the embryos were 'human beings' from the moment of fertilization, awarded 'custody' to Mary Sue Davis and directed that she 'be permitted the opportunity to bring these children to term through implantation.'" The court of appeals reversed, finding that Junior Davis had a "constitutionally protected right not to beget a child where no pregnancy has taken place," and holding that "there is no compelling state interest to justify ordering implantation against the will of either party."[54] Thus, in the absence of a contract, the court uses its judgment to balance the interests involved. While the lower court treated the embryos like children and determined custody, the appellate court held that if one party did not want to have the embryos used, they should not be. Is this fair?

Courts are split on how to resolve these cases. Some use the contract approach, where contracts are enforced as long as they do not violate public policy. One state (Iowa) uses the mutual consent approach: the courts rule that neither can use the embryos without the consent of the other (including donation, use for research, or destroyed), thus giving each an equal say. Finally, some states use a balancing approach; if there is no contract, the court must balance the interests involved. Which approach does the Pennsylvania court use in *Reber v. Reiss*[55] and what is the result?

---

51 The doctor who pioneered this technology and won a Nobel Prize for it called the medium, "'a magic culture fluid.'" Obituary of Robert G. Edwards, 87, "Nobel Prize winner's research helped lead to the birth of the first 'test tube' baby," R. O. Stein, *Washington Post*, April 11, 2013. His Nobel Prize was condemned by a Vatican official.
52 *Davis v. Davis*, 842 S.W.2d 588 (Tenn. 1992).
53 Ibid.
54 Ibid.
55 http://scholar.google.com/scholar_case?case=10257709054642909486&hl=en&as_sdt=6&as_vis=1&oi=scholarr

BRET HOWARD REBER, APPELLANT V. ANDREW LYNN REISS
42 A.3D 1131 (2012) PA SUPER 86

Superior Court of Pennsylvania
Decided: April 11, 2012

BEFORE: PANELLA, LAZARUS, and STRASSBURGER, JJ.*

Bret Howard Reber (Husband) appeals from the final divorce decree and order of equitable distribution in which the trial court awarded Andrea Lynn Reiss (Wife) the frozen pre-embryos[1] created from Husband's sperm and Wife's eggs. Upon review, we affirm.

Husband and Wife were married on October 12, 2002. The trial court summarized the relevant facts as follows (footnotes omitted by the author).

In November 2003, Wife, at the age of 36, was diagnosed with breast cancer. As a result of the diagnosis and proposed recommended cancer treatments, the parties were advised to undergo in vitro fertilization ("IVF") to preserve Wife's ability to conceive a child. To accommodate the IVF process, Wife deferred the commencement of her cancer treatment for several months. In February and March 2004, Husband and Wife underwent the IVF process resulting in the production of thirteen pre-embryos using Husband's sperm and Wife's eggs.

Following fertilization, the pre-embryos were then cryopreserved and presently remain frozen and stored with Reproductive Science Institute of Suburban Philadelphia, P.C. ("RSI").

After undergoing the IVF process, Wife proceeded with extensive breast cancer treatments including two surgeries, eight rounds of chemotherapy and 37 rounds of radiation. Wife has undergone testing with regard to her ability to have children since her recovery from cancer and testified that she "was lead [sic] to believe that I cannot have children myself as I am."

On December 28, 2006, Husband filed a Complaint in Divorce. Husband subsequently developed a relationship with another woman and on January 18, 2008, approximately 18 months after he and Wife separated, Husband's biological son was born with this other women [sic]. Husband testified that this child was conceived intentionally and that he intends to have more children.

Wife, now age 44, has no children. Wife seeks all thirteen pre-embryos for implantation. The parties agree, as does the [trial] court, that the pre-embryos are marital property subject to equitable distribution.

Husband filed an Amended Complaint in Divorce on July 7, 2008. Service of the Complaint was accepted on January 26, 2009. Husband filed an Affidavit under Section 3301(d) on July 23, 2008. The marriage of the parties is irretrievably broken and the parties have lived separate and apart for a period in excess of two years.

[Husband] filed a Motion for the Appointment of a Special Master on January 27, 2009. Master Lynn Snyder was appointed on February 9, 2009 and held a preliminary conference on February 23, 2009. Master Snyder held a settlement conference on May 14, 2009. The case did not settle and a certificate of trial readiness was filed on May 14, 2009. The trial was conducted on February 22, 2010 before Master Snyder.

On August 11, 2010, Master Snyder filed an Amended Report and Recommendation addressing the distribution of the parties' pre-embryos. [That report provided, in relevant part, that "the pre[-]embryos be awarded to Husband, who shall direct RSI that the pre-embryos be destroyed and discarded forthwith." Master's Amended Report, 8/11/2010, at 18.] Wife filed one Exception to the Master's Amended Report on August 25, 2010, [which related to the disposition of the pre-embryos]. Wife filed a Brief in Support of Exceptions on October 20, 2010. Husband filed a Brief in Response to [Wife's] Brief in Support of Wife's Exceptions on November 3, 2010. On November 10, 2010, the [trial court] heard oral argument on Wife's exception.

Trial Court Opinion, 5/6/2011, at 1–3 *(citations and footnotes omitted by the author)*.

After argument, the trial court concluded that while "ordinarily the party wishing to avoid procreation should prevail, in our balancing of the facts unique to this case, we find that Wife's inability to achieve biological parenthood without the use of the pre-embryos is an interest which outweighs Husband's desire to avoid procreation." Accordingly, the trial court entered a final decree and awarded the pre-embryos to Wife as part of the order of equitable distribution. Final Decree, 5/6/2011, at 3 (unnumbered). Husband filed a timely notice of appeal and both Husband and the trial court complied with Pa.R.A.P.1925.

On appeal, Husband presents numerous issues for review. The primary focus for Husband is that the trial court erred in finding that Wife's interests in procreating outweighed Husband's interests to avoid unwanted procreation....*(omissions on review by author)*

First, we point out, and both parties agree, that the contested disposition of frozen pre-embryos in the event of divorce is an issue of first impression in Pennsylvania. The cryopreservation of pre-embryos presents novel legal issues, "primarily because of the potential for the passage of several years between fertilization and later transfer and subsequent birth of the child." Wilder, supra. In this case, Husband and Wife have separated and now disagree on whether the pre-embryos should be awarded to Wife for implantation or be awarded to Husband for either donation to research or destruction.

In determining who should receive these pre-embryos, we find guidance in the case law from our sister states that have addressed similar issues. These jurisdictions have conducted three types of analyses: the contractual approach, the contemporaneous mutual consent approach, and the balancing approach.

Some states first look to any prior agreements between the parties regarding the disposition of cryopreserved pre-embryos. See Kass v. Kass, 696 N.E.2d 174 (N.Y.1998); Roman v. Roman, 193 S.W.3d 40 (Tex.2006); In re Marriage of Dahl & Angle, 194 P.3d 834, 841 (Or.Ct.App.2008). In all three cases, the husband and wife signed a consent form where they agreed that in the event of death or divorce, any cryopreserved pre-embryos would be destroyed or donated to research. All three courts held that such an agreement was enforceable and did not violate public policy.

When considering a similar issue, the Supreme Court of Massachusetts came out differently. See A.Z. v. B.Z., 725 N.E.2d 1051 (Mass.2000). In that case, the husband and wife utilized IVF and had twins. Prior to undergoing IVF, they filled in the portion of a consent form that provided that should the parties "separate," the wife would attain possession of any cryopreserved pre-embryos. The husband and wife subsequently separated and the wife wanted to use their cryopreserved pre-embryos for herself to have more children. Husband objected. The Supreme Court concluded that husband and wife never intended the agreement to be binding as an agreement between the two of them, the term "separation" is legally distinguishable from "divorce," and the consent form was ambiguous. Id. at 1056–7. Thus, the Court declined to enforce the agreement.

Furthermore, the Supreme Court of Massachusetts opined in dictum that "even had the husband and the wife entered into an unambiguous agreement between themselves regarding the disposition of the frozen pre-embryos, [they] would not enforce an agreement that would compel one donor to become a parent against his or her will." Id. at 1057. Enforcement of such a contract against the will of one party, the Supreme Court concluded, would violate public policy. Id. at 1058.

The Supreme Court of Iowa applied the contemporaneous mutual consent model. See In re Marriage of Witten, 672 N.W.2d 768 (Iowa 2003). In that case, the informed consent agreement allowed for the distribution of the pre-embryos only upon consent and agreement of both parties. At trial, wife wanted custody of the pre-embryos for implantation in herself or a surrogate. Husband wanted them to be donated to another couple. The Iowa court concluded that it violated public policy to enforce judicially an "agreement between a couple regarding their future family and reproductive choices." Id. at 782 (emphasis in original). The Court then held that the best approach in this case was to require the two parties to devise a new, contemporaneous agreement,[5] with the party opposing destruction responsible for storage fees. Id. at 783.

A third approach is for the court to balance the interests of the parties. The first state to do this was Tennessee. See Davis v. Davis, 842 S.W.2d 588 (Tenn.1992). In that case, the husband and wife pursued fertility treatments for many years prior to the creation of the frozen pre-embryos at issue. Upon divorce, the parties disputed who controlled the pre-embryos. The wife wanted to donate them to another infertile individual for use and husband wanted to discard them.[6] The Supreme Court of Tennessee determined that a proper analysis required it to "weigh the interests of each party to the dispute. in order to resolve that dispute in a fair and responsible manner." Id. at 591. The husband testified that he was "vehemently opposed to fathering a child that would not live with both parents" due to his own parents' history of divorce. Id. at 604. He was also opposed to donating the pre-embryos to another couple whose marriage might end in divorce.

On the other hand, wife wanted to donate them to another couple because otherwise she would have the "burden of knowing that the lengthy IVF procedures she underwent were futile." Id. The Supreme Court of Tennessee used a balancing approach and concluded that husband's interest outweighed wife's in this case, and further noted that "[t]he case would be closer if [wife] were seeking to use the pre-embryos herself, but only if she could not achieve parenthood by any other reasonable means." Id.

When confronted with a similar issue, New Jersey also applied a balancing approach. In J.B. v. M.B., 783 A.2d 707 (N.J.2001), the wife utilized IVF and had given birth during the course of the marriage. When the parties separated, the husband wanted control over the frozen pre-embryos for use by a surrogate. The wife wanted the pre-embryos to be discarded. The Supreme Court concluded that, in this instance, wife's right not to procreate or be forced into parenthood outweighed husband's right to procreate where husband could still procreate without wife's involvement (the fertility issues which led to the couple's use of IVF in the first place were due to issues associated with the wife). Id. at 717. Notably, one justice wrote a concurring opinion stating that "the same principles that compel the outcome in this case would permit an infertile party to assert his or her right to use a pre[-]embryo against the objections of the other party, if such use were the only means of procreation." Id. at 720 (Verniero, J. concurring).

In this case, we need not decide whether to adopt one approach or another. Both the master and the trial court applied the balancing approach because neither party had signed the portion of the consent form related to the disposition of the pre-embryos in the event of divorce or death of one party. Also, it was quite obvious that Husband and Wife could not come to a contemporaneous mutual agreement regarding the pre-embryos. Accordingly, we agree that the balancing approach is the most suitable test. Nonetheless, Husband argues that the trial court should have enforced a provision in the consent form that the pre-embryos would be destroyed after three years. Husband's Brief at 10. We disagree.

Prior to undergoing IVF, Husband and Wife signed a form entitled Informed Consent for Cryopreservation and Storage of Embryos. Wife signed as the Patient and Husband signed as the Partner. The form provided that the "[m]aximum duration of embryos storage for each group or partial group of embryos is not to exceed three years." Informed Consent, p. 2.

The section of the informed consent regarding the duration of storage cannot be read as an agreement between Husband and Wife to destroy the pre-embryos at the end of three years; rather, it is an agreement between the two of them and RSI about the storage of the pre-embryos. Furthermore, the contract also provided that RSI would send a notice of intent to destroy the pre-embryos via certified mail when it came time to destroy them. Both Husband and Wife testified that they had not received such notice. Accordingly, Husband had no reasonable expectation that the pre-embryos would be destroyed. Because the parties never agreed to a disposition for the pre-embryos in the event of death or divorce, Husband's contention that the trial court erred by not applying the three-year destruction provision is without merit.

We must now determine whether the trial court erred in its application of the balancing approach. To that end, we are left with the same questions the Supreme Court of Tennessee faced in Davis, supra, where "there was initially no agreement between the parties concerning disposition of the pre[-]embryos under the circumstances of this case; there has been no agreement since; and there is no formula in the Court of Appeals opinion for determining the outcome if the parties cannot reach an agreement in the future." Davis, 842 S.W.2d at 598.

We first note that "[i]n the context of an equitable distribution of marital property, a trial court has the authority to divide the award as the equities presented in the particular case may require." Schenk v. Schenk, 880 A.2d 633, 639 (Pa.Super.2005).[7] Here, the trial court held that "because Wife cannot achieve genetic parenthood otherwise, we conclude that Wife's interest in biological procreation through the use of these pre-embryos outweighs Husband's professed interest against procreation." We agree.

Wife's Interests in Procreation

This case presents a compelling circumstance not at issue in cases resolved by our sister states—the trial court concluded that Wife has no ability to procreate biologically without the use of the disputed pre-embryos. Husband disagrees with a number of aspects of this conclusion. He argues the evidence was insufficient to support this finding. He also argues that Wife should have produced medical evidence or a medical expert to verify this contention. Husband also argues that the "trial court erred and abused its discretion in making credibility determinations on [Wife's] exceptions to the Master's recommendation." Husband's arguments do not entitle him to relief.

At the Master's hearing, Wife testified that she does not "think it is possible" for her to have a biological child. Upon questioning by the Master about any results of medical testing, Wife stated, "I was [led] to believe that I cannot have children myself as I am." Furthermore, Wife testified that she underwent IVF only after she was diagnosed with breast cancer, after consultation with her doctor, and then she delayed chemotherapy by two to three weeks to undergo the process.

The Master offered the following conclusions based on Wife's testimony at the hearing:

It is recognized that opportunities of conceiving decrease after age forty. And this Master is aware of the potential ramifications of her cancer treatments. That being said, Wife did not offer any medical testimony as to her inability nor did she testify to any testing [8] that would lead her to conclude a natural pregnancy is medically unlikely. While conceiving naturally may be extremely difficult, both adoption and foster children are found to be reasonable means of achieving parenthood.

The trial court offered the following analysis:

Wife provided sufficient testimony that these thirteen pre-embryos were her only viable option to achieve genetic parenthood. Wife testified that she had Stage 3B cancer requiring a biopsy, two surgeries, eight rounds of chemotherapy and 37 rounds of radiation. After receiving her cancer diagnosis and upon suggestion of her doctor, she and Husband went through the IVF process in order to preserve Wife's ability to conceive a child. Upon questioning by the Master as to whether she had medical tests done which lead her to believe that she was incapable of having children, Wife testified that she had tests done after her recovery and that she could not have children.

Both the Master and trial court essentially concluded that Wife's doctors informed her that it would be highly unlikely, if not impossible, for her to become pregnant after undergoing chemotherapy treatments. After all, it is well known that "[l]ife-preserving treatments such as chemotherapy and radiation threaten fertility[.]" Gregory Dolin, M.D., J.D. et al., Medical Hope, Legal Pitfalls: Potential Legal Issues in the Emerging Field of Oncofertility, 49 Santa Clara L.Rev. 673, 683 (2009). Furthermore, Wife's age is a factor. Accordingly, Wife's testimony was sufficient to support the conclusion; the trial court did not make a credibility determination; and additional medical evidence or testimony was unnecessary in this case.

Husband also argues the trial court erred in concluding that Wife had no other reasonable opportunities to become a parent. Husband's Brief at 17–19. Specifically, Husband contends that both adoption and foster parenting were available to Wife. Id.

First, we point out, that our consideration is in Wife's interest to procreate as opposed to achieving any sort of parenthood. Furthermore, with regard to having a biological versus a non-biological child, Wife testified that she "always believed that [she] would have children." She stated, "I always wanted to have children. I wouldn't have gone through the whole IVF thing if I hadn't wanted children. And I wanted that experience of being pregnant and that closeness, that bond." Id.

There is no question that the ability to have a biological child and/or be pregnant is a distinct experience from adoption. Thus, simply because adoption or foster parenting may be available to Wife, it does not mean that such options should be given equal weight in a balancing test. Adoption is a laudable, wonderful, and fulfilling experience for those wishing to experience parenthood, but there is no question that it occupies a different place for a woman than the opportunity to be pregnant and/or have a biological child. As a matter of science, traditional adoption does not provide a woman with the opportunity to be pregnant.

Even if adoption was not a distinct experience from the opportunity to procreate biologically, we agree with the trial court's conclusion that adoption is not a practical option for Wife. Trial Court. At the hearing, Wife testified to the following:

I would probably have to go outside the country to adopt. And, additionally, because of my health history, a lot of birth parents or agencies in foreign countries would look down on that, despite the fact I have been given a clean bill of health.

Adoption is a complicated process. "There are three routes by which one may adopt a child. None [is] risk or burden-free and the burdens are multiplied for aging single women." Ellen Waldman, The Parent Trap: Uncovering the Myth of "Coerced Parenthood" in Frozen Embryo Disputes, 53 Am. U.L.Rev. 1021, 1056 (2004). Waldman then goes on to discuss the public, private, and international routes for adoption, all of which pose significant obstacles to Wife. She notes that in terms of public adoption, there are many more adoptive parents than children available for adoption.[9] Furthermore, when public adoption agencies do have a "child, they first look to place that child with a married couple and will only look to a single person as a secondary option." Id. at 1057. Additionally, there are issues for older, single women when it comes to private adoption. She notes that "all private agencies have their own requirements regarding age, marital status and income that may exclude older single mothers." Id. at 1058. The same holds true for foreign adoption, which leads Waldman to conclude that "[a]doption, especially for single older women, is an expensive process fraught with the potential for protracted delay and ultimate disappointment." Id. at 1059.[10]

Thus, we conclude that Wife's compelling interests in using the pre-embryos include the fact that these pre-embryos are the option that provides her with what is likely her only chance at genetic parenthood and her most reasonable chance for parenthood at all. We now turn to consider Husband's interests in avoiding unwanted procreation.

Husband's Interests to Avoid Unwanted Procreation

Husband makes several arguments that the trial court erred in the weight it applied to his reasons for avoiding unwanted procreation with the pre-embryos. Husband contends that he opposes Wife's use of these pre-embryos for procreation because he, himself, was adopted and he would not want any of his children not to know his or her biological father.

Husband's concerns, based on his own life experiences, are not unreasonable. However, we agree with the trial court that these concerns are ameliorated by the fact that "Wife has agreed to permit Husband to be involved in the child's life, if he so desires Wife's testimony at the master's hearing supports this conclusion.

Q: And [Husband] also testified if you had a child, he would want to participate, if there was a child, he would want to participate in raising it. How do you feel about that?

A: That's fine. I would want him, his parents to be involved as well. Because I feel that would be good for the child.

Q: You haven't had a lot of communication since you've separated?

A: I know, but I haven't seen any reason.

Q. But you don't have a child with him yet?

A: Correct.

Q: Even if he was not financially responsible or not paying you support, would you have any objection to him seeing the child?

A: No.

Thus, Husband will have the option to be part of the child's life, alleviating his concerns about the child not being able to find out about his or her biological father.

Furthermore, Husband argues that he only agreed to participate in IVF as a "safeguard," and he never intended actually to have a child with Wife. The trial court offered the following analysis about the weight it gave this argument.

We believe that Husband implicitly agreed to procreate with Wife when he agreed to undergo IVF, signed the consent form, provided sperm for the creation of the pre-embryos, and agreed to the fertilization causing the pre-embryos to be created. The use of the pre-embryos was never made contingent upon the parties remaining married. In fact, when provided the opportunity to resolve the fate of the pre-embryos in the event of divorce, neither party completed that portion of the IVF consent form.

Husband voluntarily provided Wife sperm when her doctors suggested she undergo IVF to preserve her fertility. To the extent Husband only considered his participation in IVF a "safeguard" for Wife, the only reason one undergoes IVF is to have a child. Clearly, Husband knew the potential result of his participation in IVF was going to be a child at some point in the future. The safeguard was to guard against the very situation where Wife could not have a biological child. That is the situation she is in now.

Husband also contends that the prospective child would be a financial burden for him, and the trial court erred in concluding it had full equity power to rely on Wife's vow not to seek financial support from Husband if a child is born. Husband's concerns must be considered in light of Wife's agreement to do her best to assure that Husband never has to pay to support the child or children.

The trial court questioned counsel for Wife extensively on this issue at argument.

[Counsel for Wife]: [Husband] is afraid of the financial repercussions, but we put it right on the record, we put over and over again that we will do whatever it takes to make sure that there will be no financial repercussions. We agree to an indefinite alimony award of a dollar a year modifiable in the event my client ever filed for child support and we specified that amount will be 30 percent higher than any child support award agreed to. I don't believe that's against public policy. I believe it would stand.

THE COURT: What if she passed away?

[Counsel for Wife]: Your Honor, [Husband] would not be obligated to take care of this child if she passed away. He would have the right to have custody.

THE COURT: How about enforcing the dollar a year modifiable alimony if she passed away?

[Counsel for Wife]: She has family and friends that could raise this child. I acknowledge that that may not be ideal, especially for [Husband], who may feel an obligation to raise his own child, not have that child raised by a third party. But she could make a life insurance award so that there was money in trust that could be payable to [Husband] as reimbursement for any child support he had to pay for a third party.

THE COURT: Is she willing to do that?

[Counsel for Wife]: Yes, absolutely, she will do whatever financially it takes to make sure that [Husband] is whole and she can—she has retirement accounts. Your Honor knows the assets from the rest of this case and she would put all of that aside in escrow in the event of her death, along with any life insurance she may have, to make [Husband] whole if any third party filed for child support.

Rather than making a determination about issues surrounding child support, the trial court concluded that "any attempt to decide these issues now would be speculative." The trial court went on to say that in its "overall balancing of the parties' interests, we have considered all the evidence presented, including Wife's 'vow' not to seek Husband's financial support for a child, but no reliance is placed on such a vow."

We recognize that "[i]n Pennsylvania, a parent cannot bind a child or bargain away that child's right to support." Kesler v. Weniger, 744 A.2d 794, 796 (Pa.Super.2000). Nonetheless, we have also held that "under Roberts [v. Furst, 561 A.2d 802 (Pa.Super.1999)], parties can make an agreement as to child support if it is fair and reasonable, made without fraud or coercion, and does not prejudice the welfare of the children." Kraisinger v. Kraisinger, 928 A.2d 333, 340 (Pa.Super.2007). Accordingly, we conclude the trial court did not err in the weight it gave to Wife's vow not to seek support-the trial court did not rely on the vow and appropriately left open such a determination until the issue becomes an actual case or controversy before the court.

Finally, Husband makes an overarching argument that it is against Pennsylvania public policy to force him to procreate with Wife when he does not want to do so. However, we agree with the trial court that Pennsylvania public policy is silent on the issue of forced procreation under these circumstances. There is no Pennsylvania case law at this time to guide us in these circumstances.

This situation, in some states, has moved from the state courts to the state legislatures.[11] However, unless and until our legislature decides to tackle this issue, our courts must consider the individual circumstances of each case. In this case, because Husband and Wife never made an agreement prior to undergoing IVF, and these pre-embryos are likely Wife's only opportunity to achieve biological parenthood and her best chance to achieve parenthood at all, we agree with the trial court that the balancing of the interests tips in Wife's favor.

Thus, we affirm the order of the trial court awarding the pre-embryos to Wife.

Order affirmed. Jurisdiction relinquished.
OPINION BY STRASSBURGER, J.

The *Reber* court was asked to resolve the issue in the context of a divorce proceeding and accepted the lower court's determination that the embryos were marital property subject to distribution, but would it make a difference if the embryos (also created for medical reasons, prior to cancer treatments) were created by an unmarried couple? In the case of *Szafranski v. Dunston*,[56] the Illinois courts were asked to decide if a woman who had created and frozen embryos before her cancer treatments could use them over her now ex-boyfriend's objection.[57]

A medical doctor, Darla Dunston was diagnosed with cancer and asked her then boyfriend, Jacob Szafranski, to donate the sperm so that she could use her eggs to create embryos. The cancer treatments would likely leave her sterile. They had only been "a few months into the relationship" and "although neither thought the relationship had long-term prospects," when requested to make the decision quickly, Szafranski agreed in "a quick phone conversation."[58] In March 2010, they signed the fertility clinic's consent form that read in part, "no use can be made of the embryos without the consent of both partners (if applicable)." The agreement also suggested they consult a lawyer for legal advice and a lawyer presented them with the option for a "co-parenting" agreement or a "sperm donor agreement." Although the woman wanted a co-parenting agreement, he refused and neither was signed. The next day, the man made the sperm donation. A month later, after Dunston had started her cancer treatments, Szafranski broke up with her (via a text message). Within four months, he sued to enjoin her from using the embryos and not "forcibly father a child against his will." The lower court ruled in favor of Dunston using the "balance" test to allow her to use the embryos saying, "her interest in being a mother outweighed Szafranski's desire not to be a father."[59] Szafranski appealed and in 2015, the state's Appellate Court affirmed the lower court's decision. Afterwards, Szafranski said, "'I don't think anyone should ever have their right to decide when and how they become a parent decided for them, and this is exactly what this is doing'."[60] The court found there was an oral agreement. Was there consent by the boyfriend to use the embryos as evidenced by the act of donating his sperm? If so, can he ever withdraw his consent, like if they break off the relationship?[61] Does it matter, as he argued in the recent appeal that this case "had spoiled his relationship with other women?"[62] During the lengthy appeals of the case, Dunston successfully adopted a child. Should that make a difference?

---

56   2013IlApp.1ˢᵗ122975.http://law.justia.com/cases/illinois/court-of-appeals-first-appellate-district/2013/1-12-2975.html

57   Tex. Fam.Code Ann. § 160.706(b) (Vernon 2011) ("The consent of a former spouse to assisted reproduction may be withdrawn by that individual in a record kept by a licensed physician at any time before the placement of eggs, sperm, or embryos.").

58   http://www.nbcnews.com/news/us-news/appellate-court-sides-chicago-woman-landmark-embryo-case-n374871

59   "Illinois appeals court hears case over Chicago frozen embryos", Tony Briscoe, *Chicago Tribune*, December 2, 2014.

60   Ibid.

61   Tex. Fam.Code Ann. § 160.706(b) (Vernon 2011) ("The consent of a former spouse to assisted reproduction may be withdrawn by that individual in a record kept by a licensed physician at any time before the placement of eggs, sperm, or embryos.").

62   "Illinois appeals court hears case over Chicago frozen embryos", Tony Briscoe, *Chicago Tribune*, December 2, 2014.

Embryo Transfers

When embryos (either fresh from fertilized egg cells or cryo-frozen then thawed) are placed in the uterus to create a pregnancy, new issues of ownership arise between the sperm and egg donors and, if different, even the woman whose womb is being used.

4. WOMB SURROGATES

Perhaps celebrities' use of surrogate arrangements has helped them become more main stream. Sir Elton John and his husband have two children by surrogacy; Sarah Jessica Parker and Mathew Broderick had twins through a gestational carrier (who was stalked by the media). Even presidential candidate and Mormon, Mitt Romney's son, Tagg, had twins (he thanked his surrogate via a tweet).

Surrogacy is when a woman contracts to bear a child for another person or persons. If prostitution is immoral (the use of a woman's body for money) why is a surrogate arrangement allowed? A minority of states allow surrogate arrangements. In a traditional surrogacy, the surrogate mother uses her own egg. In a gestational surrogacy, one woman provides the egg and another the womb. If the mother is genetically unrelated to the child (and has an embryo implanted), who is the "real" mother? While some courts have confused the issues (indeed, one court in California found that the child had *no* mother), most courts that recognize such contracts find that the "intended" mother is the one who intended to create the child. *Johnson v. Calvert*, 19 CA Rptr 2nd 494, 0.2d 776 (CA 1993.) In 2013, California passed a law that would allow children to have more than two legal parents. This would "allow courts to recognize three or more legal parents so that custody and financial responsibility can be shared by all those involved in raising a child."[63]

Ideally, when creating a surrogacy contract, it should be made between the father (who donates his sperm) and the surrogate mother and her husband (couple #2). In addition to being married (they would be more "stable"), couple #2 should already have children of their own (they would be less likely to want/need to keep this one). Under the traditional surrogacy contract, the surrogate's husband should also give up any claim to the child (who is born to his wife while he is married to her and would be presumed his marital child) under the contact. Often, the wife of the man who signs the contract with the surrogate (if she is genetically unrelated to the intended child) does not sign the contract to avoid the allegations of "baby selling" found in the seminal case of *Matter of Baby M*, 537 A.2d 1227 (NJ 1988), by the New Jersey Supreme Court in 1988. Under this arrangement, if all goes as it should, the woman has the baby, and signs the documents to relinquish any maternal rights to the child. Since the child has one half of his genetic makeup, husband #1 is the biological father of the child and takes full custody. Also, since the surrogate

---

63   Quoting California Senator Mark Leno. "Brown signs bill to allow children more than two legal parents", Patrick McGreevy and Melanie Mason, *Los Angeles Times*, October 4, 2013. http://articles.latimes.com/2013/oct/04/local/la-me-brown-bills-parents-20131005

mother has given up her rights to the child under the contract it is agreed that the contracting husband's wife can now step in and adopt the child.

The problem arises if the surrogate mother changes her mind and does not want to give up the child after she births it. In the *Baby M* case, the surrogate mother did this and the intended parents asked the court to enforce the contract. But the *Baby M* court found that surrogate contracts where the surrogate mother was paid were void. What happens if the contract is voided? The court, as in *Baby M*, made the decision whether to place the child with the surrogate mother or the intending parents, based on the traditional "best interest of the child" test. (The court gave custody to the intending parents under that standard, but recognized the rights of the birth mother, and gave the surrogate mother visitation.) In voiding the surrogate contract in *Baby M*, the court also objected that the adopting mother should be held to the same investigations as a traditional adopting mother and not be able to do so merely under the contract. Was this part of the *Baby M* case decided correctly?

Under the traditional view, surrogate contracts are void. Is there a fundamental right to procreate that is being ignored?[64] While some states, like California and Maryland, allow surrogate contracts, some, like New Jersey and Texas, do not allow such contracts based on public policy grounds. Does it make sense for people to enter into a surrogate contract if it is not enforceable in their state? Since the District of Columbia does not allow surrogate contracts, and Virginia only allows altruistic ones, is it fair for the parties to go to Maryland to enter into the contract? Would it make more sense for a court to approve an agreement before the pregnancy occurs?[65] (Contrast this with states' invalidation of a birthing mother's pre-birth consent for adoption.) Interestingly, the UPA seems to impose a penalty when it states that failure to obtain court approval of the surrogate agreement will cause the imposition of financial support if the intending parents refuse to adopt the child. Do you think this might prevent the surrogate mother from changing her mind and wanting to keep the child? If so, then what is the purpose of the law?

In the *Baby M* case, the court voided surrogacy contracts that involved payment of money to the surrogate mother, but seemed to leave open the issue of the validity of altruistic surrogacy contracts (where the surrogate mother does not receive any compensation). Should this make a difference? When Melissa Brown was diagnosed with breast cancer (which killed her mother after three hard years of treatment) "before the first toxic chemical dripped into her bloodstream, Melissa's oncologist—the same doctor who'd cared for her mother for more than 20 years—recommended a sort of insurance policy for the future. If you want children, he told her, preserve your fertility now. Along with killing the bad cells, cancer treatment can wreak havoc on a woman's ability to bear children. It can catapult you into early menopause. You may stop ovulating—or you may not—but if you know you want children, rolling the dice on whether

---

64   Generally, the right seems to include a right not to procreate in the birth control cases; see Chapters 5 and 13.

65   See generally, the National Conference of Commissioners on Uniform State Laws' Uniform Parentage Act (UPA) of 2000, recognizing "gestational agreements" which are validated by a court, based on a home study of the intended adopting mother's fitness (just as in adoption).

you'll be able to conceive post-treatment is probably not a risk you want to take."[66] When she learned her mother only had four months to live, Melissa moved her impending wedding up from June until March. The month after Melissa finished her own chemo treatments, her mother died. Now wanting children, Melissa had only four eggs she was able to freeze before her treatments began—not a lot—plus the possibility that the rise in estrogen from pregnancy could trigger new cancer concerns. Her sister Jessica offered to serve as her surrogate. "Jessica was 25, unmarried; with no children of her own—the antithesis of the ideal surrogate, actually."[67]

"As Jessica's clothes began to feel snug, she decided it would be too awkward to continue dating. She broke up with someone she'd been seeing casually rather than tell him what was going on. She was fastidious about referring to her swelling abdomen as 'Melissa's belly.' When strangers inquired about her due date, as strangers are wont to do, she'd issue her stock disclaimer: *They're not mine; they're my sister's. I'll tell her congratulations for you.* Reactions were varied. 'Some people said that's amazing,' says Jessica, 'and others were like, 'you're weird.' To keep from getting overly attached to the babies growing inside her, she would silently repeat her mantra: *I'm just the oven.* 'I will always have a different bond than just a random aunt or uncle,' says Jessica, 'but from Day One, I always said in my head that I was just a little oven.'" The healthy baby was born by C-section at 38 weeks.[68] During the delivery, Jessica asked the doctor to cover her nakedness from her brother-in-law. "Later, Steve, Melissa and Jessica would all crack up over it."[69] Was this surrogacy the kind of success that courts should enforce?

The payment of money to the surrogate made a difference to the New Jersey court but should it? Why is this better? Does the fact that money is paid (between $10,000 to $25,000 or more) mean that poor women are exploited? On the other hand, because such contracts for gestational surrogacy typically range from $40,000 to $70,000, is this elitist? In response to an article by the intended mother about her surrogacy experience in *New York Times Magazine*, the blogosphere was on fire with criticism of the disparity between the contracting mother (who skied at Olympic speeds during the surrogate's pregnancy and had three houses, including one photographed in Southampton) and the surrogate mother (a substitute teacher with a household income of $50,000 per year) who was using her $25,000 payment to help pay for her own two children in college.[70]

Is it troubling that military wives are increasingly serving as surrogates? One reason is that Tricare, the federal government insurance program for military families, does not discriminate on coverage for intended/surrogate or typical pregnancy. Military wives are also ideal because their husbands may be away on long deployments without access to the women. Many military

---

66   http://healthland.time.com/2012/05/09/my-sister-my-surrogate-after-cancer-one-sister-gives-another-the-ultimate-mothers-day-gift/, "My Sister, My Surrogate: After Battling Cancer, One Woman Receives the Ultimate Mother's Day Gift," Bonnie Rochman, May 9, 2012, *Time*.

67   Ibid.

68   Ibid.

69   Ibid.

70   http://www.nytimes.com/2008/11/30/magazine/30Surrogate-t.html?pagewanted=5&_r=0&ref=magazine, "Her Body, My Baby," Alex Kuczynski (the intended mother), *New York Times Magazine*, November 28, 2008.

wives say they need to do it to supplement their husbands' low military pay. When one military surrogate wife said she wanted to use the money to take her family to Disney World, was this wrong? Should taxpayer money fund someone's surrogate expenses? Also, many wealthy Chinese couples hire surrogate mothers from the U.S. The children, born in the U.S., are citizens. Beyond the question of baby selling, does this amount to citizenship buying?[71]

THE CONTRACT

Assuming that the contract is entered into in a state that recognizes surrogacy agreements, both the woman and her husband should sign the contract showing consent. The contract requires the woman to give up any parental rights once the child is born (and her husband too, to invalidate the presumption of legitimacy for a child born to a married woman). Contracts can be very lengthy, up to 30 pages, and may include requirements as to the woman's behavior (e.g., specify how much caffeine the mother can drink, and which hair products they can use, and state that she is subject to random drug and alcohol testing.)[72] Should the contract also require the woman's husband to have certain behaviors? What would they be? The consideration for the contract is the payment to the woman (from $10,000 and up) for her "expenses." Does that fee only cover the surrogate's expenses?

BREACH OF CONTRACT

Generally, when a problem arises in a surrogacy contract it is because the surrogate refuses to relinquish the child. What happens then? Can the parents sue for breach of contract? If they win, what is the remedy? Can the court force the surrogate to give up the child she carried for nine months and birthed? Should the court handle this kind of enforcement?

What happens if it is the intended parents who break the agreement and decide that they do not want the child? In 2005, a surrogate mother became pregnant with five babies. When the intended mother found out, she said, "I just wanted one!" What would happen if the intended parents rejected all five children? Or only took one? One of the five had a serious heart problem that would require immediate surgery—would that be the child they would reject?[73] What

---

71 A similar issue was raised by a March 2015 FBI raid in Los Angeles of several "multimillion-dollar birth-tourism businesses that enabled thousands of Chinese women to travel here and return home with infants born as U.S. citizens." "The investigations are likely to culminate in the biggest federal criminal case ever against the booming 'anchor baby'" industry, Marim Jordan, *The Wall Street Journal*, March 3, 2015, http://www.wsj.com/articles/us-agents-raid-alleged-maternity-tourism-anchor-baby-businesses-catering-to-chinese-1425404456

72 "The Making of a 'Gayby Boom': It Takes a Village," *The Washington Post*, January 18, 2005, pg. F5.

73 "Surrogate Returns Couple's Hope for a Child Five-fold," Amy Argetsinger, *Washington Post*, April 14, 2005, A1 and A7. In this inspirational story about 25-year-old Teresa Anderson, "who may be the first surrogate mother to give birth to quintuplets" to the intended parents who had tried unsuccessfully to have their own children for almost

happens if the intended parents divorce during the pregnancy? They would still be responsible for the resulting child's care and support.

A 2014 surrogate arrangement raises many issues on an international scale when an Australian couple contracted with a Thai woman to serve as their surrogate. Because commercial surrogacy is illegal in Australia, many couples seeking children go to a small number of countries like India and Thailand that allow foreigners to hire local woman for surrogates. One thing that is agreed upon is that the Australian couple agreed to pay a 28-year old mother of two (the amounts differ somewhere between $12,000 and $16,000—either a princely sum in Thailand) to act as their surrogate. When the couple learned that the woman was pregnant with twins, they gave her a bonus. But when they learned that one of the twins would have Down syndrome, the surrogate alleges that they told her to abort it (which she opposed for religious reasons). The couple said the doctors were aware, but waited until after seven months to let them know (outside of the abortion period). While the stories differ as to the reason, the end result was that the Australian parents only took the healthy twin back home with them. The story gets worse. After the story received international outrage, it was uncovered that the father was a convicted sex offender.[74] In response, in February 2015, Thailand banned commercial surrogacy by foreigners[75] and made it human trafficking to remove a surrogate child from the country. How many concerns raised in *Baby M* does this case confirm?

COMPLICATIONS FOR SAME-SEX COUPLES

Same-sex couples are increasingly using surrogate agreements. Some argue that this scientific advancement allowed recognition of same-sex marriage, having eliminated the argument that marriage is reserved for heterosexual couples who can only have genetically related children. Indeed, some surrogate agencies focus mainly on gay and lesbian clients.[76] These surrogate arrangements raise unique issues on parentage (e.g., can a child have two "intended" mothers, and if so, what

---

a decade. "Anderson originally agreed to be a surrogate to earn extra money for her husband (a postal worker) and their two young daughters. But now she says she does not feel she can accept compensation from Gonzalez and her husband, Enrique Moreno, whom she notes will be burdened enough trying to raise five children—all boys."(A1). "Anderson said she entered the surrogacy arrangement with the intention of earning $15,000.…The matter, though, has been resolved: Anderson said she determined several months ago not to accept money from the couple, who took out a second mortgage on their home just to cover the fertility treatments. It will be reward enough, she said, to see the couple go home with five babies." (A.7)

74 "Australian parents of Thai surrogate twin say they feared losing both babies", *Reuters*, August 10, 2014. The surrogate claims the agency owes her over $2,000. When the surrogate mother later sued to get back the twin that was taken to Australia, its court ruled in favor of keeping the baby with its Australian family, despite the prior conviction. "But in his decision, Justice Thackray said there was no evidence he had reoffended since his release from jail in 1999". http://www.abc.net.au/news/2016-04-14/baby-gammy-twin-must-remain-with-family-wa-court-rules/7326196

75 "Thailand bans surrogacy for foreigners with new law," Rebecca Lee, *PBS News Hour*, February 21, 2015. http://www.pbs.org/newshour/rundown/thailand-bans-surrogacy-foreigners-new-law/

76 "The Making of a 'Gayby Boom': It Takes a Village," *The Washington Post*, January 18, 2005, pg. F5.

will the birth certificate say?) and child support (financial) from two non-biologically related parents.

REGULATION

"Almost every other developed nation regulates fertility treatments more systematically than the United States does; some, such as Israel, have extensive state subsidies for certain treatments, while others, such as Germany, ban practices that are common here, such as surrogacy or anonymous sperm donation."[77] "The result is a Wild West." "[I]n most states, until recently, nothing would stop you from opening 'Sam's Sperm Bank and Delicatessen.'"[78] "In many European nations, a massive state apparatus decides who can and can't get which kind of treatment."[79] "In Italy, with the backing of the Vatican, voters failed to overturn the country's strict IVF laws, including a prohibition on freezing embryos (which will require women to use fresh embryos every time they attempt IVF, with a limit of three eggs fertilized each and requiring that 'all three must be transferred back to the woman, risking multiple births')."[80] Which regulations should the United States have, and would they work? In recent changes to its AI laws, England requires that "donors must agree to be identifiable to children who may wish to find out about them when they turn 18."[81] Should the United States require this also?

SURROGATE FATHERS

Can there be a "surrogate father?" The Wisconsin court of appeals used the term "surrogate father," in the case of *Marriage of L. M. S. v. S. L. S.*, 105 WI2d 118, 312 N.W.2d 853 (1981), which involved a husband who objected to paying child support to his wife's child at divorce. The child was born to the wife during the time she was married to the husband, but the parties conceded that the husband was sterile. According to the case facts, "[t]he husband, desirous of having

---

77 "The Stork Market: How making babies has become a $3 billion industry—and an unregulated mess," by David Plotz, reviewing the book, *The Baby Business: How Money, Science, and Politics Drive the Commerce of Conception*, by Debora L. Spar, *The Washington Post Book Review*, February 26, 2006.

78 "The Stork Market: How making babies has become a $3 billion industry—and an unregulated mess," by David Plotz, reviewing the book, *The Baby Business: How Money, Science, and Politics Drive the Commerce of Conception*, by Debora L. Spar, *The Washington Post Book Review*, February 26, 2006, quoting USC law professor Alexander Capron.

79 "The Stork Market: How making babies has become a $3 billion industry—and an unregulated mess," by David Plotz, reviewing the book, *The Baby Business: How Money, Science, and Politics Drive the Commerce of Conception*, by Debora L. Spar, *The Washington Post Book Review*, February 26, 2006.

80 "Tough Fertility Law to Stay," *New Scientist*, June 18, 2005, pg. 4.

81 "IVF waiting lists down as egg donors get 'pay' raise: Surge in hard-up women offering to sell their eggs for £750 'due to recession,'" *The Daily Mail Online*, July 17, 2012, http://www.dailymail.co.uk/health/article-2174846/Surge-hard-women-offering-sell-eggs.html

a child, often discussed with his wife different ways of having children. AI was considered but dismissed because of the required expense and travel. Attempts at adoption proved unsuccessful. The husband suggested that his wife become pregnant by another man and agreed to acknowledge the child as his own. At the husband's insistence the wife agreed, had sexual intercourse, and became pregnant." When the child, conceived under such an arrangement, was born the husband recognized the child as his own. At the divorce trial, the husband denied that he agreed to his wife becoming pregnant by another man. The lower court accepted the wife's testimony that he had; therefore, the husband had to pay child support after the divorce, which was affirmed on appeal. Is this a surrogate father? What is the difference between this and a known sperm donor?

YOU DECIDE

A Texas company "started producing batches of ready-made embryos that single women and infertile couples can order after reviewing detailed information about the race, education, appearance, personality and other characteristics of the egg and sperm donor."[82] How do you feel about this? Is it different from sperm banks? Why? Are allegations that this is leading to designer babies any different than for sperm banks? Does your opinion change if the owners say it is intended to "make it easier and more affordable for clients to have babies that match their preferences?"[83]

A 66-year-old Romanian woman, who had fertility treatments for nine years, had a premature girl baby by C-section who only weighed three-pounds, three-ounces. Should there be a law limiting the age of the mother? The father? Comedian Steve Martin had his first child at the age of 67. The oldest man to father a child was 92.[84] Is this ethically too old to become a father?

Should there be standards for doctors who work with patients that want assisted reproduction treatments? One study found that one third of AI doctors would provide services to a woman addicted to marijuana.[85]

What happens if a doctor refuses to treat same-sex couples based on religious reasons? Cases have rejected such claims by doctors, but did suggest that the doctor could refuse the treatments because the patient was a single parent (when same-sex marriage was not recognized in the state). Who would want to go to a doctor who was forced to treat her?

At a seminar in London, to drum up business, a Fairfax, Virginia, clinic gave away an attempt to get pregnant with a free cycle of in vitro fertilization from an American woman's eggs (worth about $23,000).[86] Is this nothing more than a lottery of body parts?

---

82 "Embryo Bank Stirs Ethics Fears, Firm Lets Clients Pick among Fertilized Eggs," by Rob Stein, *The Washington Post*, January 6, 2007, pg. 1.

83 Ibid.

84 *New York Times Magazine*, October 26, 2014, page 61

85 "Fit to be a mom?" by David Bjerklie, *Parade Magazine*.

86 "Fairfax clinic's giveaway of donor eggs sparks uproar," by Rob Stein, *The Washington Post*, pg. 1.

In September 2012, doctors in Sweden successfully transplanted two mother's wombs into their daughters, in two separate operations. Both recipients were in their 30s. One had her uterus removed because of cervical cancer and the other was born without a uterus. Now, the daughters are trying to get pregnant so they can give birth using the wombs from which they were born.[87]

While many argue against the "Wild West" aspect of the assisted reproductive technology field, there is no doubt that it has allowed thousands of infertile couples to have a family. Yet, concerns about exploitation of women and alleged buying and selling of human reproductive materials are valid. Surely, as the 21st century progresses, the issues raised will continue to be examined.

AS WE GO TO PRESS

The issue of who has the right to previously created embryos when a non-marital relationship dissolves was raised in 2015 and continues today between actress Sofia Vergara[88] and her ex-fiancé who sued her over two frozen embryos the couple created in 2014 while they were engaged and intended for use with a surrogate. He reportedly pays for their storage and could presumably do so for ever.[89] The question is can he use them, which is what he now wants to do but with another woman. Does it matter that these embryos were not created for medical necessity? In a non-divorce case, are the embryos property or something different? Can they be destroyed if one party wants them and the other does not want them used? Will the California courts use the guidance of the *Junior Davis* case? Does the fact that this couple is not married and not divorcing make a difference? In December 2016, a lawsuit on behalf of the embryos was allegedly filed against Vergara in Jefferson Parish Louisiana where the couple broke up. The plaintiffs named "'Emma" and "Isabella"…are…fighting for [their] right to live and to obtain an inheritance created for their benefit". "Louisiana law holds that viable embryos are people who can't be intentionally destroyed."[90] At about the same time of that suit, in California, the ex-fiancé dropped his case in state court for control of the embryos.[91]

---

87 "Mother-to-daughter womb transplant 'success' in Sweden," *BBC News*, September 18, 2012. www.bbc.co.uk/news/world-europe-19637156 In October 2014, the first baby was born to a womb-transplant recipient. "First successful birth by womb transplant in Sweden", Paula Mejia, Newsweek, October 4, 2014. http://www.newsweek.com/first-successful-birth-womb-transplant-sweden-275376. In 2016 in the U.S. the first uterus transplant failed. https://www.scientificamerican.com/article/first-u-s-uterus-transplant-fails-due-to-complications/. In 2016, the first US penis transplant was conducted for a cancer survivor with a donated penis. https://www.nytimes.com/2016/05/17/health/thomas-manning-first-penis-transplant-in-us.html?_r=0

88 Ironically, she is probably best known for her role on T.V.'s *Modern Family*.

89 "Sofia Vergara's frozen embryo fight. What's the harm in keeping them?" Maren Shapiro, *Today Show Today Health*, April 17, 2015. http://www.today.com/health/sofia-vergaras-frozen-embryo-fight-whats-harm-keeping-them-t16036. See also, his letter to the editor. "Sofia Vergara's Ex-Fiancé: Our Frozen Embryos have a right to live", Nick Loeb, *New York Times*, April 29, 2015 https://www.nytimes.com/2015/04/30/opinion/sofiavergaras-ex-fiance-our-frozen-embryos-have-a-right-to-live.html?_r=0

90 http://www.theadvocate.com/new_orleans/news/courts/article_d9f9bb12-bd9a-11e6-b460-2f455e600861.html

91 Ibid.

In another Hollywood celebrity case, Jason Patric claims that he is the father of a child created with his girlfriend, but she claims he was "just a sperm donor." Although the couple tried to have children together while they were living together, Patric volunteered to be a sperm donor[92] and the child was born via artificial insemination. Afterwards, "according to the court opinion, the actor kept in close contact with his son and Ms. Schreiber, who referred to Mr. Patric as 'Dada' when speaking to her son"[93] but he was not listed as the father on the child's birth certificate. When she ended her relationship with him a few years later, Patric filed for a custody dispute, but she said that he had no rights as the sperm donor. In California, like most states, a sperm donor has no parental rights unless there is a prior written agreement or the couple is married. In 2014, an appellate court allowed Patric to continue his case for custody.[94] If they had been married and Patric donated the sperm, there would be no contest. At this time where more children are born outside of marriage, does it still make sense to require a couple to be married for the man's sperm donation to give him parental rights to the biological children he creates?

92 "Paternity rights of sperm donors expanded in actor's custody case", Jacob Gershman, *Wall Street Journal Law Blog*, May 14, 2014 http://blogs.wsj.com/law/2014/05/14/court-expands-paternity-rights-of-sperm-donors-in-actors-custody-dispute/
93 Ibid.
94 http://people.com/celebrity/jason-patric-custody-battle-i-miss-my-son/

16

WHO'S YOUR DADDY?

Baby mama. The mother of your child(ren), whom you did not marry and with whom you are not currently involved.[1]
—Urban Word of the Day for June 13, 2008, Urban Dictionary

The gods visit the sins of the fathers upon the children.
—Euripides

Mothers are fonder than fathers of their children because they are more certain they are their own.
—Aristotle

While philosopher and scientist Aristotle could use early biological knowledge to classify the mother in ancient Greece, the case of *Amy G. v. M. W.*, below, might have given him something more to think about. In this case, a man had an extramarital affair that produced a child. Later, when the father and his wife were living with the child, the biological mother came to assert her rights, and the couple raised many claims in arguing that the wife is the child's mother.

---

1   Urban Dictionary, http://www.urbandictionary.com/define.php?term=baby%20mama

AMY G. V. M. W.
V 142 CAL.APP.4TH 1,
(CAL. APP. DIST. 2006)

142 Cal.App.4th 1, 47 Cal.Rptr.3d 297, 06 Cal. Daily Op. Serv. 7656, 2006 Daily Journal D.A.R. 10,923 (Cal. App. Dist. 2006) Cert. Denied 127 S.Ct 2252

Background: Mother of child born out of wedlock filed petition against married father, who was living with the child and his wife, seeking establishment of the parental relationship, child support, custody, and visitation. Father moved for joinder of his wife and mother's husband as necessary parties. Father's wife also filed a separate action to establish her status as the child's mother. The Superior Court, Los Angeles County, Nos. BF024437, BF023845, Mitchell L. Beckloff, Temporary Judge, denied father's joinder motion in mother's action, and granted mother's motion to quash wife's action, dismissing it with prejudice. Father filed petition for writ of prohibition to vacate court's denial of his joinder motion, father and his wife appealed dismissal of her separate action, and appeal and petition were consolidated.

Holdings: The Court of Appeal, Klein, P.J., held that:

1. given mother's prompt assertion of her legal maternity, father's wife could not be either natural or presumed mother through gender-neutral reading of provisions of Uniform Parentage Act (UPA);
2. this interpretation of UPA did not violate equal protection or due process;
3. mother was not equitably estopped from denying wife's maternity; and
4. mother's husband was not mandatory party who had to be joined in mother's action.

Petition denied, and dismissal affirmed.

KLEIN, P.J.
*4 INTRODUCTION

M. W. (hereafter Kim) and G. G. (father) are the biological parents of three year-old Nathan. Father and his wife, Amy, have raised Nathan in their home since he was one month old.

In an action brought by Kim for custody and visitation rights to her biological child, the trial court denied father's motion to join Amy as a party. Father filed a petition**299 for writ of prohibition to vacate the court's order and to join Amy in the action.

Amy also brought a separate action against Kim and father, to be declared Nathan's presumed mother; the trial court granted Kim's motion to quash and dismissed that action. Amy and father appealed that order.

*5 In this consolidated petition and appeal, father and Amy argue that Amy is Nathan's presumed mother, and therefore the trial court erred in denying Amy joinder or standing. Father and Amy's arguments present the question of whether the statutory presumptions of paternity contained in the Family Code enable the wife of a man who fathered a child in an extramarital relationship to assert status as the child's mother, when the child's biological mother has come forward promptly to assert her maternal rights.

We answer no, and affirm. We uphold the trial court's denial of father's motion to join Amy and its order granting Kim's motion to quash Amy's independent action.

FACTUAL AND PROCEDURAL BACKGROUND

1. Facts.

Father is married to Amy. During his marriage to Amy, he had an extramarital relationship with Kim, the real party in interest. That relationship resulted in a child, Nathan.

During her relationship with father, Kim was married to Steven, but they were separated at the time of Nathan's conception and birth.

Nathan is Kim's only child. Father and Amy have two daughters.

The parties disagree as to their intent and as to the circumstances of Nathan's conception and birth. Father asserts Kim offered to bear a child who would be raised as a child of his marriage to Amy. Kim contends her relationship with father was romantic, the pregnancy was unplanned, and that she expected they would raise Nathan jointly.

Kim concealed her pregnancy from business associates, acquaintances, family and friends and left California for Virginia, where she gave birth to Nathan. Kim cared for Nathan during his first month in Virginia.

In June 2003, when Nathan was one-month old, father came to Virginia to take him to California. Father met with Kim in a hotel lobby. He presented Kim with an "agreement regarding custody and adoption" (the Agreement), drafted by a Maryland law firm he had retained.

The Agreement provided: Father would have sole custody over Nathan; Kim would have no visitation; and Kim consented to a stepparent adoption by Amy. The Agreement also contained recitals to the effect that Kim acknowledged and was aware of her right to obtain independent counsel, *6 father's counsel had not provided her with any legal advice in connection with the Agreement, she was executing the Agreement freely and voluntarily, and the Agreement was not the product of any fraud, duress or undue influence. Kim and father signed the Agreement while sitting in father's limousine. FN1

FN1. Amy did not pursue a stepparent adoption of Nathan.

Kim did not have a lawyer when she signed the document. She contends she did not understand what she was signing and felt pressured to do so.

After signing the Agreement, they returned to the hotel lobby where father picked up Nathan. Kim handed father all of Nathan's clothes, formula, diapers and **300 toys. That evening, father flew with Nathan back to Los Angeles.

Since June 29, 2003, Nathan has lived continuously with father and his family and has never been alone with Kim.

2. Proceedings.

On September 29, 2003, Kim filed a petition against father to establish parental relationship, seeking child support, custody and visitation. Thereafter, Kim brought an order to show cause. Kim did not serve the papers until November 11, 2003.

Father responded, requesting the court to deny Kim the relief she requested and to enter a judgment of parentage recognizing Amy as the mother.

a. Father's initial motion for joinder of Amy as a necessary party.

On December 18, 2003, at a hearing on Kim's order to show cause, father argued that Amy was a necessary party and Kim's custody request could not be heard without Amy's joinder. The trial court denied father's request for joinder, ruling, inter alia, Amy "is completely aligned" with father and therefore her interests were adequately protected.

In a supplemental memorandum of points and authorities, father unsuccessfully argued, inter alia, Amy was the presumed natural mother of Nathan pursuant to Family Code section 7611, subdivision (d) "because she has taken him into her home, held him out as her son, and played all the social, psychological and economic roles of mother since he was one month old.... " FN2

FN2. All further statutory references are to the Family Code, unless otherwise indicated.

*7 b. Amy's independent action to establish parental relationship.

On January 26, 2004, after father failed in his attempt to join Amy in Kim's action, Amy filed a separate action, naming Kim and father, to establish her status as Nathan's mother. Amy brought the action pursuant to section 7650, which provides in relevant part: "Any interested person may bring an action to determine the existence or nonexistence of a mother and child relationship." (§ 7650, subd. (a).)

On June 23, 2004, the trial court granted Kim's motion to quash, ruling that Amy was not an interested person within the meaning of section 7650 because she was not biologically related to the child with whom she sought to establish a parental relationship.

Thereafter, the trial court granted reconsideration, again granted the motion to quash, and dismissed Amy's action with prejudice.

On March 24, 2005, Amy and father filed a timely notice of appeal from the order of dismissal.

c. Proceedings in Kim's action; trial court again denies joinder of Amy.

Turning our focus back to Kim's action, on February 9, 2004, the trial court ordered that Kim have monitored visitation with Nathan for four hours per week.

On March 12, 2004, the parties stipulated to the appointment of Dr. Jeffrey Lulow to conduct a child custody evaluation.

On August 15, 2005, father filed a written motion for joinder of Amy as well as Steven. With respect to the facts showing that Amy was either indispensable or a necessary party, the motion denied Kim's parentage and contended: Amy is Nathan's mother, Amy "has exercised actual custody of Nathan and asserted custody rights since Nathan was less than a month **301 old," and a complete and effective judgment could not be had without joining Amy as a party.

Father also sought to join Steven, Kim's husband at the time of the child's conception and birth, in order to establish father's paternity with finality.

Father argued joinder was mandatory and complete relief could not be had without joining Amy and Steven as parties.

*8 On August 30, 2005, nearly 18 months after the March 12, 2004 order appointing Dr. Lulow, he completed his evaluation.

On September 15, 2005, Steven filed a responsive declaration stating he was making no claim to parentage of Nathan, that he was willing to appear in the action solely for the purpose of entering into a binding waiver of a claim to parentage, and that he did not wish to be otherwise joined as a party to the litigation.

By way of opposition to the joinder motion, Kim argued Amy was merely a stepparent and she had no standing to allege maternity.

On October 21, 2005, the matter came on for hearing. The trial court refused to take judicial notice of the child custody evaluation for purposes of the joinder motion and stated it had not read the report. The trial court denied father's motion for joinder of Amy and Steven. FN3

FN3. This court has reviewed Dr. Lulow's report, which discusses, inter alia, the bond between Amy and Nathan. The contents of the report do not affect our legal interpretation with respect to the application of the parentage statutes.

The reporter's transcript of the hearing on the joinder motion sets forth the trial court's reasoning herein. The trial court repeatedly asked, "How is Amy... any different from a live-in nanny?" FN4 The trial court also commented, "[Amy] doesn't have custody rights. [Father] has custody rights. And she happens to live with [father]." [Author's emphasis added.]

FN4. Although we affirm the trial court's decision, we find this comment, comparing Amy to a domestic employee, unfortunate…

d. Subsequent proceedings.

d. Standing to bring maternity action under section 7650, subdivision (a).

Section 7650, subdivision (a) allows any "interested person" standing to bring a maternity action. Father and Amy argue Amy is an "interested person" because she claims to be Nathan's mother, and therefore the trial court erred in granting Kim's motion to quash Amy's independent action.

Having set forth father and Amy's theories, we now turn to the merits.

3. Father and Amy's arguments are unavailing because Amy cannot be deemed to be Nathan's mother.

As outlined above, father and Amy's arguments all are predicated on Amy's claim she is Nathan's mother. Therefore, our threshold question is whether Amy can assert status as Nathan's mother in view of the undisputed fact that Kim, a party to both actions, is Nathan's biological mother.

Amy and father advance several arguments as to why Amy can allege status as Nathan's mother. Amy and father allege Amy is Nathan's presumed mother under section 7611, subdivisions (a) and (d). They further allege Amy is conclusively presumed to be Nathan's mother under section 7540. They also take the position Amy is Nathan's natural mother within the meaning of section 7635, subdivision (b). Based on any and all of these claims, Amy and father argue Amy is entitled either to joinder in Kim's action or to standing to bring an independent maternity action. As explained, none of these theories has merit.

*12 a. Amy cannot establish status as Nathan's presumed mother under section 7611, subdivisions (a) and (d).

Section 7611 sets forth various circumstances wherein the court will presume a **304 man to be a child's father. "A man is presumed to be the natural father of the child if… [¶] (a) He and the child's natural mother are or have been married to each other and the child is born during the marriage…" (§ 7611, subd. (a).) A man is also presumed to be the natural father of the child if "[h]e receives the child into his home and openly holds out the child as his natural child." (§ 7611, subd. (d).)

The UPA specifically provides maternity may be established "by proof of her having given birth to the child, or under this part [i.e., the UPA, § 7600 et seq]." (§ 7610, subd. (a), italics added.) FN8 The UPA also provides, as discussed above, the rules pertaining to paternity actions apply equally to maternity actions. (§ 7650, subd. (a).) Therefore, the question presented is the applicability of section 7611, pertaining to presumed fathers, to Amy.

FN8. In contrast, the father and child relationship may be established simply "under this part." (§ 7610, subd. (b).)

In general, California law only recognizes one mother. (*Johnson v. Calvert* (1993) 5 Cal.4th 84, 92, fn. 8, 19 Cal.Rptr.2d 494, 851 P.2d 776.) Amy and father do not dispute that Kim gave birth to Nathan, making Kim the natural mother under section 7610, subdivision (a). However, because section 7610, subdivision (a), provides maternity may be established "by proof of her having given birth to the child, or under this part [i.e., the UPA]" (§ 7610, subd. (a), italics added), Amy and father assert Amy's maternity based on the presumed father provisions of section 7611, subdivisions (a) and (d), which they seek to apply in a gender-neutral manner. Amy and father argue Amy is Nathan's presumed mother under section 7611, subdivision (a), by virtue of her marriage to father, and under section 7611, subdivision (d), because she received Nathan into her home and held him out as her own child. Neither the case law nor the statutory framework supports this argument.

In limited circumstances, the presumptions of paternity listed in section 7611 have been interpreted to apply to women. (See, e.g., In re *Karen C.* (2002) 101 Cal.App.4th 932, 937–938, 124 Cal.Rptr.2d 677; In re *Salvador M.* (2003) 111 Cal.App.4th 1353, 1357–1358, 4 Cal.Rptr.3d 705; *Elisa B. v. Superior Court* (2005) 37 Cal.4th 108, 119–120, 125, 33 Cal.Rptr.3d 46, 117 P.3d 660.)

In *Karen C.,* the birth mother gave her child to another woman when the child was born and subsequently absented herself. (*13 In re Karen C., supra, 101 Cal.App.4th at p. 934, 124 Cal.Rptr.2d 677.) The other woman, who took the child into her home and raised the child as her own, was presumed to be the child's mother under section 7611, subdivision (d). (*Karen C.,* at p. 938, 124 Cal.Rptr.2d 677.) Similarly, in Salvador M., where the birth mother was deceased, the child's adult half-sister who raised the child since his mother's death was presumed to be his mother under section 7611, subdivision (d). (In re *Salvador M., supra,* 111 Cal.App.4th at pp. 1355–1358, 4 Cal.Rptr.3d 705.) Thus, in both Karen C. and *Salvador M.,* the birth mother was absent and there was no competing claim to maternity.

Elisa B. applied section 7611, subdivision (d), to declare a woman, Elisa, a presumed mother of the twin children born to her same-sex partner, Emily. (*Elisa B. v. Superior Court,* supra, 37 Cal.4th at pp. 113–114, 125, 33 Cal.Rptr.3d 46, 117 P.3d 660.) After the relationship ended, a county district attorney sued Elisa for child support on behalf of the twins. **305 (Id. at pp. 113, 115, 33 Cal.Rptr.3d 46, 117 P.3d 660.) Elisa had actively participated in causing the children to be conceived with the understanding that she would raise the children as her own together with Emily. Once the children were born, Elisa received them into her home and openly held them out as her own. (Id. at pp. 113, 125, 33 Cal.Rptr.3d 46, 117 P.3d 660.) Given these circumstances, the court declared Elisa a presumed mother under section 7611, subdivision (d), perceiving "no reason" why both parents of a child cannot be women. (*Elisa B. v. Superior Court,* supra, at pp. 119, 125, 33 Cal.Rptr.3d 46, 117 P.3d 660.) In reaching this conclusion, the court specifically noted there were "no competing claims to her being the children's second parent." (Id. at p. 125, 33 Cal.Rptr.3d 46, 117 P.3d 660, italics added.)

Father and Amy rely on *Elisa B.* for the proposition that section 7611 should apply in maternity cases even where the child's birth mother is present and asserts legal parenthood. However, *Elisa B.* is distinguishable. Here, Nathan's natural father is known and present in the action. Nathan only can have one additional parent. Both father and Amy concede that Kim is Nathan's biological mother. By alleging presumed maternity, Amy advances a competing claim to be Nathan's second parent. Because the absence of a competing claim to be the second parent specifically drove the *Elisa B.* court's decision, *Elisa B.* cannot control this case.

The cases cited by Amy and father where the courts applied the presumed father statute, section 7611, to recognize a presumed mother all involved circumstances where there was no competing claim to be the child's mother or second parent. (*Elisa B. v. Superior Court,* supra, 37 Cal.4th at p. 125, 33 Cal.Rptr.3d 46, 117 P.3d 660; In re *Karen C.,* supra, 101 Cal.App.4th at p. 938, 124 Cal.Rptr.2d 677; In re *Salvador M.,* supra, 111 Cal.App.4th at p. 1359, 4 Cal.Rptr.3d 705.) Here, unlike those cases, both the child's biological father and biological mother have identified themselves and come forward to assert their legal parentage. Under these circumstances, it is not appropriate to invoke a gender-neutral reading of the paternity presumptions to provide Nathan with another mother. To allow Amy an opportunity to be declared *14 Nathan's mother through a gender-neutral reading of the UPA would arrive at an impracticable result. (§ 7650, subd. (a.).)…

Here, no blood tests are required. It is undisputed that Kim, not Amy, is Nathan's biological mother. Accordingly, Amy cannot enjoy a conclusive presumption of maternity under section 7540.

d. Amy cannot assert status as Nathan's natural mother

We also reject Amy and father's additional suggestion that Amy is Nathan's natural mother, and therefore can be joined pursuant to section 7635, subdivision (b). While the word "natural" is not always interpreted as synonymous with "biological" (see, e.g., **307 In re Nicholas H. (2002) 28 Cal.4th 56, 64, 120 Cal.Rptr.2d 146, 46 P.3d 932), the language of section 7635, subdivision (b), expressly refers to the "natural mother" and also differentiates between "each man presumed to be the father under Section 7611, and each man alleged to be the natural father.… " (§ 7635, subd. (b), italics added.) Because the statutory language provides this distinction, we interpret "natural mother" here to refer to the biological mother. Thus, Amy cannot be deemed to be Nathan's natural mother.

*16 e. Preliminary conclusion: trial court did not err in refusing to join Amy or in granting Kim's motion to quash Amy's separate action.

For the reasons discussed above, we hold, whereas here, a birth mother promptly comes forward to assert her legal maternity, and the child's father is undisputed and present in the action, the father's spouse cannot be the child's natural mother or the child's presumed mother through a gender-neutral reading of either section 7611, subdivisions (a) and (d), or section 7540.

Because Amy cannot legally be Nathan's mother under these circumstances, Amy cannot "claim an interest relating to the subject of the action" which would require her joinder under Code of Civil Procedure section 389, subdivision (a). Amy is not Nathan's natural mother or presumed mother and therefore is not a person who may be made a party to the action under Family Code section 7635, subdivision (b); for the same reasons, she is not an "interested person" within the meaning of section 7650, subdivision (a); and she cannot claim custody rights under rule 5.158(a) because Nathan is not a child of the marriage between Amy and father.

For these reasons, we find no error in either the trial court's denial of father's motion to join Amy or its grant of Kim's motion to quash Amy's independent action.

4. The statutory scheme does not violate equal protection or due process.

a. Equal protection.

Amy and father contend an interpretation of the statutory scheme which denies Amy joinder or standing violates equal protection.

Father and Amy rely on *Elisa B.* for the proposition that the statutory scheme, if interpreted to deny Amy's joinder, violates equal protection on the basis of sexual orientation. Elisa B. held a woman in a same-sex relationship with the biological mother could be declared the child's presumed mother under section 7611, subdivision (d), even though the biological mother is present in the action. (See *Elisa B. v. Superior Court*, supra, 37 Cal.4th at pp. 118–119, 125, 33 Cal.Rptr.3d 46, 117 P.3d 660.) Father and Amy argue that to deny Amy a similar opportunity to establish status as a presumed mother effectively treats a heterosexual woman differently than a similarly situated woman in a same-sex relationship.

*17 Relying on *Jesusa V.*, father and Amy also argue that the statutory scheme, if applied to deny Amy's joinder, violates equal protection on the basis of gender. *Jesusa V.* held a man who received a child into his home and held the child out as his own could qualify as the presumed father under section 7611, subdivision (d), even though the biological father also was a party to the proceedings. (In re *Jesusa V.*, supra, 32 Cal.4th at pp. 603–604, 10 Cal.Rptr.3d 205, 85 P.3d 2.) Father and Amy argue that to deny Amy a similar opportunity to assert her status as a presumed mother treats a woman differently than a similarly situated man.

These arguments are also without merit. "The first prerequisite to a meritorious claim under the equal protection clause is a showing that the state has adopted a classification that affects two or more similarly situated groups in an unequal manner." (In re *Eric J.* (1979) 25 Cal.3d 522, 530, 159 Cal.Rptr. 317, 601 P.2d 549.) To prevail on either of their equal protection claims, father and Amy must first demonstrate that Amy is similarly situated to the individuals she describes who have asserted presumed parentage under the statutory scheme. As explained, Amy is not similarly situated to either the biological mother's same-sex partner in *Elisa B.* or the nonbiological presumed father in *Jesusa V.*

In a situation such as *Elisa B.*, where two women are same-sex partners, and one gives birth to a child while the other holds the children out as her own, there is no third person who claims to be the child's second parent. In contrast, a woman, such as Amy, who is married to the child's father and wishes to assert presumed maternity, is competing with the child's biological mother for maternal rights. Unlike the circumstances in *Elisa B.*, where it was appropriate to provide a second parent for the child, here two parents, Kim and father, already are present in the action. Therefore, we reject Amy's claim she is being denied equal protection based on her sexual orientation.

Likewise, Amy is not similarly situated to a nonbiological father, such as in *Jesusa V.*, who receives his wife's child into his home and holds the child out as his own. While a biological father's genetic contribution to his child may arise from nothing more than a fleeting encounter, the biological mother carries the child for the nine-month gestational period. Because of this inherent difference between men and women with respect to reproduction, the wife of a man who fathered a child with another woman is not similarly situated to a man whose wife was impregnated by another man. Therefore, it is appropriate for the Family Code to allow the birth mother's husband to claim presumed paternity when the biological father is present in the action, and not allow the wife of the biological father to do the same when the biological mother has promptly come forward to assert her parental rights. "The difference between men and women in relation to the birth process is a real one, and the principle of equal protection does not forbid *18 [the Legislature] to address the problem at hand in a manner specific to each gender." *(Tuan Anh Nguyen v. INS (2001) 533 U.S. 53, 73 [, 121 S.Ct. 2053, 150 L.Ed.2d 115] [upholding a federal law imposing different requirements for citizenship of a child born to one citizen parent and one noncitizen parent, depending upon whether the citizen parent is the mother or the father].)* Given Kim's role and presence as Nathan's biological mother, Amy is not similarly situated to a nonbiological presumed father.

Therefore, we reject father and Amy's equal protection arguments.

b. Due process.

Father and Amy also contend that the statutory scheme, as applied to deny Amy joinder or standing, violates substantive due process and infringes on family privacy and the integrity of the marital family unit. This argument is unpersuasive. Amy and father are asserting a purported right to raise a child resulting from an extramarital relationship between father and another woman, so as to displace the biological mother. It is unfortunate these proceedings already have spanned nearly three years. However, Kim first sought to assert her maternal rights shortly after Nathan was born, and Kim has **309 since enjoyed monitored visitation with Nathan. Under such circumstances, we perceive no substantive due process or other constitutional claim....

However, Nathan's paternity is not an issue in this case. G. G. asserts he is Nathan's father, and Steven concurs. While Steven has not been joined formally as a party in the action, he has received notice of the action and an opportunity to be heard via his September 15, 2005 responsive declaration. In the declaration, Steven eschewed paternity, stating he agreed to enter into a binding waiver of a claim to parentage. Unlike in Sheldon P., where there existed "the potential to deprive... the presumed father... of rights he wishes to assert," here Steven has agreed to waive all such rights. (*County of Los Angeles v. Sheldon P.,* supra, 102 Cal.App.4th at p. 1345, 126 Cal.Rptr.2d 350.) In *Sheldon P.,* there was at least a theoretical possibility that the absent party would "'claim an interest relating to the subject of the action.... '" (Id. at p. 1344, 126 Cal.Rptr.2d 350, citing Code Civ. Proc., § 389, subd. (a).) In marked contrast, Steven already has expressly waived any "interest relating to the subject of the action." (Code Civ. Proc., § 389, subd. (a).) Therefore, the trial court properly found Steven's joinder is not compulsory under Code of Civil Procedure section 389, subdivision (a).

CONCLUSION

We conclude the trial court did not err either in denying father's motion to join Amy in the action or in granting Kim's motion to quash Amy's independent action. **310 When a birth mother promptly comes forward to assert her legal maternity, and the child's father is undisputed and present in the action, the father's spouse cannot be presumed to be the child's mother under any gender-neutral reading of sections 7611, subdivisions (a) or (d), or 7540. Therefore, Amy cannot claim to be Nathan's mother. We further conclude, against father and Amy's contentions, that the trial court's refusal to treat Amy as a presumed mother does not violate equal protection or due process. Finally, we reject Amy and father's contentions that Amy has standing to assert equitable estoppel, and that Steven's joinder is mandatory.

*20 DISPOSITION

The order to show cause is discharged. Father's petition for writ of prohibition or other appropriate relief is denied. The order granting Kim's motion to quash and dismissing Amy's independent action is affirmed. Kim shall recover her costs.

Does the court in *Amy G.* make the biological mother's case easier? But is that in the child's best interest?

NONMARITAL BIRTHS

Shakespeare's *King Lear* opens with a conversation between the Earls of Gloucester and Kent, by which the audience learns that Gloucester has two sons: 1) Edgar, who is older and his legitimate heir; and 2) Edmund, his younger, illegitimate son. Despite his descriptions of them, Gloucester claims to love both his sons equally (*"who yet is no dearer in my account"*).

How does society react when unmarried people produce a child together? As Shakespeare's *King Lear* illustrates, history is replete with children born to unmarried parents and society often discriminates against these children.[2] (As Gloucester says, *"I have so often blushed to acknowledge him."*) A series of Supreme Court cases in the 1960s helped to eliminate this legal stigma. When terms like "baby mama" are the word of the day on today's Urban Dictionary, is this perhaps one area of the law where the courts are ahead of society?

HISTORICAL LEGAL TREATMENT

The general term "illegitimate" means, "not authorized by law".[3] More specifically, the term is used legally when referring to any children born to unwed parents or out of wedlock.[4] Thus, under the law, children born when their parents are married (in wedlock) are deemed "legitimate." According to the Center for Disease Control in the United States, in 2015, 40.2 percent of all births were to unmarried women.[5] A 2012 study found that more than half of the births to American women under the age of 30 occurred to unmarried women: "While out-of-wedlock births used to pertain to mostly minority and/or poor women, the study found that white women in their 20s are leading the trend."[6] While questions on the impacts of this on society and family have been looked at briefly in this book (see chapter 8) and are really beyond it, the large percentage of nonmarital[7] births may influence society's acceptance, and therefore challenge the historical legal treatment and stigmas.

---

2 Ironically, some speculate that Shakespeare, who had no biological descendants after the deaths of his own three childless wives, may have had an illegitimate son for whom Shakespeare was the godfather. http://www.william-shakespeare.info/william-shakespeare-illegitimate-son-william-davenant.htm

3 Google dictionary, first definition. https://www.google.com/search?q=illegitamte&ie=utf-8&oe=utf-8

4 Ibid., second definition.

5 Citing the CDC, http://www.cnsnews.com/news/article/terence-p-jeffrey/cdc-babies-born-unmarried-women-exceeded-40-8th-straight-year

6 Child Trends study reported in February 21, 2012, *Clutch Magazine*. Citing the *New York Times*, "One group still largely resists the trend: College graduates, who overwhelmingly marry before having children. That is turning family structure into a new class divide, with the economic and social rewards of marriage increasingly reserved for people with the most education." http://thegrio.com/2012/02/21/study-for-most-women-under-30-most-births-happen-outside-of-marriage/ Study: For most women under 30, most births happen outside of marriage.

7 Called bastards by Shakespeare (when referring to Edmund in *King Lear*) or "out of wedlock" and "illegitimate" by society and the courts, these hurtful names have largely been discarded as the court opinions attempted to bar the

Having adopted the common law (court created) to largely follow the English model, it is easy to see how the United States began to discriminate against nonmarital births. In England, where the right to the throne passes through family lines, it was necessary to know the bloodline. Thus, while many children may have been born to a king, only those who were born from his queen were in line for succession. In England, this classification was created at birth and was irremediable. Children born outside of marriage were ignored and stigmatized or worse.

In the formation of our nation, the Pilgrims' Puritan morality continued to disapprove of nonmarital sexual relations and perpetuated society's harsh treatment of nonmarital births. All children born to married parents automatically received all the rights of childhood (support, inheritance, etc.). Children born to unmarried parents did not. A child born out of wedlock was *filius nullius* (a child of no one), harshly known as a bastard. But why did society punish the children who were products of relationships when they did not commit the offending behavior themselves?

THE 1960S SUPREME COURT CASES

Based on 14th Amendment Equal Protection arguments, in a series of cases during the 1960s, the Supreme Court of the United States worked to remove that prejudice. Under the law, a child born to a married couple had full legal rights of the parent-child relationship. They could expect support and companionship and even have rights to legal remedies, such as claims for wrongful death, if a third party's wrongful acts caused the death of a parent. Nonmarital children, however, were given none of those rights. Indeed, they were given legal disabilities that prevented claims for support or other favored legal treatment.

With the 1960s Supreme Court's chain of decisions, these differences were discarded as unlawful discrimination. Thus, the law began to recognize the rights of parentage as extending to all children, nonmarital or marital. As seen below, these rights include the right to make a wrongful death claim for the loss of a parent, to obtain financial support (for the necessities) from both parents, and rights to fathers of nonmarital children. Scientific testing continues to make the establishment of the link more accurate. Today, many states rely on the Uniform Parentage Act, which extends the parent and child relationship equally to every child and to every parent, regardless of the marital status of the parents. Now, fewer and fewer people even know about this classification as the law and society abandon it.

A. Right to Make a Wrongful Death Claim

This change in the law began with the landmark case of *Levy v. Louisiana*, 391 U.S. 68 (1968). The Court was evaluating Louisiana's law for wrongful death. Under the law, children whose

---

discrimination and stigma. Now, children born from unmarried parents are referred to as "nonmarital" births by the courts.

parents were married on the day they were born could sue if someone's actions led to the death of their parent(s). However, children whose parents were not married at the time of their birth were denied the right to sue. The Supreme Court invalidated the law and found that in denying the right to sue for the wrongful death of a parent, nonmarital children were discriminated against. The court reasoned that to continue to allow the disparate treatment would mean that nonmarital births amounted to "nonpersons" under the law. If the state's purpose in making such a distinction was to discourage people (especially women) from having sex outside of marriage, does this law work?

B. Right to Support

While most people expect that both parents are responsible for financially supporting their children, this was not the case until the 1970s. Traditionally, mothers had to support their children, whether nonmarital or marital. In many states, including Texas, under the common law and by state law, a biological father of a nonmarital child did not have a duty to support that child. In another landmark case, *Gomez v. Perez*, 409 U.S. 535 (1973) citing to *Levy*, the Supreme Court found that if a judicially enforceable right to financial support exists for legitimate children, it also exists for nonmarital children. Does that judicially enforceable "right to support" extend beyond financial needs?

Still, unless the father filates (files court papers recognizing the child as his, see below), it is generally up to the mother to bring a paternity action. Traditionally, there was a short period in which such claims could be made (one year or two). Recent court decisions or federal legislation[8] have caused states to lengthen the time to make such a claim (up to 18 years if the state receives federal funds). Again, if the purpose were to discourage people from having sexual relations outside of marriage, would the denial of financial support be the carrot to do it? (See the end of this chapter.)

FATHERS' RIGHTS

In another landmark case, *Stanley v. Illinois*, 405 U.S. 645 (1972), the Supreme Court extended rights in nonmarital relationships beyond the children to the biological fathers. Under the state's law, when a biological mother died, custody of any nonmarital children did not automatically transfer to the biological father because nonmarital fathers had no duty of support. They would have to ask the court for such approval; until approval was granted, their children were wards of the state. Under this law, unmarried fathers were the only ones subject to a fitness hearing; unmarried mothers were not. Therefore, they had rights to the nonmarital children upon death of their biological father. If the biological father of the marital children died, would the children be removed from their mother?

---

8   Child Support Enforcement Amendments of 1984, 42 U.S.C. Section 666 (2006).

In this case, Joan Stanley lived on and off with Peter Stanley for 18 years and had three children with him. When she died, Peter Stanley was not allowed to keep the children. Instead, social services took them after a brief "dependency" determination. Unlike child custody cases in which the state wants to remove a marital child from a parent and must prove "unfitness" to do so, no opportunity to prove "fitness" was allowed here. Thus, the 14th Amendment's due process clause entitles both types of parents to a "fitness" hearing before the state may remove children. If, as the states had alleged, these laws were designed to protect the emotional, mental, and physical welfare of the children involved and the moral welfare of the community, presumably, does this particular law correctly punish the person involved in the unmarried sexual relationship—the man? The *Stanley* court invalidated the law and gave recognition to the father for the children he produced. As part of this case, the court stated that it was not the place of the state to meddle in a family's business.

With the increase in nonmarital births, the issue more often surrounds the involvement of the biological father in his child's life and the state's obligation to ensure it. Perhaps as a way to eliminate this responsibility, Virginia established a Putative Father Registry[9] that allows men engaged in extramarital or premarital relations to protect their parental rights to any children that may be produced. The procedure is simple and involves mailing in a completed form that allows a man to register for each sexual act or each new partner. Failure to register means that Virginia is under no obligation to try to locate the father before the mother makes decisions, including placing the baby for adoption. What are the results? For the first year of operations, 64 men registered their sexual encounters, compared with a reported 33,681 nonmarital births.[10]

Would Virginia's Putative Father Registry have helped in this case? A 20 year-old Virginia man, John Wyatt, was concerned when he could not reach his "on-and-off-again" pregnant girlfriend, who was close to delivery of their baby—she had turned off her phone. Finally, the hospital confirmed that she had a baby girl, but when he arrived at the hospital on February 11, 2009, the "administrators insisted that no such baby was there—and no such mother."[11] Records confirmed that the baby, Emma, had been born at the hospital, but for the next two weeks the mother and baby lived in hotels while an adoption was arranged to a couple in Utah. Meanwhile, Wyatt filed for custody in Virginia within eight days after Emma's birth.

So began the "highly unusual dispute [that] pits Virginia against Utah; a Stafford County judge... awarded Wyatt custody of Emma and cited a federal kidnapping statute in ordering the state to bring her back from Utah. Virginia officials say they lack the legal authority to follow the judge's order. In Salt Lake City, a Utah judge issued a competing order granting temporary custody to the adoptive couple in that state and Emma has been living with them ever since".[12] The adopting parents assert that Wyatt "failed to assert his parental rights in time to contest the

---

9   The U.S. Supreme Court case of *Lehr v. Robertson* 463 U.S. 248 (1983), approves such registries as a way to assert parentage.

10   "Virginia to Lovers: Let's Get Cynical," by Marc Fisher, "Raw Fisher," a blog, 2008.

11   http://www.washingtonpost.com/wp-dyn/content/article/2010/04/13/AR2010041302445.html, "'Baby Emma' case puts state adoption laws between father, child," by Jerry Markon. *WashingtonPost.com*, April 14, 2010

12   Ibid.

adoption. His appeal is pending in a Utah court."[13] "My daughter is being held hostage," said Wyatt.[14]

When he found out about the surprise pregnancy (to a woman he had known since second grade, began dating in seventh grade, and whose relationship continued, off and on, through high school), Wyatt was excited, "'My father died when I was 10, so I've always wanted to be there for my children.'" [15] Wyatt went with her to doctor's appointments[16] but the couple had argued about putting the baby up for adoption. A February 5, 2009, text message "has become central in the dispute. Wyatt recalls the mother texted him that she was 'receiving information' from a Utah adoption agency. He immediately called her, and says she assured him that they would make a decision jointly—and that she'd alert him the minute she went into labor. In their final conversation, about 11 hours before the birth, Wyatt [claims] the mother vowed they would raise the baby together."[17] Two days after the baby's birth, the mother relinquished her parental rights to the child and gave custody of her to the Utah couple who had traveled to Virginia to pick up the child.[18]

"At the behest of her parents, the mother also met with McDermott, an adoption attorney. He instructed Fahland [the mother] to falsely indicate on adoption paperwork that she did not know Wyatt's address, according to the court opinion. At McDermott's urging, she also made other false statements to Wyatt so that he "would not take steps to secure his parental rights and prevent the adoption."[19] The mother "did not feel she could give the baby what the baby needed… [a]nd she didn't think John could either."[20] In an affidavit in the Utah courts, the mother claimed "that she told Wyatt in the text that she 'intended' to put the baby up for adoption in Utah," implying that it would have given Wyatt time to file a court action in Utah to contest the adoption. "Frankly, he never did," said Larry Jenkins, the Utah couple's attorney.[21]

In his December order granting custody, Virginia Judge Gerald F. Daltan said that because Wyatt is Emma's "acknowledged father" and had sought custody five days before the Zarembinskis filed adoption papers in Utah, Emma could not be adopted without his consent. He called Wyatt "a

---

13   Ibid.

14   Ibid.

15   Ibid.

16   http://www.sltrib.com/sltrib/news/53956775-78/adoption-court-virginia-wyatt.html.csp. "Virginia Father Gets Green Light to Seek Damages in Utah Adoption," Brooke Adams, *Salt Lake Tribune*, April 20, 2012.

17   http://www.washingtonpost.com/wp-dyn/content/article/2010/04/13/AR2010041302445.html, "'Baby Emma' case puts state adoption laws between father, child, "by Jerry Markon. *WashingtonPost.com*, April 14,2010

18   Ibid.

19   "Virginia Father Gets Green Light to Seek Damages in Utah Adoption," Brooke Adams, *Salt Lake Tribune*, April 20, 2012. http://www.sltrib.com/sltrib/news/53956775-78/adoption-court-virginia-wyatt.html.csp.

20   "The Utah statutes can be harsh, but they are looking at what's best for the child: stable placements and two-parent families," said David Hardy, a lawyer for LDS Family Services, a Mormon Church–affiliated adoption agency that is among the nation's largest. "'Baby Emma' case puts state adoption laws between father, child," by Jerry Markon. *WashingtonPost.com*, April 14, 2010. http://www.washingtonpost.com/wp-dyn/content/article/2010/04/13/AR2010041302445.html,

21   Ibid.

good and decent person" "who is fit to raise Emma."[22] But later, in Utah, a Utah judge granted the adopting parents "temporary custody in August," and "that Wyatt cannot object to the adoption, partly because he failed to move quickly enough to assert his parental rights under Virginia law—even though the Virginia judge said he had."[23] In July 2011, the Utah Supreme Court upheld that finding, "holding that Wyatt did not meet required deadlines for asserting his parental rights under Utah law. Also, the court found that he was barred from arguing that the federal Parental Kidnapping Prevention Act required Utah to follow a Virginia judge's order granting him custody because he failed to raise that argument in the lower court."[24]

Experts say that Utah adoption laws are unusually tough on unmarried fathers. Lawyers cite at least ten recent cases in which babies were taken to or born in Utah and adopted without an out-of-state father's consent."[25] Wyatt sued in federal court in Virginia against Mark McDermott, (the girlfriend's attorney); An Act of Love, (the Utah adoption agency); Lorraine Moon (the agency employee who facilitated the adoption); Larry Jenkins, (the Utah attorney); and the adoptive parents.[26]

Three years later, on March 29, 2012, the Virginia Supreme Court ruled that Wyatt "was 'purposefully kept in the dark' about Baby Emma's Utah adoption and could argue in federal court that the proceedings interfered with his parental rights"[27] and that he "could pursue monetary damages in federal court for loss of companionship, mental anguish, loss of services and expenses incurred in his fight to recover his now 3-year-old daughter."[28] In its ruling, the Virginia court found that "while Virginia statutes do not specifically recognize 'tortious interference with parental rights,' such a cause of action has existed in common law since 1607 and continues to exist today."[29] "Failure to recognize that claim would 'leave a substantial gap in the legal protection afforded to the parent-child relationship,' the majority wrote. It said an 'overwhelming majority' of courts in 'sister states' have reached similar conclusions.[30] The court also found that the "defendants went to 'great lengths to disguise their agenda from the biological father,

22 Ibid.
23 Ibid.
24 "Virginia Father Gets Green Light to Seek Damages in Utah Adoption," Brooke Adams, *Salt Lake Tribune*, April 20, 2012. http://www.sltrib.com/sltrib/news/53956775-78/adoption-court-virginia-wyatt.html.csp
25 "In one case, the Utah Supreme Court last year ruled in favor of an unwed Wyoming mother, who falsely told the father she miscarried, traveled to Utah to deliver the baby girl, and put her up for adoption. "Utah risks becoming a magnet for those seeking to unfairly cut off opportunities for biological fathers to assert their rights to connection with their children," Chief Justice Christine Durham wrote. http://www.washingtonpost.com/wp-dyn/content/article/2010/04/13/AR2010041302445.html, "'Baby Emma' case puts state adoption laws between father, child," by Jerry Markon. *WashingtonPost.com*, April 14, 2010
26 http://www.sltrib.com/sltrib/news/53956775-78/adoption-court-virginia-wyatt.html.csp, "Virginia Father Gets Green Light to Seek Damages in Utah Adoption," Brooke Adams, *Salt Lake Tribune*, April 20, 2012.
27 Ibid.
28 Ibid.
29 Ibid.
30 Ibid.

including preventing notice of his daughter's birth and hiding their intent to have an immediate out-of-state adoption, in order to prevent the legal establishment of his own parental rights.'"[31]

While Utah's aggressive adoptions continue against unwed fathers, what is the effect on married fathers? A Texas husband's firstborn child was placed for adoption with a Utah couple while he was serving in the military.[32] "Terry Achane, 31, a drill instructor in South Carolina, says it was just days after he left his pregnant wife for his new job out of state that she quietly signed over their unborn baby to a family of seven in Utah" [this family had spent the last few years struggling to naturally expand their family of five children].[33] "The adoption agency Adoption Center of Choice told the new family that [the father] wasn't aware of his daughter's placement with them and he would most likely contest it if he had found out. The *Tribune* reports that [his wife] had given the adoption agency Mr. Achane's former address in Texas for contact, knowing full well at the time that he was not living there."[34] "Feverishly calling anyone who may know where his wife could be, while fearing she may have carried out the abortion she once threatened to do, he learned from a family doctor that his wife was no longer pregnant but they could not legally disclose what had happened to the baby."[35] "'This is a case of human trafficking'; [said Mark Wiser, Mr. Achane's attorney]... 'Children are being bought and sold. It is one thing what [adoption agencies] have been doing with unmarried biological fathers. It is in a new area when they are trying to take a child away from a married father who wants to have his child.'"[36] Unable to get confidential information from the adoption agency, Mr. Achane hired a lawyer. "When an attorney for the Frei family contacted Mr. Achane, asking him to consent to the adoption, he said no and demanded his little girl be returned to him—to the Frei family's complete surprise." "'Over the last 19 months, despite the law requiring that a father show interest in his child and at least attempt regular communication to establish a bond, the father has never shown any interest in Leah other than to hire an attorney,' the Utah family wrote in their blog."[37]

"Despite a judge's order to return the child [to Achane] within 60 days, the adopting family asked that his parental rights granting him custody of her be terminated and reached out for public financial support."[38] They accused him of abandoning both the mother and baby during her pregnancy and therefore demonstrating no capability for raising the girl.[39]

---

31 Ibid.
32 http://www.dailymail.co.uk/news/article-2242567/Terry-Achane-Married-fathers-horror-wife-places-baby-adopted-Frei-family-telling-him.html#ixzz2Owlyf4Jc, "U.S. Married Father's horror after wife places his child with an adopted family without telling him." http://www.dailymail.co.uk/news/article-2242567/Terry-Achane-Married-fathers-horror-wife-places-baby-adopted-Frei-family-telling-him.html#ixzz2Owlyf4Jc, "The Adoptive parents say they plan to appeal the judge's decision," Nina Golgowski, MailOnline, December 3, 2012
33 Ibid.
34 Ibid
35 Ibid.
36 Ibid.
37 http://www.dailymail.co.uk/news/article-2242567/Terry-Achane-Married-fathers-horror-wife-places-baby-adopted-Frei-family-telling-him.html#ixzz2Owlyf4Jc, "Adoptive parents say they plan to appeal the judge's decision," Nina Golgowski.
38 Ibid.
39 Ibid.

"'The right of a fit, competent parent to raise the parent's child without undue government interference is a fundamental liberty interest that has long been protected by the laws and constitution of this state of the United States, and is a fundamental public policy of this state,' said Judge McDade. He added that there is no law requiring the father to 'prove himself' as fit to father his own child." "'Once Mr. Achane contacted the Adoption Center of Choice… to let them know he opposed the adoption and wanted his daughter back, that should have been the end of this case,' said Judge McDade."[40]

In November 2012, despite the adoptive family's continued fight to keep her,[41] a Utah court "gave" Achane custody of his daughter and allowed the girl to reunite with her father.[42] The couple had 60 days to return her and in January 2013, "'I got my daughter back,' Achane told the *Salt Lake Tribune*, 'I'm very happy. It's 22 months too long, but the wait was worth it.'"[43]

INHERITANCE

While the *Levy* case caused the successful application of equal protection challenges to most laws that treated children differently based on their parentage, it cannot be read to do so in all cases. Inheritance, because of the potential for fraud and other confusion, is an area in which the courts are willing to allow two different treatments. Perhaps this is because anyone can be included or excluded in a will, thus allowing inheritance for nonmarital children when intended. While nonmarital children could inherent from their mother, it is only in modern times that this right extends to both parents. Still, unless the father filates (files court papers recognizing the child as his or "holding out" the child as his and living with the child during the first two years), it is generally up to the mother to bring a paternity action.

EFFECTS OF ANNULMENT

If an annulment "wipes the slate clean" as if the marriage never occurred, what is the effect on children who are born from that now "non-marriage?" Since the 19th century, most states have laws legitimizing children from annulled marriages or recognizing that their parents were married at the time the children were born (even though now no such marriage is recognized).

---

40 Ibid.
41 "Judge McDade condemned the adoption agency [already under investigation] that handled Achane's daughter's case for refusing to disclose any information to him nearly two years ago when he learned that his child had been given away without his consent, according to the *Salt Lake Tribune*." http://www.dailymail.co.uk/news/article-2268565/Terry-Achane-baby-Soldier-wins-22-month-custody-battle-finally-reunited-daughter.html#ixzz2Owv5yOBt, "Soldier wins 22-month custody battle and finally reunited with daughter, 2, who his wife gave up for adoption without telling him" *Daily Mail*, January 25, 2013.
42 Ibid.
43 Ibid.

ESTABLISHING PATERNITY

There are three ways to establish paternity: 1) Legal Presumption; 2) DNA testing; and 3) Filation, or acceptance.

1. Legal Presumption

Based on an old English law from Lord Mansfield, traditionally, the law presumed that a child born to a married couple was the legitimate child of the husband. This was designed to create certainty and to prevent unnecessary interference in the family unit. In the *Amy G.* case above, the court was asked to examine whether this ancient presumption should apply in the reverse so that the wife is presumed the mother of any children born during their marriage. How did this work out?

In cases using the legal presumption, the husband's name is specified as the father on the child's birth certificate. Does this seal the legality of the relationship? No. Like the presumption, the name on the birth certificate is still subject to rebuttal in a custody determination case.

What is the effect of divorce or death? In many states, a woman's pregnancy was a defense to a divorce action. The court would not grant a divorce while she was pregnant or until the child was born to eliminate questions of legitimacy. Most states have dropped those laws. Also, now in most states if a child is born within 300 days of a divorce, the court will use the presumption and deem the recently divorced husband the father. Is this a good idea?

Finally, can a couple get married after a child is born to legitimize it? Most states recognize marriages done within a short time (e.g., 300 days) as sufficient to find that the child was born to a married couple. Similarly, if the husband dies within a short period (less than 9 months) before the birth of the child, the court will presume that the child was his. Which part of that rule applies in this case? "They say being a bride and becoming a mother are two of the best days in a woman's life. In 2012, in France, Danielle Clewlow managed to achieve both in one day, when just after saying her vows; she gave birth to a bouncing 7lb 7oz baby boy. Incredibly, just-married Danielle and her new husband Aaron, 25, even managed to return to their evening wedding reception to show off the newborn."[44] According to the mayor, "it did rather shake us up. The bride was definitely a bit worn out, but we put that down to the stress of the wedding. I tried to hurry it up a bit so that she didn't get too tired".[45] When a baby is born at the time of its parent's wedding, is the baby legitimate because it was born to a married couple or because the couple was married shortly after its birth?

---

44   http://www.dailymail.co.uk/news/article-2140320/Bride-gives-birth-baby-boy-wedding-day--makes-time-newborn.html#ixzz2SYtnfYve, "Bride gives birth to baby boy on her wedding day… but still makes it back in time for evening reception to show off newborn," Allison Smith Squire, *Daily Mail*, May 6, 2012.
45   Ibid.

2. Recognition

A second way the law will "legitimize" a child born to an unmarried woman is when the man "[holds] himself out as the father" (including welcoming the child into his home). Or, within a short period of time after the birth, the father can file an order of filation with the court legally acknowledging the parent-child relationship.

3. DNA/Technology

Science's rapidly evolving knowledge of genetics and DNA has allowed the law to create a third way to determine paternity using blood testing and DNA. While DNA was originally used to exclude possible fatherhood, now it can also be used to show probable parenthood. Science is so precise that courts can use evidence of about 100% that a person is not the father of the child and over 99% probability that the man is the father. During the 2000s, the number of paternity tests taken every year jumped 64 percent, to more than 400,000. This figure counts only a subset of tests—those that are admissible in court and thus require an unbiased tester and a documented chain of possession from test site to lab.[46]

As the stigma/legal disability of nonmarital birth has diminished in society, should a non-husband male who believes he is the biological father of his affair partner's child be able to insist on a blood test? Who should be allowed to challenge the time-honored presumption that a child born to an intact family of a married mother and father is the child of the married husband and wife? In Colorado, which follows the Uniform Parentage Act (UPA), the 2000 case of *N.A.H. v. S.L.S.* had to balance presumptions of fatherhood between the husband (listed on the birth certificate, though his wife left because of domestic abuse allegations) and a man alleging paternity and supported by DNA testing, but opposed by the married husband and wife.[47] Which should the court pick? The courts were initially wary in allowing an outside/third party to challenge the harmony of a married family by claiming to be the true father of a married couple's child. Should the interest of preserving martial harmony still survive today?

---

46 FN 88 http://www.nytimes.com/2009/11/22/magazine/22Paternity-t.html?pagewanted=all&_r=0, "Who Knew I Was Not the Father?" Ruth Padawer, *New York Times Magazine*, November 17, 2009.

47 Unlike California's 2015 law that allows more than one person recognized in the parental role, Colorado permits only one person legally in the role (see chapter 15).

Supreme Court of Colorado, En Banc.
Justice KOURLIS delivered the Opinion of the Court.

This case concerns the interpretation of Colorado's Uniform Parentage Act (the UPA), and causes us to determine what considerations that Act directs the courts to include in making paternity decisions. Specifically, the case involves a young girl, S.R.H., who was born in 1994, when her mother was married to N.A.H. (Husband). N.A.H. was identified on the birth certificate as her father and accepted the child into his home. However, genetic tests demonstrate that, in fact, S.L.S. (Biological Father) is the biological father of S.R.H. Pursuant to Colorado statutes, both men can claim a presumption of being S.R.H.'s legal father. Because a child can have only one legal father, the court must resolve the competing presumptions afforded these two men and adjudicate paternity for the child. Colorado's UPA specifies that in the face of conflicting presumptions, courts should look to the weight of policy and logic in settling the conflict and adjudicating paternity. Accordingly, we determine that a question of paternity is not automatically resolved by biological testing, but rather calls upon the courts to consider the best interests of the child in analyzing policy and logic as directed by the statute.

We hold that the best interests of the child must be of paramount concern throughout a paternity proceeding, and therefore, must be explicitly considered as a part of the policy and logic analysis that is used to resolve competing presumptions of fatherhood.

In this case, the magistrate did not make express findings on the best interests of the child when he adjudicated Biological Father as the child's legal father. The court of appeals upheld the magistrate's adjudication, even absent such findings. *See In re S.R.H.*, 981 P.2d 199 (Colo.App.1998). Since we conclude that the court must address the best interests of the child,[1] we reverse the court of appeals and remand the case for further proceedings.

I.

A.

On June 28, 1994, A.H. (Mother) gave birth to a baby girl, S.R.H. At the time of S.R.H.'s conception and birth, Mother was married to Husband and they lived together. Husband attended the child's birth, was listed on the birth certificate as the father, and accepted S.R.H. as his own child.

During their twenty-year marriage, the couple periodically experienced marital difficulties and had a history of domestic violence. On one occasion, Mother temporarily moved out of state, and on another occasion, she visited a safe house for counseling for victims of domestic violence.

At a time when she and Husband were having difficulties, Mother became involved in an extra-marital affair with a coworker, Biological Father. Mother would visit Biological Father's home, telling him that she did not want to return to her home because **[9 P.3d 358]** she feared Husband. During this time, Mother and Biological Father conceived S.R.H. Mother told Biological Father that he was the real father and that he would be listed on the birth certificate. For approximately eighteen months after S.R.H. was born, Mother left the child in Biological Father's care for ten hours every Friday while Mother worked. Biological Father also took S.R.H. on a weeklong trip out of state to meet his relatives.

Mother and Husband separated in November 1995, and she filed for dissolution of marriage. She alleged that Husband had assaulted her, and that he had not bonded with S.R.H. Shortly thereafter, however, Mother and Husband reconciled and began attending marriage counseling. In January 1996, Mother abruptly terminated Biological Father's visits with S.R.H.

As a result, Biological Father petitioned for a determination of his parent-child relationship with S.R.H. on March 5, 1996. Husband was unaware that S.R.H. was not his biological daughter until Biological Father initiated this action.

B.

After an initial hearing on April 22, 1996, the magistrate ordered genetic testing of the parties to determine whether Biological Father was, in fact, S.R.H.'s biological father. Biological Father submitted to such testing, but Mother did not present the child for testing. As a result, Biological Father moved for a declaration that he was the child's legal father under section 13-25-126(1)(a), 5 C.R.S. (1999), which provides that if a party refuses to submit to genetic tests, the court may adjudicate the question of parentage against that party.

The magistrate held a hearing on the issue on December 30, 1996. Prior to the hearing, the parties stipulated that paternity testing would show Biological Father to be S.R.H.'s biological father with greater than ninety-seven percent accuracy. At the hearing, the Guardian Ad Litem (GAL) recommended that Biological Father be allowed to pursue his paternity claim, and that the court assess the best interests of the child after the paternity determination.

On January 3, 1997, the magistrate issued an order declaring Biological Father to be the legal father. The magistrate recognized that under state law, Husband and Biological Father each were entitled to a presumption of legal fatherhood. He also recognized that the paternity statute required him to resolve the competing presumptions by considering policy and logic. *See* § 19-4-105(2)(a), 6 C.R.S. (1999). He then stated,

In this case the logically persuasive presumption is that the DNA testing is the most accurate way to determine who the father of the child may be. That individual is [Biological Father]. Therefore, unless this presumption is outweighed by considerations of public policy, it must control. The facts in this case do not rise to the level of showing that public policy would be served by declaring the respondent, [Husband], to be the father of the child. The Court acknowledges that [Husband] is and will continue to be an excellent and committed parent. However, this is not a case in which the Court is to select which male will do a better job of being the father of the child. [Biological Father] isn't just the sperm donor. He has shown that he wishes to be actively involved in the child's life. The record reflects that, throughout the life of the child, [Biological Father] has made reasonable attempts to see the child and be a part of the child's life.... Although the Court recognizes that there continues to be a strong presumption of legitimacy, that presumption is overcome by the logic of the scientific evidence.

Mother and Husband appealed this decision to the district court. The district court held that the magistrate should not have accepted the parties' stipulation as to the results of genetic testing. The district court judge stated that, "compliance with the Magistrate's order for genetic testing may eliminate the need to weigh logic and policy considerations in resolving any conflict between presumed fathers." The district court ordered the parties to complete genetic testing, and the magistrate to hold a second hearing on the issue of paternity. **[9 P.3d 359]** Mother and Husband continued to delay genetic testing. As a result, Biological Father again moved for a declaration of paternity under section 13-25-126(1)(a). In May 1997, the magistrate repeated his order for genetic testing, and Mother and Husband then complied. The tests revealed that Biological Father could not be excluded as S.R.H.'s biological father, and that the probability of his parentage was 99.68% when compared to an untested, unrelated Caucasian male.

The magistrate held a second hearing on July 1, 1997. At the outset of the hearing, the magistrate reiterated that he was deciding between competing presumptions based on policy and logic. He then made factual findings, and again adjudicated Biological Father as S.R.H.'s legal father. The court then took additional testimony, which was directed at allocating parenting time, the reintroduction of Biological Father into S.R.H.'s life, and child support. On July 12, 1997, the magistrate issued his second order declaring Biological Father to be S.R.H.'s legal father. He also ordered S.R.H.'s name to be changed, and the parties to work with a psychologist to formulate a plan to integrate Biological Father into S.R.H.'s life.

In reviewing the magistrate's order in the context of the second appeal, the district court ruled that in "determining where the weightier considerations of policy and logic are to be found, the Court is to look closely at issues touching upon the best interests of the child." After assessing the evidence, the district court concluded that "[n]othing indicated to the magistrate that contact between [Biological Father] and [S.R.H.] would be contrary to [S.R.H.'s] best interest, nor was there any evidence indicating that for [S.R.H.] to become aware that [Biological Father] is her father would emotionally or in some other fashion harm her." Therefore, the district court held that the magistrate's decision that Biological Father should be S.R.H.'s legal father was not clearly erroneous.

The court of appeals upheld the district court's ruling that Biological Father is S.R.H.'s legal father. *See In re S.R.H.*, 981 P.2d 199 (Colo.App.1998). The court of appeals held that the presumption of legitimacy, which would favor Husband as the legal father, was not irrebuttable. *See id.* at 202. The court determined that evidence in the record supported the factual findings made by the magistrate and the district court, and that their findings as to the positive role Biological Father could play in S.R.H.'s life were not unreasonable or unfair. *See id.* at 203. Mother and Husband appealed that ruling.

II.

At the outset, we note the extraordinary importance of the outcome of a paternity proceeding. Such a proceeding determines who a child's legal father will be, and therefore, who will enjoy the rights and responsibilities of legal fatherhood. Parenthood in our complex society comprises much more than biological ties, and litigants increasingly are asking courts to address issues that involve delicate balances between traditional expectations and current realities. The determination of parenthood includes the right to parenting time; the right to direct the child's activities; the right to make decisions regarding the control, education, and health of the child; and the right to the child's services and earnings. See Michael H. v. Gerald D., 491 U.S. 110, 118-19, 109 S.Ct. 2333, 105 L.Ed.2d 91 (1989). Legal fatherhood imposes significant obligations as well, including the obligation of support and the obligation to teach moral standards, religious beliefs, and good citizenship. See id. [9 P.3d 360] Paternity proceedings are governed by Colorado's version of the Uniform Parentage Act (the UPA). See §§ 19-4-101 to -128, 6 C.R.S. (1999); see also R.McG. v. J.W., 200 Colo. 345, 349, 615 P.2d 666, 669 (1980). Under the paternity statutes, a presumption of fatherhood may arise in a number of different circumstances. See § 19-4-105(1), 6 C.R.S. (1999). These include when a child is born into an intact marriage, see § 19-4-105(1)(a); when a man and a child's mother married or attempted to marry either before or after the child's birth, providing certain other conditions are met, see § 19-4-105(1)(b), (c); when a man receives a child into his home and holds the child out as his natural child, see § 19-4-105(1)(d); when the man files a written declaration of paternity in a court registry, see § 19-4-105(1)(e); or when genetic tests show that the probability of a man's parentage is ninety-seven percent or higher, see § 19-4-105(1)(f). Thus, in a single situation, presumptions of paternity may simultaneously arise in favor of different men.

The UPA recognizes this by providing a mechanism to choose among competing presumptions: "If two or more presumptions arise which conflict with each other, the presumption which on the facts is founded on the weightier considerations of policy and logic controls." § 19-4-105(2)(a). Competing presumptions must be resolved, because although a child certainly can have emotional attachments to more than one father figure, she can have only one legal father. *See Michael H.*, 491 U.S. at 130, 109 S.Ct. 2333.

In this case, competing presumptions of legal fatherhood arise. Husband benefits from two presumptions: the presumption of legitimacy and the presumption occasioned by accepting the child into his home and holding her out as his own. The presumption of legitimacy declares that "[a] man is presumed to be the natural father of a child if: a) he and the child's natural mother are or have been married to each other and the child is born during the marriage." § 19-4-105(1)(a). A strong public policy supports this presumption. *See A.G. v. S.G.*, 199 Colo. 403, 407, 609 P.2d 121, 124 (1980) (stating that the presumption of legitimacy is "one of the strongest presumptions known to the law"); *W.C. ex rel. A.M.K.*, 907 P.2d 719, 722 (Colo.App.1995). The presumption associated with accepting the child as his own is closely related to the presumption of legitimacy and arises when a man "receives the child into his home and openly holds out the child as his natural child." § 19-4-105(1)(d).

Biological Father benefits from a competing presumption that presumes a man to be a child's legal father if genetic testing reveals that he is the biological father. *See* § 19-4-105(1)(f). Section 13-25-126 outlines the procedures for paternity testing and admission of the results into evidence:

(1)(a) In any action, suit, or proceeding in which the parentage of any child is at issue, upon motion of the court or any of the interested parties, the court shall order the alleged mother, the child or children, and the alleged father to submit to genetic testing... for the purpose of determining probability of parentage. If any party refuses to submit to these tests, the court may resolve the question of parentage against such party to enforce its order if the rights of others and the interests of justice so require.... (e) The results of such tests shall have the following effect:... (III) If the experts conducting the tests conclude that the genetic tests... show that the alleged parent is not excluded and that the probability of the alleged parent's parentage is ninety-seven percent or higher, the alleged parent is presumed to be the parent, and this evidence must be admitted. Other expert testimony can be offered to rebut the presumption, but cannot prohibit the presumption from attaching. **[9 P.3d 361]** (IV) The presumption of legitimacy of a child born during wedlock is overcome if the court finds that the conclusion of the experts conducting the tests, as disclosed by the evidence based upon the tests, shows that the husband or wife is not the parent of the child.

§ 13-25-126, 5 C.R.S. (1999).[3]

Our task in this case is to determine what the General Assembly has directed courts to do in the situation presented by the facts of this case. The first question must be whether there are genuine competing presumptions, or whether one of the men who claims fatherhood is entitled to a conclusive determination.[4]

Nowhere in the statutes does the General Assembly identify any presumption as conclusive. Specifically, section 19-4-105 does not indicate that the presumption of legitimacy automatically outweighs the presumption of biology, or that the converse is true. In fact, no section of the UPA suggests that one presumption of fatherhood should be absolute or conclusive. Rather, the paternity statute indicates that any of the presumptions may be rebutted by clear and convincing evidence. See § 19-4-105(2)(a); see also In re L.J.P., 2 P.3d 140, 142 (Colo.App.2000) (remarking that the paternity statutes "plainly state" that paternity presumptions may be rebutted).[5]

Similarly, the evidentiary statute does not conclusively elevate a biological presumption over other presumptions. That statute indicates that the presumption of legitimacy is overcome "if the court finds that the conclusion of the experts conducting the tests, as disclosed by the evidence based upon the tests, shows that the husband or wife is not the parent of the child," § 13-25-126(1)(e)(IV); it does not state that blood evidence is conclusive of fatherhood in all circumstances, or that it automatically eliminates other presumptions of fatherhood. Additionally, although the evidentiary statute states that evidence of biological fatherhood must be admitted and that a biological presumption must attach, the presumption based on biology is still rebuttable. *See* § 13-25-126(1)(e)(III).

This understanding of the statutes is in accord with the evidentiary nature of presumptions. Presumptions generally do not conclusively resolve an issue, but create a prima facie case, which "is always subject to be[ing] overcome by evidence to the contrary." *American Ins. Co. v. Naylor,* 101 Colo. 34, 36-37, 70 P.2d 349, 351 (1937) (quoting *Ward v. Teller Reservoir & Irrigation Co.,* 60 Colo. 47, 50, 153 P. 219, 222 (1915)). The purpose of a presumption is to aid the trier of fact in ascertaining the truth at trial. *See Denver Publ'g Co. v. City of Aurora,* 896 P.2d 306, 318 (Colo.1995) (stating that "we recognize that a presumption is a rule of convenience based on experience or public policy"); *Murray v. Montgomery Ward Life Ins. Co.,* 196 Colo. 225, 228-29, 584 P.2d 78, 81 (1978); *Naylor,* 101 Colo. at 37, 70 P.2d at 351.

Both the paternity statute and the evidentiary statute contemplate trials on the issue of paternity, indicating that the presumptions of fatherhood are not conclusive, but are subject to adjudication. *See* § 19-4-105(2) (stating that presumptions may be rebutted in "an appropriate action" and that a voluntary acknowledgement of paternity is considered a legal finding of paternity on the date of a judicial proceeding); § 13-25-126(1)(d) **[9 P.3d 362]** (stating that objections to blood tests should be made prior to trial); § 13-25-126(1)(e) (regarding the admissibility of evidence at trial). Indeed, substantial portions of the UPA are directed at the right to a trial on the issue of paternity, and to the proper trial and pretrial procedures. *See* § 19-4-128, 6 C.R.S. (1999) (stating that any party may demand a trial on the issue of paternity); § 19-4-114(3) (stating that a paternity action shall be set for trial if the parties refuse the judge's pretrial recommendation); § 19-4-111, 6 C.R.S. (1999) (outlining pretrial proceedings). If either the presumption of legitimacy or the presumption of biology were conclusive, then a trial on the issue of paternity would never be necessary. Thus, it is evident from the statutory scheme as a whole that presumptions of fatherhood can be the starting point for an adjudication of paternity, not the end of the inquiry.

As a result, we conclude that the statute contemplates that neither the presumption of legitimacy nor the presumption based on biology is conclusive. Rather, the statutory scheme as a whole indicates that all presumptions are rebuttable, including the presumption based on biology. The statutes allow for the creation of various presumptions in favor of men who have claims to fatherhood of a child. When those presumptions conflict, then the statute directs the courts to resolve them on the basis of policy and logic. Accordingly, the next step is to analyze what the courts must consider in the policy and logic equation.

III.

The petitioners, Husband and Mother, argue that we should reverse the magistrate's determination of paternity because the magistrate failed to consider explicitly the best interests of the child as part of the policy and logic used to resolve competing presumptions. We agree, and hold that the best interests of the child must be considered as part of the policy and logic analysis used to decide legal fatherhood. We hasten to add that we are not, in our role as an appellate court, usurping the function of the trial court by anticipating any particular outcome once the trial court rehears this matter. We are not ruling on the ultimate question of whether it is in S.R.H.'s best interests to have Biological Father declared to be her legal father. Rather, we are announcing a test of law, and determining whether the magistrate's findings reflect application of that test.

A.

Although courts previously have considered policy and logic in resolving these competing presumptions, our courts have not had an opportunity to explain what factors are encompassed within "policy" and "logic." The court of appeals used this formula to address a similar conflict between the presumption of legitimacy and the presumption based on biology in *W.C. ex rel. A.M.K.*, 907 P.2d 719. In that case, a mother engaged in an extramarital affair with the putative father, which resulted in the conception of a child. *See id.* at 720. The mother's husband believed he was the father as he was married to the mother at the time of the child's conception and birth. *See id.* After recognizing the competing presumptions, the court of appeals upheld the trial court's decision that the mother's husband should be confirmed as the child's legal father. *See id.* at 722-23. The trial court's decision was grounded in the particular facts of the case, in which the putative father made no effort to establish paternity for the first six years of the child's life, and the child had no relationship with the putative father. *See id.* at 721. In addition, the child was nine years old at the time of the paternity order, he suffered from hyperactivity and attention deficit disorder, and experts testified that the boy would suffer adverse consequences from learning that the man whom he believed to be his father was not his father. *See id.* at 722. Although the court of appeals focused on these facts, it did not employ any particular standard in resolving the case.

Clearly, the inquiry is fact-intensive, and the trial court's findings concerning paternity ultimately govern the outcome. However, today we clarify that the courts must focus on the best interests of the child and make determinations of paternity with that standard at the forefront.**[9 P.3d 363]**

B.

The UPA is replete with references to the best interests of the child. In fact, the stated policy underlying the UPA is the protection of the best interests of children. See § 19-1-102(1)(a), 6 C.R.S. (1999) (stating that one of the purposes of the Children's Code, which encompasses the UPA, is "[t]o secure for each child subject to these provisions such care and guidance… as will best serve his welfare"). Accordingly, the UPA specifically directs trial judges to consider the best interests of the child at other phases of a paternity proceeding. For example, after a paternity action is filed, a trial judge must hold an informal hearing on the issue of paternity if such hearing would be in the best interests of the child. See § 19-4-114, 6 C.R.S. (1999).[6]

Additionally, following the pretrial hearing, the trial judge "shall evaluate the probability of determining the existence or nonexistence of the father and child relationship in a trial and whether a judicial declaration of the relationship would be in the best interest of the child." § 19-4-114(1), 6 C.R.S. (1999). On the basis of that evaluation, the trial judge may make a recommendation as to paternity or as to whether the action should proceed to trial. *See id.* One of the judge's options is to recommend an agreement under which legal fatherhood is not determined, but the putative father undertakes some financial obligation for the child. See § 19-4-114(1)(b). As part of such an agreement, the judge may order that the putative father's identity be kept confidential if in the best interests of the child. *See id.* Colorado law also directs trial judges to return to the best interests of the child standard after paternity has been established, when the court resolves issues of parenting time and decision-making responsibilities. *See, e.g., In re Marriage of Francis*, 919 P.2d 776, 779 (Colo.1996); *In re Marriage of Mann*, 655 P.2d 814, 817 (Colo.1982).

If the parties refuse to accept the judge's pretrial recommendation, the court may order genetic testing if it has not already been done, and the action will be set for trial. See § 19-4-114(3), 6 C.R.S. (1999). After the genetic testing has been conducted, competing presumptions of paternity may arise.[7]

Hence, although the term best interests of the child is used numerous times throughout the legislation, at the stage of resolving competing presumptions, the UPA directs the court to use policy and logic as the dispositive criteria. *See* § 19-4-105(2)(a). Therein lies the confusion, and Colorado courts have not addressed the role that the best interests of the child should play in measuring policy and logic. See *W.C. ex rel. A.M.K.,* 907 P.2d 719 (resolving competing presumptions of legal fatherhood without referring to the best interests of the child).

However, it is clear to us that the General Assembly intended the whole paternity proceeding to be about the best interests of the child, and it is, therefore, axiomatic that the trial judge must focus on best interests in resolving the competing presumptions. The policy of the UPA is to meet the best interests of the child: such policy is necessarily a part of the final determination of paternity. Accordingly, we now hold that the best interests of the child must be part of a court's consideration of policy and logic when the presumption of legal fatherhood arises in more than one man.[8] As the Washington **[9 P.3d 364]** Supreme Court recognized, "A paternity suit by its very nature, threatens the stability of the child's world." *McDaniels v. Carlson,* 108 Wn.2d 299, 738 P.2d at 261 (1987). This is especially true if the paternity action is filed after a child has established strong family ties with one parent. The outcome of a paternity action irrevocably alters a child's current family situation and her future. Therefore, "`[d]espite the numerous burdens and benefits of being a father... it is the child who has the most at stake in a paternity proceeding.'" *Id.* (quoting *State v. Santos,* 104 Wn.2d 142, 702 P.2d 1179, 1180 (1985)). Because a paternity action significantly impacts a child, concern for her welfare should be paramount at every stage of the proceedings.

Other states agree, and require that the best interests of the child be fully considered in resolving competing presumptions of paternity. *See Ban v. Quigley,* 168 Ariz. 196, 812 P.2d 1014, 1018 (App.1990); *Department of Health & Rehabilitative Servs. v. Privette,* 617 So.2d 305, 309 (Fla.1993); *In re Marriage of Ross,* 245 Kan. 591, 783 P.2d 331, 339 (1989); *C.C. v. A.B.,* 406 Mass. 679, 550 N.E.2d 365, 373 (1990); *In re Paternity of B.J.H.,* 573 N.W.2d 99, 102 (Minn.Ct.App. 1998) (holding that the best interests of the child is part of the analysis for resolving conflicting presumptions); *In re Paternity of "Adam",* 273 Mont. 351, 903 P.2d 207, 211 (1995); *M.F. v. N.H.,* 252 N.J.Super. 420, 599 A.2d 1297, 1302 (1991); *McDaniels v. Carlson,* 108 Wn.2d 299, 738 P.2d 254, 261 (1987); *In re Paternity of C.A.S.,* 161 Wis.2d 1015, 468 N.W.2d 719, 726 (1991) (finding that state statutes explicitly direct courts to consider the best interests of the child).[9]...

C.

Having determined that the best interests of the child standard applies, we next must determine what factors the court should consider in assessing those interests when competing presumptions of paternity arise. Some states have set out exhaustive lists of factors to be considered in determining the best interests of the child. *See In re Paternity of "Adam",* 903 P.2d at 211; *M.F.,* 599 A.2d at 1302. Other states have left the determination largely to the discretion of the trial judge. *See In re Paternity of C.A.S.,* 468 N.W.2d at 728.

We believe the latter course is the wiser. The General Assembly has chosen not to define the best interests of the child in the context of a paternity proceeding, although they have done so in the context of dissolution of marriage. *See* § 14-10-124, 5 **[9 P.3d 365]** C.R.S. (1999). We defer to that choice.

We hold merely that the trial judge should take into account all the facts and circumstances of the case. Affording the trial judge significant deference recognizes the myriad relevant facts that may properly influence a trial judge's decision. It also allows the judge to assess the credibility of the parties' competing claims as to the child's best interests, and to consider expert evidence if appropriate. However, all the facts considered by the trial judge should bear directly on the child's best interests.[11] In some cases, the child's best interests may not match the best interests of any of the adults involved.[12] Perhaps, as King Solomon observed many centuries ago in a battle over parentage, the true parent is the one who can elevate the best interests of the child over his or her own best interests.

IV.

Given our conclusion that a court must apply the best interests of the child standard in weighing competing presumptions, we must now turn to the ultimate question of whether the magistrate in this case did so. We conclude that the findings are insufficient to convince us that he did apply the best interests standard, and thus, we remand the case.

At the first hearing, the magistrate took testimony from the parties, Husband and Mother's marriage counselor, S.R.H.'s day care provider, and a friend of Husband and Mother's. All of that testimony might have pertained to S.R.H.'s best interests. In his order following the hearing, however, the magistrate failed to address the best interests of the child. The magistrate instead stated that the presumption in favor of the biological father must control unless outweighed by considerations of public policy. The judge acknowledged Husband's fitness as a parent as well as the role that Biological Father had played in S.R.H.'s life, and then concluded that the scientific weight of the genetic evidence overcame the presumption of legitimacy. None of the magistrate's analysis appears to have been directed at S.R.H.'s best interests.

At the second hearing, the magistrate first stated that he would decide between the competing presumptions based on policy and logic. He went on to recognize the public policy interest in preserving marriages and intact families. The magistrate noted that Husband and Mother's marriage, although strong at the time of the hearing, had been troubled in the past. He noted that Biological Father believed he was the father, had insisted on a relationship with S.R.H., and that Mother had accommodated his relationship with the child. The magistrate then found that Biological Father's relationship with S.R.H. ended because Mother reconciled with Husband and she wanted to prevent Husband from learning of S.R.H.'s true parentage. All of the magistrate's factual findings focused on the adults, and not on the impact that the adults' actions and relationships might have on S.R.H.

The GAL recommended that the court make further inquiry into S.R.H.'s best interests before making a paternity determination. The magistrate did not do so, however, and proceeded to conclude that Biological Father should be adjudicated the legal father. Only then did the court hear expert testimony, all of which was directed at parenting time and the reintroduction of Biological Father into S.R.H.'s life.

On the whole, we find that the record of the hearings does not indicate that the magistrate made findings concerning whether it was in the best interests of the child to name Biological Father the legal father. **[9 P.3d 366]** Biological Father argues that the magistrate's determinations implicitly considered the best interests of the child, and therefore, no further action is necessary. We disagree, and find that the record contains insufficient evidence to conclude that the trial court clearly took evidence and engaged in an inquiry focused on the child's best interests. Because the magistrate did not affirmatively consider S.R.H.'s best interests, we remand this case for specific findings as to the best interests of the child.[13] In conducting the analysis, the trial judge should take into account all the facts that may bear on S.R.H.'s best interests, including those facts that have developed since this appeal began.

V.

In conclusion, we hold that when presumptions of paternity arise in more than one potential father, trial courts must take the best interests of the child into account as part of policy and logic in resolving competing presumptions. This is consistent with the statutory approach to paternity proceedings as a whole.

In this case, the magistrate's findings were not sufficient to demonstrate that he affirmatively considered the best interests of the child. Accordingly, we reverse the court of appeals and remand the case for additional findings consistent with this opinion.

Justice COATS dissents, and Justice RICE joins in the dissent.

Justice COATS, dissenting:

Today a majority of the court holds that in a paternity proceeding in Colorado, the question of paternity is not automatically resolved by establishing the genetic or biological father of the child. Rather, the majority holds that the best interests of the child are paramount and must be explicitly considered by a court in deciding which of two presumptive natural fathers should be declared the legal father of the child, even after court-ordered genetic testing has proven as a matter of scientific fact that one cannot possibly be, and the other almost certainly is, the child's biological father. Because I do not understand Colorado's statutes the same way, I respectfully dissent.

Colorado's statutory scheme specifies a number of circumstances in which a man is presumed to be the "natural" father of a child. The majority's conclusion derives from its construction of the statute's formula for resolving conflicting presumptions of paternity, particularly its use of the words "policy and logic." *See* § 19-4-105(2)(a), 6 C.R.S. (1999) ("[T]he presumption which on the facts is founded on the weightier considerations of policy and logic controls."). I reach a different conclusion for two separate but related reasons.

First, in light of the legislature's evidentiary treatment of genetic tests that definitively exclude certain individuals from the class of possible parents, I do not believe this case calls for us to resolve conflicting presumptions of paternity. Second, while I wholeheartedly agree with the majority that the best interests of the child are paramount in affixing the incidents of the parent-child relationship, including among other things the duty of support, allocation of parental responsibilities and guardianship, and parenting time privileges with the child, it seems clear to me from the statutory scheme as a whole that the first requirement of a paternity proceeding is to determine, to the extent possible, the natural[1] or biological father of the child. That being the case, the best interests of the child can be (and expressly are) taken into account in a host of other **[9 P.3d 367]** ways by the statutes, but they cannot change the fact of paternity… (footnotes omitted by the author)

In *N.A.H. v. S.L.S.* the alleged biological father intervenes in the marital relationship to claim paternity of their child. The courts were initially weary in allowing an outsider to challenge the harmony of a married family by claiming to be the true father of the married couple's child. Should that interest of preserving martial harmony still survive today?

EQUITABLE OR PUTATIVE FATHER

What is the effect on a husband who raises his non-biological child as his own based upon presumption and later finds that the child is not his? Many states recognize him as the "equitable" parent (even though non-biological) who is prevented from later disavowing his paternity. Is it reasonable that by having created a parental relationship with the child he should have to financially support it, while the biological father does not? Would it be fair for a non-biological father to have to financially support his "equitable" daughter after his wife moves in with the daughter's biological father and they are living as an intact biological family?

Compare this to a Maryland court's decision, which found that a putative father to two different women should be allowed to take a blood test to determine whether the children that he has been obligated to provide child support for are actually his. While the lower court prevents him from taking the test, on appeal, the court allows him to do so. In so doing, the court rejects that the best interest of the child should be taken into consideration when the court makes its determination.

A djudged father filed motion to obtain blood or genetic testing and to set aside declaration of paternity. The Circuit Court, Talbot County, denied motion. Mother appealed. The Court of Special Appeals, 129 Md.App. 260, 741 A.2d 553, vacated and remanded. In two other cases, second adjudged father sought review of rulings of the Circuit Court, Baltimore City, Kenneth Lavon Johnson, J., that he was not entitled to a hearing to set aside two prior paternity declarations. After grant of certiorari, the Court of Appeals, Cathell, J., held that: (1) statutory amendment permitting court to set aside or modify paternity declaration on basis of blood or genetic tests applied retroactively, and (2) blood or genetic tests are available, upon motion, to any putative father seeking to challenge a prior paternity declaration.

So ordered.

Determination of best interests of child in ordering blood or genetic testing requested by putative father, or in consideration of paternity, whether original or revised, is inappropriate. Code, Family Law, §§ 5–1029, 5–1038(a)(2)(i) 2.

CATHELL, Judge.

Three separate paternity disputes are before this Court. In each case, the man previously adjudged to be the father of a child in a prior paternity proceeding seeks to set aside that prior judgment based on alleged new evidence that he is not, or may not be, the actual father. In the first case, number 136, petitioner Danielle R. appeals from a decision of the Court of Special Appeals, which held that Tyrone R., respondent, is entitled to a court-ordered genetic or blood test and, if the test proves he is not the father of the child in question, a hearing on whether to set aside the original paternity declaration entered against him. In the cases numbered 117 and 137, appellant William Carl Langston appeals from two consolidated rulings of the Circuit Court for Baltimore City that he is not entitled to a hearing to set aside two prior paternity declarations adjudicating him to be the father of two different children. In one of those cases, he has taken a post-declaration blood test, which excluded him from being the biological father of the child in question.

I. Facts and Procedural Background

A. Case No. 136

Danielle R. and Tyrone W. were involved in a dating relationship from October 1987 to June 1988, during which time they engaged in sexual intercourse. At some point in the relationship, Danielle informed Tyrone she was pregnant and he was the father. On January 8, 1989, Danielle gave birth to a son, T. R. Based on his belief that he was the natural father of T. R., Tyrone entered into a paternity agreement on April 27, 1989, in which Tyrone acknowledged that he was T. R.'s *400 father, without requesting a blood test to determine paternity. The Circuit Court for Talbot County subsequently entered a declaration of paternity on May 9, 1989, which included an order to pay child support.

Tyrone was not aware prior to and during the paternity proceedings that Danielle **391 had been involved in a relationship with another man, James P., before she met Tyrone. Danielle testified at the proceedings below that her relationship with James had ended in 1986. Danielle and James began dating again when T. R. was three years old. Sometime after the paternity declaration was entered, Tyrone learned about Danielle's relations with James. Tyrone testified below that he confronted her on the telephone about the relationship and alleged that Danielle threatened him that, because of his accusation, she would seek an increase in the child support he was paying "if" T. R. was Tyrone's son.

On April 7, 1998, the Talbot County Bureau of Support Enforcement and Danielle filed a petition in the Circuit Court for Talbot County to increase the child support Tyrone was paying under the 1989 paternity declaration. Tyrone responded to the petition and filed a "Complaint to Set Aside Declaration of Paternity." The complaint was based on Maryland Code (1984, 1999 Repl.Vol.), section 5–1038(a)(2)(i)2 of the Family Law Article, FN1 which allows a circuit court to set aside or modify a paternity declaration "if a blood or genetic test done in accordance with § 5–1029 of this subtitle establishes the exclusion of the individual named as the father in the order." Tyrone's complaint requested blood or genetic testing to determine whether he could be excluded as the natural father of T. R.

The circuit court referred the matter to a domestic relations master. After an evidentiary hearing, the master recommended that genetic testing be conducted. The Talbot County Bureau of Support Enforcement filed exceptions with the *401 circuit court. Without a hearing, the circuit court rejected the master's recommendations on August 18, 1998, and dismissed Tyrone's complaint to set aside the original paternity declaration. The circuit court ruled that there was no authority in Maryland to set aside the paternity declaration absent fraud, mistake, irregularity, or clerical error. The circuit court also ruled that Tyrone had "failed to act with ordinary diligence" by waiting nine years to challenge the paternity declaration, and that Tyrone was "bound by the 1989 judgment."

Tyrone appealed to the Court of Special Appeals. That court vacated the order of the Circuit Court for Talbot County, holding that Tyrone was entitled to a blood or genetic test to determine whether he is T. R.'s biological father. The court also held that, if the tests excluded him as the biological father, he was entitled to a hearing on whether to set aside the original paternity declaration. *Tyrone W. v. Danielle R.*, 129 Md.App. 260, 300–01, 741 A.2d 553, 575 (1999). Danielle appealed to this Court, and we granted her a writ of certiorari.

B. Case No. 117

Appellant William Carl Langston entered into a consent decree of paternity before the Circuit Court for Baltimore City on October 27, 1987. In the decree, he acknowledged that he was the father of Angela, who was born to appellee Alice Riffe, and agreed to pay child support.

Angela subsequently moved to Harford County to live with her natural grandfather, Carl Riffe. When her grandfather requested that the Harford County Department of Social Services (HCDSS) provide Angela with benefits, the HCDSS sought a paternity declaration from the Circuit Court for Harford County against appellant in July of 1997. Apparently, the HCDSS was unaware of the 1987 declaration issued in Baltimore City. A blood test was conducted, which excluded appellant as the natural father of Angela. The Circuit Court for Harford County subsequently dismissed the HCDSS paternity complaint on December 9, 1997.

**392 *402 Appellant was brought before the Circuit Court for Baltimore City on October 18, 1998, on a show cause order for failure to pay child support for Angela. At a contempt hearing before a master on December 16, 1998, appellant introduced into evidence the blood test results from the Harford County paternity litigation. The master recommended that the contempt proceedings be postponed to provide appellant an opportunity to challenge the 1987 paternity declaration.

Appellant filed a complaint to set aside the 1987 paternity declaration on January 7, 1999, based on section 5–1038(a)(2)(i)2. Appellee sought a dismissal of the complaint, arguing that section 5–1038(a)(2)(i)2, which was adopted by the General Assembly in 1995, could not be applied retroactively. The Circuit Court for Baltimore City ultimately ruled in favor of appellee and denied appellant's complaint to set aside the paternity declaration. A master subsequently recommended that appellant be held in contempt for the child support arrears and the circuit court agreed, issuing an order on May 6, 1999. Appellant made a timely appeal to the Court of Special Appeals. This Court granted a writ of certiorari on its own motion prior to any proceedings before the intermediate appellate court.

C. Case No. 137

Appellant Langston also had entered into a paternity consent decree on March 22, 1985, before the Circuit Court for Baltimore City. In that decree, he acknowledged that he was the father of Jason L., the son born to appellee Sharon Locklear on December 24, 1984, and he agreed to pay child support.

A show cause order was subsequently issued to appellant for failure to pay child support. From the beginning, the proceedings in this case were consolidated with appellee Riffe's case (number 117 before this Court). Thus, the procedural steps in this appeal, and the dates on which they occurred, were virtually identical to the background described in appellee Riffe's case, supra. The only differ-ence between *403 the cases appears to be that appellant, at the time he filed his petition for recon-sideration, did not have any previous blood or genetic test excluding him as the biological father of

Jason L. Rather, he alleged that he learned after the original paternity declaration was entered that appellee Locklear had engaged in sexual relations with other men around the time that Jason probably was conceived. The master recommended that his request for a genetic test be granted to determine whether he is the biological father of Jason L. The circuit court denied appellant's complaint and his request for genetic testing, appellant appealed, and we granted a writ of certiorari on our own motion.

All that the 1995 amendment effectively does is to permit a man declared to be the father of a particular child or children to petition to reopen that declaration following a blood or genetic test that excludes him as the father. It is a substantive right that did not previously exist. Under our holding in *Tandra S. v. Tyrone W.*, supra, 336 Md. 303, 648 A.2d 439, once the declaration became final, in the sense that it was no longer subject to review on appeal or pursuant to a timely filed motion under Rule 2–534 or 2–535(a), the finding of paternity was immune from relitigation. Chapter 248 afforded men the right, under limited circumstances, to relitigate that determination. It gave them a cause of action, even though in the same case, **426 that previously did not exist. That is not, in my view, merely procedural....

Nor is the 1995 Act solely remedial in nature. Chief Judge Bell notes quite well the substantive aspects of the legislation. It permits the court, on the basis of evidence that, in most instances, could have been obtained earlier, to undo a legal relationship and with it, often, an emotional one as well. That was the policy choice that the Legislature made and had the right to make, but to suggest that there is no substantive aspect to the amendment is to ignore the reality of its effect. I fully understand the view expressed by the dissenting judges in *Tandra S.*, which obviously was persuasive to the Legislature, and I make no comment, one way or the other, on the merits of that view from the perspective of social policy. *464 Whether good policy or bad, the fact is that the accomplishment of its objective necessarily leaves children legally fatherless, sometimes emotionally fatherless, without an existing order of paternal support, and without an ability to inherit from a man previously adjudicated to be the child's father. It abrogates, as well, the support flowing to the mother or other custodian of the child. The hope that, someday, the "true" father may be discovered and substituted—the likelihood of which, I suspect, is largely remote—does not diminish the immediate substantive effect of setting aside an established paternity declaration.

For these reasons, I would hold that the 1995 amendment is not retroactive and does not apply to declarations of paternity that were final prior to October 1, 1995. I would reverse the judgment of the Court of Special Appeals in No. 136 and affirm the judgments of the Circuit Court for Baltimore City in Nos. 117 and 137.

Judge RODOWSKY has authorized me to state that he joins in this dissenting opinion.

359 Md. 396, 754 A.2d 389

In deciding this case, the court accepts the DNA evidence and uses it. Paternity courts have accepted DNA testing (more advanced than blood tests), blood tests and Polymerase Chain Reaction (PCR), which is most reliable with a reliability to an exclusion power of 99.99% or higher.

DNA testing can even be performed before the baby is born by taking a blood sample from the pregnant woman. The importance of establishing the biological parent and child bond has been recognized by court cases holding that someone who cannot afford the cost of a blood test to prove or disprove paternity is entitled to have the test paid for by the government.[48] While most DNA testing cases involve a mother's efforts to determine paternity for child support proceedings[49] against a biological father, occasionally a case goes the other way, with a father attempting to establish his maternity.

In July 2010, professional basketball player LeBron James and his mother Gloria James, were sued by a lawyer claiming that he was LeBron James' father. The lawyer, Princeton graduate Leicester Stovell, filed a suit in federal court asking for $4 million, claiming that he had been trying for three years to establish paternity. Although James alleges an earlier paternity test had ruled out the possibility that Stovell was LeBron's father, Stovell claimed it could have been tampered with—"and there are indications that there was a motivation." Stovell "said he had sex with James' mother, Gloria James, after meeting at a Washington bar while she was visiting from Ohio in 1984. A few months later, she told him she was pregnant, but did not say whether he was the father." Stovell also "claims she told him the child would be named LeBron, similar to Leicester Bryce, Stovell's first and middle names." "Stovell said his only request was that the child, if a boy, plays basketball."[50] Stovell also says that in a conference call, Gloria James denied ever meeting him, but the player agreed to provide a DNA [sample]." "There is a DNA test that came back with the results 99.9 percent conclusive excluding paternity by Mr. Stovell," said Fred Nance [James's attorney]."[51] U.S. District judge Colleen Kollar-Kotelly dismissed the case and "cited several problems with the suit… including a failure to show any actual damages.[52]

---

48   *Little v. Streater*, 452 U.S. 1 (1981).

49   DNA testing (through a sample of the neighbor's dog's saliva and fur) was used in Virginia to determine who had killed a woman's cat, but despite the strong link of the genetic evidence, Loudon County officials said "they need an eyewitness to close the case." "Cat Owner Turns to DNA in Pet Whodunit, but Case Isn't Closed," Karin Brulliard, *Washington Post*, January 9, 2006. In another interesting twist, in 2013, a man was convicted of murder when his cat's hair matched the cat hair found on the victim's body.

50   http://www.cnn.com/2010/SPORT/07/08/lebron.james.lawsuit/index.html, "Lawyer sues basketball star LeBron James, alleging he is his father," Bill Mears, CNN, July 8, 2010

51   http://voices.washingtonpost.com/reliable-source/2010/07/rs-_lebron.html

52   http://www.abajournal.com/news/article/judge_tosses_suit_by_dc_lawyer_claiming_to_be_lebron_james_father/, "Judge Tosses Suit by DC Lawyer Claiming to Be LeBron James' Father," Debra Cassens Weiss, ABAJournal.com, September 15, 2011

COMPLICATIONS FOR SAME-SEX PARENTS

When only one parent can be biologically related to a child in a same-sex relationship, what is the effect of the relationship between the non-biological parent and the child? In the New York case of *Jann P v. Jamie P*,[53] the court looked at this issue after New York passed its Marriage Equality Act in 2011. The Act promised that same-sex married couples would "be treated equally in all respects under the law." But does it and can it? After a lesbian couple lived together they decided to have a child through artificial insemination (without medical supervision) with one of the partners agreeing to bear the child. When the child was born in a Catholic hospital it would not allow the other partner's name on the birth certificate. Allegedly both were involved in pre-natal care and co-parenting after the baby was born (e.g., the non-biological parent was at the birth and cut the umbilical cord) including calling the non-biological parent "Daddy. Three weeks after the baby was born the couple married when the baby was two months old and the Marriage Equality Act was six months old. Within a year, the partner moved out. "Using a form she and her father found on the Internet, the couple signed a separation agreement" which called the child a "child of the marriage", gave the non-biological parent time with the child (every Saturday and other Sunday) and stipulated that no one other than the two women would raise the child. This was followed by a petition for joint custody by the non-biological parent, which was rejected by the biological parent who argued that the other was not a parent. New York law agreed and denied the non-biological parent custody or even visitation.

While it is true that the non-biological parent was not on the birth certificate and not married at the time of the birth, did she do anything else that would allow the courts to recognize her relationship with the child? First, she held herself out as the child's parent from birth and provided financial support and love to the child. Second, there is an argument for equitable or "de facto" parenthood based on the beneficial relationship between the non-biological parent and the child. (While other states have passed such laws to deal with similar issues in heterosexual cohabitations and stepparents, New York did not. The only way the homosexual parent could get parenthood was to adopt.) Third, the couple married shortly after the child was born which in many states allows a child to be a marital birth. None of this was enough. Indeed the court acknowledged that if the partner were a "man who held himself out as the...father 'for a period of time sufficient to establish a paternal bond with the boy, he would have standing to file a petition seeking a declaration of paternity'... which in turn would allow him to seek custody." But, "because she cannot claim that she is J.'s father'... the law does not provide for a proceeding to a declare paternity.'" The state's legislature would have to amend the law to make the terms gender neutral. When the non-biological partner lost her request for custody (and parental recognition), she appealed. Making matter worse, the boy was removed from the biological partner's home because of allegations of abuse and placed in foster care. Not only was the non-biological partner not given an opportunity to take in the child requiring him to go to strangers, but now she did not

---

53 *Jann P. v. Jamie P.*, NYLJ 1202664272007 (published July 23, 2014).

have contact with him or the foster mother. Complicating this case more, the biological parent then got pregnant to a man she was in a non-marital relationship with. "Since Jann and Jamie are still married, the law presumes Jann to be a parent to the child Jamie is carrying, in a way it didn't with J., who was born before their marriage."[54] Does the law only give her parental access to the child intended for another relationship and not the one she intended to have as her own?

WILL A DNA TEST ALWAYS PROVIDE ALL THE ANSWERS?

With over 99 percent accuracy, DNA testing is widely accepted in courts to determine paternity. But will it be able to supply all of the answers? With testing based on the father supplying one half of the child's chromosomes, what happens if the potential father has an identical twin with identical chromosomes?

STATE EX REL. DEPT. OF SOCIAL SERVICES, DIV. OF CHILD SUPPORT ENFORCEMENT V. MILLER 218 S.W.3D (MO. APP 2007)

B ackground: Mother filed a paternity action against two identical twin brothers to determine which brother was the biological father of child. The Circuit Court, New Madrid County, Fred W. Copeland, J., adjudicated one brother as father of child. Brother who was adjudicated father appealed.

Holding: The Court of Appeals, Phillip R. Garrison, J., held that evidence supported finding that the adjudicated father was the biological father of out-of-wedlock child.

Affirmed.

The Court of Appeals will reverse the trial court's judgment only if no substantial evidence supports it, it is against the weight of the evidence, it erroneously declares the law, or it erroneously applies the law.

PHILLIP R. GARRISON, Judge.

---

54 "Parenthood Denied by the Law", John Leland, *The New York Times*, September 14, 2014, P. 26

In this paternity action the trial court entered a judgment finding that Raymon Miller ("Appellant") was the natural father of the minor child ("K. A. A."), and that his identical twin brother, Richard Miller ("Richard") was not the natural father. The results of blood tests performed on the two brothers demonstrated that both had a 99.999% probability of being the father. The issues on this appeal relate to *4 whether sufficient evidence was presented to rebut the presumption, created by the blood tests, that Richard was the father. We affirm.

On September 13, 2004, Holly Marie Adams ("Mother"), individually and as next friend of K. A. A., as well as the State of Missouri through the Department of Social Services, Division of Child Support Enforcement (collectively "Plaintiffs"), filed suit against Appellant and Richard to determine the identity of the natural father and to obtain a declaration of paternity as to K. A. A., born April 12, 2004. After a bench trial, the court entered a judgment finding that Appellant was K. A. A.'s natural father. This appeal followed... (evidentiary rules removed)

Blood tests conducted on Appellant and Richard demonstrated that both had a combined paternity index of 814,445 and a probability of paternity of 99.999% with a prior probability of 0.5. The conclusion of those tests stated:

The alleged father [Appellant], cannot be excluded as the biological father of the child [K. A. A.], because they share genetic markers. The probability of paternity is 99.999%, as compared with an untested, unrelated Caucasian man of the North American Population. [Richard] is the twin brother of [Appellant] and an alleged father of [K. A. A.]. The probability that [Appellant] is the biological father of [K. A. A.] is identical to the probability that [Richard] is the biological father. [Appellant] and [Richard] are one billion times more likely to be identical twins than to be fraternal twins.

At trial, Mother testified that K. A. A. was born approximately three and one-half weeks prior to her due date of May 1, 2004. She said that she had a sexual relationship with Appellant that began in December 2002, and ended when they had sex on August 8, 2003, one week after her last full menstrual period ended. She said that Appellant never used any kind of birth control when they had sex. She also said that she had a sexual relationship with Richard that began in 2002 and lasted until April 2003. FN2 She first suspected that she *5 was pregnant when she began having morning sickness around the 18th to 20th of August 2003, and made a doctor's appointment. Mother testified that she again had sexual intercourse with Richard on August 22 or 23, 2003, but that he used a condom on that occasion; she did not start her period which should have begun on August 24 or 25, 2003; she went to the doctor on August 26, 2003, at which time a urine test confirmed her pregnancy; and that type of urine test requires that the person be pregnant at least two weeks before it will provide a positive result.

FN2. Mother, who at the time of trial was twenty-four years old, said that she had been around Appellant and Richard since she was fourteen or fifteen years old and could tell them apart.

Appellant's two points on appeal are inter-related and will be considered together. In one, he contends that the trial court erred in declaring him the father of K. A. A. because the party bringing a paternity action has the burden of proof, which is by a preponderance of the evidence, and in this case that burden of proof was not met because the undisputed evidence showed that the blood tests were non-determinative between he and Richard, and that both had sexual intercourse with Mother at or around the time of conception. In the other point, Appellant contends that the trial court erred in finding that Richard was not K. A. A.'s biological father because there was a conclusive presumption of his paternity pursuant to Section 210.822, FN3 and there was no clear and convincing evidence to rebut that presumption as provided in Section 210.822.2....

1. A man shall be presumed to be the natural father of a child if:

(4) An expert concludes that the blood tests show that the alleged parent is not excluded and that the probability of paternity is ninety-eight percent or higher, using a prior probability of 0.5.

2. A presumption pursuant to this section may be rebutted in an appropriate action only by clear and convincing evidence,... If two or more presumptions arise which conflict with each other, the presumption which on the facts is founded on the weightier considerations of policy and logic controls. The presumption is rebutted by a court decree establishing the paternity of the child by another man.

As indicated earlier, blood tests in this case indicated that either Appellant or Richard was the father of K. A. A., and that the probability of that being true was equal as between the two of them. It is Appellant's position that pursuant to Section 210.822, the blood test created a conclusive presumption that Richard was the father of K. A. A. and there was no evidence to rebut that presumption.

Illinois Dept. of Public Aid, ex rel. *Masinelli. v. Whitworth*, 273 Ill.App.3d 156, 209 Ill. Dec. 918, 652 N.E.2d 458 (1995), was a case involving a paternity suit against two identical twin men in which the results demonstrated an equal probability that they each fathered the child in question. That case also involved a statute creating a presumption of parentage which could be rebutted by clear and convincing evidence. Id. at 460. The Illinois Appellate Court held that when blood tests of two identical twins produces an equal probability of fatherhood, there is a rebuttable presumption that one or the other is *6 the father. Id. In such cases, the court said that the "so-called 'hard' scientific blood testing could result in competing presumptions of paternity which cancel each other out, relegating the trier of fact to the 'soft' evidence." Id. at 461. There, the "soft evidence" was that one twin had had sexual intercourse with the mother but the other had not. Id. at 459–60. The appellate court approved the trial court relying on nongenetic evidence to conclude that one of the twins was the father. Id. at 461.

The reasoning of *Whitworth* is persuasive. Otherwise, application of the statutory presumption from the blood tests under the facts here, without more, would result in neither brother being adjudicated K. A. A.'s father even though those same tests indicate that one of the two is the father.

Appellant draws our attention to Section 210.836(1), providing that evidence relating to paternity may include evidence of sexual intercourse between the mother and alleged father "during the possible time of conception." Continuing, he argues that Mother admitted having sexual intercourse with Richard on several occasions, specifically "at or around the time of conception." Although Mother testified that she had a sexual relationship with Richard that ended in April 2003, and was not renewed thereafter except on one occasion, to wit: August 20 or 22, 2003, Appellant emphasizes a portion of Mother's testimony that he seems to contend required the trial court to find that Mother had sexual intercourse with both Appellant and Richard on August 8, 2003. She had testified that she went to the rodeo in Sikeston, Missouri, on the evening of August 8, 2003, and later went to Appellant's home in Wardell, Missouri, where they had sex. During cross-examination by Appellant, Mother said she went to the rodeo alone, and that Richard was at the rodeo with a friend. She was then asked, "Did you sleep with him while in Sikeston for the rodeo?" to which she answered "yes, ma'am." She then said she went to Appellant's home where they had sex later that night or early the next morning.

In both his points on appeal, Appellant impliedly accepts August 8, 2003, as the date of conception and argues that the above evidence demonstrates that both brothers had sex with Mother on that date. FN4 That, together with the identical blood test results, he argues, dictates the conclusion that plaintiffs did not meet their burden of proof and did not rebut the equal presumption that Richard was the father.

FN4. Courts take judicial notice of the normal 280-day gestational period and the party having the burden of proof must present evidence to support a finding of a shorter or longer gestational period. *Robinett*, 770 S.W.2d at 304. Although Appellant does not argue that the normal gestational period would indicate an earlier date for conception than August 8, 2003, we note that Mother's testimony about her having had a full menstrual period beginning on July 25, 2003, along with her testimony that Appellant was the only person she had sex with until after the urine test indicated she would have been pregnant would have been sufficient to support a finding by the trial court that conception occurred in early August. Id.

Appellant's reliance on Mother's answer to the one question referred to above as requiring the conclusion that Richard and Appellant both had sex with Mother on August 8, 2003, is misplaced because it ignores the entirety of Mother's other testimony. As indicated earlier, at other points in her testimony, Mother said that she had a full menstrual period beginning July 25, 2003; she said that on August 8, 2003, she had sex with Appellant, but not Richard; she had sex with Richard a week *7 and [a] half or two weeks after she had sex with Appellant on August 8, 2003; she had morning sickness, believed she was pregnant, and made a doctor's appointment to test for pregnancy between August 18 and 20, 2003, before she had sex with Richard on August 22 or 23, 2003; Appellant did not use a condom when he had sex with Mother on August 8, 2003, but Richard did use one when he had sex with her on August 22 or 23, 2003; and a urine test administered by her doctor on August 26, 2003, not only showed she was pregnant, but also demonstrated that she had been pregnant at least two weeks.

As indicated earlier, the trial court is the judge of credibility and was entitled to believe all, part or none of a witness's testimony, and we are to review the evidence and inferences in the light most favorable to the judgment and disregard evidence and inferences to the contrary. In addition, we note that the record does not indicate that findings of fact and conclusions of law were requested or entered by the trial court. Accordingly, all fact issues are to be interpreted as having been found in accordance with the result reached. *Gerecke v. Gerecke*, 954 S.W.2d 665, 668 (Mo.App. S.D.1997).

Based on the above, Appellant's points are denied. The judgment of the trial court is affirmed.

Beyond the legal issues raised in these cases, being the keeper of the secret history of a child's origins involves many ethical issues too. What are some of these issues? They may begin at conception if the baby is the product of a clandestine extra-marital affair. This creates its own deceptions that may be coupled with allowing the husband to believe that the child is his and the child being lead to believe this also. Thus, the child is deceived as to one-half of its biological family history. Some argue that "the right to know who you are and where we come from is basic and core."[55] If you know that someone is not the true father, what should you do?

---

[55] See generally, "Secret History," Ariel Kaminer, *New York Times Sunday Magazine's The Ethicist*, August 28, 2011, Pg. 16, quoting Adam Pertman, author of "Adoption Nation".

CHILD ABUSE

All children are essentially criminal.
—Denis Diderot[1]

The first duty to children is to make them happy, If you have not made them so, you have wronged them, No other good they may get can make up for that.
—Charles Buxton[2]

INTRODUCTION

Maybe more than any other area in family law, the family's treatment of children has seen the most change; from the strictness of common law to the alleged excesses of today. Times have changed and society's view of children has changed too: from a necessary burden or indentured servant to the focus of the family to be cherished and even indulged. Yet, it is still hard to imagine the extent of brutality that parents or caregivers can impose on vulnerable children. Beginning in the 1960s, the federal government began to encourage states to protect children and prevent abuse by putting systems in place.

HISTORY

Under common law, children were lower on the pecking order than wives—who were on a par with the family's livestock.[3] It is not surprising that children learned by the rod and were

---

1   www.quotationspage.com/quote/21215.htm
2   www.brainyquote.com/quotes/quotes/c/charlesbux402278.html
3   http://family.findlaw.com/child-abuse/child-abuse-background-and-history.html, "Child Abuse Background and History," "Children under English common law were considered the property of their fathers until the late 1800s; American colonists in the seventeenth and eighteenth centuries carried this tradition to the early years of the United States."

expected to benefit the family, not to benefit from it. Indeed, the SPCA, the Society for the Prevention of Cruelty to Animals was formed over 19 years before the first such society for children.[4] In many ways, it was the case of a young foster child, Mary Ellen Wilson, which led from one to the other.

Know the Victim

Mary Ellen was born in New York in 1864.[5] After her father died, her mother worked to support them and put Mary Ellen in a boarding home. When her mother fell behind on her payments and failed to visit, the owner of the boardinghouse (without the mother's relinquishment of rights) turned Mary Ellen over to New York's Department of Charities[6], which "placed her illegally, without proper documentation of the relationship, and with inadequate oversight in the home of Mary and Thomas McCormack, who claimed to be the child's biological father."[7] When that "father" also died, his widow remarried, and Mary Ellen joined her and her new husband. It was known in their tenement neighborhood that the widow was abusive to Mary Ellen, who "suffer[ed] almost daily whippings and beatings."[8] Why did the family keep her if she appeared to be such a burden? They had little money, so perhaps they received a small foster care stipend. Only after the family moved to another tenement neighborhood did one of the old neighbors contact a church missionary worker to attempt to help Mary Ellen.

At the new tenement, the missionary worker, Etta Angell Wheeler, found a neighbor, Mary Smitt, "who confirmed that she often heard the cries of a child across the hall. Under the pretext of asking for help for Mrs. Smitt, Etta Wheeler introduced herself to Mary Connolly [the widow and "mother" of Mary Ellen]. [Once in the apartment, Wheeler] saw Mary Ellen's condition for herself. The nine-year-old appeared dirty and thin, was dressed in threadbare clothing, and had bruises and scars along her bare arms and legs."[9] "I was there only long enough to see the child and gain my own impression of her condition. While still talking with the woman, I saw a pale,

---

4   The New York Society for the Prevention of Cruelty to Children, founded in 1875, was the first child protective agency in the world. http://www.nyspcc.org/nyspcc/, "The first Society for the Prevention of Cruelty to Animals (SPCA) was organized in England in 1824, to prevent carriage drivers from overworking or beating their horses. The first U.S. SPCA was founded in 1866—nine years before an agency to protect children was formed. http://www.spcai.org/index. php/about/our-history.html

5   "No longer able to stay at home and care for her infant daughter, Francis boarded Mary Ellen (a common practice at the time) with a woman named Mary Score. As Francis's economic situation deteriorated, she slipped further into poverty, falling behind in payments for and missing visits with her daughter. As a result, Mary Score turned two-year-old Mary Ellen over to the city's Department of Charities." http://www.americanhumane.org/about-us/who-we-are/ history/mary-ellen-wilson.html citing to Watkins, S.A. (1990). The Mary Ellen myth: Correcting child welfare history. *Social Work*, 35(6), pp. 500–503.

6   Ibid.

7   Ibid.

8   Ibid.

9   Ibid.

thin child, barefoot, in a thin, scanty dress so tattered that I could see she wore but one garment besides."[10]

It was December and the weather bitterly cold. She was a tiny mite, the size of five years, though, as afterward appeared, she was then nine. From a pan set upon a low stool she stood washing dishes, struggling with a frying pan about as heavy as herself. Across the table lay a brutal whip of twisted leather strands and the child's meager arms and legs bore many marks of its use. But the saddest part of her story was written on her face in its look of suppression and misery, the face of a child unloved, of a child that had seen only the fearsome side of life. These things I saw while seeming not to see, and I left without speaking to, or of, the child. I never saw her again until the day of her rescue, three months later, but I went away determined, with the help of a kind Providence, to rescue her from her miserable life.[11] (Testimony of Mrs. Etta Angell Wheeler.)

With no organization in existence to protect abused children, Mrs. Wheeler eventually turned to Henry Bergh, the founder of the American Society for the Prevention of Cruelty to Animals (ASPCA). "Mr. Bergh was in his office and listened to my recital most courteously but with a slight air of amusement that such an appeal should be made there. In the end he said: 'The case interests me much, but very definite testimony is needed to warrant interference between a child and those claiming guardianship. Will you not send me a written statement that, at my leisure, I may judge the weight of the evidence and may also have time to consider if this society should interfere? I promise to consider the case carefully.'"[12] Mr. Bergh then sent a detective, posing as a census taker, to see Mary Ellen and her condition.

The next day, Mr. Bergh arranged the matter to be dealt with in court in front of Judge Lawrence of the New York Supreme Court "who took kindly"[13] to the case. Interestingly, the police were never involved except to pick up Mary Ellen from her house. "She was wrapped in a carriage blanket and was without other clothing than the two ragged garments I had seen her in months before. Her body was bruised, her face disfigured, and the woman, as if to make testimony sure against herself, had the day before, struck the child with a pair of shears, cutting a gash through the left eye-brow and down the cheek, fortunately escaping the eye."[14]

"The child was sobbing bitterly when brought in but there was a touch of the ludicrous with it all. While one of the officers had held the infuriated woman, the other had taken away the terrified child. She was still shrieking as they drove away and they called a halt at the first candy shop, so that she came into court weeping and terrified but waving as a weapon of defense a huge stick

---

10 http://www.americanhumane.org/about-us/who-we-are/history/story-of-mary-ellen.html, "The Story of Mary Ellen" quoting Mrs. Etta Angell Wheeler.
11 Ibid.
12 Ibid.
13 Ibid.
14 Ibid.

of peppermint candy. Poor child! It was her one earthly possession. The investigation proceeded. The child's appearance was testimony enough, little of mine was needed, and, thus, on Thursday, April 9, 1874, her rescue was accomplished. This Mr. Bergh had effected within forty-eight hours after first hearing of the case." *Mrs. Etta Angell Wheeler.*[15]

At the hearing, Mary Ellen testified:

> My father and mother are both dead. I don't know how old I am. I have no recollection of a time when I did not live with the Connollys.... Mamma has been in the habit of whipping and beating me almost every day. She used to whip me with a twisted whip—a raw hide. The whip always left a black and blue mark on my body. I have now the black and blue marks on my head, which were made by Mamma, and also a cut on the left side of my forehead which was made by a pair of scissors. She struck me with the scissors and cut me; I have no recollection of ever having been kissed by any one—have never been kissed by mamma. I have never been taken on my mamma's lap and caressed or petted. I never dared to speak to anybody, because if I did I would get whipped.... I do not know for what I was whipped—Mamma never said anything to me when she whipped me. I do not want to go back to live with mamma, because she beats me so. I have no recollection ever being on the street in my life.[16]

The judge assumed guardianship of Mary Ellen. For a while, she was placed in a home for older girls (including "wayward" girls), but Mrs. Wheeler eventually convinced the judge to allow her to take the child to live with her family. "When twenty-four she was married to a worthy man and has proved a good home maker and a devoted wife and mother to her children, two bright, dutiful daughters, it has been her joy to give a happy childhood in sharp contrast to her own."[17] In a separate trial against the "mother" "on April 21, 1874, Mary Connolly was found guilty of felonious assault and was sentenced to one year of hard labor in the penitentiary.[18]

While the myth surrounding this story is that the ASPCA's attorneys argued that laws protecting animals from abuse should not be greater than laws protecting children, in actuality, Mr. Bergh acted on his own and not representing the ASPCA.[19] (Although Mrs. Wheeler's niece was quoted as saying "You are so troubled over that abused child, why not go to Mr. Bergh? She is a little animal surely."[20]) The child abuse case that had gained national attention (Bergh used his contacts at the *New York Times* for coverage) helped cause the formation of the New York Society for the Prevention of Cruelty to Children.

---

15 Ibid.
16 Ibid.
17 Ibid.
18 Ibid.
19 http://www.americanhumane.org/about-us/who-we-are/history/mary-ellen-wilson.html citing to Watkins, S.A. (1990). The Mary Ellen myth: Correcting child welfare history. *Social Work*, 35(6), p. 500.
20 Ibid.

Child abuse captured the country's attention again in 1962, when an article appearing in the *Journal of the American Medical Association* described symptoms of child abuse and deemed child abuse to be medically diagnosable. Within ten years, every state had statutes known as "mandatory reporting" laws. Mandatory reporting laws require certain professionals who regularly work with children—doctors and teachers, for example—to report to police suspected child abuse situations. A 1974 federal law further bolstered efforts to eliminate child abuse by funding programs to help individuals identify and report child abuse and to provide shelter and other protective services to victims.[21]

TODAY'S REMEDIES: THREE STEPS

While society is better equipped to deal with child abuse as a result of Mary Ellen's case, child abuse continues unfortunately. "Each year in the U.S., an estimated 2,400 children die as a result of mistreatment and more than 500,000 are seriously injured or disabled."[22] "According to the child sexual abuse prevention organization *Stop It Now!*, as many as one in three girls and one in seven boys experience sexual abuse."[23] Perhaps one of the most horrifying cases entwining spousal abuse with child abuse occurred in Erie, Pennsylvania. In 2006, a "woman used her 4-week-old baby as a weapon in a domestic dispute, swinging the infant through the air and striking her boyfriend with the child."[24] Child abuse made the headlines in Pennsylvania (Jerry Sandusky case), Texas (Warren Jeffs' polygamy case), and Delaware (pediatrician Earl Bradley) in some of the largest or horrific child abuse cases and will be discussed below.

The federal government began a serious effort to deal with child abuse after the American Medical Association took on the issue of child abuse in the 1970s. An article in the *Journal of the American Medical Association* described the symptoms of child abuse and deemed child abuse to be medically diagnosable. A 1974 federal law further bolstered efforts to eliminate child abuse by funding programs to help individuals identify and report child abuse and to provide shelter and other protective services to victims.[25] Thereafter, encouraged by the federal government's promise of funding, states established procedures to recognize and establish safeguards for children.

---

21 http://family.findlaw.com/child-abuse/child-abuse-background-and-history.html, "Child Abuse Background and History"

22 "How best to protect children", Ilana Shere, *The Washington Post*, August 16, 2011, P. Health E5.

23 http://www.livescience.com/17031-penn-state-child-abuse-eyewitness-psychology.html, "Child Abuse: Why People So Often Look the Other Way," Stephanie Pappas, *LiveScience*, November 15, 2011.

24 Nation in Brief, *Washington Post*, October 10, 2006. "Chytoria Graham, 27, of Erie, was charged with aggravated assault, reckless endangerment and simple assault. She was held Monday in the Erie County Jail in lieu of $75,000 bail. The infant, whose name was not released, suffered a fractured skull and some bleeding in the brain, authorities said. His head hit Graham's boyfriend, the baby's father"… Authorities removed four other children from Graham's home and placed them with the Erie County Office of Children and Youth."

25 http://family.findlaw.com/child-abuse/child-abuse-background-and-history.html, "Child Abuse Background and History"

While no one condones child abuse, society's ability to regulate it is impacted by a parent's right to raise their children as they see fit. Yet, society has an obligation to protect its citizens, especially the most vulnerable, such as children. How does the state constitutionally intervene in an "intact" family relationship between a parent and child? Generally, states have established a three-step process. First, the state needs to receive notice that the child is being maltreated. Second, the government needs to assess the probability that the suspected abuse occurred and then allow the court's determination in civil or criminal proceedings. Third, if child abuse is found, a dispositional hearing must occur to determine what to do with the child.

Step 1. Reporting Requirements

In order for the state to intervene in the parent-child relationship, the child needs to come to the state's attention; someone must report the mistreatment. Within ten years of the AMA's report on child abuse, every state created mandatory reporting statutes, requiring certain people to report suspected child abuse.

Who should be required to report child abuse? Arguably, every adult should have an ethical obligation to report, but should it be a mandatory duty for all? In 18 states, anyone who suspects child abuse or neglect is required to report it. Many states allow a person to report even if he is not mandated ("permissive reporters"). About 48 states have mandatory reporting requirements[26] for professionals who deal with children regularly in the course of their work, such as school nurses, doctors, and teachers, school nurses, principals and school counselors, social workers, child care providers, mental health providers, and law enforcement.[27] If a mandatory reporter "observes a child being subjected to conditions that would reasonably result in harm," he may have an obligation to report. In Maryland, there is a 24-hour period to do so, but the period varies. While a mandatory reporter could be sanctioned for failure to report (such as losing their professional license), there is no such penalty for a permissive reporter. Generally, voluntary reporters receive immunity for any problems with a report. Some states allow anonymous reporting, while others require identification to help the investigators. Which is better?

CIVIL LIBERTIES CONCERNS

Because child abuse reporting laws are "informer" statutes, they raise civil liberties concerns. Should family members be reporting family activities to the government? Most would say yes to protect

---

26 "Mandatory Reporters of Child Abuse and Neglect" https://www.childwelfare.gov/topics/systemwide/laws-policies/statutes/Manda/?hasBeenRedirected=1

27 Twenty-seven states include members of the clergy and some, including Maryland, include mediators. Some include photograph processors (less important in the day of disc cameras), camp and youth center personnel, and in Washington, D.C., and some other states, animal control officers. Four states, Louisiana, Oregon, Virginia and Washington State, include faculty, administrators, athletic staff, and other employees and volunteers at institutions of higher learning, including public and private colleges and universities and vocational schools.

vulnerable children; the risks of irreparable danger from child abuse outweigh possible abuse by the reporter. Even so, where does this information go? In many states, even if no conviction occurs, "unofficial" reports are maintained of anyone accused of child abuse. Is that constitutional?

THE JERRY SANDUSKY CASE

Pennsylvania has been in the eye of the storm of controversy since 2011, when the Jerry Sandusky case involving Penn State University broke. "Former longtime Penn State assistant football coach Jerry Sandusky, known for his charitable work with at-risk children and for helping establish the school's 'Linebacker U' reputation, was found guilty of 45 of 48 charges that he sexually assaulted 10 boys over 15 years in Centre County, in a scandal that ended the 46-year tenure of [legendary] football coach Joe Paterno, crippled the Penn State football program, and brought far-reaching implications."[28] In 2012, Sandusky, 68 years old, was sentenced to a 30 to 60 year prison sentence.[29] Even though he was convicted on 45 counts of indecent assault and involuntary deviate sexual intercourse, he maintains his innocence and is pursuing appeals.[30]

---

28   http://www.ydr.com/crime/ci_19280635, "Jerry Sandusky case: Summary of investigation, conviction of the former Penn State defensive coordinator," *Daily Record/Sunday News*, November 8, 2012.

29   Ibid. In 2014, a court ordered that Sandusky could not continue to collect his $4,900 monthly state pension benefits because of the child abuse conviction. But in 2015 an appeals court overruled that decision and reinstated the monthly pension payments. http://www.usatoday.com/story/sports/ncaaf/2015/11/13/jerry-sandusky-pension-restored-pennsylvania-court/75702030/ Three Penn State officials also faced related charges for their actions in response to complaints about Sandusky acting inappropriately with children in Penn State showers: the university's former president, Graham Spanier, former athletic director Tim Curley, and former vice president Gary Schultz. As we go to press, on March 24, 2017, the former University president was convicted of child endangerment based in part on the testimony of the two others who plead guilty earlier in the year. http://www.npr.org/sections/thetwo-way/2017/03/24/521427407/ex-penn-state-president-guilty-of-child-endangerment-in-abuse-scandal Other sensational child abuse cases involving sports during the 2-year gap of this book's rewrite include the case of former Speaker of the U.S. House Dennis Hastert who was sentenced to 15-months after he admitted paying $3.5 million to "keep one victim quiet", but he was not charged with child abuse because the statutes of limitations had expired. During the trial, allegations were made that such crimes occurred while he was a teacher and wrestling coach, before he ran for Congress. The Judge called Hastert "a serial child molester". http://www.cnn.com/2016/06/22/politics/dennis-hastert-goes-to-prison/ During the trial, comedian Andy Richter, known as late night talk show host Conan O'Brien's sidekick, tweeted his recollection that Hastert put a "'Lazyboy-type chair" outside of the boy's shower and watched as they showered. http://www.chicagotribune.com/news/local/breaking/ct-andy-richter-hastert-lazyboy-met-20160408-story.html The case continues in 2017 with another bizarre twist; Hastert's lawyers requested $1.7 million of the money back from the victim because he "broke his silence by talking to the feds" in response to the victim's lawsuit requested the remaining money that Hastert had promised him. http://www.nbcnews.com/news/us-news/dennis-hastert-wants-sex-abuse-accuser-return-hush-money-n709116 The second, a case much like Sandusky's, involves allegations by former female US Olympic gymnasts, against their long-time team doctor and USA Gymnastics for ignoring many prior warnings. https://www.washingtonpost.com/news/morning-mix/wp/2016/09/13/gymnasts-accuse-ex-usa-gymnastics-doctor-of-sexual-abuse/?utm_term=.6d72b7c0042c.   Despite these headline cases, substantiated cases of child sexual abuse have declined 53% from 1990 to 2015. Yet the numbers are "still obscenely high"…"21% of girls and between 3 to 10% of boys are sexually victimized by age 17", according to David Finkelhor. "The overwhelming majority of sexual assaults come from father, stepbrothers, uncles, boyfriends, coaches." "Clinging to Hope amid the Horror of Captivity", E. Graff, *The Washington Post*, May 24, 2015, pg. B7.

30   Ibid.

After this case, Pennsylvania scrutinized its child abuse statutes.[31] At the time of the Sandusky case, Pennsylvania's mandatory reporters included professionals who came in contact with children "through medical, professional or other training and experience."[32] **The state law required reporting by anyone** who, in the course of employment, occupation, or practice of a profession, has reasonable cause to suspect, on the basis of medical, professional, or other training and experience, that a child under the care, supervision, guidance or training of that person or of an agency, institution, organization, or other entity with which that person is affiliated is a victim of child abuse, including child abuse by an individual who is not a perpetrator.[33] Questioning how this abuse could have occurred over many years without any report (even though it was witnessed by at least two adults, see below), the state investigated.[34]

In its report, an 11-member Pennsylvania Task Force on Child Protection called for expanding requirements regarding who must report suspected child abuse to outside investigators, increasing penalties for failure to report suspected abuse, and tracking abuse reports at the state level instead of county-by-county. The Committee recommended that the list of those required to report abuse suspicions should grow to include "coaches, attorneys, college administrators, librarians and anyone else working or volunteering in a role that brings them in regular contact with children."[35] "Schools should no longer have a different set of requirements for child abuse reporting, and instead should require teachers and personnel both to report abuse suspicions to an outside agency as well as to tell their supervisors."[36] Some states, such as Maryland, include additional adults like mediators as mandatory reporters. Who else?

---

31 http://www.ydr.com/crime/ci_19280635

32 http://www.preventchildabusepa.org/faq.php

33 Ibid.

34 Actually it was both "[t]he Sandusky and Roman Catholic priest molestation scandals that provided the impetus for the creation of the task force but the panel took a wider view. [I]n 2005, a Philadelphia grand jury issued a scathing report... accusing Archdiocesan officials of covering up for pedophile priests. But because of the statutes of limitations in place then, none of those cases could be prosecuted. Outraged, state legislators pushed through measures extending the civil and criminal deadlines for reporting rape and broadening child-endangerment laws to include those who supervised suspected molesters.... Those changes made possible this year's case against Monsignor William J. Lynn, who was convicted June 22 of endangering children in approving transfers of pedophile priests to other parishes." http://www.post-gazette.com/stories/local/state/pa-takes-time-to-create-tougher-abuse-laws-642990/, "Pennsylvania takes its time creating tougher child abuse laws, knee-jerk action could hinder child welfare agencies," Jeremy Roebuck, *Philadelphia Inquirer*, July 3 2012.

35 http://www.post-gazette.com/stories/local/state/pennsylvania-group-recommends-guides-for-reporting-child-abuse-663959/#ixzz2P2PIfJoH http://bigstory.ap.org/article/panel-recommend-child-abuse-law-changes-pa "Sweeping changes suggested for Pa. child abuse law," Mark Scolforo and Peter Jackson, AP November 27, 2012.

36 http://www.post-gazette.com/stories/local/state/pennsylvania-group-recommends-guides-for-reporting-child-abuse-663959/#ixzz2P2PIfJoH, "Pennsylvania group recommends guides for reporting child abuse", Laura Olson, *Post-Gazette.com*, November 28, 2012.

DEFINING CHILD ABUSE

States' statutory definitions of child abuse vary greatly. Like the legal definition for cruelty, the definition must be broad by nature to attempt to encompass many different scenarios. Although child abuse definitions have been challenged as "vague", and therefore violating 14th Amendment due process, the courts do not generally uphold such challenges. Most all states include abuse, neglect or abandonment in their definition of child abuse. Certain behaviors are generally included, such as battering and excess discipline, but it is impossible for the law to include every specific act. Arkansas tried to do so by including a list that is not exclusive, including (without justification) throwing, kicking, burning, biting, or cutting; striking with a closed fist; shaking or striking on the face (or if a child younger than six on the head); shaking a child younger than three; interfering with breathing; urinating or defecating on; pinching, biting or striking in the genitals; tying to a fixed or heavy object or binding or tying the limbs together; giving poisonous or noxious substances that interfere with normal physiological functions (not from a doctor) or that has the ability to alter the mood, including marijuana, alcohol (except for religious ceremonies); narcotics or over-the-counter drugs used to overdose; exposure to chemicals including those generated during the manufacture of methamphetamines; subjecting to Munchausen by proxy (confirmed by a doctor).[37] As the Arkansas code demonstrates, no matter how detailed (or how awful), it is impossible for the laws to include every specific act. While some focus on physical and/or sexual abuse, others include severe emotional injuries too. Some require the former before they will acknowledge the latter. What is the effect of Pennsylvania's child abuse statute including "mental injury which is non-accidental"? The Commission also suggested including stronger penalties for failing to report the crime and expanding the definition of sexual abuse to include sexually explicit conversations.[38]

In 2012, Florida lawmakers passed the toughest mandatory-reporting law in the nation. Florida now requires all adults to report suspected abuse and failure to do so is a felony.[39] Should a mandatory reporter go to jail if he fails to report? Now at least 17 other states have mandatory reporting requirements. The 2015 Supreme Court's ruling in *Ohio v. Clark* "was important to teachers, who are often under orders to report suspected abuse." In the case, the defendant was living with and pimping his girlfriend. He watched her two children while she worked "for him as a prostitute." After the 3-year-old came to school with bruises and identified the defendant as the abuser, the court allowed the teacher's testimony on the issues even though it did not allow the boy's testimony because he was incompetent to testify due to his young age. The Ohio Supreme Court overturned the defendant's conviction agreeing with the defendant that his 6th amendment right to confront his

---

37   Arkansas Code of 1987 Family Law Code Section **9-27-303. Definitions,** http://www.arkleg.state.ar.us/assembly/ArkansasCode/9/9-27-303.htm

38   http://bigstory.ap.org/article/panel-recommend-child-abuse-law-changes-pa? Mark Scolforo and Peter Jackson, AP. November 27, 2012.

39   Ibid.

accuser was violated. The Supreme Court overruled that decision saying that the boy's conversation with the teacher was made to protect him, not to try to convict the defendant.[40]

Step 2. Investigation

The second step in the process of reporting suspected child abuse occurs upon receipt of a report to the state's social services agency ("SSA"), which makes an immediate investigation. Once the investigation is complete, the SSA will prepare a report to give to the courts.[41] One of the Pennsylvania commission's proposals was to increase the use of investigative teams from various fields for child abuse cases. This may have prevented additional victims because Sandusky's acts drew the attention of police and child welfare workers more than a decade before.[42] Under the new recommendations, more people would find themselves subject to the child endangerment criminal statute, including anyone who knowingly acts to prevent police or child welfare workers from learning of abuse in order to protect someone.[43]

Step 3. The State Takes the Child

In the third step, the state receives the social services investigation report at a civil or criminal hearing. If it is a civil matter, the court holds a hearing to determine if the child was the subject of child abuse, neglect or endangerment. If so, the state can exercise its *parens patriae* power that allows it to protect children from harm (statistically, this is a rarely used option). In so doing, the state effectively takes over as the child's parent by declaring the child a dependent of the state. If it is a criminal matter, the court will determine if the abusive behavior requires criminal penalty.[44] In either event, the court will then need to hold a disposition hearing and determine the placement of the child (e.g., with relatives, in an institution, or in the foster care program). In some civil cases, the child may be able to return to his/her parents if there is a parenting plan in place to prevent future abuse. While the state's goal has traditionally been to remedy the problem and reunite the family, a more realistic look at the recurring nature of abuse has caused more focus on foster parenting to adoption. Is this the best course?

MOTHER'S DRUG USE AS ABUSE

Courts are mixed on whether a pregnant mother's actions while the fetus is developing in the womb should amount to abuse. In the case of *Johnson v. State*, 602 So.2d 1288 (Fla. 1992), a

---

40 "Defendant rebuffed on cross-examining 3-year-old accuser", R. Barnes, *Washington Post*, June 19, 2015, p.A4.
41 Colo. Civil Code § 19-1-303(l)
42 Ibid.
43 Ibid.
44 In criminal proceedings, the victim of the abuse may have to testify. In 2015, in the case of *Ohio v. Clark,* the U.S. Supreme Court will decide if allowing the subject of a child abuse criminal case, a 3-year-old boy, to tell his day care providers about his injuries and allowing them to testify to what he said, violates the assailant's due process class because the boy could not be cross-examined.

pregnant woman with a history of drug abuse continued to use crack on the day her child was born. After the child's birth, the state prosecuted her criminally under a law prohibiting drug dealing to child. The state argued that the drugs transferred to the child via blood in the short period before the umbilical cord was cut. The court held that the use of the criminal statute would be inappropriate here. Yet, if she had given the child drugs after it was born she would be charged with the crime. Is that fair? Now, a majority of states penalize women whose newborns test positive for a controlled substance; most are charged with child abuse or endangerment.[45] Other courts have found that children born addicted or with fetal alcohol syndrome are abused and have removed them from their mothers.

Under its 2006 chemical endangerment law, "Alabama law prohibits a 'responsible person' from exposing a child to 'an environment in which he or she... knowingly recklessly or intentionally causes or permits a child to be exposed to... a controlled substance, chemical substance or drug paraphernalia.'"[46] The law was created to protect children from the dangers of methamphetamine labs, but prosecutors have broadened its use. At least 60 prosecutions of new mothers for drug use have been charged since law was passed. The minimum sentence is ten years. Sixteen states consider a mother's substance abuse to be child abuse.[47] Amanda Kimbrough, 32, was criminally charged after the "death of her third child...born premature at 25 weeks [who] weighed 2 pounds 1 ounce, and lived only 19 minutes." "When [she] tested positive for methamphetamine, her two daughters were swiftly removed from her custody, and she was only allowed supervised visits for 90 days. Social services mandated parenting classes and drug treatment." On appeal, she argued, "[u]nder Alabama's chemical-endangerment law, pregnant women have become 'a special class of people that should be treated differently from every other citizen.'" And, she says, the law violates pregnant women's constitutional rights to equal protection under the law. Should drug use by pregnant mothers be criminal? Was it meant to apply to pregnant women's drug use? 'The words 'womb,' 'uterus,' 'pregnant women' don't appear in the law," her lawyers argue. "It was a law meant to protect children from meth labs."[48] After "the Alabama Court of Criminal Appeals upheld this expanded interpretation of the chemical-endangerment law, ruling that the dictionary definition of 'child' includes 'unborn child,'" some wonder if this is all "a back door" into passing "fetal personhood" laws.[49] Ironically, prenatal testing showed that the child would have Down syndrome, but Kimbrough chose to have him rather than abort. Do such laws cause pregnant

---

45 "The terrible war on pregnant drug users", Deborah L. Rhode, *The New Republic*, July 17, 2014. http://www. newrepublic.com/article/118681/law-protect-fetuses-actually-punishes-minority-women
46 Ibid.,
47 Ibid.
48 Quoting Emma Ketteringham, director of legal advocacy at the National Advocates for Pregnant Women, which has drafted "friend of the court" briefs for Kimbrough signed by groups like the National Organization for Women-Alabama and the American Medical Association. "The criminalization of bad mothers", *New York Times*, Ada Calhoun, *The New York Times*, April 25, 2012. http://www.nytimes.com/2012/04/29/magazine/the-criminalization-of-bad-mothers.html
49 *Ibid.*

women to lose their constitutional rights of medical privacy? No one advocates that women should use illegal drugs while pregnant, but do all drugs actually impact the developing fetus? [50] What is the effect of "[p]oor nutrition, smoking, drinking, homelessness, poverty"?[51] Drug use negatively impacts all members of the family, but should the government criminally penalize prenatal activities? Does this extend to the behavior of the father, too?

In 2014, in Virginia a woman in a restaurant/bar was breastfeeding with a shot and a beer in front of her. Afterwards, the management confronted her about breastfeeding while consuming alcohol and mentioned that some customers had complained.[52] Was it just about some uncomfortable patrons as the mother claimed, or is the restaurant acting appropriately? If a bar's employees think someone has too much to drink, they have a duty to refuse to serve any more. Should the same rule apply to a breastfeeding mom? If so what about pregnant mothers?

If addiction is a brain disease, are other kinds of behavior by an impaired mother that impact her children (such as hoarding) criminal child abuse? In *State v. Scruggs*, 905 A.2d 24 (Conn. 2006), after her son, who had been the subject of school bullying, committed suicide, the mother was charged with felony child neglect because, among other things, she was a hoarder. The Connecticut Supreme Court found that the mother would not have known that her poor housekeeping would pose a threat to her son's mental health.

PARENTS' DUTY TO PROTECT VERSUS ACTIONS OF OMISSION

In 2005, a California mother was found guilty of child abuse when she left her child with their pit bull dog who was "known to be aggressive" and it mauled her child. In some states, a parent's inaction is also a ground for child abuse when it endangers the child. While we assume a parent has a moral duty to protect, what is the legal effect of this assumption? In the case of

---

50 There are scientists who say that methamphetamines do not have a long-term impact on a developing fetus. Dr. Carl L. Hart, an associate professor of psychiatry and psychology at Columbia University and a research scientist at the New York State Psychiatric Institute, says that heavy alcohol use is potentially far more serious than a mother's use of opiates, cocaine or meth, because while these harder drugs may result in preterm labor or withdrawal symptoms that need to be managed, few babies experience long-term effects. Babies with fetal alcohol syndrome, by contrast, are likely to have lifelong physical, mental and emotional issues, including significantly delayed brain development. Ibid.

51 Quoting Dr. Stephen Kandall, a neonatologist and the author of "Substance and Shadow: Women and Addiction in the United States," Kettering is also quoted, "It starts with cocaine, and then it's cigarettes and alcohol. How much alcohol? And when? It's only a matter of time until it comes to refusing a bed-rest order because you need to work and take care of your other children and then you have a miscarriage. What if you stay at a job where you're exposed to toxic chemicals, as at a dry cleaner? What if you keep taking your S.S.R.I.'s during pregnancy? If a woman is told that sex during her pregnancy could be a risk to the fetus, and the woman has sex anyway and miscarries, are you going to prosecute the woman — and the man too?" Ibid.

52 http://fox6now.com/2014/09/04/there-is-no-law-that-says-i-cant-breastfeed-and-drink-mothers-labor-day-outing-turns-into-social-media-mess/

Commonwealth v. Raproso, 413 Mass. 182, 595 N.E. 2d 773 (1992), the mother was charged as an accessory to rape when she failed to stop her live-in boyfriend from raping her 17-year-old mentally disabled daughter. The boyfriend alleged that "she needs a man" and that this would improve her condition. The mother did not try to stop the man before he entered the girl's bedroom but she stood outside the unlocked door pounding on it and telling him to stop. After several incidents of rape, the mother finally reported it to the police. The court held that the parent had a "duty to prevent harm to the child and take reasonable steps to prevent harm to her," but the failure to do so was not a crime because she was not a conspirator; she did not want the rape to occur. Should parents be criminally liable for failing to protect?[53] Some states have found criminal liability when a mother fails to protect a child from a father's sexual abuse. In *In re Shane T.*, 453 N.Y.S.2d 590 (Fam. Ct. 1982), in which the father called his son a "fag" and other slurs and forced him to massage his feet while the mother stood by, the court found that both parents had abused their son. Surely if the other parent stands by and fails to prevent the child abuse all would agree that parent should face legal action along with the abuser.[54]

But what happens if the mother has been a victim of abuse too? What happens if the husband threatens to kill her if she intervenes? In some states the woman has received criminal sentences for failing to protect that are longer than the abusers. "In 2006, a man pled guilty to abusing his girlfriend's three-month-old daughter by breaking her ribs and femur and was sentenced to two years in prison. The infant's mother... was found guilty of failing to protect her daughter and given a sentence of 30 years in prison. Even though there was no evidence that she ever hurt her daughter, and even though there was significant evidence that she was abused by Braxton and feared him, her sentence was 15 times greater than his. In a similar case...a woman was sentenced to 45 years in prison after her boyfriend...beat her three-year-old son to death. The mother's lengthy sentence came despite a witness's testimony that she had seen Turner threaten to kill Lindley if she intervened. The witness said that, despite the threat, Lindley grabbed her son and ran outside, but Turner dragged them back in and locked the door behind him."[55] Does that make sense?

---

53 Contrast the failure to protect with the Texas father who beat a man to death with his hands after the man allegedly tried to sexually assault the father's 4-year old daughter. Should the law view this murder differently? The sheriff did not arrest the father. http://www.cbsnews.com/news/texas-father-kills-man-who-tried-to-molest-his-4-year-old-daughter-says-sheriff/

54 In 2014, a Maryland man was charged with murder for allegedly beating the 9-year-old son of his girlfriend for "eating birthday cake without permission." The mother, who was not home at the time, was also charged with murder and child abuse because the mother allegedly told the ambulance workers that "her son was fine and just "'congested'" and declined their treatment. https://www.washingtonpost.com/local/public-safety/md-man-pleads-guilty-in-case-of-9-year-old-fatally-beaten-over-birthday-cake/2016/09/13/11224994-79ce-11e6-beac-57a4a412e93a_story.html?utm_term=.fc707b9fd8e5

55 "Failure to protect laws punish victims of domestic abuse," Adam Banner, *The Huffington Post*, December 4, 2014. http://www.huffingtonpost.com/adam-banner/do-failure-to-protect-law_b_6237346.html

SHOULD PARENTS BE CRIMINALLY RESPONSIBLE FOR THEIR CHILDREN'S ACTIONS?

"Where are the parents?" It is a question often asked when children do horrific acts like school shootings. If parents are given the right to raise their children without state intervention and the child does something dangerous to others, should the law hold the parents criminally or legally liable? Is this really failing to exercise control over your children? When a man's child was murdered for her bike by a neighbor's son with a troubled history, the father sued the parents for "essentially being bad parents." On his Change.org petition the father of the murdered girl wrote, "'Parents who ignore the warning signs of their children's propensity toward violence are direct contributors to their minor children's murders" in his effort to encourage the New Jersey legislature to pass a law punishing such parents with prison time.[56] If the parents are found guilty for this, what should the punishment be? Should they do jail time too? Maryland may impose up to $10,000 in restitution if children are found guilty of a crime. Would parenting classes be more effective? At the other extreme end of parenting, should schools hold parents legally responsible if their children miss school or are late to school too many times? Unlike murder, the parents would not legally be responsible for this type of behavior. In 2014, the Virginia Supreme Court ruled that parents whose children arrive late to class cannot face criminal charges.[57] What about parents who allow their underage children to have parties with alcohol? Should the law interfere with parenting rights in these cases?

In 2014 a Texas judge sentenced a 16-year-old to no jail time (but 10 years' probation) for his drunk-driving accident that killed four people and critically injured two. The teenaged driver was allegedly drunk (three times over the legal limit) and had traces of Valium in his system at the time of the accident. The teen's defense was that he was a victim of wealth; his sense of wealthy entitlement given to him by his indulgent parents empowered the teen with such a sense of entitlement that he could not be fully accountable for his actions. This became known as the "Affluenza Defense." Did the judge go too far when he blamed the parent's overindulgences while absolving the son for responsibility?[58] The case got even weirder, when while on probation the teen was "at a beer-pong gathering, in apparent violation of the terms of his probation, [and] was captured on video and posted to Twitter." The teen then went on the run with his mother to the resort town of Puerto Vallarta, Mexico to flee the law, but not before his mother "hosted a farewell gathering"

---

56 "Is it a crime to raise a killer?" Lisa Belkin, *Yahoo News*, September 12, 2014. http://news.yahoo.com/is-it-a-crime-to-raise-a-killer--190558283.html

57 "Va. High court: Parents can't face charges for tardiness," Matt Zapotosky & Moriah Balingit, *The Washington Post*, November 1, 2014, P.B2.

58 Or was this really a case of "a combination of neglect and abuse from parents so inadequate to the task of raising him—so unable to set boundaries, or instill morals—that even Roald Dahl might have had a hard time imagining their failings"? http://www.newyorker.com/culture/cultural-comment/the-sad-lessons-of-the-affluenza-teen.

for him with his friends.[59] Both were arrested in Mexico and his mother could face prison time of up to 10 years. The teen received an almost two year sentence for violating his probation.[60]

Contrast this to Maryland where the state court of appeals ruled in July 2016 that parents who "knowingly and willfully" provide alcohol to underage drinkers (under 21) may face civil liability for any harm that their drunken children commit. [61] Thirty other states also hold parents both criminally and civilly liable in such situations.[62]

BATTERED CHILD SYNDROME

Because many abusive acts take place behind closed doors and against children too young to credibly testify (or even talk), or who are dead, many courts will admit evidence of the "battered child syndrome," or BCS. "Coined by radiologists who speculated that some unexplained traumatic injuries to children may have been inflicted intentionally by parents... the term has become a widely accepted description in the medical literature and the case law." BCS is used when a child presents multiple injuries in various stages of healing and when the parents' explanations are inconsistent with the clinical findings. When an expert's testifies that a child is the victim of BCS the expert is explaining that the child's injuries were intentionally, not accidentally caused. The testimony does not go to the issue of who did the abuse. In *Estelle v. McGuire*, 502 U.S. 62 (1991), the U.S. Supreme Court accepted BCS as evidence in the murder case of a father against his daughter. In the case, the "battered child testimony revealed evidence of rectal tearing, which was at least six weeks old, and evidence of partially healed rib fractures, which were approximately seven weeks old. The trial court instructed the jury that the prior injury evidence could be considered for 'the limited purpose of determining if it tends to show... a clear connection between the other two offense[s] and the one of which [McGuire] is accused, so that it may be logically concluded that, if the Defendant committed other offenses, he also committed the crime charged in this case.'" "The state court of appeals upheld the conviction, finding that the introduction of prior injury evidence was proper under state law to prove battered child syndrome, which exists when a child has sustained repeated and/or serious injuries by non-accidental means" (*Estelle*, p. 62). The Supreme Court felt that admission of these prior acts "parallel[ed] the use of prior act

---

59   Ibid.
60   Ibid.
61   https://www.washingtonpost.com/opinions/give-alcohol-to-an-underage-drinker-in-maryland-and-you-can-be-sued-for-what-happens-next/2016/07/16/db981e40-4abe-11e6-acbc-4d4870a079da_story.html?utm_term=.3983b3af2559 Two months before, Maryland's House of Delegates in the General Assembly moved to "stiffened the (criminal) penalty for adults who provide alcohol to people younger than 21—including a provision that would send such adults to jail." But the bill was later weaken to require jail time or a fine if the adult, "'knew or should have known' an underage drinker would drive, and if that drunk driver causes 'serious injury or death to the individuals or another.'" www.pressreader.com/usa/the-washington-post/20160420/282003261601278
62   Ibid.

evidence for the purpose of showing intent, identity, motive, or plan" (*Estelle*, p. 64), and decided there were no grounds for habeas corpus relief.

CLASS ACTION LAWSUITS

A massive child abuse case called "[t]he worst, most tragic case involving a single perpetrator in our nation's history" involved Lewes, Delaware, pediatrician, 56-year-old Earl Bradley.[63] Bradley was indicted in "2010 on 471 charges of molesting, raping and exploiting about 103 child patients (102 girls and 1 boy) in his office. Some of the victims were as young as three months old."[64] Sometimes Bradley videotaped the attacks and created a video library of hundreds of such videos, using what Judge Joseph R. Slights III described as an "elaborate" system installed in his offices.[65] Judge Slights described Bradley's "reign of abuse" against infants and children, stretching from the mid-1990s until his arrest in 2009. The judge described how Bradley allegedly drugged lollipops he gave his young patients to dull the physical and emotional pain of the attacks. "He was a monster," attorney Jonathan Schochor said.[66] Bradley was arrested in December 2009, convicted in a bench trial in 2012 of rape, assault, and sexual exploitation of a child, and sentenced to 14 consecutive life terms and an additional 164 years in prison. His lawyers appealed, but the Delaware Supreme Court upheld the conviction.

After Bradley was convicted of one of the child abuse charges, the remaining victims mediated their cases and agreed to split up a $123 million settlement. Attorneys involved in the case say it represents a new way of dealing with the fallout from sexual abuse cases with multiple victims, mediating through a class action as opposed to filing individual claims.[67] Judge Slights wrote in the final settlement agreement that a collective mediation ensured all victims could receive compensation and allowed Bradley's "already traumatized" victims to avoid lengthy court cases. He added that many of the defendants had "substantive defenses" they could have used had cases been litigated in court.[68] Bradley had no assets or insurance that could be tapped to compensate his victims. The plaintiffs in the case sued Beebe Medical Center, where Bradley had worked until 2002 and where he retained hospital privileges. Other defendants alleged

---

63 http://articles.baltimoresun.com/2012-12-09/news/bs-md-pedophile-settlement-20121209_1_delaware-pediatrician-abuse-victims-sexual-abuse-cases, "Abuse victims of Delaware pediatrician collect $123 million settlement," Ian Duncan, *Baltimore Sun*, December 9, 2012, quoting attorney Jonathan Schochor.

64 http://www.nytimes.com/2010/04/19/us/19abuse.html, "Pediatrician Charged with Rape Was Once Cleared by Hospital," AP, *New York Times*, April 18, 2012.

65 http://articles.baltimoresun.com/2012-12-09/news/bs-md-pedophile-settlement-20121209_1_delaware-pediatrician-abuse-victims-sexual-abuse-cases, "Abuse victims of Delaware pediatrician collect $123 million settlement," Ian Duncan, *Baltimore Sun*, December 9, 2012.

66 Ibid.

67 Ibid.

68 Ibid.

that the hospital and a number of doctors should have investigated reports of abuse more thoroughly. Prior to his child abuse case, there had been other allegations of child abuse, which included the accounts of three doctors and a nurse. "In the spring of 2005, the Milford police tried to charge Dr. Bradley with offensive touching after a 3-year-old patient told her parents about his kissing her too much in at least one office visit."[69] The medical center worried it would be bankrupted by a wave of lawsuits and sought a mediated settlement, according to the final agreement.[70]

SPANKING AND DISCIPLINE

At common law, parents had a "privilege to discipline" while raising their children as they saw fit. This privilege was limited by the amount and type of force that may be used. While reasonable force is acceptable, what distinguishes this from excessive discipline? Probably issues of the child's age and size could be relevant, but should they? Also, such behavior must be used in "correcting" the child's behavior—not just for punishment.[71] What is the effect of provocation by the child, if any? Is an adult using physical force in anger ever acceptable?

In 2012, Delaware became the first state to define child abuse as any act that causes a child pain (or impairment of physical condition). Penalties include up to one year in jail as a misdemeanor for causing pain to a child under 18 and two years of jail for children under three. Does this make spanking illegal? The state argues that it does not, because another state law still makes it all right to use reasonable and moderate force for disciplining a child.[72]

In 2016 the Obama administration called for an end to corporal punishment nationwide, calling it "'harmful, ineffective, and often disproportionately applied to students of color and students with disabilities.'"[73] If schools want students to resolve conflict without violence, show they use it.[74] If schools should not paddle, why should parents? Since 2007, in California, where corporal punishment (creating serious injury) is *per se* abuse, attempts have been made to outlaw

---

69   http://www.nytimes.com/2010/01/08/us/08pediatrician.html, "Arrest of Pediatrician Follows Years of Complaints," Ian Urbana, *New York Times*, January 7, 2012.

70   Ibid.

71   Interestingly, many states equate the standards for child discipline with that of elderly/adult laws, e.g., Alaska.

72   http://situationroom.blogs.cnn.com/2012/10/03/does-a-new-law-in-delaware-ban-spanking/

73   Curiously, this was on the same week that incoming President Trump nominated Betsy De Vos, a millionaire whose family fortune comes from Amway sales, among other things, and spent it on advocating for use of state education money to fund private schools. https://www.washingtonpost.com/local/education/education-secretary-calls-on-all-states-to-abandon-corporal-punishment/2016/11/22/079f496a-b02b-11e6-840f-e3ebab6bcdd3_story.html?utm_term=.9800e170fa60

74   Although the majority of schools ban paddling, 19 mostly southern public schools still use it. https://www.washingtonpost.com/news/wonk/wp/2015/10/19/in-this-part-of-the-united-states-principals-still-legally-hit-students/?utm_term=.b1bbc8897100 Will the prospect of a lawsuit stop them?

spanking. One bill proposed that spanking a child younger than four would be a misdemeanor and subject to up to a year in jail and a $1000 fine.[75] The issue of spanking remains controversial.[76]

In 2015, when the NFL began to focus on family abuse by its players, Minnesota running back Adrian Peterson was criminally indicted on charges of child abuse after disciplining his four-year-old son with a tree branch, which left marks on the child's body. The NFL suspended him indefinitely.[77] These sanctions sparked discussion on the issue of abuse. After saying, "Listen, you can't hit a woman"[78], former athlete turned sports commentator, Charles Barkley, seemed to step in it when he defended the use of "corporal" punishment by Peterson. Arguing *mos maiorum*,[79] Barkley said that, in effect, if it was good enough for his family to use a switch, then it was good enough for him. Commentator Jim Rome asked, "Can you hit a child?" Barkley replied, "I'm from the South. Whipping — we do that all the time. Every black parent in the South is going to be in jail under those circumstances. We have to be careful letting people dictate how—" Jim Rome cut him off saying, "It doesn't matter where you're from. Right is right and wrong is wrong."[80] Who is right?

Is it OK to spank? Or is that the government interfering too much in the parent-child relationship? A 2016 research study concluded that the more child are spanked, the "more likely that they are to defy their parents and to experience increased anti-social behavior, aggression, mental health problems and cognitive difficulties."[81] Yet, in the U.S. 72% of people think spanking your children is sometimes acceptable.[82] In many countries in Europe, spanking has already been outlawed, but it is not treated with criminal sanctions at first, just as a parental education tool to modify behaviors.[83] If it is acceptable to spank, what about disciplining others' children with a spank? Is that different? In a television mini-series "The Slap," based on an Australian novel, a

---

75   http://www.time.com/time/nation/article/0,8599,1581853,00.html "Should Spanking Be Banned?" *Time*, January 24, 2007, At the time, then Governor Schwarzenegger noted that although the Governor recalled being hit by his father, he said that he and his then- wife, Maria Shriver, did not practice spanking and preferred other methods of discipline, like threatening to take away playtime

76   According to the American Psychological Association, "A growing body of research has shown that spanking and other forms of physical discipline can pose serious risks to children." http://www.apa.org/monitor/2012/04/spanking.aspx See also, https://www.scientificamerican.com/article/what-science-says-and-doesn-t-about-spanking/

77   Eleven other players were arrested since 2005, but were allowed to continue to play. "NFL Arrests Database", USA Today, http://www.usatoday.com/sports/nfl/arrests/

78   "Barkley talks Rice, Peterson; says 'we spank kids in the South'", Ray Wilson, CBS Sports, September 14, 2014, http://www.cbssports.com/nfl/eye-on-football/24709288/barkley-hopes-team-gives-rice-a-chance-says-we-spank-kids-in-the-south

79   An ancient Roman concept that it is the custom of the ancestors.

80   "Barkley talks Rice, Peterson; says 'we spank kids in the South'", Ray Wilson, CBS Sports, September 14, 2014, http://www.cbssports.com/nfl/eye-on-football/24709288/barkley-hopes-team-gives-rice-a-chance-says-we-spank-kids-in-the-south

81   http://www.sciencenewsline.com/news/2016042515300068.html

82   Based on a poll conducted by *60 Minutes* and *Vanity Fair* magazine in November 2014. "Poll: Most people approve of spanking kids", Julie Crandall, ABCNEWS, November 8, 2014. http://abcnews.go.com/US/story?id=90406

83   http://www.time.com/time/nation/article/0,8599,1581853,00.html "Should Spanking Be Banned?" *Time*, January 24, 2007.

man "slaps another family's unruly child at an afternoon barbecue." The child, whose parents are "messy bohemians,"[84] "starts swinging a bat at other children when he loses his turn" in cricket. When adults try to intervene, the boy kicks one in the shins and the slap results. Afterwards, the parents of the boy sued the man that slapped him, their friend. While this example is only fiction, is it ever right to physically discipline another family's children?[85]

RELIGIOUS AND CULTURAL DEFENSES

While Colorado's child abuse code states that "Any investigation of child abuse shall take into account the child-rearing practices of the child's culture," most states do not allow a person's cultural heritage to redefine child abuse for the state.[86]

A. Religious Defense

What are the effects of religion or cultural differences on child abuse? Sometimes, a parent may argue against or defend against allegations of child abuse based on religious grounds. In one of the largest abuse cases ever alleged in the United States, the state of Texas in 2008 removed over 400 children from a "fundamentalist religious" polygamous sect. "[I]n a saga that gripped the state [and the country] with lurid tales of adolescent brides married to older men under the cloak of a secretive sect practicing its religion on an isolated ranch… Texas authorities raided the Yearning For Zion Ranch outside the small west Texas community of El Dorado…, removing over 400 children in response to an abuse complaint. The compound was run by a renegade Mormon sect called the Fundamentalist Church of Jesus Christ of Latter-Day Saints, which still practices polygamy."[87] When the police raided[88] the group's remote West Texas ranch in April 2008, they found "women dressed in frontier-style dresses and hairdos from the 19th century as well as seeing underage girls who were clearly pregnant."[89]

---

84   "At the heart…is a parenting style that we might call neglectfully obsessive." The parents are around their son "all the time but rarely seem to be paying attention." (Prior to the bat incident, the boy had pulled plants from the garden and dirtied an adult's record collection.) "Television show about a Slap Finds Resonance in Brooklyn", Ginia Bellafante, *The New York Times, Big City*, March 22, 2015, P. 22.

85   How is that punishment different than the mother who makes her child eat hot sauce as made famous in the recording on the Dr. Phil Show? Are they both designed to deter behaviors by punishment and "might makes right"?

86   Colo. Civil Code § 19-1-303(l).

87   http://www.reuters.com/article/2008/12/23/us-usa-polygamists-report-idUSTRE4BM53N20081223,   "Texas polygamist ranch report details child abuse," Jim Forsyth, *Reuters*, December 23, 2008.

88   The call to an abuse hotline that spurred the raid turned out to be a hoax, http://usatoday30.usatoday.com/news/nation/2011-08-04-polygamist-warren-jeffs-trial_n.htm, "Polygamist leader convicted of child sex abuse," *USA Today* Nation, August 4, 2011.

89   Ibid.

In its report of its conclusions from the raid, the state's authorities found that "[c]hild neglect and abuse were widespread at a Texas polygamist ranch with at least a dozen girls forced into underage marriages."[90] "Twelve girls are confirmed victims of sexual abuse and neglect because they were married at ages ranging from 12 to 15," the Texas report said.[91] The state's report went on to say that 262 other children "were subjected to neglect because parents failed to remove their child from a situation in which the child would be exposed to sexual abuse committed against another child."[92] The report said "most of the cases had been closed because of subsequent steps taken by parents."[93]

"Texas authorities have been criticized for their handling of the case and the massive show of force used in initial raids on the compound. In May [2008], a court ruled that Texas overstepped its authority when it removed the children, a ruling upheld by the state's Supreme Court... That led to the return of the children to their parents,[94] but investigations were allowed to continue."[95] Did Texas do the right thing?

From information obtained at the raid, "[t]he Texas Attorney General filed charges ranging from bigamy to sexual assault against 12 men in connection with the case. One was the group's jailed spiritual leader, Warren Jeffs, who was convicted in 2007 in Utah of forcing a 14-year-old girl to marry her first cousin."[96] That case was subsequently overturned by a Utah court. In Texas, however, prosecutors used DNA evidence found during the child abuse raid to "show Jeffs fathered a child with a 15-year-old girl and played an audio recording of what they said was him sexually assaulting a 12-year-old girl. They also played audio recordings in which Jeffs was heard instructing young women on how to please him sexually."[97]

"Much of the material [used for the conviction] was discovered in a vault at the end of a secret passageway in the temple and another vault in an annex building." "'You might have asked yourselves,'"... "'a lot of people may ask, why would someone record sex?... This individual considers himself to be the prophet. Everything he did, hour after hour, he was required to keep a record of that.'" "On one of the tapes played at the trial, Jeffs made a reference to 'drawing close' or 'being close,' which authorities testified is how church members refer to sex. Two female voices said, 'OK.'" "A good wife is trained for her husband and follows the spirit of peace," Jeffs was heard saying. Another audiotape included Jeffs and the younger girl from a recording made in August 2006 at the Texas compound, according to testimony from Nick Hanna, a Texas Ranger involved in the 2008 raid. Played in court, it was difficult to decipher, but Jeffs' voice and a

---

90   http://www.reuters.com/article/2008/12/23/us-usa-polygamists-report-idUSTRE4BM53N20081223, "Texas polygamist ranch report details child abuse," Jim Forsyth, *Reuters*, December 23, 2008.
91   Ibid.
92   Ibid.
93   Ibid.
94   Ibid.
95   Ibid.
96   Ibid.
97   Ibid.

female voice are heard. He says, "I perform this service in the name of Jesus Christ, Amen," then mentions the alleged victim by name. When she says something, he responds, "don't talk while praying." Several minutes of heavy breathing followed.[98]

Jeffs acted as his own attorney and "claimed he was the victim of religious persecution. The FLDS, which has at least 10,000 members nationwide, is a radical offshoot of mainstream Mormonism. The church believes polygamy brings exaltation in heaven and that Jeffs is God's spokesman on earth."[99] In his opening statement, Jeffs "evoked images of the civil rights movement and mentioned former Mormon leader Joseph Smith Jr. He also asked the jury to remember constitutional guarantees of religious freedom."[100] "The lone defense witness Jeffs called, church elder JD Roundy, spent about 10 minutes on the stand Thursday discussing FLDS history." In response, "the [p]rosecutors said the case had nothing to do with his church or his beliefs." "You have heard the defendant make repeated arguments about religious freedoms," said lead prosecutor Eric Nichols. "Make no mistake, this case is not about any people, this case is not about any religion. It is about one individual, Warren Steed Jeffs, and his actions."[101]

Jeffs was sentenced to life in prison for sexually assaulting an under-age follower he took as a bride in what his church deemed a "spiritual marriage" and an additional "20-year sentence for the sexual assault of a 15-year-old girl"—the maximum sentence for both.[102] Eleven other FLDS men were charged with crimes, including sexual assault and bigamy. All seven of those who have been prosecuted were convicted, receiving prison sentences of between six and 75 years.[103] One, Fredrick M. Jessop, a former polygamist bishop, was convicted of marrying the sect leader Warren Jeffs to the 12-year-old girl, and was sentenced to ten years in prison.[104]

B. Cultural Defense

On a much smaller scale, but no less horrific, an Ethiopian immigrant living in Georgia was charged with aggravated battery and cruelty to a child when he mutilated his two-year-old daughter's genitals with scissors to remove her clitoris in Atlanta in 2001. "The practice crosses ethnic and cultural lines and is not tied to a particular religion but is common (especially in the rural areas) in Ethiopia, where the defendant grew up in its capital Addis Ababa. While

---

98   Ibid.
99   Ibid.
100   Ibid.
101   Ibid.
102   http://www.nytimes.com/2011/08/10/us/10brfs-POLYGAMISTLE_BRF.html?ref=warrensjeffs, "Texas: Polygam ist Leader Gets Life Sentence," AP, *New York Times*, August 9, 2011.
103   Ibid.
104   http://www.nytimes.com/2011/11/09/us/fredrick-jessop-sentenced-for-polygamist-marriages. html?ref=warrensjeffs, "Texas: 10-YearSentence for Polygamist Marriage," AP, *New York Times*, November 8, 2011.

the procedure is banned by federal law, many states do not have a law against it."[105] Compare this to "oral suction," or *metzitzah b'peh*, where "[a]fter removing the foreskin, the mohel, who conducts the circumcision, cleans the wound by sucking blood from it."[106] "According to city health officials, the ritual may have caused three infants circumcised by the same mohel in 2003 and 2004 to contract neonatal herpes (one of the infants subsequently died)."[107] Hasidic Jews in New York have the procedure performed on their sons. Does it make a difference if the child is newborn, five, or 12?[108]

While Colorado's child abuse code states that "[a]ny investigation of child abuse shall take into account the child-rearing practices of the child's culture," most states do not allow a person's cultural heritage to redefine child abuse for the state.[109] So, if a parent raises a cultural "defense," courts generally have not been receptive. In one particularly heinous case, *In re D. H.* (2012)[110], involving physical abuse and sexual abuse, the father tried to argue that incest was within the cultural defense. Terrell, the father, challenges some—but not all—of the sustained counts in this dependency case, where the evidence supported findings that he repeatedly raped his 12-year-old daughter and beat his son with extension cords, leaving physical and emotional scars on the children. Nevertheless, he questions the court's findings that (1) the sexual abuse of his daughter places his son at risk, and (2) both children are at risk of physical abuse. Because the facts, even though accepted by the court as true, may be too shocking to repeat here, most of the case has been heavily excerpted.

---

105   http://usatoday.printthis.clickability.com/pt/cpt?action=cpt&title=Man+gets+10-year+sentence, "Man gets 10-year sentence for circumcision of 2-year old daughter," *USA Today*, November 1, 2006.

106   "Is Ritual Circumcision Religious Expression? The uneasy state of church and state," Jeffrey Rosen, *New York Times Magazine*, 2006, p. 28. In 2013, Congress "made it a crime to take a girl from the United States for the purpose of mutilating her abroad, a practice known as 'vacation cutting.'" https://www.washingtonpost.com/news/powerpost/wp/2016/08/11/with-500000-female-genital-mutilation-survivors-or-at-risk-in-u-s-its-not-just-someone-elses-problem/?utm_term=.39de33fe875c

107   Ibid.

108   In 2015, a Florida court jailed a mother for a week for contempt of court after the mother refused to sign the paperwork to allow her 4-year-old son's circumcision. The mother opposed the procedure "saying it would be physically and psychological traumatic." The father said, "it was "'the normal thing to do.'" https://www.washingtonpost.com/news/morning-mix/wp/2015/05/26/intactivism-why-a-fla-mother-took-her-son-into-hiding-to-avoid-circumcision/?utm_term=.d804c5ccf98d Probably the mother did not help her case when she hide the boy from his father for four months in a shelter where she was "out of reach of the boy's father and law enforcement," Ibid.

109   Colo. Civil Code § 19-1-303(l)).

110   Not reported in the *California Reporter*.

(Cal. App. 2 Dist. 2012)

(Not Officially Published)

BOREN, P.J.

The court sustained allegations that Father physically abused Jeremiah using extension cords and switches, inflicting marks: the abuse endangers Jeremiah and places D. H. at risk of physical harm and abuse; and Father sexually abused D. H. by forcibly raping her, causing pain and fear: this abuse endangers D. H.'s health and safety and places Jeremiah at risk of harm and sexual abuse. The court declared the children to be dependents of the court pursuant to section 300, subdivisions (a), (b) and (d).

After conceding the harm he inflicted on D. H. and Jeremiah while they lived with him in Texas—leaving physical scars on Jeremiah and emotional scars on D. H.'s psyche—Father believes that this is all water under the bridge, because the children have been safe from him since they returned to live with Mother in California a few years ago. The problem is that Father now lives in California, filed a petition in family law court to gain custody of D. H. and Jeremiah, and obtained a visitation order to see them. There is not a shred of evidence that Father no longer is an incestuous child rapist or child batterer. While the children were safe when Father lived 1,400 miles away that buffer is gone and they must be protected from him now…

Father fails to connect the dots between his past abuse, his recent custody petition, and the children's current state of distress. While admitting that he "whooped" the children, Father denies that this constituted physical abuse. The court acted well within its discretion to protect these children from Father, who requires extensive counseling to overcome his predilections for sexual abuse and violence.

Finally, the court properly asserted jurisdiction because it determined that Father's continuous sexual abuse of D. H.—while Jeremiah was in the same room—posed a risk of substantial harm to both children. (In re *P. A.* (2006) 144 Cal.App.4th 1339, 1345 *[father's sexual abuse of daughter posed a risk of harm to his sons, who were unaware of father's conduct].*) The legislative intent is to protect the siblings of sexually abused children. (Id. at p. 1347.) "[A]berrant sexual behavior by a parent places the victim's siblings who remain in the home at risk of aberrant sexual behavior." (Ibid.) A parent who sexually abuses a daughter in the presence of his son evinces "a total lack of concern for whether *[the son]* might observe his aberrant sexual behavior." (In re *Andy G.* (2010) 183 Cal.App.4th 1405, 1414.) In this case, Father, repeatedly raped D. H. at night while Jeremiah was in the same hotel room.

Father suggests that incest is not aberrant because it does not depart substantially from standards of behavior in his group, even if it is "not acceptable in the view of most Californians." Incest is criminal behavior, punishable by imprisonment, as are forcible rape and sex with a minor child. (Pen. Code, §§ 261, 261.5, 264, 269, 285; People v. Tobias (2001) 25 Cal.4th 327, 336, 337–338 *[incest is "unlawful by the nature of the acts involved" and is "highly reprehensible and abusive behavior"]; People v. Bowles* (1960) 178 Cal.App.2d 317.) We do not require expert testimony, scientific authority or empirical evidence to conclude that Father's incest with his 12-year-old daughter is atypical, peculiar, anomalous, irregular and eccentric... in a word, aberrant.

DISPOSITION
6 The judgment is affirmed.

You decide—Are the cases below child abuse, neglect, or abandonment?

Leaving your child in a car to go gambling? In Baltimore Maryland, at the New City Casino, a 25-year-old woman was arrested after leaving her 3-year-old son alone in a car in its parking garage while she played roulette.[111] Is this different than the New York mothers who left their sleeping children in the apartment while they listened on a baby monitor and dined at a restaurant down the street as discussed in the book's introduction?

Leaving your children in a car to go to a wine tasting? Parents in Washington D.C., who left their two toddlers alone (in their car seats) while they went to a wine tasting, pleaded guilty to two misdemeanor counts of second degree attempted cruelty to children and were ordered to take parenting classes. Although the children, aged 2 and 3, had on coats (no hats or gloves, one did not have shoes) the January temperature was only 35 degrees. The doors were locked and the windows were rolled up. Does it make a difference that the parents were "only 400 feet around the corner" or that they left an iPhone in the car with an open connection (that showed they had been gone about one hour)?

Attempting to leave your baby at the restaurant's coat check? "When the maître d' explained that dinner lasted at least three hours, she stared back at him, unfazed. "Yes, I know."[112]

---

111 "Woman leaves child in car to gamble at Baltimore casino", Catherine Hawley, *ABC NEWS*, April 12, 2015. http://www. abc2news.com/news/crime-checker/baltimore-city-crime/woman-leaves-child-in-car-to-gamble-at-baltimore-casino
112 https://www.nytimes.com/2015/08/23/opinion/sunday/dinner-and-deception.html?_r=0 Is that worse than the New York mothers who listen in on the monitor while they dine next door or down the street as raised in the book's introduction?

Taking your own nude photos? In Virginia, a 44-year-old woman received a one year prison sentence for having her two young children take nude photos of her. Does it make a difference that the photos were for prostitution ads? Charges of neglect charges were made after an investigation began into allegations of possible prostitution in the home.[113]

Cursing at a young child. In Brooklyn, New York, a "56-year old women with two grown children "hurled a "particularly non-PG expletive at her assailant" when walking on her sidewalk when a boy on a scooter "came hurtling toward her...at Nascar speed" causing her to jump out of the way to avoid getting hit.[114] When the mother and friend caught up, they asked, "You just cursed a child!" and did not apologize. Who should have recourse here and what would it be?

Smoking marijuana in front of your children, when it is legal to smoke, like in DC? What if the parents hide their smoking by not doing it in the house? Is the porch enough?[115]

Allowing your 4-year-old son to crawl through a barrier and fall 15 feet into the zoo's gorilla enclosure? In 2016, many were outraged when the Cincinnati Zoo shot Harambe, a 17-year-old male gorilla who had "grabbed and dragged the child" after he fell in. The boy was not hurt.[116]

Free Range Parents, who allow their children to walk home from the playground without a parental escort? The playground is about one mile from their house in Maryland. In December 2014 two children were picked up by the police after a report from a concerned citizen that they were walking alone through a busy city neighborhood. The parents believe in "'free-range' parenting, a movement that has been a counterpoint to the hyper-vigilance of 'helicopter' parenting with the idea that children learn self-reliance by being allowed to progressively test limits, make

113   "Mother in Sterling gets prison for child neglect", Dana Hedgpeth, The Washington Post, Local Digest, March 20, 2015, P. B3.

114   "Television show about a Slap Finds Resonance in Brooklyn", Ginia Bellafante, *The New York Times, Big City*, March 22, 2015, P. 22. Louise Crawford began with "'Get the' and ended with 'off the street'".

115   Even if it is legal, using it may still be a factor in custody cases. Is this the same as "parents cracking open a beer at the end of the day?" https://www.washingtonpost.com/local/even-where-its-legal-for-parents-to-smoke-pot-what-about-the-kids/2015/06/06/dd4549c8-f977-11e4-9030-b4732caefe81_story.html?utm_term=.2e8ed21c5b6e Does this lead to the drunk dad that lets his 9-year old daughter be his designated driver? At least a witness (who had called 911 after seeing the girl drive off in the van with her drunk dad) said, "'She's driving pretty good. I'm telling you. I can't believe it.'" http://www.nbcnews.com/id/44932952/ns/us_news-crime_and_courts/t/why-did-you-stop-me-i-was-driving-good--year-old-asks/#.WNx64qIpDIU

116   http://www.cnn.com/2016/05/29/us/cincinnati-zoo-gorilla-shot/ "Some even suggested the boy's parents should be held criminally responsible for the incident. An online petition seeking 'justice for Harambe' through criminal charges earned more than 8,000 signatures in less than 24 hours."

choices and venture out in the world."[117] Usually, the children carry laminated cards that say, "I am not lost. I am a free-range kid," but they did not have them that day. Would it have made a difference to the "six police officers and five patrol cars"[118] that came to the family's home? In its investigation of the child neglect report, the state relied on a Maryland law that requires children under 8 to be left with a reliable person who is at least 13 years old, but the law specifically references dwellings, enclosures and vehicles; it does not mention outdoor settings. Curiously, the country requires children to walk to school (no bus provided) if they live less than one mile from school. After the police, child protective services came immediately to conduct an investigation and required the parents (both college educated) to sign a "safety plan" pledging not to leave the children unsupervised until the next CPS follow up. After interviews at school and home, CPS later found the parents responsible for "unsubstantiated" child neglect,[119] and the file will remain open for five years by CPS (to be referred to if another allegation occurs during that time period).

In a similar case in Austin, Texas, parents were investigated for neglect when their 6-year old "lagged behind, playing on a bench, a few houses down the street" while the others were walking the dog. In Florida, "a mother of two was arrested for letting her 7-year-old son walk alone to a park and play there, about a half a mile away from their home" (he had a cellphone to keep in touch).[120] While some report unescorted children as a potential for danger, the Maryland parents researched the issue and concluded that stranger child abductions were down and their children were more likely to face a danger in a car accident.[121] Are these a failure to provide proper care and supervision? Or, is this really a case of parenting style? As this chapter discussed, there are many children that are truly subject to horrific abuse by their caretakers and parents. While all applaud the state's efforts to protect, should the state focus on the most extreme cases?

Yet, there are cases were children are being horrifically treated and concerned citizens are right not to turn away. "Of all the missed chances outlined in the grand jury report regarding the

---

117 "They want 'free-range' kids, but not all do", Donna St. George, *The Washington Post, Metro section,* January 15,2013, P. B1.
118 "Raising our children on fear", Danielle Meitiv, *The Washington Post, Sunday Opinion,* February 15, 2015, P. A21. This is an op-ed by the mother of the children who asks, "When did Americans decide that allowing our kids to be out of sight was a crime?"
119 There are three options the CPS could take: determine that nothing occurred, find it unsubstantiated, or conclude that it occurred. The finding of unsubstantiated means there was some information to support the conclusion or credible reports that differ on the issue or insufficient information for a more definite conclusion.
120 "Free-range flap feeds fire of U.S. debate on parenting", Donna St. George & Brigid Schulte, *The Washington Post Metro Section,* April 19, 2015, P. C1. Headlines noted that in South Carolina, when a mother was arrested because she "allegedly allowed her 9-year-old daughter to play at a park while she worked at a McDonald's as a shift manager" and another in Florida who left her 6 and 8 year old to play at a park while she shopped at the food bank, but these really raise more issues of economics than the free range parenting discussed here. The danger issue may stem from some highly publicized child abductions in the 1970s and 1980s, including the case of Etan Patz, who never made it the first day he walked from his house to the bus stop in New York. As this book is being written, a New York jury has been in deliberations on the issues of murder and kidnapping against a man that recently confessed to that 1979 killing.
121 "Raising our children on fear", Danielle Meitiv, *The Washington Post, Sunday Opinion,* February 15, 2015, P. A21. The mother notes that obesity risks are far more hazardous.

allegations of child sexual abuse by former Pennsylvania State University assistant coach Jerry Sandusky, two moments stand out: One, a 2000 incident when a janitor allegedly witnessed Sandusky performing oral sex on a middle school-age boy, and the other, a 2002 incident in which a graduate assistant, now a coach at the school, allegedly saw Sandusky anally raping a boy of about age 10 in the university locker room."[122]

Both men reported what they saw to their supervisors and, according to grand jury testimony, both were distraught—the janitor so much so that his co-workers thought he might have a heart attack. But neither man stepped in to stop the abuse."[123] Why not? What would you do in that situation?

CHAPTER SOURCE

Weisberg, D. Kelly. (2011). *Emanuel Law Outlines, Family Law*.

---

122 http://www.livescience.com/17031-penn-state-child-abuse-eyewitness-psychology.html, "Child Abuse: Why People So Often Look the Other Way." Stephanie Pappas, *Live Science*, November 15, 2011
123 Ibid. In 2000, the janitor cleaning the locker room who saw Sandusky performing oral sex on a young boy, according to grand jury testimony, told his co-worker that he had "fought in the [Korean] war... seen people with their guts blown out, arms dismembered.... I just witnessed something in there I'll never forget."

MEDICAL DECISION MAKING

The test of the morality of a society is what it does for its children.
—Dietrich Bonhoeffer[1]

The family is a court of justice which never shuts down for night or day.
—Malcolm De Chazal[2]

In September 2014, England sent out an international "amber alert" when parents disagreed with a hospital's prescription of chemotherapy for their 5-year old son's cancer and checked out without the doctor's consent. The hospital had successfully conducted emergency surgery on the boy to remove a brain tumor, a medulloblastoma. Afterwards, the hospital's doctors prescribed radiation and chemotherapy, but the parents wanted to use a more focused "proton beam therapy" available in Prague "which Britain's National Health Service provides only for eye cancers."[3] The father said, "Doctors in Britain refused to help him and said if [they] continued to question the [doctor's] judgment they would obtain a court order to prevent him and his wife from visiting their son in the hospital." The parents then removed the boy from the hospital and took him, with the rest of the family, to their vacation home in Spain, which they were planning to sell to pay for the treatments in Prague. Meanwhile, the hospital contacted the police. Based on the hospital's allegations of parental neglect and concerns that the boy's life was a risk, the police issued an Interpol Yellow Alert.[4] Both parents were arrested in Spain and spent two nights in jail. Their young, ill son was placed under police guard, alone, in a Spanish hospital for several hours until an older brother was allowed to stay with him. After being released from jail, the father posted a video online and said, "I just want positive results for my son"... "I just please ask, call off this ridiculous chase.... My son's smiling. He's happy. We're doing things as

---

1   www.quotationspage.com/quote/39154.htm
2   http://www.quotationspage.com/search.php3?Search=Family%20&Author=&page=4, The quotations page.
3   "British couple arrested in Spain after taking ill son from hospital", Christopher Wreth, *Los Angeles Times*, September 1, 2014. http://www.latimes.com/world/europe/la-fg-britain-treatment-cancer-20140901-story.html"
4   Out of jail, British couple reunite with ill son", Katrin Benhold, *The New York Times*, September 3, 2014. http://www.nytimes.com/2014/09/04/world/europe/british-parents-reunited-with-ill-child-after-arrests.html

a family with him. We just want to be left in peace. He's very sick. I just want to get on with his treatment, and I'm not coming back to England if I cannot give him the treatment I want. Which is proper treatment, not a little bit of chemotherapy."[5] When the case drew a public outcry, the arrest warrant was dropped and the English hospital agreed to approve the Kings' requested treatment. But, at the time it contacted the police the hospital also requested that the court have the child become a ward of the court thus allowing an English judge to make any decisions about his medical treatment. That was not removed. Was the parent's behavior neglect? Would this happen in the United States?

Under the Constitution, parents have the right to raise their families without government interference. But is this right inviolate? As one of its highest responsibilities, does the government not have the duty to protect the most vulnerable among us, including children? This is the tension created in the triangle that runs across its base, between the parent and child and upward to the state (see illustration below). What merits governmental interference in an intact family?

```
┌─────────────────────────────────────┐
│                                     │
│          State/government           │
│                 ∧                   │
│      Parents---------Children       │
│                                     │
└─────────────────────────────────────┘
```

"Daniel Hauser sat quietly in a Minneapolis courtroom while adults debated how to combat the Hodgkin's lymphoma that has invaded his body. Doctors wanted the 13-year-old boy to undergo chemotherapy and radiation. His parents were resisting: their religion advocated natural and homeopathic methods. The judge ruled... that Hauser's family must select an oncologist and that he must receive chest X-rays to determine the extent of his cancer, the results of which would help determine a new medical plan of action. By [the next week] the boy and his mother were missing, having skipped the scheduled chest X-ray appointment; a warrant has been issued for the mother's arrest."[6] Who is right?

HISTORY OF PARENTAL MEDICAL DECISION MAKING

In the case of *Meyer v. Nebraska*, 262 U.S. 390 (1923) the U.S. Supreme Court held that parents have a constitutionally protected interest in raising their children without government interference. This right, however, has limits. In *Prince v. Massachusetts*, 321 U.S. 158 (1944), the U.S. Supreme Court recognized children's rights that may limit their parents' rights. When dealing

---

5   Quoting Brett King concerning his son Ashya King, Ibid.
6   www.newsweek.com/2009/05/18/parents-rights-judges-rules.print.html, "Parents' rights, judges' rules: In the battle between families and the courts over medical treatment for kids, who has the last word?" Kate Dailey, *Newsweek*, May 19, 2009.

with medical decision making for children, the court treads carefully between these two sets of rights.

A. Absolute Parental Authority

At common law, when children were treated like cows and livestock, parents had absolute authority over how to raise them. Given the economy of the times, children were mini-workers, either used in a family business or farm or apprenticed out to learn a trade for the family's profit. If a child became sick or required any complicated medical assistance, the parents made the decision, no matter the doctor's medical recommendation. Indeed, if a doctor were to provide treatment without parental approval, it amounted to "battery" (an unlawful touching) under the law and the doctor could be held liable, even if the treatment proved beneficial to the child. To avoid this, the doctor/hospital request that the court make the sick child a ward of the court, thus taking away the parent's rights to make decisions about their child's treatment.[7] Without a finding of cruelty that the parents were withholding treatment, the courts deferred to the judgment of the parents, which they deemed to be "in the best interests" of the child.[8]

In the case of *In re Tuttendario* 21 Pa. Dist. 561 (PA 1912), when refusing a request for the state to intervene in a child's medical care, the court wrote, "[w]e are asked to supersede the child's natural guardians on the sole ground that their judgment is impaired by natural love and affection and that we should substitute for them a human society whose judgment is untainted by such emotions. We have not yet adopted as a public policy the Spartan rule that children belong not to their parents but to the state."

B. Life Threatening

Once society started to value children beyond a financial interest, the law begun to change and the government/state could exercise its responsibilities to its littlest citizens by intervening in the family medical decision-making process when it was a life-or-death decision for the child.[9] In his book *The Children Act*, Ian McEwan puts a fictional twist on this issue when asking a judge to allow a hospital to intervene in a case of Siamese twins. The twins shared only one organ, the bladder but one twin's aorta fed into the others, so that one twin's heart sustained them both. One

---

7 While society no longer views children as profit centers for parents, the same rules apply that prevent doctors treating children without the parents' consent.

8 Attitudes toward protecting children also started to turn at this time. (See Chapter 17 and the discussion of the creation of the Society for the Prevention of Cruelty to Children).

9 After graduating from Yale Law School, former Secretary of State Hillary Clinton supported deference to parental authority in "Children Under the Law" in the Harvard Educational Review in which she advocated that "the state was obligated to intervene only in the case of actual harm to children". "Only medically justifiable reasons for intervention should be acceptable. Parental behavior that does not result in medically diagnosable harm to a child should not be allowed to trigger intervention, however offensive that behavior may be to the community." "Stop Hillary! Vote no to a Clinton dynasty," Doug Henwood, *Harper's Magazine*, November 2014. P. 30, 32.

twin was "sucking, normally, feeding and breathing for both, doing 'all the work' and therefore abnormally thin." Without intervention, that twin's heart would fail (for doing the work for both) and he would die in 6 months (taking the other twin with him). The hospital wanted permission to separate the twins to save that one twin "who had the potential to be a normal healthy child." "The loving parents, devout Catholics...refused to sanction murder."[10] The judge is obligated to consider what is in the dependent twin's best interests. What should be the result?

Usually these cases involve proposing treatment designed to save a life. What happens if the doctors prescribe the removal of life support and the parents do not want it? In late December, 2013, at a hospital in Oakland, California, a 13-year-old girl was declared brain-dead after a routine tonsillectomy. Her doctors said that she "would not recover, so they want[ed] to take her off the machines that are keeping her body functioning. Her family want[ed] to continue life support, saying they have hope she will pull-through." A court granted the family's request and gave an additional week before the doctors could act.[11] Eventually, the family was able to find a nursing home to provide long-term care for the girl just before the judge's continuance expired but when the child needed two medical procedures performed to allow her to transfer (inserting a breathing tube and a feeding tube) the hospital refused. A hospital spokesman said it "does not believe that performing surgical procedures on the body of a deceased person is an appropriate medical practice."[12] Was the hospital being punitive because it lost or did it have valid reasons to refuse to insert the tubes?

A more horrific case involving an end of life decision case occurred in Boston in 2004. An 11-year-old was taken to the hospital with multiple injuries (burned chest, teeth broken, and a "brain stem partly sheared leaving her in a vegetative state.") The police said the girl's aunt, who had adopted her, and the aunt's husband (who married before the child was adopted but never adopted the child) "were responsible for the abuse." When the aunt was released on bail, she committed suicide with her mother. This left the aunt's husband to face the charges of criminal child abuse. Although the girl was in the care of the state (it was her legal guardian) and it wanted the court to give permission to remove life support, the husband petitioned the court to recognize him as the "de facto" parent and allow him to make the end of life decision to have the hospital take all extraordinary measures to keep her alive. Some argued he wanted to keep her alive to prevent the filing of murder charges against him. His attorney denies that and says that among

---

10   *The Children Act*, Ian McEwarn, Nan A. Talese/Doubleday, 2014, PP. 26-7. The main character of the book, the British family court judge decided that the twin, unlike his brother, had no interests because he had only a "rudimentary brain, no lungs, a useless heart, was probably in pain and condemned to die and soon." p. 28. The hospital argued that "separating the twins was analogous to turning off [his] life support machine (the other twin)." Yet, the judge viewed the surgery too invasive, "too much a trespass on [his] bodily integrity, to be considered a withdrawal of treatment. What about intent? If they do the operation is the court intending to kill the other twin which would be illegal?" The judge used the doctrine of necessity to make her decision.

11   "Brain-dead teen gets week's extension", Digest, *The Washington Post*, December 31, 2014, P. A3.

12   Citing David Durand, chief of pediatrics at Children's Hospital Oakland. "Facility is found for girl ruled brain-dead," A.P., *The Washington Post*, December 29, 2013, P. A2.

other things the wife's "Catholic faith might have made her opposed to ending life support." What should the court do?[13] Should the court ask the child's biological mother (who placed the child for adoption with her sister after the mother was charged with child abuse against the girl?)

C. Quality of Life

As late as mid-century, the courts continued to prevent doctors from conducting simple procedures to better the child's life and/or health when the parents objected. For example, in *In re Hudson* 126 P.2d 765, 768 (Wash. *1942*) , a mother objected to the doctor's suggested "removal of the daughter's functionally useless, congenitally oversized arm, even though it posed increasing danger to her system because there was no suggestion that if it remained, it would lead to imminent death (and the daughter wanted it removed)."[14] Generally, society intervenes in the family's medical decision making at the request of a doctor treating the child, usually through the hospital. The health organization makes a formal request to the court for the "state" to declare the child a dependent and then the state gives the doctor permission for the medical treatment he deems necessary under the Hippocratic Oath. In so doing, the state, using its *parens patria* status, steps into the parents' shoes, in effect, to make the best decision for the child's interests (overriding the decision of the parents). Once society began to protect children, compassion led courts to extend its powers even more to include decisions that would improve the child's quality of life. But is this a slippery slope? What happens if a child is unhappy with her large nose? Or her breast size?[15]

D. Child Makes the Decision

The cycle continues to evolve. Now, courts are exploring the possibility that children should be permitted to make their own medical decisions. Since the child is the one who is most affected by the medical condition and treatment, should he not make the decision? "[F]orcing a treatment on a child who doesn't want it is its own kind of ethical dilemma. 'There are some kids for whom it becomes in their mind a vicious assault every time they're treated. At a certain age and height and weight, it starts to seem inappropriate to hold them down on a regular basis to do what needs to be done.'" In ruling that a child can make his own medical decisions, the courts generally go on a case-by-case basis, looking for "mature minors," weighted with the severity of the condition and its treatments. Under the law, generally the age of majority is 18—at that point the child is

---

13   The juvenile court rejected the husband's request. "Girl's end-of-life case questions a difficulty decision and who is fit to make it," Pam Belluck, *The New York Times national Report*, December 6, 2005. P. A 18. The court did ask the birth mother who said her preference was "to let her rest and shut the machine off."
14   *Domestic Relations,* Wadlington and O'Brien, Foundation Press. 2007.
15   In 2012, a bullied 14-year-old girl got plastic surgery to fix her ears, nose and chin. "Should bullied teens be getting plastic surgery?", ABC News, August 9, 2012. http://abcnews.go.com/Nightline/video/bullied-teens-plastic-surgery-17007425

"mature" enough to make a decision on her own.[16] "Children don't always have the long-term perspective needed to consent to painful treatment. 'A child may be more concerned with how much pain they'll have in the short term... Parents can understand the big picture'"[17] to make the decision,[18] and no state has created a law with a specific age lower than this to allow a child's decision. "Bioethicists encourage adults to allow children to at least participate in decisions about their medical care, especially when those choices will cause them pain."[19]

In January 2015, the Connecticut Supreme Court unanimously affirmed a trial court's decision for state officials to take over the medical care of 17-year-old "Cassandra C," who had Hodgkin's lymphoma and refused the hospital's proscribed treatment of chemotherapy, which she referred to as poison (and wanted to try "alternative" treatments instead). Her doctors said that her disease was "highly curable" with the treatment. In making its decision, the court ruled that the patient failed to prove she was a mature minor. Thus, because the failure to take the treatment would be life threatening, the state forced her to have the treatments, which she said may leave her unable to have children.[20] Four months later, Cassandra was not allowed to leave the hospital where the chemotherapy took place, and her mother was banned from visiting her. Petitions to the court for visitation or to leave were rejected.[21]

In the case of 13-year-old Daniel, above, is he mature enough to make his own decision? He has told his parents that he does not want the treatment and has "reportedly vowed to punch, kick or scratch anyone who attempts to treat him."[22] Does such a combative treatment benefit the child and/or the disease? But at 13, is Daniel mature enough to have his choice respected? Are children really ever independent of their parents when making decisions?

Interestingly, one type of medical treatment does not allow for either absolute parental authority or the mature minor in medical decision making. A parent may not consent to a child less than 18 years-of-age obtaining a BRCA test for breast cancer which shows the mutation associated with a greater family risk for breast cancer. Why is this treated differently? Should anything else be treated this way too?

---

16   www.newsweek.com/2009/05/18/parents-rights-judges-rules.print.html, "Parents' Rights, Judges' Rules: In the battle between families and the courts over medical treatment for kids, who has the last word?" Kate Dailey, *Newsweek*, May 19, 2009 quoting Dr. Doug Diekema, director of education at the Treuman Katz Center for Pediatric Bioethics at Seattle Children's Hospital.

17   Ibid., Quoting Dr. Dennis Drotar, professor of pediatrics and director of the Center for Treatment Adherence at the Cincinnati Children's Hospital Medical Center.

18   Some exceptions exist for emancipated children, those in the military, etc.

19   www.newsweek.com/2009/05/18/parents-rights-judges-rules.print.html.

20   "Conn. High court clears forced treatment for teen", Sarah Larimer, *The Washington Post*, January 9, 2015, P. A2.

21   "Judge: Cassandra C can't go home amid cancer treatments", Bill Briggs, *ABCNews* April 1, 2015. http://www.nbcnews.com/health/health-news/judge-cassandra-c-cant-go-home-amid-cancer-treatments-n334086   Some states, however, are allowing terminally ill teens to express their "preference for their final days and afterward in a planning guide that a hospital social worker helps them fill out. It would allow a team to decided things ranging from who gets her laptop and her dog to does she want to be on life support? "Facing Early Death, on Their Terms, Teenagers Get a Voice on Their Final Days", Jan Hoffman, *The New York Times*, March 29, 2015, P. 1).

22   Ibid.

E. Religious Objection Complication

"The calls come in at all hours; patients reporting broken bones, violent coughs, deep depression, Prue Lewis listens as they explain their symptoms. Then [she] simply says, 'I'll go to work right away.' She hangs up, organizes her thoughts and begins treating her client's aliments the best way she knows how: she prays."[23] "She doesn't see most of the patients she treats. That isn't necessary, she said, for her prayers to be effective."[24] "This is health care in the world of Christian Science, where the sick eschew conventional medicine and turn to God for healing. Christian Scientists call it 'spiritual health care.'"[25, 26]

"Since the early 1900s, parents who willfully withheld medicine in the name of religion have been prosecuted and convicted."[27] Often, however, parents do not allow the recommended medical procedures out of malice, but because of deeply felt religious objections. Thus, the court's equation for determining medical intervention gets further complicated by adding in the factor of the First Amendment's free exercise of religion. In an effort to accommodate this, states have

---

23   "Praying for healing, lobbying for a provision," William Wan, *Washington Post*, p. B1, November 23, 2009.

24   Ibid.

25   Ibid.

26   Interestingly, during the "Obama Care" debates, the Church of Christ Scientist lobbied to include a provision to pay $20 to $40 [to the church's 1,400 trained practitioners] for patients to someone to pray for their ills. "Pray practitioners are trained in a 'two week intensive course' and collect 'testimonials of healing from people [they] have worked with' and who 'bandage and comfort but do not provide drugs or perform procedures as basic as setting bones.'" While it was stripped from the House's version of the bill in the Senate, the church "has some powerful allies," including former senator John F. Kerry of Massachusetts (now secretary of state), where the church is based, and Utah senator Orrin G. Hatch, who said the provision would "ensure that health-care reform law does not discriminate against any religion. But opponents of spiritual care coverage—a coalition of separation-of-church-and state advocates, pediatricians and children's health activists—say such a provision would waste money, endanger lives and, in some cases, amount to government-funded prayer." "As the health-care debate enters its final stages, the clash over spiritual care has become essentially a referendum about whether the government recognizes prayer as a legitimate and viable health-care option." Yet, it appears that no such debate occurs in the case law on medical decision making, as courts do not challenge a parent's First Amendment challenges to medical decision making for their children, but weigh the effects of it on a case-by-case basis. Also, the Internal Revenue Service "allows prayer treatments to be itemized on income tax forms as medical expenses. And a few federal insurance programs, such as those for military families, already reimburse for prayer." www.newsweek.com/2009/05/18/parents-rights-judges-rules.print.html, "Parents' rights, judges' rules: In the battle between families and the courts over medical treatment for kids, who has the last word?" Kate Dailey, *Newsweek*, May 19, 2009

27   "Suffer the Children", Abraham Verghese (reviewing "Bad Faith" by Paul A. Offit), *The New York Times Book Review*, April 12, 2015, P. 14. Offit claims that in the 1970s "when Walter Mondale was working to introduce the landmark Child Abuse Protection and Treatment Act" Capita "was about to shine an unwanted light on" faith healing way of life, so the church asked H.R. Haldeman and John Ehrlichman (of the Watergate break-ins), both Christian Scientists, for help. "Halderman and Ehrlichman inserted a religious exemption into Capita: "No parent or guardian who in good faith is providing a child treatment solely by spiritual means—such as prayer—according to the tenets and practices of a recognized church through a duly accredited practitioner shall for that reason alone be considered to have neglected the child."

tried to pass laws that balance the two competing interests: parents are permitted to use their spiritual treatment (e.g., prayer) until it is clear that it is failing, and then they are required to get "traditional" (western) medical intervention for the child. If the parents fail to do so and this results in the child's death, the parents could be charged with child abuse or even homicide. Florida had a similar statute in the case of *Hermanson v. State,* 604 So 2d 775 (1992). Laws like the Florida law in *Hermanson* draw their own constitutional challenges because it is difficult to determine the line when medical treatment becomes legally necessary. If one truly believes that God will intervene if one prays more devoutly, how can one question that it might not work out alright?

"'We live in a modern era with antibiotics, immunization, advanced diagnostic procedures. Why would you risk the life of your child when they could easily be saved?'"[28] asked "Rita Swan, who said the prayer practices put children at risk." "It is a question that has haunted Swan since the death of her son in 1977."[29] "Swan was a lifelong Christian Scientist. So when 15-month-old Matthew came down with a fever, she and her husband took him to church leaders. 'The practitioner prayed, and the fever went away,' she said. 'At first, we thought that Christian Science had accomplished something strong and real, but then he just got worse.' Soon, the toddler could not walk or sit up. Swan considered taking Matthew to a doctor, but church leaders told her that if she did, they could not pray for him anymore. By the time she took him to the hospital, it was too late. A week later, he died of bacterial meningitis, which doctors said could have been cured with antibiotics and today can be prevented with a vaccine."[30]

It has been over two decades since a Christian Scientist was prosecuted for the death of a child treated with prayer instead of medicine.[31] "'The church doesn't pressure people to avoid doctors,' said spokesman Phil Davis, and prayer treatment is now seen as a substitute for or as a supplement to medical treatment."

This statistic may be changing. Wisconsin is a state with an exemption for faith-based neglect under the child abuse laws. In 2009, the court found parents of an 11-year-old daughter criminally responsible for her death from undiagnosed but treatable diabetes. The parents are affiliated

---

28 "The reason for the continued and enormous popularity of faith healing is that, to some extent at least, it works. New research suggests that placebo response generates measurable endorphin release in the brain." Ibid.

29 Ibid. Describing how the Swans lost their 15-month-old child to untreated meningitis, a survivable illness had it been treated earlier. When she and her husband noticed he had difficulty walking, they, Christian Scientist, called a practitioner to pray for him. Prior to that, Rita had her own experience with this when "repeated prayer 'treatments' failed to give her relief from a painful ovarian cyst, she allowed physicians to operate. But she was viewed as having abandoned her faith. She was no longer permitted to lead church meetings or teach Sunday school. To Rita this loss of community was profound, and perhaps explains why, as her baby was getting worse, she did not seek medical care." See also, "When a Child Dies, Faith is No Defense," Jonathan Turley, *Washington Post,* November 15, 2009, pp. B1, B3.

30 Ibid.

31 "When a child dies, faith is no defense," Jonathan Turley, *Washington Post,* November 15, 2009, p. B1.

with a faith-healing church called Unleavened Bread Ministries and continued to pray with other members while Madeline died. They could have received 25 years in prison, but because of their religious rationale the court sentenced them each to six months (to be served one month per year and staggered so that while one parent is in prison the other is out) and 19 years' probation.[32] They kept custody of their [other] children.[33] While courts may no longer ignore the death of a child from medical neglect the courts "routinely hand down lighter sentences."[34] Is it true that in cases where "courts confront repeated faith-based fatalities in a single religious community, the legal system risks becoming a facilitator, if not an accessory, to the crimes through lenient sentencing"?[35] Does it make a difference that after the death and the trial, the mother in this case said, "'I do not regret trusting truly in the Lord for my daughter's health' and the father said, 'I am guilty of trusting my Lord's wisdom completely... Guilty of asking for heavenly intervention. Guilty of following Jesus Christ when the whole world does not understand. Guilty of obeying my God.'"?[36] Should they have shown contrition, or would that have undermined the court's leniency in the sentencing? Is it more unsettling that they retained custody of their other children?[37] At least in another case which involved the death of a 15-month-old whose cyst grew to the size of a softball causing a blood infection and pneumonia while the parents "anointed her with oil and administered small amounts of wine," the judge ordered the parents to "promise to bring [their other 5-year-old child (while the mother was also pregnant with another on the way)] to a doctor for scheduled checkups."

"At least five states have passed legislation eliminating religious exemption from child abuse laws."[38] In February of 2014, a Philadelphia judge found faith healing parents guilty of third-degree homicide, endangering the welfare of a child, and conspiracy. They were sentenced up to seven years in prison for the death of their seven-month-old infant from pneumonia and dehydration. They are members of a church that believes in "divine healing." Was the judge sending a message to parents or just influenced by the fact that this was their second child to die of an illness?[39]

The U.S. Supreme Court has never ruled on this issue. "In Canada and Britain, where there is no religious exemption for medical neglect, deaths of children from faith healing are exceedingly rare. In America the problem continues."[40]

---

32 Ibid.
33 Ibid., pp. B1, B4.
34 Ibid, p. B1.
35 As the author Jonathan Turley questioned. Ibid., pp. B1, B4.
36 Ibid., p. B4.
37 "When a child dies, faith is no defense," Jonathan Turley, *Washington Post*, November 15, 2009, pp. B1, B4.
38 "Suffer the Children", Abraham Verghese (reviewing "Bad Faith" by Paul A. Offit), *The New York Times Book Review*, April 12, 2015, P. 14.
39 "Digest", *The Washington Post*, February 20, 2014, P. A3.
40 "Suffer the Children", Abraham Verghese (reviewing "Bad Faith" by Paul A. Offit), *The New York Times Book Review*, April 12, 2015, P. 14.

MORE EXTREME TREATMENTS VERSUS LESS EXTREME TREATMENTS

Generally, the more extreme the medical treatment, the more invasive, painful, or negative the side effects, the more the state will exercise caution in intervening. "There's got to be a balancing of potential benefits against potential harm. In some situations you have a treatment where the likelihood of success is very small, and in situations like that, the courts are much less likely to order the treatment." [41] In the case of Daniel Hauser that began this chapter, "his disease has a very high rate of remission (90 percent) when treated with radiation and chemotherapy—difficult procedures, but by no means experimental or unproven. That's why when thinking about cases like this, the basic stand is not simply "What's in the best interest of the child?" but rather, "Will the refusal of the treatment cause harm to the child?" The phrase "best interest" can be interpreted in different ways. "For the parent who doesn't want their child to get a blood transfusion because they feel it's a matter of their child's spiritual salvation, their belief system tells them it's not in their child's best interest to get it."[42]

Vaccinations

In 2014, Disneyland may not have been "the happiest place on earth" when over 150 cases of measles were linked to the California Adventure Park.[43] Although no "patient zero" or the person who triggered the Disneyland-linked outbreak was discovered, "they think it's someone who caught the virus outside the country and visited one of the Disney theme parks during the holidays." Measles had been eliminated in the United States in 2000, yet, last year, there were a record 644 measles infections. Fifty-three percent of Americans believe vaccines are safe and effective.[44] Known as "the jab" in England, vaccinations are designed to inoculate children against major infectious diseases. Over the early childhood years, a panel of vaccines is recommended to prevent the child from contracting diseases like measles, mumps, etc. Generally, public schools mandate that students receive all of the required shots before they are allowed to enroll. This is a public health effort, because not only does it protect the child from the disease, but failure to do so puts the rest of society at risk, too. A debate over the effects of vaccines as related to autism caused

---

41   Quoting Alan Meisel, director for the Center of Bioethics and Health Law at the University of Pittsburgh. "Parents' rights, judges' rules: In the battle between families and the courts over medical treatment for kids, who has the last word?" Kate Dailey, *Newsweek*, May 19, 2009, p. B3.

42   Ibid. Quoting Dr. Doug Diekema, director of education at the Treuman Katz Center for Pediatric Bioethics at Seattle Children's Hospital.

43   "Measles cases in outbreak linked to Disney swell to 107", *The Chicago Tribune*, January 30, 2015. http://www.chicagotribune.com/lifestyles/health/chi-science-parents-vaccinate-kids-measles-20150130-story.html

44   Only 1 percent less than the number who believe that houses can be haunted by ghosts. *Harper's Index*, February 2015.

some families to halt vaccinations. The Centers for Disease Control and Prevention continues to deny any connection between the two.[45]

What about those who have a religious objection as discussed above in faith healers who shun western medicine? "[A]mong the major religions there is virtually no canonical basis for vaccine aversion; the Bible, the Quran and the texts of Sanskrit were obviously written before the creation of vaccines, and most religions privilege the preservation of life."[46] Some Christians raising objections to vaccines because many of the common vaccines, for rubella and chicken pox, for example, are grown in and then removed from cells descended from the cells of aborted fetuses" which were discarded about 40 years ago.[47] Why do we allow people to opt out of this part of public health? "You cannot object to a drunken-driving arrest for instance, on the grounds that you worship Bacchus."[48]

Nationwide, the measles vaccination rate is over 90 percent.[49] California law requires two doses of the measles vaccination before kindergartners can enroll, but parents may obtain exemptions for the vaccines if they say the inoculations conflict with their personal beliefs.[50] Does a

---

45   http://thechart.blogs.cnn.com/2013/03/29/vaccine-autism-connection-debunked-again/comment-page-1/   http://thechart.blogs.cnn.com/2013/03/29/vaccine-autism-connection-debunked-again/comment-page-1/, CNN Health, the Chart, March 29, 2013. See also, The United States Centers for Disease Control and Prevention study *Increasing Exposure to Antibody-Stimulating Proteins and Polysaccharides in Vaccines Is Not Associated with Risk of Autism* by Destefano et al., 2013, purports that "increasing exposure to antibody-stimulating proteins and polysaccharides in vaccines during the first 2 years of life was not related to the risk of developing an Autism Spectrum Disorder." Compare the medical advancements with doctor's experiences in the 1960s. When an outbreak of German measles caused over 20,0000 congenitally deformed babies, the doctors who performed abortions on pregnant women with rubella risked having their medical licenses revoked because abortion was illegal in 1964. T*he Law of Reproductive Rights and Technology*, by Rachel Krantz, 2002, p. 97.

46   Don Seeman, a rabbi and professor of Jewish studies and medical anthropology at Emory University said, "I don't think there's much rabbinical support for not vaccinating. What does exist in certain communities is a lot of anxiety about science and the risks we are exposed to through technology." "On shaky ground in refusing to vaccinate," Ginia Bellafante, *The New York Times*, Big City, February 15, 2015. P. 26. "When measles erupted around a megachurch in Texas two years ago, the church's pastor didn't invoke liturgical justification for why her congregants didn't immunize their children, but instead the entirely debunked connection between autism and vaccines."

47   "Vaccines' abortion connection", Lauren Markoe, *Washington Post Religion*, February 7, 2015. B2.

48   Ibid.

49   "More cases of measles linked to Disney theme parks", CBSNews, January 13, 2015. http://www.cbsnews.com/news/more-cases-of-measles-linked-to-disney-theme-parks/

50   But as a result of this measles outbreak, students at the University of California's 10 campuses will be required to be vaccinated for measles and other diseases beginning 2017. "Measles prompts change in UC policy", Steve Gorman, *The Washington Post*, February 8, 2015, P. A4. New York has twice rejected a similar proposal allowing vaccine-rejection. "On shaky ground in refusing to vaccinate, Ginia Bellafante, *The New York Times,* Big City, February 15, 2015. P. 26.

parent's deliberate decision to not get their child vaccinated amount to neglect?[51] It costs over $5 million medically a year to care for this medically preventable disease, should parents who do not vaccinate have to pay for these expenses to their children if they can afford it.[52] Should a grandmother secretly vaccinate her grandson when the mother will not?[53]

Some decried drug manufacturer Merck's T.V. commercials about its HPV vaccine during the family time of the 2016 Olympic games as an effort to shame parents into taking action The ads talked about how the disease leads to cancer that can be prevented. It ended with the haunting question, "Did you know, Mom and Dad?" Was the company just reminding parents that they are "responsible not only for our acts of commission but also for our acts of omission?" Some critics labeled the commercials "bullying" to "guilt trip parents to bolster corporate profits."[54] Was the company's motive more sinister? Was it really trying to "encourage law makers to include HPV vaccination in the schedule of vaccines required for most children to attend public school?" Only DC, Virginia and Rhode Island require it.[55]

Obesity

In a case of first impression for the New York courts, in *Kayla T. v. Linda T.*[56] in the New York Family Court, Chemung County, on February 23, 2007, the issue was a morbidly obese child, who also suffered from numerous comorbidities, and whether to remove her from her parents' care because they "consistently failed to address her severe medical concerns" and failed to ensure her proper school attendance. Social services had made a recommendation to the parents about an exercise and nutrition plan for the girl, yet during a six-month period before the hearing, her weight increased from 238 pounds to 263 pounds. She also continued to miss school. The court decided that removal was appropriate and necessary. Did the court make the right decision?

---

51   In 2015, Pakistan arrested hundreds of parents for endangering public security because they refused to get their children polio vaccinations. *The Washington Post*, The World, March 3, 2015, P. A6.

52   One of the richest counties in the U.S., Marin County, California, has one of the highest vaccine-refusal rates. "Calling the shots", Laura Hilgers, *Marin Magazine*, September 2014. http://www.marinmagazine.com/September-2014/Calling-the-Shots/

53   This question was posted to Emily Yoffe or "Dear Prudence" in Slate.com. https://www.google.com/search?q=Dear+Prudence&ie=utf-8&oe=

54   https://www.washingtonpost.com/news/to-your-health/wp/2016/08/11/do-the-new-merck-hpv-ads-guilt-trip-parents-or-tell-hard-truths-both/?utm_term=.9497b46b1ed0

55   Ibid.

56   http://ny.findacase.com/research/wfrmDocViewer.aspx/xq/fac.20070223_0002538.NY.htm/qx

Factors to Consider in Judicial Rullings
By Jenna T. Hayes and Lorie L. Sicafuse

In 2009, a South Carolina woman, Jerri Gray, was arrested and charged with criminal neglect when it was discovered that her 14-year-old son, Alexander, weighed 555 pounds.[1] Alexander was removed from his mother's care and placed in a foster home. This case ignited a national debate as to whether or not childhood obesity should be considered a form of child abuse. In recent years, courts in several states have grappled with this question. Rulings have varied, with most courts ordering that the child be immediately removed from his or her parent's custody. Other courts have initially opted for more therapeutic measures, such as providing these families with medical assistance or ordering parents to implement diet and exercise plans for their child. Yet, even when courts attempt to address childhood obesity through less punitive approaches, the child is often eventually placed in protective custody.

Arguments exist both for and against the consideration of childhood obesity as abuse. Those in favor of classifying obesity as a form of child abuse cite the immediate and long-term negative health and psychosocial effects of childhood obesity and legal definitions of abuse. Those against classifying obesity as a form of child abuse often argue that parents have a constitutional right to raise their children in whatever way they deem appropriate; they also emphasize that some cases of childhood obesity may be attributable to human genetics or other environmental influences (e.g., school and peers) beyond parental control. Based on these arguments, this article proposes that childhood obesity should be considered child abuse in only the most extreme cases in which all other court interventions aimed at addressing this problem have failed. In all cases, rulings should be based in therapeutic jurisprudence, characterized by the maximization of therapeutic outcomes for children and families without subordinating due process or other justice values.[2]

---

1   Ron Barnett, "S.C. case looks on child obesity as child abuse. But is it?" (USA Today, Jul. 20, 2009), available at http://www.usatoday.com/news/health/weightloss/2009-07-20-obesityboy_N.htm

2   Pamela Casey & David B. Rottman, *Therapeutic Jurisprudence in the Courts*, 18 Beav. Scl. L. 445, 446-448 (2000).

Obesity rates are on the rise in the U.S., with over 30 percent of children in 30 different states classified as obese.[3] In the 1970s, 5 percent of children were classified as over-weight,[4] as compared to 32 percent in 2003-2006.[5] In 2003, the U.S. Surgeon General labeled childhood obesity as an "epidemic" and called for action to address this "preventable" problem.[6] This surge in childhood obesity coupled with public outrage towards parents of morbidly obese children suggests that courts may face an increasing number of cases involving obese children and their families.

Though it is the court's job to protect children, this does not always mean that charging parents with child abuse and subsequently removing the child from their care is the best and/or only option. Scholars, judges, and the legal community as a whole should be aware of the pertinent factors to consider in such cases and make increased efforts to address this obesity epidemic through less distressful means (i.e. family counseling, nutrition education). Targeting the underlying causes of obesity within each individual family unit focuses on moving toward solutions rather than promoting punitive reactions to childhood obesity.

PAST COURT CASES

One of the first major court cases on this issue was *In re L. T.,* in which an Iowa court affirmed the decision of the trial court to have Liza, a 10-year-old weighing 290 pounds, removed from her mother's care and placed in a treatment facility.[7] The court reasoned that "the child's obesity was a potentially life-threatening condition, and that it interfered with the child's socialization." Though this case did not define the mother's actions as "child abuse," they did determine Liza was a "child in need of assistance."[8] As a result of Liza's mother's refusal to place her in a treatment facility, Liza was immediately placed in foster care.

As the recognition of obesity as a global "epidemic" became a focus of national research, cases presenting morbid obesity as child abuse became increasingly public. In 2002, a Texas court affirmed a decision that terminated the parental rights of a mother whose child was only 4 years old, but weighed 136 pounds.[9] Prior to terminating the mother's parental right, child protection services, with

---

3   Trust for America's Health (TFAH) and Robert Wood Johnson Foundation, *F as in Fat: How Obesity Policies are Failing in America (2009), available at* http://healthyamericans.org/reports/obesity2009/

4   D. Joliffe, Extent of Overweight Among US Children and Adolescents from 1971 to 2000, 28 Int. J. Obesity 4-9, 6 (2004).

5   Nanci Hellmich, *Child obesity rates are high but 'leveling off,'* USA Today (May 27, 2008), available at http://www.usatoday.com/news/health/weightloss/2008-05-27-obesity-children_N.htm

6   Richard H. Carmona, U.S. Surgeon General, *The Obesity Crisis in America, (July 16, 2003), available at* http://www.surgeongeneral.gov/news/testimony/obesity07162003.htm

7   See generally In re L. T., 494 N.W.2d 450, 451 (Iowa App. 1992).

8   Iowa Code 232.2(6) (f) (1991).

9   In re G.G., 66 S.W.3d 517, 517 (Tex. App. Fort Worth Dist. 2002).

the support of the court, tried to help the mother by providing both medical assistance and a "home-maker" to serve as a role model for the mother. Despite attempts to address the case therapeutically, the mother became noncompliant.

At trial, the judge determined that the child had been neglected, therefore expanding the state's legal definition of abuse to include morbid obesity.[10]

Over the past decade, a handful of judges have explicitly defined morbid childhood obesity as a form of child abuse or neglect. Under New York state family law, a child is deemed abused or neglected when a parent's lack of proper care subsequently impairs the child's physical, mental, or emotional well-being.[11] In 2007, a New York court cited this law after the parents of a morbidly obese teenager, Brittany T., failed to change the child's diet and ensure that she regularly attended school and visited the local gym, as the court had previously ordered.[12] Thus, the court ruled for the removal of Brittany T. from her parents' custody.

In 2000, a similar case came before an Indiana court. In this case, the parents of a 111-pound 4-year-old were charged with, and ultimately pled guilty to, a criminal charge of child neglect.[13] Though medical doctors had provided the parents with an individualized diet plan, the parents found the plan too "difficult" to follow. Instead, the parents decided to feed their child junk food, even while in the hospital seeking treatment for health issues relating to the child's obesity.

The majority of cases dealing with childhood obesity as child abuse have ruled for removal of the child from the parent's custody. However, a significant case, *In re D.K.*, discussed the role of the court in family preservation, stating that "children should be separated from their families only in cases of clear necessity."[14] The court emphasized the importance of providing support from a child social services agency as well as the need for follow-up supervision. Despite recognizing alternative means of addressing childhood obesity, the judge ultimately ruled to remove 451-pound D.K. from his mother's care. Because the mother's own morbid obesity prohibited her from leaving their home, the judge felt that allowing the child to remain in the home would only be a further detriment to the child's obese state.

A new perspective in dealing with childhood obesity cases arose in the case of Anamarie Martinez-Regino, a 131-pound, 3-year-old girl. In 2000, Anamarie was taken from her parents' care when they were charged with medical neglect.[15] Her parents claimed that their child's obese state was due to an uncontrollable genetic condition. Courts had not previously considered that obesity might have

---

10   Abigali Darwin, *Childhood Obesity: Is it Abuse?* Child Welfare League of America: Children's Voice, (2008) *available at* http://www.cwla.org/voice/0807obesity.htm.

11   In re Brittany T., 835 N.Y.S.2d 829, 830 (N.Y. Fam. Ct. 2007).

12   Id.

13   Deena Patel. *Super-Sized Kids: Using the Law to Combat Morbid Obesity in Children,* 43 Fam. Ct. Rev. 164–177, 170 (2005).

14   In re D.K., 58 Pa. D. & C. 4th 353, 358 (Pa, Com. Pl. 2002).

15   Shireen Arani. *State Intervention in Cases of Obesity-Related Medical Neglect*, 82 B.U.L. Rev, 875, 875-6 (2002).

a genetic cause. This specific court did not deny that Anamarie's obesity was genetically based, but failed to fully acknowledge this possibility. Despite this defensive tactic, Anamarie was temporarily removed from her parents' custody based on her parents' inability to implement physician ordered nutritional and exercise plans.[16]

Courts presented with childhood obesity issues have delivered various rulings that typically resulted in removal of the child from the parents' care and custody. Each court has considered different alleged causes of childhood obesity and relied on different interpretations of what constitutes "child abuse." Though some courts have tried to alleviate the problem of obesity by initially favoring more therapeutic options, none of the courts described here have comprehensively addressed such cases utilizing therapeutic jurisprudence. The majority of these rulings have ultimately favored more punitive methods. There is no common consensus among the various courts on how judges should rule in such cases. A variety of arguments exist both in favor of and against the classification of childhood obesity as child abuse.

ARGUMENTS FOR ABUSE CLASSIFICATION

The main arguments for classifying childhood obesity as child abuse focus on the physical and psychosocial health problems children experience as a result of being obese. These health problems may not only have serious consequences for obese children, but they also may undermine physical and psychosocial functioning in adulthood. Proponents of this classification also contend that the actions or inactions of parents with obese children conform to legal definitions of child abuse.

Physical Health Problems

Childhood obesity is associated with a variety of physical health-related problems. Obese children are at a greater risk for both immediate problems and other issues that will persist through and/or appear in adulthood.[17] Obesity in childhood presents cardiovascular disease risks including, but not limited to, high cholesterol and blood pressure, and abnormal glucose tolerance. Childhood obesity is the strongest predictor of the development of Type 2 diabetes in youth, and the proportion of children diagnosed with this illness has increased dramatically within the last decade.[18] Children may develop complications from Type 2 diabetes at a younger age than individuals who develop the illness in

---

16   Lisa Belkin, *Watching Her Weight*, N.Y. Times, July 8, 2001, at 630.

17   Centers for Disease Control and Prevention, *Childhood Overweight and Obesity* (n.d.), available at http://www.cdc.gov/obesity/childhood/index.html

18   Tamara S. Hannon, Goutham Rao, & Silva A. Arslanian, *Childhood Obesity and Type 2 Diabetes Mellitus*, 116 J. Pediatrics 473, 473 (2005).

adulthood; risks of this illness include kidney failure, advanced cardiovascular problems, stroke, and sudden death. Additional health risks of childhood obesity include asthma, hepatic steatosis (fatty degeneration of the liver), and sleep apnea.[19]

Though many of these health risks are typically associated with adults, it is important to remember that such chronic, long-term effects of obesity do in fact apply to children. As noted above, diagnoses of serious health conditions associated with obesity are becoming more and more common. Moreover, these health problems often persist throughout the lifespan. Though childhood obesity is a primary risk factor for obesity in adulthood, research has shown that obese children who subsequently lose weight as adults are more susceptible to health problems and premature death than adults with healthier childhood weights.[20]

Psychosocial Health Problems

Childhood obesity has been associated with a multitude of psychosocial health problems as well. Research shows that obese children are more likely to have low self-esteem and suffer from other related psychopathology.[21] These negative self-images, in some cases, do not develop until adolescence. Overweight girls have more depressive symptoms than their "normal-weight" peers; the difference in symptoms for boys is not as significant.[22] These negative self-evaluations resulting from childhood obesity have been linked to lower levels of academic achievement and social functioning.[23]

Obese children are likely to become targets of constant stigmatization and be placed on the receiving end of this social stigma at a very young age. Research shows that young children experience both peer rejection and prejudiced attitudes in the school setting. Average weight children ages 3–5 judge their obese peers by associating them with terms such as mean, stupid, ugly, and less desirable as a playmate.[24] Children ages 3–11 similarly associate unhappiness, laziness, and lacking friends with obesity.[25]

---

19 Centers for Disease Control and Prevention, *supra* n. 17.
20 See generally Richard J. Deckelbaum & Christine L. Williams, *Childhood Obesity: The Health Issue*, 9 Obesity Res. 293 (2001).
21 See generally Alan J. Zametkin, Christine K. Zoon, Hannah W. Klein, & Suzanne Munson, *Psychiatric Aspects of Child and Adolescent Obesity: A Review of the Past 10 Years*, 43 J. Am. Acad. Child Adolescence Psychiatry 387–94 (2004).
22 Sarah J. Erickson, Thomas N. Robinson. K. Farish Haydel, & Joel D. Killen, *Are Overweight Children Unhappy? Body Mass Index, Depressive Symptoms, and Overweight Concerns in Elementary School Children*, 154 Arch. Pediatric Adolescence Med. 931–35, 934 (2000).
23 See generally Howard Taras & William Potts-Datema, *Obesity and Student Performance at School*, 75 J. Sch. Health 291–295 (2005).
24 P. Cramer & T. Steinwert, *Thin is Good, Fat is Bad: How Early Does It Begin?* 19 J. Appl. Dev. Psychology 429–51, 429 (1998).
25 Jody A. Brylinskey & James C. Moore, *The Identification of Body Build Stereotypes in Young Children*, 28 J. Res. Personality 170–81, 175 (1994); J. Wardle, C. Volz, & C. Golding, *Social Variation in Attitudes to Obesity in Children*, 19 Int. J. Obesity 562–69, 562 (1995).

Such social stigma has increasingly negative psychological effects on children due to the mounting physical dissatisfaction they experience as they age. Research has shown that as a result of weight-based teasing, adolescents are 2 to 3 times more likely to think about or attempt suicide than their normal-weight peers.[26] The psychological stress of low self-esteem and social stigma in childhood can persist into adulthood, hindering social and economic success. Ultimately, persons who are obese in childhood receive less education, are less likely to marry, and have higher poverty rates.[27]

Overweight children have to battle with a multitude of physical and psychosocial health problems and stressors that their normal-weight peers do not. Not only does childhood obesity threaten the physical and psychological well-being of youth, but it also poses significant health-related risks for adolescents and adults who were obese as children. All of these negative health issues are of great concern in childhood obesity cases, and are often cited as reasons why childhood obesity should be considered child abuse.

LEGAL DEFINITIONS

In many states, the law can be used to advocate for the classification of childhood obesity as abuse. States including Texas, Pennsylvania, New York, New Mexico, and Indiana have expanded their definition of child abuse to explicitly include obesity. In all states, including those that have adjusted their abuse definition, the legal description of child abuse must, at a minimum, reflect the definition of the federal legislation Child Abuse Prevention and Treatment Act (CAPTA). CAPTA defines child abuse and neglect as "any recent act or failure to act on the part of a parent or caretaker, which results in death, serious physical or emotional harm, sexual abuse, or exploitation, or an act or failure to act which presents an imminent risk of serious harm."[28]

Many argue that the physical and psychosocial health problems caused by childhood obesity present an "imminent risk of serious harm" to children. Therefore, parents' actions, or inactions in some cases, can be interpreted as child abuse under this definition from the federal government. For instance, parents who continue to feed their obese child foods high in fat, sugar, and calories, despite physician's warnings that the child is pre-diabetic and prone to heart problems, may be charged with child abuse; parental failure to monitor their child's diet or ensure that the child engages in routine physical activity may also constitute abuse.

---

26   Marla E. Eisenberg, Dianne Neumark-Sztainer, & Mary Story, *Associations of Weight-Based Teasing and Emotional Well-being Among Adolescents*, 157 Arch. Pediatric Adolescence Med. 733–738, 735 (2003).
27   M. B. Schwartz & R. Puhl, *Childhood Obesity: A Societal Problem to Solve*, 4 Obesity Rev. 57–71, 65 (2003).
28   U.S. Department of Health and Human Services, The Child Abuse Prevention and Treatment Act: Including Adoption Opportunities & The Abandoned Infants Assistance Act, (2003) *available at* http://www.acf.hhs.gov/programs/cb/laws_policies/cblaws/capta03capta_manual.pdf, at 44.

As children cannot protect themselves, parents are easily blamed for the physical and psychosocial harms caused by childhood obesity. The implications of the health problems associated with this epidemic heighten the concern of child advocates, leading many to argue that parents' behaviors (or lack thereof) cohere with the federal legal definition of abuse.

ARGUMENTS AGAINST ABUSE CLASSIFICATION

Arguments against equating childhood obesity with abuse defend on the ground that all United States citizens have the constitutional right to parent as they see fit without governmental interference. Opponents of this classification also focus on the genetic influences of childhood obesity, effectively shifting the blame from the parents. Lastly, some critics highlight other environmental contributors to obesity that fall beyond a parent's control in maintaining that childhood obesity does not necessarily constitute abuse.

Right to Parent

In *Meyer v. Nebraska*, the court recognized parental rights as "essential to the orderly pursuit of happiness by free men."[29] The court explained that parents have the right to "bring up children... according to the dictates of his own conscience." Many courts have upheld that this privacy and autonomy of the family and the rights of parents to direct the upbringing of their children are part of the "liberty" protected under the Due Process clause of the Fourteenth Amendment. Courts have solidified this right to "parent" as they see fit without governmental interference in specific terms of childhood obesity cases as well. These courts have determined that obesity alone is not a justification for the state to interfere with the fundamental right to parent.[30]

Genetically Based Obesity

As previously mentioned, the case of Anamarie Martinez-Regino drew attention to the genetic underpinnings of childhood obesity. The onset of similar cases has heightened researchers' interest in the prevalence of genetically based obesity. Adoption and twin studies suggest that 80 percent of obesity risk is due to genetics.[31] Current research has focused on specific genes that may cause obesity, namely

---

29   Meyer v. Nebraska, 262 U.S. 390, 399 (1923).
30   In re D.K., *supra* n. 14: In re Brittany T., *supra* n. 11, at 839.
31   Richard C. Thirlby & James Randall, A Genetic *"Obesity Risk Index" for Patients with Morbid Obesity,* 12 Obesity Surgery 25-9, 25 (2002).

leptin, which plays a key role in the hormonal control of appetite.[32] Mutation of this gene can cause severe obesity in rare cases.

The most commonly cited genetic disorder associated with life-threatening childhood obesity is Prader-Willi syndrome.[33] Among other symptoms, Prader-Willi syndrome is associated with malfunctioning of the hypothalamus (the area of the brain that controls hunger sensations) and manifests itself in an insatiable appetite, which often leads to overeating, and therefore, obesity. Other endogenous causes of childhood obesity exist as well.

Environmental Factors Beyond the Parental Scope

Many opponents of the abuse classification note the presence of environmental factors outside of the home setting. The role that school plays in childhood obesity is commonly cited by researchers as a major influence on a child's weight. Many schools offer a variety of food and drinks of poor nutritional quality and school lunches are typically high in fat and calories. Legal professional Sherry Colb observed that government-sponsored programs in New York City public schools provide students with free lunches teeming with fat and processed carbohydrates; these schools also regularly distributed sugary snacks to students.[34] Further, the reduction in physical education classes and recess, limited health education classes, and overall lack of opportunities for students to participate in physical activity during school hours may also contribute to childhood obesity.[35] Though strides are being made to improve schools and their health programs, the environment in many schools remains conducive to childhood obesity, and largely beyond parental control.

With so many contributing factors, some hesitate to blame parents for their child's obesity. Removing some of the blame from the parents eliminates the need to classify childhood obesity as child abuse. Considering the constitutional right to parent and research highlighting causes of childhood obesity beyond parental control, it is hard to argue that parents of obese children should be punished.

CLASSIFIED AS ABUSE?

The legal community, health professionals, and the public continue to debate over the classification of childhood obesity as child abuse. Currently, both the medical and psychological fields are hesitant

---

32 Phyllis W. Speiser, et al., *Consensus Statement: Childhood Obesity*, 90 J. Clinical Endocrinology and Metabolism 1871-1887, 1873 (2004).

33 Merlin G. Butler, Jeanne M. Hanchett, and Travis Thompson, *Clinical Findings and Natural History of Prader-Willi Syndrome*, 3–48, In Management of Prader-Willi Syndrome (3rd Ed.) (New York: Springer, 2006).

34 Sherry F. Colb. FindLaw. *Child Obesity as Child Neglect: Is the Standard American Dangerous?* (July 22, 2009). available at http://writ.news.findlaw.com/colb/20090722.html

35 F as in Fat, *supra* n. 3.

to label childhood obesity as a form of abuse,[36] despite recent state expansions of child abuse definitions to encompass some cases of childhood obesity. Both proponents and opponents of this abuse classification present well-intended and compelling arguments. Yet, classifying child obesity as child abuse is almost always problematic, and in many cases its costs may outweigh its intended benefits.

Legal-Related Challenges

As previously discussed, classifying childhood obesity as abuse may infringe upon family privacy rights and parents' right to raise children in any manner they see fit. This argument alone suggests that child advocates and legal actors should be extremely cautious when considering whether a particular case of childhood obesity may constitute abuse. In addition, expanding the legal definition of abuse to include some cases of childhood obesity may pose legal and ethical challenges. Though childhood obesity is undoubtedly associated with serious health consequences, it may be difficult to establish that a child's weight poses an "imminent risk of serious harm."

Many parents make decisions that pose health risks to their children; in some cases, these choices are legally protected. For instance, some parents choose not to vaccinate their children against serious illnesses and 20 states currently permit parents to seek exemption from mandatory vaccination regulations on the basis of personal beliefs.[37] Yet, doing so increases children's risk of developing debilitating illnesses that in some cases can result in death. Parents may also fail to seek treatment for children suffering psychological illnesses or provide nutritionally inadequate diets that may not necessarily lead to childhood obesity, but can still result in negative health outcomes. These examples are not intended to undermine the seriousness of childhood obesity, but rather to illustrate the difficulty in maintaining a balance between parental rights and children's health and wellbeing. Classifying childhood obesity as abuse may pave the way for similar policies that can threaten fundamental rights to family privacy and the right to parent.

It may also be difficult to determine whether a parent's actions or inactions are indeed the primary cause of a child's obesity. As previously noted, many cases of obesity may be attributable to genetics and environmental factors beyond parental control. The alarming increase in both child and adult obesity rates in recent years further suggests that larger social forces may be responsible for this nationwide epidemic. For instance, childhood obesity has been attributed to technological advancements and industrialization as well as the increased availability and low cost of foods high in sugar,

---

36   Lauren Cox, *Scottish Courts Briefly Take Obese Mother's Newborn Child—Overweight Family Raises Issue: If You and Your Kids Are Obese, Is It Neglect?* ABC News, Oct. 27, 2009, available at http://abcnews.go.com/Health/Diet/courts-obese-familys-newborn-neglect/story?id=8921808.

37   Jennifer Steinhaur, Public Health Risk Seen as Parents Reject Vaccines, N.Y. Times, March 21, 2008. *available at* http://www.nytimes.com/2008/03/21/us/21vaccine.html?_r=3&coref=slogin

calories, and fat.[38] Single parents, or parents who both must work outside of the home in order to make ends meet, may have difficulty monitoring their child's diet, or they may face time and economic constraints that encourage increased reliance on prepared or highly processed foods.

Considering the myriad of factors that likely contribute to childhood obesity, it may be unfair to punish parents as if they were solely responsible for their child's condition. Further, as each case of childhood obesity has different etiological and epidemiological characteristics, it is nearly impossible to set a standard for which cases of obesity should be classified as abuse.

Negative Consequences of Abuse Classification

Though charging parents of obese children with child abuse is intended to prevent negative health-related outcomes, it also may result in some unforeseen negative consequences. Recent research confirms that childhood obesity is more common among Mexican-American boys, African-American girls,[39] and in lower-income house-holds with poorly educated parents.[40] Thus, classifying childhood obesity as abuse may unfairly target ethnic minorities or individuals from disadvantaged backgrounds when, in some cases, a child's obesity may be largely attributable to economic hardship or cultural factors. Classifying childhood obesity as abuse may also lead a parent to resort to extreme measures in order to avoid arrest and losing custody of their child. Jerri Gray fled the state with her son Alexander when faced with accusations of criminal negligence stemming from his obesity; the pair was located some days later in Maryland. Alternatively, a parent may subject their child to grueling exercise regimes which may be dangerous for an obese child with limited cardiovascular functioning, or implement an extreme diet that deprives the child of nutrients essential for healthy growth and development.

Judges and other legal actors should carefully consider these legal obstacles and potentially harmful consequences when deciding whether a particular case of child obesity constitutes child abuse. Such a classification nearly always results in removal of the child from a parent's care and offers a simplistic but dramatic "solution" to a complex social and family issue. Though the courts must address the problem of childhood obesity, it should only be classified as abuse in the most extreme cases in which all other options have been exhausted.

---

38 *See generally* Patricia M. Anderson & Kristin F. Butcher, *Childhood Obesity: Trends and Potential Causes*, 16 Future Child. 29–33 (2006).

39 Cynthia, L. Ogden, Susan Z. Yanovski, Margaret D. Carroll, & Katherine M. Flegal, *The Epidemiology of Obesity*. 132 Gastroenterology 2084-102, 2092-3 (2007).

40 Jennifer S. Haas, Lisa B. Lee, Celia P. Kaplan, Dean Sonneborn, Kathryn A. Phillips, and Su-Ying Liang, *The Association of Race, Socioeconomic Status, and Health Insurance Status With the Prevalence of Overweight Among Children and Adolescents*, 93 Am. J. Pub. Health 2105-10, 2108 (2003); see also E. Goodman, The Role of Socioeconomic Status Gradients in Explaining Differences in US Adolescents' Health, 89 Am. J. Pub. Health 1522-8, 1524 (1999).

CONSIDERATIONS FOR JUDGES

Intervention Must Occur

Intervention in childhood obesity cases must occur whether or not judges choose to rule that such cases are child abuse. Overweight children are more likely to become overweight adults.[41] The likelihood of obesity to persist into adulthood only compounds a person's risk for health problems that can ultimately lead to death. The psychosocial problems resulting from stigmatization and bias against obese children increase in intensity with age as well.

In cases of extreme obesity, intervention in the parent-child relationship is essential to protect the welfare of children who are unable to act in their own interests. Some parental judgments of the "best interest of the child" and resulting care are not sufficient for prevention, and consequently require the state to intervene.

In California, a 680-pound 13-year-old girl died of health-related issues. Her mother was later found guilty of misdemeanor child abuse due to her "inaction" in promoting her daughter's health and safety.[42] Though an extreme ruling, this case illustrates that, without judicial intervention as a method of protecting children from the harms related to obesity, it is possible that children can unnecessarily experience great harm or even death.

View Childhood Obesity From a Therapeutic Jurisprudence Perspective

In deciding how to rule in cases of childhood obesity, judges should focus on principles of therapeutic jurisprudence in which the law acts as a "therapeutic agent." Removal of the child from the parent's care is a detrimental option that should not be considered unless no other effective options present themselves. A variety of family-oriented services can and should be ordered. A comprehensive approach should be taken after analyzing each childhood obesity case through the lens of therapeutic jurisprudence.

Therapeutic jurisprudence proposes that the law can and should be used to promote well-being without subordinating due process or other important justice principles. Rulings from this approach aim to maximize therapeutic outcomes and minimize anti-therapeutic consequences for victims, defendants, families, and the community.[43] In practice, therapeutic jurisprudence requires carefully considering all aspects of each individual case to develop tailored interventions that will lead to positive physical, psychological, and social outcomes.[44] Consequently, therapeutic jurisprudence

---

41   Robert C. Whitaker, Jeffery A. Wright, Margaret S. Pepe, Kristy D. Seidel, & William H. Dietz, *Predicting Obesity in Young Adulthood from Childhood and Parental Obesity*, 337 N. Eng. J. Med. 869-73, 871 (1997).

42   Patel, *supra* n. 13.

43   *See generally* David B. Wexler & Bruce J. Winick, Law in a Therapeutic Key: Developments in Therapeutic Jurisprudence xvii (Carolina Academic Press: North Carolina, 1996).

44   Casey & Rottman, *supra* n. 2, at 445–457, 454.

incorporates knowledge and theory from a broad range of social science disciplines. Judges and other legal actors adopting this perspective may seek counsel from experts employed in a variety of domains (e.g., social workers, physicians, academic researchers) and draw on current literature as well as past experience when making case-specific decisions.

Those viewing childhood obesity cases through the lens of therapeutic jurisprudence may incorporate education-oriented methods in order to help change attitudes and improve knowledge related toward eating and exercise, as well as methods for teaching the family how to implement changes in their specific system and how to obtain necessary resources. In this way, judicial orders address the psychosocial health issues along with the physical health of the child and family. Mental health practitioners, nutritionists, and other medical professionals may all play important roles, from advising judges to counseling children and families. These basic interventions would likely benefit individuals involved in all types of childhood obesity cases. However, judges must further explore the nuances of each case in ordering additional measures to help combat child obesity across a variety of familial and social contexts.

Refrain From Implementing "Blanket Solutions"

As previously discussed, recent research has uncovered a number of trends in the prevalence of childhood obesity. A blanket solution to obesity cases would not be appropriate when the prevalence of obesity is so disproportionate across socioeconomic status, race, and parental education. Due to these trends in obesity, interventions will most likely target impoverished minorities and families lacking parental education. Steps must be taken to ensure that intervention does not take the form of selective enforcement.

To illustrate the importance of considering these contextual factors, it is helpful to review the effects of such a "blanket" treatment. In *In re Brittany T.*, the courts had ordered the parents to make sure their child attended school regularly, implement changes in the child's diet as instructed in a mandatory nutrition program, and make the child exercise at the gym 2–3 times per week.[45] After failing to institute such changes, the parents of Brittany T. cited several reasons and/or excuses for their inability to comply with the court's orders, including a lack of knowledge of the school's start time, their personal health problems relating to the dad's confinement in a wheelchair, and their inability to access necessary resources such as transportation. By not considering the low socioeconomic status of the family and the obvious limitations of the parents' level of education and parents' personal health problems, the court failed to appropriately intervene in this case. It is clear that poorer families often cannot afford healthier foods, gym memberships, and other costs that are necessary to adhere to rulings typical in childhood obesity cases.

---

45   In re Brittany T., *supra* n. 11, at 831-2.

Focus on the Underlying Causes

Rather than ordering interventions that are not appropriate and tailored to each specific case, judges should seek to effectively address each childhood obesity case individually. Therapeutic jurisprudence seeks to identify the underlying causes of each specific childhood obesity case. It is imperative to analyze the cause within the family unit as each case or childhood obesity has unique contributors. An interplay of genetic, behavioral, and environmental factors must be present in each case for obesity to manifest itself. Though genes may increase the likelihood of obesity in many children, environmental and behavioral factors also affect a child's susceptibility to obesity. A miniscule number of cases of childhood obesity are caused predominately by genetic defect,[46] but approximately 90 percent can be attributed to lifestyle and environmental influences.[47] It is important to note that these environmental influences often extend beyond the influence of the parents. Though having an obese parent more than doubles the risk of the child being obese,[48] this is clearly not the only cause of obesity.

In cases in which there is a substantial genetic foundation leading to obesity, it is especially important that families are teamed up with medical professionals. This can include the treating physician and dieticians, as well as visiting nurses. These professionals should be utilized to help the family improve the diets of the children and the family together. They are also a key resource in helping to diagnose and treat physiological conditions that may lead to obesity, such as thyroid issues. They can provide help with early onset physical problems that have already manifested themselves and ensure compliance with dietary recommendations. Individualized exercise programs can also be created in collaboration with these professionals and should be ordered by the courts.

As impoverished families are more likely to have obese children, it is likely that the families involved in these cases need economic support. In ruling from a therapeutic jurisprudence perspective, if at all possible, families should be provided with contacts which can improve their financial situation. Parents will likely benefit from financial counseling, job training, and other interventions designed to foster economic stability (e.g., G.E.D. or post-secondary classes). This will in turn allow these parents to provide their children with healthier food choices, gym passes, and other means of combating obesity.

As stated above, having an obese parent doubles a child's risk of becoming obese. In many childhood obesity cases, the parents are also obese and therefore can benefit from education as well. In all cases, families as a whole should he ordered to enroll in family counseling. This multidisciplinary approach can address the family unit as a whole. Often, social science professionals will address the issue from a family systems theoretical approach.

---

46 Rebecca Moran, *Evaluation and Treatment of Childhood Obesity*, 59 Am. Fam. Physician, 861-8, 871-3 (1999), *available at* http://www.aafp.org/afp/990215ap/861.html.

47 *Id.*

48 Whitaker, *supra* n. 41, at 871.

Family systems theory greatly influences the field of human development and family studies, yet little recognition of this approach exists in the legal system. This theory addresses the "family" (biological parents, siblings, anyone with an intimate familial-type connection) as a whole entity that is both dynamic and ever-changing.[49] In order to understand the child and all causes of their obesity, they must be viewed in terms of the collective family. Ordering families to attend counseling that incorporates diet and exercise programs for both individual and family behavior modification has been shown as one of the most successful means of treating childhood obesity.[50]

Use Removal of Child from Parent's Care as a Last Resort

Approaching childhood obesity cases from a therapeutic jurisprudence perspective often requires that family units remain intact in most cases, a balance between family preservation and child protection can be achieved without removing the child from the home.[51] Unfortunately, the majority of the cases discussed in this article resulted in removal of the child.

From a therapeutic jurisprudence perspective, it is clear that removal causes a multitude of anti-therapeutic consequences possibly more traumatic than from simply being obese. Experts note that children's identities are based on their attachment with their parents or caregiver and that short disruptions in the parent-child relationship have negative effects on children's emotional stability.

The ruling *In re D.K.* established the precedent that whenever possible, the courts should allow for a government agency to educate and supervise the parents to preserve the family.[52] It is imperative to recognize the inherent strengths of families when the family unit receives proper support, considers the home to be the ideal place for a child to be raised, and recognizes the necessity of preserving the stability of intimate familial relationships for the child's sake.[53] More importantly, the placement of an obese child in foster care may have negative effects on the child's weight itself. Though research on the topic is limited, it has been shown that children may actually gain weight while in foster care.[54]

Removal must be reserved as the most extreme solution. Situations in which parents are unlikely to change their abusive behavior and the family is the primary source of danger to children are the only cases in which removal may have therapeutic consequences.

---

49   Susan L. Brooks. *A Family Systems Paradigm for Legal Decision Affecting Child Custody*, 6 Cornell J. L. & Pub. Pol'y 1, 5-6 (1996).
50   Leonard H. Epstein, Michelle D. Myers, Hollie A. Raynor, & Brian E. Saelens. *Treatment of Pediatric Obesity*. 101 J. Pediatrics 554-570, 561 (1998).
51   *See generally* Anthony N. Maluccio, Barbara A. Pine, & Robin Warsh, *Protecting Children by Preserving Their Families*, 16 Children and Youth Serv. Rev. 295–307 (1994).
52   *In re D.K., supra* n. 14, at 358–359.
53   *See generally* Mark E. Courtney, *Reconsidering Family Preservation: A Review of Putting Families First*, 19 Children and Youth Serv. Rev. 61.76 (1997).
54   *See generally* S.C. Hadfield & P.M. Preece, *obesity in looked after children: Is foster care protective from the dangers of obesity?* 34 child: Care, health, and Dev, 710–712 (2008)

Ensure Accountability

Many critics of applying therapeutic jurisprudence to cases of childhood obesity are concerned about the longitudinal effects this approach will have in the life of an obese child. Long-term success in combating a child's obesity requires constant implementation of the behaviors modifications ordered by the court and subsequent the professionals working with these families. Judges need to ensure that families are monitored and complete all mandatory orders including attending counseling. If families are not held accountable, lifestyle modifications necessary to make a lasting change will not have the opportunity to be realized. Though the suggestions included in this article may not solve all cases of childhood obesity, these measures must be tried first.

CONCLUSION

It is clear that the childhood obesity "epidemic" must be addressed. Unless legal actors target the underlying causes of this problem, ruling in cases involving childhood obesity will continue to be ineffective. Childhood obesity, when untreated, leads to lifelong physical and psychosocial health issues. Though a parent has the fundamental right to parent as they see fit, the state has the responsibility to intervene in cases in which a child's obesity is life-limiting. Not only should care be taken to account for genetic contributions to obesity and influences beyond the parental scope, but judges should also focus on ruling from a therapeutic jurisprudence perspective aimed at supporting change within the family unit.

With education and other therapeutic means of treatment, obesity may not carry into adulthood and its negative effects can be greatly reduced. If all other means of therapeutic jurisprudence fail, removal of the child from the tare of the family should be considered as a last resort. It is imperative for judges to focus on principles of therapeutic jurisprudence and utilize the law as a therapeutic agent. Whether or not childhood obesity is considered child abuse, in each specific case education-oriented and non-punitive methods of addressing the underlying cause of obesity within the family unit must be implemented.

How can this article be reconciled with the Alabama grandmother who was convicted of capital murder and sentenced to life in prison when she "ran her granddaughter to death" as punishment for lying about eating chocolates?[57]

---

57   "Jury recommends life in prison for Ala. Woman", *Washington Post Digest*, March 27, 2015.

SIBLING DONORS

In her book, *My Sister's Keeper*, author Jody Picoult[58] raises many of the issues that occur when parents decide to have a "sibling donor."[59] If one of their children has a disease that may require organ, marrow, or tissue donation, some parents may decide to have another child, who may be a possible donor to the sick child. These cases raise medical and ethical issues like, should one child be "hurt" by a medical procedure in order to help another? (The Hippocratic Oath seems to say no.) Can a parent make a decision with both the children's best interests in mind? When a child is asked to help out by donating, what is the effect of the decision? Either way, what happens if the other sibling dies? Even this issue of creating the second child is challenging. Through the use of assisted reproductive technologies, should parents be able to select a child who will have the necessary matches to help the sick child? What is the effect of a child created as a sibling donor, even if the parents intended to have a second child anyway?

"God's been very kind."[60] Kabir Sekhri was diagnosed with T-cell acute lymphoblastic leukemia "the same week that his grandfather succumbed to throat cancer after years of grueling treatment."[61] The disease has a poor prognosis compared with other pediatric cancers, but while Kabir's body "responded well enough to the early chemotherapy to put him in remission, he had not completed the full regimen when he relapsed." His doctor advised him to travel to America for the newest drugs and best treatments, so he left behind everyone he knew and had grown up with ("his beloved sister and the aunts, uncles and cousins who make up the Sekhris' close-knit extended family, the friends he played with his entire childhood...")[62] They flew to Washington, D.C., to Georgetown's Lombardi Cancer Center, where "[f]our months of highly aggressive chemotherapy drugs ravaged Kabir but pushed his body into a second remission that made him a candidate for a bone marrow transplant. The perfect donor: his 16-year-old sister, Ridhima."[63] She flew from India to "Duke University Medical Center for the procedure. The graft took well enough that when Kabir returned to Washington in early 2006, he was out of the hospital far more than in it, giving him a chance at memories not integrally tied to pain."[64] His one year checkup "revealed a second relapse."[65] Kabir "rejected any talk of another transplant," but agreed to another attempt at chemotherapy.[66] Kabir grew weaker, "wracked by days of extreme fevers,

---

58   *My Sister's Keeper: A Novel*. Washington Square Press, 2004. Also a 2009 movie starring Cameron Diaz, Sofia Vassilieva, and Alec Baldwin.

59   In the book, the donor daughter asks a lawyer to medically emancipate her from her parents to avoid further bodily donations.

60   "Britain debates a child's right to choose her own fate," Kevin Sullivan, *Washington Post* Foreign Service, November 14, 2008, p. 16.

61   Ibid.

62   Ibid.

63   Ibid.

64   Ibid.

65   Ibid.

66   Ibid.

numbness and bleeding. He stopped eating and virtually stopped communicating. When he did talk, he'd say plaintively, in a wispy voice made almost childlike by the drugs: 'I just want to go home.'" Months later, "a bone marrow biopsy showed the unexpected—a partial remission. No matter, Kabir reminded [the doctor]; he'd said he was finished."[67] The doctor, with a son one year younger, "still is struggling with that." The next month, the family was on a plane home to India. "I made a promise I would get him home, and I need to stick to my promise," his mother said.[68]

THE SLIPPERY SLOPE OF CASES: YOU DECIDE

- In 2007, Jade Sanders and Lamont Thomas of Atlanta were convicted of malice, murder, and given life sentences for the death of their six-week-old child. The defense attorneys cited the couple's strict vegan lifestyle to explain why they fed their newborn son a diet of soy milk and organic apple juice, though during the trial, Sanders said she had also breast-fed her son, who died in an emaciated state at six weeks, weighing just three and a half pounds. The prosecutor and court had no qualms in treating this couple's beliefs as a poor excuse for murder, even though the defense called a nutritionist and vegan expert as a witness to show that a vegan diet can be safe for an infant. The prosecutor even told the jury: "They're not vegans, they're baby-killers."[69]

- Thirteen-year-old Hannah Jones of England "was diagnosed with leukemia in 1999 when she was 4. Chemotherapy sent the cancer into remission but caused her to lose hair and skin. Amid all the strain on her young body, she developed a hole in her heart. In March 2000, she came home from the hospital weighing less than 30 pounds. She had to be fed by tube and needed an oxygen cylinder to help her breathe."[70] She was already nine when she first went to school, but she needed a heart transplant by age 12. "She was fitted with a pacemaker, and doctors showed her films of a transplant operation. They told her that the surgery itself might kill her and that her weakened immune system would make her susceptible to a recurrence of leukemia. They told her she would need a constant regimen of drugs and that she would probably need a second transplant in about 10 years."[71] She refused the treatment and went home. Her parents supported her position. The hospital called her parents "and threatened to send police to forcibly remove Hannah from their care, saying they were not acting in her best interest. Hospital officials threatened to seek a court order forcing her to have the transplant."[72] Should the hospital go to court, and should the court order the

---

67   Ibid.

68   Ibid.

69   "When a child dies, faith is no defense," Jonathan Turley, *Washington Post*, November 15, 2009, p. B1.

70   "Britain Debates a Child's Right to Choose Her Own Fate," Kevin Sullivan, *Washington Post* Foreign Service, November 14, 2008.

71   Ibid., p. 16.

72   Ibid.

treatment? Does the fact that there is a shortage of hearts available for transplant influence the decision to force someone who does not want it to take it when others do?[73]

- "Our 12-year-old son has obsessive-compulsive disorder. His psychiatrist recommended a medication, but our son fears its potential side effects and refuses to take it. We could sneak a liquid version into his meals, but his physician said this could be considered child abuse. Yet under the circumstances, not doing so seems worse, considering that our son's condition prevents him from making a self-healing decision. What to do? Name withheld, Pennsylvania."[74] Would this amount to child abuse?

- A mother smokes in the car with the windows up while her newborn and two-year-old are in the backseat.[75] With marijuana legal in many states, is it abuse to smoke it in the house when your children are around? Why is this different than parents legally drinking alcohol?

- In 2004, the parents of "Ashley," a bedridden, severely mentally and physically disabled nine-year-old child had her uterus and breast tissue removed and dosed her with large amounts of hormones to stunt or stop her growth.[76] The process is known as growth attenuation. Ashley's static encephalopathy has left her with the mental ability of a three-month-old child.[77] Unable to talk, walk, or even keep her head up, Ashley is fed through a tube.[78] The parents claimed they needed to do this to keep her a manageable size in order for them to continue to treat her at home as they age.[79] The parents call her "their pillow angel 'since she is so sweet and stays right where we place her, usually on a pillow'."[80] The treatment kept her at about 65 pounds and "about 13 inches shorter and 50 pounds lighter than she would be as an adult."[81] "Ashley's parents say keeping her small will reduce the risk of bedsores and prevent her from going through puberty... [to avoid] the discomfort of periods or grow[ing] breasts that might

---

73 Ibid., p. A16.

74 "Treating a Son's O.C.D., The Ethicist," Randy Cohen, *New York Times Magazine*, April 18, 2010, p. 30. The answer begins, "When a query includes the verb 'sneak', its answer is predictable. When a physician describes a proposed action as potential 'child abuse', my facial expression is similarly predictable. Both good medical practice and good ethics urge you not to deceive your son." The article then cites Bryna Siegel, a professor of child and adolescent psychiatry at the University of California, San Francisco, that "if medication is to be included in your son's treatment, it should be employed only 'with the agreement of the boy, who by this time should have a confidential working relationship with his therapist and discuss his fears about medications.'"

75 In March 2013, Maryland's Senate passed a bill to prohibit drivers and passengers from smoking in the car while children are passengers, making it a $50 penalty for violation. Mobile homes are excepted. http://www.somdnews.com/article/20130327/NEWS/130329162/1074/senate-votes-to-ban-smoking-in-cars-with-kids&template=southernMaryland, "Senate votes to ban smoking in cars with kids: Perennial bill from Forehand inspired by her father," Holly Nunn, *SoMdNews*. Many states already have laws banning smoking in restaurants and public buildings.

76 "Treatments to Keep Disabled Girl Small Stir Debate," Bloomsburg News, *Washington Post*, January 5, 2007, p. A2.

77 Ibid.

78 Ibid.

79 "Surgery to Stunt Girl's Growth Sparks Debate," Lindsey Tanner, AP. Junomsg://0674F2000

80 Ibid.

81 Ibid., quoting the parents' blog.

develop breast cancer, that runs in the family."[82] According to the parents' blog, "Ashley's smaller and lighter size makes it more possible to include her in the typical family life and activities that provide her with needed comfort, closeness, security and love: meal time, car trips, touch, snuggles, etc."[83] Is this really treatment for the benefit of Ashley, or her parents—or both? Is that wrong?[84]

- What about giving hormone blockers to a son, who likes to dress as a girl? Or, taking away the dolls of a boy who likes to dress as a girl? Or allowing him to keep them?[85]
- Is getting a circumcision abuse?[86]
- What about parents who let their children go to tanning booths?
- How about allowing children to be in beauty pageants?[87]

CONCLUSION

What should be the outcome of Daniel Hauser's case, which opened this chapter? When the case discussion ended, the mother, Colleen Hauser of Minnesota, had gone into hiding to avoid the court's order requiring chemotherapy for her 13-year-old son's Hodgkin's lymphoma tumor growing in his chest. "She was eventually forced to yield; this month [November 2009] her son finished his final radiation treatment and his family says his cancer is gone."[88] Did ethics and the law work properly together?

Are these medical decisions making cases involving private tragedies appropriately decided by the families or the government and the courts? Should the government enforce its decisions by using the police to forcibly take a sick child to the hospital for treatment? Or even just a social

---

82   Ibid., quoting the parents' blog.

83   Ibid.

84   A case like Ashley's was the subject of a "Law and Order" episode. But, there is no empirical evidence that "correlates body size with quality of life." https://www.nytimes.com/2016/03/27/magazine/should-parents-of-severely-disabled-children-be-allowed-to-stop-their-growth.html?_r=0 Which is more important, the child's comfort or bodily integrity? Ibid., P 149. Do these cases justify non-essential medical treatment? Ibid., p. 149 Does this violate the American Disabilities Act or the right to privacy? Did the parents and/or the doctor violate her rights by sterilizing her without a court order? What separates this from eugenics as discussed in Chapter 13?

85   "I have to be patient, but sometimes I feel like an emotional hostage, because as his parent, it's my job to help him be whatever he wants to be, and I can't do that if he doesn't know where he's headed." A parent dealing with similar parenting issues for her son: "Raising a Boy who Prefers to Look and Act Like a Girl Tests Even the Most Progressive Parents," Ruth Padawer, *New York Times Magazine*, August 12, 2012, p. 23.

86   Proposed circumcision ban struck from San Francisco ballot, http://abcnews.go.com/Health/san-francisco-circumcision-ban-striken/story?id=14179024. Does the child have a right to bodily integrity?

87   "France moves to ban child beauty pageants", Angela Charlton, *The Washington Post*/The World, September 19, 2013, P. A8. "France's senate voted to ban beauty pageants for children younger than 16 in an effort to protect girls from being sexualized too early." The proposed penalty for entering a child in a contest was severe--up to two years in prison and about $40,000 in fines. "At this age, you need to concentrate on acquiring knowledge...I have a hard time seeing how these competitions are in the greater interest of the child", citing Chantal Jouanno who wrote the law.,

88   "When a child dies, faith is no defense," Jonathan Turley, *Washington Post,* November 15, 2009, p. B1.

worker to enforce the order? These decisions are just too heartbreaking to bear. While the decisions will never go away with legislation, it could help. Surely, our country could provide better help to caregivers who are already burdened by such decisions.

AS WE GO TO PRESS

After California passed a mandatory vaccine law in 2015, "kindergarten vaccination rates have risen to their highest level in more than 15 years."[89] Yet, the state was sued for removing the parental personal belief option. Despite the debunking of the vaccine/autism link, as a candidate and now as President, Donald Trump has been skeptical of vaccines' safety and tied vaccines to autism. Will a federal campaign "trump" state's decisions on vaccines?

Why do some people still challenge the medical community and the science the supports vaccines? If you do not want to take your doctor's advice to give your children the vaccines, why do you go to the doctor anyway? Is it OK for pediatricians to put up signs refusing to service unvaccinated children in their office?

---

89 http://www.sacbee.com/news/politics-government/capitol-alert/article145890544.html#storylink=cpy

19

EDUCATION

When I think back on all the crap I learned in high school,
it's a wonder I can think at all....
—Paul Simon, "Kodachrome"

Try not to have a good time... this is supposed to be educational.
—Charles M. Schulz [1]

I n addition to providing support, medical care, and shelter, part of parents' responsibilities in raising their children is to oversee their education. Once mandatory education laws were passed at the turn of the 20th century, the state inserted itself into that parent-child relationship. While adults have many rights against government interference, those same rights often do not extend to children, especially to the same extent. While in the past education cases involved parents objecting to a school's policy, now they involve parents suing on issues individual to their child such as suspensions, discipline and grades.

HISTORY OF PARENTS' RIGHTS TO RAISE THEIR CHILDREN

Parents have a right to have children and to raise them as they deem fit. In *Meyer v. Nebraska*,[2] the Supreme Court was asked to look at a state law prohibiting the teaching of foreign languages. This was during the 1920s, after the "war to end all wars" (World War I), and the country was entrenched in its isolationist foreign policy. As a result, Nebraska banned the teaching of foreign languages, including German. When a teacher ignored the rule and taught a German language class, many of the parents supported his actions, but the school board district fired him. While

---

1 www.brainyquote.com/quotes/quotes/c/charlesms109506.html
2 In *Meyer v. Nebraska*, 262 U.S. 390 (1923) (U.S. 1923).

striking down the law and supporting the parents, the Supreme Court wrote, "there seems no adequate foundation for the suggestion that the purpose was to protect the child's health by limiting his mental activities." A few years later, in 1925, the Supreme Court looked at the issue of education in *Pierce v. Society of Sisters*,[3] where the Court invalidated a state law requiring parents to send their children to public school as an overreach on the parents' constitutionally protected right to decide their children's education as part of the child's overall upbringing.

SEX EDUCATION

One area in which a parent's right to raise a child can clash with the state's responsibility to educate its citizenry is that of sexual education. While a state (generally through standards established by a department of education) can mandate the teaching of sexual education as part of the curriculum, it generally leaves up to the different counties how to implement that requirement, and to what extent. When a sex ed. class or program is imposed, what happens if it conflicts with a parent's religious or personal beliefs? First, only public schools are subject to the Constitution's freedom of religion requirements. Second, even in the public schools, the state must provide for a student to "opt" out of the offending requirement. The New Jersey case of *Smith v. Ricci* dealt with this conflict.

Under *Smith v. Ricci*, 446 A.2d 501 (N.J. 1982), when a program is mandatory, as long as the school allows the parents an option to have their children not participate in the program, it will not be invalidated. Fast forward several decades. High Schools now may have to defend against parents' lawsuits when the schools supply condoms in condom distribution programs for AIDS awareness education. Under these programs, at the student's request for a free condom, a nurse gives counseling and information on the prevention of sexually transmitted diseases. In *Curtis v. Falmouth*, 652 N.E. 2d 580 (Mass. 1995), the parents challenged the program because it did not allow them to "opt out" their children from participation. How should it be decided?[4]

CHILDREN'S RIGHTS AT SCHOOL

By entering the school's front door, a student seems to give up some of his rights. While the right to free speech is generally recognized, it is limited at school (but still exists). The cases generally hold that free speech can be limited if it is necessary for the school to keep order and fulfill its

---

3   U.S. 510,45 S. Ct. 571,69 L. Ed. 1070,1925 (U.S. 1924).

4   In 2014, Montgomery County, Maryland, expanded its sex education program to include lessons on sexual orientation as early as middle school in response to a" survey showing 11.2 percent of Maryland high schoolers reporting harassment based on perceived sexual orientation in 2011." https://www.pressreader.com/usa/the-washington-post/20140514/282205123913743 Previous attempts to modify the curriculum drew "thousands of comments" and a lawsuit over the issue of incorporating sexual orientation and condom demonstrations in 2007.

educational mission. In *Tinker v. Des Moines Independent Community School District*, 393 U.S. 503 (U.S. 1969), First Amendment protections were recognized for student speech unless it causes a disturbance.

In the case of *Morse v. Frederick*,[5] in 2007, 18-year-old Joseph Frederick held a 14-foot paper sign on a public sidewalk outside his Juneau, Alaska, school that read, "BONG HITS 4 JESUS,"[6] as the school waited outside for the Olympic torch runner to pass by.[7] When a school administrator told Frederick to take the sign down and he refused, they took the poster and suspended him. He sued. "A federal appeals court in San Francisco agreed, concluding the school could not show Frederick had disrupted the school's educational mission by showing a banner off campus" and his case eventually went up on appeal to the U.S. Supreme Court.[8] There, the majority's opinion called it a "sophomoric" banner. Chief Justice John Roberts,[9] writing for the 6-3 majority, wrote, "It was reasonable for (the principal) to conclude that the banner promoted illegal drug use—and that failing to act would send a powerful message to the students in her charge." In dissent, Justice John Paul Stevens said, "This case began with a silly nonsensical banner, (and) ends with the court inventing out of whole cloth a special First Amendment rule permitting the censorship of any student speech that mentions drugs, so long as someone could perceive that speech to contain a latent pro-drug message." After the ruling, Frederick said, "'I find it absurdly funny.'... 'I was not promoting drugs.'... 'I assumed most people would take it as a joke.'"[10] Did Frederick cause a disturbance, or is there a new rule limiting students' rights to free speech?

STUDENT LOCKERS

Since at least the days of the civil rights integration cases, schools have successfully searched students' school lockers (at that time, the administration was trying to deal with bomb threats by people opposing the Supreme Court-ordered integration of schools). These searches are generally allowed because a student should not have an "expectation of privacy" in a school-owned locker. Is this right?

Compare locker searches to searching student backpacks or purses. In Talbot County, Maryland, two families of former high school lacrosse players filed a federal civil rights claim against school

---

5   551 U.S. 393 (2007).

6   Even with its Jesus reference, no one seemed to raise a First Amendment free exercise of religion issue.

7   "Though he was standing on a public sidewalk, the school argued Frederick was part of a school-sanctioned event, because students were let out of classes and accompanied by their teachers."

8   At the Supreme Court, the school was represented by Kenneth Starr, the independent counsel for President Bill Clinton's impeachment trial (*Time* picked both Starr and Clinton as "People of the Year"). Starr then became dean of Pepperdine University's law school. He argued for the principle "that a school 'must be able to fashion its educational mission' without undue hindsight from the courts."

9   http://www.cnn.com/2007/LAW/06/25/free.speech/, "'Bong Hits 4 Jesus' case limits student rights," Bill Mears, CNN.com, June 26, 2007.

10   Ibid.

officials claiming an unconstitutional search of the students' athletic equipment bags. Based on a tip, the school searched the bags for alcohol while on a school bus. They did not find alcohol, but they did find two small knives and a lighter, for which the students were suspended. The students claimed they used them for maintaining the lacrosse equipment. After the school punished the students, the Maryland State Board of Education overruled the school and ordered the student's records expunged—a rare reversal of a zero tolerance policy.[11]

RANDOM DRUG TESTING

While adults may be subject to random drug testing to keep their jobs, should students also be subjected? Again, showing that children/students may be held to a lower standard than adults, the U.S. Supreme Court has held that it is permissible to subject student athletes to random drug tests. In *Vernonia School District v. Acton*, 515 U.S. 646, 115 S.Ct.[12] (U.S. 1995), when allegations of drug use in the student body were made, the school implemented a random student drug-testing policy including athletes, whom the school thought might be inclined to injuries while in a drugged state. In perhaps one of a few times the U.S. Supreme Court wrote about bodily functions, the majority opinion wrote, "The privacy interests compromised by urine samples are negligible since the conditions of collection are similar to public restrooms, and the results are viewed only by limited authorities. Furthermore, the governmental concern over the safety of minors under their supervision overrides the minimal, if any, intrusion in student-athletes' privacy."

ZERO TOLERANCE POLICIES

Another area where schools curtail student rights is in zero tolerance policies. Many schools have such policies against the possession of drugs or guns on campus, or even sexual harassment. Certainly, these are important topics that require serious consideration, but are those laws sometimes against common sense?

---

11 "Families sue Talbot school officials", Donna St. George, *The Washington Post Metro*, January 21, 2014, P. B1. Speaking of parents suing over student athlete issues, while not a school lawsuit, a Virginia family sued when their daughter's traveling team coach "benched her and the league told [the daughter] she could not join another team". They alleged that during her junior year not playing would impact her ability for college recruitment and that the league has lost sight of its mission to have kids play sports. The defendant league responded that she is just disgruntled and that allowing mid-season transfers would be an administrative nightmare. "The lawsuit is one of a number filed across the country in recent years as families have increasingly turned to the courts to intervene in youth sports disputes. Parents upset that their children have been cut, benched, yelled at by coaches or even fouled too hard are asking judges to referee". "Suits are filed: For benched Va. Teen, it's not just a game," Justin Joubenal, *The Washington Post*, April 1, 2015, P. 1.

12 http://www.soc.umn.edu/~samaha/cases/vernonia_sch_dist_v_acton.htm also, http://www.oyez.org/cases/1990-1999/1994/1994_94_590 Use this link to listen to the Supreme Court hearings and opinion announcement on the case.

In December 2006, in Waco, Texas, four-year-old Chris Blackwell was given an in-school suspension for engaging in "inappropriate physical behavior interpreted as sexual contact and/or sexual harassment." A teacher's aide filed a "student behavior referral," stating that as he waited in line for the school bus, "Christopher called my name, he looked at me and smiled with a great big grin on his face, he stuck his face and rubbed it across my chest and he thought it was funny."[13] "Only after Chris' father complained did the school agree to change Chris' record from sexual harassment to "inappropriate physical conduct." Was this the right thing to do?

But what about when middle school girls complain that their buttocks were slapped by fellow male classmates while in school? Does the age or behavior make a difference? When several boys "ran through the halls at school, swatting the bottoms of girls" on what is unofficially "Slap Butt Day" at Patton Middle School, where swatting butts is considered a form of greeting by kids but a violation of school policy, the boys **were put in jail** and charged with "five counts of felony sex abuse in the first degree."[14] They "were sent to the office, where the school's vice principal and police officer…questioned them and the girls who were the supposed 'victims.' After hours of interrogation, the boys were read their Miranda rights, handcuffed and taken to the juvenile detention center."[15] Is that right?

In Maryland, a seven-year-old boy was suspended for two days from elementary school when he ate his pop tart–like breakfast sandwich into the shape of a gun and then yelled, "Look I made a gun" (according to a subsequent appeal). He aimed the pastry at students in a hallway and those at nearby desks. Under the school's policy against guns or references to guns, he was expelled. It mattered not that he was originally trying to eat it into the shape of a mountain.[16] Better yet, the school sent home a letter to parents notifying them that "a student used food to make an inappropriate gesture,"—maybe to offer some counseling to the other seven-year-olds?

In appealing the suspension in the so called "Pop Tart case", the boy's father said, "The chewed pastry was not capable of harming anybody, even if thrown,"[17] and "It was harmless," his father said. "It was a *Danish*."[18] The school refused the parents' request to have the permanent record expunged.[19] The parents retained a lawyer and appealed the suspension. In March 2013, "a Maryland lawmaker introduced a bill that would forbid suspensions of young children for

---

13 http://abcnews.go.com/2020/story?id=3693516&page=1#.UWwfOkrYySo, "Sexual Abuse or Harmless Horseplay?" John Stossel and Frank Mastropolo, ABC News, *20/20*, October 5, 2007.

14 Ibid.

15 Ibid.

16 http://www.foxnews.com/us/2013/03/05/boy-7-suspended-for-shaping-pastry-into-gun-dad-says/, "Boy, 7, Suspended for Shaping Pastry into Gun, Dad says," *Fox News*, March 5, 2013.

17 http://articles.washingtonpost.com/2013-03-14/local/37711264_1_anne-arundel-schools-spokesman-pastry-gun "Appeal for Maryland 7-year-old Suspended for Nibbling Pastry into Shape of a Gun," Donna St. George, *Washington Post*, March 14, 2013.)

18 Quoting his father Mr. Welch. Ibid.

19 Ibid. In the appeal, the parents argued that the "'shape that touched off so much trouble… is similar in appearance to puzzle pieces of states such as Idaho, Florida and Oklahoma,'" which they said are "'available in every second grade classroom in the state of Maryland. The filing included photos of chewed Pop-Tarts and the three states."

imaginary guns, pictures of guns or objects that resemble a gun but serve another purpose." In September 2014, "The superintendent of Anne Arundel County Public Schools reaffirmed that 9-year-old Josh Welch's suspension had nothing to do with Pop-Tarts or guns, saying the boy is a troublemaker who frightened his classmates."[20] Calling it "political correctness run amok", the family and lawyer appealed again. [21] In March 2015, the Maryland State Board of Education upheld the suspension "because of the disruption and other previous misconduct".[22] In 2015, a Maryland Circuit Court judge upheld the school's decision.[23] Eventually, the family and the school district reached a confidential settlement. [24] The incident happened when the boy was 7. He was 11 by the time it was resolved.

"A dozen [Maryland] families have...suspensions for incidents that did not pose serious harm." "[C]hildren have been suspended from school for pointing their fingers like guns and, in one case, for talking about shooting a Hello Kitty gun that blows bubbles. In several cases, the offenses were described in harsh terms—one as a "terroristic threat"—and officials agreed, after appeals, to clear the students' permanent records.[25] In one Maryland country a "sixth grader who was suspended for making a gun gesture to a school bus...will have the incident cleared from his records according to his mother." After a one-day suspension his family appealed arguing that because "his gesture was not intended as a threat, making the infraction a part of his permanent record was too far". In another county, a "kindergartner...was suspended for having a cowboy-style cap gun on a school bus" because he wanted to show it to a friend. In Ohio, a 6-year old boy pretending to be a Power Ranger was suspended when he shot an imaginary bow and arrow.[26]

In the meanwhile, other states have cited the Maryland case in proposing "Pop-Tart" gun bills that limit student suspensions for imaginary weapons. Florida passed a law "to limit zero tolerance at schools including 'discipline for brandishing partially consumed pastry or other food to imitate a weapon.'" [27] These laws were passed after the outrage and grief of the Sandy Hook Elementary massacre. Many would support the application of these zero tolerance gun laws on a 17-year old, but should they be applied to a kindergartener?

---

20 http://www.wjla.com/articles/2014/09/family-of-md-boy-suspended-for-pop-tart-"Family of MD boy suspended for 'pop tart' gun wants his suspension record expunged", Brad Bell, WJLA ABC7, September 3, 2014. http://www.wjla.com/articles/2014/09/family-of-md-boy-suspended-for-pop-tart-"Family

21 Citing to attorney Robin Ficker. Ibid.

22 "Md. State board upholds boy's suspension in pastry gun case", Donna St. George, *The Washington Post*, March 5, 2015. http://www.washingtonpost.com/local/education/md-state-board-upholds-boys-suspension-in-pastry-gun-case/2015/03/04/782b412e-c1db-11e4-ad5c-3b8ce89f1b89_story.html

23 https://www.washingtonpost.com/local/education/resolution-years-later-in-boys-suspension-over-pastry-gun/2016/10/25/6bc337de-96f5-11e6-bc79-af1cd3d2984b_story.html?utm_term=.5e97937849e3

24 Ibid.

25 http://www.washingtonpost.com/local/education/md-state-board-upholds-boys-suspension-in-pastry-gun-case/2015/03/04/782b412e-c1db-11e4-ad5c-3b8ce89f1b89_story.html

26 http://abc13.com/education/boy-6-suspended-over-imaginary-bow-and-arrow/1069386/

27 As a result of the Pop Tart case, neighboring Calvert County Maryland school officials revised their policy too. http://www.orlandosentinel.com/features/education/school-zone/os-gov-scott-pop-tart-bill-post.html

AS WE GO TO PRESS

"'I just want people to pee where they want to pee—it's not that big of a deal." "We just want to pee in peace."[28] Is this the issue at the center of a national debate? Or is the issue really much bigger than that? When Virginia high school student, Gavin Grimm, "born a girl…changed his name…under(went) hormone therapy and identifies as a boy" came out to his school they "took it in stride, He used the boy's restroom, No big deal."[29] After school board involvement and community meetings Grimm was stopped from using the boy's restroom and given a choice between the girl's restroom or a unisex restroom. No high school student wants to stand out, but beyond that bathrooms can be places of bullying and predatory behavior. Grimm sued under Title IX which bars schools that receive federal aid (almost all of them), from discriminating against a student based on sex. The courts went back to the debate as to whether this was determined by anatomy or psyche (see Chapter 9), not considering how such a bathroom ban would be enforced (panty checks?). Meanwhile, states[30] like North Carolina passed laws "bar(ring) individuals in the state from using public bathrooms that do not correspond to their biological sex — the one listed on their birth certificate"[31]. In 2016, then Republican candidate, Donald Trump said, people should "use the bathroom they feel is appropriate."[32] In 2017, President Trump rescinded protections for transgender students that had allowed them to use bathrooms corresponding with their gender identity, overruling his own education secretary and placing his administration firmly in the middle of the culture wars that many Republicans have tried to leave behind."[33] In a similar flip flop, North Carolina's legislature hurriedly changed its mind when faced with the loss of future N.C.A.A. Division 1 basketball tournaments in the state. Where will this go from here?

CHAPTER SOURCE

Weisberg, D. Kelly. *Emanuel Law Outlines*, "Family Law." (2011)

---

28   "An issue bigger than bathrooms, VA transgender teen says national Gavin Grimm, the high school plaintiff in a nationally watched case.

29   "Beyond bathroom talk", Ruth Marcus, *The Washington Post*, April 24, 2016, A21.

30   Indeed, over 40 transgender bathroom bills were debated in16 states. "Talking points', *The Week*, April 8, 2016, 17

31   https://www.nytimes.com/politics/first-draft/2016/04/21/donald-trump-says-transgender-people-should-use-the-bathroom-they-want/ The law also removed anti-discrimination protections for lesbian, gay, bisexual and transgender people. "In other words, people in North Carolina can now be legally fired from their jobs or turned away at hotel chains for being gay." "Talking points', *The Week*, April 8, 2016, 17, citing Michael Barone in the NationalReview.com.

32   Ibid.

33   https://www.nytimes.com/2017/02/22/us/politics/devos-sessions-transgender-students-rights.html

20

CUSTODY

When it comes to determining child custody, however, sexism is the rule.
—Phyllis Schlafly[1]

I'm a pretty hands-on dad and make the most of my custody. I take care of my little one whenever I can, and she determines what I can do and where I can do it.
—Paul McCartney[2]

Given Ms. Schlafly's statement, it may be surprising that originally, at common law, custody was usually granted to the father. It was only when mandatory education laws made child-rearing unprofitable that mothers began to receive custody of their children regularly. (This is why she and most people think the mother usually gets custody over the father.) When two parents cannot agree who should raise their child, is the court the right place to resolve this issue? If so, what standards should the court impose? Also, since children are at the center of the issue, how involved should they be in the decision?

CUSTODY

The term custody actually encompasses two different concerns. The first, legal custody, determines which parent will make the major decisions for the child. This may include decisions about school and education, religion, medical and health, and issues concerning the child's general welfare (see Chapters 18 and 19). The second, physical custody, refers to where the child will live or spend periods of time. If one parent has sole physical custody of a child, the other parent will often obtain visitation. Visitation is a court-approved schedule to dictate where the noncustodial parent

---

1 www.brainyquote.com/quotes/quotes/p/phyllissch206969.html
2 www.quoteauthors.com/quotes/paul-mccartney-quotes.html

will spend time with the child(ren) and when that will occur. This can vary from long periods (over the weekend or summer break) to a weekly meal.[3]

If the parents can work out the terms of the custody arrangement themselves, they can present it to the court for approval. If not, they might seek the assistance of a family mediator to facilitate their agreement. Otherwise, the decision is made by a judge in court. Modern courts often like to presume that joint custody is best; children need both of their parents. This is only realistic, however, if the couple is amicable.[4]

HISTORY

When 20th-century courts were left to decide which of two parents would be better for children when the family unwound, the courts tried to simplify it with presumptions. The first, based on the "**tender years**" doctrine, created the maternal preference known by many. Under this determination of custody, the courts felt that when a child was very young (of tender years), the mother was the best parent to meet the child's needs. This was in keeping with a society in which the father worked outside of the home and the mother stayed home to raise the children. Under the tender years presumption, mothers were presumed the best parent and fathers either had to prove they were better or that the mother was unfit. (Perhaps this is why older generations still gasp when they hear that a father has custody of his children and assume the worse about the mother.)

With woman about half of the workforce, does this make sense today? The tender years presumption was challenged in the courts on Equal Protection grounds. The courts agreed that it amounted to gender discrimination and rejected it. Yet, how were the courts to make the decision now? In a West Virginia case, *Garska v. McCoy*, 278 S.E.2d 357 (W. Va. 1981),[5] the court

---

3   Unfortunately, in China, parents' visitation takes on a whole new meaning. China proposed a law requiring adult children "to regularly visit their elderly parents. If they do not, parents can sure them". http://www.nytimes.com/2011/01/30/world/asia/30beijing.html

4   Unfortunately, many headline-grabbing custody cases show the worst that can occur in divorce and custody battles. Some require "no verbal contact," some involve allegations of improprieties by private investigators, or some involve nasty exchanges between the divorcing spouses. "Christie Brinkley, Peter Cook divorce: Supermodel, ex-husband reach out of court settlement four years after splitting," Helen Kennedy, *Daily News*, June 25, 2012. "The settlement includes a 'no verbal contact' rule that both claimed they needed to protect themselves from the other's spite." In another supermodel divorce/custody case, Stephanie Seymour filed court papers about concerns of her estranged husband's private investigator. "'It is [Seymour's] position that the nature and scope of said surveillance was improper, entailed fabricated allegations, was calculated to harass and defame [her] and that such improper conduct may have been suborned by Mr. Brant, and therefore speaks to his character and fitness,' a lawyer for Seymour wrote in court papers." http://www.nydailynews.com/new-york/supermodel-stephanie-seymour-battles-ex-husband-peter-brant-divorce-case-nastier-article-11.202023, "Supermodel Stephanie Seymour battles ex-husband Peter Brant as divorce case gets nastier," Jose Martinez , *Daily News*, (August 19, 2010.) For his part, the estranged husband, Peter Brant "contend[ed] that Seymour, 41, has problems with booze and prescription drugs." The couple went on to reconcile.

5   http://www.iso.gmu.edu/~weitzman/garskav.htm

is very clear that it is eliminating "any gender based presumption" (by replacing the tender years presumption) when it creates the **"primary caretaker"** presumption.

GARSKA V. MCCOY
278 S.E.2D 357 (1981)

JUDGES: Neely, Justice.
OPINION BY: NEELY

The appellant, Gwendolyn McCoy, appeals from an order of the Circuit Court of Logan County which game the custody of her son, Jonathan Conway McCoy, to the appellee, Michael Garska, the natural father. While in many regards this is a confusing case procedurally, since the mother and father were never married, nonetheless it squarely presents the issues of the proper interaction between the 1980 legislative amendment to W. Va. Code, 48-2 15 [1980] which eliminates any gender based presumption in awarding custody and/or care of J. B. v. A. B., 161 W.Va. 332, 242 S.E.2d 248 (1978) which established a strong [*61] maternal presumption with regard to children of tender years.

In February, 1978 the appellant moved from her grandparents' house in Logan County, where she had been raised, to North Carolina to live with her mother. [***359] [***4]. At that time appellant was 15 years old and her mother shared a trailer with appellee, Michael Garska. In March, Gwendolyn McCoy became pregnant by Michael Gaska and in June, she returned to her grandparents' home in West Virginia.

The appellant received no support from the appellee during her pregnancy, but after she gave birth to baby Jonathan the appellee sent a package of baby food and diapers. In subsequent months the baby developed a chronic respiratory infection which required hospitalization and considerable medical attention. Gwendolyn's grandfather, Stergil Altizer, a retired coal miner, attempted to have his great-grandson's hospitalization and medical care paid by the United Mine Workers' medical insurance but he was informed that the baby was ineligible unless legally adopted by the Altizers.

In October, 1979 Gwendolyn McCoy signed a consent in which she agreed to the adoption of Jonathan by her grandparents, the Altizers. Upon learning of the adoption plan, the appellee visited the baby for the first time and began sending weekly money orders for $15. The Altizers filed a petition for adoption in the Logan County Circuit Court on 9 November 1979 and on 7 January [***5] 1980 the appellee filed a petition for a writ of habeas corpus to secure custody of his son.

Both the adoption and the habeas corpus proceedings were consolidated for hearing and the circuit court dismissed the adoption petition upon finding that the baby had not resided with the Altizers for the requisite six months before the filing of the petition, under W.Va. Code, 48-4-1(c) [1976], since Gwendolyn McCoy had moved away from their home for a short period. The circuit court heard testimony from three witnesses on the father's petition to be awarded custody of the child and then adjourned the [*62] hearing without a decision.

The hearing on the habeas corpus petition resumed on 27 May 1980 and the circuit court awarded custody of Jonathan McCoy to the appellee based upon the following findings of fact:

(a) The petitioner, Michael Garska, is the natural father of the infant child, Jonathan Conway McCoy;

(b) The petitioner, Michael Garska, is better educated than the natural mother and her alleged fiancé;

(c) The petitioner, Michael Garska, is more intelligent that the natural mother;

(d) The petitioner, Michael Garska, is better able to provide financial support [***6] and maintenance than the natural mother;

(e) The petitioner, Michael Garska, can provide a better social and economic environment than the natural mother;

(f) The petitioner, Michael Garska, has a somewhat better command of the English language than the natural mother;

(g) The petitioner, Michael Garska, has a better appearance and demeanor than the natural mother;

(h) The petitioner, Michael Garska, is very highly motivated in his desire to have custody of the infant child, and the natural mother had previously executed an adoption consent, for said child.

The appellant asserts the following errors: (1) the circuit court failed to apply the tender years presumption in favor of the mother articulated in *J. B. v. A. B.*, 161 W.Va. 332, 242 S.E.2d 248 (1978) and earlier cases since it was the operative rule of law at the time the pleadings were filed; (2) the circuit court established and applied arbitrary and inappropriate standards to determine the relative fitness for custody of the parties; and (3) the circuit court erroneously refused to allow the petitioner to withdraw her "consent for adoption" even though the adoption petition itself had been dismissed.

[*63] [***7] While the issue of adoption by the Altizers does, indeed, enter into this case, in the final analysis the entire dispute comes down to a custody fight between the natural father and the natural mother. Although Code, 48-2-15 [1980] is concerned with the award of custody in a divorce proceeding, that section is the preeminent legislative expression of policy concerning custody between natural parents in that it abolishes all gender based presumptions and [**360] establishes a "best interest of

the child" standard for the award of custody. The final order was entered after the operative date of the 1980 Amendment to W.Va. Code, 48-2-15, the relevant part of which provides:

> *In making any such order respecting custody of minor children, there shall be no legal presumption that, as between the natural parents, either the father or the mother should be awarded custody of said children, but the court shall make an award of custody solely for the best interest of the children based upon the merits of each case.*

Furthermore, the case was tried below on the theory that Code, 48-2-15 [1980] applies to this case to the extent that it obliterates the [***8] presumption of *J. B. v. A. B.*, supra, that children of tender years should be awarded to the mother.

This Amendment was enacted in response to *J. B. v. A. B.*, where we said in syl. pt. 2:

> *In a divorce proceeding where custody of a child of tender years is sought by both the mother and father, the Court must determine in the first instance whether the mother is a fit parent, and where the mother achieves the minimum, objective standard of behavior which qualifies her as a fit parent, the trial court must award the child to the mother.*
>
> *In the case before us the father, by providing fifteen dollars a week child support, probably showed sufficient parental interest to give him standing to object to an adoption. n2 However, there is no evidence before us to [*64] indicate that the mother was an unfit parent and, consequently, no justification for the trial court to remove custody from the primary caretaker parent and vest it in a parent who had had no previous emotional interaction with the child.*

n2 W.Va. Code, 48-4-1(a)(2) [1976] says that a determined father means any person who "has acknowledged his parental status by contributing to the child's support" and W.Va. Code, 48-4-1(b) (1) says that "[i]n the case of a child sought to be adopted, the written consent, duly acknowledged, of the mother and father (in the case of an illegitimate child, the mother and determined father) or the surviving parent of such child sought to be adopted must be obtained."

[***9]

It is now time to address explicitly the effect which the strong presumption in favor of the primary caretaker parent articulated in *J. B. v. A. B.*, supra has upon the equity of divorce and child custody dispositions. In this regard we must be concerned not only with those disputes which are decided by trial judges in court but also with all those cases which are settled outside of court in reliance on the rules we generate.

The loss of children is a terrifying specter to concerned and loving parents; however, it is particularly terrifying to the primary caretaker parent who, by virtue of the caretaking function, was closest to the child before the divorce or other proceedings were initiated. While the primary caretaker parent in most cases in West Virginia is still the mother, nonetheless, now that sex roles are becoming more flexible and high-income jobs are opening to women, it is conceivable that the primary caretaker parent may also be the father. If the primary caretaker parent is, indeed, the father, then under W.Va. Code, 48-2-15 [1980] he will be entitled to the alimony and support payments exactly as a woman would be in similar circumstances. Peters v. [***10] Narick, 165 W.Va. 662, 270 S.E.2d 760 (1980).

Since the parent who is not the primary caretaker is usually in the superior financial position, the subsequent welfare of the child depends to a substantial degree upon the level of support payments which are awarded in the course of a divorce. Our experience instructs us that [*65] uncertainty about the outcome of custody disputes leads to the irresistible temptation to trade the custody of the child in return for lower alimony and child support payments. Since trial court judges generally approve consensual agreements on child support, underlying economic data which bear upon the equity of settlements are seldom investigated at the time an order is entered. While Code, 48-2-15 [1980] speaks in terms of "the best [**361] interest of the children" in every case, the one enormously important function of legal rules is to inspire rational and equitable settlements in cases which never reach adversary status in court. n3

n3 For a complete discussion of this proposition see Mnookin & Kornhauser, "Bargaining in the Shadow of the Law: The Case of Divorce," 88 Yale L.J. 950 (1979).
[***11]

If every controversy which arose in this society required court resolution, the understaffed judiciary would topple like a house of cards. It is only voluntary compliance with the criminal law and the orderly settlement of private affairs in the civil law which permits the system to function at all. Consequently, anytime a new statute is passed or a new rule of common law developed, both legislators and judges must pay careful attention to interpreting it in a way which is consonant with equity in the area of private settlements.

Syl. pt. 2 of *J. B. v. A. B.*, supra, attempted to remove from most run-of-the-mi[ll] divorce cases the entire issue of child custody. Certainly if we believed from our experience that full-blown hearings on child custody between two fit parents would afford more intelligent child placement than an arbitrary rule, we would not have adopted an arbitrary rule. However, it is emphatically the case that hearings do not enhance justice, particularly since custody fights are highly destructive to the emotional health of children. Furthermore, our mechanical rule was really quite narrowly drawn to apply only to those cases where voluminous evidence would inevitably [***12] be unenlightening. We limited the mechanical rule to the custody of children who are too young to formulate an opinion concerning their own custody and, further, we limited it to cases where an initial [*66] determination had been made that the mother was, indeed, a fit parent. While in *J. B. v. A. B.*, supra, we expressed ourselves in terms of the traditional maternal preference, the Legislature has instructed us that such a gender based standard is unacceptable. However, we are convinced that the best interests of the children are best served in awarding them to the primary caretaker parent, regardless of sex.

Since trial courts almost always award custody to the primary caretaker parent anyway, establishment of certainty in this regard permits the issues of alimony and support to stand upon their own legs and to be litigated or settled upon the merits of relevant financial criteria, without introducing into the equation the terrifying prospect of loss to the primary caretaker of the children. As we noted in *J. B. v. A. B.*, supra, at 242 S.E.2d 255, "empirical findings directly or indirectly relevant to questions for which judges deciding difficult [custody] cases [***13] need answers are virtually nonexistent. Okpaku, Psychology: Impediment or Aid in Child Custody Cases? 29 Rutgers L.R. 1117, 1140 (1976)." The 1980 Amendment to Code, 48-2-15 was not intended to disturb our determination that in most instances the issue of child custody between two competent parents cannot be litigated effectively. Its intent was merely to correct the inherent unfairness of establishing a gender-based, maternal presumption which would defeat the just claims of a father if he had, in fact, been the primary caretaker parent.

II

In setting the child custody law in domestic relations cases we are concerned with three practical considerations. First, we are concerned to prevent the issue of custody from being used in an abusive way as a coercive weapon to affect the level of support payments and the outcome of other issues in the underlying divorce proceeding. Where a custody fight emanates from this reprehensible motive the children inevitably become pawns to be sacrificed in what ultimately becomes a very cynical game. Second, in the average divorce proceeding intelligent determination of relative degrees of fitness requires a precision of measurement [*67] [***14] which is not possible given the tools available to judges. Certainly it is no more reprehensible for judges to admit that they cannot measure minute gradations of psychological capacity between two [**362] fit parents than it is for a physicist to concede that it is impossible for him to measure the speed of an electron. n4 Third, there is an urgent need in contemporary divorce law for a legal structure upon which a divorcing couple may rely in reaching a settlement.

n4 According to the Heisenberg Principle in Physics it is impossible to assert in terms of the ordinary conventions of geometrical position and of motion that a particle (as an electron) is at the same time at a specified point and moving with a specified velocity for the more accurately either factor can be measured the less accurately the other can be ascertained.

While recent statutory changes encourage private ordering of divorce upon the "no-fault" ground of "irreconcilable differences," W.Va. Code, 48-2-4(a)(10) [1977], our legal [***15] structure has not simultaneously been tightened to provide a reliable framework within which the divorcing couple can bargain intelligently. Nowhere is the lack of certainty greater than in child custody. Not very long ago, the courts were often intimately involved with all aspects of a divorce. Even an estranged couple who had reached an amicable settlement had to undergo "playacting" before the court in order to obtain a divorce. Now, however, when divorces are numerous, easy, and routinely concluded out of court n5 intelligible, reliable rules upon which out-of-court bargaining can be based must be an important consideration in the formulation of our rules.

n5 "Typically, the parties do not go to court at all, until they have worked matters out and are ready for the rubber stamp." Friedman & Percival, A Tale of Two Courts: Litigation in Alameda and San Benito counties, 10 Law & Soc'y Rev. 267, 270 (1976), quoted in Mnookin & Kornhauser supra n.2.

Since the Legislature has concluded that private [***16] ordering by divorcing couples is preferable to judicial ordering, we must insure that each spouse is adequately protected during the out-of-court bargaining. Uncertainty of outcome is very destructive of the position of the primary caretaker parent because he or she will be willing to [*68] sacrifice everything else in order to avoid the terrible prospect of losing the child in the unpredictable process of litigation.

This phenomenon may be denominated the "Solomon syndrome", that is that the parent who is most attached to the child will be most willing to accept an inferior bargain. In the court of Solomon, the "harlot" who was willing to give up her child in order to save him from being cleaved in half so that he could be equally divided, was rewarded for her sacrifice, n6 but in the big world out there the sacrificing parent generally loses necessary support or alimony payments. n7 This then must also be compensated for "in the best interests of the children." Moreover, it is likely that the primary caretaker will have less financial security than the nonprimary caretaker and, consequently, will be unable to sustain the expense of custody litigation, n8 requiring as is [***17] so often the case these days, the payments for expert psychological witnesses.

n6 1 Kings 3:16 et. seq.

n7 There is very little hard evidence to support this theory that parents use the specter of custody proceedings to gain leverage in financial settlements. An interview transcript on file with the Yale Law Journal with the Assistant Clerk of New Haven County Superior Court at p.7 (Dec. 17, 1977) attests to the frequency of fathers using threats of a custody battle to gain a reduction in alimony. See Note, "Lawyering for the Child", 87 Yale Law Journal 1126, 1131 n. 21 (1978).

n8 For a discussion of decision making by the parties to litigation, see Galanter, "Why the 'Haves' Come Out Ahead: Speculatories or the Limits of Legal Change", 9 Law & Soc'y Rev. 95 (1974).

Therefore, in the interest of removing the issue of child custody from the type of acrimonious and counter-productive litigation which a procedure inviting exhaustive evidence will inevitably create, we hold today [***18] that there is a presumption in favor of the primary caretaker parent, if he or she meets the minimum, objective standard for being a fit parent as articulated in *J. B. v. A. B.,* supra n9 regardless of sex. Therefore, [**363] in any custody dispute involving children of tender years it is incumbent upon the [*69] circuit court to determine as a threshold question which parent was the primary caretaker parent before the domestic strife giving rise to the proceeding began.

n9 As we said in *J. B. v. A. B.,* supra, where the primary caretaker fails to provide: emotional support; routine cleanliness; or nourishing food, the presumption shall not apply.

While it is difficult to enumerate all of the factors which will contribute to a conclusion that one or the other parent was the primary caretaker parent, nonetheless, there are certain obvious criteria to which a court must initially look. n10 In establishing which natural or adoptive parent is the primary caretaker, the trial court shall determine which [***19] parent has taken primary responsibility for, inter alia, the performance of the following caring and nurturing duties of a parent: (1) preparing and planning of meals; (2) bathing, grooming and dressing; (3) purchasing, cleaning, and care of clothes; (4) medical care, including nursing and trips to physicians; (5) arranging for social interaction among peers after school, i.e. transporting to friends' houses or, for example, to girl or boy scout meetings; (6) arranging alternative care, i.e. babysitting, day-care, etc.; (7) putting child to bed at night, attending to child in the [*70] middle of the night, waking child in the morning; (8) disciplining, i.e. teaching general manners and toilet training; (9) educating, i.e. religious, cultural, social, etc.; and, (10) teaching elementary skills, i.e., reading, writing and arithmetic.

n10 The Oregon Supreme Court has also relied upon a determination of the primary caretaker parent in reaching custody decisions. That court awarded custody to a mother when: "The undisputed evidence in this case was that the wife was not merely the mother but was also the primary parent. During the marriage she was not working and performed the traditional and honorable role of homemaker. She cleaned the house, cared for the children, fed the family, nursed them when sick and spent those countless hours disciplining, counseling and chatting with the children that every homemaker should. For some families the husband may perform this role and be the primary parent. In other families the parents evenly divide the role and there is no primary parent. In this family the husband played the traditional role of breadwinner, working eight to ten hours a day. In his off-hours he dedicated much time and attention to the children, but the lion's share of the child raising was performed by the wife. It is undisputed that the children were happy and well-adjusted and that the relationship between the wife and children was close, loving and successful. Although the same relationship unquestionably existed to a degree with the husband, the close and successful emotional relationship between the primary parent and the children coupled with the age of the children dictate the continuance of that relationship." *Derby and Derby,* 31 Or. App. 803, 806-7, 571 P.2d 562, 1080 (1977), modified on other grounds, 31 Or. App. 1333, 572 P.2d 1080 (1977), rev. den. 281 Or. 323 (1978).

[***20]

In those custody disputes where the facts demonstrate that child care and custody were shared in an entirely equal way, then indeed no presumption arises and the court must proceed to inquire further into relative degrees of parental competence. However, where one parent can demonstrate with regard to a child of tender years that he or she is clearly the primary caretaker parent, then the court must further determine only whether the primary caretaker parent is a fit parent. Where the primary caretaker parent achieves the minimum, objective standard of behavior which qualifies him or her as a fit parent, the trial court must award the child to the primary caretaker parent.

Consequently, all of the principles enunciated in *J. B. v. A. B.*, supra, are reaffirmed today except that wherever the words "mother," "maternal," or "maternal preference" are used in that case, some variation of the term "primary caretaker parent," as defined by this case should be substituted. In this regard we should point out that the absolute presumption in favor of a fit primary caretaker parent applies only to children of tender years. Where a child is old enough to formulate an opinion about his [***21] or her own custody the trial court is entitled to receive such opinion and accord it such weight as he feels appropriate. When, in the opinion of the trial court, a child old enough to formulate an opinion but under the age of 14 has indicated a justified desire to live with the parent who is not the primary caretaker, the court may award the child to such parent.

[**364] III

In the case before us it is obvious that the petitioner was the primary caretaker parent before the proceedings under consideration in this case arose, and there is no finding on the part of the trial court judge that she is an unfit parent. [*71] In fact, all of the evidence indicates that she mobilized all of the resources at her command, namely the solicitous regard of her grandparents, in the interest of this child and that she went to extraordinary lengths to provide for him adequate medical attention and financial support. While, as the trial court found, the educational and economic position of the father is superior to that of the mother, nonetheless, those factors alone pale in comparison to love, affection, concern, tolerance, and the willingness to sacrifice—factors about which conclusions [***22] can be made for the future most intelligently upon a course of conduct in the past. At least with regard to the primary caretaker parent there is a track record to which a court can look and where that parent is fit he or she should be awarded continued custody.

Certainly the record in the case before us does not demonstrate any intent by the mother to abandon the child through permitting him to be adopted by the grandparents; it is well recognized that mothers in penurious circumstances often resort to adoption in order to make the child eligible for social security or union welfare benefits, all of which significantly enhance the child's opportunities in life. Absent an explicit finding of intent to abandon we cannot construe manipulation of the welfare system to direct maximum benefits towards this child as anything other than a solicitous concern for his welfare.

Accordingly, for the reasons set forth above the judgment of the Circuit Court of Logan County is reversed and remanded with directions to enter an order in favor of the petitioner. FNCC

Curiously, the *Garska* court makes no mention of the situation of the child's creation, in awarding custody under the "primary caretaker" presumption. What factors does the court list that should be followed when making this presumption?[6] These factors still leave the judge with a lot of discretion in making the custody determination. Is that good or bad?

BEST INTEREST OF THE CHILD

Although the court hoped to avoid making the "Solomon-like" decision referenced in *Garska* by using a non-gender-based presumption,[7] did it really succeed? Today, these presumptions have largely been abandoned. Instead, most courts use the **"best interest of the child"** test. While the specifics are set up by state law, some of the factors the courts may look at in determining a parent's fitness include: wealth (or more importantly, lack of it); careers or employment history and potential day-care issues; emotional ties to the child; home environment; and moral fitness. Court may also consider the child's age, health, sex, and emotional ties to each parent. Courts have restricted some factors that should not be considered as part of the test. The remaining factors still leave the judge with a lot of discretion in making the custody determination. Is this good or bad?

1. Nastiness

Can a parent lose custody of a child for disparaging the other parent in front of the child? How far would that parent have to go in alienating the child's affection for the ex-spouse in order to lose custody? Are repeated unsubstantiated allegations of sexual abuse against one spouse enough?

---

6   In a later West Virginia case involving application of the primary caretaker presumption, the court looks at the effect of placing a child in the father's home where there are smokers. "It is necessary, however, to address the issue of the child's exposure to second-hand smoke. Obviously, in light of Justin's respiratory problems, special consideration to smoke in his environment is merited. We do not believe, however, that the fact that the Appellant and his family members smoke, standing alone, can outweigh the bulk of the other testimony in this matter. Thus, we reverse the decision of the lower court and remand for entry of an order awarding custody of Justin to the Appellant, but with special instructions to the Appellant and his family to provide a smoke-free environment for Justin." *Michael Scott M. v. Victoria L. M.*, http://law.justia.com/cases/west-virginia/supreme-court/1994/22875.html. Is this case a precursor to Maryland's law against smoking in the car with children present?
7   How gender unbiased was it, if it merely replaced the word "mother" with "primary caretaker?"

In *Renaud v. Renaud*,[8] the father appealed a decision to give the mother sole legal and physical parental rights, even though the court found that "the mother had interfered with the relationship between the child and father" by repeatedly making false allegations that the father was sexually abusing the child. In the case, "the parties separated following father's disclosure that he was having an affair with a co-worker and wanted a divorce. At the time of trial in April and May of 1997, mother was living with the three-year-old child in the marital home, and father was living with the co-worker and her children." The court wrote that "[a]lmost immediately, [the] mother began to impede father's contact with the child, forcing father to file a number of motions to establish an emergency visitation schedule. Following a hearing in July 1996, the court established a temporary visitation schedule. Thereafter, mother filed a succession of relief-from-abuse petitions, alleging that father had physically and sexually abused the minor. The allegations ranged from evidence of diaper rash, to sunburn, cuts and bruises, and inappropriate touching. These petitions further disrupted father's contact with the child, resulting in periods of non-contact and supervised visitation."

The Vermont Supreme Court never substantiated any of the abuse allegations; the petitions were dismissed and there was never a finding of abuse by the father. Indeed, the court found that father had never abused the minor, that the factual support for the "excessive number of motions and petitions" was "weak at best," and that mother had, in fact, "imagined abuse where there was no abuse." The court further found that mother's actions were the result of a heightened distrust of father because of his marital unfaithfulness, and that her "baseless suspicions ha[d] adversely affected [the minor] in that he is no longer as loving towards [father] as he once was."[9] "A team of psychiatric experts appointed by the court observed that the child interacted well with each parent, but noted that mother's repeated accusations had damaged the child's relationship with father, and warned that if such accusations continued they could seriously compromise the father-child relationship." While citing a long string of cases upholding the proposition that a parent who tries to alienate a child from the other parent may lose custody and emphasizing that when that alienation technique includes false allegations of sexual abuse,[10] the court affirmed the sole custody to the mother in this case. Is this right? Does the court's award of substantial visitation to the father make a difference?[11] Should the father in *Renaud* be able to sue his wife for the sexual abuse allegations? How about the mother's interference with his right to visitation?

---

8   *Renault v. Renault,* 168 Vt. 306; 721 A.2d 463 (1988) at http://law.justia.com/cases/vermont/supreme-court/1998/97-366op.html

9   *Renaud v. Renaud,* 168 Vt. 306; 721 A.2d 463 (1988), http://law.justia.com/cases/vermont/supreme-court/1998/97-366op.html

10   On the issue of allegations of sexual abuse, the court cites to the case of In re *Wedemeyer,* 475 N.W.2d 657, 659 (Iowa Ct. App. 1991) (upholding change of custody where mother's 'flagrant and continuing destructive conduct,' including persistent allegations that father was 'an insane sex addict who masturbates and performs sexual acts with animals,' had interfered with children's association with father.)

11   Was the court affected by the father's extramarital affair? The appellate court claims that it was not. "Finally, father's claim that the court placed undue emphasis on fault is expressly contradicted by the court's findings, which noted that father's fault in the breakup of the marriage was fully offset by mother's dissipation of marital assets through

2. Race

Most case law interpreting the best interest of the child involves determining what factors are not appropriate for influencing a decision. In *Palmore v. Sidoti*, 466 U.S. 429 (1984), the U.S. Supreme Court held that race should not determine a custody placement. In this case, the custodial parent/mother lost custody while she had an African American boyfriend (whom she later married).[12]

3. Religion

What happens if the parents are of two different religions? Under the First Amendment's freedom of religion, a court could not make a custody determination by choosing one religion over the other. But is the effect of awarding custody almost the same when one parent with legal custody is authorized to make such decisions? Suppose the custodial parent chooses one religion in which to raise the child, but the other spouse has visitation and takes the child to worship in a different religion during this time. Is this a reason to prevent the visitation? In an attempt to not tread on the parents' free exercise rights, courts often find that it is in the child's best interest to expose him to both religions, unless a showing of harm is made. To do otherwise would cause the court to appear to prefer one religion over another in violation of the Establishment Clause of the First Amendment.

4. Sexual Conduct or Sexuality

Previously, the "scarlet letter" effect of an affair, or even extramarital cohabitation, could prevent a parent from having custody of a child. Based on more modern morality, a parent's sexual behavior must generally have a proven "adverse impact" on the child before it should impact a custody decision. Generally, these cases dealt with heterosexual infidelities. What happens if the affair is between a same-sex couple when the child was born into a heterosexual family?

5. Same Sex Couples

Would it make a difference if the child was the product of a same-sex couple? With marriage equality, the courts should apply the law equally. Previously, when such marriages were not recognized, the court would often deny custody to a non-biological parent. But what happens when neither is a biological parent. In the 2007 case of *Soo-Hoo v. Johnson* involving two Chinese children, a Minnesota court recognized the rights of the non-adopting domestic partner and awarded reasonable visitation with the adopted children (who she had lived with until the relationship ended.) The court awarded the visitation because the partner had demonstrated "established

---

the filing of excessive motions and petitions, and thus that neither factor would be considered in the property division." *Renaud v. Renaud.*

12 The court held that under the Equal Protection clause, race cannot be the determinative factor in a custody decision.

emotional ties creating a parent and child relationship."[13] Despite their committed relationship and commitment to the child, however, she did not receive custody, which remained with the mother who had adopted them. Indeed, her visitation was only granted under a law that gave similar rights to any third-party who lived with the children for more than two years but was no longer living with them.

6. Heterosexual Unmarried Couples

Even with the popularity of private ordering (see chapter 3), the law often lags behind when it comes to custody determinations. After a man and women who lived together but were not married could not have a child, they were successful in creating one through anonymous donor sperm. After the baby was born, the man was thrilled and helped out by changing diapers, bathing him and comforting him when the baby woke at night.[14] The woman left their home and moved into a new apartment in the next state but committed suicide the next month. The baby was then put in foster care by the state, even though the man wanted custody. The woman's sister did too. Who should have custody? In New York, the man was "effectively not a parent at all. He was not married to [the baby's] mother. He had no blood relationship to the child. And he did not take steps to legally adopt him after his birth."[15]

7. Military Parents

While the Soldiers' and Sailor's Civil Relief Act protects military personnel from losing their jobs or homes while they are deployed, it does not protect them from losing their children.[16] After serving 10 months in Iraq in the National Guard, when a soldier came home she was denied access to her one-year old daughter. She had left the girl with "her former companion" and made a "written family care plan… with military officials outlining shared custody" when the mother returned. But when she did, the companion claimed it was "too disruptive for the baby to spend more than a few hours… with 'a mother she doesn't really know or recognize that well."[17] "Custody disputes involving returning members of the service have long been an unpleasant fact of military life" but now that women are in combat it is creating more problems. "Some advocates say an unspoken bias against mothers who leave their young children has heightened both legal barriers and social stigma when these women try to resume their role as active parents."[18]

---

13   U.S.C.A. Const. Amend. 14; M.S.A. § 257C.08(4). Interestingly, in the case, in addition to ordering custody of the children to one of the women, the judge also ordered her to therapy. This was overruled on appeal.
14   http://www.nytimes.com/2013/02/03/nyregion/a-custody-battle-after-the-law-says-a-parent-isnt-a-parent.html?_r=0
15   Ibid.
16   http://www.nytimes.com/2009/09/01/nyregion/01guard.html
17   Ibid, quoting his lawyer, Amy Lefkowitz.
18   Ibid.

8. Disability

Should disability play a role in custody determinations? Does it matter if it is the disability of the child or the parent or if it is a physical or emotional disability? Generally, the courts will apply the "adverse impact" rule and only consider a disability to be relevant if it has a negative impact on the child. *In re Marriage of Carney*, 598 P.2d 36 (Cal. 1979) the custodial father of the children was severely injured in a car accident and became quadriplegic. The mother, living on the other side of the country and who had not had much contact with the children, asked the court to modify the custody arrangement based on the father's condition. The court refused, based on the father's heroic efforts at rehabilitation and the increased time he now has to spend with his children. Would the court have ruled the same way if the father was disabled at the time of the divorce? Contrast *Carney* with *In re Adoption of Harold H*,[19] Court of Special Appeals of MD, 0464, 2006, in which the court took custody from a mother in her 40s who had a stroke and was living in a nursing home. The woman to whom the state wanted to allow her son to be adopted was willing to let him visit his mother and sister and was open to the possibility that the son could be readopted should the situation change. Is this fair?

9. Abuse Allegations

Abuse is one factor that most courts will consider before an adverse impact must be demonstrated. Can it ever be in the child's best interest to be placed with an abusive parent? In some states, the abuse is a rebuttable presumption and the abuser has the right to refute the concerns by showing that the abuse occurred at a time far removed from the custody request. In such a scenario, how long should this have to be? What if the abuse was toward the mother (or father), and the child had never been abused? Should custody be awarded to a parent that allowed the child to witness abuse?[20] What about visitation with the sexually abusive parent, is this ever allowed? Courts generally do not like to deny visitation to a parent, but may require supervised visitation (so that the parent is never alone with the child).[21] Is this trustworthy?

---

19 http://law.justia.com/cases/maryland/court-of-special-appeals/2006/464s06-1.html

20 Across the nation, 23 states and Puerto Rico have adopted laws addressing violence committed in front of children. In at least five of these states, it is considered a separate crime. In 2014, Maryland proposed such a law which would have an additional penalty of five years. "Seeing. Suffering", Theresa Vargas, *The Washington Post*, March 9, 2014, P. C1.

21 In New Hampshire, 2013, during a supervised visitation at the YWCA, a father fatally shot his 9-year-old son and then killed himself. The YWCA was open on Sundays for supervised visitation and custody exchanges. At one point the YWCA staff used to "wand" parents with metal detectors before coming into the visitation room, but stopped doing this because, among other reasons, the staff was not sure what they would do if they found a gun. When the father set off the metal detector on previous occasions, he blamed it on some cans he brought for the boy to play with. "Final Report", New Hampshire Attorney General's Report of Investigation, August 27, 2013. http://www.google.com/url?sa=t&rct=j&q=&esrc=s&source=web&cd=2&ved=0CCcQFjAB&url=http%3A%2F%2Fdoj.nh.gov%2Fmedia-center%2Fpress-releases%2F2013%2Fdocuments%2F20131107-manchester-murder-suicide-report.pdf&ei=QdFQVdzEK4vdsAXCzIGIDA&usg=AFQjCNHXvaFxsUH8cg5qJM9LffeSxpER6Q&bvm=bv.92885102,d.b2w

10. Child's Preference

Another factor the courts may use is the **child's preference**. Most states require consideration of what the child wants in custody cases. What role should the child's opinion play in the court's decision? What factors may affect this? What if there is more than one child—what is the effect of sibling integrity? What happens if the siblings disagree?

11. Relocation

Relocation is one of the hotter issues in custody cases. Should the custodial parent be allowed to move the child away from the noncustodial parent? It depends. Some courts give the custodial parent a good faith presumption that the move is appropriate. Others require a demonstration of exceptional circumstances before allowing the move. Generally, the court should evaluate the move to determine whether it is in the child's best interest. If the parents live close to each other, relocation could have a real impact on the child. But in our mobile society, is it realistic to believe that ex-spouses will remain close by? What happens if the parent wants to move the child to another state? Or another country? In this last context, concerns of enforceability of custody orders and abduction could be genuine.

In *Sinicropi v. Mazurek*, 273 Mich.App. 149, 729 N.W.2d 256 (Mich.App.2006),[22] which follows, when the biological mother, who had joint custody, moved to another town 90 miles away, the court approved a change of custody to allow the five-year-old boy to remain in the equitable father's community where the "child had lived most of his life in the same town, where he had a good support system, where he attended school, and where he was well cared for and loved by father." In *Sinicropi v. Mazurek*, the child's interests were paramount. Yet, is it fair to limit a parent's right to move if the move is for career advancement which is probably in the child's best interest? But to allow the move could limit the other parent's easier access to the child. Maybe the best way to resolve this is to take a page out of family mediation. When parents reach an agreement on custody during mediation, a good mediator will test the agreement by working out future possibilities, based on the distance of the move. For example, the agreement might say that if the custodial parent moves more than 25 miles away, they can do so without input from the other spouse. If the move is from 25 to 100 miles, they need to pay for the other spouse's increased transportation expenses and transport the child one way of the commute. If the move is more than 100 miles away or out of state, the parties agree to come back to mediation to resolve the issue.

---

22 This case also raises issues of paternity in non-marital births that affect custody, especially when the lower court determines that the child has two fathers, biological and equitable.

SINICROPI V. MAZUREK 273 MICH.APP. 149, 729 N.W.2D 256 (MICH.APP., 2006)

Background: After man who had properly executed an acknowledgment of parentage sought custody of child born out of wedlock, mother and such acknowledger stipulated to entry of a consent order giving mother and acknowledger joint legal and physical custody of child. Biological father then filed a paternity action under the Paternity Act. Paternity action was consolidated with custody case, and the trial court entered an order of filiation recognizing biological father as child's father, but did not revoke acknowledger's acknowledgment of parentage. Following a best-interests evidentiary hearing on custody, the Circuit Court, Jackson County, John G. McBain, Jr., awarded sole physical custody of the child to acknowledger, awarded acknowledger and mother joint legal custody, awarded mother parenting time, and ordered mother and biological father to pay child support. All three parties appealed.

Holdings: The Court of Appeals, Murphy, P.J., held that:

(1) trial court was not authorized to enter order of filiation under Paternity Act where an unrevoked acknowledgment of parentage was already in place;

(2) inability to obtain filiation order due to existence of unrevoked acknowledgment of parentage did not violate due process rights of biological father who had no parent-child relationship with five-year-old child;

(3) consent order did not bar trial court from considering mother's motion for revocation of acknowledgement;

(4) mother's move to another town almost 90 miles away was a sufficient change of circumstances to warrant change of custody; and

(5) evidence supported grant of sole physical custody to acknowledger.

Reversed and remanded with directions.

MURPHY, P.J.

*152 Each of the three parties has filed an appeal in this litigation that involves issues regarding custody of a seven-year-old boy born to Holly Mazurek: paternity, an order of filiation, an acknowledgment of parentage and attempted revocation thereof, equitable parenthood, the constitutional rights of a biological father, standing, statutory construction, child support, and various other legal matters. The trial court effectively ruled that the child has, simultaneously, two legally recognized fathers. The trial court awarded Martin Powers, who executed an acknowledgment of parentage with Mazurek but who is not the child's biological father, sole physical custody of the minor child, while also entering an order of filiation in favor of Gregory Sinicropi, who is the child's biological father. The trial court rejected attempts to have the acknowledgment of parentage revoked. Mazurek, but not Sinicropi, was awarded parenting time, and both Mazurek and Sinicropi were ordered to pay child support. We hold that an order of filiation cannot be entered under the Paternity Act, MCL 722.711 et seq., if, under the Acknowledgment of Parentage Act, MCL 722.1001 et seq., a proper acknowledgment of parentage was previously executed and has not been revoked. This is because, under MCL 722.1003 and MCL 722.1004, an unrevoked acknowledgment already legally established paternity and conferred the status of natural and legal father on the man executing the acknowledgment, which in turn entitled him to **260 seek custody or parenting time if desired and obligated him to pay support if appropriate. Accordingly, the trial court erred by ruling that the child has two legally recognized fathers under both the Acknowledgment of Parentage Act and the Paternity Act. The case is remanded to the trial court for action consistent with this opinion and further *153 reflection on the issue of revocation of the acknowledgment of parentage.

I. Basic Facts and Procedural History

This case concerns a child who was born out of wedlock in 1999 to Mazurek while she was in a relationship with Powers, but Sinicropi is the biological father of the child as established by DNA (deoxyribonucleic acid) testing. Mazurek had dated Powers, then briefly dated Sinicropi, before subsequently resuming her relationship with Powers, during which time the child was born. Powers, along with Mazurek, executed an acknowledgment of parentage on the child's birth. None of the parties was aware that Sinicropi was the biological father until 2004, when the DNA testing was conducted following Mazurek's suspicion that Sinicropi might be the father given the child's developing physical characteristics and appearance. Meanwhile, Powers raised the child as his own with Mazurek.

Powers and Mazurek again split up in 2001, and Powers filed a custody action against Mazurek when the relationship ended. They immediately stipulated the entry of a consent order giving them joint legal and physical custody. In 2004, Powers sought sole custody after Mazurek moved out of Jackson, Michigan, where Powers, Mazurek, and the child had resided since the child's birth, to live with her new fiancé in Shepherd, Michigan. An ex parte order was entered granting Powers sole custody pending an evidentiary hearing. The trial court refused to dismiss Powers's custody action and to revoke the acknowledgment of parentage as requested by Mazurek on multiple occasions, not because of a failure to show that Sinicropi was the biological father, but because it would be inequitable *154 and because res judicata and collateral estoppel arising out of the consent order of joint custody would not allow it.

The trial court eventually converted the ex parte custody order into a temporary order, scheduling a full evidentiary hearing on issues of custody and parenting time. Thereafter, Sinicropi filed a paternity action under the Paternity Act. Subsequently, the trial court, after consolidating the paternity and custody cases, entered an order of filiation that recognized Sinicropi as the child's father, yet the acknowledgment of parentage was not revoked. At this stage in the proceedings, the young boy was five years old. The trial court had rejected Powers's argument that Sinicropi lacked standing to file a paternity action, and it similarly rejected renewed efforts to have Powers's custody action dismissed for lack of standing and to have the acknowledgement of parentage revoked. The trial court effectively ruled that the child had two legal fathers under the Acknowledgment of Parentage Act and the Paternity Act.

Following a best-interests evidentiary hearing on custody, the trial court awarded sole physical custody of the child to Powers, awarded Powers and Mazurek joint legal custody, and awarded Mazurek parenting time. The trial court reserved ruling on parenting time for Sinicropi and on the issue of child support. In response to postjudgment motions filed by Mazurek and Sinicropi, the trial court concluded that it should have conducted a best-interests analysis with respect to Sinicropi and custody, but the court otherwise rejected Mazurek's and Sinicropi's attack on the **261 judgment. The trial court reviewed the child custody factors and in a separate opinion decided that it would not be in the child's best interests to award shared custody to Sinicropi.*155 Subsequently, Mazurek and Sinicropi were both ordered to pay child support. All three parties now appeal, presenting various arguments... (author's omission of text)

IV. Analysis

A. Acknowledgment of Parentage Act
The best place to begin our analysis is with the Acknowledgment of Parentage Act, because Powers and Mazurek jointly executed an acknowledgment long before Sinicropi brought an action under the Paternity Act. MCL 722.1003(1) provides:

> *If a child is born out of wedlock, a man is considered to be the natural father of that child if the man joins with the mother of the child and acknowledges that child as his child by completing a form that is an acknowledgement of parentage. FN1*

FN1. "An acknowledgment of parentage form is valid and effective if signed by the mother and father and those signatures are notarized by a notary public authorized by the state in which the acknowledgment is signed. An acknowledgment may be signed any time during the child's lifetime." MCL 722.1003(2).

*158 There is no dispute that Mazurek and Powers properly executed an acknowledgment of parentage consistent with the requirements of the statute, and thus Powers was legally considered the natural father of the child. MCL 722.1004 provides:

An acknowledgment signed under this act establishes paternity, and the acknowledgement may be the basis for court ordered child support, custody, or parenting time without further adjudication under the paternity act. The child who is the subject of the acknowledgement shall bear the same relationship to the mother and the man signing as the father as a child born or conceived during a marriage and shall have the identical status, rights, and duties of a child born in lawful wedlock effective from birth.

Pursuant to the plain language of the statute, when Powers and Mazurek executed the acknowledgement of parentage Powers's paternity was established, and the child was in a position identical to one in which the child was born or conceived during a marriage. See *Killingbeck v. Killingbeck*, 269 Mich.App. 132, 143, 711 N.W.2d 759 (2005) (acknowledgment of parentage establishes paternity and gives the male acknowledger "status as a parent"). The Legislature was clearly expressing**263 a public policy position favoring legal protection of a child born out of wedlock, pursuant to which a mother and a man jointly executing an acknowledgment of parentage would be legally recognized as the child's parents without litigation, thereby allowing the parties to seek and the court to enter custody, parenting time, and support orders.

In *Eldred v. Ziny*, 246 Mich.App. 142, 148–149, 631 N.W.2d 748 (2001), this Court, discussing the status and rights conferred on a man who acknowledges parentage under the act, stated:

> *159 A plain reading of § 4 reveals that, contrary to Mr. Ziny's assertion, acknowledgement of paternity under MCL 722.1003 does not afford the father the same legal rights as a father whose child is born within a marriage, but rather … merely entitles the parties to seek custody, support, or parenting time without the need to first obtain an order of filiation under the Paternity Act, MCL 722.711 et seq. Although MCL 722.1004 affords the child the full rights of a child born in wedlock, the statute does not grant a putative father who acknowledges paternity the same legal rights as a father whose child is born in wedlock. See, e.g., Crego v. Coleman, 463 Mich. 248, 264, 615 N.W.2d 218 (2000). [Emphasis in original.] FN2*

FN2. The parties have devoted a great deal of attention to *Eldred*, but it is important to view that opinion in context. In *Eldred*, a child was born out of wedlock and the natural father and the mother signed an acknowledgment of parentage. The child lived with her mother, and the father was ordered to pay child support following a support action initiated by the county prosecutor. The mother then died in an automobile accident, and the child began living with her father, but she also stayed at times with her maternal grandparents. The maternal grandmother later intervened in the support action and filed a third-party petition for custody. Eventually, an order awarding the maternal grandmother sole legal and physical custody was entered. *Eldred*, supra at 144–145, 631 N.W.2d 748. This Court held, contrary to the father's argument, that the maternal grandmother had standing to maintain the custody action under MCL 722.26c(1)(b) (biological parents never married, custodial parent dies, third person related to child). Id. at 145–147, 631 N.W.2d 748. The father also argued that MCL 722.26c(1)(b) conflicted with his custody rights as a natural father under the Acknowledgment of Parentage Act despite the fact that he had never taken the steps to procure a court order awarding him custody of the child. The father contended that he had the same legal rights as those held by a father whose child was born in wedlock, and that it was unnecessary for him to seek custody under the Child Custody Act. The Court found that the statutes did not conflict and that, as quoted above, the father was not in the same position as a father whose child was born in wedlock. Id. at 147–149, 631 N.W.2d 748. Pertinent to our analysis, the *Eldred* panel never held that the acknowledgment of parentage failed to provide the father with standing or a right to seek custody, or that the law precluded the father from being awarded custody. Further, the *Eldred* opinion did not hold that the rights of a biological father are superior to the rights of a man who acknowledges parentage and obtains custody with respect to a child born out of wedlock. Indeed, MCL 722.1011, which we will discuss later, suggests otherwise. We note that in this case, Powers obtained an order in 2001 granting him joint legal and physical custody.

Although Powers may not have had legal rights identical to those of a father whose child is born or conceived within a marriage, the Acknowledgment of Parentage Act bestowed on Powers the designation of "natural father," MCL 722.1003(1), and entitled him to seek custody. Powers was the "legal parent" for purposes of the Child Custody Act. *Killingbeck*, supra at 144, 711 N.W.2d 759 ("Pursuant to the acknowledgment of parentage statute, Killingbeck thus became a 'legal parent' for purposes of the Child **264 Custody Act...."). FN3 Moreover, from the child's legal perspective, it was as if he were born in wedlock.

FN3. Contrary to Mazurek's arguments on appeal, Powers had standing to seek custody under the Child Custody Act as a "parent" pursuant to the language found throughout that act and the plain language of the Acknowledgment of Parentage Act, where the acknowledgment had been properly executed and not revoked. MCL 722.1004; *Killingbeck*, supra at 144, 711 N.W.2d 759.

Mazurek made multiple attempts to have Powers's custody action dismissed and the acknowledgment of parentage revoked, which the trial court rejected. With regard to revocation of an acknowledgment of parentage, MCL 722.1011(1) allows certain individuals, including Mazurek as the child's mother but not Sinicropi, to file a claim for revocation. An affidavit signed by the claimant is required and must set forth facts that constitute either a mistake of fact, newly discovered evidence, fraud, misrepresentation, misconduct, or duress relative to the acknowledgment. MCL 722.1011(2). Relevant here is mistake of fact. MCL 722.1011(3) provides:

> *If the court finds that the affidavit is sufficient, the court may order blood or genetic tests at the expense of the *161 claimant, or may take other action the court considers appropriate. The party*

filing the claim for revocation has the burden of proving, by clear and convincing evidence, that the man is not the father and that, considering the equities of the case, revocation of the acknowledgment is proper. [Emphasis added.]

In *Killingbeck*, supra at 144, 711 N.W.2d 759, this Court emphasized that even where there is clear and convincing evidence that the man who executed the acknowledgment of parentage is not the biological father, revocation of the acknowledgment must also be warranted by the equities in the case. It is plain from the language in MCL 722.1011(3) that the Legislature contemplated situations in which a man executed an acknowledgement of parentage, the man was determined not to be the biological father, but the acknowledgment of parentage would nonetheless remain valid and intact in the face of an attempted revocation if the equities of the case so dictated, thereby leaving the man who was not the biological father as the natural or legal father and shutting the door on the biological father. This scenario, which played out in the case at bar, could be viewed in a sense as creating an "equitable-like" parent because equity ultimately allows the man to retain his recognition as the natural father under the Acknowledgment of Parentage Act where revocation is rejected despite the lack of any biological connection between the child and the acknowledger. But regardless of the equitable nature of the circumstances, a man executing an acknowledgment of parentage that remains valid in the face of an unsuccessful revocation attempt is considered the natural and legal father of the child. FN4

FN4. It may well be that the Legislature, which has always been concerned chiefly with the best interests and protection of children as reflected in various legislation, made a policy decision in enacting MCL 722.1011(3), which recognized that, regardless of the lack of biological ties, a child's well-being might be better served by having a male acknowledger continue caring for the child as father, especially if he has done so for many years, rather than traumatically removing the man from the child's life and introducing a new male who is essentially a stranger.

*162 In *Van v. Zahorik*, 460 Mich. 320, 331, 597 N.W.2d 15 (1999), our Supreme Court rejected a request to extend the doctrine of equitable parenthood outside the context of marriage because "the extension of substantive rights regarding child custody **265 implicates significant public policy issues and is within the province of the Legislature, not the judiciary." Van, however, is not implicated here because, in contrast to the factual circumstances in Van, Powers executed an acknowledgment of parentage. And, furthermore, the Acknowledgment of Parentage Act reflects express legislative approval of an "equitable-like" parent by not permitting the revocation of an acknowledgment of parentage if a claimant fails to establish clear and convincing evidence that the equities of the case demand revocation regardless of the fact that another man has clearly and convincingly been shown to be the biological father. See *Killingbeck*, supra at 143–144, 711 N.W.2d 759 (similarly distinguishing Van). FN5 However, and once again, regardless of the equitable nature of such a situation, the man executing the unrevoked acknowledgment is still deemed the natural and legal father.

FN5. To the extent that the trial court here relied on the doctrine of equitable parenthood apart from MCL 722.1011, it was contrary to Van and in error. Unless there is a proper revocation, and even if a court relies on the equity provision in MCL 722.1011(3) in refusing to revoke an acknowledgment, a man who executes an acknowledgment of parentage is the natural and legal father, not the equitable father. MCL 722.1003(1); *Killingbeck*, supra at 144, 711 N.W.2d 759.

B. The Paternity Act and its Relationship to the Acknowledgment of Parentage Act

Before reviewing the trial court's handling and denial of the motion to revoke the acknowledgment of *163 parentage, we shall first discuss the Paternity Act and its relationship to the Acknowledgment of Parentage Act, given that an order of filiation was entered despite the fact that the acknowledgment was not revoked. We conclude that the trial court erred when, after refusing to revoke the acknowledgment of parentage, it nonetheless entertained Sinicropi's paternity action and entered an order of filiation recognizing Sinicropi as the child's legal father as a result of the DNA testing.

We hold that Sinicropi could not obtain an order of filiation because the Paternity Act and the Acknowledgment of Parentage Act, when read and construed together, do not permit the entry of an order of filiation where an unrevoked acknowledgment of parentage is already in place.

As noted above, the Acknowledgment of Parentage Act "establishes paternity" and provides a court with the basis and authority to enter orders regarding custody, parenting time, and support. MCL 722.1004. With respect to the Paternity Act, our Supreme Court stated that "[t]he act was created as a procedural vehicle for determining the paternity of children 'born out of wedlock,' and enforcing the resulting support obligation." *Syrkowski v. Appleyard*, 420 Mich. 367, 375, 362 N.W.2d 211 (1985); see also *Elmore v. Ellis*, 115 Mich.App. 609, 611, 321 N.W.2d 744 (1982) (purpose of act is to provide child support to children born out of wedlock). Thus, the Acknowledgment of Parentage Act and the Paternity Act provide two separate procedures by which to establish paternity and provide support for children born out of wedlock. In Aichele, supra at 154–155, 673 N.W.2d 452, this Court, comparing the two acts, noted:

> [T]he acts simply provide different means to the same end. Under the Paternity Act, a party can seek a judicial determination of paternity; under the Acknowledgment of *164 Parentage Act, a man and a woman can essentially stipulate the man's paternity. Under either act, paternity can be properly established only if the child is "born out of wedlock[.]" [Emphasis in original.]

It is evident to us that the Paternity Act and the Acknowledgment of Parentage Act constitute legislation envisioning alternative mechanisms to establish paternity where a child is born out of wedlock, i.e., an acknowledgment of parentage is executed or an order of filiation is entered. But the Legislature did not intend the creation of two legal fathers for one child through utilization of both acts, one by acknowledgment and one by order of filiation. FN6 A court cannot recognize both. As stated by our Supreme Court in In re KH, 469 Mich. 621, 624, 677 N.W.2d 800 (2004), "where a legal father exists, a biological father cannot properly be considered even a putative father."

FN6. The Paternity Act and the Acknowledgment of Parentage Act contain provisions that lend support to the conclusion that both acts cannot be implemented to recognize two legal fathers for one child. See MCL 722.714(2) ("An action to determine paternity shall not be brought under this act if the child's father acknowledges paternity under the acknowledgment of parentage act."); MCL 722.1004 (signed acknowledgment establishes paternity "without further adjudication under the paternity act").

With the enactment of the revocation provision contained in MCL 722.1011 of the Acknowledgment of Parentage Act, the Legislature astutely envisioned cases in which it is discovered that the biological father is not the same individual who executed the acknowledgment of parentage, yet the Legislature did not provide that the acknowledger is then automatically no longer deemed the natural father and that an order of filiation can be entered in favor of the biological father if known. Rather, the Legislature provided for revocation proceedings that took into consideration biology *165 and equity. Construing the Acknowledgment of Parentage Act and the Paternity Act together and harmoniously, there can only be one conclusion with respect to the legislative intent in the context of the facts presented in this case. If an acknowledgment of parentage has been properly executed, subsequent recognition of a person as the father in an order of filiation by way of a paternity action cannot occur unless the acknowledgment has been revoked. Were we to accept Mazurek's and Sinicropi's contention that a biological father is always entitled to commence a paternity action and obtain an order of filiation where a child is born out of wedlock, the revocation provision in the Acknowledgment of Parentage Act, and especially the language regarding the equities of revocation, would be rendered meaningless in a legal battle between a biological father and an acknowledger. FN7 Such a position is contrary to the legislative intent as outlined in this opinion. FN8

FN7. MCL 722.717(5), which provides, in part, that "[a]n order of filiation supersedes an acknowledgment of parentage," supports our conclusion that a father cannot be legally recognized under both the Acknowledgment of Parentage Act and the Paternity Act. Further, this statutory provision does not negate our ruling that a previously existing and unrevoked acknowledgment of parentage controls, because a challenged order of filiation under the circumstances presented would be vacated and treated as if it never existed.

FN8. Under the position advocated by Sinicropi and Mazurek, a man who has physically, emotionally, and financially cared for a child after acknowledging paternity must always step aside for a biological father even if the acknowledger had cared for the child 5, 10, 15, or more years. This intent cannot be discerned from a harmonious reading of the acts.

A case that draws many parallels and comparisons to the facts presented in the instant action is *Killingbeck*, supra, in which a child was born out of wedlock to the plaintiff mother. The plaintiff mother had a long-term relationship with Dennis Killingbeck, a brief relationship with Tony **267 Rosebrugh, and then resumed the *166 relationship with Killingbeck, which eventually led to marriage and divorce. The child, however, was born before the marriage. Killingbeck had signed an acknowledgment of parentage following the child's birth and acted as his father for four years until DNA tests revealed that Rosebrugh was the biological father. The plaintiff filed a divorce action against Killingbeck and, about a year later, the plaintiff and Rosebrugh filed a paternity petition to revoke the acknowledgment of parentage. The parties' rights to file the paternity petition were not at issue. FN9 The trial court revoked the acknowledgment of parentage because Killingbeck had not fathered the child, and it amended the birth certificate to reflect that Rosebrugh was the biological father, but the court also awarded Killingbeck the rights of a de facto parent on equitable theories. Eventually, the trial court awarded Rosebrugh and the plaintiff mother joint legal custody, awarded the plaintiff sole physical custody, awarded both Rosebrugh and Killingbeck specific parenting time, and ordered Rosebrugh to pay child support. *Killingbeck*, supra at 135–139, 711 N.W.2d 759.

FN9. Here, there was no need for Mazurek to file a separate action to revoke the acknowledgment of parentage because an ongoing custody action was in place, and thus a simple motion sufficed. MCL 722.1011(1) allows a claim for revocation to be filed as an original action or as a motion in an existing custody case. Although in Killingbeck a paternity petition was filed, the nature of the action focused on revocation of the acknowledgment. This Court did not address the propriety of the plaintiff and Rosebrugh filing a paternity action under the Paternity Act where an acknowledgment of parentage had been signed, nor did the Court examine the propriety of Rosebrugh joining with the plaintiff mother in requesting revocation of the acknowledgment.

On appeal, the *Killingbeck* panel addressed Rosebrugh's and the plaintiff's argument that Killingbeck should not have been afforded parental rights concerning the child on the basis of the equitable parent doctrine or equitable estoppel. The Court held, consistent*167 with Van, supra, that, to the extent that the trial court relied on equitable parenthood or equitable estoppel, the order awarding Killingbeck parenting time was erroneous. *Killingbeck*, supra at 142–143, 711 N.W.2d 759. The Court also stated, however, that "[h]ad the trial court not revoked the acknowledgment of parentage, an order granting parenting time to Killingbeck would have been authorized." Id. at 143, 711 N.W.2d 759. The *Killingbeck* panel ruled that the acknowledgment of parentage established paternity and gave Killingbeck the status of a legal parent, making him eligible for parenting time under the Child Custody Act. Id. at 143–144, 711 N.W.2d 759. The Court continued by ruling that the trial court acted on a mistaken understanding of law when it "revoked the acknowledgment only because it thought that, nonetheless, Killingbeck could be granted parenting time." Id. at 144, 711 N.W.2d 759. The panel proceeded to discuss the "equity" provision in the acknowledgment revocation statute, and it vacated the trial court's order revoking the acknowledgment, stating:

The record here evidences the trial court's conclusion that, notwithstanding the repeated protestations of plaintiff and Rosebrugh, the equities of this case justified Killingbeck's continuing right to parenting time. At the very least, the trial court might well have weighed the equities of this case differently in determining the motion to revoke Killingbeck's acknowledgment of parentage had it realized that Killingbeck's right to seek parenting time was at issue.

**268 Accordingly, while we reverse the order granting Killingbeck parenting time as a "de facto father," we also vacate the order revoking the acknowledgment of parentage as it may have been based on a mistake of law. On remand, the trial court shall reconsider the motion to revoke the acknowledgment in light of this opinion. [Id. at 144–145, 711 N.W.2d 759.] [FN10]

FN10. The Court declined to address how Rosebrugh's rights and status would be affected should the trial court decide not to revoke Killingbeck's acknowledgment on remand as no one challenged Rosebrugh's rights on appeal and the issue was not raised. *Killingbeck*, supra at 149–150, 711 N.W.2d 759. The Court left that issue for another appeal if necessary. Id. at 150, 711 N.W.2d 759. Here, there was no revocation by the trial court, leaving two fathers, and the issue of Sinicropi's rights and status has been raised.

*168 The *Killingbeck* decision in no way precludes our analysis and holding here. Rather, it provides us with support for the proposition that Powers's execution of the acknowledgment of parentage, in which Mazurek joined, gave Powers the status of legal father and gave him the opportunity and right to request custody and parenting time. *Killingbeck* further supports our position that revocation of the acknowledgment, despite clear and convincing evidence that Powers was not the biological father, still required consideration of the equities.

C. Constitutional Claims

[20] The next issue we address is the constitutionality of precluding entry of an order of filiation in favor of Sinicropi under the facts presented. Sinicropi and Mazurek argue that Sinicropi's constitutional due process rights would be violated if he is deprived of the opportunity to litigate paternity and obtain an order of filiation, along with being deprived of any custodial claims to the child, despite the lack of any assertion or finding that he is unfit. We note that Sinicropi was not entitled to initiate a claim for revocation of the acknowledgment of parentage under MCL 722.1011 because under subsection 1 of the statute only the mother, the man who signed the acknowledgment, the child, or a prosecuting attorney can file a claim for revocation.

Sinicropi's constitutional arguments are premised on the single fact that he is the child's biological father. In *169 *Hauser v. Reilly*, 212 Mich.App. 184, 536 N.W.2d 865 (1995), this Court held that in the absence of a substantial parent-child relationship that stretches beyond a mere biological link, the plaintiff could not claim that he was deprived of his due process rights when he was denied standing to bring an action under the Paternity Act. Id. at 187–189, 536 N.W.2d 865. Hauser involved a child born in wedlock and a paternity action brought by the plaintiff who claimed that he, not the mother's husband, had fathered the child. The plaintiff in *Hauser* had never engaged in the daily supervision, education, protection, or care of the child. Id. at 185–186, 190, 536 N.W.2d 865. The Court, rejecting the plaintiff's constitutional claims, reasoned:

> *While we sympathize with plaintiff* [biological father], *who was allegedly denied access to his child by defendant mother, we cannot agree that any putative father who could establish paternity by scientific means has a liberty interest in all proceedings concerning that child.*

It is true that both parents and children have a due process liberty interest in their family life. In re *Clausen*, 442 Mich. 648, 686, 502 N.W.2d 649 (1993). The protected interest, however, is in the family life, not in the mere biological link between parent and child. A rapist has a biological link with a child conceived **269 by that rape. If we held that a mere biological link would ensure a father of a liberty interest in the rights to a relationship with the child, the rapist would be entitled to due process protections. *[Hauser, supra* at 188–189, 536 N.W.2d 865.]...

*172 D. Issues Related to Revocation of an Acknowledgment of Parentage

We next examine the trial court's decision not to revoke the acknowledgment of parentage and revocation proceedings in general. As indicated earlier, MCL 722.1011(3) provides, in part, that "[t]he party filing the claim for revocation has the burden of proving, by clear and convincing evidence, that the man is not the father and that, considering the equities of the case, revocation of the acknowledgment is proper." The plain and unambiguous language of the statute makes clear that simply because the man who signed the acknowledgment of parentage is shown by clear and convincing evidence not to be the child's biological father, the revocation inquiry is not at an end. Rather, the trial court must also determine whether there is clear and convincing evidence that revocation is proper given the equities of the case. See *Killingbeck*, supra at 144, 711 N.W.2d 759.

Here, DNA testing provided clear and convincing evidence that Powers was not the biological father, and the parties present no argument to the contrary. Our discussion regarding the equities of the case first requires*173 us to look at the nature of the trial court's rulings. In the fall of 2004, Mazurek filed a motion to dismiss Powers's custody action and to revoke the acknowledgment of parentage. The trial court denied the motion in a written opinion and order. However, the focus of the court's ruling was not on the "clear and convincing" and equity language contained in MCL 722.1011(3). Instead, the trial court first discussed equitable parenthood and *Van*, supra, which it found distinguishable because here there was an acknowledgment of parentage and a court order providing Powers with joint legal and physical custody. The trial court further determined that Powers was the legal parent and had standing to pursue custody. The trial court then proceeded to rule, on the basis of *Hawkins v. Murphy*, 222 Mich.App. 664, 565 N.W.2d 674 (1997), **271 that the doctrines of collateral estoppel and res judicata precluded dismissal of Powers's custody action and precluded revocation of the acknowledgment. The trial court essentially ruled that the issue of paternity could not be revisited. Apparently, the trial court was relying on the 2001 consent order of joint custody as support for invoking those doctrines. The trial court did not address the revocation motion as required by MCL 722.1011, specifically subsection 3.

We first note that *Hawkins* is easily distinguishable. In *Hawkins*, a child was born out of wedlock, and the plaintiff mother commenced a paternity action against the defendant, resulting in an order of filiation naming the defendant as the father. The parties subsequently married, but divorced soon afterwards. A consent judgment of divorce gave full custody to the plaintiff mother, and the defendant was allowed liberal visitation. The parties' contentious relationship resulted in several postjudgment court proceedings, and the plaintiff mother eventually moved to set aside the order of *174 filiation and to amend the judgment of divorce, claiming that the defendant was not the child's father. DNA testing revealed that the defendant was not the father, and the court suspended his visitation rights and support obligations. *Hawkins*, supra at 666–667, 565 N.W.2d 674.

The Hawkins panel held that res judicata barred the plaintiff mother's relitigation of paternity "when the parties had had a full and fair opportunity to litigate the issue in the paternity and divorce proceedings." Id. at 671, 565 N.W.2d 674. The Court stated that "the parties cannot raise the issue of paternity if it has already been conclusively determined in a prior adjudication." Id. (citation omitted). This Court further held that the doctrine of collateral estoppel barred relitigation of paternity "when the prior proceeding culminated in a valid final judgment, and the issue was actually and necessarily litigated." Id. at 671–672, 565 N.W.2d 674 (citation omitted).

Here, the consent order of joint custody was not the result of litigation over the issue of paternity and therefore did not determine paternity. Paternity was not an issue when Powers filed the motion for custody in 2001 because the acknowledgment of parentage had already established paternity. MCL 722.1004. Of course, the acknowledgment of parentage itself did not constitute prior litigation that could give rise to res judicata and collateral estoppel. And the acknowledgment was expressly subject to revocation under MCL 722.1011. Thus, the trial court erred in analyzing the revocation motion in terms of res judicata and collateral estoppel instead of taking into consideration the necessary analysis set forth in MCL 722.1011.

The trial court touched on the issue of revocation of the acknowledgment at a later hearing in May 2005 on Powers's motion to dismiss Sinicropi's paternity action. The trial court stated that it was not changing its *175 previous ruling with respect to Powers and the acknowledgment, noting that Powers was operating under a good-faith belief that he was the child's father. However, the court also found that Sinicropi had standing relative to his paternity complaint. In a June 2005 hearing on a motion by Powers for child support based on the order of filiation that had now been entered with respect to Sinicropi, Mazurek, now joined by Sinicropi, argued that Powers's custody case should be dismissed because Sinicropi was the child's father and Powers recognized Sinicropi's status as father by requesting child support. In a written opinion and order, the trial court reviewed the facts of the case, again distinguished *Van*, determined that Powers was the legal father pursuant to the acknowledgment **272 of parentage and the consent order of joint custody, and acknowledged that it was effectively ruling that the child had two fathers, i.e., Powers as the legal father and Sinicropi as the biological father. FN12 The trial court also again employed the doctrines of res judicata and collateral estoppel under Hawkins. Moreover, the trial court stated, "It would be manifestly inequitable to allow [*Mazurek*] to repudiate [*Powers's*] legal rights as a father in these circumstances and allow her to revoke her acknowledgment of parentage that was in effect for years." FN13

FN12. We point out that at the hearing on which the order was based, the trial court at times referred to Powers as the legal and equitable father of the child, and stated that it was applying the equitable parenthood doctrine.

FN13. At the hearing, the trial court noted:

> *Now, I recognize that Mr. Sinicropi had no idea that he was the biological father of this child until many years later. But, the reality was ... Mr. Powers carried on, believing himself to be the father, acting, paying support,* [and] *acting in his role of father. So, really what you would have* [is an argument] *that at this point in time the Court should eliminate an equitable father* [in favor] *of* [a] *late coming legal father that no one had any idea about until the last few months.*

We remand this case so that the trial court can revisit the issue of revocation of the acknowledgment of parentage.*176 We do so because the trial court never squarely addressed the issue of revocation within the four corners of the language of MCL 722.1011(3), which requires, in part, that Mazurek prove by clear and convincing evidence that revocation of the acknowledgment is proper "considering the equities of the case." FN14 While the trial court's comments in prior proceedings clearly demonstrate the court's position that equity favors Powers, we nevertheless conclude that remand is proper, not only to allow the court to address the issue within the parameters of MCL 722.1011(3) without consideration of res judicata and collateral estoppel, but also for the court to render a decision knowing and appreciating full well that if revocation is not permitted this time, Sinicropi shall have absolutely no rights as a father because the order of filiation will be vacated consistently with this opinion. FN15

FN14. There is no need to review whether there was a mistake of fact regarding paternity or whether there is clear and convincing evidence that Powers is not the biological father given the unchallenged DNA evidence and the parties' agreement that Sinicropi fathered the child.

FN15. Sinicropi argues that the trial court erred in denying his motion for disqualification. He did not, however, request a referral to the chief judge after the trial judge denied the motion for disqualification, and thus the issue is not preserved. MCR 2.003(C)(3)(a); *Welch v. Dist. Court*, 215 Mich. App. 253, 258, 545 N.W.2d 15 (1996). Moreover, Sinicropi's arguments fail because there is no record support for his claims, the arguments are speculative and lack specifics, there has been no showing of actual bias or prejudice, and he has not met the heavy burden of overcoming the presumption of impartiality. MCR 2.003(B)(1); *Cain v. Dep't of Corrections*, 451 Mich. 470, 495–497, 548 N.W.2d 210 (1996).

E. Custody Determination

For purposes of judicial expediency, we shall address the arguments regarding the trial court's custody decision *177 should the court again decline to revoke the acknowledgment of parentage. Our discussion in this section is to be read in the context of Powers's standing in the position of a man who has executed an unrevoked acknowledgment of parentage, with Sinicropi no longer having rights pursuant to the order of filiation. Numerous arguments are presented with respect to the trial court's rulings at the evidentiary hearing on the child's best interests and with regard to the custody determination.

**273 First, we find no merit to Mazurek's assertion that the trial court should have applied the presumption in MCL 722.25(1) and determined that custody with her was preferable to custody with Powers. MCL 722.25(1) provides that "[i]f the child custody dispute is between the parent or parents and an agency or a third person, the court shall presume that the best interests of the child are served by awarding custody to the parent or parents, unless the contrary is established by clear and convincing evidence."

Mazurek's argument is based on the premise that Powers is a third person, not a parent. As we concluded earlier, the acknowledgment of parentage bestowed on Powers the status of natural parent. Thus, the custody dispute between Mazurek and Powers was between two parents and the standard best-interests analysis applies without the parental presumption. MCL 722.25(1). Sinicropi is a third person who does not have standing under the Child Custody Act because he cannot meet the third-party standing requirements of MCL 722.26b and MCL 722.26c.

Mazurek next argues that her move to Shepherd, Michigan, did not constitute a sufficient change of circumstances to warrant the trial court to entertain a change of custody. Pursuant to MCL 722.27(1) (c), a court may "[m]odify or amend its previous judgments *178 or orders for proper cause shown or because of change of circumstances." See *Foskett*, supra at 5, 634 N.W.2d 363. We conclude that the move was sufficient for the trial court to consider a change in custody because the move had or could have had a significant effect on the child's life. *Vodvarka*, supra at 511–513, 675 N.W.2d 847. This case involves the move of a custodial parent 89 miles from the other custodial parent, which would have changed the child's living environment and forced the child to attend two different schools.

Next, Mazurek contends that the trial court's factual findings are against the great weight of the evidence. We first note that when a modification of custody would change the established custodial environment of a child, there must be a showing that the change is in the child's best interests by clear and convincing evidence. MCL 722.27(1)(c). The trial court found that there was an established custodial environment with both Mazurek and Powers. Accordingly, in order to support the award of sole physical custody to Powers, there needed to be clear and convincing evidence that it was in the child's best interests to award custody to Powers. See *Foskett*, supra at 8, 634 N.W.2d 363 (Where there is a joint established custodial environment, neither parent's custody may be disrupted absent clear and convincing evidence.). The trial court found by clear and convincing evidence that the factors favored physical custody with Powers.

The best-interests factors are set forth in MCL 722.23 and provide that the court must consider:

(a) The love, affection, and other emotional ties existing between the parties involved and the child.

(b) The capacity and disposition of the parties involved to give the child love, affection, and guidance and to continue the education and raising of the child in his or her religion or creed, if any.

*179 (c) The capacity and disposition of the parties involved to provide the child with food, clothing, medical care or other remedial care recognized and permitted under the laws of this state in place of medical care, and other material needs.

(d) The length of time the child has lived in a stable, satisfactory environment,**274 and the desirability of maintaining continuity.

(e) The permanence, as a family unit, of the existing or proposed custodial home or homes.

(f) The moral fitness of the parties involved.

(g) The mental and physical health of the parties involved.

(h) The home, school, and community record of the child.

(i) The reasonable preference of the child, if the court considers the child to be of sufficient age to express preference.

(j) The willingness and ability of each of the parties to facilitate and encourage a close and continuing parent-child relationship between the child and the other parent or the child and the parents.

(k) Domestic violence, regardless of whether the violence was directed against or witnessed by the child.

(l) Any other factor considered by the court to be relevant to a particular child custody dispute.

[*Mazurek*] attacks each of the trial court's findings on the factors, raising various points. On many factors, Mazurek simply identifies facts that she believes the trial court did not consider. Presumably, then, Mazurek is asserting that had the trial court considered the evidence, it would have weighed the factor differently. Mazurek first contends that the trial court did not consider the fact that she was a stay-at-home mother or address the issue of religion under factor b (capacity and disposition of parties to give the child love, affection,*180 and guidance and to continue the education and raising of the child in his or her religion). The trial court, however, did address religion and found that the parties had an equal capacity and disposition to raise the child as a Catholic, but found that this factor slightly favored Powers because of his sacrifices and efforts to put the child first. Although the trial court did not specifically mention that Mazurek was a stay-at-home mother, it did not need to comment on every matter in evidence. *MacIntyre v. MacIntyre* (On Remand), 267 Mich.App. 449, 452, 705 N.W.2d 144 (2005).

Mazurek next contends that the trial court made its finding regarding factor c (capacity and disposition of the parties to provide material needs) without any discussion of the testimony. The trial court stated, "I think that both parties clearly have an ability where they could provide the children with those." The court was only required to explicitly state its findings, not discuss the testimony. See *Foskett*, supra at 9, 634 N.W.2d 363. And Mazurek does not identify any evidence to indicate that the trial court's finding that Mazurek and Powers were equal under the factor was against the great weight of the evidence.

Mazurek also takes issue with the trial court's finding regarding factor d (length of time child had lived in stable environment and desirability of continuity) because it allegedly found in favor of a city, not a person. Although the trial court did not expressly state that the factor favored Powers, it is clear from the court's comments that it viewed the factor in favor of Powers. The trial court stated that it was desirable to maintain continuity by having the child be with Powers and his extended family in Jackson. The court did not find in favor of a city. Mazurek also contends that the trial court's consideration of school and community under *181 this factor constituted impermissible double weighing. However, the trial court did not mention school, and its reference to Jackson was in the context of discussing the child's ties to Powers and his extended family. In this **275 regard, the community consideration of factor h naturally overlapped this factor and does not constitute impermissible double weighing. *Fletcher*, supra at 25–26, 581 N.W.2d 11; *Carson v. Carson*, 156 Mich.App. 291, 299–300, 401 N.W.2d 632 (1986).

Mazurek additionally asserts that the trial court again found in favor of a location rather than a person under factor e (permanence of family unit of existing or proposed custodial home). The trial court stated, "I think he's had a degree of permanence with respect to that family unit here in Jackson County." It is readily apparent that the trial court was referring to Powers and presumably found that this factor favored him. We find that the trial court's finding under factor e was not against the great weight of the evidence.

Mazurek next contends that the trial court did not address Powers's acknowledgment of the danger of drinking while he was taking antidepressants under factor g (mental and physical health of the parties). The trial court found that the factor weighed equally. Again, the trial court need not comment on every fact in evidence. *MacIntyre*, supra at 452, 705 N.W.2d 144. But the trial court did mention Powers's depression and that it did not appear to interfere with his ability to effectively parent. And there was no evidence that Powers actually drank regularly or that his depression was not under control. Further, Mazurek knew Powers was on depression medication and would sometimes drink, yet she had no concerns about his ability to parent. The trial court's finding was not against the great weight of the evidence.

*182 Mazurek also maintains that the trial court did not make a specific finding regarding factor h (the home, school, and community record of the child). The trial court noted that the child did very well in school and had received an award for turning in his homework on time for the entire year. It also stated that when a child did not do well that it was a possible indicator that the custodial placement was not the best place for the child. Implicitly, this indicated that the court found in favor of Powers, who had the child enrolled in a Jackson school. We conclude that the trial court's comments were sufficient to discern its finding, and its failure to more explicitly state its finding was not error requiring reversal.

Mazurek also takes issue with the fact that the trial court did not consider the child's preference under factor i (child's preference). The trial court stated that it could not consider the child's preference because none of the parties presented him for an interview. We note that the parties stood mute when the trial court made this statement, and there is no indication in the record that Mazurek wished or requested that the trial court speak to the child regarding his preference. This fact distinguishes the case from *Flaherty v. Smith*, 87 Mich.App. 561, 564–565, 274 N.W.2d 72 (1978), *Lewis v. Lewis*, 73 Mich. App. 563, 564, 252 N.W.2d 237 (1977), and In re *Custody of James B*, 66 Mich.App. 133, 134, 238 N.W.2d 550 (1975), in which the trial court either declined or refused to interview the children on request. We recognize that "[a] trial court must consider, evaluate, and determine each of the factors contained in [MCL 722.23]" when determining a child's best interests. *Mann v. Mann*, 190 Mich.App. 526, 536, 476 N.W.2d 439 (1991). Assuming that the child, who was six years old when the custody hearing was conducted, was of sufficient age to express a preference, and assuming *183 that the trial court erred in not interviewing the child when neither party apparently wished to have the child appear, reversal is not warranted because **276 had the child expressed a preference, it would not have changed the trial court's ruling, given the court's overall statements and strong feelings regarding what was best for the child, nor would it lead us to conclude that the court erred in awarding sole physical custody to Powers.

Mazurek next argues that the trial court's finding under factor j (willingness of one parent to foster child's relationship with the other parent) is against the great weight of the evidence because the evidence demonstrated that Powers was unwilling to accept the child's affection for people outside his own family. We disagree. Mazurek makes much of Powers's attitude regarding the child's siblings and the fact that he stated that she kidnapped the child when she took him to Shepherd. The latter statement is not an indication that Powers was unwilling to foster the child's relationship with Mazurek. He simply viewed as egregious Mazurek's act of removing the child to a town almost

90 miles away. Regarding the child's siblings, this factor only involves the parent-child relationship. MCL 722.23(j). Powers testified that he believed Mazurek and the child loved each other, and he made sure that the child called Mazurek when important events occurred during his parenting time. The trial court's finding that the factor did not favor Mazurek or Powers is not against the great weight of the evidence.

Mazurek next asserts that the trial court did not address factor k (domestic violence). This is incorrect. The trial court found that the factor favored neither Mazurek nor Powers as evidenced by its statement, "I didn't find any evidence of domestic violence." *Mazurek* mentions past behavior by Powers that she contends *184 should have been addressed by the trial court under this factor. But again, the trial court need not comment on every fact in evidence. *MacIntyre*, supra at 452, 705 N.W.2d 144. The trial court's failure to comment cannot be construed to mean that it did not consider the evidence. And we conclude that the alleged incidents, if true, did not constitute evidence of domestic violence such that the trial court's finding was against the great weight of the evidence.

Ultimately, Mazurek's primary complaint appears to be that the trial court gave undue weight to the consideration of the child's school, which the court considered as another factor under factor l (other relevant considerations), contrary to Mazurek's assertion that the trial court made no findings under this factor. A court need not give equal weight to all the factors, but may consider the relative weight of the factors as appropriate to the circumstances. *McCain v. McCain*, 229 Mich.App. 123, 130–131, 580 N.W.2d 485 (1998). The *McCain* panel, quoting *Heid v. AAASulewski* (After Remand), 209 Mich.App. 587, 596, 532 N.W.2d 205 (1995), stated:

> "We disapprove the rigid application of a mathematical formulation that equality or near equality on the statutory factors prevents a party from satisfying a clear and convincing evidence standard of proof. We are duty-bound to examine all the criteria in the ultimate light of the child's best interests." [*McCain*, supra at 130, 580 N.W.2d 485.]

The trial court placed considerable emphasis on the child's ties to his family, friends, and school in Jackson, and the desirability of maintaining stability for him. Mazurek and Powers agreed that the joint custody arrangement had worked fairly well when Mazurek lived in Jackson. The trial court believed that it was not in the child's best interests to keep the arrangement *185 and have him attend two different schools. Thus, it decided that there was clear and convincing evidence that it **277 was in the child's best interests to remain with Powers in Jackson, where he had lived most of his life, where he had a good support system, where he attended school, and where he was well cared for and loved by Powers. In sum, we hold that the trial court did not abuse its discretion in awarding sole physical custody to Powers.

V. Conclusion

We hold that an order of filiation cannot be entered under the Paternity Act if, under the Acknowledgment of Parentage Act, a proper acknowledgment of parentage was previously executed and has not been revoked. This is because, under MCL 722.1003 and MCL 722.1004, an unrevoked acknowledgment already legally established paternity and conferred the status of natural and legal father upon the man executing the acknowledgment, which in turn entitled him to seek custody or parenting time if desired and obligated him to pay support if appropriate. Accordingly, the trial court erred by ruling that the child has two legally recognized fathers under both the Acknowledgment of Parentage Act and the Paternity Act. The case is remanded to the trial court for further reflection on the issue of revocation of the acknowledgment of parentage. The trial court is directed to address revocation solely under MCL 722.1011(3), which requires, in part, that Mazurek prove by clear and convincing evidence that revocation of the acknowledgment of parentage is proper considering the equities of the case. Should the trial court again rule to reject revocation, the court shall pronounce Powers as the child's legal father, vacate the order of filiation and any orders based *186 thereon, including the child support orders relative to Sinicropi, and let stand the custody determination as between Powers and Mazurek because we find no errors warranting reversal with respect to that determination. Should the trial court decide to revoke the acknowledgment of parentage on remand, the court shall pronounce Sinicropi the child's legal father consistent with the order of filiation, vacate any orders based on Powers's status as the father, including the order granting him joint legal and sole physical custody, and enter any appropriate orders, upon hearing if necessary, in regard to custody and support as those matters relate to Sinicropi and Mazurek.

Remanded for proceedings outlined in and consistent with this opinion. We do not retain jurisdiction.

PARENT VERSUS NONPARENT

In this "it-takes-a-village" world of raising children, many children are raised by a nonbiological "parent" or a grandparent. Sometimes this occurs because the biological parent cannot be with the child and sometimes it results from abandonment. No matter what the circumstances, generally, when a custody decision comes down to a biological parent and a nonbiological parent, the biological parent is presumed the fit parent. Is this right?

What about a grandparent who has raised the child while the biological parents did not because of drug use or some other type of "abandonment?" Again, the courts will generally have a presumption favoring the biological parent when he returns and requests custody, provided the court can deem him fit (even with assistance of a parenting plan). In one of the first cases dealing with grandparents' rights, the U.S. Supreme Court, in *Troxel v. Granville*, found that a parent had the right to limit a grandparent's visitation with a grandchild. In this case, the couple had children, but never married. After they separated, the grandparents regularly visited with the children when the father had them on the weekends. After the father's suicide, the mother limited the grandparents' visits to once per month and they challenged this in court. In denying the grandparents visitation rights, the Court spurred many state legislatures to limit who can request visitation.[23] Recall that in Minnesota's *SooHoo* case, above, the court referred to *Troxel*, but distinguished it. Why?

In a case with a twist, under a lower court ruling, a nonbiological father won custody of a child and was paid child support by the biological parents, when the court found that the child had three parents. Which previously discussed Pennsylvania case does this seem to be the reverse of? Does this result seem any fairer?

DISAGREEING WITH THE CUSTODIAL PARENT'S DECISIONS

In the case of *Smith v. Smith*, 2007-Ohio-1394,[24] a mother lost custody of her older son "twelve years old, who has exhibited signs from a very early age that he wanted to be treated as a girl." "While the child was in her care, she supported and encouraged him in his belief that he is a girl. She allowed him to wear girl's clothing, to go by the name Christine, to participate in transgender support groups, and to be generally treated as a girl." When she relocated in order to enroll her son in a transgender school, her husband filed for custody, even though he had not had much contact with the children since the separation. The Ohio court granted him custody. On appeal, the mother argued that the court's decision "interfered with her right to make medical decisions concerning her child, failed to find that she was harming her son, and failed to consider the impact of the change of custody on the parties' younger son." The court found no reversible error and allowed the father to retain custody.

In an ideal world, children will have both parents to raise them. Even with a divorce, a presumption of joint custody can give them that opportunity to have both parents in their lives. But is it realistic that a couple who could not stay together can raise a child together while separated? Often, divorce brings out the worst in parents. Yet, parents and the courts continue to struggle with ways to make it work in the best interest of the child.

---

23 *Troxel v. Granville*, 530 U.S. 57 (2000).
24 http://www.sconet.state.oh.us/rod/docs/pdf/7/2007/2007-ohio-1394.pdf

CHILD SUPPORT

CHILD SUPPORT

In the relationship between the parent and child, parents are expected to support their children. Although a definition of parental support should include emotional support, support is limited to financial support under the law. Encouraged by federal laws, all states have statutes detailing the amount of child support necessary and the remedies for a parent's failure to provide it.

HISTORY

Historically, under common law or by state law, only the father/husband was responsible for child support. Over time, biological fathers were required to support all of their children, both marital and nonmarital (see Chapter 16). Similarly, under equal protection challenges, both the mother and father are expected to provide financial support to their children.

---

1 http://www.nypost.com/p/pagesix/ethan_hawke_warns_dads_gala_pay_H99rm7MPkWrpvav8xzmyPN "Ethan Hawke Warns Dads to Pay their Child Support," October 29, 2010.
2 www.brainyquote.com/quotes/quotes/s/susanfalud166873.html

While the terms of this support are determined by the couple during an intact marriage, the court will oversee and intervene to accomplish this once the couple has divorced. More and more cases involve challenges by custodial fathers to obtain child support payments from their ex-wives.

Equal protection has also been applied when state laws provide two different ages of majority for male and female children. In *Stanton v. Stanton*, the Supreme Court of the United States reinforced the application of equal protection on gender equity in child support when reviewing a Utah statute that established two different ages of majority: 21 for males and 18 for females when payments were due from the mother. Ironically, in making its ruling, the Supreme Court in 1975 (with no women sitting on it), takes judicial notice that, "Coeducation is a fact, not a rarity. The presence of women in business, in professions, in government and in all walks of life where education is desirable" was used in determining whether there was a "reasonable basis for the classification."

STANTON V. STANTON
421 U.S. 7, 95 S.CT. 1373,
43 L.ED.2D 688

Supreme Court of the United States (1975)

Supplementary proceedings were brought by a divorced wife for judgment for support payments accruing after her daughter reached the age of 18. The Third District Court, Salt Lake County, denied the petition and plaintiff appealed. The Utah Supreme Court affirmed, 30 Utah 2d 315, 517 P.2d 1010. On notation of probable jurisdiction, the Supreme Court, Mr. Justice Blackmun, held that the difference in sex between children did not warrant a distinction in the Utah statute under which girls attained majority at 18 but boys did not attain majority until they were 21 years of age, and the statute could not, under any test, survive an attack based on equal protection.

Reversed and remanded.

Mr. Justice BLACKMUN delivered the opinion of the Court.

This case presents the issue whether a state statute specifying for males a greater age of majority than it specifies for females denies, in the context of a parent's obligation for support payments for his children, the equal protection of the laws guaranteed by s 1 of the Fourteenth Amendment.

Appellant Thelma B. Stanton and appellee James Lawrence Stanton, Jr., were married at Elko, Nev., in February 1951. At the suit of the appellant, they were divorced in Utah on November 29, 1960. They have a daughter, Sherri Lyn, born in February 1953, and a son, Rick Arlund, born in January 1955. Sherri became 18 on February 12, 1971, and Rick on January 29, 1973.

During the divorce proceedings in the District Court of Salt Lake County, the parties entered into a stipulation as to property, child support, and alimony. The court awarded custody of the children to their mother and incorporated provisions of the stipulation into its findings and conclusions and into its decree of divorce. Specifically as to alimony and child support, the decree provided:

> 'Defendant is ordered to pay to plaintiff the sum of $300.00 per month as child support and alimony, *9 $100.00 per month for each child as child support and $100.00 per month as alimony, to be paid on or before the 1st day of each month through the office of the Salt Lake County Clerk.' App. 6.

The appellant thereafter remarried; the court, pursuant to another stipulation, then modified the decree to relieve the appellee from payment of further alimony. The appellee also later remarried.

When Sherri attained 18 the appellee discontinued payments for her support. In May 1973 the appellant moved the divorce court for entry of judgment in her favor and against the appellee for, among other things, support for the children for the periods after each respectively attained the age of 18 years. The court concluded that on February 12, 1971, Sherri 'became 18 years of age, and under the provisions of (s) 15–2–1 Utah Code Annotated 1953, thereby attained her majority. Defendant is not obligated to plaintiff for maintenance and support of Sherri Lyn Stanton since that date.' App. 23. An order denying the appellant's motion was entered accordingly. Id., at 24–25.

The appellant appealed to the Supreme Court of Utah. She contended, among other things, that Utah Code Ann. s 15–2–1 (1953)FN** to the effect that the period of minority for males extends to age 21 and for females to age 18, is invidiously discriminatory and serves to deny due process and equal protection of the laws, in violation of the Fourteenth Amendment and of the corresponding *10 provisions of the Utah Constitution, namely, Art. I, ss 7 and 24, and Art. IV, s 1. On this issue, the Utah court affirmed. 30 Utah 2d 315, 517 P.2d 1010 (1974). The court acknowledged: '*There is no doubt that the questioned statute treats men and women differently,*' but said that people may be treated differently '*so long as there is a reasonable basis for the classification, which is related to the purposes of the act, and it applies equally and uniformly to all persons within the class.*' Id., at 318, 517 P.2d, at 1012. The court referred to what it called some '*old notions,*' namely,**1376 '*that generally it is the man's primary responsibility to provide a home and its essentials,*' ibid.; that '*it is a salutary thing for him to get a good education and/or training before he undertakes those responsibilities,*' id., at 319, 517 P.2d, at 1012; that '*girls tend generally to mature physically, emotionally and mentally before boys*'; and that '*they generally tend to marry earlier,*' ibid. It concluded: [Author's emphasis added.]

Period of minority.—'The period of minority extends in males to the age of twenty-one years and in females to that of eighteen years; but all minors obtain their majority by marriage.' As is so frequently the case with state statutes, little or no legislative history is available on s 15–2–1. The statute has its roots in a territorial Act approved February 6, 1852. Comp.Laws of Utah, 1876, s 1035…

'(I)t is our judgment that there is no basis upon which we would be justified in concluding that the statute is so beyond a reasonable doubt in conflict with constitutional provisions that it should be stricken down as invalid.' Id., at 319, 517 P.2d at 1013.

If such a change were desirable, the court said, 'that is a matter which should commend itself to the attention of the legislature.' Id., at 320, 517 P.2d, at 1013. The appellant, thus, was held not entitled to support for Sherri for the period after she attained 18, but was entitled to support for Rick 'during his minority' unless otherwise ordered by the trial court. Ibid., 517 P.2d, at 1014.

We noted probable jurisdiction. 419 U.S. 893, 95 S.Ct. 170, 42 L.Ed.2d 137 (1974). (arguments on mootness and portion of standing deleted by author)…

In addition, the Uniform Civil Liability for Support Act has been in effect in Utah since 1957. Laws of Utah, 1957, c. 110, now codified as Utah Code Ann. ss 78–45–1 through 78–45–13 (Supp.1973). Section 78–45–4 specifically provides: 'Every woman shall support her child.' This is in addition to the mandate contained in s 78–45–3: 'Every man shall support his wife and his child.' 'Child' is defined to mean 'a son or daughter under the age of twenty-one years.' s 78–45–2(4). And s 78–45–12 states:…

The test here, then, is whether the difference in sex between children warrants the distinction in the appellee's obligation to support that is drawn by the **1378 Utah statute. We conclude that it does not. It may be true, as the Utah court observed and as is argued here, that it is the man's primary responsibility to provide a home and that it is salutary for him to have education and training before he assumes that responsibility; that girls tend to mature earlier than boys; and that females tend to marry earlier than males. The last mentioned factor, however, under the Utah statute loses, whatever weight it otherwise might have, for the statute states that 'all minors obtain their majority by marriage'; thus minority, and all that goes with it, is abruptly lost by marriage of a person of either sex at whatever tender age the marriage occurs.

Notwithstanding the 'old notions' to which the Utah court referred, we perceive nothing rational in the distinction drawn by s 15–2–1 which, when related to the divorce decree, results in the appellee's liability for support for Sherri only to age 18 but for Rick to age 21. This imposes 'criteria wholly unrelated to the objective of that statute.' A child, male or female, is still a child. No longer is the female destined solely for the home and the rearing of the family, and only the male for the *15 marketplace and the world of ideas. See *Taylor v. Louisiana*, 419 U.S. 522, 535 n. 17, 95 S.Ct. 692, 700, 42 L.Ed.2d 690 (1975). Women's activities and responsibilities are increasing and expanding. *Coeducation is a fact, not a rarity. The presence of women in business, in the professions, in government and, indeed, in all walks of life where education is a desirable, if not always a necessary, antecedent is apparent and a proper subject of judicial notice.* If a specified age of minority is required for the boy in order to assure him parental support while he attains his education and training, so, too, is it for the girl. To distinguish between the two on educational grounds is to be self-serving: if the female is not to be supported so long as the male, she hardly can be expected to attend school as long as he does, and bringing her education to an end earlier coincides with the role-typing society has long imposed. And if any weight remains in this day to the claim of earlier maturity of the female, with a concomitant inference of absence of need for support beyond 18, we fail to perceive its unquestioned truth or its significance, particularly when marriage, as the statute provides, terminates minority for a person of either sex. *[Author's emphasis added.]*

Only Arkansas, as far as our investigation reveals, remains with Utah in fixing the age of majority for females at 18 and for males at 21. Ark.Stat.Ann. s 57–103 (1971). See *Petty v. Petty*, 252 Ark. 1032, 482 S.W.2d 119 (1972). Furthermore, Utah itself draws the 18–21 distinction only in s 15–2–1 defining minority, and in s 30–1–9 relating to marriage without the consent of parent or guardian. See also s 30–1–2(4) making void a marriage where the male is under 16 or the female under 14. Elsewhere, in the State's present constitutional and statutory structure, the male and the female appear to be treated alike. The State's Constitution provides that the rights of Utah citizens to vote and hold office 'shall not *16 be denied or abridged on account of sex,' and that '(b)oth male and female citizens… shall enjoy equally all civil, political and religious rights and privileges,' Art. IV, s 1, and, since long before the Nation's adoption of the Twenty-sixth Amendment in 1971, did provide that every citizen 'of the age of twenty-one years and upwards,' who satisfies durational requirements, 'shall be entitled to vote.' Art. IV, s 2. Utah's statutes provide that any citizen over the age of 21 who meets specified nonsex qualifications is 'competent to act as a juror,' Utah Code Ann. s 78–46–8, may be admitted to the practice of law, s 78–51–10, and may act as an incorporator, s 16–10–48, and, if under 21 and in need, may be entitled to public assistance, s 55–15a–17. The ages at which persons may serve in legislative, executive, and judicial offices are the same for males and females. Utah Const., Art. VI, s 5, Art. VII, s 3, and Art. VIII, s 2. Tobacco may not be sold, purchased, or possessed **1379 by persons of either sex under 19 years of age. ss 76–10–104 and 76–10–105 (see Laws of Utah, 1974, ss 39–40). No age differential is imposed with respect to the issuance of motor vehicle licenses. s 41–2–10. State adult education programs are open to every person 18 years of age or over. s 53–30–5. The Uniform Gifts to Minors Act is in effect in Utah and defines a minor, for its purposes, as any person 'who has not attained the age of twenty-one years.' s 75–15–2.11 (Supp.1973). Juvenile court jurisdiction extends to persons of either sex under a designated age. ss 55–10–64 and 55–10–77. Every person over the age of 18 and of sound mind may dispose of his property by will. s 74–1–1. And the Uniform Civil Liability for Support Act, noted above and in effect in Utah since 1957, imposes on each parent an obligation of support of both sons and daughters until age 21. ss 78–45–2(4), 78–45–3, and 78–45–4 (Supp.1973).

We therefore conclude that under any test—compelling state interest, or rational basis, or something in between—s 15–2–1 in the context of child support, does not survive an equal protection attack. In that context, no valid distinction between male and female may be drawn.

Our conclusion that in the context of child support the classification effectuated by s 15–2–1 denies the equal protection of the laws, as guaranteed by the Fourteenth Amendment, does not finally resolve the controversy as between this appellant and this appellee. With the age differential held invalid, it is not for this Court to determine when the appellee's obligation for his children's support, pursuant to the divorce decree, terminates under Utah law. The appellant asserts that, with the classification eliminated, the common law applies and that at common law the age of majority for both males and females is 21. The appellee claims that any unconstitutional inequality between males and females is to be remedied by treating males as adults at age 18, rather than by withholding the privileges of adulthood from *18 women until they reach 21. This plainly is an issue of state law to be resolved by the Utah courts on remand; the issue was noted, incidentally, by the Supreme Court of Utah. 30 Utah 2d, at 319, 517 P.2d, at 1013. The appellant, although prevailing here on the federal constitutional issue, may or may not ultimately win her lawsuit. See *Harrigfeld v. District Court*, 95 Idaho 540, 511 P.2d 822 (1973); *Commonwealth v. Butler*, 458 Pa. 289, 328 A.2d 851 (1974); *Skinner v. Oklahoma*, 316 U.S. 535, 542–543, 62 S.Ct. 1110, 1113–1114, 86 L.Ed. 1655 (1942).

The judgment of the Supreme Court of Utah is reversed and the case is remanded for further proceedings not inconsistent with this opinion.

It is so ordered.

Judgment reversed and case remanded.

HOW MUCH?

Previously, the court had wide discretion in determining the necessary amount of child support. Encouraged by the federal law, states have developed systems for standardizing this determination and a system to collect it if it goes unpaid.[3] Most states use the **"income shares"** model of child support. This model is based on the idea that after the divorce (or if the unmarried parents live apart), the children should get the same proportion of the parents' income as if they had stayed together. The rationale is generally along the lines that the children should retain the same economic standard of living after their parents' divorce. Under this system, both parents' incomes are included in the calculation of the child support, and their combined income is then proportioned for the total payment of the child's support. Luckily, states using this model often have computer programs that will assist in making the calculations once the basic amounts are entered. Another model is the percentage of income; child support is calculated by a percentage

---

3   In 2009, Maryland's legislature made the first increase in the recommended amount for child support payments in over 20 years. Those outdated child support guidelines "are based on the economic realities of 1988, when a gallon of gas cost $1.08 and a first-class stamp was 22 cents." The state estimated at that time that child support affected 500,000 children in Maryland. "Md. Child support amounts might rise", Donna St. George, *The Washington Post Metro*, November 4, 2009.

of the parent's income that increases by the number of children. The other parent's income is irrelevant.

While the state establishes the payments under its guidelines they are presumptions and, in extraordinary cases, a court can deviate from them. In California, a Los Angeles family court judge ordered movie star Halle Berry to pay $240,000 a year—or $20,000 per month—in child support to her ex-boyfriend, model Gabriel Aubry, for their five-year-old daughter.[4] Actor Tom Cruise agreed to pay his ex-wife Katie Holmes $400,000 per year—or $33,333 a month—in child support for the next 12 years, until their daughter turns 18, for a total of $4.8 million.[5,6] In what was thought to be the largest request ever made in the New York courts, fashion model Linda Evangelista asked for $46,000 per month in child support[7] for the child she had with François-Henri Pinault, but a confidential settlement was reached between them.

STEPPARENTS

While biological fathers may have avoided child support in the last century,[8] many states and cases have now extended the responsibility of child support from not only biological fathers, but to stepparents and their stepchildren. What if the stepparent has not adopted the stepchild—should financial support still be imposed? If the stepparent is living with the stepchild, it may be imposed. Another factor may be the length of time that they lived together. What happens if support is imposed on a stepparent, but the stepfather/mother divorces the biological parent? Does the support obligation continue? It would seem logical that if a stepparent had a duty to provide financial support, it should continue; some courts have imposed it after divorce.

EQUITABLE PARENTS

How far should this support obligation go? Suppose that a husband and wife have a child together and raise her as their own. Later, when the man becomes suspicious that the child is not his biologically and confirms that she is not, his wife leaves and moves in with the biological father. Should the husband still have to pay child support to the woman and man living together with their biological child? In a Pennsylvania case, the court said yes. Under the doctrine of the

---

4   http://newsfeed.time.com/2012/06/21/halle-berry-ordered-to-pay-240000-in-child-support/, "Halle Berry Ordered to Pay $240,000 in Child Support," Melissa Locker, *Time*, June 21, 2012.

5   Cruise will also pay for medical expenses, insurance, and college costs.

6   http://www.huffingtonpost.com/2012/08/24/katie-holmes-tom-cruise-settlement_n_1827494.html, "Katie Holmes Tom Cruise Settlement: Actress to Receive Just $400,000 per Year," August 24, 2012.

7   http://www.huffingtonpost.com/2011/08/02/linda-evangelista-francois-henri-pinault-child-support_n_915809.html. "*Linda Evangelista Asks François-Henri Pinault For $46,000,*" www.huffingtonpost.com/... /linda-evangelista-francois-henri-pinault-, Hillary Moss, October 2, 2011.

8   *Gomez v. Perez*, 409 U.S. 535 (1973).

equitable parent, the court found that the husband had acted for so long as the child's father, and the child had relied on him as her father, that it would be unfair to her to allow the father to deny the obligation of financial support now.

"It was in July 2007 when Mike L. asked the Pennsylvania courts to declare that he was no longer the father of his daughter. For four years, Mike had known that the girl he had rocked to sleep and danced with across the living-room floor was not, as they say, 'his.' The revelation from a DNA test was devastating and prompted him to leave his wife—but he had not renounced their child. He continued to feel that in all the ways that mattered, she was still his daughter, and he faithfully paid her child support. It was only when he learned that his ex-wife was about to marry the man who she said actually was the girl's biological father that Mike flipped.[9] When Mike went to court to try to end his paternal rights, for the girl that he 'still loves' and who has regular visitation with him, the court required him to make child support payments to the girl. 'I pay child support to a biologically intact family,' Mike told me, his voice cracking with incredulity. 'A father and mother, married, who live with their own child. And I pay support for that child. How ridiculous is that?'"[10]

"Mike wondered just what the word 'father' really meant. Was he the father and Rob the stepfather or the other way around? Most galling to Mike was that he was expected to subsidize this man's cozy domestic arrangement. Mike's wages would be garnished because he was the legal father—even though, in this case, the biological father had more of the benefits of fatherhood and none of its obligations."[11]

In Mike L.'s case, his ex-wife made the argument that the biological father loved the daughter and acted as her father and "the hearing officer ordered, Rob [the biological father] should help pay her support, too."[12] While the biological father was named in the lawsuit, he never appeared in court. The ex-wife's attorney argued on appeal of this determination "that parenthood shared by one mother and two fathers 'would lead to a strange and unworkable situation' so, the lawyer reasoned, Rob should not be forced to help pay for L.'s care." The Pennsylvania Judge, David Wecht, wrote in his opinion that "Pennsylvania law did not allow for the recognition of two fathers of the same child." Mike L., who had acknowledged paternity, was responsible for support payment.[13]

Should Mike have to pay support? Is it in the child's best interest to require him to pay support? Will it only drive a wedge in the relationship the law is trying to preserve? In 2003, a Pennsylvania appellate court bluntly applauded William Doran—who had been by all accounts

---

9   "Who Knew I Was Not the Father?" Ruth Padawer, *New York Times Magazine*, November 17, 2009, also at http://www.nytimes.com/2009/11/22/magazine/22Paternity-t.html?pagewanted=all&_r=0
10   Ibid., Quoting Mike L
11   Who Knew I Was Not the Father?" Ruth Padawer, *New York Times Magazine*, November 17, 2009, also at http://www.nytimes.com/2009/11/22/magazine/22Paternity-t.html?pagewanted=all&_r=0
12   Ibid.
13   "Who Knew I Was Not the Father?" Ruth Padawer, *New York Times Magazine*, November 17, 2009, also at http://www.nytimes.com/2009/11/22/magazine/22Paternity-t.html?pagewanted=all&_r=0

a loving father to his 11-year-old son—for cutting off ties with the boy, once DNA showed they were not related. The judges found that Doran had been tricked by his former wife into believing he was the father of their son, and he was allowed to abandon all paternal obligations.[14] In a similar case, the non-biological father said, "The courts insist on the best interest of the child… but it was in the child's best interest for [the biological mother and father] not to do this [have the affair] in the first place. So why is that burden all of a sudden put on me?"[15] Does this make sense?

COLLEGE

While the income shares model gives the child a share of the parents' income as if the divorce never occurred, does it really do more than this? Traditionally, a parent's duty to support a child ends at the child's age of majority—in most states, age 18. Yet, when parents divorce, some states (through agreement, case law, or state statute) require the parents to pay the child's college tuition. Often, in the separation agreement, the parents will resolve this issue too—even if the state does not require college tuition and expenses as support, the court may enforce the terms of the agreement and require it.

The case of *Christopher v. Christopher* (—So.3d—, 2012 WL 6634435 (Ala.Civ.App. 2012)), combines many of the above issues (viz., gender equality requiring both men and women to pay support, stepparent/new spouse's responsibility for support, and paying for college after divorce). In the case, the woman remarried after a divorce. Although she did not make much as a part-time hairdresser, the court felt that it was appropriate to make her pay for part of her daughter's college. The court said she may have to make some personal sacrifices to make the payments, but felt that such payments would not meet the undue hardship standard. If she makes $400-500 a month from her job and $1,000 per month as a hairstylist, could she pay about one quarter of her daughter's college expenses, totaling almost $10,000 per year? Does the fact that she used the $100,000 from the divorce as a down payment on a house with her new husband make a difference? How about that fact that the new husband makes a decent wage? Should he have to contribute to support? Does her new husband effectively pay support? If his wife is forced to make the child support payment, it will drain their income for household expenses.

---

14 Ibid.
15 Ibid.

CHRISTOPHER V. CHRISTOPHER—
SO.3D—, 2012 WL 6634435
(ALA.CIV.APP. 2012)

Only the Westlaw citation is currently available (NOT YET RELEASED FOR PUBLICATION).

Background: Father filed post-divorce petition for postminority educational support. The Circuit Court, Limestone County, No. DR–10–279.02, granted petition. Following denial of her motion to alter, amend, or vacate the Judgment or, in alternative, for new trial, mother appealed.

Holdings: The Court of Civil Appeals, Moore, J., held that:

(1) trial court did not impermissibly include income or assets of mother's new husband as source for payment of postminority educational support;...

(2) mother lacked standing to assert argument that Judicial mechanism facilitating receipt by children of divorced parents of parent-funded post-secondary education resulted in impermissible discrimination against children of nondivorced parents;...

(4) trial court's imposition of postminority-educational-support obligation on mother did not unconstitutionally usurp mother's parental role by depriving her of her fundamental right to condition financial aid on adherence to her code of conduct;...

(6) trial court did not plainly and palpably err in finding that mother was able to pay postminority educational support without undue hardship.

Affirmed.
MOORE, Judge.

*1 Carolyn Sue Christopher ("the mother") appeals from a judgment of the Limestone Circuit Court ("the trial court") requiring her to pay postminority educational support on behalf of her child, C. C.

Procedural History

The mother and Charles Phillip Christopher ("the father") were divorced by a judgment of the trial court in 2010. At the time the divorce judgment was entered, the mother and the father had one adult child and two children who were still under the age of majority, C. C. and Ca. C. On April 18, 2011, four days before C. C.'s 19th birthday, the father filed a petition requesting that the trial court order the mother to pay a portion of C. C.'s postminority educational expenses. The mother filed an answer, in which she asserted that she was financially unable to contribute to C. C.'s college education and that the application of our supreme court's holding in Ex parte *Bayliss*, 550 So.2d 986 (Ala.1989), was unconstitutional. The mother served a copy of her answer upon the state's attorney general. See Ala. Code 1975, § 6–6–227. After a trial, the trial court entered a judgment requiring the mother to pay 25% of C. C.'s college expenses. On January 29, 2012, the mother filed a motion to alter, amend, or vacate the judgment or, in the alternative, for a new trial; that motion was denied on February 7, 2012. The mother filed her notice of appeal on February 19, 2012.

Facts

At the commencement of the trial, the parties stipulated that C. C.'s net estimated college expenses total $9,435 per semester and that an existing college fund would be utilized before any contribution would be required from either parent.

The mother testified that C. C. is a student at the University of Alabama. She admitted that, during their marriage, she and the father had anticipated that their children would attend college. The mother testified that she is employed at "Growing Younger" earning between $400 and $500 a month and that she also earns $1,000 per month as a self-employed hairdresser. She testified that she had earned more as a hairdresser before the parties' divorce but that, due to the divorce, many clients had stopped using her as their hairdresser.

The mother testified that she had received $100,000 as her part of the equity in the marital home in the parties' divorce judgment but that she was using that money as the down payment on a new house that she would own with her new husband. She testified that the cost of the new house was more than $300,000. She further testified that she and her husband would be equally dividing the monthly mortgage payment on the new house but that he was not putting any money toward the down payment on the house. The mother testified that, in the parties' divorce judgment, she had also received $120,000 from one of the father's retirement accounts and an additional $10,000 in lieu of receiving any interest in another account. She also testified that she does not have a separate retirement account and that her only other asset is an automobile. The mother testified that she does not earn enough income to contribute to C. C.'s college education.

*2 The mother testified further that, during the parties' marriage, the parties had not been able to afford to send their oldest child away to college, so he had attended Calhoun Community College his first year. She testified that the parties had put their oldest child's college expenses on a credit card. She testified that the father had been earning approximately $85,000 a year at that time and that she had been earning between $1,600 and $2,000 a month. She testified that, during the marriage, the father's income had paid the parties' bills and her income had been used simply for entertainment.

The mother testified further that, at the time of the trial, her monthly expenses totaled $2,475 and that she does not live an extravagant lifestyle. She testified that, when she and her family move into the new house, their monthly utility payments would increase and the house payment would be more than the rent she was paying at the time of trial. She later testified that she hoped the new house payment would be between $1,100 and $1,200 a month and that she would be paying one-half of that amount (between $550 and $600), as opposed to the $675 she was paying for one-half of the monthly rent at the time of the trial. She stated, however, that they had not yet obtained insurance on the house.

The father testified that his annual income from his primary employment had increased since the time of the parties' divorce from approximately $90,000 to almost $100,000 and that he had also earned an additional $3,000 per year working for an auction company. The father testified that, although the parties had stipulated at the divorce proceedings that the mother's monthly income was $2,100, the mother had testified that she was making more than that. He also testified that he had believed at that time that the mother was earning $2,100 a month based on the lifestyle they had lived and on their not having had to borrow money to send their oldest child to college. He admitted that he did not know what the mother's income was at the time of the trial of this matter. He testified, however, that he did not agree with the mother's testimony regarding her present monthly income and that he believed she is capable of contributing to C. C.'s college expenses.

The father admitted that the mother had lost customers when their "situation" became public before he actually filed for a divorce. He testified that she still had done "a lot of hair" while he was still living with her before filing for a divorce but that the number of clients had been somewhat reduced. He testified that he believed she was making more than $1,100 a month at the time of trial and that, to reach that level, her business must have dropped off "a lot" after the divorce. *He testified that he had told some of the mother's clients what he thought had caused the parties' marriage to end, but, he said, he had also told them that he was fine with them continuing to go to her to get their hair done. [Author's emphases added.]*

*3 The father testified further that, when the parties' oldest child was in college, the father's income had been used to pay the house payment, the utilities, and other necessities. The father testified that he pays all three children's automobile-insurance premiums and cellular-telephone bills. He also testified that he does not pay any additional money above his child-support obligation for the parties' youngest child but that he usually gives her $20 when she visits. He testified further that, since the parties' divorce, he had purchased a house for $192,000 and that he had made a down payment of slightly more than 20% of the purchase price...

The father testified that he could use the mother's assistance in paying for C. C.'s college education. He testified, however, that he would work additional jobs in order to make sure C. C. obtained a college education.

Issues

On appeal, the mother argues (1) that the trial court erred in considering her remarriage to her current husband in ordering her to pay postminority educational support; (2) that § 30–3–1, Ala.Code

1975, discriminates against children of nondivorced parents as a class, making it unconstitutional; (3) that the trial court's judgment requiring the mother to pay postminority educational support unconstitutionally discriminates against her, as a divorced parent, as to the exercise of her rights; (4) that the trial court did not have jurisdiction to order the mother to pay any support for the benefit of C. C. because C. C. had reached the age of majority and has no mental or physical disability and, therefore, the award violates the separation-of-powers doctrine; and (5) that the trial court's judgment ordering postminority educational support resulted in an undue hardship for the mother.

Discussion

I.

In its judgment, the trial court stated, in pertinent part: "This court has examined the income of the parties, the potential earnings of the parties, distribution of assets by the parties following their divorce, the remarriage of the [mother] and whether this Order shall impose an undue hardship on the parties." (Emphasis added.) The mother argues that the trial court erred in considering her remarriage to her current husband in ordering her to pay postminority educational support because, she says, "[a]t no time has any appellate court of the State of Alabama made the remarriage of the parent a factor to be considered in the award of a post-secondary education support for a child." (Mother's brief, p. 23.)

*4 In Ex parte *Bayliss*, supra, the supreme court held that one of the primary considerations a trial court must consider when awarding postminority educational support is "the financial resources of the parents." 550 So.2d at 987. In *McCarthy v. Popwell*, 915 So.2d 56, 59 (Ala.Civ.App.2005), a plurality of this court reasoned that, because a stepparent has no legal obligation to support a child of his or her spouse's former marriage, the income of a noncustodial parent's new spouse could not be considered part of the financial resources of the parents of the child in determining whether to award postminority educational support; however, McCarthy does not stand for the proposition that a trial court cannot consider a parent's economic arrangement with a new spouse in assessing that parent's independent ability to contribute financially to the postminority educational expenses of his or her child of a former marriage...

*5 "'Following divorce the noncustodial parent, most frequently the father, often establishes a new life for himself, possibly including a new spouse, stepchildren, and new children. One result is that the interest, concern, care, and money of the noncustodial parent that is available for the children of the original marriage often declines or vanishes altogether. This is particularly true in such matters as the cost of education for their post-majority children. By imposing an educational support obligation on these parents, at least one of the disadvantages caused children by divorce can be reduced or eliminated. It is true that the imposition of this burden on divorced noncustodial parents establishes a classification with discriminatory obligations. However, as the *Childers* [v. Childers] [89 Wash.2d 592, 604, 575 P.2d 201, 208 (1978)] court pointed out, instead of an arbitrary, inequitable, unreasonable, or unjust classification, what exists is a package of special powers in equity that the courts, regardless of legislation, have long used to protect the interests of children of broken homes and to assure that the disadvantages of divorce on these children are minimized. In short, the courts have found a reasonable relationship between this classification and the legitimate state interest in minimizing the disadvantages to children of divorced parents....'"

[6] We note that the mother's argument regarding discrimination against children of nondivorced parents was not specifically raised in Exparte *Bayliss*; however, the mother lacks standing to assert that argument because she is not a child of an intact family,...

As the father argues in his brief to this court, the courts of this state and the United States Supreme Court have concluded that a parent has a fundamental right to direct the education of only minor children,... not children who have reached the age of majority. Generally speaking, once a child attains the age of majority, that child is emancipated under the law. See § 26–1–1(a), Ala.Code 1975.

The mother maintains, however, that her dispute with the father involves not just the funding of C. C.'s education, but her right to control the behavior of C. C. while he is receiving that funding. The mother argues that she, like any married parent in this state, has a fundamental right to raise her child according to her value system and to withhold or reduce financial aid for that child as a means of punishing the misconduct of the child or coercing the child to comply with that value system. See Judith G. McMullen, Father (or Mother) Knows Best: An Argument Against Including Post-Majority Educational Expenses in Court-Ordered Child Support, 34 Ind. L.Rev. 343, 363 (2001) (noting that "a divorced parent may choose not to pay college or other post-majority expenses for children of a former marriage... because the child's behavior is unacceptable to the parent"); Huitink, 93 Iowa L.Rev. at 1441 (noting those and similar circumstances and stating that, "[w]hen a child goes to college, financial support may be the most important, if not the only, influence parents can exert on their children"). According to the mother, Ex parte *Bayliss* divests her of that right by requiring her to financially aid C. C. without conditioning that responsibility on C. C.'s compliance with the mother's code of conduct. In that regard, the mother complains that the trial court has unconstitutionally usurped her role as a parent.

or not, "this court is bound by the decisions of our supreme court." TenEyck, 885 So.2d at 158.

*9 Based on the foregoing, we cannot conclude that the trial court's imposition of a postminority-educational-support obligation on the mother is unconstitutional.

[18] [19] [20] The mother's final argument is that the trial court's judgment ordering the mother to pay postminority educational support creates an undue hardship on the mother. ,,,"A parent has a legal duty to provide or aid in providing a college education for his/her child if the child demonstrates the ability and willingness to attain a higher education and the parent has sufficient estate, earning capacity, or income to provide financial assistance without undue hardship to himself....*10 *Thrasher v. Wilburn*, 574 So.2d 839, 841 (Ala.Civ.App.1990). Specifically, the mother argues that because

her monthly expenses exceed her income, she should not be required to contribute to C. C.'s college education. The mother, however, testified that she was awarded $100,000 in the divorce judgment and that she was using the entirety of that award as a down payment on a new house. The trial court could have determined that the mother could have used some of those funds to offset her postminority-educational-support obligation instead of paying the entire amount down on the new house. Considering our standard of review on this issue, we cannot reverse the trial court's judgment.

Conclusion

Based on the foregoing, we affirm the judgment of the trial court.

AFFIRMED.

While parents are required to support their children, should this include payment for college? The evidence shows that the wife in *Christopher* is making less money because the local gossip about the reason for her divorce has discouraged some of her customers from returning to her hair salon. The husband acknowledges that he may have contributed to this loss of business through his conversations about why the marriage failed. Should this impact the court's determination?

SAME-SEX PARENTS

As the Pennsylvania case discussed above shows, courts may recognize several parents for a child: a biological father, mother, and equitable parent. So, while children in a heterosexual relationship are entitled to support from all parents, should this apply to children of same-sex couples? Should both moms or both dads have to pay? In California, the court said yes. In *Elisa B. v. Superior Court*, 117 P.3d 660 (Cal. 2005), twins were born to one of two lesbians and the two women raised the twins together as a family. When one woman left the relationship, she said she did not have to provide financial support because she was not the child's parent. The court disagreed, saying that a child may have two parents, both of whom are women. Probably the fact that the woman who ended the relationship helped raise the children, established a family relationship with them, and even supported her partner's artificial insemination attempts to create them, is in keeping with the Pennsylvania case's equitable parent finding, too.[16]

---

16 https://www.courtlistener.com/opinion/2629934/elisa-b-v-superior-court/. See also, *Emanuel Law lines, Family Law*, by D. Kelly Weisberg, 2011.

UNTIL WHEN?

Most states say that a child is considered an adult and able to make their own decisions at the age of 18. This is referred to as the age of "majority," and the child is deemed "emancipated" from the parent-child relationship under the law. As a result, generally, parents are no longer required to provide the "necessities" for their children. Combine this with the principle that the government generally does not interfere with the parent-child relationship, and the question arises of how long a parent can be required to pay child support. Cases like *Christopher v. Christopher*,—So.3d—, 2012 WL 6634435 (Ala. Civ. App. 2012), above, show that a child engaged in full-time study in college may be able to expect child support, but with what restrictions? Or expectations? Is it really about age or is it about what the "emancipated" child is doing with their life? What if the child is living with her boyfriend, working, and taking classes at college? Should she be deemed unemancipated and due support?

ANDERSON V. LOPER
689 SO.2D 118
(ALA.CIV.APP., 1996)

Father filed petition to modify child support and requested that obligations be terminated based on minor child's graduation from high school, employment, and moving in with boyfriend. The Washington Circuit Court, J. Lee McPhearson, J., denied father's petition. Father appealed. The Court of Civil Appeals, Crawley, J., held that trial court's judgment that minor child was not emancipated was not plainly and palpably wrong.

Affirmed.

Monroe, J., concurred specially and filed opinion.

Minor child was not emancipated, and thus father was not relieved of child support obligations, where mother could still make reasonable demands on minor child and be obeyed and child was still utilizing financial support from parents, even though child had moved out of mother's home and in with boyfriend over objections by both parents and currently was living on her own and even though father had strained relationship with her.

For purposes of child support, age of majority is 19 and parent has duty to support child who is under age 19; however, once child is emancipated, parent no longer has duty of support. Code 1975, § 26-1-1.

Emancipation of minor child is governed by statute and commonly occurs when minor child has reached age of 18. Code 1975, § 26-13-1.

In determining if minor child is emancipated for purposes of child support, court must base its decision on best interests of minor child; multitude of factors are proper for consideration and there are no specific rules or guidelines that control every case. Code 1975, § 26-13-1.

Trial court is entrusted to make ultimate decision on contested issues in determining emancipation of minor child, and its judgment will not be set aside unless Court of Civil Appeals finds that judgment is plainly and palpably wrong.

CRAWLEY, Judge.

In October 1995, Gary Lee Anderson (the "father") filed a petition to modify child support and requested that his obligation to provide support to his minor child, Denina Anderson, be terminated and that he be allowed to recover child support payments made in June, July, August, and September 1995. As grounds for his motion, the father alleged that the minor child had graduated from high school, become employed, and moved from the home of Cynthia Loper (the "mother") to reside with her boyfriend and his parents. These facts, he alleged, proved that his minor child was emancipated and that his support obligation should be terminated. The mother answered the petition, and the trial court set the matter down for hearing on January 24, 1996. After hearing the testimony presented, the trial court denied the petition. The father appeals. We affirm.

The trial court's order is thorough. The judgment makes clear the basic facts of this case; therefore, we will quote the trial court's findings.

"It is the finding of this Court as follows:

"1. That the minor child, Denina Marie Anderson, currently eighteen (18) years of age, graduated from high school in May of 1995; and,

"2. That the minor child moved from the home of the [mother] in June of 1995 to live with her boyfriend and his family apparently over the objections of [both the mother and the father]; and,

"3. That while the minor child was living with her boyfriend and his family, she attended, on a full time basis, Alabama Southern Community College in Gilbertown, Alabama on a Pell Grant and worked at the Family Dollar Store on a part-time basis; and,

"4. That the prior child support paid by the [father] has gone to the [mother] and [was] then forwarded to the child and applied toward the child's automobile loan for the vehicle the child purchased after she moved from the home of the [mother]; and,

"5. That in December of 1995 the minor child moved from her boyfriend's family home to Mobile to begin a new job at a fitness center as her work at the Family Dollar Store had been reduced and to begin preparation for attendance at the University *120 of South Alabama beginning in February or March of 1996 on a Pell Grant; and,

"6. That said child is not 'self-supporting' as the child is receiving child support from the [father] as set out above and also receives financial help from the [mother] for living expenses. That while the child is a student and working on a part-time basis, the child would not be independent as defined in Alabama case authority.

"7. That the minor child is not 'emancipated' and free of parental control although the child has often acted contrary to the wishes of her parents. During the time the child is dependent, in part, on her family for financial support, reasonable demands can be expected to be made on the child. While the Court is aware of the strained relationship between the minor child and the [father], it appears that the [mother] still can make reasonable demands on the minor child and be obeyed by the minor child. The Court is not aware of case authority that says that the [father] is entitled to relief from paying child support while the minor child is still subject to parental control, in part, from one of the parents."

While we are not unsympathetic to the father's objections to the path the minor child has taken, we agree with the trial court that the minor child is not emancipated and that the father still has a duty to support her in her minority. See State ex rel. *Shellhouse v. Bentley*, 666 So.2d 517, 518 (Ala.Civ.App.1995). The age of majority in this state is 19, Ala.Code 1975, § 26-1-1, and a parent has a duty to support a child who is under the age of 19. *Shellhouse*, 666 So.2d at 518. However, once a child is emancipated, a parent no longer has a duty of support. *B. A. v. State Department of Human Resources* ex rel. R.A., 640 So.2d 961, 962 (Ala.Civ.App.1994).

Emancipation of a minor child is governed by statute and can occur only when a minor child has reached the age of 18. Ala.Code 1975, § 26-13-1. The trial court must base its decision on emancipation on the best interest of the minor child. Id. "The best interest standard affords freedom for the trial court to consider numerous and varied factors.... A multitude of factors are proper for consideration when the trial court is determining what is in the best interest of the child, and there are no specific rules or guidelines that will control every case." *Hodge v. Hovey*, 679 So.2d 1145, 1148 (Ala.Civ.App.1996) (citations omitted). The trial court heard the testimony of and observed the demeanor of the mother, the father, the minor child, and other witnesses; it is entrusted to make the ultimate decision on contested issues, and its judgment will not be set aside unless this court finds that the judgment is plainly and palpably wrong. *Swann v. Swann*, 627 So.2d 429, 430 (Ala.Civ.App.1993). We cannot say that the trial court's judgment that the minor child is not yet emancipated is plainly and palpably wrong.

In addition, the father argues that the child has not spoken to him or visited with him for over two years and that, therefore, his duty to support the child should be abrogated. The father has cited an

Alabama case that holds that a trial court can condition the payment of child support upon compliance with visitation directives in a divorce judgment. See *Snellings v. Snellings*, 272 Ala. 254, 130 So.2d 363 (1961). However, the petition to modify did not contain this argument, and the record on appeal does not indicate that the argument was presented to the trial court. An argument not presented below cannot be considered on appeal. *West Town Plaza Assocs. v. Wal-Mart Stores*, Inc., 619 So.2d 1290, 1294 (Ala.1993).

The judgment of the trial court is affirmed.
AFFIRMED.
MONROE, Judge, concurring specially.

I cannot say that the trial court's judgment was plainly and palpably wrong under the law as it stands now; therefore, I have no choice but to concur, albeit reluctantly, with the majority's opinion. However, I believe that when a "child" who has already graduated from high school sees fit to move out of *121 the house to live with her boyfriend in defiance of her parents' wishes, the law is doing no favors to either the "child" or the parents by requiring the parents to continue to support that "child" under the guise of child support. The daughter has no reason to accede to her parents' wishes because she knows that, regardless, she will receive monthly financial support from her father. In essence, we make it possible for her disobey her parents. Even though I disagree with the outcome of this case, the law binds me to that outcome; therefore, I am concurring specially.

Should the father have to pay for his daughter, who is living with her boyfriend at his parents' house? Would it make a difference if she was married to the boyfriend?

MODIFICATION OF CHILD SUPPORT

Once a child support award is made, is it set in stone? Child support awards can be modified generally based on a **"substantial and material change of circumstances."** What kinds of changes should this include? During the recent financial recession, courts were flooded with requests for modification of support payments because of lost jobs. Is this fair? Certainly, if a man has no or limited money when his job is "downsized" due to a bad economy, it does seem fair to reduce the amount of child support he pays; most courts grant this request. While courts may be receptive to reducing the amount of support because of an undue hardship, they will expect that the parent make some personal sacrifice when they assess the hardship (see the *Christopher v. Christopher* case above). Where should the court's involvement end in making a determination of personal sacrifice? An expensive car? What about a home? What about cable TV, a cell phone, or a weekly pedicure? Also, what is the impact on the ex-wife and children who had anticipated this income in making their own expenses?

What happens if the spouse voluntarily changes her occupation, causing a reduction in her income—should this make a difference? Courts are generally unreceptive to a reduction in child support payments caused by a voluntary job change. Does this seem fair? Suppose the wife quit her high-pressure job as a lawyer to become a yoga teacher—does she lose that liberty interest to pursue her dreams after she divorces? What about if the job change is necessitated by a health condition? The court may be sympathetic to this request, assuming it amounts to a substantial change. But what are the limits? If the health condition can be remedied by surgery—will the court require the obligor to get it? What about a health condition brought on by obesity or cigarette smoking? Is this a reason to take away money from the children? Finally, if the father may be able to reduce his child support payments when he loses his job, what happens if he is put in prison?

As discussed above in the *Christopher* case, sometimes the recipient has changed circumstances. In the case of a new stepparent, remarrying may reduce the mother's child support from her ex-spouse.[17] Some jurisdictions automatically terminate child support as a material change of circumstance upon the custodial parent's remarriage. Is this fair? Why should the father no longer have a duty to his child? Some states even allow reductions when the custodial parent cohabitates with another person.

In the *Gowins v. Gary* case in Georgia, the courts looked at the issue of modifying a child support award based on the mother/custodial parent's alleged extravagant behavior. In this case, twins were born to Diana Gowins and W. E. Gary, "who were not married to each other, entered into a July 2002 settlement agreement placing sole legal custody of the children with Gowins and obligating Gary to pay, inter alia, child support in the amount of $14,000 per month per child."[18] "In November 2005, Gary petitioned to modify his monthly support obligation for the twins, asserting that a change in circumstances authorized a payment reduction."[19] "Gary subsequently sought to modify the agreement and reduce this payment, arguing, among other things, that Gowins was using the money to sustain her own lifestyle and finance questionable investments, rather than to support the twins.[3] The trial court denied Gary's request by enforcing the settlement agreement and its $28,000 monthly obligation through an April 2005 child support judgment. In its order, the trial court found that although Gowins had not been 'a good steward of the monies provided her,' she was 'attempting to provide the twins with a life-style as nearly comparable as possible to the lifestyle [Gary's other children] enjoyed.' The trial court further found that Gowins was unemployed at the time and had no monthly income."

"Approximately seven months later, Gary filed the petition at issue in this case, seeking a downward modification of his monthly support payment. He again asserted that Gowins was misusing the child support payments and spending the money to improve her own lifestyle, as

---

17 Not to mention remove her alimony; see discussion in Chapter 12.

18 *Gowins v. Gary*, 654 SE 2d 162—Ga: Court of Appeals, 2007, http://scholar.google.com/scholar_case?case=1366 7595966791878273&hl=en&as_sdt=2&as_vis=1&oi=scholarr

19 Ibid.

well as the lifestyle of an older child fathered by another man. He further argued that the $28,000 monthly support obligation greatly exceeded the twins' needs."

"Following a hearing, the trial court reduced Gary's monthly support payment. The trial court found that Gowins was still unemployed, but that her gross monthly income equaled $28,240—the support payment from Gary plus $240 she received in child support from her older child's father. It also found that the value of Gowins's home had appreciated, that her credit rating had improved, and that she had received a capital gain from an investment in 2005. The court expressed dismay at Gowins's spending habits and her inability to manage the money received from Gary, and it noted that she spent a significant amount of that money on herself and her older child."[20]

"Ultimately, the trial court concluded that Gowins did not need $28,000 per month to support the twins. It also determined that her financial status had improved and that she was capable of obtaining employment. It thus reduced Gary's direct monthly payment to Gowins from $28,000 to $5,000." Gowins appealed to the Georgia Court of Appeals, which reversed the lower court's reduction in support, for, among several reasons, the fact that the court failed to find that the twins' needs had changed, so that "overpayment is not a basis for modification. Rather, the focus must be on a change in circumstances."[21] On the issue of whether the mother's failure to work should be taken into consideration in changing the amount of child support, the appellate court wrote that, "the trial court noted that Gowins had not attempted to secure employment, despite her ability to work. Gowins, however, was not working when the trial court entered its April 2005 order," and went on to say that the lower court did not indicate the necessary change in circumstance and that her lack of employment "simply maintained the status quo."[22]

"[T]he trial court found that Gowins' credit rating had improved. It is unclear whether this finding impacted the modification determination. But unless the improved credit rating is linked to a change in income or financial status, this rating should not factor into the trial court's decision."[23]

The appellate court concluded, "[u]ndoubtedly, the trial court was concerned about Gowins' spending habits, failure to obtain employment, and mismanagement of the significant sums paid by Gary. But it initially approved the $28,000 support payment in April 2005, despite many of these same concerns. And although Gary claims that the monthly obligation—to which he agreed through settlement—is excessive, it cannot be altered unless he shows that a change in circumstances requires reconsideration."[24] The appellate court then vacated the lower court's judgment and remanded the case with direction.[25]

---

20 Ibid.
21 Ibid.
22 Ibid.
23 Ibid.
24 Ibid.
25 Ibid.

This case makes clear that modification of a child support order requires the demonstration of a material change in circumstance. But should the custodial parent be penalized if he uses the child support for an investment that generates a profit? How about if the custodial parent lives a lavish lifestyle? Or raises a non-biological sibling in the home, too? Should the court consider a custodial parent's unemployment in determining child support? Does a mother of two young twins have a right to be a "stay-at-home mom" without the court penalizing her?[26]

ENFORCEMENT

"Howard Veal, of Michigan, fathered 23 children with 14 women, including one baby a year for 10 years from 1988 to 1998, according to the Michigan attorney general. Problem is, Veal also racked up $533,000 on late child-support payments. So on Sept. 24, a local judge sentenced him to two to four years in prison, a much stricter penalty than the guidelines suggest."[27] Veal, who is on unemployment, lives with a woman who "has a newly built home and two cars, one of which is a Mercedes."[28]

The term "**deadbeat dad**"[29] was coined because, statistically, a high percentage of noncustodial fathers do not pay their child support. Federal laws have made it easier for parents to cross state lines to force an out-of-state obligor to pay child support.[30] Also, federal and state laws working together have helped to enforce child support payment obligations. Under state laws, a person who fails to make child support payments (in some cases, even one), may have wages garnished which then go directly to the custodial parent for payment. Also, a lien may be placed on real estate (which prevents selling without repayment of the debt first). Most effective are laws that suspend a license for failing to pay support. Licenses can range anywhere from a driver's license, a business or professional license (e.g., plumber, lawyer, or stylist), to possibly even a hunting or fishing license. Tax refunds can also be diverted from the obligor to the custodial parent. Finally, since child support is court ordered, a judge can find an obligor in contempt, either civilly or criminally, for failing to make payments. Under this method, the parent is put in jail until they pay the debt or agree to do so. Should this be the enforcement remedy of last resort? If a parent is in jail, will they be able to earn money to pay off the debt?

Beyond the traditional remedies of taking away licenses and using wage garnishments, is there anything else that would be effective to combat this problem? Why is it that a parent thinks it

---

26 Contrast this with the recent British cases that may allow stay at home mothers to gain some of their partner's economic windfalls years after their divorces are final (see chapter 12). Which is right?

27 http://healthland.time.com/2010/10/04/man-owes-half-a-million-in-child-support/, "Michigan Man Owes Half a Million Dollars in Child Support," Belinda Luscombe, *Time* Health and Family, October 4, 2010.

28 Ibid. According to the attorney general's memo.

29 Indeed, Congress passed a bill in 1998 called the "Deadbeat Parents Punishment Act" (18 U.S.C. Section 228) (2006).

30 The Full Faith and Credit for Child Support Orders Act, 28 U.S.S. Section 1738 (2006).

is acceptable to pay the cable or car payment while ignoring child's support when faced with a variety of bills? In Ohio, Judge James Walther, saying that, "[i]t's your personal responsibility to pay for these kids," ordered a father to "stop having children."[31] In that case, Asim Taylor, 35, had failed repeatedly failed to pay child support for his four children. When he was indicted in 2011, he owed back child support of over $78,000,[32] which had ballooned to $96,000 when he finally pleaded guilty to failure to pay child support. Taylor's attorney said, "It's not a question whether or not he wants to have more kids. It's a question of whether or not the government should be telling somebody that they can or they can't."[33] What is the effect of the *Redhail v. Zoblicki* case (Chapter 5) on this type of penalty?

When a parent fails to take financial responsibility for a child, everyone loses: the child, the custodial parent, and the taxpayer. But in cases like *Veal*, should women who continue to have children with men who have already not provided financially for their other children also be blamed? Beyond this, while financial support helps, can society ever get parents to provide more, such as a relationship with their children?

Limited to money issues?

At the hearing for child support for their seven-month-old boy, Messiah Martin, the father requested that the baby's last name be changed to his family name of McCullogh. The Judge agreed to the last name change but also unilaterally changed the child's first name to Martin from Messiah, "saying the religious name was earned by one person and 'that one person is Jesus Christ.'"[34] Her decision was overturned in chancery court a month later, she resigned and was censured by the Board of Judicial Conduct.[35]

AS WE GO TO PRESS

Should parents who are in prison pay child support? "Of the 2.2 million people incarcerated in the United States about half are parents, and at least 1 in 5 have a child-support obligation."[36] How will they pay it when prisoners often make $40 per month in prison jobs? A 2010 administration survey found 51,000 federal prisoners had child support orders, with almost 29,000 of the prisoners behind on payments. The average amount owed was nearly $24,000.[37] When they do

---

31 http://newsfeed.time.com/2013/01/28/judge-orders-man-owing-96k-in-child-support-to-stop-having-kids/, "Judge Orders Man Owing $96K in Child Support to Stop Having Kids," Erica Ho, January 28, 2013, *Time* newsfeed.
32 Ibid.
33 Ibid.
34 "Judge changes boy's name from Messiah", *The Washington Post, The Nation*, August 12, 2013, P.A3.
35 "Magistrate censured for 'Messiah' ruling," *The Washington Post*, Digest, March 3, 2014.
36 https://www.washingtonpost.com/politics/for-men-in-prison-child-support-becomes-a-crushing-debt/2015/10/18/e751a324-5bb7-11e5-b38e-06883aacba64_story.html?utm_term=.54f454b97183
37 http://www.reuters.com/article/us-usa-criminaljustice-childsupport-idUSKBN12E0X2

not make their child support payments, penalties and interests start to build up and federal law prohibits retroactive child support debt reduction. While most states allow prisoners to modify their child support payments to amounts that reflect their status, fourteen states do not. In those states incarceration is a form of "'voluntary impoverishment'".[38] As his administration wound down in the fall of 2016, President Obama worked to finalize regulations to classify incarceration as "'involuntary'" and thus allow modifications of the amount of child support due to accurately reflect a prison salary.[39] Prisoners who accrue huge debts have a harder time finding legal jobs. They can even be put back in jail because of child support debts.

Yet, some Republicans objected arguing it undercut welfare reform, with its emphasis on collecting child support so tax payers would not have to pay. Speaker of the House of Representatives Paul Ryan introduced a bill to block the Obama change, but it did not pass into law.[40] Now that Representative Ryan and the Republicans are in control what will happen on this issue?

CHAPTER SOURCE

Weisberg, D. Kelly. (2011). *Emanuel Law lines*, Family Law.

---

38   https://www.washingtonpost.com/politics/for-men-in-prison-child-support-becomes-a-crushing-debt/2015/10/18/e751a324-5bb7-11e5-b38e-06883aacba64_story.html?utm_term=.54f454b97183
39   http://www.reuters.com/article/us-usa-criminaljustice-childsupport-idUSKBN12E0X2
40   Ibid.

PARENTAL RIGHTS TERMINATION AND ADOPTION

22

These considerations are why domestic relations pose the hardest problems for judges. If we could appoint King Solomon, who was the first domestic relations judge, as special master, we could do it. But we can't do it.
—U.S. Supreme Court Justice Anthony M. Kennedy,[1]
at the oral argument on the case of
Adoptive Couple v. Baby Girl, April 16, 2013

There are times when the adoption process is exhausting and painful and makes you want to scream. But, I am told, so does childbirth.
—Scott Simon[2]

Adoption involves the termination of a parent's rights to his child so that another person can step into the parent's shoes and become the parent. Unlike custody arrangements, a decision to sever parental rights cannot be undone. Sometimes, this termination is voluntary, and sometimes it is done at the direction of the state through a court order, often because of neglect, abuse, or endangerment.

HISTORY

Adoption is one area in Family Law that is truly American law. In keeping with its emphasis on illegitimacy and blood lines, England did not have an adoption system. The British housed their unwanted children in large orphanages notoriously depicted by Charles Dickens in *Oliver Twist*, with the line, "Please sir, I want some more." In America, as with other family law issues, adoption laws are driven by state statute.

---

1 At the oral argument on the case of *Adoptive Couple v. Baby Girl*, April 16, 2013.
2 *Baby, We Were Meant for Each Other: In Praise of Adoption*, Random House, 2010.

One common rule is that adoptions must be made in the "best interest of the child." Also, blood relatives are favored over non-blood relatives. Beyond this, the decision is left to the court. As a result, issues like the prospective adopting parents' ability to have a child (and issues of sterility and infertility) can sway some court's favorable decisions. Is this fair? What about divorcing parents, should the court disfavor them? What is the effect of the proposed parent's age—is it discriminatory to consider their age? Should a court allow a 70-year-old to adopt a child? Should a 57-year-old be able to adopt a younger adult? What about stepparents—should it be assumed they will adopt when they marry the biological mother? What happens when a biological father has not terminated his rights before the adoption? Finally, what happens if the adopting parents want to void the adoption? Can the adoption agency be held responsible for a misrepresentation? Although adoption is a relatively "new" area of the law (around since the mid-19th century), the problem it deals with is a diminishing one. In the United States and many countries, there are shortages of newborn children who need families and are available for adoption. Would a foreign country pass a law banning Americans from adopting?

TYPES AND FACTORS

There are two general types of adoption. The first, **private adoption**, occurs when the biological parent(s) arrange with a lawyer (or some other intermediary) to allow the adoption of their child to another person(s). The second, **agency adoption** is when a licensed adoption agency puts a baby up for adoption. Remember, as the *Baby M* case stressed, it is illegal to sell a baby; a mother may only be reimbursed financially for her "medical expenses." (Chapter 15)

Because the biological parents must terminate their parental rights to the child before an adoption may take place, generally, parental consent is necessary. If a relative is available for the adoption, the court will prefer the relative to a nonrelative. Often, with a shortage of available children (especially newborns), biological parents are able to select the adopting parents from a "beauty pageant"–like display of information. Ten years ago, prospective parents created elaborate photo albums detailing all the benefits of an adoption with them, including information on careers, assets, and school systems. Now, prospective parents post elaborate profiles on adoptive websites.

Like custody determinations, the standard for determining an adoption placement is the "best interest of the child." Unlike custody, issues of the child's age, sexual orientation (often of the parents), race, ethnicity, and religion may dictate an adoption determination. Courts have discretion in making the adoption. Sometimes a factor can be deemed relevant, but not conclusive.

1. RACE

Should race have anything to do with adoption cases?

White foster parents brought action to challenge on constitutional grounds the refusal of a county adoption agency to allow them to adopt a child of mixed racial parentage. The foster parents alleged that the county agency's denial of their application was based solely on racial grounds and therefore violated their rights to equal protection and due process. The United States District Court for the Northern District of Georgia, Charles A. Moye, Jr., J., 408 F.Supp. 382, dismissed the complaint, and plaintiffs appealed. The Court of Appeals, Tuttle, Circuit Judge, 547 F.2d 835, reversed and remanded. A rehearing en banc was granted, and the Court of Appeals, Roney, Circuit Judge, held that: (1) under the circumstances, the consolidation of the hearing on the preliminary injunction with trial on the merits was a responsible exercise of judicial discretion; (2) the district court's finding that race was not used in an automatic fashion to reject plaintiffs' adoption application was not clearly erroneous; (3) the difficulties inherent in interracial adoption justified the consideration of race as a relevant factor in placing children for adoption; (4) the relationship between plaintiffs and their foster child was not within the constitutionally protected familial right to privacy; (5) the facts did not give rise to a constitutional claim for harm to reputation; (6) the child had no constitutionally protected due process right to a stable environment which would preclude his being moved from home to home without a prior hearing, and (7) under all the circumstances, the procedures used by the adoption agency struck a constitutionally adequate compromise among the various interests involved and rendered whatever process was due.

Decision of the District Court affirmed.

Godbold, Circuit Judge, concurred in part and filed statement.

RONEY, Circuit Judge:

Plaintiffs, Robert and Mildred Drummond, a white couple, acted as state-designated foster parents of a mixed race child for over two years. When the defendant state adoption agency decided to remove the child for permanent placement in another home, plaintiffs commenced this action under 42 U.S.C.A. s 1983. Alleging denial of their rights under both the equal protection and the due process clauses of the Fourteenth Amendment, they sought preliminary and permanent injunctive relief, which was denied by the district court. Although a panel of this Court reversed, Drummond v. Fulton

County Department of Family & Children's Services, 547 F.2d 835 (5th Cir. 1977), the full Court finds no deprivation of constitutional rights and affirms the dismissal of plaintiffs' complaint.

Initially, the en banc Court adopts the discussion, reasoning and result contained in the dissenting opinion to the panel decision in this matter as the correct statement of the law in this case. That opinion is reported in 547 F.2d at 857–861. We further address the issues here, however, in view of the oral argument before the full Court, a subsequent case decided by the United States Supreme Court, and supplemental briefs filed with this Court.

The factual background of this dispute is set out in full in Judge Tuttle's thorough opinion for the panel which considered this case. 547 F.2d 835–857. A brief recapitulation will suffice to place the following discussion in context.

In December 1973 in an emergency situation, a one-month-old mixed race child named Timmy was placed for temporary care in the home of Mr. and Mrs. Drummond by the Fulton County children's service agency. Lengthy proceedings were commenced to determine whether the child should be permanently removed from his natural mother's custody and placed for adoption.

Within a year, the Drummonds had become sufficiently attached to Timmy to request permission to adopt him. The Drummonds had not signed an agreement that they would not try to adopt their foster child, as is common practice with many placement agencies. Although the level of care provided by them as foster parents had consistently been rated excellent, there was an emerging consensus within the defendant child placement agency charged with Timmy's care that it would be best to look elsewhere for a permanent adoptive home. When this was explained to the Drummonds *1204 in March 1975 they appeared to acquiesce. By August of that year, however, they had renewed their request to adopt Timmy.

The child was not legally freed for adoption by the Georgia courts until September 1975. Because this signaled the end of any attempt to return Timmy to his natural mother, the agency began a more focused consideration of what ultimate placement would be best for Timmy. After a number of discussions with the Drummonds, a final decision-making meeting was held in November 1975 with 19 agency employees present. Although the Drummonds were not present at this meeting, caseworkers who had dealt with them during the past two years did attend. As a result of that meeting a final agency decision was made to remove Timmy from the Drummond home and to deny the Drummonds' adoption application. It is clear that the race of the Drummonds and of Timmy and the racial attitudes of the parties were given substantial weight in coming to this conclusion. The agency employees were also aware that as Timmy grew older he would retain the characteristics of his black father. A few months later the plaintiffs filed suit....

After hearing six witnesses and arguments of counsel the court, by verbal order, dismissed the complaint on the merits. In rendering that decision, the court made the following finding:

It is obvious that race did enter into the decision of the Department.... (I)t appears to the Court...
that the consideration of race was properly directed to the best interest of the child and was not an
automatic-type of thing or of placement, that is, that all blacks go to black families, all whites go to
white families, and all mixed children go to black families, which would be prohibited.

On appeal counsel was appointed to represent Timmy's separate interest in this litigation.

The case as now presented to the en banc Court formulates four major issues for resolution: (1) did the action of the defendant constitute a denial of equal protection; (2) do the Drummonds have a protected liberty or property right in their relationship with Timmy; (3) does Timmy have such a right; and (4) if such rights exist, how much procedural protection is required in order to safeguard them?

I.

The Drummonds and counsel for Timmy contend that the state denied them equal protection of the laws because of the extent to which race was considered in making the adoption decision. Although the complaint alleged that race was the sole determining factor, the district court found that this was not the case, and the finding was not clearly erroneous. The argument has thus centered on the question of whether a state agency, charged with the responsibility of placing for adoption a child in its custody, may take into consideration the race of the child and the race of the prospective adoptive parents without violating the equal protection clause of the United States Constitution...

The manner in which race was considered in this case frames the precise issue before us. The district court found that race was not used in an automatic fashion. The Drummonds' application was not automatically rejected on racial grounds. This finding may not be disturbed*1205 here because not clearly erroneous. Fed.R.Civ.P. 52(a); *United States v. United States* Gypsum Co., 333 U.S. 364, 68 S.Ct. 525, 92 L.Ed. 746 (1948). But can race be taken into account, perhaps decisively if it is the factor which tips the balance between two potential families, where it is not used automatically? We conclude, as did another court which grappled with the problem, that "the difficulties inherent in interracial adoption" justify the consideration of "race as a relevant factor in adoption,..." *Compos v. McKeithen*, 341 F.Supp. 264, 266 (E.D.La.1972) (three-judge court)...

In this regard, the Supreme Court has recently provided some guidance. It appears that even if government activity has a racially disproportionate impact, the impact alone does not sustain a claim of racial discrimination. "Proof of racially discriminatory intent or purpose is required to show a violation...." *Arlington Heights v. Metropolitan Housing Corp.*, 429 U.S. 252, 265, 97 S.Ct. 555, 563, 50 L.Ed.2d 450 (1977). There has been no suggestion before this Court that the defendants had any purposes other than to act in the best interest of the child when it considered race. Furthermore, the Supreme Court has recently stated in the sensitive area of voting apportionment that the consideration of race is not impermissible. *United Jewish Organizations of Williamsburgh, Inc. v. Carey*, 430 U.S. 144, 97 S.Ct. 996, 51

L.Ed.2d 229 (1977). As the plurality opinion in that case remarks, where race is considered in a non-discriminatory fashion and there is "no racial slur or stigma with respect to whites or any other race," there is no discrimination violative of the Fourteenth Amendment. 430 U.S. at 165, 97 S.Ct. at 1009.

In concluding that there has been no denial of equal protection in these circumstances, we note the following factors.

First, consideration of race in the child placement process suggests no racial slur or stigma in connection with any race. It is a natural thing for children to be raised by parents of their same ethnic background.

Second, no case has been cited to the Court suggesting that it is impermissible to consider race in adoption placement. The only cases which have addressed this problem indicate that, while the automatic use of race is barred, the use of race as one of the factors in making the ultimate decision is legitimate. In re *Adoption of a Minor*, 97 U.S.App.D.C. 99, 101, 228 F.2d 446, 448 (1955); *Compos v. McKeithen*, 341 F.Supp. 264, 266 (E.D.La.1972)...

Third, the professional literature on the subject of transracial child placement stresses the importance of considering the racial attitudes of potential parents. The constitutional strictures against racial discrimination are not mandates to ignore the accumulated experience of unbiased professionals. A couple has no right to adopt a child it is not equipped to rear, and according to the professional literature race bears directly on that inquiry. From the child's perspective, the consideration of race is simply another facet of finding him the best possible home. Rather than eliminating certain categories of homes from consideration it avoids the potentially tragic possibility of placing a child in a home with parents who will not be able to cope with the child's problems.

Fourth, in the analogous inquiry over the permissibility of considering the religion of would-be adoptive parents, numerous courts have found no constitutional infirmity. See generally, Annot. Religion as a Factor in Adoption, 48 A.L.R.3d 383 (1973). Those cases make the same distinction as this Court makes in the racial context. So long as religion is not an automatic factor, its consideration as one of a number of factors is unobjectionable.

Finally, adoption agencies quite frequently try to place a child where he can most easily become a normal family member. The duplication of his natural biological environment is a part of that program. Such factors as age, hair color, eye color and facial features of parents and child are considered in reaching a decision. This flows from the belief that a child and adoptive*1206 parents can best adjust to a normal family relationship if the child is placed with adoptive parents who could have actually parented him. To permit consideration of physical characteristics necessarily carries with it permission to consider racial characteristics. This Court does not have the professional expertise to assess the wisdom of that type of inquiry, but it is our province to conclude, as we do today, that the use of race as one of those factors is not unconstitutional...

AFFIRMED.

JOHN R. BROWN, Chief Judge, concurring:

While I agree with the views expressed by Judge Roney and concur fully in the result and opinion, I feel that some comment is warranted focusing on the practicalities and realities of the unfortunate situation which confronts us...

As to the last of these topics, not only do I agree with Judge Roney's conclusion that race may be considered as "a" factor in adoptions without violating the equal protection clause, but I would state that as a practical matter, it should be so considered. Indeed, adoption personnel would be blinking at reality if they failed to consider the race of the adoptive parents vis-a-vis the child. I would also go so far as to state that they could give substantial weight to race as a factor including consideration of such things as the geographical location and area attitudes involved without treading dangerously on equal protection rights. Indeed, agency personnel, without violating the Fourteenth Amendment, could expressly declare that the racial difference between the child and the "adoptive" parents was the primary reason for making the child placement decision. Granted that society and the community should not harbor attitudes against interracial mixture, the subject of the foster home placement and even adoption is the child, whose life will be affected by community values and prejudices *1212 as they exist, not what they ought to be.

Lastly, it would be unwise, and to my mind, an arrogation of power for Federal Judges to voyage into the supersensitive realm of state adoption matters. To set standards as the dissent would require sounds easy. But inevitably that process involves policy choices which go to the heart of the welfare of the child, probably for the rest of the child's life. On what do we draw in making these choices? Are we, as Federal Judges, endowed with sufficient prescience to decide such delicate issues? We should remind ourselves that we do not possess the wisdom of Solomon and that Timmy's adoption is not as blissfully simple as cutting the baby in half.

As this case shows, race may be relevant to the adoption determination. Should it be? "Since 1996, it has been illegal to consider race when determining whether families are suitable to raise adopted children—the law was intended to increase adoptions of black children, who are disproportionately represented in the foster care system, by making it easier for whites to take them home."[3] A 2008 study said that [4] "transracial adoptees report struggling to fit in with their peers,

---

3 The 1996 Multiethnic Placement Act—Interethnic Adoption Provision (MEPA—IEP), which Congress passed in response to headlines about white parents who wanted to adopt black children but were thwarted by race-matching policies prohibited any adoption agency receiving federal funds from factoring race into decisions on foster care and adoption, was meant to widen the pool of prospective permanent homes for black children. http://www.time.com/time/health/article/0,8599,1809722,00.html#ixzz2QazoyU4R, "Should Race Be a Factor in Adoptions?" Jeninne Lee-St. John, *Time* Health and Family, May 27, 2008.
4 "Finding Families for African American Children," a 2008 study by the Evan B. Donaldson Adoption Institute, that studies and provides education on adoption, based on review of national statistics and studies on transracial adoptions in the U.S. over the past two decades, in which "the institute argues that race should be a factor in adoption placement, and that agencies should be allowed to screen non-black families who want to adopt black children—for their ability to teach self-esteem and defense against racism, and for their level of interaction with other black people." Ibid.

their communities and even with their own families. The study also says that minority children adopted by white parents are likely to express a desire to be white, and black transracial adoptees have higher rates of behavioral problems than Asian or Native American children adopted transracially; they also exhibit more problems than biracial or white adoptees, or the biological children of adoptive parents." Arguments have been made that transracial adoptions are not in a child of color's best interest because, among other things, it deprives the child of their cultural heritage and created a backlog of available black children. Yet, under the law adoption agencies are prohibited "them from preparing white parents for race-specific challenges they might face raising black children." "Black children are adopted less frequently and more slowly than kids of any other race. Fifteen percent of U.S. children are black, but they account for nearly a third of children in foster care and a third of those awaiting adoption." Are these policies in the child's best interest?[5]

2. RELIGIOUS MATCHING

Similarly, many states support a match of religions between the child and the adopting parent(s). Religious matching generally means that "whenever practicable" or "if possible," an adoption should occur to prospective parents who are of the same religion. Similar arguments of cultural history are raised as in transracial adoptions. Assuming that the adoption agency is faith-based, this policy is understandable. However, when the state is the adoption agency, is it still appropriate to use the religious matching rule, or does this run contrary to the Establishment clause as discussed in the custody cases? Moreover, is a child's religious preference the issue, or is it really about the biological parents' preference? Does a newborn child have a best-interest concern that is protected by a religious preference?

3. GAY ADOPTION

When states were still mixed on recognizing and allowing marriage equality, the law was also mixed on whether to allow gay couples to adopt. After the *Obergefell v. Hodges* decision (see Chapter 6), only one state, Mississippi, specifically barred gay and lesbian couples from adopting children.

"The one-sentence Mississippi law—which reads, simply, 'Adoption by couples of the same gender is prohibited'—was adopted in 2000. While several other states, including Alabama, Florida, Nebraska and Michigan, had similar bans, all have since been overturned."[6] In March 2016, "U.S. District Judge Daniel Jordan issued a preliminary injunction against the ban, citing the

---

5   http://www.time.com/time/health/article/0,8599,1809722,00.html#ixzz2QazoyU4R, "Should Race Be a Factor in Adoptions?" Jeninne Lee-St. John, *Time* Health and Family, May 27, 2008.

6   http://www.huffingtonpost.com/entry/mississippi-same-sex-adoption_us_56fdb1a3e4b083f5c607567f

Supreme Court's decision legalizing same-sex marriage nationwide last summer… The Supreme Court ruling 'foreclosed litigation over laws interfering with the right to marry and rights and responsibilities intertwined with marriage,' Jordan wrote. 'It also seems highly unlikely that the same court that held a state cannot ban gay marriage because it would deny benefits—expressly including the right to adopt—would then conclude that married gay couples can be denied that very same benefit.'[7] "Some states still have restrictions on fostering children."[8]

Before federal law required all states to recognize marriage equity, some same-sex couples used the law of adoption to give their partners some of the benefits of marriage. Again, because adoption is driven by state law, many states refused to allow same-sex couples to use adoption as "a quasi-matrimonial vehicle to provide non-married partners with a legal imprimatur for their sexual relationship, and because adoption is entirely statutory and is in derogation of common law, the legislative purposes and mandates must be strictly observed."

MATTER OF ROBERT PAUL P. (N.Y. 1984.)
63 N.Y.2D 233

---

471 N.E.2d 424, 481 N.Y.S.2d 652, 42 A.L.R.4th 765, 53 USLW 2224

OPINION OF THE COURT
Jasen, J.

We are asked to decide whether it was error for Family Court to deny the petition of a 57-year-old male to adopt a 50-year-old male with whom he shares a homosexual relationship.

Appellants are two adult males who have resided together continuously for more than 25 years. The older of the two, who was 57 years of age when this proceeding was commenced, submitted a petition to adopt the younger, aged 50 at the time. The two share a homosexual relationship and desire an adoption for social, financial and emotional reasons. FN1 Following a hearing at which both parties to the prospective adoption testified, and upon receipt of a probation investigation that was favorable to the parties, Family Court denied the petition. That court concluded that the parties were

---

7   Ibid.
8   Ibid.

attempting to utilize an adoption for the purposes properly served by marriage, wills and business contracts and that the parties lacked any semblance of a parent-child relationship.

The parties' affidavit, attached to the petition, states the following reasons for the proposed adoption:

> *The Appellate Division unanimously affirmed, without opinion, and granted leave to appeal to this court. We now affirm for the reasons that follow.*

> "2. *The two of us have lived together for a period of over 25 years. We consider ourselves to be a family, though this might not be true in the traditional sense. Though not the only reason for our petition, our present living arrangements, in a leased apartment, are not formalized and we fear the possibility of eviction; our financial and personal lives are entwined together and though it is not expected, we are concerned about the disposition of our estates upon death and lastly, though not least, we expect to live out our lives together and are concerned about the ability and right under the law for each of us to take care of the other should unexpected events occur.*

> "3. *Though the above reasons indicate financial, economic and practical considerations for our petition, not of any lesser extent and perhaps of more importance, are the many personal, emotional and sentimental reasons for which we present our petition. Simply stated we are a family and seek to formalize such.*" *236

Our adoption statute embodies the fundamental social concept that the relationship of parent and child may be established by operation of law. (Matter of Upjohn, 304 NY 366, 373.) Despite the absence of any blood ties, in the eyes of the law an adopted child becomes "the natural child of the adoptive parent" with all the attendant personal and proprietary incidents to that relationship. (*Carpenter v Buffalo Gen. Elec. Co.*, 213 NY 101, 108.) Indeed, the adoption laws of New York, as well as those of most of the States, reflect the general acceptance of the ancient principle of adoptio naturam imitatur—i.e., adoption imitates nature, which originated in Roman jurisprudence (Wadlington, Minimum Age Difference As A Requisite for Adoption, 1966 Duke LJ 392, 392–396), which, in turn, served as a guide for the development of adoption statutes in this country. (Howe, Adoption Practice, Issues and Laws 1958–1983, 17 Family LQ 173, 173–177; Wadlington, Adoption of Adults: A Family Law Anomaly, 54 Cornell L Rev 566, 567; Huard, Law of Adoption: Ancient and Modern, 9 V and L Rev 743, 748; Matter of Livingston, 151 App Div 1–2.)

In imitating nature, adoption in New York, as explicitly defined in section 110 of the Domestic Relations Law, is "the legal proceeding whereby a person takes another person into the relation of child and thereby acquires the rights and incurs the responsibilities of parent." (Emphasis supplied.) It is plainly not a quasi-matrimonial vehicle to provide nonmarried partners with a legal imprimatur for their sexual relationship, be it heterosexual or homosexual. (See, e.g., *Stevens v Halstead*, 181 App Div 198.) Moreover, any such sexual intimacy is utterly repugnant to the relationship between child and parent in our society, and only a patently incongruous application of our adoption laws—wholly inconsistent with the underlying public policy of providing a parent-child relationship for the welfare of the child (Matter of *Malpica-Orsini*, 36 NY2d 568, 571-572, app dsmd sub nom. *Orsini v Blasi*, 423 US 1042; Matter of Upjohn, supra; Howe, op cit , 17 Family LQ, at pp 176–179; Huard, op cit , 9 V and L Rev, at pp 748–749)—would permit the employment of adoption as the legal formalization of an adult relationship between sexual partners under the guise of parent and child. *237

While the adoption of an adult has long been permitted under the Domestic Relations Law, there is no exception made in such adoptions to the expressed purpose of legally formalizing a parent-child relationship. Adoption laws in this State, first enacted in 1873, initially only provided for the "adoption of minor children by adult persons". (L 1873, ch 830.) As early as 1915, however, the statute was amended to allow adoption of "a person of the age of twenty-one years and upwards" (L 1915, ch 352) and presently the law simply provides that an unmarried adult or married adults together "may adopt another person" without any restriction on the age of the "adoptive child" or "adoptee". (Domestic Relations Law, §§ 110, 109, subd 1.) Despite these and other statutory changes since adoption came into existence in New York, the basic function of giving legal effect to a parent-child relationship has remained unaltered.

Indeed, although the statutory prerequisites may be less compelling than in the case of the adoption of a minor, an adult adoption must still be "in the best interests of the *[adoptive]* child" and "the familial, social, religious, emotional and financial circumstances of the adoptive parents which may be relevant" must still be investigated. (Domestic Relations Law, § 116, subds 2, 3, 4.) Neither the explicit statutory purpose nor criteria have been diluted for adult adoptions, and this court has no basis for undoing what the Legislature has left intact.

Moreover, deference to the narrow legislative purpose is especially warranted with adoption, a legal relationship unknown at common law. (*Betz v Horr*, 276 NY 83, 86-87; Matter of Thorne, 155 NY 140, 143.) It exists only by virtue of the legislative acts that authorize it. Although adoption was widely practiced by the Egyptians, Greeks and Romans, it was unknown in England until the Adoption of Children Act of 1926, more than 50 years subsequent to the enactment of adoption laws in New York. (See, generally, Huard, op cit, 9 V and L Rev 943; see, also, Matter of *Clark*, 87 Cal 638, 641—adoption was "unknown to the common law" and "repugnant to *[its]* principles".) Adoption in this State is "solely the creature of, and regulated by, statute law" (Matter of *Eaton*, 305 NY 162, 165) and ""[t]he Legislature has supreme control of the subject"". (*Carpenter v *238 Buffalo Gen. Elec. Co.*, supra, at p 107, quoting Matter of *Cook*, 187 NY 253, 260.) Consequently, because adoption is entirely statutory and is in derogation of common law, the legislative purposes and mandates must be strictly observed. FN2 (See Matter of *Malpica-Orsini*, supra, at p 570; Matter of *Santacose*, 271 App Div 11, 16; 2 NY Jur, Adoption, § 3.) FN2 It is true, as the dissent notes (dissenting opn, at p 241), that this court has stated in the past that "the adoption statute 'has been most liberally and beneficently applied'" (Matter of *Malpica-Orsini,* 36 NY2d 568, 572). However, a closer look at this court's opinion in that case reveals that the statute is thusly to be applied only "[i]n harmony with the legislative policy" which is the "fundamental social concept that the relationship of parent and child*** may be established" (id., at pp 571–572). It is clear that we were addressing only the beneficent promotion of the "humanitarian principles" involved in "establishing a real home for a child" (id.)—not a liberal expansion of the underlying purposes and application of the adoption statute beyond that intended by the Legislature.

Here, where the appellants are living together in a homosexual relationship and where no incidents of a parent-child relationship are evidenced or even remotely within the parties' intentions, no fair interpretation of our adoption laws can permit a granting of the petition. Adoption is not a means of obtaining a legal status for a nonmarital sexual relationship—whether homosexual or heterosexual. Such would be a "cynical distortion of the function of adoption." (Matter of *Adult Anonymous II,* 88 AD2d 30, 38 *[Sullivan, J. P., dissenting].*) Nor is it a procedure by which to legitimize an emotional attachment, however sincere, but wholly devoid of the filial relationship that is fundamental to the concept of adoption.

While there are no special restrictions on adult adoptions under the provisions of the Domestic Relations Law, the Legislature could not have intended that the statute be employed "to arrive at an unreasonable or absurd result." (*Williams v Williams,* 23 NY2d 592, 599.) Such would be the result if the Domestic Relations Law were interpreted to permit one lover, homosexual or heterosexual, to adopt the other and enjoy the sanction of the law on their feigned union as parent and child.

There are many reasons why one adult might wish to adopt another that would be entirely consistent with the basic nature of adoption, including the following: a childless individual might wish to perpetuate a family name; *239 two individuals might develop a strong filial affection for one another; a stepparent might wish to adopt the spouse's adult children; or adoption may have been forgone, for whatever reason, at an earlier date. (See Wadlington, Adoption of Adults: A Family Law Anomaly, 54 Cornell L Rev 566, at p 571, n 26, and p 578.) But where the relationship between the adult parties is utterly incompatible with the creation of a parent-child relationship between them, the adoption process is certainly not the proper vehicle by which to formalize their partnership in the eyes of the law. Indeed, it would be unreasonable and disingenuous for us to attribute a contrary intent to the Legislature. FN3

FN3 The dissent's reliance on *People v Onofre* (51 NY2d 476) is misplaced. (Dissenting opn, at pp 239, 241, 241–242.) The issue in this case is not whether private consensual homosexual conduct is legally proscribable—this court has already answered that question in the negative (id.) and the decision today in no way affects or conflicts with that holding. The sole issue addressed today is whether adoption under the Domestic Relations Law is an appropriate means to legally formalize an indisputedly and entirely nonfilial relationship between sexual partners—regardless of whether their relationship is homosexual or heterosexual. The decision today in no way imposes or chooses a "concept of private morality" nor in any way judges the propriety or morality of the parties' "individual conduct".

If the adoption laws are to be changed so as to permit sexual lovers, homosexual or heterosexual, to adopt one another for the purpose of giving a nonmatrimonial legal status to their relationship, or if a separate institution is to be established for the same purpose, it is for the Legislature, as a matter of State public policy, to do so. Absent any such recognition of that relationship coming from the Legislature, however, the courts ought not to create the same under the rubric of adoption.

Accordingly, the order of the Appellate Division should be affirmed, with costs.
Meyer, J.
(Dissenting).

Having concluded in *People v Onofre* (51 NY2d 476, 490) that government interference with a private consensual homosexual relationship was unconstitutional because it would not "do anything other than restrict individual conduct and impose a concept of private morality chosen by the State", the court now inconsistently refuses to "permit the employment of adoption as the legal formalization of an adult relationship between sexual partners under the guise of parent and child." (Majority opn, at p 236.) *240

The history and background of the adoption laws is sufficiently spelled out by Justice Sidney H. Asch in Matter of *Adult Anonymous* II (88 AD2d 30) and Family Court Judge Leon Deutsch in Matter of *Anonymous* (106 Misc 2d 792) and need not be further developed here. I write, therefore, essentially to emphasize the extent to which, in my view, the majority misconceives the meaning and purpose of article 7 of the Domestic Relations Law.

Under that article the relationship of parent and child is not a condition precedent to adoption; it is rather the result of the adoption proceeding. This is clear from the provisions of sections 110 and 117. The second unnumbered paragraph of section 110 defines "adoption" as "the legal proceeding whereby a person takes another person into the relation of child and thereby acquires the rights and incurs the responsibilities of parent in respect of such other person," (emphasis supplied) and section 117, which spells out the "effect of adoption," provides in the third unnumbered paragraph of subdivision 1 that, "The adoptive parents or parent and the adoptive child shall sustain toward each other the legal relation of parent and child and shall have all the rights and be subject to all the duties of that relation including the rights of inheritance from and through each other and the natural and adopted kindred of the adoptive parents or parent" (emphasis supplied). FN1 From those provisions and the statement in the opening sentence of section 110 that, "An adult unmarried person *** may adopt another person", no other conclusion is possible than that the Legislature has not conditioned adult adoption upon there being a parent-child relationship, but rather has stated that relationship to be the result of adoption. Indeed, had it intended to impose limitations of age, consent of others, sexual orientation, or other such condition upon adult adoption, it could easily have done so. FN2 *241

FN1 Reference in the latter provision to "adoptive parent" and "adoptive child" does not require a contrary conclusion, for subdivision 1 of section 109 defines the former to "mean a person adopting" and the latter to "mean a person adopted."

FN2 (Cf. Cal Civ Code, § 227 p, subd [a] ["Any adult person may adopt any other adult person younger than himself or herself"]; Conn Gen Stats Ann, § 45–67 ["Any person eighteen years of age or older may by written agreement with another person at least eighteen years of age but younger than himself"]; Mass Gen Laws Ann, ch 210, § 1 ["A person of full age may *** adopt as his child another person younger than himself"]; Nev Rev Stats, § 127.190 ["any adult person may adopt any other adult younger than himself"]; see 1953 version of the Uniform Adoption Act, 9 ULA [Master ed.], p 14; Wadlington, Minimum Age Difference as a Requisite For Adoption, 1966 Duke LJ 392, 404–406.)

Nor will it do to argue, as did Justice Joseph P. Sullivan dissenting in Matter of *Adult Anonymous II* (88 AD2d, at p 38), that because the Legislature that provided for adoption of adults continued the proscription against homosexuality, it did not envision adoption as a means of formalizing a homosexual relationship. The wording of section 110 being sufficiently broad to permit such formalization once the prior criminal proscription has been declared unconstitutional, to deny it that effect is to ignore the rule that a court is "not at liberty to restrict by conjecture, or under the guise or pretext of interpretation, the meaning of" the language chosen by the Legislature (*Department of Welfare v Siebel*, 6 NY2d 536, 543, app dsmd 361 US 535; accord *Allen v Minskoff*, 38 NY2d 506, 511). It is "incumbent upon the courts to give effect to legislation as it is written, and not as they or others might think it should be written" (*People v Woman's Christian Assn.*, 56 AD2d 101, 104, on further appeal 59 AD2d 1005, affd 44 NY2d 466; *Lawrence Constr. Corp. v State of New York*, 293 NY 634, 639).

Contrary to the suggestion of the majority that the adoption statute must be strictly construed (majority opn, at p 238), it "has been most liberally and beneficently applied" (Matter of *Malpica-Orsini*, 36 NY2d 568, 572, app dsmd sub nom. *Orsini v Blasi*, 423 US 1042). True, *Stevens v Halstead* (181 App Div 198) held its use for the purpose of passing property from a 70-year-old physically infirm man to a married 47-year-old woman with whom he was living in an adulterous relationship to be improper. But that holding was predicated on the conception that it was "against public policy to admit a couple living in adultery to the relation of parent and child" and because "[t]his meretricious relationship, and the undue influence which imposed the will of defendant on decedent, condemn the adoption." (Id., at p 201.) Here, however, there is no suggestion of undue influence and the relationship, which by the present decision is excised from the adoption statute's broad wording, has, since the Onofre decision, been subject to no legal impediment. That it remains morally offensive to many cannot justify imposing upon the statute a limitation *242 not imposed by the Legislature (*People v Onofre*, 51 NY2d, at p 490; *Department of Welfare v Siebel*, 6 NY2d, at p 543).

What leads to the majority's conclusion that the relationship of the parties "is utterly incompatible with the creation of a parent-child relationship between them" (at p 239) is that it involves a "nonmarital sexual relationship" (at p 238). But nothing in the statute requires an inquiry into or evaluation of the sexual habits of the parties to an adult adoption or the nature of the current relationship between them. It is enough that they are two adults who freely desire the legal status of parent and child. The more particularly is this so in light of the absence from the statute of any requirement that the adoptor be older than the adoptee, for that, if nothing else, belies the majority's concept that adoption under New York statute imitates nature, inexorably and in every last detail.

Under the statute "the relationship of parent and child, with all the personal and property rights incident to it, may be established, independently of blood ties, by operation of law" (Matter of *Malpica-Orsini*, 36 NY2d, at pp 571–572); existence of a parent-child relationship is not a condition of, but a result of, adoption. The motives which prompt the present application (see n 1 to majority opn) are in no way contrary to public policy; in the words of Mr. Justice Holmes, they are "perfectly proper" (*Collamore v Learned*, 171 Mass 99, 100). Absent any contravention of public policy, we should be "concerned only with the clear, unqualified statutory authorization of adoption" (*Bedinger v Graybill's Executor*, 302 SW2d 594, 599 [Ky]; Matter of Berston, 296 Minn 24, 27) and should, therefore, reverse the Appellate Division's order.

Judges Jones, Simons and Kaye concur with Judge Jasen; Judge Meyer dissents and votes to reverse in a separate opinion in which Chief Judge Cooke concurs; Judge Wachtler taking no part.

Order affirmed, with costs. *24

For those gay couples lucky to successfully adopt, marriage equality created problems. Now, when gay marriage was legal, were they prevented from marrying because they were a legal father and son or mother and daughter? Should the courts void their adoptions to allow marriage? In Pennsylvania, an 80 year-old man who had adopted his 69-year old partner wanted to void the adoption in order to marry but the state law prevented it unless there was evidence of fraud In December 2016, a *Pennsylvania Superior Court panel agreed to void the adoption, paving the way for the couple's marriage after almost fifty years of being in a relationship.*[9]

4. OPEN ADOPTION

A more recent option in adoption is an open adoption. This is an arrangement in which the biological parent(s), usually the mother, has an agreement with the adopting parents that she will remain in the child's life. Often, this includes scheduled or open visitation. In such arrangements, the child is aware of the role of the biological parent in their life. Some who practice this

---

9 http://www.post-gazette.com/local/north/2016/12/21/Pennsylvania-court-ruling-clears-way-for-gay-Fox-Chapel-couple-to-marry/stories/201612210196?pgpageversion=pgevoke

type of open adoption believe it is in "the vanguard of reshaping domestic American adoption, transforming it from a clandestine, stigma-laden arrangement into a more open and collaborative one. They believe it's healthy, if possible, for an adoptive child to know where he or she came from; to have access to his or her medical background and genetic history; and to know that he or she was not abandoned or 'given away.'"[10]

What is the status of the biological mother in an open adoption? Is she a second mother? What happens if the adopting family changes its mind and does not want to allow the biological mother's continued contact? In *Michaud v. Wawruck*, 551 A.2d 738 (Conn 1988), the lower court treated visitation as a side agreement as contrary to public policy because the biological parents' rights must be terminated under the state adoption law, but the Connecticut Supreme Court held that if it was in the child's best interest, it is not, per se, void.

5. FATHER'S RIGHTS

Biological fathers are seeing increased legal rights in matters of the adoption of their biological children. In cases when the father recognizes the child as his own, biological fathers are required to give up their parental rights and consent before his child may be adopted by another person(s). If the biological father's rights are not terminated, problems can arise years later after the adoption is completed.

KRUKEMYER V. FORCUM
475 FED. APPX. 563, 2012 WL
1139007 (C.A.6 (OHIO 2012)

Background: Biological father brought action against adoptive father, and adoptive father's attorney, alleging failure to comply with certain procedural requirements of Indiana law during the adoption. The United States District Court for the Northern District of Ohio, James G. Carr, J., 2011 WL 9344, granted attorney's motion to dismiss. Plaintiff appealed.

Holdings: The Court of Appeals, McKeague, Circuit Judge, held that:

(1) adoptive father's attorney was not a state actor;

---

10   "In Open (Secret)", by Liza Mundy, *Washington Post*, May 6, 2007, pg. 18.

(2) attorney did not have actual knowledge that biological father would be affected by the adoption proceedings;

(3) biological father failed to identify any alleged misrepresentation made by adoptive father's attorney to biological father; and

(4) attorney's alleged failure to comply with procedural requirements for providing public notice was not with the intent to cause biological father severe emotional distress.

Affirmed.

*564 On Appeal from the United States District Court for the Northern District of Ohio...
McKEAGUE, Circuit Judge.

**1 Plaintiff Terry R. Krukemyer is the biological father of Lena Rosalie Krukemyer, who was born in Bowling Green, Ohio, on April 2, 1994. FN1 That Krukemyer is Lena's biological father was confirmed by DNA testing on October 30, 2007. Krukemyer did not learn he is Lena's father until some thirteen years after Lena's birth, as the mother, Jessica R. Jackson, did not inform him of either the conception or the birth. In April 1998, Lena had been adopted under Indiana law by David G. Jackson, who was married to Jessica from June 1996 to August 2008. Approximately five months after David and Jessica Jackson were divorced, Krukemyer married Jessica Jackson. Krukemyer's paternity and adoption of Lena were established under Ohio law in July 2009. The three—Krukemyer, Jessica, and Lena—have continued to live together as a family ever since. (footnotes omitted) Yet, the reunited family's happiness is not complete. Krukemyer commenced this action in January 2010 in the Northern District of Ohio. Named as defendant, in relevant part, is James S. Forcum, the attorney who represented David Jackson in the Indiana adoption proceedings. All the claims stem from defendant Forcum's alleged failure to comply with certain procedural requirements of Indiana law. Forcum's nonfeasance allegedly had the effect of denying Krukemyer notice of the impending adoption, thereby contributing to the prolongation of his ignorance of Lena's existence. On January 3, 2011, the district court granted Forcum's motion to dismiss the complaint under Fed.R.Civ.P. 12(b)(6) for failure to state a valid claim. Krukemyer appeals...

II

Krukemyer alleges his due process rights were violated as a result of Forcum's failure to comply with state law procedural requirements in the adoption proceedings. Specifically, Forcum's alleged failure to make a diligent search for the father and serve notice of the adoption proceedings in the county of the father's last known address is said to have deprived Krukemyer of eleven years' *566 enjoyment of his father-daughter relationship with Lena. The district court dismissed the claim for lack of an allegation that Forcum was a governmental actor.

Indeed, there is no constitutional right to be free from harm inflicted by private actors. A due process claim lies only against a governmental defendant. It is well-settled that a lawyer representing a private client is not a state actor acting "under color of law." See *Polk Cnty. v. Dodson*, 454 U.S. 312, 318 n. 7, 102 S.Ct. 445, 70 L.Ed.2d 509 (1991); *Powers v. Hamilton Cnty. Pub. Defender Comm'n*, 501 F.3d 592, 611 (6th Cir.2007); *Catz v. Chalker*, 142 F.3d 279, 289 (6th Cir.1998), amended on denial of reh'g, 243 F.3d 234 (6th Cir.2001); *Horton v. Martin*, 137 Fed.Appx. 773, 775 (6th Cir.2005); *Dallas v. Holmes*, 137 Fed.Appx. 746, 752 (6th Cir.2005). Krukemyer has not identified any contrary authority. Nor does the complaint contain allegations from which it could be reasonably inferred that Forcum's alleged nonfeasance was attributable to the state. We find no error in the district court's dismissal of the due process claim...

IV

Krukemyer asserts a claim for fraud, alleging Forcum made material misrepresentations to the Indiana court in the adoption proceeding with the intent to defraud him of his paternal rights. The district court held this claim fails for lack of an allegation that Krukemyer had detrimentally relied on any misrepresentation by Forcum. The court cited *Adoptive Parents of M. L. V. and A. L. V. v. Wilkens*, 598 N.E.2d 1054, 1058 (Ind.1992), for the proposition that, under Indiana law, "[t]o maintain an action for fraud, there must be a material misrepresentation of past or existing fact made with knowledge of or reckless disregard for the falsity of the statement; and the misrepresentation must be relied upon to the detriment of the relying party." The court observed that Krukemyer's allegations arguably made out a claim that fraud had been perpetrated on the Indiana court, but held that they failed to make out a claim on which Krukemyer could recover. FN3. Count III sets forth a claim for recovery for alienation of affection. Krukemyer has not challenged the dismissal of this claim and any objection is deemed forfeited.

Krukemyer acknowledges that his reliance on Forcum's alleged misrepresentation is an essential element of his fraud claim. Yet, he fails to identify in the complaint any allegation of misrepresentation (or even of silence in the face of a duty to speak) by Forcum to Krukemyer on which Krukemyer relied to his injury. Krukemyer struggles to contort the facts into a form meeting the required elements of a fraud claim. He insists Forcum's actionable fraud consists of his inaction—i.e., his failure to instruct Lena's mother that she had a duty to inform Krukemyer of Lena's existence, and his failure to properly publish notice of the adoption proceeding. By virtue of this inaction, Krukemyer contends, "reliance was imposed" on him by operation of law by virtue of his having remained ignorant of the adoption proceeding and failing to exercise his right to object.

To be sure, if Forcum and Krukemyer were in a relationship by virtue of which Forcum had a duty to speak to Krukemyer, then Forcum's alleged silence or inaction in derogation of that duty, if detrimentally relied upon by Krukemyer, could conceivably amount to actionable fraud. See *Allison v. Union Hosp., Inc.*, 883 N.E.2d 113, 122–23 (Ind.App.2008). However, Forcum and Krukemyer were in no such relationship. They did not know each other and had not had any contact with each other. There is no allegation that Forcum had knowledge of the biological father's identity. At all times pertinent, Forcum was in an attorney-client relationship with David Jackson. Forcum was thus in a fiduciary relationship with Jackson by virtue of which he owed certain duties to Jackson. And in representing Jackson as an "officer of the court," Forcum had certain duties under Indiana law. Yet, none of these duties was owed to Krukemyer personally, such that he, in the event of a breach thereof, could sue *568 Forcum for fraud. Accordingly, the fraud claim was properly dismissed.

V

Finally, in Count V, Krukemyer asserts a claim for intentional infliction of emotional distress. The district court properly identified the elements of such a claim as requiring Krukemyer to allege that Forcum engaged in extreme and outrageous conduct which intentionally or recklessly caused him severe emotional distress. See *Cullison v. Medley,* 570 N.E.2d 27, 31 (Ind.1991). It is the intent to harm the plaintiff emotionally which constitutes the basis for the tort of intentional infliction of emotional distress. Id. In the appropriate case, the "extreme and outrageous" question can be decided as a matter of law. *Lindsey v. DeGroot,* 898 N.E.2d 1251, 1264 (Ind.App.2009). The district court held that Krukemyer's claim fails for lack of allegation of conduct by Forcum that can be reasonably character-ized as "extreme and outrageous." Further, the court held implausible the allegation that Forcum failed to comply with the procedural requirements of the law with intent to cause Krukemyer severe emotional distress. We agree.

Our survey of Indiana case law shows that the Indiana courts have not construed the intentional-infliction-of-emotional-distress cause of action, newly recognized in *Cullison,* so broadly as to encom-pass facts such as those alleged here. See e.g., *Curry v. Whitaker,* 943 N.E.2d 354, 361 (Ind.App.2011) (noting that the requirements to prove this tort are "rigorous"); *Beauchamp v. City of Noblesville, Ind.,* 320 F.3d 733, 747 (7th Cir.2003) (observing that the Indiana courts have sustained summary judgment for defendants in more extreme cases); *Collins v. Purdue Univ.,* 703 F.Supp.2d 862, 871–73 (N.D.Ind.2010) (collecting cases and recognizing that Indiana courts have required "conduct so outrageous in char-acter, and so extreme in degree, as to go beyond all possible bounds of decency, and to be regarded as atrocious, and utterly intolerable in a civilized society").

Where the alleged tortious conduct consists essentially of an adoptive father's attorney's failure to ensure in 1998 that proper public notice was given in the county of the presumed biological father's last known address; and the biological father was not even aware that he may have fathered the child or even that she existed until 2007; and the attorney's nonfeasance was ostensibly consonant with the wishes of the child's mother (wife of the attorney's client), who had never disclosed the conception or birth of the child to the biological father; and there is no allegation that the attorney knew of the bio-logical father's identity or knew whether the biological father had any potential interest in asserting his paternal rights; and the attorney's alleged nonfeasance in 1998 caused no conceivable emotional distress to the biological father before 2007, when he learned of his role in the child's conception from the mother; we hold that the alleged facts do not make out the sort of extreme and outrageous conduct that can be deemed, under Indiana law, to have been undertaken intentionally or recklessly to inflict emotional harm on the biological father. We therefore find no error in the district court's dismissal of the intentional-infliction-of-emotional-distress claim.

VI

**5 None of the foregoing should be construed as condoning the alleged misfeasance of Attorney Forcum in his handling of the 1998 adoption proceedings. We find simply, on de novo review of the district court's order of dismissal, that none of the claims for relief asserted by plaintiff Krukemyer *569 states a valid claim on which relief can be granted under the governing substantive law. The district court's order is therefore AFFIRMED.

---

6. WEIGHT AND HEALTH ISSUES

If the Chinese government began considering the body mass index of American parents when screening couples' eligibility for international adoption, would it stand up in court here in the United States?[11,12] Courts are increasingly denying adoptions to prospective parents whom the court deems too obese or unhealthy. In Texas, 558-pound Gary Stocklaufer, a 34-year-old truck driver, and his wife were rejected in their attempt to adopt a child, related to him, who had lived with them from a week old. In so doing, the judge gave four-month-old Max to another couple for possible adoption. "The Stocklaufers have been married 15 years and are licensed by the state of Missouri as foster parents and have cared for children. In November 2000, they adopted another relative, eight-year-old Robert. The same judge who denied their petition to adopt Max approved Robert's adoption after multiple house visits and background checks," Cindy Stocklaufer said. Even then, her husband weighed more than 500 pounds. "They never even mentioned it when we adopted Bobby, and he was the same size," she said.[13] Is this in the

---

11   8   http://www.cbsnews.com/2100-201_162-3203710.html, "Man Denied Adoption Has Gastric Bypass," *CBS News*, February 11, 2009.

12   The Chinese did actually start such screenings in May 2009. Similar decisions have been made in Canada and in the U.K. There, a man was told to get his body fat index lower before he could be considered a potential adoptive parent. http://news.bbc.co.uk/2/hi/uk-news/7823707.stm "Man told he is too fat to adopt," Louise Birt, *BBC News*, January 12, 2009.

13   http://www.cbsnews.com/2100-201_162-3203710.html, "Man Denied Adoption Has Gastric Bypass," *CBS News*, February 11, 2009.

best interest of the child, "considering the Stocklaufers are the boy's relatives chosen as parents by the birth mother with a previous successful adoption"?[14]

In Mr. Stocklaufer's case, he decided to fight for the child by undergoing surgery, a gastric bypass, in order to lose the weight. Stocklaufer was quoted as saying that the judge felt "I wouldn't live long enough to see the child grown, to raise the child."[15] A hospital performed the surgery for free.[16]

WRONGFUL ADOPTION

Under the common law torts of fraud and misrepresentation, an adoption agency can be held liable for misrepresenting important/material facts about an adoption or for withholding/concealing important information. What kinds of things would be considered important?

ROSS V. LOUISE WISE SERVS.
8 N.Y.3D 478, 868 N.E.2D 189, 836 N.Y.S.2D 509,
2007 N.Y. SLIP OP. 03793 (2007)

OPINION OF THE COURT
Chief Judge Kaye.

Plaintiffs, adoptive parents Arthur Ross and Barbara Ross, have asserted three causes of action against Louise Wise Services: wrongful adoption/fraud; negligence and breach of fiduciary duty; and intentional infliction of emotional distress. On defendants' motion for summary judgment, we conclude that, while plaintiffs may seek compensatory damages, punitive damages are not available for the first claim in this case, and statutes of limitations bar the second and third claims.

*482 **2 Facts

In 1960 plaintiffs applied to Louise Wise (the Agency) for assistance in adopting an infant. FN1 They told the Agency that they preferred a "healthy infant from a healthy family," and that "it would be

---

14 Ibid.
15 Ibid.
16 Ibid.

nice if the baby's birth family had an artistic background." Mr. Ross was nationally recognized in the advertising field, had won awards and made a good salary, and the couple were engaged in various cultural activities. According to one social worker who had interviewed them, plaintiffs were mature, seemed comfortable about adopting a child and could handle the situation "better than the average couple with whom we place a child."

In the spring of 1961 plaintiffs were offered a boy, born January 11, 1961. In response to plaintiffs' question about the health of the baby and his biological family, the social worker told plaintiffs this was "a demanding baby who likes attention." She described the physical appearance and artistic interests of the birth parents and indicated that they were healthy but the birth father was allergic to penicillin and the maternal grandfather had died of heart disease. The Agency did not, however, disclose that either of the birth parents or members of their families had suffered from emotional disturbance.

According to Agency files, the biological mother never had a "normal" home life. In 1952, her father, the baby's biological grandfather, was hospitalized for 1 1/2 years for schizophrenia when he was in his mid-60s. The report also indicated that the birth mother was worried that her feelings of stress could affect the baby. She and the biological father married only because she was pregnant. She had seen a psychiatrist, who wrote to the Agency that the mother "presented as a girl who was failing in her major adjustments to life: late to school with the result that she failed to maintain matriculation at two colleges; few friends; hostility to most people; and demanding dependency." The biological father, according to the files, saw a psychiatrist, who, after one meeting, stated that the father was "a seriously disturbed young man, classified him as a paranoid, schizophrenic, and felt he had married purely for her [the birth *483 **3 mother's] money." The doctor also noted that, while the birth father could use treatment, "there was no rush."

Plaintiffs accepted the child, and on March 30, 1961, took home the baby they named Anthony. Although he was an active, difficult infant who could not sleep well, Ms. Ross attended to him and he was a happy baby. The adoption was finalized in 1962, and in 1964 plaintiffs adopted a daughter from the Agency. By the time Anthony was four, his troublesome behavior led plaintiffs to seek professional help.

Postadoption Events

In 1970, when Anthony was nine years old and the difficulties increased, plaintiffs called the Agency and were directed to Barbara Miller, head of the Post-Adoption Service. Plaintiffs told Miller that Anthony was experiencing "night terrors," cursed at the family, hit his parents and threatened people with objects. Ms. Ross suspected that he was hyperactive and might have brain dysfunction. Plaintiffs asked whether there could have been problems with the birth mother, whether she had taken drugs, whether she attempted to abort the pregnancy or whether there was birth trauma. Miller recommended that plaintiffs see a psychiatrist, Dr. Anne-Marie Weil, associated with the Agency. Miller's letter to Weil noted that Anthony's birth mother and grandfather "had histories of emotional instability"; however, Miller did not give Weil any specifics of the schizophrenia, and neither Miller nor Weil told plaintiffs of any emotional instability. Weil never saw Anthony himself, and her suggestions for behavior modification were to no avail.

While Ms. Ross wished to get treatment for Anthony, Mr. Ross disagreed and hoped that Anthony would grow out of his disruptive behavior. In 1973, after Anthony's school advised plaintiffs that Anthony needed a special school, they called Miller again to ask that she send a summary of Anthony's "birth history, background and foster home experience to Dr. Stella Chess," a well-known child psychiatrist plaintiffs had engaged. Although Miller mentioned in her report to Chess that Anthony was a tense, active baby, she did not tell the doctor of the birth parents' history of schizophrenia. In the same call to Miller, Ms. Ross indicated that she suspected more and more that Anthony's difficulties were organically based and divulged that she was forced to separate herself from her son as much as possible since his violence was getting progressively worse.

When she phoned the Agency in 1981, Ms. Ross told Miller that, fearful of her own and her daughter's physical well-being, *484 she had moved out of her home in 1978 when Anthony had finished a special high school. Plaintiffs divorced in 1979. The daughter then lived with her mother and Anthony with his father. Though Miller stated in her notes that Anthony **4 remained disturbed and undiagnosed, she mentioned nothing to plaintiffs about his biological background. FN2

Anthony continued to live with his father and graduated from college. Over the years, he did see several doctors, none of whom could assist him. He had some odd jobs but could not keep any. Ms. Ross called the Agency in 1994 and told them that she thought Anthony had ADHD. The Agency again did not disclose any information, including that it had received a call in 1984 that Anthony's birth mother had committed suicide in 1973. Anthony's behavior became more erratic, and he started to see a psychiatrist again. In 1995, when Anthony was 34, Mr. Ross woke up to find his son about to hit him with a large flashlight. Anthony was taken to Bellevue, where he was diagnosed as a paranoid schizophrenic.

The Action

The *New York Times Magazine* on March 14, 1999, published an article, "What the Jumans Didn't Know About Michael," describing a family who adopted a boy from the Agency and learned years later that the birth family's history included schizophrenia. As a result, plaintiffs sought Anthony's medical records. These were sent in April 1999, and plaintiffs filed suit on June 25, 1999. Plaintiffs testified in their depositions that much as they love Anthony, they would not have adopted him before they saw him if they had been told about the schizophrenia in his biological family, and that psychiatrists might have treated him differently had disclosure been made earlier. Further, they claimed that the stresses in their family resulted in both plaintiffs' clinical depression, the dissolution of their marriage and lost employment.

*485 Agency Policies in the 1960s and 1970s

In the 1960s and 1970s, the belief among the social workers and psychiatrists who worked for the Agency was that, in the development of a child, nurture played a far more **5 significant role than nature. For that reason, the policy of the Agency was not to disclose certain information about a birth family's medical history if the doctors were unsure whether the factors were hereditary. Anita Longo Sorensen, the Agency's expert witness, expressed this opinion in an affidavit and added:

> "Moreover, it was the belief and general opinion of social workers and other professionals in the adoption field at those times that mental illness would not be passed on if a child were placed in a loving environment.
>
> "It was also the general opinion and belief of social workers and other professionals in the adoption field at those times that the disclosure of certain information to prospective adoptive parents would interfere with the bonding between adoptive parent and child and prove detrimental to the child, the parents and their relationship. Therefore, it was the practice of social workers and other professionals in the adoption field in the 1960s and into the early 1980s not to disclose information that could be viewed as negative and which was not believed to be hereditary for fear that it would influence the family adversely on how they would nurture the adopted child. This practice remained in effect until changes were made in the Social Services Law and the Public Health Law in the early-mid 1980s."

Specifically, psychiatrists were unsure about the hereditary factors of mental illness and therefore would not discuss with adoptive parents mental disturbances of the biological family. Florence Kreech, Executive Director of the Agency during that period, testified that their psychiatrists "felt for many, many years we knew so little about schizophrenia and they felt very strongly about not putting labels on people." Kreech knew that studies were underway, but the Agency's psychiatrists "knew too little about hereditary factors," and had no certain information that a child of a parent or parents who had schizophrenia had a greater risk of developing it. "[T]here were children that may have come from parents—and, again, they wouldn't put labels on them—whose parents were disturbed, but it did not necessarily follow that the children were going to be disturbed."

*486 Miller conceded that she concealed the biological information from all adoptive parents, including plaintiffs, when they called with postadoptive questions. She followed what the Agency considered normative policy. Generally, the Agency might have told a couple that there was some disturbance in the family background, but more likely the Agency, without divulging aberrant history, would find an adoptive couple who could be accepting of emotional **6 problems. Social workers and psychiatrists were concerned that the child not be stigmatized.

"[I]f there were a history of mental illness which we understood to be noninheritable at that time—and I couldn't find a psychiatrist in New York at the time who would have told you that it was inherited—we would not mention that, simply because our psychiatrist felt that it had no meaning and it would only cause anxiety or might cause anxiety in the parents."

A "healthy baby" at that time meant a physically healthy child.

The Agency has included in the record extracts from literature published in the 1960s through 1980s to underscore the divergent views on the etiology of schizophrenia. For example, Herbert Weiner, M.D., wrote in 1967 that "In psychiatry, the nature-nurture controversy continues to rage.... " (Schizophrenia III: Etiology, in Freedman and Kaplan, Comprehensive Textbook of Psychiatry § 15.3, at 604 [1967].) The author concluded that "The environment may continuously interact with the genotype to elicit certain kinds of general potentialities and more specific dispositions to react to certain categories of environmental stress that lead to the illness" (id. at 620).

Plaintiffs too presented the affidavit of an expert, Dr. Dolores Malaspina, whose work concentrates on schizophrenia. She indicated that as far back as 1911 a study showed that schizophrenia "arose from a hereditary taint," and even in the 1920s, studies demonstrated elevated risks for the disease in close relatives. Malaspina affirmed that "[a]lthough a number of American practitioners theorized in the post-World War II era that schizophrenia could arise from a dysfunctional family, the evidence of its genetic familial nature was never questioned." Studies indicated that the likelihood of getting schizophrenia for someone with one affected parent is 12%, and the risk for bi-lineal inheritance is 46%. A doctor's not knowing the family history could make diagnosis "correspondingly difficult."

*487 It was not until 1983 that the Legislature enacted Social Services Law § 373-a (L 1983, ch 326, amended by L 1985, chs 103, 142), which provides that medical histories should be disclosed to pre-adoptive parents and adult adoptees. In 1985, the statute was amended to include adoptive parents. The Legislature also enacted Public Health Law §§ 4138-b, 4138-c and 4138-d, effective December 6, 1983, establishing an Adoption Information Registry in the Department of Health to allow adult adoptees to obtain nonidentifying medical information.

Decisions of the Lower Courts

In Supreme Court, the Agency moved for an order granting summary judgment dismissing plaintiffs' complaint; granting partial summary judgment dismissing plaintiffs' second and third causes of action as time-barred; dismissing plaintiffs' claim for emotional distress and recovery of business or other losses from that emotional distress, and limiting potential recovery of compensatory damages to extraordinary out-of-pocket expenses of raising plaintiffs' adopted **7 child to age 21; and dismissing plaintiffs' claim for punitive damages. Refusing to grant summary judgment as to the first count (wrongful adoption/fraud), the court found triable issues of fact as to whether the Agency concealed or misrepresented material facts at the time of the adoption and in subsequent years about the child's biological history. The court dismissed the claims for negligence and intentional infliction of emotional harm on statute of limitations grounds, limited potential recovery of compensatory damages to out-of-pocket expenses before the child reached 21 and allowed the claim for punitive damages to proceed.

The Appellate Division affirmed. The Agency did not appeal Supreme Court's refusal to dismiss the cause of action for wrongful adoption. All five Appellate Division Justices agreed that the statute of limitations had run on the negligence and intentional infliction of emotional distress claims. As to the punitive damages, two Justices determined that plaintiffs had raised sufficient issues of fact based on the Agency's initial as well as subsequent failures to disclose the child's family history of mental illness. The two other Justices in the majority concluded that the issue concerned the conduct surrounding the adoption and consequences of the initial concealment, not the Agency's subsequent action or inaction. The dissent, while not questioning plaintiffs' cognizable claim of wrongful adoption, stated that punitive damages could rest only on conduct at the time of the adoption and on the Agency's motivation—which, *488 from the extensive record evidence, was not to hurt maliciously or inflict pain but to find a good home for the child. The Appellate Division granted leave.

The Agency appeals from the order allowing the issue of punitive damages to proceed; plaintiffs cross-appeal from the order dismissing their second and third causes of action. We agree with the trial court and Appellate Division on the statute of limitations issue, agree with the dissent on the punitive damages issue and accordingly modify the order of the Appellate Division.

Analysis

(1) As a threshold matter, the Agency, in failing to challenge the order leaving in place the action for wrongful adoption, acknowledges that plaintiffs have raised a cognizable claim under common-law fraud principles in the adoption setting (see *Juman v Louise Wise Servs.*, 159 Misc 2d 314, 316-317 [NY County 1994], affd 211 AD2d 446 [1st Dept 1995]).FN3 The **8 court in Juman indicated that the tort concerned not simply an agency's silence but "'the deliberate act of misinforming'" a couple who were deprived of their right to make informed parenting decisions (id. at 318 *[citation omitted]*). To establish a prima facie case for fraud, plaintiffs would have to prove that

"(1) defendant made a representation as to a material fact; (2) such representation was false; (3) defendant[ ] intended to deceive plaintiff; (4) plaintiff believed and justifiably relied upon the statement and was induced by it to engage in a certain course of conduct; and (5) as a result of such reliance plaintiff sustained pecuniary loss" (id. at 320).

Thus, plaintiffs here will have the opportunity to show that the Agency's admitted policy to withhold information from them concerned material facts on which they relied and as a result of which they sustained monetary losses.

The questions we are called upon to answer are whether plaintiffs may seek punitive damages for wrongful adoption/fraud as alleged, and whether equitable estoppel bars the Agency from asserting the defense of statute of limitations on the second and third causes of action.

*489 Punitive Damages

Compensatory damages are intended to have the wrongdoer make the victim whole—to assure that the victim receive fair and just compensation commensurate with the injury sustained. Punitive damages are not to compensate the injured party but rather to punish the tortfeasor and to deter this wrongdoer and others similarly situated from indulging in the same conduct in the future (*Walker v Sheldon*, 10 NY2d 401, 404 [1961]; see *Krohn v New York City Police Dept.*, 2 NY3d 329, 335 [2004]; *Sharapata v Town of Islip*, 56 NY2d 332, 335 [1982]). Subjecting a wrongdoer to punitive damages serves to deter future reprehensible conduct. Hence the term "exemplary damages" is a synonym for punitive damages.

Punitive damages are permitted when the defendant's wrongdoing is not simply intentional but "evince[s] a high degree of moral turpitude and demonstrate[s] such wanton dishonesty as to imply a criminal indifference to civil obligations" (*Walker*, 10 NY2d at 405; see *Rocanova v Equitable Life Assur. Socy. of U.S.*, 83 NY2d 603, 613 [1994]). In *Prozeralik v Capital Cities Communications* (82 NY2d 466, 479 [1993]), the Court wrote that punitive damages may be sought when the wrongdoing was deliberate "'and has the character of outrage frequently associated with crime'" (citation omitted). The misconduct must be exceptional, "as when the wrongdoer has acted maliciously, wantonly, or with a recklessness that betokens an improper motive or vindictiveness... or has engaged in outrageous or oppressive intentional misconduct or with reckless or wanton disregard of safety or rights" (**9 *Sharapata*, 56 NY2d at 335 [*citations and internal quotation marks omitted*]; see also *Wilson v City of New York*, 7 AD3d 266, 267 [1st Dept 2004] [*misconduct lacked "the character of spite, malice or evil motive"*]).

Plaintiffs in *Juman* brought suit for wrongful adoption on facts analogous to those here. The prospective adoptive parents had been told certain information about the birth parents but not that they had met in a psychiatric hospital and that the mother had undergone a frontal lobotomy years before the child was born. The child became paranoid schizophrenic. The First Department found that the plaintiffs were entitled to seek compensatory damages but not punitive damages—conduct subsequent to the enactment of Social Services Law § 373-a setting standards for disclosure was irrelevant to the wrongful adoption claim "since the operative facts are those that occurred*490 at and around the time of the... adoption" (3 AD3d at 310).

In *Jeffrey BB. v Cardinal McCloskey School & Home for Children* (257 AD2d 21 [3d Dept 1999]), also a wrongful adoption case, the Third Department similarly dismissed a claim for punitive damages. Although the prospective parents, who had five other children, specifically asked about problems in the child's background, the agency withheld that she had been sexually abused. She would, thereafter, allegedly abuse two of the other children. The court determined that the agency's actions did not rise to the level of culpable conduct necessary to award exemplary damages.

(2) In this case, the Agency has conceded that it intentionally misrepresented facts about Anthony's background. We are troubled by such concealment, and sympathetic to the suffering plaintiffs have endured. They have presented sufficient triable facts to proceed on their fraud claim for compensatory damages.

(3) In its motion for summary judgment, however, the Agency has shown that, even if its failure to disclose may have been tortious, its conduct in connection with the adoption did not evince the high degree of moral turpitude required for punitive damages. Nor would punitive damages be warranted against the Agency for deterrence.

First, nothing in the record disproves what the Agency's own social workers and its expert stated— in the 1960s and even into the early 1980s the policy was not to disclose certain information about the child's biological background if the professionals were unsure whether the factors were hereditary. Many thought that mental illness could be avoided if a child were placed in a loving environment and that disclosure of birth parents' emotional disturbances would negatively affect the child's bonding with the adoptive parents. While it may be difficult for us in the twenty-first century to envisage not discussing mental or physical illness with prospective parents, and while such normative conduct may be deemed tortious even for that **10 time, we cannot say that the record shows that the Agency's motivation was malicious or vindictive.

Not until 1983 did the Legislature enact Social Services Law § 373-a to require disclosure of medical histories to prospective adoptive parents and adult adoptees. Although we address common-law tort and not violation of the statute, that the statute was enacted only in the 1980s is a factor in determining that punitive damages are inappropriate here.

*491 As to deterrence, section 373-a now requires agencies to provide to prospective adoptive parents and, upon request, to adoptive parents "the medical histories of a child legally freed for adoption… and of his or her natural parents, with information identifying such natural parents eliminated." Medical histories include "psychological information" (id.). Thus, the statute assures that agencies do not conceal relevant history of birth parents. Moreover, defendant Agency no longer acts in placing children for adoption, and its records are now housed at a different agency.

The complaint here includes a single cause of action for wrongful adoption and fraud at the time of the adoption. There are no separate counts of fraud concerning conduct in later years. Thus, even though no justification may exist, for example, for the Agency's failure to disclose information to the doctors plaintiffs consulted for Anthony in the 1970s, the fraud of wrongful adoption must center on the conduct that induced the prospective parents to accept the child. Because we cannot conclude from the record that the initial concealment was motivated by malice so as to warrant punitive damages, or that these damages would deter future reprehensible conduct, we limit plaintiffs' potential recovery to compensatory damages…

Accordingly, the order of the Appellate Division should be modified, without costs, by granting defendant's motion to dismiss plaintiffs' demand for punitive damages and, as so modified, affirmed. The certified question should be answered in the negative.

Judges Ciparick, Graffeo, Read, Smith, Pigott and Jones concur.

- *In June 1982, Anthony, 21, unexpectedly appeared at Dr. Weil's office and asked for a report that she had written 10 years earlier. Weil had no recollection of the report but called Miller, who wrote in her notes that the doctor was frightened by Anthony's demeanor and felt he was a paranoid schizophrenic, capable of violence. Miller wrote back saying that she appreciated the caution, but neither Miller nor Weil alerted the plaintiffs. In 1984, when Anthony was 23, he made an appointment at the Agency to learn about his birth history. He was told what plaintiffs had been told at the outset—that the medical information was good.*

The parents in *Ross* claimed that the adoption negatively impacted their entire family structure. So what happens if an adoption just does not work out? Can you return an adopted child? In April 2010, Torry Hansen of Tennessee did. Claiming that the Russian adoption agency from which she had obtained Artyom Saveliev had lied to "get rid of the boy" and that "[h]e is violent and has severe psychopathic issues," she put the boy on a plane, alone, to Russia, with a letter that said, in part, "I am sorry to say that for the safety of my family, friends, and myself,… I no longer wish to parent this child. As he is a Russian national, I am returning him to your guardianship."[17] The event caused outrage in the international community, prompting Russia to consider halting all American adoptions from their country. Hansen went to counseling over the situation, but "never brought Saveliev to see a psychiatrist or psychologist." Afterward, the World Association for Children and Parents, the agency that helped Hansen adopt the child, filed a lawsuit seeking child support. In May 2012, a Tennessee court ordered her to "pay $150,000 plus an additional $1,000 a month in child support… until the boy turns 18."[18] "According to an Associated Press update on his story in April 2012, Saveliev now lives in a village made up of foster families outside of Moscow. When asked if he wanted to return to America, he shivered and yelled 'No!' He refuses to speak in English, and has had to go through extensive counseling and speech therapy to start communicating again.'"[19]

---

17 "Tennessee Mother Ships Adopted Son Back to Moscow Alone," Netter & McGee, *ABCNEWS*, April 9, 2010, http://abcnews.go.com/WN/anger-mom-adopted-boy-back-russia/story?id=10331728.
18 "Mom who sent adoptive child back to Russia ordered to pay child support", *CBSNews*, May 18, 2012, http://www.cbsnews.com/8301-201_162-57437258/mom-who-sent-adoptive-child-back-to-russia-ordered-to-pay-child-support/.
19 Ibid.

INTERNATIONAL ADOPTIONS

Due to the shortage of available newborn children for adoption in the United States, many families go abroad to adopt.[20] Generally, children from Asian countries and Russia are popular choices. According to the State Department, over 45,000 Russian children have been adopted by American families since 1999.[21] In 2012, President Vladimir Putin of Russia signed a law banning Americans from adopting Russian children. The adoption ban[22] was named after a 21-month-old boy, Dima Yakovlev, who died of heatstroke in Virginia in 2008 when his adoptive father left him in a parked vehicle for nine hours. Anger over American adoptions was revived in 2010 when Artyom Saveliev, discussed above, was sent alone on a flight back to Russia by his adoptive mother, Torry Hansen, along with a note saying the boy was "violent and has severe psychopathic issues."[23] The bill also imposes sanctions on Americans accused of abusing Russian children, especially if the parents received "lenient sentences."[24] "Scores of families were hoping to complete adoptions that were in their final stages."[25]

Then, in January 21, 2013, "Russian officials accused a Texas woman [Laura Shatto], of fatally beating a 3-year-old boy she had adopted from Russia, setting off a new wave of outrage in a country already focused on American adoptions that have culminated in neglect or abuse." "Reports of Max's death...prompted a number of new measures—most notably a temporary halt to all adoptions in the Pskov region, from which both Max and Dima Yakovlev had been adopted."[26] Prior to his death, the Shattos' two adopted brothers were playing in the backyard.

---

20 Since the early '90s, 100,000 children have been adopted from China. "The Returned" Maggie Jones, *the New York Times*, January 18, 2015. P. 30, 37.

21 http://abcnews.go.com/blogs/headlines/2012/12/putin-will-sign-ban-on-adoptions-to-united-states/. "Putin Will Sign Ban on Adoptions to United States", by Kirit Radia, *ABC News*, December 27, 2012.

22 Others claim that the ban was the result of the U.S.'s passage of the Magnitsky Act, which seeks to punish a group of Russian officials who have been implicated in the torture and death of a Russian lawyer named Sergei Magnitsky. In 2008, Magnitsky "discovered that a group of Russian officials had stolen $230 million from the Russian treasury. When he blew the whistle on the scheme, some of those same officials allegedly conspired to get him arrested, and he died in a prison cell a year later, having been reportedly beaten and denied medical treatment." http://world.time.com/2012/12/20/why-has-moscow-passed-a-law-to-ban-u-s-adoption-of-russian-orphans/#ixzz2QbANz6n4, "Why Has Moscow Passed a Bill to Ban U.S. Adoption of Russian Orphans?" Simon Shuster, *Time International*, December 20, 2012. Since this was written about in the last edition, this footnote has featured prominently in international news. This has become a major focus in the special prosecutor's investigation of the Trump administration because both the president and his son Donald Trump Jr. said they were discussing "adoption" with a Russian agent during the campaign.

23 http://www.nytimes.com/2013/02/20/world/Europe/adopted-boys-death-in-us-stirs-outrage-in-russia.html?pagewanted=all&_r=0 "After Adopted Boy Dies In U.S., Russian Officials Accuse Texas Woman" Ellen Barry, *The New York Times, Europe*, February 19, 2013.

24 http://abcnews.go.com/blogs/headlines/2012/12/putin-will-sign-ban-on-adoptions-to-united-states/ "Putin Will Sign Ban on Adoptions to United States", by Kirit Radia, *ABC News*, December 27, 2012.

25 http://www.nytimes.com/2013/02/20/world/Europe/adopted-boys-death-in-us-stirs-outrage-in-russia.html?pagewanted=all&_r=0 "After Adopted Boy Dies in U.S., Russian Officials Accuse Texas Woman" Ellen Barry, *The New York Times, Europe*, February 19, 2013.

26 Ibid.

When Mrs. Shatto came back outside she found the younger, Max, "lying in the grass... not breathing". "It seemed like a terrible accident—a severe allergy attack or perhaps a seizure—until the doctors saw the muliticolored collage of bruises on Max's body. They marked his chest, his groin, his thigh, his left arm, his right arm, his chin, his neck, his face. Suddenly, Mrs. Shatto was no longer a grieving mother struck by calamity. She was a murder suspect, a symbol of the worst fears about adoption."[27] In a twist, Texas' investigation concluded that Max's death was "an accident resulting from internal injuries probably caused by a fall from the swing set and that Max's bruises were self-inflicted... by a deeply troubled child who clawed his skin raw, banged his head against walls and hurled his body on the floor".[28] Russian authorities did not accept that finding and moved to annul the adoption. Russia also demanded the return of Max's body. "They accused the couple of fabricating Max's history of self-injury to cover up their mistreatment." The U.S. would not have to accept Russia's order of annulment.

Before adoptions from Russia, China, and Korea were popular, Americans went to Ireland to adopt a baby. In 1952, the Irish government tried to "end the transatlantic traffic in Irish babies" through a law that would forbid adoptions of children less than seven-years-old. Subsection 2, however, allowed removal of illegitimate children with approval of their mothers. This clause was highlighted in the book *Philomena*[29] which focused on Sean Ross Abbey, a convent that ran a "mother and child home" where Philomena Lee's illegitimate son was taken from her and placed for adoption with an American family who called him Tommy Kavanagh. The Irish government was concerned not only about the high number of Irish children that were adopted out of the country, but that the Catholic Church, who coordinating those adoptions, determined the parent's suitability based only on their statements that they were religious (Catholic). Because unwed mothers were often shamed and coerced into terminating their parental rights, the new law did little to stop the international adoptions. In June 2013, the Irish government apologized that it had taken so long to compensate the women who worked in the laundries of these church-run homes—"an estimated 770 survivors out of more than 10,000 who lived in the dozen facilities from the 1920s to 1996"[30] and agreed to pay out $45 million in compensation.

---

27   "World of Grief and Doubt After an Adoptee's Death," Rachel L. Swarns & David M. Herszenhorn, *The New York Times*, September 1, 2013, P. A.

28   Ibid., P. 16. "Child welfare officials...have not disputed the finding about Max's death, said they could not determine who caused the bruises on his body, leaving the Shattos under a cloud of suspicion. Leaving the file open may prevent Mrs. Shatto from continuing her job as a teacher." In its article, *The New York Times* reviewed Max's autopsy report, adoption and medical records and others involved in the case, including the child's doctor and wrote, that "Those reports and interviews helped bolster the Shatto's account".

29   Martin Sixsmith, Penguin Books, 2009. The book was later made into an Oscar nominated movie starring Dame Judi Dench in the titular role. In real life, Philomena went on to marry and have two children. Her adopted son was successful in American, having graduated from Notre Dame and "who became the chief legal counsel to the Republican National Committee in the 1980s before dying of AIDS-related complications at 43". "The real Philomena, Anne Midgette", *The Washington Post*, February 4, 2014. http://www.washingtonpost.com/lifestyle/style/the-real-philomena-lee-finds-hollywood-ending-to-adoption-story/2014/02/04/a907b510-8db7-11e3-95dd-36ff657a4dae_story.html

30   "Ireland to pay 45 million to Catholic laundry workers", *CBSNews*, June 26, 2013. http://www.cbsnews.com/news/ireland-to-pay-45-million-to-catholic-laundry-workers/

In South Korea, a group of adults who were adopted children advocated for ending international adoption—to "make [themselves] extinct." During the 1980s South Korea "sent overseas for adoption 8,800 mostly illegitimate children." Indeed, "South Korea had earned the reputation as the Cadillac of adoption programs because of its efficient system and steady supply of healthy babies...The number of adoptions reached unsettling heights, with an average of 24 children leaving South Korea each day." "Over the past six decades, at least 200,000 Korean children—roughly the population of Des Moines—have been adopted into families in more than 15 countries, with a vast majority living in the United States."[31] Hundreds of these adopted children have now moved back to South Korea, including about 300 to 500 in "ASK," Adoptee Solidarity Korea, which "began as a reading group who began to discuss why Korean single mothers felt pressure to give their children." "Most [of those returning to South Korea] lack fluency in the language and possess no memories of the country they left when they were young. But they are back, hoping for a sense of connection—to South Korea, to their birth families to other adoptees." Growing up in foreign countries, these children never felt connected, wondered about their kin in Korea, and wanted to return. To facilitate the transition for those returning, the government "offers F-4 visas, which allow them to live and work in the country indefinitely," and they can apply for dual citizenship. Agencies help them to find "language classes and translation services and organize social events."

While ASK has now backed away from advocating prohibiting adoptions as too polarizing, the group has "emerged as leaders in a movement to question the very concept of international adoption, one that has galvanized other adoptees around the world." Said one member, "I don't think it's normal adopting a child from another country, of another race and paying a lot of money. I don't think it's normal to put a child on a plane away from all its kin and different smells." The group has "succeed[ed] in enacting an amendment to South Korea's adoption law." "Women must now receive counseling and wait seven days before placing a child for adoption. All adoption must be registered through the courts, which gives adoptees, who often struggle to make contact with their families (only a small percentage of Korean adoptees who search for birth families ever find them), an avenue for tracing their history."

"While the predominant narrative of adoption focuses on what is gained, each adoption also entails loss for both the child and her biological family."[32] These all are sad endings to the new beginning of adoption.

---

31 "The Returned" Maggie Jones, *The New York Times*, January 18, 2015. P. 30. "Though only 7,000 children were adopted into the United States in 1990, by 2004—the peak of international adoption—that number had risen to 23,000." In the 2000s "adoption experts shifted from telling parents to 'assimilate' their adopted children ... to acknowledge racial differences and to embrace their children's birth culture. Some parents signed up for 'homeland tours' to Korea or sent their children to Korean summer 'culture camp'".

32 Ibid., P. 34.

23 TECHNOLOGY AND FAMILY LAW

This cyber world is sort of the wild, wild west. To some degree we are asked to be the sheriff.
—President Barack Obama[1]

In short, it is okay to love your technology. Just don't use your technology for love.
—Kira Sabin[2]

INTRODUCTION

Remember when phones were only used to make phone calls? With daily advances that have transformed phones into computers, technology has become ubiquitous.[3] In a world where we are always plugged in,[4] technology has altered familial interactions, yet, it remains mostly unregulated. The law simply cannot keep up with the pace of technological development. While this is

---

1 Said at Stanford University where President Obama was speaking at a White House Summit on Cybersecurity and Consumer Protection. "Obama calls for New Cooperation to wrangle the 'wild west' Internet," Nicole Perlroth and David E. Sanger, February 13, 2015. http://www.nytimes.com/2015/02/14/business/obama-urges-tech-companies-to-cooperate-on-Internet-security.html

2 "Don't let technology ruin a new relationship," *Huffington Post,* November 17, 2011.

3 A 14-year-old boy was convicted of plotting to bomb a Vienna train station after downloading the bomb-making instructions from an al Qaeda site onto his PlayStation. *The Week,* June 5, 2015, P. 8.

4 "Americans spend an average of about three hours a day looking at their smartphones." "Talking points", *The Week,* July 24, 2015, p. 14. "The cornucopia of technology that we are accepting into our lives, with little or no self-reflection or thoughtful examination, may very well come back and bite us." These family law cases raised issues that are the tip of the iceberg for those who invite technology into every waking hour without thinking about the affects it creates on privacy and other liberties (not to mention the frequency that the information is compromised. "600,000 Facebook accounts are compromised each day"). One study that analyzed the Facebook profiles of college students accurately guessed their sexual orientation most of the time. While that study occurred in 2009, ages ago in terms of the advances in technology, it is still disturbing that something so private can become so public. "You've been hacked," Jenna Wortham, *The New York Times Book Review,* May 17, 2015, P. 14, citing *Future Games,* by Marc Goodman, Random House Audio, 2015.

a book on family law, there is not much law to fill a technology chapter due to few regulations. This chapter, however, does contain cases, including an occasional US Supreme Court case. It also contains examples of how families use technology (or how it is used against them), from the collection of evidence in divorce cases to monitoring teenagers by cell phone. Perhaps the chapter's best value is the many cautionary tales it provides. But to prove I am not just a Luddite, this chapter also includes positive ways how technology has affected the family. The materials are presented in the order they impact the topics of previous chapters to allow the reader to bring the book's materials full circle.

LOVE NOTES (CHAPTER 4)

As evidenced by the forthcoming materials included in this chapter, hidden recordings or copies of texts and emails are revealed much more frequently during domestic relations legal cases. As a result, "lawyers are starting to recommend digital-privacy clauses for prenuptial and postnuptial agreements. Such clauses aim to prevent spouses from using personal texts, e-mails, or photos against each other should they wind up in divorce court."[5]

Should such a prenup clause include the old school methods of "surreptitious conversation recordings"? This might have been helpful when 7th *Heaven* star Stephen Collins purportedly confessed to molesting underage girls (years prior) during a therapy session that was recorded and the recording given to the police by the actor's estranged wife during their divorce case.[6] The release of the recording caused cancellation of his reruns on cable and damaged the longtime actor's career. What was the benefit? Now that he cannot work, his assets will be worth less, with less available to divide with his ex-wife of twenty-five years during their divorce. Indeed, as his court filings pointed out, "As a result of the audio's release, Collins' future earnings have been reduced to only what he can earn off investments."[7]

Moreover, the increased use of recorded phone conversations by handheld technology creates ethical issues that include complicating the duty to preserve evidence. On the one hand, covertly recording another's conversation may be an invasion of state or federal privacy laws. In some states, it is okay to press "record" without telling the other person as long as you are one of the people in the conversation. In other states, you must always disclose before recording a

---

5   "The adultery arms race," Michelle Cottle, *The Atlantic*, November 2014, P. 58, 60.

6   http://www.foxnews.com/entertainment/2014/11/09/damaging-tapes-hang-over-stephen-collins-divorce-case/"damaging tapes hang over Stephen Collins' divorce case," AP, November 9, 2014.

7   Ibid. The allegations were investigated but no charges were filed. http://www.foxnews.com/entertainment/2014/11/09/damaging-tapes-hang-over-stephen-collins-divorce-case/"damaging tapes hang over Stephen Collins' divorce case," AP, November 9, 2014. The tapes raise many legal concerns such as how they were recorded, what is the effect of the doctor/patient privilege, etc. "Since [the wife] provided the audio to authorities, it is unlikely she will face any criminal charges…. She might face a civil lawsuit from Collins over damage to his career," said Alison Triessl, a California attorney. The recordings would probably not have been admissible in the divorce court over evidentiary objections, so did they serve their purpose?

conversation. Should similar rules be put in place for recording video on a phone? How about printing written text or email messages or tweets? What is the effect of a voicemail message someone leaves? Should that be treated similarly to the permanent record created by a text or email? Does there seem to be a different standard of privacy expectation or has the law just not kept up with technology? Yet on the other hand, parties in court cases have a duty to preserve evidence. Attempts to "hide" or delete electronic accounts (such as email), or to wipe a hard drive clean, may violate it. All of these involve real penalties, financial or worse.

TECHNOLOGY, THE FAMILY, AND THE CONSTITUTION (CHAPTER 5)

First Amendment Internet Free Speech?

"People say pretty inflammatory things online, shielded by a computer screen," but determining "what is a threat and what is a rant is not the simplest thing."[8] "Harassment happens all the time on Facebook from inappropriate messages, comments or persistent behaviors. From sexual harassment to assault threats, there has been a significant increase in the number of harassment cases happening on Facebook. It is not uncommon for sex offenders and sexual predators to prey on unsuspecting victims on Facebook and even pose as a teen or college student."[9]

Cyber-harassment usually pertains to threatening or harassing email messages, instant messages, blog entries, or even websites created for the sole purpose of tormenting another person.[10] Some states approach cyber-harassment by including language that addressed electronic communications in general harassment statutes, while others have created stand-alone cyber-harassment laws.[11] Other states apply traditional laws of harassment when people harass, threaten, or bully others online. Is this old school method sensible, or would specific language make the laws easier to enforce? It is often said that cyber-harassment differs from cyber stalking in that cyber-harassment may generally be defined as not involving a credible threat.[12] Also, cyberbullying

---

8   Quoting Seattle Police Detective Drew Fowler. "On social media, when is a rant also a threat?" Katie Zezima, *The Washington Post*, December 26, 2014, A3.

9   http://www.wsj.com/articles/cyberbullying-law-challenged-in-court-1401925445

10   In *The Dark Net*, Jamie Bartlett "reveals what we are capable of when we're shielded by the computer screen, and presents a revelatory portrait of the Internet's strangest subcultures where he writes about trolls and pornographers, drug dealers and hackers, political extremists and computer scientists, bitcoin programmers and self-harmers, libertarians and vigilantes," 2015, Random House.

11   National Conference of State Legislatures. http://www.ncsl.org/research/telecommunications-and-information-technology/cyberstalking-and-cyberharassment-laws.aspx

12   Also, cyberbullying and cyber-harassment are sometimes used interchangeably, but cyberbullying generally refers to electronic harassment or bullying among minors within a school context and, as such, will be addressed in the section on education. https://m.facebook.com/notes/exposing-the-human-predator-created-by-trish-p/state-cyberstalking-and-cyberharassment-laws/1524820937789885/ "Exposing the Human Predator," a note by Trish P on Facebook. See also, http://www.ncsl.org/research/telecommunications-and-information-technology/cyberstalking-and-cyberharassment-laws.aspx

and cyber-harassment are sometimes used interchangeably, but cyberbullying generally "refers to electronic harassment or bullying among minors within a school context" and as a result will be addressed below in the section on education.[13]

In 2015, it looked like the US Supreme Court might define free speech for the internet when deciding the issue of "whether violent images and threatening language posted on Facebook and other social media constitute a true threat to others or simply the protected rants of someone imbued with what one advocate called 'digital courage'"?[14] But, in the case of *Elonis v. U.S.*, 575 U.S. _ (2015), the Court avoided the internet free speech issue and merely rejected the lower court's standard "of the defendant's subjective intent to threaten, as required by the Ninth Circuit and the supreme courts of Massachusetts, Rhode Island, and Vermont; or whether it is enough to show that a 'reasonable person' would regard the statement as threatening, as held by other federal courts of appeals and state courts of last resort."[15]

In the case, Anthony D. Elonis of Pennsylvania was convicted on four counts of violating the federal threat statute and sentenced to forty-four months in prison for posting ominous photos and making violent rants on his Facebook page against former coworkers, law enforcement officials, and especially his estranged wife (who had already obtained a restraining order against him). "Elonis speculated about blowing up elementary schools and threated co-workers." He posted about his estranged wife, "There's one way to love you but a thousand ways to kill you. I'm not going to rest until your body is a mess, soaked in blood and dying from all the little cuts." After an FBI agent talked to Elonis about the posting, he later wrote on his Facebook page, "Little agent lady stood so close, took all the strength I had not to turn the [expletive] ghost. Pull my knife, flick my wrist and slit her throat." In his defense, Elonis argued that these postings, "which included the lyrics of songs by the rapper Eminem, were free speech—were attempts to deal with the pain of his personal problems and not specific threats to harm anyone." He also argued that although the language was violent, he had "posted explicit disclaimers in his profile explaining that his posts were 'fictitious lyrics' and he was 'only exercising [his] constitutional right to freedom of speech.'"

"The court for years has held that 'true threats' to harm another person are not protected speech under the First Amendment."[16] Is there a difference when they are made via technology where the threats become so public and reach a large audience so quickly? Does the fact that the threats via technology create a written record make a difference compared with threats made between two shouting people? Should this difference require "the government to prove that the

13 National Conference of State Legislatures. http://www.ncsl.org/research/telecommunications-and-informationtechnology/ cyberstalking-and-cyberharassment-laws.aspx
14 "Justices agreed to consider whether social-media threats are free speech," Robert Barnes, *The Washington Post*, June 17, 2014, A16.
15 SCOTUS Blog, http://www.scotusblog.com/case-files/cases/elonis-v-united-states/
16 "Justices agreed to consider whether social-media threats are free speech," Robert Barnes, *The Washington Post*, June 17, 2014, P. A16.

defendant purposefully intended to threaten the victim"?[17] In situations such as this one, in which Elonis's wife already had a protective order against him, why would she not be terrified by his postings? What more could she do? Elonis's attorney argued that a victim should be required to make the harasser aware that he or she (the victim) feels threatened before the harasser is required to stop. Did not the wife do this when she obtained the protective order?

While awaiting the court's decision in *Elonis*, a similar situation occurred in Maryland. An Army veteran was arrested after he sent various texts threatening to shoot his wife and others at the US Capitol, where she worked. When the husband accused his wife of having an affair with a Capitol police officer, he "threatened to shoot the officer in the face."[18] She replied, "You come to my job on some crazy PTSD, I will file for divorce. Your choice." He wrote back, "When I come divorce won't help. Cause I'm making the news today.... Probably won't make it all the way up but u will get my last point I will ever make. Someone is going on be grieving for their family members today. Including my family. I PROMISE YOU THAT." The police took the husband to the hospital for an emergency medical evaluation and then arrested him for making treats to commit violence (which carries a maximum sentence of five years), saying, "[c]onsidering we found two guns in the search... and considering that he has extensive combat training, this was a pretty credible threat. Had we not intervened, I'm a little bit afraid of what could have possibly happened."[19] Does using violent rap lyrics differentiate these two cases? Does possessing guns make the threat more credible? If so, how is that influenced by the Second Amendment "right to bear arms"?

Second Amendment Right to Bear Arms?

When a New Jersey father posted a photo on his Facebook page of his eleven-year-old son holding what appears to be an automatic weapon (it was a .22-caliber rifle manufactured to look like an automatic weapon), what should have happened? Was the father using his First Amendment free speech rights along with his Second Amendment rights as he claimed?[20] When the local police and child protective services came to investigate after receiving "anonymous calls expressing concern about the safety of a child," the governor called for an investigation of those investigations. Should he have done this? Did New Jersey overreact?[21] Does it make a difference if both father

---

17 "The menace in a threat," Kevin Reed, *The Washington Post*, February 16, 2015, A3.

18 "Police: Army Veteran threatened to carry out attack at Capitol," Lynh Bui and Peter Hermann, *The Washington Post*, February 6, 2015.

19 Ibid., quoting Cheverly Police Detective Bernard Jones.

20 "Facebook photo of 11-year-old with a rifle send New Jersey child welfare authorities to father's home," Erik Ortiz and Daniel Beekman, *New York Daily News*, March 20, 2013. http://www.nydailynews.com/news/national/facebook-photo-n-boy-holding-rifle-draws-outrage-article-1.1293868

21 "New Jersey to investigate state response of Josh Moore with gun," *News12 New Jersey*, March 28, 2013. Governor and presidential candidate Chris Christie requested an investigation on those investigations. http://newjersey.news12.com/news/nj-to-investigate-state-response-to-photo-of-josh-moore-with-gun-1.4926610

and son have state licenses regarding gun use?[22] What if the photo had shown a father holding his baby and a gun? What is the extent of the Second Amendment when it involves children? When a father shoots his daughter's laptop with his pistol in response to her "bratty" Facebook posts and then posts the video to YouTube, what should happen?[23] Should the police investigate? Should child protective services? Is there a lack of threat to the children involved?

COURTSHIP (CHAPTER 7)

Is texting to blame for dating's demise? "Instead of dinner-and-a-movie, which seems as obsolete as a rotary phone," young people today "rendezvous over phone texts, Facebook posts, instant messages and other 'non-dates' that are leaving a generation confused about how to land a boy-friend or girlfriend."[24] Clearly, the influence of technology is everywhere when it comes to modern courtship; from online dating to online stalking technology—all have changed the mating dance.

Online, not in Person, Interaction

"Romeo, Romeo, Where art thou Romeo?[25] is a line delivered from a balcony, not a text message, in an immortal message of courtship. Does romance or courtship require face-to-face interaction? For this generation, technology drives courtship. "Relationship experts point to technology as another factor in the upending of dating culture. Traditional courtship—picking up the telephone and asking someone on a date—required courage, strategic planning, and a considerable invest-ment of ego (by telephone, rejection stings). Not so with texting, e-mail, Twitter or other forms of 'asynchronous communication,' as techies call it," one author argues. "In the context of dating, it removes much of the need for charm; it's more like dropping a line in the water and hoping for a nibble."[26] Yet many readers would argue the vulnerability still exits. Today, people really agonize over the first email or text message they send to someone who stirs their romantic interest. Many budding Shakespeareans have become experts in composing Spartan texts that minimize misin-terpretation. While adolescents and adults may easily dash off texts when they are comfortable, the first message may go through many drafts. The beauty of the text message is that, like Cyrano,

---

22 The father is a hunting firearms safety instructor and the son has a state hunting license. "Facebook photo of 11-year-old with a rifle send New Jersey child welfare authorities to father's home," Erik Ortiz and Daniel Beekman, *New York Daily News*, March 20, 2013. http://www.nydailynews.com/news/national/facebook-photo-n-boy-holding-rifle-draws-outrage-article-1.1293868

23 "Fed-up North Carolina Father shoots daughter's laptop," Kevin Dolack, ABC News, February 14, 2012. While the father became an Internet sensation with more than twenty-two million viewers, according to his Facebook post-ing, the police and child protective services both investigated. In her Facebook postings the daughter "complained about her parents making her do chores around the house." http://abcnews.go.com/blogs/technology/2012/02/fed-up-north-carolina-father-shoots-daughters-laptop/

24 Alex Williams mourns the "End of Dating" in the "End of Courtship," Alex Williams, *The New York Times*, January 11, 2013. http://www.nytimes.com/2013/01/13/fashion/the-end-of-courtship.html

25 Romeo and Juliet, Act 2, Scene 2, William Shakespeare.

26 Ibid.

you can confer with friends on how to phrase it, which you cannot do when making a phone call. "In a world where 'courtship' is quickly being redefined, women must recognize a flirtatious exchange of tweets, or a lingering glance at a company softball game, as legitimate opportunities for romance, too."[27] If courtship requires at least some live communication, is phone sex enough?[28]

A 2015 Pew Research Center study on teen dating looked at the impact of technology and found it omnipresent, from flirting ("putting a 'bunch of emojis' under a girl's photo"), to an expectation of "hearing from a partner at least once a day (38%), to once an hour (11%). [29] Yet, old-school traditions still exist. The majority of teens still ask someone out in person and 78% will break up in person too.[30] Still, 7% of teens are OK with breaking up by changing your social media status to "'single'".[31]

"A lot has changed since Match.com launched on April 21, 1995. Then, only 14% of American adults were Internet users, and online dating options were scarce. Today, nearly nine-in-ten Americans are online" and "online dating has lost much of its stigma. A majority of Americans now say online dating is a good way to meet people, when that hasn't always been the case."[32] "[A]t least 40 million Americans are looking for love on the Web."[33] "One-in-five adults ages

---

27 Said Jessica Massa and Rebecca Wiegand, founders of a dating commentary and advice site. "The end of courtship," Alex Williams, *The New York Times*, January 11, 2013. http://www.nytimes.com/2013/01/13/fashion/the-end-of-courtship.html

28 "In the age of Tinder and self-curated dating profiles, where image and first impressions hold sway," is going old school, and asking deep questions face-to-face, going to work? In 2015, Mandy Len Catron's essay "To Fall in Love With Anyone, Do This" appearing in *Modern Love* "told how to find love" by replicating a twenty-year-old experiment by psychologist Arthur Aron where two strangers "asked each other 36 increasingly personal questions followed by a four-minute staring session to see if doing so would lead to intimacy and love. Afterward, over 8 million people worldwide tried it." Ironically, in the ultimate defeat of its purpose, "[o]ne man even posed the questions to his disengaged cat in a YouTube video which amassed nearly 40,000 views." Perhaps the success of simply talking directly to each other says more about the social implications of our world in which we are plugged in, yet oblivious to the humanity of others. "The 36 Questions: An Answer to their Prayers?" Daniel Jones, *The New York Times Modern Love*," February 15, 2015, P. 6. In a snarky parody of the test, substituted questions included, "[o]n average, how long do you spend composing tweets before you post them? Do you realize that they don't matter? Before responding to a text, do you wait a few minutes to make it seem like you're doing something more important? Why? Answer me now." "To Fall Out of Love, Do This," Susanna Wolff, *The New Yorker*, January 26, 2015. http://www.newyorker.com/magazine/2015/01/26/fall-love Is that more accurate for the technology generation?

29 "Social media, the ever-present wingman in teen relationships", Hayley Tsukayama, Washington Post, October 2, 2015, P. A18

30 Ibid.

31 Ibid.

32 "Five facts about online dating," Aaron Smith and Monica Anderson for the Pew Research Center, April 20, 2015. ttp://www.pewresearch.org/fact-tank/2015/04/20/5-facts-about-online-dating In 2017, a new dating app called "Hater" matches people up by "mutual objects of loathing". https://www.washingtonian.com/2017/03/24/washington-loves-hate-according-new-dating-app/ Tops on the hate list, "uber surge pricing". Really, of all the things to hate? And how romantic is that?

33 "Five Myths Online dating", Christian Rudder, Washington Post, October 4, 2015, B2. Mr. Smith is the "head of OkCupid". The article also mentions the "'Craigslist killer'" who murdered a woman he met online (and later committed suicide in jail) and the case of a man who came to the home of a woman he met on line with a knife and the intention of killing her, but claims "that the numbers suggest that online dating is very safe."

25–34 years old have used online dating, but it's also popular with older singles, too." Indeed, "5% of Americans who are in a marriage or committed relationship say they met their significant other online."[34] With so many options and easy accessibility, courtship may involve speed dating or meeting as many of the online matches as possible. Does all this Internet dating feel like a job search where one prepares a profile (which is like creating your resume for the job search), joins an online dating site such as Match.com (which is like filling out a job application), and sets up some "interviews" or first dates, which require online background research (see below) to prepare for the face-to-face meeting? "It's like online job applications, you can target many people simultaneously—it's like darts on a dart board, eventually one will stick." Under common law, a woman's "job" was to find a husband, but as women joined the workforce, her options broadened. Have the advances of technology returned us to a society where finding a mate is a job?[35] Has online dating taken away the mystery and romance?[36]

"Harassment on dating apps is a common problem." According to a 2013 study, "28 percent of online daters reported feeling harassed, with more female online daters (42 percent) saying they had experienced harassment than male online daters (17 percent)."[37] In response, some cyber-vigilantes have begun to shame cyber-harassers. Shortly after joining Tinder, a thirty-one-year-old woman began receiving "creepy messages. Married men propositioned her for sex. Guys lashed out if they didn't get a reply in a timely fashion. Various men sent naked selfies."[38] She tried blocking them and reported them to Tinder,[39] but they just came back with new screen names. So, she "took screen shots of the offending messages, superimposed them with remarks like 'Tinder is not the solution to your marital problems' and uploaded them to her profile as a warning to future matches." Another woman compiled "abusive messages from men on OKCupid and other sites" on her Instagram account, "Bye Felipe." She invited other women to submit screen shots to call out "dudes who turn hostile when rejected or ignored" and had 318,000 followers and four thousand submissions, including text messages that quickly devolved "into misogynistic outbursts, explicit photographs and tirades like, 'You deserve something worse than death.'" Curiously, "[t]he site's name is based on the urban slang term 'Bye Felicia' which is used to dismiss

---

34   "Five facts about online dating," Aaron Smith and Monica Anderson for the Pew Research Center, April 20, 2015. ttp://www.pewresearch.org/fact-tank/2015/04/20/5-facts-about-online-dating

35   Ibid. Quoting Joshua Sky, 26, a branding coordinator in Manhattan, describing the attitudes of many singles in their 20s.

36   Is this "job" mind-set of romance why some Manhattan Upper East Side wives receive year-end "wife bonuses" from their husbands for the wives' performances in running the family household and presumably other wifely activities? *Primates of Park Avenue*, Wednesday Martin, Simon & Schuster, 2015.

37   "Women Turn Table on Online Harassers," Alyson Krueger, *The New York Times*, May 3, 2015, P. 14, citing a study by the Pew Research Center.

38   "Ibid.

39   Tinder and other sites are aware of the harassment problem and will shut down a site. Twitter acknowledges its "online-abuse problem" and has worked to combat it. "Twitter tightens its policy against online harassment," Hayley Tsukayama, *The Washington Post Economy & Business*, April 22, 2015, A14.

someone insignificant." What does that say about a society where there exists such a term for this now daily occurrence of alienating someone?

But should these cyber-vigilantes be careful? "Lawsuits over negative reviews have risen in recent years with the popularity of sites such as Yelp, Angie's List and TripAdvisor that allow users to rate and provide feedback on businesses."[40] Reviewers are finding themselves in court, including the unhappy dog owner who posted negative reviews on Yelp and Angie's List over dog obedience classes ("In a nutshell, the services delivered were not as advertised and the owner refused a refund"),[41] which was met with the company's $65,000 defamation lawsuit against her, claiming the "statements were false and damaged her small business, which had great reviews until that point."[42] In another case, in Virginia, a homeowner filed a "scathing review" of the work done by the contractor she had hired, including that he billed her for work he did not do and implied he was involved with jewelry that had disappeared, calling the experience a "nightmare,"[43] to which the contractor responded that it was she who "stole his goods and services" since she did not pay him for the job and prevented him from entering the property to pick up his equipment. These cases raise the question whether the reviews are really that defamatory or are the businesses retaliating because of the importance online reviews have on their businesses? Does this have a "chilling effect on First Amendment rights"? In these cases the courts decided that each of the parties defamed the other and no one had received compensation. What about complaints about a child-care provider, or a date, would these cases with the threat of a countersuit of defamation that includes substantial financial penalties prevent posting? Some states (including Maryland) have anti-SLAPP laws ("strategic lawsuits against public participation") that "allow for the quick dismissal of cases a judge deems to be targeting First Amendment rights."[44] Is there a difference

---

40   "Panned on Yelp, business bites back," Justin Jouvenal, *The Washington Post*, March 26, 2015, B1. In 2012 in Fairfax, Virginia, a contractor sued a client for $750,000 but the jury found that both defamed each other and gave no money awards. "In suit over online reviews neither side wins damages," Justin Jouvenal, *The Washington Post*, February 2, 2014, C5. In another case a DC carpet business asked the court to turn over the names of negative reviewers who posted anonymously.

41   "Negative Yelp, Angie's List reviews prompt dog obedience business to sue," Justin Jouvenal, *The Washington Post*, March 25, 2015. http://www.washingtonpost.com/local/crime/negative-yelp-review-of-dog-obedience-class-spurs-lawsuit/2015/03/25/eb92dab6-d183-11e4-8fce-3941fc548f1c_story.html

42   Ibid.

43   "In suit over online reviews, neither side wins damages," Justin Jouvenal, *The Washington Post*, February 2, 2014, C5. The court said both sides defamed each other.

44   The District of Columbia also has one. What would be the effect when teenage girls at the all-girls National Cathedral School in Washington "'created an online document to share anecdotes about "'negative social and sexual experience.'" It started out as cooperative educational program in a health and human sexuality class with the neighboring all-boys school, but it soon became a forum for painful accounts of "'unwanted sexual advances at parties, of inappropriate sexual comments, and of sexual and social behaviors that our schools do not condone," wrote a school official in a letter to students' parents. While the letter "suggest[ed] that debate on the nation's college campuses about sexual misconduct is reverberating in high schools as well," the school shut the online document down. Should it have done this? At the all-boys school, St. Alban's, officials apologized "to any student who has been hurt or insulted" by responses from the school's students, and the boys were asked to "stop immediately." Via email, parents were asked to speak to their sons over the school break and to "clearly define appropriate behavior for him." Both schools reminded

between reviewing/outing a harassing online dater and outing/giving a negative review on services or goods?

Background Checks; not Personal Introductions

"There's another reason web-enabled singles are rendering traditional dates obsolete. If the purpose of the first date was to learn about someone's background, education, politics and cultural tastes, Google and Facebook have taken care of that."[45] But does this cyber background check take the place of actually meeting a person? Maybe Europe's "right to be forgotten" laws would again require an in-person meeting?

"The Internet may never truly forget, but Google is starting." An EU court requires Google to filter its search engine results when requested under Europe's "right to be forgotten" law whereby people have the right to request the removal of embarrassing Internet search results tied to their names. Google has begun removing offending user data only in Europe.[46] Google argues the law puts the company "in the uncomfortable position of making what are essentially censorship decisions," such as whether results "include outdated information about your private life" and whether "there's a public interest in the information remaining in search results—for example, if it relates to financial scams, professional malpractice, criminal convictions or the public conduct of a government official." The company will run a blanket disclaimer on all European sites to state that some of the search results may have been removed under the "right to be forgotten."[47] What is the effect of this law on the perceived reliability of the Internet? Is there a public interest in keeping such information online?

Sex Offender Registration in Teen Dating

States have good laws that punish sexual acts against minors. But sometimes internet dating has caught teens hooking up with teens under these laws which place them on the state's sex offender registry for life. Such registration often requires "regular contact with authorities", allows "searches of his home every 90 days" by the government and requires him to live "far from schools, parks and other public places."[48] In 2015 in Indiana, a 19-year-old boy "met a girl through Hot or Not, a dating app, and after some online flirting, he drove to pick her up at her house in Michigan, just miles over the state line. The had sex in a playground... The girl, who by her own account told [him] that she was 17---a year over the age of consent in Michigan—was

---

"parents to be sure that parties in private houses are supervised and that alcohol is not served to students at those events." "Online exchange roils two schools," Nick Anderson, *The Washington Post, Metro*, December 23, 2014, B1.

45 http://www.nytimes.com/2013/01/13/fashion/the-end-of-courtship.html

46 "Google begins removing user data under 'right to be forgotten law.'" Andrea Peterson, *The Washington Post,* June 27, 2014, A17. Since then, some European countries have asked Google to remove language on its citizens on the US web, but Google has yet to comply or agree to it.

47 Ibid.

48 https://www.nytimes.com/2015/07/05/us/teenagers-jailing-brings-a-call-to-fix-sex-offender-registries.html

actually 14".[49] The boy pleaded guilty, received a 90-day sentence and was ordered to register. Does this serve the public? During his sentencing, the judge "criticized online dating in general and berated [the defendant] for using the Internet to meet women."[50] As part of his sentence, the defendant was prohibited from using the Internet for 5 years, even though he was a computer science student. In an interview, a state senator and "one of the authors of the state's ex offender registry law said, "'In my opinion, society, over several decades, has become looser. People are meeting online, and that creates all sorts of problems. Now, people have all these crazy apps where you can locate people in your vicinity where people want to have a relationship. You should be very careful."[51] The boy's father said, "No computer for five years, no smartphone?... To me, that's wrong. That's like taking away electricity or heart or gas to somebody in today's world."[52] Who is right?

The Engagement Ring

After the Buffalo Bills' defensive end Mario Williams sued his former fiancée to recover a $785,000 ten-karat engagement ring, she responded by "releas[ing] his alleged text messages in which he talked about having suicidal thoughts, including, 'No money in the world should leave me with suicidal thoughts.'" The 2014 settlement of the case included this joint statement: "Ms. Marzouki regrets that after the lawsuit was filed, certain text messages were released by her lawyer without her knowledge that were taken out of context by the media," and "Ms. Marzouki believes that the media reports do not reflect the good character of Mr. Williams" and included public apologies by both.[53] Did the "accidental" release of personal text messages help resolve this domestic relations matter? As asked in prior cases of released personal communications during a legal matter, should that happen? Here text messages were made public. Is there a difference between the admissibility of a text message or a recording as evidence in a courtroom?

Dating Violence

Dating violence has always been a problem and technology has made it easier than ever for abusers to reach their victims.[54] "Dating violence refers to any kind of abuse—emotional, physical, or sexual—between dating partners. Young people are particularly vulnerable to dating violence; one in four adolescents reports having been in an abusive relationship." Technology enables this abuse. **Textual harassment** is abusive text messaging when one partner continuously texts the

---

49   Ibid.
50   Ibid, quoting Judge Dennis M. Wiley of the Michigan District Court.
51   Ibid, quoting Rick Jones, a Michigan state senator.
52   Ibid, quoting Lester Anderson.
53   "Mario Williams, former fiancée agree to settlement on $785K ring," Josh Katowitz, CBSSports, January 3, 2014. http://www.cbssports.com/nfl/eye-on-football/24396478/mario-williams-former-fiancee-agree-to-settlement-on-785k-ring
54   "Dating violence takes technological leap," Petula Dvorak, *The Washington Post*, March 5, 2013, B1.

other to demand their location or plans for the evening, or when a partner refuses to stop texting the other until receiving a response. "Social networks can also become tools for control. One in ten teens have had a boyfriend or girlfriend demand a password for email or social network accounts... and one in ten teens have had a boyfriend or girlfriend demand they un-friend someone on a social network. One Rhode Island teen was forced by her boyfriend to delete every male contact on her account, and then coerced to close it altogether."[55] Are these controlling behaviors precursors to physical violence?

Cyberstalking

New technologies have made us "Ph.D.s in Internet stalking," but amateurs in love.[56] "The term 'stalking' is often jokingly used when someone views a Facebook page so often that he knows *a little* too much about that person's recent life." Cyberstalking, however, is a serious crime on a social networking site and can result in criminal penalties. "**Cyberstalking** generally refers to a pattern of threatening or malicious behaviors"[57] and typically involves harassing a person with messages, written threats, and other persistent online behavior that endangers a person's safety. "Although cyberstalking may seem like nothing more than annoying behavior, it is a legitimate cause for concern. In many cases, it can lead to in-person stalking or endangerment if not taken seriously."[58] Because of its threatening nature, cyberstalking is usually considered the most dangerous of the three types of Internet harassment. Yet sanctions range from a misdemeanor to a felony.[59] An estimated 1.4 million people are stalked annually in the United States.[60]

California was the first state to pass a law in 1990, which criminalized stalking behavior. Since then, all states and the federal government have passed such laws, including an amendment to extend the law to stalking via electronic communications. In 1996, the federal government defined interstate stalking as a federal offense.[61] In Seattle, Washington, a college student was

---

55 Centers for Disease Control and Prevention. (2010). Understanding Teen Dating Violence: Fact Sheet. Retrieved from: http://www.cdc.gov/violenceprevention/pdf/TeenDatingViolence_2010-a.pdf

56 Alex Williams mourns the "End of Dating" in the "End of Courtship," Alex Williams, *New York Times*, January 11, 2013. http://www.nytimes.com/2013/01/13/fashion/the-end-of-courtship.html

57 http://www.ncsl.org/research/telecommunications-and-information-technology/cyberstalking-and-cyberharassment-laws.aspx

58 http://www.wsj.com/articles/cyberbullying-law-challenged-in-court-1401925445

59 Ibid.

60 Citing the National Violence Against Women Survey in http://www.ncsc.org/Topics/Children-Families-and-Elders/Domestic-Violence/Resource-Guide.aspx

61 Cyberstalking is usually thought of as being committed against the person who has not reciprocated the stalker's affections. In a twist, one woman alleged she was the victim of cyberstalking in an extramarital affair by another woman and the director of the CIA, which lead to his resignation and a later guilty plea to the federal charge of removing and retaining classified information because he had improperly shared classified information with her. General David Petraeus and his biographer Paula Broadwell were having an affair, in which the FBI discovered that Broadwell had been sending emails disparaging another woman to four-star General John Allen. After the FBI traced the emails to Broadwell, she admitted having sent them (as well as another from "Tampa Angel" to the woman's husband, Dr. Scott Kelley, which also disparaged his wife and promised "embarrassment for all, including spouses, such as info

sentenced to a six-month suspended term and deported[62] after he was convicted of cyberstalking for making threats on social media to carry out a campus shooting, and "to seriously injure or kill women" at the University of Washington and "other women." Another Seattle man, a former human resources officer, pleaded guilty to cyberstalking for making more than four thousand obscene and threatening phone calls to twelve hundred people, some of whom he had worked with. "The records showed that [he] had called hundreds of women, including one woman in his apartment complex, who received 177 calls. The woman filed numerous police reports, saying she believed the caller could see inside her apartment when he was talking to her.... Federal prosecutors say many of the victims altered their lives. Some moved, others quit jobs and still others canceled their cellphone numbers, only to start receiving calls at work or home."[63]

In 2014, the US Justice Department arrested the creator of the "stalker app" called StealthGenie, which, for one hundred to three hundred dollars a year, allowed "buyers" to track nearly any movement or utterance of their target. This app underscores the remarkable surveillance capabilities of iPhones, BlackBerrys, and Android devices. It "requires that a user gain physical access to a targeted smartphone. Once StealthGenie is installed, it continuously reports information back to the user without the phone owner's knowledge."[64] This is all done surreptitiously, without the person's knowledge or consent. The inventor was charged with "conspiracy, sale of a surreptitious interception device and advertising a surreptitious interception device." In the first prosecution of its kind, federal officials said StealthGenie violated the law by "offering the ability to secretly monitor phone calls and other communications in almost real time, something typically legal only for law enforcement." "Selling spyware is not just reprehensible, it's a crime.... Apps like StealthGenie are expressly designed for use by stalkers and domestic abusers who want to know every detail of a victim's personal life—all without the victim's knowledge."[65] The manufacturer argued that, "any legal issues were limited to the users of the device." Is it correct

in national headlines"). All charges against Broadwell were dropped in December 2012. The case goes on, however, because the woman and her husband have sued certain government agencies and departments for allegedly defaming their character. "FBI agent testifies in Paula Broadwell cyberstalking case," Jake Tapper, CNN, April 20, 2015. http://www.cnn.com/2015/04/19/politics/david-petraeus-paula-broadwell-fbi-case/

62 In addition, he will not be able to return to the United States for ten years. He has also "posted comments on several YouTube videos related to Elliot Rodger, the man who killed six people and then himself near the University of California, Santa Barbara, [in 2014]... some of [his] comments were posted only a few days after the June 5 shootings at Seattle Pacific University that left one student dead and two wounded." Posting under the Google username "Foss Dark," he defended Rodger's actions, and in one comment on June 9 said, "I live in Seattle and go to UW, that's all ill give u. Ill make sure I kill only women, and many more than Elliot accomplished [sic]." http://blogs.seattletimes.com/today/2014/12/ex-uw-student-convicted-of-cyberstalking-deported-to-india/ See also, http://www.washingtontimes.com/news/2014/dec/26/ex-seattle-student-convicted-of-cyberstalking-depo/#ixzz3bq2q6ucp

63 "Man guilty of cyberstalking: 4,000 calls to 1,200 people," Mike Carter, *The Seattle Times*, September 24, 2010. http://www.seattletimes.com/seattle-news/man-guility-of-cyber-stalking-4000-calls-to-1200-people/

64 "Maker of StealthGenie, an app used for spying, is indicted in Virginia," Craig Timer and Matt Zapotosky, *The Washington Post*, September 30, 2014, P. 14.

65 "Pakistani Man Indicted for Selling StealthGenie Spyware App," FBI. September 29, 2014, quoting Assistant Attorney General Leslie R. Caldwell of the Justice Department's Criminal Division.

that the consumer who uses it for devious purposes is the problem? The manufacturer claimed it advertised the app "as a system for monitoring small children or suspicious employees."[66] In 2015, the StealthGenie creator plead guilty and admitted, "he broke the law, albeit unknowingly, in advertising and selling" the StealthGenie and was ordered to pay a $500,000 fine.[67]

A study showed that one in four stalking cases nationwide involved some type of tracking technology.[68] In response to this statistic, the federal cyberstalking law was again amended in 2006 to include surveillance of a victim by a GPS (global positioning system).[69] Most people use their GPS to get directions or to find the nearest restaurant, but a GPS can also be used by stalkers to track their victims from a distance. While the US Supreme Court ruled police cannot use a twenty-four-hour tracker such as a GPS without a warrant,[70] the ruling did not apply to private citizens. It is left to the states to prohibit such behavior.

New York amended its laws, in October 2014, to prevent private citizens from using tracking devices or "electronic following." In one of the first cases to use the new law, in 2015 a New York man was arrested and charged "for allegedly using a GPS device to stalk his ex-girlfriend."[71] When the woman took her BMW in for service, the mechanic found a GPS on the car. She contacted the state police who removed the tracker that had allowed her ex-boyfriend "to follow the BMW's every move on a smartphone for two months." With such inexpensive and accurate technology, it is unlikely this will be the last case.

Revenge Porn

How should society deal with the sexual extortion that is facilitated by technology? **Revenge porn** (also known as nonconsensual pornography) occurs when a person posts naked pictures of another person online, usually as retaliation against that person for a prior action, such as a breakup. Often the photos were made and obtained consensually, but posted and disseminated without consent. "Until recently, [such] actions would have been outside the reach of the law,

---

66 "Maker of StealthGenie, an app used for spying, is indicted in Virginia," Craig Timer and Matt Zapotosky, *The Washington Post*, September 30, 2014, P. 14.

67 "Maker of smartphone spying app pleads guilty in federal court," Matt Zapotosky, *The Washington Post*, November 25, 2014. http://www.washingtonpost.com/local/crime/maker-of-smartphone-spying-app-pleads-guilty-in-federal-court/2014/11/25/a211d506-74b6-11e4-bd1b-03009bd3e984_story.html

68 "Ossining Man Charged With Stalking After Allegedly Putting GPS On Ex's Car," Kenneth Martin, NewYorkCBS, February 11, 2015. http://newyork.cbslocal.com/2015/02/11/ossining-man-charged-with-stalking-after-allegedly-putting-gps-on-exs-car/

69 Ibid.

70 *U.S. v. Jones*, 132 S. Ct. 945, 565 U.S. (2012), http://www.oyez.org/cases/2010-2019/2011/2011_10_1259 Interestingly, in that case, Justice Samuel Alito aligned with three of the court's liberals and accused conservative Justice Anthony Scalia's analysis of the case as relying on eighteenth-century trespass law to solve a twenty-first-century privacy problem.

71 The GPS was a "Sky Patrol" tracker that sells for about $300. "Ossining Man Charged With Stalking After Allegedly Putting GPS On Ex's Car," Kenneth Martin, February 11, 2015. http://newyork.cbslocal.com/2015/02/11/ossining-man-charged-with-stalking-after-allegedly-putting-gps-on-exs-car/

because victims were not offered protection from people who intentionally posted their nude photographs without their consent." New Jersey was one of the first states to pass a law to prosecute people for posting "revenge porn." Today, "the District (of Columbia) and 34 states have laws criminalizing the publication of explicit images and videos without the subject's consent." In August 2016, Congress debated whether a federal law was needed.[72] "The laws are receiving more support nationwide, and Facebook, Twitter and Reddit recently banned nonconsensual sexual images and videos."

In New Jersey it is a third-degree invasion of privacy to "post sexually explicit photos without the other's consent." In December 2014, former New York Jets' football player Jermaine Cunningham was arrested in New Jersey after "sending naked pictures of a woman to the victim's friends and family following a 'domestic incident' in New Jersey."[73] He was charged under the state's revenge porn law along with invasion of privacy and a gun offense.

Under California's first "revenge porn" law it was a "misdemeanor to post identifiable nude pictures of someone else online without permission with the intent to cause emotional distress or humiliation. That law was expanded [in 2014] to make it a misdemeanor to distribute a naked photo of someone, often in the act of revenge, even if the photo was originally taken by the naked person."[74] In 2014, the first California case to successfully prosecute under its 2013 "revenge porn" law involved a man's breakup with his girlfriend. After their relationship ended, "that is when he decided to get even" by posting a "topless photograph of his ex-girlfriend on her employer's Facebook page along with messages calling her a 'drunk' and a 'slut' and encouraging her firing."[75] After his conviction, he was sentenced to a year in jail. The California attorney general said, "She has a problem with the term 'revenge porn,' saying that it suggests consent and that the perpetrators were vengeful ex-lovers, which is not always the case. Cyber exploitation... is a more accurate term to describe the crime."[76] Is she correct?

Also in California, in 2014, a man *Rolling Stone* magazine "once dubbed the 'most hated man on the Internet' because of his posting of explicit photos and information about the people portrayed in them on his website plead guilty to identity theft and computer hacking" (and could face from two to seven years in federal prison). In addition to hiring "someone to hack hundreds of email accounts and steal photos," he also posted images from "jilted lovers to get even with former partners."[77] The man then charged the women $250 to remove the naked pictures. "As

---

72   "Taking on revenge porn", *The Washington Post*, August 21. 2016, A 18.

73   Ibid.

74   "Revenge porn site founder pleads guilty hacking, ID theft," Jonathan Lloyd, NBCLosAngeles.com. http://www.nbclosangeles.com/news/local/Revenge-Porn-Case-Hunter-Moore-Guilty-Plea-294199191.html

75   "'Revenge porn' conviction is the first under California law," Veronica Rocha, *Los Angeles Times*, December 4, 2014. http://www.latimes.com/local/crime/la-me-1204-revenge-porn-20141205-story.html

76   Ibid.

77   Hunter "Moore, who was dubbed the 'king of revenge porn,' later told a *Los Angeles Times* reporter who asked about those who wanted their photos removed: 'I understand it can hurt your reputation, and your job and yadda yadda yadda.'" "Revenge porn site founder pleads guilty to hacking, ID theft," Jonathan Lloyd, NBCLosAngleles.com. http://www.nbclosangeles.com/news/local/Revenge-Porn-Case-Hunter-Moore-Guilty-Plea-294199191.html

part of a plea agreement, all of his future online activities will be monitored once [he] is released from prison. He must register devices capable of accessing the Internet with his probation officer, agree to have those devices searched, and agree not to encrypt any files without permission."

A Seattle man was "charged with cyber-stalking for allegedly uploading nude photos of a woman on a revenge porn website and allegedly threatening to show them to her friends and family if she didn't 'play along.'" The woman had hired the man, a computer technician, off of Craigslist to transfer data between two of her computers, one of which had some nude photos. He "is accused of posting dozens of naked pictures of the woman on a revenge porn website." The "calls got more and more alarming, the victim said, with the computer tech allegedly threatening to 'tie her up and rape her.'"[78] While this case clearly shows the need for laws against cybercrimes given the impacts on the victims, does it confuse cyber stalking with revenge porn? Should they be two separate crimes?

Some say this is the risk a person takes in taking nude photos. But is it similar to victim shaming/blaming in a sexual assault case?[79] Just remember: if you send a photo to anyone, you cannot be sure what they might do with it.[80] If it is posted online, your family, your children, and even your employer may see it. When on the other side of the camera lens, remember: if you want to post a photo, make sure you have the person's permission to post it—not just possess it.

Positive Note #1

A 2016 study found that the internet's "vast online dating pool is breaking down social barriers and helping people meet—and marry—others of different races, religions and education."[81] Maybe the internet will fulfill its goal of increasing globalization.

Positive Note #2

In Japan, Japanese artist Yasushi Takahashi—aka Yassan—used GPS (global positioning satellites) to create a marriage proposal one could see from space. Yassan quit his job, traveled for

---

78   "Seattle man charged with cyberstalking for allegedly posting naked pics of woman on revenge site," Hana Kim, Q13Fox, July 3, 2014. http://q13fox.com/2014/07/03/computer-tech-posts-naked-pictures-of-woman-he-barely-knows-on-revenge-porn-website/

79   One author compared the "shame of cyber-security violations to the rationale behind why rape survivors often don't report the crimes to the police." "You've been Hacked," Jenna Wortham, The New York Times Book Review, May 17, 2015, P. 14, citing Future Crimes, by Marc Goodman, Random House Audio, 2015.

80   Even just keeping a nude selfie can be a crime. In North Carolina, a 16- and 17-year-old couple made a plea deal to charges of child pornography to avoid jail time of up to 10 years and registration on the sex offenders registry. When investigators were investigating a statutory rape claim not involving the couple, the investigators found the pictures on their phones. The boy had a naked picture of himself taken on his phone and another naked picture of the girl (given consensually) and she had a nude picture of herself on her phone. Each was charged with sexually exploiting a minor. "The U.S. at a glance", The Week, October 2, 2015, P 7.

81   https://www.pressreader.com/usa/the-washington-post/20160919/281840053136380 referring to a study done by Gina Porarca of the University of Lausanne, Switzerland.

six months through Japan, and covered more than 4,349 miles (mostly on foot and sometimes by car, ferry, or bicycle). GPS tracking followed his every step; at the end, the GPS records of his travels spelled out the phrase "Marry Me"—with an arrow through the heart sign.[82] According to Guinness Records, it is the world's largest proposal. By the way, she said yes.

HOW MARRIAGE AFFECTS WOMEN (CHAPTER 10)

Under the fiction of oneness, at common law, a married woman "merged" with her husband to become "one," the husband, in the eyes of the law. Some recent technology cases seem to uphold that outdated concept. In 2009, a Minnesota man "installed a GPS tracker on [his wife's] car and allegedly downloaded spyware onto her phone and the family computer. His now ex-wife "had a mechanic search her car. The tracker was found." The husband was sentenced to a month in jail but a second conviction for "illegally tracking her car, was overturned on appeal." The judge ruled that "joint ownership [between the husband and the wife] gave [the husband] the right to install the GPS tracker."[83] Also, to avoid liability, manufactures of spyware apps warn consumers to get permission before installing them. But the Minnesota case shows that "… questions of ownership and privacy get messy between married partners, and the landscape remains in flux as courts struggle to apply old laws to new technology."[84]

DIVORCE (CHAPTER 11)

"It may seem surprising that a Facebook profile, a relatively small factor compared to other drivers of human behavior, could have a significant statistical relationship with divorce rates and marital satisfaction. It nonetheless seems to be the case."[85] A 2014 study published in a computer journal, *Computers in Human Behavior, in Law & Daily Life,* found a link between Facebook/social media use and divorce rates, finding a 2 to 4 percent increase in the divorce rate with every 20 percent growth in Facebook users (e.g., Facebook accounts per capita).[86]

---

82 It will be part of a new documentary about walking leading to extraordinary things, the "Walkumentary Series." "The most romantic proposals ever," Catherine Eade, "Mail Online," December 4, 2014. http://www.dailymail.co.uk/travel/travel_news/article-2860396/The-romantic-proposal-Artist-spends-six-months-trekking-3-000-miles-Japan-GPS-tracker-spell-Marry-islands.htmlv

83 "The adultery arms race," Michelle Cottle, *The Atlantic*, November 2014, P. 58, 61.

84 Ibid.

85 Quoting Sabastian Valenzuela and Daniel Halpern of the Catholic University of Chile and James Katz of Boston University, from their study reported in the journal *Computers in Human Behavior, in Law & Daily Life* in "Social networking link to divorce, marital unhappiness" in "Facebook, Twitter Usage Linked to Higher Divorce Rates," Tom Jacobs, *Pacific Standard*, May 2, 2014. http://www.psmag.com/books-and-culture/facebook-twitter-usage-linked-higher-divorce-rates-80579

86 "Social networking link to divorce, marital unhappiness," Everette Rosenfeld, CNBC, July 8, 2014. In the study they compared state-by-state divorce rates to per capita Facebook accounts. In a separate analysis, they also used data from a 2011–2012 survey that asked individuals about marriage quality and social media use.

While the study "found a link between social media use and decreased marriage quality in every model... analyzed," the researchers made clear this does not prove that Facebook caused the increase in marital dissatisfaction or that marital dissatisfaction causes people to join Facebook. The study also saw that "participants who spent more time on online social networks reported, on average, lower levels of marital happiness" and that "heavier use of social networking sites was a 'strong, positive predictor' of thinking about walking away from one's marriage."[87] They wrote, "Excessive use of social networking sites could leave ignored spouses feeling abandoned. If people are using such sites to follow former lovers—or people who could conceivably turn into romantic partners—such behavior 'may evoke feelings of jealousy.'"

"Technology continues to change the nature of relationships. Social networking and messaging apps make it easier for people to misbehave, where previously alcohol was often the mitigating factor in dubious behavior."[88] Courtrooms see increased use of social media and technologies, especially in divorce and child custody proceedings. The availability of lives shared on social media is an excellent and inexpensive source of information when investigating fault-based claims in divorce. Through the use of inexpensive technology such as spycams or hidden cameras in the home (including in bathrooms and bedrooms) estranged spouses can gain access to the other's most private moments via spyware programs that relay the moment to the other's computer, tablet, or cell phone and/or that intercept emails and Internet searches.[89]

Spying, however, is often unnecessary in the world of over sharing when estranged spouses share photos and all the details of their lives on Facebook or other social media sites. (If the ex does not post the info, someone on her friends' list may). They also provide an easy way to record a conversation or print a text to create a permanent record.[90] All of this has provided divorce lawyers with a treasure trove of evidence that previously required hours of private investigation by costly detectives. "Cloud-based software, such as Apple's iCloud, provide a way for information to be shared wirelessly between people's laptops, cell phones, and tablets. Any device connected to the cloud software will have access to the pictures, messages, applications, and many other things that are on the other devices. This software is now providing a new way for people to learn whether their partners are cheating on them." This allows partners to discover

---

87   While the media was ablaze with "research claims that one in five of online divorce petitions cited Facebook," that has been debunked (see "Irreconcilable Claim: Facebook Causes 1 in 5 Divorce," Carl Bialik, *The Wall Street Journal*, March 12, 2011.) "In fact, both the marriage and divorce rates in the United States have declined as Internet usage has risen, according to the Centers for Disease Control and Prevention's National Center for Health Statistics" according to Bialik.

88   Quoting a family law lawyer in England, Sam Hall, in "Apple iCloud sparks divorce cases," Sophie Curtis, *The Telegraph*, April 18, 2014. http://www.telegraph.co.uk/technology/apple/10770335/Apple-iCloud-sparks-divorce-cases.html

89   http://www.ncsc.org/Topics/Children-Families-and-Elders/Domestic-Violence/Resource-Guide.aspx

90   Even when you think you have "hidden" or deleted your online dating history, forensics examiners can uncover it during a divorce to show adultery, even if the divorce and separation has already occurred (in many states, including Maryland). Moreover, it may be a duty to preserve such data in a court case; an attempt to wipe the computer's hard drive could be sanctionable behavior subject to financial or other penalties.

incriminating messages or photos when their devices sync to the cloud if accounts are shared between partners. In one case, "a married man in his early forties was out for the night with male friends, who encouraged him to download Tinder and 'look up' nearby single women looking for dates. He also used Snapchat to exchange explicit photos with women, which continued in the weeks following the night out. Unfortunately for the man, the photos and messages synced to the iCloud account he shared with his wife—which could also have been viewed by his iPad-literate son, aged just seven."[91]

Many people take for granted that they can control who sees what in their cloud accounts, even when they have shared these accounts with family and friends. In reality, it is unclear how this privacy works when trying to apply the law. Some people try to discuss their expectations for online privacy by making real-world comparisons (e.g., their cloud account becomes a "locked room"). Do these real-life analogies work for technology? How should privacy work in these cases?

Online Affairs

While cell phone pictures and selfies and other uses of technology are providing the documented evidence for a divorce request, what happens if no adulterous sexual relationship occurs—or even no physical meeting at all? Should adultery include a purely cyber-based affair?[92] One Australian study found that "more than half of the respondents believed an online relationship constituted unfaithfulness, with the numbers climbing to 71 percent for cybersex and 82 percent for in-person meetings."[93] "Women usually feel more threatened by the emotional betrayal of a partner's online affair, while men are more concerned about physical encounters... but the gender differences are lessening."[94] "Online affairs can contribute to divorce and child custody fights as the involved partner becomes more enmeshed in the online relationship."[95] One review of studies on Internet

91   "Apple iCloud sparks divorce cases," Sophie Curtis, *The Telegraph*, April 18, 2014. http://www.telegraph.co.uk/technology/apple/10770335/Apple-iCloud-sparks-divorce-cases.html

92   In *The Enlightenment of Nina Findlay*, by Andrea Gilles, Other Press, 2015, the author "plumbs the heart of marital infidelity. Is it the flesh or the sprit, she asks, that commits true adultery? And if the spirit, what does that reveal about the charged gray area of extramarital friendship—especially in the Facebook age, when texts may fly and laptops hide secrets, their sparks flaring?" "The Boys Next Door," Dylan Landis, May 17, 2015, *The New York Times Book Review*, P. 22.

93   Based on a 2008 Australian study into Internet affairs of 183 adults who were currently or recently in a relationship, which found that more than 10 percent had formed intimate online relationships, 8 percent had experienced cybersex, and 6 percent had met their Internet partners in person (*Australian Journal of Counselling Psychology*, Vol. 9, No. 2) in the *American Psychological Association's Monitor on Psychology*, March 2011. http://www.apa.org/monitor/2011/03/Internet.aspx

94   Quoting Katherine Hertlein, PhD, an associate professor at the University of Nevada in Las Vegas who studies online affairs in the *American Psychological Association's Monitor on Psychology*, March 2011. http://www.apa.org/monitor/2011/03/Internet.aspx

95   Citing a 2008 article in the *Journal of Marital and Family Therapy* (Vol. 34, No. 4) by Hertlein and a colleague who reviewed eight studies of Internet affairs, in the *American Psychological Association's Monitor on Psychology*, March 2011. http://www.apa.org/monitor/2011/03/Internet.aspx

affairs documented many negative effects, "including less interest in sex in the committed relationship and neglect of work and time with children. Almost two-thirds of the participants in one study reported they had met and had sex with their Internet partners; only 44 percent of them reported using condoms."[96]

Taking this line of thought to an extreme, is it "cheating" when one partner "abides by the marital commitment to wait until she and her husband can co-watch [a TV show] but her husband has found it tougher to abide by this media fidelity"? Is it true that "in modern-day romance, resisting the impulse to binge so that you may watch (a TV show) with a lover is the new equivalent of meeting the parents or sharing a sober kiss"? Was actress Molly Ringwald correct when she tweeted, "The definition of devotion: waiting until the end of the day to listen to the last episode of @serial with your husband"?[97] Has the immersion in constant access to programming expanded relationship fidelity to not bingeing alone?

ASSISTED REPRODUCTIVE TECHNOLOGIES (CHAPTER 15)

The speed of advancements in assisted reproductive technologies and technology exceed the law's ability to keep pace. Some examples:

In Tennessee, in 2014, a woman placed her four unused pre-embryos[98] on Facebook for adoption. She had used two, but was now too old to use the remaining four. The eggs were still usable; they remain viable for less than ten years. When placing the pre-embryos on Facebook, she "detailed the kind of family she and her husband were looking for: married several years, in a steady loving relationship, strong Christian background, roots in Tennessee."[99] Should the families who adopt the pre-embryos have a relationship with the "donor" family? If so, what kind? Should they act like friends, cousins, or more?

In 2016, a man answered a *Craigslist* ad to donate sperm that was placed by a lesbian couple. When the couple broke up they sued the donor for child support. Although Kansas law protects donors who give their sperm to a doctor for insemination from being recognized as the legal father, in this case the woman did not use a doctor. Still, the court ruled that the donor was not the child's father and ruled that the woman who did not give birth was the second parent.[100]

In 2015, pregnant women began selling their urine on eBay. Other than their intent to make money in an unsavory way, the purpose is unclear. Another ad suggests it is a way to "make that

---

96 "While there is no universally accepted definition, an Internet affair frequently involves intimate chat sessions and sexually stimulating conversation or cybersex, which may include filming mutual masturbation with a Web camera." Ibid.

97 "Cheating with 'The Good Wife,'" Katherine Rosman, *The New York Times*, February 15, 2015, P.2.

98 A human embryo or fertilized ovum in the first fourteen days after fertilization, before implantation in the uterus has occurred. https://www.google.com/search?q=what+is+a+preembryo&ie=utf-8&oe=utf-8

99 "Family turns to Facebook to find home for unused embryos," Kelly Wallace, CNN, January 14, 2015. http://www.cnn.com/2015/01/07/living/feat-family-facebook-unused-embryos/

100 http://wqad.com/2016/11/30/kansas-judge-rules-sperm-donor-not-on-hook-for-child-support/

man yours" by providing a fake positive pregnancy test to persuade him to propose?[101] Possibly, this scam is also designed to embezzle money for the cost of an abortion? Women regularly sell their breast milk online. All of this is done without regulation.

US businesses now offer "fetal keepsake images and videos using ultrasound. Some of this imaging requires an hour-long session to video the fetus, or even several sessions." Ultrasound imaging is a technique that uses high-frequency sound waves to examine tissues inside the body. Medicine has used this method for years to monitor a baby's development in the womb or even to determine its sex. The problem with this new commercial ultrasound imaging is that it can produce "physical effects in tissue" and the "long-term consequences are unknown." Also, "it may cause unnecessary anxiety… if images, videos or monitor readings are misinterpreted. The point is ultrasound is an invaluable medical tool in pregnancy. It's not a gimmick. Use it wisely."[102]

NONMARITAL BIRTHS (CHAPTER 16)

Tweet Serves as Recognition of Nonmarital Child

While a non-married biological father can "hold out" his child as his own and legitimize the child as his by such public recognition, usually this results from telling people that this is his child and/or doing parental activities with the child. In a modern-day twist, Representative Steve Cohen from Tennessee "held out" his nonmarital twenty-four-year-old daughter as his own via a series of public tweets. It "began when [she] tweeted the 56-year-old bachelor Congressman just before President Obama's State of the Union address… to say she saw him on television." "Pleased u r watching. ilu," he responded, before deleting the tweet just three minutes later. The next day, on Wednesday, he sent the young woman another tweet. "Nice to know you were watchin' SOTU [state of the union]." "Happy Valentines beautiful girl. Ilu."[103]

This caused some to be suspicions[104] and "a media inquiry began as to the recipient's identity." In response to media questions, "[a]n aide to the 64-year-old Memphis Democrat said he had accidentally exchanged a couple of public tweets with a woman who is the daughter of a friend, but removed them when he realized they weren't private." Later, Representative Cohen confessed that the woman was "his daughter whom he learned about three years ago." "Cohen, who has never been married, said… that he decided to publicly acknowledge Victoria Brink

---

101 "Selling fake positive pregnancy tests, no questions asked," Ben Axleson, Syracuse.com http://www.syracuse.com/news/index.ssf/2013/09/women_sell_fake_pregnancy_tests_craigslist.html"Woman

102 "Prenatal Tests Unsound Practices," Nancy Szokan, *The Washington Post*, February 17, 2015, E3, citing an article in the *Lancet*.

103 http://www.nydailynews.com/news/politics/congressman-flirty-tweets-college-student-raise-eyebrows-article-1.1264230, "Congressman's tweets to bombshell blonde lead to bombshell announcement—she's his daughter!" Kristen A. Lee, *New York Daily News*, February 14, 2013.

104 Following the tweets, the Tennessee Republican Party's executive director issued a news release comparing Cohen to former US Representative Anthony Weiner, who resigned in 2011 in disgrace after tweeting lewd pictures of himself.

as his daughter after bloggers and the media tried to make the exchanges appear salacious."[105] But in another twist, it turns out that she is not. A subsequent DNA test showed they were not related. Cohen, who is 64, said he was "stunned and dismayed" that the tests "disproved what Victoria and I believed about our relationship."[106]

CHILD ABUSE (CHAPTER 17)

"A Korean couple's compulsive video gaming led to the starvation of their newborn."[107] The child's name was Sarang, which means "love" in Korean.[108] More ironically, during this time they were "raising a virtual child in an online fantasy game." The Korean court gave them a two-year sentence, which was suspended for the female defendant because she was again pregnant.[109] Was this the only case, it would be extreme. In 2013, in Oklahoma, however, "[i]nvestigators believe [that a] couple spent so much time playing with their avatars in a life-simulation video game that they let their daughter starve."[110] The couple was charged with child abuse and neglect when they left their starving three-year-old daughter, who weighed thirteen pounds, at the hospital "and went back to their Tulsa home to go back to playing the online game." Although the child was not able to walk or move and had "very limited vocal skills," she was expected to survive.[111] Technology's addictive nature does not bode well for some parents or their children.

In 2015, in Virginia, a forty-four-year-old woman received a one-year prison sentence for having her two young children take nude photos of her. But is taking pictures of mom nude really

---

105   "Steve Cohen, Victoria Brink Twitter Exchange Reveals Father-Daughter Relationship," Lucas L. Johnson, *Huffington Post*, November 15, 2013.

106   Cohen said, "I still love Victoria, hold dear the time I have shared with her, and hope to continue to be a part of her life. It's been a roller-coaster ride these last three and a half years, from which I have learned something about parenting and some more about love, life and heartache." "Tests show Rep. Steve Cohen's daughter is not his," Catalinia Camia, *USA Today*, July 18, 2013. http://www.usatoday.com/story/onpolitics/2013/07/18/steve-cohen-daughter-paternity-twitter/2551031/

107   "Do new technologies pose an existential threat?" Matthew Wisnioski, *The Washington Post*, February 15. 2014, reviewing *Mind Change* by Susan Greenfield, Random House, 2015.

108   The story was the subject of the HBO movie *Love Child*, July 28, 2014. "A Korean Couple let a baby die while they played a video game," Sean Elder, *Newsweek*, July 27, 2014. http://www.newsweek.com/2014/08/15/korean-couple-let-baby-die-while-they-played-video-game-261483.html

109   "Jail for couple whose baby died while they raised online child," Andrew Salmon, CNN, May 28, 2010. http://www.cnn.com/2010/WORLD/asiapcf/05/28/south.korea.virtual.baby/

110   "Oklahoma parents so engulfed in Second Life they allegedly starved their real 3-year-old daughter," Joe Kemp, *New York Daily News*, October 12, 2013. http://www.nydailynews.com/news/national/oklahoma-parents-engulfed-online-fantasy-world-allegedly-starved-real-3-year-old-daughter-cops-article-1.1483479

111   Social services had taken custody of the girl when she was a few weeks old because the couple was not "spending time" with her. She was returned a year later but returned "malnourished just a couple of months later." While continuing to reunite the family, the mother "allegedly requested to keep the visits limited to the afternoon hours, because she claimed to have a late-night gig as a deejay." "When officials found the famished child… they learned that the job Pester mentioned was only a computer game in which she played a deejay." Ibid.

neglect? Does it make a difference that these pictures were for her online prostitution ads? The child-neglect charges were made after an investigation began on possible prostitution in the home allegations.[112]

Beyond such obvious cases of child abuse, the Internet has opened the floodgates for other forms of abuse; from YouTube videos of parents who encourage their toddlers to get high on their marijuana smoke[113] to videos of child pornography. "Omnipresent in 2007, a quarter of all Internet searches were related to pornography. Nielson ratings showed that in January 2010, more than a quarter of Internet users in the United States, almost 60 million people visited a pornographic Web site. That number represents nearly a fifth of all the men, women, and children in this country."[114] While discussion of the effects of such statistics on morality, dating, and sex are beyond this book; this section focuses on the Internet as a tool for the illegal distribution of child pornography, which provides a financial incentive for its creation. Child pornography includes sexual abuse, and it is a crime to distribute or watch it. Laws against making and viewing child pornography are strong and clear. The more difficult issue is how to penetrate the Dark Web to prosecute and stop it.

"In 1978, Congress made child pornography illegal and then the Supreme Court upheld a state's ban on the sale of it amounting to the death knell of businesses that made or sold it... But then came the Internet,"[115] which enabled a black market in the industry. One issue the courts have wrestled with involves restitution to the child victims of pornography. While the law requires restitution payments from the perpetrator of the crime, should such payments extend to those who view it? Does the cybercrime reoccur each time the scene is viewed? "Studies link child sexual abuse to psychological trauma, addiction and violent relationships in adulthood." But there is no research on possible additional harm that comes from knowing that pictures of your sexual abuse are online.[116] When the issue was raised legally in the context of restitution demands, "[in] at least a dozen cases, defendants have appealed restitution decisions and mostly won." Five federal courts have "expressed skepticism" on requests beyond nominal restitution while two other appeals courts "allowed the young women to recover from individual defendants as members of the group of viewers but only for amounts of $10,000 or less."[117] Only a few child-pornography victims have sued for restitution. The 2014 US Supreme Court case of *Paroline v.*

---

112 "Mother in Sterling gets prison for child neglect," Dana Hedgpeth, *The Washington Post, Local Digest*, March 20, 2015, B3.

113 Along with various YouTube videos, a Washington woman's cell phone showed her twenty-two-month-old toddler inhaling from a bong. "Washington mother accused of letting her toddler inhale marijuana from a bong," March 13, 2013, Fox News. http://insider.foxnews.com/2013/03/13/jarring-video-washington-mom-accused-of-letting-toddler-inhale-marijuana-smoke-from-bong

114 "Nielson ratings showed that in January 2010, more than a quarter of Internet users in the United States, almost 60 million people visited a pornographic Web site. About one-quarter 'Hard Core,'" Natasha Vargas-Cooper, *The Atlantic*, January/February 2011, P. 97.

115 "The Price of Stolen Childhood," Emily Bazelon, *The New York Times Magazine*, January 27, 2013, P. 24, 25.

116 Ibid., P. 29.

117 Ibid., P. 29.

U.S.,[118] involving a nine-year-old girl (called "Amy"), who was sexually abused by her uncle who lived across the street with her mother's sister, looked at this issue. "When [the victim] was 17, she learned that images of her abuse were being trafficked on the Internet, in effect repeating the original wrongs, for she knew that her humiliation and hurt would be renewed well into the future as thousands of additional wrongdoers witnessed those crimes." Defendant Doyle Randall Paroline was one of those who viewed her videos and he pled guilty in federal court to possessing about "300 images of child pornography, including two of an 8- or 9-year-old girl identified in court documents as 'Amy Unknown.'"[119]

"Under the 2004 Victim Notification System at the Justice Department, a crime victim must receive notice every time a suspect in that crime is arrested or has a court appearance.[120] If the child is still a minor that notice goes to her parents."[121] The girl's attorney read the Violence Against Woman Act, which "gave victims of sex crimes, including child pornography, the right to restitution or compensation for the 'full amount' of their losses"—which meant restitution was mandatory.[122] "Each time a letter arrived [that involved viewing of an "Amy" picture], her attorney would investigate to see if the defendant had assets to pay restitution. Based on financial projections 'Amy' claimed $3.4 million as a lifetime claim,"[123] including compensation "for psychological damage and lost income after she discovered the images" were on the Internet."[124] Amy's attorney then looked for "wealthy defendants" based on the victim letters. One, Alan Hesketh, a former vice president at Pfizer, a pharmaceutical company, "was charged with trading nearly 2,000 child pornography photos online—among them four pictures of Amy." When the state filed its criminal case against him, Amy's attorney filed a request for restitution.[125] Hesketh plead guilty and was sentenced to six and a half years in prison. "With the judge's encouragement, he agreed to pay $130,000 in restitution to Amy."[126] Another defendant, a sixty-five-year-old sheriff's deputy from Virginia, "was caught with more than 600 pictures on his computer," including Amy's. He was sentenced to seventeen and a half years, and the judge ordered him to "pay all

---

118   *PAROLINE v. UNITED STATES* (2014) 701 F. 3d 749, vacated and remanded. https://www.law.cornell.edu/supremecourt/text/12-8561 See also, the lower court case from the 5th Circuit.

119   The uncle plead guilty to one count of rape and two counts of child sexual abuse in state court and was sentenced to the minimum for each one, which totaled twelve and a half years in prison. In federal court, he pleaded guilty to one count of production of child pornography and received a twelve-year sentence. Both sentences were served concurrently. "Money is No Cure," Emily Bazelon, *The New York Times Magazine*, January 27, 2013, P. 24, 26.

120   Ibid., P. 24, 25.

121   In one child pornography victim's case, "she received so many of the letters that 'We stacked them in a laundry basket in a walk-in closet so I wouldn't have to see them. Then there were more baskets, and we had to move them to the garage.'" Ibid., 25.

122   Ibid., P. 26.

123   Ibid., P. 26.

124   "Court limits payment in child porn case," Robert Barnes, *The Washington Post*, April 24, 2014, A4.

125   Ibid. Amy attended his hearing to prove that this was not a "victimless crime," as he alleged. "I thought, I want him to look at me and know that I'm not a picture; I'm a person."

126   Ibid., P. 27.

of Amy's claim." When he turned out to have $2 million in assets, he paid $1.2 million to Amy[127] and because the defendant had agreed not to appeal, Amy was able to keep all of it. In other cases, other "courts denied her request for restitution, stating that 'there was not enough proof that any one man who viewed her pictures was responsible for the harm she has suffered.'" Amy won more than one hundred fifty cases, totaling $1.6 million, usually in small amounts of $100 or $1,000 and "paid out in checks as small as $7.33."[128]

On appeal of some of the restitution awards, in October 2012, the Fifth Circuit Court of Appeals allowed "Amy to obtain restitution from one or all of the defendants who downloaded her pictures. In making his ruling, Judge Garza wrote, 'Defendants collectively create the demand that fuels the creation of abusive images' and returned a restitution check of $529,000 back to the lower court on remand because the check did not provide for full restitution as the VAWA allows—it was too small."[129] This decision created a split between the appeals courts on the VAWA's restitution provisions, allowing the US Supreme Court to hear the appeal.

In a 5–4 ruling in April 2014, the US Supreme Court took away Amy's $3.4 million restitution award from Paroline when it ruled "a person convicted of possessing child pornography must pay restitution to the victims," but limited the damages to be "proximate to the harm that a specific offender has caused."[130] In writing for the majority, Justice Anthony M. Kennedy said the law was flawed and invited Congress to rewrite it. While he acknowledged that victims should receive restitution, he said defendants are only "liable for the consequences and gravity of their own conduct, not the conduct of others." He said there were three options: 1) Give nothing because it was "impossible to tell how the [defendant's] possession of two images affected her"; 2) Make the defendant pay for all damages; or 3) Take a middle ground. That is what the majority did.[131] (None of the justices believed that option one, no payment, was the correct answer.) Wrote Justice Kennedy: "Every viewing of child pornography is a repetition of the victim's abuse." So, as Justice Kennedy questioned, how does a judge determine the amount of money that reflects a defendant's "relative role"? "This cannot be a precise mathematical inquiry." The court suggested factors to look to in determining the amount of restitution to contribute, including: "the number of other defendants who have paid restitution, the number of future offenders likely to be caught, and whether the defendant reproduced or distributed images of the victim." Amy's lawyer estimates that "more than 70,000 people have seen" the images. In the arrest of the StealthGenie manufacturer cited above, he argued that "any legal issues were limited to the users of the device." Thus, does shifting the blame from the creator of the technology to the users of the technology work?

---

127   The court allowed his wife to keep the remainder of the estate. Ibid., P. 28.

128   Ibid., P.28. Amy's uncle paid about $6,000 in restitution.

129   Ibid., P. 47.

130   Ibid.

131   Ibid. In her dissent, Justice Sonia Sotomayor agreed with the 5th Circuit that the law allowed all defendants liable for the full amount and allowing one to pay it all, and then allowing him to sue the others for their share. This allows the victim not to have to relitigate the issue (and relive the crime) over and over again with each defendant and makes it easier for the victim to collect from one wealthy defendant.

Trolling

"Trolling and social media seem to go together like YouTube and cat videos." Beyond the use of technology in committing a crime, it also shapes the dialogue on it. "To **troll**, by definition, is to write something that provokes a target into an angry or emotional response—and in the process to attract attention and reframe a debate in a way that is more favorable to one's own viewpoint."[132] In a tragic case, in 2015, a concerned citizen called the police on a twenty-four-year-old mother who was observed pushing her dead child on a playground swing in Prince Georges County, Maryland, for many hours and possibly overnight. Surprisingly, about three-fourths of the comments were supportive, but there were the usual trolls who wanted to ignore the obvious mental health issues and move directly to draconian criminal punishments.[133]

In 2015, a family filed a lawsuit after their son attempted suicide from "trolls" on-line. Harassment included accusing the victim of "rape, posting mass bombing threats in his name" and "'swatting'" him (reporting a crime so the police SWAT unit arrives) and then "his parents' house was vandalized, he received death threats, his car was broken into, and his mother's job was put in jeopardy."[134] In 2016 a Virginia court awarded the family $1.4 million, "one of the largest in an Internet trolling case in the nation's history."[135] Attempts and successful suicides are becoming more common as on-line harassment increases.

Over-sharing

"We live, it has been said many times, in the era of over-sharing. Sometimes this produces awkward situations. Other times it produces something worse. A woman wrote a letter to "The Haggler," David Segal, in the *New York Times* about her online argument with her husband "about moderating [their] use of marijuana," which also showed up on their son's linked account. Because the son had a learning disability, his teachers saw the arguments as they popped up during times the son used his iPad at school for an educational accommodation. "They immediately reported my husband and me to the child protection division of the Alabama Department of Human Resources," wrote the woman, requesting the Haggler's advice. According to the woman, two weeks later a rep from the D.H.R. came to her house and interviewed all three of the couple's children and asked the mother "if I feed and bathe my children." The social services representative

---

132 "Antisocial media," Daniel W. Drezner, *The Washington Post*, May 17, 2015, B3. Trolling is not limited to social media and can include editorials in the newspaper.

133 "She's recovered from a breakdown she told a court. Then her 3-year-old was found dead on a park swing," Ian Shapira, DeNeen L. Brown, Keith L. Alexandar, *The Washington Post*, May 30, 2015. http://www.washingtonpost.com/local/shed-recovered-from-a-breakdown-she-told-a-court-then-her-3-year-old-was-found-dead-on-a-park-swing/2015/05/30/3b189e50-056d-11e5-bc72-f3e16bf50bb6_story.html

134 https://www.washingtonpost.com/local/crime/reign-of-terror-online-trolls-destroy-a-virginia-familys-offline-life/2015/07/20/a467f9bc-19ba-11e5-93b7-5eddc056ad8a_story.html?utm_term=.cf2fcb194be9

135 urn-table-on-internet-troll-wins-13-million-verdict/2016/11/03/a2e5c098-a1df-11e6-8d63-3e0a660f1f04_story.html?utm_term=.155fa1993a0e

also required the husband and wife to submit to a drug test the next day and several more were required over the next few months. Three months later, child services sent a "letter stating the accusations of child abuse and neglect against [the couple] were 'indicated,' which translates to 'true' in D.H.R.'s terminology." After an administrative review, the parents were eventually cleared by the D.H.R. but both of their names "were kept in the 'system,'" where they remain for five years.[136]

Let us look at this case without the technological impact. In the old days, parents might have talked face-to-face about problems in their marriage. Indeed, in the old days, the teacher would not "see" the parents' discussion of marital issues; or, if a teacher came across a piece of personal correspondence she would probably have respected its privacy. Or, in real life, if a child and teacher barged into a parents' conversation, the parents would just stop talking—the teacher would not be able to scroll through a written record of their conversation. Private family matters would have stayed private and not disrupted the family. In our current age of over-sharing, people do not think much before writing and sharing the minutiae of their lives. Email and Facebook used to seem so casual—now they come up in court!

Positive Note #1

"Having a robust social media presence can help solve crimes."[137] "Police departments across the country are moving quickly to harness the reach and transparency of these networks as tools to investigate and, they hope, neutralize the potential for violence." Police have used "Pinterest" to disseminate mug shots and photos of missing persons. "When the time comes and there's a child missing, we put it out on Twitter, and we find them in 10 minutes."[138] In 2015, "Homeland Security Investigations arrested or assisted in the arrest of 2,394 child predators worldwide… an increase of 150 percent since 2010" through better use of technology. This included reviewing social media accounts, and using smartphone apps "to seek the public's help" in locating predators, and by reviewing vast amounts of data quickly.[139]

---

136 "When a Shared ID leads to a Grim Predicament," David Segal, "The Haggler," *The New York Times*, June 8, 2014, P. 3. The wife wrote to ask The Haggler "Does Apple really think about these kinds of potential consequences?" His response was to verify it was not a hoax but true (it was) and that "it sounded like the sort of tale Franz Kafka would have written had he lived in the age of cloud computing." By the way, Apple's response was "the company would soon make it easier for families to communicate and share purchases, photos and calendars within the same household… each with their own Apple ID,'" called family sharing.

137 "On social media, when is a rant also a threat?" Katie Zezima, *The Washington Post*, December 26, 2014, A3, quoting Detective Drew Fowler, Seattle Police Department.

138 Ibid. Quoting Detective Drew Fowler, Seattle Police Department. Police also use social media as part of their "media relations arm" of the force. During the aftermath of the Boston Marathon bombing, the police used Twitter to keep the public informed.

139 "U.S. turns tables on online predators", Jerry Markon, *The Washington Post*, A17. The article mentions successes like catching a predator "seen on video molesting an 8-year old girl" through "1.6 million views on Facebook and Twitter led to more than 80 tips."

Positive Note #2

On another positive note, "There is evidence that technology has already made household chores much less time-consuming. Parents together now spend 27.6 hours a week on chores, down from 36.3 in 1965," per the American Time Use Survey and the Pew Research Center. "Some of their new free time is spent on their children.[140]

In addition, the Internet allows for creation of a "village" for raising children without having to leave the house by going online to "Internet communities." "Copious evidence online suggests that dads want their own space there... to talk about their larger roles in the family (and to sometimes joke about them)." For example, sites such as Daddit, which has more than thirty-four thousand subscribers (almost twice that of Mommit), meet the "growing demand of fathers seeking their own cozy corner of the web. On Daddit, you get the geekier side of the Internet, where people have done technical research about why this product is better than another product, but I think it also shows that dads are taking on more roles and responsibilities when it comes to parenting."[141] While there are many "Daddy bloggers" that have large followings, there is also a "growing number of Internet communities, networks, forums and email lists delving into the joys, trials and even public-policy aspects of being a father." When his daughter's premature birth caused a stay in the neonatal intensive-care unit, one father used "an invitation-only email list of hundreds of fathers from the technology and media worlds, called Nuevo Dads," to hear others' similar NICU experiences. "No one teaches you how to be a dad. It made me feel less alone."[142] Another website created 940 Saturdays—the number of Saturdays between when a child is born and when he or she turns eighteen to answer the often asked father's question of what to do with their child today. "The brotherhood of fathers has migrated to Twitter, where there were 112 million dad-related tweets in 2014, compared with 212 million about moms. (And about 2.5 million active Twitter users mention dad or father in their Twitter bio...)"[143] Even celebrities use social media to share their family experiences. Ashton Kutcher famously posted on Facebook to his millions of followers that "there are NEVER diaper changing stations in men's public restrooms. The first public men's room that I go into that has one gets a free shout out on my FB page!" It lead to the popular hashtag "#pottyparity."[144]

---

140   "An app for all your chores," Claire Cain Miller, *The New York Times*, September 28, 2014, P. 3.

141   "Making Room (on the Internet) for Daddy," Hannah Seligson, *The New York Times*, May 3, 2015, P. 10, quoting Avi Moskowitz, who volunteers as a moderator for Daddit. Both Daddit and Mommit are a part of the social networking site Reddit, formed to meet the growing demands of fathers.

142   Ibid. Quoting Bre Pettis.

143   Ibid. They can provide "advice from other dads on what instrument to get a 4-year-old to what basketball league to join."

144   Ibid.

MEDICAL DECISION MAKING (CHAPTER 18)

While the research is not settled, there is much of it that says too much technology can be harmful to a child, affecting everything from sleep to depression and self-esteem. Also, "children tend to disappear through the looking glass when they get their first phone. They become vulnerable to the dark side of the Internet."[145] Given this, are parents negligent in giving their child a cell phone?[146] If not, at what age should a child receive a cell phone or other technology? "Seventy-two percent of children age 8 and under had used a mobile device. These figures include a third of children under age 2."[147] Is one way to be a responsible parent to require a contract with your child governing cell phone use? The "Internet is bursting with dozens of multi-plank contracts for parents to execute with their children."[148] One "family contract" reads: "We will have weekly technology-free retreats, like hiking, biking or walking the dogs."[149] Have we really come to this as a society where parental decisions are written into contracts that are signed off on by family members, including children? If the parent is so uncomfortable with the decision because of the inherent problems and/or the maturity of the children, maybe the parent just needs to say "no." Other parents give their children the devices but then secretly monitor them with spyware. Assumedly, when the spyware picks up an infraction, the children will learn about the monitoring. What lesson will that teach the children about trust?

Will this create a next generation that does not trust parents in a relationship while itself also using spyware? (See above discussion on cheating in adult relationships.) Or if you are upfront about it, what is the effect of requiring your child to allow you to "join any social network they join and know their passwords and check their texts?"[150] If your children add you as a friend on their social media sites, what should you do if you see that one of their friends engages in risky behavior?

New parenting issues are arising as "millions of American families buy robotic voice assistants to turn off lights, order pizzas and fetch movie times, [and] children are eagerly co-opting the gadgets to settle dinner table disputes, answer homework questions and entertain friends at sleepover parties."[151] "But psychologists, technologists and linguists are only beginning to ponder the possible perils of surrounding kids with artificial intelligence, particularly as they traverse important

---

145   "Talk to Me, Not the Screen," Bruce Feiler, *The New York Times*, March 22, 2015, P. 2.

146   Prior New York City Mayor Michael Bloomberg prohibited students from carrying cell phones to city public schools but the current mayor, Bill de Blasio, lifted the ban. Ibid.

147   "The Eye-to-Eye Challenge," Bruce Feiler, *The New York Times*, April 19, 2015, citing a Common Sense Media study. Ironically, a Common Sense Media study showed that "parents spend more than nine hours a day looking at media screens yet believe they are good technology role models for their children." "When should my child get a smartphone? Survey says... ", *The Washington Post Magazine*, January 15, 2017.

148   Ibid.

149   The contract also required a weekly movie night and said that "When Mom watches horror or fantasy films, she's not allowed to say, 'Ewww,' 'Oh no!' or 'Gasp!'" Ibid.

150   Ibid.

151   "The know-it-all robot playmates", Michael S. Rosenwald, *The Washington Post Sunday, March 5, 2017 G1*.

states of social and language development."[152] As I write, the trending YouTube video of the day is a toddler talking to a mailbox because it looks like a robot, telling it, "I love you, robot."[153] A reporter writes that her "2-year-old son has been so enthralled by Alexa, that he tries to speak with coasters and other cylindrical objects that look like Amazon's device."[154] Is this worrisome?

Sexting

Since common law, the courts have recognized parents' responsibilities to raise their children, but when combining that with supervision of their technology use (called "digital parenting") that responsibility becomes even more complicated.[155] Sexting is one of the more troubling concerns to arise from adolescent technology use. While most think of sexting as teens texting nude selfies, the legal definition of **sexting** is "the sending of digital text messages containing suggestive, provocative, or explicit sexual photographs."[156] Should sexting be limited to provocative pictures or should it also include provocative language?

"Millions of teens send nude selfies to other kids, with unpredictable consequences."[157] "The speed with which teens have incorporated the practice into their mating rituals has taken society by surprise."[158] "At least 20 states have passed... laws [on sexting], most of which establish a series of relatively light penalties,"[159] from paying a fine to doing community service to taking a class. Other states, like Massachusetts, consider it child pornography and will prosecute both the recipient and the sender (even though "in most states it is perfectly legal for two 16-year-olds to

---

152 Ibid.

153 https://www.youtube.com/watch?v=h1E-FlguwGw "Rayna meets a "'robot'".

154 Quoting the author, Michael S. Rosenwald in "The know-it-all robot playmates", Michael S. Rosenwald, *The Washington Post Sunday, March 5, 2017 G1.*

155 When President Obama's daughter Malia's private photo became public on Instagram (it is unclear whether it was meant to be made public) and then "was widely circulated online, she is posing with her hands behind her head, wearing a wrinkled T-shirt emblazoned with the emblem of Brooklyn rap group Pro Era." The group used the image to promote their work. The White House had no comment on the picture. While presidents have always tried to keep their young children out of the media, this is probably much more complicated with the ubiquity of social media, where an Obama family picture posted online can "garner 63,000 Instagram likes." "They do walk the line of giving people a sense of who they are as people, which is a really important part of relating to a public figure, and also keeping their private lives private." (Quoting Laura Olin the social media director of the Obama 2012 campaign.) Having an "Office of Digital Strategy" would be nice for any parent. "The First Mom's Next Social Media Challenge: Sasha and Malia," Krissah Thompson, *The Washington Post Style*, January 15, 2015, C1.

156 Duhaimes's Law Dictionary. http://www.duhaime.org/LegalDictionary/S/Sexting.aspx

157 "Why kids sext," Hanna Rosin, *The Atlantic*, November 24, 2014, P. 65, 66. In an investigation of a sexting problem involving more than one hundred pictures of high schoolers (and even middle schoolers as young as fourteen) at a Louisa County High School in central Virginia, boys interviewed told the deputies, "It's nothing unusual. It happens all the time." (Quoting Major Donald Lowe of the county police department who lead the investigation.) After confiscating phones from every student they interviewed who had a naked picture on the device, "after just a couple of days, the deputies had filled multiple evidence bins with phones, and they couldn't see an end to it."

158 Ibid.

159 Ibid. P. 69.

have sex. But if they take pictures, it's a matter for the police."[160]). Boys and girls are equally likely to have sent a sext, but girls are much more likely to have been asked to do so—68 percent have been.[161] Most teens sext because their girlfriend or boyfriend wanted them to do it. In a study of eighteen-year-olds, 77.7 percent said "the picture they sent caused no problem for them."[162]

So is it a crime?[163] Is there a difference if an adult is involved? Should it make a difference whether the sext was voluntarily sent to another person? How should society respond? Is a high school student who takes a naked picture of her own body and sends it to her high school boyfriend creating child pornography? Does school or police involvement make this more of an issue than it is to the kids involved (viz., embarrass the girls whose nude pictures are posted)? Is this involvement necessary because society needs to protect children from their own outrageous behaviors? Is a senior high school girl's *Roe* argument that "it is my body and I can do whatever I want with it" correct? When parents or the police make a big deal about sexting, does it send a bad message to young girls about being "proud of my body"?[164] Are the girls being exploited? Are the girls just victimizing themselves?[165]

If intentionally sending a naked picture to a partner or potential partner falls within the crime of sexting, how is upskirting not a crime? Also called photo voyeurism, upskirting occurs when a person secretly takes a photo of another person's "private areas" in public. For example, when the police observed a man "snapping photos of women sitting on the steps" of the Lincoln Memorial, they arrested him.[166] The police found "images of women's buttocks on the camera and hundreds of comparable shots from other outings on a computer in his car" and charged him with two counts of attempted voyeurism. The DC Superior court agreed with the man that "the women did not have a reasonable expectation of privacy in such a public place and that they had positioned themselves in ways that made their intimate areas visible to any other passerby." In other words, the court made it very clear that a stranger surreptitiously taking pictures of people's underwear (or more) is legal—even when the judge said the "conduct was 'repellant and disturbing.'"[167] Yet, when a high school girl takes a provocative picture of herself, this is a crime?

How does a parent prevent a child from sexting or posting something inappropriate? "One parent... requires her children to put potential posts on the refrigerator and get a majority vote

---

160   Ibid.
161   Ibid. Referring to a study of seven public high schools in East Texas that found 28 percent of sophomores and juniors had sent a naked picture of themselves by text or email, and 31 percent had asked someone to send one. P. 68.
162   Ibid. Referring to a study by Elizabeth Englander, a psychology professor at Bridgewater State University. P. 68.
163   In one unbelievable case in Pennsylvania, in 2014, "two popular girls persuaded an autistic boy to share a picture of his penis with them, then forwarded the picture to a wide circle of schoolmates." They prosecuted the boy. Ibid., P. 69.
164   Ibid.
165   Ibid.
166   When the police approached the man, "he became nervous and attempted to remove the memory card from the camera." "Photo voyeurism case is dismissed," Justin Jouvenal and Miles Parks, *The Washington Post*, October 10, 2014, B4.
167   Quoting DC Superior Court Judge Juliet J. McKenna. Ibid.

from the family."[168] How well do you think this would work for teens? Another suggests "The Grandmother Rule"; would you want your grandmother to see this? What would be the penalty for violations? One suggested consequence is to "Actually show the post to Grandma!"[169]

PARENTAL DECISION MAKING—EDUCATION (CHAPTER 19)

Cyberbullying

"**Cyberbullying** is the willful and repeated use of cell phones, computers, and other electronic communication devices to harass and threaten others. Instant messaging, chat rooms, emails, and messages posted on websites are the most common methods of this new twist of bullying."[170] Cyberbullying and cyber-harassment are sometimes used interchangeably, but cyberbullying generally refers to electronic harassment or bullying among minors within a school context.[171] The diamond and the curse of technology is that anything posted to the Internet quickly spreads to a "vast audience" while the cyberbully remains anonymous and difficult to locate.[172] "Cyberbullying on Facebook has contributed to the deaths of several teens who either committed suicide or were killed by a peer."[173]

Cyberbullying that involves hacking or password and identity theft may be punishable under state and federal law.[174] More than a dozen states have passed cyberbullying laws since "the 2006 death of 13-year-old Megan Meier…[who]committed suicide after a neighbor pretending to be a teenage boy on MySpace sent her cruel messages."[175] Albany County New York's law, passed in 2010, "makes it a crime to communicate 'private, personal, false, or sexual information'" intended to "'harass, annoy, threaten, abuse, taunt, intimidate, torment, humiliate, or otherwise inflict significant emotional harm on another person.'"[176]

In one of the first challenges to a cyberbullying law under First Amendment free speech and other issues, New York's highest court reviewed the case of a fifteen-year-old high school student

---

168   "Talk to Me, Not the Screen," Bruce Feiler, *The New York Times*, March 22, 2015, P. 2.
169   Ibid. But some family contracts cut both ways, prohibiting Mom from posting that embarrassing picture of the family, including teenagers, with Santa and might include the plank, "If Mom wants to post a photo with a kid in it, she needs to ask."
170   National Conference of State Legislatures. http://www.ncsl.org/research/education/cyberbullying.aspx
171   National Conference of State Legislatures. http://www.ncsl.org/research/telecommunications-and-information-technology/cyberstalking-and-cyberharassment-laws.aspx
172   Ibid.
173   This is distinguished from "self-cyberbullying" where teens "post mean things about themselves on social-media sites, usually to get sympathy or attention." "Why kids sext," Hanna Rosin, *The Atlantic*, November 2014, P. 65, 74.
174   When adults engage in this kind of online behavior it is called cyber-harassment or cyberstalking. http://security-affairs.co/wordpress/4891/cyber-crime/7-most-common-facebook-crimes.html
175   "CyberBullying law challenged in court," Joe Palazzolo, *The Wall Street Journal*, June 4, 2014. http://www.wsj.com/articles/cyberbullying-law-challenged-in-court-1401925445
176   Ibid.

who created on Facebook a "'Cohoes Flame' page and posted photos of other teenagers with captions that included graphic and sexual comments." "In one of the less offensive posts, he wrote that one 15-year-old girl 'Kisses Like A Dog,' and has 'Cottage Cheese Legs.'" In others, "he listed alleged sexual partners and specific sex acts under the photos, according to court documents." Police located him "through his IP address and charged him as an adult with eight counts of violating the Albany cyberbullying law, as well as eight counts of harassment." The student said "he intended the pages to be funny."[177]

The trial "judge threw out the harassment charges but not the cyberbullying counts, which carry a punishment of up to one year in prison and a fine of up to $1,000." The student "pleaded guilty to a single count of cyberbullying, on the condition that he could challenge the law's constitutionality in higher state courts. He was sentenced to three years of probation." In 2013, "an Albany County judge ruled that the law was constitutional as applied to speech directed at minors, but not speech directed at adults."

In 2014, however, "the New York Court of Appeals, in a 5–2 ruling invalidated the Albany County cyberbully law under the First Amendment because it 'prohibit[ed]' a vast swath of speech 'far beyond the cyberbullying of children.'"[178] "Judge Victoria Graffeo, writing for the majority, described the posts as 'repulsive and harmful' but declined the county's request to uphold the law in a form that would have barred narrow categories of electronic communications, including sexually explicit photographs and private or personal sexual information, sent with the intent to harm." In his dissent, Judge Robert Smith said "the majority made too much of the flaws in the law's draftsmanship. 'The crux of the case, in my view, is whether Albany County constitutionally may do what it is trying to do: to prohibit certain kinds of communication that have no legitimate purpose and are intended to inflict significant emotional injury on children.'"[179]

In 2013, "Rebecca Ann Sedwick, 12, jumped to her death from the top of a silo at a derelict cement plant."[180] A Florida sheriff arrested two of her classmates, girls 12 and 14, on felony charges of aggravated stalking—bullying that he alleged was "a contributing factor" to the suicide. The two girls had urged Sedwick to kill herself; they told her to "drink bleach and die." The older girl told the younger one to beat up Sedwick. Sedwick "became increasingly desperate... tried to run away from home and... cut her wrists." Although she started at a new school, "she continued to receive abusive message on her phone." "After Sedwick's death, the older girl posted on her Facebook page: 'Yes ik [I know] I bullied Rebecca and she killed herself but IDGAF [I don't give a f—].'" Is this case really an example of cyberbullying?

Is charging young children with a crime the right response? Some argue it "will help draw attention to the problem of online bullying, a growing dynamic among the nation's youth as more

---

177   Ibid.
178   "New York judges strike down cyberbullying law," Joe Palazzolo, *The Wall Street Journal*, July 1, 2014. http://www.wsj.com/articles/new-york-court-strikes-down-cyberbullying-law-1404239912
179   Ibid.
180   "Bullying charges called 'uncharted territory,'" Robert Barnes, *The Washington Post*, October 17, 2013, A3.

of them spend time on mobile gadgets." But is bullying a felony? Are "adolescents too immature to understand the consequences of bullying "and does that take away from the adult's (parents and school officials) obligations to intervene earlier?" Is it true that if "they were old enough to be on social media sites, or mature enough to be using the language that they were using... they should be held accountable"?[181] Also, does it only "prolong the pain in this case?"

Positive Note

Students use technology devices such as smartphones (which are increasingly smaller and easy to conceal, much as the Apple Watch) to cheat on their exams. In China, however, drones are used to monitor high school-aged children taking their college entrance tests to prevent cheating.[182]

CUSTODY (CHAPTER 20)

"The digital world is changing at too rapid a pace for individuals or government regulations to keep up."[183] The uses for technology create some interesting issues in custody determinations today. In 2015, when a mother "took her two daughters" to Mexico to avoid a custody battle with her husband, their "digital footprints" gave them away when she used Spotify to stream music and movies. "As technology gets better and more companies come out, there are more opportunities to go get search warrants and figure out where people are."[184] While the courts generally have broad discretion in determining how to apply today's technology in custody hearings, one state has passed a law that gives the courts a specific dictate.

Disparaging the Other Parent

Judges have punished parents who disparage the other parent to their children during or after a divorce. Over-sharing via technology could inadvertently put a parent in this position. If one parent vents his or her feelings about the "ex" on social media, and the child has access to it, is this

---

181   Ibid. Quoting Sue Scheff, a parental advocate for those with "troubled youths," who runs Parents' Universal Resource Experts.

182   "China monitors university entrance exams with drones to catch cheating students," ABCNews Online, June 9, 2015. http://www.abc.net.au/news/2015-06-09/china-monitors-university-entrance-exams-with-drones/6530958 "Officials in Luoyang, in Henan province, purchased a drone designed to search for radio signals that could indicate cheating students, according to the *Dahe News*, the official provincial newspaper. It would monitor signals from five hundred meters above the test site, the paper said. The drone already uncovered college students taking the high school exams for pay. Would a drone be distracting while taking a test?

183   "Do new technologies pose an existential threat?" Matthew Wisnioski, *The Washington Post*, February 15. 2014, reviewing *Mind Change*, by Susan Greenfield, Random House, 2015.

184   Quoting Drew Webber involved in the case. "A wanted woman's use of Spotify is music to Colorado investigators' ears", Jacob Bogage, *Washington Post*, July 16, 2015, A9.

a violation? Moreover, what is the effect on a child (or any relatives of the "ex") still connected on social networks?

Pornography

Courts are more commonly hearing allegations of a parent (usually the father) using Internet pornography when assessing custody and risk to children. This issue ranges from excessive viewing of adult pornography to requesting the children to view pornography with the parent. A simple allegation that a parent watches pornography will probably not affect the parent's chance for custody because of First Amendment free speech concerns (and the fact that pornography is legal). But if the allegations state the viewing was excessive, that might trigger a more comprehensive review before custody could be considered. The court would consider whether it is an addiction that could interfere with caregiving. Also of concern is whether the frequency of viewing would likely cause the child to unintentionally view it as well? At the other end of the issue: parents who view pornography with a child. In 2014, Utah modified its child-custody factors to deal with parents who "intentionally" expose a child to pornography. The Utah law already required the court to include "the past conduct and demonstrated moral standards of each of the parties" when determining what is best for the child in custody evaluations. This new law now requires the court to factor in "whether the parent has intentionally exposed the child to pornography."[185] At the other end of the porn/custody spectrum: if the parent watches child pornography, that is illegal and should be reported to the police.

TERMINATION OF PARENTAL RIGHTS/ADOPTION (CHAPTER 22)

Text Message Serves as Termination of Interest

One father waived his rights to his child by a text message. The case of *Adoptive Couple v. Baby Girl*, No. 12–399 (2013), involved a father who gave up his parental rights to his child "Baby Veronica" via text message. Two years later, the father asked to have the child back after she had been adopted by another couple and was living on the other side of the country. The lower court agreed with him and ordered the return of his daughter.

While it is generally true that the courts prefer a biological parent for an adoption, this case involves setting aside an adoption. Certainly, taking the child from its adoptive parents raises some concerns about whether this is in the child's best interest. The reason the lower court decided in

---

185 SB0227 30-3-10 (1)(a)(1)(iv). "There are cases in Utah—and I'm saddened and embarrassed to report this to you—where a father will sit down with a young boy and say, 'You've got to watch this to be a man,' and they're showing them pornographic videos," said bill sponsor Senator Todd Weiler. "House passes bill making child exposure to porn a custody factor," Mike Terry, *Deseret News*, March 13, 2014. http://www.deseretnews.com/article/865598611/House-passes-bill-making-child-exposure-to-porn-a-custody-factor.html?pg=all

the father's favor is that Baby Veronica is about "3/256th% Cherokee."[186] The biological father, Dusten Brown, is a member of the Cherokee Nation. In 1978, Congress passed the Indian Child Welfare Act to remedy the regular removal of Native American children from their families and tribes by placing them with non-Native adoptive families.[187] It is estimated that about one-third to one-fourth of Indian children were so removed.[188] To remedy this, the "ICWA established a chain of adoptive preferences for children with Indian heritage. In the event that neither parent could take custody, other Indian family members were to have priority, and after that, tribal adoptive parents."[189]

Baby Veronica's adopting family challenged the law as inapplicable in this case because Brown is "not a parent" (arguing that he gave up his parental rights when he sent that text message) and that, as such, the Indian parent did not have custody.[190] In addition to the text message, "A month prior to the birth, [the biological mother], through her lawyer, sent a letter notifying the Cherokee Nation of her adoption plans, giving them a chance to intervene under the Indian Child Welfare Act. The tribe said it had no record of Brown as a tribal member. So the adoption went forward.

---

186   "Which family is Baby Veronica's?" Robert Barnes, *The Washington Post*, April 15, 2013, A10. Quoting the adopting family's lawyer, Lisa S. Blatt.

187   This shameful period of American history probably has roots from the 1870s when Native American children were "assimilated" into white schools.

188   http://www.npr.org/2013/04/16/177327391/adoption-case-brings-rare-family-law-dispute-to-high-court?ft=1&f=1001&sc=tw&utm_source=twitterfeed&utm_medium=twitter "Adoption Case Brings Rare Family Law Dispute To High Court," Nina Totenberg, NPR, April 16, 2013.

189   Ibid.

190   The birth mother is not an Indian, but a Hispanic casino worker/single parent with two other children, who put the child up for adoption and approved the adopting parents in an open adoption. She claims she did so after Brown (whom she was engaged to for a month before she became pregnant) refused to support the child. (See also, "Justices Conflicted by Baby Veronica Case," *The Washington Post*, April 17, 2013 (A3), which described the situation as "Brown and [the mother] became engaged in December 2009 and learned a month later that she was pregnant. But she called things off after Brown pressured her to get married right away, and he later texted, in response to her question that he would rather give up parental rights than pay child support." According to the National Indian Child Welfare Association, Brown, the biological father, acknowledges he was engaged to the mother "when [Victoria] was conceived, but her mother broke off the engagement while the father, Dusten Brown, was serving in the U.S. Army and stationed at Fort Sill, Oklahoma. Unbeknownst to Brown, she began the process of placing her child up for adoption. In the final months of pregnancy, the mother cut off all communication with Brown and worked closely with an agency and attorney to adopt the child to a non-Indian couple from South Carolina, the Capobiancos. Brown was not informed of Veronica's birth on September 15, 2009. Veronica was placed with the Capobiancos three days after her birth in Oklahoma, and they relocated her to South Carolina shortly thereafter. Four months later, the couple finally served Brown with notice of their intent to adopt Veronica. Immediately, he went to court to request a stay of the adoption until after his deployment (which, because of his military status, is provided for by federal law). He also began the legal steps to establish paternity and gain custody. He was then deployed to Iraq. Because the Capobiancos waited until just days before Brown was deployed, the adoption hearing was not completed until he returned home." http://www.nicwa.org/BabyVeronic/ NICA, National Indian Child Welfare Association. The NICA asserts that Brown did not knowingly waive his rights to the child but admits that he did sign, mistakenly, an "Acceptance of Service and Answer of Defendant, which stated he was not contesting the adoption of Baby Girl and that he waived the thirty-day waiting period and notice of the hearing. Father testified he believed he was relinquishing his rights to the Mother and did not realize he consented to Baby Girl's adoption by another family until after he signed the papers." (NICA)

Four months after the birth of the baby girl—as Brown was about to deploy to Iraq, and as the adoption was about to become final—he was served with papers notifying him of the adoption. Brown signed off on them, inadvertently, he claims. But within days he filed a formal objection, invoking the Indian Child Welfare Act."

After the lower court ruled in favor of Brown based on the ICWA, the adoptive parents appealed to the US Supreme Court based on the federal ICWA. At the oral argument before the Supreme Court, "The birth mother's[191] lawyer… argued that if Indian fathers can sweep in this way, based only on biology, and override the birth mother's decision, why couldn't sperm donors or rapists who are Indian do the same?" "No other set of men can choose to kind of sit back, renounce all responsibility but hold a back-pocket veto to an adoption choice."[192]

In a 5–4 decision, the Supreme Court reversed the lower court's decision and remanded it based on the finding that the father never had custody. In writing the opinion, Justice Alioto said, "This case is about a little girl who is classified as an Indian because she is 1.2% (3/256) Cherokee. Because Baby Girl is classified in this way, the South Carolina Supreme Court held that certain provisions of the federal Indian Child Welfare Act of 1978 required her to be taken, at the age of 27 months, from the only parents she had ever known and handed over to her biological father, who had attempted to relinquish his parental rights and who had no prior contact with the child. [H]ere, the parent abandoned the Indian child before birth and never had custody of the child." It seems the Supreme Court was influenced by the father's initial waiver of parental rights via a text message as support of his termination of interest in the child. Finally, is there a conflict of interest in this case, if both Chief Justice Roberts and Justice Thomas have adopted children?

As these last two cases ask the question, has society become so programmed to share that we forget what the effects of it may be? Were the fathers too cavalier about tweeting/texting messages in a moment that later greatly affected their future and their relationship with a possible child?

Conclusion

You can tell, I am resistant to technology, probably because as this chapter illustrates, I am pessimistic that society has not really used it for its potential, but more for the bad than it seems for the good. As I write this, "Chicago police have arrested two juveniles in connection with a group sexual assault on a teenage girl that was broadcast on Facebook Live."[193] As many as six rapists may have been involved. Moreover, "[a]t least 40 people were watching the live stream, but none of them reported it, police said."[194] Should they arrest the viewers too? Lastly, the "victim

---

191   Christy Maldonado.
192   http://www.npt.org/2013/04/16/177327391/adoption-case-brings-rare-family-law-dispute-to-high-court?ft=1&f=1001&sc=tw&utm_source=twitterfeed&utm_medium=twitter. "Adoption Case Brings Rare Family Law Dispute To High Court." Nina Totenberg, NPR, April 16, 2013, quoting Lori Alvino McGill.
193   http://www.cnn.com/2017/04/02/us/chicago-facebook-gang-rape-arrest/
194   Ibid.

has received online taunts and harassment during the course of their investigation".[195] There is nothing more that can be said about this other than to hope that justice is swift for the victim.

For years I have told my classes that monkeys could do more with this gift of technology than we humans have. I think I envisioned chimpanzees using Spotify as Mozart wafted over the jungle. Two months ago, however, the "Netherlands announced how it is hoping to find a partner for an orangutan named Samboja: through "'Tinder for orangutans.'"[196] The Zookeepers "will use a tablet to show the orangutan pictures of available males from a breeding program… While there may not be any swiping left or right involved, researchers will pay attention to how Samboja responds to the images. Maybe my theory on the monkeys was wrong.

As this chapter's sampling shows, examples of technology's influence on families are endless. I will close with one cautionary tale on the use of technology that is near to my heart and written by a law school professor: "When a Web site broke the news on April 3 that, instead of posting an Internet link to an article about writing legal briefs, I had inadvertently sent my law school students a link to a porn site, I thought I would never recover."[197] "Unsurprisingly, some students spread word of the incident through social media and anonymous e-mails to the media." The professor complained that while everyone attacked her, no one investigated the students who passed on the error.[198] "Everyone was talking about me. Everyone was speculating about whether I watched porn, or used sex toys, or like kinky sex. Some people were calling for my job and law license."[199] She is a tenured faculty member at Drexel University, which conducted a short internal investigation and "found [no] violat[ations] of Title IX or Drexel's sexual harassment and misconduct policy." To one of her teenage daughters, she said, "What I had to tell her about myself was not nearly as bad as a cancer diagnosis—and my chances of recovery… [were] one hundred percent." As she points out, "there is nothing newsworthy about it…. My students are adults. The link was quickly removed. There was nothing illegal in the video. The post occurred in the same two-month period when the movie 'Fifty Shades of Grey' grossed almost $570 million worldwide." The law professor wrote," Seemingly, private citizens do not have the right to that one simple thing: privacy." She argues that she reclaimed her dignity, and wrote, "Here's what I've learned: Losing your dignity is not like losing your virginity (and, yes, I understand the loaded nature of those words)."

Reading her op-ed piece brought many of the problems of technology's easy use into focus for me. Unlike her, my initial thoughts were that she should apologize to her students, and then everyone should calm down and get back to work. But it is a chilling reminder of how, through our use of technology, we allow our own privacy to be invaded in many ways. I suspect that she,

---

195   Ibid.

196   "Thanks to 'Tinder for orangutans,' Samboja will have chance to pick her mate" Amy B Wang, *The Washington Post,* February 1, 2017, A3.

197   "Reclaiming my dignity," Lisa T. McElroy, *The Washington Post Sunday Opinion*, April 26, 2015, A15.

198   Ibid. She asked, "No one asked why, if they found it so offensive, students opened the link, with its unmistakable Web address, and watched the video long enough to know what it contained."

199   Ibid.

too, would agree that this attitude clearly contrasts with that of the founding fathers in writing the Constitution.

But this unwinding of society is a bigger issue left for another day. I end with my own pet peeve: stay off your technology when you are around your children—tender years, or older. Over two decades ago, I was shopping in a baby store and was horrified when a toddler picked up a toy cell phone, put it to her ear, and said, "Not now, I'm on my cell." Years later, when I would take my young son for a stroll, I was disheartened to encounter other mothers pushing a stroller while on their cell phones and their own child received no interaction. I guess this is how that toddler on the toy cell learned those first words. The message these mothers were sending to their children was that whoever was on the phone was more important than their children. When those children grow up, I thought, they too will be immersed in the same technology their parents had modeled for them. "The data use among children is staggering." "Media use among 8- to 18-year-olds [is] more than 7.5 hours a day."[200] "A quarter of teenagers are online 'almost constantly.' Among 12- to 17-year-olds, texting has become the primary means of communication, outstripping direct human contact." [201] There are concerns that so much use of technology impacts children's sleep habits, self-esteem, social success, feelings of normalcy, and ability to read other's nonverbal emotional cues.[202] There are only 940 Saturdays, so even without definitive research, my parental instinct tells me, why not hang up the phone and talk to your child instead?[203] Really, spend some time together, before it's gone.

---

200 "The Eye-to-Eye Challenge," Bruce Feiler, *The New York Times*, April 19, 2015, P.2. Citing a Kaiser Family Foundation study.

201 Ibid. Citing a Pew Research Center study.

202 Ibid. Citing an old study by Clifford Nass, at Stanford University and others. A University of Basel student found that teenagers who kept their smartphones on at night were more likely to watch videos, text, and have poor sleep habits and higher depression. "Talk to Me, Not the Screen," Bruce Feiler, *The New York Times*, March 22, 2015, P.2. In contrast, other research argues that technology has demands on social intelligence and that video games and watching TV have cognitive benefits. "The Eye-to-Eye Challenge," Bruce Feiler, *The New York Times*, April 19, 2015, P.2.

203 Maybe I am not so old school, the "Obamas, for example, said they did not give their daughters cellphones until they were 12, barred their use during the weekdays, kept the girls off Facebook until 17." "Talk to Me, Not the Screen," Bruce Feiler, *The New York Times*, March 22, 2015, P.2.

GLOSSARY

A

Adultery—voluntary sexual relations between an individual who is married and someone who is not the individual's spouse.

Agency Adoption—occurs when a licensed adoption agency puts a baby up for adoption after it has been relinquished from its biological parents.

Alienation of affection—an action brought by a deserted spouse against a third party alleged her spouse to be responsible for the failure of the marriage.

Analysis—reasoning in deciding a case that summarizes relevant facts.

Annulment—a judgment by a court that retroactively invalidates a marriage to the date of its formation.

Answer—gives the plaintiff notice of the issues the defendant will raise as the case progresses and enables the plaintiff to adequately prepare a case

Appellant—a person who, dissatisfied with the judgment rendered in a lawsuit decided in a lower court or the findings from a proceeding before an Administrative Agency, asks a superior court to review the decision.

Appellee—a party who has won a judgment in a lawsuit or favorable findings in an administrative proceeding, which judgment or findings the losing party, the appellant, seeks to have a higher court reverse or set aside.

Assisted Reproductive Technology—the technology used to achieve pregnancy in procedures such as fertility medication, artificial insemination, in vitro fertilization and surrogacy.

B

Battered Spouse Defense—raised by a wife against her spouse.

Battered Woman Syndrome (BWS)—a mental disorder that develops in victims of domestic violence as a result of serious, long-term abuse.

Bigamy—the act of going through a marriage ceremony while already married to another person.

Black-letter law—the well-established technical legal rules that are no longer subject to reasonable dispute.

C

Circuit Court—a court holding sessions in different sections of a judicial district.

Civil Matters—part of the law that encompasses business, contracts, estates, domestic (family) relations, accidents, negligence, and everything related to legal issues, statutes, and lawsuits, that is not criminal law. In a few areas civil and criminal law may overlap or coincide.

Civil Union—a legally recognized union of a same-sex couple, with rights similar to those of marriage (started in Vermont).

Code—a systematic and comprehensive compilation of laws, rules, or regulations that are consolidated and classified according to subject matter.

Cohabitation Agreement—contract between a couple that is living together but not anticipating marriage.

Collusion—a pact between two people to deceive a court with the purpose of obtaining something that they would not be able to get through legitimate judicial channels.

Comity—the acceptance of a decision or law by a court of another jurisdiction, either foreign or domestic, based on public policy rather than legal mandate.

Common Law Marriage—also known as sui juris marriage, informal marriage, or marriage by habit and repute, is a legal framework in a limited number of jurisdictions where a couple is legally considered married, without that couple having formally registered their relation as a civil or religious marriage.

Complaint—the pleading that initiates a civil action; in Criminal Law, the document that sets forth the basis upon which a person is to be charged with an offense.

Confidential Marriage—formalities are carried out with no public records of personal information or licensing regarding the union.

Conclusion—in a trial or court hearing, a final determination of the facts by the trier of fact (jury or judge) and/or a judge's decision on the law

Condonation—may be made when an accuser has previously forgiven or *condoned* (in some way or at some level supported) the act about which they are complaining.

Connivance—tacit encouragement of or assent to another's wrongdoing, esp. (formerly) of the petitioner in a divorce suit to the respondent's adultery.

Constitution—a body of fundamental principles or established precedents according to which a state or other organization is acknowledged to be governed.

Constructive Desertion—the end of marital Cohabitation brought about when one spouse, by his or her conduct, forces the other to leave home.

Covenant Marriage—a legal union of husband and wife that requires premarital counseling, marital counseling if problems occur, and limited grounds for divorce.

Criminal Matters—those statutes dealing with crimes against the public and members of the public, with penalties and all the procedures connected with charging, trying, sentencing and imprisoning defendants convicted of crimes.

Criminal Conversion—treating another as one's own.

Cruelty—the intentional and malicious infliction of physical or psychological pain on another often accepted as one of the three major fault-based grounds for divorce.

Cyberbullying—willful and repeated use of cellphones, computers, and electronic devices to harass and threaten others, usually done in the context of minors and/or in a school environment.

Cyber-harassment—threatening or harassing email messages, instant messages, blog entries, or even a website created for the sole purpose of tormenting another person.

Cyberstalking—a pattern of threatening or malicious behaviors with messages, written threats, and other persistent online behaviors that endanger another person's safety.

D

Defendant—the person defending or denying; the party against whom relief or recovery is sought in an action or suit, or the accused in a criminal case.

Defense of Marriage Act (DOMA)—is a United States federal law that originally allowed states to refuse to recognize same-sex marriages granted under the laws of other states but is now limited to not requiring states to recognize valid same-sex marriages from another state.

Domestic Partnership—a legal or interpersonal relationship between two individuals who live together and share a common domestic life but are neither joined by marriage nor a civil union.

Domiciled—the status or attribution of being a permanent resident in a particular jurisdiction

Dowry—property or money brought by a bride to her husband on their marriage.

F

Federalism—a political concept in which a *group* of members are bound together by covenant with a governing representative head.

Fiction of Oneness—common law concept that the wife becomes "one" with her husband after marriage and gives him all of her rights and property.

Form Family—a group that is created by its connections through blood (biologically), marriage, or adoption.

Full Faith and Credit—concept that one state will accept a legal judgment or status from another state (unless it is immoral)

Functional Family—members are together based on a commitment to each other while they function like form families.

G

Geriatric Marriage—marriage with special allowances for older/retired people.

H

Holding—any ruling or decision of a court.

I

Issue—identify the conflict that the court will resolve.

J

Joint Custody—both parents share the ability to have access to educational, health, and other records, and have equal decision-making status where the welfare of the child is concerned.

Jurisdiction—determination of which court has the authority to hear a case.

L

Legal Custody—gives one parent the authority to make major decisions for a child without the consent of the other.

M

Marriage Equality—Same-sex marriage, the union of two people of the same sex.

Mootness—of an issue in the case is still ripe for review

Motion—a formal request made to a judge for an order or judgment.

N

Non-marital Birth—child born to an unmarried couple (formerly called illegitimate)

P

Parties—persons who are directly involved or interested in any act, affair, contract, transaction, or legal proceeding; opposing litigants.

Physical Custody—the legal and practical relationship between a parent and his or her child, such as the right of the parent to make decisions for the child, and the parent's duty to care for the child.

Plaintiff—the party who initiates a lawsuit by filing a complaint with the clerk of the court against the defendant(s) demanding damages, performance and/or court determination of rights.

Polygamy—the practice or custom of having more than one wife or husband at the same time.

Post-marital—an agreement made between spouses after marriage concerning the rights and responsibilities of the parties upon Divorce or the death of one of the spouses.

Postnuptial Agreement—written contract executed after a couple gets married (or have entered a civil union) to settle the couple's affairs and assets in the event of a separation or divorce or possibly death

Precedent—judicial decision that is binding on other equal or lower courts in the same jurisdiction as to its conclusion on a point of law, and may also be persuasive to courts in other jurisdictions, in subsequent cases involving sufficiently similar facts.

Prenuptial Agreement—written contract made in anticipation of marriage to determine asset allocation in the event of termination of the marriage or possibly death. Also called a 'prenup' or premarital agreement.

Private Adoption—occurs when the biological parent(s) arrange with an intermediary to allow the adoption of his/her child to another person(s).

Protective Orders—used to help victims/survivors of domestic violence keep attackers away to prevent future attacks also known as peace orders and restraining orders.

Putative Marriage—contracted in good faith, and in ignorance of the existence of those facts which constituted a legal impediment to the intermarriage.

Q

Quantum Meruit—"as much as he deserves", in equity, the law infers to pay a reasonable amount for what has been done.

R

Recrimination—a charge made by an individual who is being accused of some act against the accuser.

Relationship Agreement—contract between a couple that is not living together or anticipating marriage

Revenge Porn (aka nonconsensual pornography)—posting naked pictures of another online, usually in retaliation for the other person's actions, such as ending the relationship

Ruling—an official or authoritative decision, decree, statement, or interpretation (as by a judge on a point of law) that answers the question raised by the issue.

S

Separation Agreement—written agreement between two married people who have agreed to live apart for an unspecified period of time in anticipation of marriage. It may address alimony, child support, custody arrangements, bills, and bank accounts etc. Also called a **Settlement Agreement.**

Sexting—sending digital text messages with suggestive, provocative, or explicit photographs

Stare Decisis—policy of courts to abide by or adhere to principles established by decisions in earlier cases.

Statutes—laws enacted by a legislature.

T

Temporary Restraining Order—court order that protects a person or persons from physical, mental, verbal, or other abuse. E.g., it can require the abuser to keep at least 100 yards away from the victim, enforceable by arrest.

Term Marriage—is on its face unlawful and therefore legally has no effect.

Textual harassment—abusive text messages persistently demanding locations or plans, or a person's refusal to stop texting until he or she receives a response

Troll—to write something online that provokes a target into an angry response and to attract attention or reframe the debate so that it is more favorable to the writer's position

V

Viability—time period after a fetus could live independently.

Visitation—court approved schedule where the non-custodial parent spends time with the child(ren).

Void Marriage—is a marriage which is unlawful or invalid under the laws of the jurisdiction where it is entered.

Voidable Marriage—is valid but is subject to cancellation if contested in court by one of the parties to the marriage.

W

Writ of Certiorari—a written order for a superior court to call up to review the record of a proceeding in an inferior court.

Sources:
Blacks' Law Dictionary
Google Dictionary
Law.com
Wiktionary

SPECIAL THANKS

As always, thanks to my family for their support in keeping me motivated and ignoring the endless clutter created when researching and writing this book. Special thanks to Tommy Tripp for contributing his astute copyedits and creative research during his breaks from Johns Hopkins University. A big shout-out to my fantastic University of Maryland undergraduate TA Carly Hanft, who took my upper-level family law class as a freshman and was such a dynamo that I hired her as my research assistant for the past three years. I am grateful for her long nights she put in editing, researching, and overseeing the technology during this re-write. I appreciate her intelligence, enthusiasm, and commitment to this project and already miss her as she graduates next month. Thanks, too, to everyone at Cognella for all their patience. I wish to thank everyone at the University of Maryland College Park's Department of Family Studies; I have always felt like part of the "family." Finally, while I have learned it takes many to write a textbook, mostly it involves long hours alone by the computer, so any errors in the text are mine.

CPSIA information can be obtained
at www.ICGtesting.com
Printed in the USA
LVHW06s0634170718
583960LV00001B/1/P